"This well-produced,
easy-to-read
Bible compendium
is a basic book for all
would-be disciples
of Jesus Christ.
I commend it most
heartily."

Dr J.I. PACKER
PROFESSOR OF THEOLOGY,
REGENT COLLEGE,
VANCOUVER

"An invaluable handbook for
those who want to have
both an integrated overview
of the message and grand
themes of the whole Bible
and a better understanding
of each book of the Bible."

LINDSAY BROWN
INTERNATIONAL DIRECTOR, LAUSANNE
COMMITTEE FOR WORLD
EVANGELIZATION,
IFES EVANGELIST AT LARGE

"It is my prayerful hope that these
studies will introduce thousands of
new believers to the thrill of
discovering what the Bible says ..."

BILLY GRAHAM
(ON THE BIBLE TEACHING SECTION)

This book is dedicated with
great appreciation to Les Coley,
a former CLC UK National Director.
Les is a very knowledgeable lover of books
and of The Book. He was an inspiration
and an example to the creator of
this project – Robert Hicks.

CLC
BIBLE
COMPANION

Martin H. Manser • *Editor*
Tony Cantale • *Designer*
Robert F. Hicks • *Project director*
Larry Stone • *International development*

DISCOVER • UNDERSTAND • APPLY
the contents   the truths   the message

CLC
PUBLICATIONS

PUBLISHER

CLC International, P.O. Box 1449,
Fort Washington, PA 19034, U.S.A.
www.clcinternational.org
www.CLCBibleCompanion.com

A catalogue record for this book
is available from the British
Library

ISBN-13 978-1-936143-13-9
ISBN-10 1-936143-13-5

Produced by
Creative 4 International:
Martin H. Manser · *Editor*
Tony Cantale · *Designer*
Robert F. Hicks · *Project director*
Larry Stone · *International
development*

Editorial assistant
Nicola L. Bull

Cover design
Cristi Cotovan

Introductory article
Andrew Stobart

Knowing Jesus
Andrew Stobart

The Bible Book by Book
David Barratt, Mike Beaumont,
Pieter Lalleman, Richard
Littledale, Debra Reid,
Andrew Stobart, Derek Williams

*Extracts at Mark, 1 Corinthians,
Galatians, Ephesians, Philippians,
Colossians, 1 and 2 Thessalonians,
1 and 2 Timothy, Titus,* from *Critical
Companion to the Bible,* edited by
Martin H. Manser (Facts on File,
2009) by permission of Facts on
File

Bible Teaching
Richard Bewes, Robert F. Hicks

Discovering God's Way
John Balchin, John Benton,
Richard Bewes, Rosalind Bradley,
Julian Charley, Peter Grainger,
Erroll Hulse, Gilbert Kirby,
Ada Lum, Alec Motyer,
Stuart Olyott, Roger Salisbury,
Derek Tidball, Peter White

Living the Christian Life
Derek Williams, Robert F. Hicks,
Andrew Stobart

Miracles and *Parables of Jesus Christ*
from *Collins Bible Dictionary* by
Martin Selman and Martin
Manser (Harper Collins, 2005).
Prayers of Jesus Christ adapted from
Collins Bible Dictionary by
permission of the publishers.
Definitions in the section "Bible
Themes" adapted from *Collins
Bible Dictionary* by permission of
the publishers, and *Dictionary of
Bible Themes* edited by Martin
Manser.

Unless otherwise stated, all
Scripture references are from
the Holy Bible, New International
Version, copyright © 1973, 1978,
1984 by International Bible
Society. Used by permission of
Hodder & Stoughton Publishers,
an Hachette UK company

Contents
CONTINUED

THE BIBLE
BOOK BY BOOK

Pages 116–405
An overview of each book of the Bible

BIBLE
TEACHING

Pages 406–539
The essential truths of Christianity

Contents

KNOWING
JESUS

POWERPOINT AND PRESENTATIONS

How to use the material in this book

This book is a resource for those who want to study the Bible and for those who seek to teach others.

Material is presented throughout using headings, subheadings and explanation. It can be adapted for PowerPoint or overhead projection by copying or extracting the headings and subheadings for display.

You will find that some material is presented in "bullet points"; other material readily subdivides into teaching points. By listing and displaying what is suitable for display and using your own notes for explanation, a teaching session can easily be developed. Because of the consecutive nature of the material whole teaching programmes can be created relatively simply.

Material in this book may be freely used for such study and teaching purposes in a non-commercial personal, church or teaching setting.

Those who have worked on this book want people to be helped in their faith and understanding of God and his ways.

USING POWERPOINT

For guidance on preparing PowerPoints, see the section on page 824. In that section, we have also included sample PowerPoints from the main parts of this book. For PowerPoints on all the studies in the main sections of this book, see www.CLCBibleCompanion.com or the DVD that is available separately. The PowerPoints are free for you to download and use as you wish.

ABBREVIATIONS

Abbreviations for the books of the Bible used in this book are:

Old Testament		New Testament	
Genesis	Ge	Matthew	Mt
Exodus	Ex	Mark	Mk
Leviticus	Lev	Luke	Lk
Numbers	Nu	John	Jn
Deuteronomy	Dt	Acts	Ac
Joshua	Jos	Romans	Ro
Judges	Jdg	1 Corinthians	1Co
Ruth	Ru	2 Corinthians	2Co
1 Samuel	1Sa	Galatians	Gal
2 Samuel	2Sa	Ephesians	Eph
1 Kings	1Ki	Philippians	Php
2 Kings	2Ki	Colossians	Col
1 Chronicles	1Ch	1 Thessalonians	1Th
2 Chronicles	2Ch	2 Thessalonians	2Th
Ezra	Ezr	1 Timothy	1Ti
Nehemiah	Ne	2 Timothy	2Ti
Esther	Est	Titus	Tit
Job	Job	Philemon	Phm
Psalms	Ps	Hebrews	Heb
Proverbs	Pr	James	Jas
Ecclesiastes	Ecc	1 Peter	1Pe
Song of Songs	SS	2 Peter	2Pe
Isaiah	Isa	1 John	1Jn
Jeremiah	Jer	2 John	2Jn
Lamentations	La	3 John	3Jn
Ezekiel	Eze	Jude	Jude
Daniel	Da	Revelation	Rev
Hosea	Hos		
Joel	Joel		
Amos	Am		
Obadiah	Ob		
Jonah	Jnh		
Micah	Mic		
Nahum	Na		
Habakkuk	Hab		
Zephaniah	Zep		
Haggai	Hag		
Zechariah	Zec		
Malachi	Mal		

Foreword

The Bible is the most remarkable book in human history. An international bestseller since the printing press was invented, the Bible was written thousands of years ago and yet it is wonderfully relevant in our day and age. It claims to be the very Word of God. What could be more engaging than to hear and understand God speaking to you and me?

And yet ... so often the Bible is left unread on the bookshelf, because it appears a difficult book to understand. Therefore we need a friend, a *Companion* to help us discover, understand and grapple with the wonderful truths in its pages.

The *CLC Bible Companion* sets out to achieve the aims described on its cover:

- **DISCOVER the Contents.** What does the Bible say? Why does it comprise 66 books written by 40 different authors? Why are different styles used? "The Bible book by book" section will open this up to you.
- **UNDERSTAND the Truths.** The section "Bible Teaching" introduces the essential truths of the Christian faith. With more than 300 individual studies, it is designed in such a way that the material can be used for personal devotion, small group study or as the basis for preaching.
- **APPLY the Message.** Ultimately the Bible remains as any other book unless the wonderful truths are applied and lived out. The *CLC Bible Companion* will challenge and encourage you to live out your faith.

But this is far more than just a book. It is our desire that the *CLC Bible Companion* be an open-ended resource. With this in mind, PowerPoint presentations of all 300+ studies are available on our website **www.CLCBibleCompanion.com**. Alternatively, the material – both the book and the presentations – is available in DVD format.

It has been a pleasure to work with our friends from Creative 4 to make this project a reality. Resources from their version of this book, *Open Your Bible*, co-published with CLC in the UK, are available via **www.openyourbibleresources.com**

CLC is an international organisation working in over 50 countries to make the Bible and Christian books available via publishing, wholesale distribution and through our 200 bookshops. Our deep desire is to see people from all parts of the world discover, understand and apply the message of the Word of God. We believe that the *CLC Bible Companion* achieves this purpose and we warmly commend it to you.

Neil Wardrope
CLC International Director
www.clcinternational.org

Introduction

Welcome to the *CLC Bible Companion*. This book is an all-in-one guide to the Bible that is both a comprehensive reference book and an exciting companion. Here you will have opportunity to:

· know Jesus Christ
· discover the contents of the Bible
· explore the truth of the Bible
· believe and experience the message of the Bible

In all, your life will be enriched as you allow God to speak to you through his word. But we want more for you than that: this book's special task is to enable teachers and preachers around the world to communicate the message of the Bible to others effectively.

The text is user-friendly to enable the busy teacher to grasp subjects in an accessible way and to make the most of their time. Whether you teach in a church service, a student group or home group, we know that you will find life-giving information in these pages. Pass it on!

As those involved in creating this book, we believe it to be unique. Its various approaches all have one underlying aim: to help you know your Bible more thoroughly.

We believe the Bible is an essential ingredient of the Christian life – to appreciate the content of the whole sweep of the books of the Bible, to know its basic doctrines and to know how to apply its message – there is enough here for a lifetime of study!

The core parts of the *CLC Bible Companion* are:

· **Knowing Jesus** (see pages 16–115) – a guide to the person of Jesus Christ: his identity, teaching, encounters and salvation. This section provides an opportunity to explore the impact of Jesus' life, death and resurrection so that we can know him for ourselves.
· **The Bible Book by Book** (see pages 116–405) – provides an overview of the essentials of each book of the Bible. Sometimes we can be so immersed in the details of a particular verse that we do not realise the purpose and importance of each Bible book, so this summary of each whole book of the Bible gives a summary, an outline and

the key teachings, plus application to work out its relevance for today.

· **Bible Teaching** (see pages 406–539) – explores the essential truths of Christianity, such as God, Jesus Christ, the Holy Spirit and Humanity, in a clear and methodical way, to lay and develop a solid foundation for your Christian life.

· **Discovering God's Way** (see pages 540–671) – provides teaching on helping us go deeper in our Christian faith. The teaching is grouped under four main headings: Discovering Jesus Christ, Discovering Prayer, Discovering Discipleship, and Moving on as a Christian. The aim of this section is to develop growth in our Christian life.

· **Living the Christian Life** (see pages 672–787) – shows how we are to work out and apply the message of the Bible at every stage in our Christian life.

· **Resources for the Journey** (see pages 788–845) – provides a listing of key themes with Bible references, a guide to using the teaching in this book on PowerPoint, and an index to the whole book.

We've also included many other resources to help you get even more out of your Bible: maps and charts as background information, for example, maps of Abraham's travels; the exile; charts such as Old Testament festivals; lists of the miracles and parables of Jesus Christ.

As you read through this book, you will find it helpful to open your Bible and look up the references: this will help reinforce the words of the Bible in your heart and mind. This book is designed for use with any translation of the Bible such as the New International Version.

The contemporary approach and design of this book will help make the Bible as accessible as possible. We live in a visual age, so the use of full-colour text and illustration is an important aspect of this book's preparation.

For many people, the Bible is a closed book: it does not mean anything. As you use this book next to your Bible, our hope is that you will be challenged: you will see the way God wants you to live and we trust this book will equip you to serve him even more effectively in his world. Our prayer and hope is that you will hear God speak in a fresh way as you explore and apply its message, first to yourself and then to the lives of those you teach.

Tony Cantale
Martin Manser
Robert Hicks
Larry Stone

The Authority and Inspiration of the Bible

THE terms "authority" and "inspiration" together help us to understand the significance of the Bible for the Christian faith.

The term "authority" describes the fact that the Bible is uniquely capable of leading people from every generation and situation to faith in God through Jesus Christ. No other book in the world has this authority. The Bible, in both the Old and New Testaments, faithfully presents the character of the creator God and declares his invitation for the world to come to him for salvation. The Bible is said to be authoritative in all matters of faith, which means that when it comes to finding out about having a relationship with God, the Bible can be trusted.

The Bible's authority was recognised by the early church. The New Testament documents were originally collected together because they were considered to be an accurate account of the events and significance of the life, death and resurrection of Jesus Christ. The church realised that when the apostles who had been with Jesus and seen him after his resurrection had themselves died, it was vital that the young church was able to pass on their testimony about God's good news. From the beginning, the church also accepted the Jewish Scriptures as an authority for their faith. These were the Scriptures that Jesus himself had known and quoted from, and as the first Christians studied the writings and prophecies, they discovered that they also pointed faithfully to what had happened in Jesus Christ. The

Jewish Scriptures became the "Old" Testament, while the new documents became a "New" Testament. Together, these Scriptures were the official documents of the church, called a *canon* (from the Latin and Greek for "rule", which referred to the church's decision to recognise the authority the documents already had in church life and thought).

Thus, the Bible is said to have authority because God's people have already identified it as being a faithful (written) messenger of God's good news. This is why the Bible is often called "the word of God". Christians understand that the Bible is not filled simply with human messages or accounts of religious experiences, but that through the different human authors of the various books, God declares his word. The authority of the Bible for faith thus leads straight to our second term. The fact that God's message is heard through human words is called the Bible's "inspiration".

Using the term "inspired" about the Bible does not mean that God dictated the words of Scripture to the human authors, who simply acted as secretaries. In that case the human authors would have contributed nothing at all. But on the other hand, calling Scripture "inspired" does not mean that the human authors merely had a good idea, which they wrote down as being a message from God. In actual fact, the inspiration of the Bible does not say much about how the text itself came about. There may have been many different ways by which the authors received God's

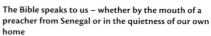

message and wrote it down. This variety would fit well with the multiple genres we find in Scripture.

Inspiration is not so much a theory of the Bible's composition as an affirmation of what the Bible is. Inspiration describes the Bible by referring to both its divine and human authorship at the same time. The Bible is inspired because the message we receive from it is both a collection of human words – with cultural, literary and stylistic characteristics – and the words of the eternal God! The term "inspiration" helps Christians to affirm equally that the Bible is human, and so requires study and effort in order to be understood, and that it is divine, so its message can only be received as the Spirit of God enables faith and understanding.

The terms "inspiration" and "authority" help us to understand what our relationship with the Bible should be. By calling the Bible inspired, we recognise that the Bible is given to us by God and through it he meets with us today. Because God himself speaks through the human words, the Bible really does reveal God's character and his works in the world. As this unique revelation, the Bible is supremely authoritative for the Christian life. By recognising the Bible's authority, we are acknowledging that it is God's word, and not ours, and that is decisively significant for our lives and for the world. We must therefore listen to Scripture, and seek the enlightenment of God's Spirit, to help us understand and apply God's message to our lives.

Understanding the Message

The Bible was written centuries ago over a long period of time by many different people from all walks of life, in a setting different from our own.

When we read a portion of Scripture we should consider:
· the type of writing
· the context it was written in and for
· the reason it was written
· what can it now say to me?

We will discover the joy of reading the Bible:
· if we read while dependent on the Holy Spirit to help us understand it
· if we sincerely want to know more about God and his ways
· if we prayerfully read it to discover its message, rather than primarily as literature or for information
· if we allow our reading to lead us to worship God through prayer and praise and apply what we have learnt, with God's help, to our daily life.

When reading a portion of Scripture we must:
· not take a verse or one part of Scripture out of its context
· not create an opinion based only on one verse or portion – this is the error of cults and those who want to twist the meaning for their own ends
· not think of it as anything other than the word of God – the Scriptures were written by real people in many real situations, under the Holy Spirit's inspiration.

OLD TESTAMENT

"What am I reading?"

NEW TESTAMENT

> " *The unfolding of your words gives light; it gives understanding to the simple.*"
>
> PSALM 119:130

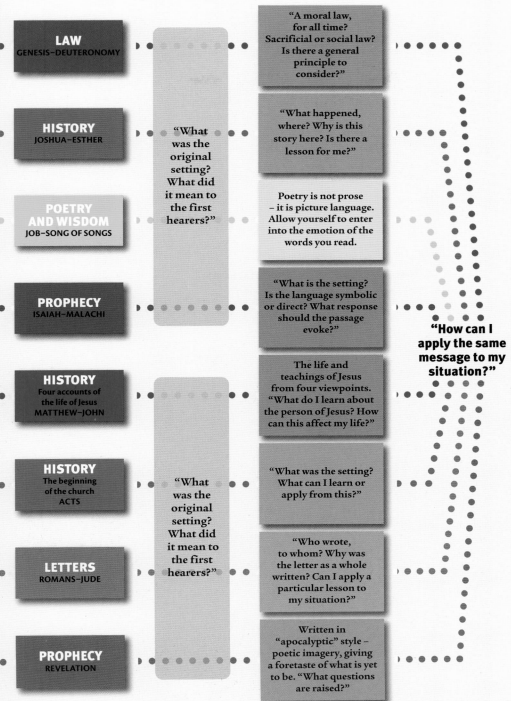

LAW
GENESIS–DEUTERONOMY

HISTORY
JOSHUA–ESTHER

POETRY AND WISDOM
JOB–SONG OF SONGS

PROPHECY
ISAIAH–MALACHI

HISTORY
Four accounts of the life of Jesus
MATTHEW–JOHN

HISTORY
The beginning of the church
ACTS

LETTERS
ROMANS–JUDE

PROPHECY
REVELATION

"What was the original setting? What did it mean to the first hearers?"

"What was the original setting? What did it mean to the first hearers?"

"A moral law, for all time? Sacrificial or social law? Is there a general principle to consider?"

"What happened, where? Why is this story here? Is there a lesson for me?"

Poetry is not prose – it is picture language. Allow yourself to enter into the emotion of the words you read.

"What is the setting? Is the language symbolic or direct? What response should the passage evoke?"

The life and teachings of Jesus from four viewpoints. "What do I learn about the person of Jesus? How can this affect my life?"

"What was the setting? What can I learn or apply from this?"

"Who wrote, to whom? Why was the letter as a whole written? Can I apply a particular lesson to my situation?"

Written in "apocalyptic" style – poetic imagery, giving a foretaste of what is yet to be. "What questions are raised?"

"How can I apply the same message to my situation?"

Knowing Jesus

Jesus Christ has influenced millions of people throughout history. Today over 2 billion people – about one in three of the world's population – claim some allegiance to him. But who is he? Where did he come from? What did he do? What can we learn from his teaching and life? What do his death and resurrection mean today? In this section of the book, we explore Jesus' unique identity and his radical teaching, his powerful encounters and his perfect salvation. Each study consists of the key truth, the main teaching and questions to think about, with the aim of us encountering and knowing Jesus for ourselves.

Knowing Jesus

CONTENTS

See also "Jesus Christ", p.434–445 and
"Discovering Jesus Christ", p.546–587

JESUS' UNIQUE IDENTITY
Jesus in history

KEY TRUTH

Jesus lived in a specific time and place in history, so we can discover many reliable facts about his life, death and resurrection.

THE WORLD OF JESUS

Jesus was born into the Jewish world of first-century Israel. Although some aspects of the first century world were similar to life in today's world, other aspects now seem strange and unfamiliar. To understand Jesus and his message better, it is important to get to know this time and place. Helpfully, it is well documented in various historical sources.

- **Jewish writings after the Old Testament.** At the end of the Old Testament, some of the Jews had returned to their land after exile in Babylon (see Nehemiah and Ezra). The period of time before the start of the New Testament is known as the intertestamental period. A number of Jewish books written during this time can be found in the Apocrypha section of some Bibles. These include the two books of Maccabees, written around 100 BC. 1 and 2 Maccabees tell the story of Judas Maccabeus and his companions, who led a Jewish revolt in 167–164 BC against Antiochus Epiphanes, their Syrian ruler. Later, when the Romans took over the region in 63 BC, many Jews longed for another revolutionary leader like Judas to rescue them from foreign power. These writings record some of the stories and events from the Jews' recent history that would have been well-known and important in Jesus' day.
- **Dead Sea Scrolls.** In 1947, a shepherd found a collection of ancient scrolls in a cave near the Dead Sea. The scrolls from this and ten other caves (also known as the Qumran texts, because the caves are near

the site of Qumran) include copies of every book of the Old Testament except Esther. There are also some commentaries on the Old Testament and other writings that describe the beliefs of some Jews, a group often known as the Essenes. They wrote about a great Messiah who they believed would save them from their troubles. The scrolls help us to understand the beliefs of some Jewish people at the time of Jesus, and remind us that there were many different groups believing different things in the ancient world, much like in society today.

> " *The Word became flesh and made his dwelling among us. We have seen his glory, the glory of the One and Only, who came from the Father, full of grace and truth.*"
>
> JOHN 1:14

- **Josephus.** The Jewish historian Josephus lived from AD 37 to shortly after AD 100. He wrote *The Jewish War*, which recounts what happened to the Jews after the Maccabean revolt. Josephus is the most important source of information outside the New Testament about life in Palestine during the time of Jesus.
- **Roman historians.** During the time of Jesus, Palestine was under the control of the

Bethelehem, birthplace of Jesus, is today a troubled place: a Jewish roadblock on the road to Jerusalem

Roman Empire. Roman historians, such as Tacitus and Suetonius, record how the empire viewed the Jewish people, and also occasionally mention the early Christian movement.

· **Archaeology.** Jesus lived alongside other people with homes and jobs. Archaeologists have found buildings and other items of interest that show what life was like in first-century Palestine. They have also discovered specific locations that match the record of the New Testament, such as the village of Bethany (eg John 11:18) or the Praetorium, the official residence of the Roman governor in Jerusalem (eg John 18:28).

THE LIFE OF JESUS

It is essential to remember that the story of Jesus' life is grounded in real history. By comparing the historical information given by the Gospels (eg Luke 2:1; 3:1) with what is known about the officials they mention, Jesus' birth can be dated about the year 4 BC. He was born in Bethlehem, just south of

Jerusalem, but spent his early years in Nazareth, near the Sea of Galilee, in the north. When he was around thirty years old, he began a ministry of teaching and healing, which took him all over the land. He had many followers, but there were twelve special disciples who were with him throughout his ministry. Jesus' teaching and actions frustrated the Jewish leaders, who were afraid he would disrupt the fragile peace they had with the Romans. In AD 30 or 33, Jesus was arrested by the Jewish authorities and handed over to the Romans to be crucified. On the third day after his burial, some of his followers found that his tomb was empty, and met with him again, alive from the dead (see especially 1 Corinthians 15:1-11).

This account of Jesus' life, drawn from the Gospels, can be matched with other ancient historical sources. For instance, the Jewish historian Josephus recorded the following information about Jesus:

> "At this time there was a wise man who was called Jesus, and his conduct was good, and he was known to be virtuous. And many people from among the Jews and the other

nations became his disciples. Pilate condemned him to be crucified and to die. And those who had become his disciples did not abandon their loyalty to him. They reported that he had appeared to them three days after his crucifixion, and that he was alive. Accordingly they believed that he was the Messiah, concerning whom the Prophets have recounted wonders."

Josephus' work was written around AD 90, so it was within living memory of the life of Jesus. Josephus also tells his readers about John the Baptist and James, the brother of Jesus. The life of Jesus, and the other people and events recorded in the Gospels, were not closely kept secrets, but public knowledge.

THE GOSPELS ABOUT JESUS

Most of our information about Jesus comes from the New Testament, and especially from the four Gospels: Matthew, Mark, Luke and John. "Gospel" means "good news". These books were written to tell the world what was important about the life, death and resurrection of Jesus. They are not complete biographies of Jesus, and they do not give us all the information that we might wish we had. However, they contain all that we need to know in order to understand the significance of Jesus and what he has done for us.

The Gospels in the New Testament can be relied upon as accurate pictures of Jesus. Many of the people and places mentioned in the New Testament Gospels have been verified by other historical documents and archaeology. Luke points out that he had spent much time researching his Gospel and speaking to eyewitnesses (Luke 1:1-4). All the Gospels were written within living memory of Jesus' life, and so the first readers would have been able to check that they were accurate. It is interesting to note that later on, many years after Jesus' time, other stories containing

TO THINK ABOUT

Make a list of the ways in which you normally think/sing/talk about Jesus (eg "Lord", "teacher", etc.).
· How easy do you find it to connect Jesus to his historical time and place? Do you think it is important to make these connections? Why?
· What would you like to know about Jesus that the Gospels do not speak about? Why do you think Matthew, Mark, Luke and John did not write about this?

Choose one of the Gospels and read through it in one sitting.
· What picture of Jesus do you think this writer wanted to give you? Now do the same for the other Gospels.

Read the four accounts of the discovery of Jesus' empty tomb: Matthew 28:1-15; Mark 16:1-8; Luke 24:1-12; John 20:1-18.
· Are there any notable differences in detail? How do you feel about the differences between the Gospels? Are they important? Why or why not?
· What would you say to someone who suggested that the story about Jesus was not true?

It is essential for the Christian faith that Jesus was an historical figure. John 1:14 sums up our message that in Jesus, God came to live among us. If Jesus were not real, our message would not be true. But the New Testament story about Jesus is supported by other historical data. Thank God that we can know him because of Jesus, who lived in a specific time and place in history.

imaginative and fanciful ideas were written about Jesus, such as the Gospel of Thomas, from the second century AD. However, the early Christians refused to believe them and these documents did not become part of the New Testament. On the other hand, the four Gospels were accepted because they gave a clear and unembellished account of Jesus' life and ministry.

It is significant that there are four Gospels in the New Testament, rather than only one. This can sometimes seem confusing, especially when the Gospels contain differences in detail about the same event. For instance, John says that Jesus overturned the money-changers' tables in the temple when he began his preaching and healing ministry (John 2:13-21). Matthew, Mark and Luke say it happened shortly before the end of his life (Matthew 21:12-13; Mark 11:15-17; Luke 19:45-46). Did the event happen twice? Or did one or more of the Gospel writers put it in the wrong place? We must remember that the Gospels do not intend to give us a diary of the events of Jesus' life. The authors arranged their material about Jesus in their own ways in order to help their readers understand the significance of these events. John placed this episode at the beginning of his Gospel because it illustrates how Jesus' ministry was replacing the religion of the temple. Matthew, Mark and Luke want to show how this event led the Jewish authorities to put Jesus to death (see, eg, Luke 19:47). However, this difference does not make their writing less accurate. Good history is not simply a list of facts, but is also a knowledge of why the facts are important. Sometimes the facts need to be arranged in a certain way, or particular elements need to be stressed, so that the significance of Jesus can be understood. The Gospel writers are like film editors, who cut and paste the story of Jesus so that we too can understand him in the way they did. Because Jesus was a living historical figure, we should not be surprised that his life cannot be confined by a single account (see John 21:25). The fact that there are four accounts of his life is something to be celebrated, not ignored. Each Gospel writer provides a unique perspective on Jesus' person and work. Together, the four Gospels help us to meet with the Jesus who lived, died and rose again two thousand years ago.

JESUS' UNIQUE IDENTITY

Jesus the Messiah

KEY TRUTH

Jesus is called "the Messiah" or "Christ" because of his unique role in fulfilling the promises that God made to the Jewish people long ago.

OLD TESTAMENT PROMISES

Throughout the Old Testament, God made it clear that his people Israel were to play a special part in his plan to rescue and restore the world. When God called Abraham, he promised him that his descendants would be a blessing to everyone on the earth (Genesis 12:1-3). As the prophet Isaiah said over 1,000 years later, Israel were supposed to be a light to the nations, revealing the way to worship and serve the true God (eg Isaiah 60:1-3). Through Israel, God would invite the whole world to discover his salvation.

However, the people of Israel kept wandering away from the true God. Instead of being a light to the nations, they copied the practices of the nations around them and worshipped idols. Because they were not faithful to him, God allowed the Israelites to be defeated by their enemies and eventually carried into exile. It was clear that Israel needed to be saved too.

In the Old Testament, God used many individuals to rescue his people from their difficulties: for example, Moses led the Israelites out of slavery in Egypt (see Exodus 1–15); wise and brave leaders like Deborah and Gideon helped the Israelites to defeat their enemies (see Judges); kings like David and Solomon brought honour and wealth to the nation (see 1 Chronicles 29); prophets called on the people to repent and follow the ways of God; and after the exile, a governor named Nehemiah and a priest called Ezra helped to rebuild Jerusalem and the temple.

Despite these, it was never long before Israel needed to be saved again. The great leaders in Israel's history were not able to bring about permanent salvation and blessing for Israel and the world. But still God promised that a day would come when Israel would be saved once and for all. Some of these prophecies spoke about a wonderful leader who would be sent by God to accomplish this salvation. This leader would be greater than Moses (Deuteronomy 18:15-18) and David (2 Samuel 7:12-16). Isaiah's prophecy describes this mysterious person as a just and wise ruler (Isaiah 9:6-7), and as a faithful servant of God (42:1-9) who will deal with Israel's sin (52:13–53:12) and so reveal God's light and salvation to the whole world (42:6; 49:6), just as God had promised.

This servant will be able to accomplish all these things because he will be anointed with God's Spirit (Isaiah 61:1). In the Old Testament, a person was anointed with oil in order to be set apart to do special tasks for God, particularly as a king or priest (eg 1 Samuel 16:13; Leviticus 8:12). Prophets too were set apart by God (eg Jeremiah 1:5). At the end of the Old Testament period, some people in Israel were looking for the greatest prophet, priest and king – the greatest "anointed one" – to come to establish God's permanent kingdom of peace (Zechariah 9:9-10).

JEWISH EXPECTATIONS

In the years between the Old and New Testaments, the expectation that an "anointed one" would come to save Israel grew. Ever since their return from exile, apart from the short period between 140 and 63 BC, the people of Israel had been ruled by a succession of foreign empires: first Persian, then Greek, then Egyptian, then Syrian and finally Roman. Jews longed to be free to rule themselves, and some began regularly using the Hebrew term for "anointed one" – our word Messiah – to describe a coming leader who would liberate them and restore their former glory.

There were many different ideas about what this Messiah would be like. Generally, people thought he would be a king greater than King David, who would lead a successful revolt against foreign powers. In the Dead Sea Scrolls two different Messiahs are expected, one a king and the other a priest. The priestly Messiah would clean out and rebuild the temple in Jerusalem. This was necessary because the temple had been defiled by Israel's foreign rulers – particularly by Antiochus Epiphanes the Syrian, who had built a pagan altar in the temple in 167 BC. Even though Judas Maccabaeus had led a successful military revolt and had reconsecrated the temple in 164 BC, other Jews still looked for the true Messiah to come and bring God's salvation once and for all. What connected these expectations was a belief that the Messiah would fulfil Jewish dreams of greatness.

THE REALITY OF JESUS

The New Testament declares that Jesus is the Messiah who was promised in the Old Testament (Mark 1:1; John 20:31; Acts 18:28). However, while Jesus fulfilled Old Testament prophecies (eg Matthew 1:21-23), he also challenged some Jewish expectations.

· **The birth of Jesus.** Jesus' birth clearly pointed to his unique role as Messiah. The angel Gabriel told Mary that she would give birth to the great king of Israel (Luke 1:32-33). The birth itself took place in Bethlehem, to fulfil the prophecy of Micah

5:2 (Matthew 2:3-6). Angels told some shepherds that the Messiah had been born in Bethlehem (Luke 2:11), and wise men from the east travelled to find the "king of the Jews" (Matthew 2:1-11). When Jesus was first taken to the temple in Jerusalem, Simeon and Anna recognised that he was the Messiah of Israel (Luke 2:25-38), although Simeon also spoke of unexpected suffering (34,35).

· **John the Baptist.** John was sent to prepare the way for Jesus (Luke 1:67-79), by his preaching and baptism (Matthew 3:1-6). He was so popular that people began asking if he was the Messiah, but John told them that the Messiah was coming after him, and pointed them to Jesus (John 1:19-31).

· **Jesus' ministry.** Jesus knew that his ministry of preaching and healing was a fulfilment of Isaiah's prophecy about the Messiah (Isaiah 61:1-2; Luke 4:16-21; 7:18-23). He spoke with greater authority than the leaders of the day (Matthew

> " *But what about you?* " he asked. "*Who do you say I am?*" Simon Peter answered, "*You are the Christ, the Son of the living God.*"

MATTHEW 16:15-16

7:28-29), and declared that he was greater than the prophet Jonah and King Solomon (Matthew 12:38-42). Just like the expected Messiah, he spoke about establishing God's kingdom (Mark 1:14-15).

· **Peter's declaration.** Jesus' twelve disciples had followed him more closely than any others during his ministry. One day, Jesus asked them who they thought he was. Peter exclaimed, "You are the Messiah!" (Matthew 16:13-16; Mark 8:27-29; Luke 9:18-20). People followed Jesus because they

believed he was the one God had promised to send to rescue Israel (Luke 24:21).

- **The Messianic secret.** In the Gospels, when people recognised that Jesus was the Messiah, Jesus often told them not to tell anyone else (Matthew 16:20; Mark 8:30; Luke 4:41; 9:21). He referred to himself as "Son of man" rather than as "messiah". Jesus knew that people would misunderstand what he had come to do. They thought that the Messiah would be a great political leader who would deal with the Romans and set up a new national government (John 6:15). Instead, Jesus taught his disciples that, as the Messiah, he would suffer humiliation and death and then rise again in order to deal with Israel's greatest enemy: not Rome, but sin and death (Mark 8:31; John 12:31-36; Matthew 26:26-28). The disciples did not fully understand this until after the resurrection.
- **Jesus' trial and crucifixion.** In the week before his death, Jesus was welcomed into Jerusalem as a king (Luke 19:29-40), and he cleared the temple of merchants and money-changers (19:45-46). He was acting as God's promised Messiah! However, the Jewish authorities saw him as a threat to their way of life (see John 11:47-53), so they worked out a way to get rid of him. They arrested and tried him for pretending to be the Messiah (Luke 22:66-71). They accused

The River Jordan, where Jesus was baptised by John the Baptist, and the Golden Gate, Jerusalem, through which Jesus entered to the acclaim of the crowds

him of trying to lead a revolt against the Roman emperor (23:2), and asked the Roman governor Pilate to crucify him. On the cross, a notice was placed over Jesus' head that read, "This is the King of the Jews". Many people mocked Jesus, because they could not believe that God's true Messiah would be killed on a cross. (23:35-39).
- **The resurrection.** The disciples thought that the crucifixion was the end of their hope that Jesus was the Messiah. But on the third day, Jesus was raised from the dead. When he appeared to them, he explained that they had misunderstood the prophecies of the Old Testament (Luke 24:25-27,44-47). Jesus had not failed in his role as Messiah; rather, by his death and resurrection, Jesus had accomplished what God had promised!

THE PREACHING OF
THE EARLY CHRISTIANS

After Pentecost, the disciples proclaimed the good news that Jesus is God's Messiah (eg Acts 2:36; 18:5). Jesus sent his disciples into all the world, not just to Jews (Matthew 28:19). The message for Jews is that their

TO THINK ABOUT

Read some of the Old Testament passages about the Messiah (eg 2 Samuel 7:1-16; Psalm 110; Isaiah 42:1-9; 49:1-6; 52:13–53:12; Zechariah 9:9-10).

· If you did not know that Jesus was the Messiah, what type of person would you be expecting to fulfil these prophecies? What would he do? How would he do it?

John the Baptist had pointed other people to Jesus, yet he still wondered if Jesus really was the Messiah (Luke 7:18-23).

· Why do you think this was?
· Knowing what you know now, after the crucifixion and resurrection, how would you respond to John?

The Jews expected their Messiah to be the greatest prophet, priest and king.

· Think about what a prophet did in the Old Testament. How was Jesus the greatest prophet? Now do the same for priest and king.
· How did Jesus fulfil Jewish hopes? How did he change them?
· What does it mean for you to call Jesus "Christ" or "Messiah"? How has your understanding changed through this study?

The Christian message is rooted in the prophecies and hopes of the Old Testament. Jesus came as God's Messiah to fulfil these prophecies, and open God's kingdom to the whole world. Thank God that in Jesus Christ both Israel and the world have been rescued from sin, and have the opportunity to share his salvation.

Messiah has come to fulfil all God's promises, even if he has done so in a surprising way (2 Corinthians 1:20). The message to non-Jews is that because the Messiah has come, God's light and salvation are now available to everyone (Ephesians 2:11-22).

The Greek form of Messiah – our word "Christ" – became the most common way for early believers to refer to Jesus. But remember that "Christ" is a title, not a surname. Followers of Jesus Christ were soon called "Christians" (Acts 11:26).

JESUS' UNIQUE IDENTITY
Jesus, the true human

KEY TRUTH

Jesus was fully human in every way; in fact, he shows us what it really means to be human.

THE MAN FROM NAZARETH

From the second century AD, some people claimed that Jesus had not really been human, but that he had only seemed to do human things, suffer and die. This idea may be reflected in 2 John 7. They could not understand how Jesus, the divine Son of God, could ever have been a man with flesh and blood. These views are known as "Docetism", from the Greek word "to appear" or "to seem". Early church leaders, such as Ignatius and Irenaeus, argued against Docetism, and the church's creeds clearly affirmed that Jesus was a human. It is important to note that Docetism arose around the second century, well after the events of Jesus' life. The people who met Jesus during his earthly life had no reason to doubt that he was a human being, just like them. The New Testament consistently describes Jesus in human terms:

- **Birth and early years.** Although Jesus was conceived in Mary by the power of the Holy Spirit (Matthew 1:20; Luke 1:35), he still had a very human birth (Luke 2:6) and required his mother's care and attention (Luke 2:7) and Joseph's protection (Matthew 2:13-15). Over the following years, Jesus grew up in age, strength and wisdom, just like any child would (Luke 2:40,52). We do not know very much about Jesus' family life; however, it is clear from the Gospels that his parents, brothers and sisters were well known in their home town of Nazareth (Matthew 13:54-56; Mark 6:1-3). Jesus' early years were so normal that the people who had seen him grow up were

surprised that he could teach about God with authority (see also Luke 2:46-47) and do great miracles – they thought he was just a carpenter, as Joseph had been before him. In the mid-second century AD, imaginative stories began to be written about Jesus' early life, claiming he had superhuman powers. For instance, in the Infancy Gospel of Thomas, he moulds some birds out of clay and then brings them to life! While these stories were quite popular at the time, the church never accepted them as true. As the New Testament suggests, until the beginning of his public ministry, Jesus seems to have grown up just like any other first-century Jewish boy.

- **Physical, emotional and spiritual life.** Jesus was fully human in every way. He had bodily needs for food (Matthew 4:2; 21:18; Luke 4:2), water (John 4:7; 19:28), and rest (Matthew 8:24; Mark 4:38; Luke 8:23; John 4:6). He accepted the hospitality of others during his ministry (John 12:1-2, also Luke 8:1-3), and was often found at a party! He experienced the full range of human emotions, including joy (see Luke 7:34), friendship and love (John 15:12-15), compassion (Matthew 9:36; Mark 1:41; Luke 7:13), grief (John 11:33-35), anger (Mark 3:5; John 2:13-17) and anguish (Luke 22:44). In his spiritual life, Jesus had to draw strength from God in prayer (Luke 6:12; 9:28) and resist the temptations of Satan (Matthew 4:1-11, also Luke 4:13). The first Christians knew that Jesus' work of salvation was effective for them because he had been completely human, just like them in every way except for sin (Hebrews 2:14-18; 4:15).

- **Jesus' miraculous power.** Sometimes we think that Jesus' miracles prove that he was divine. However, the people who saw them did not automatically think this. They presumed he was a human who was able to use heavenly or demonic power (Luke 11:15-16). Jesus explained that he worked miracles by "the finger of God" (Luke 11:20); he was a human being filled with the Holy Spirit of God (Luke 4:18-21). Other humans also performed miracles (eg 1 Kings 17:17-24; Acts 3:1-10).

- **Death and burial.** The Gospels describe the agony Jesus endured on the cross (Matthew 27:33-50; Mark 15:33-37; Luke 23:44-46). John records that he saw blood and water flowing out of Jesus' side after his death, proving that he really was dead (John 19:33-35). Jesus was buried in a tomb, and everyone expected that his body would rot away (the women brought spices for it on the third day, Luke 24:1).

- **Bodily resurrection.** After his resurrection, Jesus remained a real human being, even though his resurrected body was able to do extraordinary things (Luke 24:31,36). He ate with his disciples and invited them to touch his body to prove he was not a ghost (Luke 24:37-43; John 20:27).

The message of the first Christians was grounded in the knowledge that Jesus, who had brought God's life and salvation, was a real human being (1 John 1:1-3), both before and after his resurrection (Acts 17:31; 1 Corinthians 15:17).

THE SON OF MAN

Jesus knew that he had a special status among other humans. In the Gospels, he refers to himself over fifty times as "the Son of Man" (eg Mark 2:10; 10:45). The Aramaic phrase that stands behind this title can simply mean

> "*That which was from the beginning, which we have heard, which we have seen with our eyes, which we have looked at and our hands have touched – this we proclaim concerning the Word of life. The life appeared; we have seen it and testify to it, and we proclaim to you the eternal life, which was with the Father and has appeared to us.*"

1 JOHN 1:1-2

"a human being", but it has special significance because of its use in Daniel 7:13. There, Daniel sees a vision of "one like a son of man" approaching the throne of heaven and being given authority by God to rule the whole world. By calling himself "the Son of Man", Jesus is referring both to the fact that he belongs to the family of humanity and to his unique status within that family.

When Jesus calls himself "the Son of Man", he claims that he is the one human being to whom God has given authority over everything (see Mark 14:62). Jesus uses this power and authority to seek out and save the lost (Luke 19:10). He brings salvation through the weakness of his humanity – ultimately through his suffering and death in Jerusalem (Mark 8:31; 14:41). In the future, as the Son of Man, Jesus will be the standard of judgement for all other humans (Luke 18:8).

THE SECOND ADAM

The role of the Son of Man – to exercise responsible authority over the earth – was nothing new. In Genesis 1, humans were created on the sixth day, after everything else,

as the pinnacle of God's work. God gave humans a task appropriate to their lofty status – he instructed them to act as good stewards of his world (Genesis 1:28). Adam (whose name simply means "man") and his wife Eve were supposed to be role models for the rest of humanity, living with God in fellowship and obedience. However, through their distrust of God's word (Genesis 3:1-5) and disobedience (Genesis 3:6), this good order was disrupted (Genesis 3:14-19). The Old Testament does continue to speak of God's vision for humanity (eg Psalm 8); however, in reality, humans are now incapable of living in the way God intended. Sin and death get in the way.

If the story of Adam reveals what went wrong, the story of Jesus is the story of humanity as it should be. Jesus lived in constant fellowship with his heavenly Father. He exercised responsible authority over the world around him (eg calming the storm, Mark 4:39; feeding the crowds, Matthew 14:19-20). Jesus was not just another member of the human race; he was the one true human, the one who revealed human life as God had always intended it.

One of the ways the first Christians expressed this was by calling Jesus "the second Adam" or "the last Adam". Paul contrasts the disobedience of Adam with the obedience of Jesus, and then he contrasts the effects of their lives: whereas Adam's disobedience brought death to all, Jesus' obedience brought life to all! (1 Corinthians 15:45; Romans 5:12-21). It is sometimes suggested that John's Gospel envisages Jesus as the second Adam too. Just before his crucifixion, at the climax of John's Gospel, Jesus is presented by Pilate to the crowds with the words, "Here is the man!" (John 19:5). Whatever Pilate himself may have thought about Jesus, Christians have rightly seen a deeper level of meaning in these words: "Here is the true man! Here is the second Adam!"

THE IMAGE OF GOD

Humans were created in the image of God (Genesis 1:27). This means that among all creatures, humans were to embody the kind of life that God has, and reflect his glory in the rest of creation (Psalm 8:5). Since the fall, the image of God in humanity has been broken and marred by sin. However, Jesus is the perfect and complete image of God (Colossians 1:15; Hebrews 1:3), fully reflecting God's glory in his humanity (John 1:14).

Of course, Jesus is much more than the perfect human being. But we must remember that Jesus resists sin and reflects God's glory because he is being truly human, not superhuman. Jesus reveals that sin is not a normal part of humanity as God intended it; it is abnormal. As a human being, Jesus lived in dependence on God's Holy Spirit, and was raised from the dead. This is what it means for us to be human too (Philippians 2:5-8). Jesus' perfect humanity is the hope of our salvation – we can be truly human as we join his family and are made in his image, which is the image of God (Romans 8:29).

TO THINK ABOUT

Read one of the following passages: Matthew 4:1-11; John 11; Luke 22:39-46.

· In what way does this passage reveal Jesus' humanity?
· How is Jesus' response different from the one you might make?
· What does this passage teach you about living a truly human life? Now do the same for the other passages.

The first Christians believed that Jesus revealed what true humanity looked like. Think about the ways in which our society describes human life. Make a list of any key descriptions. Now make a list of the main characteristics of Jesus' life. You may find it helpful to look at some Bible passages: Philippians 2:5-8; Hebrews 2:14-18; 4:15.

· What differences can you see between the two lists?
· Why is Jesus different? Is it because he is divine? Or because he is more fully human?

There is an old saying: "to err is human, to forgive is divine".

· Is the first part of this saying correct? Why, or why not?
· What about death? What place does death have in human life?
· How has this study on Jesus' humanity changed your understanding of your own humanity?

One of the early church fathers explained that Jesus became like us, so that we can become like him! Thank Jesus that he has shared our humanity completely, and that he has revealed what humanity is really supposed to be. Ask for the strength of his Holy Spirit, to live a life of obedience and responsible authority, just like Jesus.

JESUS' UNIQUE IDENTITY
Jesus, the Son of God

KEY TRUTH

Jesus' understanding of his mission and the events of his life reveal his unique relationship with God and his true identity as the Son of the Father.

"JESUS IS THE SON OF GOD"

The declaration of Jesus as the Son of God was central to the faith and preaching of the first Christians, and continues to be so to this day. Mark tells his readers at the beginning of his Gospel that the Jesus whose story he is about to recount is "the Son of God" (Mark 1:1). The first message preached by Paul after his encounter with the risen Jesus on the road to Damascus was that "he is the Son of God" (Acts 9:20). In 1 John, the confession that Jesus is God's Son is seen as the key to the whole Christian life (1 John 4:15; 5:5,10,12). However, the first Christians did not invent this belief; it is grounded in the life, teaching and mission of Jesus himself.

BACKGROUND

Jesus' disciples would already have been familiar with the term "son of God" from two main contexts.

- **The Old Testament.** The people of Israel knew that they had a special relationship with the true God. When God had rescued them from slavery in Egypt, he had sent a message to Pharaoh through Moses, saying, "Israel is my firstborn son. Let my son go so that he may worship me" (Exodus 4:22-23; see also Hosea 11:1). In the ancient Middle East, as in many places today, the firstborn son had a special status within family life: he enjoyed the closest relationship with his father and often spoke and acted on the father's behalf. Among all the nations of the world, Israel was God's firstborn son, enjoying his lavish love and blessing and

being called to act on his behalf in the world (eg Deuteronomy 7). Later, the king of Israel was also seen as the "son of God", because of God's promise to David in 2 Samuel 7:14. The king represented in one individual what the whole nation was supposed to be. Psalm 2, which was possibly sung at the coronation of kings in Israel, mentions the close relationship with God that the king enjoyed, as well as his special responsibilities to act on God's behalf (see also Psalm 89:19-37). Of course, it soon became clear that neither the nation of Israel nor the king were fulfilling their responsibilities as God's "son". Passages in the Dead Sea Scrolls indicate that at least some Jews expected the coming Messiah to be the true "son of God".

- **Pharaohs, kings and emperors.** Israel was not the only nation to use the term "son of God" to describe their ruler. In the ancient Near East, both Egypt and Babylon also gave this title to their pharaohs and kings. For them, it highlighted the special relationship the king was thought to enjoy with the gods, and so underlined his authority to rule. Whereas in Israel the use of the term did not mean that either the king or the nation was in any sense divine (but merely a human representative of God), this distinction was not as clear for other nations, who thought that the gods might adopt heroic leaders as divine sons. For instance, in the fourth century BC, Alexander the Great declared himself to be a son of the god Zeus, and expected actually

Ancient olive trees in the Garden of Gethsemane

to become a god after his death. He asked his subjects to worship him as divine during his lifetime! In the Roman Empire it was commonly believed that an emperor became a god at his death; his successor was then called a "divine son", or a "son of god". This belief was inscribed on some Roman coins, which have been discovered by archaeologists. For instance, the penny that Jesus asked to see in Mark 12:13-17 was probably marked with the inscription "Augustus Tiberius Caesar, Son of the Divine Augustus".

The early Christians proclaimed Jesus to be the true "son of God" written about in the Old Testament. They did so in a world where the term was used as a political title for emperors who demanded worship. However, they also knew that Jesus had transformed the meaning of the term, because he was the Son of God in a new and unique way.

THE SON'S MISSION

In one of his parables, Jesus tells the story of a man who owned a vineyard. He leased the vineyard to some tenants and then went away for a long time. When it came to the harvest, he sent servants back to the vineyard to collect his share of the produce. However, the tenants attacked his servants and chased them away. Eventually, the man sent his own son, thinking the tenants would respect him. But instead they murdered the son, and so faced the owner's judgement (Matthew 21:33-39). Jesus' hearers knew from the Old

Testament that the nation of Israel was the vineyard (see Isaiah 5:1-7; Psalm 80:8-18), and the Jewish leaders could tell that they were the tenants who were supposed to care for it (Matthew 21:45). The owner was, of course, God himself; his servants were the prophets who had been sent to warn Israel to produce a crop of righteousness for God (see John the Baptist's message in Luke 3:8). In the parable, Jesus is the owner's son: he has been sent after all the prophets to turn the tenants from their wicked ways and make the vineyard productive once more.

Just as the Old Testament background suggests, Jesus as the Son of God came to accomplish the Father's work. The Son is the Father's chief representative who can act with the Father's authority. Peter recognised that Jesus was not just another prophet, but that he was "the Messiah, the Son of the living God" (Matthew 16:16) – Peter had recognised that Jesus had a unique role in bringing God's plan to its climax. Jesus was the Father's Son! Sometimes people called Jesus the "son of David", which is a reminder of God's promise in 2 Samuel 7:14 that the great coming king in the line of David would be the son of God (eg Mark 10:47). In John 1:49 Jesus is declared to be both "the king of Israel" and "the Son of God", showing the clear connection between these two terms.

From the earliest days of his earthly life, Jesus was aware that he had been sent to work in his Father's business, just as a firstborn son would be (Luke 2:49; John 8:42). To call Jesus "the Son of God" is a recognition that Jesus acts completely on his Father's behalf (John 10:36-37), so that whatever he does, it is what the Father wants (John 5:19). As God's Son, Jesus fulfils all God's promises from the Old Testament (2 Corinthians 1:19-20).

THE SON'S RELATIONSHIP WITH THE FATHER

Jews have always been careful about the terms they use to speak to and about God. Although

> " *And when the centurion, who stood there in front of Jesus, heard his cry and saw how he died, he said, 'Surely this man was the Son of God!'* "
>
> MARK 15:39

God's personal name (in Hebrew, YHWH) was revealed to Moses in Exodus 3:14, Jews tended to avoid using it in case they broke the third commandment (see Exodus 20:7). In Jesus' day, they used other less personal terms, such as "God", "Lord", "the Blessed One" (Mark 14:61), or simply "Heaven" (Mark 11:30).

Jesus, however, used the most intimate language to speak about his relationship with God. In the four Gospels, he consistently speaks of God as "Father" around 150 times (around 100 times in John's Gospel alone). In the garden of Gethsemane, just before his arrest, Jesus prayed using the term "Abba", which is an everyday Aramaic term meaning "Daddy" that expresses the closest relationship of love and trust between a child and his father (Mark 14:36). As the Son of God, Jesus has seen the Father (John 6:46), and so is able to make him known to others (Luke 10:22; John 1:18).

Just as Jesus trusts the Father, so the Father trusts Jesus as his Son to do his will (Matthew 11:27). At two key points in Jesus' ministry, God's voice is heard saying, "This is my beloved Son with whom I am well pleased": at his baptism (Matthew 3:17; Mark 1:11; Luke 3:22) and his transfiguration (Matthew 17:5; Mark 9:7; Luke 9:35).

THE SON'S TRUE IDENTITY

Key aspects of Jesus' life helped the first Christians to realise that he was the "Son of God" in a new and unique way.
· **His incarnation.** Jesus was conceived by the power of the Holy Spirit of God, rather

The Roman soldier who watched Jesus die exclaimed, "Truly this man was God's Son" (Matthew 27:54; Mark 15:39).
· What might he have meant by this?
· What did the Gospel writers mean when they used this term? Did it have a different level of meaning for them?

The apostle John describes Jesus as the Son more than any other writer in the New Testament. Read through the letter of 1 John.
· How does John use this title for Jesus?
· Why do you think he uses it, rather than any other?
· How has your understanding of Jesus as the Son of God changed through this study?

Read Romans 8:12-17 and Galatians 4:1-7.
· What is the significance of the term "Abba" in these passages?
· How is our relationship with God similar to Jesus'? How is it different?

Jesus taught his disciples to pray using the term "Father". He enables us to relate to God in a completely new way. Thank God that he sent his Son Jesus to be our Saviour, so that we too can be his children. Then pray the prayer that Jesus taught his disciples (Matthew 6:9-13; Luke 11:2-4).

---

than by a human father (Matthew 1:18,20; Luke 1:35). Jesus also consistently spoke of how he had "come from the Father" (eg John 16:28). Whereas for other humans, birth is the beginning of life, Jesus' birth was an incarnation – he had existed as the Son of God before his human birth. Unlike the pagan rulers, Jesus was not an adopted son of the gods, but the eternal Son of God.
· **Recognition by Satan and demons.** Whereas Jesus' true identity was hidden from his disciples during his earthly ministry, it was recognised by Satan (Matthew 4:3,6; Luke 4:3,9) and by demons (eg Luke 8:28).
· **His resurrection and ascension.** Jesus was put to death because of his claim to be speaking and acting as the Son of God (see Luke 22:70-71). His resurrection was God's confirmation that Jesus had spoken the truth about himself. Paul pointed to the resurrection as the revelation, or declaration, of Jesus' true identity as the Son of God (Romans 1:4). After his resurrection, Jesus returned to the Father (John 16:28; 20:17) to be in the place of honour at his right hand (Acts 7:56; Hebrews 1:2-3).
· **His work of salvation.** The first Christians knew that Jesus had given them a new, intimate relationship with God (eg Galatians 4:4-6). As they made sense of this, they realised Jesus could only do this if he himself were God's Son in a unique way – if he fully shared the same divine nature as his Father. When they looked back over his life and teachings, they saw that this was in fact what Jesus was all along. The term "Son of God" had been enriched and transformed. Jesus the Son is to be trusted and worshipped just like his Father.

JESUS' UNIQUE IDENTITY
Jesus, wisdom and Word

KEY TRUTH

The New Testament proclaims Jesus as the one through whom the whole of creation has life and salvation: he is the human embodiment of the wisdom and Word of God!

WORDS OF WISDOM

Throughout history, people have recognised and valued the practical knowledge that has enabled them to live life well. This wisdom has been handed on from one generation to the next, often within the family context, but also through formal education and religious teaching. Wise men and women have usually enjoyed honoured positions in their societies. Their wisdom was not simply an accumulation of facts, but rather a deep understanding of the way the world works, and of how to live successfully in it. Sometimes these wise words were written down, as in the ancient Egyptian document *The Instruction of Amenemope* from around 1100 BC, just before the time of Solomon. At other times, groups of wise people have gathered together to share ideas and discuss their understanding of the world, such as the Greek philosophers (the word "philosopher" means "lover of wisdom"). Often travelling religious teachers would share their wise sayings with their followers and hearers.

God's people have their own tradition of wisdom, stretching back into the Old Testament. King Solomon was known as the wisest king who ever lived (1 Kings 4:29-34). Some of his sayings were collected, along with others, into the book of Proverbs. The books of Job and Ecclesiastes are also wisdom literature, as are some Psalms and some of the prophets (eg Psalm 37; Isaiah 28:23-29). A key message of Old Testament wisdom is that the way to live well in the world is to live in the knowledge of God's holy presence: the fear of the Lord is the beginning of wisdom (eg Job 28:28; Psalm 111:10; Proverbs 1:7; 9:10). (Fear here means great respect, not dread.) Wisdom was pictured as a woman, standing on a street corner warning people of what would happen to them if they refused to listen to her teaching (Proverbs 1:20-33). If they did listen to her, then they would find happiness and life (Proverbs 3:13-18). In one of the inter-testamental Jewish works, called Sirach or Ecclesiasticus, readers are invited to put wisdom's yoke on their necks in order to find life and rest (Sirach 51:26-27).

When people met Jesus they were amazed by his wise teachings (Matthew 13:54) and called him a rabbi (eg John 1:38; 3:2) – a travelling Jewish teacher, often regarded as being wise. They had never heard such teaching as his. He was able to confound the Jewish religious leaders with his wise answers to their questions (Mark 12:13-34). Jesus knew that he was a messenger of wisdom (Luke 11:49), and just like the wisdom tradition, he sometimes spoke in riddles (eg Matthew 22:41-46), while his parables were meant to puzzle people and make them think (Mark 4:11-12). However, Jesus did not just repeat the wisdom of the world around him, or of the Old Testament; he taught new things with authority (Matthew 13:52; Mark 1:22). His stories and teachings revealed the way the world really is, and what life lived in God's holy presence should look like. Jesus described those who listened to him as wise, while those who rejected him were foolish (Matthew 7:24-27). Jesus' own words and

A Jewish Torah. Jesus told his listeners that the scriptures spoke of him and his relationship with his Father God

completion (8:31). Wisdom is understood as God's agent of creation.

Incredibly, Paul uses the same language to describe Jesus' role in creation! In Colossians, Jesus is described as "the firstborn of all creation", who was before all things so that all things might be created through him (1:15-17; also Hebrews 1:2). Jesus has taken the place, the role, of wisdom: it is Jesus who was with God in the beginning and who is God's agent of creation. The wise ordering of the cosmos, in all its immensity and detail, was accomplished by God through Jesus Christ. As wisdom, Jesus is the source of good order within creation.

· **Wisdom and salvation.** Since the world was created by the wisdom of God, the way to live in harmony with both God and the

teachings have taken the place of those of Wisdom. It is now Jesus' yoke that brings life and rest (Matthew 11:28-30). As Peter once said to Jesus, "You have the words of eternal life!" (John 6:68). When placed alongside even the wisest king from Israel's history – King Solomon – Jesus is far wiser! (Matthew 12:42).

THE WISDOM OF GOD
Jesus was not just a wise man who spoke wise words; the New Testament declares that he is the human embodiment of God's own wisdom (1 Corinthians 1:24,30).

· **Wisdom and creation.** Wisdom language is used in the Old Testament to describe the way in which God created the world (Psalm 104:24; 136:5; Proverbs 3:19-20). When God's people look at creation, they know that it has not been thrown together randomly, but that it reflects the wise ordering of God. In Proverbs, wisdom is seen as the first of all God's works, brought forth before all the rest of creation (8:22,26). Wisdom was with God, standing right beside him as he created the world (8:27-30), and rejoicing with him at its

> " *I*n the beginning was the Word, and the Word was with God, and the Word was God. He was with God in the beginning. Through him all things were made; without him nothing was made that has been made."
>
> JOHN 1:1-3

world is to live wisely. The book of Proverbs constantly contrasts wise people, who enjoy God's favour, with foolish people, who will end up in destruction (eg 1:32-33). However, because of sin, humans are unable to find wisdom themselves. The Old Testament sees wisdom as a gift of God (see 1 Kings 3:5-28), which had been especially given to the nation of Israel in their law so that they could show the rest of the world how to live in fellowship with God

(Deuteronomy 4:5-8). Of course, Israel also went astray, and needed to be rescued themselves. In another inter-testamental Jewish work called the Wisdom of Solomon, wisdom is praised for rescuing God's people from their troubles: God's wisdom even led the Israelites out of their slavery in Egypt (Wisdom of Solomon 10:1-21). "God loves nothing so much as the person who lives with wisdom" (Wisdom of Solomon 7:28)!

Jesus is the embodiment of this saving wisdom. In Colossians, Paul goes on from noting Jesus' role in creation (1:15-17) to describe his role in salvation (1:18-20). Just as Jesus was "the firstborn of all creation", so too he is the "firstborn from the dead" – he leads the way from sin and death into God's kingdom, just as wisdom led the Israelites out of slavery into freedom. He does this through his death and resurrection, which is considered foolishness by unbelievers, but is in fact the very wisdom of God (1 Corinthians 1:18-25; see also the reaction of the Greek philosophers in Athens to Paul's preaching, Acts 17:32). This wise plan of salvation was kept hidden for ages past, but has now been revealed to all (Ephesians 3:8-10). Jesus as the Wisdom of God shows us that to be saved means to be set free to live in the way God always intended (see Matthew 11:28-30).

· **Wisdom and God.** How can you separate God's wisdom from God himself? For the Jews, God and his wisdom had the closest possible relationship. Wisdom was "with God" at the beginning (Proverbs 8:30). In the Wisdom of Solomon, wisdom is described as "a breath of the power of God, and a pure emanation of the glory of the Almighty ... a reflection of eternal light, a spotless mirror of the working of God, and an image of his goodness" (7:25-26). To say that God's wisdom has done something or that God has done something is the same thing.

The first Christians realised that because Jesus was God's Wisdom he had the closest possible relationship with the Father. Hebrews calls him "the reflection of God's glory and the exact imprint of God's very being" (1:3). As Wisdom, Jesus shares the being of the Father so completely that whatever Jesus says and does reveals exactly who the Father is and what he wants for his world.

THE WORD OF GOD

The first chapter of John's Gospel famously introduces Jesus as "the Word of God". For John, this term had a very similar meaning to the concept of wisdom. God's Word is the way in which God accomplishes things: he created everything by his Word (eg Genesis 1; Psalm 33:6), and his Word was given to Israel in the law and the prophets to guide them in the way of salvation (eg Psalm 119:105). God's Word is the reason and purpose of creation; to hear and respond to God's Word is to be saved. Just like Wisdom, it is difficult to distinguish God's Word from God himself.

John declares that Jesus is God's Word: he was with God in the beginning (John 1:1-2); he was the agent of creation (1:3) and continues to give light and life to the world (1:4,9); he brings knowledge and salvation that is even greater than that of Moses and the law of Israel (1:17). Moreover, with Jesus, God's Word is no longer simply a message that is spoken and heard: God's Word becomes flesh, and so can be seen too (1:14). Jesus' human life completely embodies the life-giving Word of God. This is what the church means when it speaks about the incarnation: God's eternal Word has become a human life – the life of Jesus.

Just as words are carried out of our mouths by the force of our breath, so Jesus, the Word of God, came from the Father in the power of the Spirit. The first Christians used the idea of God's "Word" being spoken to describe the activity of the three persons of

TO THINK ABOUT

Think about the different ways in which you use words in your daily life.
- What can words do? Do they always do what you want them to do? Why, or why not?

Isaiah 55:11 reminds us that God's word always accomplishes what he intends.
- Where do we hear about God's word in the Old Testament? (Try starting with Genesis 1; Deuteronomy 30, especially verse 14; and Ezekiel 37:1-14.)
- What does God intend his word to do? What does it in fact accomplish?

Now read John 1:1-18 and Hebrews 1:1-2.
- What does it mean to call Jesus "the Word of God"? How does Jesus relate to the words of God you looked at in the Old Testament?
- What does it mean to call Jesus "the Wisdom of God"? Does this add anything to our understanding of him? If so, what?

- How does this understanding of Jesus as the Wisdom and Word of God help to make sense of his teachings?
- What would you say to someone who claimed that Jesus was just a very wise teacher, and no more?

As the Word and Wisdom of God, Jesus is the one who first brought life to the world in creation, and still brings life to it in salvation – all things were made through him and for him! He is able to do this because he completely shares God's being: as John says, he is with God, and he is God. Thank God that because his Wisdom and Word are fully embodied in Jesus, we can know him personally and live in the way he always intended. Ask for forgiveness for the times you have lived foolishly, and pray for the strength of his Spirit to live wisely, following Jesus the Wisdom of God.

the Trinity: the Father speaks; Jesus the Son is the Word that is spoken; the Spirit is the breath of God which carries forth his Word. The doctrine of the Trinity is essential to understand the way in which God communicates his Word with his world – he does so as a Father, through his Son, in the power of the Spirit.

JESUS' UNIQUE IDENTITY
Jesus the Lord

KEY TRUTH

Jesus is the true Saviour and rightful ruler of the world, who is worthy of worship and obedience.

"JESUS IS LORD"

Along with the term "Messiah" or "Christ", "Lord" is the most common title given to Jesus in the New Testament. In the letters, Jesus is repeatedly referred to as "the Lord Jesus Christ" (eg Romans 1:7; 5:1; 15:6; 1 Corinthians 1:2,7-8,10; James 1:1; 1 Peter 1:3 etc.). In fact, the confession that "Jesus is Lord" was seen by Paul as the distinctive mark of Christian faith, along with belief in Jesus' resurrection (Romans 10:9). The recognition of Jesus' lordship is a sure sign that God's Spirit is at work in a person's life: no one can say "Jesus is Lord" except by the Holy Spirit (1 Corinthians 12:3).

BACKGROUND

The word "lord" (in Greek, *kyrios*) was common in New Testament times, and was used in a number of contexts.

- **Social world.** Most simply, the word "lord" is a term of respect, used to address someone who is superior in status, knowledge or power. In the Gospels, the word is often used for Jesus in his role as teacher (eg Luke 11:1), and is sometimes translated simply as "Sir" (eg Mark 7:28). It was also commonly used by slaves or servants to address their owners or masters (see Ephesians 6:5), and so was a term indicating submission to authority.
- **Religious world.** Many ancient religions, especially in Egypt, Syria, Asia Minor and Greece, spoke about their gods and goddesses as "lords". It was used as a term of address in prayer, and referred to the

power and authority the gods were thought to have over the lives of their worshippers, who were often seen as slaves. Paul refers to these "many gods and lords" in 1 Corinthians 8:5.

- **Political world.** It was common to refer to political rulers as "lords" (see Jesus' comment in Mark 10:42). However, in the first-century Roman world, there was only supposed to be one lord – the Roman emperor, or Caesar. He was the one who held the position of authority over everyone else in his empire, and he demanded the loyalty of his subjects by asking them to confess "Caesar is Lord". Some early Christians were persecuted and killed because they refused to make this confession.
- **Biblical world.** The Jewish people had a particular use for the word "lord". Although God had revealed his personal name to them as YHWH (see Exodus 3:13-15), his people usually tried to avoid using this name in their speech because they were afraid of breaking the third commandment (Exodus 20:7). Instead, when Jews read the Hebrew Scriptures, they substituted God's name YHWH with the word *adonai,* which means "my Lord". When the Hebrew Scriptures were translated into Greek around the third century BC, the Greek word kyrios was used to translate YHWH, because it also meant "lord", just like *adonai.* In many English translations of the Old Testament, the presence of the Hebrew YHWH is signified by "LORD", all in upper

case letters. Many of the first Christians were Jews, who would have been familiar with both the Hebrew Bible and its Greek translation, the Septuagint. For them, the title "Lord" brought to mind both God's personal name, and the fact that God was indeed the rightful ruler of Israel (Exodus 20:2) and of the whole world (Psalm 24:1).

Calling Jesus "Lord" draws on all of these backgrounds. Jesus is the good and wise master of his disciples; he is the true ruler of all the world; and most amazingly of all, he is God!

LORD OF CREATION

Jesus demonstrated through his miracles that he has authority over the created world. When he calmed the sea, saving his disciples' boat from sinking, they wonder, "Who is this, that he commands even the winds and the water, and they obey him?" (Luke 8:22-25). The answer, which we discover as we continue to read the New Testament, is that Jesus is the

> " *Thomas said to him,*
> *'My Lord and my God!'* "
>
> JOHN 20:28

Lord, to whom God has given authority over everything (Matthew 28:18; see also Psalm 89:9). Whereas other lords may damage creation or hoard its resources for themselves, Jesus is the good Lord who is able to bring order back into creation (eg healings) and use its resources to provide generously for all (eg Mark 6:41-44). He is able to exercise this good authority because creation was made through him and for him (Colossians 1:16).

LORD OF SALVATION

When the first Christians confessed "Jesus is Lord" they were not only referring to Jesus' lofty position above creation; they were also referring to Jesus' ability to bring salvation – the world is safe when it is in his hands!

- **Miracles.** Satan claimed that he is the lord of the world (Luke 4:6), and it certainly seems sometimes that the world is enslaved by sin and evil. However, Jesus is a stronger Lord (Luke 11:22) who is able to command sickness (Luke 4:39), demons (Luke 4:35) and even death itself (John 11:43), and they obey him!

- **Suffering and death.** Jesus is the true Lord who will not stand by and watch Satan spoil his good world; however, Jesus' lordship was not a display of sheer power, but rather of suffering service. As Jesus said, he did not come to be served, but to serve, and to give his life for the life of the world (Mark 10:45; Galatians 1:3-4). In John's Gospel, Jesus rules as Lord from the cross, not from a throne (John 12:32). And even in Revelation, where there is a throne, Jesus the Lord is pictured as a Lamb that looks as if it had been slaughtered (Revelation 5:6). Whereas the Roman emperor may have brought peace to his empire through military might, Jesus brought true peace to the world through his own suffering and death (see John 18:36). The distinctive meal of the church is known as "the Lord's supper", which clearly connects Jesus' lordship with his broken body and shed blood (1 Corinthians 11:23-32).

- **Resurrection.** When Jesus met his disciples after the resurrection, their use of "Lord" took on a new meaning (eg Luke 24:34; John 20:28). He was not just their revered teacher, but he was now recognised as the one who has power to banish sin and death and bring new life. In Peter's sermon on the day of Pentecost, the resurrection is seen as God's confirmation that Jesus truly is the Lord of the world (see Acts 2:36).

- **Jesus' return.** One of the earliest confessions of the church was *maranatha*, an Aramaic expression which can mean either "the Lord comes" or "Come, our Lord!" The

Sunset over the Great Plains, Colorado, USA.
A reminder of the vastness and glory of God's creation, accomplished through Jesus

early church probably used it to mean both, since they recognised that while Jesus the Lord had come, he also will come in power on a future day to bring God's kingdom and its justice in full (2 Thessalonians 1:7). The phrase *maranatha* therefore became a prayer, as at the end of the book of Revelation (22:20) and in 1 Corinthians 16:22, expressing the longing that Jesus will come to complete the work of salvation that he has begun.

LORD OF THE SPIRIT

Just before he ascended into heaven, the risen Jesus told his disciples that he had been given all authority on earth and in heaven (Matthew 28:18). When he went to heaven, he said, he would send to the disciples the gift of the Holy Spirit (Luke 24:49), and this happened on the day of Pentecost (see Acts 2). What amazed the disciples was that Jesus himself had sent the Spirit of God to them (Acts 2:33)! In this, Jesus was unlike any of the great leaders of God's people from the Old Testament – God's Spirit had come upon them (eg David in 1 Samuel 16:13), but they had never been able to control the Spirit themselves. In contrast, Jesus is the Lord of the Spirit: he is able to send the Spirit upon his disciples (see also John 20:22), and the Spirit is now the presence of Jesus with them

(Matthew 28:20; John 14:26).

As Lord, Jesus directs the Spirit to give different gifts to different people within the church so that his followers will be equipped for their mission and service in the world (1 Corinthians 12:4ff). In this way, Jesus is the Lord of the church – he is the one we obey and serve (1 Corinthians 15:58; Luke 6:46), and as servants we should be like our master (eg Colossians 3:13). Jesus is still the Lord of the church today; he guides and directs it so that it can do his will.

LORD AND GOD

When Thomas met Jesus after the resurrection, he exclaimed, "My Lord and my God!" (John 20:28). The early Christians realised that Jesus was doing the things that only God could do. So, if Jesus had authority over creation, was able to defeat sin and death and bring new life, and could give the Spirit of God to his people, then Jesus must in fact share the being, nature and glory of God himself! And if Jesus is God, then he should be worshipped. Jews had always insisted that it was idolatry to worship anyone other than YHWH, their God (eg Exodus 20:3). In Isaiah, for instance, YHWH is seen as the only source of life and salvation, to whom every knee should bow and every tongue swear allegiance (Isaiah 45:22-24). However, Paul applies these same words to Jesus in Philippians 2:9-11. It is Jesus to whom every knee will one day bow, and the confession of allegiance will be the words "Jesus is Lord". Jesus the Lord *is* God, together with the Father and the Spirit (see 1 Corinthians 8:6; Ephesians 4:4-6).

"Jesus is Lord" is thus politically and religiously explosive! If Jesus is Lord, then neither Caesar nor anyone else is truly lord; if Jesus is Lord, then he is fully God, worthy to be worshipped and obeyed.

TO THINK ABOUT

Paul and the other early missionaries went around the ancient world with the message that "Jesus is Lord". Read about Paul's visit to Thessalonica in Acts 17:1-9, especially noting verse 7.
· How might the Thessalonians have understood the term "lord" (remembering that Thessalonica was a Roman city in Macedonia, and that Paul first preached to the Jews there)?

Now read through 2 Thessalonians, noting Paul's references to Jesus as "Lord".
· How does Paul use the term? Would anything Paul said have shocked the Thessalonians, or challenged their understanding of lordship?
· Why do you think Paul's message was so controversial?

We may not always use the word "lord" today, but we do have people and ideas that exercise authority over us. Make a list of the "lords" that try to influence your life.
· How powerful is their influence? Are you able to break their power yourself?
· What does it mean for you that Jesus is a "stronger Lord", who can set you free?
· How should this understanding affect the way you live?

The most basic Christian confession is that "Jesus is Lord". Our lives should be living proof that there is a true Lord of the world, who governs and directs it in righteousness and justice. Pray to Jesus the Lord now, thanking him that he has used his lordship to bring grace and peace. Ask for strength to live a life worthy of him now, and pray for his return with the ancient words of the church: *Maranatha*, Come, Lord Jesus!

JESUS' RADICAL TEACHING
Teaching in parables

KEY TRUTH

The parables Jesus told are challenges to understand God's action within the world – God's kingdom – in a profoundly new way, making clear the urgency of a definite response to Jesus' own ministry.

JESUS, A GREAT STORY-TELLER

Jesus is rightly regarded as a skilful story-teller. Ever since he told them, his stories have been retold and enjoyed by countless generations of Christians, and have often been known and loved outside the church too. Many have been the subject of great works of art, such as Rembrandt's *Return of the Prodigal Son* and some of the phrases he used have passed into common usage, such as "killing the fatted calf" (Luke 15:23) for an extravagant feast.

Jesus' stories were engaging and often entertaining (for instance, the image of a man wandering around with a plank in his eye in Luke 6:41-42!); however, he did not tell them to make people smile and laugh. These stories embody Jesus' deeper message about God's activity within the world. For this reason they are often called parables, which indicates that they have a deeper meaning. In Jesus' parables, a profound understanding of God's kingdom is placed side by side with stories about fathers and sons and seeds and feasts.

About one third of Jesus' teaching recorded in the Gospels is in this story form. Not all parables are long stories with multiple characters (such as Luke 15:11-32); some are very short (eg Mark 2:21). One was even acted out by Jesus over two days (Mark 11:12-24). Other "parables" are simply brief proverbs, questions or riddles (eg Mark 3:23-26; Luke 6:39). Even when Jesus did not tell complete stories, his teaching was full of images that use everyday objects and events to illustrate his point: eg salt (Matthew 5:13); light (Matthew 5:14); bread (John 6:35); sheep and shepherds (John 10:11). Mark records that Jesus did not speak to people except in parables (Mark 4:34)!

Today, Jesus' parables can seem very familiar, perhaps even harmless. However, in Jesus' day they were new and often shocking. Jesus did not just repeat old stories, but he picked up familiar themes and retold them, giving them a surprising new twist – the prodigal son returns home and is welcomed by the father rather than punished (Luke 15:11-24); even more remarkable, the older

The Return of the Prodigal Son, by Rembrandt van Rhyn

son disagrees and becomes an outsider. The wounded Jew is helped by a despised Samaritan, while his fellow Jews pass by on the other side of the road (Luke 10:30-37). While the crowds hung on Jesus' words, not everyone liked his parables. After one particular parable, the Jewish leaders were so enraged that they wanted to arrest him (Matthew 21:45-46; Mark 12:12; Luke 20:19). Many of Jesus' parables were told in the context of debate and controversy with his opponents (eg Mark 3:22-27; Luke 15:1-3). In order to understand the true genius of Jesus' stories, they must be read in this light: they were revolutionary!

WHY DID JESUS USE PARABLES?

It is often suggested that Jesus told parables in order to make complex theological concepts more understandable for his ordinary hearers. There is some truth in this – Jesus did want to bring the message of God's kingdom to everyone, not just the well-educated religious leaders. However, the problem with this suggestion is that the meaning of Jesus' parables was not always obvious to his hearers. Even Jesus' closest disciples were sometimes confused, and needed them to be explained (Mark 4:10,13,34). According to Jesus himself, he did not use parables in order to make his teaching more accessible to people, but less so (Mark 4:11-12)! To understand what Jesus meant by this, it is important to note the background to his parables.

- **Old Testament parables.** There are a number of parables recorded in the Old Testament, usually told by a prophet in order to challenge whoever is listening to respond to God's word. In 2 Samuel 12 the prophet Nathan goes to King David, who has just sinned by arranging for Uriah the Hittite to be killed and then taking Uriah's wife Bathsheba to be his own. Nathan tells David a parable about a rich man, who has many flocks of sheep, and a poor man, who has just one little lamb. One day, the rich man takes the poor man's lamb in order to prepare a feast, because he did not want to kill one of his own flock (12:1-4). This parable provokes the anger of David, who immediately wants to punish the rich man (12:5-6). Then Nathan delivers the punch line of the parable: 'You are the man!' (12:7). The judgement that David passed on the rich man is in fact what David himself deserves (12:10-12). Here, the parable confronts David with the reality of his own sin and so gives him the opportunity to respond in repentance (12:13). Just a few chapters later, the wise woman of Tekoa tells David another parable, with a similar purpose (2 Samuel 14), and in 1 Kings 20:38-42 King Ahab is presented with an acted parable. Many of the prophets either told or acted out parables in order to challenge the Israelites to see the reality of their sin against God and return to him (eg Isaiah 5:1-7; Hosea 1:2-11; 3:1-5, where Hosea's marriage itself becomes a parable).

- **Old Testament imagery.** Although Jesus told parables using everyday objects and images, he did not choose them at random. Instead, he told stories about themes that had special significance in the history of God's people. In the Old Testament, Israel was commonly pictured as a vineyard or vine (Isaiah 5:1-7; Ezekiel 19:10-14) and as a fig tree (Jeremiah 8:13). Similarly, Israel was the firstborn son of God's family (Exodus 4:22). God was the shepherd of his people, who were sheep (Psalm 23:1; 100:3; Ezekiel 34). By telling stories about sheep and sons and fig trees and vineyards, Jesus was therefore telling stories about the nation of Israel. His first hearers would have recognised that he was telling stories about them! (see Matthew 21:45).

Through his parables, Jesus was overturning the accepted understanding of God's activity within the world. His hearers – both then and now – do not just need new information in order to belong to God's kingdom; they need an entirely new way of life. For this, they need to be confronted with the reality of their own sin, and of God's judgement and grace, and so be given an opportunity to respond with repentance and faith. This is exactly what Jesus' parables do.

When the disciples asked Jesus why he taught in parables (Matthew 13:10), he replied by quoting Isaiah 6:9-10, which is a reminder that it is possible to see and hear, but not to truly understand. The kingdom of God is only accessible to those who are open to being challenged and transformed. These people will be able to see themselves as characters within the parables, and so will find the grace and hope that God offers. Those who are unwilling to be changed by God will never be able to understand the meaning of the parables, because they will not see that they are invitations to a new way of life. In fact, for them, not only Jesus' parables but also the whole of life will seem like a perplexing riddle ("everything is in parables", Mark 4:11). Interestingly, this conversation comes in the middle of the parable of the sower, which is a perfect picture of Jesus' use of parables – Jesus gives the word of the kingdom to everyone, but only some will allow the seed to take root in their hearts and bear a good crop (Matthew 13:1-9,18-23).

UNDERSTANDING JESUS' PARABLES

Throughout the history of the church, many preachers and teachers have seen Jesus' parables as complex allegories, in which every character and element has a direct counterpart in the life of faith. For instance, in an early interpretation of the parable of the Good Samaritan, the wounded man is Adam; Jerusalem is the garden of paradise; Jericho is the world; the priest is the Old Testament law; the Levite stands for the message of the prophets; the Samaritan is Christ; the donkey

is Christ's crucified body; and the inn is the church! There may be some value in these interpretations, but they should be approached with caution. Jesus' first hearers would have understood his parables in a different way, which is still profound and breathtaking today.

In his parables, Jesus is redefining the people of God around himself. Jesus dared to take the familiar images of Israel from the Old Testament, and weave them into new stories about God's kingdom in the present. A common theme of his parables is that the people who expected to be part of the feast, or who thought that the vineyard belonged to them, end up being thrown out, and others take their place (eg Matthew 22:1-14; Luke 20:9-16). To belong to God's kingdom, it is no longer sufficient to be part of the nation of Israel; now it means to build on the foundation of Jesus' words (Matthew

> " *With many similar parables Jesus spoke the word to them, as much as they could understand. He did not say anything to them without using a parable.*"

MARK 4:33-34

7:24-27), to serve others in his name (Matthew 25:31-46), and to wait for his return to put the world to rights (Matthew 13:24-30,36-43).

Jesus' parables are difficult to understand because they are not just entertaining stories told to illustrate spiritual truths; rather, they challenge the whole way we view the world, ourselves, and even God, and invite us into a new way of life, which requires repentance and faith. The parables only make sense because Jesus himself tells them. He is not

TO THINK ABOUT

Find one of your favourite parables in the Gospels and read it a couple of times. Try working through the following questions to understand it better.

· What is the context of this parable? To whom is Jesus speaking? Is there a question Jesus is answering, or a point he is wanting to make?
· What are the main images in this parable? Do any come from the Old Testament? If so, how are they used there? (A concordance might be a useful tool here.)
· Is there a surprising twist in the way Jesus tells this story? What is it? How else do you think it might have ended? Why does Jesus tell it like this?
· How might this parable have challenged Jesus' hearers? Which of the characters in the parable (if there are any) might they have thought themselves to be?

· How does it challenge you? Are you in the parable? If so, where?
· What is your response to this parable?

Now find a less familiar parable and work through the same questions. You may like to try one or more of the following: Matthew 25:1-13; Mark 4:26-29; Luke 18:9-14.

· How would you respond to someone who told you they thought Jesus' parables were "just good stories"?
· What parables do you think Jesus would tell today? What images would he use?

Jesus' parables bring the kingdom of God into sharper focus, and challenge us to consider our own response to Jesus' ministry. Thank God that Jesus has prepared the way for you into the kingdom of God, and ask for help to properly understand and respond to Jesus' parables – in repentance, faith and obedience.

---

just a story-teller, but he is on his way to die and rise again in Jerusalem, in order to bring about the very kingdom of which he speaks. The parables are a summons to respond to

Jesus before it is too late. For this reason, parables are at the heart of Jesus' ministry.

See also Parables of Jesus Christ, page 305.

JESUS' RADICAL TEACHING
Teaching on the Mount

KEY TRUTH

In the Sermon on the Mount, Jesus announces that his disciples can live in a radically different way, because the blessing of belonging to God's kingdom has overtaken them!

A BETTER MOSES, A BETTER *TORAH*

One of the greatest figures in the Old Testament is Moses, who had been sent by God to lead the Israelites out of slavery in Egypt and bring them to their new land. The book of Exodus records how, along the way through the wilderness, Moses went up Mount Sinai to receive the Ten Commandments and other instructions from God himself (Exodus 19–31). These commandments and instructions became the foundation for the new nation of Israel, and along with the rest of the Pentateuch (Genesis–Deuteronomy) were known collectively as *Torah* (the Hebrew word for "law"). It is preferable to use the term *Torah* because whereas "law" sometimes gives the image of cold, oppressive or impersonal commands, God's *Torah* is a gift of love – a law that expresses Israel's close covenant relationship with him and enables them to respond to his faithfulness towards them with their own (see also Psalm 119, a song of delight in God's *Torah*).

The New Testament presents Jesus as a better Moses (see the promise in Deuteronomy 18:18 and the reality in John 1:17; 5:46; Hebrews 3:3). Jesus came to take God's people a huge step forward, not by abolishing the law of Moses, but by fulfilling its purpose (enabling covenant relationship with God), widening its scope (to all who follow him, and not just to those who are physically Jews) and deepening its demands (to include even the desires of the heart).

Jesus' teaching is a new and better *Torah*!

The block of teaching found in Matthew 5–7 is a concise summary of this new *Torah*. At the end of the fourth century AD, Augustine wrote a commentary on these chapters, coining the title "The Sermon on the Mount", by which we now know it. There is a similar, but shorter, block of teaching in Luke 6:20-49, which has more recently been called "The Sermon on the Plain" because of its different location (Luke 6:17). Jesus probably repeated his teaching numerous times, and so the two versions of the Sermon should not be a cause for concern. In Matthew's Gospel the Sermon is introduced in a way that specifically echoes the Old Testament story of Moses receiving the *Torah*. Jesus "went up the mountain" (Matthew 5:1, probably one of the hills beside the Sea of Galilee), just as Moses had gone up Mount Sinai. He sat down, which was the position of authority for teachers (see Matthew 23:2, also note 7:29), and taught his disciples, among whom there were twelve particular followers, symbolising the renewal of the twelve tribes of Israel.

It must be remembered that this is not a moral code telling people generally how to live a good life, as it is sometimes seen today. Instead, the Sermon is a specific message for Jesus' followers, challenging them to behave in a way consistent with the rule of God that Jesus was bringing into the world. It is significant that Jesus first delivered this teaching to Jewish people. They already were God's people, but Jesus was challenging them to become part of the true, renewed people of

God – to go beyond Moses' *Torah* to the better *Torah* of Jesus the Messiah.

GOOD NEWS: YOU'RE BLESSED!

Jesus begins with a set of nine statements that start with the Greek word *makarios*, which means "blessed". In Latin, "blessed" is *beatus*, and so this section of the Sermon is often called the Beatitudes. Sometimes the word "blessed" is translated as "happy" or "fortunate"; however, in order to understand Jesus' message properly it is essential to note the use of the word throughout Scripture. Importantly, when God called Abraham to follow him, it was God's intention that through Abraham's descendants, all the nations of the world would be blessed (Genesis 12:3). To be "blessed" means to enjoy the intimate family relationship with God that he offers to his people. In particular, in the Old Testament, blessing was associated with obedience to the *Torah*, by which God's people Israel could stay within their covenant relationship with God. When the Israelites were on the edge of their new land, Moses told them that if they obeyed God's law, then "blessings shall come upon you and overtake you" (Deuteronomy 28:1-2).

In the Beatitudes, Jesus announced that the blessing of life in God's family and kingdom had already "come upon and overtaken" his followers! In a sense, they are a more detailed version of Jesus' key message: "The time is fulfilled and the kingdom of God has come near; repent, and believe the good news" (Mark 1:15). The kingdom has come near – its blessings are available – in the person of Jesus himself. In Jesus' new *Torah*, God's blessing is no longer dependent upon perfect obedience of the commandments, but rather is freely given to all those who come to him through Jesus.

This is good news: God's blessing has come upon and overtaken Jesus' disciples. These beatitudes are counter-cultural, because the world calls people who are rich

Extreme law enforcement in London, UK. God's laws were given to set boundaries that enable people to live in peace and harmony

and successful in the present "blessed". Jesus' disciples, on the other hand, display none of the characteristics of success or wealth: they have no claim to material wealth (Matthew 5:3, see also Luke 6:20), they are distraught at the absence of God's kingdom in the world around them (5:4), they do not try to impress God or others (5:5), they are not satisfied with the way things are (5:6), they show mercy rather than clinging to their rights (5:7), their lives are completely open before God and the world (5:8), they work to bring peace because there is no peace at the moment (5:9) and they are persecuted rather than honoured by the world (5:10-11). These characteristics are not "blessed" in the world's eyes, yet they describe what Jesus' disciples are, both then and now. Nonetheless, Jesus announces that God's blessing has overtaken them. By following Jesus they have already begun to experience the life and joy of God's kingdom, and they are promised that they will experience it in full when God puts the world to rights.

LIFE IN GOD'S KINGDOM

Jesus continued by giving examples of what life is to be like, given that God's blessing has been freely given to his disciples.

- **Salt and light (5:13-16).** God's people were always supposed to exist for the sake of the rest of the world (Genesis 12:3; Isaiah 60:3). By their difference from the world, they were to be light and salt, revealing the truth about God and his ways, and restoring the flavour of the world. The temptation, however, had always been to shut themselves away from the rest of the world and keep the blessing for themselves. Now that Jesus' disciples have experienced God's

> " *Now* when he saw the crowds, he went up on a mountainside and sat down. His disciples came to him, and he began to teach them. "

MATTHEW 5:1-2

blessing through the ministry of Jesus, they must not fall into the same trap, but rather fulfil the role that God had always intended for his people: they must salt the earth and light it up! Jesus will show them what this means in the rest of his Sermon.

- **Radical demands (5:17-48).** Jesus stressed that he had not come to do away with the law and prophets that had shaped the life of God's people until then, but rather to fulfil (5:17) and deepen them (5:20). His disciples were not just to observe the outward form of the commands, but allow God's good *Torah* to sink deep into their hearts so that

their every action flowed from their relationship with God (see Jeremiah 31:33). Six times he used the formula, "You have heard that it was said …, but I tell you …" – Jesus' disciples are to go beyond the letter of the law and be forgiving (5:21-26), self-controlled (5:27-30), faithful (5:31-32), honest (5:33-37), generous (5:38-42) and loving (5:43-47). There is an obvious parallel with the fruit of the Spirit, described by Paul in Galatians 5:22-23. This cannot be generated by strict adherence to a moral code, but can only grow as "fruit" from a renewed heart. The only way to "be perfect" (Matthew 5:48) is by keeping close to the heavenly Father, through Jesus, in the Spirit.

- **Worship from the heart (6:1-18).** (See also "Teaching on prayer") Jesus challenged his disciples about every aspect of their religious life: holiness (6:1), charity (6:2-4), prayer (6:5-15) and fasting (6:16-18). His key point is that in God's kingdom, these things flow naturally from the heart as an expression of love to God; they are never done to impress others.

- **Trusting the Father, living in the family (6:19–7:12).** Jesus continues with a series of instructions about wealth (6:19-21,24), worry (6:25-34), and relating to others (7:1-6,12). Holding these instructions together is a recognition that Jesus' disciples now belong to the family of God; therefore, their heavenly Father will provide everything they need (7:7-11). They do not need to search for life from any other source, but must keep their eyes focused on him (6:22-23). This simple, childlike trust that God will provide for their needs means they do not need to put others down (7:1-6) or pretend they are better than anyone else (7:12).

HEARING AND DOING

When Moses gave Israel the *Torah* in the Old Testament, he spoke about the connection

TO THINK ABOUT

Read Deuteronomy 28:1-15, and then Matthew 5:1-12.
- Are there any similarities between these two passages of blessings? Are there any differences? If so, why?
- How would you translate the word "blessed" to bring out its full meaning?
- How do you think Jesus' disciples felt when they heard the Beatitudes? How do you feel? How is it good news?

Matthew 7:12 has been known as "the Golden Rule" since the 18th century, and is often highly regarded by people who don't know anything else about Jesus.
- Other people have said a similar thing, but is there anything different about Jesus' version of the "Golden Rule"? In what context does Jesus give it?

Read through the whole Sermon slowly, reminding yourself that this is the kind of life that is possible because of Jesus!
- Are there any particular parts of the Sermon that stand out for you?
- Are there aspects of kingdom life that you need to renew in your own life? How will you do this?

The Sermon is not for some elite group of Christians, but for everyone who follows Jesus. It is Jesus' new *Torah*, expressing the intimate family relationship that his disciples can enjoy, and describing the kind of life that flows from it. Thank God that his blessing has come upon and overtaken you, and ask him for the courage to allow the fruit of his kingdom to grow in your life.

between obedience and blessing, and disobedience and curse (eg Deuteronomy 11:26-28). Similarly, Jesus concluded his Sermon by stressing the consequences of taking him at his word: if his disciples receive God's free blessing and live in it, their blessing will increase, but if they simply hear Jesus' words and go on living as they did before, then their lives will come crashing down around them (Matthew 7:24-27). Jesus reminded them that following him is strenuous (7:14) and sometimes dangerous

(7:15). Many people, even today, are impressed by the sentiments of the Sermon on the Mount and try to follow its teaching, but do not want to know the Jesus who gave it (7:21-23). Without him, though, following the Sermon is pointless and impossible. Jesus did not set out a series of steps for people to take in order to enter God's kingdom: he announced that they were already blessed by being with him, and then told them to go and live like it in the world!

JESUS' RADICAL TEACHING
Teaching on prayer

KEY TRUTH

Jesus taught his disciples to pray in the light of his own example and mission, emphasising the privilege and responsibility that they now have as God's children to pray to God as Father.

GOD'S PEOPLE PRAY!

From the very beginning of history, people have wanted to communicate with God in prayer (Genesis 4:26), whether to praise him for all he has done, or to ask him for help and guidance. When people turned away from the true God, they did not stop praying, but instead their prayers became frantic and empty, because their gods could neither hear nor answer (see 1 Kings 18:26-29; Isaiah 45:20). On the other hand, Israel insisted that the true God of the world, YHWH, was ready and willing to listen to their prayers, and come to their aid (eg 2 Chronicles 6:18-40). The book of Psalms contains prayers that were used by individuals and groups in Israel through all their experiences of life, including times of joy (eg Psalm 96) and despair (eg Psalm 22). There are even prayers for times when it seems God is not listening (eg Psalm 88) – he still hears then!

While God's people knew they could pray at any time, it became common to pray regularly in the morning and the evening, and sometimes in the middle of the day too (see Daniel 6:10). The morning and evening prayers coincided with the hours of sacrifice in the temple. The temple itself was known as a house of prayer (Isaiah 56:7), because it was the particular place where God lived among his people. An important element of pilgrimage to Jerusalem was prayer in the temple (eg 1 Samuel 1:9-18).

To this day, Jews have a regular form of prayer, one of which is called the *Shema*. This begins with the words of Deuteronomy 6:4, "Hear, O Israel; the Lord our God, the Lord is one" (*Shema* is the Hebrew word for 'hear') and continues with Deuteronomy 6:5-9, 11:13-21 and Numbers 15:37-41. Another common prayer from around the time of Jesus was called the Eighteen Benedictions. In these prayers, God's people celebrated their relationship with God, committed themselves to serve him and asked for his blessing on their lives.

JESUS' LIFE OF PRAYER

As a Jew, Jesus would have shared the familiar pattern of praying at least twice a day, reciting the *Shema* (see Mark 12:29) and using the temple in Jerusalem as a "house of prayer" (see Mark 11:17). However, Jesus' prayer life was not confined to these regular times, words and places. The Gospels record how he occasionally spent extended periods of time on his own in prayer, often in a deserted place away from the crowds (eg Luke 5:16). Jesus spent time in prayer before particularly important events, such as the choosing of the disciples (Luke 6:12-13), Peter's confession of him as the Messiah (Luke 9:18) and the transfiguration (Luke 9:28). He prayed to bless the food before he miraculously fed the crowds in Matthew 14:19. Just before his arrest and crucifixion, Jesus agonised in prayer in the garden of Gethsemane (Luke 22:41-46), and he also prayed to his Father from the cross (Luke 23:34,46). These prayers show Jesus' dependence on his Father for strength and wisdom, and his complete trust in his Father's will.

Jesus' prayers were not just like other prayers, however. He expressed the most intimate relationship with God, calling him "Father" (see Matthew 11:25-27, and also the use of "Abba" in Mark 14:36). Jesus' prayer for his disciples in John 17 is bold and confident because he knows the Father will listen to him and grant his request. The later New Testament speaks about Jesus' continuing ministry of prayer for Christians (Hebrews 7:25). Jesus' use of prayer provides an example for all Christians: prayer has been given to us to help us remain in constant fellowship with God, to draw strength from him and to bring our requests for others (see 1 Thessalonians 5:17; Hebrews 4:16).

TEACHING ABOUT PRAYER

In addition to Jesus' example in prayer, his teaching provided helpful instruction to his disciples. In particular, a number of his parables deal with the nature and practice of prayer.

- **Confidence in prayer.** A major theme of Jesus' teaching on prayer is the confidence that his followers can have in the goodness of God the Father. Because of this, they should be bold in asking for good things from him, since he delights to give generously to his children (Matthew 7:9-11). Jesus even makes the astonishing claim that his disciples can ask for "anything" in prayer, and they will receive it (Mark 11:24; Matthew 21:22)! This does not mean that God will always fulfil his children's wildest dreams. Jesus' disciples must ask "in faith", "believing that they will receive it", and so it follows that they can only truly ask in faith for things that are consistent with God's character and kingdom. However, within the will of God there are still many good things that can be sought in prayer – and Jesus promises that God will hear and answer!

- **Simplicity and humility in prayer.** The confidence of Christian prayer is not in a form of words, or a particular technique, but in the character of the God to whom prayer is made: he is always good. This means that prayer does not need to be an elaborate construction of fine phrases intended to make God take notice of the prayer, but can be a simple, childlike request. Jesus warns against piling up empty phrases, as in other religions (Matthew 6:7). Some pagan prayers began with endless terms of address, describing all the attributes of the god to whom the person was praying, but Christian prayer can simply begin, "Father, ...''! Similarly, those who pray to God do not need to offer excuses for their behaviour, or present themselves in a better light. Jesus told a

> " *This, then, is how you should pray:*
> '*Our Father in heaven,*
>   *hallowed be your name,*
> *your kingdom come,*
>   *your will be done on earth*
>   *as it is in heaven.*'"

MATTHEW 6:9-10

parable to remind his hearers that God listens to those who are humble – who simply state the truth about themselves, and trust in God's mercy and grace (Luke 18:9-14).

- **Persistence in prayer.** Jesus told a couple of parables about the need to be persistent in prayer. In one, a man gets out of bed to give his friend a loaf of bread because of his friend's persistence (Luke 11:5-8). In another parable, an unjust judge grants a widow's request because she refuses to leave him alone (Luke 18:1-8). The point of these parables is not to suggest that God is either unjust or unwilling to grant his people's requests. The point is rather about the persistence of the one who is seeking bread or justice. They refuse to go away, or turn to anyone else, because they know that the man in bed and the unjust judge are the only people who can solve their problems. Persistence in prayer does not just mean praying a lot; it means refusing to look anywhere else for the things that only God can give. Praying is a matter of asking,

As the Son of God, Jesus' relationship with his Father was one of total intimacy and dependence

seeking and knocking (Matthew 7:7) – it can often be a hard discipline to maintain.
· **Authenticity in prayer.** Jesus made a connection between the activity of prayer and the rest of life. In particular, he noted that it is useless for his disciples to pray for forgiveness from God if they are not willing to forgive one another (Matthew 6:14-15; 18:23-35). Jesus' disciples are not to be "hypocrites" – people who love to pretend that they are very close to God through loud public prayers and visible fasting (Matthew 6:2,5,16). Such people only pray and fast because of the effect it has on other people's view of them. This is hypocritical, because prayer is supposed to be about complete dependence on God. Jesus' disciples are to remember that prayer and fasting can be done in secret, and God knows, which is what really matters (Matthew 6:3-4,6,17-18).

THE LORD'S PRAYER

Christian prayer is part of the new relationship with God that has been made possible by Jesus. In prayer, Christians enter into the childlike relationship with God the Father that characterised Jesus' own life (note Romans 8:15-17; Galatians 4:6). The classic Christian prayer is thus the Lord's Prayer (Matthew 6:9-13; Luke 11:2-4), since it was given to the disciples by Jesus himself as a pattern for their own prayer (Luke 11:1). Throughout the ages and across the world, the Lord's Prayer (sometimes called the "Our Father", *Pater Noster* in Latin) is used regularly to enable God's people to express their trust in God, and seek his help.

Jesus' prayer is set firmly within his Jewish tradition, while also being new and unique. The prayer begins by addressing God as Father, which expresses the intimate relationship that Jesus' followers can enjoy with God. Since it is addressed to "our Father" (Matthew 6:9), this prayer is to be shared with all Christian brothers and sisters. The rest of the prayer flows out of this close family context. God's children long for his name and reputation to be honoured (see the third commandment, Exodus 20:7), and for the world to come completely under his loving and gracious rule, just as it is in heaven. God has always provided bread for his people (eg manna in the wilderness, Exodus 16:4), and in the future kingdom, there will be a huge feast to satisfy the world's hunger (Isaiah 25:6); for now, God's children ask for

TO THINK ABOUT

Think about your own practice of prayer.
· How did you learn to pray? Were there particular people, or places, or words that helped you?

Now think about Jesus' prayer life. Read one or more of the following passages: Luke 6:12-13; Luke 9:28; Matthew 26:36-44.
· Jesus was the Son of God; so why do you think he needed to pray?
· How did Jesus pray? What aspects of prayer do you notice from these passages?
· What did prayer enable Jesus to do? Did it change anything? If so, how?

Go through the Lord's Prayer slowly, phrase by phrase (Matthew 6:9-13; Luke 11:2-4). Use the following questions to come to a deeper understanding of what the prayer is about.

· What might this phrase have meant for Jesus' disciples?
· Are there any other aspects of Jesus' teaching that say a similar thing? Can you think of any relevant parables?
· What does the phrase mean for you today?
· Can you think of another way of expressing the phrase, so that someone unfamiliar with the rest of Jesus' teachings would understand it?

Prayer is a gift and a privilege. It is also a responsibility, because it is the means by which we lay ourselves and our world open to God's transforming power. Thank God that you can know him as Father, and then use your version of the Lord's Prayer to pray for yourself, your community and the world.

---

enough bread for this day, confident that God will provide all the good things they need. In celebrating their own free forgiveness by God, they commit themselves to forgive others also – a reminder that relationship with God must be worked out in other relationships too. Living in this way will not be easy, since it attracts the attacks of Satan and the scorn of the world. The prayer thus continues with a request that these trials will not be overwhelming, but that God's deliverance will be experienced instead (see Matthew 26:41). In

the church's use of Jesus' prayer, a final sentence is added, acknowledging that "the kingdom, power and glory" belong to God – surely a fitting end to this magnificent prayer. Whenever this prayer is used, it is to be remembered that it is a gift from Jesus – he has taught us to pray!

In addition to repeating it literally, the Lord's Prayer can be used as a model which we can elaborate. True prayer thus begins with God and his interests before asking for our own needs and the needs of the world.

JESUS' RADICAL TEACHING
Teaching about God and his kingdom

KEY TRUTH

Jesus revealed the true identity of God to his disciples, and taught them that God's royal rule over the world was present and active through his ministry.

MAKING GOD KNOWN

Religions around the world have come up with a vast array of gods, goddesses, spirits and forces to explain the world around them. All these attempts, however, are much like a person stumbling around a room in darkness, unable to describe accurately what is really there. As John's Gospel says, "No one has ever seen God" (1:18), so all the images of the divine are at best wishful thinking, and at worst deception and slavery. In the Bible, God's people have always insisted that they know what God is like, not because they have made up a better story about him, but because he has told them about himself and has confirmed that he is speaking the truth by being faithful to his promises (eg Exodus 3:13-17; 20:2). Jesus' teaching picked up the Old Testament understanding of God and took it much deeper and further. He taught his disciples about God with an entirely new confidence and authority. As John 1:18 explains, Jesus is able to make God known to others because he came from the Father, so he has seen God and knows him.

- **Creator.** God's people Israel confessed that their God YHWH was in fact the God of the whole world, who had brought a good, ordered creation out of the chaos of nothing (Genesis 1; Isaiah 42:5). The universe was not a collaborative effort from a number of different divine beings, who each had their own particular area of expertise (eg the god of wind, the god of fire, etc.). Rather, everything was the good work of the one God of the universe (eg Job 38:4–39:30). Jesus' teaching assumes that his hearers held this Jewish belief that their God was the creator. He challenged them to think through the implications of this: if God has created something, then it must be good (eg marriage, Mark 10:6-9); if God has given such beauty to his creation, then there is no reason to doubt his willingness to give other good gifts (Luke 12:28).

- **Father.** Jesus' distinctive teaching about God is his message that God, the creator, is in fact the "Father" of his people. Although in the Old Testament Israel had sometimes seen their relationship with God in this way (eg Hosea 11:1-4), Jesus consistently taught that God is his own Father (Matthew 11:25-27), and, because of what he has done for them, the Father of his disciples also (see John 14:7; 20:17). When Jesus uses this term for God, he does not mean that God is just a greater version of earthly fathers, since they are sometimes far from perfect, perhaps even evil. Instead, for Jesus, God is the true Father, who defines what being a "father" really means (eg Matthew 7:11). As Father, God does not leave creation on its own to fend for itself: he cares constantly for it, its plight is never out of his attention (Luke 12:6-7,30), and he longs for it to turn to him for help (Matthew 18:14; Luke 15:20). Jesus teaches his disciples to have complete confidence in the fair generosity of their Father in heaven (Matthew 5:45), and to come boldly to him with their requests (Luke 11:13). Jesus' disciples can pray to God as Father (eg Matthew 6:9; also Jesus'

A young Slovakian girl hears words of truth and life over the airwaves

own prayer in 26:39,42), because Jesus has shared his own intimate family relationship with them. Jesus teaches his disciples that they will one day experience the full glory of the Father (eg Mark 8:38; Luke 9:26) – his overwhelming and unmissable presence that will transform the world into all he intends it to be, and which will confirm his people as his true family. The Father's glory was glimpsed in the transfiguration of Jesus (Luke 9:28-36), and is seen in his work in and through believers now, ahead of the future fullness of the kingdom (eg John 15:8; Matthew 5:16). Jesus' teaching about his Father gave early Christianity its distinctive creed: we believe in God the Father, with the Son and the Spirit.

· **Source of salvation.** Jesus taught his disciples that he was not acting on his own behalf, but was fulfilling his Father's will (eg John 4:34, 6:38). Throughout Jesus' teaching, he refers to God as the one who sent him to the world to accomplish the work of salvation (John 3:17). God is intimately concerned to put the relation-ship of the world to him to rights: salvation is not something that needs to be wrestled from God, but something that flows freely from him, if only people will recognise it! In his parables Jesus often describes the watching and waiting (eg Matthew 13:30; Luke 15:20), preparing and inviting (eg Luke 14:17) that God does in order to share the joy of his kingdom with the world.

"THE KINGDOM IS NEAR!"

When Jesus began his ministry, he announced that "The time is fulfilled, and the kingdom of God has come near; repent, and believe in the good news" (Mark 1:15; also Matthew 3:2 and Luke 4:43). In the synoptic Gospels (Matthew, Mark and Luke), Jesus uses the term "the kingdom of God" or the similar phrase "kingdom of heaven" around 90 times.

· **Background: God's royal rule.** "Kingdom" language is a way of talking about how God is active within the world. In the Old Testament, it soon became clear that although God had created the world to be a place of good order and blessing, humans refuse to live in that order and try to control their own lives instead (see Genesis 3). God called Abraham and his descendants to live under his authority, to show the rest of the world what life under him looks like. Later, God's people Israel understood that God had delivered them from slavery in Egypt so that they could live under his divine rule instead, which was the way of life and freedom (Exodus 19:5-6). Although the whole earth belongs to God (Psalm 24:1), God's people are his particular kingdom because they live as God intends the whole world to live – in close fellowship with him, and at peace with one another. Just like the rest of the world, however, Israel too refused to live under God's good rule. They eventually appointed human kings to rule over them (see 1 Samuel 8), who often led them astray. The prophets continually reminded them that only God was their true king (eg Isaiah 43:15; 44:6). Towards the end of Old Testament times, the faithful in Israel looked forward to a coming day when God's kingdom would come in full – the coming Messiah, the true descendant of King David, God's appointed agent, would bring God's justice and peace to Israel and the whole world (eg Daniel 7:13-14; Zechariah 9:9-10). Through this judgement and renewal, the Lord himself would become king over all the earth (Zechariah 14:9): everyone will acknowledge his right and authority to establish his order in the world (see Psalm 97).

At the time of Jesus, the hope for God's kingdom was strong. Israel had lived under occupation for centuries, and they longed to be free of their political and military over-lords. The Jewish historian Josephus recorded the slogan of one of the revolutionary groups around the time of Jesus: "no King but God!" For Jesus' hearers, the "kingdom of God" was a way of describing what life would be like set free from Roman occupation, living under God's rule alone, and so experiencing the blessings of being his special people. The picture of this kingdom included geographical (the land of Israel) and political (free from Roman rule) hopes, as well as religious (worship at the Temple) and ethical (perfect obedience to God's *Torah*) renewal.

- **Arrival of the kingdom: Jesus' ministry.** Much of Jesus' teaching and many of his parables summon his hearers to recognise that God's kingdom is not a long way off in either time or distance, but that it has "come near" in his own ministry, and so the time has come for them to decide to enter into it (Mark 1:15). In Luke 17:21, Jesus tells the Pharisees that the kingdom is already among them, within their grasp, if only they could recognise it. The "nearness" or "presence" of God's kingdom was demonstrated through Jesus' encounters with people, especially his healings and exorcisms (Matthew 12:28; Luke 11:20). God's royal rule came upon people as they were set free from the slavery of sickness or demon possession. When Jesus sent his disciples out to prepare the way for him in nearby towns (Luke 10:1), he instructed them to imitate his own ministry – to preach the news that "the kingdom of God has come near" and to demonstrate it with healings (Luke 10:9). God's kingdom was coming near because Jesus himself was the king (see Luke 19:38). However, Jesus challenged the expectations of his hearers. The kingdom would not be the great geographical and political state that they had imagined, with the whole world being ruled from Jerusalem. There would be no dramatic, military clash with the Roman Empire. In many of his parables, Jesus taught that the kingdom will grow gradually, almost unnoticed, like a small seed growing up into a field of wheat, or a great tree (Mark 4:26-32). Nor would the kingdom be for the people they imagined: Jesus ate with outcasts and welcomed children, who were often disregarded – the kingdom of God is for them (Mark 2:17; 10:14; see also parables, eg Luke 14:16-24).

Even the thief who died alongside Jesus was accepted into his kingdom (Luke 23:42-43)! Jesus transformed his hearers' hopes for the kingdom: God's royal rule was no longer confined to the land of Israel, the political state centred around Jerusalem, worship at the Temple or obedience to the *Torah*. God's rule, which was fully embodied in Jesus himself, now comes upon all who trust in Jesus and commit themselves to follow him (Matthew 6:33). Belonging to this kingdom would involve immense cost (Luke 14:25-33), but it is in fact a great treasure (Matthew 13:44-45) which will be enjoyed in full when Jesus the king returns to throw a great, everlasting celebration (eg Matthew 25:34). Matthew uses the term "kingdom of heaven" alongside "kingdom of God" to explain the nature of the kingdom further. Since heaven is the part of reality where God's rule is already obeyed fully by the angels, the "kingdom of heaven" is the part

> *" 'The time has come,' he said. 'The kingdom of God is near. Repent and believe the good news!' "*
>
> JOHN THE BAPTIST: MARK 1:15

of earth that has already been brought into God's good order. At the moment the kingdom of heaven grows alongside the kingdom of the world but in the future Jesus will remove all sin and evil so that his kingdom fills the whole earth (Matthew 13:41-43). Jesus taught his disciples to pray that God's royal rule would come "on earth as it is in heaven" (Matthew 6:10). Jesus himself – in his teaching and healings, and especially his suffering, death and resurrection – is the embodiment of the kingly rule of God.

TO THINK ABOUT

Make a list of the ways in which you, or people you know, often think about God.
· Do any of these match Jesus' teaching about God? Are any different from Jesus' teaching, or even contrary to it? If so, where do they think they come from?
· How would you summarise Jesus' teaching about God?

Read Matthew 13, noting the different parables and images Jesus uses to explain the kingdom of heaven to his hearers.
· What do you think Jesus means by "the secrets of the kingdom of heaven" (verse 11)? Why is it secret? From whom is it hidden?
· What does this chapter teach you about God's kingdom?
· Why do you think Jesus uses images of growing (seeds/yeast)?

· What is the relationship between the nearness of the kingdom now, and the fullness of the kingdom in the future?

Jesus demonstrated the kingdom of God through his friendship with outcasts and his healings. The kingdom is not just an inward experience of God's rule, but includes an outward expression of it.
· How do you live in God's kingdom today? What could you do to make God's good order more evident in the world around you?

The task of the church is to proclaim the kingdom of God by inviting people to live under the good order of Jesus, the King (see Acts 17:7). Thank God that his kingdom is not far off, and pray that his rule would become a reality in your life, and the world around you.

JESUS' RADICAL TEACHING
Teaching about the future

KEY TRUTH

Jesus reworked Old Testament expectation of the future around himself: as the Son of Man, he will one day come to gather God's people together and usher them with the rest of creation into God's future age.

THE FUTURE OF GOD'S WORLD

Jesus' teaching about the future was firmly rooted in the prophetic hopes of Israel from the Old Testament. These hopes had accumulated throughout Israel's life, but especially during the exile, when they were away from their own land. God's message to Israel through his prophets contained promises that were only partially fulfilled by the return from exile, so the Jews looked forward to a day when they would be fulfilled completely. This vision of the future contained a number of aspects:

- **Renewal of Israel's life.** In the middle of the exile, the prophet Ezekiel was given a vision of a restored land, with a new temple at the centre (Ezekiel 40:2). This temple will be the residence of Israel's God and because of his presence among his people they will be completely holy (43:7-9, also 48:35). The moral life of the nation will be renewed (see 45:9-10) and God will provide healing and food (47:12). Elsewhere in the prophetic books, the future is described as the ending of exile (Isaiah 40:1-2), when the faithful of Israel will be gathered together from where they were scattered (Jeremiah 31:7-14). God will make a new covenant with his people, in which all their sins will be forgiven and they will know him intimately (Jeremiah 31:31-34).
- **Judgement of God's enemies.** Many of the prophets spoke about the coming "day of the Lord", when God would fulfil his promises by bringing judgement upon his enemies. Israelites typically understood God's enemies to be the pagan nations around them, especially the nations who had persecuted and oppressed them. However, God's prophets warned Israel that the "day of the Lord" would bring judgement to people within Israel too – to those who refused to live by the light of God's *Torah* (eg Amos 5:18-24). Many Jews felt that they had already been judged through exile, and so it simply remained for the rest of the world to experience God's judgement on their sin.
- **Resurrection of the dead.** Understandably, death is often seen as the end of all life. However, Israel's experience of God's covenant love and faithfulness was so strong that they began to hope that God would continue to care for them even after death (Psalm 16:9-10). In Ezekiel 37, God spoke of the coming restoration of Israel in terms of a resurrection from the dead – dead corpses coming to life again by the power of his word (Ezekiel 37:1-14). When God renewed Israel's life, it was inconceivable that the faithful saints who had died previously would not also be present. So, in Daniel, when Israel are renewed, then there will be a general resurrection, and God will gather into his kingdom all those who have been faithful to him (Daniel 12:2-3).
- **Reordering of creation.** The end of Isaiah's prophecy provides a glimpse of the universal scope of God's future salvation. It

is not just for Israel, or the nations surrounding Israel, but for the whole world! The whole of creation – heavens and earth – will be renewed (Isaiah 65:17) and all the disruption that was caused by sin will be forgotten (65:19-23). This good order will extend even to the natural world: the wolf and the lamb will feed together! (65:25). Heaven, for both the Jewish and the Christian faith, is not a disembodied spirit world somewhere else, but rather this physical earth, brought completely under God's loving rule.

REWORKING THE VISION

Jesus' teaching about the future coincided with many of the themes of Jewish eschatology (teaching about the last things, from the Greek word *eschatos*, meaning "last"). For instance, he spoke about a coming judgement, at which the righteous would be rewarded, but the wicked would find themselves excluded from God's kingdom (eg Matthew 25:31-36), and he affirmed the resurrection of the dead (Mark 12:24-27). However, Jesus had reworked the Jewish vision in two main ways:

· **The coming of the Son of Man.** In the Old Testament, passing reference is made to a "son of man" who comes to the throne room of God to receive authority over the whole world (Daniel 7:13-14) after a period of intense evil and suffering (see the four beasts in 7:1-12). Jesus puts this image in the centre of his eschatology by consistently referring to himself as the "Son of Man" (eg Mark 14:21). In Jesus' clearest teaching about the future, he says that the Son of Man (that is, Jesus himself) will be central to the fulfilment of God's promises (Luke 21:27-28): he will gather together God's faithful people (Matthew 24:31; Mark 13:27) and bring about God's righteous judgement (Matthew 16:27; John 5:27). Jesus interprets his own suffering and death in Jerusalem as the suffering of the Son of Man (Matthew 17:22-23), through which he will go to God's throne to receive authority over the whole world (Matthew 26:64; Mark 14:62; Luke 22:69). The "coming" (Greek, *parousia*) of the Son of Man is the moment when all will realise that Jesus is indeed God's appointed Messiah, the one who really does have authority over all creation (see Matthew 24:30). This image has parallels in the Roman world – a Roman emperor might "come" to a subject city, to display beyond doubt that he is its lord and master. In his teaching, Jesus placed himself

Jesus stated that even he did not know when the Father would usher the world into the future age

at the centre of the vision of the future: God's future will arrive when the Son of Man, who has died and risen again, comes in unmistakable glory to bring justice and peace, resurrection and life.

- **The future now; the future then.** Most Jews believed that God's future would arrive all at once – there would be a cataclysmic event through which God would defeat his enemies, reorder the world and re-establish his people. The present age would give way at a single moment in time to the future age. Jesus taught his disciples that the relationship between the future and the present was more complicated than that. The future was already beginning to take place in the present; the "birth pangs" of the future age were already being felt (Mark 13:8) and his disciples were to watch for the signs of it. Through Jesus' work, the future was already rushing upon his disciples (eg resurrection, John 11:23-26), even though it would also come fully soon (Matthew 24:42).

PROPHECIES AND INSTRUCTIONS

Some of Jesus' teaching was very specific to his first hearers but all of it has a wider application today. He did not intend to give his disciples a detailed timetable for the future, but rather to prepare them for what would take place.

- **Times of tribulation.** In Jesus' major session of teaching on the future (see Matthew 24 and Mark 13), he spoke of the great troubles and suffering that his people would face ahead of the final coming of God's kingdom. In particular, he prophesied that Jerusalem and the Temple would be turned into rubble (Mark 13:2), and that the citizens would have to flee to the hills (13:14-18). This in fact happened in AD 70 when the Roman army sacked Jerusalem and levelled the Temple. This in itself vindicated Jesus and his message – the Temple could no longer be the way to have fellowship with

God; Jesus was. Jesus tells his disciples that they will face much suffering before his final coming. His teaching gives a picture of a world spiralling out of control; but Jesus' disciples must not become alarmed (13:7) or desert their faith (13:21). They can pray for God's strength and deliverance (Matthew 6:13; 26:41), and look for the coming of the Son of Man, who will certainly eventually come and bring with him God's salvation and universal order.

> "*No one knows about that day or hour, not even the angels in heaven, nor the Son, but only the Father.*"
>
> MATTHEW 24:36

- **The urgency of decision.** Jesus commented that even he did not know when the Father would usher the world into his future age (Mark 13:32). For this reason, since it could come at any moment, Jesus warns his hearers to be ready (13:33-37; also Matthew 24:36–25:13). In order to be part of God's kingdom then, it is vital to be part of his kingdom now, watching and waiting and working for his return (eg Luke 19:11-27).
- **Finality of judgement.** Many of Jesus' parables speak about a moment of final judgement, when the owner of the house, or the master of the servants, or the farmer of the field returns. At the coming of the Son of Man, his judgement will distinguish between those who have received the news of God's kingdom gladly and set about serving King Jesus, and those who have rejected the news and only served their own ends (eg Matthew 22:1-10; 25:31-46). According to Jesus, this judgement is final (see Luke 16:26). Those who have rejected the kingdom message are sent away from the Father's presence into "darkness" and

TO THINK ABOUT

Read through Matthew 24.

· What is the context of Jesus' teaching here? (24:1,3) What do you think is going through the disciples' minds?

· Does Jesus answer their question? Why, or why not? What is he trying to say?

· How does Jesus use the imagery of the Son of Man from Daniel 7?

· Remember that God's future comes in stages. Might any of this refer to Jesus' death and resurrection in Jerusalem? The Fall of Jerusalem in AD 70? The coming judgement? Or a combination of the above?

Think about the common images people have about heaven, hell and the future.

· How do these images compare with Jewish eschatology (teaching about the future)?

· How do they compare with Jesus' view of the future?

· Are there any elements that we often miss? Or elements that we add?

· How would you respond to someone who said that "everyone goes to heaven when they die"? To which bits of Jesus' teaching might you point them?

Jesus taught his disciples about the future so that they would not become alarmed, but remain strong in their faith, and urgent in their mission. His message about judgement is always a warning for us, reminding us that true life is only ever found in him. Thank Jesus for the glimpse of the future that he has given, and for the firm hope we have that he will come soon. Now ask him for the strength and time to serve him well.

"fire" (eg Matthew 25:30,41). One of the words commonly used in the Gospels is *Gehenna*, sometimes translated as "hell", which referred to a valley on the south of Jerusalem (Valley of Hinnom, Joshua 15:8). During the reigns of the wicked kings Ahaz and Manasseh, this valley was used for sacrificing humans to the god Molech by fire (2 Chronicles 28:3; 33:6). God condemned the practice, and spoke of the valley as a place of utter death and destruction (eg Jeremiah 7:30-33). It therefore became a symbol of God's rejection and judgement. By Jesus' day, it was a rubbish dump, probably always smouldering with fire. Jesus used this image

to speak of the terrible judgement that would overwhelm those who reject God's invitation of life in his kingdom, just as it would the devil and his angels (Matthew 25:41). The shock of Jesus' teaching was that he told his Jewish listeners that they were not safe from this judgement; they too would end up in *Gehenna* if they did not see that he was reforming God's true people around himself! It is unclear whether Jesus taught hell to be a place of eternal conscious torment, or of the utter annihilation of life – either way, Jesus has made clear the finality of judgement and the urgency of entering his kingdom now.

JESUS' RADICAL TEACHING
Teaching about himself

KEY TRUTH

Jesus taught his disciples to trust in him as the true focus of all their hope and devotion: he himself is the subject of his message.

JESUS IN JOHN'S GOSPEL

John's Gospel provides the clearest picture of Jesus' teaching about himself. From the very beginning of the Gospel, John is concerned to show his readers not just what Jesus did, but also who he is (eg John 1:14). Interestingly, unlike the synoptic Gospels (Matthew, Mark and Luke), John's Gospel hardly ever uses the term "kingdom of God", because John wants to emphasise the significance of Jesus himself, who is of course the essential figure in the kingdom of God. John remembers and records statements Jesus made about himself, which bring into focus who he is and how his disciples should relate to him. Jesus' teaching about himself in John's Gospel is crystal clear: he is the one true hope of the world, who satisfies the deepest longings of his people.

SEVEN IMAGES OF JESUS

Early in John's Gospel, Jesus meets a Samaritan woman at a well (4:7). In conversation with her, Jesus tells her that the age-old controversy between Samaritans and Jews about where to worship God (4:20) is no longer necessary – all people everywhere can worship God "in spirit and in truth" (4:23-24). The Samaritan woman replies that she expects the Messiah will clear up all the confusion (4:25). Jesus' response is simple, "I am – the one who is speaking to you!" (4:26). In Greek, his statement begins *ego eimi*, "I am". On one hand, Jesus is simply saying, "It's me!" But these specific words recur throughout John's Gospel at key moments, hinting at their significance for Jesus in his teaching

about himself. In particular, John's Gospel contains seven "I am" statements through which Jesus explains who he is to his followers.

· **I am the bread of life** (6:35,48,51). The previous day, Jesus had fed the crowd with five loaves and two fish (6:1-13), and now they had returned to him wanting more miraculous food (6:26,34). They thought that Jesus was the promised prophet like Moses (Deuteronomy 18:18; John 6:14), so they asked him for a sign to prove himself (6:30), just as Moses had provided "bread from heaven" for the Israelites for forty years during their exodus journey from slavery in Egypt to the promised land (6:31; Exodus 16:4,35). Jesus corrected them: it was not Moses who had given the Israelites bread, but God (6:32). Now God was providing a much better bread for them – Jesus himself – which would feed them on a much more profound exodus: the journey from sin and death to eternal life (6:35). Jesus is not just a prophet like Moses who can ask God to send provision; Jesus himself is that provision! God sent bread from heaven during the first exodus because that was what was needed then. But Jesus has been sent "from heaven", because he is the essential provision for the new exodus: no one can come into the eternal life promised by God except by him (6:50-51). Jesus' teaching about himself as the bread of life is echoed in the Lord's Supper (6:52-57; Luke 22:19), and in the prayer he taught his disciples (Matthew 6:11).

- **I am the light of the world** (8:12; 9:5). Throughout Scripture, light is an image of God's activity of creation (see Genesis 1:3) and salvation (see Exodus 13:21; Psalm 27:1). The world has become a dark place because of sin, so God set his people in the middle of the world to reflect his own light, revealing the way to him (see Isaiah 42:6; 49:6; 60:1-3). Israel often failed to be the light of the world because they also were affected by the darkness of sin. Jesus declared that he is what Israel were always supposed to be (8:12). However, Jesus is not just a reflection of God's light; he is the source of light itself and so is able to give it to others, as he demonstrates by healing a blind man (9:1-7). As John comments at the beginning of the Gospel, Jesus is the true light, who was at work in both creation and salvation (1:3-5,9). Just as Israel were to reflect God's light, so Christians are to reflect Jesus' (see Matthew 5:14; 2 Corinthians 4:6; 1 John 1:7).

Lighthouse at Portofino, Italy. As Jesus is the very source of light, we are to allow his light to reflect from us

- **I am the door of the sheep** (10:7,9). Gates or doors in sheepfolds are important for the safety and security of the sheep; they prevent the sheep from wandering away and predators from attacking the flock. A flock of sheep was a common image for God's people in the Old Testament (eg Psalm 100:3). The gate, for them, was God's Torah, entering through which they would experience salvation and blessing (note Deuteronomy 6:9). Jesus declares that he is the new Torah – he is the new gate of the flock of God's people, entering through which they will discover life in abundance (John 10:9-10). There is no other legitimate way into God's fold (10:1). Jesus will watch over the coming and going of the sheep (10:9), which echoes the constant watchful care of God himself in Psalm 121:8.

- **I am the good shepherd** (10:11,14). If Israel were seen as sheep in the Old Testament, then God was their shepherd (Psalm 23:1). However, God shared his care of the flock with Israel's leaders (eg Joshua in Numbers 27:17; also 2 Samuel 7:7), and in particular the king (especially David, 1 Chronicles 11:2). Apart from David and a few other good leaders, these "shepherds" did not take care of Israel, but led her into idolatry and wickedness, and allowed her to become prey for other nations, all the while making themselves comfortable with warm clothing and rich food (see Ezekiel 34:1-6). So God promised through Ezekiel to take the flock back under his control and rescue his sheep (34:11-16). He would appoint a new David to care for his renewed flock (34:23-24). Jesus announces that he is this new good shepherd – he is the true ruler

> " *Jesus answered, 'I am the way and the truth and the life. No one comes to the Father except through me.'* "
>
> JOHN 14:6

over God's people (John 10:11-16). Unlike the wicked leaders of Israel, Jesus is prepared even to go to his death in order to rescue his sheep from destruction (10:11). Jesus teaches his disciples that his suffering and death are God's means of gathering his people together. Far from being a failure, Jesus is the good shepherd who bring health and care to his wandering sheep (note also Luke 15:3-7; 1 Peter 2:25).

· **I am the resurrection and the life** (11:25). Israel knew that only God held the power of life (eg 2 Kings 5:7). Death, as the ultimate result of sin, disrupts God's good creation and threatens to remove even God's own people from their awareness of him (see Psalm 6:5; 88:10-11). In one of the greatest visions of the Old Testament, God promises to speak to the dead and dry bones of his people and raise them up to new life and fellowship with him (Ezekiel 37:1-14).

Israel's resurrection hope was not just new spiritual life, but new physical life too, in God's renewed world. In John 11:25, Jesus tells the grieving Martha that he is "the resurrection and the life": he is the powerful Word of God who has come to breathe new life into the world. He raised Martha's brother Lazarus to show the truth of his words (John 11:41-44). Jesus' teaching pointed forward to his own death and resurrection, by which he defeated sin and death. He brings new spiritual life now, but will completely fulfil his promise in the future when he will return to bring "resurrection and life" to all his followers.

· **I am the way, the truth, and the life** (14:6). "Way", "truth" and "life" are all images that spring directly from the Old Testament's teaching about obedience to God's Torah. If the Israelites were careful to walk in the way of God's commands, then they would enjoy blessing and life as God intended (Deuteronomy 5:32-33). Since God's law is the way to life, it was celebrated by the Israelites as truth (eg Psalm 25:5; 119:43). Jesus tells his disciples that they can follow him to God's new creation, where they will live in perfect fellowship with the Father (John 14:2-3). The way to get there – the way of truth that leads to life – is no longer God's Torah but Jesus himself (14:6). Jesus defines what it means to live in the kingdom of God, both now and forever. Jesus' words still speak powerfully today of his uniqueness: there is no other way to true life than through him.

· **I am the true vine** (15:1,5). The vine, or vineyard, was a common image for the whole nation of Israel in the Old Testament (eg Psalm 80:8; Jeremiah 2:21). They were supposed to produce fruit of righteousness for God, the vine-keeper. But instead, they produced little fruit – and what fruit they did produce was bad. Jesus teaches his disciples that he is the true vine (John 15:1): he is all Israel were ever supposed to be. His disciples are branches on the vine (15:5), which means that as long as they remain connected to him they will receive the pruning discipline of the Father (15:2-3), and bear good fruit from the resources of Jesus' life that will flow into them (15:5). Remaining in Jesus is all his disciples need in order to be pleasing and productive for the Father.

"I AM"

Jesus' use of the words "I am" has an even deeper significance. In John 8, Jesus stated, "you will die in your sins unless you believe that I am" (8:24), and then again, "when you have lifted up the Son of Man, you will realise that I am" (8:28). These sentences only make sense if Jesus is using "I am" as a title. At the end of the chapter, he claimed that "before Abraham was, I am" (8:58). At that, the Jews

were about to stone him (8:59), which was the usual punishment for blasphemy (see Leviticus 24:16), indicating how serious an offence Jesus had committed in their eyes. So how are his words blasphemy? The personal name for God in the Old Testament, YHWH, is translated "I am who I am", or "I am" (see Exodus 3:14). Jesus applies this divine name to himself in order to explain his origin (8:58), his suffering (8:28; 13:19), and his saving significance (8:24; see also 6:20). The Jews rightly recognised that Jesus was making a claim to share in the being and identity of the one true God of Israel! The Christian faith affirms that Jesus' teaching about himself was true: he is the great "I am", he shares the being and identity of YHWH, and so he is able to give life and hope to the whole world.

TO THINK ABOUT

Choose one of Jesus' seven "I am" statements and read the whole chapter or chapters in which it is found. Use the following questions to come to a deeper understanding of his teaching.
· Who is Jesus speaking with? Does the statement come as part of a conversation with his disciples or controversy with his opponents?
· Are there any miracles ("signs" in John's Gospel) that illustrate Jesus' statement about himself?
· What Old Testament imagery was Jesus using? How did he transform it?
· What was Jesus saying about himself in the statement you have chosen? How would you express this today?
· How do people in John's Gospel respond to Jesus' teaching about himself? How do you think people today respond to it? How do you?

Now choose one or more of the other statements and work through the same questions.
   Read John 8:31-59 slowly, and try to follow the discussion between Jesus and the Jews.
· What is their problem with Jesus? What have they misunderstood?
· How does Jesus respond? Try to imagine what it would have been like as one of the Jews to hear Jesus say this to you.
· How does verse 58, and Jesus' claim to be "I am", draw the discussion to its climax?
· How do you respond (see verse 59)?

Jesus' claims about himself were profoundly disturbing to many of his hearers, and some people still find them so today. He is the source of God's new creation, and the unique way to life within it. Think about how Jesus' claims make you feel. Now pray to God, expressing your trust in Jesus as the great "I am", and asking for the boldness to share this knowledge with others.

JESUS' POWERFUL ENCOUNTERS
Crowds and disciples

KEY TRUTH

Many people went to see Jesus out of curiosity, but Jesus called them to the greater commitment and cost of discipleship.

JESUS AND THE CROWDS

From the beginning of Jesus' public ministry, news about his healings and teachings spread quickly through the towns and villages of Palestine, first in the area of Galilee where Jesus began his work (Mark 1:28) but soon also further afield, including Judea and Idumea in the south, beyond the River Jordan (Decapolis) in the east, and the northern regions around Tyre and Sidon (Mark 3:8). Wherever Jesus went, crowds of people came to find him. They had different reasons for doing so: many were sick and wanted to be healed (Matthew 19:2; Mark 3:10); others came with the sick, perhaps simply out of curiosity to see if the stories about Jesus' miracles were true (Matthew 15:30-31; Mark 1:32-33; John 12:18); some had already experienced a miracle and wanted to see what the next would be (John 6:2,22-25,30); still others came to listen to his teaching (Mark 2:13; 10:1). These crowds were often large and rowdy, jostling to get near to Jesus and trampling on each other (Mark 5:24; Luke 12:1), so much so that he sometimes had to escape from them (eg Mark 3:9; 4:1). The Gospels portray the crowds as unstable in their attitude towards Jesus. At times they were delighted with him (eg Mark 12:37), but at other times they complained about him (John 7:12) and wanted to kill him (eg Luke 4:29-30). As Jesus came towards the end of his ministry, and headed towards Jerusalem, a growing crowd followed him. At first, they celebrated his arrival in Jerusalem with singing and palm branches (Matthew 21:8-11), but then just a few days later some of them were involved in his arrest (Matthew 26:47) and were stirred up by the Jewish leaders to demand his death (Mark 15:11-15). They gathered for his crucifixion (Luke 23:48), and ridiculed him.

When Jesus saw the crowds, he was filled with compassion. He taught them (Matthew 15:10; Mark 6:34), fed them (Matthew 15:32) and healed those who were sick (Matthew 14:14), because he recognised that they were "harassed and helpless, like sheep without a shepherd" (Matthew 9:36). The image of helpless sheep, wandering around lost without a shepherd, is familiar from the Old Testament; in Ezekiel 34, God declares that the leaders of Israel have led God's flock astray and then deserted them. The undisciplined, unruly crowds who followed Jesus would have been mainly made up of these Israelites, whom Jesus calls "the lost sheep of Israel" (Matthew 10:6). They have been misled by their leaders, and no longer enjoy the blessings of God's kingdom. As the Good Shepherd who cares for his sheep, Jesus wants to bring them back into God's fold (John 10:9,11).

Although the crowds did follow Jesus around, they were not true disciples, and were quick to disperse or turn against him. Jesus certainly did not measure the success of his ministry by the size of the crowds who followed him. Much of Jesus' preaching to the crowds invited them to move from casual curiosity to committed discipleship (eg Luke 9:23,57-62). Belonging to the crowd was easy;

Jesus had compassion for the crowds – "sheep without a shepherd". Takeshita Street, Tokyo

learn the teachings of their rabbi by living with him and following him wherever he went. A phrase from the time described disciples as those "covered in the dust of the rabbi", because they had been literally following their teacher so closely!

- **Followers.** Just like any rabbi, Jesus had a group of followers known as disciples. Unlike the crowds, who came and went, these followers stayed with Jesus for extended periods of time in order to learn from him. The early chapters of the Gospels suggest that there were large numbers of people who followed Jesus in this way (eg Luke 6:17). Some were John the Baptist's disciples who had decided to follow Jesus instead (see John 1:35-39). Others were people whom Jesus had met in their places of work (eg Matthew 4:18-22; 9:9). For them, not being professional religious people (eg like the scribe in Matthew 8:19), the prospect of being the disciple of a rabbi was so wonderful that they immediately left their work and followed Jesus. Jesus' followers came from all classes of society – for instance, Joseph of Arimathea was a rich man (Matthew 27:57) – and even included women, some of whom were also rich and played an integral part in Jesus' mission by supporting the other disciples from their resources (see Luke 8:1-3; 23:49).

belonging to Jesus as a disciple would be hard, but it was the only way to be part of the kingdom of God that Jesus was bringing.

JESUS AND HIS DISCIPLES

"Disciple" was a common term in the first century for a person who was a committed follower of a political, philosophical or religious leader. Within the Jewish world, it was particularly used for the students of a rabbi, or religious teacher. In the Gospels, John the Baptist and the Pharisees have groups of disciples (eg Mark 2:18; Matthew 22:15-16). These disciples would often be the most promising students who had come through the Jewish education system – they would have already memorised the Hebrew Scriptures and displayed the potential to learn their rabbi's particular teaching about the law and the prophets in order to go and teach it to others. It was therefore both a great honour and a great duty to be called by a rabbi to become his disciple. Disciples would

- **The Twelve.** Early in Jesus' ministry, he chose twelve followers out of the wider group to form a core band of disciples (Mark 3:13-19; Matthew 10:2-4; Luke 6:12-16). As he reminded them later, in becoming a part of this intimate group, they had not chosen him, but rather he had chosen them (John 15:16). They had two main purposes: to be "with" Jesus as followers, and also to be "sent out" by Jesus as representatives (Mark 3:14). The word "sent", in Greek, is *apostolos*, and so the Twelve also became known as "the apostles". They were to be with Jesus throughout his ministry, to hear his message and learn his way of life; then they were sent out by Jesus into the towns and villages of Israel, to spread Jesus' message about the kingdom, and to demonstrate it with the same miraculous signs that Jesus had used (Mark 3:14-15; see Matthew 10:1-42). After his resurrection, these disciples (without Judas, who had betrayed Jesus) were to take the message about him into the world (see Matthew 28:19).

Jesus' choice of twelve disciples is significant, given that there were originally twelve tribes in Israel, coming from the twelve sons of Jacob (see Genesis 49). After the exile, only the tribe of Judah had remained visibly intact. When Jesus chose

> *" Then he [Jesus] said to them all: 'If anyone would come after me, he must deny himself and take up his cross daily and follow me.'"*

LUKE 9:23

twelve disciples, he was announcing the restoration of God's people, now reconfigured around himself. The disciples were a diverse group of people. Simon, who was named "Peter" by Jesus, and his brother Andrew, and the two sons of Zebedee, James and John, were all fishermen from Galilee. Peter, James and John were closest to Jesus, being with him at key times such as the transfiguration (Mark 9:2) and Jesus' prayer in the Garden of Gethsemane (Matthew 26:37); and among these, Peter was the most prominent of all the disciples. Matthew, or Levi, was a tax collector (Matthew 9:9), who would thus have been considered a social outcast because of his employment with the despised authorities. On the other hand, Simon was a member of the Zealots (Matthew 10:4; Mark 3:18), who were

zealous nationalists prepared to fight the Roman authorities. It is possible that Judas Iscariot was also a member of the Zealots, since "Iscariot" could mean a "Sicarian", a radical group of Zealots; or it could simply designate his home town. Either way, Judas became the treasurer of the group, but later fell into theft (John 12:6) and finally betrayed Jesus to the authorities. Although Thomas is known for his doubting of Jesus' resurrection (John 20:25), he was actually a disciple of great courage (eg John 11:16). Along with the other disciples – Philip, Bartholomew, James the son of Alphaeus, and Thaddaeus (known as Judas the son of James in Luke 6:16) – these twelve represented a spectrum of Jewish life and belief. What brought them together was the call of Jesus, which transcended all their other commitments (eg Matthew 19:27) and gave them the new, uniting purpose of heralding the kingdom that Jesus was bringing.

- **The Seventy.** A final notable group were the seventy that Jesus sent out to prepare the ground for him in the towns he would visit on his way to Jerusalem (Luke 10:1). If the twelve disciples mirror the twelve tribes of Israel, then perhaps these seventy reflect the elders that Moses appointed to assist him in leading the nation of Israel (Numbers 11:16,24,25).

THE CALL TO DISCIPLESHIP

Jesus' message was that God's true people were all those who gathered around him. He summoned his hearers to move from the "harassed and helpless" crowd to become his disciples. Unlike other rabbis, who only wanted to have the most promising students as disciples, Jesus welcomed anyone who would come to him (John 6:37). However, his preaching made clear the costs involved – the disciples could only expect to be treated in the same way as their rabbi (Matthew 10:24-25; Luke 14:26-27; John 15:20). So Jesus

TO THINK ABOUT

Read Jesus' instructions to the Twelve before he sent them out in Matthew 10.

- What does it mean to be a disciple and an apostle in this passage? What is the basis of the Twelve's discipleship (see 10:1)?
- What challenges will Jesus' disciples face as they go out? Why might this be?
- How does Jesus encourage them (see especially 10:26-31)?
- Do Jesus' instructions about discipleship still apply today? Were any specific to that particular occasion? What is different about being a disciple now (after the resurrection of Jesus)?

Think about the crowds who followed Jesus.

- Are there any "crowds" today? Why are people attracted to Jesus?
- How about you: are you ever like the crowds?

- How do you respond to Jesus' call to become a disciple? Do you ever think of Jesus as your "rabbi"?
- What might it look like for you to be "covered in the dust" of rabbi Jesus?
- A disciple must both be with Jesus, as well as be sent out by him. Which do you find easier?

Jesus' first disciples were aware of the cost and commitment involved in following Jesus in a way that we are often not. However, it is still a hard thing to follow Jesus today, whether in parts of the world where there is persecution for being a Christian, or because living "covered in the dust" of Jesus provokes ridicule from a disinterested world. Thank Jesus that he is a good rabbi, who has called you to be with him as a follower, and be sent out into the world as his representative. Pray for the strength to do both things well.

instructed his hearers to consider if they were willing to reorder their lives completely around him before they began to follow him (Luke 14:28-33). For those who did respond to Jesus' call, however, there was the joy of being part of God's kingdom now (eg Luke 10:17) and the promise of enjoying God's renewed world forever (eg Matthew 19:28-29).

JESUS' POWERFUL ENCOUNTERS
Acts of healing

KEY TRUTH

Jesus' acts of healing confirmed and illustrated the truth of his announcement that the kingdom of God was arriving among people through his ministry.

JESUS, THE HEALER

All four Gospels record that acts of healing were central to Jesus' public work. Healings were present from the very beginning of his ministry; just after his temptation by Satan in the wilderness (Matthew 4:1-11), Jesus went through the region of Galilee "proclaiming the good news of the kingdom and curing every disease and every sickness among the people" (Matthew 4:23). News of these wonderful, liberating healings soon spread throughout the whole land, and crowds of sick people began to gather around Jesus wherever he went (eg Matthew 4:24; Mark 1:32-34; Luke 5:15). About one third of Mark's Gospel is devoted to recounting Jesus' miracles and healings, but we can be sure that there were many more that were never written down, yet still brought relief and joy to the people who experienced them (see John 21:25).

Jesus' healing miracles seem so wonderful that many people through the ages have presumed they were simply stories made up by the early Christians. Some people today are sceptical that God's power could intervene in a person's life to bring about physical healing and wholeness. However, there is very good reason to accept the Gospel accounts as true, and affirm that Jesus healed people. For a start, Jesus' opponents in the Gospels did not try to deny that Jesus had healed people – knowledge of the healings was too widespread for them to be able to claim that. Instead, they tried to suggest that Jesus healed by using demonic power rather than divine power (eg

John 9:16). Non-Christian writings about Jesus also confirm that he did miraculous things. Josephus, a first-century Jewish historian, referred to Jesus as a "doer of wonderful deeds" (*Antiquities of the Jews* 18.63, published around AD 90). A Jewish teaching document (part of the Talmud), records that Jesus was condemned to death because he "practised sorcery" (*b.Sanhedrin* 43a). So the historicity of Jesus' miracles was not in question – he was undoubtedly a great healer. The real question surrounded their source and meaning: were they from God, or not?

WHO JESUS HEALED

Jesus' healing of a person was not dependent on the nature of that person's illness. He was not a "specialist", who worked with only certain kinds of sickness, but healed all who came to him. The Gospels record that Jesus cured fevers (Mark 1:30-31), serious skin diseases (Mark 1:40-42; Luke 17:11-19; the term "leprosy" could cover a number of different infections), paralysis (Matthew 9:2-7), disfigurement (Matthew 12:10-13), deafness and dumbness (Mark 7:31-37), blindness (Mark 8:22-26; John 9:1-7), and dropsy (Luke 14:1-4). There were even occasions when he brought a dead person back to life, shortly after their death from illness (Mark 5:35-43; Luke 7:11-17; John 11:38-44).

Sick people came into contact with Jesus from many different sections of first-century society: many would have been ordinary Jews, but some were despised Samaritans (eg Luke

17:16) and even Gentiles (eg Matthew 8:5-13; Mark 7:26). Jesus healed the daughter of a prominent synagogue leader (Matthew 9:18), as well as a beggar (Mark 10:46) – what mattered to him was a person's need, not their social status.

Some of the people whom Jesus healed had sought him out, coming with an already deep faith that he could bring healing (Mark 5:27-28); others were people who met him on his journeys, recognising in that moment their opportunity for healing and seizing it gladly (Mark 10:47); still others simply happened to be in the same place as Jesus and found themselves being healed by him! (Mark 3:1-5; Luke 13:10-13). Not all came to Jesus by themselves: once, a paralysed man was brought to Jesus by his friends (Luke 5:18-20), while on other occasions the sick person remained at home while someone else went to Jesus (eg Matthew 8:5-6).

Jesus certainly healed in response to faith (Matthew 9:28-29), but sometimes he healed as an act of utter compassion, when there could have been no evidence of faith before the miracle occurred (eg Luke 7:11-15). Jesus did not even seem to heal people on the basis of what their response to him would be after their healing: in Luke 17:11-19 Jesus healed ten lepers, but only one came back to thank him. Jesus' healing was free and generous – just like God's grace.

HOW JESUS HEALED

There was no set pattern or method for Jesus' healings. Often Jesus healed with a simple word that declared the healing had already taken place through a person's encounter with him, such as "Stand up, take your mat and go home" to the paralysed man (Mark 2:11) or "Receive your sight" to the blind men (Luke 18:42). Sometimes, in addition to his words, he also made physical contact with the sick person (eg Luke 13:13). On a couple of occasions, Jesus used his own saliva in the healing (Mark 8:23; John 9:6), but he could

also heal from a distance, with no contact at all (eg Matthew 8:5-13). In Mark 5:25-34, the haemorrhaging woman was healed by touching Jesus' cloak before he had even become aware of her in the crowd!

This variety of stories shows that Jesus' healings were not the work of magic, requiring complicated rituals or a specific form of words. There was only one occasion when Jesus prayed to God before a healing, and even then he declared that his prayer was only for the crowd's benefit (John 11:41-42). Unlike prophets of the Old Testament, who

> "*Jesus went throughout Galilee, teaching in their synagogues, preaching the good news of the kingdom, and healing every disease and sickness among the people.*"
>
> MATTHEW 4:23

relied on prayer to God (eg 2 Kings 4:32-35), or the first Christians, who healed using Jesus' name (see Acts 3:6), Jesus healed people on his own authority. It was as if Jesus was so full of health and wholeness – the blessing of God's kingdom – that he was able to give it away to others! Although this healing was given freely and generously, it was not without personal cost to Jesus (see Mark 5:30), and he would sometimes withdraw from the crowds to rest and pray (Luke 5:15-16). Those healed by Jesus, even from a distance, would have known that they had experienced the power of Jesus' ministry, and not some vague miraculous power.

DEMONSTRATION OF JESUS' MESSAGE

Jesus' acts of healing were not dramatic stunts intended to amaze people and attract large crowds. Rather, they were intimately connected with his central message that God's kingdom was arriving among people through his ministry (Mark 1:15). Without the healings, the truth of Jesus' message could have been called into question.

- **The need for healing.** For the people of Israel, sickness was not simply an annoying personal misfortune that accidentally happened to some people – it was a social and spiritual disaster. Genesis identifies sickness as one of the consequences that sin has within God's good creation (Genesis 3:16-19 – though not necessarily a direct consequence of a person's own sin, see John 9:2-3). Within the Jewish system of worship, priests who had physical imperfections – of whatever nature – were forbidden from entering the temple to offer sacrifices to God, lest God's holy perfection was thought to be tainted by association (see Leviticus 21:16-24). Even for ordinary worshippers, physical deformities rendered a person "unclean", and there were elaborate rituals that needed to be followed if they were to be accepted back into the worshipping community of God's people. Leprosy was dealt with by exclusion – lepers would find themselves excluded not only from worship in the temple, but also from normal society (Leviticus 13:45-46). By Jesus' day, it was a common assumption that someone who was blind, deaf, dumb, lame or otherwise sick or unwell, could not be a full member of God's people. Sickness or deformity was like a plague to be avoided; it affected the individual person as well as the people around them, who were in danger of becoming "unclean" by association too.

- **The hope of healing.** In the Old Testament, physical illness was often used as a symbol of Israel's experience of broken fellowship with God. When God's people went into exile, the prophets spoke about a coming day when God would renew the life of his people, delivering them from their enemies and bringing them back to their

Jesus' acts of healing showed no boundaries – rich and poor were blessed. Leprosy treatment, Burma

land. This renewal would come as a great healing, which would be so amazingly powerful that it would incorporate even the blind, deaf, lame and dumb back into God's people (see Isaiah 35:1-6). The agent who would bring this healing was God's anointed ruler, the Messiah (the "servant" in Isaiah 53:4 and 61:1-4). Although Israel had returned to their land under Nehemiah and Ezra, in Jesus' days they still experienced the oppression of foreign rule, and so still hoped for God's full liberation to come.

- **The reality of the kingdom.** When Jesus announced that the kingdom of God was arriving in his ministry, he demonstrated the truth of his message by healing people. In particular, Jesus healed the types of people mentioned by Isaiah: the blind, the lame, the deaf and the dumb. For those who were willing to realise it, Jesus' healings were unmistakable signs that the prophecies about God's kingdom were now being fulfilled by Jesus (Matthew 11:2-6) – he was bringing the peace and wellbeing (the *shalom*) of God's kingdom to all who would receive it. His healing did not just relieve people of their personal distress and enable them to return to normal community life; most importantly, it signalled that God's kingdom was now fully open to them, and

TO THINK ABOUT

Read some of the background on "uncleanness" in Leviticus 13:45-46 and 22:1-9. Now read Luke 5:12-13 and 7:11-15.

· What do you notice about Jesus' actions?
· What normally happened (in Jewish thought) when a clean person touched an unclean person/thing? What happened when Jesus did?
· What does this tell you about Jesus' acts of healing?
· How do you think Jesus' first followers might have felt?

Choose one of your favourite healing accounts (or use one of these: Matthew 9:2-7; Mark 3:1-5; Luke 17:11-19; John 4:46-54). Now explore it with the following questions:

· Who needs to be healed? From what? How might the illness be affecting wider life and worship?
· Does the person come to Jesus alone, or with others? What attitude does the person have towards him? Who else is watching?
· How does Jesus respond?
· How is this a demonstration of the arrival of God's kingdom in Jesus' ministry?
· Is healing like this possible today? Why, or why not? If it happened, what would it demonstrate?

Jesus' acts of healing revealed the nature and reality of God's coming kingdom. Whenever God's kingdom is announced today, it should not be too surprising if healing sometimes occurs, though for full healing we must of course wait until God's kingdom finally comes. Thank Jesus for the glimpse of the kingdom's reality in his ministry, and pray that you may experience more of that reality in your own life, both now in part, and fully in the future.

---

they could be established as members of God's renewed people! In Luke's Gospel, when the crowds experience one of Jesus' acts of healing, they exclaim that Jesus must be God's great prophet, whose ministry demonstrates that God has not forgotten his promises (Luke 7:16). Of course, Jesus is much more than a prophet. He is the "servant" from Isaiah, who takes the infirmities of God's people upon himself, in order to liberate them (Matthew 8:16-17; Isaiah 53:4). Ultimately, Jesus' healing power springs from his death and resurrection, by which he defeated the powers of sin and death, and so opened the way to God's *shalom* for all who come through him. Although the whole world must still wait for God's kingdom to come in its fullness, Jesus' healings brought the kingdom into particular moments of time and space, as signs of the reality of his message.

See also Miracles of Jesus Christ, page 304.

JESUS' POWERFUL ENCOUNTERS
Nature miracles

KEY TRUTH

Jesus' nature miracles revealed the deep significance of his mission in the world: through Jesus, God was providing salvation and rescue just as he had done in the past.

GOD'S POWER OVER CREATION

In the Old Testament, one of Israel's central convictions was that their God YHWH was not a small tribal god, like many of the gods of the nations around them – he was the great creator who had lovingly brought the whole universe into existence! (eg Isaiah 40:28). Although the created world had been caught up in the consequences of human sin (Genesis 3:17-19), it was not ultimately opposed to God's good purposes, but in fact declared his glory (Psalm 19:1) and obeyed his commands (see Job 38). So, when God was at work, rescuing his people from their enemies,

he was able to use creation to fulfil his purposes. In the great exodus from Egypt, God revealed his power to Pharaoh and the Israelites through various miraculous acts, from the plagues in Egypt (Exodus 7–11) to the parting of the Red Sea (14:21-29). Time after time through Israel's history, God did miraculous things within the created world in order to bring blessing and deliverance to his people (eg Exodus 17:1-7). Many of Israel's songs contained reminders of these mighty acts, as a prompt to praise and thank him (eg Psalm 105). Israelites recognised that the power of God they had experienced in the great acts of salvation was the same power that had brought the universe into existence in the first place; just as he had spoken it into

A miraculous catch of fish from the Sea of Galilee caused Peter to wonder who Jesus really was

being, so God could speak again and direct it to make a way for his people's salvation.

Jesus' nature miracles took place against this background. For the people who experienced them, these miracles were not merely astonishing tricks designed to get their attention. First-century Jews would have instinctively associated Jesus' miracles with God's mighty acts of salvation and deliverance from the Old Testament. At the very least, these miracles signalled that God was at work again, directing even nature itself

> " *They were terrified and asked each other, 'Who is this? Even the wind and the waves obey him!'* "
>
> MARK 4:41

to come to his people's aid. Sometimes they functioned as acted parables, illustrating Jesus' message about the kingdom of God (eg the miraculous catches of fish illustrated the task of the disciples, Luke 5:1-11 and John 21:1-11; the withering of the fig tree illustrated the judgement and destruction of the temple, Matthew 21:18-21 and Mark 11:12-25). But they also prompted a deeper question: if Jesus has this power over creation, then who is he? (Mark 4:41).

FEEDING THE CROWDS

The Gospels record two occasions when Jesus provided food for a crowd that had gathered to hear him teach (Mark 6:35-44; 8:1-9; also recorded in Matthew 14:15-21; 15:32-38; Luke 9:12-17 and John 6:5-13). Only the number of men in each crowd was recorded: first five thousand, then four thousand, besides women and children – and Jesus fed them all from a few loaves and fish, with plenty left over. It is a clear indication that Jesus provides for those who gather around him.

But there is a deeper significance. On both occasions, the miracle happened out in the wilderness, away from towns and villages (Mark 6:35; 8:4). Back in the Old Testament, the people of Israel had experienced many years of wandering in the wilderness, during their exodus from Egypt. At that time, as in Jesus' day, they grew hungry and were unable to provide for themselves, given that the wilderness was no place to find or buy food. In Exodus 16:3 they grumbled to Moses and Aaron about their hunger: God should not have brought them out into the wilderness, only to let them die of starvation. If God's deliverance from Egypt were to be real and complete, he would need to feed them on their journey too. In response, God promised to "rain down bread from heaven" in order that they could eat their fill (Exodus 16:4-8). The "manna" that God gave them was essential provision for their journey to the Promised Land. In the Gospels, the disciples are concerned that the crowds have no food and ask Jesus to send them home. However, Jesus refuses to send them away – they have already experienced something of the kingdom of God through his teachings, and now they would experience it in their stomachs! Jesus instructs the crowds to sit down in an orderly fashion (Mark 6:39), perhaps a reflection of the organisation of the Israelite camp in the wilderness (see Numbers 2). He then blesses the small amount of food he has and gives it to the twelve disciples for distribution. Jesus was providing abundant food in the wilderness, just as God had done before. Jesus is leading God's people in a new exodus – not from slavery in Egypt, but from the greater slavery of sin and Satan. Jesus is able to carry his people through the whole journey. Those who stay with him (see Mark 8:2, the crowd had been with Jesus for three days) will find that he provides everything they need.

Jesus' miracle did not only look back to the exodus, it also looked forward to the coming of God's kingdom. It was commonly understood that when God's Messiah came to put the world to rights, he would throw an extravagant feast for the nations (see Isaiah 25:6-9), known as the messianic banquet. This was a common theme in Jesus' parables (eg Luke 14:15-24). By feeding the crowds, Jesus was bringing a foretaste of the great messianic feast. In particular, the second crowd, gathered in Gentile territory, probably included not only Jews, but also people from "the nations". If he was doing that, then he must be the Messiah!

WATER TO WINE

Jesus' miracle at the wedding in Cana, where he turned water into wine (John 2:1-11), also had close connections with the messianic banquet. In Isaiah 25:6, the menu at the coming great feast included an abundance of "well-matured wines" (see also Amos 9:13). Jesus certainly supplied an abundance of wine for the wedding: the six water jars together would have produced around seven hundred litres of wine (John 2:6)! The chief steward who was in charge of the feast was also amazed by its quality (2:10). In John's Gospel, this is the first of Jesus' miracles, or "signs", which revealed who he was and what he had come to do (2:11). Jesus' ministry is the "new wine" of God's kingdom (see Mark 2:22).

JESUS AND THE SEA OF GALILEE

Even today, the Sea of Galilee is well known for its sudden and ferocious storms, resulting from its particular geographical location and climate. On a couple of occasions Jesus' disciples, despite including experienced fishermen in their number, were caught out in a boat in the middle of the sea when a storm engulfed them. On one occasion, Jesus was with them in the boat, and he calmed the violent wind and waves with a simple command (Matthew 8:23-27; Mark 4:37-41; Luke 8:22-25). Another time, Jesus was not in the boat, but came walking over the water to meet them as they were battling against the weather (Matthew 14:24-33; Mark 6:48-52; John 6:18-21). More than any other miracles, these nature miracles on the Sea of Galilee seemed to provoke the disciples to wonder about the true identity of Jesus (eg Matthew 8:27).

In the Jewish mind, the ability to control the wind and waves of a storm belonged to God alone. This image went back to creation itself, where God spoke over the chaos of the waters to bring his good, ordered creation; by his word, the seas were gathered in one place, and the dry land in another so that life could flourish (Genesis 1:2,9-10). Israelites associated the sea with the chaos and disorder of evil that tries to resist God's good purposes: the Red Sea had been in their way during their escape from Egypt (Exodus 14:1-12); and in Daniel's prophecy, the four evil, beastly kingdoms rise up from the sea (Daniel 7:1-12). The Babylonians, who had carried Israel into exile, believed in a goddess called Tiamat, who was thought to embody the chaotic seas, and was sometimes associated with great sea dragons. In the Babylonian story of creation, she had been killed and cut open in order to form the heavens and the earth. In the Old Testament, the Israelites affirm that their God has complete control over these chaotic waters. In an echo of his separation of water from land at creation, God drove back the Red Sea to let Israel pass on dry ground (Exodus 14:21-31; Psalm 77:16-19). In Daniel, the four beastly kingdoms were followed by the reign of God's appointed "son of man" (Daniel 7:13-14). God is praised for having defeated the great sea dragons (Psalm 74:13-14) – he is more powerful than all the Babylonian gods – and calming the chaotic waters, whether literal or metaphorical (Jonah 1:15-16; Job 26:12; Psalm 65:7; 89:9; 107:23-30).

Against this background, Jesus' ability to walk over the waves and command the sea to be still was a clear indication of his true

TO THINK ABOUT

Read the accounts of Jesus' feedings of the crowds in Matthew 14:13-21 and 15:29-39.

- What are the similarities between the two occasions? Are there any differences?
- What would it have been like to be part of the crowd that day? One of the disciples?
- Why do you think the disciples responded as they did in 15:33? Would you have responded differently?
- How does the background of "bread from heaven" (Exodus 16) and the messianic banquet (Isaiah 25:6-9) help you to understand this miracle?

The calming of the storm echoes the Old Testament's description of God's power in creation and salvation over the forces of chaos and evil.

- What are the forces of chaos in the world today?

- What significance does Jesus walking on the water have for you?
- Read Matthew 14:22-33. Why do you think Peter wants to go to Jesus?
- Is it possible to experience nature miracles today? If so, what significance do they have?

Jesus' nature miracles show that he has the authority to use creation to accomplish God's good purposes. He can bring the blessing of God's kingdom into any situation. Thank God for the storms he has stilled in your life. Now commit yourself to trust him to provide for you, as you journey from death to life with the risen Christ!

identity. In Matthew 14:33, the disciples recognise that the one who stills the storm must be God's supreme representative, his Son. When Jesus walks across the water to the disciples, he greets them with the words "It is I", which in Greek is simply *ego eimi,* "I am", the personal name of God from Exodus 3:14 (Mark 6:50; John 6:20). These miracles also

indicate the significance of Jesus' ministry – his power over the chaos of the sea is evidence that God is at work through him to defeat the greater chaotic forces of sin and Satan, and bring the peace of his kingdom. The God of Israel was at work once more!

See also Miracles of Jesus Christ, page 304.

Satan and demons

KEY TRUTH

During his ministry, Jesus encountered the greatest enemy of God –
Satan, with his demons – and consistently demonstrated that God's power
is greater and ultimately victorious!

THE ENEMY OF GOD AND HIS PEOPLE

Since the beginning of creation, there has always been opposition to God's good purposes. In Genesis 3, a serpent interrupts the harmony of the Garden of Eden and tempts the first humans to turn away from God. The following chapters describe the evil that resulted: jealousy and anger (4:5), murder (4:8,23), wickedness (6:5), pride (11:4). Just when it seemed the world was spiralling out of control, God called Abraham (12:1-3) and promised that through Abraham's descendants, he would restore his good order to the world. However, time after time, Abraham's descendants – the nation of Israel – found themselves being dragged away from God's good rule and blessing, back into the evil and suffering of the world around them: first slavery in Egypt, then attack from foreign nations, then being carried away into exile. Throughout it all, they found it impossible to stay in close fellowship with God, but were themselves constantly riddled with cruelty, injustice and sin. Behind the armies of their foreign oppressors lay the greater hostile power of the worldwide forces of evil.

Israel came to understand that these hostile forces were personal in nature, and were directly opposed to their God YHWH. Since they were God's special people, chosen to reveal God's good order to the rest of the world, the attention of this evil being was turned purposefully towards them – if it could, it would disrupt YHWH's relationship with the people of Israel. The Hebrew term they used for this figure was *satan*, which means "the adversary" or "the accuser". Satan was a mysterious figure in the Old Testament, but he seemed to have access to God's heavenly courtroom, where he would attempt to bring accusations against God's faithful people (eg Job 1:6–2:7; 1 Chronicles 21:1; Zechariah 3:1). His sole purpose was to disrupt God's good plans, by destroying God's people; he was the serpent in the Garden of Eden. In later Jewish writings, Satan had angels and powers at his command, through which he could instigate evil in the world.

Satan is a conspicuous character in the New Testament, appearing as the personal enemy of Jesus and his divine mission (see Luke 4:2-13). He is often called "the devil" – when the Hebrew Scriptures were translated into Greek, the word *diabolos* ("devil") was used since it means "a slanderer", just like *satan*. He is also called "the evil one" (eg Matthew 5:37), "the tempter" (Matthew 4:3), "the enemy" (Luke 10:19), "Beelzebul" (Matthew 10:25, probably meaning "lord of heaven", using a version of the Hebrew word Baal, one of the Canaanite gods), "the ruler of demons" (Matthew 9:34) and "the ruler of this world" (John 16:11). All these names bring out aspects of his hostile work among people. The extraordinary number of demons that Jesus encountered during his ministry suggests that Satan was particularly and visibly active, trying to work against Jesus and God's kingdom.

AN INITIAL VICTORY

At the very beginning of his ministry, Jesus had a private confrontation with Satan (Matthew 4:1-11; Mark 1:12-13; Luke 4:1-13). After his baptism and affirmation by God (Matthew 3:13-17; Mark 1:9-11; Luke 3:21-22), Jesus was led into the wilderness by God's Spirit, where he fasted for 40 days and nights. There is a direct parallel with God's people Israel in the Old Testament. After they had come through the Red Sea (baptism) and been given a covenant with God (affirmation of mission and identity), the Israelites spent 40 years in the wilderness, where their faith and obedience to God was tested (see Deuteronomy 8:2). Now God's true Son was also to experience this testing, but unlike Israel, he would trust and obey his Father perfectly (Hebrews 4:15).

Matthew and Luke record three specific temptations that Satan brought to Jesus, yet in each case Jesus resisted by quoting verses from Deuteronomy (8:3; 6:16,13). Satan's temptations had made the first humans doubt God's words, but Jesus stood by the truth of them. In each of Jesus' temptations, he was being challenged about his understanding of his mission and identity ("if you are the Son of God ...").

- First, Satan tempts Jesus to provide bread for himself, but Jesus replied by quoting Deuteronomy 8:3. The Israelites in the wilderness had grumbled about having no bread, and had only reluctantly trusted God's word to provide them with the manna they needed. Jesus gladly trusts God to provide for him and will not allow his physical need for bread to come before his faithfulness to God.
- In another temptation, Jesus is challenged to throw himself off the top of the temple, in order to be rescued by God's angels in full view of the crowds of Jerusalem (see Psalm 91:11-12). This would certainly have given Jesus an instant following, but it would not have matched his mission of service and suffering. Jesus quoted Deuteronomy 6:16 in response, confirming that he would not force God to prove his care for him in the way that the Israelites had in the wilderness. There, despite God's constant provision, they had still doubted that he would give them water, asking "Is God among us or not?" (see Exodus 17:1-7). Jesus had already received God's affirmation at his baptism, and he needed no more proof that God really was with him in his ministry.

- In a final temptation, Satan promised to give Jesus all the kingdoms of the world, in return for Jesus' worship. Jesus recognised, however, that the world was not Satan's to give. As God's Son, he could ask the Father,

> " *Jesus said to him, 'Away from me, Satan! For it is written: "Worship the Lord your God, and serve him only." ' Then the devil left him, and angels came and attended him."*
>
> MATTHEW 4:10-11

who could rightly give him the nations (see Psalm 2:7-8). He quoted Deuteronomy 6:13, a reminder that Israel's God was the only one worthy of worship and obedience, because he was the one who had fulfilled his promise of bringing Israel out of slavery in Egypt. This same LORD God was now about to achieve a greater rescue – of the whole world from slavery to Satan, and his evil forces – and Jesus committed himself fully to this task, even though it would mean his own suffering and death.

After this, Satan went away from Jesus, his plans to tempt Jesus away from his mission utterly defeated. Jesus had won the victory over "every temptation" that Satan could throw at him (Luke 4:13) by his persistent trust in God and his willingness to obey him. While there would be other confrontations between Satan and Jesus – most notably in Jesus' exorcisms – the initial and decisive victory had already been won.

CASTING OUT DEMONS

As Jesus went about his ministry, he encountered numerous individuals who had been overcome, or possessed, by evil spirits or demons. People who doubt the existence of such spirits suggest that these "demoniacs" were in fact suffering from severe psychological disorders that would now be treated through medicine or therapy. However, around the world today Christians are aware of psychological illness and demon possession as two distinct phenomena. There is no good reason to doubt that demons are real and sometimes have the ability to torment and destroy a person's life. The demoniacs in the Gospels were not simply suffering from psychological disorder, but had been possessed by forces of evil outside of themselves. Demons are in Satan's control, and their sole aim is to frustrate God's good purposes in the world, and particularly in an individual's life.

For Jesus, casting out demons was a key indication that God's kingdom was really arriving in his ministry (Matthew 12:28; Luke 11:20). The coming of God's kingdom in this way meant that Satan himself was defeated (Luke 10:18) and had already been bound in advance of his ultimate destruction (Mark 3:27). In fact, exorcism was so integral to Jesus' mission that when he sent his disciples out to spread the news in the surrounding towns and villages, he also gave them power to cast out demons (eg Matthew 10:1; see also Luke 10:17). For the people who had been possessed, Jesus' exorcism was itself the coming of the kingdom – God had set them

A Shona witchdoctor, Zimbabwe

free by his liberating rule, just as he had promised.

Typically, the demons could recognise both the true identity of Jesus as the Son of God, and his superior power over them, so that they were afraid he would destroy them (eg Mark 1:24; 5:7). They were obviously extremely powerful, since they were able to kill an entire herd of pigs (Matthew 8:31-32) and leave a young boy looking as if he were dead (Mark 9:26). Yet, as with his other healings, Jesus was able to cast out these strong demons with a simple word of command. This contrasts with other exorcists of the day who would spend time invoking the power of God, and often used special forms of words and other magical parapher-nalia, such as bowls of water and finger rings, amulets and other objects. Jesus' opponents suggested that Jesus could only exercise such authority over the demons if he was himself

TO THINK ABOUT

Read the story of one of Jesus' exorcisms in Mark 5:1-20. This takes place on the eastern shore of the Sea of Galilee, which was primarily Gentile, rather than Jewish, territory.

· How do you think Jesus' disciples felt when they stepped out of the boat? Remember what they have just been through (4:37-41), and that they are now on Gentile land (5:1), close to some tombs (5:2) and a great heard of pigs (5:11, considered by Jews to be unclean).
· What had Satan's demons done to the man they met?
· How do the demons react to Jesus? Why do you think this is?
· How did Jesus' exorcism affect the man who had previously been possessed? The demons? The local people? The disciples?
· How did this exorcism bring God's kingdom? In what wider ways does it illustrate what the kingdom is like?

Try working through another of Jesus' exorcisms: Luke 9:38-42.

In the New Testament, the power of Satan and his demons was unmistakable. Jesus confronted it head on.

· In what ways do you experience the reality and power of evil today?
· Is it important to recognise a personal source to evil (ie Satan)? Why, or why not?
· What does Jesus' ministry of exorcism teach today's church? Note Mark 16:17.

Although Satan's evil power is still strong and dangerous today, we must affirm that Jesus has bound Satan, and has already won the victory over him, supremely in his death and resurrection. The kingdom of God comes among us when demons are cast out, and God's liberating rule begins. Thank Jesus for his strong, resurrected power. Use Ephesians 6:10-17 to pray for God's strength as you face the evil in the world around you, whatever form it takes.

in league with them (Matthew 12:24). But as Jesus pointed out, Satan would never work against himself in that way (Matthew 12:26). Demons can only be driven out by a stronger power, and since Jesus did not use any authority except his own (Mark 9:25), he himself must be that stronger power. In a parable he told, he was the stronger man who had overpowered a strong man in order to plunder his possessions (Luke 11:21-22, see also Matthew 12:29). Through his exorcisms, Jesus was plundering Satan's domain, indicating that God's kingdom of peace and order was already arriving in part, and would certainly triumph in the end!

Forgiveness of sinners

KEY TRUTH

Jesus claimed that forgiveness was freely available to all through him, and he demonstrated this at the meal table by eating with sinners, welcoming them into the fellowship of God's family!

"SINNERS" IN THE GOSPELS

Throughout his ministry, Jesus constantly associated with "tax collectors and sinners", not only as he went about in the streets, but also in the most intimate context of the meal table (eg Mark 2:15-16). Jesus clearly saw this fellowship as central to his mission (Mark 2:17), but his opponents found it infuriating (eg Luke 15:2).

It is important to be clear about what the term "sinner" meant in the first-century Jewish context. It was not primarily a moral category, as it is often used today. The "sinners" who met with Jesus were not necessarily people who had led lives of great immorality, though of course some were (eg the woman caught in adultery, John 8:3). Rather, for the Jews of Jesus' day, a "sinner" was simply anyone who was considered to be outside the covenant with the God of Israel, for whatever reason.

- **Gentiles.** Technically, "sinners" included all Gentiles, who simply by being born outside the nation of Israel could not belong within God's covenant (eg Psalm 9:17). However, since Jesus' ministry in the Gospels was mostly among Jews, this usage is not frequent; Gentiles are referred to by their various nationalities (Canaanite, Greek, Roman, etc.) and are understood to be automatically outside the Jewish covenant (see Matthew 15:24-26).
- **Unfaithful or unobservant Jews.** In the Gospels, the term refers primarily to "sinners" within Israel herself – Jews who

had not remained loyal to the covenant or its way of life; people who had transgressed, or stepped over, the boundary of their relationship with God as it had been spelled out in the *Torah*. This group certainly included those who persisted in moral sin, such as prostitutes; but it also referred to a wider group of people who simply failed to obey rigorous religious standards. In Jesus' day, the Pharisees were the champions of this ceremonial purity. The Pharisees had added strict guidelines to the code of life set out in the *Torah* for nearly every area of life, including, for instance, whom they associated with, how they washed before meals (eg Mark 7:3-4) and many extra days of fasting. In the eyes of the Pharisees, many of the common Israelites were "sinners", since they were either unwilling to keep such strict standards, or unable to do so because of their physical health or work. Falling short of such standards (the original meaning of "sin" is "to miss the mark") made a person unclean.

- **Tax collectors.** Tax collectors are often mentioned alongside sinners in the Gospels. They were minor government officials or customs officers who worked for King Herod in Galilee or the Romans in Judea. They were collecting taxes for the Roman Empire, and so they were often spurned for collaborating with the occupying force. This collaboration with Gentiles meant they were unable to keep the strict purity laws. They may even have engaged in usury (lending money at interest), which was forbidden in the Old Testament (eg Leviticus 25:35-37; Deuteronomy 23:19-20). In addition, some tax collectors were corrupt (eg Zacchaeus, Luke 19:8), which firmly placed them in the "sinners" group.

Within the covenant, sin could be dealt with through the sacrificial system centred in the temple in Jerusalem. The book of Leviticus outlined the sacrifices that were appropriate for different types of sin (see especially Leviticus 4–6). In every case, at the end of the

> *" When the teachers of the law who were Pharisees saw him eating with the 'sinners' and tax collectors, they asked his disciples: 'Why does he eat with tax collectors and "sinners"?' "*
>
> MARK 2:16

ritual, the "sinner" was declared to be forgiven (eg Leviticus 4:26,31,35), which meant being accepted back into covenant relationship with God. Anyone who failed to follow this means of grace remained in sin, cut off from God. Many Jews expected that when God's Messiah came, the "sinners" would be sent away from God's presence in judgement, while the "righteous" (those who had kept the laws and offered the sacrifices) would enjoy the blessings of the kingdom.

THE SCANDAL OF JESUS' FORGIVENESS

Jesus angered the Jewish religious leaders by declaring God's forgiveness to "sinners" without requiring them to go through the sacrificial system. The words Jesus used –

"Your sins are forgiven" (eg Mark 2:5) – were the same words that the priest would have used at the end of a sacrifice in the temple, yet Jesus was proclaiming them on his own authority, rather than as a result of a carefully followed procedure. The leaders understandably responded with outrage: "This is blasphemy! Who can forgive sins except God alone?" (Mark 2:7; Luke 7:49). They were, of course, partially right – only God has the authority to accept people back into covenant with himself. But, in their minds, this forgiveness could only be received through the temple. Jesus was bypassing the temple by declaring God's forgiveness directly to sinners. He could do this because he is God's true representative and because he would die on the cross as the perfect, once-for-all sacrifice. As such, he can accept sinners back into covenant with God entirely on the basis of their relationship with him, rather than their adherence to the sacrificial laws (Mark 2:10).

The free availability of forgiveness outside the temple system was central to Jesus' message. In the Old Testament, the prophets had looked forward to a day when God would make a new covenant with his people. In this covenant, all their past sins would be swept away by a powerful forgiveness, and they would experience a new intimacy with God (eg Jeremiah 31:31-34). Jesus proclaimed that this new covenant had already arrived, and would be sealed once and for all by his own sacrificial death (see Luke 22:20). Jesus' healings illustrated the reality of his declaration of forgiveness (eg Matthew 9:2-8). Through healing, a person was visibly made clean and readmitted to the community of God's people. This demonstrated the deeper reality: God had accepted them into his kingdom, which was gathering around Jesus.

JESUS' TABLE FELLOWSHIP

Jesus did not just declare God's forgiveness to people; he embodied it in his actions. In

**Accused by his critics for eating with "the wrong crowd",
Jesus openly declared by his actions that God's mercy
extended to all**

particular, the Gospels recount that Jesus was
often found eating and drinking with tax
collectors and sinners, so much so that he was
accused of being "a glutton and a drunkard"
(Matthew 11:19). As far as the Pharisees were
concerned, this was unacceptable behaviour
for a rabbi who spoke about the kingdom of
God (eg Matthew 9:11).

The meal table was a significant place in
Jesus' world. In particular, it was where
fellowship with God was expressed. In the
Jewish sacrificial system, when a peace
offering was made, after part of the sacrifice
had been burnt on the altar, the rest was given
back to the worshipper so that they and their
family and friends could have a feast (see
Leviticus 3:1-17; 7:11-21). The temple in
Jerusalem was supposed to be a place for
joyful feasting in the presence of God
(Deuteronomy 12:5-7). For Pharisees, who

wanted to extend the regulations of the
temple into everyday life, every meal reflected
these temple meals – eating together was a
sign that the people around the table
belonged in God's kingdom. For this reason,
they had strict regulations about their eating
practices, and especially about whom they
could and could not eat with. Such table
fellowship was also an anticipation of God's
future kingdom, which had been described by
Isaiah as a great feast in God's presence (eg
Isaiah 25:6-9).

Jesus announced that God's kingdom had
come near in his ministry (Mark 1:15). But
who was it for? By eating with tax collectors
and sinners, Jesus clearly declared that God's
kingdom was open to those who had
previously been considered outside God's
grace, for whatever reason. Jesus came to
bring God's forgiveness to "sinners" – people
who knew they had stepped over the
boundary of covenant with God (Mark 2:17).
For these people, Jesus' table fellowship was a
great joy and delight! But for the Pharisees,

TO THINK ABOUT

Read the story of Jesus in Simon the Pharisee's house, in Luke 7:36-50.

· Given the importance of the meal table for Pharisees, what did Simon's invitation say about his attitude toward Jesus?
· What did Simon find so unwelcome about the interruption by the woman (see verse 39 especially)?
· How does Jesus respond to Simon?
· How does Jesus respond to the woman?
· Why do the other guests respond as they do (verse 49)?
· How would you have felt if you were a guest of Simon that day? What about if you were the woman?

Jesus' three parables in Luke 15 were given in response to the grumbling of the Pharisees about his table fellowship. Read them now.

· How does this context help you to make sense of the parables? What point is Jesus making?

Many fathers of the day might have preferred to kill the rebellious son, rather than the fatted calf!

· What does Jesus' table fellowship and his announcements of forgiveness say about God?
· What does it mean to be a "sinner" today?
· How do we move from being a sinner cut off from God to being an intimate family member?

The forgiveness of sins through Jesus Christ is central to the Christian message (see Acts 2:38). Through what Jesus has done, all may come into God's kingdom and share in his feast – both now (our daily provision, Matthew 6:11) and fully in the future (Luke 14:15; Revelation 19:9). Thank Jesus that he has forgiven you, so that you are no longer a sinner but a friend. Pray for those you know who need God's forgiveness. How could you invite them to Jesus' table?

Jesus' open welcome undermined their whole system of regulations and sacrifices. Jesus often warned them that their "righteousness" was in danger of keeping them away from God's kingdom (eg Luke 11:37-41). He told parables about great feasts where the invited guests stayed away, while the outcasts from the streets were brought in (eg Luke 14:16-24, also 13:28-29). The Pharisees should have rejoiced that God was at last opening his kingdom to all and bringing the blessing of forgiveness and fellowship to those gathered around his Son, Jesus. But instead, they grumbled (Luke 15:1-2), which revealed that they themselves had not truly experienced God's intimate covenant relationship (Luke 15:25-32).

Jesus' last supper with his disciples was the ultimate example of his table fellowship. As they shared the bread and wine, Jesus declared that his disciples would soon experience the new covenant promised by the prophets, which he was about to bring through his death and resurrection (Luke 22:14-20; see also 1 Corinthians 11:23-26). When he shared a meal with them again after his resurrection, they knew that Jesus had been faithful to his word: the kingdom of God really was open to all who come to him, and the possibility of forgiveness was now to be preached to all nations (see Luke 24:30-31,47)!

JESUS' POWERFUL ENCOUNTERS
Authorities and opponents

KEY TRUTH

In the context of first-century Jewish society, Jesus' announcement about God's kingdom brought him into opposition with many different groups who claimed political and religious authority.

THE ROMANS

The Roman Empire was the superpower of Jesus' day, with vast provinces stretching from the city of Rome west to Spain, north to the English Channel, south to northern Africa and Egypt, and east to Syria. The first emperor, Augustus (27 BC–AD 14), famously established peace after the years of civil war that had brought the Roman Republic to an end. Augustus' stepson Tiberius succeeded him as emperor (AD 14–37), but his reign ended in a period of tyranny and unpopularity.

Palestine had been under Roman authority since the latter days of the Republic (Pompey's army arrived in 63 BC). Initially, it was simply a client kingdom – retaining its own government, but being dependent on Rome. However, following civil unrest around AD 6, the southern area of Judea came under direct Roman control as a Roman province with its own appointed governor. During Jesus' ministry, Pontius Pilate was governor of Judea (AD 26/27–37). On a number of occasions, Pilate showed his contempt for Jewish customs: he brought standards with the image of the emperor (a clear symbol of emperor worship) into Jerusalem; he used money from one of the temple funds to build an aqueduct; and he had been involved in a number of suspicious massacres (eg Luke 13:1), one of which led to his being recalled to Rome at the end of AD 36. The Jewish people were increasingly restless and rebellious under their Roman rulers, eventually leading

to the Jewish War of AD 66–70, which resulted in the siege and fall of Jerusalem (AD 70).

The Romans are mostly in the background in the Gospels, though their pervasive influence can be seen in issues such as the payment of taxes (Mark 12:13-17) and in the presence of soldiers (eg Matthew 8:5, and the allusion in Matthew 5:41 to the forced carrying of a soldier's baggage). The Jewish authorities had to collaborate with the Romans in order to have Jesus executed. Jesus was brought before Pilate on a false charge of treason (Luke 23:1-2), and although Pilate was convinced that Jesus was innocent of this charge (Luke 23:4,14,20), he authorised Jesus' crucifixion to satisfy the crowd and for fear of his position (John 19:8). Jesus remained respectful throughout his questioning by Pilate (John 18:28–19:16), and endured the mockery of the soldiers who flogged and crucified him. Unlike some other Jews who claimed to be "messiahs", Jesus never attempted to organise a revolutionary army to fight the Romans and restore Jewish political sovereignty. Indeed, he explicitly rejected the way of violence (eg Matthew 26:52). As he told Pilate, his kingdom was different (John 18:36).

HERODS AND HERODIANS

The Herodian family were important rulers over Palestine in the first century.

· **Herod the Great (37–4 BC).** Herod was originally governor of Galilee (47–37 BC) in a complicated arrangement of power, with his father as administrator of the Roman client kingdom of Judea, his brother as governor of Jerusalem and a powerful high priest in charge at the temple. The family came from Idumea so he was not a full Jew. In 40 BC Jerusalem was captured by the Parthians, who enslaved the high priest and Herod's brother. Herod fled for his own safety, and eventually went to Rome, where the Senate appointed him as King of Judea. He returned to Palestine and recaptured first Galilee and then, in 37 BC, Jerusalem itself. In 20 BC Herod began to rebuild the temple in Jerusalem. The work on the temple was not finished until AD 63, but it was described as the most lavish and beautiful building that people had seen. Despite this work, Herod was not universally accepted by the Jewish people, since he had mixed ancestry and was obviously friendly with the Romans. He was a violent ruler, executing any who opposed or threatened him – including his first wife and other members of his own family (note Matthew 2:16 in this context). When he died, his kingdom was divided between three of his sons.

- **Archelaus (4 BC–AD 6).** After Herod the Great's death, Archelaus ruled over Idumea, Judea and Samaria. However, like his father, he was violent (see Joseph's concerns about him in Matthew 2:22), and soon the Jews rebelled against him. To keep the peace, Augustus deposed him and set up Judea as a Roman province controlled by a Roman governor.
- **Philip the Tetrarch (4 BC–AD 34).** Philip ruled over the far north-eastern parts of Herod the Great's kingdom, which were mainly Syrian and Greek rather than Jewish. He built up and named the cities of Caesarea Philippi and Bethsaida, which were visited by Jesus during his ministry (eg Matthew 16:13; Mark 8:22).
- **Herod Antipas (4 BC–AD 39).** Antipas ruled over Galilee, where much of Jesus' ministry took place, and Perea. Antipas was responsible for arresting then executing

John the Baptist (Mark 6:17-28). When he heard about Jesus, he was first afraid that John had come back to life (Luke 9:7-9), but then wanted to kill him too (Luke 13:31). The political context was volatile, and Antipas wanted to quell any potential disturbances. Since Jesus was from Galilee, Pilate consulted Antipas during his questioning before Jesus was condemned (Luke 23:6-12). Jesus remained silent before him and, in response, Antipas mocked him.

While many Jews detested the Herodian dynasty because of their close connections with Rome, some believed that this complicated political arrangement was the best way forward for Israel. In the Gospels, these people appear as the "Herodians" (see Mark 3:6; 12:13; Matthew 22:16). They helped the Pharisees to plot Jesus' death, since they saw him as a threat to the fragile political peace.

THE SANHEDRIN

The Sanhedrin in Jerusalem was the ruling body for all Jewish affairs, covering religious, political and legal issues. It had a working relationship with the Romans. It was a body of 71 members ("elders"), presided over by the high priest, and predominantly made up from chief priests and scribes. They heard the most important cases of law, and could condemn someone to death; however, the Romans had taken away their power to actually execute a person, so people condemned by the Sanhedrin were handed to the Romans for execution, as in Jesus' case. John 11:47-53 records that the Sanhedrin had decided to put Jesus to death in order to avoid social unrest. They had their own police, who were used to arrest Jesus (John 18:3).

In the mind of the Sanhedrin, Jesus was a threat to their authority. The Sanhedrin simply wanted to hang on to their own power, and would do anything – including fabricating evidence (Matthew 26:59) – in order to get rid of Jesus. They could not accept

Jesus' message because they did not believe he was God's Messiah, and so they accused him of blasphemy, and sentenced him to death (Matthew 26:59-67). Jesus calmly declares the truth to them by pointing to the evidence of his whole ministry (John 18:19-23).

PRIESTS AND SCRIBES
Within the Jewish world, to be a priest or a scribe was a professional occupation.

- **Priests.** Priests were members of the family of Aaron within the tribe of Levi. They normally lived throughout the land, but would go to Jerusalem on a rotation system in order to provide worship and perform sacrifices at the temple. Because of their connection with the sacrificial system, they were highly regarded in their local communities, where they often exercised a teaching role (see Leviticus 10:11). The high priest held great power and influence in both religion and politics, and presided over the Sanhedrin in Jerusalem. For some time this role had been given to the highest bidder or to a politically useful person. Around the high priest were "chief priests" who were members of the Sanhedrin, and highly regarded in Jewish life. The chief priests were strongly opposed to Jesus – not least because even though he was not a Levite, he was teaching in the temple (see Matthew 21:23) and declaring forgiveness of sins! Most of the chief priests were Sadducees.
- **Scribes.** Scribes were specialists in the law of Israel, and carried out the essential work of drawing up marriage and business contracts. Their work covered the social, legal and religious aspects of the law. They saw themselves as guardians of Israel's way of life, and had built up "hedges" around the law to help people avoid inadvertent sins (see Luke 11:45-52). The scribes questioned Jesus about his interpretation of the law (Mark 12:28), and joined with the Pharisees in trying to trip him up. Jesus

> " *Then the Pharisees went out and began to plot with the Herodians how they might kill Jesus.*"
>
> MARK 3:6

warned his disciples not to be like them: concerned to appear knowledgeable and respectable, but in fact full of corruption (Luke 20:46-47).

PHARISEES AND SADDUCEES
The Pharisees and Sadducees were two opposing religious and social movements within Israel, representing different visions of what it meant to belong to God's people.

- **Pharisees.** Pharisees had widespread support in Israel throughout the first centuries BC and AD although there were no more than several thousands of them. They were particularly concerned to extend the purity laws of the temple into everyday life. They believed that if they surrounded themselves with strict regulations, they would be more likely to keep the commandments of the law, and thus remain in covenant with God. Because of their concern for purity, Pharisees were often at the forefront of political resistance against their pagan rulers, and they despised the collusion of the Herodians and Sadducees. Many Pharisees were rabbis, who travelled around with disciples, teaching their understanding of God's *Torah*. Others were scribes also. Because their understanding of what it meant to be God's people did not depend heavily on the temple, but rather on the study and obedience of God's commands, this movement was able to survive the destruction of the temple in AD 70 and to form the basis of later rabbinic Judaism.

  Some Pharisees were open to Jesus' message (eg Nicodemus, John 3:1), but

An Orthodox Jew binds tefillin – small boxes attached to strips of leather – around his head and arm. Jesus reprimanded the Jewish leaders of his day for being too concerned with ceremony

many found his message about the kingdom too radical ("He eats with tax collectors and sinners!", Mark 2:16). Throughout his teaching, Jesus accused the Pharisees of making entry into God's kingdom too difficult (Matthew 23:4). He warned them that unless they realised that Israel was being re-established around him, they would find themselves cast out of God's kingdom.

· **Sadducees.** Unlike the Pharisees, the Sadducees were happy to collaborate with the Romans. They came mostly from privileged priestly families in Jerusalem, and were strongly represented in the Sanhedrin. They focused almost entirely on the five books of the Pentateuch for their teachings, and famously denied the resurrection of the dead (see Matthew 22:23). On this point, Jesus rebuked them for not knowing the Scriptures (presumably a reference to their focus only on the Pentateuch) or the power of God (22:29). At this, they joined forces with the Pharisees to seek Jesus' downfall (22:34).

TO THINK ABOUT

By the end of his ministry, Jesus' message about the kingdom of God had brought him into confrontation with nearly every group in Palestine.
· Work through the list of groups again. What did Jesus say or do that challenged or offended them?
· How important is it to understand this background in interpreting the ministry of Jesus?
· What were the political implications of Jesus' message?
· What were the religious implications?

Read the account of Jesus' trial in Luke 22:63–23:25.
· Which groups were involved in Jesus' conviction?
· What did each group have to gain from Jesus' death? (See John 11:47-53 also.)
· How did Jesus act toward these authorities and opponents?

There is a similar complicated mix of authorities in today's world.
· Can you identify any particular "groups"?
· Do they oppose Jesus? How?
· What would it look like to announce God's kingdom to them?

Jesus was not afraid to speak the truth about God's kingdom, even when it challenged people's entire outlook on life. Some people responded with faith, but many others became his enemies, and conspired to put him to death. Even then, Jesus continued to love them (Matthew 5:44), and spoke to them about God's kingdom. Tell God about your own response to Jesus' message – how you have faith, and how you also sometimes side with his opponents. Thank Jesus for loving and challenging you, and ask for courage and wisdom to announce the kingdom today, whatever the opposition.

JESUS' PERFECT SALVATION
Rejection in Jerusalem

KEY TRUTH

Jesus' betrayal, arrest and crucifixion came at the climax of his ministry, revealing
the complete human rejection of Jesus and his mission.

BETRAYAL BY JUDAS

The Gospels record the terrible truth that
Jesus' arrest and subsequent crucifixion were
made possible by the actions of one of his
closest disciples. Judas Iscariot was one of the
Twelve, whom Jesus had chosen near the
beginning of his ministry to be with him and
share in his mission of announcing the
kingdom (Mark 3:14-19). Like the other
disciples, Judas would have seen Jesus' many
miracles and heard his teachings. He had even
been sent out with the others to preach Jesus'
message, heal the sick and cast out demons
(see Matthew 10:1-8).

Judas' reason for betraying Jesus is not
entirely clear. He negotiated a financial
reward from the chief priests (Matthew 26:14-
16), which may have appealed to his existing
habit of taking money from the common
purse of the disciples (see John 12:6). Or, it
may be that Judas thought that Jesus had
betrayed him and his country – in his mind, a
Jewish messiah was supposed to be a
nationalistic champion fighting against the
Romans, and so Judas found Jesus' version of
God's kingdom disappointing. After the
jubilation of the triumphal procession into
Jerusalem (Matthew 21:1-11) and his
dramatic actions in the temple (21:12-13),
Jesus was back to speaking about his own
suffering and death again (26:2). Or, Judas
may have wanted to provoke Jesus into action,
perhaps by engineering a showdown with the
chief priests. Perhaps then Jesus would at last
call down fire from heaven (Luke 9:54) or
summon a legion of angels (Matthew 26:53).

Judas may not have intended Jesus to be
killed: after he saw that Jesus had been
condemned to death, he was filled with regret,
and killed himself (Matthew 27:3-5).

Behind these suggestions, however, there is
one certainty: Satan was at work in Judas'
betrayal (Luke 22:3; John 13:2,27). The enemy
of God and God's people was not just out
somewhere else in the world; he had made
inroads into the closest of Jesus' companions.
Judas had allowed himself to accept the lies
and deceit that Satan always sows, and in the
end, instead of carrying out the mission of
Jesus as he had been called to do, he helped
the evil work of Satan. Judas' actions were a
betrayal of everything he had experienced
through his time with Jesus. He led the
guards to a private garden in Gethsemane, on
the slopes of the Mount of Olives, where Jesus
and his disciples had often gathered (John
18:1-3). In this most intimate location, Judas
betrayed Jesus with a greeting and a kiss
(Mark 14:44-45). The close friendship that
Jesus had invited Judas to share with him, had
become the opportunity for his betrayal (see
Luke 22:6); Jesus' love was being thrown back
in his face.

THE JEWISH CHARGE

Jesus was taken under guard to the house of
the high priest Caiaphas, where the
Sanhedrin had assembled (Luke 22:54;
Matthew 26:57). The timing and location of
this council (at night in Caiaphas' residence,
rather than during the day at the temple) were
highly unusual, indicating the extreme haste

of the Jewish authorities to have Jesus executed before the festival of Passover (Matthew 26:5). In any case, the Sanhedrin had already decided that Jesus would be sentenced to death (John 11:47-53); all they needed now was to settle upon a legitimate charge to justify the sentence (eg Matthew 26:59).

In Jewish law, two of the most serious crimes were false prophecy and blasphemy, both punishable by death (see Deuteronomy 13 and Leviticus 24:13-16). The charge of false prophecy was to be brought against any

> " *Then* one of the Twelve – the one called Judas Iscariot – went to the chief priests and asked, 'What are you willing to give me if I hand him over to you?' So they counted out for him thirty silver coins. "
>
> MATTHEW 26:14-15

person who tried to lead Israel astray from their obedience to the LORD and his commands. In the eyes of the Sanhedrin, this was exactly what Jesus had been doing (see John 11:48; Luke 23:5). Throughout his ministry, Jesus had presented a message about God and his kingdom that overturned their own understanding of what it meant to be God's people. Jesus had welcomed tax collectors and sinners to his meal table, and had proclaimed forgiveness outside the sacrificial system. Ultimately, he had prophesied the destruction of the temple itself, the central symbol of Israel's relationship with God (Matthew 26:61; Mark 14:58; see John 2:19). Jesus, with his twelve disciples, was claiming to create a new Israel based around loyalty to himself; he was acting as if he were God's Messiah, the true son of

David. Jesus' popularity with the crowds just a few days before was of great concern to the Sanhedrin (see Luke 19:47-48). In their minds, they had to charge him with false prophecy in order to prevent ordinary Jews from going after him.

For the charge to be confirmed, all Caiaphas needed was to get a confession out of Jesus. He asked Jesus directly, "Are you the Messiah?" (Matthew 26:63). Since Caiaphas was sure that Jesus was not the Messiah, but a false prophet, if Jesus were to answer positively then he would have condemned himself. However, in reply, Jesus not only confirmed his identity, but also prophesied that he would sit on a throne beside the God of Israel (Matthew 26:64). The Sanhedrin responded in horror: now, Jesus was not only a false prophet, but also a blasphemer, claiming equal power with God. For them, this was a solid legal basis for his death (Matthew 26:65-66), and they concluded the session by mocking him as a false prophet (Matthew 26:68; Mark 14:65; Luke 22:64).

The Jewish charge against Jesus was that he was leading people astray from a true understanding of what it meant to be God's people ("perverting our nation", Luke 23:2). However, this charge rested on the blindness of the Jewish authorities to the true identity of Jesus. He really was God's Messiah, who shared in divine power and authority; his teaching about God's kingdom was the truth. But by refusing to believe this, the Jewish authorities had to condemn him to death.

THE ROMAN CHARGE

Under Roman rule, the Sanhedrin had no authority to carry out the death sentence. It was therefore essential that they persuaded Pilate, the Roman governor, to have Jesus killed. Pilate, however, was not known for his respect towards Jewish customs and laws, and the Sanhedrin knew it was unlikely he would sentence Jesus to death for being a wayward prophet. So, when they brought Jesus to

Pilate, they expanded their accusation to include a claim that Jesus was a political revolutionary, who was intent on fighting the Roman Empire (Luke 23:2). Pilate quickly realised that the claim was unfounded, and that Jesus had no intention of mobilising a revolutionary army (John 18:33-38), and he was ready to let Jesus go free. But then the Sanhedrin put Pilate in a political corner. If he refused to execute Jesus, he would find himself being accused of disloyalty to Emperor Tiberius, which was a dangerous position to be in (John 19:12). Caught in this dilemma, Pilate put his self-interest before the truth of the matter. He washed his hands of the responsibility that was rightfully his (Matthew 27:24-26), and handed Jesus over to be crucified to avoid being accused of treason himself. Roman soldiers mocked Jesus as a failed king (Mark 15:17-20), and Pilate hung the charge against Jesus above his head on the cross: "This is the King of the Jews" (John 19:19).

Crucifixion was a powerful and gruesome symbol of the might of the Roman Empire. Death on a cross was painful, slow and public. It was a clear warning that those who rebelled against the authority of Rome would be routed out and destroyed, overwhelmed by the sheer brutality of Rome's military power. As a general rule, Roman citizens did not have to face crucifixion, unless they were convicted of the most extreme case of treason. The cross was reserved for non-citizens, provincial subjects who were dangerous criminals, revolutionary leaders and slaves. It was the fate of those who were discarded by the Empire. By executing Jesus for revolution despite the lack of evidence, Pilate had put him in this category: against the grand scale of the Roman Empire and in comparison to the progression of Pilate's own career, the life of Jesus was considered worthless. Jesus was

simply a disposable pawn in the power games of politics.

JESUS, ALONE

From the moment of his arrest in the Garden of Gethsemane, Jesus is presented by the Gospels as a lone figure. His disciples desert him (Mark 14:50) and Peter, who had promised to follow Jesus to the end, denies even their acquaintance to a servant girl at the high priest's house (14:66-72). In Matthew and Mark, by the time Jesus is hung on the cross, he cries out that it seems even God has

Jesus spent his last hours deserted by his followers, to face his fate alone

TO THINK ABOUT

Read the account of Jesus' betrayal and arrest in Mark 14:10-11,17-21,26-50,66-72.

· How did Jesus prepare his disciples for what would happen?
· How do you think Jesus felt on this night? How does he express this?
· What is the difference between Jesus and his disciples?

Now read the account of Jesus on the cross in Mark 15:25-37.

· Who rejects him in this passage? Why?

Jesus' cry in verse 34 is a quote of the first verse of Psalm 22. Read the whole psalm now.

· How does this psalm express Jesus' situation?
· What is the note of hope in the psalm?
· Do you think Jesus might have had this in mind? If so, why?

· How did Jesus think his rejection and suffering would bring the kingdom to others?

Jesus was betrayed by one of his disciples, deserted by his friends, rejected by the Jewish authorities and discarded by the Roman Empire on a cross.

· Is your attitude to Jesus ever like this? How?

The account of Jesus, alone on a cross, is sobering for us. We too easily resist the good news of God's kingdom and reject the One who brings it to us. Pray to God now, confessing your part in the rejection of Jesus. Thank him that Jesus suffered your rejection willingly and then rose again so that you may be his friend.

---

forsaken him (Matthew 27:46; Mark 15:34). Bystanders mocked him, and even one of the criminals who was crucified along with him joined in the taunt (Luke 23:35,39). Along his way to Jerusalem, many of those who were following him had fallen away (eg John 6:66), and now, at the climax of his work, he was utterly rejected by humans (note Isaiah 53:3). No one shared his mission.

This rejection did not come as a surprise to Jesus. Many times throughout his ministry, he had told his disciples that he would face betrayal and rejection when they reached Jerusalem (eg Luke 9:22; 13:33; 18:32-33; 22:22). The authorities had already rejected his message about God's kingdom and Jesus knew that rejection of his message would ultimately turn into rejection of himself.

Despite knowing this, however, Jesus remained committed to his mission. At any moment, he could have turned around and avoided the suffering he would face, but he did not (see Luke 9:51; 22:42). He continued to proclaim God's kingdom and demonstrate it with miracles and actions, even while knowing it would lead to his death. In a profound way, Jesus willingly brought rejection upon himself, because he knew that this was the only way to establish God's kingdom and open the way for many to become children of God. The kingdom that he had proclaimed in word and action throughout his ministry would now be established through his death and resurrection, alone.

New Passover, new Exodus

KEY TRUTH

In order to explain his approaching death to his disciples, Jesus infused the traditional Passover meal with fresh meaning: his death was to be the beginning of a new exodus for God's people!

REMEMBERING RESCUE

The faith and life of God's people Israel was built around the practice of remembering. In their songbook of psalms, while there are a few outbursts of praise to God for his universal goodness (eg Psalm 104), the vast majority of songs are joyful recollections of the mighty acts of God in their history (eg Psalm 136), or pleas to him that he would rescue them again just as he had in the past (eg Psalm 80). Their annual worship was punctuated by a number of festivals, at which they would gather together to remember particular episodes from their history: for instance, at Passover, they would remember their escape from Egypt; at Pentecost, they would remember the giving of God's *Torah* at Mount Sinai; at the Feast of Tabernacles, although largely a harvest festival, they would remember their 40 years of wandering through the wilderness on their journey from Egypt to the Promised Land. Through these festivals, they were supposed to remember who they were – a people chosen and rescued by God, and called to live differently in the world (see Exodus 12:24-27).

By New Testament times, of all the festivals, Passover (which included the seven-day Festival of Unleavened Bread) was the most significant. At Passover, the Israelites remembered how they had been slaves in the land of Egypt. But God had heard their cries for help and had come to their rescue (the story is in Exodus 1–15). Despite experiencing nine miraculous plagues, the Egyptian

Pharaoh refused to let the Israelites go free. So God warned of one final plague, in which every firstborn son of every family would die. God gave instructions to the Israelites about how they were to be kept safe from this plague (Exodus 12:1-13). They were to gather in households, dressed ready for their journey out of Egypt, and kill an unblemished lamb. Some of the blood would be smeared on the doorposts of the house, while the rest of the lamb would be prepared for the household to eat. When God sent the plague on every firstborn son in Egypt, he would see the blood on the doorposts of the Israelites and "pass over" their houses. Everything happened as God had said: the firstborn sons of the Israelite families were safe and the Egyptians let the Israelites go free at once. God's "pass over" had been the source of their salvation.

The Passover meal was to be "perpetual ordinance" for God's people (Exodus 12:14). By celebrating it at the beginning of every year, they were to remember that their life as a nation had begun when God brought them out of slavery in Egypt by a great act of judgement (on the Egyptians) and grace (on them). In Jesus' day there were a number of key elements to its celebration, including:

- **Timing and location.** Jewish days began at sundown, and so the Passover meal, eaten after dark, would have begun the day of Passover and the week-long Feast of Unleavened Bread. Jewish pilgrims would travel into the walled city of Jerusalem and share the Passover meal together there.

- **Lamb and bread.** The Passover lamb would be roasted over a fire, and had to be eaten completely. The lamb's bones were not to be broken. The meal also included unleavened bread, which was a reminder of the speed of God's deliverance – the "pass over" had happened so quickly that they had no time to bake leavened bread.
- **Cup.** There were four cups of wine, which were passed around and shared, reminding them of God's promises of deliverance and blessing.
- **Remembering.** The meal was explicitly intended to recall the story of exodus, so the host would take time to explain the meaning of the elements of the meal to the gathered family.
- **Anticipation.** As well as looking back, the meal looked forward to God's great coming rescue. For many Jews in Jesus' day, this particularly meant rescue from their oppression under Roman rule. They prayed that God would send the Messiah.

JESUS' LAST SUPPER

The Gospels record that Jesus celebrated a last Passover meal with his disciples before his betrayal and arrest (Matthew 26:17; Mark 14:12; Luke 22:8,15). This would have taken place after dark within the city walls of Jerusalem (note Luke 22:8-14), marking the beginning of the first day of the week-long Passover (Unleavened Bread) festival. That year, the first day of Passover was also a Friday, which is the Jewish "day of Preparation" for the Sabbath (see Mark 15:42). This explains the comment in John's Gospel that Jesus died on "the day of Preparation of Passover" (John 19:14). Some have thought this refers to the day before the whole Passover festival began, which would mean that Jesus could not have celebrated a Passover meal the night before. However, "the day of Preparation of Passover" most likely means "Friday during Passover", especially since John later says that the Sabbath was simply "a day of great solemnity" (19:31 – because it was the Sabbath during the festival; see also Luke 23:54,56), and does not call it the Passover itself. Jesus' last supper, arrest, trial and crucifixion all happened during the first 24 hours of the Passover festival.

In any case, Jesus specifically called the meal with his disciples in the upper room a Passover meal (Luke 22:15). There, in the context of remembering God's great act of deliverance in the past, Jesus explained to his disciples that God was about to accomplish another deliverance, more profound even than the exodus from Egypt. As host, it was Jesus' role to explain the meaning of the

> "*And he said to them, 'I have eagerly desired to eat this Passover with you before I suffer. For I tell you, I will not eat it again until it finds fulfilment in the kingdom of God.'*"
>
> LUKE 22:15-16

elements of the meal. Usually this explanation would have referred back to the events of the exodus, but Jesus reinterpreted them in a striking new way.
- **Bread.** The unleavened Passover bread had symbolised the urgency of Israel's escape from Egypt. For Jesus, the urgency was his own approaching death – the bread was his body, which would soon be broken in order to bring about God's great deliverance.
- **Cup.** The cups of wine had referred to the blessing of covenant life which the exodus would bring to the Israelites (see Exodus 6:5-7). Jesus took one of these cups and associated it with the blessings he was about to bring – forgiveness of sins and the new covenant (Jeremiah 31:31-34). To bring these blessings, however, he would have to

The act of remembrance in taking bread and wine is an acknowledgement that Jesus offered himself as the sacrifice for our sin – his body "broken for us"

the Messiah to come, for he was that Messiah! Instead, Jesus looked forward to the fulfilment of his work when he would share the meal again with all God's rescued people in the renewed creation (Luke 22:16,18). Jesus certainly shared a meal with his disciples again after his resurrection (eg Luke 24:30), and the first Christians celebrated this meal in anticipation of the great messianic banquet when Jesus will bring God's kingdom in full (1 Corinthians 11:26).

JESUS, OUR PASSOVER

Although Jesus' last supper probably did include a roasted lamb (the disciples would have known how to prepare a proper Passover meal, Luke 22:13), the Gospel writers do not record Jesus referring to it. The omission is intentional. In the new exodus of God's people – not from slavery to Egypt, but from slavery to the most overwhelming powers of Satan, sin and evil – it is not a lamb whose death marks God's act of deliverance and liberation, but Jesus himself. As Paul declared later, "Christ, our Passover, has been sacrificed!" (1 Corinthians 5:7).

Jesus wanted his disciples to understand that his death was not a terrible mistake. Throughout his ministry, he had been teaching them about God's kingdom. To belong to this kingdom was to experience forgiveness of sins, healing and restoration, and the joy of intimate fellowship with God and one another around his meal table. This was the life of the new covenant, which God had promised in the Old Testament (eg Jeremiah 31:31-34; Ezekiel 37:26-28). However, just as the blessings of God's old covenant with Israel had only come after Israel had been delivered from slavery in Egypt, so now the blessings of God's new covenant could only arrive through a new act of deliverance and rescue. God's enemies were to be defeated and his people set free on a journey to his new creation! Jesus' death was

pour out his own blood, just like the Passover lamb (see also Exodus 24:8 and Zechariah 9:11).

- **Remembering.** The great event of deliverance that Jesus explained to the disciples was not the Passover and exodus of long before, but his own approaching death. For them, this meal was to take on a new significance, as they remembered Jesus' suffering and death, which had brought about the new exodus of God's people.
- **Anticipation.** Jesus did not need to pray for

TO THINK ABOUT

Read the regulations for the Passover in Exodus 12–13.

- Who could share in the Passover meal? Why was this?
- How were they to eat the meal? Why?
- What would it have been like to be a firstborn son that night?
- What did the Passover accomplish? For Israel? For Egypt? For God (see 12:12)?
- Why did God instruct the Israelites to celebrate the Passover meal at the beginning of every year?

Read Matthew's account of the Last Supper in Matthew 26:17-30. The Last Supper is one of the sacraments (human actions that embody God's great story of salvation) celebrated by Christians today.

- How do its roots in the Passover meal help you to understand the meaning of Jesus' death?

- How was Jesus' death like that of the Passover lamb? How was it different?
- Do you think the Last Supper is in any way like the Passover meal? How? How is it different?
- If you have ever shared in a Last Supper celebration, think about it now. In what ways was it like the meal Jesus shared with his disciples? How was it different?
- What is the significance of sharing the Last Supper with others (see Acts 2:46)?

Jesus' death was God's great act of deliverance, through which he defeated his enemies and brought his people out of slavery in a new exodus. Thank Jesus that he died to set you free, and that you can now belong to his kingdom of grace and peace. Pray for strength as you live out the great exodus in your daily life.

that act of deliverance. God had provided Jesus as the new Passover lamb, whose death would mark God's defeat of his people's enemies and their safe escape from slavery. Far from being a mistake, Jesus' death was necessary if his disciples were to be set free to be God's true people. By his death, all who come to Jesus can be rescued from the kingdom of darkness and brought into the kingdom of God's light (Colossians 1:13).

The Passover meal was a constant reminder to the Israelites of God's great act to deliver them and of their identity as his chosen, loved and rescued people. The disciples who shared the new Passover meal with Jesus, along with all those who continue to do so today, celebrate God's greatest act of deliverance – the defeat of his enemies through the death of Jesus – and express the joy and commitment of being part of his people. By gathering around the table of the Last Supper until Jesus comes, Christians demonstrate and celebrate that they belong to his kingdom.

Dealing with sin

KEY TRUTH

By his death, Jesus dealt with the sin that has so devastatingly disrupted the life of God's world and its fellowship with him.

UNDERSTANDING SIN

The early Christians expressed their understanding of the significance of Jesus' death with a simple summary statement: "Christ died for our sins, according to the Scriptures" (1 Corinthians 15:3). This short summary, however, called to mind a whole world of meaning from the Old Testament, which helped the first Christians to understand what Jesus had done for them. For a start, Jesus had done something about "sin".

- **A history of sin.** In the Old Testament, sin was not a vague term referring to general moral failings, as it is sometimes used today. Sin could only be named as "sin" within a particular context: the context of relationship with God. God had established the world as a place where humans could flourish in life as they remained in constant, obedient fellowship with him (Genesis 2:15-17). But, no sooner had this relationship been established, than humans stepped outside its boundaries by disobeying God's command (3:6), and so losing the blessings of life with him (3:16-24). From then on, sin was always "lurking at the door" (4:7), disrupting the peace of God's creation, and turning humans away from him.

  Throughout the Old Testament, God called a particular people to come back into fellowship with him. He rescued the nation of Israel from slavery in the land of Egypt so that there would once again be people who would enjoy life as he had intended. He made a covenant with them, committing himself to them and asking them to commit to him. To help them live constantly within this covenant, he gave them the gift of a law, known as the *Torah*, which described the kind of life that remained within the boundaries of his covenant. Obeying God's *Torah* was not supposed to be a heavy burden, but a joyful delight – it affirmed that God wanted his creation to be blessed. As Israel stayed close to him, they would show the rest of the world what God's life-giving holiness looked like (Exodus 19:5-6). However, sin was still "lurking at the door", and the people of Israel were quick to go out to it, and let it into their midst. Time after time, sin disrupted God's covenant, and turned his people away from him.

- **A definition of sin.** Simply put, sin is missing the way of life that God intends. Within the context of Israel, this way of life had been clearly described by God's good commands in the *Torah* (see Psalm 119, a song of praise to God for his law). Sin in Israel, therefore, was to disobey God's law and step outside his holy way of life. It could happen deliberately, as God's people intentionally turned away from him, or unintentionally, as they were simply caught up in the waywardness of the world around them (see Leviticus 4). Importantly, sin is not simply an action – failing to live up to a list of do's and don'ts – but an attitude of the heart: human life that is out of step with God from the very centre of its being.

The result of sin. The Old Testament had many different ways to describe the consequences of sin, all of them negative. It caused banishment from God's blessing (Genesis 3:24); it created uncleanness that spread like a malicious virus through society (see Leviticus 5:2); it brought guilt and shame and despair (Psalm 6:1-7); it grew unchecked into whole systems of evil and injustice (eg Amos 1–2); and it resulted in the ultimate banishment from God's presence – death. God's constant judgement about sin was that it had to be removed if people were to live. If it were not removed, then they would die, both now and eternally.

UNDERSTANDING SACRIFICE

The first Christians proclaimed that Jesus had "died for sin". The background to this was the sacrificial system of the Old Testament. Through sacrifice, God had provided a way for sin to be dealt with, so that his people would not be swept away by his judgement about sin and its disastrous consequences, but rather be restored to life and fellowship with him.

The sin offering. Leviticus 4:1–5:13 describes the procedure for presenting a sacrifice for sin to God. To us today, the amount of bloodshed involved in these sacrifices may seem excessive, but in the ancient context where animals were sacrificed by all societies in their thousands and millions, God's instructions were in fact restrained and gracious – there was a standard procedure and by following it closely the worshipper could know that they were back in fellowship with God. They did not need to sacrifice for the same sin twice. The procedure was clear: if a person sinned, they were to bring an animal to the priest, confess the sin and lay their hand on the head of the animal as it was slaughtered. This signified that this costly sacrifice had died in the place of the sinner. Blood was sprinkled inside the sanctuary, signifying that God had accepted the offering and the carcass of the animal was completely burned up. The sin had been removed from

The Scapegoat, **by Holman Hunt. Each year the high priest laid his hands on a goat, confessing the sins of the people. The goat was driven out into the wilderness and left to die, paying the price for sin on behalf of the nation**

the sinner, so that it could no longer riddle the fellowship of God's people with its devastating consequences. The priest would declare the sin "forgiven", which meant that God and his people were once again "at one" (atonement, Leviticus 4:20,26,31, etc.). The death of the sacrifice meant the life of the worshipper.

- **The Day of Atonement.** Once a year, all Israel observed the Day of Atonement, on which the whole nation was cleansed (Leviticus 16:34). Central to the proceedings were two goats. On this day alone, the high priest entered the Most Holy Place, with a bowl of blood from one of the goats. He came out of the Most Holy Place and made atonement for each area of the sanctuary in turn, in order to show clearly that forgiveness and cleansing had been initiated by God himself (16:15-19). Then the high priest laid hands on the second goat and confessed over it all the sins of Israel. It would be sent out into the wilderness, where it would die, signifying that God had removed sin from the people completely – the goat had borne it away (16:22). Free of sin, God's people were re-established in their relationship with him, and could go in peace to live out his covenant in their lives. Once again, a sacrifice had died in order to let God's people live.

JESUS, THE SACRIFICE FOR SIN

The first Christians understood Jesus' death as a sacrifice for sin against this Old Testament and contemporary Jewish background.

- **The sacrifice of the new covenant.** Jesus' death brought God's covenant with Israel to its climactic end (Romans 10:4) and ushered in a new, better covenant. The old covenant, which included the sacrificial system, had been intended to cleanse Israel from their sin so that they could demonstrate to the nations what it meant to live in intimate fellowship with God. But

> " *The* next day John saw Jesus coming toward him and said, 'Look, the Lamb of God, who takes away the sin of the world!' "
>
> JOHN 1:29

throughout their history, God's people had struggled to stay in fellowship with him, time and again being overwhelmed by sin and its consequences. The constant sacrifice of animals was not working – sin was still rampant among God's people.

The writer of Hebrews had grasped the profound significance of Jesus' death. Unlike the sacrifices in the temple, which had to be offered time after time because they never really cleansed the worshipper (10:4), Jesus "has appeared once for all at the end of the age to remove sin by the sacrifice of himself" (9:26). Jesus was the reality of atonement, of which all the Old Testament sacrifices had just been shadows and anticipations ("sketches of heavenly things", 9:23). His sacrificial death had brought about a new covenant relationship with God.

- **The universal sacrifice.** As part of the new covenant, Jesus' sacrifice was not just for Israel, but for the whole world. John the Baptist had said, recalling the imagery of the Day of Atonement, that Jesus was "the Lamb of God who takes away the sin of the world" (John 1:29). Certainly, he had been crucified as a direct result of the sin of those who rejected him; but in a profound sense, he had died with the weight of the whole world's sin on his shoulders. The world is the sort of place where the Son of God, who brings only grace and truth, can be crucified (John 1:10-11,17). But because of Jesus' sacrifice, it is also the sort of place that can be freed to live with God.

Read Hebrews 9. Remember that the "tent" is the tabernacle, which preceded the temple in Jerusalem as the place where God lived among his people.

· What does the writer of Hebrews say about the old sacrificial system?
· What is unique about Jesus? What role/s does he have in the "greater and perfect tent"?
· What does Christ's sacrifice do?

Now read Hebrews 10. Remember the role that the sacrificial system played in the Old Testament: to keep the Israelites in constant fellowship with God by removing the stain of sin.

· How should we live in light of Christ's sacrifice?
· What encouragement do you find here? What challenges you?

Many people today find the idea of sacrifice distasteful or simply perplexing.

· Why do you think this is? Are there any deeper reasons than merely the amount of blood involved?
· How would you explain the sacrifice of Jesus to someone who had no knowledge of the Bible? How about the concept of sin?

Jesus' willing sacrifice of himself for our sins is a constant source of love, wonder and praise for Christians. Spend time now thanking Jesus for his sacrifice, and that your sins are now dealt with, certainly and forever. Pray for courage to put sin behind you and live in the freedom he has given.

· **A liberating and cleansing sacrifice.** As Jesus explained to his disciples at the Last Supper, he was going to his death to bring about the forgiveness of sins (Matthew 26:28). He would bear the devastating agony of sin's true consequences in his own body, so that others would not have to. At the moment he died, the curtain into the Most Holy Place in the temple was torn in two (Matthew 27:50-51). The way in to fellowship and new life with God – the way that had been blocked by sin – had now been opened for all (see Ephesians 2:18; Hebrews 10:19-20; 1 Peter 3:18). But also, as pictured by the Day of Atonement, God's cleansing power could sweep out of the temple into the world. Through Jesus, all can be cleansed and purified, so that they may worship God with the life he always intended (Hebrews 9:14).

Jesus' sacrificial death is, in fact, central to his announcement of the kingdom. Without being set free from sin, it would be impossible for his followers to share in the life of God's promised kingdom. Without a sacrifice for sin, God's judgement about sin would remain over them – their lives would end in death (Romans 6:23). However, because he died "for our sins" (1 Corinthians 15:3), bearing them away in his own body (1 Peter 2:24), people who come to him are set free from sin to live in God's new covenant, looking forward to the fulfilment of their salvation in his new creation. Jesus' death as a sacrifice for sin enables a great, gracious exchange to take place: he took our sin, so that we might share in his righteousness (2 Corinthians 5:21; Romans 3:21-26)!

JESUS' PERFECT SALVATION
The triumph of resurrection

KEY TRUTH

Jesus did not remain in the tomb: he was raised on the third day, triumphing decisively over all God's enemies and declaring that God's new world has begun, starting with him!

DEATH AND RESURRECTION

In the first-century world, to be executed on a Roman cross was the greatest, most humiliating defeat imaginable. The whole might of the Roman Empire had turned against the person who was nailed to the cross – they were powerless and crushed. In the Jewish world, crucifixion carried an additional stigma. Jewish law pronounced that "anyone hung on a tree is under God's curse" (Deuteronomy 21:23), and by Jesus' day the "tree" was understood to include the wooden cross of Roman execution. When Jesus was killed, therefore, it would have been difficult to see his crucifixion as anything other than utter defeat. His message had been rejected, and he himself had been beaten, mocked, humiliated and executed.

Yet, in just a few weeks, his disciples were announcing that this same Jesus was in fact the true ruler of the world, and that his message was the hope for the nations (see Acts 2:36,38-39) – and they were doing so in the very city where Jesus had been arrested and put to death! Many of these disciples, who had deserted Jesus upon his own arrest, would soon endure arrest, persecution and death themselves, rather than renounce their new faith in him (eg Stephen, Acts 6:8–7:60). For them, the crucified Jesus was not a humiliating failure or evidence of God's curse, but rather the "power and wisdom of God" (1 Corinthians 1:22-24), a great victory (Colossians 2:15) and the source of God's blessing (Galatians 3:13-14).

This change did not come about because the disciples had simply reinterpreted the facts. It was not based on wishful thinking, that perhaps Jesus' death by crucifixion was not so bad after all. The disciples were transformed by something that had happened. Their central claim was that the Jesus who had been crucified had not remained in the tomb. He had risen – and they had seen him with their own eyes! As Peter said in his sermon to the crowds on the day of Pentecost: "God raised him up, having freed him from death, because it was impossible for him to be held in its power ... This Jesus God raised up, and of that all of us are witnesses" (Acts 2:24,32). Jesus' death makes no sense on its own, without his resurrection. If Jesus were not raised from the dead, then it would be both pointless and foolish to commit one's life to him and to the message about him (1 Corinthians 15:14,17-19). But, because of his resurrection, Jesus can be proclaimed throughout the whole world as "Lord and Christ" (Acts 2:36) – the one who rightfully rules all things, and pours out God's blessing on the world.

AN EMPTY TOMB

In Jesus' Jewish tradition, burials normally had two stages. First, the body would be washed and anointed, the mouth bound up, and the body wrapped up in linen cloth and laid out on a shelf in a cave. The warm climate would have led to quick decomposition, and sometimes the cave might have been used for more than one body, so spices were added to counter the stench of decay. Then the cave would be blocked off. Secondly, after a period of twelve months, when the flesh had decomposed, the bones would be gathered up together, placed in an ossuary ("bone-box") and buried in an ancestral tomb.

After his crucifixion, some of Jesus' disciples wrapped Jesus' body up in accordance with these Jewish customs and laid him in a nearby tomb (John 19:38-42).

> *"But God raised him from the dead, freeing him from the agony of death, because it was impossible for death to keep its hold on him."*
>
> ACTS 2:24

Perhaps due to the haste with which this had to be completed before the Sabbath began, some of the women who had followed Jesus decided to go to the tomb as soon as the Sabbath was over to bring more spices (Luke 23:56; 24:1). They expected to attend to Jesus' body and then leave the tomb, presumably for a year until they could gather Jesus' bones up into an ossuary. They found, however, that the cave was open and that Jesus' body had gone! (Luke 24:2-3).

Throughout history, many sceptics have set out to find the body of Jesus, thinking that it must have been either moved or stolen. Perhaps Jesus' disciples pulled off an elaborate hoax. Or perhaps, after the trauma of the crucifixion, they did not remember in which tomb Jesus had been laid. However, none of these theories make sense of the facts. Both the women (Matthew 27:61) and the authorities (27:62-66) had carefully noted the location of the tomb. If the authorities had stolen the body, then they would surely have produced it to prove that the disciples'

message about Jesus' resurrection was a lie. And it is highly unlikely that the disciples would be willing to be persecuted and killed for a hoax they knew was untrue. If they had just made up the story of the empty tomb, anyone from Jerusalem could have simply gone out to the tombs and exposed Jesus' body. But all of Jerusalem knew that Jesus' body was not in the tomb! (Luke 24:18).

MEETING JESUS AGAIN

On its own, the empty tomb would be odd, but it could not have produced the shockwave that would soon travel across the whole world. The message of the first Christians was not that the tomb was empty (though they knew it was), but rather that the Jesus who had been crucified and buried was in fact alive, having risen from the dead! They had met with him, over a period of 40 days (Acts 1:3).

Again, many people find this hard to believe, and so have tried to account for the disciples' message in others ways. Some suggest that Jesus must have merely fainted on the cross, appeared dead, and so been buried in the tomb, where he revived and came out to meet his disciples. Or perhaps the disciples were simply hallucinating. But none of these theories make sense of the facts. The Romans were extremely thorough in their practice of execution (see John 19:33-34). Even if Jesus had somehow survived the beating, whipping and crucifixion, and then been revived in the tomb, he would have been a broken man when he met the disciples, and would have died at some point later – but they experienced him as someone more full of life than they were! The Gospels also insist that the risen Jesus was not a hallucination or a ghost. The disciples themselves had a hard time believing that Jesus was really, physically alive again, so he provided "many convincing proofs", including eating food with them (eg Luke 24:36-43; Acts 1:3). When they began to spread the message of Jesus' resurrection, they were absolutely sure that he had not been left in the decay of death but that he had risen to new life!

THE MEANING OF THE RESURRECTION

Jesus' disciples did not expect Jesus to rise from the dead on the third day after he was crucified. So, once they had met with the risen Jesus, they quickly realised that his resurrection completely overturned and reworked all their expectations about what God was doing in the world.

- **The vindication of Jesus.** For a start, the resurrection was divine confirmation that Jesus truly was Israel's Messiah (Romans 1:3). It was inconceivable to the disciples that a crucified Messiah could be any sort of Messiah at all: how could a dead man liberate God's people from their enemies and bring about an everlasting kingdom of freedom and peace? (Luke 24:21). Throughout his ministry, Jesus had declared that God's kingdom was present where he was (Mark 1:15). He was the true Son of God who could act on his Father's authority. He could bring forgiveness and healing directly from God, without the need for sacrifices in the temple. His death apparently shattered all these claims. But now, God had raised Jesus up (Acts 2:24), declaring in power that Jesus is who he claimed to be: Lord and Messiah (Acts 2:36). Jesus has God's authority to bring his kingdom to the world!

- **The defeat of God's enemies.** From the point of view of the resurrection, the disciples had to rework their understanding of Jesus' death. They already knew that Jesus had suffered and died under the full weight of God's enemies: he had been crucified because of the betrayal, greed, injustice, sin and evil that riddled the whole world, and even his own closest friends. His

death had looked like a triumph for Satan. But the resurrection told a different story. Jesus had not been overwhelmed by those things; instead, he had overwhelmed them – not by meeting violence with greater violence, but through suffering. In light of the resurrection, Jesus was the suffering servant promised by Isaiah 40–55, whose terrible afflictions brought about the rescue of God's people. Jesus had stemmed the tide of sin and death, in his own body, on the

The resurrection of Jesus is final proof that Jesus truly is the Messiah

TO THINK ABOUT

Read the story of Resurrection Day in Luke 24.

· How had the discovery of the empty tomb affected Jesus' followers?
· When did they finally believe that Jesus had been raised to life?
· What do you think Jesus told the disciples on the road to Emmaus (verse 27)?
· Why do you think the disciples were joyful in verses 52,53?

Now read Peter's sermon on the Day of Pentecost in Acts 2:14-36. Remember: the resurrection was not an isolated event, but it was part of a whole world of thought and belief.

· How does Peter link the resurrection of Jesus back to the promises of the Old Testament?
· What did the resurrection mean for the people listening to Peter?

In Romans 10:9, Paul notes that the basic confession of the Christian faith includes two elements: "Jesus is Lord", and "God raised him from the dead".

· Why is belief in the resurrection of Jesus so important?
· Have we lost the context within which the resurrection makes sense?
· How would you go about explaining the resurrection of Jesus to someone who had no knowledge of the Bible? (Acts 17:22-32 may give some help.)

The whole message of Christianity is encapsulated in the claim that Jesus is risen from the dead. To be a Christian means to trust that God really has done through Jesus what the New Testament says he has – begun the work of new creation that will be brought to completion someday soon. Thank God that he has triumphed over all his enemies, by raising Jesus from the dead. Now pray that the power of his resurrection would be seen in your life (Philippians 3:10).

---

cross. And his resurrection was the joyful triumph over them – he had left them in the tomb; death was defeated; sin's power was broken; God's enemies were humiliated (1 Corinthians 15:55-56; Colossians 2:15; Revelation 1:18).

· **The beginning of new creation.** God's people Israel had, of course, always believed that God would accomplish such a great victory over his enemies. But they had thought it would happen all at once, at the end of the age. Some Jews believed that when the end came, there would be a general resurrection of all faithful Israelites, so that none of God's people would miss out on his great triumph (based on prophecies in Ezekiel 37:1-14; Daniel 12:2; see also John 11:24). Jesus' resurrection, on his own, right in the middle of history, was

simply astounding! Somehow, God's new world had come forward from the future to meet them in the present! The first Christians called Jesus the "first-fruits" of God's new creation (1 Corinthians 15:20) – the first crop of harvest, which is the sign and promise that the rest will follow. They had to rework their whole understanding of God's activity in the world around this. Jesus is the pioneer of faith (Hebrews 12:2), who has gone on ahead of the rest of creation into God's new creation, to show the way. The early church knew that as they gathered together, living and working in the Spirit of the risen Jesus, he was already bringing his new creation about in their midst (2 Corinthians 5:17). By his risen power, he would go on doing so until the day when all things will be made new.

The gift of the Spirit

KEY TRUTH
The risen Jesus brings his followers into a new, lasting covenant with God, by pouring out on them the Holy Spirit.

NEW FOR OLD
In the Old Testament, God's covenant with Israel was a declaration of his faithful commitment to them, to which they were expected to respond with trust and obedience. The terms of this covenant had been given at Mount Sinai, where it was engraved on the stone tablets of the law that God gave to Moses (see Exodus 31:18). Through this covenant, God and his people would live together as he had always intended them to, experiencing intimacy, joy and blessing (eg Deuteronomy 28:1-6). However, as the history of Israel made clear again and again, God's people were less committed to this covenant than God himself was. They were either unable or unwilling – or both – to stay within it. (For a brief summary of Israel's history, see Nehemiah 9:6-37.) Time after time, God delivered his people from their enemies, and restored them to fellowship with himself after periods of judgement in exile. By his grace, God kept the covenant with his people, even when they were faithless to him. The covenant was good, but God's people could not keep it.

Throughout the Old Testament, though, there was a glimmer of hope. The prophets spoke of a coming day when God would make a new covenant with his people, which would end their constant wavering between half-hearted obedience and disobedience. In Jeremiah, it was promised that this new covenant would not be like the old covenant, where the law was engraved on tablets of stone; instead, God's commands would be engraved on his people's hearts (Jeremiah 31:31-33). Ezekiel's prophecy went further: God's people would be given a new heart altogether – a heart of flesh that would be sensitive to God's voice, replacing their old, stony heart (Ezekiel 36:26). In other words, the covenant with God would move from being outside God's people, in words written on stone tablets, to being inside, within and among them. This would be nothing less than a new creative act of God! When God created the world, his Spirit had been active (Genesis 1:2); and so too the new hearts of God's people would be a work of his Spirit: "I will put my Spirit in you and move you to follow my decrees and be careful to keep my law" (Ezekiel 36:27). In the Old Testament, God's Spirit had come upon particular people to enable them to accomplish his work (eg David in 1 Samuel 16:13). But the longing cry of God's faithful people was for his Spirit to be poured out on all Israel, so that they would all live and move completely within the joy and intimacy of his covenant (eg Numbers 11:29; Joel 2:28-29).

THE DAY OF PENTECOST
After Jesus had risen from the dead, he spent 40 days with his disciples, teaching them about the kingdom of God (Acts 1:3). At the end of this period, Jesus "withdrew" from them, returning to the presence of his Father in heaven (Luke 24:51). After this ascension, they would no longer have his bodily presence with them. However, Jesus told them that it was to their advantage that he left them like this (John 16:7). By going away, back to the

place of authority with the Father, he would be able to send them a gift that would be even more beneficial to them than his bodily presence – the Holy Spirit.

- **The promise.** The way Jesus described this coming gift would have left the disciples in no doubt that he was speaking about the Spirit of the new covenant: "I am sending upon you what my Father promised" (Luke 24:49); "wait for the promise of the Father" (Acts 1:4). The disciples would "receive power" when the Spirit came upon them (Acts 1:8). Just as the prophets had said,

> " *But I tell you the truth: It is for your good that I am going away. Unless I go away, the Counsellor will not come to you; but if I go, I will send him to you."*

JOHN 16:7

they would be able to live in intimate fellowship with God and do his work in the world. So the disciples waited in Jerusalem. They knew from Jesus' resurrection that God was already beginning to fulfil some of his promises that they had thought would only occur at the end of the age. New creation had already burst into the present in the form of Jesus' risen body. But when would they themselves experience this new life? Would they have to wait until God's kingdom came in full some day in the future (see Acts 1:6)?

- **The significance of Pentecost.** Pentecost, or the Feast of Weeks, was a significant festival in the Jewish calendar. It was primarily a harvest festival, marking seven weeks after the first-fruits of the harvest had been gathered (Leviticus 23:9-21; seven weeks is 49 days, and the Feast was on the following day; "Pentecost" is Greek for

The Holy Spirit was poured out on the disciples 50 days after Jesus had risen from the dead

"fiftieth"). By the time of Jesus, however, this feast was also a celebration of the giving of the *Torah* (law of the covenant) at Mount Sinai, since this was thought to have happened 50 days after the exodus from Egypt. On that occasion, Moses had ascended the mountain in order to speak with God, and had received from him the stone tablets inscribed with the law (Exodus 31:18; 34:27-32). It is no coincidence, then, that the Holy Spirit filled the disciples on the day of Pentecost (Acts 2:1-4). There is an implicit echo of the story of the giving of the law in Peter's sermon. Jesus had not ascended to the top of Mount Sinai, but into heaven itself, and had received the promise of the Holy Spirit from the Father (Acts 2:33). This Spirit was now being poured out by Jesus on his disciples – just as Moses had come down the mountain with the tablets of stone. On the day of Pentecost, when Israel were celebrating the giving of the old covenant at Mount Sinai, Jesus' disciples were experiencing the gift of the new covenant – the Holy Spirit poured out on them!

- **Power to witness.** The disciples experienced the Spirit on the day of Pentecost as a rushing, enlivening, creative presence in their midst (Acts 2:2-4). The Spirit was certainly the "power" about which Jesus had spoken in Acts 1:8! There, Jesus has said that the Spirit would provide power for the disciples to be witnesses to the whole world. "Witnesses", of course, were what the people of the old covenant were always supposed to be: a light to the nations, drawing people to the truth and ways of the true God. However, the stony hearts of God's people had meant that they were never the witnesses they should have been, and the message about God had got garbled and lost among their own words and deeds. The promised Spirit of the new covenant changed all of this. Because the Spirit brought new hearts of flesh, God's

new covenant people were no longer hampered in their witness for God. Their lives were set free and empowered to show the reality of God's kingdom through word and deed. On the day of Pentecost, Jesus' disciples spoke freely to a multinational crowd, boldly declaring "God's deeds of power". Miraculously, every person understood in their own language! (Acts 2:5-11). Later, there were miracles of healing too (see Acts 3:1-10). As Peter explained to the crowds, these strange happenings were signs that God's promises were being fulfilled (Acts 2:16-21, quoting Joel 2:28-32). The new covenant had clearly arrived, brought about by Jesus through his death, resurrection and ascension; and so it was time for all to join in (Acts 2:37-42).

THE SPIRIT AND SALVATION

The gift of the Spirit is essential to Jesus' saving work. Without the Spirit, the claim that Jesus has initiated the new covenant with God for his disciples would be empty. For the first Christians, both the ministry, death and resurrection of Jesus, and the gift of the Spirit were integral aspects of God's great salvation (see Acts 11:17).

- **The Spirit makes Jesus present.** Throughout Jesus' earthly ministry, it was clear that he himself, in his words and actions, was the presence of God's kingdom. But what would happen to that kingdom once Jesus had ascended into heaven? If the kingdom required the presence of Jesus, then surely it would no longer be available. Would the memory of it simply be kept alive by a small band of followers?

  On the contrary, by going away from his disciples, Jesus said that he would be able to send the Spirit, who would take Jesus' kingdom presence and make it known to and through the disciples, wherever they were (John 16:12-15). The book of Acts describes how the Spirit brought Jesus'

TO THINK ABOUT

The Spirit is sometimes described as the "forgotten" person of the Trinity!
· Why do you think this is?
· How easy do you find it to talk about the work of the Spirit?

Read Ezekiel 36:22-38.
· What is the big picture of this prophecy?
· How important is the promise of the Spirit?

Now read Romans 8:1-17.
· What is the relation between the work of Jesus and the work of the Spirit in this passage?
· Does this passage describe the fulfilment of the prophecy of Ezekiel in any way?

The Spirit is the gift of Jesus to his people, in order to establish them in the new covenant. All who have put their trust in Jesus are given the Spirit.
· How do you see the Spirit at work in your life?
· How could you live more in step with the Spirit?
· If the Spirit has been given to you as a "power for witness", how could you exercise this in your own life?

Jesus' work of salvation is not just a piece of information; it is a new intimate relationship with God that is characterised by childlike confidence. This is only possible through the Spirit, who has been poured out by Jesus into the lives of his disciples. Thank Jesus for this gift, and ask for strength and discernment to live today in step with the Spirit.

---

kingdom presence into surprising places, often working far ahead of Jesus' own disciples (eg Acts 10). Jesus' forgiveness and blessing are still available today, through his Spirit.

· **The Spirit establishes Jesus' disciples in his kingdom.** The major mark of the new covenant with God is that those who belong to God through Jesus are given a new heart, which will enable them to live constantly in intimate fellowship with him. The first Christians recognised that this was the work of the Spirit in their lives. Through the Spirit, God had applied to them all the blessings of the kingdom about which Jesus had spoken. The Spirit brought into their present lives the new creation that had begun with Jesus' risen body! They could

call God "Father" (Romans 8:15-16; Galatians 4:6); their lives would produce good fruit (Galatians 5:22-23). They used the phrase "living in the Spirit" as shorthand for belonging to Jesus' kingdom and experiencing his life and power at work in their lives (see Romans 8:1-5).

Those who are marked by the Spirit in this way know that they belong securely to God. The Spirit is thus a "seal" on a Christian's life, guaranteeing that they will be part of God's kingdom when Jesus finally brings it in all its fullness (eg Ephesians 1:13-14). Those who belong to God through Jesus, and keep in step with his Spirit, have nothing to fear, but can look forward in hope to the new creation!

New creation

KEY TRUTH
Jesus will complete his saving work when he comes again to usher in God's new creation, for which his church now lives in expectant hope.

THE FRUSTRATION OF CREATION
In the beginning, God's intention was that the whole of creation would flourish under the careful stewardship of the humans he had created in his own image (Genesis 1:28; 2:15). He gave them freedom to use their abilities to tend and shape the world around them, so that their creative work within his creation would reflect back to God his own glory (see Psalm 8). Creation was to be a place of life and love, creativity and joy, abundance and satisfaction!

However, the first chapters of the Bible make it clear that this good order suffered a profound disruption. In Genesis 3, the very humans God had made and set within such a world of blessing turn away from him, and so sin breaks their fellowship with God. But sin did not just affect human relationships with God and one another; its repercussions were felt within creation itself (Genesis 3:17-19). Instead of cooperating with human stewardship, the created world went its own way, just like the first humans themselves had done. Sin, by its nature, gets out of control. The act of creation resulted from God's good order triumphing over formless chaos (eg Genesis 1), but sin tries to drag creation back into that chaos – sin un-creates. Alongside the goodness of creation, because of sin creation is also a place of death and rivalry, decay and despair, scarcity and poverty.

The wellbeing of the whole of creation is bound up with that of the humans whom God has placed in stewardship over it. In Romans, Paul writes that all creation has been "subjected to frustration" until the time when God's people themselves are fully set free (Romans 8:18-23). Without the freedom of God's people, the whole of creation must suffer together with them under the "bondage of decay". Creation is frustrated – it cannot flourish as God intends it to, until sin is finally banished.

THE LIBERATION OF CREATION
The story of salvation told throughout the Bible is thus not simply about how humans can move back into fellowship with God. It has a much wider scope – how will the whole of creation, galaxies and insects included, be all that God intended it to be?

- **Israel's hope.** The people of Israel were keenly aware that they had been set free by God from slavery in Egypt. What they sometimes remembered (but mostly forgot) was that God had rescued them because he wanted to rescue all the nations of the earth too – Israel were always supposed to be blessed in order to be a blessing (see Genesis 12:1-3). God's love towards Israel in her waywardness was a sign to the world that he wanted all people to turn back to him. They were to be a light to the nations, so that God's salvation would reach to the ends of the earth (eg Isaiah 49:6).

But God's vision for the world through Israel went even further! For if the whole of humanity was going to be purified and brought back into fellowship with God through a great work of salvation, then the repercussions of that salvation would be felt throughout the cosmos. If the power of sin were to be broken, and God's people were to become who they were always supposed to be, then creation could once again be brought under the good and wise stewardship of humans created in God's image. The prophet Isaiah looked forward to the day when not only God's people would be saved and the nations of the world come to worship God, but also wolves and lambs and leopards and goats would live together in harmony (Isaiah 11:6-9). Under the good rule of God's Messiah, the mountains and the hills would burst into song and the trees clap their hands! (Isaiah 55:12). God's salvation would reverse the effects of Adam's sin – the thorns and weeds that had sprung up in the ground would turn into productive trees (Isaiah 55:13; see Genesis 3:18). Finally, God's salvation will be so complete, that it will in fact be the creation of a "new heavens and a new earth" (Isaiah 65:17), from which sin and chaos are banished, and all things reflect the good order of Israel's God.

· **Jesus' resurrection.** When Jesus' first disciples met him again, after his crucifixion, risen from the dead, they caught a glimpse in his resurrected body of what the renewal of all creation would be like. He still had a real body, but it was transformed in ways they could never have imagined and could hardly describe (eg John 20:19; 1 Corinthians 15:35-49). They recognised, though, that his resurrection was a kind of "first-fruits" – the sign and promise of what would happen to all who believed in him (1 Corinthians 15:20) and, indeed, would happen to all things. God's new creation will be the sort of place where Jesus' risen body (and those of his people) is at home! (see 2 Peter 3:13).

· **Jesus' coming.** The first Christians knew that the history of salvation had not yet reached its conclusion. Although Jesus had already won the decisive victory over sin and death, and had defeated the power of Satan, this great triumph still needed to be applied to the whole of creation. As Paul said, the world is still subjected to frustration. But because of Jesus' resurrection, all creation is holding its breath, knowing that at any moment God's future may overtake the present, and it will be transformed into the home for God's resurrected people (Romans 8:19; see 1 Corinthians 15:50-55).

The key figure in this final, dramatic moment in the history of salvation will, of course, be the risen Jesus. Throughout his teachings, Jesus had spoken rather

> " *Therefore keep watch, because you do not know the day or the hour.*"
> MATTHEW 25:13

cryptically of the "coming of the Son of Man" (eg Mark 13:26) and told parables about masters returning unexpectedly to their servants (eg Mark 13:34-37). After his resurrection, the disciples were able to understand and spell out more clearly what this meant in terms of God's promised future. In Acts, Peter tells his hearers that Jesus "must remain in heaven until the time of universal restoration that God announced long ago" (Acts 3:21). At the moment, the world remains in frustration because Jesus is simply not here (in body, though he is by the Spirit). But at some unexpected moment in the future, Jesus will "appear"; he will "come"; he will be "revealed" (eg Philippians 3:20; 1 Thessalonians 4:16; 1 John 2:28). When he arrives, he will be bodily present in his glory as the true Lord of all, and the whole world will be judged by its relation to him. Those who belong to him will become fully part of God's new world, as he already is (eg

Colossians 3:4), and creation will be set free from death and decay (Romans 8:21). Jesus will gather up the whole creation under his good rule and will hand it back to God the Father (1 Corinthians 15:24). Jesus' coming will be the final destruction of all God's enemies, and the transformation of all creation – he will complete his saving work as he ushers in God's new heavens and new earth!

ANTICIPATING LIBERATION

In the meantime, Jesus instructs his people to live in expectant hope. The church is the gathering of those who wait eagerly for the coming again of the risen Jesus. They rest their lives on the conviction that Jesus has dealt with their sin, so that when he comes to usher in God's new world, they will not be swept away with God's judgement of sin, but

Not just the church, but the whole of creation, is waiting for the return of Jesus. Eruption of Mount Etna, Sicily, 2002

rather be established for ever in the eternal kingdom of God (eg Romans 5:9). While the church waits with expectant hope, it must watch and work.

· **Watching for Jesus' coming.** Many of Jesus' parables presented a warning to his disciples: "Watch! Stay alert!" (eg Matthew 25:1-13). There have been two thousand years of history since Jesus ascended into heaven, and it is tempting to forget that Jesus could come with God's kingdom at any moment. This warning is a reminder that the church must always look towards God's great renewal in the future. Whatever blessings it experiences now through the Spirit are simply foretastes and anticipations of the fullness that Jesus will bring! When God's people forget to watch, their gatherings begin to look like any other human society (1 Thessalonians 5:6). But when they remain alert, watching for Jesus' coming, they live differently – expectantly, living in the present to show that the

coming Jesus is truly Lord of all. Just before his arrest, in the Garden of Gethsemane, Jesus told his disciples, "Watch and pray so that you will not fall into temptation" (Matthew 26:41). As they watch for his coming, Jesus' disciples have been given the gift of prayer, so that they will not lose their way as they depend on him. Sometimes this prayer will not be for themselves, but for others, that they too may come to watch for Jesus (see Romans 8:26).

· **Working with resurrection power.** "Blessed is the servant whom his master will find at work when he arrives" (Matthew 24:46). Although Christians must wait for Jesus' coming in order to experience God's kingdom in full, they must not be idle in the meantime. Indeed, Jesus' resurrection from the dead means that God's new creation has already begun to burst into the present age! Jesus sends his Spirit upon his people so that they too can experience outbursts of new creation in their lives and relationships – sometimes even through healing of their bodies and minds. God's people must set about cultivating this new creation, preparing the ground of lives and situations for God's new life to burst forth, always celebrating the good things that he is doing. This work, even in our daily occupations, done before Jesus comes, has lasting value because it is the work of God's kingdom and so will be carried over into new creation (see 1 Corinthians 3:12-15; 15:58).

By waiting, watching and working, God's people live constantly within Jesus' saving work. They look back to his death and resurrection which has set them free; they live in the new covenant by his Spirit now; they look forward to his coming, when he will finally destroy sin, death and Satan, and usher in God's new creation.

TO THINK ABOUT

Make a list of the things you enjoy in the created world.
· How have these things been affected by the disruption of sin?
· How do you think they will be transformed in God's new creation?
· What can you do to preserve or restore them?

Read Isaiah's vision of the renewed creation in one or more of the following passages: 11:1-10; 55:1-13; 65:17-25. Now use the following questions to come to a deeper understanding.
· What is the vision of the renewed created order in this passage?
· How does Isaiah's vision of the new creation fit alongside his other vision – eg of a new covenant with Israel?
· How has this passage been fulfilled by Jesus? What still remains to be fulfilled?

Read Romans 8:18-27.
· What is the "hope" about which this passage speaks?
· How are we to wait for this hope?

Read 1 Corinthians 15:20-28.
· How does this passage speak about the completion of Jesus' saving work?
· How does it make you feel? Why?
· What does it mean for you to wait, watch and work?

As Christians, we live in hope, because we know that we live within Jesus' saving work – his work is behind us, with us now and ahead of us. Thank Jesus that his saving work is so complete, and that no part of your life is outside his power to save and heal. Now pray that he will come soon to usher in God's new creation (Revelation 22:20).

shouted with a great shout, that
the wall fell down flat, so that
the people went up into the
city, every man straight before
him, and they took the city.

21 And they utterly destroyed
all that was in the city, both
man and woman, young and
old, and ox, and sheep, and ass,
with the edge of the sword.

22 But Joshua had said unto
the two men that had spied out
the country, Go into the har-
lot's house, and bring out thence
the woman, and all that she
hath, as ye sware unto her.

23 And the young men that
were spies went in, and brought
out Rahab, and her father, and
her mother, and her brethren,
and all that she had; and they
brought out all her kindred, and
left them without the camp of

...they burnt the city
...and all that was
...the silver, and
...the vessels of
...they put into

...of the house of the

...Rahab
...her father's
...all that she had
...in Israel even
...because she hid

the son of Z...
the tribe of Judah...
accursed thing: and
of the LORD was kind...
the children of Israel

2 And Joshua sent
Jericho to A-i, which
Beth-a-ven, on the
Beth-el, and
...saying, Go
the country. And
up and viewed A-i.

3 And they return
and said unto h...
the people go up
two or three th...
up and smite
not all the p...
thither; for th...

4 So there w...
the people ab...
men: and th...
men of A-i.

5 And the...
...about...
for they ch...
fore the...

The Bible Book by Book

The following pages give a summary of each book of the Bible. Our aim has been to introduce the key teaching and practical application of the Bible in a readable and accessible way.

Each outline contains the following features:

- Background giving an overview, summary and context of the book
- Outline giving the structure of the book
- Key themes showing some of the major distinctive emphases of the book
- Relevance for today: showing how the message of the book can be worked out in our own lives.

The Bible Book by Book

CONTENTS

This page shows the 66 books of the Bible arranged in order.
An alphabetical list is given on the facing page.

THE OLD TESTAMENT

THE NEW TESTAMENT

THE BOOKS OF THE BIBLE IN ALPHABETICAL ORDER

MAPS AND CHARTS

The Calendar Year

The Jewish calendar, as in all early civilisations, grew out of the agricultural cycle and the phases of the moon. Religious rites and festivals were associated with both the farmer's year and commemoration of the great events in Jewish history.

In order that the lunar calendar would relate to the solar year an extra month (Second Adar) was added about every three years.

Late summer harvest: grapes and ripening figs

A limestone "notepad" found at Gezer in central Israel shows the calendar inscribed in Hebrew. Dated at around 900 BC, it is known as the "Gezer Calendar"

Spring harvest: lemons

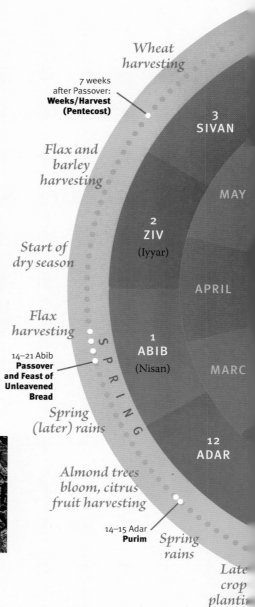

Wheat harvesting

7 weeks after Passover: **Weeks/Harvest (Pentecost)**

3 SIVAN

MAY

Flax and barley harvesting

2 ZIV (Iyyar)

APRIL

Start of dry season

Flax harvesting

1 ABIB (Nisan)

MARC

14–21 Abib **Passover and Feast of Unleavened Bread**

SPRING

Spring (later) rains

12 ADAR

Almond trees bloom, citrus fruit harvesting

14–15 Adar **Purim**

Spring rains

Late crop planti

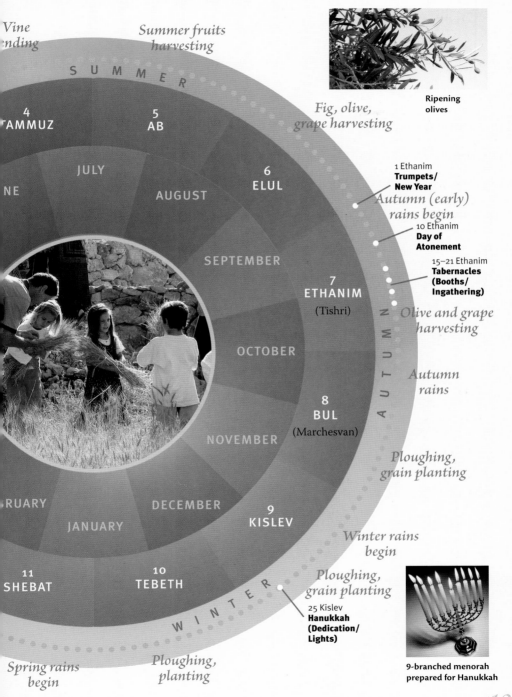

Vine
~~nding~~

Summer fruits
harvesting

SUMMER

Fig, olive,
grape harvesting

Ripening
olives

4
~~T~~AMMUZ

5
AB

JULY

AUGUST

~~N~~E

6
ELUL

1 Ethanim
**Trumpets/
New Year**

Autumn (early)
rains begin

10 Ethanim
**Day of
Atonement**

SEPTEMBER

15–21 Ethanim
**Tabernacles
(Booths/
Ingathering)**

7
ETHANIM
(Tishri)

Olive and grape
harvesting

OCTOBER

A
U
T
U
M
N

Autumn
rains

8
BUL
(Marchesvan)

Ploughing,
grain planting

NOVEMBER

DECEMBER

9
KISLEV

Winter rains
begin

JANUARY

Ploughing,
grain planting

11
SHEBAT

10
TEBETH

25 Kislev
**Hanukkah
(Dedication/
Lights)**

WINTER

~~F~~RUARY

9-branched menorah
prepared for Hanukkah

Spring rains
begin

Ploughing,
planting

Festivals and Feasts

	Time	Description	Reason	Bible reference
Sabbath	7th day of the week	Day of rest, no work	Rest for people and livestock	Ex 20:8-11
Sabbath year	Every 7th year	Year of rest, fields left fallow	Rest for the land, help for the poor, debts cancelled	Ex 23:10-11 Dt 15:1-6
Year of Jubilee	Every 50th year	Debts cancelled, slaves liberated, land returned to its rightful owner	Help for the poor, social stability, rest for the land	Lev 25:8-55
Passover	14 Abib (1st month)	Slaying and eating a lamb with bitter herbs and bread without yeast, in each household	To remember the sparing of Israel's firstborn and the nation's deliverance from Egypt	Dt 16:1-7
Unleavened Bread	15–21 Abib (1st month)	Eating bread without yeast, assemblies, offerings	To remember how the Lord brought out Israel from Egypt in haste	Ex 12:15-20; 13:3-10; 23:15
Firstfruits	16 Abib (1st month)	A wave offering of a sheaf from the first of the barley harvest, a burnt offering and a grain offering	To recognise God's provision	Lev 23:9-14
Weeks (Pentecost/ Harvest)	6 Sivan (3rd month)	A time of joy. Freewill and compulsory offerings, including the firstfruits of the wheat harvest	To joyfully give thanks for God's blessing in the harvest	Ex 23:16
Trumpets (Rosh Hashanah/ New Year)	1 Ethanim (7th month)	Assembly on a day of rest, marked by trumpet blasts and sacrifices	To present all Israel as a people before the Lord	Lev 23:23-25
Day of Atonement (Yom Kippur)	10 Ethanim (7th month)	Day of rest, fasting, sacrifices of atonement for priests and people	To cleanse people and priests from their sin and to purify the Holy Place	Lev 16; 23:26-32

Observing feasts and festivals is an important part of Hebrew religion. They were viewed as gifts from God, regulating the people's communal life as God's people, and have preserved the memories of God's interaction with his people throughout their history, especially in terms of his miraculous deliverance or his daily provision for their physical and spiritual needs.

Times of joy: children dressed up for Purim celebration; gathering firstfruits of wheat for the Festival of Weeks

	Time	Description	Reason	Bible reference
Tabernacles (Booths/ Ingathering)	15–21 Ethanim (7th month)	Week of celebration for harvest, building and living in temporary shelters, offering sacrifices	To remember the journey to the Promised Land and to give thanks for the bounty of Canaan	Ex 23:16
Sacred Assembly	22 Ethanim (7th month)	A day of gathering together, rest and sacrifices	To close the cycle of feasts	Lev 23:36; Nu 29:35-38
Hanukkah (Dedication/ Festival of Lights)	25 Kislev (9th month)	Family celebration of lighting of oil or candles in a 9-branched menorah	To celebrate the rededication of the temple and altar by the Maccabees	(Referred to in Jn 10:22)
Purim	14, 15 Adar (12th month)	Day of happiness, feasting and giving presents	To remember the preservation of the Jews under Persian rule in the time of Queen Esther	Est 9:18-32
	The first day of each month was designated as new moon, and was celebrated with sounding of trumpets and festivity			Nu 10:10; 1 Sa 20:5

Sacrifice

SACRIFICE AND OFFERING IN THE OLD TESTAMENT

Sacrifice and offering are woven into the fabric of the Jewish way of life. Rules for sacrifice were given to Moses by God himself, with provision for all aspects of life. Each sacrifice was to be carried out in a specified way outlined in Leviticus 1–7. But the annual sacrifice of the Day of Atonement (16:1-34) reminds us that none of these sacrifices could ever atone for sin (only unintentional sin was provided for; there was no sacrifice for deliberate sin). The New Testament sees this as anticipating Christ's sacrifice, which alone can do away with all sin (Hebrews 9:1–10:14).

IN THE NEW TESTAMENT

All the writers in the New Testament stress the significance of Jesus' death as superseding the sacrifices of the Old Testament. As God's perfect high priest, Jesus Christ himself became the perfect sacrifice – one offering for sin, valid for all time. Human sin is atoned for once and for all. The former system could not do this. His sacrifice has made the way open for people to come to God, so that now no further sacrifice is required.

Israelite practice and observance was distinct from that of the nations around them because:

· Jews believed in one God;
· people were to seek to live pure lives in obedience to God's law and to respect others;
· repentance and atonement were necessary because sin created separation between God and humanity;
· practices of magic and sorcery were forbidden;
· there was to be no human sacrifice, sexual deviation or frenzied activity.

In Jesus' time sheep from the Shepherds' Fields at Bethlehem were used for ritual sacrifice in the temple at Jerusalem

The law was sympathetic to people's situation, so that an offering would be within the means of the giver. The sin offering for a poor person could be a pigeon or dove

	Description	Purpose	Bible reference
Burnt offering	A bull, ram or male bird, without defect, or for the poor a dove or young pigeon. (The only offering where the whole animal was consumed)	A freewill act of worship, an atonement for unintentional sin, a token of devotion and dedication to God	Lev 1; 6:8-13
Cereal or grain offering	Grain, fine flour, olive oil, incense, baked bread, salt, often offered with a burnt or peace offering	A freewill act of worship recognising God's goodness and provision	Lev 2; 6:14-18
Peace or fellowship offering	An animal from the herd or flock, without defect	A freewill act of worship to re-establish fellowship with God or others, or a thank offering. Accompanied by a communal meal	Lev 3; 7:11-36
Sin offering	Either a young bull (for the high priest and gathering); a male goat (for a senior figure); a female goat or lamb (for a commoner); a dove or pigeon (for the poor); a tenth of an ephah of fine flour (for the destitute)	A requirement to obtain forgiveness for unintended sin, to be accompanied by confession; and for cleansing from defilement	Lev 4:1–5:13; 6:24-30
Guilt or repayment offering	A ram or a lamb	A requirement for atonement for unintended sin needing restitution: to be accompanied by making good the wrong and paying a fine	Lev 5:14–6:7; 7:1-10
The Day of Atonement	Once each year, on the 10th day of Ethanim, the high priest was allowed into the Most Holy Place, where the ark of the covenant was. He was to obtain forgiveness and cleansing for his own sin, then offer on behalf of the sins of the nation. A bull and a goat would be sacrificed, while another goat would have the sins of the people confessed over it and was then released in the desert		Lev 16; Heb 9–10

Money and Values

The exchange of goods gradually gave way from around the 7th C BC to the exchange of precious metals by weight, then much later to coinage that represented weight and worth. There was no constant standard, and values varied according to time, place and personal honesty. International trade brought a degree of understanding of values across cultures. Some coinage bore the mark or seal of the local overlord.

In New Testament times, Roman standards took hold, although money-changers in Israel did a brisk business due to the circulation of Roman, Greek and local currencies.

OLD TESTAMENT VALUES
(Measured by weight which eventually related to value)

	Approx weight	
Shekel	11.5g	(50 shekels = 1 mina)
Mina	500g	(60 minas = 1 talent)
Talent	30kg	

There was a silver standard and a gold standard for the wealthy

NEW TESTAMENT VALUES IN ISRAEL
Showing comparative values across the currencies, approximate

Roman	Greek	Jewish
		Lepton
Quadrans		= 2 lepta
As		= 4 lepta
4 asses (= 1 sestertius)		
Denarius (= 16 asses)	Drachma	
2 denarii =	Didrachma (2 drachmae)	Half-shekel
4 denarii =	Stater/tetradrachma	Shekel
Aureus (gold)	(25 drachmae)	
100 denarii =	Mina*	= 30 shekels
240 aurei =	Talent* (60 minas)	

*An amount of money, not a coin

Money was minted in brass, copper, silver and gold.
A lepton was the widow's offering: Mk 12:42
One as was the value of two sparrows: Mt 10:29
A denarius was a day's wages: Mt 20:9-10
A half-shekel was the standard temple-tax: Mt 17:24

Silver shekel of Darius 1, Persian, c. 500 BC; Roman copper quadrans, c. 230 BC; legionary denarius of Marc Antony, 32 BC; Jewish copper lepton (a "widow's offering"); Jewish half-shekel; tetradrachmae from Antioch, Syria, showing the busts of Nero c. AD 68 and Claudius c. AD 52

Weights and Measures

Most transactions in ancient times would have been by exchange of goods. For paying in silver, scales and weights were used. These had to be standardised, although the system was open to abuse by the unscrupulous. Many weights were formed into shapes and marked.

Measures were used for selling and storage of harvest produce and liquids. A fair and full measure of grain was said to be "running over".

All equivalents shown are approximate.

WEIGHT

Old Testament
Gerah (0.6g)
Bekah (6g)
Shekel (11g)
Royal shekel (13g)
Mina (600g)
Talent (34kg)
Double standard talent (60kg)

New Testament
Litra/pound (327g)
Talent (20–40kg)

DRY MEASURES

Old Testament
Log (0.3 litres)
Kab (1.2 litres)
Omer (2.2 litres)
Seah (7.3 litres)
Ephah (22 litres)
Lethek (110 litres)
Cor, Homer (220 litres)

LIQUID MEASURES

Old Testament
Log (0.3 litres)
Kab (1.2 litres)
Hin (4 litres)
Bath (22 litres)

Liquid container, Egyptian, holding a hin

Amphorae, discovered near Athens, dated c. 500 BC

Duck-shaped basalt weight from Mesopotamia, c. 1000 BC. Part of a set of standardised weights

Bronze lion-weight from Nimrud. Assyrian, inscribed with the king's name

The World of the Old Testament

Black Sea

Adriatic Sea

Rome •

ITALY

MACEDONIA

THRACIA

PONTUS

LYDIA

Hattusha •

Aegean Sea

PHRYGIA

CAPPADOCIA

ACHAIA

Athens •

CILICIA

CARIA

Taurus Mountains

Haran •
Genesis 12

Sparta •

SICILY

KITTIM

Riv.
Euph.

CAPHTOR

The Great Sea
(Mediterranean Sea)

ARAM

• Damascus
Isaiah 7

Cyrene •

CANAAN
Jerusalem •
2 Samuel 6

Jericho
Joshua 6

PUT

Alexandria •

• Rameses
Exodus 1

KEDAR

LIBYA

Memphis •

Sinai
Exodus 19–20

MIDIAN

DEDAN

EGYPT

River Nile

Red Sea

O

Thebes •

Abu Simbel •

ETHIOPIA
(CUSH)

With an ongoing rise and fall of dominant powers
country, regional and place names changed.
The map shows selective place names to aid
identification with various biblical accounts.

0   100   200 miles

0   100   200 kilometres

0 10 20 miles
0 10 20 kilometres
Mt Hermon
Tyre
Laish (Dan)
Kedesh
Misrephoth-maim
Hazor
R Jordan
Merom
Acco
Aphek
Chinnereth
Sea of Chinnereth
The Great Sea
R Kishon
Mt Carmel
BASHAN
Shunem
Dor
Megiddo
CANAAN
Taanach
Beth-shean
Migdal
Dothan
Jabesh Gilead
PLAIN OF SHARON
Socoh
River Jordan
Tirzah
THE ARABAH
Mt Ebal
Shechem
Succoth
Mt Gerizim
Penuel
Joppa
Aphek
Shiloh
Gath
Beth-horon
Bethel
Gilgal
Gezer
Jericho
Shittim
AMORITES
Ashdod
Ekron
Aijalon
Gibeon
Mt Nebo
Makkedah
Kiriath Jearim
Jerusalem
Beth-jeshimoth
Libnah
Bethlehem
Ashkelon
Adullam
Ataroth
Eglon
THE SHEPHELAH
Lachish
Gaza
Hebron
Salt Sea (Sea of the Arabah)
Kiriathaim
Debir
HILL COUNTRY
R Arnon
Beersheba
THE NEGEV
Hormah
MOAB
SCYTHIA
Caspian Sea
SCYTHIA
Caucasus Mountains
ARMENIA
Ararat Genesis 8
Kara Kum
MEDIA
PARTHIA
Nineveh Jonah
Ecbatana
Asshur
Zagros Mountains
River Tigris
ELAM (PERSIA)
BABYLONIA
Babylon Genesis 10
Susa Nehemiah 1
Ur Genesis 10
Lower Sea
GANDHARA
River Indus
INDIA
Erythraean Sea
JOKTAN
Arabian Sea
HAZARMAVETH
SHEBA

Genesis
GREAT BEGINNINGS

THE LAW

OVERVIEW
Genesis reveals how everything began, and what went wrong with it. The problems started when humanity made wrong choices, ruining a perfect world, but a loving God had a plan to bring people back to himself and restore his creation.

SUMMARY
Genesis ("origins" or "beginnings") is a story of beginnings. Most major Bible themes are first found here.

The beginnings of everything
Genesis begins with creation and early human history (1:1–11:32). It doesn't explain how things were made, simply who made them and why. Creation (1:1–2:3) climaxes with the first humans, Adam and Eve, created to know God (1:26-27) and rule everything (1:28-30). Their freedom was limited by just one command: not to eat from a particular tree (2:2-17). Yet this was the very thing they did, leading to expulsion from the Garden of Eden (3:1-24). Human society continued to develop but, without God's presence, deteriorated rapidly (4:1–11:32). Even God's judgement through a flood (6:1–9:29) didn't restrain human arrogance and sin (11:1-4). But God had a plan.

The beginnings of a family
Through Abram, God would build a new family who would love and obey him. Although Abram's wife was barren (11:30) and, being Chaldeans (11:31), they were moon-worshippers, God nevertheless revealed himself, promising to bless him and make him into a nation that would bless all nations (12:1-3). Abram responded in faith (15:1-6) and God made a covenant with him (15:7-20; 17:1-22). Abraham – see 17:5 for the change of his name from Abram – wasn't perfect (12:10-20; 20:1-18) and tried to help God's plan (16:1-16); but he finally learned that God does things in his own way and time. Only then was Isaac, the promised son, born (21:1-7).

Under Isaac and his son Jacob, God's people grew in numbers and prosperity, living as nomads in Canaan (chs. 24–36). Jacob's twelve sons became the twelve tribes of Israel, the name Jacob was given after wrestling with God (32:22-32). Through one of those sons, Joseph (37:1-36; 39:1–41:57), Israel went to Egypt to avoid a famine (42:1–50:26). The growing family was now safe, but in the wrong place! It would be centuries before they returned to the Promised Land, a key feature in Old Testament history.

Author
The traditional view is that Moses wrote the Bible's first five books ("the Pentateuch" or "five-volume book"), though some think his stories were only written down much later. But since Moses kept written records (Exodus 17:14; 24:4; 34:27), there seems no good reason for doubting his authorship, as Jesus himself confirmed (Mark 7:10; 12:26).

Date
Although recording events from much earlier in history, Genesis was probably written during the wilderness wanderings (c.1446–1406 BC), though some later editing may have taken place.

OUTLINE – GENESIS

The beginnings of everything

1:1–2:25 The beginning of the world in fellowship with God

3:1-24 The beginning of sin and its effects

4:1-26 The mixed beginnings of Adam's family

5:1-32 Adam's family tree

Beginning again with Noah

6:1–8:19 The destruction of the world by the flood and Noah's salvation

8:20–9:17 God's new covenant with Noah

9:18-27 Another mixed beginning

9:28–10:32 Noah's family tree

11:1-9 The world's sin at the tower of Babel

The beginnings of God's family

Abraham's story

11:10-32 Abraham's ancestors

12:1-9 God calls Abram

12:10-20 Abram's mixed beginning in Egypt

13:1–14:24 Abram and Lot

15:1-21 God's new covenant with Abram

16:1-16 Ishmael is born

17:1-27 God gives Abram a new name and the sign of circumcision

18:1-15 God reaffirms his promise to Abraham and Sarah

18:16–19:29 The destruction of Sodom and Gomorrah and Lot's salvation

19:30-38 Interlude: Lot and his family

20:1-18 Abraham deceives Abimelech

21:1–21:21 Isaac is born and Ishmael is sent away

21:22-34 Abraham's treaty with Abimelech

22:1-19 Abraham's obedience is tested

22:20–24:67 Abraham's wife dies and Isaac marries Rebekah

25:1-10 Abraham's death and burial

Isaac's story

25:11-26 The families of Abraham's sons, Ishmael and Isaac

25:27-34 Esau sells his birthright to Jacob

26:1-35 Isaac deceives Abimelech and makes a treaty

Jacob's story

27:1-40 Jacob deceives Isaac to gain Esau's blessing

27:41–28:9 Jacob flees home and Esau marries a Canaanite

28:10-22 Jacob meets God in a dream

29:1–30:24 Jacob's marriages and children

30:25–31:55 Jacob cheats Laban of his wealth and leaves

32:1–33:20 Jacob wrestles with God and is reunited with Esau

34:1-31 Interlude: Dinah and the Shechemites

35:1-15 God promises to bless Jacob and gives him a new name

35:16-29 Jacob's family

36:1-43 Esau's family tree

Joseph's story

37:1-11 Joseph dreams of greatness

37:12-36 Joseph's brothers sell him into slavery

38:1-30 Interlude: the story of Judah and Tamar

39:1-23 Joseph is wrongly accused and imprisoned

40:1-23 Joseph interprets dreams in prison

41:1-57 Joseph reveals the coming famine to Pharaoh and is made ruler of Egypt

42:1–44:34 Joseph's brothers travel to Egypt for food

45:1–47:12 Joseph is reunited with his brothers and father in Egypt

47:13-26 Joseph's greatness in Egypt

47:27–50:14 Jacob blesses his sons and dies

50:15-26 The last days and death of Joseph

God

The Bible's opening verse focuses us on God – *eternal* (21:33), *unique* (1 Timothy 1:17), *all-powerful*, creating everything from nothing (Hebrews 11:3). However, he is no mere force or power, but *personal*, making humans in his image (1:26-27) for relationship with him (2:7-24). As Genesis unfolds, we see that he is also gracious (12:1-3), caring (16:7-16), sovereign (50:20), and yet he judges sin (3:23; 6:7; 11:8; 19:23-29).

Humanity

Although made on the same day as animals, humans are distinct and superior, reflected in their separate creation (1:24-26), dominion over the animal world (1:28), and creation in God's image (1:26-27) – an image reflected fully and equally in both sexes.

Creation

Creation is "good" (1:4,10,12,18,21,25,31) and to be enjoyed, but not to the exclusion of its creator, nor by being made into god (Exodus 20:4-5). As God's stewards, humanity is to care for creation on his behalf (1:28; 2:15; 9:1-3; Psalm 8:3-8; 115:16).

Sin

Adam and Eve's disobedience had widespread consequences, affecting relationship with God (3:8-10), one another (3:7,12), and creation itself (3:17-19), yet excusing its guilt by hiding and explaining things away (3:7-13). Their sin spread deeply into their descendants (eg 4:1-8) and the rest of humanity (6:1-6) so that "every inclination of his heart is evil from childhood" (8:21). The Bible says that "all have sinned and fall short of the glory of God" (Romans 3:23).

Covenant

While covenants (solemn, unbreakable contracts between two parties) were common, biblical covenants were distinct by being entirely at God's initiative. So all Abraham could do when God made covenant with him was stand by and watch (15:1-21). Only after it was made could he respond. God made covenants with his people at key times (eg 9:8-17; 15:9-21; 17:1-27; 19:3-8), but the prophets looked forward to a new covenant, written in people's hearts (Jeremiah 31:31-34; Ezekiel 37:25-27), which the New Testament says happened through Jesus (Matthew 26:26-28; Hebrews 9:15-28).

ABRAHAM'S JOURNEYS

Abraham and his family group's journey from Ur in southern Mesopotamia took him through the fertile river plains where their flocks could find pasture. While most of the group settled in Paddan-Aram, Abraham obeyed God's call and travelled on with his own family to Canaan. A visit to Egypt provided respite during a time of famine.

Election

Election is God's gracious and sovereign calling of people for his greater purpose. In Genesis he chooses Israel through Abraham (12:1-3; 15:1-18; 17:1-16) rather than another nation, Isaac rather than Ishmael (17:19-21; Romans 9:6-9), Jacob rather than Esau (25:23; 27:1-40; Romans 9:10-16). This choice isn't out of favouritism, but love (Deuteronomy 7:7-8), in order to bring about his bigger salvation purposes. Those chosen can therefore never be proud (Romans chapters 9–11), and even those not chosen can still find blessing, as Ishmael (21:17-20) and Esau (36:6-8) discovered.

RELEVANCE FOR TODAY – GENESIS

Sin is always exposed

Sin's deceitfulness makes us think we can hide sin; but we can't. Adam and Eve tried to hide (3:8-10); Cain claimed to know nothing of what had happened to Abel (4:8-12); Abraham lied about Sarah (12:10-20; 20:1-18); but all were exposed. We don't find forgiveness for sin by hiding it, but by confessing it (eg 1 John 1:8-9).

Faith is always rewarded

Abraham wasn't perfect; what put him right with God was not behaviour, but faith (15:6). Despite setbacks and mistakes, he kept faith in God's promise and was therefore blessed (21:1-5; 22:1-18). The New Testament sees him as an example to follow (eg Romans 4:1-25; Galatians 3:1-18; Hebrews 11:8-19).

Promises are always fulfilled

God promised Abraham he would be "very fruitful" (17:6) and become a great nation. Genesis shows how this promise was kept, as Abraham's descendants grew in numbers and wealth, eventually becoming twelve tribes. When Canaan experienced a famine, God took them to safety in Egypt where they "were fruitful and increased greatly in number" (47:27). This continued until, by Exodus, Pharaoh was fearful of their size (Exodus 1:1-10).

Obedience is always blessed

Abraham responded to God's call to "Go to the land I will show you" (12:1) even though he didn't know where it was, trusting God's

> " *You intended to harm me, but God intended it for good to accomplish what is now being done, the saving of many lives."*
>
> GENESIS 50:20

promise that he would be blessed and be a blessing (12:2). This mission call to "go" is still relevant today for all God's people (Matthew 28:18-20). As Jesus' followers obeyed it, they too were blessed (eg Mark 16:20; Acts 2:38-41; 8:4-8), as we ourselves will be.

Purposes are always worked out

Right from the Garden of Eden, Satan has tried to oppose God's purposes, but Genesis shows how God's providence – his unceasing watch over his people and his shaping of all events and circumstances for his own purposes – ensures that things always come out right in the end. While we see this at several points in the lives of the patriarchs, nowhere is it clearer than in the story of Joseph. He trusted God was at work even when everything seemed to go wrong (37:36; 39:1–41:57), assuring his fearful brothers that God had been working through everything (50:20-21). Still today God is the one who "in all things works for the good of those who love him" (Romans 8:28).

Exodus
A PEOPLE FREED, A NATION FORMED

OVERVIEW
Oppressed by Egypt's Pharaoh and forced into slavery, God's people cried out for freedom. But God's plan was far bigger than theirs. They were simply hoping for freedom from a cruel nation, but God planned to transform them into a nation of his own.

SUMMARY
Exodus (meaning "exit" or "way out") opens with Abraham's descendants still in Egypt, where we left them in Genesis. 430 years have passed (12:40) and new rulers (1:8), who knew nothing about how Joseph had saved Egypt from famine, felt threatened by their growing numbers. So they made them slaves (1:9-14) and killed their firstborn sons (1:15-22).

Responding to their cries (2:23-25), God called Moses to free them. Moses felt inadequate (3:10–4:17), but was just the man God needed. Although born a Hebrew, he grew up in Pharaoh's palace (2:1-10) learning skills like leadership and writing. However he would also have worshipped Egypt's gods, so first needed to meet the living God. God revealed himself to Moses when he was 80 (7:7) in a burning bush, not just as his ancestors' God, but also as "I AM", and sent him back to Egypt (3:1–4:31).

Pharaoh refused to free his slaves (5:1-21); but through ten plagues (7:14–12:30), climaxing in the death of Egypt's firstborn sons, his hardened heart was broken. He freed the Israelites, then changed his mind and pursued them, trapping them by the Red Sea. However God miraculously parted the waters, letting them escape (14:1-31).

The joy of freedom quickly gave way to grumbling because of desert hardships, despite God's miraculous provision (15:22–17:7). Three months later, they arrived at Mount Sinai where they stayed for almost a year. Here God made a covenant with them (19:1-8; 24:1-18), giving them the Ten Commandments (20:1-17) and other laws (20:22–23:19). This Law was placed in the ark of the covenant and kept in a special tent (the tabernacle). In the courtyard surrounding it, priests could offer sacrifices (27:1–30:38) to re-establish the covenant when people broke it.

While Moses was still up Mount Sinai, Aaron made a golden calf (a pagan symbol) which the people worshipped in a wild party (32:1-8). It was only because of Moses' prayer that God didn't abandon them (32:9–33:22). God honoured Moses' faith by revealing what he is really like: a God who wants to forgive rather than judge (34:6-7). This revelation transformed Moses (34:29-35).

With the ark and tabernacle completed (35:4–40:33), God visited his people in a cloud of glory (40:34-38). Now the journey could continue.

Author
Traditionally seen by both Jews and Christians as Moses. There are suggestions within the text itself that this is the case (see 17:14; 24:4; 34:27). See Genesis, p.130.

Date
Written some time after the exodus, usually dated c.1446 BC, during the wilderness wanderings, though some later editing may have taken place.

OUTLINE – EXODUS

The Israelites in Egypt
1:1-14 The Egyptians enslave the Israelites
1:15-22 The cruelty of Pharaoh and the kindness of the Egyptian midwives

Moses' story
2:1-10 Moses is born and adopted by Pharaoh's daughter
2:11-25 Moses escapes to Midian
3:1–4:17 Moses receives God's call at the burning bush
4:18-31 Moses and Aaron bring God's message to the Israelites in Egypt
5:1-23 Pharaoh refuses to free the Israelites and forces them to work harder

God's deliverance of the Israelites from Egypt
6:1-8 God's promise to the Israelites
6:9–7:13 Moses and Aaron are ignored by the Israelites and by Pharaoh
7:14–10:29 Nine plagues on Egypt
11:1-10 Moses warns Pharaoh of the tenth plague
12:1-27 Instructions for the Passover
12:28-42 The Passover and escape from Egypt
12:43–13:16 Further instructions for celebrating the Passover
13:17–14:31 The Israelites cross the Red Sea and the Egyptian army is defeated
15:1-21 A song celebrating God's deliverance

God's new nation is formed
The Israelites in the wilderness
15:22–17:7 God provides water and food
17:8-16 Israel defeat the Amalekites with God's help
18:1-12 Jethro visits Moses with some advice
18:13-27 The beginnings of Israel's legal system
God's covenant with Israel
19:1-25 God comes to the Israelites at Mount Sinai
20:1-21 God gives the Ten Commandments
20:22–23:19 Instructions for Israel's way of life
23:20-33 God's promise to be with his people
24:1-18 The Israelites agree to the covenant
25:1–31:18 Instructions for Israel's worship and religious life
32:1-35 The Israelites sin by making a golden calf
33:1–34:35 God reestablishes the covenant with the Israelites
35:1–40:33 The Israelites obey God's instructions and build the tabernacle
40:34-38 God's glory comes and fills the tabernacle

MOSES AND THE EXODUS

Under Joseph's patronage Jacob and his family were welcomed into Egypt and settled there (Ge 39–50). A later pharaoh pressed his descendants into bondage and slavery. An order to dispose of all male Hebrew infants could not prevent the birth and survival of Moses, who was raised in the royal court as an Egyptian noble.

After killing an Egyptian who was beating a Hebrew, Moses fled for his life to Midian, where he lived and raised a family. God called him to return to Egypt to lead his people out of slavery (Ex 3:1–4:20). Eventually, after God's power had been evidenced through plagues (Ex 7–10), the Hebrews left, after 430 years in Egypt.

The route taken is open to debate and some place names are uncertain. Because the Hebrew people both questioned Moses' authority and continually disobeyed God, their journey from Egypt to their promised home took a further 40 years, allowing the generation who left Egypt to die and their children to inherit the Promised Land.

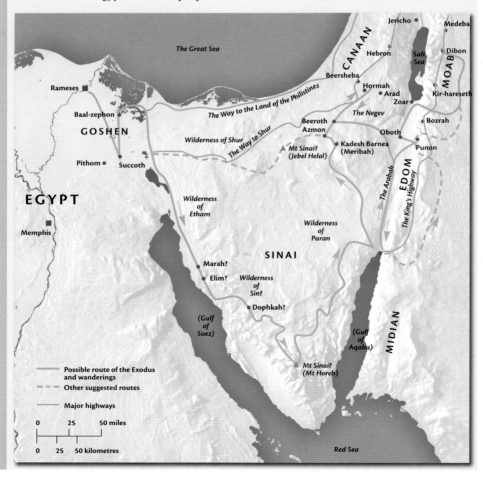

Revelation

God's appearing to Moses through the burning bush (3:1–4:17) is an expression of *revelation* – God revealing himself, entirely at his own initiative, to people not looking for him and without hope of finding him (eg Genesis 12:1-4; 35:6-7; Ezekiel 1:1–2:2; Acts 9:1-18; Hebrews 1:1-3). Revelation is essential because God is so transcendent and so holy that we ourselves could never find him or discover his character and purposes.

God revealed not only himself, but his name – the Lord, or Yahweh (3:15) – which is a play on words with the Hebrew "I am" (3:14) – showing he is both a personal God and one who is always "there".

Remembering

Knowing how easily people forget, God commanded Israel to remember the exodus through the annual festival of *Passover* (12:1-20), still celebrated by Jews today. In this key Old Testament festival, they remembered how God "passed over" their homes, spared their firstborn, and freed them (12:21-42).

Passover (or *Feast of Unleavened Bread*) was one of three annual festivals God established to help Israel remember him (23:14-17). The other two were *The Feast of Harvest* (or *Feast of Weeks* or *Pentecost*), celebrating God's provision through the grain harvest in May/June, and *The Feast of Ingathering* (or *Feast of Tabernacles*), celebrating the fruit harvest in September/October and recalling their life in "tabernacles" (tents) in the wilderness.

Redemption

God described his freeing Israel as a *redemption* (6:6-8), which becomes a model of salvation for God's people. The Bible often looks back to this event as the greatest redemption in Israel's history (eg Deuteronomy 7:7-8; 15:12-15; 2 Samuel 7:22-24; Isaiah 43:1-4).

In the New Testament Jesus' death is seen as the ultimate price to redeem humanity from their sin (eg Romans 3:23-24; Galatians 3:13-14; Ephesians 1:7).

Response

Having established his covenant with Israel and made them his people, a holy God expected them to now lead holy lives (19:3-8; 22:31). The Ten Commandments (20:1-17), the very heart of the covenant he made with them, sum up fundamental responses to God and one another, and are still a sound basis for any society. The laws that follow (20:22–23:19) unpack these basic commandments, governing Israel's life in the wilderness and the Promised Land, and establishing a pattern of worship for them (chapters 25–40). Trying to live by these laws would reveal the impossibility of living up to God's holy standards.

RELEVANCE FOR TODAY – EXODUS

The God of history

Exodus shows that God acts within history to save his people. No circumstance is outside his control.

· Israel's slavery was transformed by God who always remembers his people (2:23-25; 3:7-10) and works all things together for good (Romans 8:28).
· Jesus holds the scroll of history, not Satan (Revelation 5:1-10). When Satan tried to destroy the Jewish babies, God intervened and protected Moses right under Pharaoh's nose (2:1-10; Acts 7:20-22).

" I will free you ... I will redeem you ... I will take you as my own people, and I will be your God."

EXODUS 6:6-7

The God of promise

No matter how long we might wait, God always keeps his promises. He revealed himself as the God of Abraham, Isaac and Jacob (3:6) because the promises to them were about to be fulfilled (3:15-17). It was this promise that kept Moses going (eg 33:14; Numbers 10:29), together with God's constant promise that he was with him (eg 3:12; 4:15).

The God of power

More miracles happen in Exodus than probably any other Old Testament book, reminding us that God doesn't just speak, he

also acts. When Pharaoh didn't respond to his word (7:8-13), God demonstrated his power though ten plagues (7:14–12:30), each one challenging an Egyptian god (for everything struck either represented a god or was seen as a god). God's power always prevails.

The God of grace

Although containing God's laws, Exodus is also full of God's grace: his undeserved kindness. We see this in:

· God's revelation and call to Moses (3:1-10)
· God's provision of co-leaders through Jethro's wise counsel when Moses was weary with the responsibilities of leadership (18:13-27)
· God's forgiveness of Israel when Moses prayed (32:17–33:17)
· God's revelation of himself as, first and foremost, "compassionate and gracious" (34:6).

The God of guidance

God did not free Israel and then let them get on with life. He carefully guided them, both by his presence (the cloud and fiery pillar, 13:21-22) and his word (the Law). God never leaves us alone. All we have to do is follow, even when it looks like a wilderness ahead.

The God of hope

Exodus is full of hope in the midst of hopeless situations (eg 3:7-10; 14:15-18; 15:22-25; 33:12-23). The prophets often looked back to the exodus as a model of hope for God's people (eg Isaiah's seeing the return from exile as a new exodus, Isaiah chapters 40–55). The New Testament focuses our ultimate hope in the return of Jesus Christ.

Leviticus
HOLY GOD, HOLY PEOPLE

OVERVIEW

The nation that a holy God had redeemed from slavery in Egypt now needed
to learn what it meant to be holy (different) themselves, not just in their worship
and religion, but in the whole of life.

SUMMARY

Leviticus ("relating to the Levites") was given
this title because much of it concerns the
work of the Levites and the priests that
assisted in worship. In Exodus the holy God
had made Israel his "holy nation" (Exodus
19:6) and given them instructions for
building the tabernacle. Now in Leviticus he
gives them laws regulating worship in that
tabernacle and describing the holy lifestyle
that should follow. These instructions were
given during the year that Israel was camped
at Mount Sinai.

God describes to Moses the sacrificial
system (chapters 1–7) through which fellowship with him could be maintained or restored. Five key sacrifices are outlined: the
burnt offering (1:1-17; 6:8-13), expressing
devotion to God; *the grain offering* (2:1-16;
6:14-23), expressing gratitude for God's
provision; *the fellowship offering* (3:1-17;
7:11-21), re-establishing friendship between
the worshipper and God or others; *the sin
offering* (4:1-35; 6:24-30), covering unintentional sin against God; *the guilt offering*
(5:14–6:7; 7:1-6), covering unintentional sin
against others. Each sacrifice was carried out
in different and precise ways, underlining that
sinners couldn't rush into a holy God's
presence. Only *unintentional* sin was covered;
there was no provision for *deliberate* sin. The
annual sacrifice of the Day of Atonement
(16:1-34) reminded God's people that none of
these sacrifices were ever sufficient to really
deal with sin. The New Testament sees this as a
foreshadowing of Christ's sacrifice, which
alone can atone for sin (eg Hebrews 9:1–10:14).

Holy sacrifices to a holy God needed holy
priests to offer them, and so God outlined
the qualifications and characteristics of the
priesthood (8:1–9:24). Throughout Leviticus,
God's people are reminded that because God
is holy they too must be holy. One important
reminder of this comes in the deaths of
Aaron's sons Nadad and Abihu because of
their disobedience. In this instance God
speaks to affirm that he will be show his
holiness (10:1-3).

The need for holiness was further stressed
by excluding anything unclean or imperfect
from God's presence (11:1–15:33). Only when
ritually cleansed could the defiled person
return. The New Testament says that Jesus
has now done this cleansing for us (eg
Hebrews 9:11-14).

Chapters 17–27 describe how the national
life of Israel was to reflect their holiness. They
were to be seen as different from the people
around them. Practical issues are specified
including sexual relationships (18:1-30), the
poor (19:9-10), gossip (19:16), respect for the
elderly (19:32), honesty in business (19:35-36)
and care for the land (25:1-7).

Author

Traditionally seen by both Jews and Christians
as Moses. See Genesis, p.130.

Date

Written some time between 1446 and 1406 BC,
during the wilderness wanderings, though
some scholars think later editing may have
taken place. See Genesis, p.130.

OUTLINE – LEVITICUS

Instructions for holy sacrifices
1:1-17 Instructions for burnt offerings
2:1-16 Instructions for grain offerings
3:1-17 Instructions for fellowship offerings
4:1–5:13 Instructions for sin offerings
5:14–6:7 Instructions for guilt offerings
6:8–7:21 Further instructions to the priests about offerings
7:22-27 Prohibition against eating fat and blood
7:28-36 Instructions allowing priests to have part of the fellowship offering
7:37-38 A summary of the offerings

The institution of a holy priesthood
8:1-36 Aaron and his sons are ordained as priests
9:1-24 The priests begin their ministry
10:1-20 The importance of following God's instructions

Instructions for a holy life
11:1-23 Clean and unclean meat
11:24-47 Clean and unclean animals
12:1-8 Instructions for purification after childbirth
13:1–14:57 Instructions for the purification of diseased skin, clothes and houses
15:1-33 Instructions for purification after bodily discharges
16:1-34 The annual Day of Atonement
17:1-9 Israel's sacrifices must be made at the tabernacle
17:10-16 Prohibitions against consuming blood and the meat of animals that have died naturally
18:1-30 Instructions for sexual practices
19:1–20:27 Further instructions for holy living, and the results of disobedience
21:1–22:16 Further instructions about the priesthood
22:17-33 Further instructions about the purity of sacrificial animals
23:1-44 Instructions for annual festivals
24:1-9 The provision of oil and bread for the tabernacle
24:10-23 Instructions about just punishment
25:1-55 Special years of Sabbath and Jubilee
26:1-46 The consequences of obedience and disobedience
27:1-34 The valuation and redemption of gifts dedicated to God

Holy priests

God permitted only certain people to work in the tabernacle. These people were priests, Aaron's descendants (Numbers 3:10), to offer sacrifices and Levites, Levi's descendants, to assist them (Numbers 3:5-9). Priests, ordained for their work (8:1–9:24), stood between sinful people and holy God.

Christ alone is now our High Priest (Hebrews 2:17; 3:1; 4:14–5:10; 10:19-23) and so we need no other. *All* Christians are now priests (eg 1 Peter 2:4-10).

Holy sacrifices

What made these sacrifices different was that they were not *people's gifts* to the gods (like in other religions), but *God's gift* to them (17:11). This was *God's* way of dealing with sin. Adam and Eve had tried to hide sin (Genesis 3:7-11); sacrifice brought it into the open.

The sinner killed the sacrifice himself (eg 1:3-5; 3:1-2), underlining that "the wages of sin is death" (Romans 6:23). The priest then took its blood to the altar (eg 1:5; 3:2) to "make atonement" (eg 1:4; 4:20). The Hebrew word means "to cover". It is only as sins are covered or dealt with that sinners can approach a Holy God and become "at one" with him.

Sacrifices were always:

· *Animals* (eg 1:2; 4:3), substituting for humans through the laying-on of hands (eg 1:4)
· *Male* (eg 1:3; 4:3), underlining the cost because males, with their breeding potential, were more valuable
· *Perfect* (eg 1:3; 4:3), reflecting God's perfection and that only the best was good enough.

The inadequacy of these sacrifices, however, was shown by the Day of Atonement (16:1-34) when atonement was made for the nation's sins. The high priest killed one goat, sprinkling its blood on the ark in the Most Holy Place (which he could enter only once a year), and then laid hands on a second goat, confessing the people's sins and sending it into the desert. Through these two aspects – wiping away and sending away – the assurance of God's forgiveness was declared.

Holy living

Much of Leviticus concerns the way that God wanted his people to live – different (the meaning of "holy") from those around. No area of life was exempt – worship, health, work, sex, attitudes, justice, business – all expressions of the command to "love your neighbour as yourself" (19:18).

The way we live

A holy God wants holy people, and holiness must affect the *whole* of life, Leviticus shows; and the New Testament agrees (eg 1 Corinthians 6:9-20; Ephesians 4:17–5:20; 1 Peter 1:13–2:12). If people claim to be saved but are not changed, we may doubt whether they are truly saved.

Holiness is not a list of behaviours that must be followed or avoided, however. Jesus rejected this approach to holiness (adopted by the Pharisees), stressing that it was primarily a matter of the heart (Mark 7:1-23).

> " '*C*onsecrate yourselves and be holy, because I am the LORD your God. Keep my decrees and follow them. I am the LORD, who makes you holy.' "

LEVITICUS 20:7-8

The way we worship

Sacrifices were costly (animals were not cheap!), bringing home that sin cannot be dealt with cheaply and that true worship will always cost us. We no longer need to bring animal sacrifices, for Christ's sacrifice fulfilled them all. They were just shadows, while his was the real thing (Hebrews 10:1-14). We can now freely enter God's presence to worship at any time (Hebrews 4:14-16).

The way we care

Leviticus shows the need to demonstrate our love for God through practical expressions of love for others (19:18). This is reflected in laws about gleaning (19:9-10) and the Jubilee Year (25:8-55), when all land was to be returned to its original owner every fiftieth year to give everyone a fresh start in life.

Jesus commanded his followers to demonstrate their love for God in practical care for others (Luke 10:27) and James doubted the reality of anyone's faith who didn't (James 2:1-17).

The way we rest

The holy God gave his people a holy day, the Sabbath (23:3) which was to be different from other days. Everyone had to stop work so they could be refreshed and remember God.

By Jesus' day, the Pharisees had made the Sabbath a burden rather than a blessing by filling it with rules, something Jesus criticised (Mark 2:23-28; Luke 14:1-6; John 9:13-34). However, he never undermined the Sabbath itself, and its principle of rest and refreshment remain part of God's wise pattern for life, going back to creation itself (Genesis 2:2-3; Exodus 20:8-11).

The first Christians changed this day of rest and remembrance from Saturday to Sunday to celebrate the resurrection.

Numbers
FROM GRATITUDE TO GRUMBLING

OVERVIEW

Continuing the journey begun in Exodus and Leviticus, Numbers describes how the Israelites moved on from Mount Sinai towards the Promised Land. Sadly they didn't respond with gratitude, but with grumbling, and so forfeited the right to enter it. A two-week journey would now take 38 years, and only their children would ever reach it.

SUMMARY

After a census (1:1-54) the twelve tribes were assigned positions around the ark (2:1-34). God assigned responsibilities to the Levites (3:1–4:49; 8:5-26), gave instructions for keeping the camp pure (5:1-31), and established a trumpet-alert system (10:1-10). Now they could leave Sinai (10:11-36). But they quickly grumbled about their hardships, idealising life in Egypt and wishing they were back (11:1-6). God provided manna (11:7-9) and quail (11:31-34) and gave Moses 70 elders when he found the burden of leadership too great (11:10-35). Even Miriam and Aaron joined in the criticism (12:1-16). Clearly life in the desert was a strain.

Spies were sent into Canaan and returned with mixed reports (13:1-33). The land was fertile, they said, but its inhabitants were too strong to dislodge. Their report prompted a desire to return to Egypt (14:1-4), and only Joshua and Caleb stood firm (11:6-9). Moses and Aaron prayed (11:5), appealing to God's reputation (11:13-16) and character (11:17-19) as reasons for him not abandoning Israel.

God heard their prayer but said everyone over 20 years old, except Joshua and Caleb, would die in the desert and never enter Canaan (11:29-30; Hebrews 3:7-11).

The journey was a mixture of good and bad. On the bad side, a rebellion had to be crushed (16:1-50); Edom refused permission to cross their territory (20:14-21); Aaron died because of disobedience (20:22-29). On the good side, Aaron's rod blossomed as a sign (17:1-13); water miraculously gushed from a rock (20:1-13); God provided healing from snake bites (21:4-9; John 3:14-15). God might have been judging his people, but he had certainly not abandoned them.

The opposition of Moab, east of the Dead Sea, was overcome as the prophet Balaam, hired to curse them, found he could only bless (23:1–24:25). Temptations to sexual immorality were not as easily overcome however (25:1-17).

God appointed Joshua to succeed Moses, excluded from entering Canaan because of his own disobedience (27:12-23). Two tribes were allowed to settle east of the Jordan provided they helped the others take their land first (32:1-42). Moses made a record of their journey (33:1-55) and God defined the boundaries of the land (34:1–36:13). Now they were ready for the final stage of the journey.

Author

Traditionally seen by both Jews and Christians as Moses. See Genesis, p.130.

Date

Written some time between 1446 and 1406 BC, during the wilderness wanderings, though some scholars think later editing may have taken place. See Genesis, p.130.

OUTLINE – NUMBERS

Preparations for the journey to the Promised Land

1:1-49 The first census of Israel

1:50–2:34 The organisation of Israel's camp

3:1–4:49 The Levites and their duties

5:1-31 Instructions for the purification of Israel

6:1-21 Instructions for Nazirites

6:22-27 The priestly blessing

7:1–8:26 The consecration of the tabernacle and the Levites

9:1-14 The second Passover is celebrated

9:15–10:10 Information about moving the camp of Israel to follow the fiery cloud of God's presence

The journey through the wilderness

10:11-36 Israel begin their journey from Mount Sinai

11:1–12:16 The grumbling of Israel and the answer of God

13:1-24 Twelve spies explore Canaan

13:25–14:45 The Israelites disobey God and are forbidden from entering Canaan for 40 years

15:1-41 Instructions about offerings, sins and tassels on clothing

16:1-50 The rebellion of Korah, Dathan and Abiram

17:1-13 Confirmation of Aaron's priesthood

18:1–19:22 Further instructions about priests and purification

20:1-13 Moses and Aaron disobey God at Meribah

20:14-21 Israel cannot pass through the land of Edom

20:22-29 Aaron dies and Eleazar takes his place

21:1-35 Israelite victories and complaints, and the bronze snake

22:1–24:25 The prophecies of Balaam

25:1-18 The Israelites are seduced

Preparations for journeying to the Promised Land (again)

26:1-65 The second census of Israel

27:1-11 The petition of Zelophehad's daughters

27:12-23 God chooses Joshua to succeed Moses

28:1–30:16 More instructions about offerings and vows

31:1-54 The Israelites defeat the Midianites

32:1-42 Reuben, Gad and half the tribe of Manasseh given land on the east side of Jordan

33:1-49 A summary of Israel's journey

33:50–35:5 Plans for inheriting the land of Canaan

35:6-34 Instructions for cities of refuge

36:1-13 Instructions about the inheritance of daughters

The kingdom of God

Israel left Sinai not as a bunch of escaping slaves, but as an advancing army with God in their midst, symbolised by the ark of the covenant at the centre (2:1-31; 10:11-33). Here is a picture of God's kingdom advancing, about to invade part of fallen humanity and from which God would expand that kingdom into the whole world. The heart of Jesus' message was that God's kingdom is here, advancing, and cannot be stopped (Matthew 4:17,23; 9:35-38; 13:1-52; 16:18-19; 24:14).

The discipline of God

God had made a covenant with Israel at Sinai, but that didn't mean they could now do as they pleased simply because God was with them. Grumbling and rebellion was a breach of that covenant and a lack of trust; so God, like any good father (Hebrews 12:5-11), disciplined his children (11:1-10; 12:1-15; 14:35; 16:1-50).

The promises of God

Hundreds of years earlier God had promised Canaan to Abraham (Genesis 12:1; 15:12-20; 17:1-8). Now at last his descendants were on their way to possess that promise. Their constant disobedience and lack of faith in the desert could have led God to abandon his promise, however, for they had failed to keep their part of the covenant – to "obey me fully" (Exodus 19:5). But Numbers shows us how God stays faithful to his promises even when we aren't faithful. Those who had not trusted would be excluded from entering the Promised Land; but God would maintain his part of the promise and fulfil it through their children (14:29-35).

The miracles of God

Like in Exodus, there are many miracles in Numbers, for this was a crucial time when God's power needed to be experienced. There are significant miracles of provision – some of them supernatural, like the mysterious manna (11:4-9), some an overruling of natural forces, like the wind blowing quail towards them (11:31-32). God is the sovereign God of both.

One of the strangest miracles is Balaam's talking donkey (20:21-35). Whether this was (impossible as it may seem) a literal talking donkey (after all, there is a talking snake in the Garden of Eden, Genesis 3:1-4), or whether it was what Balaam thought was happening (for magicians from this part of the ancient world believed in animal divination), it brings home the fact that God is prepared to do anything to get his message across to people.

Beware of grumbling

Grumbling occurs often in Numbers (11:1-10; 12:1-15; 14:1-2,27-45; 16:1-50; 17:1-13) and each time God judges it. Paul told the Corinthians, "Do not grumble", referring back to these stories (1 Corinthians 10:1-11). See also Hebrews 3:17-19; James 5:9.

Beware of living in the past

Whenever life got hard, the Israelites wished they were back in Egypt, forgetting what life had been like there and idealising the past (11:4-6; 14:1-4). It is always easy to think the past was better, but it rarely was. And anyway, God does not want us living in the past but in the present.

Beware of thinking God's rules don't apply to you

No one is exempt from obeying God, not even (especially) leaders. Both Aaron (20:23-29) and Moses (Deuteronomy 34:1-12) learnt this the hard way. God wasn't prepared to let them require certain behaviour of others but then not live up to that themselves. The New Testament says leaders will be judged by higher standards (James 3:1).

Beware of jealousy in ministry

Miriam and Aaron became jealous of Moses, feeling they were as good as him (12:1-3). While their criticism had some basis (he had married a Cushite woman), it was really a cover for their jealousy of his prophetic ministry (12:2). But God saw through this and rebuked them (12:4-15). God wants leaders who aren't jealous of others but who see their need of one another and work together (1 Corinthians 3:3-7; 12:27-31; Ephesians 4:7-13).

Beware of getting in a rut

Once we have experienced God working in a particular way, it is easy to think this is how he will work next time. This is what Moses did. He had seen God provide water previously (Exodus 17:1-7). That time God had told him to *strike* the rock; surely that was how God would do it again. But in fact, this time God told him to *speak* to the rock, not strike it (20:8). In doing it like he had before, he disobeyed God, out of frustration with the people it seems (20:10-11). But God rebuked him and said he could not now enter the Promised Land.

" *We* should go up and take possession of the land, for we can certainly do it." But the men who had gone up with him said, "We can't ..."

NUMBERS 13:30-31

Deuteronomy
FINAL PREPARATIONS

OVERVIEW

With the journey from Egypt completed, Moses made his farewell speech.
Forbidden to enter Canaan himself, he encouraged the people to occupy the land
God had promised long before and prepared them for their new life by reminding
them of God's laws and renewing the covenant. His work done, Moses then died.

SUMMARY

Deuteronomy (meaning "second law")
follows the ancient pattern of a covenant
renewal document:

Recollection

Covenant renewal treaties began by
recounting the history of the parties involved,
just like here. Moses looked back over the 38
years since leaving Mount Sinai, recalling key
events, both good and bad (1:1-3:29), and
urging continued obedience to God (4:1-40).

Requirements

Moses then outlined the terms Israel must
follow as their part of the covenant. The Ten
Commandments were given central place
(5:1-33) and were then summed up in one
short commandment: "Hear, O Israel: The
LORD our God, the LORD is one. Love the LORD
your God with all your heart and with all your
soul and with all your strength" (6:4-5). Jesus
himself would say that this commandment
summed up all the others (Mark 12:28-31).

This absolute allegiance to God was then
underlined by instructions to destroy the
Canaanites who might otherwise turn their
hearts to their gods (7:1-26). (In fact, this was
exactly what would happen.) Warned not to
forget God and all he had done (8:1-20), they
were reminded that they would conquer
Canaan, not because of their own goodness or
abilities, but because God was with them. If
they feared God alone (10:12-22) and

remained obedient, they would indeed be
blessed (11:1-32).

Chapters 12–26 then give a wide range of
religious, social and legal laws governing life
in the Promised Land.

Ratification

Having outlined the terms of the covenant,
Moses listed curses that would follow if they
disobeyed (27:1-26; 28:15-68) and blessings if
they obeyed (28:1-14). The covenant was then
ratified (renewed) (29:1-30:20).

The covenant renewed, Moses' work was
complete and he handed over leadership to
Joshua, who had been alongside him since
leaving Egypt, encouraging him to be strong
and courageous for the task ahead (31:1-8).
He praised God for all he had done (32:1-43),
blessed the twelve tribes (33:1-29) and then
died, being buried on Mount Nebo on the
very edge of the Promised Land (34:1-12) – so
close, and yet so far.

Author

Traditionally seen by both Jews and
Christians as Moses, apart from the final
chapter which records his death. See Genesis,
p.130.

Date

Written some time between 1446 and 1406 BC,
during the wilderness wanderings, though
some scholars think later editing may have
taken place. See Genesis, p.130.

OUTLINE – DEUTERONOMY

The recollection of Israel's covenant with God

1:1-5 Introduction to Moses' speeches
1:6-8 Israel begin their journey
1:9-18 Tribal leaders are appointed
1:19-25 The twelve spies explore the land of Canaan
1:26-48 The Israelites rebel and cannot enter the land
2:1–3:11 The Israelites' wanderings in the wilderness
3:12-20 The land east of the Jordan is divided among Reuben, Gad and half the tribe of Manasseh
3:21-29 Moses is forbidden entry to the Promised Land because of his disobedience
4:1-14 Moses urges Israel to obey God's laws
4:15-31 Moses warns the Israelites not to turn to other gods
4:32-40 The greatness of God in heaven and earth
4:41-43 Moses establishes cities of refuge

The requirements of Israel's covenant with God

4:44-49 Introduction to the law
5:1-33 A repetition of the Ten Commandments
6:1–11:32 A call to obey God wholeheartedly and so experience his blessing in the land of Canaan
12:1-32 Instructions for worship in the land
13:1-18 Instructions about false prophets and idolaters
14:1-21 Instructions about clean and unclean animals
14:22–15:18 Tithes, debts and slaves
15:19–16:17 Instructions for sacrifices and festivals

16:18–17:20 Justice and kings
18:1-8 Gifts for the priests and Levites
18:9-14 Call to holy living in the new land
18:15-22 True and false prophets
19:1-13 Instructions about the cities of refuge
19:14–25:19 Various instructions about justice, war, family quarrels, sexual purity and general integrity
26:1-15 Offerings and tithes
26:16-19 The terms of the covenant between God and his people
27:1-8 Instructions about building an altar on Mount Ebal
27:9–28:68 The consequences of obedience and disobedience

The renewal of Israel's covenant with God

29:1-29 The covenant is for Israel and her descendants
30:1-10 God's commitment to his covenant people
30:11-20 Moses explains the choice between life and death

The end of Moses' life and ministry

31:1-29 Moses hands over leadership to Joshua and urges the Israelites to keep obeying God
31:30–32:47 Moses recites to Israel the song God had given him
32:48-52 God tells Moses of his approaching death
33:1-29 Moses blesses the tribes of Israel
34:1-12 Moses dies and is buried by God

Deuteronomy is one of the most quoted books in the New Testament, with almost 100 quotations and references to it. Jesus himself quoted it to resist the devil (Luke 4:4,8,12). Clearly Deuteronomy was much loved by Jesus and the first Christians.

A unique God

Yahweh, the living God, is the one and only God (eg 4:35-39; 6:4-5), something that needed emphasising before Israel entered Canaan with its many gods and idols. Israel was to have no other gods (5:6-7) nor make any idols (4:15-19; 5:8-10). Monotheism (belief in one God), not polytheism (belief in many gods), is upheld for God's people.

A loving God

Deuteronomy is about the people's relationship with God. God and his people are bound together not just by a treaty, but by love. Love led God to choose Israel, rescue them and bring them to the Promised Land (4:35-38; 7:7-9; 10:14-15; 23:5). Thirteen times Israel is called to love God in return, and to show their love for him through love for one another and through obedience to the detailed laws governing every aspect of life.

A blessing God

God wants to bless his people (eg 1:11; 7:13-15; 15:4-6,10,18; 28:1-14); but to experience this, they must live a life of total commitment to him. Only obedience will lead to blessing (28:1-14) while disobedience will lead to curse (27:1-26; 28:15-68).

A holy God

All this talk of God loving and blessing people could lead them think they could do as they like and God would turn a blind eye. But Deuteronomy shows this is not the case, as we see in the command to destroy the Canaanites (7:1-6; 9:1-6). To human thinking, this seems unjust. But it was to do with both God's holiness (7:6) and human wickedness (9:5). Canaanite religion, which was not only idolatrous but also included temple prostitution and child sacrifice at times, was an offence to the holy God. But God knew it was also attractive to sinful people and would be a snare to Israel (9:16). God wanted to stop the infection of Canaanite religion getting in to them, for through Israel salvation would come for all the nations.

The blessing of serving God

Once we realise there is only one true God, it is logical to love and serve him alone (6:4-5). No room is left for other gods or idols (4:15-19), whether literal or metaphorical; all are empty, false and should be destroyed (12:2-4).

The blessing of obedience

God blesses those who say, "We will listen and obey" (11:27). While his blessings are often material, we cannot assume they will always be so, or that they will come immediately. Even Jesus, who obeyed God like no other, experienced homelessness (Matthew 8:20). God's blessing may sometimes be spiritual rather than physical, and may even be delayed until heaven (eg Mark 10:21; Hebrews 11:24-26; Revelation 22:12).

> " *Hear, O Israel:*
> *The* LORD *our God,*
> *the* LORD *is one.*
> *Love the* LORD *your God*
> *with all your heart*
> *and with all your soul*
> *and with all your strength.*"
>
> *DEUTERONOMY 6:4-5*

The blessing of having a successor

Moses' faithful service for 80 years would have been of little value if he had no successor. Joshua had been alongside Moses all that time and had witnessed first hand how he had prayed, trusted God, performed miracles, and led God's people. Now it was his turn (31:1-8).

Real success is not simply doing things yourself, but producing others who can continue after you, taking God's work to its next stage, just like Joshua. Success is producing successors.

The blessing of purity

God's purity should be reflected in the purity of our own lives. The world says we are missing out if we stay pure, especially in the area of sexual relationships, but God says that sex is special, solely for one man and one woman within marriage. Every sexual relationship outside of this – sex before marriage, outside of marriage, instead of marriage – is impure in God's eyes (22:13-30) and cannot bring his blessing. Thinking we can live in sexual impurity and still be blessed is to deceive ourselves (eg 1 Corinthians 6:9-10).

The blessing of compassion

While underlining God's compassion to us, Deuteronomy shows that if we want to experience that compassion we ourselves must demonstrate it. Chapters 17–25 therefore contain laws calling for compassion in matters as varied as law (16:18-20; 17:8-11; 21:1-9), provision for God's servants (18:1-8), warfare (20:1-20) and even nature itself (22:6-8).

PALESTINE IN THE EARLY OLD TESTAMENT

0   10   20 miles

0   10   20 kilometres

Sidon

Zarephath

Mt Lebanon

Damascus

ARAM (SYRIA)

Mt Hermon

Tyre

Laish (Dan)

Kedesh

Hazor

Merom

Acco

Chinnereth

Sea of Chinnereth

Ashtaroth

The Great Sea

Aphek

BASHAN

Mt Carmel

R Kishon

Jokneam

Dor

Megiddo

Shunem

Edrei

Ramoth Gilead

CANAAN

Beth-shean

Migdal

Dothan

River Jordan

Socoh

HILL COUNTRY OF ISRAEL

Tirzah

Mt Ebal

Shechem

Mt Gerizim

Succoth

R Jabbok

Penuel

Mahanaim

THE ARABAH

PLAIN OF SHARON

Joppa

Aphek

Lod

Bethel

Ai

Jericho

Gilgal

Shittim

Rabbah

AMMON

Beth-horon

Gezer

Ekron

Aijalon

Gibeon

Jerusalem

AMORITES

Mt Pisgah

Heshbon

Ashdod

Beth-shemesh

Timnah

Bethlehem

Beth-jeshimoth

Medeba

Ashkelon

Socoh

Lachish

Adullam

Mamre

Ataroth

Kiriathaim

THE SHEPHELAH

Eglon

Debir

CANAAN

Hebron

HILL COUNTRY OF JUDAH

Salt Sea (Sea of the Arabah)

R Arnon

City of Moab

Gaza

Rapha

Beersheba

Ar

MOAB

Hormah

The Valley of Siddim

Kir-hareseth

THE NEGEV

Rehoboth

Zoar?

Possible region of cities of Sodom, Gomorrah, Admah, Zeboiim, Zoar.

Ziph

Brook Zered

EDOM

Beeroth

Hazazon-tamar

WILDERNESS OF ZIN

Joshua
TAKING THE LAND

OVERVIEW

After Moses' death, Joshua ("the Lord saves") succeeds Moses as leader of
the Israelites. His task to lead them into the Promised Land was not easy.
Canaan was occupied by many independent states and fortified cities. It was
therefore only through dependence on God that he could lead God's people to
claim their inheritance.

SUMMARY

Call

With Moses dead, God called Joshua to his
new task (1:1-2), promising him success
(1:3-5) and challenging him to be courageous
and obedient (1:6-9). Joshua then prepared
the Israelites (1:10-18) and sent spies to
reconnoitre Jericho (2:1-24).

Crossing

The spies had forded the river the previous
day (2:23), but it was now in flood (3:15),
which the Canaanites probably interpreted as
Baal (their weather god) protecting them.
God told the priests to carry the ark into the
river, and as they did, the water stopped so
people could cross (3:14-17). Stones were
erected to remember what God had done
(4:1-24).

Circumcision

Before fighting, the men needed circumcising
(something neglected in the wilderness) to
remind them they were God's people (5:2-9).
Once the Passover was celebrated (5:10-12)
they were ready for battle. Joshua was
reminded that this was God's battle (5:13-15).

Conquest

Joshua began by capturing cities along the
road that cut Canaan into two. Jericho was
taken, not by fighting but through a noisy
religious procession (6:1-27). Moving west,
they found themselves unexpectedly defeated

at Ai (7:1-9). The reason was sin: Achan had
taken plunder from Jericho designated for
God alone. With his sin exposed (7:10-26), Ai
was taken (8:1-35).

In phase two, Joshua turned south. The
Gibeonites tricked Israel into becoming allies
(9:1-27) and five Amorite kings marched
against them (10:1-6). God miraculously
defeated them (10:7-15), allowing Joshua to
conquer the rest of the south (10:16-43).

In phase three, Joshua turned north,
defeating the King of Hazor and his allies
(11:1-23). The conquest was now over, some
30 years after it began, and God allocated
land to each tribe (13:8–21:45), but pockets of
resistance remained for many years (13:1-7).

For map of the division of the land into
tribal territories, see p.168.

Covenant

The conquest over, Joshua made his farewell
speech (23:1-16) and led the people in an act
of covenant renewal (24:1-27), reminding
Israel of all God had done and urging
wholehearted obedience. His work complete,
he died, aged 110 (24:28-33).

Author

The book does not give the author, but the
word "we" (eg 5:1) indicates an eye-witness.
While Joshua kept records (eg 18:8; 24:25), the
frequent use of "to this day" (eg 7:26) suggests
the final version was written later, perhaps
during the monarchy, by an unknown author.

Date

Traditionally, the invasion of Canaan is dated as beginning in 1406 BC and lasting some 30 years. Some archaeological evidence has been interpreted as making a date as late as 1250 BC possible for Joshua's invasion. The surrounding nations – Hittites, Egyptians and Babylonians – were weak by this time, leaving Canaan (situated between them) vulnerable to Joshua's army.

THE CONQUEST OF CANAAN

1 Moses dies in sight of the Promised Land (Dt 34)

2 God commissions Joshua (Jos 1)

3 Spies are sent from Shittim to Jericho (2)

4 The nation cross the Jordan on dry ground (3–4)

5 Jericho falls (6)

6 Ai attacked – Israelites routed (7)

7 Ai attacked again and destroyed (8)

8 Words of the law read at Mt Ebal and the covenant restored (8)

9 Gibeonites deceive Joshua (9)

10 The sun stands still at Gibeon to prolong the light for battle (10)

11 Five Amorite kings routed and put to death at Makkedah (10)

12 The southern cities overcome (10)

13 Coalition of northern kings defeated at the Waters of Merom (11)

14 The land is divided between the tribes of the nation (13–19)

15 The covenant renewed yet again at Shechem (24)

16 Joshua dies and is buried at Timnath Serah (16)

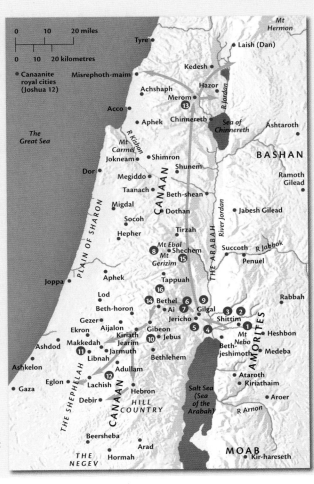

OUTLINE – JOSHUA

Entering the Promised Land
1:1-18 Joshua takes charge of the Israelites
2:1-24 Joshua sends two spies into Canaan to report on the land
3:1–5:1 The Israelites cross the river Jordan on dry land
5:2-12 The circumcision of male Israelites and the celebration of the Passover

The conquest of the Promised Land
5:13–6:27 The destruction of Jericho
7:1–8:29 Achan's sin and the battle for Ai
8:30-35 The covenant with God is declared at Mount Ebal
9:1-27 The Israelites are deceived by the Gibeonites
10:1-43 The conquests of southern Canaan
11:1-15 The conquest of northern Canaan
11:16-23 A summary of Joshua's conquests
12:1-24 A list of the kings defeated by the Israelites

The allocation of the Promised Land
13:1-7 Land still to be conquered
13:8–19:51 The division of the land among the tribes of Israel
20:1-9 Instructions for establishing cities of refuge
21:1-45 Towns and land given to the Levites

Life after the conquest
22:1-34 Reuben, Gad and half the tribe of Manasseh return home
23:1-16 Joshua urges the Israelites to obey God who has kept his promises
24:1-27 Joshua leads the Israelites in renewing their covenant with God
24:28-33 Joshua and Eleazar die and are buried in the land

KEY THEMES – JOSHUA

The God of faithfulness
It was almost 600 years earlier that God had promised to make Abraham into a great nation and to give him Canaan (Genesis 12:1-2; 15:7-21; 17:3-8). God hadn't rushed to fulfil that promise, but it had now surely happened, as Joshua reminded the people (24:2-15). God always keeps his promises.

The God of battle
Joshua contains some hard stories, with commands to wipe out whole peoples – genocide. Why was this?

First, God had given the Canaanites a long time to repent, just as he promised (Genesis 15:16); but they had continued with their corrupt religion and morality. God is patient; but his patience doesn't last for ever and judgement eventually comes.

Second, these were commands for specific times and purposes, limited in *extent* to Canaan (they weren't allowed to attack neighbours or build an empire) and in *execution* (they weren't allowed to use captured chariots to fight more aggressively, 11:6). God wanted Canaan, and only Canaan, as a base for his people from whom Messiah would come to save *all* the nations.

Third, in those days, victory in battle reflected the greatness of your God. A God who wasn't victorious was considered weak; so God was demonstrating who he was in the language of that time.

Fourth, the taking of the Promised Land is a picture of God's advancing kingdom that cannot be stopped and that one day will overcome all the peoples of this world (eg Daniel 2:44; 7:13-14). God is a God of battle; but that battle is now spiritual (John 18:36).

These stories cannot be taken as justification today for every fight we think is right. When Joshua asked the angel if he was on their side or their enemies, he replied "Neither!" God is on his own side, not ours (5:13-14).

The God of detail

Joshua contains much material that we might (if we are honest) consider boring: lists of defeated kings (12:1-24), descriptions of how the land was to be divided (13:1–19:51), cities of refuge (20:1-9), towns for the Levites who had no land of their own (21:1-45). While we might not see this as the most inspiring part of Scripture, they bring home God's infinite care for the details of life, no matter how trivial they might seem. God wanted to ensure that no one was left out in experiencing his promise.

RELEVANCE FOR TODAY – JOSHUA

Be obedient

The key to success, Joshua was told, was absolute obedience to God and his word, something God underlined to him at the beginning (1:7-8). The fact that the people were quick to obey Joshua (1:17-18) probably reflects the fact that they saw obedience in his own life first. Leaders cannot ask of others what they will not do themselves.

Be strong

Three times God tells Joshua to "be strong and courageous" (1:6-7,9), just as Moses had told him (Deuteronomy 31:6-7), and even the people say this to him too (1:18). This appeal is based on God's presence "for I will be with you" (see also 8:1; 10:8; 11:6). Presumably this was because Joshua didn't feel very strong and courageous at that moment. His life-long mentor, Moses, was dead, and only Caleb and himself remained of those who had left Egypt 40 years earlier and had seen God's power in overcoming an enemy. Would people believe God could do it again – and through him? Little wonder he felt anxious. But leadership means taking hold of God yourself in order to inspire confidence in others.

Be radical

Israel failed to completely drive out the Canaanites, as God had commanded. Pockets of resistance were left in the shape of towns they felt unable to conquer (13:1-7), and these would prove to be a source of trouble and temptation to Israel for many years to come. When we are not radical in removing potential problems from our lives, we can guarantee things will go wrong at some point in the future. Jesus urged his followers to be radical in dealing with things that might lead them astray (Mark 9:43-48).

> "... *Choose for yourselves this day whom you will serve.*"
> JOSHUA 24:15

Be fair

Joshua cast lots to divide the land between the tribes (18:1-10) so no one could accuse him of unfairness or favouritism. While every family was given their own plot of land, the Levites were excluded to remind them that their inheritance was their service to God (18:7). So Joshua provided towns where they could live and pasture lands for their flocks (21:1-45). He also provided cities of refuge, spread across the country, where anyone guilty of manslaughter could flee to ensure a fair trial before the elders (20:1-9). Although he was responsible for the whole nation, Joshua was thoughtful in recognising particular needs. We too should always be fair concerning the needs of others, especially if we are a leader.

Judges
THE SAD DECLINE

OVERVIEW

By the end of Joshua's life, Canaanite power had been broken, but the Canaanite presence still remained. The people of Israel needed to complete their work, cleansing Canaan of its godless people and religion. But with no clear leader to unite them, Israel's life fragmented and spiralled downhill for the next 300 years. They forgot their God, but God had not forgotten them.

SUMMARY

Setting the scene

Judges begins by showing that the conquest was incomplete (1:1–2:5) and the Israelites were beginning to accept Canaanite life, rather than destroy it (2:6-13). God didn't abandon them, however, first disciplining them through attacks from enemies (2:14-15), then delivering them as they called to him (2:16). He did this through "judges" (2:16), Spirit-anointed leaders whose task was to judge God's enemies by overcoming them. However, the people always reverted to wicked ways (2:6-23), and this cycle of disobedience, distress and deliverance continued for over 300 years.

Stories of twelve judges

The author tells of twelve judges, from Othniel (1367–1327 BC) to Samson (1075–1055 BC). He constructed his story very carefully, selecting the judges he wrote about. Right in the centre are two contrasting stories: Gideon, who didn't want to be king (6:1–8:35), and Abimelech his son, who did (9:1-57). On either side come Deborah (4:1–5:31), from the west, and Jephthah (10:6–12:7), from the east, both of whom were not highly regarded in their culture, the first because she was a woman and the second because he was a prostitute's son. And then on either side of these stories come two loners: Ehud from the south (Benjamin) and

Samson from the north (Dan). The point the author is making is that right across Israel, the nation had gone astray, going round in ever-descending circles. But although Israel had abandoned God, God had not abandoned Israel.

Spiritual and social decline

Chapters 17–21 show how bad life had become. Micah established an idolatrous shrine and unofficial priest (17:1-12), and the Danites stole both (18:1-31). A homosexual gang demanded sex with a visiting Levite (19:16-22) and raped and murdered the woman with him (19:23-29), leading to civil war among God's people (20:1–21:24). The concluding verse sums up the darkness: "In those days Israel had no king; everyone did as he saw fit" (21:25).

Author

While the author is unknown, the expression "in those days Israel had no king" (17:6; 18:1; 19:1; 21:25) indicates it was written during the monarchy and looking back to life before it. Samuel may have gathered some of the original material.

Date

Judges covers the period between the Joshua's death (around 1375 BC) and Saul's rise as king (around 1050 BC). This fits in with Jephthah, a later judge, saying that Israel had been in Canaan for 300 years (11:26).

OUTLINE – JUDGES

Life in the Promised Land after Joshua
1:1-36 Military successes and failures
2:1-5 Israel have disobeyed God by failing to complete the conquest of the land
2:6-10 The death of Joshua and the forgetfulness of Israel
2:11-23 The recurring cycle of disobedience and deliverance in the period of the judges
3:1-6 A list of the other nations who remained in the land

The stories of twelve judges
3:7-11 Othniel and the king of Aram
3:12-30 Ehud and the king of Moab
3:31 Shamgar and the Philistines
4:1–5:31 Deborah and Jabin, the Canaanite king
6:1–8:32 Gideon and the Midianites
8:33–9:57 Apostasy and Abimelech's evil
10:1-2 Tola the judge of Israel
10:3-5 Jair the judge of Israel
10:6–12:7 Jephthah and the Ammonites
12:8-10 Ibzan the judge of Israel
12:11-12 Elon the judge of Israel
12:13-15 Abdon the judge of Israel
13:1–16:31 Samson and the Philistines

The religious and moral decline of Israel
17:1-13 The idolatry of Micah
18:1-31 The tribe of Dan worship Micah's idol
19:1-30 The rape and death of a Levite's concubine
20:1-11 Israel gather an army to avenge the concubine's death
20:12-25 The Israelite army is defeated twice by the tribe of Benjamin
20:26-48 Benjamin is defeated by the Israelites
21:1-25 The defeated Benjamites take wives for themselves

THE JUDGES OF ISRAEL

Once the nation of Israel was settled in the land of Canaan, they soon forgot that God had brought them there and established them. They started to become like the nations about them, so God allowed neighbouring nations to discipline them. Each time the nation recognised their wrongdoing and cried to God for help, he raised up individuals to protect and guide his people in the power of his Spirit.

1. Othniel (of Judah) drove out invading nomads from the east led by Cushan-Rishathaim (Judges 3:7-11).

2. Ehud (of Benjamin) defeated the Moabite king Eglon (3:12-30).

3. Shamgar was victorious over the Philistines (3:31).

4. Deborah the prophetess (of Ephraim) and Barak (of Naphthali) led the northern tribes to defeat the Canaanites led by Jabin and Sisera (4–5).

5. Gideon (of Manasseh) drove out Midianite and Amalekite invaders (6–8).

6. Tola (of Issachar) led the nation (10:1-2).

7. Jair (of Gilead) led Israel (10:3-5).

8. Jephthah (of Gilead) led the people to drive out the Ammonites (11:1–12:7).

9. Ibzan (of Zebulun) led the nation (12:8-10).

10. Elon (of Zebulun) led the nation (12:11-12).

11. Abdon (of Ephraim) led Israel (12:1-15).

12. Samson (of Dan) warred against the Philistines (13–16).

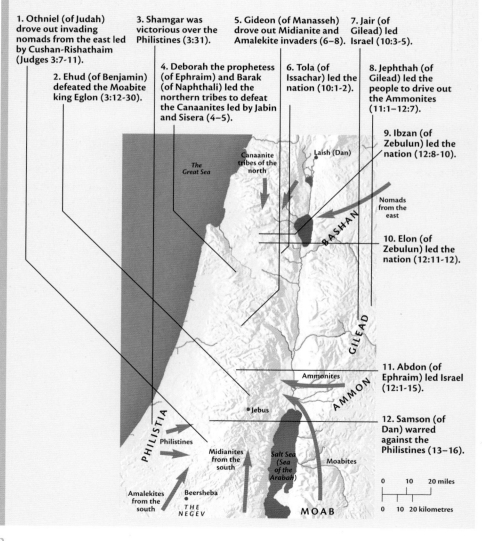

KEY THEMES – JUDGES

The king they forgot

A central theme is that Israel had forgotten that God was their king and they were bound to him by covenant. When they wanted to make Gideon king (thinking this would solve their problems), he had to remind them of this (8:23); but they constantly forgot and "everyone did as he saw fit" (17:6), a clear breaking of the covenant (Deuteronomy 12:8). They therefore forfeited the covenant's blessings (Deuteronomy 28:1-14) and experienced its curses instead (Deuteronomy 28:15-68). It was only God's mercy and patience that kept them from being completely destroyed.

The leaders they followed

Although sometimes fulfilling legal functions (eg 4:4-5), the judges were primarily leaders God raised up and empowered by his Spirit to rescue Israel from its current enemy. Even the best had weaknesses, however: Gideon was fearful (6:11) and unbelieving (6:13); Ehud was deceptive 3:15-27); Samson was ruled by sexual passions (14:1-7; 16:1,4) and was angry (14:19) and vindictive (15:1-5). The fact that God used such people was not a sign of his approval, simply a reflection of how bad things had got. These were the best God could find!

The gods they embraced

While the Canaanites were a very cultured civilisation (contrary to common belief), they practised fertility religion in which nature's powers were worshipped. Baal, the son of El (the chief god) was a god of fertility and weather. He was often portrayed on a bull's back with a lightning spear. Together with Asherah (El's wife) and Ashtoreth (Baal's wife) they were worshipped through ritual prostitution, which was thought to bring fertility to the land. It is therefore easy to see why Canaanite religion was so attractive and why God commanded its removal. It was Israel's failure to do so that led to problems for over 300 years.

The discipline they experienced

Israel's apostasy (turning from God) broke the covenant and was grounds for God abandoning them, but he didn't. Rather, he used loving discipline through permitting surrounding peoples to attack Israel, trying to bring them to their senses and bring them back to him. While they did return, it was always short-lived, and as soon as the latest crisis was over, they went back to their old ways. But God never gave up; he kept disciplining them for their good (eg Hebrews 12:5-11).

Called to live differently

God called Israel to be "a holy nation" (Exodus 19:6), living differently from those around. But rather than change the world, they were distracted from their allegiance to Yahweh. They began to worship other gods and as a consequence, the downward spiral of religious, moral and social decline gained momentum.

Christians too are told not to love the world or anything in it (1 John 2:15), but to live a holy life, different from the culture around (eg Ephesians 5:3-16; Colossians 3:1-17; 1 Thessalonians 4:3-8). We are here to influence the world, not the other way around.

> " *In* those days
> Israel had no king;
> everyone did as
> he saw fit."
>
> JUDGES 21:25

Called to live by the Spirit

The judges were empowered for God's work by God's Spirit (eg 3:10; 6:34; 11:29; 13:25; 14:6,19; 15:14). When his Spirit was working, they were not dependent on human resources, as Gideon discovered when God reduced his army from 32,000 to just 300 (7:1-7), nor limited by human abilities (14:5-6; 15:11-17). Their anointing was only temporary, however, the Spirit coming on them for the occasion and then leaving again. By contrast, since Pentecost, Christians can experience a permanent anointing of God's Spirit (1 John 2:27), empowering them for Christ's work (Acts 1:8).

Called to trust God

Gideon didn't feel up to the task, making excuses and full of doubt, despite God's reassurances (6:11-16). Yet God called him to trust, and patiently bore with his requests for signs (6:17-18,36-40). God didn't see his doubt as sin, however; he patiently dealt with it, just as he did with Moses (Exodus 3:10-17).

We too are called to trust God (Proverbs 3:5-6; Isaiah 26:3-4; John 14:1) and he may even graciously give us signs to encourage and guide us along the way (Isaiah 30:21). Note however that Gideon's fleece was a lack of trust, rather than a measure of faith!

Called to keep going

Judges brings home the importance of keeping going, especially when the work is not yet completed, something the Israelites failed to do. When the Promised Land wasn't taken as quickly as they thought it might be, many got discouraged and never possessed their possessions, settling for less than God's best. By contrast, Caleb was a man who wouldn't give up and so got what he was promised (1:20; Joshua 14:6-15).

God calls his people to keep going (Hebrews 10:35-39; 12:1-2; James 1:2-12), especially when things don't happen overnight.

Ruth

FAITHFULNESS REWARDED

OVERVIEW

Named after one of its main characters, Ruth shows how things never get too bad for God to come and change them. In the dark days of the judges (1:1), a ray of sunshine breaks out through this story of love, faithfulness and redemption.

SUMMARY

Ruth begins with a prologue of 71 words in Hebrew (1:1-5) and ends with an epilogue of 71 words. In between there are four scenes, with a turning point right in the middle: "That man is our close relative; he is one of our kinsman-redeemers" (2:20). This is the key to the story: it is a story of redemption.

Scene 1: The return (1:1-22)

A famine led Elimelech, Naomi and their two sons to leave Bethlehem, seeking refuge in Moab (1:1-2). Elimelech died there, so Naomi married her sons to Moabites, Orpah and Ruth; but the sons also died and the three women were left abandoned (1:3-5). Naomi decided to return to Bethlehem, urging her daughters-in-law to stay in Moab (1:6-9). Orpah stayed, but Ruth insisted on accompanying Naomi home (1:10-18), with a wonderful expression of commitment (1:16). Naomi arrived home bitter from her experiences (1:19-22).

Scene 2: The reunion (2:1-23)

Quite accidentally (humanly speaking), Ruth went gleaning (picking up harvest leftovers) in the field of a kind landowner who was Naomi's relative (2:1-18) and therefore able to be a kinsman-redeemer (2:19-23).

Scene 3: The request (3:1-18)

Naomi told Ruth to visit Boaz (3:1-6). That night, Ruth lay at his feet and, when he awakened suddenly, requested his protection (3:9) – an invitation to marriage. Boaz saw

this as kindness, for although younger than him (3:10), Ruth had put Naomi's needs first. But there was a problem: a closer relative had rights before Boaz (3:11-18).

Scene 4: The redemption (4:1-12)

Before the elders, Boaz explained Naomi's situation to this relative (4:1-3). At first he was eager for marriage since he would get Elimelech's land; on discovering it carried responsibilities for Ruth too, and any future children, he quickly declined (4:5-6). This released a delighted Boaz to marry Ruth (4:7-12).

The epilogue (4:13-17) tells how their marriage was blessed with a son (4:13-17). Not only had Ruth been redeemed, along with Naomi, but also she had become the ancestor of Kind David, from whom Jesus, the great Redeemer, would come – an amazing story of redemption, underlined in a final genealogy (4:18-22).

Author

While Jewish tradition points to Samuel, this is unlikely since the story mentions King David. We simply do not know the author.

Date

The mention of David (4:17,22) and the style of writing suggests that Ruth was written during the period of the monarchy.

OUTLINE – RUTH

Scene 1: The return to Bethlehem after disaster

1:1-5 Naomi's husband and sons die

1:6-18 Naomi's daughter-in-law Ruth decides to return to Judah with Naomi

1:19-22 Naomi and Ruth arrive in Bethlehem

Scene 2: The reunion with Naomi's relative

2:1-7 Ruth goes to work in Boaz's fields

2:8-16 Ruth is shown unexpected kindness by Boaz

2:17-23 Ruth and Naomi rejoice at Boaz's kindness

Scene 3: The request of Naomi and Ruth

3:1-8 Naomi plans for Ruth to ask Boaz to fulfil his responsibilities as kinsman-redeemer

3:9-15 Boaz agrees to do so if a closer relative will not

3:16-18 Naomi and Ruth wait for news

Scene 4: The redemption is complete

4:1-8 The closer relative refuses to redeem Ruth as well as the land

4:9-12 Boaz declares he will redeem Naomi's land and marry Ruth

4:13-17 Ruth and Boaz have a son called Obed

4:18-22 The family line of David, the grandson of Ruth and Boaz

KEY THEMES – RUTH

God's remnant

No matter how bad things get, God always keeps some who stay faithful to him. This "remnant" is represented by Boaz who was faithful and did things God's way, even in these dark days. Not only was he personally rewarded for his faithfulness, but through him came Jesus, the Saviour of the world.

God always has a faithful remnant through whom he works his purpose (Genesis

45:7; 2 Kings 19:1-4; Ezra 9:5-15; Isaiah 10:20-22; Jeremiah 23:1-4; Romans 11:1-5).

God's grace

God's grace is shown not just to Naomi, a daughter of Israel, but also to Ruth, a Moabite. The Moabites had been enemies ever since forbidding Israel to pass through their territory on the way to the Promised Land (Judges 11:14-18), and the Law excluded them from God's presence (Deuteronomy 23:3-6; Nehemiah 13:1-3). But Ruth shows that Gentiles too can experience God's grace, as Jesus' ministry would show (Matthew 28:19; Mark 7:24-30). Becoming part of God's people has nothing to do with our race, circumstances or efforts, but everything to do with God's grace received by faith (Romans 1:5; Ephesians 2:8-18).

God's covenant love

God's covenant love (NIV, *kindness*) is a recurring theme (1:8; 2:20; 3:10). It is reflected in the commitment Ruth makes to Naomi: "Where you go I will go, and where you stay I will stay. Your people will be my people and your God my God" (1:16) – a commitment to stand by another come what may. Boaz shows the same kindness to his distant relatives when he acts as their kinsman-redeemer, reflecting God's covenant love to his people when they didn't deserve it.

God's redemption

In ancient literature, the key to understanding a book was often right at the centre. The centre of the Hebrew text in Ruth is 2:20, "That man is our close relative, he is one of our kinsman-redeemers", showing that redemption is the key theme. The word occurs (in various forms) 23 times in this short story. It is significant in various ways: Naomi is redeemed from bitterness to joy; Ruth is redeemed from being an outsider to being part of God's people; Boaz is redeemed from being alone to having his own family; Bethlehem is redeemed from famine to plenty. Everything in the story shouts out the message that God is a redeemer God (Exodus 6:6-8; 2 Samuel 7:22-24; Job 19:25; Isaiah 43:1-13; Galatians 3:13-14; 1 Peter 1:18-19).

Looking across the Judean hills to Bethlehem, home to Naomi and Ruth and birthplace of Jesus

Be patient

Naomi and Ruth had to patiently wait and trust Boaz to act (3:18); Boaz too had to wait and see whether the nearer kinsman-redeemer would act instead of him. They may well have felt anxious, wondering whether things would turn out right; but none of them tried to make things happen by manipulating the circumstances. If God is going to act, we can wait patiently for him; he does not need our help. The Bible commends patient waiting for God to act (Proverbs 8:34; Isaiah 64:4; Hebrews 6:15; James 5:11).

Be redemptive

Nothing and no one is ever beyond God's ability to redeem them, as the story of the desolate Naomi and Ruth show us. In hundreds of stories in the Bible we see God redeeming or rescuing people from their situations (Exodus 3:7-10; Deuteronomy 4:32-40; Psalm 34:22; Isaiah 41:10-14; Jeremiah 50:34; Luke 1:67-75; 1 Peter 1:18-19). As his people, therefore, we too should never write off anyone or anything, but rather always look to bring the best out of every situation.

Be committed

Naomi's situation was transformed through Ruth's commitment to her. Her expression of commitment – "Where you go I will go, and where you stay I will stay. Your people will be my people and your God my God" (1:16) – is one of the most beautiful expressions of commitment in the Bible and is still a powerful example for Christians to follow in their commitment to one another. If we are members of Christ's body, how can we not be committed to one another (Romans 12:4-5; 1 Corinthians 12:12-27; Ephesians 4:3-16)?

Be trusting

No matter how bad things look, this story shows us that we can trust in God who is always at work behind the scenes and who "in all things works for the good of those who love him, who have been called according to his purpose" (Romans 8:28). Nothing can separate us from the love of God in Christ (Romans 8:32-39). Trusting him in the hard times isn't always easy, but it is always blessed (Psalm 40:1-5; 84:5-12; Jeremiah 17:5-8).

Be considerate

Putting others first is more important than our own personal comfort, as Ruth demonstrated. Jesus did not consider himself when he went to the cross, but rather us (Philippians 2:3-11). We are therefore called to always be considerate towards others (Titus 3:1-2; James 3:13-18; 1 Peter 3:7).

> " *That man is our close relative; he is one of our kinsman-redeemers.*"
>
> RUTH 2:20

1 Samuel
THE SEARCH FOR A KING

OVERVIEW

Named after the man God used to establish kingship in Israel, Samuel describes Israel's transition from theocracy (ruled directly by God) to monarchy (ruled by a king). But Israel's king also had a king – the Lord God. Saul, their first king, forgot that fact and was destroyed; David, the second, remembered it and was blessed.

SUMMARY

Samuel's story

Miraculously born to godly parents (1:1-20) at the end of the period of the judges, Samuel was handed over to God's service (1:21–2:11). It was while serving Eli the priest that he was called to be a prophet (3:1-21). Around this time the Philistines, coastal dwellers who were pressing inland for more territory, fought Israel and captured the ark (4:1-22), though quickly returning it (5:6–7:1). This increased Philistine threat, the failure of Eli's sons and Samuel's increasing age, led Israel to ask for a king (8:1-5).

Saul's story

Although Samuel was angry with the people's request, God told him to proceed (8:6-21). God chose Saul, an ideal man, at least according to their standards (9:2), and Samuel anointed him king (9:3–10:7), but tested his obedience (10:8). While making a good start (11:1-15), Saul became independent, and Samuel rebuked him when he disobeyed God's command. Saul claimed it was because his soldiers were afraid and Samuel had not come to offer the sacrifice on time (13:5-12), but Samuel said this disobedient action meant God had taken the kingdom from him (13:13-14). Even when given a second chance, Saul failed the test, once again protesting his innocence (15:1-21). So Samuel abandoned him to his fate (15:22-35).

David's story

In looking for Saul's replacement, Samuel looked for the wrong qualities initially (16:1-7). God led him to David, probably just 15 years old, and anointed him as Israel's new king (16:13). David quickly proved himself, as a musician (16:14-23), fighter (17:1-58) and friend (18:1-4). This made Saul jealous and he tried to kill David (18:5–19:24). For the next ten years, David was on the run from Saul, hiding in the hills and even among the Philistines (27:1-12; 29:11). Amazingly he spared Saul's life twice (24:1-22; 26:1-25). Abandoned by God, Saul resorted to a witch (28:1-25). Defeated in battle, he killed himself, (31:1-13) ending a life once so full of potential.

Author

The author of 1 and 2 Samuel, originally one book but separated when translated from Hebrew into Greek, is unknown. It was not Samuel since he dies in 1 Samuel 25; the books are simply named in honour of him.

Date

Written after Solomon's death (930 BC) as the author refers to "Israel and Judah", names used only after the nation divided (1 Kings 12:1-20).

OUTLINE – 1 SAMUEL

Samuel's story
1:1-8 Hannah's misery at having no children
1:9-18 Hannah prays for a son and promises to give him to God
1:19-28 Samuel is born and dedicated to God at the tabernacle
2:1-11 Hannah's prayer of thanksgiving
2:12-36 The wickedness of Eli's sons
3:1-21 God gives Samuel a message of judgement for Eli's family
4:1-11 The Philistines capture the ark of the covenant and kill Eli's sons
4:12-22 Eli hears the news and dies
5:1–7:1 The ark of the covenant is returned to Israel
7:2-17 Samuel leads Israel to victory over the Philistines

Saul's story
8:1-22 Israel asks Samuel to give them a king
9:1–10:8 Saul is chosen and anointed as king
10:9–11:15 Saul's kingship is confirmed by victory over the Ammonites
12:1-25 Samuel's warning to Israel
13:1-14 Saul disobeys God and Samuel prophesies his doom
13:15-23 Israel's military situation
14:1-52 Saul's victories over the Philistines
15:1-9 Saul's victories over the Amalekites
15:10-35 God rejects Saul as king of Israel

David's story
16:1-23 Samuel secretly anoints David as king
17:1-58 David kills Goliath the Philistine
18:1–19:24 David's time in Saul's court
20:1-42 Jonathan discovers Saul's plot against David
21:1–23:29 David runs from Saul
24:1-22 David spares Saul's life
25:1 Samuel dies
25:2–27:12 David's life as a fugitive
28:1-25 Saul consults a medium and is told of his own death
29:1–30:31 David's victory over the Amalekites
31:1-13 The Philistines defeat the Israelites and kill Saul and Jonathan

KEY THEMES – 1 SAMUEL

The king

Until now, Israel had been ruled directly by God, through his appointed spokesmen (like Moses), but now, kings would govern Israel on his behalf. Unlike the nations around, however, their king was not free to do as he pleased; he too was subject to God's Law and God's prophetic word. It was when Saul showed he would not do this that God replaced him with "a man after his own heart" (13:14) – David.

Samuel felt that God didn't want Israel to have a king (8:8), though this may simply have been self-pity, for God assured him it is not him they have rejected (8:7). However, God had already made provision for kingship in the Law given to Moses 400 years earlier (Deuteronomy 17:14-20); so it may have been, not that Israel asked for the wrong thing, but they asked it for the wrong reason – to bring them security.

The prophet

Miraculously born to a barren woman (1:1-20), Samuel quickly grew in faith (2:26) and prophetic gifting (3:19-21). His first prophetic word was really hard to deliver: he had to tell Eli, his friend and mentor, that his godless family would be judged (3:11-14). But Samuel was not only a prophet but also the last of the judges (7:15-17) and he led Israel in a significant battle against the Philistines (7:2-14). He was not afraid of challenging disobedience to God's word, even disobedience by the king (13:13; 15:22-26). Throughout the Bible the prophet is given the task of boldly proclaiming what he believes God is saying, and God's people, having tested it, are then to obey (Deuteronomy 18:14-21; 1 Corinthians 14:29-33).

The covenant

The appointment of a king was not the end of the covenant God made with Israel at Sinai, but rather a new *expression* of it. That was why Samuel called Israel to renew their allegiance to God when Saul was appointed king (11:14–12:25). Israel's first obedience was still to God, but through the king; but the king himself also had to obey God and was not above the covenant. This is why Samuel wrote down rules for kingship, explaining them to both king and people and placing them before the LORD in the sanctuary as a covenant act (10:25). When Saul failed to obey that covenant, he was removed from office, for no one is higher than God's word.

God's servant

True servants don't simply start the race well, they also finish it well. Saul began well, with every advantage: physically strong, popular, Spirit-anointed; under pressure, however, he yielded to others' fears (13:7-9) and ideas (15:13-15) and so was disqualified.

Meanwhile, despite many obstacles during his

TRIBAL TERRITORIES

Under Joshua, the land of Canaan was divided into regions and allotted to each of the tribes. The main bulk of the land was taken including the Negev, the Shephelah, the Arabah, from Kadesh Barnea in the very south to beyond Laish in the north, but much remained unconquered, including the land of the Philistines.

In the allotment of land, the region east of the River Jordan was given to Reuben, Gad and half the tribe of Manasseh. To the west of the Jordan the regions given to Judah, Ephraim and Manasseh were decided by casting of lots at Gilgal. The remaining regions were decided at Shiloh. As the priestly tribe, Levi was allotted 48 cities across the land, of which six were appointed as cities of refuge.

Because Joshua had not been able to drive out all other nations from the land, they became an ongoing problem for the new nation of Israel, continually at war and attempting to reclaim territory. Further, inter-marriage with the surrounding nations led to religious compromise and led the people away from observing the law given to Moses. As a result, the nation suffered God's judgement at the hand of invaders throughout its history.

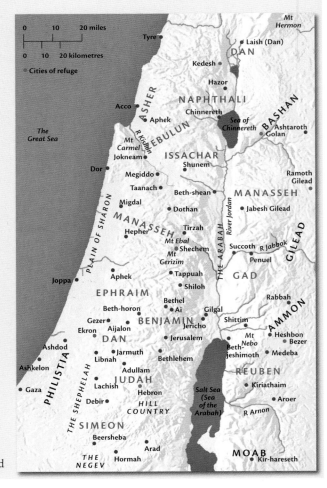

ten years on the run, David kept going, which is what all God's servants are encouraged to do (Hebrews 12:1-3).

God's voice

The living God speaks (15:10; Job 33:13-14), in contrast to dumb idols (12:21; Isaiah 44:12-20). However, God does not waste his words, and God stops speaking when we stop listening. He gave Saul repeated opportunities to hear and obey his voice, but when he would not listen, Samuel abandoned him to his fate (15:34-35). At the end, Saul was desperate to hear God, but God wouldn't answer (28:5-6). "Today if you hear his voice, do not harden your hearts" (Hebrews 3:7,15; 4:7).

God's timing

God's timing is generally much slower than ours. Hannah had to wait for many years, living under provocation (1:6-7), before

> " *The* LORD *has sought out a man after his own heart.*"
>
> *1 SAMUEL 13:14*

God heard her prayer and gave her Samuel (1:17-20). David, although anointed king (16:12-13), had to wait for ten years before seeing that become reality. But their waiting was not wasted. Hannah learned how to pray; David learned how to endure, fight and lead. With God, waiting time is never wasted time.

God's boundary

It is understandable when people want to know their deceased loved-ones are at peace or want to contact them, but this is a boundary God says we must not cross. The Bible forbids all spiritism, divination, mediumship and sorcery (Leviticus 19:31; 20:6; Deuteronomy 18:9-13; Isaiah 8:19-22; Acts 13:6-12; Galatians 5:19-20), for they open us up to demonic powers.

Saul knew this, and had previously outlawed mediums and spiritists (28:3). However, in his hour of desperation, he ignored God's command and consulted a medium, with terrifying results (28:4-25). Was it Samuel he saw, permitted by God, as an exception, to return from the dead? Or a deceiving spirit (1 Kings 22:21-23; 1 Timothy 4:1) impersonating him? Whatever it was, the medium was terrified (28:12) and Samuel went home even more afraid and depressed (28:20-23).

We engage with evil spiritual powers to our peril, as Saul was about to discover. In crossing this final boundary, the ultimate one of many he had crossed, he stepped towards a shameful death (31:1-4), his life ruined by fear, greed and jealousy – so much potential, wasted.

2 Samuel
THE MAN AFTER GOD'S HEART

OVERVIEW

Continuing where 1 Samuel finished, this book shows how Saul's death opened the way for David to become king, at first of Judah, then later of all Israel. Unlike Saul, here was a man after God's heart who wanted to rule God's way. But that didn't mean he was perfect, as we often discover.

SUMMARY

New king

David was heartbroken to hear of Saul and Jonathan's death (1:17-27), killing the Amalekite who claimed (falsely) to have killed Saul (1:1-16). This reverent attitude towards kingship made David seek God (2:1) rather than hastily claiming what God had promised. Although welcomed as king by Judah at this point (2:2-4), it was seven antagonistic years before Israel accepted David (5:1-5) – after Saul's son, Ishbosheth, was murdered (4:1-12).

New capital

David captured Jerusalem, strategically situated on the border between north and south, making it his new capital (5:6-12). He strengthened its importance by bringing the ark there (6:1-5). However, disobedience in transporting it (Exodus 25:12-14) led to disaster and David became angry with God (6:6-11). It was months before David brought it back to Jerusalem, with great rejoicing (6:12-23).

New victories

God's favour was seen in David's military victories (5:17-25; 8:1-14; 10:1-19). He established the kingdom in a way Saul never done and honoured God for it (22:1-51).

New covenant

David felt it strange that, while he lived in a palace, God had only a tent (7:1-2). So he decided to build a temple. But God said that he didn't want David to build a house for him; rather he would build a house for David (7:4-11), promising him an eternal kingdom (7:12-16). These words of promise are known as the Davidic covenant. David responded to God's words with a prayer of humble gratitude and praise (7:18-29).

New problems

Even the greatest leader is only human, and the second half of 2 Samuel is all about David's failures.

- **Failure in his personal life**, through adultery and conspiracy to murder (11:1-27). Through confessing quickly, however (in contrast to Saul who excused sin or blamed others), David was forgiven (12:1-25).
- **Failure in his family life**, through weak fathering. David failed to discipline Amnon when he raped Tamar (13:1-21), and Absalom when he avenged her (13:23-39). When David eventually allowed Absalom to return from self-imposed exile (14:1-33), Absalom interpreted this as weakness and gathered people (15:1-6), finally leading a coup (15:7-12). David fled, leaving his country in civil war (15:13–17:29). It fell to Joab to deal with Absalom (18:1-18) and persuade David to return (18:19–20:26).

- **Failure in leadership**, through counting his soldiers. Whether an act of pride, or lack of trust in God, he was judged for it (24:1-25). Not even the king was exempt from God's discipline (7:14).

Author
See 1 Samuel, p.165.

Date
See 1 Samuel, p.165.

OUTLINE – 2 SAMUEL

The beginning of David's rule
1:1-16 David is told of the death of Saul and Jonathan
1:17-27 David mourns for Saul and Jonathan
2:1-7 David crowned king over Judah
2:8–3:39 War between David and Ish-Bosheth king of Israel
4:1-12 Ish-Bosheth is murdered
5:1-5 David becomes king over all Israel
5:6-15 David captures the city of Jerusalem
5:16-25 David's victory over the Philistines
6:1-23 David brings the ark of the covenant to Jerusalem

Successes and failures
7:1-29 God's new covenant with David
8:1-18 David's military victories
9:1-13 David's kindness to Mephibosheth
10:1-19 David's victory over the Ammonites and their allies
11:1-5 David's affair with Bathsheba
11:6-25 David arranges Uriah's death
11:26-27 David marries Bathsheba and a son is born
12:1-14 Nathan the prophet rebukes David for his sin
12:15-25 The child dies, but Solomon is born
12:26-31 The end of the conflict with the Ammonites

Absalom's rebellion
13:1-22 Amnon rapes his half-sister Tamar
13:23-29 Absalom murders Amnon in revenge
13:30-39 David mourns for Amnon and Absalom flees
14:1-33 David and Absalom are reunited
15:1-12 Absalom organises a rebellion
15:13–16:14 David and his supporters flee from Jerusalem
16:15–17:14 Absalom plans to kill David and his army
17:15-29 David is warned of Absalom's plans
18:1–19:8 Absalom is killed and David mourns

The final years of David's rule
19:9-43 David's return as king to Jerusalem
20:1-26 The rebellion and death of Sheba
21:1-14 The Gibeonites are avenged by killing seven sons and grandsons of Saul
21:15-22 Battles against the Philistine warriors
22:1-51 David's song of praise to God
23:1-7 David's last words
23:8-39 David's mighty men
24:1-17 David disobeys God by taking a census of Israel and a plague is sent on Israel
24:18-25 David builds a new altar and the plague is stopped

The Davidic king

David is the focal point in 2 Samuel, presented as the ideal king who took his responsibilities before God seriously, unlike Saul who so often put his own interests first. Under his godly leadership, Israel reached the boundaries that God had promised his ancestors long before and experienced security and blessing. The Bible presents him as a "type" or model of the coming Messiah (eg Jeremiah 23:5-6; Ezekiel 34:23-24). Jesus' kingship is often linked with David's (eg Matthew 22:41-46; Luke 1:31-33) and Jesus is even called the Son of David (eg Matthew 12:22-23; 21:9).

The Davidic covenant

God would not allow David to build a house for him because of the blood on his hands from battle (1 Chronicles 28:2-3). Nevertheless, God recognised the integrity of David's devotion to him and promised to build a house for David instead – a house not of stones but of descendants. God covenanted with David that, in contrast to Saul, he would always have a descendant on the throne (7:11-16).

At a purely human level, this promise seems to have failed, for there has not been a descendant of David on Israel's throne for well over 2000 years. However, the New Testament says this descendant is Jesus, the Son of David, who reigns on an eternal throne in heaven (eg Luke 1:32-33; Revelation 22:16).

The Davidic city

Knowing the jealousies that could have arisen if he had chosen a capital in either the northern or southern territories, David wisely chose a city on the boundary between the two, a city that had not been taken when Joshua entered the Promised Land or since. Entering Jerusalem by its water shaft, David overcame its inhabitants, the Jebusites, and made it his capital and personal property, calling it the City of David (5:6-9). It was also known as Zion (5:7), after the hill on which it was built.

Because the temple would be built here, Zion became known as "the city of God" (eg Psalm 46:4-5; 87:1-7) and also as a symbol for the people of God (eg Hebrews 12:22-23; 1 Peter 2:4-6; Revelation 14:1).

DAVID'S CONQUESTS

Under David's kingship, the kingdom of Israel was extended from the Gulf of Aqaba in the south to the upper Euphrates River in the north.

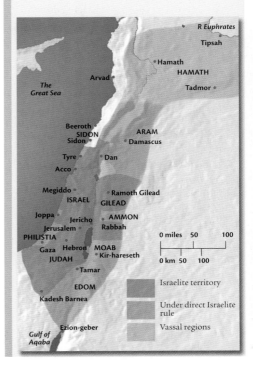

Don't be presumptuous

God had promised David the throne (1 Samuel 16:1-13), but David didn't assume Saul's death meant this was his moment. Rather he prayed, asking if this was God's time and only proceeding when God spoke (2:1-4). He then waited seven years before Israel asked him to be their king too (5:1-3). If God is at work, we don't need to make things happen, as David discovered.

Don't be judgemental

David expressed his delight at the ark's return to Jerusalem (6:9-19) through extravagant worship. However, his wife Michal despised what she felt was his undignified behaviour (6:20). But David said he would "become even more undignified than this" (6:22), such was his love for God. Michal's judgemental attitude was itself judged: she remained childless (6:23) and David was vindicated. The Bible often warns us against judging others (Matthew 7:1-5; Romans 2:1-4; 14:1-23; James 2:1-4, 4:11-12).

Don't be casual about temptation

None of us can ever afford to be casual about temptation, like David was (11:1-5). When he should have been fighting, he took it easy and stayed home (11:1). From his roof he caught sight of Bathsheba bathing and, rather than turning away quickly, he slid down the spiral of temptation into sin ("saw ... sent ... get ... slept with her"). At any point he could have turned away, but didn't; and so Bathsheba became pregnant and her husband ended up dead (11:6-27).

Temptation is common to everyone (Luke 17:1; Romans 7:15-25; 1 Corinthians 10:12-13), so we should always be alert and flee temptation quickly when it comes (1 Corinthians 6:18-20; 1 Timothy 6:9-12; 2 Timothy 2:22; James 4:4-10).

Don't be slow to confess

While David's sin (11:1-27) seems worse than anything Saul did, David was forgiven while Saul wasn't. Why? Because Saul never took responsibility for his sin, always blaming others (1 Samuel 13:11-12; 15:15-21), while David confessed quickly (12:13). Hidden sin cannot be forgiven; but if brought into the light, God will forgive it, as David experienced (Psalm 32:1-5; 51). Hiding sin harms me; confessing sin frees me (Proverbs 28:13; 1 John 1:6-9).

> " *The LORD himself will establish a house for you.*"
>
> 2 SAMUEL 7:11

Don't be disloyal

Despite experiencing David's forgiveness and being allowed to return to Jerusalem, Absalom started to secretly gather supporters around himself with the specific aim of stealing their hearts from David and taking over the kingdom (15:1-6). Such deceptive and ungodly behaviour should never be part of how we live, especially if we are a leader. God hates disloyalty (Numbers 12:1-15; Psalm 78:56-59).

1 Kings
FROM BLESSING TO DIVISION

OVERVIEW

Looking back over history, 1 Kings surveys the events that led Israel from Solomon's glorious reign (970–930 BC) to division, decline, and (in 2 Kings) disaster, asking: "How did we end up here in exile?" The author's answer is simple: because we were disobedient.

SUMMARY

Years of blessing

The transition of kingship from David to Solomon, just as promised (1 Chronicles 22:6-10), was somewhat unsteady (1:1–2:46). Solomon's reign was characterised by:

- **Wisdom.** When invited to choose his blessing, Solomon chose wisdom (3:5-15). His wisdom was both down-to-earth (3:16-28) and far-reaching (4:29-34). Proverbs records many of his sayings.
- **Worship.** Solomon built the temple David had planned (5:1–7:51). God's presence filled it as Solomon dedicated it to God (8:1-66). God reaffirmed his covenant, but reminded Solomon to obey him (9:1-9). The temple remained the focus of worship until destroyed by Babylon in 586 BC.
- **Wealth.** Solomon became extremely wealthy (10:14-29), as the Queen of Sheba witnessed (10:1-13). Some wealth came from trade, but some from taxes.
- **Wives.** Solomon showed his wealth by having 700 wives and 300 concubines. This inability to rule his sexual appetite would be his downfall, for his foreign wives brought their foreign gods which stole Solomon's heart (11:1-13).

Years of division

Sadly, Solomon sowed the seeds of Israel's destruction, through crippling taxes and compulsory labour, which bore fruit in the reign of his son, Rehoboam. Rejecting the elders' wisdom, he threatened to make things even harder for the northern tribes, on whom the greatest burden had fallen (12:1-15). They therefore rejected him, crowning instead Jeroboam, one of Solomon's officials, and established a separate kingdom (12:16-24). God's people split into two – Judah in the south and Israel in the north – never to come together again. To prevent people going to Jerusalem to worship, Jeroboam established shrines (12:25-33), a sin rebuked by prophets (13:1–14:20) and known thereafter as "the sin of Jeroboam".

The author then deals with these two kingdoms in parallel – Judah first and then Israel. Israel's kings were wicked; most of Judah's were good.

Years of challenge

A major focus is Elijah (17:1–21:29; 2 Kings 2), who challenged Israel for adopting Baal worship, or at least trying to blend worshipping Baal with worshipping the living God. Miracles are associated with Elijah's ministry, showing God's provision (17:1-6), compassion (17:7-24; 21:1-29) and supremacy (18:16-46).

Author

Originally one book, 1 and 2 Kings were written by an unknown author who based his accounts on court sources (11:41; 14:19; 14:29) and probably prophetic records (referred to in Chronicles).

Date

Written some time after the fall of Jerusalem (586 BC), during Israel's exile.

OUTLINE – 1 KINGS

Years of blessing and the rule of Solomon

1:1-53 Solomon becomes king

2:1-12 David's final advice to Solomon before his death

2:13-46 Solomon rule is established

3:1-28 God gives Solomon wisdom and greatness

4:1-34 Summary of Solomon's administration, prosperity and wisdom

5:1–6:38 Solomon builds a temple for God in Jerusalem

7:1-12 Solomon builds a palace for himself

7:13-51 The furnishings for the temple

8:1-21 The ark of the covenant is brought to the temple

8:22-66 Solomon dedicates the temple

9:1-28 God's promise to Solomon and Solomon's achievements

10:1-13 The Queen of Sheba visits Solomon

10:14-29 Summary of Solomon's possessions

11:1-13 Solomon's many wives lead him to sin against God

11:14-25 Solomon's enemies Hadad and Rezon

11:26-40 Jeroboam rebels against Solomon and receives a promise from God

11:41-43 Solomon's death

Years of division and decline

12:1-24 The northern tribes of Israel rebel against Rehoboam and crown Jeroboam as king

12:25-33 Jeroboam's idolatry

13:1–14:18 Prophecies against Jeroboam

14:19-20 The death of Jeroboam king of Israel

14:21-31 Rehoboam rules in Judah

15:1-8 Abijah rules in Judah

15:9-24 Asa rules in Judah

15:25-31 Nadab rules in Israel

15:32–16:7 Baasha rules in Israel

16:8-14 Elah rules in Israel

16:15-20 Zimri rules in Israel

16:21-22 Tibni rules in Israel

16:23-28 Omri rules in Israel

16:29-34 Ahab becomes king of Israel

Years of challenge and the ministry of Elijah

17:1-24 Elijah and God's provision

18:1-40 The contest with Ahab and the prophets of Baal

18:41-46 God answers Elijah's prayer for rain

19:1-8 Elijah flees from Queen Jezebel

19:9-18 God encourages Elijah and gives him a new commission

19:19-21 Elisha follows Elijah

20:1-34 King Ahab's victory over the king of Aram

20:35-43 Ahab is condemned for his disobedience

21:1-29 Naboth is murdered so that Ahab can have his vineyard

22:1-28 Ahab's downfall is prophesied

22:29-40 Ahab is killed in battle

22:41-50 Jehoshaphat rules in Judah

22:51-53 Ahaziah becomes king of Israel

The message

The underlying message of Kings is that *obedience leads to blessing*. Not a social or political history, but rather a spiritual one, Kings focuses on one key truth: that whenever a king obeyed the covenant, Israel was blessed; whenever he didn't, or simply observed it in theory, it was cursed. The dividing line is always between kings who were faithful to God and the covenant and those who were not. Most attention is focused on kings that demonstrate this "Deuteronomic principle", so called because it is the principle God gave to Moses in Deuteronomy 28. It is the guiding light of our author's analysis of Israel's history.

The messengers

This message is reinforced by the prophets who challenged the kings when they disobeyed the covenant and encouraged them when they obeyed. Most important is Elijah, with his challenge to obey God alone; but other prophets are also mentioned, including Ahijah (11:29-39; 14:1-18), Shemaiah (12:22-24), Micaiah (22:1-28), and in 2 Kings Jonah (14:25), Isaiah (19:1–20:19), and Huldah (22:14-20), and Elisha (2:1–9:1; 13:14-21). As God's messengers, the prophets were to be listened to and obeyed.

Elijah and Elisha's authority was underlined by the miracles they performed, the most significant outbreak of the miraculous since the exodus. These were needed because these were very dark days, and true worship was in danger of disappearing, especially in the north.

The mess

Solomon's sowing of the seeds of the nation's destruction (both through his importing of foreign gods and his unreasonable demands for the building of his palace and temple), together with his son Rehoboam's lack of wisdom, led the country into a complete mess from which it never recovered. God's one people divided into two nations, Judah and Israel, never to come back together again, and often to be at odds with one another.

The books of Kings show us how Israel was unstable, with 20 different rulers from nine different dynasties over 210 years, before being finally destroyed by Assyria. Meanwhile Judah had 20 rulers from just one dynasty (David's) over 345 years, making it much more stable. Judah, with its temple to help focus on the living God, stayed for the most part true to Yahweh, but Israel was constantly seduced to the worship of Baal with its sensuous fertility rituals.

The need for obedience

The constant message is that obedience leads to blessing and disobedience leads to curse. We cannot expect blessing if living in disobedience. Obedience is the first call on God's people (eg Leviticus 25:18; Deuteronomy 26:16-19; 1 Samuel 15:22-23; John 14:15; Romans 6:15-18; 1 Peter 1:13-16).

The need for wisdom

Solomon was famous for his wisdom (10:24), but he was also foolish. In marrying foreign wives, he not only disobeyed God (11:2), his heart was stolen as they introduced their gods to him (11:1-13). His son, Rehoboam, was unwise for not listening to the elders' advice (12:1-15), with catastrophic results (12:16-24) which never healed.

The Bible encourages us to seek wisdom above everything else (eg Proverbs 1:7; 2:1-22; 3:13-20; 4:1-9; 8:1-36; 24:3-6; James 1:5).

The need for dedication

Although initially passionate for God, Solomon became lukewarm after marrying unbelieving wives, something the Bible forbids (Deuteronomy 7:3-4; 2 Corinthians 6:14-18). Solomon's desire for personal pleasure, sexual satisfaction and a comfortable life gradually became more important than God and he end up drifting away. No one suddenly decides, "I think I'll become lukewarm today"; it is something we gradually drift into, usually by explaining away God's word. The Bible warns us about becoming lukewarm (Revelation 3:14-22).

The need for unity

When Solomon died, disunity erupted. Both sides were in the wrong: Rehoboam for not being a servant to his people (12:7), the northern tribes for rejecting their God-appointed ruler (12:16). The results of their disunity lasted for 350 years and led to Israel being destroyed by Assyria.

It is so easy to divide when things don't go the way we think they should; but God hates

> " *The LORD became angry with Solomon because his heart had turned away from the LORD ...*"
>
> *1 KINGS 11:9*

division, and the Bible urges us to maintain unity (Romans 15:1-7; 1 Corinthians 12:21-26; Ephesians 4:1-13; Philippians 4:2-3; Colossians 3:12-14). Jesus prayed for unity among his followers (John 17:20-23) for it carries the blessing of God (Psalm 133:1-3).

The need for wholeheartedness

The Ten Commandments reveal that there is only one God and he alone is worthy of our devotion (Exodus 20:1-6). However, many kings in this period tried to blend worship of God with worship of other gods (syncretism). The Bible says that God finds this utterly unacceptable (Deuteronomy 7:1-6; Joshua 23:16; Jeremiah 19:1-15; Hosea 2:2-15; 1 Corinthians 8:1-13; 10:21).

2 Kings
JUDGEMENT TIME

OVERVIEW

Continuing the story of 1 Kings, the divided people of God continued to reject his call through the prophets. For Israel, this led to destruction by Assyria; for Judah, exile in Babylon. But the reason for both lay, not in the rise of these superpowers, but in the judgement of God.

SUMMARY

Elisha picks up Elijah's mantle (2:1-18) and a series of miracles, mostly personal rather than national, confirm his God-given authority (2:19-22,23-25; 3:14-20; 4:1-7,8-37,38-41, 42-44; 5:27; 6:1-7,8-23; 6:24-7:20; 8:1-6,7-15). The author then returns to the history of Judah and Israel and, as in 1 Kings, alternates between the two.

Israel

Israel's godlessness continued, characterised by:

- **religious syncretism**, as they "persisted in all the sins of Jeroboam and did not turn away from them" (17:22). (See 10:28-31; 13:1-3,10-11; 14:23-24; 15:8-9,17-18,23-24, 27-28). They also blended worship of God with worship of Baal (17:7-17).
- **political instability**, as one dynasty replaced another, often through bloodshed (eg 10:1-17). Every northern king, except Omri and Jeroboam II, was weak, and even these two are dismissed in a few verses because of their godlessness. Several kings tried to prop up the nation through political alliances with other nations.

Prophets like Jonah (785-775 BC), Amos (760-750 BC) and Hosea (750-715 BC) challenged both king and nation, reminding them of God's character and covenant, denouncing sin, and warning that unless people repented, judgement would come. That judgement came through Assyria.

Assyria wanted more territory and, after several years of dominating Israel from a distance, it finally besieged its capital Samaria in 722 BC (17:1-4). Israel was conquered and many citizens were deported across the Assyrian empire (17:3-6; 18:9-12). The history of the ten northern tribes was now over, the deportees being scattered among other races and religions to be lost without trace.

Judah

Meanwhile down south, David's descendants continued to rule, challenged and encouraged by Obadiah (855-840 BC, or 605-586 BC), Isaiah (740-681 BC), Micah (750-686 BC) and Jeremiah (628-585 BC). Two good kings were Hezekiah (715-687 BC), who reformed worship and trusted God when Assyria attacked Jerusalem (18:1-20:21), and Josiah (640-609 BC), who refurbished the temple, rediscovered part of God's Law, and renewed the covenant (22:1-23:30). Especially bad was Manasseh (687-642 BC), who returned to Baal worship, erecting pagan altars in the temple and even sacrificing his son (21:1-18).

Jeremiah (626-585 BC) warned that judgement was coming. If Judah didn't repent, it would be judged, like Israel, and even the temple would be destroyed. No one believed him, but when Babylon conquered Assyria (605 BC), it invaded Judah and appointed Zedekiah as king (24:1-17). When he tried to rebel, Babylon marched against Jerusalem, capturing it in 586 BC. The city and temple were destroyed and the population exiled to Babylon (25:1-21; 2 Chronicles 36:15-21; Jeremiah 52:1-30).

Author
See 1 Kings, p.174.

Date
See 1 Kings, p.174.

>>>

KEY THEMES – 2 KINGS

The God of miracles

Many miracles happened through Elijah and Elisha. With Elijah, they generally demonstrated God's supremacy over Baal; with Elisha, God's compassion for those in need. Miracles are generally restricted in the Old Testament to crucial moments, like at the exodus and during these dark days when the prophets were fighting for the survival of Israel's faith. In the New Testament, miracles become much more common, not only in Jesus' and the apostles' ministry, but throughout the early church.

The God of judgement

Kings shows that, while God loves his people, if they continue in sinful ways he has no alternative, as a holy God, but to judge them. We see this, first in the destruction of Israel by Assyria, and then in the exile of Judah by Babylon.

Jeremiah, prophesying at the end of this period, described God's wrath – his righteous anger against sin – as being stored up in a goblet, ready to be poured out in judgement (Jeremiah 25:15-29), not just on God's enemies, but also on God's people unless they changed. It is this cup that Jesus saw himself drinking for us at the cross (Matthew 26:39).

The God we can trust

Hezekiah showed how God can be trusted (18:5). When Assyria, now only a few miles from Jerusalem after its invasion of Israel, threatened to invade Judah too (18:17-37), Hezekiah turned to God, rather than Egypt, spreading out Assyria's threatening letter before God in the temple (19:14-19). Isaiah encouraged him to stand firm (19:20-34) and "that night the angel of the LORD went out and put to death a hundred and eighty-five thousand men in the Assyrian camp" (19:35). Whenever the kings trusted God, and returned to his covenant like Josiah did (eg 22:1–23:25), he rescued them; whenever they depended on themselves or human resources, he left them to experience the consequences.

What happened to Israel?

Many Israelites were dispersed across the Assyrian Empire, while other conquered peoples were transported to Israel, thus mixing up these nations and destroying any powerbase that might rebel. Many fanciful ideas grew up about what happened to the ten lost tribes of Israel. However, while some probably fled to Judah, most were either dispersed (and we have no idea what happened to them) or were left behind and intermarried with other peoples. These eventually became the Samaritans, despised by Jews in New Testament times because of their racial and religious impurity.

RELEVANCE FOR TODAY – 2 KINGS

God's people

God uses all kinds of people. **Elijah** ("My God is the LORD") was from Gilead, a backwater, and his rough manner and blunt message made him look like a nobody. He preferred to work alone, and could be something of a depressive (1 Kings 19:1-5). By contrast, **Elisha** ("My God saves") was a quieter character who came from a wealthy family and gave up everything to respond to God's call. While sometimes involved in national affairs, he was more concerned with individuals, wanting them to know that God, not Baal, was their provider.

God still uses different characters and personalities. We don't have to imitate others to be used by him.

God's portion

Before Elijah was taken into heaven, Elisha asked for "a double portion" (2:9). He wasn't asking to be twice as powerful or anointed, but rather to be his successor. When a father died, the eldest son received a double share of the inheritance because he was now responsible for the wider family. Elisha was saying he was now ready to pick up Elijah's responsibilities.

God is looking for those who are not eager to get special anointing for themselves, but for others. His portion is for service not for selfishness.

God's perspective

God wants us to look with spiritual eyes. When Elisha's servant saw the Arameans who were sent to capture his master, Elisha asked God to open his eyes "and he looked and saw the hills full of horses and chariots of fire all around Elisha" (6:17). Elisha understood that God's angels are always around, always protecting us. See Psalm 91:9-13.

> *"... the LORD removed them from his presence, as he had warned through all his servants the prophets..."*
>
> 2 KINGS 17:23

God's love

The story of the healing of Naaman (chapter 5), an Aramean commander with leprosy, shows that God's love reaches beyond those who are already his people. Damascus was a proud city and Elisha challenged his pride by telling him to bathe in the Jordan, a river much inferior to the rivers of Damascus. While at first he struggled with this, the wisdom of a young Israelite girl prevailed and he obeyed. He was healed and became a believer (5:14-15).

God wants us to always be ready to look beyond our own kind – whether people, tribe, town or nation – remembering that his salvation really is for all.

1 Chronicles
UNDERSTANDING YOUR HISTORY

OVERVIEW

1 Chronicles (originally one book with 2 Chronicles, but separated by the Greek translators of the Old Testament) tells the history of Israel with a particular emphasis on the role of the temple and its priests. It emphasises God's ongoing purposes for his people in the light of his promises in the past, especially to David.

SUMMARY

The history of God's people

To establish the identity of God's people, 1 Chronicles opens with long genealogies (chapters 1–9). For people returning from exile to reclaim their heritage, this was immensely important. Going right back to Adam, through the development of twelve tribes from Jacob's twelve sons, and right up to their recent experience of God's judgement (9:1-2), the Chronicler sets the scene for new hope.

The history of God's king

Having dealt quickly with Saul (10:1-14), the Chronicler focuses on Israel's ideal king, David. Omitting Saul's opposition (1 Samuel chapters 18–31) and David's seven-year rule over just Judah (2 Samuel 2:1-4; 5:1-5), he tells how David became king over "all Israel" (11:1) because both God and Israel wanted it (11:2-3). David demonstrated his leadership by capturing Jerusalem, making it his capital (11:4-9), and gathering warriors (11:10–12:40). Bringing the ark there reinforced Jerusalem's importance, though disaster interrupted the process (13:1-14). Realising this was because they had violated God's holiness by not having Levites carry it (15:1-2,13; see Exodus 25:12-14), the ark was returned properly, amid great rejoicing (15:1–16:43). The irony of God's ark being in a tent while David lived in a palace provoked a desire to build a temple (17:1-2). However, God turned David's desire

on its head: God would build a "house" for him instead (17:3-10), one that would last for ever (17:11-14), and David responded with gratitude (17:16-27). David's victories (18:1–20:8) were followed by Satan's attack, provoking David to pride by taking a military census (21:1-6). God was angry with David and sent a plague as judgement (21:7-14). However, the place where God stopped the plague – where his judgement and mercy met – was designated as the future temple's site (21:15–22:1). The remaining chapters are devoted to David's preparations for building the temple: his charge to Solomon and explanation of why he himself couldn't build it (22:2-19); the Levites' roles (23:1–26:32); arrangements for military and administrative service (27:1-34); David's plans (28:1-21) and gifts (29:1-9) for the temple. The book closes with David's prayer of amazement (29:10-20) and the anointing of Solomon as king (29:21-25). This done, David's life work is over (29:26-30).

Author

The author of Chronicles ("the Chronicler") is unknown, although ancient Jewish tradition suggests Ezra wrote Chronicles, and Ezra and Nehemiah, which complete the story.

Date

Written after Judah's return from exile in Babylon in the 5th or 4th century BC.

OUTLINE – 1 CHRONICLES

KEY THEMES – 1 CHRONICLES

God's purpose

While Kings, written in exile, answers the question, "How did we end up here?" Chronicles, written after the return from exile, answers the question, "Is God still with us?" The Chronicler answers, "Yes!" For even though there was no Davidic king ruling and Israel was subject to Persia, God still had a purpose for them. Assuming his readers knew Samuel and Kings (eg 2 Chronicles 27:7), he focuses on events that demonstrated this ongoing purpose to provoke them to faith for the future.

God's covenant

David acknowledged that God "remembers his covenant for ever, the word he commanded, for a thousand generations" (16:15). It was this covenant, rather than present circumstances, that was Israel's basis of hope. When this covenant was obeyed, its blessings were experienced; when it wasn't, disaster came (eg 15:2,13). The consequences of obedience and disobedience are seen especially in 2 Chronicles.

God's king

The Chronicler sees David as the ideal king. Whereas in 2 Samuel we see his failures (eg his adultery and weak fathering), Chronicles presents him in a better light, omitting his bad points and highlighting his good ones. The prophets saw David as a "type" of the Messiah who would fulfil God's promises to David (eg Isaiah 9:6-7; Jeremiah 23:5-6; Ezekiel 34:23-24), and the Chronicler also sees David as typifying that messianic king.

God's temple

The Chronicler emphasises David's preparations for the temple, and 2 Chronicles Solomon's actual building of it. He draws parallels between David-Solomon and Moses-Joshua, the "preparer" and the "doer" (eg compare 22:11-16; 28:2-10 with Deuteronomy 1:37-38; 31:2-8). When the Chronicler was writing, the temple was probably still in ruins; but his work ends with Cyrus' edict about its rebuilding (2 Chronicles 36:22-23), demonstrating hope for its future. The temple represents continuity with the past. It, rather than king, is now the focus of Israel's identity.

God's people

The term "all Israel" is used repeatedly, even when referring to the divided kingdom. This is because the returned exiles were now all that was left of God's people. In 2 Chronicles he records how, after the kingdom divided, godly people left Israel for Judah (eg 2 Chronicles 11:14; 15:9; 30:1-20; 34:9). So the post-exilic remnant could truly be called "all Israel" since representatives from the other tribes were among them.

RELEVANCE FOR TODAY – 1 CHRONICLES

The Chronicler underlines keys to our moving into God's future at a time of change and challenge:

Knowing who we are

Although genealogies (like the one in chapters 1–9) can seem quite boring to us (if we're honest!), they were important to people

> " *Now, who is willing to consecrate himself today to the LORD?*"
>
> *1 CHRONICLES 29:5*

at the time. Here, at the beginning of Chronicles, they establish the identity of the returning exiles, for people can only know where they are going when they know who they are and where they have come from. Jesus himself underlined this principle. "Jesus knew ... that he had come from God (*identity*) and was returning to God (*destiny*), so he got up ... and began to wash his disciples' feet" (John 13:3-5). His security in his identity and destiny meant he could undertake any task, even washing feet, for neither was affected by it. We cannot serve God and move ahead into his future for us unless we are secure about who we are in Christ. It was Jabez' confidence in who he was that enabled him to confidently ask God for more (4:10).

Learning from history

By retelling Israel's history (to people who already had Samuel and Kings) the Chronicler was showing that we can always learn from the past, especially from different perspectives, and if we don't learn, we will commit the same errors again. By emphasising some facts and omitting others, he underlined his message that only obedience leads to ongoing blessing. Comparing Chronicles with Samuel and

KINGS OF ISRAEL AND JUDAH
Dates are approximate; overlapping dates indicate periods of co-regency

The united kingdom		Israel		Judah	
1050–1010	Saul	931–910	Jeroboam I	931–913	Rehoboam
1010–970	David			913–911	Abijah
970–931	Solomon	910–909	Nadab	911–870	Asa
(931 The kingdom divides)		909–886	Baasha		
		886–885	Elah		
		885	Zimri		
		885–880	Tibni		
		880–874	Omri		
		874–853	Ahab	873–848	Jehoshaphat
		853–852	Ahaziah		
		852–841	Jehoram	848–841	Jehoram
		841–814	Jehu	841	Ahaziah
				841–835	Queen Athaliah
		814–798	Jehoahaz	835–796	Joash
		798–782	Jehoash	796–767	Amaziah
		793–753	Jeroboam II	792–740	Uzziah
		753–752	Zechariah	740–735	Jotham
		752	Shallum		
		752–742	Menahem		
		742–740	Pekahiah		
		740–732	Pekah	735–715	Ahaz
		732–722	Hoshea		
		(722 Israel falls, people exiled)		715–687	Hezekiah
				687–642	Manasseh
				642–640	Amon
				640–609	Josiah
				609	Jehoahaz
				609–598	Jehoiakim
				597	Jehoiachin
				597–586	Zedekiah
				(586 Jerusalem falls)	

Kings often highlights what important lesson he was trying to underline.

Needing one another
Despite his gifts and calling, David was not a "one-man ministry". He not only gathered great warriors (11:10–12:40), he also released them in their gifting (eg 11:14,20-21,22-25; 12:1-2,8,14). This in turn produced loyalty as they "gave his kingship strong support" (11:10) and committed themselves to his success (12:18). Good leaders do not do everything themselves but release the gifts in all God's people. The Chronicler knew that, in this period after the return from exile, God's people desperately needed that.

Planning for the future
Most politicians (and many pastors) think only of their own immediate success, but David thought to the future and made plans for the success of his son Solomon. David prepared everything for the building of the temple, but he knew it would be Solomon who built it. Good leaders plan for the future and for their successor's success, not simply their own.

2 Chronicles
FROM DEDICATION TO DISASTER

OVERVIEW

Continuing the history of Israel begun in 1 Chronicles, the book surveys the kings of Judah from its third king, Solomon, to its last one at the time of the exile showing that, despite the hard time God's people have been through, there is still hope for the future.

SUMMARY

Solomon

Invited to choose a blessing, Solomon chose wisdom, but was given wealth too (1:1-17). He built the temple (3:1–5:1), brought the ark there (5:2-14) and dedicated it (6:1-42). Fire fell (7:1), showing God's acceptance. God appeared to him in a dream (7:11-12), promising that repentance and obedience would produce blessing (7:13-18) but disobedience would always bring curse (7:19-22), a principle seen throughout Chronicles. In Solomon the writer sees temple and throne coming together, which is why he avoids mentioning his errors, noted in Kings.

The divided kingdom

Lacking Solomon's wisdom, Rehoboam ignored Israel's plea for relief (10:1-15). Israel therefore split away, crowning Jeroboam (10:15-19). Rehoboam strengthened Judah by reinforcing its border towns (11:5-12), and some northern priests and Levites joined him because of Jeroboam's idolatry (11:13-17). But Judah too adopted idolatry (12:1,5) and was punished by Egypt robbing the temple (12:1-11). Rehoboam repented and Judah was spared (12:12).

The Chronicler then recalls Judah's succeeding kings, ignoring Israel completely except where its story affected Judah. The message is clear: only obedient kings were blessed.

Good kings

These include:

- Jehoshaphat (17:1–20:37), who taught God's word and defeated his enemies through praise, but who later allied with Israel and didn't remove high places.
- Joash (24:1-16), who restored the temple and worship, but who later adopted Baal worship (24:17-27).
- Uzziah (26:3-23), who was a great soldier, farmer and administrator, but who became proud and contracted leprosy.
- Hezekiah (29:1–32:33), who restored both temple and worship and followed Isaiah's counsel when Sennacherib threatened Jerusalem, seeing it spared, but who became proud.
- Josiah (34:1–35:27), who purged Judah of idolatry and refurbished the temple. During repair works "the Book of the Law" (probably Deuteronomy) was found (34:14-15) which Josiah immediately implemented.

Wicked kings

These include:

- Ahaz (28:1-27), who developed pagan worship and was judged through military defeats. His appeal to Assyria ended in humiliation, but this didn't turn him back to God.
- Manasseh (33:1-20), the longest reigning (52 years) and most wicked of Judah's kings, who utterly embraced Baal worship, including child sacrifice (33:1-9). He finally repented in exile in Assyria.

End of the kings

With Assyria's overthrow, Judah was eyed up by both Egypt and Babylon. After years of uncertainty, God allowed Babylon to destroy Jerusalem (36:15-19). Many were massacred, while the rest were taken into exile (36:20) to give the land rest from the people's wickedness (36:21).

The author concludes with a summary of the return from exile, which is expanded further in Ezra.

Author

See 1 Chronicles, p.182.

Date

See 1 Chronicles, p.182.

THE DIVIDED KINGDOM

After Solomon died, his son Rehoboam was appointed king over Judah, continuing the same overbearing hold over the country as his father. Jeroboam returned from Egypt and led demands for a less oppressive approach. Rehoboam refused, causing Jeroboam to be appointed king over the tribes of the north.

Shechem became the capital of Israel in the north while Jerusalem ruled over Judah. During Jeroboam's reign he relocated his capital to Tirzah, but years later Omri had Samaria built as his seat of power.

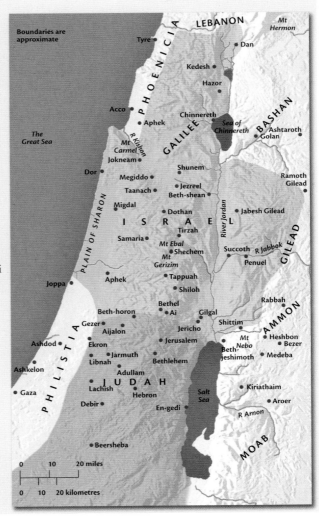

OUTLINE – 2 CHRONICLES

Solomon's rule

1:1-6 Solomon rule is established

1:7-17 God gives Solomon wisdom and wealth

2:1–3:17 Solomon builds the temple for God in Jerusalem

4:1–5:1 The furnishings for the temple

5:2-14 The ark of the covenant is brought to the temple

6:1–7:22 Solomon dedicates the temple and God promises to be with him if he remains faithful

8:1-18 The achievements of Solomon

9:1-12 The Queen of Sheba visits Solomon

9:13-28 Solomon's great wealth and wisdom

9:29-31 Solomon's death

The history of the kingdom of Judah

10:1-19 Solomon's kingdom is divided

11:1–12:16 Rehoboam rules in Judah

13:1-22 Abijah rules in Judah

14:1-7 Asa becomes king of Judah

14:8-15 Asa defeats the Cushites

15:1-19 Asa renews the worship of God in Judah

16:1-10 Asa makes a treaty with the king of Aram

16:11-14 Asa becomes ill and dies

17:1-19 Jehoshaphat becomes king of Judah

18:1-34 Jehoshaphat makes an alliance with Ahab king of Israel against the Arameans

19:1–21:3 Jehoshaphat rules in Judah

21:4-20 Jehoram rules in Judah

22:1-9 Ahaziah rules in Judah

22:10-12 Athaliah, mother of Ahaziah, rules in Judah

23:1-21 Jehoiada the priest rebels against Athaliah and makes Joash king

24:1-16 Temple worship is restored and the temple is repaired

24:17-22 Joash reverses the reforms after Jehoiada's death

24:23-27 The end of Joash's life and rule

25:1-28 Amaziah rules in Judah

26:1-23 Uzziah rules in Judah

27:1-9 Jotham rules in Judah

28:1-27 Ahaz rules in Judah

29:1-36 Hezekiah becomes king of Judah and rededicates the temple

30:1-27 Hezekiah celebrates the Passover in Jerusalem

31:1-21 The religious reforms of Hezekiah

32:1-23 King Sennacherib of Assyria invades Judah

32:24-33 Hezekiah's sickness, recovery, foolishness and death

33:1-20 Manasseh rules in Judah

33:21-25 Amon rules in Judah

34:1-33 Josiah becomes king of Judah and rediscovers God's Law

35:1-19 The Passover is celebrated in Jerusalem

35:20-27 Josiah's death in battle

36:1-4 Jehoahaz rules in Judah

36:5-8 Jehoiakim rules in Judah

36:9-10 Jehoiachin rules in Judah and is taken to Babylon, along with treasures from the temple

36:11-13 Zedekiah becomes king of Judah

36:14-21 Jerusalem falls to the Babylonians, the temple is destroyed and the people are taken into exile

36:22-23 Cyrus allows the exiles to return to the land

See 1 Chronicles, p.183.

God's temple

The temple is given priority because the writer wants to encourage the returned exiles to give priority to it as a symbol of the priority God must have. Although based on the tabernacle, Solomon wanted the temple to reflect God's greatness in size and magnificence (3:3–5:1). God's acceptance of it was shown in his coming in cloud (6:13-14) and fire (7:1), symbols of his presence at the exodus.

God's priests

The Chronicler records faithful work by priests, like preparing the temple and bringing the ark to it (4:1–5:14). Northern priests and Levites are commended for abandoning idolatrous Israel and coming to Jerusalem (11:13-17). Priests were involved in praising in battle (13:13-18; 20:18-23) and collecting offerings (24:4-5,8-11; 31:4-13). The work of the chief priest Jehoiada as counsellor to Joash is particularly noted, and he was rewarded by being buried alongside kings (22:10–24:16).

God's law

Whether the temple existed or not, it was according to their allegiance to the covenant that every king was judged. Those who "did what was right in the eyes of the LORD" (eg 20:32; 24:2; 26:4; 27:2; 29:2; 34:2) were blessed; those who didn't were judged, as God said (7:14-22). The rediscovery of "the Book of the Law" (probably Deuteronomy) is highlighted (34:14-33), with Josiah quick to implement its requirements, leading to another reform.

God's prophets

The prophets' role was not primarily to predict the future, but to call people back to the covenant and encourage them in face of difficulties. Their importance is reflected in the many prophets mentioned, including: Shemaiah (12:5,15), Iddo (13:22), Azariah (15:8), Micaiah (18:1-27) and Oded (28:9-11). Canonical prophets linked with kings were:

· Micah (750–686 BC) – Jotham, Ahaz, Hezekiah
· Isaiah (740–681 BC) – Hezekiah
· Jeremiah (628–585 BC) – Josiah, Jehoiakim, Jehoiachin, Zedekiah
· Zephaniah (640–609 BC) – Josiah
· Nahum (663–612 BC) – Josiah
· Habakkuk (640–598 BC) – Josiah, Jehoiakim
· Daniel (605–530 BC) – Jehoiakim and exile
· Ezekiel (593–571 BC) – Jehoiakim, Jehoiachin, Zedekiah and exile
· Obadiah (possibly 855–840 BC) – Jehoshaphat, Jehoram; (or 605–586 BC) – Jehoiakim, Jehoiachin, Zedekiah

God's kings

Kings were appointed by God, but they couldn't do as they pleased. They were constrained by God's Law (eg 7:17-22), and were judged by whether they lived according to it. For the Chronicler, kings' disobedience always met with immediate retribution (eg 12:5; 16:7-9; 19:1-2; 21:12-15; 24:20; 25:14-15; 28:1-5; 34:22-25).

Understanding God's promises

God's promises aren't always worked out as we expect. The Chronicler (and prophets like Haggai, Zechariah and Malachi) saw that God's promise of an eternal Davidic kingdom (1 Chronicles 17:10-14), apparently now broken, wasn't dependent on David's descendants reigning. Rather, "ideal" kings, like David, Solomon, Jehoshaphat, Hezekiah and Josiah, were "types" of the coming Messiah and his everlasting kingdom. God's ways of working things out is often different (eg Isaiah 55:8-9).

" *If my people,*
who are called by
my name, will humble
themselves and pray and
seek my face and turn from
their wicked ways,
then will I hear from heaven
and will forgive their sin
and will heal their land."

2 CHRONICLES 7:14

Seeking God's resources

Invited to choose any gift (1:7), Solomon chose wisdom (1:10); and because he didn't grasp for things for himself, God added wealth too (1:11-12). Good leaders seek nothing for themselves, only for those they lead; so it is sad when they prioritise personal prestige or possessions. God's blessing of prosperity is for others through us, not for us through others.

Finding God's heart

No matter how far we have drifted from God, there is always a way back. Even Manasseh, one of Judah's worst kings, discovered this. Although involved in idolatry, child-sacrifice, sorcery, witchcraft and spiritism (33:6), he made a dramatic U-turn when taken into exile (33:12). Despite all he had done and led others into doing, God not only forgave him, but restored him (33:13), as he promised (7:14). His repentance shows it's never too late for anyone to find God's heart.

Building God's house

Solomon wanted his temple to reflect God's greatness (2:5) and impress unbelievers (9:6), and it did. But it was also a snare, eventually becoming a source of pride. Judah thought that, as "God's house", God was bound to protect it and Jerusalem; but they were wrong (36:15-19), as Jeremiah warned (Jeremiah 7:3-15). Buildings are not God's house; we are (eg 1 Peter 2:4-5). Buildings make good servants but poor masters.

Experiencing God's revival

Revivals are exciting times; but for them to be long-lasting, the change in lives must be profound; when it isn't, the revival is shallow and short-lived, as Hezekiah discovered. While revival led to the speedy renewal of the temple (29:36) and even touched people's pockets (31:4-10), the change was not deep: priests weren't ready for the challenge (30:2-3), Hezekiah became proud (32:24-26), and his son Manasseh, clearly untouched by the revival, quickly led the nation back into paganism (33:1-9), showing how superficial the revival had been. Revivals are not about superficial excitement, but deep and lasting change. Key principles for revival can be found in Solomon's prayer (7:14).

Ezra
GOD'S PROMISE IS KEPT

OVERVIEW

Picking up where 2 Chronicles finished, Ezra tells how God's people returned to Judah and how, despite many struggles and obstacles, they succeeded in rebuilding the temple and re-establishing themselves in the land God had promised them so long before.

SUMMARY

Return

Having conquered Babylon, Cyrus allowed the Jews in 538 BC to return to the home from which Babylon had exiled them 70 years earlier (1:1-4), fulfilling Jeremiah's prophecy (Jeremiah 25:8-14; 29:4-14). They were given resources and livestock to begin life again (1:6) and Cyrus returned the temple's treasure (1:7-11). The returning exiles, under Zerubbabel, are carefully listed (2:1-70).

Rebuilding

Three months after their return, they rebuilt the altar and recommenced sacrifices (3:1-6) "despite their fear of the peoples around them" (3:3). Then the temple's foundation was relaid, a moment of great emotion (3:7-9).

Resistance

Their return was resented by those Assyria had resettled, for this was now their home. So, with offers of help to rebuild the temple rejected (4:1-3), they turned against the Jews, undermining them (4:4-5) and warning the Persian king how dangerous a restored Jerusalem would be (4:6-22). Further work was then prohibited (4:23-24) and stopped for 16 years – too long for Haggai and Zechariah who stirred them into action (5:1-2). Further threats in the form of opposition represented by the governor of the Trans-Euphrates (Tattenai) and Shethar-Bozenai and their associates (5:3) and an appeal to Darius followed (5:3-17), but God frustrated this and Darius confirmed Cyrus' permission (6:1-12),

leading to the completion of rebuilding and dedicating the temple (6:13-22) on March 12, 516 BC, almost 70 years exactly after its destruction.

Renewal

Between chapters 6 and 7, 30 years pass about which we know nothing. But in 458 BC Ezra, an expert in God's Law (7:10), returned with another group (7:1-10; 8:1-14), with authority to implement God's Law (7:11-28). Having fasted before the journey to seek God's protection (8:15-23) and entrusted resources to twelve priests and twelve Levites (8:24-30), he celebrated their safe arrival with sacrifices (8:31-36). He was appalled at the spiritual state of God's people, especially how many, including priests and leaders, had married unbelievers (9:1-5), prayerfully recalling that this was the root of the backsliding that had led to exile (9:6-15). All the men were called to Jerusalem (10:1-8) where, in pouring rain (10:9), Ezra confronted them (10:9-17). Over the coming days (10:12-17), a list of those who had intermarried was drawn up (9:18-44).

While most of Ezra is written in Hebrew, parts quoting official documents or letters (4:8–6:18; 7:12-26) are written in their original Aramaic, the international language of the day.

Author

Literary parallels suggest the same author as Chronicles, possibly Ezra himself.

Date

Written after Judah's return from exile around 440 BC.

OUTLINE – EZRA

The return to Jerusalem

1:1-4 Cyrus allows the exiles to return and to rebuild the temple

1:5-11 The exiles prepare to return with the treasures from the temple

2:1-70 A list of the exiles who returned to Jerusalem

Rebuilding and resistance

3:1-6 The temple altar is rebuilt

3:7-13 The temple foundations are relaid

4:1-24 The enemies of God's people oppose and frustrate the work

5:1–6:12 King Darius approves the rebuilding of the temple

6:13-15 The temple is completed

6:16-18 The rebuilt temple is dedicated

6:19-22 The Passover feast is celebrated

The renewal of moral and religious life

7:1-26 Ezra's commission to return to Jerusalem

7:27-28 Ezra praises God

8:1-14 A list of the exiles who returned with Ezra

8:15-20 Ezra finds Levites to return with him to serve in the temple

8:21-30 Ezra prepares for the return

8:31-36 Ezra arrives in Jerusalem

9:1–10:44 Ezra leads the people to renew their moral and religious life

KEY THEMES – EZRA

God's sovereignty

Ezra opens with a great declaration of God's sovereignty. Cyrus, King of Persia, may have conquered Babylon and swallowed its empire, but what really lay behind his victory was the sovereign timing of God who had counted the 70 years Jeremiah had prophesied and had determined that now was the time for his people to go home, just as promised (1:1). Cyrus may not have known God, but God knew Cyrus and moved him to do what he wanted.

God's temple

The importance of the temple, as the new focus of religious and cultural identity, is underlined by detailing the long and difficult process of rebuilding it in the face of constant opposition (4:1-24; 5:3-17). The opposition almost succeeded, the people becoming so discouraged that they stopped work for 16 years. It took the provocation of Haggai and Zechariah to stir them into action again (5:1-2; see Haggai and Zechariah, p.286, 289). The mixed emotions at the foundation-laying (3:10-13) show how important re-establishing the temple was to them.

God's word

Ezra was a scribe (religious teacher) who was "well versed in the Law of Moses, which the LORD, the God of Israel, had given" (7:6). His knowledge led King Artaxerxes to send him to Judah to teach this law to God's people. His desire to give God's word first place is seen in his challenging people to put right their disobedience to it concerning mixed marriages (9:10-15; Exodus 34:15-16) and his later week-long reading it to them (Nehemiah 8:1-18). Reading the Scriptures had found new importance during the exile when they did not have the temple and its sacrifices, and it helped shape modern Judaism.

God's people

God's people are called to be holy – distinct and different – even as God himself is (Leviticus 11:44-45; 19:2; 20:26; 1 Peter 1:15-16). The first group of returning exiles had intermarried with the residents of the land put there by Babylon. No doubt it was with good intentions, perhaps because there weren't enough Jewish women to provide every Jewish man with a wife to have children to continue the nation; however, good intentions are no substitute for obedience, so Ezra challenged this fundamental breach of holiness. God's people are called to maintain their holiness, their distinctiveness through everything – worship, lifestyle, character and beliefs.

RELEVANCE FOR TODAY – EZRA

Keeping holy

While most Christians genuinely want to lead lives that are pleasing to God, it gets harder to be holy in times of pressure. The lack of

> " *There is still hope for Israel ...* "
>
> EZRA 10:2

Jewish women led many Jewish men, and even some leaders, to forget the demands of holiness in marriage – that God's people may only marry believers (eg 2 Corinthians 6:14-18) – in favour of "being practical". After all, without children, they no doubt thought, how would the Jewish race ever continue? But following God's holiness will always be for our best, even though we may have to trust God on the way.

Keeping going

It's hard to keep going when everything is against us, and even harder when God's promises aren't working out as quickly or easily as we had hoped. That's what the returning exiles experienced. Discouraged by opposition and lack of progress, they eventually gave up and focused on their homes instead of God's house. So God sent Haggai and Zechariah to stir them up (5:1-2). God wants his people to learn stickability and not give up (Galatians 6:9; Hebrews 12:1-13).

Keeping focused

Ezra believed in the value of fasting – abstaining from food to focus on God. It was practised at crucial times in the Bible or on solemn occasions to show complete dependence on God. Ezra fasted before undertaking the long and hazardous journey back to Judah (8:21-23). Others who fasted include David (2 Samuel 12:16), Daniel (9:3), Esther (4:3,16), Nehemiah (1:4), Paul (Acts 13:2-3) and Jesus (Matthew 4:2). When prayer doesn't seem to be working, or the challenge ahead seems great, fasting still helps us focus on God and his ability to provide a solution to our needs.

Keeping sincere

Sincerity and integrity are important for God's people, and even more so for leaders. There is nothing more shameful than leaders being exposed for having secretly done the very things they have been preaching against. Jesus condemned the Pharisees for living this way (eg Matthew 23:1-39). Ezra, by contrast, was very careful to keep his integrity. "Ezra had devoted himself to the study and observance of the Law of the LORD, and to teaching its decrees and laws in Israel" (7:10). Notice that studying and observing (for himself) came before teaching (for others).

Nehemiah
BUILDING FOR GOD

OVERVIEW

Continuing the story begun in Ezra, Nehemiah recounts the story of the amazing rebuilding of the walls of Jerusalem and the reorganising of the life of God's people under the inspiring leadership of Nehemiah.

SUMMARY

Requesting permission

On hearing of the returned exiles' struggles (1:1-3), Nehemiah, a Jew in Persian royal service, was devastated and immediately fasted and prayed (1:4-11). While wanting an answer "today" (1:11), it was four months (2:1) before it came. Noticing his sad face, the king asked what was wrong (2:1-2). Nehemiah explained about Jerusalem, seeking permission to go and rebuild it (2:3-5). The king agreed, but made it clear he wanted Nehemiah to return to his job as king's cupbearer (2:6).

Rebuilding walls

Having inspected the walls by night to keep his plans secret (2:11-16), Nehemiah challenged the leaders (2:17-18). As the work began, they faced opposition: threats (2:19-20), ridicule (4:1-3), anger (4:7-8), rumour-mongering (6:1-9) and intimidation (6:10-13), but Nehemiah encouraged them to keep building.

Dividing the task between 42 groups, he involved everyone, assigning them sections near their homes (3:1-32) and ensuring they were protected (4:16-18). Through his single-minded determination, the work was completed in just 52 days (6:15), an amazing timescale after 90 years of relative inactivity. With guards placed on the gates (7:1-3), the city was at last secure and censuses could be taken (7:4-73; 11:1-24,25-36; 12:1-26).

Re-ordering life

Nehemiah never lost sight of people in the midst of the project, implementing social reforms for the poor. Not only had many sold land, some were now selling their children to raise money (5:1-5). Nehemiah demanded an end to interest on loans and the return of family land (5:6-13), setting a self-restrained example (5:14-19).

With the walls secure, Ezra read God's Law in a great ceremony (8:1-18), leading to immediate recognition of the need for repentance (8:9) and the restoration of the week-long Festival of Tabernacles (8:13-18). Two weeks later, they gathered again for a ceremony of repentance and rededication (9:1-38). Finally the walls were dedicated to God (12:27-43).

Returning home

Nehemiah's first tour of duty lasted twelve years (5:14) after which he returned to Persia. But he then came back, discovering many abuses: mixed marriages (13:1-3,23-29), an Ammonite living in the temple (13:4-5,8-9), the Levites not supported (13:10-14), and Sabbath observance neglected (13:15-22). He took swift action to correct all this, so restoring Israel's distinctiveness.

Author

The opening words suggest the author was Nehemiah. However the book was combined with Ezra in the earliest Jewish manuscripts, suggesting the same editor, possibly Ezra, worked on both.

Date

Written almost 100 years after the return of the first exiles, around 430 BC.

EXILE AND RETURN

The story of the middle eastern nations was one of continually fluctuating power.

From c. 1350–625 BC Assyria held the ascendancy. During this time Tiglath-pileser III claimed Syria, Phoenicia and Galilee as Assyrian provinces.

King Hoshea of Israel revolted but was attacked and defeated by Sargon II in 721. The whole of the northern kingdom was exiled, never to return: foreign peoples from Syria and Babylonia were imported to replace them.

In 701 Sennacherib overran Phoenicia and many of the cities of Judah; Hezekiah in Jerusalem was forced to pay a heavy tribute.

In 626 Babylon won independence from Assyria but in 614 became part of the Medes and Babylonian empire.

In 597 Nebuchadnezzar conquered Jerusalem: Jehoiachin and the leading men of Judah were exiled to Babylon and Zedekiah installed as puppet king. Ten years later Zedekiah revolted – Jerusalem was besieged again and destroyed (587/6).

The nation remained in exile until the decree of Persian king Cyrus allowed many to return with Zerubbabel in 538. Haggai and Zechariah encouraged rebuilding of the temple in Jerusalem (520).

In 458 Ezra returned with a large group. He reinstated the Law and marriage reforms. Nehemiah followed from Susa in 445. The walls of Jerusalem were rebuilt and life began again in their homeland.

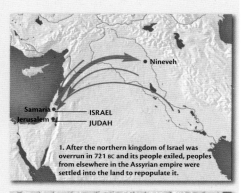

1. After the northern kingdom of Israel was overrun in 721 BC and its people exiled, peoples from elsewhere in the Assyrian empire were settled into the land to repopulate it.

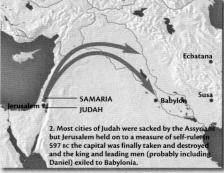

2. Most cities of Judah were sacked by the Assyrians but Jerusalem held on to a measure of self-rule. In 597 BC the capital was finally taken and destroyed and the king and leading men (probably including Daniel) exiled to Babylonia.

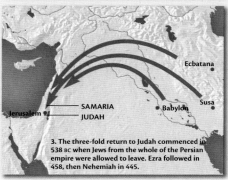

3. The three-fold return to Judah commenced in 538 BC when Jews from the whole of the Persian empire were allowed to leave. Ezra followed in 458, then Nehemiah in 445.

OUTLINE – NEHEMIAH

Nehemiah requests permission to return to Jerusalem

1:1-4 Nehemiah hears about the situation in Jerusalem

1:5-11 Nehemiah's prayer for God's help

2:1-10 King Artaxerxes allows Nehemiah to return

Rebuilding the walls of Jerusalem

2:11-16 Nehemiah's inspection of the city walls

2:17-18 Nehemiah and the people agree to rebuild the walls

2:19-20 The ridicule of Sanballat, Tobiah and Geshem

3:1-32 The workers who rebuilt the wall

4:1-15 Opposition to the work and the tiredness and fear of the workers

4:16-23 Nehemiah's solution to the security problem

5:1-19 Nehemiah's solution to economic problems

6:1-19 The city walls are completed

7:1-3 The appointment of officials and security guards

7:4-73a Nehemiah makes a register of the exiles who had returned

The re-ordering of religious life

7:73b–8:12 Ezra reads the Book of the Law to the people

8:13-18 The Feast of Tabernacles is celebrated

9:1-38 The people confess their sin and recommit themselves to God

10:1-27 The names of those who signed the binding document of dedication to God

10:28-39 The promise of the people to obey God

The returned exiles resettle

11:1-24 The new residents of Jerusalem

11:25-36 The new residents of the land of Judah

12:1-26 Priests and Levites who returned from exile

12:27-43 The city walls are dedicated

12:44-47 Information about the provision for the priests and Levites

Nehemiah's reforms

13:1-3 Those in mixed marriages are expelled from the community

13:4-9 Nehemiah removes Tobiah's belongings from the temple quarters

13:10-14 Nehemiah reintroduces tithing

13:15-22 Nehemiah brings back Sabbath regulations

13:23-29 Mixed marriages are prohibited

13:30-31 Nehemiah assigns duties to the priests and makes provision for them

KEY THEMES – NEHEMIAH

God's man

Nehemiah shows us that it's not just religious leaders (prophets and pastors) that God can use. He had a "secular" job in Persia as "cupbearer to the king" (1:11) – in other words, the poison tester! His faithful and trusted service over the years opened a door for God to use him for much bigger purposes.

God's city

Nehemiah was appalled at Jerusalem's condition and gave himself unstintingly to its restoration. The detailed description of who built various sections of the wall (chapter 3) underlines the Jerusalem's importance for re-establishing the identity of God's people. With no Davidic king ruling, the restored city

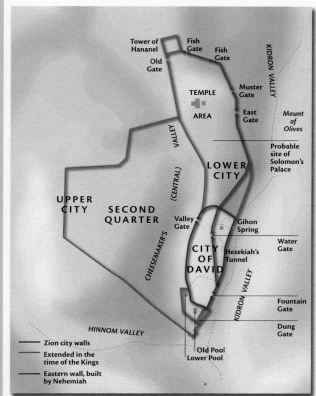

JERUSALEM IN THE OLD TESTAMENT

Jerusalem was founded by David on the site of Jebus. It was extended to the north by Solomon then westward by later kings. King Hezekiah provided added security by cutting a hidden tunnel to bring water from the Gihon Spring inside the city walls. The city was destroyed by the Babylonians in 586 BC. Rebuilding started after the return from exile, most notably under Nehemiah. Further fortification was added to the west by the Maccabees. The exact siting of the city walls is disputed.

and temple took on new importance, as Nehemiah understood.

God's remnant

With only a small remnant of God's people returning to Judah (many decided to stay in Persia), it was crucial they maintained a distinct lifestyle to mark them out as God's people. This was why Nehemiah was so shocked when he returned for a second period of office (13:6-7) and found the Jews had disregarded Ezra's teaching and backslidden in many areas, such as mixed marriages (13:1-3,23-29) and neglecting the Sabbath (13:15-22). His swift, firm action was designed to re-establish the distinctiveness of God's people, crucial to their future survival.

God's justice

True faith, the Bible says, will always overflow into social justice and compassion (eg Jeremiah 22:2-3; Amos 5:21-24). Nehemiah understood this, and so was quick to act when the poor were being abused by the rich (5:1-13), setting a personal example of simple living (5:14-19). Jesus said that it was impossible to love God without loving those in need (eg Luke 10:25-37).

God's Law

As in Ezra, God's Law has a central place in Nehemiah. Having completed his task of getting the wall and gates rebuilt, Nehemiah gave way to Ezra for him to bring God's Law to God's people. An initial morning's reading from the Law (8:1-12) turned into a week-long reading (8:13-18). But just hearing the word of God isn't enough; it's important that people understand it, which is why the Levites were involved in "making it clear and giving the meaning so that the people could understand what was being read" (8:8). This central place of God's Law was crucial to establishing and maintaining the identity of the people of God.

RELEVANCE FOR TODAY – NEHEMIAH

The importance of being prayerful
Nehemiah was clearly a man of prayer, knowing both how to spend lengthy times of prayer (1:4) and how to send up "arrow prayers" in moments of need (2:4; 6:9). Both are needed if we are truly to keep dependent on God and not ourselves or our own abilities.

> " *Come, let us rebuild the wall of Jerusalem, and we will no longer be in disgrace."*
>
> NEHEMIAH 2:17

The importance of being ready
Between Nehemiah praying (1:4) and God answering his prayer (2:1), four months passed. God doesn't always answer our prayers immediately so it is important to be ready at the time when he does.

The importance of good administration
Some people seem to think that it isn't spiritual to prepare or plan, but Nehemiah wouldn't have agreed. He prepared by making a secret night-time survey of the wall (2:12) which enabled him to win over the leaders the next day (2:17-18). He then organised the workforce, with everyone working on a section of the wall near their home to ensure the work was done well (chapter 3). With the work completed, he then made careful listings of people and things. Good administration does not need to quench the Spirit; indeed good administration is a gift of the Holy Spirit (1 Corinthians 12:28).

The importance of team work
Nehemiah was not a "one-man ministry". He knew the importance of getting everyone involved and making them feel part of the team. He did this by carefully assigning people to work together on areas of the wall near their home. Note the recurrence of the phrase "next to him/them" in chapter 3 (3:7,17,18,19,20,21,22,23,24,25,27,29,30,31). "Team" ensures that "Together Everyone Achieves More". (See also 1 Corinthians 12.)

The importance of clear teaching
Ezra was keen that people should not only hear God's word but also understand it. He involved the Levites in instructing the people in the word and in "making it clear and giving the meaning so that the people could understand what was being read" (8:8). "Making it clear" can also mean "translating it", probably from classical Hebrew into the local language. This and the teaching almost certainly happened in small groups around the temple courtyard. The true measure of teaching is not how well teachers feel they have taught but how well the listeners have learnt.

Esther
THE POWER BEHIND THE THRONE

OVERVIEW

While some Jews went home after the exile, others chose to stay in Persia where they had established new lives. Esther tells how a Jewish orphan there became Queen of Persia and, through her position, foiled a plot to exterminate the Jews.

SUMMARY

A new queen

When King Xerxes' wife refused to be displayed as royal treasure (1:1-12), he deposed her, to teach both her and all wives a lesson (1:13-22). Esther, a Jewish orphan, was chosen to replace her (2:1-18), though her uncle Mordecai told her not to reveal her Jewish nationality (2:10,19-20). She established her new position as queen by passing on Mordecai's warning concerning an assassination plot (2:21-23).

A new problem

Four years later, Haman became chief courtier, but Mordecai refused to bow down to him (3:1-4). Furious, Haman decided to exact revenge by destroying not just him but all Jews (3:6) and persuaded the king to issue a decree for their extermination (3:7-15). Mordecai appealed for Esther's intervention (4:1-14), saying that perhaps this was the very reason God had made her Queen (4:14).

A new deliverance

Esther organised a banquet for Haman and the king (5:1-8). Haman's delight that he was honoured in this way was spoilt when he saw Mordecai at the king's gate. So Haman built a gallows for Mordecai's execution (5:9-14). That night the king couldn't sleep and sent for the royal records and discovered he had never rewarded Mordecai for saving his life (6:1-3). The king asked Haman what should be done for a man he wanted to honour and,

thinking it was for himself, Haman suggested a procession (6:4-9). He was devastated to find it was for Mordecai (6:10-14). That evening at the banquet, Esther explained what Haman had planned against her people, the Jews (7:1-6). The king was angry, and even angrier when he thought Haman was molesting her. He ordered Haman's execution on the very gallows built for Mordecai (7:7-10). Haman's job was given to Mordecai who immediately issued a law allowing Jews to defend themselves (8:1-17). Since Persian laws couldn't be repealed, the earlier decree permitting their extermination still stood; but with permission to defend themselves, they took this opportunity to deal with their enemies (9:1-17).

A new remembrance

The Festival of Purim was instituted to remember this example of deliverance (9:18-32). Mordecai himself would be remembered as a Jew who served the secular authorities but who through it had "worked for the good of his people" (10:3).

Author

Unknown, though clearly someone who understood both Judaism and life at the Persian court.

Date

Shortly after the events narrated, around 460 BC.

OUTLINE – ESTHER

A new queen
1:1-22 Queen Vashti is deposed by King Xerxes

2:1-18 Esther finds favour with the king and is made queen

2:19-23 Esther's uncle Mordecai uncovers a conspiracy to kill the king

A new problem
3:1-15 Haman plots to destroy Mordecai and all the Jews

4:1-17 Esther agrees to help Mordecai stop Haman's plot

A new deliverance
5:1-8 Esther provides a banquet for the king and Haman

5:9-14 Haman plans to hang Mordecai the next morning

6:1-14 In the night, the king hears about Mordecai's loyalty and decides to honour Mordecai

7:1-10 Esther uncovers Haman's plot, and Haman is hanged on the gallows he had built for Mordecai

8:1-17 The king reverses Haman's plot and gives the Jews freedom to defend themselves

9:1-17 The Jews are victorious over their enemies

A new remembrance
9:18-32 Mordecai institutes the Festival of Purim

10:1-3 Mordecai becomes great in the royal court

King Xerxes of Persia ruled over his kingdom from the twin capitals of Susa and Persepolis. He built the Gate of All Nations in Persepolis as the grand entrance to the city

God's presence

While God is never mentioned in Esther, it is clear that he is at work on every page. His apparent absence is the author's technique for showing that God is in control of life – everything in life – even when it isn't obvious. For example, the "coincidences" in chapter 6: the king not being able to sleep, his requesting the court records to read, his discovering what Mordecai had done for him, Haman's entering the court – all this speaks of a God at work at just the right moment.

God's people

Archaeological discoveries show that Jews were still in Persia long after the exile. It is estimated that only 50,000 returned to Judah, a handful compared to those who left. Many stayed where they were because they had settled into a new life, while others moved to other parts of Persia. This dispersion (the "Diaspora") helped the rapid spread of Judaism and, ultimately, of Christianity too, since Christian missionaries often began their evangelism at the synagogues.

God's protection

Haman's edict was the final attempt in the Old Testament period to exterminate the Jews. Haman was an Agagite (3:1), meaning he was probably descended from Agag, King of the Amalekites. This would explain his intense hatred of Jews, since the Amalekites had been Israel's traditional enemy ever since the exodus (Exodus 17:8-16; Deuteronomy 25:17-19). Haman clearly saw this as his moment to "get even", but the God who neither slumbers nor sleeps (Psalm 121:3-4) had his watchful eye on his people to protect them. God's complete reversal of this situation for his people is still celebrated by Jews today in the Festival of Purim, as commanded in this story (9:23-32). In this joyful festival, the story of Esther is read, people dress up in costumes representing the key people in the story, and a celebratory meal is enjoyed together.

God's parallels

The Bible contains a number of remarkable parallels, as God repeats things he has done in the past. The author of Esther seems to have noticed the parallels between Esther and Joseph (Genesis chapters 37–50), parallels reflected in both the language used and the details given. For example, both stories are set in foreign royal courts and both have heroes who rise to a significant position within it which God was then able to use for the deliverance of his people.

Jews celebrate the feast of Purim each year in honour of Queen Esther. Children dress up and special food is prepared

Aligning your life

God wants us to line up our lives completely with him and his purposes, even if that seems risky. Both Mordecai and Esther were prepared to stand and be counted for God, and God honoured them both. Jesus himself underlined this principle (eg Matthew 10:26-33).

Acknowledging your rulers

Esther, like Joseph and Daniel, acknowledged the authority of her ruler, because that was where God had placed her. It can't have been easy because women in the Persian court were merely royal playthings, but she trusted Mordecai's counsel that God had brought her here for a greater purpose (4:14-16). Before the exile Jeremiah urged the Jews to seek the good of the nation they were being taken into because if it prospered, they too would prosper (Jeremiah 29:4-7). Paul urged Christians to submit to secular authorities, support them, pay taxes and pray for them (Romans 13:1-7; 1 Timothy 2:1-4; Titus 3:1).

Appreciating your workplace

Joseph's gifts of administration and dream-interpretation were developed in Egypt; Moses' gift of leadership was learnt in Pharaoh's palace; Daniel's prophesying grew in the service of Babylon; Nehemiah's servant-heart was learnt in Persia – all underlining that God's training of us happens as much in the secular sphere as among God's people. If Esther had despised her position and tried to escape it, it is highly likely the Jews would have been almost exterminated.

Accepting your delays

Most of us hate delays, wanting to rush in and get things done now, but Esther learned how to wait for God's moment. She didn't tell the king immediately she was Jewish (2:10); she didn't rush to tell him of Haman's plan but called people to prayer (4:15-16); when he asked what he could give her, she didn't tell him straight away (5:3-4). She knew that "there is a time for everything, and a season for every activity under heaven" (Ecclesiastes 3:1). Waiting and delays are hard, but they are always worth it, bringing us in line with "the God who acts on behalf of those who wait for him" (Isaiah 64:4).

> " *The tables were turned and the Jews got the upper hand over those who hated them.*"
>
> ESTHER 9:1

Affirming your joy

Our author loved feasting, there being ten banquets in Esther (1:3-4; 1:5-8; 1:9; 2:18; 3:15; 5:1-8; 7:1-10; 8:17; 9:17; 9:18-32). In fact, every key point happens at banquets – probably to underline the importance of Purim, one of Judaism's most joyful holidays. Jesus himself was not afraid to express his joy in life through feasting (eg Matthew 9:10-13; John 2:1-11), despite the Pharisees' objections (eg Matthew 9:14-15). Jesus knew how to feast, just as he knew how to fast.

Job
DEALING WITH DISASTER

OVERVIEW

When Job's life fell apart, he dared to question God. Job's suffering ultimately leads him to a deeper and first hand understanding of God (42:5). This enables him to accept his period of suffering rather than to be obsessed by trying to understand the reasons for it.

SUMMARY

The book of Job begins with two scenes. The first is on earth: Job is a godly man who has a large family and many possessions (1:1-5). The second is in heaven: Satan talks to God about Job, and suggests that Job only follows God because life is going well for him (1:6-11). God allows Satan to test Job (1:12) by taking away all his possessions and his children (1:13-19). However, Job remains faithful to God (1:20-22). Satan then tries to test Job's trust in God by giving him a painful skin disease (2:1-8).

Job still did not lose faith in God (2:9-10), but tries to understand what has happened to him (3:1-26). Much of the book is in the form of a conversation with his friends (2:11-13; 32:1-5). Eliphaz, Bildad and Zophar try to convince Job that he is suffering as a result of some secret wickedness (eg 8:1-22; 11:1-20; 15:1-35; 22:1-30). Job should accept his suffering as the discipline of God (eg 4:1–5:27). However, Job maintains his innocence and accuses God of bringing suffering on him unjustly (eg 6:1–7:21; 9:1–10:22; 23:1–24:25).

A fourth friend, Elihu, rebukes Job and the other friends (32:1-5). For Elihu, Job's suffering is a warning, to keep Job close to God, and so Job should not have complained (32:6–35:16).

Finally, God speaks (38:1). He overwhelms Job with his ability to create and sustain the world, and asks Job a series of unanswerable questions to show that his wisdom and power are beyond human understanding (38:2–41:34).

These questions leave Job with nothing to say (40:3-5). But after God has finished speaking, Job reaffirms his complete trust in God (42:1-4). Eliphaz, Bildad and Zophar are rebuked by God for their unwise counsel (42:7-9). In the final scene, God blesses Job with another large family, great wealth and a long life (42:10-17).

Author
An Israelite, but otherwise unknown.

Date
The date when Job was written down is unknown – probably between 7th and 2nd centuries BC, though the story itself is much older.

Job is set a long time ago, perhaps in the age of the patriarchs of Genesis. Its story, however, is relevant for everyone who struggles with seemingly unjust suffering.

OUTLINE – JOB

Introduction
1:1-5 Job's godly life
1:6–2:10 Satan's plan to test Job
2:11-13 Job's three friends
3:1-26 Job's lament for his situation

Job's conversation with his three friends
4:1–5:27 Eliphaz: if Job is innocent, suffering will not last long
6:1–7:21 Job protests his innocence and asks God to leave him alone
8:1-22 Bildad: God will restore Job if he is innocent
9:1–10:22 Job complains that God has been unjust
11:1-20 Zophar: Job is suffering because of some secret sin
12:1–14:22 Job wants to speak with God to declare his innocence
15:1-35 Eliphaz: Job must not pretend to be innocent
16:1–17:16 Job thinks he will die without being proved righteous
18:1-21 Bildad: the wicked will be destroyed
19:1-29 Job laments that everyone has turned against him
20:1-29 Zophar: destruction will come to the wicked
21:1-34 Job complains that the wicked do well while the righteous suffer
22:1-30 Eliphaz: Job has been wicked
23:1–24:25 Job complains that he cannot find God to complain to him
25:1-6 Bildad: it is impossible for humans to be righteous before God
26:1-14 Job dismisses his friends' advice: God's ways remain hidden
27:1–31:40 Job sums up his situation

Elihu's speeches
32:1-5 Elihu is introduced
32:6–33:33 Elihu: suffering is a warning
34:1-37 Elihu: God is not unjust, as Job says
35:1-16 Elihu: Job should not have complained to God
36:1–37:24 Elihu: God is powerful and wise, beyond human understanding

God's response
38:1–40:2 God's first speech: God's great power and wisdom
40:3-5 Job cannot give a reply
40:6–41:34 God's second speech: God's great power and wisdom

Conclusion
42:1-6 Job's repentance and faith
42:7-9 Job's friends are rebuked
42:10-17 Job is blessed by God

Understanding God's justice

Like other wisdom literature in the Bible (such as Proverbs, Ecclesiastes, and James), the book of Job is interested in reflections on the right way to live in "the fear of the Lord" (wisdom). Job's friends express the standard understanding of God's justice: God punishes the wicked but rewards the righteous (eg 4:7-9; 8:3,20; 20:1-29). Job's suffering, however, causes him to question this understanding. Job is convinced that he is innocent of any wrongdoing (see 31:1-40) and so it appears that God is bringing disaster to the godly while letting the wicked prosper (eg 10:2-3; 12:4). Job cries out in complaint to God that God is being unjust: God is treating the righteous Job as if he were wicked (9:22). Job wishes he could confront God and present his complaint in person (13:22-27; 23:1–24:12).

In the end, God confronts Job and declares that he remains just (40:8). Although God does not explain to Job why he has been suffering, Job accepts God's response and confesses that he should not have spoken about God's ways when he did not know them (42:1-6). The standard view of God's justice remains: God rewards Job for his faithfulness (42:10-17). However, the book of Job has shown that understanding God's justice is not straightforward. Suffering and wickedness, and blessing and righteousness are not always automatically linked.

The mystery of suffering

Despite his righteous life, Job experiences great suffering: he loses all his possessions (1:13-17), his children are killed (1:18-19) and he is struck down with a painful skin disease (2:7-8). As a result of this, Job wishes he had never been born (3:1-19; 10:18-19) and he experiences the darkness of depression (eg 3:20-26; 6:1-3), feeling that he has been rejected by both God (6:4; 16:7-14; 19:7-12) and his friends (6:14-23; 19:13-22). Job's friends presume that Job must have sinned in order to bring this suffering upon himself as the discipline of God (eg 22:4-11). However, Job is sure that he is right with God, and his woes are undeserved (eg 27:2-6).

When God speaks, he does not accuse Job of being an evildoer. All suffering does not come as a result of sin. But neither does God answer Job's complaint and tell him why he has suffered so much. God does not even mention that he had allowed Satan to test Job (1:6-12; 2:1-6). Suffering remains a mystery. What Job does learn, though, is that God is wiser and far more powerful than Job had ever imagined (42:2-5).

Staying faithful through suffering

Throughout his sufferings, Job was unaware of the conversation that had taken place between God and Satan (1:6-12; 2:1-7). The readers of the book, however, know that Job's terrible circumstances are the result of Satan's desire to test Job's faith (1:9-11; 2:4-5). Satan expects Job to curse God, once his possessions, family and health are taken away – and Job's wife agrees (2:9)!

Job, however, remains faithful to God throughout his troubles. Although Job does not understand why he is going through suffering, and even accuses God of some injustice in allowing him to suffer, he still declares that God is the creator of the universe (9:4-10; 10:8-12), full of wisdom (12:13; 21:22), and the only hope for the future (19:25-27). Job's faithfulness is

> " *The* LORD *gave and the* LORD *has taken away; may the name of the* LORD *be praised."*
>
> JOB 1:21

ultimately revealed by the end point he reaches: he seals his lips (40:4-5), confirms his faith, confesses his sin (42:1-6) and forgives those who have accused him of wrong (42:7-9).

The honesty of prayer

At the end of the book, God commends Job for how he has spoken of God (42:7-8). God did not agree with all that Job had said in the rest of his conversation with his friends (see eg 38:2; 40:8), but he is pleased that Job has been honest. Job did not curse God (2:10) or give up on God, but rather expressed his bewilderment at his suffering and complained that God did not seem to be listening to him (19:7).

God wants us to be honest in our relationship with him. Job teaches us that God allows himself to be questioned. He may not give the answers we expect (Job was overwhelmed by God's answer in 38:1–41:34), but our questions and complaints show that we are still holding on to our faith in him, and struggling to relate what we know of God's justice and goodness to the suffering we are experiencing.

The danger of speaking out about God's ways

In another situation, the advice of Job's friends may have been entirely appropriate. Their belief in God's justice (eg 8:2-22; 34:10-30) was admirable. However, they failed to recognise that their rigid beliefs did not apply in every situation: in this situation, Job was innocent and his suffering was simply a mystery. God rebukes Job's friends for what they had said to Job (42:7-8).

The book of Job reminds us that God's ways can never be contained by simple human formulas. Whenever we speak out about God's ways – especially in pastoral situations – we should remember that our understanding is always limited.

Psalms
THE HEARTBEAT OF FAITH

OVERVIEW

A relationship with God embraces all human emotions and experiences.
The book of Psalms is the songbook of God's people – through the Psalms they can
find words to express their hope, trust, despair, thanks, sorrow and praise to God.

SUMMARY

Psalms is a collection of 150 poems, arranged into five books.

Book 1 (Psalms 1–41) is a collection of David's psalms. It begins with an introduction to the entire collection, describing the blessing of those who delight in God rather than following evil (1). Most of the psalms in Book 1 are personal prayers for help (eg 5, 10, 22) or expressions of confidence in God (eg 3, 18, 23, 27). Some give praise to God for his greatness in the world (eg 8, 29, 33).

Book 2 (Psalms 42–72) is a compilation of psalms from different authors. They include personal prayers of praise and thanksgiving (eg 46, 47, 66), petition (eg 51, 55, 64) and devotion to God (eg 42, 62, 63).

The psalms of Book 3 (Psalms 73–89) are mainly written by Asaph, the worship leader in Jerusalem. They seem to refer mostly to the life of Israel as a nation (eg prayer for restoration in 85).

Psalms 90–106 (Book 4) give praise to God for his faithfulness to Israel, particularly around the time of the exodus from Egypt (eg 105).

The final book (Psalms 107–150) includes a meditation on God's law (119) and a small collection of songs for pilgrims on the way to Jerusalem (120–134). Although there are a few petitions (eg 102, 140), most of the psalms in this section are hymns of praise to God (eg 100, 103, 134, 144–150).

Author

The Psalms were written by a number of different authors. Around half are attributed to David, but other authors include Moses (90) and the leaders of worship at the temple in Jerusalem – the sons of Korah (eg 42; see 1 Chronicles 6:31-33) and Asaph (eg 50; see 1 Chronicles 6:39; 15:17; 16:5). The authors of other psalms remain unknown.

Date

The Psalms were written over most of the Old Testament period – from the time of Moses and the exodus from Egypt to the exile in Babylon (c. 1300–586 BC). Some Psalms might even come from the period after the exile. Most, however, were probably written after David's reign as king in Jerusalem (c.1000 BC).

The book of Psalms spans nearly the whole of Israel's history, and touches upon almost every major event from creation, the patriarchs, and the exodus to the exile. Some relate to a specific incident, which is noted in the psalm's title (eg 3, 30, 34).

OUTLINE – PSALMS

Book 1

1	The righteous and the wicked
2	The king is enthroned
3	Trust in the middle of trouble
4	Confidence in God's goodness
5	Assurance of acceptance by God
6	Prayer for healing
7	Prayer for deliverance
8	Praise of God's majesty in creation
9	Praise for God's justice
10	Lament of the oppressed
11	God is the only refuge
12	Prayer to be kept safe
13	Call for God to answer prayer
14	Reflection on foolish people
15	Reflection on the righteous person
16	Confidence in God
17	Prayer to be kept close to God
18	The great ways of God
19	The glory of God's creation and law
20	Confidence that God will save
21	The king praises God
22	Prayer for help in distress
23	Confidence in God's guidance
24	Entering God's house
25	Celebration of God's character
26	Prayer for vindication
27	Putting trust in the Lord
28	Prayer for mercy
29	God is awesome!
30	Praise to God for salvation
31	Trust in times of distress
32	Encouragement to trust in God's forgiveness
33	Praise for God's faithfulness
34	God's deliverance
35	Prayer for God's help
36	Godlessness and God's love
37	Trusting in the Lord
38	Prayer for forgiveness
39	Prayer for wisdom, help and forgiveness
40	Prayer and thanks for rescue
41	Prayer for healing

Book 2

42	Putting hope in God
43	Prayer for rescue and guidance
44	Prayer for God to come to Israel's aid
45	Praise for the king at his wedding
46	The strength of God's presence
47	Praise to God the King
48	God and his city
49	Wealth and wisdom
50	Acceptable sacrifices
51	Confession and cleansing
52	The wicked and the righteous
53	Reflection on foolish people
54	Prayer for salvation
55	Deliverance from enemies
56	Fear of enemies and God's salvation
57	God's love and faithfulness
58	The judgement of the wicked
59	Deliverance from the wicked
60	Lament over God's rejection
61	Prayer for safety, and for the king
62	Finding rest in God
63	Seeking God
64	Complaint about the wicked
65	Praise for God's creation
66	Declaration of God's power in salvation
67	Prayer for blessing
68	The great majesty of God
69	Prayer for salvation from enemies
70	Prayer for help
71	God is refuge and hope
72	Prayer for the king to rule with justice and blessing

Book 3

73	The wicked perish but the righteous are held by God
74	Lament because of enemies' success
75	Thanks for God's judgement
76	God is great and to be feared
77	Calling to God in time of need
78	The history of Israel

SONGS OF PRAISE AND THANKS

The book of Psalms is best known for its songs of praise and thanks to God, many of which are still used regularly in the worship of God's people today. The Hebrew title for this book means "praises".

KEY THEMES

Praise for who God is

Hymns of praise declare the majesty and greatness of God. There are a number of common themes:

· **God is awesome.** In many hymns of praise, the psalmist is overwhelmed by the greatness of God. God's power is able to make the earth shake (29:3-8), and he sits on the throne of the universe, surrounded by fire and thick cloud and lightning (97:2-4) – symbolising his unapproachable majesty!

· **God is creator.** The world and everything in it belong to God because he has created it all (24:1-2). The psalms of praise delight in the wonders of God's creation (104:2-26).

· **God is King.** Compared to the heavenly angels and the gods of other nations, the God of Israel is the mighty King of kings and Lord of lords (89:6-7; 135:5). God rules over the nations (47:7-9) – to him alone belongs all authority and power.

· **God is near.** The songs of praise often contrast the majestic power of God in creation with his gentle tenderness to his people. God is praised for his grace, compassion, mercy, and love (145:8-9). He is faithful and righteous (145:13,17) and is especially close to those who are in need (145:14-16,18).

Thanks for what God has done

God's people always have so much to thank God for! The songs of thanks are declarations of the mighty deeds of God:

· **The salvation of Israel.** Many psalms give thanks to God for rescuing Israel out of difficult situations. In particular, God is

> " *Shout with joy to God, all the earth!*
> *Sing the glory of his name;*
> *make his praise glorious!*"
>
> PSALM 66:1-2

thanked for bringing Israel out of Egypt at the Exodus (136:10-15) and giving them the land of promise (136:16-22).

· **Personal deliverance.** God kept safe not only the nation of Israel, but also individuals. David and his fellow Israelites could be personally thankful to God for delivering them out of many different situations: despair, danger, sickness and sin (see eg 30:1-12).

· **Faithfulness, justice and care.** God's people thank him for being faithful to them (117:2) and listening to their prayers (118:21). God especially cares for those who are helpless, such as the oppressed, the poor and the lonely (146:7-9).

RELEVANCE FOR TODAY

Joining with creation

The Psalms make it clear that humans are not alone when they give praise to God. The whole of creation – including heavenly angels and all the creatures of the earth – is already praising God for his great goodness (148:1-2,7,10). The natural world of the skies, the stars and the mountains declare God's glory (19:1; 148:3-4,8-9). Even the rivers clap their hands (98:8)!

Our praise may often seem to be very small in comparison with the greatness of God. But by our songs of thanks and praise we join with the rest of creation, both heavenly and earthly, to worship the Lord our God. Praise reminds us that we are not the only people who have been blessed by God: he has a worldwide family and an entire universe to praise him!

A celebration of praise

The Psalms give us a glimpse of the worship of the Israelites. Some psalms would have been read by a leader, others included responses for the congregation to join in (see eg 136). Many were songs to be sung (108:1). The hymns of praise mention dancing, tambourines, harps, trumpets, flutes, strings, and cymbals (149:3; 150:3-5) – this worship was joyful and enthusiastic, encouraging the whole congregation of Israel to join in praise of their God.

There are certainly times for quietness and solemnity in our worship. But the Psalms teach us to praise God with reverence and joy. We must avoid losing either aspect in our worship today: God is great and to be feared, but he is also so wonderful that we must burst out in joy!

The worthiness of God

There is always something for which we can be thankful. Even when our situation seems bleak, the Psalms teach us that we can still bring praise to God for who he is and what he has done. God never ceases to be worthy of worship (48:1).

The focus of praise should always be God. So, whatever we may feel like, it is always fitting for us to praise him (33:1). In the Psalms, praise will always be pleasant to us also (135:3; 147:1)! Our praise should be overwhelmed by the sheer awesomeness and greatness of God.

Joyful celebration, Ghana

PRAYERS TO GOD

The most common type of psalm is a prayer to God. These psalms cover the whole spectrum of human experience.

KEY THEMES

Crying out to God

Many of the Psalms are passionate cries to God from the middle of difficult and distressing circumstances. These psalms come from almost every imaginable situation – from being attacked by enemies (25:2,19) to suffering from a deadly sickness (41:8). The psalmist feels alone (31:11-12), close to death (31:10), and full of anxiety (31:9). At times, the psalmist goes through the darkness of depression. On occasion, even faith in God seems to falter, and the psalmist feels abandoned by the very God to whom the prayer is made (22:1-2).

These psalms plead for God's intervention and help, whether for help, whether in the form of protection from enemies (25:20), healing (41:4) or guidance (27:11). Some ask God to save the psalmist because of his righteous life (26:1,11) and to destroy the enemies who ridicule and attack them (35:4-8). Others simply make a complaint to God, because of evil in the world (64:1-6) or because God himself seems to be far away (22:1).

Confessing sin

Sometimes, the problem the psalmist faces is not something external, like trouble or sickness, but internal – the guilt and power of sin. Many psalms speak about Israel's rebellion against God, which has led to God's rejection of them (74:1). Others refer to the personal sins of the psalmist (6:1-7). In Psalm 51, David confesses his sin with Bathsheba (see 2 Samuel 11:2-27). In each case, the psalm recognises that sin destroys relationship with God, and so asks for God's forgiveness and cleansing (51:1-2,9-10). The psalmist prays

that God will also restore the life of Israel, after her rebellion (85:4-7).

Trusting and hoping

A common theme in the prayer psalms is the confidence that the psalmist has in God. God is a place of safety and security (18:2), who can always be trusted to be good, just, merciful and faithful (86:15-17). The Psalms express a deep longing to be with God (63:1), and constantly encourage the reader to trust and hope in him (43:5).

RELEVANCE FOR TODAY

Expressing life to God

The diversity of the prayer psalms shows that all the experiences and emotions of life can be expressed to God. The Psalms range from great joy and confidence in God (31:7) to deep despair about life (55:4-5). Some psalms even express frustration at God, complaining that he seems far away (22:1). Others speak about the desire for revenge on enemies and oppressors (eg 58:6; 137:8-9), about which we might feel uncomfortable. However, it is appropriate for God's people to call out to him whatever their situation and feelings, because he is their loving Father who cares for them. It is certainly better to direct our desire for revenge against evildoers to God in prayer, rather than to take God's justice into our own hands.

Reading the Psalms regularly can help us to express the depths of human experience in our faith and worship.

Appealing to God's faithfulness

According to the prayers of the book of Psalms, the basis for confidence that God will help in the present is his past faithfulness. The Psalms often recount scenes from the history of Israel – particularly the exodus from Egypt and entry into the Promised Land – as a way of reminding both the users of the psalm and God himself of God's mighty acts to help his people in the past (eg 44:1-4; 80:8-11). If God is to be true to himself, and to the covenant he has made, he will surely come to rescue his people in their present trouble. This gives the psalmist confidence to appeal directly to God for help (83:1-18).

The psalmist's confidence in the face of difficulty is an example for Christian prayer also. After the death and resurrection of Jesus Christ, we have even more reason to appeal to God's faithfulness and ask for his strength for our problems and weaknesses. The basis of our present help is what God has already accomplished in Jesus Christ.

Being transformed by prayer

The Psalms are difficult to categorise, because the emotions and experiences they express can change in the space of one psalm. Petition can turn into praise (compare 28:1-5 and 6-9,

> *"Hear my voice when I call, O LORD, be merciful to me and answer me. My heart says of you, 'Seek his face!' Your face, LORD, I will seek."*

PSALM 27:7-8

or 69:1-29 and 30-36), while initial confidence and thanksgiving can lead to further petition (compare 40:1-10 and 11-17). Prayer is truly a conversation with God, in which we both express our own feelings and also receive an assurance of God's faithfulness, holiness or justice. The Psalms show that prayer itself can lead to relief from trouble, or to deeper reflection on the mystery of life or to a fresh acknowledgement of our need for God's help.

PSALMS OF INSTRUCTION

Some psalms instruct the reader in the type of life that is pleasing to God. To know God's blessing, there are both things to avoid and things to do.

KEY THEMES

God's life-giving law

The book of Psalms begins with a meditation on the goodness of God's law (1:2). In fact, the division of the Psalms into five books could be a way of accompanying the five books of the law (Genesis to Deuteronomy) with five books of songs. Whether or not this is so, God's law recurs throughout the Psalms as the way to enjoy life with God (19:7-11). Psalm 119, the longest chapter in the Bible, is a long poem of delight in God's law. The law is God's eternal word (119:89) that gives direction to life (119:105,133). By obeying this law, God's people will be pure and righteous

(119:9). It is therefore very precious (119:127) and evokes the love of God's people (119:167). This picture of God's law corrects the image many people have of dry, meaningless commands.

Wisdom and purity before God

As with wisdom literature, some Psalms make a contrast between foolish and wise people. Foolish people are those who turn away from God's law and do not seek him (14:1-3; 53:1-3). Wise people, on the other hand, desire to follow God's will (1:2; 40:8) and so are righteous. God will watch over the righteous while letting the wicked go to their destruction (1:6).

> *"Direct me in the path of your commands, for there I find delight."*

PSALM 119:35

The wise person will seek to be pure before God. Wisdom shows that real purity is not ritual obedience to the letter of the law, and does not come from simply offering sacrifices (40:6). The purity God delights in is purity of the heart (51:6). This can only come as humans confess their sin to God (51:3-5) and receive God's cleansing (51:7,10). This purity is expressed by a righteous life, which is marked by honesty, integrity, mercy and kindness (15:1-5).

The Psalms show that true righteousness is a matter of the heart, and not of following the right rituals.

Warnings from Israel's history

Some psalms were written in order to pass on the history of Israel to future generations (78:1-6). This history was not simply a repetition of historical facts, but was also a warning to avoid the sins of previous generations and instead to trust in God (78:7-8; 95:7-11).

RELEVANCE FOR TODAY

Singing and learning

The book of Psalms may have been Israel's songbook, but it was also her textbook too. By memorising and reciting these songs, Israelites learned to express their relationship with God. Alongside the rest of Scripture, the Psalms have a valuable role in Christian nurture and education. Sung worship and poetry have a huge role to play in informing and shaping each new generation. The Psalms should inspire us to be creative in expressing our relationship with the eternal God, as we find new songs to praise him (96:1)!

The faith of God's people

The Psalms remind us that God's people in the Old Testament were not simply a political nation, with civic and social laws – they were also a worshipping people. The Psalms found their place in Israelite corporate liturgical life. Other parts of the Old Testament focus on the historical rise of the nation, or the specifics of laws for religious practices. The Psalms, though, are the heartbeat of God's people. They remind us that God's people in every age have a living faith: they were real

> *"Your throne, O God, will last for ever and ever; a sceptre of justice will be the sceptre of your kingdom."*

PSALM 45:6

people with real struggles, doubts, joys and hopes. This faith may not be expressed in dry history books, but it can be found in the songs, poems and prayers they write and use. The book of Psalms encourages us to appreciate and learn from the spirituality of our forefathers in the faith (78:5-8).

Learning and loving

The Psalms are about devotion – faith in and love for God that leads to an overflow of praise, or petition, or thanks, or confession. Whether a psalm was written by the great King David, or an unknown poet, its value is not in who wrote it, but in its ability to lead us to a deeper understanding of and trust in God. The Psalms teach us to love God's law (119:167), because it is pleasing (119:103).

SONGS FOR SPECIAL OCCASIONS

Some psalms were written with a particular occasion in mind, including the royal psalms and the songs of pilgrimage.

ROYAL PSALMS

Key theme

The royal psalms (eg 2, 45, 110) focus on the king of Israel. Some celebrate the enthronement of the king (2:6-7; 110:1), while another celebrates the king's wedding (45:17). The king is described as just and righteous (72:1-7); he trusts in God (21:7) and his kingdom will become great and will last for ever (72:8-11). The psalmist prays for the king to be blessed (20:9; 72:15-17).

Relevance for today

Although these psalms were originally written for David and his successors in Jerusalem, some of the statements made about the king were not fulfilled by the Old Testament kings (eg 72:17; 110:4). These words look forward to the true king and Son of God, Jesus Christ. Jesus used the words of Psalm 110 to describe his own relationship with his heavenly Father (110:1; see Matthew 22:43-45). Early Christians used quotations from the royal psalms to show that Christ was the true king promised by the Old Testament (eg see Acts 2:34-35; Hebrew 1:5,13). These psalms help us to express our worship of Christ as king of the universe.

SONGS OF PILGRIMAGE TO ZION

Key theme

Psalms 120–134 are known as the "songs of ascent". They were probably sung by faithful Israelites on their way to Jerusalem for the major religious festivals at the temple. Other psalms also speak of coming to worship at Jerusalem (eg 24:3-4; 100:4). Others declare the greatness of Jerusalem, because it is the city where Zion, the temple mount, is situated, and so for the Israelites the earthly location of God's heavenly rule (eg 87:1-6).

> " *I* rejoiced with those who said to me, 'Let us go to the house of the LORD.'"
>
> PSALM 122:1

Relevance for today

We no longer worship God in a particular location (see John 4:21,23). These psalms, however, are not just about the temple in Jerusalem, but about the seriousness in which Israelites came to worship. They wanted to prepare themselves to be in God's presence (15:1-5), and they sang songs of joy as they looked forward to being in God's house (122:1-5). We should approach worship of God with the same deep and joyful faith.

Proverbs
WISDOM FOR LIFE

OVERVIEW

How can you learn to live well in the world? Proverbs is full of practical advice to help you in all kinds of situations. Readers of Proverbs will gain insight about life if they pursue wisdom by fearing the Lord.

SUMMARY

Proverbs introduces itself as a useful instruction manual for gaining wisdom (1:1-6). After identifying the basic principle of wisdom (1:7), Proverbs continues with a long poem in which the reader is persuaded to follow the path of wisdom rather than the way of folly (1:8–9:18). Wisdom and Folly are both described as women, who invite the reader to come to them (1:20-33; 8:1–9:12; 9:13-18). The reader should go to Lady Wisdom, because wisdom is the most valuable possession you can acquire (2:1–4:27). By contrast, adultery (5:1-23; 6:20–7:27), laziness (6:1-11) and corruption (6:12-19) are to be avoided at all costs.

The rest of Proverbs (10:1–31:9) contains collections of short pieces of wisdom on a wide range of topics: wealth, work, eating and drinking, family life, conversation, education, friends, marriage, reputation, ruling a nation, generosity, charity and many other topics. Most are short, two-line couplets, which compare, contrast or highlight wise and foolish actions. There is often no discernible order between the sayings, and many repeat the same idea, but the reader is encouraged to take them all to heart in order to become wise and godly (eg 23:19,22-26). Proverbs ends with a description of a godly woman, who is worthy of great honour (31:10-31).

Author

Proverbs is mainly a collection of Solomon's wise sayings (1:1; 10:1–22:16; 25:1–29:27), but some sayings from Agur (30:1-33) and King Lemuel (31:1-31) are also included. Other sayings are simply from "the wise" (22:17–24:22; 24:23-34). It is likely they were collected together by unknown scribes (see eg 25:1).

Date

Most of the proverbs come from the time of King Solomon (c. 961–922 BC), but were probably collected at a later date – some at the time of King Hezekiah (c. 715–687 BC) and some even later after the exile.

Proverbs seems to have been written in the royal court in Jerusalem. The court would have had international contacts, so it is not surprising that some parts of Proverbs are similar to other works of wisdom in the ancient world. Proverbs, however, sets wisdom within the context of faith in Israel's God. It may have first been used to train the children of important courtiers, but its value for those in all walks of life was soon recognised outside the court.

OUTLINE – PROVERBS

1:1-6 Introduction to the book
1:7 The basic principle of wisdom

Parental advice on wisdom
1:8-33 The result of folly and wisdom
2:1-22 The benefits of being wise
3:1-20 Wisdom and God
3:21-35 Instructions on making decisions and being a good neighbour
4:1-27 The great value of wisdom
5:1-23 Warnings against adultery
6:1-19 Warnings against folly, laziness and corruption
6:20-35 More warnings against adultery
7:1-27 The seductive lure of adultery
8:1-36 The reward of finding wisdom: life
9:1-18 The choice between wisdom and folly

The collections of proverbs
10:1–22:16 The proverbs of Solomon
22:17–24:22 The sayings of the wise
24:23-34 More sayings of the wise
25:1–29:27 More proverbs of Solomon
30:1-33 The sayings of Agur
31:1-9 The sayings of King Lemuel
31:10-31 The value and greatness of a noble woman

KEY THEMES – PROVERBS

The fear of the Lord

Wisdom, knowledge and understanding begin with the fear of the Lord (1:7; 9:10). "Fear", in this statement, does not mean being frightened of God, but rather being aware that the whole of life is lived in his presence and that carefully following his ways leads to blessing. To fear God means to respect him, as a child would respect loving parents who know what is best. To live in the fear of God means to avoid sin (3:7; 14:16) and to do what is right (14:2). This is more important than great wealth (15:16).

According to Proverbs, fearing God leads to long and blessed life (10:27; 14:27; 19:23; 22:4). Those who fear God can be confident that he will keep them safe (14:26; 29:25) and should receive honour from others (31:30).

Proverbs shows the reader that wisdom can only be gained as the gift of God to those who fear him (2:1-8).

Wisdom and foolishness

Proverbs contrasts the way of wisdom (8:1–9:12) with the way of foolishness (9:13-18). The difference between these ways is not in the amount of information a person knows, but in whether or not a person is able to live well in the world. In Proverbs, foolishness is a moral problem: the foolish person rejects God's wisdom (1:7,29-30), despises

instruction (15:5), is controlled by anger (12:16; 14:16-17) and is deceitful (11:3), lazy (6:9-11), dishonest (17:23) and proud (13:10). A fool brings dishonour to their family (10:1) and harm to their friends (13:20). A fool does whatever they think is right.

A wise person, by contrast, is always willing to listen to advice (1:2-6; 4:1,10; 5:1-2; 12:15; 23:22). They will learn from the experiences of others and from observing the natural world (eg 6:6). Most of all, the wise person will trust in God's judgements rather than their own (3:5-6). This type of wise life pleases God (3:4), and leads to success and contentment (24:3-6,14).

Proverbs describes many more differences between the wise and the foolish person in order to encourage the reader to seek wisdom.

The rewards of wisdom

The proverbs act as mini parables that teach a general straightforward observation of God's character and how life works: wisdom and the fear of the Lord bring life and success, while foolishness brings death and hardship (eg 1:32-33; 8:35-36). Although the rewards of wisdom may often seem to be missing at the moment, Proverbs expresses strong faith in the just judgement of God (eg 15:3), expecting the foolish to end in disaster while the wise will enjoy God's blessing.

Faith and life

Proverbs does not make a distinction between a person's attitude toward God and their behaviour in the world. It is taken for granted that a godly person will be wise, and an ungodly person will be foolish (1:7). Proverbs assumes that faith is not just for special occasions or special places, but is to be lived out in every situation. We should not pretend that our faith is only important in church!

Wisdom in the world

Although our world may seem very different from that of Solomon and the other authors, Proverbs gives wise advice on many contemporary issues:

- **Work and wealth.** Proverbs encourages diligence and hard work (6:6-11; 10:4-5). Those who work hard should be allowed to enjoy what they have earned, while those who are unwilling to work will not stay rich (eg 10:4; 12:27). Wealth itself is not as important as what you do with it (11:4): a wise person will be generous (11:25).
- **Authority.** Proverbs expects wise people to respect authority and to receive instruction willingly (eg 13:13). When a wise person is in a position of authority, they will not abuse that position but act justly and do what is right (eg 28:2-3,16). Proverbs warns against the abuse of power.
- **Friends.** Friends are very important, and a wise person will choose their friends carefully (13:20). Wise friends will not lead one another astray.
- **Speech.** Proverbs reminds its readers to avoid malicious (11:12), angry (12:16) or deceitful (12:19) conversations. Sometimes, it may be better to say nothing at all, than to speak untruthfully or without proper thought (10:19).

Wisdom in the home

Proverbs also has much to say about the intimate relationships of family life:

- **Marriage.** Marriage is the closest of human relationships. It is therefore important that the husband or wife we choose is godly (31:10-31), so that this relationship can be blessed by God (18:22). Because of the importance of marriage, Proverbs is very concerned that its readers avoid adultery (5:1-20; 6:24-29). However appealing it may seem, it is the worst form of foolishness (7:10-27).
- **Parents and children.** Parents and children should respect each other (17:6). Parents are responsible for the wellbeing and instruction of their children (19:18; 22:6; 23:13-14), and children should receive this gladly (23:22). Other people, such as Solomon himself, also act as instructors in wisdom. Proverbs shows the importance of wise and godly teachers and mentors, who will show how to live a faithful life by their example.

" *Trust in the LORD with all your heart and lean not on your own understanding; in all your ways acknowledge him, and he will make your paths straight.*"

PROVERBS 3:5-6

Ecclesiastes
THE TENSION OF FAITH

OVERVIEW

Ecclesiastes encourages us to take a long, hard look at the world. What we find is often not very comforting: people build up wealth and wisdom, only to lose it when they die; sometimes the wicked do better than the wise and the good. There seems to be no discernible order to life; it is meaningless. Ecclesiastes helps us to face up to this reality of life.

SUMMARY

Ecclesiastes begins with a description of how the author, who is known as "Teacher" (Hebrew, *Qoheleth*) sees the world: life is meaningless, and is full of repetitive experiences (1:1-11). The Teacher had become wise through much study and learning, but his knowledge of the world only made him more certain that it is meaningless (1:12-18). He tried to find meaning in many things: pleasure (2:1-3), great building projects (2:4-6), wealth and greatness (2:7-10), and hard work (2:17-26), but he realised that all these things were worthless, because despite them he would die, just like everyone else (2:11-16).

The Teacher reflects on the seasons of life (3:1-8) and suggests that people should enjoy life because it would soon be over (3:9-22). It is pointless to strive to accumulate great wealth; it is better to be content and to enjoy what is already possessed (4:7-8; 5:10–6:12).

Although it is good to be wise and righteous (7:11-12), the Teacher notes that it often does not bring the expected reward: wicked people live long while righteous people die early (7:15; 8:14). So he encourages people simply to be obedient citizens (8:2-8), neither being overly wicked or overly righteous (7:16-17)! They should enjoy this life, because death is the end of everything (9:1-12).

Ecclesiastes ends with a series of short proverbs about wisdom (9:17–11:6), and a call to remember that God will judge all people (11:7–12:14).

Author

Qoheleth, often translated as "the Teacher". He claims to be king of Israel, with his court in Jerusalem (1:1,12). Whoever it was, this anonymous author was building upon the tradition of Solomon's wisdom.

Date

Ecclesiastes was probably compiled after Israel's exile, sometime in the 5th to 3rd centuries BC.

The first readers of Ecclesiastes were Israelites who knew the promises of God and the type of wisdom found in the book of Proverbs. Ecclesiastes reminded them that despite their faith in God, life was sometimes confusing and meaningless. Many of the Teacher's observations of life are true of every generation and culture.

OUTLINE – ECCLESIASTES

Introduction

1:1-11 The meaninglessness of life

1:12-18 The Teacher's great wisdom cannot make sense of life

Observations of the absurdity of life

2:1-23 Observations from human achievements and hard work

2:24-26 The importance of enjoying life

3:1-11 Observations from the seasons of life

3:12-13 The importance of enjoying life

3:14-21 Observations from God's judgement of all

3:22 The importance of enjoying life

4:1-16 Observations from human life

5:1-7 The danger of speaking foolishly

5:8-17 Observations about wealth

5:18-20 The importance of enjoying life

6:1-12 Observations about prosperity

7:1–8:1 Observations about wisdom

8:2-14 Observations on government and justice

8:15–9:12 Enjoy life, because the future is in God's hands

Conclusion

9:13–11:6 Be wise but acknowledge life's uncertainties

11:7–12:14 Enjoy life but remember God's judgement

Life is meaningless!

Throughout Ecclesiastes, the Teacher exclaims that life is meaningless (eg 1:2,14; 2:11,15,23,26; 4:4,7,16; 5:7; 6:2,9; 7:15; 8:14; 12:8). "Meaningless" is a translation of the Hebrew word *hebel*, which expresses the Teacher's deep confusion about life. He has looked at life "under the sun" (1:14) and realised that all the things humans busy themselves doing come to nothing in the end (2:11).

Observations of the world

The Teacher's conclusion that life is meaningless is not an irrational outburst, but the result of his careful observation of the world (1:13-14) and study of conventional wisdom (1:17). Like other wisdom literature, Ecclesiastes places great weight on human experience, but in the Teacher's case, he is unable to find a discernible order. His honest observation of life led him to note several things that seem to call the meaning of life into question:

- **The reality of death.** Death comes to everyone, whether they have been wise or foolish, wealthy or poor, wicked or godly (2:14,16; 9:2). For the Teacher, living before the knowledge of the resurrection of Christ, there is nothing beyond death – it is the end of all hope and knowledge (9:4-6). Whatever advantage a person may have enjoyed in life, whether riches or wisdom, it is all taken away by death (2:16; 5:15). When death comes, someone else will receive the riches that a person has worked hard to gain (5:18,21). For the Teacher, the finality of death means that all the effort humans put into their lives is meaningless. At death, humans are no better than animals (3:18-20).

- **The reality of human inadequacy.** Although humans are able to do great things (2:4-5), amass huge wealth (2:7-9), and gain much wisdom (1:16), their power and knowledge is limited (1:15). All humans, whatever their status in life, are subject to time and chance (9:11). Even the wisest person cannot explain the mystery of life (8:17; 11:5) or tell what the future will hold (7:14; 11:2,6). Complete wisdom, according to the Teacher, is unattainable (7:23-24), and it is impossible to understand the ways of God (3:11).

- **The reality of injustice.** Faith in Israel's God includes the belief that he will bring all people to judgement (3:17; 11:9; 12:14). However, experience shows that often the wicked enjoy success in life while the righteous suffer (7:15; 8:14). Oppressors appear to get away without judgement (4:1-2) and wicked rulers pervert justice (3:16; 5:8-9). If death is truly the end, as the Teacher thinks, then the lack of judgement in this world makes faith in God's justice meaningless.

Being honest

We might be surprised that the book of Ecclesiastes is in the Bible! Its message seems to be very different from the confident tones of faith we find in other books. The repeated statement that "everything is meaningless" (1:2; 12:8) is perhaps a little disconcerting for our faith. But that is the value of Ecclesiastes for us. It is a reminder that God allows us to be honest in our faith. We do not have to pretend that we can make complete sense of the world, when in fact our experience of it leads us to confusion. As Christians, we cannot ignore the horrors of natural disasters, terrible illnesses or intense emotional or physical suffering. Sometimes we will want to cry out with the Teacher that life is meaningless!

Living with tension

The Teacher writes as a believing Israelite. His exclamation of the absurdity of life does not come from a rejection of faith. In fact, it is because of his faith in God and God's justice, and his refusal to give that faith up (see 12:13-14), that he finds the injustice of the world so troublesome (8:13-14).

When the promises of faith and the experiences of reality contradict each other, it is tempting to resolve this tension by either denying the problems are real, or by denying God himself. The Teacher takes neither of these routes. He can speak one moment of the meaninglessness of life (3:9-10), and the next moment of the beauty of God's creation (3:11). For the Teacher, faith lives with a real tension: our experience of the world throws surprising things in our way (9:11), but God is still worthy of worship and obedience (3:14; 12:13). We must learn to live with the same tension.

Enjoying life

Throughout Ecclesiastes, the Teacher encourages his readers to enjoy their lives (2:24; 3:12-13,22; 5:18-19; 8:15; 9:7-10; 11:9). He has observed that many people spend so much of their time striving for wealth or success that they do not have time to enjoy what they have worked for before they die (eg 4:8; 6:3). Instead of this meaningless activity, the Teacher tells his readers to be content with what they have (4:6) because it comes from God (7:14). God wants us to enjoy what

> "When times are good, be happy; but when times are bad, consider: God has made the one as well as the other."
>
> ECCLESIASTES 7:14

he has given us (9:7), and our enjoyment and contentment is a gift from him (2:24-26; 3:13; 5:19).

Of course, Christians can look forward to resurrection life after death, which was not a part of the Teacher's faith. However, it is a good thing for us also to enjoy our lives now. However meaningless life may seem, we still have much to be thankful to God for.

Song of Songs
THE JOY OF LOVE

OVERVIEW

Love and romance are important aspects of all human life – but do they have a place within the life of faith? Song of Songs answers "yes", with a dramatic celebration of the romantic love between a man and a woman.

SUMMARY

Song of Songs, which means "the best song", is a dramatic poem about a developing relationship. The exact plot of the unfolding drama is a little unclear, and even the identity of the speakers is uncertain. The male character appears to be very important and wealthy, and is possibly even the king (see 1:4,12; 6:8-9; 7:5). Some scholars have seen him as a dramatic representation of Solomon (see 1:1; 3:7,9) while others think he is just a wealthy shepherd (eg 1:7). The other main character is a young Shulammite woman (6:13). There is also a chorus of friends.

The drama begins with the young woman entering the king's court in Jerusalem. She is anxious to attract the attention of the man and win his love (1:2-7). When he sees the young woman, he is immediately impressed (1:9-11).

The young woman tells her friends how amazing her lover is (2:3-7), and she is delighted when he comes to her again (2:8-11). It is now obvious that they are committed to each other (2:16). When the man is away, the young woman longs for his presence (3:1-3).

Next, the man is seen on his wedding day, dressed in all the splendour of Solomon (3:6-11). He praises the beauty of the young woman (4:1-15). They delight in their union with each other (4:16–5:1).

In the next scene, the husband apparently arrives home late, to find his wife already in bed. She delayed opening the door for him, and he leaves (5:2-6). She goes to search for him (5:7) and asks her friends to help her find her lover (5:9-16). Eventually, the couple are reunited and delight once more in each other (6:4–8:7). The book ends with a meditation on the delight of pure love (8:8-14).

Author

The book is linked to Solomon (1:1; see also 3:7,9,11; 8:12), though it was not necessarily written by him. It is likely that an unknown author was using Solomon's royal court as the setting for this dramatic poem.

This style of dramatic literature would fit well in the high society of the royal court in Jerusalem. It also makes many references to the surrounding countryside.

Date

Date of composition is unknown, but it was at least not before the reign of Solomon (mid 10th century BC), and could have been much later.

OUTLINE – SONG OF SONGS

The first scene: the table
1:1 The title
1:2-8 The young woman and the daughters of Jerusalem
1:9–2:2 The man and the young woman talk

The second scene: the spring fields
2:3-7 The young woman describes her experience
2:8-13 The man comes to meet the young woman
2:14-17 The lovers delight in each other

The third scene: the city in the night
3:1-3 The young woman's search
3:4-5 The meeting in the night

The fourth scene: the wedding
3:6-11 The entrance of the groom
4:1-15 The man's song of praise for his bride
4:16–5:1 The wedding night

The fifth scene: the young woman's bedroom
5:2-6 The young woman delays opening the door for her husband
5:7-8 She searches for him in vain
5:9-16 She describes him to the daughters of Jerusalem
6:1 The daughters of Jerusalem help in the search

The sixth scene: the garden and the road
6:2-3 The young woman and the man meet
6:4-9 The man accepts and praises his wife
6:10-12 The young woman is at the side of the man in his chariot
6:13 The couple leave the city

The seventh scene: the countryside
7:1–8:4 The lovers delight in each other
8:5-7 The strength of love
8:8-12 The purity of love
8:13-14 A final delight in each other

KEY THEMES – SONG OF SONGS

Celebrating love

The central theme of the Song of Songs is love. The colourful descriptions the book uses have caused embarrassment for some readers, who have interpreted it simply as a picture of God's love for Israel, or Christ's love for the church. However, the love that is the main theme of the book is really romantic human love, including its sexual expression.

- **Love has a rich language.** Song of Songs is full of lively descriptions of the delight lovers find in each other's bodies. Most of the imagery comes from the worlds of shepherding (eg 1:8; 4:1-2) and gardening (eg 4:12-15), and while some references may seem a little obscure today, it is obviously a very exuberant way of describing human love.

- **Love itself is passionate.** From the very beginning, the relationship described in the Song of Songs is full of passion. The young woman longs to kiss the man (1:2), and sets out to win his affection (1:7). Once he sees the young woman, he is captivated, and lavishes her with gifts (1:11). They long for each other when they are apart (2:9; 3:1) and delight in each other when they are together (eg 4:1-7).

Loving exclusively

It seems strange that this celebration of the exclusive relationship between the man and the young woman is set in the royal court and associated with Solomon. 1 Kings records that Solomon had 700 wives and 300 concubines, who between them led Solomon astray from the Lord (1 Kings 11:1-4). Here in the Song of Songs, it is noted that there are 60 wives and 80 concubines in the royal court (6:8).

In contrast to Solomon's many marriages, Song of Songs holds on to the importance of exclusive relationship. Both the man (6:8-9) and the woman (5:10) think that their lover is beyond all comparison with other people. The young woman is even better that the many wives and concubines of the royal court (6:9)! The couple say that they have given themselves to each other completely (2:16; 4:9; 6:3).

Whoever wrote Song of Songs wanted to celebrate exclusive love. Perhaps it was also a way of criticising Solomon himself, whose accumulation of wives had led him astray from God (1 Kings 11:3-4)!

Sexuality and faith

The existence of the Song of Songs as part of Scripture shows that the passion of sexual love is part of God's good creation. God himself is not mentioned in the Song of Songs, but the background for the work is the royal court in Jerusalem, and so faith in Israel's God is presumed. It is important to emphasise, particularly in today's society, that delighting in sexuality is not incompatible with Christian faith. The moral boundary for sexual activity – marriage – does not deny the goodness of intimacy, but rather affirms that it is God's gift to be enjoyed in the proper context.

Lessons in love

Although an ancient poem, the reality of human love does not change, and so Song of Songs has much to say to today's world:

· **Patience and strength.** Three times in Song of Songs, the young woman comments, "Do not arouse or awaken love until it so desires" (2:7; 3:5; 8:4). This is simple advice to be patient with the development of a loving relationship, and the advice is repeated throughout the book as the man and his beloved grow closer together. Despite the pressure of society to jump immediately into a sexual relationship, Scripture advises giving a relationship time and space to grow so that when the sexual element is added within marriage, it is fulfilling (5:1). In this way, love will grow strong, and will not fail (8:6-7).

· **Purity.** The young woman is seen as a locked garden, to which the husband has exclusive access (4:12,16). It is revealed at the end of the book that the young girl has been protected from sexual activity (8:8-9) until she can give it exclusively to her husband (8:12). This standard of purity, of course, applies to both men and women.

The love of God and Christ

While the Song of Songs is actually speaking about a human relationship, it has been understood to refer also to God's relationship with his people. It was often read at the beginning of the celebration of the Jewish Passover, as a reminder that God's covenant with Israel was not simply a matter of words and laws, but a relationship of passionate love. Christians have often seen the Song of Songs as a picture of Christ's love for the church, which is compared in the New Testament to the marriage relationship (see eg Ephesians 5:25). The richness of human love should remind us of the God who has created it – and of his great, passionate love for the world.

"*Love is as strong as death, its jealousy unyielding as the grave. It burns like blazing fire, like a mighty flame.*"

SONG OF SONGS 8:6

Isaiah
PROPHET OF SALVATION

OVERVIEW

Isaiah's comprehensive message to God's people addresses them in prosperity, exile and restoration. He brings to them messages of warning, comfort and hope in some of the deepest insights into God's character and purposes in the Old Testament, insights that proved to be foundational to New Testament thinking about Jesus and the nature of salvation.

Isaiah is the longest of the prophetic books, slightly longer than Jeremiah. It is the prophetic book most quoted in the New Testament. Its poetic language suggests deep revelation and great inspiration of the human spirit

SUMMARY

Part one (chapters 1–39)

The book falls into two parts. The first part (chapters 1–39) covers the time of four major reigns in Judah, the southern kingdom of the divided country of Israel. The opening section (chapters 1–12) includes an account of the prophet's own calling (chapter 6), probably the most dramatic of all accounts of prophetic calling (see also 1 Samuel 3, Ezekiel 1 and Jeremiah 1).

Interestingly, however, this account is preceded by five chapters that outline many of the main themes of the book: God is "the Holy One of Israel". He is deeply offended by the immoral behaviour of his people, for which there will be punishment in terms of invasion and devastation of the now prosperous land. But after punishment will come restoration and good government. The delay in giving an account of Isaiah's calling has the effect of concentrating our minds on the message and its authenticity, not on the messenger.

Isaiah's prophecies have a political dimension in warning against any sort of alliances with other countries. Instead they must trust in God alone for political as well as spiritual salvation (chapters 7–11). The

section concludes with a psalm (chapter 12).

The second section of the first part is a series of oracles against neighbouring countries (chapters 13–24). This is a common prophetic practice. Parallels can be found, for example, in Jeremiah 46–51 and Ezekiel 25–32. God is Lord of the whole earth and his people's destiny is not separate from other nations, though different from theirs. In Isaiah's day, the dominant threat to Judah's security was Assyria (14:24-27); its false security was Egypt (19:1–20:6).

But the strongest woes and denunciations seem to be against Babylon (13:1–14:23; 21:1-10), which in Isaiah's time was for some periods an independent but small state (see chapter 39). Only in the following century did Babylon rise to be a devastating force enabling it to destroy Jerusalem. The taunting language used against its pride (14:12-23) reminds us of Ezekiel's language against Tyre (Ezekiel 28).

In chapter 22, Isaiah turns the denunciations back on his home city, Jerusalem. In the final chapter of the section, there is a concluding apocalyptic description of worldwide destruction, and the restoration of God's kingly rule from Jerusalem.

The third section (chapters 25–35)

elaborates on the preceding themes. Chapters 25–26 form an apocalyptic bridge with the preceding section. The fourth section is a historical one, narrating three interventions into King Hezekiah's life (chapters 36–39), including a threat to Jerusalem by the Assyrians. Some of this material also occurs in 2 Kings 18:17–20:19.

Part two (chapters 40–66)
The second part of the book can be further divided into two sections. The first section (chapters 40–55) deals with Judah in exile in Babylon and the promise of restoration, not in terms of a great king or future leader, but in terms of Israel as servant. This section includes the famous servant songs that are often related to the ministry of Jesus Christ. The Persian king, Cyrus, is mentioned as deliverer, but only as a minor player in the drama of salvation.

The final section (chapters 56–66) paints a picture of universal deliverance and justice. At the same time it acknowledges that return from exile had not or would not mean perfect spirituality. The same old faults are all too likely to recur. In fact, the final chapter parallels the opening chapter in placing the hope of a new rule of God alongside the destruction on those who had rebelled. We are reminded that holiness is both glory and fire.

Author
Isaiah is mentioned in 2 Kings 19:2-7,20-34 and 20:1-19. These chapters, together with Isaiah 6 and 36–39, give us a picture of a prophet in the mainstream of national life. This has led some scholars to think he was well-born, unlike his village contemporary, Micah. He was married, his wife possibly having a prophetic ministry in her own right. They had two boys, both symbolically named.

The shift of emphasis between the first and second parts has led to the supposition that Isaiah only wrote the first part, and the second part was written by someone living in the exile some 150 years later. Isaiah is not mentioned by name in the second part. However, if this is the case, then someone had obviously immersed himself in the writings of his predecessor. While some of the language and ideas are different, much is similar.

Date
Isaiah lived through the reigns of Uzziah (or Azariah, 792–740 BC), Jotham (740–735 BC), Ahaz (735–715 BC), and Hezekiah (715–687 BC). This is the period of Assyrian domination. For example, Sennacherib reigned 705–681 BC. The northern kingdom fell to the Assyrians in 722 BC and Sennacherib besieged Jerusalem in 701 BC. It is supposed Isaiah died during the reign of Manasseh (687–642 BC). The second part of the book covers the period of the exile in Babylon (from 598 BC), ending when the Persian King Cyrus allowed the Jews to return to Jerusalem in 538 BC after his conquest of Babylon.

Tile frieze of the Babylonian god Marduk from the Ishtar Gate, Babylon. The city was denounced by Isaiah for its idolatry and pride

OUTLINE – ISAIAH

KEY THEMES – ISAIAH

The Holy One of Israel

This phrase is distinctive to the book of Isaiah. It forms one of the unifying key phrases of the prophecy, being found in every part (eg 1:4; 5:19,24; 8:13; 10:17,20; 12:6; 17:7; 37:23; 47:4; 57:15; 60:9,14). Most of the prophetic books speak of God's holiness, but it is Isaiah who perhaps has the deepest sense of it. For modern people, it is a much harder concept to understand than, say, the New Testament teaching "God is love" and therefore close attention has to be paid to this book in order to understand what the phrase means.

Isaiah's great vision (6:1-7) is a good starting place. The otherness and transcendence of God is stressed, as it is in 40:12-14. His ways are not our ways (55:8-9), as Job 38 also reminds us. However, that does not prevent him from forming the closest relationships with humans, either as individuals or as a chosen nation.

But holiness is more than otherness: it is also purity and freedom from all sin and imperfection. That is why holiness is typically associated with God's anger, since that is part of the divine reaction to deliberate sin, especially pride, rebellion and false religion. False religion lowers standards, covers over sin too easily (1:13-17). However, God's anger does not prevent him from approaching sinful people (1:18-20). Isaiah 53 in fact is a startling revelation of the lengths God will go to deal with people's sinful behaviour or "transgressions".

Holiness is also closely linked to God's sovereignty, in that there is simply "no other god" (43:10; 45:5-6; 46:9). This is the offence of idolatry, which claims that there are other gods (40:18-20). Chapter 40 stresses God's unique creative power and his rule of the cosmos, including the nations of the earth. But it finishes on a profoundly personal note of promise, that his greatness does not prevent his appreciation of human weakness nor his desire to provide help for it (40:28-31).

The Holy City

The concept of holiness is applied to an earthly city, variously called Jerusalem or Zion, the capital of Israel. In the book, we see it actually besieged and then miraculously saved (chapters 36–37). In fact, this becomes a metaphor for the spiritual deliverance from earthly power and pride that God desires. He wants his kingdom to have an earthly basis, but one that shares in his own nature of holiness. This theme again runs through the book (eg 1:26; 2:3; 4:3; 25:6; 52:8; 54:11; 60).

As such, the holy city can become a spiritual centre for the whole world. It is a provision for all who seek God, not just the Jewish people. Its approaches are spoken of as "the way of holiness" (35:8) which needs preparation (42:16), the turning of spiritual darkness into light. This holy city is the place where the remnant will return from exile (37:32; 51:11). In the New Testament, the book of Revelation speaks of this as the "new Jerusalem" and sees it as the new paradise of God (Revelation 21–22).

The Servant

The second part of Isaiah contains a group of "Servant Songs", the most famous of which is 52:13–53:12, which became central to early Christian formulations of who Jesus Christ was and how his death had been redemptive.

These songs represent one of the most

significant shifts between the two parts of the book. In the first part, there are prophecies of a king from the line of David who will become God's chosen leader or *Messiah* (meaning, literally, "the anointed one") (eg 9:1-7; 11). In the second part, specifically chapters 40–55, these are replaced by this figure of the servant. At first, the servant appears to be the whole nation (41:8-9; 43:1-13), but then becomes an individual (42:1), whose mission is to bring justice and understanding (42:4,7), "release from the dungeon". In 49:5-6 and 50:10 he appears to be the prophet himself, as representative of the nation, with a mission of being "a light for the Gentiles".

However, in the last servant song, 52:13–53:12, he is portrayed as an individual who can bring actual salvation "for the transgression of my people". His suffering leads to an actual death, which becomes a substitute death, allowing comparison with animal sacrifices laid down in the Mosaic rituals of guilt offerings (53:10). The notion of justification is introduced, which became so important for Paul in the New Testament (see Romans 6), as he sees Christ as the embodiment of the suffering servant.

Redemption and salvation

Though other prophets speak of redemption, ransoming and salvation, it is Isaiah who speaks most coherently and fully on these. 43:1-28 is perhaps one of the most poetic expressions of this. The simplest notion is that of deliverance from punishment, as in conquest, captivity and exile. However, the book extends the notion from return from exile to a holy city and fertile land, with a restored covenant with God, to an inner state of salvation. In this inner state there is righteous living, joy (35:10; 52:8-9), peace (57:2), and justice (56:1). God himself takes on the title "Saviour" (43:3; 60:16) and "Redeemer" (43:1,14; 44:6), and the terms are human and personal, not legal (46:3-4; 61:10). This is a personal, loving act of God (54:5,8).

A new thing

Like the Psalms, Isaiah speaks to us about a whole range of human experience of God as well as a whole range of God's attributes. Our spiritual experiences often find themselves defined by the images and expressions to be found among the many prophecies of the book. This is its relevance for today.

One such experience is that of the new birth of salvation and redemption. Isaiah is emphatic in its sense that God wants to do "a new thing" (43:19, compare 42:9; 48:6). The first part of the book traces the failure of God's people, despite threats of punishment and promises for reform. The exile becomes a sort of death experience, out of which new hope, a new thing arises. In this new thing, God wants to draw a line under the past. This is expressed in various ways. For example, 43:25 talks of "I am he who blots out your transgressions ... and remembers your sins no more." The only thing we need to remember is that "I am God, and there is no other" (46:9). Another way is in terms of healing and peace (57:18-19); another the sense of being born in the new holy city, as part of a redeemed citizenship (66:7-11).

A new spirit

But to be able to live in the light of this we need a new spirit within us. Isaiah prefigures New Testament teaching on the Holy Spirit in various passages. 44:3 promises the outpouring of "my Spirit on your offspring" and the new covenant is defined in terms of the Spirit being on us in 59:21 (see also 32:15). Both the new Davidic leader and "the servant" are promised the Spirit (11:1-2; 42:1), the former passage giving a formulation of the Holy Spirit which is still used today as the "sevenfold Spirit". The prophet himself senses the Spirit on him to preach the message of deliverance and comfort (61:1-2), quoted by Jesus in Luke 4:18. Ezekiel follows Isaiah in promising a new spirit (Ezekiel 11:19; 18:31; 36:26).

Living waters

In the Gospels, the Holy Spirit is likened to springs of running waters (John 4:10-14; 7:38-39). The imagery comes largely from Isaiah, "I will pour water on the thirsty land" (44:3). Water imagery is central to all the Old Testament prophets: the land was typically fertile but arid. Water would therefore bring prosperity and fruitfulness, but the failure of rains or irrigation would mean desert-like conditions.

Many people have described times of their life as deserts: a lack of fruitfulness, joy, life even. Conversely, many have described their experience of the Holy Spirit in their lives as being showered, baptised, flooded – all words that refer to water (see also John 7:37-39).

Isaiah speaks to all these conditions. In 55:1-3, the prophet invites the thirsty to drink of "the waters", which are then linked to "the everlasting covenant" and "my faithful love promised to David". 35:1-7; 41:18-19 and 44:3-4 describe a new fertility in the desert, an image literally fulfilled in the state of Israel today, but for most people, a metaphor of emotional and spiritual renewal (32:2). 48:21 takes us back to when God led the Israelites out of Egypt and did not allow them to go thirsty. The many images of God as "the Rock" in the book have a subtext rooted in this time, when Moses struck the rock for water to gush out.

Peace

One of the water images refers to peace: "your peace would have been like a river" (48:18). Peace is a concept with which we identify readily – both as an inner state and an outer one. Isaiah talks of "the covenant of peace" (54:10). This implies not just that God will protect his people from wars, but that he is no longer at enmity with them. It is both the

" *Fear not, for I have redeemed you.*"

peace of God and peace with God that we need, and is here promised (see also 26:12). Elsewhere, the Messiah is called "Prince of Peace" (9:6-7; see also 32:16-18; 60:17). His reign will be marked by peace when swords shall become ploughshares (2:4) and wolves shall lie down with lambs (11:6; 65:25).

Deep waters

Isaiah also uses the image of water to express our experience of being overwhelmed by circumstances: that is, rivers in flood and "waters of affliction" (30:20). 43:2 describes passing "through the waters" in parallel with walking "through the fire". Both are images of testing and trial. The promise of God's presence in such circumstances is one that many Christians have held on to rather like a rescue rope or life belt. The following verses suggest not just a survival by the skin of our teeth, but a divine love that allows these experiences as "a ransom". Such verses are a small aspect of the whole theme of deliverance running through the book, expressed here as redemption, calling and summoning.

Jeremiah
THE HEART-BROKEN PROPHET

OVERVIEW

Jeremiah lived through the last days of the southern kingdom of Judah. He consistently warns of impending disaster, brought about by the nation's neglect of true religion, its turning to pagan practices and its social injustice. Its blind trust in its covenant relationship with God is a delusion, as are its false prophets with their messages of peace. But no one listens to the prophet. He is heartbroken and argues with God about his seemingly impossible mission to make people listen. He also believes the Babylonians are God's instrument of punishment and advises cooperation with them. This is seen as treasonable, and he is thrown into prison, in danger of his life. His last warning is not to trust Egypt. Ironically, this is where he ends up, forced there after Jerusalem's destruction.

SUMMARY

Jeremiah's ministry

Jeremiah's ministry extended through the reigns of five kings, in a constantly deteriorating spiritual and political situation. However, the many prophecies contained in the book are not arranged in any chronological order. They were first given orally; but at some point, Jeremiah felt the need to write them down with the help of Baruch his assistant, and show them to the king (chapter 36). The king cynically took each page as it was read, cut it up with a knife and threw the fragments into the fire. It took Jeremiah and Baruch a year to rewrite them, adding a number of other prophecies at the same time. Then they had to flee the fall of Jerusalem, the written scrolls ending up in Egypt or Babylon. The wonder is that so much has survived, not that it appears chaotically arranged!

Included in the book are a series of denunciations against surrounding nations (chapters 46–51), and a historical account of the last days of Jerusalem (chapters 34–45; 52), the last chapter containing the same material as 2 Kings 25 and 2 Chronicles 36.

These two topics form discreet sections in the latter part of the book.

Jeremiah's pleadings to a deaf city

The first ten chapters introduce some of the book's central themes. Chapter 1 is an account of Jeremiah's young calling, and the signs to confirm it, similar to the callings of Isaiah and Ezekiel. The remaining nine chapters speak against the fashionable syncretistic religion. It is not that the people had abandoned their traditional worship of God; they had added all sorts of pagan elements, the worst feature of which was child sacrifice (2:1–3:6; 7:16–8:17).

The people had a false sense of security from the presence of Solomon's temple in Jerusalem. It was seen as where God literally dwelt and while it was there, they felt safe (7:1-15). But there was no moral sense to this, and social injustice ran rife (5:1-31; 6:13-21; 9:3-26). In some prophecies, Jeremiah suggests there was still time to repent, return to true worship and restore justice (3:11–4:4; 5:18). In this, Jeremiah is similar to many of his predecessors, Amos, Hosea, Isaiah and Micah, for example. But if they did not repent, then God had appointed the

DOMINANT POWERS OF BIBLE TIMES

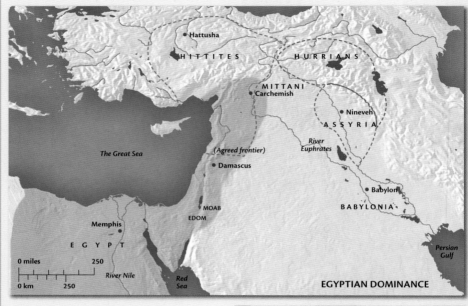

EGYPTIAN DOMINANCE

c. 3000–1200 BC
Egypt had dominated since around 3000 BC and, with its extensive trade interests, was at its height at this period. Other great nations were attempting to expand their borders. Later the decline of Egypt and the absence of one supreme power enabled the people of Israel to settle in Canaan.

c. 1350–650 BC
The Assyrians arose as the leading power from c. 1350 BC until the capture of Nineveh by King Nabopolassar of Babylon in 612 BC. Despite their aggression towards other nations, they built great cities, palaces and temples. Literature too played a significant part in Assyrian life.

THE ASSYRIANS

c. 600 BC
By around 1850 BC Babylonia was one of the earliest centres of civilisation in the Middle East and had developed sophisticated skills like writing and irrigation. After 612 BC the empire expanded to take control of the area from the Persian Gulf to the border with Egypt. The reign of supreme power was relatively short-lived, with Cyrus II of Persia taking Babylon in 539 BC.

THE BABYLONIANS

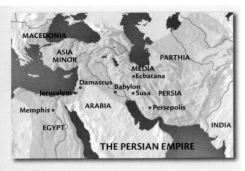

539–333 BC
Cyrus the Great established Persian domination west into Babylonia, Egypt and Asia Minor, expanding into Macedonia, and east to India, using wise administration and rule to control the vast area. Magnificent buildings and skilled craftsmanship are testament to the Persian love of beauty and refinement. Alexander the Great of Macedonia conquered the empire in 333 BC.

333–167 BC
Alexander the Great was a brilliant general, but he was also keen to unify the peoples he ruled by imposing Greek culture and ideals on them. In twelve years he changed the face of the whole Middle East. After his death the empire was divided into four regions which eventually fought against themselves, bringing about their own downfall to Rome.

167 BC–AD 475
Rome's power increased steadily, gradually expanding from Italy into surrounding nations, including north Africa, and establishing a provincial system to control its interests. The prevailing Greek culture was absorbed into the Roman way of life. Soon the whole of the Mediterranean area was under Roman rule.

Babylonians, the enemy from the north, to wipe Jerusalem from the map and disperse its people (4:5-31; 6:1-12,22-30).

This message was really heartbreaking for him to give, and in this he reflected God's heart (4:9; 8:18–9:2; 10:19-25). Other prophets, especially Hosea, had spoken similarly. But Jeremiah allows us to see his own emotions much more: we sense the drama and the anguish of his own soul.

Jeremiah's inner conflict

The second group of chapters (chapters 11–20) shows this inner conflict even more, where growing outer conflict parallels it. The section has five utterances beginning "The word of the LORD came to me" or something similar (11–12; 13; 14–15; 16–17; 18–20). The themes of the first section are repeated, though in chapters 11–12, Jeremiah introduces specific reference to the covenant relationship between God and his people. We also hear about the plot against Jeremiah by his fellow-villagers and Jeremiah's complaint to God about them. This was the first of many attacks on the prophet. Another occurs in 20:1-18, where one of the priests attacked Jeremiah physically.

We also see a number of enacted prophecies, where Jeremiah was told to do some rather strange action, which was then interpreted symbolically. So here he had to bury some brand-new linen undergarments (13:1-11); take a vow of celibacy (16:1-4); go to a potter's workshop (18:1-11) and buy a jug and take it to the city gates (19:1-13).

Denunciation of faithless kings and false prophets

The third section comprises a series of denunciations against faithless kings and false prophets (chapters 21–29). Jeremiah's uncompromising message to the people, who wanted to hear only that God would save them from Nebuchadnezzar, the

Babylonian king, was that Nebuchednezzar was God's chosen instrument over all the immediate nations, and so it was useless to resist him. He also writes to those already in exile (Jerusalem was attacked twice), telling them to expect 70 years of exile. Jeremiah's condemnation of kings and the prophets who gave false messages of security is quite specific.

The promise of restoration

However, chapters 30–33 counterbalance this with promises of restoration. Though such promises are typical of the prophets, what is here remarkable is that they were made while Jeremiah was in prison and the city under siege. At one point, there was a brief respite and Jeremiah went out to buy a field, to show there would be a future life in the land (32:1-25).

The last days of Jerusalem

The prophecies against Jerusalem cease at this point, to be replaced by a historical account of its siege and fall, and the chaotic conditions after. Jeremiah was carried off against his will to Egypt, where he must have died. He had actually seen many of his prophecies come true, including the death of a number of his opponents.

Judgements against surrounding nations

A series of woes and denunciations against neighbouring states is then added (chapters 46–51), including a major one against Babylon herself. Though she had been God's instrument, she was condemned because of her pride. The final note, however, is that the Davidic kingship had survived in exile (52:31-34). A remnant had been kept safe. God's purposes with his people continued.

Author

Jeremiah was born in the village of Anathoth, where his father Hilkiah was a priest. The village lay in the territory of Benjamin, north of Jerusalem, and part of the southern kingdom of Judah. He was called to be a prophet at a young age, in the reign of the reforming king Josiah, over whose untimely death he wrote a lament (2 Chronicles 35:25).

He is often referred to as the "weeping prophet" (9:1). He is revealed as a complex character, uncompromising and consistent, realistic yet visionary, pessimistic yet hopeful of the future. He is worn down by constant opposition and rejection, and laments his calling. Yet heroically he continues at great danger to himself, suffering beatings, imprisonment and near death, finally being carried off against his will to Egypt, after having refused safe passage to Babylon. As a true prophet, he wishes to intercede for his people, but is forbidden to pray for them. As a "prophet to the nations" (1:5) he also speaks out against the surrounding nations.

Date

The book describes events from shortly before the death of King Josiah in 609 BC till several years after the fall of Jerusalem in 586 BC. Jeremiah's ministry lasted some 30 years, following Nahum's and Zephaniah's, and then contemporary with Ezekiel's and Daniel's, these two already being in exile.

In 612 BC the Babylonians defeated the Assyrians, and in 605 BC, at the battle of Carchemish, the Egyptians, though the Egyptians would make comebacks. The Egyptians replaced Josiah's son, Jehoahaz, with their own puppet king, Jehoiakim (609–598 BC). He rebelled against the Babylonians in 602 BC, but died before they could respond. His son Jehoiachin (or Jeconiah or Coniah) was seized with a large number of leading families and deported to Babylon in 598 BC (Jeremiah 52:31). The Babylonians put in Zedekiah as their puppet, but he too rebelled in 587 BC, leading to the final siege and burning of the city of Jerusalem.

OUTLINE – JEREMIAH

Jeremiah's pleadings to Israel and Judah

1:1-19 God calls Jeremiah to be a prophet

2:1–3:5 God's charge of unfaithfulness against Israel

3:6–4:2 God pleads for Israel to return to him

4:3–6:30 Judgement is coming on Judah and Jerusalem

7:1–8:3 Jeremiah condemns false worship and idolatry

8:4–9:26 Jeremiah's grief at God's judgement of the people's apostasy

10:1-25 Idol worship is futile and will lead to destruction

Jeremiah's inner and outer conflicts

11:1-17 Judah has broken the covenant with God

11:18–12:17 Jeremiah complains to God and God answers

13:1-27 The parables of the linen belt and the wine jars

14:1–15:21 Jeremiah is forbidden to pray for Judah

16:1–17:27 The coming exile because of the people's disobedience

18:1–19:14 Two parables from the potter

20:1-18 Jeremiah is humiliated and complains to God

Denunciation of faithless kings and false prophets

21:1–22:30 God's message of judgement for Judah's kings

23:1-40 God's righteous ruler and the destruction of false prophets

24:1-10 The parable of the good and bad figs

25:1-38 Judah's captivity will last for 70 years and the other nations will also face judgement

26:1–28:17 Jeremiah's dramatic messages

29:1-32 Jeremiah's letter to the exiles

The promise of restoration

30:1–31:40 God will bring restoration and a new covenant

32:1-44 Jeremiah buys a field as a sign of hope

33:1-26 God's messages of promise while Jeremiah is in prison

The last days of Jerusalem

34:1–35:19 The people of Judah do not keep their word, while the Recabites remain faithful to their word

36:1-32 King Jehoiakim burns the scroll of Jeremiah's prophecies

37:1–38:28 Jeremiah is imprisoned but still brings God's message to King Zedekiah

39:1-18 The fall of Jerusalem to the Babylonians

40:1–41:15 Chaos in Judah after the Babylonians leave

41:16–43:13 Jeremiah is taken to Egypt against his advice

44:1-30 Those who fled to Egypt will not escape the Babylonians

45:1-5 A message for Baruch, Jeremiah's assistant

Judgement against surrounding nations

46:1-28 A message of judgement against Egypt

47:1-7 A message of judgement against Philistia

48:1–49:22 Messages of judgement against Moab, Ammon and Edom

49:23-39 Messages of judgement against Damascus, Kedar and Hazor, and Elam

50:1–51:64 A message of judgement for Babylon and of hope for Israel and Judah

52:1-34 An account of the fall of Jerusalem and the exile

KEY THEMES – JEREMIAH

False security

7:1-15 is a key passage in the book. The Israelites, in their spiritual confusion, were imagining that because "the temple of the LORD" was in the centre of their capital, Jerusalem, God was actually living in it and therefore they were invulnerable to outside attack. This sense of false security enabled them to "steal and murder, commit adultery and perjury" without any scruples on the one hand while on the other they "burn incense to Baal and follow other gods", the whole time saying "we are safe".

Jeremiah demolishes this security by pointing out the fate of Shiloh, the place where the precursor of the temple, the tabernacle, was given a temporary home (Judges 18:31). Shiloh was now deserted, the northern tribes from around the area were already in exile. Sacred space may be necessary for the divine presence (see Haggai), but that presence is dependent on a holy people as much as on a God who wishes to dwell among them. There can be no security outside a holy God *and* a holy people. 9:23-24 pushes this even further: there can be no dependence on anything except a true understanding of who God is, that is a God who loves justice and righteousness.

Social injustice

The exposure of social injustice runs through many of the prophetic books (see Isaiah, Joel, Amos, Micah, Habakkuk and Zephaniah). Chapter 5 is a dramatic plea for it. 6:13-21 sets God's hatred of injustice against the vain attempts by the people to mask it by making ritual offerings, again a central theme of other prophets. Whilst social and personal morality are not the same as holiness, they are not separate, either. This is what Jeremiah's audience could not understand. They felt as long as they made the required sacrifices in their ritual worship, it didn't matter how they

behaved to each other. It became a "buying God off" – but we cannot buy God off. The message is that social justice and personal morality authenticate worship and sacrifice and render it acceptable.

Punishment as refinement

9:7 is typical of many verses. Such is the spiritual blindness of the people that they need their eyes opening. Only drastic punishment will bring this about. If they are willing to accept such punishment, that is to accept the Babylonians as God's instrument of punishment, and accept the consequent exile as its form, then there will be a continued promise and future. Otherwise, punishment moves from being refinement to being a sentence of death. That is not God's purpose, but a realistic consequence.

What may amaze us is that even in the nearness of Babylonian attack, King Zedekiah imprisoned Jeremiah rather than receive his message (37:16). But then having imprisoned him, he secretly asked Jeremiah if he had a word from God (37:17; 38:14). At first, Jeremiah merely asked him where the false prophets were who had prophesied peace (37:19) but then urged him again to surrender and take his punishment (38:17). God was willing to have mercy till the last moment. Even so, the king refused (compare 18:12).

Restoration and the new covenant

Like other prophets who prophesied exile and punishment, for example Isaiah, Jeremiah also prophesied restoration (eg 30:3-24). But he went further. He saw that God's people needed a new covenant. The old one had not led to any permanent change of heart (11:1-13). 31:31-34 are the crucial verses here. The law is now to be written on their hearts, rather than on stone tablets, as given to Moses on Mount Sinai; and put "in their minds" – an internalised covenant. Judgement gives way to salvation here (chapters 30–33), and is Jeremiah's consolation.

The New Testament means the new covenant, so we can see Jeremiah's prophecy anticipates God's plan for the future. Jeremiah's verses are, in fact, quoted in the Letter to the Hebrews (Hebrews 8:8-12) as a central part of the writer's argument about this new and better covenant. What the New Testament shows is that it needs the revelation of Jesus Christ to the individual believer by the Holy Spirit to bring about this new "writing" on our hearts (2 Corinthians 3:3-18). This revelation brings about inner transformation (the new birth), made possible by the once-for-all perfect sacrifice of Christ (Hebrews 9:11-15).

The promise of restoration, therefore, can be interpreted at two levels. Firstly, in terms of the Old Testament, there was indeed a return from exile and a return to the Holy Land. Secondly, in terms of the New Testament, there was a new return to a covenant relationship with God, not in terms of a geographical sacred land, but still as a new people of God, a holy nation (1 Peter 2:9).

RELEVANCE FOR TODAY – JEREMIAH

Complaints

The Bible shows us prophets arguing with or complaining to God on several occasions. In Habakkuk, for example, the prophet cannot understand God's purposes in using the Babylonians as his instrument of justice (Habakkuk 1:12-17). So he argues it out with God, the result being a deeper understanding of God's immediate and his long-term purposes. The point is, God does not mind our arguing (called a "complaint" in literary terms), as long as we accept the answer when it comes.

Jeremiah makes a number of complaints. The most relevant, perhaps, is that voiced in 12:1-4, a complaint repeated in Gerard Manley Hopkins' famous sonnet "Thou art indeed just, Lord". Hopkins talks of his failure to prosper in his ministry, while the wicked seem to have successful careers. Jeremiah offers some of this complaint: why do the ways of the wicked prosper? People are then saying, "God will not see what happens". The psalmist had similar problems (eg Psalm 73:12-14).

God's answer to Jeremiah is not quite what he expected. It is basically that problems like these are training to toughen up Jeremiah in his prophetic role. The image is of an athlete (12:5), an unusual image for the Old Testament, when athletic competitions were not known. Athletes need tough courses to train on to build up their stamina. Jeremiah will have to get used to problems like this: there are far harder ones down the road (12:7-13). Certainly, we can see Jeremiah's life as a prophet was exemplary in the mental toughness required over a sustained period of time.

A second complaint was in 15:10, enlarged upon in 20:7-18: Jeremiah had simply had enough! No one listened to him, he was attacked and his ministry seemed to be having no effect. He says at first he delighted in it (15:16) but now it is a pain (15:18). If he tries to keep quiet, the message burns like a fire inside him (20:9).

To the second complaint there is no easy answer given. He is promised his life, that is, he will know God's protection. 1 Corinthians 4:2 provides some sort of answer: God requires faithfulness in ministry, not success. Jeremiah stuck at a hopeless task, and is quite rightly viewed as one of the greatest prophets, even though in terms of audience response he must seem the least. But God's word is truth, and it is the truth-tellers whom history vindicates.

This leads to the answer to the first complaint: evildoers did not prosper. All they had was eventually looted and burned, and they were hauled into exile if they were lucky. Again, the long-term purposes of God are the ones that have to be looked to.

The potter and the clay

Another way of expressing some of the dilemmas discussed in the previous section is through the extended analogy used in chapters 18–21. God is the potter; we are the clay. The clay cannot demand anything of the potter; and if the potter decides to rework the clay, that is entirely up to him. In the end, therefore, we do have to submit to the will of

" *I will put my law in their minds and write it on their hearts.*"

JEREMIAH 31:33

God. This is not fatalism, however, since fate is blind and unfeeling, whilst God is loving and creative, like the potter. A pot has some purpose and some beauty to it, some order and design. Ultimately, Jeremiah needed to give the prophecy to himself, as we often need to.

Plans to prosper

Despite the many prophecies of impending judgement and destruction, the book makes clear that this is not God's purpose for his people. 29:10-14 give a summary of what those plans are: to restore and to prosper. The condition is that the LORD is sought with the whole heart.

Such promises are relevant to any time. We have an inbuilt need to "prosper", to receive some fruit for our labours. The irony is that only the prophet himself seemed excluded, in that his prophecies did not seem to prosper but brought him into trouble. However, in the long term, his words too have prospered, because we prosper by believing them as truth. Isaiah 55:11 reinforces this: "my word ... will accomplish what I desire".

There is always a choice

Jeremiah's prophecies were often given in extreme conditions, for example, with the Babylonians closing in on a besieged city. But even in the most extreme conditions, Jeremiah insists we always have a choice. 21:8 is the clearest expression of this: "the way of life and the way of death" – this is the most basic choice possible. The choice did seem extreme: stay in the city and die; surrender and live (38:17-19). The "no surrender" brigade won the vote over Jeremiah and duly died, for no good purpose. Those who made the right choice lived to take God's purposes into exile. In such difficult circumstances, we need to trust God to give us a prophetic word as to what the choice is set before us.

Lamentations
DEATH OF A CITY

OVERVIEW

The book of Lamentations mourns the death of the holy city, Jerusalem.
Her people have gone into exile as part of the punishment God has sent them
for their sins. Sometimes the city herself speaks; sometimes the writer.
The last chapter pleads with God to remember the survivors and to restore them.

SUMMARY

There are a number of examples of laments in
the Old Testament, for example 2 Samuel
1:19-27; Psalms 38, 79, 88; and Amos 5:2. This
is the only book of the Bible given wholly over
to lamentation. Its five chapters are separate,
carefully crafted poems. The first four
chapters are acrostics, each verse of chapters
1, 2 and 4 beginning with a successive letter of
the Hebrew alphabet, 22 in all. Chapter 3
devotes three verses to each letter, whilst
chapter 5 retains 22 verses, though not the
acrostic form.

The tight structure gives form to what
would otherwise be a devastating grief that
would overwhelm the writer. The acrostic
form is used, it has been suggested, to show
that the grief is all-inclusive, omitting
nothing. Chapter 3 reaches a climax at the
book's mid-point as the writer is able to catch
a glimpse of a compassionate God behind the
force of his destruction of the city (3:22-30).
There is no protest to God: the reasons for the
punishment are too well known, too
obviously deserved. But the implications are
enormous: the enemies of God's people scorn
them (2:16; 3:46); the whole ritual of worship
has been abandoned (2:6); the survivors have
suffered dreadfully (5:10-13) and are having
to do dreadful things, even eat their dead
children (2:20; 4:10).

Author

No writer is mentioned by name. The
commonest assumption is that he is the
prophet Jeremiah, who certainly saw the
destruction of Jerusalem, and was not
immediately taken into exile to Babylon. He
would therefore have had time to have seen
the aftermath of the burning of the city, and
to have composed this lament then or soon
afterwards. There are many echoes of the
book of Jeremiah, in terms of the city's
failures and its predicted doom, as well as
various verbal echoes (eg Jeremiah 4:27-31; 6;
9; 13:18-27). And we know Jeremiah had
written other laments (2 Chronicles 35:25; see
Jeremiah 9:10f.; 14:17f.)

Date

The destruction of Jerusalem was in 587 BC, so
the composition of this book must have been
shortly after this time. The destroyed city is
named variously *Jerusalem*, *Zion* and *daughter of
Zion*.

OUTLINE – LAMENTATIONS

The first lament

1:1-11a Mourning for the devastated city of Jerusalem

1:11b-22 The city calls out for comfort, but no one responds

The second lament

2:1-10 God has become the enemy of Jerusalem

2:11-22 Astonishment at the severity of Jerusalem's punishment

The third lament

3:1-20 A lament because of the suffering God has inflicted

3:21-33 Hope in God's unfailing love, even when he brings judgement

3:34-66 A plea for justice

The fourth lament

4:1-10 The misery of the people

4:11-22 Jerusalem has been judged by God, but the other nations will not escape it either

The fifth lament

5:1-18 Jerusalem has suffered enough

5:19-22 A prayer for restoration

KEY THEMES – LAMENTATIONS

God as enemy

There is a saying, "With friends like these, who needs enemies?" The poet here feels much the same: "The LORD is like an enemy" (2:5). The whole section 2:1-5 deals with God's hostility towards the city. However, there is a difference between "like an enemy", as here, and "the enemy", as in 2:7. The poet feels there is also a human enemy, who should be punished, too, for their destructiveness and mockery (1:21; 3:61-66).

This builds on the viewpoint of the book of Jeremiah: that God is using the Babylonians to punish Jerusalem for her wickedness. Yet in turn, the Babylonians will be punished for their pride. But here, the sense is that God is first and foremost the enemy, the first cause of the destruction, the Babylonians only the second cause. That is why here the enemy is left anonymous and unnamed. What matters is God's enmity. So does God actually send evil, or merely permit it?

We need to realise this is a human, academic question. From God's standpoint,

in this case, the alternatives are meaningless. What we need to realise is that God is both friend and enemy at the same time. "Faithful are the wounds of a friend" (Proverbs 27:6) is the nearest we can get to this paradox in human terms, but the truth is stronger even than this. The behaviour and attitudes of God's covenant people have outraged him. God's people have, in fact, become his enemies, declaring war on him. So he responds. This is terrible, but in God's mercy, such anger does not last for ever (3:31-32). Enmity is not his permanent disposition, but compassion is. So in the final verse, when the poet asks, "Unless you ... are angry at us without measure", we know, even if it is only from the pages of history, that God never is.

Failure of priests and prophets

In any catastrophe, we usually want to know who is to blame. Here, the prophet-poet singles out the priests and prophets (4:13). This fits in with the book of Jeremiah, which attacks the false prophets for their saying "peace, peace, where there was no peace" (Jeremiah 6:14; 8:11; see also 23:1-40), and the priests, who at one point physically attack Jeremiah (Jeremiah 20:1-2; 26:8).

In other words, the failure is one of spiritual leadership. The very people appointed by God to keep the people in covenant faithfulness are the ones who have led them astray in a false security and into syncretism, or false worship. In biblical terms, judgement must always start with the household of God (1 Peter 4:17).

RELEVANCE FOR TODAY – LAMENTATIONS

Crying from the depths

At some time in our lives, it is almost certain we will feel like we are crying to God "from the depths" (3:55). It is difficult to imagine a more devastating scenario than that which faced the poet: the whole present and future seemed wiped out; the survivors suffering dreadful things (5:8-13) and doing dreadful things (2:20; 4:10).

At such times, it is only too easy to see God as our enemy, or as indifferent to our prayers. Our suffering seems uniquely terrible (1:12). We are reminded of the book of Job, whose afflictions seemed more than he could bear, or of Jonah, crying from the belly of the great fish, or of the psalmist, at his wits' end (Psalm 130:1). In such circumstances, all we can do is to cry out. The one note of assurance that comes from this book is that God does hear such cries (3:57-58), just as he heard Christ's desolating cry on the cross: "My God, my God, why have you forsaken me?" (Matthew 27:46). In a very real sense, it is because of Christ's cry of desolation, that our similar cries *are* heard. He has gone down into the depths and has risen again from them.

Unfailing compassion

The climax of the book is undoubtedly 3:22-23, since it represents a moment of faith in the midst of despair. It is a moment that is given to the poet in God's mercy, and so is part of the compassion that he witnesses.

The secret is acceptance (3:26). This is a just punishment; it is not outside what God said he would do. Not all our depths will be because of this, of course. Many depths come from outside ourselves, perhaps the behaviour of those we love dearly, or they are caused by natural disasters. But after all the cries, laments and anger we need to come to a place of acceptance. This is where the divine compassion must envelop us, to save us from our own self-despair, bitterness or hopelessness.

Significantly, the poet cannot hold this

> " *For his compassions never fail. They are new every morning ...*"

LAMENTATIONS 3:22-23

moment for long – but the very fact he does reach it at all is a triumph of faith. Other prophets (especially Isaiah and Ezekiel) take up the story of God's compassion.

Grieving and restoration

In a sense, the book is incomplete. "What happened?" we ask. Later books of the Bible (Daniel, Ezekiel, Zechariah, Malachi) tell us. Life does go on; God's purposes are not thwarted by even the direst catastrophe.

This book does not tell us these things. But what it does do is show us how we must enter into the grief of the situation without losing all our faith. Such grieving will allow God to continue to work out his compassionate purposes. This is the new morning.

Ezekiel
STANDING IN THE GAP

OVERVIEW
Ezekiel, in exile in Babylon, addresses his fellow exiles and the remnants of
Jerusalem before its final fall. In a series of visionary statements, he denounces the
failure of its moral and spiritual life, but also offers hope for the future. In an
apocalyptic conclusion, he foresees God's kingdom established in a perfect form.

SUMMARY
The book of Ezekiel may be divided into two
parts, with a transition between both parts.
The first part consists of a series of powerful
visions, appearances of God in his glory
(chapters 1–3), which affected Ezekiel
powerfully. They lead to a series of woes
spoken against the priests still ministering in
the Jerusalem temple, and then against the
inhabitants of the doomed city, the capital of
Judah. Their failures were both historical and
present (chapters 8–21). God's glory was seen
to leave the city. Ezekiel's language is
dramatic, often emphasised by acting out his
message (chapters 4–7).

The transition passage condemns in
equally forceful terms those nations round
about Judah who were eagerly awaiting its
downfall (chapters 25–32). The strongest
denunciations are against Tyre and Egypt.
Both would fail even more completely than
Judah.

Finally, Ezekiel offered hope for the future
in terms of a renewed covenant with God
(chapters 33–39) and a restored holy temple,
city and land (chapters 40–48). The tone here
is eschatological, looking towards the end
times, after a restoration from exile in
Babylon and further battles, after which
God's glory would be seen to have returned.

Author
Ezekiel was both a priest and a prophet, hence
his concern with both present and future
temples in Jerusalem. At the opening of the
book, he was probably about 30, the age when
priests began their service. At the end, he
would be about 50. During the book, his wife
died, though he could not mourn her death,
any more than he could mourn the death of
Jerusalem.

Date
The book's prophecies are very precisely
dated. The period indicated is from the time
of the first Babylonian assault on Judah and
the taking of a first group of exiles to
Babylon, about 593 BC, to 571 BC. This would
make him contemporary with Jeremiah, who
stayed behind in Jerusalem, and perhaps the
young Daniel. His wife's death is dated to the
final fall of Jerusalem in 586 BC.

OUTLINE – EZEKIEL

>>>

KEY THEMES – EZEKIEL

Visions of glory

Of all the written prophets, Ezekiel was, with Daniel and Zechariah, the most visionary. Some of his visions recall those of Elisha's vision of the horses and chariots of God (2 Kings 6:17), especially the opening vision which is as spectacular as any SciFi film. They reveal God in his heavenly glory, veiled in unapproachable light.

However, typically, God's glory was linked to the Jerusalem temple, such as when it was dedicated by Solomon (2 Chronicles 7:2). This is where Isaiah had his commissioning vision (Isaiah 6:4). The significance of Ezekiel's opening vision was that God's glory was universal, not confined to the temple. One could have glimpses of it anywhere. The significance of his vision of the glory leaving the temple (10:1-22) is that neither God's presence nor his glory was automatically fixed there. He would not leave his glory in a polluted building. However, Ezekiel has a further vision of the future, when that glory returns (43:1-27). God wants his glory to be in the midst of his people, though it cannot be contained there.

Prophetic responsibility

The book of Ezekiel gives clear teaching on the responsibilities of prophecy, both in terms of its giving and reception. In its giving, the responsibility is to declare it, no matter what the reception. The prophet is he who stands in the gap or breach for God, when the spiritual walls would otherwise be broken (3:4-27; 22:30). Interestingly, the book of Nehemiah literally shows just such a man.

The responsibility of reception is not just to hear, repent and obey, but to remain in that obedience (33:1-20). Even last-minute repentance will be acceptable, just as last-minute reneging will lead to death. But reception is individual (18:1-32). Here, Ezekiel modifies the older teaching of punishment extending to later generations (Exodus 20:5, but see also Deuteronomy 24:16; Jeremiah 31:29-30). The effect of sin may be generational, but the responsibility – the guilt – is on the present individual.

Dry bones

One of the most well-known visions of Ezekiel is that of the Valley of Dry Bones (37:1-14). God asks Ezekiel in a rhetorical question: "Can these bones live?" (verse 3). The answer is re-enacted in the vision, at the end of which God tells Ezekiel: "I will put my spirit in you and you will live." At the literal level, this refers to God's promise of restoration to the scattered exiles, a promise made in many other prophecies and by many other prophets, and fulfilled, as the Ezra-Nehemiah account tells us.

> " *The name of the city from that time on will be:* THE LORD IS THERE."
>
> EZEKIEL 48:35

However, the promise of renewal is an ongoing spiritual one in God's plan. At one level, our natural life needs God's spirit to make us a spiritual person, that is, regeneration. But even as believers, we have periods when our spiritual life feels dried up and in need of renewal. Water is the commonest symbol of such renewal, standing at the opposite extreme to the arid valley of Ezekiel's vision. In John 4:14, Jesus promises us a spring of water "welling up to eternal life". We need to hold to this as an ongoing promise, not just a once-off experience of grace.

Apocalyptic writing and the fall of the great city

Chapters 26–28 have puzzled many scholars and ordinary readers. They appear to be woes directed against a fairly small city and its trading empire. Why should the prophet use such poetic and forceful language at such length on these small objects?

One of the answers is that Ezekiel was speaking to more than he knew, in an apocalyptic way. Put simply, it means that Tyre becomes a type of the modern, commercial (or secular) world empire, which in its pride thinks it is self-sustaining and unconquerable, as also in Isaiah 23. In Ezekiel's day, this would have been Babylon, but Ezekiel could not easily have said this directly. In the book of Revelation, it *is* called Babylon (Revelation 18). In its pride and self-sufficiency, it comes under God's judgement (see Isaiah 14 for a similar prophecy).

But interpretations have gone further. In the language used of the King of Tyre in Ezekiel 28, we have references that can be applied to Satan himself, who is elsewhere called the prince of this world (John 12:31). He, too, is judged (John 16:11), along with the great city. Behind such imperial forces lies this satanic power, always doomed, but always needing to be recognised and opposed.

Daniel
ORDEALS AND VISIONS

THE PROPHETS

OVERVIEW

Daniel was an exile in Babylon after the fall of Jerusalem. He found favour with a
series of kings during the course of a long and distinguished life, even though he
was a Jew and even though he refused to compromise his beliefs. At times he and his
three friends underwent terrible ordeals; at other times he was given terrifying
visions of the future. But in every conflict situation, God's truth and kingdom
emerged triumphant.

SUMMARY

In this highly literary book, the twelve
chapters fall neatly into two halves. Chapters
1–6 deal with Daniel and his three friends in a
series of memorable stories. Over a lifetime,
they underwent a series of ordeals, which
tested their faith to the limits. Firstly, they
refused as Jews to go against their strict
dietary laws (chapter 1). Daniel's three friends
then refused to worship an idol and were
thrown into a furnace (chapter 3). The final
ordeal for Daniel came when he refused to
pray to King Darius. He was thrown into a
den of lions, but again survived (chapter 6).

In between these chapters, Daniel is
presented with a series of tests, which
challenge his ability as a wise man. In one case
he actually had to reveal the content of a
dream before interpreting it (chapter 2). In
another dream interpretation, he had to
predict the future disgrace of the king
(chapter 4). Finally, he interpreted a sign
about the fall of King Belshazzar, after he had
used sacred drinking vessels from the
Jerusalem temple (chapter 5).

Chapters 7–12 are more apocryphal,
interpreting dreams of future kingdoms and
their fall. Here, Daniel becomes the dreamer,
needing an angelic helper to interpret. The
second part again divides into two: the first
three chapters (7–9) are three distinct but
fairly general visions, not dissimilar to that in
chapter 2. The second part (chapters 10–12) is
one long detailed vision of the future world
kingdoms, until God's kingdom breaks in.

The two parts of the book illustrate that
the God who is in control of the nations is
also the God who cares for and protects
individuals in times of need.

Author

Daniel was a well-born young man at the
beginning of the story, who was trained in all
the wisdom of the Babylonians. Much of this
wisdom is to do with dreams and signs, as
well as the more practical wisdom of law and
administration.

Date

There exists a great deal of controversy over
the date. The exile period from 605–530 BC is
the traditional date, but some scholars have
suggested the period of the Maccabees
around 175–160 BC, another period of great
suffering for the Jewish people.

OUTLINE – DANIEL

Stories about Daniel and his friends
1:1-5 Background information about King Nebuchadnezzar's court
1:6-21 Daniel and his three friends refuse the king's food and become his chief advisors
2:1-12 Nebuchadnezzar asks his wise men to describe and interpret his dream
2:13-49 Daniel's prayer to God and interpretation of the dream
3:1-7 Nebuchadnezzar's golden statue
3:8-30 Shadrach, Meshach and Abednego are delivered from the furnace
4:1-18 Nebuchadnezzar describes his second dream
4:19-27 Daniel's interpretation and warning to the king
4:28-37 The king is humbled, and then praises God
5:1-5 King Belshazzar's feast with the temple cups
5:6-29 The mysterious writing on the wall and Daniel's interpretation
5:30-31 Belshazzar is overthrown by Darius the Mede
6:1-15 Daniel's greatness and King Darius' command
6:16-28 God protects Daniel in the den of lions

Daniel's visions of the future
7:1-14 Daniel's vision of four beasts and a figure like a son of man
7:15-28 The interpretation of Daniel's vision: the triumph of God's people
8:1-14 Daniel's vision of a ram overcome by a mighty goat
8:15-27 The interpretation of Daniel's vision: Greece will overcome the Medes and Persians
9:1-19 Daniel prays for the forgiveness of Israel's sins and the end of exile
9:20-27 A message about the end of exile and the Anointed One
10:1–11:1 Daniel receives a vision about Persia and Greece
11:2-35 The interpretation: war between the kings of the south and the north and the persecution of God's covenant people
11:36-45 The rule and final battle of the northern king
12:1-13 Daniel's vision about the end times

KEY THEMES – DANIEL

Deliverance

The theme of deliverance is seen in two ways in the book. Firstly, there is actual physical deliverance, from the furnace (3:27) and the den of lions (6:20-22). These deliverances are as miraculous as the crossing of the Red Sea, when God delivered the Israelites from the Egyptian army (9:15; see Exodus 14:14-31). The mysterious presence of the fourth person in the furnace (3:25) suggests God's direct intervention.

But the theme of deliverance runs right through the second part also. Daniel sees a time when God's people, the "saints" (7:18), will be persecuted (7:21; 8:24; 9:26; 11:31-35; 12:7). However severe the persecution, deliverance is promised (7:22; 8:25; 9:27; 12:1). The strength of apocalyptic writing is to give hope to God's people when their enemies seem to have the upper hand completely. And indeed history shows also that no period of persecution goes on for ever: the tyrants are overthrown and God's people are delivered.

The term "deliverance" is used specifically in the Bible in regards to evil. Sometimes today the term is used where the Bible would use the term exorcism or the "throwing-out" of evil spirits (eg Matthew 7:22).

Repentance for the past

The exile happened as a result of Israel's failure to follow God. Jeremiah prophesied a 70-year exile (9:2; see Jeremiah 25:11; 29:10). Daniel comes to terms with this in a remarkable chapter (9:1-19). Though he personally was faultless, he repents for the sins of his people in the past. Nehemiah does the same (Nehemiah 1), as does Ezra (Nehemiah 9), all in the same situation. So Daniel shows us that we need to repent not only of our personal sins: repentance has corporate dimensions too.

An everlasting kingdom

One of the main messages of apocalyptic writing is that although earthly kingdoms, whether Babylon, Persia, Greece, or even Rome (probably meant by the fourth beast), might seem impregnable, in the grand scheme of things they are short-lived and will inevitably fail. Only God's kingdom, the final kingdom, will last for ever (2:44; 7:14,27). This is our historical perspective as believers. The point is its certainty.

Angels

Although angels are mentioned throughout the Bible as messengers from God, they are seen in a wider context in Daniel as interpreters and revealers (8:16), and also as fighters (10:13). At his trial, Jesus acknowledges this (Matthew 26:53).

Don't compromise

Daniel and his three companions, Hananiah, Mishael, and Azariah, find themselves in exile, having lost everything, it would appear. Even their names are taken from them, being replaced by Babylonian ones. Then suddenly, they are given an opportunity to make good in a strange culture with a strange religion and a tyrannical ruler. But the demand is always to obey the rules of the conquerors, rather than their own religious beliefs.

The temptation must have been overwhelming, but the book makes it clear that no temptation to compromise beliefs is overwhelming. It is possible to withstand, even on pain of death, whether from burning, execution or wild animals. But the book goes much further in its stories: God will vindicate those who refuse to compromise, not only by delivering them, but also by honouring them and giving them victory over their enemies. In the end, Daniel lives to a ripe old age, respected and honoured. This is the consequence of true wisdom.

But Daniel also refuses to compromise in regards to his message. Despite its unpopular content he delivers it. He tells Nebuchadnezzar to his face (4:27) to repent otherwise he will go mad. He tells Belshazzar his kingdom has been judged and found wanting. He could have watered down the message. He didn't and such is the authority of truth that his message was received, even if it was not believed.

Serve God in an alien culture

Daniel proves it is possible to serve God fully in an alien culture without compromising your beliefs and practices. Daniel continued praying towards Jerusalem till he was an old man (6:10). Yet he was honoured and promoted by no fewer than three kings (2:48; 5:29; 6:28).

For all his uncompromising attitude, however, Daniel is shown to be wise and tactful. In 1:12 he suggests a way out for the nervous official; 2:20 shows due humility and deference; in 4:19 he tries to soften the blow. It is God who caused Daniel to find favour. But he still had to do his part by displaying a caring and truthful attitude.

> " *Daniel,*
> *I have now come*
> *to bring you insight*
> *and understanding."*
>
> DANIEL 9:22

God gives wisdom

James 1:15 tells us that God will willingly give us wisdom if we ask. This is what the book of Daniel shows in practice. For example, 2:23 shows wisdom given at a crucial moment. In this case it was by direct revelation (2:19,28), but this is not necessarily the only way. Patient thinking and praying about a situation or person will often bring a new love or sympathy, which will then bring its own wisdom. Taking advice from people who are more godly or less involved in a situation than we are can also bring wisdom.

Hosea
THE DIVINE LOVER

OVERVIEW

Hosea, the first of the twelve Minor Prophets, was a prophet primarily to the northern kingdom of Israel, like his predecessor Amos. Whereas Amos stresses God's justice and righteousness, Hosea presents God as divine lover. Thus, Israel's sinfulness is seen in terms of unfaithfulness as much as unrighteousness; and he uses terms of complaint, wooing and pleading as much as terms of denunciation. Remarkably, his own marriage becomes an enactment of the message he preaches: motivated by love, God will restore Israel just as Hosea takes back his faithless wife.

SUMMARY

The book falls into two somewhat unequal parts. The first part (chapters 1–3) tell of Hosea's unhappy marriage. Hosea is told to marry a woman, Gomer, who proved to be unfaithful to him. She bore him three children, all of whom were symbolically named. The first was a son called Jezreel, after the incident recorded in 2 Kings 9:13-37, prefiguring a final wiping out of the royal line of Israel. The second child, a daughter, was named Lo-Ruhamah, ("not loved"), signifying the withdrawal of God's love to Israel; and the third, a boy, was named Lo-Ammi ("not my people"), meaning that Israel was no longer to be considered the people of God. Hosea is then told to reclaim Gomer from the prostitution she had fallen into, but to set her apart for a time to prove her faithfulness (chapters 1 and 3). Chapter 2 summarises the themes and prophecies that run through the second part of the book.

The second part (chapters 4–14) consists of a series of highly poetic prophecies to Israel and sometimes Judah, the southern kingdom. These prophecies outline both the nature and possible consequences of Israel's unfaithfulness, which includes idolatry and a whole range of moral, social and political wrongs, and hold out the promise of God's forgiveness and restoration when Israel truly repents. Running through the descriptions of present failings are accounts of God's faithfulness in history.

Author

Nothing much is known about Hosea. Unlike Amos, he was a native of the northern kingdom. His imagery is entirely natural, whereas Amos' is partly urban, suggesting Hosea lived and worked on the land. His prophecies were most likely given over a number of years.

Date

The kings mentioned as reigning in the southern kingdom of Judah in 1:1 are the same as named in the book of Isaiah. Jeroboam II, the northern king, lived 793–753 BC, and is mentioned by Amos also. No reference is made to the eventual fall of Samaria, Israel's capital, which was in 722 BC, so the general conclusion is he was writing between 755–725 BC.

OUTLINE – HOSEA

Hosea's unhappy marriage and its message

1:1 Historical background

1:2-3 Hosea marries the prostitute Gomer at God's instruction

1:4–2:1 The birth and names of Hosea's three children

2:2-13 God's judgement on Israel for her adultery and idolatry

2:14-23 God's promise of restoration

3:1-5 Hosea redeems Gomer from her prostitution

Hosea's messages for God's people

4:1-19 God's complaint against Israel's idolatry

5:1-15 A message of judgement for Israel and her leaders

6:1–7:16 Hosea's call to repentance is ignored

8:1–9:9 Coming destruction for Israel

9:10-17 Israel's history of sin and unfaithfulness

10:1-15 Israel's wealth of sin and God's judgement

11:1-4 God's past deliverance of Israel

11:5-11 God's longing for unfaithful Israel to follow him

11:12–12:14 Israel and Judah have turned away from God and rejected his prophets

13:1-16 God offers salvation, but Israel rejects it

14:1-9 A promise of restoration if Israel repents

KEY THEMES – HOSEA

Spiritual adultery

Hosea's marital experiences, commented on initially in chapter 2, form the basis for his messages. The foremost theme in them is that of Israel's unfaithfulness to God, seen in terms of covenant breaking (4:1; 5:7; 6:4-7; 9:1,10). He speaks of a "spirit of prostitution" (4:12f.; 5:4; 6:10). This is then more specifically defined as idolatry (8; 9:15; 13:1-2), which is helped on by the priests (4:6-9; 5:1f.;10:5) in their refusal to hear the prophets (9:7-8; 12:10). This has led to a failure of true repentance (6:1-3; 8:2,11; 11:5,7), and instead to seeking outside help in their need for assistance and protection (5:13; 7:11; 8:9; 12:1; 14:3). The linking of idolatry to sexuality was more natural than we might think today. The worship of Baal, which was the prevalent form of idolatry in Israel, was basically a fertility cult, and there would be temple prostitutes (4:14) and a man and his son could lie with the same girl. Hence the curse of barrenness (9:11,14) and images of difficult birth (13:13) and illegitimacy (5:7). The word *Baal* itself can mean either "lord" or "husband".

God's faithfulness

Balanced against Israel's failings is a list of God's responses. Firstly, God longs to redeem and be merciful (6:11; 7:13; 11:4-9;14:4f.); but if there is no response to him, then punishment will inevitably follow (5:10-14; 9:7-9; 10:2-15; 13:7-8). This may be in the form of ecological disaster (5:7f.; 8:7; 9:2), military defeat (5:8-9; 11:5-6; 13:16) or exile (9:17; 10:5-6). Included in this theme is a series of reviews of God's faithful dealings in the past (9:10; 10:9; 12:3-10; 13:4-6). For the Old Testament writers, history is covenant history, and covenant is based on *hesed*, the Hebrew term meaning faithfulness, promise-keeping. Marriage, too, is a form of covenant (2:18-20); hence, again, the centrality of the marriage analogy in Hosea's writings.

God as divine lover

The previous theme, then, leads naturally into seeing God as divine lover. Hosea literally has to model this first by marrying Gomer, then rescuing her, literally redeeming her as he has to buy her out of prostitution. God is then seen doing the same thing: marrying Israel, and then having to woo her again out of her Baal prostitution (11:8). Chapter 2 has some ambiguity: does it refer to Hosea and Gomer, or God and Israel? The answer is both. Israel's other acts of unfaithfulness have been to trust Egypt and Assyria to protect her, instead of the LORD alone (8:9,13; 9:3).

RELEVANCE FOR TODAY – HOSEA

God's heart of mercy

One of the striking features of Hosea is the constant interchange between God's anger and frustration at Israel's unfaithfulness, and his pleas for her to turn back to him. Thus in chapter 2, we begin with "Rebuke your mother" (2:2) and "I will take back ... and I will expose" (2:9-10). But then in 2:14 comes "Therefore I am going to allure her" and "I will respond ..." (2:21). At the end of the book there is a final appeal (14:1) and a final promise of unconditional love (14:4). Similar promises of restoration close other prophetic books (eg Amos 9:11-15; Joel 3:17-21). The LORD's last word is one of mercy, forgiveness and restoration.

This should encourage us. In the prophetic writings, Israel is typically a stubborn and faithless nation, and so divine anger is turned full force on it. But there is no need for us to be like this. God wishes, far more than we do, a covenant relationship of intimacy and love. His yearning heart reaches out to gather us in. We tend to see our failings in a disproportionate way, either as huge or quite minor. Sin is sin to God, but what should matter to us is the greatness of his merciful love.

Cheap grace

On the other hand, it is possible to repent too superficially. This is what Hosea sees Israel doing in 6:1-3. God responds, "Your love is like the morning mist" (6:4). The term "cheap grace" was termed by the German theologian Dietrich Bonhoeffer to describe this sort of attitude. God's grace in forgiving us our sin freely was obtained at tremendous cost, the death of his own Son, Jesus Christ. True repentance, then, is to realise what it actually cost God. This is not to prevent us from

> " *Maintain love and justice, and wait for your God always.*"
>
> HOSEA 12:6

repenting, but to cause us to mean it as deeply as we can and seriously change what caused our sin in the first place.

The church as the bride of Christ

Although the intimate language of love might not always be associated with Old Testament prophecy, it is part of an ongoing revelation of God's covenant relationship with his people that culminates in the New Testament image of the church as the bride of Christ (Revelation 21:2,9; 22:17). A number of Christ's parables are about wedding feasts or bridegrooms (Matthew 25:1-13; Luke 5:34-35; John 3:29).

At present, it would be difficult to see the present-day church as a pure and beautiful bride. We are all too aware of spots and stains and ugly blemishes. But we need to see that for all its imperfections, Christ loves the church and is seeking to present her spotless and faultless at the day of his coming again. We should pray for it in that light.

Joel
DISASTER TO BLESSING

OVERVIEW
A dreadful plague of locusts becomes for Joel a picture of the coming Day of the LORD. He calls for national repentance. As the nation truly repents, then God pronounces judgements against the nations that have oppressed them, an outpouring of his Spirit, and a restoration of all they have lost and more.

SUMMARY
Joel's message has three parts. The first is a vivid and dramatic description of the worst plague of locusts experienced by Judah in living memory. Although locusts were a recurring menace in the Middle East (for example, Amos 7:1-2), this was obviously far worse than the normal experience. It seemed to have been accompanied by an equally devastating drought (1:1-20). Such a natural calamity needed to be met by a national call to prayer and repentance.

The second part interprets this plague as a type or picture of the Day of the LORD. The stage is widened from the local to the cosmic. The scenario becomes apocalyptic. The need for true repentance is even greater (2:1-17).

The final part has two elements. As the nation repented, the LORD promised to "repay for the years the locusts have eaten" (2:25), manifesting itself in both material restoration (3:17-21) and in spiritual gifts (2:28-32). But also there would be a day of judgement on the nation's enemies (3:1-16). The place of judgement is located as "the Valley of Jehoshaphat" (3:2) lying outside the walls of Jerusalem. God promises that "never again" would the land be devastated (3:17).

Author
Nothing is known at all about the writer apart from 1:1, where he is named as the "son of Pethuel". None of the other prophets mention him, though there are many echoes of his message scattered throughout the other prophetic books, including Zephaniah, Zechariah, Isaiah, and Daniel.

Date
There is no decisive clue within the text to give an accurate dating of the book. The compilers of the Hebrew Bible felt it should go between Amos and Hosea, presumably because they thought it belonged to the time around 770–740 BC. Some scholars agree. Some put it a generation earlier, which would make the book the first of the written prophets in time. By contrast, others put it much later, after the exile round 450 BC, the time of Malachi, or even later. There are good reasons for all these dates, but none is decisive.

KEY THEMES – JOEL

National repentance
Many prophets attacked specific sins and failings in the people of God. Zephaniah, for example, attacked spiritual apathy, syncretism and idolatry, social injustice and oppression. Repentance, therefore, had to include those sins specifically. Joel, however, makes no mention of any specific sins on the part of the nation. Instead there is general repentance. Its manifestations are sackcloth

A plague of locusts and a call for prayer

1:1 Joel receives a message from God

1:2-4 Joel's description of the plague of locusts

1:5-8 A lament because there is no wine

1:9-10 A lament for priests because there is nothing to offer at the temple

1:11-12 A lament for farmers because their crops are destroyed

1:13-14 Joel calls for repentance, fasting and prayer

1:15 The Day of the LORD is near and will bring destruction

1:16-18 The effects of plague and drought on the land

1:19-20 A plea to God for help

A message about coming judgement on the Day of the LORD

2:1-2a The alarm is sounded for the Day of the LORD

2:2b-11 The coming of a mighty destructive army led by God

2:12-14 God promises mercy and grace to those who truly repent

2:15-17 Joel calls the nation to repentance

God's message of promise and hope to his people

2:18-20 God will have mercy on his repentant people

2:21-24 A call to rejoice in God's salvation

2:25-27 God will restore what the locusts destroyed

2:28-32 God will pour out his Spirit on all people

3:1-16 The Day of the LORD will bring destruction to the enemies of Judah and Jerusalem

3:17-21 The future blessing of God's people

(1:13), a fast (1:14), weeping and mourning (2:12), tearing garments (2:13). This is in the context of a sacred assembly (1:14; 2:15). However, Joel realises God will not be impressed by these physical acts alone. They must be accompanied by a genuine inner repentance, figuratively expressed as "rend your heart" (2:13; compare Zechariah 7:5). Such repentance must include the sense of utter dependence on God, and human unworthiness.

Apocalypse now

The national calamity is expressed very dramatically in terms of an invading army (2:2-9) as the locusts advance inexorably. They are so thick that they darken the sky (2:10-11). Such cosmic manifestations are a picture of the Day of the LORD – a wake-up call to the nation that God's final intervention will be *the* decisive culmination of history (see also Zephaniah).

Judgement against the nations

Again, many of the prophetic books envisage specific judgement on other nations (see for example, Zephaniah 2:4-15). Joel is more general, mentioning by name only Tyre and Sidon, and Philistia (3:4). Nations are judged according to how they have treated Israel, that is, God's covenant people (3:4-8). Joel reverses Isaiah's picture of beating swords into ploughshares (3:10; see Isaiah 2:4; Micah 4:3). The images of the harvest and vintage of wrath (3:13) are truly disturbing. Only after such judgement can true prosperity come (3:18-19).

Never again

This apocalyptic time will also be different from the present by being a time of eternal security for God's people (3:17). Joel shares this conviction with many other prophets: there does really come a time when God brings a full end to his people's suffering and/or punishment (2:18,26; compare Amos 9:15). Here Joel makes it seem like an Eden, once lost (2:3), now regained (3:18). The book of Revelation closes with the same note (Revelation 22:1-5).

RELEVANCE FOR TODAY – JOEL

The years the locusts have eaten

One of the most widely quoted verses in Joel is 2:25, sometimes translated "I will restore ..." rather than "repay" as in the NIV. Locusts wipe out the land in an unimaginably devastating way: literally nothing remains. The word that is striking here is "years" rather than "places". Many people feel that their life has had periods of total devastation, where they have nothing to show except barrenness

> *"Everyone who calls on the name of the LORD will be saved."*

JOEL 2:32

and waste. This promise then becomes particularly important. Restoration is something God will do for them. A similar biblical image is of the barren woman rejoicing more than those women with children (Isaiah 54:1-3).

The generosity of God

The book begins with total poverty – nothing is left economically. The second part of the book not only restores this lost prosperity, but also reveals God's heart as overwhelmingly generous. The promise of restoration is filled out in detail (2:19,22-24; 3:18). Such images of plenty and fertility remind us of God's original promise to the Israelites to give them a land overflowing with milk and honey (Exodus 3:8). We tend to see God as someone who has to be persuaded to measure out his blessings one by one. This reflects our poverty of spirit rather than a true picture of the generous God who gives feasts to his returning prodigals (Luke 15:23).

Pouring out the Spirit

The promise of the outpouring of the Spirit was one of the key passages quoted at length by Peter on the Day of Pentecost (Acts 2:17-21), which was seen by the early church as the fulfilment of this prophecy. But each generation has to reclaim this prophecy for itself.

Three things need to be noted about it:
· The promise was to "all people", not just to Israel
· There were to be supernatural prophetic manifestations
· God would do the "pouring".

The Acts of the Apostles is full of such manifestations, which extend beyond the prophetic to healing and exorcisms also. Most obvious, perhaps, is the prophetic boldness of the early apostles; the outpouring was a transforming experience (Acts 2:37–3:10).

Different churches have different explanations of how this outpouring of the Spirit should be experienced today. Whatever explanation is made, it should line up with Joel's prophecy as interpreted through the New Testament.

Amos
A FAILING STATE

OVERVIEW

Amos prophesied to the northern kingdom of Israel, even though he was a southerner, from Judah. He spoke out against the luxurious lifestyle of the ruling classes, the moral and spiritual apathy this had brought about, and the injustice and corruption he saw. He viewed the exile as God's judgement on this, resulting in the near total destruction of the nation. Only a handful would be saved. Amos' message was not well received and he was told to go back to Judah (7:12-13).

SUMMARY

The prophecy falls into three sections: chapters 1–2, 3–6 and 7–9. The first two chapters consist of a brief introduction, followed by a series of woes directed at Israel's seven neighbours (1:3–2:5). The climax of this series of denunciations is one against Israel, the northern kingdom of the once unified country (2:6-16). Such attacks on other countries are common in the prophetic writings (see also Isaiah 13–23; Jeremiah 46–51; Zephaniah 2:4-15). Amos focuses on the atrocities against other countries.

The second section consists of a series of oracles, or prophecies, again mainly denunciations of evils in the land, with the retribution God is placing on them. To Amos, God is a God of righteousness, so all forms of injustice come under his judgement. Amos speaks out particularly against a corrupt legal system, bribery and failure to distribute wealth (5:11-12). Moneymaking took precedence over a true practice of religion. In fact, religion had become an empty shell of ritual with no moral force to it at all. Amos warns people to change their ways.

The final section consists of a series of five visions or pictures (7:1-9; 8:1-3; 9:1-5). The warning of judgement is rather more apocalyptic this time (8:9-14). The book finishes with the promise of a remnant and their future restoration (9:13-15).

Author

Amos came from the village of Tekoa, in the plateau south of Bethlehem, where he was both a shepherd and a tender of sycamore-figs (1:1; 7:14-15). He emphasises he was not a professional prophet. Amos was thus an outsider twice over. Nevertheless, his language is highly rhetorical.

Date

Amos preached in the reigns of Uzziah of Judah (792–740 BC) and Jeroboam II of Israel (793–753 BC). The earthquake of 1:1 cannot be dated, though it was remembered two hundred years later (Zechariah 14:5). The prophecy was received two years before it, though obviously the book was not written till after. The likeliest date for Amos' ministry is thus 775–755 BC, a little before Hosea, Micah and Isaiah.

OUTLINE – AMOS

Messages of judgement for Israel and her neighbours

1:1-2 Amos is given a message from God
1:3-5 A message of judgement for Damascus (Syria)
1:6-8 A message of judgement for Gaza (Philistia)
1:9-10 A message of judgement for Tyre (Phoenicia)
1:11-12 A message of judgement for Edom
1:13-15 A message of judgement for Ammon
2:1-3 A message of judgement for Moab
2:4-5 A message of judgement for Judah
2:6-16 A message of judgement for Israel herself

Amos' message for Israel

3:1-15 Judgement is coming on guilty Israel
4:1-13 Despite God's past judgements, Israel has not returned to him
5:1-15 God calls Israel to repent, return to him and find life
5:16–6:14 The Day of the LORD will bring judgement for Israel, not salvation

The visions of Amos

7:1-3 Amos' vision of a plague of locusts, and his prayer for mercy
7:4-6 Amos' vision of judgement by fire, and his prayer for mercy
7:7-9 Amos' vision of a plumb-line
7:10-13 Amaziah, the high priest in Bethel, sends Amos away from Israel to Judah
7:14-17 Judgement will come on Amaziah and Israel because they refuse to listen to Amos
8:1-3 Amos' vision of a basket of ripe fruit
8:4-10 Judgement will come on those who do injustice
8:11-14 A coming famine of the word of God
9:1-6 Amos' vision of God giving judgement from the temple altar
9:7-10 God's judgement will not completely destroy Israel
9:11-15 God promises he will restore and bless Israel

What God wants in a nation: justice

Israel was what is termed today a "failing state", almost a "failed state". But unlike today, the reasons were not economic or administrative. Quite the contrary, for the state was prosperous, made so by taking over much of the trade from its defeated northern neighbour, Syria. Marks of luxury, for example, the expensive houses and furnishings (6:4-6) and lush vineyards (5:11), struck the itinerant shepherd Amos forcibly. There was a legal system and religious ritual was observed (5:21-23).

Israel was failing because its very prosperity had blinded the people to the demands of justice and true worship demanded by God. Amos saw God's righteousness should be reflected in a righteous nation (3:2-3; 5:24). This should be seen in a fair legal system (5:15), and in fair treatment of the poor. Israel's failure is denounced by Amos (5:7,11-12; 6:12; 8:4).

Such failure will meet with God's judgement. Unfortunately, a corrupt society becomes morally blind, and unable to see possible judgement coming from God. Amos points out examples of other formerly prosperous states now in ruins (6:1-3). 9:1-6 paints a terrible and dramatic picture of the inevitable result of such blindness.

What God wants in a nation: true spirituality

The prophets did not simply denounce idolatry, the worship of false gods (5:26), nor syncretism (mixing worship of God with worship of idols). They also denounced worship meant for God which was mere gesture and outward show. God abhors this (8:10; compare Isaiah 1:11-17). For Amos and the other prophets, worship is a moral activity as much as a spiritual (5:24). The plumb-line image is the clearest expression of this (7:7-9): the plumb-line is a symbol of uprightness and honesty. Israel fails the test and so her high-places and sanctuaries, that is, her spiritual centres of worship, will be destroyed.

The inevitability of judgement

The first two visions show Amos pleading with God not to impose punishment (7:5). We are reminded of Abraham pleading for Sodom and Gomorrah to be saved (Genesis 18:16-33). God agrees yet in both cases judgement came. God is willing to show mercy (5:14-15), but he sees more clearly than the prophets that the unrighteous, blind inhabitants are not in a position to receive such grace. The inevitability, therefore, is as much a law of human moral blindness as God's imposition of a punishment after repeated warning. There seems to be a point of no return. Grace can then only be given after judgement (9:11-15).

Hong Kong fish market. Amos and other prophets spoke out strongly against injustice and unfair dealings against the poor

Setting lifestyle priorities

The clearest picture of the Israelites' lack of true spirituality lies in the corruption depicted in 8:5-6. The people cannot wait to get back from worship service to make more money as dishonestly as possible.

But a society or an individual does not just get to such a position at once. At some stage, wrong decisions about priorities must have been taken. Making money and grasping the economic opportunities suddenly made available must have been a decision, at some level, made consciously. Today we too can be lured by moneymaking as a prestigious undertaking. We need to take heed of the warning of Amos to avoid the moral progression downwards. From prosperity comes a carelessness over moral standards,

> " *Seek me and live.*"
>
> AMOS 5:4

cutting corners, manipulating the legal system, stepping over those who are weaker, bribery. As material rewards come, a love of luxury is developed. Formerly positive religious acts can become meaningless, a front, even a false security. Warnings, either from other people's failure, or more direct confrontations, are ignored. Ultimately, spiritual bankruptcy and God's judgement come.

Speaking out for justice

A prophet's ministry is likely to be confrontational; deafness and rejection the likely response. Jonah's preaching was quite unusually successful; Haggai's likewise. But more typical is Jeremiah's ministry with no obvious positive results, only repeated rejection. Amos suffered similarly, being told to go back home. However, his prophecies were fulfilled and the northern kingdom was wiped out some 30 years later, when the people were taken into exile by the Assyrians, disappearing without trace – the "ten lost tribes of Israel".

When Amaziah told Amos to stop prophesying, it was something Amos simply could not do: he was so conscious of God calling him (7:15) and speaking to him (3:7-8). But the Israelites had a tradition of silencing their prophets (2:11-12) and thought they could do the same to Amos. After all, "the prudent man keeps quiet in such times, for the times are evil" (5:13). In God's grace, Amos was not prudent, and we have his book as record of his imprudence and a permanent judgement against a society that wants to shut its prophets up.

Our own society does not care for any Christian prophetic voice. It discusses whether such prophets are mad, "hearing voices". But we have to speak out against those things we know offend God's righteousness if we are to keep our integrity as Christians.

Obadiah
FALL OF A PROUD NATION

OVERVIEW

Obadiah condemns the nation of Edom for its pride. Edom feels impregnable in its mountain fortress. Worse, it has betrayed Judah when Jerusalem fell, cutting off its refugees. It will be devastated in even worse measure, whilst Jerusalem will be restored as the centre of God's blessing.

SUMMARY

Obadiah predicted the fall of Edom (verses 1-7). At present, they felt invincible, giving rise to pride and false wisdom. The prophet foretold the breaking of this pride. But God was not just simply punishing pride: Edom as a nation was related to Judah, but had now betrayed Judah by siding with the invading enemy, cutting down those fleeing the burning city of Jerusalem, plundering and invading the territory of Judah (verses 8-14).

The Day of the LORD was now upon all nations: there would be divine retribution and restoration (verses 15-18). Edom and Philistia would both disappear as nations, whilst Judah would be restored as exiles repossess their stolen territories (verses 19-20). Jerusalem would once more be the city of God (verse 21).

Author

Obadiah's prophecy is the shortest of all the Old Testament prophets. We know nothing about him outside this single chapter. He sees himself as a mouthpiece of God only; his name meaning "servant of God", could be a name he gave himself. His language is both poetic and passionate.

Date

Six of his verses are very close to some in Jeremiah (verses 1-6 = Jeremiah 49:9,14-16). This leads many to presume Obadiah is referring to the fall of Jerusalem in 586 BC. Ezekiel, writing at much the same time, refers to the misdeeds of the Edomites as well (Ezekiel 25:12f.; compare Psalm 137:7; Lamentations 4:21). The prophecy is usually therefore dated within the exilic period.

A message of judgement for Edom
1a God gives Obadiah a vision about Edom
1b-9 Complete destruction will come upon proud Edom
10-14 The reason for judgement: Edom had betrayed Judah in her time of need

The great day of reversal is coming
15-16 Israel's enemies will be destroyed
17-21 Israel will be restored under God's rule and will occupy their enemies' lands

KEY THEMES – OBADIAH

Pride will be brought down

The boast of impregnability is not new to Edom. In 2 Samuel 5:6-7 we read of the Jebusites boasting that Jerusalem was impregnable. That did not prevent King David capturing it and then using it as his new capital. Edom, a little nation on the edge of the Negev desert, part of modern-day Jordan, thought its mountains were its protection. But God says, "The pride of your heart has deceived you" (verse 3). It is God himself who "will bring you down" (verse 4).

This is a theme common to other prophets also. Isaiah talks of "the pride of men brought low" (Isaiah 2:11). To the Greeks, pride was termed "hubris" and meant putting oneself beyond the reach of fate. It was considered the worst of sins. The Bible does not list sins in rank order quite like this, but certainly no one and no nation is beyond the reach of God's judgement.

Chaos and God's sovereignty

The Babylonian invasion, which led to the destruction of Jerusalem, produced a chaotic aftermath, well described in Jeremiah 39–44.

It is amazing any prophetic writing survived. Its survival is symbolic, however, of God's order being established in the middle of chaos and the breaking of relationships. Obadiah is able to see a return to order in terms of restoration, of exiles returning to their land, and Jerusalem once again being established as the centre of God's rule (verses 19-21).

Justice and fulfilment

Part of God's judgement is the equalising of guilt and punishment. The phrase "in the day of their (Judah's) disaster" is repeated as the reason for God's punishment, leading to the climax "your deeds will return on your own head" (verse 15).

As a matter of history, Edom did not fall quickly, probably not till the time of the Maccabees (1 Maccabees 5:3), some 400 years later, though they were displaced from the mountains earlier than that. God does not put a timetable on the execution of his justice. But history has proved how complete the punishment was. By New Testament times, there was no sign left of Edom.

Wasting the inheritance

It might appear that Edom had always been enemies of Israel. But in fact, the Edomites were descended from Esau, Jacob's brother (Genesis 25:24-26; 36:1). As such, there was potentially a residual blessing available for them. But they opposed Israel, especially when the Israelites were escaping Egypt (Numbers 20:18-21). Although later incorporated into King David's empire (1 Kings 11:14-22), they soon rebelled (2 Kings 8:20-21). Even so, their betrayal of Judah is seen as a brotherly betrayal by Obadiah (verse 10).

> " *But on Mount Zion will be deliverance.*"
>
> OBADIAH 17

Many people think that because their country has had a Christian past, it will still enjoy God's blessing. But actually it is possible for that country to oppose God's laws and rule and to waste its inheritance actively, not just passively. At that stage it will certainly come under God's judgement.

Courage and trust

World affairs sometimes seem chaotic, and certainly out of God's control. That may be true for our personal lives, including even betrayal by close family members. Like Obadiah, we need to re-assert our vision of God's control, order and restoration. This takes courage, especially when discouragement becomes our greatest enemy. It also takes trust in God's purposes, looking afresh at our circumstances with a view to seeing God's purposes.

Jonah
MAN WITH A MISSION

OVERVIEW

The book of Jonah is quite unlike those of the other Minor Prophets, since it tells a story of a prophet, rather than gives his message. The story itself becomes the message. Jonah is given a commission, runs away from it and almost dies as a consequence. He is recommissioned, has great success, but still cannot find fulfilment in what he has accomplished.

SUMMARY

The story divides into two halves, both of which can be subdivided to form the four chapters of this dramatic little book. The story line is not difficult – it is often retold as a children's story – but the meaning has been argued over. It contains different layers of meaning, and uses irony as a central device.

Jonah is given a commission from God to preach judgement to the city of Nineveh, the main city of the great Assyrian Empire. Unlike other prophets, such as Nahum, he is to give his denunciation in person in the country (1:2). Jonah ran away as far as he could, to Tarshish, generally supposed to have been a Phoenician colony in Spain (1:3-4).

The boat he sailed in ran into a massive storm. The superstitious sailors saw this as divine in origin and sought its cause. Eventually Jonah's disobedience came to light, and he told the sailors to throw him overboard (1:4-12). They hesitated at first, but eventually had to (1:13-15).

The storm abated at once, causing the sailors to believe in Jonah's God. Meanwhile, a great fish swallowed Jonah (1:17). Within the fish's stomach, Jonah worshipped God (2:1-9). Finally, Jonah was vomited up on dry land (2:10).

Jonah now went to Nineveh, and such was the force of his preaching, the whole city repented. God's judgement was averted (3:1-10). But instead of being pleased, Jonah became very angry with God, wishing to die. In the final chapter, God and Jonah argue about God's apparent change of mind. Jonah is challenged for his inconsistency: he is more upset at a plant dying than with the thought of a whole city's population being destroyed.

Author

There is no general agreement about the author. There is a prophet named Jonah son of Amittai mentioned once in 2 Kings 14:25 during the reign of Jeroboam II of Israel. But there is no certainty that the writer of the book and the prophet are one and the same person.

Date

Nor is there any general agreement about the date. The earliest date would have to be between 793–753 BC, the dates of Jeroboam II. It was a period of Assyrian weakness. But 3:3 suggests Nineveh's greatness was in the past, which would suggest a date after 612 BC, when the city fell (see Nahum).

Jonah's mission to Nineveh

Jonah runs away from God's commission

1:1-2 God gives Jonah a message of judgement for Nineveh

1:3 Jonah runs away and boards a boat to Tarshish

1:4 The boat sails into a great storm

1:5-10 The sailors discover that Jonah is the cause of the storm

1:11-15 Jonah persuades the sailors to throw him overboard

1:16 The sailors worship God

1:17 God sends a great fish to swallow Jonah

Jonah's prayer to God from inside the great fish

2:1-9 Jonah thanks God for rescuing him from death and declares that he will fulfil his vows

2:10 The great fish deposits Jonah on a beach

Jonah's mission to Nineveh (again)

Jonah delivers God's message to Nineveh

3:1-2 God sends Jonah to Nineveh again

3:3-4 Jonah preaches in the city of Nineveh

3:5-9 The Ninevites repent and pray to God for mercy

3:10 God has mercy and does not destroy Nineveh

Jonah's reaction to God's mercy

4:1 Jonah is angry at God's decision to have mercy

4:2-4 Jonah complains to God and God questions Jonah's right to be angry

4:5-8 God provides a vine for Jonah but it withers

4:9 God questions Jonah's right to be angry at the vine

4:10-11 God declares his concern for Nineveh

KEY THEMES – JONAH

The mercy of God

The most obvious book to compare is that of Nahum. Nahum preaches judgement over Nineveh; Jonah preaches judgement, too, but sees God's mercy. The two books together reveal "the kindness and sternness of God" (Romans 11:22): once the people repent then God "relents from sending calamity" (4:2).

Such an act is entirely in keeping with what the earlier books of the Old Testament show about God's character. Time and again, Israel disobeyed God, often abandoning the faith altogether, yet when they do eventually turn again and repent, God continues to have mercy on them and restore them.

This is the single most difficult thing for Jonah. In 4:2 he finally states why he fled: he was afraid that God would "change his mind" and leave him looking foolish. The irony here is that Jonah is the faithless prophet, not for running away, but for understanding only half his message – or rather, understanding what God was like, yet refusing to accept it. It is the same attitude as the older brother's in the parable of the prodigal son (Luke 15:25-32).

The universality of salvation

It could be argued that God's mercy to Israel was because of his covenant relationship with them as his special people. But here it is clearly shown that God has mercy on other people who were outside this covenant – in other words, God's offer of forgiveness for sins is available to everyone.

It is sometimes pointed out that this would have been the real difficulty for the original Jewish readers of the book. Their belief that God only had a plan of salvation for one nation would have been challenged. Certainly, the New Testament teaching is that "Christ died for all" (2 Corinthians 5:14).

Prophecy as a warning

Jonah wanted his message to be predictive, just as Nahum's apparently was. But in fact, any prophetic utterance of judgement is meant to pronounce a warning, not a fate. This distinction is not as easy as it sounds. The great prophet Ezekiel wrestled with understanding this (Ezekiel 18). What emerges from Jonah and the other prophets is that prophecy is a function of God's mercy (4:2); and the desired end is always repentance and faith.

RELEVANCE FOR TODAY – JONAH

Mission and motives

One of the great ironies of the book is that Jonah brought people to repentance despite his best efforts not to! His actions convinced the mariners that his God was the one to worship (1:16); and his preaching brought the Ninevites to repentance in a quite spectacular way (3:5-9).

The calling was the key element, rather than his willingness or right motive. If God calls us, he will anoint us, and it is his anointing. There is therefore no room for pride in our individual endeavours, even in our obedience.

But if we do want some personal sense of fulfilment in serving God, then right motives are essential. Jonah only got misery from his reluctance and his unloving attitudes.

> " *Should I not be concerned about that great city?*"

JONAH 4:11

Second chances

God is often said to be the God of second chances. Jonah proves the point here, just as Peter proved the point after his denial of Jesus (John 21:15-19). The great fish is a sign of mercy rather than judgement, and the time spent in its stomach was the space Jonah needed to find God's presence and purposes. In the parable of the prodigal son, it is a pig-sty (Luke 15:15-17). Second chances are given, and in his grace he provides the heart space for us to receive them.

Death and resurrection

Jesus Christ refers to the book of Jonah once in connection with repentance (Luke 11:29-32), and in connection with death and resurrection, using the three days in the fish's stomach as a sign of his time in the grave (Matthew 12:39-41; 16:4).

The whole structure of the book reinforces this. In chapter 1, Jonah descends deeper and deeper into death: he sleeps (a type of death) in the bowels of the ship; is thrown into the sea to sink; is swallowed by what could be symbolic of death. But then in the grave he comes to, and begins to rise again, thrown on to the beach as new-born. This then also signifies our rebirth, for which baptism is another water sign.

In your anger do not sin (Ephesians 4:26)

Interestingly, the end of the book is not another rising. The book finishes in an open-ended way: will Jonah come to personal sorrow for his anger against God? We don't know.

What can we do when we have anger, especially when it is against God for being seemingly "unfair" to us? The book suggests anger hurts no one but ourselves. God will argue with us, but he always has the last word (4:11). We have to give our anger to God for him to transform it.

270 THE BIBLE BOOK BY BOOK · JONAH

Micah

HUMAN INJUSTICE: GOD'S JUSTICE

OVERVIEW

Micah sees the many failings rampant in his society, naming perversions of power, money, false prophecy and false religion. This is not only his case, but God's, and God pronounces judgement, like for like. But in his mercy, God does not stop there: he promises a generous restoration and a renewed hope for his people's future.

SUMMARY

Chapters 1–3 and 6 deal with the deep failures within the societies of the northern and southern kingdoms of the Holy Land. The northern kingdom is called variously Israel, Ephraim, and Samaria, the name of its capital. The southern kingdom is called Judah or Jerusalem, its capital. Sometimes the term Israel is used of the whole country, north and south.

The book particularly singles out for repeated mention sins of social injustice, maladministration by corrupt leaders, idolatry, and false priests and prophets (1:3-7; 2:1-11; 3:1-3,8-11; 6:9-12). Such failures would lead to dire consequences, which God would either bring about or allow to happen, namely lack of prosperity, military defeat, destruction of towns and finally exile (1:8-16; 2:3-4; 3:4-7,12; 6:13-16). But even in the prediction of destruction, a promise of hope in a restored remnant is given (2:12-13).

This latter promise is then expanded in the other chapters (4-5,7). Restoration (4:6-8; 5:7-9; 7:18-20) would be accompanied by power over other nations (4:11-13; 5:10-15; 7:11-17). But the power will be primarily

spiritual. In his most exalted vision midpoint in the book, Micah saw a restored Jerusalem as the centre for worldwide worship of God (4:1-5). These chapters also contain references to the same failures as the other chapters (4:9-12; 5:3; 7:1-10). The first and last chapters book-end the prophecy, summarising the main themes and emphases.

Author

The book contains a selection of the prophecies of Micah of Moresheth-Gath (1:14), a village lying in the hilly country west of Jerusalem. Unlike Isaiah, Micah seems to have more of a country background and to have travelled widely in both kingdoms.

Date

Micah lived through the reigns of Jotham (740–735 BC), Ahaz (735–715 BC) and Hezekiah (715–687 BC). This makes him a younger contemporary of Isaiah, and a generation or so after Amos and Hosea. Some scholars think that certain small sections, which talk of the enemy as Babylon rather than Assyria (4:10), may have been added later.

OUTLINE – MICAH

A message of judgement for Israel and Judah
1:1-2 Introduction to Micah's prophecies
1:3-7 God is coming to judge Jerusalem and Samaria
1:8-16 A lament for the sin of Judah and God's coming judgement
2:1-11 God's judgement will certainly come on unjust oppressors
2:12-13 A promise of deliverance for a remnant
3:1-7 God will not answer the cries of corrupt leaders and prophets
3:8-12 The result: Jerusalem will be destroyed

A message of hope for the future
4:1-5 God will bring peace and blessing to the world from the temple in Jerusalem
4:6-8 God will rule over the returned exiles in Jerusalem
4:9-13 A promise of rescue and restoration after exile
5:1-6 The ruler from Bethlehem will shepherd God's people
5:7-9 The future strength of God's remnant
5:10-15 The coming destruction of all weapons and idols

God's complaint against Israel
6:1-5 A reminder of how God has cared for Israel
6:6-8 A reminder of what pleases God: act justly, love mercy, walk humbly
6:9-16 God's judgement is a result of Israel's social sins
7:1-6 A lament for the sins of Israel

The coming restoration of Israel
7:7-10 God himself will rescue Israel after her judgement
7:11-13 Israel will be rebuilt
7:14-15 God will be the shepherd of his people
7:16-17 The nations of the world will submit to God
7:18-20 God is faithful and merciful

KEY THEMES – MICAH

God the just judge

The book begins and ends with a courtroom drama: "the Sovereign LORD may witness against you" (1:2); "until he pleads my case"(7:9). 6:2 states "the LORD has a case against his people" (see also Malachi for this structure). The need for a just judge is especially acute when "rulers of the house of Israel ... despise justice" (3:9). Only God, and the prophet as God's mouthpiece (3:8), can make the case against his people fairly, and give a right judgement (4:3). This is because in the past God has shown himself to be merciful. 6:3-5 is the evidence for this, based on the covenant oath taken long ago (7:20).

The punishments are like for like, and therefore in due measure. The elaborate series of puns on place names in 1:8-15 in a strange way demonstrates this. The punishment fits the place, symbolic of the actual crime. Thus pride and arrogance (2:1-2) are punished by humiliation and despoliation (2:2-5). Exile (4:10) is fitting in that God's people have exiled themselves from him; they have dispossessed themselves by their robbery of land from those weaker than themselves. God's justice is truly seen in "a man reaps what he sows" (Galatians 6:7), as shown most clearly in 6:9-16.

The future shepherd

There are some passages in Micah that have a striking similarity with Isaiah. Just as Isaiah, and other prophets, attacked the country's injustices, so they also prophesied future restoration under a leader appointed by God. These prophecies were later seen as "messianic", that is, predicting a future great leader to bring salvation and deliverance. The New Testament writers quote many such prophecies as being fulfilled in Jesus Christ.

For example, Matthew 2:6 quotes Micah 5:2, which parallels Isaiah 11:1. The shepherd image of Micah 5:4 echoes that in Isaiah 40:11, and is taken up, with other Old Testament references, in Jesus' claim to be the good shepherd (John 10:14). Micah 4:1-3 parallels Isaiah 2:2-4 in predicting this future restoration, using the image of God as judge, and the peaceful one of beating swords into ploughshares. But that is after the shepherd has brought victory over his enemies (5:5-6).

God's continuing purposes

These predictions of restoration are always linked in the Old Testament prophets with prophecies concerning a righteous remnant. This is because human failure and its punishment cannot ultimately derail God's purposes. God is not at the mercy of human sin! Thus future purposes are seen as brought about by his forgiveness, intervention and provision of divine leadership – all anticipating the new covenant in Jesus Christ. In Micah we have many passages that emphasise this: 4:1-8; 5:1-15; 7:8-20.

RELEVANCE FOR TODAY – MICAH

True prosperity

Micah, like Haggai (Haggai 1:5-10) and
Malachi (Malachi 3:8-12), spells out why
God's people do not prosper. Most people
want to prosper, and feel that God should
somehow help them in this. It certainly is
God's will for us to know prosperity of some
sort (Psalm 35:27), even though the preaching
of the so-called "Prosperity Gospel" recently
has given the concept a bad name. We cannot,
of course, reduce it to simple material terms,
"paying God in order for him to pay you
back". Micah suggests the failure of
prosperity in terms of human efforts
achieving nothing. It is a moral failure, in that
we try to achieve success in wrong ways. 2:1-2
is a blatant example of this; 6:9-15 almost as
obvious a list.

If the verse "You will store up but save
nothing" (6:14) seems to describe our

> " *And he will be
> their peace.*"

MICAH 5:5

situation, the first place to seek redress is to
check our ways of "storing up" against the
prophetic checklists. There are other reasons,
of course, from practical mismanagement to a
"spirit of poverty", but Micah gives us
somewhere to start.

What does God want?

6:6-8 is a prophecy backed up by statements
from other prophets about what God truly
wants. Here, Micah makes it clear God is not
really interested in our sacrifices as such, as if
somehow he needed them. The system of
sacrifices in the Old Testament was partly to
deal with sin and partly as an expression of
gratitude. What had happened in Micah's day
was that sacrifices were made more as an
insurance policy, or to keep God on their side;
that is from wrong motives, with no intention
of moral reform.

Micah makes it clear the three true
requirements God wants are:
· To act justly
· To love mercy
· To walk humbly.

Today, sacrifices could, for example, be seen
as giving money or hours of working hard,
even hours of prayer. But if these do not come
from a merciful, humble and just heart, they
are of no real value.

What is God like?

However much Micah has expressed his
message in terms of charges, evidence,
sentencing, he returns at the end to what is
most deeply on his heart: God's pardoning
and merciful nature. "You delight to show
mercy" (7:18; see also 7:20) is something we
need to hang on to, whether in the middle of a
sense of our own failures, or in the middle of
other people's. Again, Micah echoes Isaiah,
this time Isaiah 43:25. Such mercy is true
evidence of God's loving purposes for us.

Nahum
AN EVIL EMPIRE OVERTHROWN

OVERVIEW

The prophet Nahum delivers a series of blistering attacks on the evil empire of Assyria and announces that its capital, Nineveh, will soon be unexpectedly and utterly destroyed by God. The result will be that Judah will have respite.

SUMMARY

The prophecy of Nahum is unusual in that it consists almost entirely of a series of mocking denunciations of a foreign power, rather than messages directed to the spiritual life of God's people. Although Nineveh is often addressed directly, obviously the main audience would have been the Israelites, probably living in mortal dread of this foreign power. The prophecy thus becomes a source of hope for them.

The book opens with a song of praise to God as divine warrior (1:2-14). This sets the theme of warfare and victory. For Judah this meant hope, but for Nineveh it meant total destruction. "Who can endure his fierce anger?" Nahum asks (1:5).

The second chapter consists of a vivid and dramatic description of Nineveh's final destruction, with the battle raging within its walls. Although the Assyrians might summon their picked soldiers, it would make no difference. Nahum uses images of lions, an animal the Assyrians often used symbolically: "Where now is the lions' den?" he asks rhetorically (2:11).

The final chapter is addressed to the city itself. In a highly poetic, impressionistic description, Nahum paints a picture of chaos and the humiliation of defeat.

Author

All we know about Nahum is that he came from the village of Elkosh, which was probably in Judah. He has a "burden" (1:1), as the KJV puts it, which means a heavy message of impending doom, and he gives it in a dramatic and poetic style, full of literary devices and vivid description.

Date

The Assyrians had previously attacked Jerusalem in 701 BC (2 Kings 18:17–19:36), and before that had destroyed the northern kingdom of Israel in 722 BC (2 Kings 17:1-5; 18:9-10). At the time of the writing of the prophecy, Assyria still seemed invincible and was dreaded.

However, it did fall in 612 BC, when it was attacked from the north by the Medes, and from the south and east by the Babylonians. Nahum must have been writing before this, but after the fall of No-Amon, or Thebes (in 663 BC) mentioned in 3:8.

OUTLINE – NAHUM

Nahum's message about the judgement of Nineveh

1:1 God gives Nahum a message about Nineveh

1:2-8 Nahum declares God's justice, righteous anger, power and goodness

1:9-15 Assyria will be destroyed and Judah will be set free from oppression

2:1-13 Nineveh will fall and never recover because God is her enemy

3:1-7 God will judge Nineveh because of her idolatry

3:8-13 Nineveh will be destroyed as it had destroyed Thebes

3:14-17 Destruction will come before the city is prepared

3:18-19 The Assyrians will be destroyed because of their cruelty, and the world will rejoice

KEY THEMES – NAHUM

God as warrior

This is a theme that runs through much of the Old Testament. Its commonest form is in the use of the title "Lord of Hosts", which is the term Nahum uses in 2:13. The NIV translates this phrase as "Lord Almighty".

"Hosts" is an older English word meaning "armies", "military forces". Instances of this phrase are in 2 Kings 19:31, where Isaiah predicts the defeat of the Assyrian army when besieging the city of Jerusalem, and in Isaiah 37:32, where Isaiah predicts a remnant of Israel surviving. In both cases, the meaning is that God will literally fight for his people against the enemy.

Elsewhere, God as a strong warrior is described in Habakkuk 3:5-15, and in Zechariah 9:1-15; 14:1,3,5. Zechariah forms the theme into two hymns, which include references to a theophany (or appearance of God to humans) and the cosmic disturbances brought about as God fights for his people. Psalm 98 contains similar pictures, in a tradition that goes right back to Exodus 15:3 and Joshua 5:13-15.

Nahum mentions similar disturbances to Habakkuk and Zechariah (1:3-5). He fights for his people (1:8,13) to bring them peace (1:15)

and restoration (2:2). The whole book is perhaps the most military one of all the prophets.

The severity of God

Nahum was writing about the same time as the young Jeremiah, a little after Zephaniah and a little before Habakkuk. However, the most obvious prophet to link him with is Jonah. Both prophets devoted their prophecies to Nineveh, which is the centre of power of the brutal Assyrian regime.

What is immediately striking is how different Nahum and Jonah are. In Jonah's case, the message is a message of salvation to a wicked city, a message that appears to have been received. Nahum brings a message of punishment and judgement. Taken both together, the two books represent "the goodness and the severity of God" (Romans 11:22 KJV).

God does not punish Nineveh just because they have attacked his people. Their cruelty in their own day was notorious and mentioned specifically by Nahum (2:1-4; 3:19). The taunt in 3:4 suggests they were deeply involved in witchcraft and sexual immorality.

Who writes history?

Many great empires feel themselves invulnerable. It is said that conquerors write history. Clearly Assyria thought so. Nahum reminds them of the fall of another great empire, Egypt, and one of its main cities (3:8-11). It is not the conqueror who writes history; it is God.

Over the last century, we have seen great evil empires defeated, often quite catastrophically. The feeling of relief at, for example, the defeat of Nazi Germany and Hitler's death, or the breaking of the Berlin Wall, must be similar to what Nahum was seeking to convey to his listeners. The relief is that there is a God who does bring down evil.

History continues to be written. It is almost inevitable other evil empires and leaders will emerge, thinking their destiny is in their hands, that they can write history to their will. We need to have Nahum's vision that at some stage, God will demonstrate his judgement over them. We look to him today to deal with countries that govern with brutality and injustice.

> " *The* LORD *is good,*
> *a refuge in times of trouble.*"
>
> NAHUM 1:7

Spiritual warfare

The prophecy focuses our minds on battle and fighting. What is the spiritual relevance of this? At one level, we are all too aware of inner forces at war within ourselves, just as Paul was in Romans 7:23. We cannot escape this battle between good and evil within ourselves.

The New Testament, however, suggests a much wider arena for such warfare. Interestingly, the lion image is used again to describe it: "your enemy the devil like a roaring lion" (1 Peter 5:8). That is why Paul tells us to wear armour (1 Thessalonians 5:8) and fight back against an evil which is a cosmic principle, not just a set of inner urges.

But there is also a realm of warfare at a "national" level, where countries and cultures, at certain times at least, are engaged in warfare that has a spiritual and cosmic dimension. God does fight for his people and for godly nations, to bring down mighty powers that oppose his purposes of righteousness and justice.

Proclaiming peace

In the middle of the fighting language, Nahum can still talk of proclaiming peace and protection (1:15). In this he echoes Isaiah 52:7. God fights for the peace, protection and deliverance for his people. We need to realise how much Nahum's vision was a great step of faith for him. But we need that same sort of faith, to know that God is for us, for our peace and our deliverance. Otherwise we become overwhelmed by the sheer amount of evil in this world.

Habakkuk
HARD QUESTIONS

THE PROPHETS

OVERVIEW

Habakkuk asks hard questions of God, questions about injustice and corruption in his society. He receives even harder answers. At first he is shocked by God. Then, as he waits, the answers begin to make sense. Finally, he comes to understand God's purposes and finds faith again despite what appears an uncertain future.

SUMMARY

Habakkuk the prophet found himself living in an unjust society. He cried out to God about this, asking God to send justice and punishment, but God did not seem to be listening. The book opens with Habakkuk's lodging a serious complaint against God (1:2-4).

God answered, but in a way that Habakkuk was totally unprepared for: God planned to send the Babylonians to destroy Habakkuk's society (1:5-11). The Babylonian army is vividly described in images of leopards, vultures, a desert wind. It is a terrifying picture of an unstoppable force.

Habakkuk was appalled (1:12-17). His moral sense was outraged: however bad his own society, the Babylonians were far worse. The Babylonians' victims are described as shoals of fish that have no leader and can be scooped up helplessly in nets. It would seem might is right. In a sort of challenge to God, Habakkuk set himself to wait for a full explanation (2:1).

The answer came. Habakkuk must take the long-term view. In the end, all unjust societies and nations will fail, and the oppressed will have the last word (2:2-20). Meanwhile, Habakkuk needs to live as a man of faith: he might not see the end result, but he must believe in God's plans and purposes. In a series of four woes, God universally condemns all forms of injustice and idolatry.

In a concluding prayer, Habakkuk asked God to renew his people (3:2). He remembered how God often reveals his power through nature, and how he saved his people out of Egypt (3:3-15). So whatever might happen in the immediate future, however terrible the coming invasion, Habakkuk would rejoice in God, his justice and his purposes (3:16-19).

Author

Habakkuk was a prophet (1:1; 3:1) about whom nothing is known outside this book. His name means "someone who clings or embraces". His prophecy is technically known as an "oracle". Unusually, he is told to write it down, rather than deliver it orally, as many of the prophets did (2:2). The fact that he finished with a psalm may mean that he was a "singing prophet" connected to the temple in Jerusalem (see 1 Chronicles 25:1).

Date

The Babylonians (or Chaldeans) came to power in the region after the battle of Carchemish (605 BC), when they defeated the hitherto dominant Assyrians and Egyptians. But they did not invade Judah, that is, the surviving southern kingdom of Israel, until 598 BC (2 Kings 24:1-4,8-17). This places Habakkuk between these two dates, living at the same time as the prophet Jeremiah, perhaps under King Jehoiakim. Jeremiah, too, spoke out against injustice, in considerably more detail, and predicted the coming invasion of the Babylonians (Jeremiah 5:1-13; 27:6-11).

OUTLINE – HABAKKUK

Habakkuk's conversation with God

1:1 Habakkuk receives a vision from God

1:2-4 Habakkuk complains that God has not judged the sin, violence and injustice around him

1:5-11 God replies that he is going to use the Babylonians to bring judgement

1:12-17 Habakkuk complains that the Babylonians are more wicked than God's unfaithful people

2:1 Habakkuk waits for God's reply

2:2-8 God replies that the Babylonians themselves will be judged one day

2:9-17 No injustice will escape God's judgement

2:18-20 Idols are worthless, but God is living and powerful

Habakkuk's prayer of submission to God

3:1-2 Habakkuk prays for God's help and mercy

3:3-15 God's mighty acts of deliverance in Israel's history

3:16-19 Habakkuk will wait for God's salvation with joy and trust

Protesting against injustice

Habakkuk, like most of the other Bible prophets, was revolted by his society's evil ways. His immediate concern is with the violence, injustice and conflict all around him. Wrongdoers are not brought to justice; the system is run by the wicked. Some prophets, such as Isaiah or Jeremiah, directly speak to their corrupt society. Habakkuk, it seems, has cried out to God for divine intervention.

For Habakkuk, the problem is compounded when God tells him that the Babylonians will be sent as punishment on this corrupt society. Yet "they are a law to themselves"(1:7), their "own strength is their god"(1:11). They are merciless to their enemies (1:17).

Habakkuk keeps protesting to God. The book's message is that God does hear these protests against injustice. He does not remain passive: in the long term his purposes will be revealed to those who passionately seek him.

God's strange purposes

These purposes, however, are not what Habakkuk expected. It is always good to know that injustice will be punished, but the prophet cannot dictate the mode of punishment. Being a prophet involves commitment to the people of God, however off-track. Their punishment has, to some extent, to be shared by the prophet. It also involves being prepared to lay aside previous convictions about how God works. It is not comfortable being a prophet, either physically or spiritually.

Isaiah realised this when he preached the coming of the Assyrians (Isaiah 10:5-10). Jeremiah realised this too, though his discomfort was more in the total rejection of his message (Jeremiah 36:20-32). Jonah's discomfort was more with the idea that God would forgive the very people he had been denouncing (Jonah 4:1).

For Habakkuk, the core of the problem lay in his idea of God's holiness (1:13). But God's holiness sometimes expresses itself in strange ways (Isaiah 55:8-9). All such expressions prefigure God's purposes in Jesus Christ. His own death was the strangest expression of God's holiness of all, the use of tremendous injustice to bring about justice and deliverance for humankind (Acts 2:22-39).

Living by faith

God's strange and mysterious purposes will be revealed eventually (2:3). In the meanwhile, the wicked may be "puffed up", but the righteous must hang on to their faith, and that is how they will live (2:4). The New Testament writers found in this verse the very essence of our relationship with God and they quote it three times (Romans 1:17; Galatians 3:11; Hebrews 10:38-39). For them it implies both faith in Jesus Christ and faith in God's good purposes. Hebrews states that God is not pleased with those who hang back because they cannot trust God. The choice is between allowing our faith to be constantly challenged, and receiving the revelation of God that comes with that, or "playing it safe", refusing to go beyond what can be understood.

Arguing with God

Habakkuk's dialogue with God is technically known as a "complaint". Jeremiah complained to God, too (Jeremiah 12:1-6), as did Job (Job 3:1-26), and Jonah (Jonah 4:1-3). The Bible suggests that God does not mind his servants arguing, as long as they are prepared to sit still and wait for an answer. So often in our complaining we are so full of self-pity, we only want to rehearse a list of grievances.

God answered Habakkuk twice, and through his complaints, Habakkuk actually received a deeper revelation than if he had kept quiet. However, at some point, we do have to keep quiet (2:20, also in Zechariah 2:13). Injustice and evil will inevitably baffle us; as will God's ways of dealing with them. We have to accept that we live in a fallen world, but that God is in charge of all nations and of history. This can lead us to a place of trust, even if only at the end of a process of arguing and listening.

Discerning God's purposes

If arguing is one way to gain revelation, watching is another. The prophets saw themselves as watchmen (2:1; Isaiah 21:8-12; Ezekiel 3:17; 33:1-20). When every city had walls, they were only as good as the watchmen on them. Hence the imagery the prophets used. Habakkuk uses the image not in terms of an approaching enemy, but of waiting for God's revelation or answer. It is when he

> " *The* Sovereign LORD
> is *my strength;*
> *he makes my feet*
> *like the feet of a deer,*
> *he enables me to go*
> *on the heights.*"

HABAKKUK 3:19

receives this that he is committed to communicate it.

Habakkuk discerns that God is actively in control of the whole world. He intervenes. So we have the choice as watchmen. Either we believe what the media tell us is happening in the world, or we discern what God is doing. The Bible record, especially in the prophetic writings, helps us to do this. But we have to wait in prayer, too. In that way we become people of faith, knowing what to say in troubled times.

Longing for renewal

Habakkuk cries out for renewal (3:2). He wants God's deeds to become obvious to everyone. Then he wants God's glory to be seen (2:14). That is what we should still want. Above all, God will be known through his church, the society of God's people. We need to cry to God for his church to be renewed. The KJV expresses 3:2 as "O LORD, revive thy work in the midst of the years."

Habakkuk also prays for mercy rather than anger, or even mercy out of anger. Sometimes in our prayers against injustice, we want punishment and our hearts become angry. We need to plead for mercy as we pray that our hearts would be kept tender and responsive.

Trusting God no matter what

Habakkuk's final statement is that he will rejoice in God whatever happens (3:16-18). Even if he has to suffer the devastation of Babylonian invasion, with no crops, no harvest, nothing left, he will still keep rejoicing in God.

This is tough. But this is what living by faith actually means: however hard the circumstances, yet we still rejoice. After the arguing, after the silence, after the discernment, Habakkuk reaches the stage of rejoicing unconditionally.

Zephaniah
THE DAY OF THE LORD

OVERVIEW

This book is a forthright condemnation of the spiritual state of Judah and Jerusalem. Zephaniah preaches the Day of the LORD as a day of catastrophic judgement. However, those who turn to God will be saved as a treasured and protected remnant.

SUMMARY

The book of Zephaniah can be divided into two rather unequal parts. First comes a series of judgements (1:1–3:8); which is then followed by a promise of restoration for a remnant (3:9-20).

The judgements are focused on Jerusalem, but begin as a worldwide judgement (1:2-3), then narrowing down to Judah, the southern kingdom of Israel (1:4–2:3). The book then delivers a series of judgements on Judah's neighbours (2:4-15), before returning to focus on Jerusalem, the capital of Judah, and the centre of its religious life (3:1-7). This part of Zephaniah concludes by a further brief worldview (3:8).

The judgements are delivered as woes and denunciations of specific sins, delivered as if God were speaking directly, using the prophet as his mouthpiece. The sins range from social injustice and oppression to idolatry and spiritual apathy. The coming judgement is spoken of in terms of "the Day of the LORD", which is depicted in hyperbolic terms of total destruction and cataclysm.

However, the message is tempered by the possibility of safety and deliverance in this day if the "humble of the land" seek God (2:3). These would be sheltered and become a righteous remnant, who would not only be rescued, but would also know God's pleasure and prosperity. There would be a total restoration for them.

Author

The only information we have of Zephaniah is given in 1:1, where he traces his ancestry back four generations, to Hezekiah, presumably the righteous king of Judah who reigned 715–687 BC, which would mean Zephaniah is one of the upper class of Jerusalem upon whom his prophecies pronounce judgement.

Date

The opening verse established the date as within the reign of King Josiah (640–609 BC). However, the widespread idolatry associated with the two intervening kings between Hezekiah and Josiah, Manasseh and Amon, still seems to be prevalent. Josiah introduced widespread reforms from 622 BC, though they may not have been immediately effective. The denunciation of Assyria (2:13-15) suggests a date before 612 BC, which is when that country fell. A date between 639–612 BC would make Zephaniah a contemporary of Nahum, preceding the ministry of Jeremiah.

OUTLINE – ZEPHANIAH

Messages of judgement
1:1 Zephaniah receives messages of judgement from God
1:2-3 Universal judgement
1:4-13 God declares his judgement on Judah and her people
1:14-18 The Day of the LORD will be a day of judgement
2:1-3 A call to repent before God's judgement comes
2:4-7 A message of judgement for Philistia; their land will be given to God's remnant
2:8-11 A message of judgement for Moab and Ammon; the whole world will then worship God
2:12 A message of destruction for Ethiopia
2:13-15 A message of judgement for Assyria
3:1-4 A message of judgement for Jerusalem and its leaders
3:5-7 Jerusalem does not take notice of God's righteous judgements on other nations
3:8 God's universal judgement is coming

A message of hope and restoration
3:9-10 Universal worship
3:11-20 Blessing and restoration for Judah because of God's salvation and forgiveness

The Day of the LORD

Each of the Minor Prophets has some emphasis which makes them unique. Zephaniah's emphasis is "the Day of the LORD" (1:7), a phrase which recurs some 14 times in the next 15 verses, either in that form or as "that day", "a day", "the great day of the LORD" or "the day of the LORD's wrath".

The phrase is used in earlier prophets, such as Amos (Amos 5:18-20), Joel (Joel 1:15), and Isaiah (Isaiah 2:6-22), but it is Zephaniah who uses it most emphatically and centrally in his message. Through Zephaniah, it became an accepted and widely understood phrase for later writers to use, often in an apocalyptic context.

Basically, the term means the time when God will intervene directly in some obvious way. Typically, it means a day of judgement, but as the last section demonstrates, it can also refer to an intervention of deliverance and restoration.

The remnant

The idea of a righteous remnant to be restored by God is absolutely central to Old Testament prophetic writing. Isaiah 1:9 states "Unless the LORD Almighty had left us some survivors, we would have become like Sodom". This points out two things:

· At times the Israelites were no better than the wicked nations that surrounded them and fully deserved the same judgement
· God's relationship with Israel was different. They were the people chosen by him to demonstrate his purposes to the world, and established by covenant.

This means that God chooses to preserve a people through whom he makes himself known. The pattern of Noah is similar: a remnant had to be preserved from the flood (Genesis 8:21). In Zephaniah, the remnant of Israel will be virtuous (3:12-13), and God will actively rejoice over them (3:17). The idea of gathering from exile is also typical, as in Joel 3:1-2 and Jeremiah 31.

God's anger

Again, God's anger is central to an understanding of his nature as revealed throughout the Old Testament. In Zephaniah, the emphasis is on a holy God in an unholy city (3:5). God's choice of Jerusalem as his holy city, where his temple would be situated, meant that in some sense it was his earthly dwelling place. Though he was God of the whole world (1:2-3), Jerusalem was the place where evil would be especially repugnant to him, since his presence would give it special holiness. Zephaniah's description of particular places within the city (1:10-12) shows that God's anger is not just of a general nature, but quite specific. Jesus' cleansing of the temple shows something of this anger (Matthew 21:13). In 3:8 God's anger is directed towards the whole world, for the sake of giving all the opportunity to "call on the name of the LORD" (3:9).

The reality of judgement

Many people today shudder at the whole idea of God's anger. Either they reject the whole Christian idea of God, because they see anger in terms of arbitrary force or emotion or they reject the Old Testament depiction of God, as they see it opposing a concept of God as love. Even some Christians are guilty of this, failing to see the necessary connection between divine (in contrast to human) anger, judgement, justice, and discipline.

In terms of the reality of Zephaniah's prophecy, Assyria was devastated soon afterwards, and Judah and the city of Jerusalem a generation later. The typical attitude towards Zephaniah's message is seen in 1:12 – God will not get involved in our lives. But he did – and does. We need, then, to keep a clear sense of sin and judgement to keep our moral and spiritual senses sharp, as well as being God's instruments of righteousness in a society increasingly indifferent to moral absolutes.

No judgement without hope

The language used by the Old Testament prophets is dramatic, provocative and often deliberately exaggerated to make people listen, as in chapter 1. It does not mean it is harsh, cruel or inexorably negative. It is Satan who is "the accuser of our brothers" (Revelation 12:10). In Zephaniah, there is both promise (2:3; 3:9-12) and a picture of God rejoicing over his righteous remnant (3:17). This is followed by promises of restoration (3:18-20). "I will bring you home" (3:20) has very deep resonance, implying not only acceptance in the Father's household, but also coming to a right state of mind and heart – finding ourselves, too. This is what is often called the "father heart" of God.

> " *The* LORD *has taken away your punishment.*"
>
> *ZEPHANIAH 3:15*

The same old sins

The list of sins in Zephaniah shows us that the same sins occur in every generation even if they find new variations and expressions. Even what may seem the oddest of sins, "avoiding stepping on the threshold" (1:9) is a pagan variation of acts to avoid bad luck (see 1 Samuel 5:5). The syncretism of today is seen in 1:5: a bit of God and a bit of Molech, one of the local pagan gods, to live by. The pride of the rich and the betrayal of those who are meant to be spiritual leaders (3:4) are similarly, unfortunately, only too familiar to us.

Haggai
RIGHT PRIORITIES

OVERVIEW

Haggai urges the exiles who have returned from Babylon to get their priorities right. At present, they are putting their efforts into their own affairs, whilst the temple of God still lies in ruins. The people respond and Haggai encourages them with promises of God's blessings on their lives and their leaders.

SUMMARY

The book of Haggai consists of four separate prophecies, addressed variously to Zerubbabel, the prince; Shealtiel, the high priest; and the people in general. The prophecies are given over a very short time span, and we can trace the progress of the task Haggai urged them to carry out.

The first prophecy (1:1-11) is an explanation of why the people's lives had not prospered since their return from exile in Babylon. God had withheld blessing on their crops and commerce because they had failed to put his affairs first. This meant that the temple, burnt down at the destruction of Jerusalem in 586 BC, still lay in ruins, when it should have been their first priority.

Haggai's words had an instant effect and work was restarted (1:12-15). Haggai promised that God really was with them and would bless them. In his second prophecy (2:1-9), Haggai encouraged those especially who remembered the previous temple, which was a much bigger construction. Nevertheless, God's glory would be greater in this temple than the previous one.

In the third prophecy, addressed to priests and in the form of a series of questions and answers, Haggai reminded the people of the strict rules of ceremonial holiness. The implication is that the people have been even more defiled by the presence of the ruins (2:10-14).

Before the final prophecy addressed to Zerubbabel, which assured him of God's favour (2:20-23), Haggai asked the people to consider whether God had blessed their affairs since they had started the rebuilding programme (2:15-19).

Author

Haggai was one of two prophets who had accompanied the first group returning from exile, the other being Zechariah. The two prophets both urged the same thing, but in very different ways. Haggai is practical and direct; Zechariah is visionary and poetic. Their inspiration led to the temple being finished in five years. Haggai is mentioned in this connection in Ezra 5:1-2; 6:14.

Date

The writer is very particular to give exact dates for each prophecy. The exiles returned in 539 BC, and began some reconstruction work (Ezra 1–3). Then they ran into local opposition (Ezra 4:1-5), effectively halting the building for the next 16 years, till the second year of the Persian King Darius (522–486 BC). The prophecies were thus delivered in 520 BC.

Haggai's first message:
a call to rebuild the temple

1:1 God gives Haggai a message for Zerubbabel and Joshua
1:2-11 God has withheld blessing because his temple is still in ruins
1:12-15 The people respond with obedience to Haggai's message

Haggai's second message:
God's promise about the new temple's splendour

2:1-3 The new temple looks inferior to the old temple
2:4-5 A message of encouragement: God is with his people
2:6-9 God promises that his glory and peace will be greater in the new temple

Haggai's third message:
God's promise to the people

2:10-13 Haggai's questions to the priests about ceremonial cleanliness
2:14 The people have been defiled by the ruins of the temple
2:15-19 God promises to bless the people because of their rebuilding work

Haggai's fourth message:
God's promise to Zerubbabel

2:20-22 God will soon overthrow foreign powers
2:23 God has chosen to bless Zerubbabel

KEY THEMES – HAGGAI

Sacred space

In the Old Testament, there was a deep sense that God's presence should be visibly in the midst of his people. For this to occur, there needed to be sacred space: a building set apart entirely for God to inhabit and for his worship to take place in. At first, a tabernacle was built when the Israelites were in the desert, fleeing from Egypt. This was a tent-like structure with fencing around it. In Solomon's time, a temple was built and set apart in an awesome ceremony.

When the Babylonians captured the city and exiled its people, the Israelites learnt to live without a temple. On their return from exile, the urgency to recreate this sacred space was further lessened by opposition and their own need to make a living. It was Haggai's task to instil again into their consciousness this sense of the vital importance of the temple if God was really going to be with his people. Not till Jesus' time was this consciousness again displaced, when he stated his body was now the new temple (Matthew 24:2; 26:61; 27:40).

Covenant faithfulness

Zerubbabel was in the lineage of King David, and so inherited the Davidic covenant, as it was known (2:23, see 1 Kings 9:5). But there was a longer standing covenant, too, made during the exodus from Egypt (2:5, see Exodus 24:8), that God would be with his people. God is faithful to his covenant promises. The other aspect of covenant faithfulness is what is demanded of the people in terms of purity (2:10-14).

RELEVANCE FOR TODAY – HAGGAI

Re-ordering priorities

We all want God's blessings in our lives. We know we cannot earn them, for all blessings are by grace. Yet there are certain things that can hinder us from knowing God's blessing. The returning exiles were finding this out: whatever they tried to do to prosper failed (1:6,10; 2:16-17). Haggai's message is clear: get your priorities right. Honour God first, a message repeated by Jesus (Matthew 6:33). Malachi gave the same message in terms of giving (Malachi 3:8-12), as did Micah (Micah 6:14). Haggai widens the concept to include all our best efforts and endeavours (2:18-19).

> " *From this day on I will bless you.*"
>
> HAGGAI 2:19

Don't procrastinate

It wasn't as if the exiles were consciously refusing to rebuild the temple. But because of wrong time priorities, they were merely putting it off. But Haggai suggests this is, in effect, a refusal of God's purposes, and a dishonouring of God, since the temple, the most obvious sign of his presence, remains a ruin (1:9). The relevance in today's hectic and disordered world is clear: we are to stop making excuses and resisting God's purposes and we are to honour him by getting on with what we know he wants us to do.

Zechariah
THE CITY OF TRUTH

OVERVIEW
The prophecy of Zechariah looks towards the future of Jerusalem after the return from exile. He sees the temple rebuilt and a high priest firmly established. He also sees God's presence and blessing on the whole city and that all nations will be drawn to it. However, there will also be fierce conflict around the city before the final Day of the LORD.

SUMMARY
The book divides into two parts. Chapters 1–8 describe eight visions the prophet Zechariah received. He was in the presence of an angelic being, who gave the interpretation for each one of the visions. They vary widely in topic and symbolism, but most deal with the immediate future of Jerusalem and its temple, which was in urgent need of rebuilding after the 70-year exile in Babylon.

God promised favour again to his holy city (1:12-17), and favour and authority to the high priest, Joshua (3:1-10; 6:9-15). The city would attract many nations (2:11; 8:23) because of God's presence (2:10-13). But it needed to become a city of truth and righteousness for it to enjoy God's blessing (8:1-23).

The second part (chapters 9–14) is somewhat different. There is no named prophet and there are no angel interpreters. Instead, the series of prophecies is more apocalyptic, about the Day of the LORD. Some of the themes of the prophecies are as the first part: nations would come to Jerusalem (14:16-21); God would protect the city (9:14-17; 12:8; compare 2:4-5). But there are

also negative prophecies: nations would attack Jerusalem (12:1-5; 14:1-2), and spiritual leadership would fall into the wrong hands (11:4-17; 13:7-9). These prophecies should not be seen as sequential.

Many verses are used by New Testament writers in relation to the coming of Jesus Christ (6:13; 9:9; 11:12-13; 12:10). The prophecies also echo earlier prophecies found in the Old Testament (for example, 1:2-6,12,17; compare Hosea 14:1-7; Isaiah 54; Jeremiah 3:15).

Author
Zechariah is mentioned in Ezra 5:1 as one of the two prophets urging Joshua, Zerubbabel the governor, and the people, to rebuild the temple. The other prophet is Haggai. Both Ezra and Haggai show that their encouragement was successful.

Date
1:1,7; 7:1 help us date the first part of the book precisely to 520 BC. The second part was probably written some 40 years later, since Greece is mentioned, a power that arose around 480 BC.

Zechariah's eight visions about the restoration of Jerusalem

1:1-6 God gives Zechariah a message for his people: return to God

1:7-17 Vision 1. The angel among the myrtle trees: Jerusalem's judgement is over and restoration will begin

1:18-21 Vision 2. Four horns and four craftsmen: Judah's enemies will be destroyed

2:1-13 Vision 3. The man with the measuring line: the restored Jerusalem will be full of many people and of God's presence

3:1-10 Vision 4. Joshua the high priest is given new clothes: God's promise of cleansing for the land

4:1-14 Vision 5. The golden lampstand and two olive trees: Zerubbabel's work will be successful

5:1-4 Vision 6. A flying scroll: God's judgement of evildoers

5:5-11 Vision 7. A woman in a basket: sin is carried away to Babylon

6:1-8 Vision 8. Four chariots: God's presence goes out over all the earth

6:9-15 God tells Zechariah to crown Joshua as a sign of the restoration of both temple and monarchy

7:1-14 God desires justice and mercy instead of fasting

8:1-23 God promises to return to Jerusalem and turn mourning into feasting and celebration

Messages about the Day of the LORD

9:1-8 Israel's enemies will be destroyed and the Philistines will join the tribe of Judah

9:9-17 God's king is coming to Jerusalem and will deliver his people

10:1-12 God himself will be the shepherd of his people

11:1-17 A parable about good and worthless shepherds

12:1-9 The enemies of Judah will be destroyed

12:10-13 Israel's mourning for the one they have pierced

13:1 A fountain is opened for Jerusalem's cleansing

13:2-6 The coming end of idolatry and false prophecy

13:7-9 A remnant of God's people will be saved and purified

14:1-2 The gathering of nations against Jerusalem on the Day of the LORD

14:3-5 The LORD will fight for his people

14:6-11 The LORD will rule over all the earth from Jerusalem

14:12-19 God will send a plague on the enemies of Jerusalem who refuse to come to worship in the city

14:20-21 A promise of future holiness

Rebuilding Jerusalem as the city of truth

Much of the first part of Zechariah has to do with rebuilding after the devastation of the Babylonian attack on Jerusalem in 586 BC (1:12). Haggai concentrates on the practicality of getting the work restarted after the returned exiles had lost heart. Zechariah is more mystical and apocryphal as he envisions a wider context and wider purposes (eg 1:10-14; 6:5-8).

He sees that the city will be repopulated (2:4; 8:4-8), but lessons have to be learnt from the past for this renewal to be permanent (1:1-6). So true justice must be dispensed (7:9-10). The city must become a city of truth (8:3,16-17), then it will be a witness to the whole world (8:20-23). Zechariah is moving towards the image of the Holy City, the new Jerusalem, which fills the final pages of the Bible (Revelation 21–22).

The kingly priest

Whereas Haggai is content to encourage the existing high priest, Joshua, Zechariah has a loftier vision of what the role of high priest is to become (3:8). The enacted prophecy of fashioning a crown (6:9-15) is symbolic of the priest actually reigning, something that had never happened before. Here the term "the Branch" is used (3:8; 6:12), a term used in earlier prophecies to denote messianic rule in the line of King David (Isaiah 4:2; 11:1; Jeremiah 23:5-6; 33:15-16).

In the New Testament, the concept of the royal priest is taken to refer to Jesus Christ in the Letter to the Hebrews, by using the figure of Melchizedek (Hebrews 5:6,10; 6:20; 7:1-21; see Genesis 14:18; Psalm 110:4).

The true shepherd

Whereas the first part of the book sees the need for truth, the second part shows it has to be fought for. The rather mysterious account of the true and false shepherds depicts such a struggle. Typically at this period of the Old Testament, the term "shepherd" meant kings and rulers, rather than pastors. The true shepherd is rejected (11:8-15), prophetically being paid off with thirty pieces of silver (11:12). Later, the people "look on me, the one they have pierced" (12:10), which could be identified with the rejected shepherd, as Revelation 1:7 suggests. Christ's claim to be the true or good shepherd (John 10:14) is thus a claim to be the Messiah.

The divine warrior

The victory of good over evil will not just be gained by establishing the true city. It has to be defended, and in such a cosmic battle that only the revelation of God as the divine warrior fighting for his city will bring victory (12:1-9; 14:1-5). For further material on the divine warrior, see Nahum.

Not by power

Zechariah 4:6 is an often quoted verse. In the context of the book, it does not mean no power is required. Far from it: the real question is, whose power? The words are addressed to Zerubbabel, the governor or secular head of the tiny state re-established in the midst of hostile neighbours. It is not going to be by his power or might that the city will be established, but by the Spirit of God.

This is a fundamental biblical principle. There are many examples in the Bible of small forces, humanly speaking, overcoming much

> " *Not by might nor by power, but by my Spirit,' says the* LORD *Almighty.*"

ZECHARIAH 4:6

more powerful enemies, solely because God was fighting for them by the power of his spirit (eg Gideon in Judges 7). Thus, we must not look simply in human terms at the spiritual battle that we often feel rages round us, or at the opposition we have to face at times to advance God's kingdom.

Marks of leadership

Of all the Minor Prophets, Zechariah and Haggai address the need for firm leadership. Joshua needs to see himself standing in the righteousness given to him by God, and not in his own guilt (3:1-5): this is to be his confidence and source of courage. Zechariah needs to see himself standing in the power God will give him, not his own (4:1-6). Both need to see their anointing from God (4:11-14). No reliance on human competence alone will withstand Satan's accusations and undermining (3:2).

Fasting and feasting

The book spends nearly two chapters discussing this topic, so it must be of some real importance. The question given to Zechariah was whether the old traditions of fasting should be continued in the new city (7:3). Zechariah's answer is unequivocal. He asks what good their fasting did in the past, since it was done out of habit and tradition (7:4-7). He chimes in with the older prophets in declaring what God is really looking for is justice and truth (7:9-10; compare Isaiah 58:4-5). But he goes further: fasting will give way to feasting (8:18-19). It is this joy, combined with truth and peace, which would attract outsiders to God's people. It still does.

The end of prophecy

13:2-6 seems a rather strange set of verses. How can a prophet welcome the end of prophecy? Some interpreters see it as referring to the false shepherds of 10:17. False shepherds bring false prophecy. Some see it as anticipating 1 Corinthians 13:8, that when full knowledge and revelation come, there will be no need of prophecy. However we understand these verses, to be a prophet now needs to be done in humility by people who are pure, certainly not by anyone who promotes themselves and considers it their "job".

Malachi
SECOND-RATE RELIGION

OVERVIEW

Malachi holds the post-exilic nation to account for its second-rate religion. Its priests are leading the people poorly, offering substandard sacrifices in the temple rituals. The people are failing to give God his due; they are intermarrying with non-believers and divorcing without the slightest scruple. The book predicts the coming of a great messenger who will restore true religion.

SUMMARY

The book of Malachi stands as a bridge from Old to New Testament by anticipating the coming of a new messenger, taken later to be John the Baptist. It also brings together two great sections of the Old Testament, the Law, personified in Moses, and the Prophets, personified in Elijah.

Its 55 verses can be divided into seven sections, with a brief prologue and epilogue. Most sections can be taken as a courtroom investigation: a statement is made, it is questioned and evidence is brought. A verdict is given and a likely sentence. God is both judge and prosecutor, the prophet his recorder and mouthpiece. Rhetorical questions are a central stylistic feature.

The first section establishes Israel as his chosen people, with whom he has formed a covenant. The evidence comes from looking at Edom (or Esau), Jacob's (or Israel's) twin (1:2-5). Edom has fared, and will fare, badly, just because it was not loved by God in the same way that God loved Israel. The next two sections form accusations against the priests, who both offered substandard sacrifices (1:6-14) and failed to be true messengers for God to the people (2:1-9).

Malachi then turns to the people. They have broken faith by allowing easy divorce (2:13-16) and intermarriage with non-believers (2:10-12). A new messenger would come to bring God's verdict on their sins of injustice and witchcraft (3:1-5; 4:5). The people have failed to give God his due, the tithe or tenth part of their income, as the law of Moses requires (3:6-12). They see religion purely as something they can benefit from (3:13-18). But judgement will come. A righteous remnant will be restored (4:1-6).

Author

The name means "My Messenger", and so it is not entirely clear whether that is his real name, his title or his pen-name. Some traditions equate him with the priest Ezra, but this is not generally accepted. Nothing else is known about him.

Date

References to a governor suggest a post-exilic time, when the temple has been rebuilt in Jerusalem. The failures of the Israelites are similar to those exposed by Ezra and Nehemiah, so it is generally assumed the book was written about their time or just before, some time between 520–458 BC.

1:1 Prologue: God gives Malachi a message for Israel

1:2-5 God's love for Israel, shown in his choice of Jacob over Esau

1:6-14 God accuses the priests of offering substandard sacrifices

2:1-9 The priests have failed to instruct people in God's covenant

2:10-17 Warnings to God's people about intermarriage and divorce

3:1-5 God will suddenly come to the temple and judge his people

3:6-15 God's people are warned about their failure to obey God's laws

3:16–4:3 The Day of the LORD will bring judgement on the wicked, but healing and restoration to those who love and serve God

4:4 A call to observe the law

4:5-6 The promise that Elijah will come on the eve of the Day of the LORD

KEY THEMES – MALACHI

God's elective love

The whole emphasis of the Old Testament is that God has chosen a people for himself, to be called his people. He entered into a covenant with them, which was renewed in various forms. The concept of covenant is mentioned a number of times in the book, in connection with marriage (2:14) and the Levites, or priestly clan (2:4). The covenant, whilst a mutual agreement, is not a covenant of equals. God offered the terms of the agreement, he did the choosing (or electing), and there was no merit on the part of the Israelites to be somehow more worthy of the election than any other nation.

The argument of 1:2-5 establishes this principle by using Esau, the forefather of the Edomites, as an example. Esau and Israel were twin brothers (Genesis 25:24-26; 27:36; 28:6; 36:43), but it was Israel that enjoyed the blessing and the promise. However, Edom was not punished because it was not chosen; rather it was punished because of its unbrotherly acts against Israel, as the book of Obadiah demonstrates (see also Isaiah 34; 63:1-6; Jeremiah 49:7-22; Ezekiel 25:12-14; Amos 1:11-12). The rest of the book goes on to show that covenant blessings require responsive accountability, not a half-hearted fulfilment of duties.

The priests' responsibility

Numbers 18:21-24 is the clearest expression of the covenant with the Levites. Clearly the people have been failing in giving them their tithes, but the Levites also failed the people by not giving clear teaching (2:8-9), and they failed God by not presenting the best animals to sacrifice (1:13-14).

Malachi presents a picture of the ideal priest (2:5-7), which includes the function of teaching and being God's messenger, a role usually reserved for the prophets. In the case of Ezra, we see priests were willing to give instruction of the law (Nehemiah 8), and in the case of Ezekiel, acting as prophets (Ezekiel 1:3).

True messages

These days, our lives are full of texts and messaging. The importance of texts as true messages from God is central in this book, as is the equally important emphasis on the truth of the messenger. The prophet is messenger; so is the priest. And significantly, so is the one who is to come, to proclaim the Day of the LORD. 3:1 echoes Isaiah 40:3. It is not clear whether 3:2 refers to the appearance of the messenger or that of God. However, 4:5-6 gives a fuller account of this messianic messenger. He is seen as Elijah, the great prophet. In the New Testament, John the Baptist, the messenger of Jesus Christ, is seen as fulfilment of this verse (Matthew 11:7-15; 17:1-13; Mark 6:14-16).

RELEVANCE FOR TODAY – MALACHI

Divorce and family life

There is clear teaching on several aspects of family life in this book. The secular world sees marriage more and more as a contract. Obviously breaking a contract leads to penalties, but it is not seen as more than a legal and financial matter. Malachi teaches clearly that marriage is covenant, part of the wider covenant God establishes with his people. God therefore regards divorce as he would other acts of covenant-breaking such as idolatry: something sacred has been defiled.

This does not mean there is a total ban. But it does suggest repentance and the need for forgiveness from God. Above all, it suggests marriage should not be entered into lightly, but as a sacred trust. And it should not be with unbelievers (2:11). One of the messenger's most significant tasks will be to turn "the hearts of the fathers to the children" and the reverse. Divorce, above all, alienates. If there is no reconciliation, the land is liable to be cursed (4:6). This is strong language indeed and we need to take due note of it. It is the Old Testament's last word.

Tithing

Tithing, the giving of a tenth of your income to God, is another principle the book talks very specifically about. In the Old Testament instructions over the tithe, it was to be both the first and the best tenth. Nehemiah 13:10-14 suggests failure had become acute and was affecting the whole spiritual life of the community. The principle outlined in 3:10-12 is an echo of Haggai 1:5-6. A failure to give to God will mean lack of prosperity for the person; a willingness to give will mean God's blessing financially. It is a simple covenant equation.

Worship and covenant faithfulness

Whilst failure to tithe may seem less serious than divorce, both are symptomatic of a failure to see the Christian life in covenant

> " *To guard yourself in your spirit, and do not break faith."*
>
> MALACHI 2:15

terms. We are under the new covenant of grace, sealed by Christ's blood, and therefore we are under something even more precious than the old covenant, to which Malachi is referring.

True heart worship is also part of this covenant. Ideally, worship should bring glory to God among the nations (1:11). But a half-hearted, second-rate worship brings dishonour (1:12-14). For us, worship services should be a witness to our deepest responses to God's love. Covenant faithfulness means living the Christian life with a hundred per cent commitment to the "great king", our God.

The World of the New Testament

BRITANNIA

BELGICA

GERMANIA

NORICUM

RHACTIA

GAUL

PANNONIA

Genua

ILLYRICUM

NARBONENSIS

Sea of
Adria

CORSICA

Rome • ITALIA

Appian Way

Puteoli •

Brun

HISPANIA

SARDINIA

Tyrrhenean
Sea

S
A

• Rhegium

SICILIA

Syracuse

Malaca

Carthage •

MALTA

The Great Se
(Mediterranean

AFRICA

NUMIDIA

(Lesser
Syrtis)

Atlas Mountains

• Lepsis Magna

TRIPOLITANIA

(Gr
Sy

By the time of the birth of Jesus the Roman Empire had all
but conquered the "known world" and a time of uncertain
peace ensued – the *pax Romana*. Judea was at this time a
client kingdom of Rome – allowed a modest level of
independence. The road-building programmes that the
Romans introduced made travel easier, aiding the spread
of the good news of the kingdom.

Sahara Desert

Roman empire at AD 14, at the death of
Emperor Augustus

Later expansion

| 0 | 100 | 200 miles |

| 0 | 100 | 200 kilometres |

SARMATIA

DACIA

MOESIA

THRACE

IIA

Philippi

Thessalonica

ALY

Troas

Aegean
Sea

Athens

Corinth

Aegean
Sea

CRETE

Fair
Havens

ene

CA

LIBYA

Byzantium

Egnatian Way

MYSIA

Pergamum

LYDIA

Ephesus

CARIA

Miletus

LYCIA

SCYTHIA

BOSPORAN KINGDOM

Euxine Sea
(Black Sea)

PONTUS

BITHYNIA

PHRYGIA

PISIDIA

PAMPHYLIA

A   S   I   A   M   I   N   O   R

GALATIA

LYCAONIA

Lystra

CILICIA

COLCHIS

ARMENIA

CAPPADOCIA

Tarsus

CYPRUS

Paphos

Salamis

SYRIA

Antioch

Caucasus
Mountains

MESOPOTAMIA

Dura-Europus

River
Euphrates

Caspian
Sea

MEDIA

River
Tigris

PHOENICIA

Tyre

JUDEA

Jerusalem

Alexandria

Memphis

E   G   Y   P   T

River Nile

Thebes

Damascus

Jericho

NABATAEA

Petra

Arabian
Desert

Babylon

A   R   A   B   I   A

Red
Sea

Persian
Gulf

THE BIBLE BOOK BY BOOK 297

Matthew
THE DISCIPLES' GOSPEL

OVERVIEW

Matthew, written for Jewish Christians, focuses on who Jesus is, why he came, and how he fits into God's bigger purposes, showing he is the long-expected Messiah, the bringer of God's kingdom.

SUMMARY

Who Jesus was (1:1-17)

Matthew begins by recording Jesus' key ancestors, starting with Abraham and going through King David (1:1-17), to show he had the legal right to fulfil God's promises to them.

How Jesus came (1:18–3:17)

Matthew describes Jesus' miraculous conception and the events surrounding his birth (1:18–2:23). Passing over the next 30 years in complete silence, he comes to John the Baptist who prepared the way for Jesus (3:1-12). At his baptism, God confirmed Jesus as his Son and filled him with his Spirit (3:13-17), empowering him for his mission.

What Jesus taught (4:1–25:46)

Having overcome the devil (4:1-11), Jesus moved to Capernaum where he began his ministry and called his disciples (4:12-25). Matthew records Jesus' key teaching, organising it thematically into five main blocks (chapters 5-7; 10; 13; 18; 24-25) and interspersing this teaching with accounts of what Jesus did. Jesus' focus was always God's kingdom, his miracles serving as a *demonstration* of it and his parables an *explanation* of it. But while the Jews were expecting Messiah to establish God's kingdom with a sword, Matthew shows Jesus came to do it through a cross.

Why Jesus died (26:1–28:20)

Angered by Jesus' teaching, his religious and political opponents plotted together to get rid of him (26:3-5), finding the perfect opportunity when Judas agreed to betray him (26:14-16). Having shared the Passover with his disciples (26:17-29) and predicted Peter's denial (26:31-35), Jesus went to Gethsemane where he prayed and was betrayed (26:36-56). After several trials through the night (26:57–27:26), Jesus was crucified and buried (27:27-65). This wasn't the end of the story, however, for Jesus rose from the dead (28:1-15), proving that he was truly the Messiah. He then sent his disciples into the whole world to share his good news with others (28:16-20).

Author

Since the days of the early church it has been believed that this Gospel was written by the tax collector who appears in 9:9. This is supported by other evidence. Matthew is the only Gospel writer who identifies this tax collector as "Matthew". Furthermore, his writing shows both the interest in numbers and the local knowledge that you would expect of a tax collector living in that place at that time. This Matthew was one of the twelve disciples of Jesus (10:2-4).

Date

Since Matthew quotes extensively from Mark, it seems obvious he wrote his Gospel later, probably in the 60s, but almost certainly before the destruction of Jerusalem in AD 70.

OUTLINE – MATTHEW

KEY THEMES – MATTHEW

Jesus the Messiah

Matthew demonstrates that Jesus was the Messiah through his genealogy (1:1-17), titles (like Son of David and Messiah), parallels with Israel (eg 2:15), and fulfilment of prophecy. He quotes the Old Testament extensively, showing how events in Jesus' life fulfilled what was written (1:22; 4:14; 8:17; 12:17; 21:24), authenticating his messianic claims. He also draws parallels between Moses and Jesus. For example, just as Moses left Egypt, so did Jesus; just as Moses received God's commandments on a mountain, so Jesus explained those commandments on a mountain (the Sermon on the Mount).

Jesus the King

Matthew portrays Jesus as the ultimate King, descended from David (1:1-17) and honoured by the Gentile Magi seeking the King of the Jews (2:2), underlining the global nature of his kingship. Jesus claimed the King's right to judge everyone at the End (25:31-46) and he delegated his kingly authority over all nations to his disciples (28:16-20).

This kingship is also seen in Matthew's emphasis on "the kingdom of God"; writing for Jewish readers, he generally calls it "kingdom of heaven" since Jews avoided using God's name. The Jews believed God's kingdom would come powerfully at the End, bringing judgement on God's enemies; but Jesus said it had started to come right now, because he the King was here. His kingdom has both present (eg 12:28) and future (eg 24:36-51) dimensions.

Jesus the fulfilment and foundation

Matthew's extensive quotations from the Old Testament (eg 2:5-6; 3:3; 4:4,6-7,10; 11:10; 13:13-15; 15:7; 21:4-5,9,13,16) together with his use of the phrase "in order to fulfil" (eg 1:22-23; 4:14-16; 8:17; 12:17-21; 21:4-5) confirm his view of Jesus as the fulfilment of the Jewish hopes for a Messiah, that is, a liberator sent by God himself. He further emphasises this belief about Jesus as the fulfilment of that hope by drawing parallels, both explicit and implicit, between Moses as the bringer of the Old Covenant and Jesus as the bringer of the new. Thus, just as Moses leaves Egypt, so Christ comes from there. Just as Moses receives the Ten Commandments on a mountain (Exodus 19:20–20:1), so Jesus explains those commandments through the Sermon on the Mount. Just as Moses encountered a shocking lack of faith (Exodus 32:1-20), when he descended from the mountain, so did Jesus (17:14-20).

Jesus the Teacher

Matthew gathers Jesus' teaching into five main sections, recalling Moses and his five books of the Law and showing that Jesus is not just a teacher but a new Moses who would bring about a new deliverance. These five main sections cover:

- Kingdom living – the Sermon on the Mount (5:1–7:29). For more on the Sermon on the Mount, see p.48 and p.628-638.
- Kingdom mission – instruction on mission (10:1-42)
- Kingdom principles – the parables of kingdom (13:1-58)
- Kingdom attitudes – caring for the weak and forgiving others (18:1-35)
- Kingdom perspective – God's plan for history, including the imminent destruction of Jerusalem and Christ's return at the end of the age (24:1–25:46)

The centre of gravity in Matthew's Gospel, therefore, both in the straightforward teaching and in the parables, is the new community of the kingdom of God. Whilst Jewish mystics were talking about the location and physical appearance of heaven, Christ was talking about the essence of the kingdom of heaven, especially in the parables

THE BE-ATTITUDES

Matthew 5:1-16: the distinctive, inner, spiritual qualities that are to mark us out as citizens of the kingdom.

"Blessed are the poor in spirit, for theirs is the kingdom of heaven" (verse 3)
Are we humble? What is our response when we meet God (Isaiah 57:15)?

"Blessed are those who mourn, for they will be comforted" (verse 4)
Are we aware of our own inner corruption (Romans 7:24)?

"Blessed are the meek, for they will inherit the earth" (verse 5)
How much do we assert ourselves; how sensitive are we (Numbers 12:3)?

"Blessed are those who hunger and thirst for righteousness, for they will be filled" (verse 6)
Do we have a supreme desire to know God and have fellowship with him (Philippians 3:10)?

"Blessed are the merciful, for they will be shown mercy" (verse 7)
Are we merciful to others (Luke 10:36-37)?

"Blessed are the pure in heart, for they will see God" (verse 8)
Do we have a sincere, undivided heart that seeks God above all else (Psalm 86:11)?

"Blessed are the peacemakers, for they will be called sons of God" (verse 9)
How "touchy" are we, insisting on our own rights? Are we prayerful, doing all we can to bring peace, including being silent at times (Hebrews 12:14)?

"Blessed are those who are persecuted for righteousness, for theirs is the kingdom of heaven" (verses 10-12)
Are our lives different from those around us (2 Timothy 3:12)?

Jesus said that as citizens of the kingdom we should build our lives, not just by listening to his teaching but by putting it into practice

of chapter 13. As that kingdom's true king, he calls others to his royal service. This communal focus shows itself, too, in that this is the only Gospel to mention the church itself (16:18; 18:17). Readers of Matthew's Gospel will find themselves developing a keen awareness of their own place within God's timeless and eternal plan.

Jesus the Judge
Because Jesus is the King, he is also the ultimate judge. While Jesus' message is good news, he was not afraid to speak of God's coming judgement on those who did not believe his message (eg 11:20-24; 12:22-42; 23:1–25:46). This judgement underlines the need to make good decisions about Jesus right now or to risk losing our life for ever (eg 10:32-33; 16:24-27).

Using God's word

Many preachers today just use the New Testament, but Matthew shows how Old and New Testaments fit perfectly together. Jesus didn't come to abolish the Old Testament but to fulfil it (5:17-18), as Matthew shows by often quoting from it. He wanted us to see the unbroken line of God's activity in history, stretching back to Abraham and Moses and forward to the end of this age. Wise preachers will reflect that in their preaching.

> "*Jesus went throughout Galilee, teaching in their synagogues, preaching the good news of the kingdom, and healing every disease and sickness among the people.*"

MATTHEW 4:23

Depending on God's word

For Jesus, God's word was not something to be preserved and locked up like the Pharisees did, but a dynamic reality that changes life. He modelled his trust of it (5:18) and dependence on it (4:1-11). God's word is still living and active.

Teaching God's word

While Matthew gives us five main blocks of Jesus' teaching, it is clear Jesus taught much more, backing it up with his miracles (4:23-25) and amazing the crowds with his authority (7:28-29). He used simple illustrations to teach profound truths (eg the parables) and made them memorable through simple structures (eg the Beatitudes, 5:3-11). Good teaching is concerned for the needs of those who are taught.

Following God's word

Jesus said we should build our lives, not just on listening to his teaching but putting it into practice (7:24-27). Matthew constantly stresses the demands of discipleship, involving seeking God's kingdom first (6:25-34) and risking everything to follow Jesus (eg 4:19; 8:18-22; 10:32-39; 16:24-25). But those who do will find they are richly rewarded (eg 19:27-30).

Trusting God's word

We don't always see the fruit of what we sow immediately, and so it is with God's word (13:1-23). However, because it is *God's* word, the word of his kingdom, there is power within it and it *will* grow (13:31-33). If we live by the principles of God's kingdom, God will always vindicate what we do, just as he did in Jesus' life.

Sharing God's word

Although Matthew focuses primarily on Jesus' mission to the Jews (eg 10:5-6), he knew that Jesus' message was for everyone, whatever their racial or social background (2:1-12; 8:5-13; 21:43; 28:18-20). Our preaching the gospel can never be just kept to "our kind" of people.

PALESTINE IN NEW TESTAMENT TIMES

- - Political division

• City of the Decapolis
(the Ten Cities): self-governing
city

0   10   20 miles

0   10   20 kilometres

Sidon

Mt Lebanon

ITURAEA

ABILENE

• Damascus

Zarephath

Mt Hermon

PROVINCE   OF SYRIA

Tyre

PHOENICIA

• Caesarea Philippi

Lake Huleh

Mediterranean Sea

Ptolemais

GALILEE

Chorazin

GAULANITIS

TRACHONITIS
TETRARCHY OF PHILIP

Capernaum

• Bethsaida-Julias

• Raphana

Cana

Gennesaret

Sea of Galilee

?Dion

AURANITIS

Sepphoris

Mt Carmel

Tiberias

Hippos

GALILEE

Nazareth

Abila

Dor

Nain

Gadara

Caesarea

The Great Plain

Scythopolis

DECAPOLIS

Salim

Pella

Hill Country

Aenon

SAMARIA

Sebaste (Samaria)

Mt Ebal
Mt Gerizim

Sychar

River Jordan

• Gerasa

The Arabah

AND PEREA

R Jabbok

Joppa

Aphek

Alexandrium

J U D E A

Lydda

Bethel

Ephraim

Beth-horon

Jericho

• Rabbah
(Philadelphia)

Ekron

?Emmaus

Jerusalem

Azotus

Bethlehem

Herodium

Mt Pisgah

• Medeba

Ashkelon

JUDEA

Machaerus

Gaza

The Shephelah

Hebron

Hill Country of Judea

En-gedi

Dead Sea

R Arnon

• Rapha

Wilderness of Judea

IDUMEA

Beersheba

Masada

• Areopolis

• Malatha

Rehoboth

The Negev

NABATEAN KINGDOM

• Beeroth

• Hazazon-tamar

WILDERNESS OF ZIN

MIRACLES OF JESUS CHRIST

HEALING MIRACLES

Groups of those who were ill
Matthew 12:15; 15:29-31; Mark 7:31-37

Man with a skin disease
Matthew 8:2-4; Mark 1:40-44; Luke 5:12-14

Roman centurion's servant
Matthew 8:5-13; Luke 7:1-10

Peter's mother-in-law
Matthew 8:14-15; Mark 1:29-31; Luke 4:38-39

Paralysed man
Matthew 9:2-8; Mark 2:3-12; Luke 5:18-26

Woman with bleeding
Matthew 9:20-22; Mark 5:25-34; Luke 8:43-48

Two blind men
Matthew 9:27-31

Man with a shrivelled hand
Matthew 12:10-13; Mark 3:1-5; Luke 6:6-10

Two blind men at Jericho
Matthew 20:29-34; Mark 10:46-52; Luke 18:35-43

Deaf and mute man
Mark 7:31-37

Blind man at Bethsaida
Mark 8:22-26

Man with dropsy
Luke 14:1-4

Ten lepers
Luke 17:11-19

Malchus' ear
Luke 22:50-51

Official's son at Capernaum
John 4:46-54

Invalid man beside pool
John 5:1-9

Man born blind
John 9:1-41

EXORCISMS

Two men living among the tombs
Matthew 8:28-34; Mark 5:1-17; Luke 8:26-37

A mute man
Matthew 9:32-34

A blind and mute man
Matthew 12:22; Luke 11:14

Canaanite woman's daughter
Matthew 15:21-28; Mark 7:24-30

Boy with seizures
Matthew 17:14-19; Mark 9:14-28; Luke 9:37-42

Man in a synagogue
Mark 1:21-28; Luke 4:31-37

A crippled woman
Luke 13:11-13

NATURE MIRACLES

Calming the storm
Matthew 8:23-27; Mark 4:36-41; Luke 8:22-25

Feeding 5,000 men
Matthew 14:13-21; Mark 6:32-44; Luke 9:10-17; John 6:1-13

Walking on the water
Matthew 14:22-33; Mark 6:45-51; John 6:15-21

Feeding 4,000 men
Matthew 15:32-39; Mark 8:1-10

Coin in a fish's mouth
Matthew 17:24-27

Withering of fig-tree
Matthew 21:18-22; Mark 11:12-14,20-24

Catching fish
Luke 5:1-11

Water turned into wine
John 2:1-11

Catching fish for breakfast
John 21:1-14

RESURRECTION MIRACLES

Jairus' daughter
Matthew 9:18-19,23-25; Mark 5:22-24,35-43; Luke 8:41-42, 49-56

Widow's son at Nain
Luke 7:11-15

Lazarus
John 11:1-44

See also "Acts of healing", page 72 and "Nature miracles", page 76

PARABLES OF JESUS CHRIST

Lamp under a bowl
Matthew 5:14-16; Mark
4:21-22; Luke 8:16-17; 11:33

Wise and foolish builders
Matthew 7:24-27; Luke
6:47-49

**New cloth on an old
garment**
Matthew 9:16; Mark 2:21;
Luke 5:36

New wine in old wineskins
Matthew 9:17; Mark 2:22;
Luke 5:37-38

Sower and the seed
Matthew 13:3-8,18-23; Mark
4:2-8,13-20; Luke 8:5-8,11-15

Weeds among the wheat
Matthew 13:24-30,36-43

Mustard seed
Matthew 13:31-32; Mark
4:30-32; Luke 13:18-19

Yeast
Matthew 13:33; Luke 13:20-21

Hidden treasure
Matthew 13:44

Pearl of great value
Matthew 13:45-46

The fishing net
Matthew 13:47-50

Lost sheep
Matthew 18:12-14; Luke
15:4-7

Unmerciful servant
Matthew 18:23-35

Vineyard workers
Matthew 20:1-16

Two sons
Matthew 21:28-32

Vineyard tenants
Matthew 21:33-46; Mark
12:1-12; Luke 20:9-19

Wedding banquet
Matthew 22:1-14

The fig-tree and its leaves
Matthew 24:32-33; Mark
13:28-29; Luke 21:29-31

Wise servant
Matthew 24:45-51; Luke
12:42-46

Ten virgins
Matthew 25:1-13

Talents
Matthew 25:14-30

Sheep and goats
Matthew 25:31-46

Growing seed
Mark 4:26-29

Money-lender
Luke 7:41-43

Good Samaritan
Luke 10:30-37

Friend at midnight
Luke 11:5-8

Rich fool
Luke 12:16-21

Watchful servants
Luke 12:35-40

Unfruitful fig-tree
Luke 13:6-9

Seats at the wedding feast
Luke 14:7-14

Great banquet
Luke 14:16-24

The cost of discipleship
Luke 14:28-33

Lost coin
Luke 15:8-10

Lost (prodigal) son
Luke 15:11-32

Shrewd manager
Luke 16:1-8

Rich man and Lazarus
Luke 16:19-31

The master and servant
Luke 17:7-10

Unjust judge
Luke 18:1-8

Pharisee and tax collector
Luke 18:9-14

Ten minas
Luke 19:12-27

See also "Teaching in parables", page 44

Mark

JESUS FOR BEGINNERS

OVERVIEW

The shortest and earliest Gospel, Mark is written in simple language and is an action-packed, fast-moving account of the life and teaching of Jesus, the Messiah (8:29) and Son of God (15:39), who was rejected by his own people but vindicated by God through his resurrection.

SUMMARY

In his Gospel, Mark paints a vivid picture of Jesus as a Messiah (Saviour) whom we dare not ignore. He has largely organised his material chronologically, with much emphasis on Jesus' work in Galilee and on the final week of his life. He was writing for those who were not of Jewish background, as he often explains Jewish history and traditions. In fact, his may well have been a Roman readership.

Mark is the only Gospel to contain the actual word *Gospel*, which means "good news", and he clearly sees Christ as good news for all: good news prophesied by Isaiah (1:2-3) and prepared for by John the Baptist (1:2-8). After his baptism and overcoming Satan's temptations (1:9-13), Jesus started to announce this good news: God's kingdom had arrived; and that demanded a response (1:14-20). This kingdom would affect the whole of life, as Mark immediately demonstrates through a string of stories showing Jesus' authority over everything: demons (1:21-28), sickness (1:29-34), uncleanness (1:40-45), sin (2:1-12), exclusion (2:13-18), religious traditions (2:18-22), even the Sabbath (2:23–3:6). All this drew huge crowds (3:7-12), and Jesus now called 12 apostles to work alongside him (3:13-19). Continuing his ministry, first in Galilee and around the lake (3:20–7:23) and then in Gentile territory (7:24–9:32), he reached pagan Caesarea Philippi where he asked his disciples who they thought he was. Peter acknowledged him as the Christ, or Messiah (8:27-30). From this

point, Jesus began explaining what sort of Messiah he would be, establishing God's kingdom not through force, but through suffering and death (8:31-38).

After his transfiguration (9:2-13), Jesus moved south (10:1), teaching about discipleship and predicting his death with increasing clarity (10:32-34). The final third of Mark's Gospel is devoted to the last week of Jesus' life: his triumphant entry into Jerusalem and cleansing the temple (11:1-19), his teaching and opposition to him (11:20–13:37), his anointing (14:1-11), the Last Supper (14:12-26), his arrest in Gethsemane (14:32-52) and his trials, crucifixion and burial (14:53–15:47). The Gospel ends on a note of hope, however, as the women find the tomb empty and angels proclaiming Jesus has risen (16:1-8).

The final section (16:9-20) was probably not written by Mark (the Greek is different) but added by an early church leader.

Author

The early church was unanimous that the author was John Mark (see Acts 12:12; 15:37-40; Colossians 4:10; 2 Timothy 4:11; Philemon 24; 1 Peter 5:13). Tradition says he recorded Peter's preaching in Rome. Some think he is the man mentioned in 14:51-52.

Date

Most believe this was the first Gospel, written in the late 50s or early 60s when Roman persecution of Christians was increasing.

OUTLINE – MARK

An introduction to Jesus
the Messiah

1:1 The beginning of the good news about
Jesus

1:2-8 John the Baptist prepares the way for
Jesus

1:9-11 Jesus' baptism and God's message
about him

1:12-13 Jesus is tempted by the devil

1:14-20 Jesus begins his ministry and calls
the first disciples

1:21–2:12 Jesus' authority shown in his deeds
and preaching

2:13-14 Jesus calls Matthew to follow him

2:15–3:6 Disputes with the Jewish leaders

3:7-19 Jesus' growing popularity and the
appointing of his twelve disciples

3:20-35 Growing controversy about Jesus'
ministry

4:1-34 Parables about God's kingdom

4:35–5:43 Miracles around Galilee showing
Jesus' authority

6:1-6 Jesus is rejected in Nazareth

6:7-13 Jesus sends out the twelve disciples to
continue his work

6:14-29 John the Baptist is executed by Herod

6:30-56 Jesus feeds a crowd, walks on water
and heals many people

7:1-23 Jesus' teaching about inner cleanliness

7:24–8:10 Jesus' miracles in Gentile territory

8:11-21 The Jewish leaders and the disciples
do not understand Jesus

8:22-26 Jesus heals a blind man

8:27-30 Peter confesses Jesus to be Israel's
Messiah

The kind of Messiah Jesus is

8:31–9:1 Jesus tells the disciples about his
coming suffering and death

9:2-13 The transfiguration of Jesus

9:14-29 Jesus heals a boy possessed by an evil
spirit

9:30-50 Jesus' teaching about greatness and
service in God's kingdom

10:1-12 Jesus' teaching about divorce and
marriage

10:13-16 Jesus welcomes children and blesses
them

10:17-31 Teaching about discipleship and
wealth

10:32-45 Jesus teaches his disciples again
about suffering and service in God's
kingdom

10:46-52 Jesus heals Bartimaeus

11:1-11 Jesus' triumphal entry into Jerusalem

11:12-26 Jesus drives the merchants out of
the temple

11:27–12:44 Jesus' disputes with the Jewish
leaders

13:1-37 Jesus' teaching about the end times

14:1-11 Judas agrees to betray Jesus

14:12-26 Jesus and his disciples celebrate the
Passover

14:27-31 Jesus predicts Peter's denial

14:32-52 Jesus' prayer and arrest in
Gethsemane

14:53–15:15 Jesus' trials and Peter's denial

15:16-47 Jesus' crucifixion and burial

16:1-20 The resurrection of Jesus and the
disciples' commission

The person of Jesus

Mark introduces his Gospel by focusing on "Jesus Christ, the Son of God" (1:1), immediately declaring who he was:

- *Christ* (Greek) or *Messiah* (Hebrew), meaning "anointed one", God's deliverer. While Jesus' contemporaries expected a military Messiah, Jesus would bring deliverance in a very different way (8:27-32).
- *Son of God*, just as God himself declared (1:11; 9:7) and the soldier at the cross recognised (15:39).

Jesus' favourite title for himself, however, was *Son of Man* because its meaning wasn't immediately obvious. Drawing together two key Old Testament ideas – the Son of Man as a glorious heavenly figure (Daniel 7:13-14) and as a lowly earthly figure (Psalm 8:4) – this summed up exactly both aspects of Jesus' nature as God and man.

The problem of Jesus

Jesus was a problem to many. His family thought he was mad (3:20-21), religious leaders thought he was demonised (3:22), his townsfolk were confused by him (6:1-6), and even his disciples didn't understand him (4:13; 8:14-21,31-34). Only the demons grasped who he was (1:24,34; 5:7)! But this

Pedestrian crossing, Japan. Mark tells us that the good news of God's kingdom is here and the door to it is open to everyone

was no accident. Jesus didn't make his identity obvious, and often told those who worked it out *not* to tell others (1:44; 5:43; 8:30) because of current wrong expectations of what Messiah would be and do. Only when it was unmistakable what sort of Messiah he was claiming to be did he openly acknowledge it (14:60-64). Of course, after the resurrection, this messianic secret need remain secret no longer.

The power of Jesus

Jesus backed up his claims by demonstrating his authority. He defeated demons (1:21-28), healed sickness (1:29-45), forgave sin (2:1-12), controlled nature (4:35-41) and even overcame death (5:35-43). Even in his encounter with Pilate, he maintained his quiet authority – the prisoner ruling over his captor (15:1-15, especially verse 5). His ultimate power was displayed at the resurrection where death itself could not hold him.

The passion of Jesus

While Mark doesn't over-dwell on the details of Jesus' "passion" (sufferings), summing up the crucifixion in the simple words "and they crucified him" (15:24), it is clear this is the focus and climax of his Gospel and of all that Jesus predicted (8:31; 9:12; 10:33-34; 14:21).

The path of Jesus

The disciples are often reminded that they too must walk the path of Jesus, ready to resist the attraction of greatness (9:33-36) and to suffer like him (8:34-37). When Mark was read across the Roman Empire, where many Christians suffered for their faith, his words must have had a great impact.

RELEVANCE FOR TODAY – MARK

Jesus' authority

Mark presents Jesus as the powerful Saviour with authority over every aspect of life. Nothing is greater than him, whether

" *Surely this man was the Son of God.*"

MARK 15:39

sickness, sin, nature or death. Yet he never used this authority for selfish advantage (eg 14:44-50). Our use of God's authority should be the same.

Jesus' challenge

Mark shows that those who believe in Jesus must be ready to deny themselves and follow him with their whole being (8:34-35; 12:29-31). When Jesus asked his disciples about different perceptions of him (8:27-29), he was interested in what they themselves believe, rather than the opinions they had gathered from other people. Mere admiration of Jesus is insufficient; only a costly and wholehearted following of him would do, as the rich young man discovered (10:17-31).

Jesus' message

Mark opens his story by describing it as "the beginning of the gospel about Jesus Christ" (1:1). The word *Gospel* means "good news": the good news that God's kingdom is here and the door to it is open to everyone. As Jesus' followers, we too are called to focus on his good news as we share his message with others.

Jesus' love

Jesus mixed with all kinds of people, especially those that the religious leaders avoided and whom they described as "sinners", meaning either immoral people or simply those who didn't keep all their religious rules and rituals. They despised Jesus for this, but he said these were the very

MARK'S USE OF THE WORD "IMMEDIATELY"

Mark writes his account of Jesus in direct, forceful language. He includes relatively long stories and a limited amount of teaching by Jesus. The Gospel is action-packed and often uses the word "immediately" ("at once") to connect scenes. Another indication of rapid movement is the fact that many phrases begin with the conjunction "and", although this is not normally translated into English. The colloquial character of language and style matches the types of people who join Jesus in this story: they are mainly ordinary persons such as fishermen, women (who in those days were seen as inferior to men), and outcasts like lepers, tax collectors, and other sinners.

The narrator in this record is external to the events and never appears in the story itself. At the outset he reveals who Jesus is in his opinion, the Christ (Messiah) and the Son of God (1:1,11). The book's leading question is if the characters in the story will agree with the narrator. As presented by Mark, Jesus' public life is characterised by conflicts with his relatives and fellow inhabitants of Nazareth (3:21,30-35; 6:1-5), his followers (8:14-21), the Jewish authorities (eg 3:1-6; 8:11-13; 12:1-44) and the powers of evil (1:12-13,21-27; 5:1-13; 9:14-29). They all somehow fail to recognise or to acknowledge Jesus for who he is. The powers of evil do recognise Jesus as "the Holy one of God" (1:24, cf. 1:34; 5:7) but the value of that recognition is limited because they do not submit to him voluntarily. However, it does show us that true insight is supernaturally given.

ones who needed him (2:15-17). Our ministry should reach out to all kinds of people, not just nice people or the sort we like.

Jesus' way

Jesus' message wasn't just preached by words, but was backed up with clear demonstrations of God's love and power through his miracles of healing, and he sent out his disciples to do the same (3:14-15; 6:6-13). In the longer ending of the Gospel, this challenge is repeated (16:15-18), and even if that section wasn't written by Mark himself, it shows that such things were still expected in the early church and are a challenge to us today.

Jesus' action

Mark presents Jesus as a real man of action who doesn't sit around thinking about things but who gets on with it. One of Mark's favourite words is "immediately", which connects one story to the next and keeps things moving rapidly. His action appealed to ordinary people who had no time for the long religious debates of the scribes and Pharisees. How active are we?

JERUSALEM IN JESUS' TIME

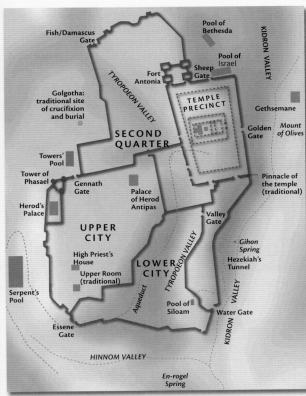

Herod the Great was responsible for a vast rebuilding programme, turning Jerusalem into a beautiful Roman-style city. The temple was rebuilt on an extended precinct overlooking the two north-south valleys, but with a Roman fortress adjoining. Some wall positionings are uncertain.

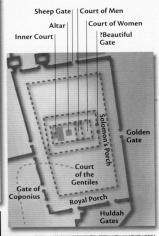

The garden tomb, Jerusalem, traditional site of Jesus' burial and resurrection

The Via Dolorosa, on the route that Jesus was taken to be crucified

Luke
THE GOSPEL FOR ALL

OVERVIEW

Based on Mark but expanded through careful research (1:1-4), Luke is the only Gospel with a sequel (Acts), taking Jesus' message from Jerusalem to Rome, underlining it is for all people everywhere.

SUMMARY

Luke's ordered account of Jesus' life takes us on a journey:

From heaven to Bethlehem

Against the background of the coming of Messiah's forerunner (1:5-25,39-80), Luke shows that Jesus was no mere man but "Son of the Most High" (1:32), God himself miraculously coming to us (1:26-38). Born in David's city of Bethlehem (2:1-7), Jesus was welcomed by ordinary people (2:8-20) and acknowledged by the spiritually faithful (2:21-38).

From Bethlehem to Galilee

The family returned home to Galilee where Jesus grew up (2:39-40). Revealing nothing about these years other than a visit to Jerusalem (2:41-52), Luke jumps ahead to John the Baptist's ministry of preparation and to Jesus' baptism (3:1-20) and temptations (4:1-13). Back in Nazareth, through a reading from Isaiah, Jesus proclaimed the sort of ministry he was beginning, one of freedom for captives (4:14-21). But Nazareth rejected him, so he relocated to Capernaum (4:22-31) from where he taught, healed, did miracles and trained his disciples (4:31–9:50). Peter at last grasped that Jesus was the Messiah and it was from this point onwards that Jesus began to tell his disciples about the death that awaited him and the challenges that faced them (9:18-26).

From Galilee to Jerusalem

Jesus then began a long journey to Jerusalem (9:51ff.), teaching all who would listen, but also encountering increasing opposition (11:14-23,37-54; 20:1-26). The journey climaxed with his triumphal entry into Jerusalem and its temple (19:28-44), which made the religious leaders even more determined to get rid of him (19:47-48). They succeeded by falsifying charges and having him crucified (22:1–23:56). While this seemed the end of the story, it wasn't: Jesus rose again and appeared to his disciples (24:1-49).

From Jerusalem to heaven

The journey was completed as Jesus returned to heaven (24:50-53). But the story wasn't over, as Luke goes on to show us in Acts.

Author

Luke, a doctor (Colossians 4:14) and travelling companion of Paul (2 Timothy 4:11) wrote Luke and Acts, both books being dedicated to the same wealthy patron, Theophilus (Luke 1:3; Acts 1:1).

Date

It is likely that Luke was written after Mark, since he quotes so much of his material. It is hard to be more exact; whereas some date the Gospel to the 60s of the first century AD, others think of a date towards 80. This suggests a date somewhere between AD 60 and 70.

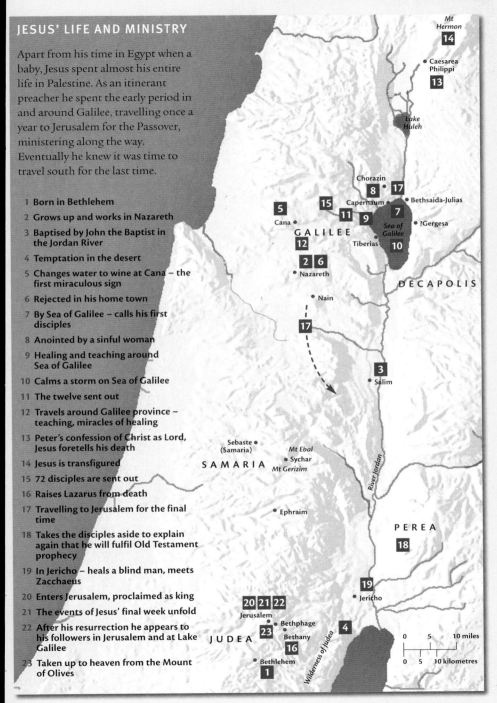

JESUS' LIFE AND MINISTRY

Apart from his time in Egypt when a baby, Jesus spent almost his entire life in Palestine. As an itinerant preacher he spent the early period in and around Galilee, travelling once a year to Jerusalem for the Passover, ministering along the way. Eventually he knew it was time to travel south for the last time.

1 **Born in Bethlehem**
2 **Grows up and works in Nazareth**
3 **Baptised by John the Baptist in the Jordan River**
4 **Temptation in the desert**
5 **Changes water to wine at Cana – the first miraculous sign**
6 **Rejected in his home town**
7 **By Sea of Galilee – calls his first disciples**
8 **Anointed by a sinful woman**
9 **Healing and teaching around Sea of Galilee**
10 **Calms a storm on Sea of Galilee**
11 **The twelve sent out**
12 **Travels around Galilee province – teaching, miracles of healing**
13 **Peter's confession of Christ as Lord, Jesus foretells his death**
14 **Jesus is transfigured**
15 **72 disciples are sent out**
16 **Raises Lazarus from death**
17 **Travelling to Jerusalem for the final time**
18 **Takes the disciples aside to explain again that he will fulfil Old Testament prophecy**
19 **In Jericho – heals a blind man, meets Zacchaeus**
20 **Enters Jerusalem, proclaimed as king**
21 **The events of Jesus' final week unfold**
22 **After his resurrection he appears to his followers in Jerusalem and at Lake Galilee**
23 **Taken up to heaven from the Mount of Olives**

Mt Hermon
14
Caesarea Philippi
13

Lake Huleh

Chorazin
8 **17**
Bethsaida-Julias
5 **15** Capernaum
Cana **11** **7**
9 ?Gergesa
GALILEE Sea of Galilee
12 Tiberias **10**
2 **6**
Nazareth
DECAPOLIS

Nain
17

3
Salim

Sebaste (Samaria)
Mt Ebal
Sychar
SAMARIA Mt Gerizim

River Jordan

Ephraim

PEREA
18

19
Jericho

20 **21** **22**
Jerusalem
23 Bethphage
JUDEA Bethany
16
Bethlehem
1

Wilderness of Judea

0   5   10 miles
0   5   10 kilometres

JESUS' LAST WEEK

1
SUNDAY

Jesus enters the city through the Golden Gate, riding on a donkey. Hailed by the people as Messiah

Matthew 21:1-11
Mark 11:1-11
Luke 19:28-44
John 12:12-19

2
MONDAY

Jesus drives out the money-changers and stall holders from the temple precinct

Matthew 21:12-17
Mark 11:12-19
Luke 19:45-48

3
TUESDAY

Teaching in the temple. At Bethany a woman anoints him "in preparation for burial"

Judas agrees to hand Jesus over to the priests

Matthew 26:6-16
Mark 14:1-11
Luke 22:1-6
John 12:1-8

4
WEDNESDAY

A quiet day with friends in Bethany

5
THURSDAY

The Last Supper: Jesus shares a final passover meal with his disciples

Matthew 26:17-30
Mark 14:12-26
Luke 22:7-38

Jesus struggles in prayer to accept the ordeal he faces

Matthew 26:36-46
Mark 14:32-46
Luke 22:39-46

Betrayed by Judas, taken captive by soldiers

Matthew 26:47-56
Mark 14:43-52
Luke 22:47-53
John 18:1-4

The last days of Jesus' life were spent in Jerusalem at Passover week. He travelled to Jerusalem knowing he would die.

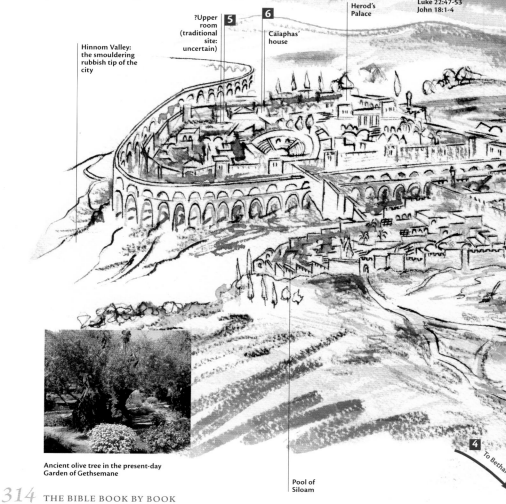

Hinnom Valley: the smouldering rubbish tip of the city

?Upper room (traditional site: uncertain)

5

6

Caiaphas' house

Herod's Palace

4
To Bethany

Ancient olive tree in the present-day Garden of Gethsemane

Pool of Siloam

6
FRIDAY

Peter denies knowing
Jesus

Matthew 26:69-75
Mark 14:66-72
Luke 22:54-62
John 18:15-18,25-27

Jesus is tried by the Jewish
Council, accused of
blasphemy

Matthew 26:57-58
Mark 14:53-65
Luke 22:63-71
John 18:19-24

Taken to Pilate, the
Roman Governor, tried
and condemned to death

Matthew 27:11-26
Mark 15:1-15
Luke 23:1-25
John 18:28–19:16

Jesus is tortured, taken to
Golgotha, crucified and
dies

Matthew 27:27-56
Mark 15:16-41
Luke 23:26-49
John 19:17-37

Jesus' body is buried and
sealed in a new tomb

Matthew 27:57-66
Mark 15:42-47
Luke 23:50-56
John 19:38-42

7
SATURDAY

The Sabbath – the Jewish
day of rest

8
SUNDAY

The risen Christ is seen by
Mary Magdalene, then
the disciples

Matthew 28:1-20
Mark 16:1-18
Luke 24:1-49
John 20:1-23

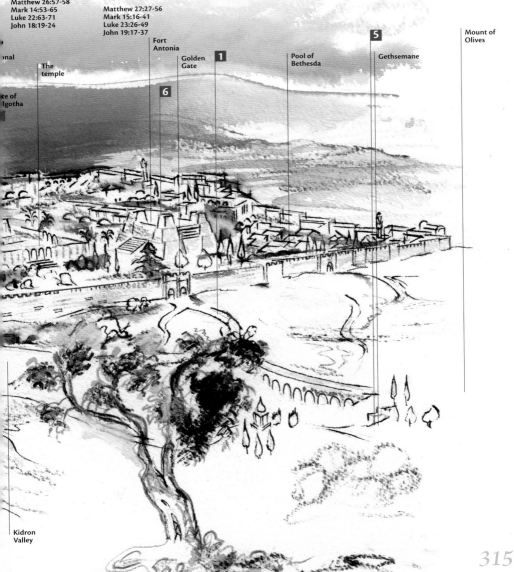

onal

The
temple

e of
lgotha

Fort
Antonia

Golden
Gate

1

6

Pool of
Bethesda

5

Gethsemane

Mount of
Olives

Kidron
Valley

315

> " *D*o not be afraid.
> I bring you good news
> of great joy that will be
> for all the people."

LUKE 2:10

KEY THEMES – LUKE

A Gospel of truth

Luke tells us that he "carefully investigated" his facts so that the reader could know "the certainty of the things you have been taught" (1:1-4). Wherever we can check his details (historical, political, social or geographical), they are always amazingly accurate, which gives us confidence to believe the rest of his story. In particular, Luke emphasises both the incarnation and resurrection in his Gospel, wanting us to know the truth of these two events as the firm foundation for our faith.

A Gospel of inclusion

From beginning to end, Luke shows that Jesus' message was for everyone. Early in his Gospel he traces Jesus' genealogy right back, not to Abraham as in Matthew, but to Adam (3:23-38), showing he had come for the whole human race. Jews found this hard to grasp; so while Nazareth was happy with Jesus' claim that he had come to bring God's promised freedom (4:14-22), they quickly turned against him when he suggested this included non-Jews (4:24-30). In one of his parables (10:29-37) Jesus dared suggest that there could be such a thing as a good Samaritan (a hated people as far as Jews were concerned). However, Luke also includes rich and influential people, such as Joanna in 8:3. At the end of the Gospel, Jesus is still under-lining that his message was for "all nations" (24:47).

A Gospel of compassion

Luke's background as a doctor is reflected in his recording many healing miracles of Jesus and his compassion for those in need, reflected for example in his tender words to the leper (5:12-13). In the miracles he shows a tenderness for the healed and a deep respect for the power of the healer, with Jesus saying that he can drive out demons by the mere touch of his "finger" (11:20)!

Luke has a strong emphasis on Jesus

AN INCLUSIVE GOSPEL

Luke writes an inclusive Gospel – including men and women, rich and poor, Jew and Gentile.

A Gospel for the curious

In an era where we are caught between scepticism on the one hand and curiosity on the other, Luke's serious piece of commissioned research is a powerful tool for introducing the curious to Jesus. Luke includes many well-known parables such as that of the prodigal son (15:11-32). These apparently simple stories contain deep truths about Jesus, God and humanity.

Nepali girls, high in the Himalayas

A Gospel for the cautious

Today many believe that Christianity has little room for those who do not fit in. Luke's Gospel, peopled with corrupt tax collectors, hesitant lepers, uncertain disciples and strong-minded women provides the ideal reading material for them. Its pages will not put them off, but rather extend an invitation to them to find out more. Not only that, but there is another book to follow on with the story of the inclusiveness of the early church: see Acts.

A Gospel for children

In former times, children were valued very little. Greeks and Romans controlled the size of their families by abandoning children. Out of all the evangelists, Luke pays most attention to children (1:41,44; 2:40-52; 9:46-48; 15:11-32; 18:15-17); 9:47 would suggest that there was one wherever Jesus was.

A Gospel for the critical

Luke's frankness makes him appealing to the sceptical and the critical. His picture of Jesus stands out against a dark background of shabby and shallow religion. He shows how our faith should influence our handling of money and possessions. Like the characters in several parables we are all managers, servants who look after our master's property (12:42; 16:1,3,8).

A comprehensive Gospel

No single description of Jesus stands out in this Gospel. Luke emphasises Jesus' humanity (eg his frequent praying) but also describes him as Son of God (1:32,35; 4:41; 10:22). Jesus is the *saviour*, a word used for kings, gods, doctors and philosophers. He is king in the line of David (1–2), a prophet but also the suffering servant of Isaiah 53.

reaching out to everybody, especially those whom society excluded: the poor (16:19-31; 21:1-4), the outcasts (17:11-19; 18:9-14), women (7:36-50; 10:38-42) and children (9:46-48; 18:15-17). Not even the religious were excluded by him, even though many of them excluded him, and he would often eat with them (7:36-50; 11:37-54; 14:1-24).

A Gospel of the Spirit

There is a strong emphasis in Luke (and in Acts) on the work of the Holy Spirit. The Spirit was active, after centuries of silence, even before Jesus' birth (1:15,17,35,41,67; 2:25-27); but once filled with God's Spirit at his baptism (3:21-23), Jesus could begin Isaiah's prophesied Spirit-anointed ministry (4:18-19). Jesus is marked out as a man of the Spirit (10:21) who said God wanted to show his extraordinary generosity and goodness and give this same Spirit to all his children (11:13).

RELEVANCE FOR TODAY – LUKE

A passion for growth

Jesus was a well-rounded man who "grew in wisdom and stature, and in favour with God and men" (2:52) – that is, intellectually, spiritually and socially. God wants us to grow in each of these dimensions too and not be imbalanced, as the Pharisees were.

A passion for the Spirit

If Jesus needed God's Spirit to live and minister, how much more do we. Jesus said that God is a good Father who gives the Spirit to those who ask him (11:13) to help them in their need (12:11-12). Blasphemy against the Spirit – resisting his work – is dangerous (12:10).

A passion for prayer

Prayer had a central place in Jesus' life, especially at key times (3:21; 5:16; 6:12; 9:28-29; 11:1; 22:39-46). He taught his disciples to pray (11:1-4) and underlined the importance of never giving up in prayer (11:5-13; 18:1-5). We need the same passion today, knowing we can do nothing without our Father's help.

A passion for the lost

While the Pharisees liked spending time with "the found", Jesus "came to seek and to save what was lost" (19:10), for finding the lost brings great joy, as the parables of the lost sheep, lost coin and lost son remind us (15:1-32). Jesus calls us, not to spend all our time with "the found", but to go and find "the lost", just as he sent his disciples to do (9:1-6; 10:1-2).

A passion for the unloved

Jesus modelled the importance of loving the unlovely, deliberately reaching out to those that the Pharisees avoided – sinners, tax collectors, prostitutes – and telling his followers to do the same (14:12-14). God's love is for everyone, and so must ours be. If we find ourselves only spending time with "nice" people, we are not being true to Jesus' call.

A passion for learning

Luke wrote his Gospel so that Theophilus, and others, "may know the certainty of the things you have been taught" (1:4). Simply believing in Jesus isn't enough; we need firm foundations of his truth in our lives, letting that challenge and change us (6:46-49). Luke particularly draws attention to the areas of religious ritual (5:33–6:5; 11:37-53) and money (12:13-34; 16:19-31; 18:18-30), both important to the Pharisees, as areas of important change for Jesus' followers.

JESUS' PRACTICE

"The Lord's prayer"
Matthew 6:9-13;
Luke 11:1-4

Praying to his Father
Matthew 6:9;
Mark 14:36; 11:25-26; 14:19;
Luke 23:46; 24:30;
John 11:41-42; 12:27-28;
17:1-26

Praying alone
Matthew 14:23;
Mark 1:35;
Luke 5:16; 9:18

Praying for others
Luke 22:32;
John 17:6-26;
Romans 8:34;
Hebrews 7:25

Praying for children
Matthew 19:13

Praying for his persecutors
Luke 23:34

Prayers of thanksgiving
Matthew 11:25-26; 14:19;
26:26-27;
John 11:41

PRAYING AT OR BEFORE MAJOR EVENTS

Praying at his baptism
Luke 3:21-22

Praying before choosing the apostles
Luke 6:12-13

Praying before he was transfigured
Luke 9:28-29

Praying in Gethsemane
Matthew 26:36-46;
Hebrews 5:7

SEVEN WORDS FROM THE CROSS

About the ninth hour Jesus cried out in a loud voice, *"Eloi, Eloi, lama sabachthani?"*– which means, "My God, my God, why have you forsaken me?"
Matthew 27:46

Jesus said, "Father, forgive them, for they do not know what they are doing."
Luke 23:34

Jesus answered him [the thief on the cross], "I tell you the truth, today you will be with me in paradise."
Luke 23:43

Jesus called out with a loud voice, "Father, into your hands I commit my spirit."
Luke 23:46

When Jesus saw his mother there, and the disciple whom he loved standing near by, he said to his mother, "Dear woman, here is your son," and to the disciple, "Here is your mother."
John 19:26-27

Later, knowing that all was now completed, and so that the Scripture would be fulfilled, Jesus said, "I am thirsty."
John 19:28

When he had received the drink, Jesus said, "It is finished." With that, he bowed his head and gave up his spirit.
John 19:30

John
FINDING LIFE

OVERVIEW

Different in approach to the other three Gospels, John selected some key incidents and teachings from Jesus' life to explore and explain them in more depth so that people might understand more of Jesus and the life they had through him (20:31).

SUMMARY

John begins his Gospel, not with the Christmas story, but in eternity (1:1-18). Seeing Jesus as the fulfilment of both ancient hopes and contemporary thought, he calls him "the Word" (a term understandable to both Jews and Gentiles) who had been with God for ever (1:1-2) but who at a moment in history "became flesh" (1:14), the most succinct summary of the incarnation in the Bible. John then divides his account of Jesus' life into two halves: his public ministry (1:19–12:50) and his private ministry (13:1–20:31).

In the first half he alternates *seven signs* (John's word for Jesus' miracles) with *seven sayings* (lengthy teachings or "discourses" explaining those signs to his disciples or others) backed up by *seven statements* about who he claimed to be (the "I am" sayings), building towards the conclusion that "Jesus is the Christ, the Son of God" (20:31). From Jesus' three Passover visits to Jerusalem, it is possible to work out that this ministry covered just over three years.

The second half records Jesus' private ministry (13:1–20:31), covering the final week of his life and his preparing his disciples for his death, including washing their feet (13:1-17), predicting his betrayal (13:18-30) and Peter's denial (13:31-38), telling them of his departure and the Spirit's coming in his place (14:1–16:33) and praying for them (17:1-26). Like the other Gospels, John then records Jesus' arrest in Gethsemane (18:1-11), his trials (18:12–19:16) and his crucifixion and burial (19:17-42), followed by the empty tomb

and Jesus' resurrection appearances (20:1-31).

In an epilogue he records two later resurrection appearances, and Jesus' recommissioning of Peter after his disastrous denial of Jesus (21:15-19).

Author

Strictly speaking, the text is anonymous. The name John in this Gospel always refers to John the Baptist. Yet the tradition of the church unanimously ascribes it to John, James' brother and one of the sons of Zebedee. The author probably introduces himself in 1:37-40 and 18:15-17 as an unnamed disciple. He may also be the "disciple whom Jesus loved" mentioned in 13:23, 19:25-27, 20:2 and 21:20-23. This is more a statement at his wonder that Jesus loved him than a measure of his own importance. The Gospel is more about its subject than its writer. A comparison between the style of this Gospel and the letters of John the apostle certainly suggests that they were written by the same person.

Date

The tradition of the church tells us that John's Gospel was written last of the four. The great sophistication of John's Gospel also made many scholars ascribe a late date to it. However, the discovery of an early papyrus fragment dating from the first quarter of the second century AD means that it cannot have been written after AD 100. The author does not allude to the destruction of the temple in AD 70 so that some even date the book during the AD 60s. The majority still think it was written at the end of the first century AD.

Who Jesus was

While the other Gospels gradually reveal Jesus' identity, John reveals immediately that he is the Lamb of God (1:29,36), Messiah (1:41,45), Son of God (1:34,49), indeed no one less than God himself (1:1-3). Jesus makes open claims about his relationship with the Father, leading to many debates and conflicts with religious leaders and even attempts to kill him for his blasphemy (5:17-18; 8:58-59; 10:33). But Jesus was clear that to reject him was to reject the Father (8:19; 14:6).

What Jesus did

John knew many of Jesus' miracles (20:30) but chose just seven, for Jews the perfect number. John calls these "signs": not just

OUTLINE – JOHN

Prologue
1:1-5 The eternal Word
1:6-15 The coming of the Word to the world, and John the Baptist's message
1:16-18 The blessings brought by the Word, who is Jesus

Jesus' public ministry: seven signs and teachings
1:19-34 John the Baptist prepares the way for Jesus' ministry
1:35-51 Jesus' first disciples follow him
2:1-11 The first sign: Jesus turns water into wine at Cana
2:12-25 Jesus clears the merchants out of the temple
3:1-21 The first teaching: Jesus discusses new birth with Nicodemus
3:22-36 John the Baptist's declaration of Jesus' greatness
4:1-42 The second teaching: Jesus discusses true worship with the Samaritan woman
4:43-54 The second sign: Jesus heals an official's son
5:1-15 The third sign: Jesus heals a lame man
5:16-47 The third teaching: Jesus tells the Jewish leaders about his relationship with the Father

6:1-15 The fourth sign: Jesus feeds a crowd
6:16-21 The fifth sign: Jesus walks over the water to his disciples
6:22-71 The fourth teaching: discussions about Jesus as the bread of life
7:1-52 The fifth teaching: discussions in the temple about Jesus as Israel's Messiah
7:53–8:11 Jesus saves a woman caught in adultery
8:12-59 The sixth teaching: discussions about Jesus' ministry and his relationship with God
9:1-41 The sixth sign: Jesus heals a man born blind
10:1-42 The seventh teaching: Jesus describes himself as the good shepherd of God's people
11:1-44 The seventh sign: Jesus raises Lazarus from the dead
11:45-57 The Jewish leaders plan to kill Jesus
12:1-11 Mary anoints Jesus with expensive perfume
12:12-19 Jesus' triumphal entry into Jerusalem
12:20-50 Jesus' message about his own ministry and death, and the people's response

demonstrations of power but pointers to who Jesus is. The *seven signs* are: turning water into wine (2:1-11), healing an official's son (4:43-54), healing a cripple (5:1-15), feeding the 5,000 (6:1-15), walking on water (6:16-21), healing the man born blind (9:1-41), and raising Lazarus (11:1-44).

What Jesus said

From Jesus' many public teachings, John again selected just seven: discussing new birth with Nicodemus (3:1-21), talking with the Samaritan woman (4:1-42), his relationship with the Father (5:19-47), Jesus as the Bread of Life (6:22-70), teaching at the Feast of Tabernacles (7:1-52), true relationship with God (8:12-59), and Jesus as the Good Shepherd (10:1-42).

What Jesus claimed

Another "seven" is found in Jesus' "I am" sayings. This was God's name, revealed to Moses (Exodus 3:14); so in using this and linking it to Old Testament symbols, Jesus was making huge claims. He said, I am the bread of life (6:35); the light of the world (8:12); the gate for the sheep (10:7); the good shepherd (10:11); the resurrection and the life (11:25); the way, truth and life (14:6); the true vine (15:1). His final use was absolute, with no qualification or description, which caused enormous reaction (8:58).

Why Jesus died

Right at the beginning John the Baptist recognised Jesus as "the Lamb of God who takes away the sin of the world" (1:29) and Jesus told Nicodemus that "the Son of Man must be lifted up" (3:14). Caiaphas, prophesying more than he knew, said "it is better for you that one man die for the people than that the whole nation perish" (11:50). For John, it was his death and resurrection that made it clear that "Jesus is the Christ the Son of God" (20:31).

Jesus teaches his disciples

13:1-17 Jesus washes the feet of his disciples

13:18-38 Jesus predicts his betrayal and denial

14:1-31 Jesus explains he is about to leave the disciples but will send the Holy Spirit to them

15:1–16:4 Jesus teaches about obeying his commands and facing opposition

16:5-33 Jesus promises the Holy Spirit and explains how the disciples' grief will turn into joy

17:1-26 Jesus prays for his disciples and other believers

18:1-27 Jesus' arrest and Peter's denial

18:28–19:16a Jesus on trial before Pontius Pilate is sentenced to death

19:16b-42 Jesus' crucifixion and burial

20:1-29 The empty tomb and the risen Jesus

20:30-31 The purpose of the book

Epilogue

21:1-14 The risen Jesus prepares breakfast for his disciples

21:15-23 Jesus recommissions Peter to serve him

21:24-25 Conclusion: there is more that could be said

I am the bread of life (6:35-51)
Do we draw on his resources – "the inexhaustible riches of Christ" (Ephesians 3:8)?

I am the light of the world (8:12)
As we follow Jesus Christ, may our light be seen in the world (Matthew 5:14-16).

I am the gate for the sheep (10:7,9)
We are to remember that the only way to become part of God's family is through Jesus Christ (14:6).

I am the good shepherd (10:11)
We are to listen to Christ and follow him; we can feel secure in his loving care. We may enjoy his provision. We are to stay close to, not wander away from, him.

I am the resurrection and the life (11:25)
We can bring "impossible" situations, people and relationships to Jesus; we are to ask him to bring life, new life, to show his power in healing and other miracles. Do we believe this (11:26)?

I am the way, the truth and the life (14:6)
We are to focus on him, trusting that he has our future safe in his hands. He is the way through all the twists and turns of life.

I am the true vine (15:1-8)
We are to receive Christ's life — his resources — into our lives. We are to obey the command to remain in Christ: keep communication channels open.

See also "Teaching about himself", page 64.

RELEVANCE FOR TODAY – JOHN

God's presence
The one who was with God and was God from the beginning (1:1-2) "became flesh and *made his dwelling* among us" (1:14), literally "pitched his tent". Just as God's tabernacle was pitched among his people during the exodus, so God "pitched his tent" among us through Jesus. Our challenge is to now "pitch" that presence where he is not known.

God's love
God sent his Son into the world because he loves it so much (3:16). He calls us to respond, not just by loving him but also by loving one another (13:34-35), reflecting the unity and love within the Trinity itself, not in theory but in reality, so that the world may believe (17:20-26).

God's action
Knowing that miracles need *explanation* and words need *demonstration*, John interwove Jesus' teaching and miracles. Still today, God's word needs demonstrating in action, and our actions need explaining in words so people will understand the gospel.

God's message
The life Jesus offers is available to all, as the contrasting stories of Nicodemus and the woman at the well demonstrate. Whether religious or sinner, enquirer or excuser, male or female, Jew or non-Jew, Jesus can make a difference. We should never doubt that anyone is beyond his reach.

God's truth
In a world of many viewpoints, John proclaims the importance of absolute truth, seeing Jesus as the true light (1:9), true bread from heaven (6:32), true vine (15:1), even truth itself (14:6). Jesus' followers need not be ashamed of claiming they have the truth, but they must also ensure there is no place for un-truth or half-truth in their lives.

God's Spirit
The Holy Spirit is needed not only to begin the Christian life (3:5) but also to live it (14:15-27). In the chapters that cover Jesus' last evening with the disciples, there is a great deal recorded about the role of the Holy Spirit in the disciples' ongoing lives. They are told that he will act as their illuminator, shining a new light on the truths which Jesus has taught them (14:26). He will act as their Counsellor, coming alongside with his help and expressing the presence of Jesus to them (14:16). When they move out into the world to spread the gospel, he will bring spiritual conviction on those who listen (16:8-10).

> " *These are written that you may believe that Jesus is the Christ, the Son of God, and that by believing you may have life in his name."*
>
> JOHN 20:31

Jesus wants every believer to experience his Spirit like streams of living water flowing from within (7:38-39).

God's restoration
Peter was devastated by his denial of Jesus (18:15-18,25-27), at last seeing how his big words weren't matched by big actions. His return to fishing (21:3) reflected his discouragement, but Jesus kindly restored him, letting him cancel his three denials with three affirmations of love (21:15-19). Peter had to learn that failure did not disqualify him, providing he handled it properly.

Acts
ADVENTURES OF THE EARLY CHURCH

OVERVIEW

With Jesus ascended and the Spirit now given, the gospel began to spread, just as Jesus promised. Acts describes the church's birth and its rapid progress across the known world.

SUMMARY

Pentecost

After the ascension, Jesus' disciples returned to Jerusalem to pray and await the promised Holy Spirit (1:1-26). Coming at Pentecost (2:1-4), he transformed the previously fearful followers and produced 3,000 conversions that first day (2:41) and a new way of living (2:42-47). Acts then records the church's subsequent advance "in Jerusalem, and in all Judea and Samaria, and to the ends of the earth" (1:8).

Jerusalem (chapters 1–7)

The apostles' ministry (3:1-26) brought not only conversions (4:4; 5:12-16) but also persecution (4:1-22; 5:17-42; 6:8–7:60). However nothing could stop them, though Ananias and Sapphira's deception almost destroyed the very thing the church was becoming known for and was ruthlessly dealt with (5:1-11). The persecution climaxed in Stephen's martyrdom (7:54-60).

Judea and Samaria (chapter 8)

The church got stuck in Jerusalem and Judea, enjoying success but failing to push out further; so God used the persecution to drive them out of their comfort zone (8:1). Philip preached so successfully in Samaria (8:4-13) that the apostles had to go and see what was happening and pray for the new believers to receive the Spirit (8:14-25). At last, the gospel had escaped its Jewish confines. An African eunuch's conversion was another step in the church reaching out to everybody (8:26-40).

The ends of the earth (chapters 9–28)

A huge turning-point was Saul's conversion (9:1-18), leading to the gospel reaching Damascus and Tarsus (9:20-31). Meanwhile Peter's vision prepared him for God giving his Spirit to Gentiles (10:1–11:18). Another breakthrough came when Saul (now Paul) made Antioch his base, from which his missionary travels stretched ever-deeper into the Roman empire, with churches planted in Asia Minor, Greece and even Rome itself (chapters 13–28). Acts has an open-ending, underlining that the work of the gospel still continues.

Author

1:1 links this book to the Gospel, also written by Luke for Theophilus. Luke's use of the first person plural in 16:10 reveals that from this point onwards he was largely writing on the basis of his personal recollections of the events. Subsequent passages containing the word "we" may well indicate events of which he had particularly vivid memories. These include the departure from Philippi in 20:5 and the journey by sea from Caesarea to Rome in 27:1.

By the time Luke tells about Paul's arrival in Rome in the final chapter, he has probably brought the story to the point where his wealthy sponsor Theophilus knows the details for himself.

Date

The events described in the book last for some thirty years, up to Paul's arrival and stay in

Rome in AD 60–62, so it must have been written after that date. Scholars are divided over the exact time of writing, some placing it around AD 70–80. Yet the fact that Acts makes no mention of the Jewish revolt in AD 66–70 or Nero's campaign of persecution in AD 64 makes it likely that it was written earlier, immediately after Luke's Gospel. Whilst Paul was awaiting his trial in Rome, Luke, his travelling companion, probably used the time to write down the remarkable events that had happened.

The key to Paul's letters
The book of Acts represents vital background reading for the letters of Paul and the other apostles. All the churches to whom Paul wrote letters appear in the book of Acts. From this book we can learn about the circumstances in which those particular churches were founded, the kind of opposition they faced and their initial response to the gospel. This makes our reading of those letters easier and richer. All the theology in Paul's letters is applied theology. In other words, it represents the principles of the gospel as applied to particular settings. Understanding those settings can help us to read his theology, and then apply it to our own particular circumstances.

KEY THEMES – ACTS

Spirit and effort
Acts underlines the importance of cooperation between God's Spirit and human effort. The church couldn't be launched until the Spirit came (2:1-4,42-47), but it was only as Christians responded to him that it grew. Believers took huge risks and endured real hardship to spread the gospel, but it was the Spirit alone who empowered them (4:8) and convicted their hearers (2:37). Luke stresses the importance of receiving the Spirit as the hallmark of real faith (2:1-4; 8:14-17; 9:17; 10:44-48; 19:1-7).

Jew and Gentile
Although the Jesus movement started within Judaism, Jesus' heart had always been for it to spread to all nations (eg 1:8). It wasn't until after Stephen's martyrdom that it began to spread more widely, initially to Samaritans as persecution forced the believers out from Jerusalem (8:1-3). However, Peter needed a divine vision to take the step of visiting a Roman household and was shocked when they too received the Spirit (10:44-46), leaving him with no choice but to baptise them (10:47-48). The church had to grapple with the implications of this (11:1-18), discussing it at special council in Jerusalem (15:1-29) where it was decided that Gentiles didn't need to become Jews and be circumcised to be saved.

Empire and kingdom
Paul often clashed with the Roman authorities. In 16:35-40 he insisted that the authorities in the city of Philippi treat him properly under Roman law. In Corinth a landmark ruling was issued by the Roman proconsul which regarded Christianity as an offshoot of Judaism and therefore protected it under Roman law (18:14-15). When threatened with flogging in Jerusalem, he claimed his legal rights as a Roman citizen to prevent it (22:25) and he later insisted on his right to stand trial before the emperor himself (25:10-11). Chapters 22–26 show that Christianity is harmless to a proper civil government.

Obstacle and opportunity
Each time the church encountered an obstacle, it was turned into an opportunity. So, the persecution in Jerusalem led to a spreading of the gospel (8:4-8); a night in jail for Paul brought the jailer and his family to

faith (16:25-34); a disagreement between Paul and Barnabas led to a multiplication of missionary endeavour (15:36-41); and Paul's shipwreck gave an opportunity to witness to Malta's governor (28:1-10).

Peter and Paul

Acts focuses largely on Peter and Paul rather than all the apostles, drawing several parallels between them, perhaps to underline they were both foundational in the development of the church and to emphasise the unity of the

OUTLINE – ACTS

Pentecost in Jerusalem

1:1-14 Jesus promises to send the Spirit and ascends into heaven

1:15-26 The disciples choose Matthias to replace Judas

2:1-13 The disciples are filled with the Spirit at Pentecost

2:14-41 Peter preaches to the crowd and many believe

2:42-47 Living as believers

The apostles' ministry in Jerusalem

3:1-26 Peter and John heal a lame man in Jesus' name and Peter preaches in the temple

4:1-31 Peter and John's controversy with the Jewish leaders

4:32-27 Living as believers

5:1-16 Judgement of Ananias and Sapphira and healing miracles

5:17-42 Opposition from the authorities

6:1-7 The appointment of deacons to help the apostles' ministry

6:8–7:60 Stephen's arrest, address to the Jewish leaders and martyrdom

Christianity spreads in Judea and Samaria

8:1-3 Persecution scatters the Jerusalem church into Judea and Samaria

8:4-25 Philip's ministry in Samaria and the gift of the Holy Spirit

8:26-40 Philip's ministry to the Ethiopian eunuch

9:1-31 Saul meets the risen Jesus and becomes a believer

9:32–11:18 God directs Peter to preach to the Gentiles

11:19-30 A church is established among Gentiles in Antioch

12:1-4 Herod persecutes the church, kills James and imprisons Peter

12:5-25 An angel releases Peter from prison, and Herod dies

Paul's missionary outreach to the Gentiles

13:1–14:28 Paul's first missionary journey with Barnabas

15:1-35 The Council of Jerusalem instructs Gentile believers

15:36–18:23 Paul's second missionary journey with Silas

18:24-28 The ministry of Apollos

19:1–20:38 Paul's third missionary journey

21:1–22:29 Paul travels to Jerusalem and is arrested

22:30–23:11 Paul is brought before the Jewish authorities

23:12-35 Paul is transferred to the Roman authorities in Caesarea

24:1-27 Paul speaks to the governor Felix

25:1-12 The new governor Festus questions Paul, and Paul appeals to Caesar

25:13–26:32 Paul speaks to Festus, King Agrippa and others

27:1–28:10 Paul's voyage to Rome and shipwreck on Malta

28:11-31 Paul preaches the gospel in Rome, under house arrest

Jewish and Gentile missions. While we learn much about Paul's movements in Acts (after all, Luke accompanied him at times), Peter disappears by chapter 15, although the New Testament contains other clues of what he did. He started to travel further, developing links with Christians in "Pontus, Galatia, Cappadocia, Asia and Bithynia" (1 Peter 1:1) and, according to tradition, ending up in Rome where he became a significant figure in the church and where both Peter and Paul were martyred.

RELEVANCE FOR TODAY – ACTS

The need for prayer

Acts not only starts with prayer (1:14); it also continues with prayer. Prayer characterised the church's meetings (2:42), was their first response to every situation (4:23-31) and guided their decisions (6:6; 13:1-3) and ministry (9:40). God doesn't need our prayers, but he loves to respond to them as he draws us into establishing his will in the world. In our age of instant communication, let's not forget that prayer takes us right to the throne room of heaven itself.

The need for the Spirit

Acts, like Luke, is a book of the Spirit. Nothing could happen for the disciples until the Spirit came, and nothing happened without the Spirit thereafter. Luke shows how different people groups all received the Spirit; none were excluded. Still today the church needs the Holy Spirit if it is to be as effective as the church in Acts.

The need for courage

The early church was born out of the courage of the first Christians. They crossed oceans and mountains, faced beatings, stoning, imprisonments, shipwreck and worse, driven on by their love for Jesus and a passion to share his gospel. Acts challenges us: are we ready to share the gospel, wherever God puts us and whatever the cost?

The need for wisdom

Acts reveals the challenge of accommodating people from different religious backgrounds, who speak different languages and come from different social strata. It wasn't always easy, but God gave them wisdom, as when they solved the tensions between the widows from Palestinian and Greek backgrounds concerning food distributions (6:1-7). In today's multicultural world, the church still needs wisdom to live genuinely as one, knowing it cannot accept divisions and still be the church.

A pastor, Nicaragua. The gospel is good news for all peoples and cultures

The need for sharing

Luke describes with apparent approval the sharing by the earliest Christians of their goods as need arose (2:44-45; 4:31-37) and mentions the well-known Barnabas as an example of this generosity. In the church today those who can afford it should support those who are in need, at home and abroad.

The need for mission

Antioch, 300 miles north of Jerusalem, lay on a major trade route. It was a cosmopolitan city where many races met – Jews, Romans, Greeks, Persians, Central Asians, Indians – and so was an ideal location for a mission-minded church. While Jerusalem stayed

> " *So the word of God spread.*"

ACTS 6:7

entrenched in its Jewish roots, Antioch's cosmopolitan mix and missionary outlook made it far more significant in the Christian mission. God is still looking for churches that will be constantly ready to look beyond themselves.

The need for strategy

Much of the church's success came down to Paul's missionary strategy, targeting key regional cities (eg Ephesus and Corinth) as bases for new church plants from which future evangelistic effort could develop. Still today the best missionary and evangelistic strategy is thought out rather than ad hoc, as Antioch discovered.

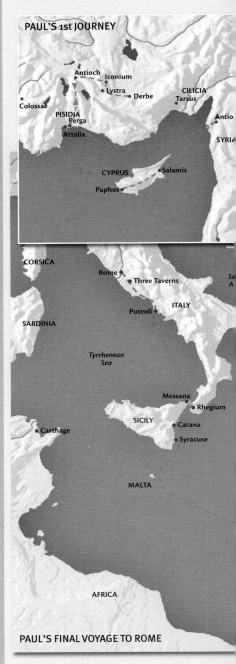

PAUL'S TRAVELS

PAUL'S 1st JOURNEY

Antioch · Iconium · Lystra · Derbe · CILICIA · Tarsus · Colossae · PISIDIA · Perga · Antio · Attalia · SYRIA · CYPRUS · Salamis · Paphos

CORSICA · Rome · Three Taverns · S... A · Puteoli · ITALY · SARDINIA · Tyrrhenean Sea · Messana · Rhegium · SICILY · Catana · Carthage · Syracuse · MALTA · AFRICA

PAUL'S FINAL VOYAGE TO ROME

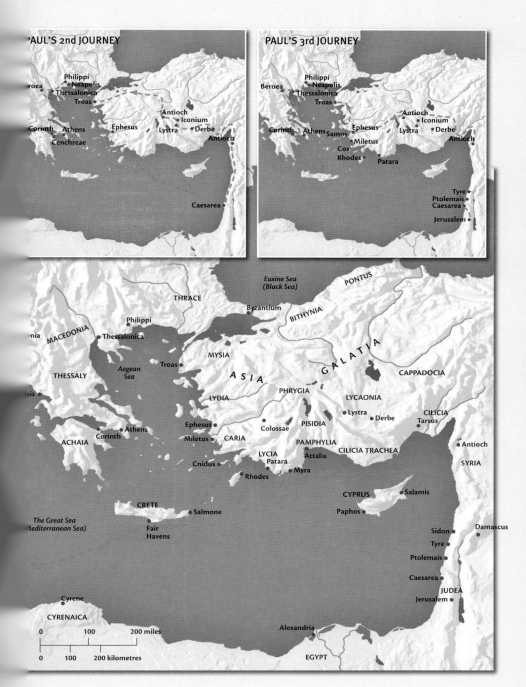

PAUL'S 2nd JOURNEY

Beroea
Philippi
Neapolis
Thessalonica
Troas
Corinth Athens Ephesus
Cenchreae
Antioch Iconium
Lystra Derbe
Antioch

Caesarea

PAUL'S 3rd JOURNEY

Beroea
Philippi
Neapolis
Thessalonica
Troas
Corinth Athens Ephesus
Samos
Miletus
Cos
Rhodes Patara
Antioch Iconium
Lystra Derbe
Antioch

Tyre
Ptolemais
Caesarea
Jerusalem

THRACE
Euxine Sea
(Black Sea)
PONTUS
Byzantium
BITHYNIA
Philippi
MACEDONIA Thessalonica
MYSIA
GALATIA
Troas
THESSALY Aegean
Sea
ASIA
CAPPADOCIA
LYDIA
PHRYGIA
LYCAONIA
Ephesus
Colossae PISIDIA Lystra
Derbe
CILICIA
Tarsus
Athens
Corinth Miletus CARIA
ACHAIA
PAMPHYLIA
Cnidus
LYCIA
Patara Attalia
CILICIA TRACHEA
Antioch
Rhodes Myra
SYRIA
CRETE
Salmone
CYPRUS Salamis
Paphos
The Great Sea
(Mediterranean Sea)
Fair
Havens
Sidon Damascus
Tyre
Ptolemais
Caesarea
Cyrene
JUDEA
Jerusalem
CYRENAICA
0   100   200 miles
0   100   200 kilometres
Alexandria
EGYPT

Romans
THE HEART OF THE GOSPEL

OVERVIEW

In this letter Paul sets out important truths about the Christian gospel in a detailed and systematic form. Romans focuses on how sinful people can be restored to a right relationship with a holy God through the atoning death of Jesus Christ. Paul then explains how this gospel can be expressed in daily life.

SUMMARY

See "Salvation: In the Letter to the Romans", p.492.

Author and date

Paul had long wanted to visit Rome (1:10-12). He planned a mission trip to Spain and intended to stop in Rome en route (15:23-24,28). Not all the Christians in Rome would have heard of him, so this is a letter of introduction setting out the insights (a spiritual gift, 1:11), that he hopes to share. Paul knew a lot about the church in Rome (1:8; 16:1-20) and expected them to encourage him too (1:12).

He probably wrote this letter while working in Corinth during his third missionary journey. He refers to Phoebe, a deacon at Cenchrea (a port for Corinth) in 16:1, and also Timothy (16:21) who we know accompanied him from Corinth to Jerusalem (15:25; Acts 20:4). This dates the letter to about AD 57. There has never been any doubt that Paul wrote it.

Background

Paul did visit Rome, but not in the way he expected. During his stay in Jerusalem he was rescued by Roman soldiers from a riot, and then arrested. He used his Roman citizenship to appeal for a fair trial before the Emperor (or Caesar) in Rome, and he was eventually taken there and kept under house arrest. This is recorded in Acts 21-28.

Rome, in Italy, was the capital of the Roman Empire which stretched across most of Europe, North Africa and the Near East. Rome was a prosperous city, housing about a million people, many of them in multi-storey apartment blocks. It had spectacular public administrative, religious, cultural and sporting buildings, some of which survive as tourist attractions today.

Rome had a large Jewish community. Visitors from Rome heard Peter preach in Jerusalem on the Day of Pentecost (Acts 2:10) and they may have been converted and formed the first church back home. Other Christians travelling to Rome would have joined and supported them later.

The Jews were expelled from Rome in about AD 50 (referred to in Acts 18:2). The historian Suetonius says this was because of riots relating to "Chrestus" – probably the Jewish community had been split by teaching about Christ. In later traditions the apostle Peter is often associated with Rome, but his precise relationship and possible visits are unrecorded in the New Testament.

OUTLINE – ROMANS

Introduction

1:1-7 Paul's opening greetings

1:8-17 Paul's plan to visit Rome and a summary of his message

Sin and judgement

1:18-32 God allows people to sin and face the consequences

2:1-16 God's judgement of sin

2:17–3:8 Jews are guilty of unfaithfulness to God

3:9-20 Both Jews and Gentiles face God's judgement

Grace and faith

3:21-31 God's new way of righteousness in Jesus Christ

4:1-25 God's promise and Abraham's faith

5:1-11 Faith brings peace and joy

5:12-21 As Adam's sin brought death to all, so Christ's sacrifice brings reconciliation and life to all

Death and new life

6:1-23 Baptism symbolises death to sin and life with God

7:1-25 The law cannot bring righteousness and life

8:1-17 Life in the Spirit: freedom in Christ and sonship

8:18-39 God's universal plan and Christian assurance

Israel and the Gentiles

9:1-5 Paul's heartache over unbelieving Jews

9:6-29 Belonging to Israel was always a matter of God's promise, not human birth

9:30–10:21 The Jews have rejected God's promise of salvation for all through Christ

11:1-24 Both Jews and Gentiles can belong to God's family if they believe

11:25-36 God's wonderful plan of salvation for Jews and Gentiles

Service and love

12:1-21 Instructions for living a life pleasing to God

13:1-7 Instructions about obedience to the government

13:8-14 Living in the light of God's coming kingdom

14:1–15:13 Living in harmony with other believers

Concluding remarks

15:14-33 A summary of Paul's mission and travel plans

16:1-27 Personal greetings and Paul's final message

Human sinfulness

The letter opens with a powerful exposure of human corruption. People have an instinctive awareness of God's existence (1:19-20) and of his requirements (2:14-15). Yet everyone has chosen to go their own way ("all have sinned", 3:23). Jews (who had received God's detailed law) and non-Jews are equally guilty before God (chapter 2). As a result, the human race has gone from bad to worse and is under the judgement of God (1:21-32).

Christ's sacrifice

God has provided a wonderful answer to this impossible situation. The death of Jesus Christ is "a sacrifice of atonement" (3:24-25). Because he, a perfect man, "died for the ungodly" (5:6) he reconciled us to God (5:10). Jesus is the "second Adam". The first Adam introduced sin into the world and was the author of spiritual death. Jesus has brought forgiveness and renewal into the world and is the source of eternal life (5:12-19).

Faith's submission

This letter is about God's offer of salvation by grace, which we appropriate through faith – that is, trust in God – and not by our failed attempts to keep God's law (3:21-31). So even Abraham, the founder of the Jewish nation, was justified by faith (chapter 4) and not by his works. But the submission of faith doesn't end there. It continues through discipleship, which includes personal sacrifice to God's purposes (12:1-2) and generous and loving conduct towards both Christians and non-Christians (chapters 12–14).

God's supremacy

No one deserves God's forgiveness and salvation. We can't earn it by what we do. But God is gracious enough to offer forgiveness and eternal life as a free gift. Grace (5:15-16) is sometimes spelt out today as "God's Riches At Christ's Expense". Grace does not mean that God overlooks sin. Because of Christ's sacrifice, God remains just (punishing sin which was laid on Christ) while at the same time justifying (putting right with God) sinners who put their faith in him (3:25-26).

Israel's status

Paul was a Jew but he had become the apostle to the Gentiles (non-Jews, 1:5). Naturally, people were puzzled by the relationship of Jews to God now that the church was equally open to all races and cultures. Christianity was not a sect of Judaism but a branch that had grown from it. In chapters 9–11 Paul emphasises God's faithfulness and says that God will indeed save a remnant of Jews (9:27-29). Many will join Gentiles in God's kingdom (11:1-6,25-27).

River baptism, Portugal. Paul teaches that salvation is ours through faith in God alone. The act of baptism signals that we have been put right with God and intend to follow his way

GOD SPOKE TO THEM THROUGH ROMANS

Paul's letter to the Romans has had a profound effect on individuals and through them the church and the whole world.

Martin Luther: one of the founding fathers of the Reformation

Augustine

In the summer of 386, Augustine sat in a friend's garden. He was in tears because he lacked the will to break with the old life and begin the new. On his lap he had the book of Romans, and having read a passage, he said: "A clear light flooded my heart, and all the darkness of doubt vanished away." He became a great leader of the church and one of its most influential thinkers.

Martin Luther

In 1513, Martin Luther, an Augustinian monk and a professor at Wittenberg University, became deeply concerned about his own salvation. He thought deeply about Romans: "Night and day I studied until I grasped the truth – what being right with God really means. It is when in his loving kindness and great mercy, God makes us right with himself through our faith," he said. "From that moment I felt reborn – as if I had gone through an open door into heaven." Luther was one of the great architects of the Reformation.

St Augustine, from a medieval illuminated manuscript

John Wesley travelled around the country by horse to take the gospel to the people

John Wesley

One day in 1738, Luther's introduction to Romans was being read at a meeting in London. It was May 24 and about 8.45 in the evening. A young man in the audience, John Wesley, was very interested. The words from Luther were describing how God changes our hearts when we put our trust in Jesus Christ. John found his heart "strangely warmed". He wrote, "I felt I did trust in Christ, Christ alone for salvation. An assurance was given me that he had taken *my* sins and saved *me* from the law of sin and death." John Wesley was able to speak to many and bring many to faith in Jesus Christ.

Powerful influence

Romans has a great influence on church history and is worth studying for that reason. Augustine (4–5th century) Martin Luther (16th century) John Wesley (18th century) and Karl Barth (20th century) all rediscovered the truths of Romans and their teaching remains powerful and relevant today.

Profound teaching

Romans is like a systematic theology. It sets out the doctrine of salvation in careful detail, explaining the relationships between Christ's death, Jewish law, God's grace and human faith. However, it has virtually nothing about the resurrection or the return of Christ, both of which are also key doctrines. Therefore, profound as it is, Romans needs to be read alongside other Bible books if we are to have a complete understanding of Christian beliefs.

Pressing questions

The question of how theology impacts on behaviour is important. Paul knew that his teaching could be misunderstood. So having explained justification by grace through faith, he asked, if God's grace is revealed because of human sin, shall we go on sinning so we can experience more divine grace? No! he says. When you trusted Christ, you died to sin so your behaviour should change (6:5-7,23).

Positive assurance

But that raises another question: I do sin, however hard I try not to! Yes, says Paul – and so do I. In chapter 7 he explains the inner battle and failure he (and everyone) experiences. The reason, he says, is that while we are being renewed by God's Spirit, we're still fallible people, so our old and new

> " *Therefore, since we have been justified through faith, we have peace with God through our Lord Jesus Christ.* "
>
> ROMANS 5:1

natures struggle with each other. But God is great and saves us in our struggle (7:24-25). Our salvation is secure despite our failings (5:1-5) and once we are in Christ no one can condemn us (8:1-2) nor separate us from God's love (8:38-39). Indeed, God is working positively for his own purposes in all our circumstances (8:28-29).

Practical discipleship

12:1 launches one of Paul's most searching passages about personal and community conduct. Among his challenges are these:

- Stick to God's standards, not the world's (12:1-2).
- Be humble; don't pretend you're super-spiritual (12:3-8).
- Love each other sacrificially and express it by helping people (12:9-13).
- Act lovingly to people outside the church who mock or attack you (12:14-21).
- Be a good citizen, obey the law and pay your taxes (13:1-7).
- Be consistent and don't backslide into your old ways (13:8-14).
- Be gentle and considerate; don't bully or boss each other (14:1–15:13).

See also "God's rescue operation", p.641.

1 Corinthians

ADVICE TO A DIVIDED CHURCH

OVERVIEW

The church in Corinth suffered from many problems as people who had been used to a carefree self-centred lifestyle came to terms with the demands of Christian discipleship. In this letter Paul deals with such urgent matters as personal morality, public worship, and splits in the church.

SUMMARY

Despite the difficult issues Paul needed to discuss, he opened the letter with positive greetings and thanksgiving. The first issue he tackles is that of the party strife within the church (1:10–4:21). This is followed by matters relating to sexuality and marriage (chapters 5–7), legal disputes between Christians (6:1-11), the attitude towards idolatry (chapters 8–10), women in Christian worship, the Lord's Supper (chapter 11), the use of spiritual gifts in particular in worship (chapters 12–14), and the resurrection of Jesus Christ (chapter 15). The final chapter contains brief notes on the collection for the church in Jerusalem, personal plans, and greetings.

Author and date

The New Testament contains two letters of Paul to the Corinthians. From these, it appears that he also wrote at least two others which no longer exist. Tracing the sequence of these letters helps us to understand what was going on, and to date the existing letters accurately. It seems to go like this:

· Corinthians A (now lost) written because Paul heard of serious problems. See 1 Corinthians 5:9.
· Corinthians B (our 1 Corinthians) written partly in response to questions sent to Paul by the church (1 Corinthians 7:1).
· Corinthians C (now lost), which was a sharp telling-off because the church hadn't changed (see 2 Corinthians 7:5-12).

· Corinthians D (our 2 Corinthians) written to encourage them after news came that the church had reformed. See the introduction to 2 Corinthians for more detail about this.

Between these letters a number of visits to Corinth were made by apostolic delegates who were also Paul's sources of information (for example, 1 Corinthians 16:17). From all the available evidence, it seems that 1 Corinthians was written by Paul while he was working in Ephesus, about AD 55 (16:8).

Background

Corinth was a large cosmopolitan city in southern Greece. It was well known for the loose morality of its occupants and visitors, and for the ready availability of prostitutes, most of whom were associated with religious cults. There was also great social mobility and the church was apparently quite mixed.

Corinth owed its prosperity to two ports nearby, making it a trading centre. The city that Paul visited had been built by Julius Caesar in 46 BC, after a previous city had been destroyed a century earlier.

Paul had founded the church there in about AD 51–52, and stayed there for about two years (Acts 18:11,18). This makes the Christians' behaviour even more surprising: they had received a long spell of good teaching. Paul visited them at least once again (2 Corinthians 2:1; 13:1-2) but this is not recorded in Acts.

OUTLINE – 1 CORINTHIANS

KEY THEMES – 1 CORINTHIANS

Church unity

The church had divided into factions each "following" a leader (1:12; 3:4). Paul says that as Christ is not divided (1:10,13), Christians should be united. Leaders are servants of God, each contributing to church development, but ultimately God alone makes the church flourish, and he is its focus of unity (3:5-9; 4:9-17).

The diversity of human talents and spiritual gifts demonstrates our interdependence in one "body of Christ". This should strengthen, rather than weaken, unity (12:12-31). In his famous description of Christian love, Paul provides a recipe for self-sacrificing unity (chapter 13).

Personal morality

Corinth was notorious for its loose sexual culture. New Christians may not change their habits overnight, but to Paul's dismay some still showed little evidence of change. This was not a matter of occasional sexual lapses, but of gross immorality. He said the church had to disassociate itself from such members (5:1-13).

Paul explained that sex unites two people in body and soul, and the body is a "temple of the Holy Spirit", so sexual relations outside marriage are wrong (6:12-20). Sex has a rightful place in marriage, and while Paul advocated celibacy for the sake of the gospel he recognised that marriage was better than burning sexual frustration (chapter 7).

Freedom and responsibility

In Corinth, most meat sold in butchers' shops had been slaughtered in cult rituals. Some Christians believed eating it was sinful. Paul disagreed, because an idol is nothing and God is supreme (8:4; 10:25-26). However, for the sake of Christians with sensitive consciences believers like him should respect their views and if necessary refrain from eating such meat. It is wrong to encourage someone with a weaker conscience to do something they feel is sinful. Paul says we should put the spiritual wellbeing of others first, and not insist on everyone adopting our views (10:24,31-33). This is especially relevant today where Christians disagree over cultural details.

Public worship

Paul insists that public worship events should be orderly, reflecting the orderly nature of God (14:33). In Corinth, there were two major problems:

· The Lord's Supper had degenerated into a party. At this time, the communion service recalling Christ's death on our behalf was part of a shared fellowship meal. But the rich refused to share their food with the poor, and others started before everyone had arrived. Having scolded them for disorderly conduct (11:17-22), Paul explains the origins and meaning of communion (11:23-26). Light-hearted participation is spiritually dangerous (11:27-30)
· The use of spiritual gifts such as tongues and prophecy had become self-indulgent displays. Paul provides detailed guidance for the church's worship meetings (chapter 14).

Resurrection hope

Some people could not understand the resurrection, perhaps because they were so fixated on the material elements of this life. In chapter 15 Paul explains that:

· There's no doubt Christ rose from the dead.
· Therefore people can rise from the dead, and we all shall when Christ returns at the end of time.
· Indeed, if we have nothing to look forward to in the next life, our faith is a waste of time.
· We will have a different resurrection body which won't be perishable.
· This is great news: death, our greatest "enemy", is defeated for ever!

Most of the key themes of 1 Corinthians are directly relevant to major issues faced by Christians in all cultures today. They can be summed up like this:

Don't split your church over secondary matters

Such secondary matters could include the particular emphasis or method of a leader, or the way in which worship is conducted and spiritual gifts manifest. The important thing is that the basic truths of the Gospel – Christ's death and resurrection – are taught, believed and applied.

> " *I* did not come with eloquence or superior wisdom ... so that your faith might not rest on men's wisdom, but on God's power."

1 CORINTHIANS 2:1,5

Recognise God-given boundaries to sex

There are boundaries to human sexual conduct which are for the good of individuals and society as a whole. Ignoring the boundaries can lead to the disintegration of relationships and families. Christians are called to model God's standards, not to mimic the world's standards.

Put other people's interests first

This is the cardinal principle of Christian love. If you are a leader, or have a specific spiritual gift or ministry, don't use your authority or influence for personal gain. Even when you don't agree with someone's view on a secondary or cultural matter, respect it and don't rubbish the person.

Think about the impact of public worship

We are to think about the impact of our public worship on other people – both committed Christians and interested visitors. Make the most of people's special gifts but make sure everything is well conducted and honouring to God. Worship should witness to the reality and presence of God, and be intelligible to all those present.

2 Corinthians
COMFORT IN SUFFERING

OVERVIEW

The problems that Paul had dealt with in his first letter to the Corinthians had improved, so he wrote to express his relief. However, another more personal issue had arisen: Paul's integrity was being questioned. So he set out his track record of faithful discipleship and intense suffering for the Gospel.

SUMMARY

Although initially Paul received good news (chapters 1–9), it appears that one of the factions he had encountered in the church (1 Corinthians 1:10-12; 3:1-4) developed into a rival church which rejected Paul as an apostle. They were doing what people often do: they asserted their presumed superiority by rubbishing someone else (chapters 10–13). Paul was hurt. The criticism was unjustified. In response he detailed all that he had endured for Christ.

Author and date

Paul had written to the Corinthians at least three times before this letter (see the introduction to 1 Corinthians for details). This letter was probably written about AD 56, a year or so after 1 Corinthians, from northern Greece (Macedonia), which is implied in 2:12-13. In between he had paid them an unsuccessful visit (12:14; 13:1-2).

However, many scholars believe that 2 Corinthians contains two separate letters, which were probably united for convenience into a single scroll early in the history of the church. The first letter, full of encouragement and relief, is chapters 1–9. The second letter,

much more downbeat, is chapters 10–13. The reason for believing this is the sharp change of tone in chapter 10. In the earlier chapters Paul had expressed his joy that his advice had been taken, an offender disciplined, and that Titus had returned from Corinth greatly encouraged (7:5-16). Paul was so delighted that he wrote "I can have complete confidence in you" (7:16)!

Sadly, his confidence was misplaced. He had heard that the Corinthians consider him weak (10:10) and foolish (11:16). His authority was being challenged by people he called "false apostles" who are agents of Satan (11:13-15). In response, he renewed his warning to unrepentant sinners (13:2-3) and challenged his readers to consider if they had left the faith (13:5).

This additional letter (Paul's fifth to Corinth) was probably sent after chapters 1–9 and the unsuccessful second visit, before Paul made his planned third visit to Corinth (13:1) which is probably implied in Acts 20:1-3.

Background

For information about the city and the church, see 1 Corinthians, p.337.

OUTLINE – 2 CORINTHIANS

KEY THEMES – 2 CORINTHIANS

Paul's consistency

- **He was consistent in his plans.** Some people accused him of changing his mind about visiting them, throwing doubt on his authority. Paul explained why he changed his plans (1:12–2:4). During the delay he continued to be anxious about them, and sent Titus to gather information (7:2-16). Later he set out his revised plans for the third visit (13:1-10).

- **He was consistent in his preaching.** Paul rarely defended or justified himself but the Corinthians' jibes forced him to. He protested that he never gained financially from his preaching (2:17; 11:8-9). He claimed that his was a God-inspired consistency and competence (3:1-6) and he never changed his message or his methods (4:1-6). In chapters 10–11 he denounced as false apostles those who spread lies about him (such as his alleged timidity in person and boldness in writing). They were preaching another gospel. He may not have been a trained preacher (11:6) but he did have the Spirit of God (3:17-18).

- **He was consistent in his patience.** Paul had been on the brink of death (1:8-9) and it was never far from him (4:7-12). He listed his troubles in 6:8-10 and expanded on them in 11:23-29. He suffered from a "thorn in the flesh" (12:1-10) which may have been a sight impediment or other physical disability. Was he bitter? No way! He knew God's help, maintained his hope, and so bore it patiently as the cost of discipleship (1:10; 4:8; 12:10).

God's comfort and glory

This letter has lots of teaching about God. It opens with praise for God's comfort (1:3-11). Paul, unselfish as ever, adds that such an experience isn't for his personal benefit alone but is meant to be shared. So too is God's glory, which shines on us and which we reflect to others around us (4:16-18). That thought leads Paul into a joyful section on the hope of heaven (5:1-10) before he later praises God again for his support in the most amazing and horrific situations (12:7-10).

Churches' charity

Giving money is often a touchy subject, but Paul wasn't afraid to broach it. He commended the Macedonian churches which were a great example to everyone for their sacrificial giving to mission and the relief of suffering. And then he says that the Corinthians, who some while before had also proved very generous, should continue to give as evidence of their genuine love for the Lord (chapters 8–9).

Submit gently

Paul's robust defence of his ministry has a subtle undercurrent. All the time, he is urging people to be humble and not self-assertive, to be gentle with each other rather than boasting about their achievements. You see this especially in 10:12-18 where he refuses to compare himself with others. Making comparisons can either depress us (because we can't match their achievement) or make us feel proud because we think we're better than they are. What's important, he says in 10:18, is God's commendation. Our aim is to please God, not gain a human reputation. That means submitting to him and fulfilling our calling.

Start again

Paul's teaching about reconciliation in 5:1–6:2 is often used in evangelistic talks, but it applies equally to believers as to unbelievers. The answer to disunity in society or the church is to seek reconciliation. God is the great reconciler: through Christ's death sinful people have been brought into fellowship with a holy God, and Christians now share in his work of reconciliation. "We are ... Christ's ambassadors" (5:20). Amazing: each Christian is a valued diplomat in God's service with the special task of bringing peace where there is dissension. We can start again after a row; and so can others, with Christ's help.

> " *We live by faith, not by sight.*"
>
> *2 CORINTHIANS 5:7*

Share generously

How we hate to part with our worldly wealth and goods! But it isn't ours, it's God's. He gives us all we have, and all we need; we won't suffer if we give some away (9:8-11). Paul's memorable phrases are easy to repeat and hard to apply: "God loves a cheerful giver" (9:7); though Jesus "was rich, yet for your sakes he became poor" (8:9) – thus giving us an example to follow. You can't be expected to give what you haven't got, Paul adds (8:12). And he challenges the attitude which applauds the accumulation of wealth at others' expense, suggesting that God's will is equality and "enough" for all (8:13-15). He is surely angry at the inequality in the world today.

Suffer graciously

Christianity does not bring a prosperity gospel but realism. Paul knits his persecution for the gospel with his "thorn in the flesh" into a single thought: we all suffer. His positive attitude refuses to allow his faith to be rocked by personal discomfort. It is a great example in our age that expects quick fixes for all ills. God is bigger than our pain. And yes, Paul prayed to be free of it. But when he wasn't, he accepted the verdict and carried on serving, expecting a better life in the future.

Galatians
THE GOSPEL OF FREEDOM

LETTERS

OVERVIEW
The churches to which this letter is addressed had caved in to teachers who said that you cannot be a Christian unless you also observe the Jewish ceremonial law. Paul wrote to correct this "false gospel". He said it led to spiritual slavery, in contrast to the freedom brought by the death of Jesus Christ and the indwelling presence of the Holy Spirit.

SUMMARY
Whereas most of Paul's letters begin with praise to God and thanksgiving for the readers and their faith, Galatians has only a short introduction (1:1-5) after which Paul immediately goes on the attack and states his point: what others after him have preached in Galatia is not the true Gospel (1:6-9). He takes much time to establish his credentials as an apostle, the credentials of the Gospel that he received from Jesus Christ himself (1:10–2:10). He recalls an earlier controversy over the issue of the law, an incident in Syrian Antioch which brought him head to head with his fellow apostle Peter (2:11-14), and he rounds off the first part of the letter with a statement of the Gospel (2:15-21).

A second round of polemics begins with the blunt address "you foolish Galatians" and continues to remind them of the work of the Holy Spirit among them as evidence for the truth of the Gospel as preached by Paul (3:1-5). Twice Abraham is introduced as an example of true faith (3:6-14,15-18). Paul explains that the role of the law was to prepare the Jewish people for the Gospel (3:19-29) so that Christians by definition are not subject to it (4:1-7). A series of personal utterances of concern for the readers follows in 4:8-20, underscored once more with reference to Abraham, this time in relation to his wives Hagar and Sarah (4:21-31). 5:2-6 applies the entire argument to the specific issue of circumcision and 5:7-12 is one more

personal appeal. A discussion of the relation between the law and the freedom in the Spirit follows in 5:13-26, with 6:1-10 offering practical suggestions for mutual relations within the fellowship. A final time Paul sums up his appeal (6:11-15) before he closes with a few words of blessing (6:16,18).

Author and date
This letter includes the themes and emphases that are a common feature of Paul's ministry and writings. What is less certain is to whom it was addressed and when it was written.

In Paul's time, two areas were called "Galatia", both within modern Turkey.

The most likely view is that Paul wrote to churches in the Roman administrative area called Galatia, in the south. Here were the cities of Antioch, Iconium, Lystra and Derbe which Paul visited and where he started churches (Acts 13–14). That makes Galatians the earliest of Paul's letters, probably written about AD 47–48 soon after his visit (1:6). He doesn't mention the Council of Jerusalem (Acts 15) which was about AD 48–49, and which he would have referred to had it happened because it strongly supported his position. Alternatively, Paul may have written to people in the north of the region at a later date (c. AD 55).

Background
The Jewish people had been given laws in the Old Testament, to which their leaders had added still more detailed legislation. Now

that non-Jews came to faith in the God of Israel, it was logical to assume that they too should abide by these rules. Yet God had revealed to Paul that he accepts believers in Jesus Christ without observance of the law.

This was the gospel Paul preached but his adversaries wanted to make all Christians subject to the law. They had arrived in the new churches soon after Paul had departed (1:6-9).

OUTLINE – GALATIANS

The Galatian problem
1:1-5 Paul's opening greetings
1:6-9 Paul's concern that the Galatians are deserting the gospel

The authenticity of Paul's gospel
1:10-24 Paul's message came directly from Christ
2:1-10 Paul's credentials as an apostle
2:11-21 Paul's argument with Peter over the inclusion of Gentiles in the church

An explanation of the gospel
3:1-5 Paul's appeal to the Galatians against legalism
3:6-9 Abraham's children are those who have faith
3:10-14 The way of the law and the way of faith

3:15-22 The relationship between God's promise and the law
3:23–4:7 The role of the law for God's children
4:8-20 Paul's concern for the Galatians
4:21-31 A picture of law and promise: Hagar and Sarah

The freedom brought by the gospel
5:1-12 Paul pleads for the Galatians to avoid slavery to the law
5:13-26 The life of freedom in the Holy Spirit
6:1-10 Various instructions for Christian living
6:11-15 Warnings against Judaisers
6:16-18 Paul's final comments

KEY THEMES – GALATIANS

Paul's personal experience
What we know about Paul's life from Acts 8–14 is supplemented in Galatians. He describes what happened after his conversion: his visits to Arabia and Damascus (1:14-17; Acts 9:19-25), then Jerusalem (1:18; Acts 9:26-30). His time in Syria (1:21) probably refers to Tarsus, which is where Barnabas found him and drew him into a wider ministry (Acts 11:22-26).

The visit to Jerusalem in 2:1 is probably that of Acts 11:27. There, the other apostles accepted Paul's ministry to the Gentiles

without imposing Jewish regulations (2:1-10), a decision later reinforced by the Council of Jerusalem (Acts 15). His argument with Peter (2:11-21) is unrecorded in Acts and is ironic because it was Peter who was first convinced of God's acceptance of Gentiles (Acts 10:1–11:18). It's a complex jigsaw, but it does fit together!

The promise of salvation
Paul stresses that God's approval and our eternal salvation is mediated only by Jesus Christ and depends on faith in Christ, not on

fulfilment of religious regulations (eg 2:15-16,20-21). No one kept all the Old Testament rules anyway so that all were under God's curse (3:10). Jesus took this curse on himself so that by trusting in his atoning death and resurrection we can be saved (3:11-14). As a result, all racial and cultural distinctions are swept aside and all believers are on an equal footing (3:26-29).

The purpose of the law

By "the law" Paul means the Jewish ceremonial law, not the moral law summed up in the Ten Commandments. The rules about food, methods of worship, and certain cultural matters are no longer compulsory. He uses the shorthand "circumcision" (5:6) to mean the whole ceremonial law, because that aspect of it was a key part of the false apostles' teaching.

However, Old Testament people weren't misguided. The law gave them a framework for understanding and relating to God while faith was in its infancy, like a guardian protecting them until the full revelation of Christ (3:19–4:7). The law points forward to Christ and is fulfilled by him.

God's power for living

We're free to be the people God intended us to be, without being enslaved to the burden of having to fulfil meticulous religious rituals! Such freedom is also what Jesus taught (John 8:31-36). We have been adopted into God's family. We're no longer domestic servants; we're heirs of the Father (4:4-11; 5:1). We have a new dynamic, God's Holy Spirit, and a new responsibility – to live in harmony with and obedience to our loving God (5:13-26).

RELEVANCE FOR TODAY – GALATIANS

Avoid legalism

An important part of biblical interpretation is to look for the principles behind the teachings. In Galatians, the principle is "legalism": the insistence that every Christian should conform to certain rituals or practices.

Such practices vary hugely from culture to culture, however! For some Christians, not drinking alcohol is almost an article of faith; for others, it is a natural thing to do, provided it isn't taken to excess. The problem is that such regulations can become "primary" issues that define a Christian. The only primary issues that Scripture allows are those which Paul emphasises in Galatians: the life, death and resurrection of Christ. If our faith is firmly in those, then issues not directly associated with the moral law are "secondary" matters over which we may disagree, but should not divide.

Argue carefully

Paul's arguments in 3:15-19 and 4:21-31 can be puzzling. Paul was a Jewish rabbi, and in

this letter was combating people from a Jewish background. Therefore he uses the allegories and accepted Jewish beliefs of his day to show that his teaching isn't contrary to God's word.

This is a good example to follow. In our discussions with people from many backgrounds, it is important to start where they are in their understanding and background knowledge. We may be able to find points of contact, as Paul did, which lead people towards a fresh and more complete understanding of the gospel. Indeed, this is the main principle of cross-cultural mission.

Act consistently

The argument with Peter (2:11-21) illustrates a common problem. We believe we should act in a certain way, but cave in under pressure and don't act consistently. That Peter could fall this way may be some comfort; everyone is vulnerable. That is why at the end of the letter Paul stresses the need to "live by the Spirit" (5:16). The Holy Spirit can give us the courage

THE GOSPEL SPREADS

One effect of persecution – driving Christians away – plus missionary work by the apostles and others combined to spread the gospel throughout the Roman world and eventually beyond.

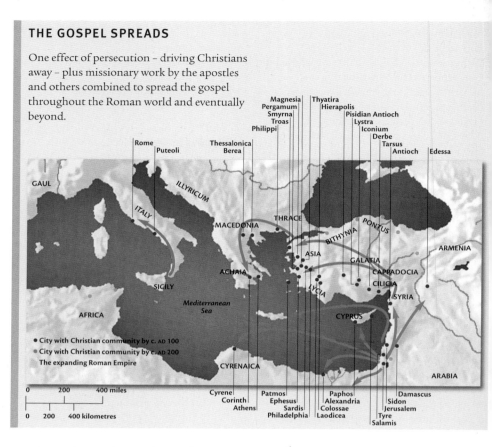

- City with Christian community by c. AD 100
- City with Christian community by c. AD 200
- The expanding Roman Empire

to be consistent when our human hearts fail us.

Apply the gospel

Christianity is a framework for living. Paul sets out the difference between "the acts of the sinful nature" (what human beings tend towards) and "the fruit of the Spirit" which is a list of virtues reflecting God's character being formed in us (5:19-26). It's a challenging list. Jealousy, rage and envy afflict all of us even if immorality and idolatry don't. None of us can read Galatians 5 lightly. The world around us expects us to demonstrate the fruit of the Spirit – and so does God.

> " *I* have been crucified with Christ and I no longer live, but Christ lives in me."
>
> GALATIANS 2:20

Ephesians
INSPIRED BY GOD'S ETERNAL PURPOSES

OVERVIEW

Ephesians is full of inspiring language. It describes God's eternal purposes for the rescue of humanity from the clutches of sin and death through the death and resurrection of Jesus Christ. Punctuated by prayers and praises, it urges readers to live out in practice the changed life that God has graciously given them.

SUMMARY

Ephesians falls neatly into two equal parts: chapters 1–3 have a doctrinal content whereas chapters 4–6 are ethical. The letter includes many topics which would have been covered in an introduction to the Christian faith but at quite a high level.

After a brief introduction and greetings (1:1-2) Paul praises the grace of God in Jesus Christ, then he mentions the Holy Spirit (1:13-14). The second half of chapter 1 addresses God directly in prayer, asking for the work of the Holy Spirit and for certainty of the believers' hope of the future. In chapter 2 attention shifts further to the position of the believers, with verses 1-10 spelling out how they were saved and verses 11-22 explaining that they belong to God's holy people, the church which consists of believers from Jewish and Gentile backgrounds. Paul then discusses the contribution of his own ministry to the church (3:1-13) and prays once more for it (3:14-21).

The second half of the letter addresses the unity, growth and development of the church (4:1-16) before it moves on to the individual believer. Here Paul considers the consequences of being a Christian. Specific topics include the roles of husband and wife (5:21-33) and other groups (6:9). The letter ends with a discussion of spiritual armour (6:10-20) and the usual personal notes and blessings (6:21-24).

Author

Ephesians is unlike any of Paul's other letters. It contains few personal reflections or greetings, apart from identifying the author as Paul (1:1; 3:1) and the final mention of Paul's messenger Tychicus (6:21-22). The subject matter is typically that of Paul, but the language is not. The original Greek contains over 40 words not used anywhere else in the New Testament, and a similar number of other words used in the New Testament but never in Paul's other letters. However, the early church accepted Paul's authorship without question. The language differences could be due to a different scribe taking Paul's dictation, and no real alternative to Paul has ever been suggested.

Date

The lack of personal data makes it difficult to date Ephesians, but it was clearly written while Paul was in prison (3:1,13; 4:1; 6:20). Ephesians has a number of similarities to Colossians, although the ideas are more developed in Ephesians and were therefore probably written after Colossians. But it probably wasn't long after, as it is usually grouped with Colossians, Philippians and Philemon as the four "prison epistles" written by Paul when he was under house arrest in Rome (see Acts 28:16,30,31), about AD 60.

Background

This "letter" is more like a sermon, an inspirational talk at a conference, or even an essay, rather than a personal letter. Paul doesn't deal with any specific issues in the local church, as he does in his other letters. The destination of Ephesus (1:1) is missing from some important early copies which has led scholars to suggest that 'Ephesians' was a circular letter (with perhaps several copies being sent at the same time) which was taken around the churches of Asia Minor (modern Turkey). Ephesus was the chief city in the area at that time. Paul wrote the letter to encourage Christians to persevere in their faith and to remind them of some basic truths and responsibilities of being a Christian.

OUTLINE – EPHESIANS

Understanding God's purposes

1:1-2 Opening greetings
1:3-14 Praise to God for his great plan for the world
1:15-23 A prayer for understanding
2:1-10 God's gift of new life in Christ
2:11-22 Jews and Gentiles become one family in Christ
3:1-13 Paul's place in God's great plan
3:14-21 Paul's prayer for the church and praise of God

Living in God's purposes

4:1-16 The unity, growth and maturity of the body of Christ
4:17–5:20 Coming out of darkness and living in the light of Christ
5:21–6:9 Guidance about family and work relationships
6:10-20 Resisting the devil with the armour of God
6:21-24 Closing greetings

Chosen people

Paul focuses on the idea of adoption (1:5) to stress the privilege of belonging to God. Roman citizens adopted sons not because they were orphaned but because they had potential as servants. Jews went further: they gave adopted children the full rights and benefits of natural children. Christians are chosen by God because he recognises our worth, and gives us full rights in his worldwide family.

The benefits are huge:

· sharing in the limitless riches of heaven (1:3-4)
· enjoying the freedom and forgiveness of grace (1:7-8)
· receiving insight into God's purposes (1:9-10)
· being integrated into God's plans and family (1:11-12)
· receiving the Holy Spirit as a sign of God's faithfulness (1:13-14).

And that's just the start! This is more than a theological principle; it's a living experience. Paul prays that we will feel and know this dynamic love and living presence of God (3:16-19).

Changed lives

Becoming a Christian is a wholesale change of life. It starts on the inside – a complete re-orientation of heart and mind – and is expressed in a radically new lifestyle. Paul describes the inner change in stark terms in 2:1-10. However "alive" we felt in our pre-Christian state, we were in fact dead to God and alienated from his heavenly riches. But out of his grace, through no merit or effort of our own, he made us alive: a spiritual resurrection. There is no greater contrast than life and death: that is the magnitude of the change.

With the privilege comes responsibility. We are not saved *through* our good deeds but we are saved *in order to do* good deeds and express God's life to others in the world (2:9-10). Paul describes the duties of the Christian in 4:17–6:23. The old self has been put off (4:22-24), and so our speech, work, and relationships are all to be transformed (4:25-32). Out goes impurity and immorality (5:3-7) and in comes the renewal of the Spirit (5:15-20), with the requirement to be considerate rather than selfish in relationships (5:22–6:9).

Church unity

How can people from different cultures work and worship together? In God's purposes there is no longer a distinction between Jew and Gentile: racism and cultural superiority of one group over another is banished for ever (2:11-18). We are all part of the same "temple" (2:19-22), and God has given the church gifted people to help maintain the unity of the Spirit (4:1-16).

How to pray for others

Ephesians contains two of Paul's prayers which are a great example to follow when we pray for other people. In 1:15-19 he:

· Thanks God for them
· Asks that they may have wisdom
· Prays they will know God better
· Prays that they will know real hope and experience God's power.

In the second, 3:14-19 (it concludes in 3:20-21 with a doxology that is often used at the end of worship services), Paul:

· Expresses adoration of God
· Prays for the inner spiritual strengthening of his readers

> " *For it is by grace you have been saved through faith – and this not from yourselves, it is the gift of God – not by works, so that no-one can boast."*

EPHESIANS 2:8-9

· Prays that they will be totally loving
· Asks that their understanding of Christ's love will be complete
· Prays that they will be filled with the fullness of God.

How to live in harmony

Conflicts easily arise through "personality clashes". These are not really any different from the racial and cultural clashes that Paul refers to. The secret of dealing with them is for both sides to recognise their unity in Christ. Through him we have been reconciled to each other as well as to God (2:14-22).

The key to putting unity into practice is love. If we love God, we should be able to deal lovingly with other members of the body of Christ. In 4:25-6:9 Paul notes some principles:

· Share your possessions (4:28)
· Talk positively, not negatively (4:29)
· Control your temper and learn to forgive (4:31-32)
· Be humble and submit to each other (5:21)
· Let mutual love rule in the home (5:33)
· Treat workers well and don't antagonise employers (6:5-9).

How to witness in the world

The world watches to see if we reflect the life of God that we speak about. So honest work (4:28), being kind rather than nasty to or about people (4:31-32), avoiding immorality and impurity (5:3-7) and drunkenness (5:18) are vital components of effective witness.

How to deal with the devil

There is a malignant spiritual power seeking to destroy the work of God. But the power of God is much stronger, and in God's armoury Christians have all they need to resist attack and defeat the enemy. The passage about the armour of God (6:10-18) draws on the image of a Roman soldier (to whom, perhaps, Paul was chained in prison) and he repeats his confident assertions to stand firm and keep praying!

Philippians
JOY IN CHRIST

OVERVIEW

Paul wrote this letter for two reasons. He wanted to thank the Christians in Philippi for a gift they had sent him (4:10), and to commend to them Timothy (2:19-24) and Epaphroditus (2:25-30), whom he was sending to Philippi. Paul also updates his readers on his current news. He includes a poem about the divinity of Christ which is one of the most famous New Testament passages.

SUMMARY

After the usual greetings, Paul begins with a warm thanksgiving to God for the church and its faith, which leads to a prayer that their love will increase even further (1:1-11). He then gives ample attention to his personal circumstances (1:12-26). It is unclear to him if he will be released or convicted, but he is open to both possibilities. Paul next encourages the readers to lead worthy lives, despite the fact that they also have to cope with some form of persecution (1:30). His appeal becomes more specific when he sets Jesus Christ as an example of humility and readiness to serve (2:1-18). The letter seems to be coming to a close with Paul's announcement that he will send Timothy to Philippi and also hopes to come in person (2:19-24). First, however, Paul will send Epaphroditus back to his home town, presumably with the letter (2:25-30). Both missionaries are warmly commended. The phrase beginning with "Finally" (3:1) could be the letter's final line, but for some reason Paul continues with some warnings against unspecified troublemakers mixed with testimonies about his own faith (3:1-4:1). Whereas they are proud of their achieve-ments, Paul refuses to boast; he puts all his trust in Jesus Christ. A few specific exhortations follow (4:2-9) before Paul discusses the relation between the church and himself (4:10-20) and concludes the letter with warm greetings.

Author and date

There has never been any doubt that the apostle Paul wrote this letter. It contains a number of personal references which tie it in with other New Testament writings and with what we already know of Paul.

However, the date at which he wrote it is unclear, because scholars are divided over where he wrote it from. Clearly, Paul was in prison (see 1:7,13,14). Many believe that this refers to his house arrest in Rome (Acts 28:16), which dates the letter at about AD 61. This would link Philippians with Ephesians, Colossians and Philemon as the four "prison epistles" written by Paul from Rome.

But there are also some good reasons for suggesting that he wrote it when he was in prison in Caesarea before being transported to Rome. That would date the letter about AD 58–59. A third view is that he was imprisoned in Ephesus about AD 53–55, but this is deduced from inferences in the New Testament; there is no direct evidence that such an imprisonment actually happened.

Background

There was a strong bond of friendship and love between the Philippian Christians and Paul, which comes across in the letter. He had not spent a long time with them, but they had taken him to their hearts and continued to support his ministry.

Philippi was a prosperous city in Macedonia (modern north-eastern Greece). A

Roman colony, it was organised by the Romans as if it was a city on Italian soil. Paul went there, having seen a vision of "a man of Macedonia" begging him to preach the Gospel (Acts 16:9-12). Some scholars believe this man to have been Luke, the author of Acts, who then began to accompany Paul on his travels as can be seen from the "we" form in Acts 16:10-11.

Paul had started preaching to the strong Jewish community in Philippi when he arrived (Acts 16:13). The conversion to Christ of a fortune teller stirred up opposition and Paul and Silas (his companion) were jailed. Released by an earthquake, they were pardoned by the authorities who had not realised that the apostles were also Roman citizens (Acts 16:35-40).

OUTLINE – PHILIPPIANS

Introduction
1:1-2 Opening greetings
1:3-11 Paul's thanksgiving and prayer for the Philippian church
1:12-26 A report of Paul's circumstances and ministry

Marks of life in God's kingdom
1:27-30 Paul encourages the Philippians to stay faithful
2:1-4 A call to unity and humility
2:5-11 The example of Christ's life and work
2:12-18 An encouragement to live as God's children
2:19-30 Examples of faithful servants: Timothy and Epaphroditus
3:1-11 Paul's confidence is in Christ, not in works of the law
3:12-14 The goal of Paul's Christian life
3:15-21 Following Paul's example and looking for the future hope
4:1-3 An appeal for unity in the church
4:4-9 Characteristics of the Christian life

Concluding remarks
4:10-20 Thanks to the Philippians for their support
4:21-23 Paul's closing greetings

KEY THEMES – PHILIPPIANS

Delight in fellowship
Paul was a pioneer church planter who was always on the move, but he also had a deep pastoral heart for the churches he had started. This short letter is full of pastoral concern for, and encouragement to, people he clearly loves: "I long for all of you with the affection of Jesus Christ" (1:8).

He recalls his joy at their response to the gospel and their work with him (1:3-8) and prays for their continued spiritual growth (1:9-11). He urges them to remain united in

fellowship, caring for one another (2:1-4; 4:2-3), not complaining (2:14-18).

Above all, he is delighted at the gift of money they sent to help him survive. He thanks them for it and for what it represents: a loving act of fellowship to a fellow Christian who is in trouble far away (4:10-20).

Determination to keep going

When Paul had been imprisoned in Philippi he had praised God, rather than cursing his luck (Acts 16:25). Now suffering a longer sentence, he continues that example. He has witnessed to soldiers and visitors, and encouraged local Christians to be bold (1:12-18).

Always optimistic, he hopes to carry on serving Christ, and expects to visit Philippi again (1:19-30). In a memorable passage, he announces his determination never to rest on his achievements. His Jewish background had prepared him for Christ, but is now superseded (3:1-11). Paul has a great passion for Christ: he longs to know him more and more (3:8-10). He realises that he still has

Coming out of church, Burkina Faso. Paul was a great believer in the importance of the local church

more to learn, do, and discover: so he presses on (3:12-15).

Divinity of Christ

In a great hymn, Paul sets out the uniqueness of Christ's divinity (2:5-11). He shows that Jesus gave up the glory of heaven in order to live as a human being. Jesus obeyed God by accepting a humiliating death, and is now exalted to the highest place in heaven as ruler of all. The context of the hymn shows that Paul sets Christ as an example for all believers.

Desire for news

Paul was never "parochial" nor was he a "hit and run" preacher! He was always keen to exchange news with other churches. So here, he tells the Philippians his news, to encourage them (1:12-26). Then he prepares them to receive his assistants Timothy and Epaphroditus (2:19-30), clearly expecting Timothy to bring back to him news of how the Philippians are faring (2:19).

Coping with pressure

Paul's positive outlook while physically chained to a Roman guard is an example and inspiration to anyone who is facing pressure or feeling "chained" to a situation they would prefer not to be in. The whole letter revolves around this. Paul sees every situation as an opportunity to witness for Christ (1:12). He is clearly aware that God is present with him always to support and inspire him. He knows Christ will give him strength in everything (4:13) and provide for all their needs (4:19).

Living purely

The Philippians were under pressure as well (1:29-30). We can be tempted to compromise our faith and act in ways that do not honour Christ. Paul urged his readers to maintain the highest standards always (1:27). Among the risks he warns against are lapsing into selfishness (2:3), giving up (2:12), arguing among ourselves (2:14-15), and letting our minds be dragged down to the world's level (4:8-9).

Maintaining priorities

Christians have two key priorities. We are to maintain our relationship with, and worship of, God. A person under pressure can become depressed and self-pitying. So Paul tells us to rejoice in who God is and what Christ has done and is doing (1:18; 3:1; 4:4) because praise liberates the spirit if not the body.

He urges the Philippians to pray for and about everything, knowing that they will receive peace of mind as a result (4:6-7). He values their intercession and believes that such prayer will be answered positively (1:19).

A second priority is to maintain good relationships with other Christians. Divisions can easily occur but they hinder the gospel (2:14-15). Paul identifies a running feud in the church, asking not only that the people involved will be reconciled but also that others will actively help them (4:2-3). Real unity means giving practical support as well as enjoying spiritual fellowship (2:1-4).

" *I press on towards the goal to win the prize for which God has called me heavenwards in Christ Jesus.*"

PHILIPPIANS 3:14

Keeping perspectives

Life on earth is important: everyone has work to do for God. But Paul also knows that life with God after death will be even better. At times, he would rather welcome death, but he recognises that it's not yet God's time – so he decides to carrying on working (1:20-26), and thus sets an example for all. This is further emphasised in 3:12-15. Knowing that there is more to do and discover, looking forward to the end, helps us see today's pressures in God's eternal perspective.

Colossians and Philemon
JESUS CHRIST IS LORD OF ALL

OVERVIEW

The thriving church in Colossae was being diverted from the Gospel by some "superspiritual" teachers who claimed insight into additional "mysteries". Paul sought to correct that error in Colossians, and at the same time wrote separately to a friend (Philemon) in that church concerning a runaway slave who had become a Christian. Note: references are to Colossians, except where stated.

Author and date

Paul's authorship of these two letters has rarely been questioned, and most scholars continue to agree that they are genuinely from him.

Both letters were written from prison (4:10,18; Philemon 9-10,23). This was almost certainly Paul's house arrest in Rome (Acts 28:16,20), which dates the letters from about AD 60. This was the same period as for the other "prison epistles", Ephesians and Philippians.

Background

Paul had not visited Colossae as far as we know. The church there began as a result of Paul's ministry in Ephesus (Acts 19:1-12). One of the converts there was Epaphras, who took the Gospel back to his home city of Colossae (1:7; 4:12-13; Philemon 23).

Colossae was about 110 miles east of Ephesus. It had once been a prosperous city on an important trade route. But by this time it was declining because the trade route had shifted north to nearby Laodicea which was becoming richer as a result (see Revelation 3:17). Laodicea is mentioned in 4:13,16 as having had a letter from Paul which is now lost.

Philemon, an inhabitant of Colossae and a church member, like many people at the time owned a slave called Onesimus. He had run away, found his way to Rome, and in prison there had heard Paul preach and had become a Christian. The letter contains Paul's plea for Philemon to be merciful to the returning and repentant slave. (It would have been customary to torture or execute him.)

SUMMARY

Colossians

After the formal opening salutation (1:1-2), Paul gives his attention to the faith of the church, indicating that he both thanks and prays for it. His reference to salvation by Christ in 1:14 brings him to a hymn in praise of Christ (1:15-20), which he subsequently applies to the readers. In 1:24–2:7 he discusses his own efforts as messenger of the good news

about Christ; the final two verses of this passage are transitional as Paul moves on to the issues at stake in the church which he discusses in 2:8-23, the central passage of the letter. The second half of the letter is the practical application. In 3:1-17 we find general guidance for the life in Christ in contrast to the readers' old lifestyle, followed in 3:18–4:6 by specific guidance for different groups of people. Finally, 4:7-18 consists of greetings and personal notes.

Philemon

In his letter, Paul plays on the meaning of the name Onesimus, which means "useful" (Philemon verse 11): "Formerly he was useless to you, but now he has become useful both to you and to me."

It is possible that this Onesimus is the same Onesimus who was bishop of Ephesus, whom Ignatius, the bishop of Antioch early in the 2nd century AD, mentioned in a letter, even referring to the same pun on the meaning of his name "Useful" ... so it may be that the runaway slave became a bishop!

OUTLINES

COLOSSIANS

The good news about Christ and the Colossian Christians
1:1-2 Greetings from Paul and Timothy
1:3-8 Thanksgiving for the faith, love and hope of the Colossians
1:9-14 A prayer for understanding, strength and joy
1:15-20 A hymn to celebrate Christ's supremacy
1:21-23 The inclusion of the Colossians in Christ's work
1:24–2:5 Paul's ministry among the churches

Paul's message for the Colossians
2:6-23 An appeal to grow to Christian maturity and avoid legalism
3:1-17 Leaving old ways of life and embracing new life in Christ
3:18–4:1 Guidance about family and work relationships
4:2-6 An encouragement to prayer and mission
4:7-18 Closing instructions and greetings

PHILEMON

1-3 Greetings from Paul and Timothy
4-7 Paul's thanksgiving and prayer for Philemon
8-21 Paul's request about Onesimus
23-25 Closing remarks

KEY THEMES

Christ's supremacy

Colossians 1:15-20 contains one of Paul's two great hymn summaries of the person and work of Christ (the other is in Philippians 2:6-11). His precise language lifts readers into worship and praise and stresses truths of cosmic dimensions:

· Christ is the exact human representation of the eternal God (1:15) and is himself fully God (1:19)
· He is the creator of everything (1:16)
· He sustains the whole universe (1:17)
· He rose from the dead and is Lord of the church (1:18)
· His redemption embraces the whole of creation (1:20).

Paul also teaches about Christ's rescue of us from sin and death in 1:13 and God's sovereign choice of Gentiles as well as Jews to share in his riches (1:27). Some of these truths are repeated in 2:9-15.

Colossians' heresy

This is not identical with any heresy known by name but we learn a lot about it by the way Paul refutes it. It suggested (2:2-4) there were deep spiritual mysteries to which the teachers had access (perhaps like some eastern mysticism today). It advocated harsh personal discipline or asceticism with restrictions on food and sex (2:21-23). There were detailed rules about worship ceremonies and an unhealthy interest in angels (2:16,18). Paul said it was deceptive (2:8); it sounds like a "pick and mix" religion of works intended to influence spiritual powers.

Christian holiness

Paul never teaches theology without also encouraging its application in daily life. So he gives the whole of chapter 3 to the marks of Christian living. In 3:12-17 he lists virtues we are to embrace, from compassion to forgiveness. They are in stark contrast to the vices we are to avoid (3:5-9). Note there that greed is identified with idolatry (3:5), something which people in western countries especially tend to overlook.

Charity for a slave

In a fascinating insight into Christian ethics, Paul urges Philemon to be merciful to the runaway slave Onesimus who had become a Christian (Philemon 10). Paul was doing the right thing in sending Onesimus back, even though Paul could make use of him (Philemon 11-14) and Philemon might punish him. So Paul calls on Philemon's sense of Christian forgiveness to welcome Onesimus back as a brother (Philemon 15-16). Paul then offers to pay personally any compensation for the slave's absence which Philemon might require (Philemon 18). That's Christian charity. The fact that the letter was preserved suggests that Philemon accepted it!

RELEVANCE FOR TODAY

Focus on the big picture

Paul's treatment of the Colossian heresy is very instructive. He focuses first on Jesus Christ and shows us exactly who he is. Then he deals with the heresy in some detail. This method reminds us that it is very easy to lose sight of the big picture – the main truths about God and Jesus – by becoming side-tracked by speculations, traditions, and debates about secondary issues. Human ideas won't last (2:22), but Jesus is eternal (1:18). So we focus on the main truths about Jesus (3:1-2) in order to keep everything else in perspective. That makes it much easier to assess the truth or otherwise of fresh ideas.

Fulfil your calling

If we set our minds on Jesus (3:1-2) we will begin to see how we are to live in the world. Notice in ch. 3 that Paul shows an act of will is involved in changing our behaviour. The supernatural inner change brought by the Holy Spirit is ongoing: our nature is being renewed (3:10). It's not fully renewed yet. Therefore Paul urges deliberate actions: put to death (3:5), rid yourself (3:8), don't lie (3:9), clothe yourselves (3:12). Discipleship is a partnership; God changes us only as far as we will allow him to.

Find purpose in your work

For some Christians, work in the secular world is a necessary drudge, but not the "real" work of the gospel. Paul would disagree. In 3:17,23 he restores to human work the dignity and purpose with which God originally endowed it (see also Genesis 2:15). All work can be done for the Lord, he says. It follows that slaves (employees) should do their best for their masters (employers) and staff should be treated by their bosses with respect and fairness (3:22–4:1). Being a good worker or boss is part of Christian witness in the world (4:5).

> "[Jesus Christ] is the image of the invisible God, the firstborn over all creation."
>
> COLOSSIANS 1:15

Friends are to be valued

Paul was very mobile – unusual in his day, but common in ours. He moved around a lot, made friends and moved on. But he kept in touch with them, and prayed for them. Tychicus had a special role as a messenger, keeping everyone in touch (4:7-9). The list of greetings and comments in 4:10-15 is not one to gloss over. These were valued people. Their mention tells us they were valued by God as well as Paul. God values those we no longer see, too; remembering them in prayer draws us closer together in the body of Christ.

Early-morning commuters, Paris. Paul taught that all work can be done for the Lord so should be done with all our heart

1 Thessalonians
KEEP UP THE GOOD WORK

OVERVIEW

The church in Thessalonica was a joy to Paul. He wrote to encourage the Christians to continue to be a shining witness to Christ despite their suffering. The letter contains many personal comments and deals with issues about Christ's return which were confusing some people.

SUMMARY

After the usual greetings, Paul brings thanks to God for the change in the readers from pagans to followers of Jesus Christ. The example of their conversion and Christian lifestyle has become known in other places and they eagerly await Christ's return (chapter 1). Paul then rehearses his time in the city, emphasises his friendly relationship with the readers, and lays his personal behavior down as an example (2:1-16). He tells how, unable to travel himself (2:18), he sent his co-worker Timothy back to Thessalonica and how he rejoiced when Timothy came back with positive information about the faith of the congregation (2:17–3:13). A section with mixed practical instructions introduces the second half of the letter (4:1-12). Subsequently Paul addresses a particular concern of the congregation about the death of some their members (4:13-18) and adds more general instructions about how to prepare for the return of Jesus (5:1-11). The final teaching is again more general (5:12-22). Good wishes and a blessing bring the letter to a close (5:23-28).

Author and date

Paul's authorship has been accepted throughout church history. The letter has all the hallmarks of Paul's ministry and teaching. It was probably written in AD 50–51, making it one of the earliest of Paul's letters. (Galatians was probably the first.) Paul wrote it while he was staying in Corinth (Acts 18). It is possible to be precise about the date and place because Paul's movements at this time are easy to pinpoint by comparing various New Testament passages (see below).

Background

Paul visited Thessalonica after fleeing Philippi on his second missionary journey. His time there is described in Acts 17:1-10. There was a good response to his preaching, especially among the majority Gentile population (Acts 17:4). However, he had begun preaching to Jews (as was his custom) and jealous Jews stirred up trouble and he had to flee (Acts 17:5-10). Acts 17:2 may imply he was only there for three weeks, but the time gap between verses 4 and 5 in that chapter could be longer than that.

From Thessalonica Paul went to Berea (Acts 17:10-15) then Athens (Acts 17:16-24) and finally Corinth (Acts 18:1). During this time Timothy was sent back to Thessalonica (3:2,6; Acts 17:15; 18:5). Timothy's report prompted Paul to write this letter.

We know that Paul was in Corinth AD 50–51 because Acts 18:12 mentions Gallio as being the proconsul there at the time. An inscription found at the site of the city confirms that Gallio was indeed there for that year.

Unlike many New Testament cities, Thessalonica still exists and flourishes today. It is in north-eastern Greece. In Paul's time it was home to about 200,000 people. It was set at the junction of two major trade routes and had a fine harbour. It provides a good example of how Paul chose strategic locations for his ministry. Thessalonica drew many visitors and travellers from a wide area; those who responded to the gospel there would take it wherever they travelled (see 1:8).

OUTLINE – 1 THESSALONIANS

An account of the life of the Thessalonian church

1:1 Greetings from Paul, Silas and Timothy
1:2-10 Thanksgiving for the birth and growth of the Thessalonian church
2:1-12 A report of Paul's work in Thessalonica
2:13-16 The Thessalonians' response and early persecution
2:17–3:5 Paul's deep concern for the Thessalonians
3:6-10 Timothy's report and Paul's thanksgiving
3:11-13 Paul's prayer for the church

Guidance for the life of the Thessalonian church

4:1-12 An appeal to keep growing in holiness and love
4:13-18 The Christian hope of resurrection from the dead
5:1-11 A reminder to be ready for the coming of Jesus Christ
5:12-22 General teaching about the Christian life
5:23-28 Closing prayer and greetings

KEY THEMES – 1 THESSALONIANS

Paul's example

The apostle reminds his readers of how he operated in order to encourage them to continue following his example (1:6). This isn't pride; it's a way of saying, God's power is sufficient for us if we keep faithful (1:5; 3:12-13; 5:23).

Paul had suffered in Philippi (Acts 16:22-24) before visiting Thessalonica, and had continued to suffer afterwards (Acts 17:5,13). Suffering, he says, is part of discipleship (3:3-4). The fact that he endured it showed that his motives for preaching were pure; he didn't preach for personal gain,

power over people, or prestige (2:3-5). He even took a job in order not to depend on their gifts (2:6-9). His concern for them (2:17–3:2) reveals Paul as a pastor as well as an evangelist. He cared greatly about the spiritual welfare of people who had come to faith through his ministry.

The church's model

What Paul praises them for here is enough to tell us that they were Christians who, like Paul, took their responsibilities seriously whatever the cost. So they became a shining example to others (1:7). This what they were like:

- · They worked for God (1:3)
- · They endured hardship (1:3)
- · They rejoiced in the gospel (1:6)
- · They spread the message (1:8)
- · They were wholehearted in their commitment (1:9).

Listening to the gospel over the airwaves in Swaziland. The good news of Jesus brings real hope

Christ's return

This was clearly puzzling some in Thessalonica. Paul ends every chapter with a reference to it (1:10; 2:19; 3:13; 5:23) and gives detailed teaching from 4:13 to 5:11. There were two big issues:

Assurance about the dead

Some Christians thought that if you died before Jesus Christ returned you would miss out on the new creation. So they were grieving not only the human loss of people they loved, but also what they thought was an eternal

loss too. Paul corrects this view in 4:13-18. Dead Christians have "fallen asleep". When Christ returns, they will rise from the dead before anything else happens (4:15-16).

Challenge for the living

We will never know when Christ is about to return. Paul repeats here what Jesus himself taught (Matthew 24:36-44). We have two options, he says. We can please ourselves, assuming that Christ won't come for ages, or we can live as if he was coming tonight. He urged the latter, because we are called to keep spiritually awake, alert to the work of God in and around us (5:5-7), and therefore living pure and holy lives (4:1-12; 5:12-22).

1 Thessalonians is an intensely practical letter and all the key themes are relevant in every age and culture. So let's take those themes another way, asking ourselves some searching questions.

Set an example to others

The challenge is both personal and corporate. Paul was leading from the front, showing by his personal dedication and his willingness to suffer that God isn't defeated by human opposition or difficult circumstances. But the church as a whole was also setting an example through its faithfulness and witness. It is often the joint activity of a group of Christians that makes the biggest impact on others. So: Is my personal life setting an example to encourage fellow-Christians and to show Jesus to the world? Is our church life harmonious and dedicated to serving Christ in word and deed?

Stay focused on Jesus

It isn't very fashionable today to think about the return of Christ – or even the journey through death which each of us must make. Yet it provided a focus for Paul's ministry and the lives of many persecuted or deprived Christians. But Paul did not simply offer a promise of future blessing just to help people cope with present stress. It was much more than that.

By focusing on the return of Jesus we have a goal, an aim. We have a task to do – help build the kingdom of God – in a limited (and

> " *We believe that Jesus died and rose again and so we believe that God will bring with Jesus those who have fallen asleep in him.*"
>
> 1 THESSALONIANS 4:14

unknown) time-frame. Jesus will hold us accountable for what we've done when he returns. So Paul is really saying get on with the job while we've got time! So:

Am I so focused on serving Jesus in thought, word and deed that I would be ready for him if he came back tonight?

Show your faith by your life

Christian witness is in deed as well as word. Non-Christians look at us and ask if we are consistently applying what we say we believe. Paul knew this, and so included his two sections on practical Christian living. They include sexual morality (4:3-8), love for one another (4:9-10) and being a good citizen (4:11-12). The many brief commands in 5:12-22 provide a good checklist for Christian discipleship, and include supporting full-time Christian workers, being patient and kind and keeping joyful and balanced in worship. So: When I read these instructions, am I keeping all of them fully in all circumstances?

2 Thessalonians
WAIT PATIENTLY FOR CHRIST'S RETURN

OVERVIEW

The Christians in Thessalonica continued to be confused about the promised return of Jesus Christ to earth. Paul told them that Jesus would return after a period of lawlessness. Meanwhile, Christians should not opt out of their social and family responsibilities while waiting for Jesus to come.

SUMMARY

After the formal opening words (1:1-2), Paul adds prayers for the church. There is thanksgiving in 1:3-4 but only in 1:11-12 is it specified what Paul is praying for; in between he assures them of God's judgement over their enemies, which is a comfort to them. The main topic is the return of Jesus Christ and Paul emphatically explains that this has not yet happened (2:1-2); on the contrary, before it takes place "the man of lawlessness" (2:3,8-9) must come and draw people away from God (2:3-12). However, despite the prospect of hard times the readers are safe in the protection of the God they are worshipping (2:13-15) and Paul blesses them (2:16-17). The practical section begins with a request for prayer for Paul and assurances of God's faithfulness (3:1-5). Paul then addresses those in the church who have left their occupations in eager anticipation of the return of Jesus Christ, and urges them to resume normal life (3:6-13). Some notes on disobedient members are appended (3:14-15) before Paul brings the letter to a close with a prayer for peace in his own hand (3:16-18).

Author and date

There was no doubt in the early church that Paul wrote this letter. In modern times, doubts have been expressed because there are a number of unusual words in the letter that Paul does not use elsewhere, and some of the subject matter (such as the "man of lawlessness") is rare in both Paul and the rest of the New Testament. Some have also suggested that this letter was written before what we know as 1 Thessalonians.

However, the teaching does not contradict the rest of the New Testament, and in many respects complements it. And 2:15 implies that Paul has indeed already written to the Thessalonians. It is therefore likely that Paul wrote this up to six months after 1 Thessalonians, perhaps when Timothy and Silas returned from having delivered it. Paul would still have been in Corinth at the time.

Background

See 1 Thessalonians, p.361 for details of Paul's visit to the city and subsequent travels.

We know from Acts, and from Galatians assuming that was the first of Paul's letters, that false teachers arose in the early church only a decade or so after the death of Jesus. In 2 Thessalonians Paul reveals a related disturbing problem: people were forging letters supposed to come from Paul, and others were spreading false rumours that Jesus had already returned to earth (2:2). Today's scams and false news stories had their counterparts 2,000 years ago!

Paul was anxious about the impact of these rumours and forgeries on the very young Christians in Thessalonica. So he wrote 2 Thessalonians to counter the false teaching. In so doing he has provided us with some clear teaching about the return of Christ, which helps us to interpret Christ's teaching and parts of the book of Revelation. And, practical as ever, Paul suggests how his important theology should be applied in difficult daily life.

OUTLINE – 2 THESSALONIANS

Dealing with persecution and false teaching
1:1-2 Greetings from Paul, Silas and Timothy
1:3-4 Thanksgiving for the faith of the Thessalonian church
1:5-12 Encouragement and prayer for the Thessalonians during their persecution
2:1-12 Teaching about the coming again of Jesus Christ
2:13-17 Encouragement and prayer for the Thessalonians to persevere

Dealing with spiritual and social responsibilities
3:1-5 A request for prayer for the ministry of the gospel
3:6-15 A warning for the idle
3:16-18 Paul's concluding prayer and greeting

KEY THEMES – 2 THESSALONIANS

Jesus' return
Paul's teaching about the second coming resembles that of Jesus in Matthew 24:26-31 and 25:31-46. Jesus will come to judge the earth (1:8-9) with the great rejoicing of the saints (1:10). The time of his coming is unknown (2:2) but will be after a period of confusion and suffering (2:4,9-12).

God's justice
When life seems unfair, people ask how a just God can allow it. They may have been doing that in Thessalonica, where Christians were persecuted for their faith. Paul reassures them that God is indeed just. While his justice may not be obvious in this life, it will be seen when Jesus Christ returns. Then, God will punish evil people and save those who suffer (1:5-10).

Satan's attack
Paul's description of the deceptive "man of lawlessness" (2:1-12) has no parallel elsewhere in the New Testament. However, it ties in with Jesus' prediction of great evil to come, and of false prophets demonstrating deceptive signs and wonders (Matthew 24:15-25). It also reminds us of passages about the antichrist such as Revelation 13.

It is pointless trying to identify this figure with any single person in history. People who combine despotic political power with false religious appeal arise at various times, and Christians always have to be ready to battle against evil. Paul assured his readers that there is a restraining power at work (2:7). God keeps Satan on a long lead but never lets him off it. Paul does not specify what the restraining power was; he may mean the *Pax Romana*, the peace and order of the Roman Empire. Despite the excesses of some emperors, the Romans generally restricted the widespread abuse of power.

The Spirit's power
Christians can cope with intense suffering and persecution because the Holy Spirit makes us more like Jesus ("sanctifies us", 2:13). We are to share in Jesus' kingdom (2:14) and he will support and encourage us until that day (2:16-17; 3:5).

Christians' responsibility
Whether Jesus returns sooner or later, we are not to be idle. Paul stresses the need for honest work (3:6-15). People were created to work, and God calls us to play a full part in the development of his world. Paul set an example by working while he preached; he didn't sponge off others, and neither should any other Christian.

RELEVANCE FOR TODAY – 2 THESSALONIANS

Be patient when suffering
This is easy to say and hard to apply. The Thessalonians' endurance is a sign of the genuineness of their faith (1:4-5). Their suffering itself was a calling from God, not (as some might suggest) a curse from God. Because of their endurance, their faith and love was growing (1:3). Difficult circumstances can nourish faith, rather than destroy it. God loves us dearly, but he may not always smooth our path through life.

Be confident when tempted
As Paul was to tell the Corinthians later (from his own experience and, perhaps, from having observed the Thessalonians), God will never allow us to be tested (or "tempted") beyond our endurance (1 Corinthians 10:13). He is still in control and will protect us from Satan (3:3). He does that by focusing our minds on his love and imparting to us the same strength that Jesus had (3:5). Our part is to keep trusting him, so that we can draw on his strength when we need it.

Be careful in what you believe
All Christians can be misled. Sadly, we are more likely to be convinced that others are wrong than entertain the possibility that we are mistaken! Paul warned the Thessalonians not to believe the false letters and rumours (2:2). Evil can appear good (2:9). But how could they know they were false? Paul's teaching at the time was incomplete – this letter fills out what he had taught in person. Paul implies here what he later said explicitly to the Corinthians: think carefully about prophecies before accepting them as true (1 Corinthians 14:29). We have the benefit of the whole of Scripture against which to test fresh ideas. Searching the Scriptures with others, prayerfully and thoughtfully, will enlarge our understanding and protect us from error.

> " *As for you, brothers, never tire of doing what is right.*"
>
> *2 THESSALONIANS 3:13*

Be tireless in doing right
Paul's first readers were very excited about their new-found faith – as "young" Christians often are. Their excitement led them into lifestyles that didn't reflect God's will, and which were a poor witness to the world. Some had given up work to prepare for Christ's return. Idleness and dependence on others isn't right (3:6-13). God doesn't usually call us to give up our day jobs; rather, he sends us back into the world to "do right" (3:13) by honouring him in all our work and relationships.

1 Timothy
INSTRUCTIONS FOR CHURCH LIFE

OVERVIEW

Timothy had been left in charge of a church in Ephesus. Paul reminded him of some basic principles governing church life which Timothy was to enforce. These include matters relating to the conduct of worship and social welfare, the behaviour of church leaders and handling false teachers.

SUMMARY

Chapter 1 is an introduction, containing greetings typical of any letter of the time (1:1-2). The purpose of the letter is to lay down ground rules for Timothy to use in the church at Ephesus. Such rules are a type of law which Timothy must use with authority against false teachers who also claim to be teaching the law.

The main body of the letter (2:1-6:2) sets out rules for dealing with the various pastoral problems outlined in the introduction. Thus, false teachers, mentioned in the first chapter, probably because that seemed the most urgent problem, are spoken of again in 4:1-4. Marks of good leaders are listed in 3:1-13, and are more personally applied to Timothy himself in 4:6-5:3. The falling away of converts is addressed in 4:1 but more in the conclusion. Matters of church discipline are set out in 5:17-22 and elsewhere, as these various problems do not form neat boundaries but overlap. Other problems concern church prayer meetings (2:1-8); women (2:9-15); widows (5:3-16); and slaves (6:1-2).

The conclusion (6:3-20) is a mixture of last-minute advice about problems, especially the falling away of converts, personal exhortation to live a godly and exemplary life, doxology (praise to God), and a real farewell.

Author

There was little doubt in the early church that Paul was the author. Serious doubts have been raised in the last 200 years. These rest partly on the differences in language used here compared with that used in Paul's undisputed letters. However, Paul was well educated and would have had a wide vocabulary, and this is not itself a conclusive argument. Another argument concerns the nature of the heresy which Paul counters and the structure of church life which he outlines. Both are said to reflect situations known later than the first century. However, Paul's descriptions suggest the early beginnings, rather than settled beliefs and practices. There is also an issue about personal allusions (see below). Paul's authorship is still highly likely.

Date and background

1 Timothy has to be considered alongside 2 Timothy and Titus, and together they are called the three "Pastoral Epistles", because they deal largely with matters of church order and leadership. They were probably all written after Paul's imprisonment in Rome (Acts 28:16,30).

It would seem that after his initial house arrest, Paul was freed for a while and went on a journey not recorded in Acts, visiting some of the churches he had previously planted. It is clear from 1:3 that he had been to Ephesus again (his first visit is recorded in Acts 19:1-41 and he met again with the church leaders in

Acts 20:13-39). In 3:14 he says he hopes to return there but we cannot be sure that he did. See the introductions to 2 Timothy and Titus for possible visits to other churches he made at this time.

Timothy was not an apostle and is best described as an apostolic delegate, or Paul's friend and assistant. Paul endorsed Timothy's authority over the church in Ephesus, so that in effect when Timothy spoke, it was Paul speaking. Perhaps Timothy used the letter itself to reinforce his authority (see 3:14-15). You will find more about Timothy in the introduction to 2 Timothy.

OUTLINE – 1 TIMOTHY

Introduction
1:1-2 Greetings from Paul
1:3-11 The problem of false teaching
1:12-17 Paul's conversion is an example of God's grace
1:18-20 Timothy's responsibility to keep the faith

Dealing with pastoral problems
Worship in the church
2:1-8 Instructions about prayer
2:9-15 Guidance for women in the church
Leadership in the church
3:1-7 Essential personal qualities for elders
3:8-13 Essential personal qualities for deacons
Timothy's role in the church
3:14-16 Paul's instructions to Timothy about proper behaviour in God's household
4:1-5 Paul's message about the false teachers and their teachings
4:6-16 Timothy's responsibilities as a servant of God
Various groups in the church
5:1-2 Respecting people of different ages
5:3-16 Guidance about the care of widows
5:17-20 Guidance about elders
5:21-25 Paul's advice to Timothy
6:1-2 Instructions for slaves who are Christians

Conclusion
6:3-10 A final warning about the false teachers and their way of life
6:11-16 An encouragement to Timothy to persevere
6:17-19 Paul's advice for the wealthy
6:20-21 A concluding message for Timothy

KEY THEMES – 1 TIMOTHY

Instructions for Timothy

There are several explicit passages of instructions to the young assistant. Especially he is to:

Oppose false teachers (1:3-11; 4:1-10)
These were people obsessed with speculations and controversies that distracted others from the true gospel. They were legalistic, imposing heavy disciplines on people, and taught that the material world is evil. This may be an early form of what developed into Gnosticism in the second century AD. Paul counters it by saying that the law of God is to rebuke sinners, not restrict saints (1:8-11). He also says that the material world is part of God's good creation and is therefore to be received gratefully rather than treated with scorn (4:3-5).

Fight the good fight (1:12-20; 4:11-16; 6:11-21)
Paul reminds Timothy of the gospel of God's grace and urges him to keep it by recalling the prophecies about his ministry (1:18; see also 6:12). This would also help Timothy overcome his natural shyness (2 Timothy 1:7) and so deal with people who looked down on him because he was young (4:12). He was simply to get on with study and ensure that he set a good example (4:12-13).

Instructions about church life

Church worship had not taken on a widely accepted liturgical pattern at this time, but here (and in 1 Corinthians 12–14) Paul indicates that certain disciplines are to be observed:

· Prayer for authorities (2:1-7). Paul often urged good citizenship (eg Romans 13:1-7) and here he urges intercessions for secular leaders. Prayers for peace help everyone; peace promotes human welfare and enables the unhindered spread of the gospel.
· Observation of cultural boundaries (2:8-15). The New Testament church existed within a patriarchal society in which men were the dominant leaders. Although Paul appreciated the ministry of women (eg Romans 16:1-4,12) he did not encourage them to take on traditional male roles; that would have been too radical for the infant church. Today, some Christians say such male dominance was a reflection of a passing culture and is not mandatory. Others suggest it is part of God's creation order and remains mandatory for the church.

Instructions about church ministers

Again, the pattern of ministry was not finally established. Today some regard the elders referred to by Paul as the equivalent of priests or presbyters – ministers in charge of a church. However, the principles Paul lays down for them and for deacons apply to all who exercise responsibility in the church. They are personal qualities, not precise definitions of roles (3:1-12).

How to serve

Paul's advice to Timothy and his instructions to church leaders gives us principles we can apply to any form of Christian activity.

- Our lives should be exemplary (3:2-4,7; 4:12). Leaders cannot exempt themselves from the standards they encourage in others; they must practise what they preach.
- Leaders are responsible for pointing out error (1:3; 4:6,11); they cannot stand by if the faith is compromised or false teaching is given.
- Leaders should not be domineering or throw their weight about, but treat others with respect (5:1-2; 6:1-2).

How to share

Christians in Ephesus seem to have been as naturally lazy and selfish as people anywhere! We all like to take the easy option. Paul has some strong words to say about sharing, in different contexts.

- In Paul's day widows might become destitute without help from the church as women generally couldn't work outside the home (5:3). Supporting fellow-Christians less well-off than we are is an important part of discipleship.
- Families should look after their needy relatives (5:8,16). This is taken for granted in many developing countries, but not necessarily in the west where families break down and the elderly are put into care homes.
- Paul is scathing of those who become "ladies of leisure" instead of accepting greater responsibility for their lives (5:13). We can apply this to anyone who can, but

doesn't, work (for whatever reason); our time and resources are to be used for others and for the church if we do not need to work in order to survive.

- People who are better off than others should find ways of using their money for the good of others and not make a god of it (6:9,17-19).

How to stand

Timothy was clearly vulnerable in Ephesus because he was an outsider, and young. It would have been easy for him to fail in his responsibilities because of the pressure he felt. Paul showed him (and us) how to stand firm in difficult situations where we are not fully accepted by others, by:

- Remembering his call which God had confirmed (1:18; 4:14)
- Holding onto the faith he had received and not swerving from it (1:19; 4:16; 6:20)
- Living consistently in a way that pleases God (6:11-14)
- Above all, holding onto God himself (4:9-10).

" *Godliness with contentment is great gain. For we brought nothing into this world, and we can take nothing out of it.*"

1 TIMOTHY 6:6-7

2 Timothy
PAUL'S FAREWELL ENCOURAGEMENTS

OVERVIEW

Paul was in prison with little hope of release. He had left Timothy to look after the church in Ephesus and wrote to encourage his young helper to stand firm in the face of opposition, false teaching and suffering. This is an intensely personal letter from a Christian leader who knows that his days are numbered.

SUMMARY

The letter begins with a standard greeting (1:1-2), which already sets the warm relational tone of the letter. Timothy is his child (Greek *teknon*), a word used both for masters to disciples and as a term of endearment to an adult (rather like "dear boy"). The main body of the letter can be divided into four heads, following the chapter divisions. 1:3-18 asks Timothy not to distance himself from Paul's suffering in prison. Chapter 2 exhorts Timothy to teach others and warn them, suggesting a continuing public ministry for Timothy, but at the same time, he needs to teach and warn himself. The issue of sound teaching as opposed to false is the one continuing concern from the first to the second letter. Chapter 3 sees this more in terms of a battle between truth and falsehood, teaching and deceiving, where practically, Timothy needs to live in the truth and resist falsehood. The final chapter (4:1-8) urges him to live in the light of Jesus Christ's second coming. The farewell greetings paint a picture both of Paul's loneliness in prison and yet the ability he still had to direct a number of people in the affairs of the young church. The bottom line of the letter is that he wants Timothy's presence, and before winter, when all travelling by sea stops (4:9,21). As in many of his other letters, he sends greetings to friends and forwards greetings from fellow-Christians in Rome.

Author and date

It is likely that Paul wrote this letter, and the serious doubts that have been raised by some scholars are dealt with in the introduction to 1 Timothy.

Some time elapsed between the writing of 1 and 2 Timothy. Paul had been travelling but was now a prisoner again in Rome, this time in a common gaol (1:8; 2:9) rather than under house arrest (Acts 28:16). His location may have been hard to find (1:17), which could account for the loneliness reflected in the letter. Paul refers to a number of friends, and asks for visitors and items to make him more comfortable (4:9-13,16). He clearly expected to be executed (4:6-8).

This probably dates the letter about AD 66 during the crackdown on Christians by the Roman Emperor Nero who – according to later traditions – executed both Peter and Paul. As he saw the end coming, Paul wrote to Timothy to urge him to keep going; he wanted to ensure that the work he had given his life for would continue.

Background

We cannot work out Paul's movements after he was released from house arrest in Rome. We know from 1 Timothy 1:3 that he had been to Ephesus. In 2 Timothy 4:13,20 he refers to recent visits to Troas, Miletus and Corinth. Other visits are referred to in Titus 1:5; 3:12.

Timothy was one of Paul's converts in Lystra (Paul visited it and other places in Acts 13:14–14:23, which he refers to here in 3:11). Timothy's father was Greek but his mother and grandmother Jews who became Christians (1:5; Acts 16:1). He joined Paul on missionary journeys, having first been circumcised in order not to offend Jews (Acts 16:2-4). From then on he is frequently cited as a close companion of Paul (eg 1 Thessalonians 1:1) and was sent as Paul's delegate to Corinth (1 Corinthians 4:17) and then Ephesus (1 Timothy 1:3).

Paul was very fond of Timothy ("my dear son", 1:2; 2:1) who had been set apart for ministry (1:6), despite being timid (1:7) and young (1 Timothy 4:12).

OUTLINE – 2 TIMOTHY

Introduction
1:1-2 Opening greetings

Be faithful
1:3-5 Paul's thanksgiving for Timothy and desire to see him again
1:6-14 A reminder to stay faithful in ministry
1:15-18 Examples of Paul's loyal and disloyal helpers

Be obedient
2:1-13 Timothy is instructed to continue Paul's ministry
2:14-19 Advice about teaching the truth
2:20-26 Personal instructions for Timothy

Be careful
3:1-9 The marks of false teachers
3:10-17 Timothy is to follow Paul's ministry and remain faithful to Scripture

Be ready
4:1-5 Paul's command to Timothy to preach the word
4:6-8 A summary of Paul's own ministry

Conclusion
4:9-18 Instructions for Timothy's journey to see Paul
4:19-22 Closing greetings

KEY THEMES – 2 TIMOTHY

Persevere through suffering

Paul's prison was clearly uncomfortable (1:8; 2:9). But suffering had been predicted for him at his conversion (Acts 9:15-16) and had become a way of life. He concluded that it was part of discipleship for many Christians (3:12). So in 2:3-7 he encouraged Timothy to endure suffering, using two common images.

A soldier on active duty would have to face hardship and possible death; an athlete going for gold would have to break through the pain barrier and keep the rules. Whenever he wrote about suffering, Paul also wrote about God's faithful help and support (3:11; 4:17); he never lost his faith.

Preserve God's truth

False teachers and godless people were everywhere in the early church, just as they are today (3:1-9; 4:3-4). Here, Paul took the unusual step of naming some false teachers and Christians who had betrayed him or deserted the faith (1:15; 2:17-18; 4:10,14-15). In the face of this varied opposition, Timothy's task was to guard the gospel (1:13-14). Paul suggested four ways he might do this, by:

· Reminding people of it (2:14)
· Keeping his own life exemplary (2:22)
· Avoiding needless petty disputes over minor details and controversies (2:14,16,23)
· Teaching Christians gently in order not to inflame opposition (2:24-26).

Preach the word

Several times Paul urged Timothy to preach the word of God (2:2,25; 4:2) but he could only do that if he was himself a careful student of it (2:15). Paul returns to the theme in 3:14-16, and 3:16 is a key verse for our understanding of the nature and purpose of Scripture. Paul says it is "God breathed" (sometimes translated "inspired" but the word is literally "ex-spired"). It means that the Holy Spirit led the writers to write down eternal truths in their own words through which future generations would be able to hear God speaking. The writers' unique personalities were not taken over. The resulting Scripture not only tells us about God and his mighty works, but also challenges our behaviour and attitudes.

Paul's hope

Nearing the end of his life, Paul faced what lay beyond the grave. He was not now concerned about the end of the world and the second coming of Christ; but about the individual's hope. He was assured of being kept safe (1:12), confident of salvation (2:10), and looked forward to "the crown of righteousness" (4:8). Above all, he had fulfilled his calling; he had no regrets (4:7).

Discipleship group, Bulgaria. Paul urged Timothy to guard against false teaching by concentrating on and teaching the basic truths of the gospel

Stay focused

There were many distractions, temptations and problems for Timothy to deal with, as there are for us. Throughout this letter Paul urges him to stay focused on:

- **His preparation and calling** (eg 1:5-6; 3:14). Looking back to those who taught us the faith, and at our conversion, spiritual growth and calling to service, can help us to face difficulties with determination and faith.
- **The gospel** (eg 1:13-14; 2:10-13). Twice Paul urges Timothy to have nothing to do with pointless debates (2:16-17,23). Instead he is to focus on, and teach, the basic truths of the gospel, such as the life, death, resurrection and atonement of Jesus. It is easy, but wrong, to let secondary matters take on the status of primary matters.
- **The Scriptures** (2:15; 3:15-17). Timothy had our Old Testament and some of Paul's writings to keep him focused on God's purposes and in tune with God's will. Bible study is important even when we know Scripture well; God speaks through it into our current circumstances.
- **The power of God.** Timothy was quiet and sensitive, easily discouraged. Paul urged him to draw on the power of the Spirit to keep going (1:7), just as God had assisted Paul (3:11).
- **His task in the church.** In 4:5 Paul tells him in effect: "Just get on with it, and leave the problems to God!"

Support your friends

We will never know why so many people deserted Paul (1:15; 4:10,16). It must have been partly because some had departed from the faith, and others were afraid of "guilt by association" – of incurring the anger of the authorities and getting arrested themselves. Paul longed for his friends as he became aware of his vulnerability and mortality in prison. He even feared that Timothy might be ashamed of him (1:8).

Like Jesus, deserted in the Garden of Gethsemane (Matthew 26:56) and crying in

> " *All Scripture is God-breathed and is useful for teaching, rebuking, correcting and training in righteousness.*"
>
> *2 TIMOTHY 3:16*

utter loneliness on the cross, "My God, why have you forsaken me?" (Matthew 27:46) Paul knew the reality of divine support (4:17) but desperately needed human comfort. He was grateful for visits from Onesiphorus (1:16) and Luke (4:9), and longed to see Timothy and Mark (4:11). Such support can be costly for those who give it, but which is more important: showing practical love for someone, or abandoning them out of fear or laziness? One day, we might be the person who needs support.

Titus
CONTROL THOSE PASSIONS!

LETTERS

OVERVIEW

The new church on the island of Crete was presenting a poor witness to the gospel. Its members hadn't brought their passionately selfish lives into line with the demands of love and kindness. Paul had sent Titus there to sort them out (1:5). In this letter Paul directs him, using blunt language, concerning the standards of behaviour he expects from leaders and church members.

SUMMARY

The letter sets out greetings in 1:1-4. Titus, like Timothy, is Paul's child (Greek *teknon*), his faithful disciple. Chapter 1 deals with the appointing of elders, Titus' first priority in the new churches set up in Crete. The problem of divisive people in the church is addressed. They are mainly Jewish "converts," if they have truly been converted, but seem to be guilty of those vices the Cretans were renowned for especially lying. Chapter 2 deals with what Titus should say to whom: young and old, men and women, and slaves. There is a simple statement of the message of salvation that is to be delivered to all. Chapter 3 contains a list of the practical and behavioural virtues Titus should teach the church as a whole, and he touches briefly on church discipline. The final few verses (3:12-15) are the farewells, personal and administrative instructions and greetings.

Author and date

There is little doubt that Paul wrote this letter which is grouped with 1 and 2 Timothy as the "Pastoral Epistles". What doubts have been raised are dealt with in the introduction to 1 Timothy.

It was written after Paul's release from house arrest in Rome (Acts 28:16), when the apostle embarked on further journeys. These are not recorded in Acts, and we cannot put together a clear itinerary. The introductions to 1 and 2 Timothy both indicate some places

he visited, and Titus adds two others. One was Crete (1:5) where Paul and Titus had recently planted a church. Paul had previously visited Crete while on his way to Rome as a prisoner (Acts 27:7-12), but the ship appears to have stayed only a short while not leaving enough time for a mission then. The other was Nicopolis in Greece (3:12) to which Paul appeared to be heading when he wrote this letter.

Paul probably wrote Titus between 1 and 2 Timothy, from Corinth which is mentioned in 2 Timothy 4:20. The date would be about AD 65.

Background

Titus, like Timothy, was converted through Paul's ministry ("my true son in our common faith", 1:4) and became a trusted assistant. Like Timothy, he was a Gentile although unlike Timothy Paul never saw the need to have him circumcised so as not to offend the Jews to whom they often ministered (Galatians 2:1-3). And unlike Timothy, he was probably a robust character not easily frightened by difficult people.

Although Titus is never mentioned in Acts, his name does appear in Paul's letters. These may not provide an exhaustive list of his postings, but clearly he was Paul's choice for trouble spots:

· Jerusalem, to explain the Gentile mission (Galatians 2:1)
· Corinth, several times including acting as

Paul's messenger (2 Corinthians 7:6,14-15; 8:6,16-21)
· Crete, to sort things out (1:5)

· Dalmatia, to churches otherwise unknown (2 Timothy 4:10).

OUTLINE – TITUS

Introduction
1:1-4 Greetings from Paul

Titus' first task: appointing elders
1:5-9 Titus' task on Crete: the appointment of elders
1:10-16 A warning about false teachers and their deception

Titus' second task: instructing the church in faith and life
2:1-10 Instructions for men, women and slaves
2:11-15 God's grace enables us to lead godly lives
3:1-8 Living in response to God's kindness and love
3:9-11 A warning about divisiveness in the church

Conclusion
3:12-15 Paul's personal requests and closing greetings

KEY THEMES – TITUS

Summaries of the gospel

The church in Crete appears to have been new (see "Author and date" above). Part of Titus' task there was to remind the Christians of the heart of the Gospel. The letter contains three classic summaries of the gospel which remain useful reminders of the most important Christian truths.

· **God's eternal plans** (1:1-3). Paul always began letters with some acclamation of God's greatness and this is no exception. Here, he tells us that God planned from the beginning of time the full revelation of his purposes through Christ.
· **The purpose of Christ's death** (2:13-14). Paul stresses the divinity of Christ ("our great God and Saviour, Jesus Christ"), which some false teachers may have been questioning. His death was to redeem us from sin and to form a community of God-centred people.

· **The nature of renewal** (3:4-7). We did not deserve God's forgiveness, Paul says, but in his generosity he saved us and renewed us so that we could live a completely new life now, and inherit eternal life after death.

Standards for leaders

Church structures had not been put in place when Paul left Crete, so Titus was to set them up (1:5). Paul's lifestyle requirements for church leaders given in 1:6-9 are briefer than but similar to the lists in 1 Timothy 3:1-13. They cover not only an understanding of Christian doctrine (verse 9) but especially an exemplary personal and home life.

What is different here is that Paul uses the word "overseer" (from which our word "bishop" comes) as well as "elder". However, he is clearly writing about the same role. This tells us that the threefold structure of ministry (deacon, elder/presbyter, bishop) which characterised the church in later times was not yet in existence.

Standards for church members

Six times Paul uses what for him is an unusual phrase and emphasis on personal conduct: Christians are "to do what is good" (1:16; 2:7,14; 3:1,8,14), and teach what is good (2:3). This is partly so that our witness is consistent – we practise what we preach (2:5,8) and to make the faith attractive to others (2:10). Among the ethical standards Paul stresses are:

· Self-control (2:2,5-6,12)
· Careful and moderate speech (2:3,8-9; 3:2)
· Honesty and integrity (2:12; 3:1; see also 1:11-12 for the opposite vice).

RELEVANCE FOR TODAY – TITUS

Be controlled

Self-control isn't easy, and some people are naturally more hot-headed than others. Many Cretans had short tempers and found it hard to turn off their passionate natures. Paul says we can change because of God's grace (2:11-14). We can infer from the letter three ways to help us:

· Jesus saved us in order that we might reflect God's character and purpose (2:14). Therefore, it is right that for every action we should ask, what would Jesus do?
· The Holy Spirit has given us a fresh start (3:5-6). The images of being "washed", "born again" and "renewed" all show us that God can and does change us for the better.
· However, changing our behaviour also involves an act of will. God doesn't do it all for us; his grace "teaches us to say 'no'" (2:12).

Be good

The Christian faith is not just a matter of believing certain doctrines. For Paul, right belief was important, but so too was faith in action. Paul is sometimes compared unfavourably with James who stressed that "faith without works is dead" (James 2:17). This is unfair on Paul because even in his most theological letters, he stresses that we are saved by faith for good works (see Ephesians 2:8-10).

In Titus, Paul stresses this more than in any of his other letters because the gospel hadn't made a noticeable difference to Cretans' lives. Doing good is not always attractive. It takes time and resources that you could otherwise spend on enjoying yourself. People can take advantage of you and presume on your kindness. Paul wants the Cretans to know that this isn't the issue. God is good, and his goodness cost him the life of his Son. Christians are to be good and do good, whatever the personal cost.

> " *When the kindness and love of God our Saviour appeared, he saved us, not because of righteous things we had done, but because of his mercy.*"
>
> TITUS 3:4-5

Be an example

If people see us behave in bad ways, when we claim that God is good, or if they see us being hateful when we say that God loves us, they will conclude that Christianity is a delusion and doesn't work. Paul urges the Cretans to show the gospel as well as tell it. This will silence critics (2:8) and draw others in (2:10). It also ensures that we are productive – we achieve something worthwhile (3:14). The key is humility (3:2), a virtue that was lacking in Crete and is rarely in abundant supply in any church.

Hebrews
CHRIST IS GREATER

OVERVIEW
When life gets tough, it is tempting to want to give up on Christianity. Hebrews is an encouragement to persevere with faith – it is pointless to return to an old way of life because only Jesus Christ can bring God's forgiveness and great promises of hope.

SUMMARY
Hebrews begins with a powerful statement of the greatness of Christ as God's Son and bringer of salvation (1:1-4). He is greater than the angels (1:5–2:4), but he became a human being, who has shared in suffering and death (2:5-18).

Christ is next seen to be greater than Moses, who led the Israelites out of slavery (3:1-6). Many Israelites, however, did not enter into God's Promised Land because of their disobedience, and Christians must not be like them (3:7–4:11).

In the next long section (4:14–10:18), the author shows that Christ is greater than the Jewish sacrificial system and its regulations. Jesus was called by God (5:1-10) to be the great high priest (4:14-16). Readers must not fall away from faith (5:11–6:8) because Christ is the high priest who enables us to inherit God's promised blessing (6:9-20). Christ is not like the other priests, but like Melchizedek, is a priest for ever (6:20–7:22). Because Jesus lives for ever, he is able to offer complete salvation to all who come to God through him (7:23-28). Jesus therefore brings a new covenant between God and his people (8:1-13). In this covenant, Jesus sacrifices his own life to bring about God's forgiveness and blessing (9:11-15). In this single sacrifice, Jesus fulfilled the old covenant (9:1-10; 9:16–10:18).

In the light of this, the readers of Hebrews must persevere with their faith in Jesus Christ (10:19-39). The Old Testament contains countless examples of faith (11:1-38). They, however, looked forward to the time when Christ would come (11:39) – so Christians have even greater reason to persevere (11:40–12:3). Readers are encouraged to resist sin (12:4) and to submit to God's fatherly discipline (12:5-13).

Hebrews closes with instructions and encouragements for the Christian community, to hold fast to true faith in Jesus Christ (12:14–13:25).

Author
Unknown. The apostle Paul, Barnabas (Acts 4:36; 9:27; 11:25-30; 13–14) and Apollos (Acts 18:24-28) are commonly proposed, but no suggestion is entirely convincing.

Date
Difficult to specify as we have no information; possibly late AD 60s.

Background
The readers were well acquainted with Jewish Scriptures and practices. Many were probably Jewish Christians who were being tempted to return to the Jewish faith because of threat of persecution. The readers may have been in Rome (see 13:24).

OUTLINE – HEBREWS

The greatness of Jesus, God's Son

1:1-4 Introduction: God's Son is his final word

1:5-14 God's Son is greater than the angels

2:1-4 A warning not to drift away from salvation

2:5-18 Jesus can bring salvation because he shares human life

3:1-6 Jesus is greater than Moses

3:7–4:13 Only the faithful will enter God's rest

4:14–5:10 Jesus is the great high priest

5:11–6:12 A call to grow in faith and a warning against falling away

6:13-20 The certainty of God's promise

7:1-25 Jesus is an eternal high priest in the order of Melchizedek

7:26–9:28 Christ's ministry is greater than the priests and sacrifices of the old covenant

10:1-18 Christ's ultimate sacrifice for sin is once and for all

The life of faith

10:19-39 Encouragement to persevere in faith

11:1-40 Examples of people of faith from the Old Testament

12:1-13 Encouragement to remain faithful and receive God's discipline

12:14–13:17 Final warning and instructions

13:18-25 Closing greetings and blessing

KEY THEMES – HEBREWS

The Old and the New

Throughout Hebrews, the author makes a contrast between the covenant God made with his people in the Old Testament and the new covenant that has been established by Jesus Christ. At every point, the new covenant based on Jesus Christ is greater and better (7:22; 8:6,13):

· The messengers of the old covenant were prophets (1:1), including Moses (3:2-5), and angels (2:2); the messenger of the new covenant is Jesus Christ, the Son of God (1:2-4; 3:6).

· The priests of the old covenant could only serve until they died (7:23); Jesus, the great high priest, lives for ever (7:24, see 6:20–7:21). Other priests were weak and sinful; Christ is perfect and sinless (7:28).

· The old sacrifices for sin had to be repeated regularly, first for the priest and then for the people (7:27; see also 10:1-3,11); Jesus offered his own life (9:11-14) once for all as a sacrifice for the sins of others (7:27; 9:28; 10:10,12).

· The old covenant could not transform human lives (7:18-19); the new covenant is able to bring forgiveness and make believers holy (10:14-18; see also 8:8-12 and 12:24).

· The old covenant brought people to Mount Sinai, where they received a terrifying revelation (12:18-21); the new covenant brings believers to God's heavenly kingdom, which is full of life and joy (12:22-24).

God's promises

Although there is a contrast between the old covenant and the new, the two covenants are held together by God's promises. In the old covenant, God promised rest to his people if they obeyed him (3:7-19). Many did not enter this rest because of their disobedience, but God still promises to bring rest to those who come to him through the new covenant of Jesus Christ (4:1-11). God's promise to bless Abraham's descendants (6:13-14) is now being accomplished through the ministry of Jesus (6:18-20). The new covenant is God's way of bringing the promised forgiveness and transformation (8:7-12). If Christians hold onto their faith in Christ, they will receive what God has promised (9:15; 10:36; 11:39-40). The final promise of God is to give his people an unshakeable kingdom (12:26-29).

Christ's obedience

Hebrews sees Christ as the obedient Son of God (1:2-3). Christ accepted the call of God to become a priest (5:5-6) to serve God and provide a way of salvation (2:17). Christ's obedience is more astounding because it led him through intense suffering and death in order to be a sacrifice for sin (eg 2:14-18; 5:7; 9:26; 12:2-3; 13:12). Christ's obedience through suffering makes him the perfect Son of God (2:10; 5:8; 7:28), who is able to save others (2:18; 5:9) and be an example for Christian perseverance (12:2-3).

RELEVANCE FOR TODAY – HEBREWS

Turn to Christ as our only hope

The readers of Hebrews were in danger of giving up on their faith in Jesus Christ (2:1-3; 3:12-14; 10:35-39). They were experiencing persecution (10:32-34), and some were tempted to go back to the familiar old covenant. Hebrews is a reminder that the Christian faith is much better than the angels (1:4), prophets (1:1-2; 3:1-6), priests (4:14-15; 7:23-28), sacrifices (9:11-14; 10:4,11-14) and law (7:19; 12:18-24) of the old covenant. Unlike these other things, Christ is able to bring believers to God and purify them (9:14; 10:22; 13:12).

> " *So do not throw away your confidence; it will be richly rewarded. You need to persevere so that when you have done the will of God, you will receive what he has promised.* "
>
> HEBREWS 10:35-36

We may not be tempted by the same Jewish customs today, but there are many other distractions to our faith. It can be easy to look for salvation by following self-help books or motivational therapists, rather than by looking to Jesus Christ. We must trust in Christ's unique position as the only one who can truly bring us to God.

See also "Jesus in the Letter to the Hebrews", pages 583–587.

Take in the Old Testament imagery

Many of the images from Hebrews sound strange to us. However, it is important for us to understand the person and work of Jesus against the background of the old covenant.

· As a high priest, Christ knows what we are going through (4:14-15), and is at God's right hand, praying for us (7:25), which is a source of great encouragement.

· As a sacrifice, Christ makes atonement for sin, removing the stain of sin from our lives and making us pure (eg 9:13-14; 13:11-12). In the light of Christ's suffering and sacrifice, we should be ready to make our own sacrifice of praise (13:15) and good works (13:16).

Trust in God continually

Hebrews has a lot to say about faith. The Israelites wandering in the wilderness were an example of unbelief (3:7-12,19). By contrast, Hebrews 11 gives a long list of people who lived by faith. They had faith in God's ability to fulfil his promises, even though they couldn't see how this would happen (11:1,39). Their trust in God remained strong, even though they experienced hardship and persecution (eg 11:32-38). These Old Testament characters should be an encouragement to readers who are thinking about giving up their Christian faith (12:1).

Hebrews warns that those who turn away from Christ will not receive salvation (2:2-3; 6:4-6). Christians must persevere with their faith (4:11; 6:11), avoiding deliberate sin (10:26-31; 12:14-17), and drawing strength from other Christians (10:24-25) and from the example of Jesus Christ (12:3).

WHAT IS HOLINESS?

Commenting on Hebrews 12:14, J C Ryle wrote:

Holiness is the habit of being of one mind with God. A holy person will:
· endeavour to shun every known sin and to keep every known commandment
· strive to be like our Lord Jesus Christ
· pursue long-suffering, gentleness, patience, kind temper, control of the tongue, moderation and self-denial
· seek to mortify the desires of the body
· follow after love and brotherly kindness, after a spirit of mercy and benevolence towards others
· seek purity of heart
· follow after the fear of God, like the fear of a child, who wishes to live and move as if he was always before his father's face, because he loves him
· seek humility
· pursue faithfulness in all the duties and relations in life
· strive for spiritual-mindedness.
   (updated from J C Ryle, *Holiness*)

OLD TESTAMENT ALLUSIONS

Hebrews uses Old Testament concepts to explain Christ's work. There are references to:
· a Sabbath rest. According to Hebrew tradition, God "rested" on the seventh day of creation, and expected his people to keep the seventh day holy by not doing any work. Hebrews uses this as a picture of the salvation which Christ brings.
· the covenant. The contract or agreement that God gives to his people. For the Jews, this agreement was expressed in the law of Moses. But now God has given a better agreement to his people through Christ.
· Christ as a high priest. Under the law of Moses, the high priest represented the people to God ... and sacrificed animals to secure forgiveness of their sins. God has provided a perfect high priest who offered, not animals, but himself.
· the Most Holy Place. A room within the tent of meeting (or tabernacle) which contained the ark of the covenant. Only the high priest was allowed to enter it, once a year, to offer sacrifices. Hebrews sees it as a picture of heaven, where Christ enters into God's presence.

James
PRACTICAL FAITH

OVERVIEW

What does the Christian life look like? James answers this question by giving a collection of clear instructions on some important issues. His letter is packed full of practical wisdom for living a godly life.

SUMMARY

After a short introduction and greeting (1:1), James launches into a call to his readers to persevere in the face of trials (1:2-4), reminding them to trust in God's ability to provide help (1:4-8) rather than in their own resources (1:9-11). God will reward those who stand firm (1:12), but those who give in to temptation will be trapped by sin and led to death (1:13-15).

James is particularly concerned about the way his readers speak. He wants them to avoid talk that is angry (1:19), uncontrolled (1:26), slanderous (4:11) or boastful (4:13-17). Instead they should learn to be controlled in their conversation (3:1-12), and to speak the truth without resorting to swearing (5:12).

A central message of the letter is that Christians must do the word of God, and not just hear it (1:22-25). James says that "faith without deeds is dead" (2:14-26).

A couple of passages deal with wealth in the church: wealthy people are not to be treated with more respect than poorer people (2:1-13), and rich business-owners are warned not to oppress their workers, because they will face God's judgement (5:1-6).

All of James' readers are warned against greed (4:1-10), encouraged to be patient in suffering (5:7-11) and reminded to pray together for forgiveness and healing (5:13-18).

Unlike other New Testament letters, there is no closing greeting. Instead, James urges his readers to look out for wayward Christians, and bring them back to the truth (5:19-20).

Author

James, the brother of Jesus. James met the risen Jesus (1 Corinthians 15:7), was with the other disciples at Pentecost (Acts 1:14) and became the recognised leader of the Jerusalem church (see Acts 15:13-21, Galatians 2:9,12).

Date

This is uncertain but could be as early as AD mid 40s, in which case this is one of the earliest New Testament writings.

Background

James wrote with many congregations in mind and intended the letter to be passed around the churches. The introduction (1:1) and various Old Testament allusions (eg 2:21-24-25; 5:11,17-18) suggest the readers were mainly Jewish Christians. Some were facing pressure to give up on their faith (eg 1:2-4), while others were struggling to live out the commandments of Jesus (eg 2:8).

OUTLINE – JAMES

KEY THEMES – JAMES

James is often described as "wisdom literature", similar to Proverbs and Ecclesiastes. Like these, James uses short examples from history (eg 2:21-24,25; 5:10-11,17-18) or from the observable world (eg 1:11,23-25; 3:3-8) to highlight God's eternal truth. Yet James has the directness of prophets like Jeremiah and Amos, and there is also much that reminds us of Jesus' Sermon on the Mount (Matthew 5–7). Unlike other New Testament letters, James does not follow a clear argument from beginning to end, but reads more like a series of short stories – or even sermons – that indicate the type of life that pleases God (1:12).

Wisdom

Wisdom is the main theme of James. If we lack wisdom, we can ask God to give it to us (1:5). Wisdom is not measured by the amount of knowledge a person has, but by their ability to live a good life (3:13) – a life that shows the fruit of a relationship with God (3:17-18). A wise person will match words with actions, but an unwise person is a hypocrite who says one thing but does another (3:14-16; see also 2:1-11).

This "heavenly wisdom" (3:17) is behind James' appeal to put into practice what the word of God says, and not simply to listen to it (1:22). The wise person actually obeys God's commands, and so doesn't forget them (1:25). Faith without deeds is not only dead (2:17,26) but also foolish (2:20); wise people will become mature by accompanying faith with action (2:22).

God as Lawgiver and Judge

Like other wisdom literature, James focuses on God's character as the just judge. God has given numerous instructions to show us how to live in the way he wants (1:20,27; 4:12). Christians who have experienced the grace of God in conversion (1:18) must not forget that their works will still be judged by God (2:12-13). As judge, God hears the complaints of those who are oppressed (5:4), as well as the slander (4:11) or grumbling (5:9) of Christians. God is ready to give generously to all who ask in faith (1:5,17; 5:15-16). He will ultimately reward those who have lived for him (1:12; 2:21-24; 4:10).

The pressures of life

James is fully aware of the difficulties of living for God in an unbelieving world. He mentions many pressured situations his readers would be facing: trials (1:2,12), temptation (1:13-15), poverty (1:9; 2:15-16), quarrels and slander within the church (4:1-12), oppression by the rich (2:6-7; 5:1-8), illness (5:13-16) and apostasy (5:19-20).

RELEVANCE FOR TODAY – JAMES

James is an excellent example of applying Jesus' teaching to the challenges of day-to-day Christian life. Although James does not often quote Jesus, much of what he writes has roots in Jesus' own teaching (eg 5:12 is similar to Jesus' words in Matthew 5:34-37). Like James, we should reflect on Jesus' teaching to help us live wise and godly lives. This is how Christians should make a real difference to the world.

" Who is wise and understanding among you? Let him show it by his good life, by deeds done in the humility that comes from wisdom."

JAMES 3:13

Believing and praying

James wants his readers to believe in the goodness of God, and not to doubt that God will give good gifts to them if they ask in faith (1:5-8,17). Elijah is an example of someone who prayed in faith (5:17-18), and James encourages his readers to pray in times of trouble, joy, sickness and sin (5:13-16). If we have faith in God, we should always be praying.

Doing

"Faith without deeds is dead" (2:26). True faith must be practical. If we have received God's grace, we must make sure we provide for the needs of others (1:27; 2:15-16) and keep ourselves away from sin (1:21,27; 4:8). True faith is obedience to God's "royal law" (2:8) and an eagerness to do God's will (2:21-25). We should take every opportunity to put our faith into practice.

Money

James has strong words about equal treatment of rich and poor (2:1-9) and for rich people who think their possessions are not subject to God (5:1-6). Much social injustice would be avoided by listening to James!

Speaking

James is very concerned about the way Christians speak. Although the tongue is so small (3:3-5), it can ruin the testimony of a Christian if it is not kept under control (3:6-8). However, if it is used carefully to praise God and bless other people, God is honoured and the Christian is considered mature (3:2,9-12). We should not curse (3:10), quarrel (4:1-2), slander (4:11), boast (4:16) or swear (5:12). Instead, we should use our tongues to pray for each other and sing songs of praise (5:13).

Persevering

Some of James' readers were in danger of giving up because of the pressures they were facing. James encourages them to trust in God's generous provision (1:5), to seek him for forgiveness and renewal when they fail (4:8-10; 5:16) and to be patient in their trials because God the Judge will come soon to deal with evildoers (5:8-9) and reward the righteous (1:12). Whatever our circumstances, God will help us to persevere, if we ask him in faith.

1 Peter
GOD'S GRACE IN DIFFICULT DAYS

OVERVIEW
Living a Christian life can lead to difficulties and suffering. Peter wants his readers to be ready for these challenges, so he writes to remind them about the grace of God which they have already received in Jesus Christ. This grace will give them the strength and hope they need.

SUMMARY
The letter begins with a short introduction and greeting (1:1-2). Peter is aware of the difficulties his readers are facing (1:6), but knows that God is keeping them safe by his power (1:5) and will bring them through their trials to full salvation (1:4-5,9).

Even though they are suffering, Peter's readers must remember that they are in fact very blessed: Jesus has redeemed them (1:18-21) and now they have been born into God's living kingdom (1:3-4,23). This salvation is so great that prophets looked forward to it (1:10-12) and the angels long to look into it (1:12)!

Those who have been born into God's kingdom must live holy lives as children of God (1:13-16), and become mature in faith (2:2-3). As this happens, Christians grow together into a people who honour God (2:4-10).

Peter is particularly concerned that Christians live good lives in every area of society (2:11–3:7). They are to be careful how they live, so that if they suffer, it is because they are doing good and not because they are evildoers (3:8-17; 4:12-16).

Christ's death and resurrection have declared God's victory over sin and death, making salvation and cleansing possible (3:18-22). Christ is the example for Christian living (4:1-2) and the standard of judgement for the world (4:5,17).

Peter reminds the church to live in harmony, and to serve one another in the strength God gives (4:7-11). Leaders, in particular, are to serve the church (5:1-4).

Peter closes with a reminder to resist the devil (5:8-9) and to trust in God, who will give grace and strength to help in times of suffering (5:10-11).

Author
Peter, one of Jesus' closest disciples. Peter is probably writing from Rome (called "Babylon" in 5:13).

Date
Probably in the early AD 60s – just before the Roman Emperor Nero's persecution of Christians, which broke out in AD 64.

Background
Peter wrote to a number of congregations in Asia Minor (1:1 – modern-day Turkey). Many were suffering insults and difficulties for their faith in Jesus Christ (eg 1:6; 4:12-15; 5:9). The letter could also have been for new Christians at their baptism (3:21, and language of "new birth" throughout).

OUTLINE – 1 PETER

KEY THEMES – 1 PETER

Suffering

Throughout the letter, Peter refers to the suffering of his readers. They have been facing all kinds of difficulties (1:6), from physical harm (2:19) to slander (3:16) and insults (4:14). Some of Peter's readers were surprised that the Christian life had led to suffering (4:12), but Peter reminds them that Jesus himself had suffered the same things and more (eg 2:21-23; 4:1). Other Christians throughout the world were also facing the same difficulties (5:9).

Christians must make sure that they are suffering for doing good, and not because they are evildoers (2:20; 4:15-16). God will bless them (3:14; 4:14) and give them strength (5:10), and suffering will make their faith stronger and purer (1:7; 4:1).

Full salvation

Christians have already received salvation through the death and resurrection of Jesus (1:3-5; 2:24; 3:18). They have entered into God's kingdom (1:3,23). Christ has saved them from their empty way of life (1:18). This salvation was predicted by the prophets (1:10-11), and was part of God's plan from the very beginning (1:20).

Christians can also look forward to future salvation (1:5). When Jesus is revealed, the whole world will see that the Christian life pleases God (1:7; 2:12). Those who suffer for their faith now will receive God's reward (5:4), and will inherit the blessings of his kingdom (1:4).

In the present, Christians can count on the grace and strength of God (1:9; 4:11; 5:10,12).

The church as God's family

Peter reminds his hearers that they have been chosen by God (1:1-2) to be obedient children of their heavenly Father (1:14). Together with all Christians, they have become living stones in God's house (2:4-5). As God's special people, they have inherited the blessings of Israel (2:9-10) – they belong to "the family of God" (4:17). They must learn to live together with love, and to use their gifts to serve one another (4:8-11). The leaders of the church are to be caring shepherds (5:1-3, see John 21:15-17).

The life of Christ

Jesus is the centre of Peter's thoughts. Peter often refers to events in Jesus' life and ministry, which Peter knew about as a first-hand witness (5:1). He speaks of Christ's suffering and death (eg 2:21-24; 4:1), his resurrection (1:3,21; 3:21) and his ascension (3:22). Christ is now the foundation (2:4-8) and Chief Shepherd (2:25; 5:4) of the church. He will come again (1:7,13; 5:4) to be judge of the world (4:5).

Old Testament Scriptures

For its length, 1 Peter has more quotes and allusions from the Old Testament than other books in the New Testament. The Scriptures

> "*Dear friends,*
> *I urge you, as aliens*
> *and strangers in the*
> *world, to abstain from*
> *sinful desires, which war*
> *against your soul.*"
>
> 1 PETER 2:11

are particularly relevant because both Peter's readers and ancient Israel lived in hostile environments and struggled to behave as God's people.

RELEVANCE FOR TODAY – 1 PETER

Imitating Christ

When Peter's hearers are suffering for their faith, they must remember that they are simply following in the steps of Christ (2:21). He is an example of patience under persecution and trust in God (2:23, see also 3:9). When faced with suffering, we should have the same attitude as Christ (4:1) and live entirely for God (4:2).

Being good citizens

Christians should be model citizens in society, by showing respect to the civil authorities (2:13-14) and their neighbours (2:17). They are resident foreigners and should not withdraw into ghettos (1:17; 2:11). Peter calls for humility and submission in the household from slaves (2:18), wives (3:1-6), and husbands (3:7). Within the church, leaders should be servants rather than lords (5:1-3) and young people should submit to them (5:5). All Christians should serve each other (4:10) and show mutual love, humility, hospitality and respect (4:8-9; 5:5). We should behave like this so that no one outside the church can accuse us of doing wrong (2:12,15). Most of all, humility and service please God, who will bless us for it (5:6).

Living in hope

Peter encourages his readers to be hopeful. Even though they are suffering in the present, their future is secure because of the resurrection of Jesus (1:3,21). Christ has already redeemed us from our sins (1:18), and is now enthroned as Lord in heaven (3:22). We wait for him to be revealed (1:7), when he will reward his faithful people (5:4) and bring them their full inheritance as God's children (1:4-5).

Because of this hope, we must make sure we do not get caught up in the sins of the world (1:13; 4:4) or the tricks of the devil (5:8). We should use every opportunity to explain our hope to other people (3:15).

Being joyful

Throughout the letter, Peter reminds his readers that they have good reason to be joyful. Even though we may have difficulties in the present, we can rejoice that God will use our sufferings to complete his work of salvation in us (1:6-9). We will be overjoyed when Christ is revealed (4:13)!

2 Peter
GROWING IN GRACE

OVERVIEW

False teachers were trying to lead Peter's readers away from Christian truth. Peter's letter warns them that false teaching leads to destruction, and he urges them to remember the true promises of God. By doing so, the readers will become stronger Christians.

SUMMARY

In the short greeting (1:1-2), Peter notes that his readers have received a precious gift of faith (1:1). God gives rich resources to his people (1:3-4) so that their faith will grow (1:5-9). If they work at their faith (1:10), they will be welcomed into God's eternal kingdom (1:11).

Peter wants to make sure that his readers will remember the truth of Christianity after he has died (1:12-15; 3:1-2). They can be sure he has told them the truth because he was an eyewitness of Jesus' life, even the transfiguration (1:16-18; see also Matthew 17:1-8). The prophecies of the Old Testament (1:19-21) also show that Peter was not making up stories about Jesus (1:16).

In contrast to Peter, false teachers invent stories and doctrines that can lead Christians astray. These false teachers will be destroyed in the judgement of God while those who hold on to the truth will be saved (chapter 2).

Christians should not be surprised that there are false teachers (3:3). These people laugh at God's promise, because they think that God will never come to create a new, righteous world (3:4-7,13). However, God works to his own timescale (3:8). He is patiently waiting for the right moment to fulfil his promise (3:9-13,15). Peter notes that the apostle Paul says the same thing in his letters (3:15-16).

In the light of all this, Peter's readers should be careful to lead holy lives, so that when God fulfils his promise he will be pleased with them (3:11-12,14). They must avoid the errors of the false teachers (3:17) and grow in the grace and knowledge of Christ (3:18).

Author

The apostle Peter (1:1) at the end of his life. 1:14 could refer to the conversation between Jesus and Peter in John 21:18-19. The author was present at the transfiguration (1:18) and mentions a first letter in 3:1.

Date

Mid AD 60s, shortly before Peter's death.

Background

The letter was written to a wide group, including the recipients of the first letter (3:1, see section at 1 Peter). The readers are facing challenges from false teachers. Among the first readers was probably Jude who used chapter 2 as a basis for his own letter.

OUTLINE – 2 PETER

KEY THEMES – 2 PETER

The danger of false teaching

Peter's main reason for writing was the threat of false teaching in the church (3:17). False teachers were deceiving the believers (2:1). Their teaching may have seemed appealing and persuasive (2:9-19), but Peter shows his readers how to identify the false teachers:

· They invent stories (2:1,3), unlike Peter, who has told them the truth (1:16-21).
· Their lifestyle does not match the gospel, but is full of shameful practices (2:2,13-14,19).
· Their motivation for teaching is greed (2:3,14; and the example of Balaam in 2:15, see Numbers 22).
· They despise authority (2:10) and are proud and arrogant (2:10-11).
· They especially try to trap weak or young Christians (2:18).
· Their teaching contradicts Scripture (2:21; 3:5,16).

The certainty of salvation

Unlike the false teachers, Peter bases his teaching on the truth about Jesus (1:16-18; 3:1), the prophecies of the Old Testament (1:19-21; 3:1) and the promises of God (1:4; 3:9,13). God's promise is to give salvation to those who believe in Christ, by rescuing them from the evil of the world and giving them life in his kingdom (1:4,11). Peter points to examples from Old Testament history to show that God is able to keep his promises. In particular, he mentions Noah (2:5) and Lot (2:6-8) to show that God is able to save the godly. This should give Peter's readers confidence that God can also act on their behalf (2:9).

The Day of the Lord

Peter tells the believers to expect the "Day of the Lord" to come at any moment (3:10). This was the day promised in the Old Testament and spoken of by Jesus (3:2). It will be the day of final judgement for the ungodly, when all that is unholy will be consumed by fire (3:7,10,12). But it will also bring God's new heaven and new earth, which will be filled with righteousness (3:13).

The false teachers denied that God would ever intervene (3:4). But for Peter, it is a certain promise (3:9,13), and the hope of believers (3:12,14; 1:11).

RELEVANCE FOR TODAY – 2 PETER

Watch out for false teachers

Peter reminds us that there will always be false teachers around (3:3) who teach their own invented stories rather than the truth of the gospel (2:1). In order to be able to recognise error, Peter's readers must study the true teachings about Jesus Christ (1:12-15,19; 3:1-2). By growing in the knowledge of Christ (3:18) and the Scriptures (3:2), Christians can be on their guard against false teachers (3:17) and will not be led away from true faith.

Be ready for Christ's coming

Peter's readers must look forward to the future God has promised (3:12). We may have been waiting a long time (3:4,8), but the delay is because God is patient and wants more people to be saved (3:9,14). When the Day of the Lord comes, it will be sudden and surprising, like a thief in the night (3:10). God's people will have a new home in the new heaven and new earth (3:7,13). Because we do not know when it will happen, we must always be ready. This means we should get rid of all sin from our lives, and make every effort to be holy and right with God (3:11,14).

> " *Therefore, dear friends, since you already know this, be on your guard so that you may not be carried away by the error of lawless men and fall from your secure position. But grow in the grace and knowledge of our Lord and Saviour Jesus Christ.*"
>
> 2 PETER 3:17-18

Grow as a Christian

Peter begins the letter by reminding his readers that their faith is a precious gift from God (1:1). God has given Christians all the resources they need (1:3), along with the promise and hope of salvation (1:4). If God has given us such great gifts, we must make every effort to nurture our Christian lives (3:18). We must grow in Christian qualities like goodness, knowledge, self-control, perseverance, godliness, kindness and love (1:5-7), so that we will be productive servants in God's kingdom (1:8). If we keep growing like this, we are unlikely to be led astray by false teaching (1:10; 3:17).

1 John
LIVING IN LIGHT AND IN LOVE

OVERVIEW

The message of 1 John is easy to understand: God is light and God is love. However, it is much more difficult to put this understanding into practice. John's letter shows us what it means to live in the light and love of God.

SUMMARY

Unlike other New Testament letters, 1 John does not begin with a greeting. Instead, John tells his readers that they can trust his message about Jesus because he himself saw, heard and was with Jesus (1:1-3). John is now passing on what Jesus had taught him (1:4-5).

God is light (1:5), so everyone who wants to be in fellowship with God must also live in the light (1:6-7). This means we must not hide our sin, but confess it to God and receive his forgiveness (1:8–2:2). To live in the light, we must obey God's commands (2:3-8), especially to love our fellow Christians (2:9-11).

John's readers already live in fellowship with God (2:12-14), but John reminds them that they cannot also love the world (2:15-17). Some people have left the church and are trying to lead others astray (2:18-19,26), but John encourages his readers to keep hold of the truth they already know (2:21-27).

In God's great love, he has made us his children (3:1), so we must become like Jesus Christ (2:29; 3:2-3). God's children will get rid of sin from their lives (3:4-10). They should also love one another (3:11-18) so that they will please God (3:19-24). John urges his readers to learn to recognise truth from error (4:1-6).

God is love (4:16), so everyone who wants to be in fellowship with God must also live in love (4:7-21) and obey God's commands (5:1-5).

John's readers know their faith is real because God lives in them by his Spirit (5:6-15). John ends by encouraging his readers to keep away from sin and hold on to true faith (5:16-21).

Author

Strictly speaking, this letter is anonymous. As it has much in common with the fourth Gospel, the church has always accepted it as being written by the same author, the apostle John. The author clearly has a position of authority in the group of churches he addresses and they will have known him well.

Date

There are no hard facts about this but most people think of a date towards the end of the first century AD.

Background

The readers of the letter were well known to the apostle John. Some of the congregation had recently left them (2:19), perhaps to follow false teaching (2:26). John writes to reassure them that their faith in Jesus Christ is true (5:13). As tradition tells us that John spent his later life in Ephesus, the readers probably lived in the same area, the west of modern Turkey.

OUTLINE – 1 JOHN

1:1-4 The truth of John's testimony
1:5–2:11 Living in God's light
2:12-14 A description of God's people
2:15-17 A warning: don't love the world
2:18-27 A warning: don't be led astray
2:28–3:3 The hope of God's children
3:4-10 Resisting sin
3:11-24 Loving one another as a mark of true Christianity
4:1-6 Learning to listen to God
4:7–5:5 Living in God's love
5:6-15 Assurance of faith in Jesus Christ
5:16-21 Final encouragement to avoid sin and live in God

KEY THEMES – 1 JOHN

God is light

John uses the contrast between light and darkness to speak about the difference between holiness and sin. Just as there is no darkness in light, so there is no sin in God (see 3:5): he is light (1:5). Christians must therefore walk in the light and avoid the darkness of sin (1:7). If we do not walk in the light, we are hypocrites, who say that we are in fellowship with God, but do not act as if we are (1:6). The test for living in the light is loving other Christians (2:9-11).

Those who live in the darkness do not know the truth, either about God (1:10; 2:4-5) or themselves (2:11). However, God is able to rescue us from darkness and sin through the work of Jesus Christ (2:1-2; see also eg 3:5). If we follow Jesus (2:6) then he will shine his light into our lives (2:8) and purify us from sin (1:7,9).

God is love

God is love (4:16), and he has showed that love to us by sending Jesus to give us new life (3:16; 4:10). God's love is generous (3:1), dependable (4:6) and universal (see 2:2; 4:14).

God's love for us is the reason (4:11,19) and pattern (3:16) for our love for one another. Those who belong to God must live a life shaped by love, just as God does (4:16,21).

God's children

1 John is full of terms of family relationship. John calls his readers "dear children" (eg 2:1,12-13,18,28; 3:7,18; 4:4; 5:21) and "dear friends" (eg 2:7; 3:21; 4:1,7,11). The warmth of their relationship is because both John and his readers are God's children (5:19).

God has made them his children because of his great love (3:1). They have been born again into God's family (3:9; 4:7; 5:1) and God's Spirit now lives in them (3:24; 4:4,13). God's children are given the gift of eternal life (5:11-12). One day, they will become like their heavenly Father (3:2). Unlike the children of the devil, God's children do what is right (3:10).

God's truth

John is concerned that his readers continue to believe the truth that they already know (2:20-21,24). They must especially keep hold of the truth about Jesus Christ (2:22; 5:5) – that he came as a real human being to bring God's salvation to the world (4:2-3; 5:6).

Living with God

Christians live in fellowship with God – with the Father and the Son (1:3; 2:24) and the Spirit, who lives in them (eg 3:24; 4:13). They are God's dearly loved children (3:1), and God listens to their prayers (5:14-15). God lives with them and gives them eternal life (2:24-25; 5:11).

We must nurture this valuable relationship with God by avoiding all sin (1:6; 2:1) and following his commands (1:7; 2:6; 5:3). If we do sin, we must not hide it, but confess it to God, who will forgive and cleanse (1:8-9). It is a great privilege to live in fellowship with God. But it is also a great responsibility: we need to take sin seriously, so that we can be pure like our loving Father (3:3).

Living with others

Christians are born into God's family, so they now have brothers and sisters in the faith (see 5:19). John's readers must make sure they are in fellowship with other Christians (1:3,7). Christians will know that their faith is real because of their love for their brothers and sisters (3:14). They cannot claim to love God if they do not also love his children (eg 4:20-21; 5:1)!

Love for one another is a central part of the Christian message (3:11). Jesus commanded his followers to love one another (3:23). Love is not a warm feeling, though. John wants us to love one another in practical ways (3:17-18). If we want to follow Christ, we must serve our fellow Christians with love.

> " *If we walk in the light, as he is in the light, we have fellowship with one another, and the blood of Jesus, his Son, purifies us from all sin.*"
>
> 1 JOHN 1:7

Living in the world

John contrasts the life of God's children with life in the world (2:15). For John, the world is a place of darkness (see 1:5-6; 2:11) and sin (2:16). People in the world follow their own desires rather than God's will (2:17). The world is under the control of the devil (5:19): his children do evil (3:10) and refuse to acknowledge Jesus Christ (4:3). The world hates God's children (3:13).

John reminds us that the evil desires of the world will not last (2:17). Jesus came into the world to be its Saviour (4:14), by defeating the devil (3:8) and by revealing God's love (4:9). No one can love both the world and God, so we should not love the world (2:15). Instead, our faith in Jesus will set us free from the evil desires of the world (5:4-5). If we truly desire this, God will help us (5:18).

2 John and 3 John
LOYALTY TO THE TRUTH

OVERVIEW

These two letters are very short, but their message is clear and direct: Christians must be loyal to the truth they have received in the good news of Jesus Christ.

SUMMARY

2 John was written to a local church (2 John 1). John is pleased that some members of the church are still walking in the truth (2 John 4) and he reminds them that this means they should love one another (2 John 5-6). John warns them about false teachers in the church (2 John 7-9). They should be careful not to welcome people who follow this teaching (2 John 10-11). Once again, John notes that he will deal with particular issues in the church personally when he visits them (2 John 12).

3 John is addressed to Gaius, a personal friend of the apostle John (3 John 1-2). Some travelling missionaries have recently visited John and told him many good things about Gaius (3 John 3-4). These missionaries had resolved to stay only in the houses of Christians on their journeys (3 John 7), and Gaius had made them very welcome and given them his support, even though he did not know them at first (3 John 5). The visitors have returned to Gaius from John, carrying this letter, and John asks Gaius to look after them again (3 John 6,8). In contrast to Gaius, another member of the church called Diotrephes did not welcome the visitors (3 John 10). John tells Gaius that he is aware of the trouble Diotrephes is causing in the church (3 John 9-10). Gaius should follow the example of good people like Demetrius (3 John 12) rather than evil people like Diotrephes. John notes that he will deal with the problem personally when he visits the church in the near future (3 John 10,13-14).

Author

"The Elder" (2 John 1; 3 John 1) who does not give his name. Traditionally seen as the apostle John, who also wrote 1 John and the fourth Gospel.

Date

Uncertain; possibly in the AD 80s or 90s.

Background

As John's ministry took place in Asia Minor (present Turkey), the readers probably lived in that area. 2 John was written to "the chosen lady and her children" (2 John 1). This was a way of referring to a congregation of Christians.

3 John was written to Gaius, a member of an otherwise unknown congregation, and a personal friend of the apostle John (3 John 1).

OUTLINE

KEY THEMES

Truth

John is delighted that members of the church fellowship are still living in the truth (2 John 4; 3 John 3-4). This truth is the message about Jesus Christ (2 John 9) and his human life (2 John 7), which they have known from the beginning of their faith (2 John 5).

Truth holds the Christian community together (2 John 1). Truth is not, however, just an intellectual understanding of the teaching of Jesus. For John, truth means a commitment to staying close to Jesus and obeying the Father's commands (2 John 4). Truth here is almost a personification of Jesus. This is why John can say that truth lives within the Christian (2 John 1) and lasts for ever. As his readers continue to walk in the truth, they will know the grace, mercy and peace of God (2 John 3).

Love

Christians cannot claim to live in the truth if they do not love one another. This message, which was central to 1 John, is repeated in 2 John. Loving one another is the defining mark of the Christian community. John's readers have heard this command from the beginning of their faith (2 John 5-6), so they should put it into practice.

Hospitality

Hospitality is a particular example of Christian love for one another, and an illustration of the way Christians are brought together by the truth. In 3 John, Gaius is commended because he showed hospitality to some travelling missionaries (3 John 5). Hospitality was especially important for Christian missionaries in the first century, who could suffer much hardship on their travels. It was not just a nice thing to do, but, more importantly, it showed a love for the truth and a commitment to helping the kingdom of God to grow (3 John 8). In contrast to Gaius, Diotrephes had refused to show hospitality to the visitors, and had gone further by trying to stop others from doing so too (3 John 10). This was not just bad manners, but showed that Diotrephes was also refusing their message. Since the visitors were connected to the apostle John, Diotrephes was therefore refusing John's teaching (3 John 9).

In 2 John, John reminds the church that

they must be careful to whom they show hospitality. While they should welcome everyone who shares the truth with them, they should refuse to welcome false teachers (2 John 10). Showing hospitality to false teachers is as bad as the false teaching itself (2 John 11).

RELEVANCE FOR TODAY

Be discerning

Christians have to discern between true and false teaching. This was and is especially important when travelling teachers arrive, who are not known by the community. Only teachers who follow the truth can be received and given an open platform (2 John 10-11; 3 John 8).

In order to discern the difference, Christians need to know the truth themselves. It is not wise to simply accept every teaching that we hear. Rather, we must be discerning and make sure that the teaching we receive is consistent with the teaching of Christ (2 John 9).

"I have no greater joy than to hear that my children are walking in the truth."

3 JOHN 4

Be hospitable

If teachers are bringing the truth, then John insists they should be welcomed with open arms (3 John 8). Hospitality is, in fact, a Christian duty. Christian workers should be treated in "a manner worthy of God" (3 John 6). By helping Christian workers, John's readers and we are in fact becoming part of their work too (3 John 8; see as a contrast 2 John 11). The care, love and acceptance we show to our leaders and other Christian workers and missionaries is an indication of our attitude towards God and his good news.

The personal touch

It is obvious that there were significant problems in the communities to which John wrote these letters. There appears to have been a rival group within Gaius' church, perhaps led by Diotrephes, which was refusing John's teaching (3 John 9-10). The other church was under threat from false teachers (2 John 7). John, however, does not deal directly with these situations in these letters. He gives general instructions to the church to continue in the truth and to watch out for error (2 John 8; 3 John 11). However, he promises that he will deal with the specific situations personally, when he comes to visit (2 John 12; 3 John 13-14). He apparently did not want to deal with them by letter.

This is good advice for dealing with pastoral problems in the church today. In an age of many different methods of communication, meeting face to face remains a wise, Christian way of resolving conflict. It helps to avoid many misunderstandings.

Jude
GOD'S JUDGEMENT

OVERVIEW

Jude's letter is a solemn warning of God's judgement on those who claim to be Christians but who do not live in a godly way. However, God will show mercy to those who trust in Jesus Christ and make every effort to keep themselves spiritually healthy.

SUMMARY

Jude had originally intended to write a general letter about the Christian faith (verse 3); however, the appearance of "godless men" in the Christian community (verse 4) made him change his plans and write about the danger of turning away from true faith instead.

After a short introduction (verses 1-2), Jude warns his readers that godless people have managed to slip unnoticed into their fellowship. These people claimed that God's grace allowed them to sin, and so made no effort to live under Christ's lordship (verse 4). They ignored the warnings of God's judgement from the Old Testament (verses 5-7) and the example of the archangel Michael (verse 9). Instead, they continued to do evil (verses 8,10) and follow the way of Cain, Balaam and Korah (verse 11). Jude describes the spiritual emptiness of their lives (verses 12-13,16) and notes that they will receive the judgement that they deserve (verses 14-15).

Jude's readers should remember that ungodly people will always be around the church (verses 17-19). They must therefore concentrate on their own spiritual healthiness (verses 20-21). They should make every effort to save those who are in error and encourage those who doubt (verses 22-23).

Jude ends with an outburst of praise to God the Father and to Jesus Christ (verses 24-25).

Author

Jude, brother of Jesus (named Judas in the Greek and in Matthew 13:55 and Mark 6:3), who was with the disciples in Jerusalem after the resurrection (Acts 1:14). He was also brother of James (verse 1), the author of the New Testament letter by this name.

Date

Possibly late AD 60s.

Background

Jude knew his readers well (verse 3, see also "beloved" in verses 17 and 20), which suggests he was writing to particular congregations with whom he had a special relationship, rather than more generally. His readers had heard at least a couple of apostles in person (verses 17-18).

OUTLINE – JUDE

KEY THEMES – JUDE

False Christianity

The main section of the letter (verses 4-19) describes the sin of godless people in the congregation to whom Jude was writing. The list of their characteristics is unpleasant:

- They are immoral (verse 8), acting like wild animals (verse 10).
- They reject God's authority (verses 4,8) and so slander his angels (verse 8).
- They are abusive (verse 10).
- They grumble and find fault with others, while doing whatever they themselves want (verse 16).
- They boast about being spiritual (verse 16).
- They flatter other people to gain their support (verse 16).
- They are divisive (verse 19).

Jude compares them to three Old Testament examples: Cain, who was jealous of his brother (Genesis 4); Balaam, who was greedy for money (Numbers 22–24); and Korah, who rejected God's authority (Numbers 16).

The worst part of their sin was that they still claimed to be true Christians, and so had deceived the rest of the church (verse 4). They were living as members of the Christian community, taking part in the fellowship meals and possibly even having some authority in the church (they are called "shepherds", verse 12). They claimed God's grace, but refused to live under the lordship of Christ (verse 4) and did not have God's Spirit (verse 19). Jude exposes these people as false Christians. They do not produce the good fruit they should (verse 12) and so are only fit for shame and judgement (verse 13).

Certainty of judgement

Although the false Christians had managed to slip into the church unnoticed (verse 4), Jude wants his readers to know that God did not overlook their sin. Jude uses examples from the Old Testament and other Jewish writings to illustrate this:

- The unbelieving Israelites were destroyed in the wilderness, even after being saved from Egypt (verse 5; see Numbers 14).
- God judged the rebellious angels (verse 6).
- Sodom and Gomorrah were destroyed (verse 7; see Genesis 19).
- Enoch's prophecy spoke of the certainty of God's judgement (verses 14-15, referring to a non-biblical Jewish writing, *The Book of Enoch*).

The false Christians will be destroyed by their sins (verse 10) and be cast out of God's presence into woe (verse 11) and darkness (verse 13).

God's keeping power

In contrast to the false Christians, Jude's readers can celebrate that they are being kept safe by Jesus Christ (verse 1). If they keep themselves in his love (verse 21), then he will bring them safely to his glorious future kingdom, purified of all their sin (verse 24). This is a cause for great joy for both God and us (verses 24-25)!

Hypocrisy in the church

The false Christians who are described in this letter had managed to become part of the church family without being challenged about their behaviour (verse 4). They had no problem with being fully involved in the church's life (verse 12), even though they did not really live under Christ's lordship. Jude's letter was a wake-up call to the church to be aware that false Christians were among them (verses 17-18).

This letter shows that heresy (false teaching) was not the only danger for the early church. Here in Jude, the danger is hypocrisy (claiming to be Christians but not living a holy life). Jude's letter urges his readers to fight for the true faith which they had received (verse 3) and not to allow the hypocrites to divide the church (verse 19) by leading others astray.

We too should be alert to the danger of hypocrisy in our own lives and in our church fellowships. God's amazing grace does not mean we can continue in sin (verse 4; see also Romans 6:1-2).

Staying healthy

Jude encourages his readers to stay spiritually healthy, which will help them to avoid the errors of the godless people. He gives a series of instructions (verses 20-21):

· Learn more about the true faith
· Pray in the Holy Spirit
· Stay within God's love
· Wait for the return of Jesus Christ.

In addition to these things, which focus on a personal relationship with God, Christians also have a responsibility for others (verses 22-23):

· Help those who have doubts about their faith
· Save those who do not know the danger they are getting into
· Warn those who are deliberately going their own way.

While Jude celebrates God's power to keep Christians in his care, he also notes the responsibility of Christians to keep themselves healthy and ready to serve God. The best way for us to avoid the error of godlessness is to keep ourselves spiritually healthy and active in mission.

" *Keep yourselves in God's love as you wait for the mercy of our Lord Jesus Christ to bring you to eternal life.*"

JUDE 21

Using stories

Jude uses a wide range of examples from both the Old Testament (verses 5,7,11) and from other Jewish writings (verses 6,9,14-15) to illustrate his teaching. He also uses examples from nature (verses 12-13) and reminds his readers of what they have already heard from the apostles (verses 17-18).

Good Christian teaching will use a variety of illustrations from many different sources to add clarity to the points being made.

Revelation
THE VICTORY OF CHRIST

OVERVIEW

Is God able to triumph over evil? The book of Revelation answers "yes", by giving its readers a view of what is going on behind the scenes of world history: the risen Christ is on the throne and is at work to bring his glorious kingdom to earth.

SUMMARY

Revelation begins with a declaration of God's greatness (1:4-8) and a description of the vision that the author John received (1:1-3,9-18). The risen Christ instructs John to write the vision down, and to send letters to seven churches, giving specific messages of warning and encouragement (1:19–3:22).

John is next given a picture of the worship of heaven (4:1-11). At the centre of this worship is the Christ the Lamb (5:6), who is praised because his sacrificial death has given him authority to open the scroll which holds God's purposes for the future (5:1-5,7-14). As the seals of the scroll are opened, terrible events take place which act as warnings of God's coming judgement (6:1-17). God's people, however, are marked out to preserve them through these troubles (7:1-8; 9:4) so that they will give praise to God (7:9-17). When the final seal is broken (8:1), another series of terrible events occur as seven angels blow seven trumpets (8:2–11:19).

John's vision continues with a scene of conflict between God's people and Satan (12:1-18). John sees two beasts which represent Satan's evil power (13:1-18), while the people of God are kept safe (14:1-5). Three angels (14:6-11) bring God's message of judgement (14:14-20). Seven final plagues are brought by seven more angels (15:1–16:21), before the kingdom of Satan, called Babylon, is brought to judgement (17:1–18:24).

This brings a great shout of praise from heaven (19:1-10) before a final great battle between heaven and Satan (19:11-21). At last, both the righteous and the wicked receive their judgement (20:1-15). In a final scene, John glimpses the glory of the new heaven and the new earth (21:1–22:5). Revelation ends with an encouragement to be ready for the coming of Jesus (22:7-21).

Author

The author calls himself John (1:1; 22:8) and is in exile on the island of Patmos (1:9). Many believe he is the apostle John, author of the Gospel and three letters, although in these writings his name does not occur.

Date

Most scholars think about AD 95, during the Roman emperor Domitian's persecution of Christians. Others think of AD 69, just after the reign of Nero.

Background

Revelation was written to seven churches in Asia Minor (now western Turkey, 1:4). Some were suffering persecution for their faith in Jesus Christ (eg 2:3,10,13), others dealing with false teaching (eg 2:2,14-15,20-25), others with lukewarm Christianity (eg 3:1-3,15-18).

OUTLINE – REVELATION

Introduction
1:1-3 An introduction to John's revelation
1:4-8 John's greetings to the seven churches
1:9-20 John's vision of the risen Christ

Letters from Christ to the seven churches in Asia
2:1-7 The message to the church in Ephesus
2:8-11 The message to the church in Smyrna
2:12-17 The message to the church in Pergamum
2:18-29 The message to the church in Thyatira
3:1-6 The message to the church in Sardis
3:7-13 The message to the church in Philadelphia
3:14-22 The message to the church in Laodicea

John's vision of worship in heaven
4:1-11 All heaven worshipping around God's throne
5:1-14 The scroll of God's purposes and the worship of the Lamb

The coming of God's judgement
6:1-17 The opening of the first six seals and the warnings of judgement
7:1-8 God's people are marked with God's own seal

7:9-17 The praise of the great multitude in heaven
8:1 The seventh seal is opened and heaven is silent
8:2–11:19 The seven trumpets announce God's judgements
12:1-17 Conflict between Satan and God's people
13:1-18 The blasphemy and deception of the two beasts
14:1-5 The song and the holiness of the 144,000
14:6-20 God's message of judgement to the earth
15:1–16:21 Seven angels bring seven plagues in seven bowls
17:1–18:24 The judgement of evil Babylon

The victory of Christ
19:1-10 A shout of praise from heaven
19:11-21 The coming of Christ and the great battle
20:1-15 The final defeat of Satan and the judgement of the righteous and the wicked
21:1–22:5 The glory of the new creation
22:6-21 Conclusion and encouragement to be ready for the coming of Christ

KEY THEMES – REVELATION

The Lamb's victory and sovereignty

Christ is the one who has secured God's victory over the powers of Satan and now sits on the throne with God (5:13; 11:15). In the first scene of John's vision, he appears as an awesome figure (1:10-16) who has authority over death and Hades, the realm of the dead (1:18). Later, he appears as a Lamb in the centre of God's throne, who is able to open the seals on the scroll which contains God's purposes for the world (5:5-10). Then he is a

mighty warrior, leading God's army to victory (19:11-21). The source of Christ's power and authority is his sacrificial death and resurrection (1:5,18; 5:9-10,12).

Satan's schemes

John shows his readers that the evil they were facing was not simply human, but demonic. The evil in the world is an attack on God and his people by Satan. Satan is the source of the false teachings and persecutions that threaten

LETTERS TO THE SEVEN CHURCHES

The letters written to the seven churches of Revelation appear in the order that a messenger travelling from the island of Patmos would deliver them.

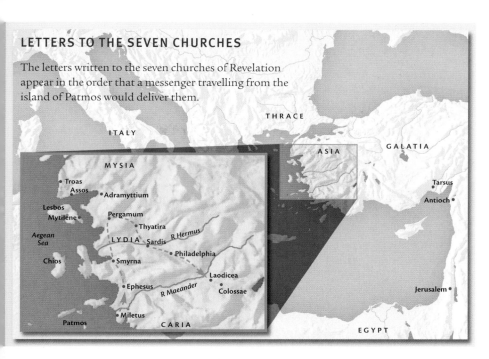

the life of the church (2:9,13,24; 3:9) and is responsible for deceiving the nations (20:3,7-10). He is represented as a dragon (12:3-9; 20:2) who seeks to frustrate God's purposes by leading people astray (12:9). His forces are described in terrifying ways: terrible beasts (13:1-18), a huge army (20:8-9), and a city drunk on the blood of Christian martyrs (17:3-6).

God's judgement

Much of the imagery of Revelation points to God's judgement of Satan's evil schemes. In the main part of John's vision, a series of terrible disasters occur as the seven seals on God's scroll are opened (6:1–8:1), seven angels blow seven trumpets (8:6–11:19), and seven bowls of God's wrath are poured out as plagues on the earth (15:1–16:21). These events appear to be warnings of God's final judgement, which happens with the seventh of each series (8:1-5; 11:15-19; 16:17-21). Yet John explicitly adds that humanity did not repent of its sins (9:20; 16:9,11). In the final

judgement, Satan is captured and thrown into a lake of fire (19:20; 20:10). All who had followed him are also destroyed (14:6-11, 19-20; 19:21; 20:11-15). This final destruction is called the second death (2:11; 20:6), but is also seen as a lake of fire (14:10; 19:20; 20:10,14). Once destroyed, Satan and his forces can no longer threaten God's kingdom.

The faithful's reward

Revelation gives a picture of the reward God will give to his faithful people:

· Safety from the worst tribulation (3:10; 7:14)
· Eternal life with God in his new creation (eg 2:7,10; 7:15-17; 21:1–22:5)
· Clean robes, symbolising purity (3:5; 7:14)
· Authority within God's kingdom (2:26-27; 3:21; 20:4).

God's faithful church is seen as the bride of Christ (19:7-9; 21:9) who will live for ever in God's new world, in which heaven and earth are joined together (21:1-3)!

Revelation is full of rich symbolism and strange images. Many people have tried to use the book to produce a timeline for the future of the world. However, John's vision does not follow a chronological order, and many of the images are simply different ways of talking about the same reality. The purpose of Revelation is not to give a schedule for God's plans, but to encourage Christians who are experiencing hardship and persecution.

God's power

Revelation's central message is the certainty of the power of God to defeat the forces of evil and bring about his new creation. John's readers were facing difficult times, and they may have begun to wonder if God was really able to save them. Revelation shows that by his death and resurrection, Jesus Christ has power and authority over all other forces in the world (see 1:5,17-18; 3:21; 5:9; 19:13). While Satan may seem powerful, he has already been defeated by Jesus, and will soon be utterly destroyed. In difficult and confusing times, it is vital to remember that the throne of the universe is occupied by God and by the Lamb, Jesus Christ (4:1–5:6; 11:15).

Christian patience

Until God's power is finally revealed, Christians must have patience. In the letters to the churches, Jesus encourages his people to remain faithful to him and to persevere through trials (2:3,10,25-26; 3:2-3). Christians are to patiently endure the disasters and judgements that are brought upon the world (13:10; 14:12), so that they will be part of the great multitude worshipping around the

> " *We give thanks to you, Lord God Almighty, the One who is and who was, because you have taken your great power and have begun to reign.*"
>
> REVELATION 11:17

throne of God (7:9-17; 14:1-5; 15:2-4). We are reminded that Christ will bring his kingdom soon, so we must always be ready (22:7-20). When persecution, hardship or confusion comes to us, we should remember that God has promised to bring us to his glorious kingdom, if we patiently persevere.

Eternal praise

The book of Revelation is punctuated with outbursts of praise. Praise is given to God by the angels, creatures and elders in heaven (3:8-11; 5:9-12,14; 7:11-17; 11:15-18; 16:5-7; 19:1-8), the multitudes of faithful Christians (7:9-10; 14:1-3; 15:2-4) and even the whole of creation (5:13). God is praised for his glorious character (4:8,11; 7:12) and the Lamb is worshipped for the salvation he has accomplished (5:9-10,12; 7:15-17). These outbursts are declarations of who God is (16:5-7) and what he has done (11:15,17-18; 19:1-8), and are filled with joy, love and thankfulness. As Christians, we join in this great symphony of praise to our great God!

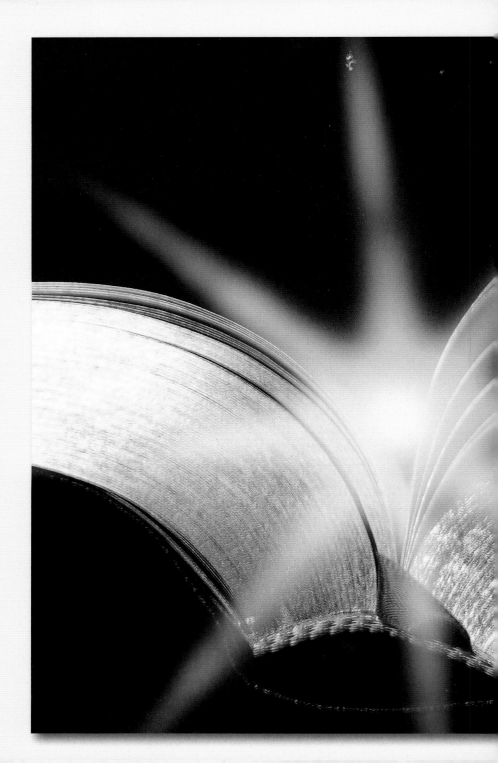

Bible Teaching

The material is arranged under ten major subject headings: the Bible, God, Jesus Christ, the Holy Spirit, Humanity, God's Messengers, Salvation, the Christian, the Church and the Last Things. Each major subject is divided into six sections and each section contains up to six separate studies.

This teaching material can be used for personal study or as a resource to aid Bible teaching in a group or in a church programme.

Bible Teaching

CONTENTS

See also "Knowing Jesus", p.16–115 and
"Discovering Jesus Christ", p.546–587

HUMANITY
1. Our Uniqueness
2. Our Diversity
3. Our Rebellion and Fall
4. Our Rebellion and Condemnation
5. Our Quest and Dilemma
6. Our Enemies
p.458–469

GOD'S MESSENGERS
1. Angels
2. Patriarchs
3. Priests
4. Prophets
5. Apostles
6. Evangelists
p.470–481

FOCUS ON ...

MAKING THE MOST OF THIS STUDY MATERIAL

Personal study

This Bible Teaching study material can be used as a companion to the Bible: as a resource to aid Bible teaching and for personal, regular study of the Scriptures.

The material is arranged under ten major doctrinal headings. Each doctrine is divided into six sections. Each section consists of up to six studies. If the whole series is completed, studying one section each week, all the material will be covered in just over one year. Each study is contained in two pages.

· **The main text** gives the theological overview. The Key Truth text summarises the subject. The Postscript text draws out a significant conclusion.

· **The Bible Study section**, while having a multiple use, is ideal for home study groups. This gives a passage of the Bible, selected to convey the main emphasis of the main study, with questions that are purposely designed to open up discussion.

· **The Reflection section** is a further aid to meditation and personal response.

This whole section concludes with a thought for each day (pages 530–539).

Group study

Study groups of all ages will benefit from the teaching they discover as they follow the guidelines within the course. Group leaders should prepare by: becoming familiar with the passages provided, being ready to support them with cross references; carefully reading the study material; being prepared to ask questions as a basis for discussion, and preparing further questions of their own.

Church programme

Ministers, pastors and teachers will find this material an invaluable reference source when preparing programmes for the church. The headings have been phrased so that the truth of the Bible is contained within the words of the headings themselves.

1. Its Main Sections

THE OLD TESTAMENT

History

The historical books of the Old Testament (from Genesis to Esther) show how God is involved in human history. He created the world, he chose a people to carry out his plan for saving all humanity and he provided them with laws for correct living.

These books of the law and the story of the nation of Israel provide the foundation for New Testament Christianity.

Poetry and Wisdom

Proverbs, riddles, songs, parables and allegories all occur in the wisdom and poetry books (from Job to the Song of Solomon). These books mirror the human response to God and to life. Despair, love and joy; the emptiness of life without God; bitterness, anger and triumphant faith – every emotion and situation has purpose when God is in the picture.

Prophecy

The prophets were men whom God called to speak for him to his people. They explained the past, reminding the people of God's law and his promises; they challenged the evils of the present; they also declared the future acts of God. Although these 17 books often speak of judgement and doom, they also tell of a future hope – the coming of a Messiah and of a new relationship with God.

THE NEW TESTAMENT

History

The four Gospels are based on the accounts of eyewitnesses who heard and saw Jesus of Nazareth, and they identify him as the Messiah, in fulfilment of the Old Testament.

The book of Acts goes on to show what took place after the death and resurrection of Jesus, and how the Christian church grew within the Jewish and Gentile worlds.

Letters

The New Testament letters were addressed to individuals, churches or groups of churches. They give the reader a vivid impression of the life of the first Christians, and the problems they faced.

These letters often show us the mistakes that Christians made, alongside the teaching of the apostles that gave correction and guidance in Christian living. Because Christians still have similar needs and weaknesses, the 21 New Testament letters have relevance for the church in every age.

Prophecy

The final book in the Bible consists of a series of visions seen by the apostle John, which reveal the situation affecting believers, unbelievers and the whole created order.

The book of Revelation is written in the language of symbolism and prophecy. It has inspired Christians down the ages with its message of the God who controls history, and who finally defeats all the powers of evil.

BIBLE CHECK

KEY TRUTH

There are 66 books, collected
in two "libraries". They were
written over a period of some
1,500 years. These books can
be placed into the six sections
in the following pages.

POSTSCRIPT

One of the remarkable things
about the Bible is that
although it is a very old book,
written to guide people in
their lives centuries ago, it is
still able to answer the needs
of people today.

BIBLE STUDY Psalm 119:1-32

Whether in a home group, student circle or simply on your
own, use these questions to help you in the study of this
passage.

1 The great Baptist preacher, C.H. Spurgeon, described Psalm
  119 as "an ocean of fire". As you read these verses, ask
  yourself what there is in them that caused this reaction.

2 Already you will have noticed that every verse has some
  reference to the word of God: laws, statutes, precepts,
  decrees, etc. What can be learnt about the character of God's
  word from these different terms?

3 Although Psalm 119 has no title, its style suggests that it
  originated with David, the shepherd boy who became Israel's
  king. Can you identify sentences in this passage which
  would have had relevance to episodes in David's life? Look,
  for example, at verses 9,14,19,23-24,28.

4 What does verse 18 have to teach us about our attitude, on
  coming to God's law? Why do we need our eyes to be
  "opened" in any case?

5 "Meditate" (verse 23). 250 years ago a Yorkshire preacher,
  William Grimshaw, defined meditation as "the soul's
  chewing". How is this to be done with God's word?

6 When the Psalms were written there was no New Testament.
  Look up Galatians 3:29. What may we learn there about the
  relationship of the Old Testament to the New?

7 Identify the four personal resolves of the psalmist in verses
  30-32. All of them are active. How can these become your
  own? Spend, now, some time in prayer and personal
  application of this great psalm.

REFLECTION

A Read Luke 24:13-35. What
does this tell us about the
Bible's power to banish fear
and aid understanding?
Notice the number of
sections in the Old Testament
referred to in verses 27 and
44.
B While all Scripture is
inspired by God, some books
may be of more importance
than others. Which do you
think these are, from both the
Old and New Testaments?
C Look at 2 Timothy 3:16-17.
Why has God given us the
Bible?
D Look at Galatians 3:29.
What does this teach us
about the relationship of the
Old Testament to the New?

THE BIBLE
2. Its Inspiration

The identity of its divine author

The Bible claims that God is its ultimate author. The conviction that God was speaking through the messages of the Old Testament is expressed many hundreds of times.

Both the Jewish people and the New Testament writers accepted that the Old Testament was inspired by God. Jesus himself upheld this view.

He believed the Scriptures, and by the way he quoted them showed that they were more important than human opinions and traditions.

The New Testament writers, for their part, were also aware that they were not teaching human wisdom, but rather God's message to humanity.

The diversity of its human writers

The biblical writers came from many different cultures and eras and represented a very wide range of intellects and abilities.

There was a diversity of circumstance. Some wrote as prisoners in exile, while others ruled kingdoms. There was a diversity of employment. Some were ordinary bakers, shepherds or tent-makers, while others enjoyed high positions in society. There was a diversity of character – from the despairing to the joyful.

The unity of its many themes

This unique library of books confronts the reader with its unity, although written over some 1,500 years. It is ancient, yet modern in its relevance to human needs. It is diverse, yet one – held together by its common theme of God's people and their desire and need of a coming Saviour. The Old Testament finds its fulfilment in the New Testament. The New Testament has its roots in the Old Testament. The library is one.

The authority of its inspired truth

From early times the value of these books so impressed itself on God's people that they acknowledged their authority and received them into the category of inspired Scripture. They recognised that it was God who was speaking.

It was not the act of binding the books into the Bible that gave them their inspiration. This they already possessed. The authority of the Old Testament was recognised by the Jews, by Jesus himself, and also by the New Testament writers, who frequently quoted the Old Testament. The New Testament writings were also accepted by the church from its early days as having the final say in everything that Christians believe and do.

The reality of its moral impact

The Bible is not afraid to portray evil honestly, even when some of its finest characters are involved in it. But in contrast, it also shows us the highest moral standard in history – the life of Jesus Christ.

This is the book that consistently challenges evil, transforms lives and exalts Christ.

BIBLE CHECK

Identity: Jeremiah 1:9; 2 Peter 1:21; 2 Timothy 3:16-17

Diversity: Amos 7:14-15; 1 Kings 4:29-32; Acts 18:3

Unity: Matthew 5:17-18; Luke 24:25-27,44

Authority: Joshua 1:7-8; Matthew 22:29; Psalm 19:7-11

Reality: Deuteronomy 32:45-47; Hebrews 4:12

KEY TRUTH

When we say that the Bible is "inspired" we mean that God spoke his message through the people that he chose. These people did not become like robots under God's control, but kept their own identities, while being guided by God.

POSTSCRIPT

Like any other book, the Bible was written by human authors. But, unlike any other book, it was guided and planned by God from beginning to end. It is because God stands behind the Bible that all Christians owe it their loyalty and their obedience to its demands.

BIBLE STUDY 2 Timothy 3:10–4:8

Here is the apostle Paul, encouraging his junior fellow-worker Timothy to be confident of God's word in all his ministry, whatever the difficulties and opposition. These questions will help in the study of this passage:

1 Reflect on the opposition that the faithful teaching of the word of God invites (verses 10-13). Why is this so? What does this have to do with Scripture's central focus (John 5:39-40)?

2 Look at verses 14 and 15. How and when were you first introduced to the Scriptures? Compare experiences.

3 What are the Scriptures uniquely qualified to do for us? Look at verses 15-17.

4 "God-breathed", "inspired by God" (verse 16). How is the "inspiration" of the Bible different from the 'inspiration' of, say, the works of Shakespeare? Compare Luke 24:27 and 2 Peter 1:21.

5 Consider the solemn responsibility of communicating "the word" to others (4:1-2). What should be our true motivation? What should be our attitude?

6 What are we up against in the proclaiming of God's revelation (4:3-4)? In what ways do you see these tendencies at work today?

7 Four direct commands are given to Timothy in 4:5. How do they apply to modern representatives of God's truth? What are our encouragements from Paul's words in verses 6-8? Finish the study by praying for people you know, worldwide, engaged in spreading the message of the Bible.

REFLECTION

A Read Exodus 3:1-14 and 4:1-17. Why was Moses reluctant to speak for God? What reasons did God give for trusting him?

B When the prophets spoke God's message they were often attacked or even killed by the people. Why? Does this still happen today?

C How did Jesus regard the Scriptures? See Matthew 5:17-19. How can we best learn from his example?

D God spoke through the writers of the Bible without robbing them of their individuality. Consider some of these writers. What do we learn from this about the way in which God uses people?

THE BIBLE
3. Its Interpretation

THE BIBLE MUST BE:

Seen in its historical setting

One of the ways in which we can understand the meaning of a Bible passage is to gain an understanding of its original meaning to the earliest readers. The more we know about the customs and politics of Bible times, the clearer its meaning will be.

For example, the New Testament commands that slaves should obey their masters. We must understand this in the light of the fact that slavery was generally accepted at that time (even though it was seen as part of the order that was passing away because of Christ).

Similarly, a knowledge of customs at that time helps the modern reader to understand the meaning of Jesus' command to his disciples to wash one another's feet – which might otherwise seem irrelevant today.

Consistent with its surrounding passage

We can better understand the meaning of a Bible word when we examine the sentence in which it occurs. In the same way, we can only truly understand a sentence when we look at the surrounding paragraph.

The leaders of many false cults and sects often twist the truth of the Bible by taking a sentence out of its context. In this way they use the Bible to support their own beliefs. Christians must be careful to find out what the Bible is really saying – even when it hurts.

In harmony with the rest of Scripture

Individual passages of Scripture are to be interpreted in the light of the whole Bible. When this is done, no one part of Scripture will be found to conflict with another. When we are confronted with apparent contradictions in the Bible, it is probably because we do not know the consistent teaching of the Bible as a whole.

The challenge to the reader of the Bible is to develop a truly biblical way of thinking.

Consistent with the purpose of God's revelation

The Bible tells us all that we need to know about God's plan for his creation and for humanity. There are many questions which we might want answered, about which the Bible says very little or nothing. But God's word tells us all we need to know about him and his plans.

We must recognise that the Bible is first of all a book of salvation. Therefore, we should avoid making clever interpretations on matters outside its main purpose.

Understood in changing cultures

The Bible has a living message, with power to transform lives and characters. Although it was given in cultures far removed from those of modern times, its relevance to life is undiminished today.

As we interpret the Bible, however, we must be prepared to wrestle with the words and terms used by the biblical writers, and to translate them in ways that the modern reader can understand.

BIBLE CHECK

Seen: Ephesians 6:5; John 13:14

Consistent: Nehemiah 8:8; 2 Corinthians 4:2

In harmony: Matthew 22:29; 2 Timothy 2:15

Consistent: Deuteronomy 29:29; 2 Timothy 3:14-15

Understood: Acts 8:34-38; Acts 17:11

KEY TRUTH

Interpretation means the discovery of the true meaning of the Bible. Several things are important to remember as we try to understand the Bible's teaching.

POSTSCRIPT

The Bible is not a scientific textbook, nor a history book. Yet it will not conflict with scientific findings nor with historical facts. Its purpose is different – that of portraying God's plan for humanity, in Christ.

BIBLE STUDY Nehemiah 8:1-12

Here is a passage that describes God's ancient people, the Jews, in the 5th century BC. They have been restored from the terrible days of exile in Babylon. Although now under Persian domination, they have an opportunity, not only to restore Jerusalem's shattered walls, but to rebuild their life – around the Book of God. Focus now on these questions:

1 "The Book of the Law of Moses" (verse 1). This was probably Deuteronomy. What are the advantages of studying the Scriptures together?

2 Picture the scene described in verses 1-6. This was a national occasion. How far has the Bible's message given a foundation to modern-day civilisations?

3 Study the key to the whole chapter (verse 8) and discuss the importance of such words as "clear", "meaning" and "understand".

4 Why is it unsatisfactory when numerous different "meanings" are forced onto a passage? (Compare 2 Corinthians 4:2). What was the result when the one true interpretation was made known to Ezra's listeners (verses 9,12)?

5 In the light of this passage, consider the reaction of others when God's message became clear to them (eg Jeremiah 15:16; 1 Thessalonians 1:6).

6 Scripture elsewhere gives warnings against false teachers who use the Scriptures wrongly (eg 2 Timothy 3:6-8; 2 Peter 2:1-3). To what extent is this a problem in your society?

7 Look at verse 5: Ezra opened the book. What resolves will you make for yourself, as you take the lessons of this passage to heart? Pray about them now. Make 2 Timothy 2:15 your motto.

REFLECTION

A Read John 13:1-15. In the time of Jesus, to wash someone's feet was an act of humility and kindness. In what ways can we obey Jesus' command in verse 14 today?

B Some words used in Bible translations are not a part of everyday speech. Find out what words like "salvation" or "repentance" mean, and put them in your own words.

C What should our reaction be when we find Christian people equally divided over the correct interpretation of a Bible passage?

D What is the strength of knowing individual verses of the Bible by heart? What is the limitation?

4. Its Application

Read prayerfully

The Bible is not simply an interesting book to read: it is a book to get involved in. It deals with issues that vitally concern the reader's life, character and destiny.

To read the Bible with prayerful dependence on the Holy Spirit is a safeguard against hardness or pride – it also shows that the reader is willing to submit to God's moral direction.

Listen personally

The Bible is not a book of abstract philosophy – it is a book about life and about people in real situations. Isaiah spoke specifically to the people of Jerusalem. The apostle Paul often greeted friends by name in his letters. The book of Revelation was written to Christians who were suffering persecution.

But we must go on to say that the Bible's rewards and promises are for every reader, of whatever century. As we open our lives to the Bible's message, we can expect God to communicate with us.

Look expectantly

As we read the Bible, we will be surprised and even shocked by some of the events that act as warnings within its pages. There will be other passages that challenge or puzzle us. We must expect to be stretched to the limit of our capacity by this book.

Apply regularly

When we read and apply the Bible regularly, one of the great benefits is that we start to see the world in a Christian way. We also see the Bible as a whole, and not as unconnected fragments.

As young children need a regular diet for proper growth, so the Christian needs to feed spiritually upon the Scriptures, applying their truths to daily living. As a result, our characters are transformed.

Act obediently

The Christian will repeatedly be confronted with the Bible's commands. The Bible challenges us to obey God's word, and not only to listen to it.

Jesus said that it is not enough merely to hear his words. It is only when we hear and obey that our lives are like a house built on rock – safe and secure.

Read totally

The Bible reader should aim at a full and balanced appreciation of all that the Bible may teach on any given topic. To rely on individual verses or on favourite selected passages (valuable though these are) will not lead us to spiritual maturity.

As we persist in reading the Bible thoroughly, worship becomes a living force, our work for God becomes a vital activity, and Christ becomes a daily companion.

BIBLE CHECK

Read: Psalm 119:33-40; Matthew 7:7-8

Listen: 1 Samuel 3:10; Revelation 1:3

Look: Jeremiah 23:29; 1 John 5:13

Apply: Psalm 1:1-2; 1 Peter 2:2-3

Act: James 1:22-25; Matthew 7:24-27

Read: 2 Corinthians 4:2; Colossians 3:16

KEY TRUTH

The Bible is meant to change the way in which we live. As we apply the Bible, God instructs, supports, cleanses and directs us in our daily lives.

POSTSCRIPT

God gave us the Bible, not just for us to enjoy its stories or learn about him. He gave us the Bible so that we may live in the way that he wants. Applying the Bible can be challenging and uncomfortable – but it must be done.

BIBLE STUDY James 1:19-27

It is all very well to understand the Bible's message, but is it being put into practice? This is a great theme of James, the half-brother of Jesus Christ (Matthew 13:55). It is a letter addressed to believers in general; this passage has a relevance for all time. The following questions will help in its understanding:

1 What sentence in this passage most clearly sums it up?
2 What is the best attitude with which we should come to the word of God?
3 Why is mere listening the way of self-deception (verse 22)? Compare your findings with Matthew 7:26-27.
4 Reflect on the phrase "the word planted in you" (verse 21). What does this mean? How does it happen? Think of the parable of the sower (Luke 8, eg verse 15).
5 What is the point of the illustration in verses 23-25? How would you apply this to your own actions?
6 Verses 26 and 27 raise an obvious question regarding our intake of God's word; how has it changed our lives? This applies to the words we are speaking, and the things we are doing. From these verses, describe a religion that is real in today's world.
7 Is it time to learn a sentence of the Scriptures by heart, as a result of reading this passage? Before you turn to prayer, look up, and start to learn Joshua 1:8 ... the reference, the words, and then the reference again, to make it stick!

REFLECTION

A Read Psalm 119:97-112. Try to list some of the benefits that result from meditating on the Scriptures.
B Christ once told a parable about the different kinds of soil into which the good seed fell (Mark 4:1-20). Try to describe the kind of life that is "good soil", in which the seed of God's word can grow.
C Discuss with your friends in practical terms the times of day when you find it best to read the Bible.
D Hebrews 4:12 describes the power of the Scriptures. Try to enumerate some of the instances in the Bible where this power is demonstrated.

5. Its Central Theme

The continual conflict

The conflict in the Bible began when Adam and Eve questioned God's authority. From this simple beginning stemmed the entrance of sin into the world, and the revolt of humanity against God's rule.

The Bible traces the spread of this conflict between humanity and God.

It shows how people soon became hostile to each other, as well as to God. The need of humanity to be reconciled to God becomes the central theme of the Bible.

The promised Saviour

The Old Testament speaks clearly about the longing for a future deliverer from sin and guilt. However, this is more than a mere hope. The prophets, particularly, speak of God's promise of a Saviour, who will establish a new agreement with God's people – with forgiveness and liberated service at its heart.

The New Testament points unmistakably to Jesus Christ as being this promised Saviour.

The work of Christ

The coming of Jesus Christ in history fulfils all the hopes of the Old Testament, and provides the basis for the New. In Jesus, God himself entered human history, and opened the way for forgiveness and holy living. This was done through Christ's death, his resurrection and his gift of the Spirit. Death is defeated, the power of Satan is broken, and the ascended Christ rules.

The new community

The New Testament portrays the followers of Christ as the society of the saved – called to be members of his world-wide church. Wherever the rule of Christ operates in people's lives, there his church is found.

This new community worships its reigning Lord, and is called upon to fulfil its mission of evangelism and practical service to the whole world. Jesus Christ personally upholds it in every experience. When he comes again, its membership and task will be complete.

The ultimate victory

The whole of creation will be involved in the final triumph of God. His love and justice will be upheld for everyone to see, and the whole empire of evil will be overthrown.

The great landmark of the future is the return of Jesus Christ, personally, historically, visibly and triumphantly. He will come as Judge of the whole world as well as Saviour of his people. The date of his coming cannot be predicted, although calamities, wars and the appearance of false Christs confirm the approach of this final event of history.

Christian believers look forward to a new heaven and a new earth. They look forward to a day when they will receive new bodies which will never age or die. Then sin and sorrow will be banished for ever, and their salvation will be complete.

BIBLE CHECK

Conflict: Genesis 3; Titus 3:3
Saviour: Isaiah 53; Jeremiah 31:31-34; Luke 24:44-45
Work: Mark 1:15; Luke 2:28-32; Titus 3:4-7
Community: Matthew 16:18; 28:19-20; Ephesians 2:18-22
Victory: 1 Thessalonians 4:13-18; Revelation 21:1-4

KEY TRUTH

Although humanity has rebelled against God and ignored his laws, God has a plan for rescuing us. This plan is centred around Jesus Christ, and concludes in God's ultimate victory over sin, Satan and death.

POSTSCRIPT

It is important for the Bible reader to understand, by consistently reading the whole Bible, that God is at the centre of all things, and is in ultimate control of the universe.

BIBLE STUDY Revelation 5:1-14

Written around AD 95, towards the end of the reign of the emperor Domitian, the book of Revelation presents the oppressed believers of every generation with a series of visions, first given to the exiled apostle, John. In this passage the theme of all the ages is opened for us. Use these questions to help in the study:

1 The "scroll" of John's vision contains not Scripture as such, but rather the secrets, the explanation of all history and its meaning. Can you think of some of the candidates who have stepped forward in their claim to be a universal teacher?

2 "I wept and wept" (verse 4). Why this failure on the part of great leaders and movements to unravel the meaning of life? Compare your findings with Daniel 2:27-28.

3 The one successful candidate is then announced (verse 5). What is special about his title? See Isaiah 9:6-7; 11:1-2. Who is this figure?

4 What is significant about this royal leader turning out to be a Lamb that has been slain (verses 6,7)? Genesis 22:8, Exodus 12:21-23 and 1 Corinthians 5:7-8 will help.

5 Discuss, from verses 8-10, this central theme of the universality of Christ's redemption of the world. When were you first caught up in this?

6 It is now the turn of the angels to sing (verses 11,12). What do we learn here about the position of Jesus Christ?

7 Verses 13,14. Is this universal song your song? What does this passage do for your own world-view? Turn now to prayer.

REFLECTION

A Consider Titus 3:3-7. How far are the major themes of the Bible summed up in this passage? Are Paul's words true of your own experience?
B A Chinese person once said of the Bible, "Whoever made this book made me." Do you agree with this? What lies behind such a sentence?
C What is the most important reason for having a biblical way of looking at life? Because the Bible brings comfort and hope? Because society needs belief of some kind? Because the Bible is true? Try to give your reasons.
D How does a biblical view of life help a person to grapple with the issues of wrongdoing, strife and injustice?

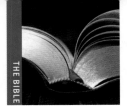

THE BIBLE
6. Its Contents

THE OLD TESTAMENT

Genesis The start of God's plan for his people.

Exodus God's people are freed from slavery.

Leviticus Preparing God's people for worship.

Numbers God's people wander in the wilderness.

Deuteronomy God's people called to obedience.

Joshua Success in the Promised Land.

Judges Failure in the Promised Land.

Ruth The story of a faithful daughter-in-law.

1 Samuel The emergence of Israel as a kingdom.

2 Samuel Israel's greatest King – David.

1 Kings Solomon – the temple – the division.

2 Kings The divided kingdom, and the prophets.

1 Chronicles God's faithfulness to his people.

2 Chronicles The fall of Israel as a nation.

Ezra The return from exile, and the new start.

Nehemiah Danger as Jerusalem is rebuilt.

Esther Esther's courage saves the exiled Jews.

Job Dialogues on the sufferings of a godly man.

Psalms Humanity's honest response to God.

Proverbs Wisdom for living.

Ecclesiastes The world's philosophy exposed.

Song of Songs A poem of love.

Isaiah The prophet of hope.

Jeremiah The prophet of tragedy.

Lamentations The prophet of sorrow.

Ezekiel The prophet of God's glory.

Daniel The prophet of confidence in God.

Hosea The prophet of love.

Joel The prophet of the Day of the LORD.

Amos The prophet of justice.

Obadiah The prophet of doom.

Jonah The prophet of repentance.

Micah The prophet of restitution.

Nahum The prophet of retribution.

Habakkuk The prophet of doubt and faith.

Zephaniah The prophet of judgement.

Haggai The prophet of dedication.

Zechariah The prophet of restoration.

Malachi The prophet of expectation.

THE NEW TESTAMENT

Matthew The teaching of the promised Messiah.

Mark The work of a powerful Saviour.

Luke The concern of a loving Saviour.

John The belief in a personal Saviour.

Acts The witness to a risen Saviour.

Romans God's righteousness upheld and applied.

1 Corinthians A church's problems corrected.

2 Corinthians The ministry of the church.

Galatians The gospel and Jewish law contrasted.

Ephesians Christ's relationship with the church.

Philippians The love and loyalty of a church.

Colossians The person of Jesus exalted.

1 Thessalonians New converts encouraged.

2 Thessalonians The second coming of Christ.

1 Timothy Instructions for church behaviour.

2 Timothy The pastor of a church encouraged.

Titus Christian self-control.

Philemon To the owner of a runaway slave.

Hebrews The greatness of Christ exalted.

James Practical instructions for a living faith.
1 Peter The suffering of the church explained.
2 Peter The perils of the church foretold.
1 John The reality of divine fellowship.
2 John Walking in the truth exhorted.
3 John Living in the truth practised.
Jude Apostasy in the church condemned.
Revelation The triumph of God over all evil.

Please note The themes opposite are only a guide. Each theme should not be seen as the only theme of any particular book, but as a distinct emphasis of that book.

KEY TRUTH

Each book of the Bible has its own distinctive central themes. The list here is a sample of some of these themes.

POSTSCRIPT

Each book of the Bible should be read as a whole, so that an overall view is gained of its contribution to God's message to humanity.

BIBLE STUDY Deuteronomy 4:32-40

The children of Israel are poised at the border of their Promised Land. The 40 years of wandering come to an end. Our passage is part of a great address in which Moses is summarising the adventure with God – which is really the story of the Bible. Use these questions for your study:

1 The sweep of God's dealings with the human race goes back to Creation itself (verse 32). What is the value of reviewing the road by which we have come?
2 "... the voice of God speaking" (verse 33). What is the great truth behind these words? Compare them with Hebrews 1:1-2.
3 How far does the overall message of the Bible's 66 books tie in with what you read in verse 34?
4 Try to itemise, in this passage, the different actions of God that have led to his people knowing and acknowledging him (verse 35,39).
5 Verse 40 concerns the keeping of God's commands. Discuss those books of the Scriptures that have so far helped you significantly.
6 Reading the Bible may seem a formidable prospect. Examine and think through the best way of arranging a programme of regular Bible reading.

REFLECTION

A Look at Matthew 4:1-11. Consider each of the temptations that confronted Jesus. Why did he make use of the Old Testament so much to resist the devil? What may we learn from this?
B Discuss with your friends which biblical book has helped you most, so far. How has it helped? Which book do you look forward to reading next? Why?
C Why is it important to read the Bible? Look up 1 John 5:13 and John 20:31.
D Perhaps you feel daunted by the thought of getting to know the books of the Bible. What is the best way of arranging your Bible reading programme?

1. The Trinity

Revealed in the Old Testament

The Old Testament stresses that God is one. The prophet Isaiah, in particular, says that there is only one God, and that all other "gods" are false. And yet at the same time, the opening sentence of the Bible uses a plural form for God's name (Elohim) and does so hundreds of times subsequently. Thus, at no point is it right to think of God in a unitarian way.

There are enough indications in the Old Testament for us to recognise the idea of three persons within the Godhead. For example, God sometimes refers to himself as "us", and there are appearances and visions of him which suggest different members of the Trinity.

Asserted in the New Testament

In the New Testament Jesus gives us some very clear teaching about the Father and the Spirit. Jesus shows us the wonderful truth that there is one God, and the Father, the Son and the Holy Spirit are all together this one God.

The New Testament does not give us a formula about the Trinity but the evidence is unavoidable. In the unity of the one God there is a Trinity of persons achieving human salvation, and in whose name we baptise.

Known by faith

Proof texts are not enough for a clear understanding of the Trinity. We must study all the teaching of Jesus and of his apostles, and observe the threads of truth that run through the Bible which relate to the will of the Father, the work of the Son and the inner working and witness of the Holy Spirit.

God the Father

The first person of the Trinity is called Father, not primarily because of his relationship to his creatures, but because of his relationship to the eternal Son.

Because of our union with Christ, the Eternal Son, we are brought to share in that dynamic relationship between the Father and the Son.

God the Son

The second person of the Trinity is called the Son. He became a man, Jesus Christ, in order to rescue humanity from the domination of sin. As Son of God he was involved with the Father in the creation of all things and shared in his eternal glory.

Within the Trinity the Son is obedient to the Father in all that he does. Thus the Son was sent by the Father and only acted under his Father's authority.

God the Holy Spirit

The third person of the Trinity was sent from the Father in Christ's name, to make personal in the lives of Christians all that Christ had made available through the cross. Just as Jesus once lived among us, so the Spirit now lives in us.

Although he was active in the Old Testament, a distinctive task of the Spirit began after the ascension of Jesus. He is the one who points attention to Christ, who speaks to the church in every age and who equips Christians with abilities to serve God.

BIBLE CHECK

Revealed: Isaiah 44:6-8;
Genesis 1:26; 18:1-15
Asserted: John 14:15-26;
16:5-15; Matthew 28:18-20
Known: John 16:12-13;
2 Corinthians 13:14;
1 Peter 1:2
The Father: Matthew 11:27;
Luke 10:21; Acts 2:32-36
The Son: John 1:1-18;
Colossians 1:15-20;
Hebrews 1:8
The Holy Spirit: Romans
8:9-11; 1 Corinthians
2:10-11

KEY TRUTH

There is only one God. But
God consists of three persons,
the Father, the Son and the
Spirit, who are all equally
God.

POSTSCRIPT

The Trinity must not be a
truth that has no relevance to
our lives. We will understand
the truth of the Trinity best as
we experience the work of the
Father, Son and Holy Spirit in
our lives.

BIBLE STUDY John 14:8-21

The teaching of the Bible that relates to the three Persons
within the Godhead is never presented as a formula, a neat
doctrine or as a philosophical system. The Trinity is always
alluded to in the most natural way. Study these verses now,
and allow the following questions to help:

1 What do we learn from Jesus' dramatic reply to Philip's
question (verses 8-10)?

2 In verse 12 Jesus declares that in the future, his followers will
accomplish things greater in dimension than what was
possible when Jesus was here on earth. How could this be so,
and why? For an illustration look at Acts 2:38-39. Look too
at the context of Christ's words (verses 16 and 17.)

3 Notice in verses 16-18 how the three Persons of the Trinity
all feature; at some points the titles seem interchangeable.
Try to think through the different roles or activities of the
Father, Son and Holy Spirit. For further clarification, see
Romans 8:3-4,11.

4 A Christian convert once wrote, "It became quite obvious to
me that by the Trinity, 'Father, Son and Holy Spirit,'
Christians meant one God in three Persons, and not three
separate deities." Discuss this in the light of John 17:11.

5 It is probably through Christian experience that the truth of
the Trinity is most easily understood (verse 21). How should
that affect the way in which we speak to inquirers about the
Trinity?

6 In your prayer time, use Ephesians 3:14-19 as an example of
a thoroughly Trinitarian prayer. Then end with "the grace"
of 2 Corinthians 13:14.

REFLECTION

A Read John 14:8-21. Go
through this passage carefully
and try to see how the
different persons of the
Trinity relate to one another,
both in who they are and
what they do.

B Why did God not reveal the
truth of the Trinity as clearly
in the Old Testament as he
did in the New? What does
this tell us about the way God
reveals himself?

C Read Exodus 3:1-6. What
can we learn from Moses'
response to God as we think
about the Trinity?

D The teaching of the Trinity
is much more than mere
discussion over certain words.
How can people make sure of
benefiting practically from
the teaching?

2. The Creator

God the creator

The universe has not always existed. The consistent teaching of Scripture is that the cosmos had a beginning. It was not formed from any matter that already existed. God, the one and only creator of the universe, brought the world into being by the unaided power of his word.

God did not need to create the universe, for he is self-sufficient. He decided to bring all things into being for his own glory. The creation involved all three persons of the Godhead. The opening chapter of the Bible records our beginnings in majestic and timeless language that communicates to every culture and era.

God the sustainer

The Bible teaches that God the creator is also the provider and sustainer of all that he has brought into being. He is not an absentee God who made the world and then left it to run itself.

Far from remaining aloof and remote from his creation, God continues to work in it. He is intimately involved in the running of the universe and the forces of nature, and he is in overall control of governments and communities. Christ also taught of the Father's concern for the least of his creatures.

God is achieving his purpose

God is in ultimate control of all that he has created. This does not mean that we are unable to decide things freely for ourselves. God has given us that freedom, even though we chose to rebel against him. But it does mean that God is active, and is bringing about the things he wants to happen.

He is achieving his purpose.

God's purpose may be stated very simply. It is to restore fallen humanity and the creation itself to the freedom and perfection that have been lost because of humanity's rebellion. God the creator is also God the redeemer.

Earth as a focal point

The earth is a very small planet in a vast universe, and it could not be argued that our world occupies any central position in creation. But it is apparent from the Bible that the creator of the cosmos has set his loving concern upon this earth.

As human beings we are physically dwarfed by the immensity of our surroundings, but the universe should hold no terrors for us, because of the place the world has in God's purpose. Ours is the visited planet, the part of creation where a special relationship has been planned between God and ourselves, who have been formed in his image. Human beings are central to God's plan for the whole universe.

BIBLE CHECK

Creator: Nehemiah 9:6;
   Hebrews 11:3; Genesis 1
Sustainer: Acts 14:17;
   Hebrews 1:3
Achieving: Daniel 2:20-22;
   Romans 8:18-25
Earth: Psalm 8:3-9;
   Revelation 21:1-3

KEY TRUTH

God has brought into existence the whole of creation, which he sustains and upholds by his power. He created the universe out of nothing, and did this for his own purpose and glory.

POSTSCRIPT

A person who is in rebellion against the creator will inevitably have a human-centred view of God and creation. The Christian learns to see creation as it really is, with God at the centre and in control.

BIBLE STUDY Genesis 1 and 2

Here is the grand "overture" to the Bible. It lays the first mighty plank of the biblical revelation, and we must remember Christ's words of Matthew 19:4-5 that by implication confirm these chapters, along with all Scripture, as coming from the mouth of God himself. Although it is hardly possible to do justice to these two chapters in a single study, the following questions may help to identify the main teaching:

1 What can you learn from these chapters about the God of creativity? Why is there no place in them for Pantheism (in which God and Nature are understood as identical)?

2 Someone has once said, "God's first rule is order." What are the indications here of a God of regularity?

3 What can be understood from chapter 1 about the God of variety? Concentrate on the occurrences of the word "separate". Note also the separation of the human race from the animal kingdom in 1:26, and the separating of ourselves into the two sexes (1:27 and 2:21-24).

4 Notice the establishing of the foundational one-day-in-seven principle in 2:2. How can this pattern of creation be preserved?

5 "The image of God", 1:27. How are we to understand this separation of ourselves from animals? Look on at verse 28, and 2:7. Compare with Psalm 8:3-9. Reflect on the personality of God, and how it is that we are not described as "which" but as "who".

6 There is much to be learnt here about the God of responsibility and our appropriate care of the environment. Read 2:8-17 and discuss.

REFLECTION

A Read Genesis 1, and think about its description of the world's beginnings. Where does this chapter place you, as a person, in the universe? See Psalm 8:3-8.

B The Bible gives us reasons to feel happy with ourselves as human beings, but also reasons to feel unhappy. Why is this?

C What features in our world do you most appreciate, and give thanks for?

D Why is the truth of creation important today? Is it enough to say that God is the creator, or should we regard the details of how he created important as well?

3. God's Being

God is everywhere (omnipresent)

God is the creator of nature and is therefore not to be confused with it (the mistake of the Pantheists). At the same time we should not separate God from his creation and think of him as absent (the mistake of the Deists).

The Bible teaches us that there is no place in creation to which we can go that will put us at a distance from God. He is present everywhere in the universe. We must be careful not to limit God in the way that he is present among us. He is present creatively in his works; he is present morally in the area of human behaviour; he is present spiritually among his people; he is present sovereignly in nations, governments and systems.

God is all-powerful (omnipotent)

The Bible gives us many examples of God's power. He brings the designs of powerful nations to nothing. He is in control of nature – and this comes out especially in the miracles Jesus performed.

However, all these instances might suggest to us that God is just a lot more powerful that we are. The fact that he is all-powerful is shown by his role as the creator of all things, the judge of all humanity, and the one who will subdue all the forces of evil. The Bible tells us he is the only God, and all power belongs to him.

God knows everything (omniscient)

God's knowledge follows from his universal presence. Because he fills heaven and earth, all things are open to his view and knowledge. He is completely aware of the past, present and future. He knows about all events, thoughts, feelings and actions.

The knowledge gained by other beings must be built up and learned. God's knowledge is eternal and is entirely his own – he has learned it from nobody.

This teaching is vital to our understanding of God. If God did not know everything, it would not be possible to believe in the justice of his judgements in history and at the end of time. This is also true in the realm of worship. The Christian prays to a God who fully understands our state and our needs, who hears and perceives not only our words but our secret thoughts and desires, and who knows the end from the beginning.

God is eternal and unchanging

The Bible describes God as the first and the last. He always has existed, and he owes his existence to no one. In contrast to the ever-changing and decaying world, the Scriptures teach us that God is unchanging in his person and purposes.

He neither increases nor decreases. He can never be wiser, holier or more merciful than he has ever been or ever will be.

For the believer, limited by a temporary body and a changing environment, the eternal God provides a permanent foundation and a secure home and resting place.

BIBLE CHECK

Everywhere: Psalm 139:7-12;
  Jeremiah 23:23-24
All-powerful: Genesis 17:1;
  Job 42:1-2; Jeremiah 32:17
Knows: Psalm 139:1-6;
  Hebrews 4:12-13
Eternal: Isaiah 44:6; Malachi
  3:6; James 1:17

KEY TRUTH

There are certain aspects of
God's being that are unique to
him, and can never be shared
with any other being.

POSTSCRIPT

These descriptions of God
only give us half of the biblical
picture of him. It is the moral
aspect of God which
completes the picture and
shows us that goodness is at
the heart of the universe.

BIBLE STUDY Psalm 139

"In its essential burden," wrote Dr Campbell Morgan, "this is
the greatest song in literature." Read the passage prayerfully,
and then try to take in something of the nature of the God we
follow, with the help of these questions:

1 The passage seems to be divided into four sections; verses
  1-6, 7-12, 13-18 and 19-24. Try to establish the dominant
  thought of each section. All of them point to some aspect of
  God.
2 "I", "me", "my". These words that run through the psalm tell
  us that God, in his different attributes, may be experienced
  personally. How did this happen for David? Compare, for
  example, verse 11 with 2 Samuel 12, especially verses 12-13.
3 We learn from verses 7-12 that there is no hiding place from
  God. Think first of a biblical example of this fact (eg Jonah
  1:3), then of some modern instances. Have you known of
  this experience?
4 Some modern theories about humanness maintain that
  person-hood does not belong to infants, either in the womb
  or newly-born. How does this psalm run counter to these
  theories?
5 Look at verse 19 onwards. Although we note that there is
  nothing actually personal about the psalmist's
  condemnation of the ungodly, there is evidently a challenge
  that he is obliged to face up to. What is it?
6 Look at the beginning and end of the psalm (verses
  1-4,23-24). Why is it such a tremendous discovery to learn
  of God's intimate knowledge of our lives?

REFLECTION

A Read Psalm 139:1-18. What
major truths about God are
expressed in verses 1-6, 7-12
and 13-18? How does the
writer see his relationship to
God? Try to list all that God
has done for him.
B How should our
understanding of God's being
affect the way that we pray?
After thinking about this,
turn to Psalm 139:23-24.

C Look at Deuteronomy
29:29. How do these words of
Moses help us in matters
where our knowledge (eg of
the future) is limited?
D Try and make the praises of
the apostle Paul your own, as
you worship God in the
words of Romans 11:33-36.

4. God's Character

God's truth is inseparable from his character

The truth of God is the foundation of all knowledge. Truth is unalterable.

It will not change or accommodate itself to varying cultures and standards. Truth is essential to God himself – it always has existed and always will exist.

Thus our existence is not a delusion, as some people claim, and the laws of the universe will not shift. Truth comes from God and is consistent with his character. We see this supremely in the person of Jesus, who as Son of God claimed to be the centre of all truth.

God's holiness reacts against all impurity

God is holy. There is no statement in the Bible which is more demanding than this. God's holiness means he is totally committed to goodness and is at war with evil.

The Bible teaches that God alone is completely pure and free from evil. As a result it is impossible for wrongdoers to live in God's presence until they have been made clean.

God's love extends to all humanity

The Scriptures are full of the love, mercy, grace and faithfulness of God. Human love is seen as an imperfect reflection of the love that characterises God.

This is the love that longs to pardon the evildoer while yet satisfying the demands of divine justice. Its highest expression is seen at the cross.

God's mercy holds back what we deserve

God's holiness and moral purity demand that those who revolt against his authority should face judgement and be overthrown. However, the Bible is full of examples of the restraining hand of God's mercy.

Thus the Bible shows us that God is slow to punish sin. He prefers to give people the opportunity to turn from wrong.

God's grace gives us what we do not deserve

The word "grace" means that "God is generous towards us even though we deserve his anger." There are two kinds of grace. On one level there is common grace where God's gifts in nature (the seasons, our natural abilities and human relationships) are given to the human race, regardless of the attitude of those who receive.

On a spiritual level we receive God's saving grace. He has given his assurances and promises to the human race throughout history, sending his messengers to raise the standards of societies and to free them from slavery to evil. Supremely, he has given his Son to the world so that the gift of eternal life might be freely available – to those who respond.

God's faithfulness provides for daily life

The writers of the Psalms constantly refer to the faithfulness of God, illustrated in the ceaseless cycle of nature and in the return of the morning each day. It is God's world and his resources are around us.

Humanity has to face danger and hardship in a world which is imperfect because of the intrusion of sin – and the Christian is as liable to face illness and testing as the non-Christian. But those with a trust in God are assured of his overall care and control of events.

BIBLE CHECK

Truth: Jeremiah 14:14;
  Numbers 23:19; John 14:6
Holiness: Isaiah 6:1-5;
  Habakkuk 1:13; Revelation
  15:4
Love: Psalm 103:13; John
  3:16; 1 John 4:7-11
Mercy: Nehemiah 9:16-17;
  Hosea 11:8-9; 2 Peter 3:9
Grace: Matthew 5:43-45;
  1 Corinthians 1:4-8;
  Ephesians 2:8-10
Faithfulness: Psalm 89:1-2;
  1 Thessalonians 5:23-24

KEY TRUTH

The truth, holiness and
goodness of God find
expression in his works and
actions, extending even to
those in rebellion against his
rule.

POSTSCRIPT

It is important to see all the
aspects of God's character.
If we only see God as holy,
he will appear harsh and
demanding. If we only see him
as loving, he will seem to be
unjust and powerless.

BIBLE STUDY Hosea 11:1-11

Here is the character of God, displayed within the great
romance of the Old Testament; his relationship with Israel.
The context is the broken marriage of the prophet Hosea.
Told by God to take back his wayward and now enslaved wife
Gomer, the whole prophecy revolves around the theme of love
that agonises between righteous judgement and free
forgiveness. It is, ultimately, God's dilemma with his people.

1 Begin with verses 1-4. How is God pictured here? What was
  the response to his attitude? Has the situation changed
  down the ages?
2 How would you summarise the result of turning from God,
  in verses 5-7? What is the challenge to modern-day
  Christians?
3 We come to the heart of Hosea's entire prophecy in verses 8
  and 9. (Admah and Zeboiim were two cities coupled with the
  immoral Sodom and Gomorrah. For their fate, look up
  Deuteronomy 29:23.) What is the dilemma that causes God
  such agony? Note, at the end of verse 8, that it is in the
  character of God himself that the solution is found, where
  righteous justice and forgiving love can meet. Look up
  Psalm 85:10; Romans 3:25-26; 1 John 3:1.
4 Like the faithless Gomer, Israel's sin would lead to slavery,
  but there was a way of restoration. Look at verses 10 and 11.
  Can you think of examples in Christian history when similar
  restorations and times of revival have taken place? What
  were the secrets of these revivals?
5 Reflect on the remark that God is the greatest sufferer in the
  universe.

REFLECTION

A Consider the teaching of
Psalm 103, and try to list
some of the qualities of God's
character that are featured
there. Which of these
qualities have you felt to be at
work in your own life?
B What is the biblical answer
to those of us who carry on
sinning, taking it for granted
that God will forgive us?
Consider your reply in the
light of Romans 2:4-5.

C What is the difference
between God's common grace
and his saving grace? Who are
the receivers of God's gifts in
each case?
D How can we best express
our gratitude to God for the
goodness that we have
received from him?

5. The Fatherhood of God

GOD IS FATHER:

By creation – of all things

Although the Bible never designates God directly as "Father of the creation", nevertheless his creativity is frequently linked with his character as Father. The universe is under his care and fatherly authority.

In the Scriptures God is portrayed as Father of human beings only in a general sense – because he created us. The close and intimate relationship that could exist between God and the individual believer was not fully revealed until it was taught and made possible by Jesus Christ. God is the Father of all people but only in a very limited sense. This is because of the universal rebellion against God's authority that has characterised the human race throughout history.

By covenant – of Israel

In the Old Testament, God initiated a solemn agreement with Israel by which he would be their God, the people of Israel would be his people and would submit to his rule and authority.

It was in this national sense that God became the Father of Israel, giving to his people guidance, protection – and discipline on the many occasions when he was disobeyed.

By adoption – of Christian believers

It was Jesus Christ who revealed the fatherhood of God towards believers in an intimate sense unknown in any other faith. He taught his followers to speak to God as their heavenly Father.

As the New Testament teaching develops we learn that salvation firstly includes giving the new believer forgiveness and the right to stand before God. But secondly, we are adopted into the circle of God's family with all the privileges that follow. Thirdly, and better still, we are given the spirit of sonship and a change of heart that encourages us to speak to God as a child would to its own father.

Such a relationship knows no human parallel. Those who have entered into such a relationship can truly be said to have been born of God. They are his children.

From eternity – of Jesus Christ

It is true that Jesus addressed God in his prayers as Father, but he never joined in prayer with his friends, nor spoke to them about 'our' Father.

The exception was the Lord's Prayer, but even then it was made clear that the prayer was for them to pray, not for himself.

Evidently, Jesus was God's Son in a way that the disciples were not. It is in the Gospel of John that the eternal relationship between the Father and the Son is most clearly seen.

BIBLE CHECK

Creation: Acts 17:24-29;
Ephesians 4:6
Covenant: Isaiah 63:16;
Malachi 2:10
Adoption: Romans 8:14-17;
Galatians 4:4-6
Eternity: Luke 11:1-3; John
20:17; John 17:5,24

KEY TRUTH

God is Father, generally, of the creation he has made. He is also Father to all Christians, whom he has adopted into his family. But uniquely, he is the Father of Jesus Christ.

POSTSCRIPT

Because of human weakness, we must distinguish between the standards set by our own father and God's perfect fatherhood. The fatherhood we have known, at its best, can only faintly mirror God's care and concern.

BIBLE STUDY Luke 11:1-13

This passage is one of the reasons why "Father" is the name by which Christian believers know God the best. It was Jesus, above all, who taught his followers to understand their relationship with God in a close and intimate sense that had never been understood before, and that knows no parallel in any other faith.

Use these questions to highlight this truth:

1 What was different about Jesus' praying that provoked the request of verse 1? Compare Matthew 6:5-8.
2 Father (verse 2). There was a Father term used of God in the Old Testament, but it was more of a national title. This new use of "Father" no longer puts us at a distance. It is a learnt truth. When did members of the group first begin to discover it?
3 The Lord's Prayer of verses 2-4 gives us a model or pattern for prayer, rather than a rigid formula. Try to identify the areas of faith and life covered by these petitions.
4 Look now at verses 5-8. Here is a cameo of life that demonstrates one massive point – that our heavenly Father is utterly unlike the man in bed. In what respects? What then should be our encouragements?
5 From verses 9 and 10, what main attitude should characterise our praying?
6 Verses 11-13 give us a yardstick from which to define true fatherhood. What does this say to a generation whose image of fatherhood has often become twisted in today's fallen world? Compare your findings with Ephesians 3:15. Then have some prayer together.

REFLECTION

A Study Galatians 4:1-7, which shows the contrast between slaves and sons (see verse 7). Trace, from verse 4, the processes by which the Christian has been made a child of God. What are the privileges that the Father gives to his children.

B How should our view of God as our Father affect the way that we pray? After thinking, check your reply with Matthew 7:9-11.

C How should you answer a person who wasn't a Christian who claimed that God was the Father of all, and that there was no need to worry about prayer, the Bible, or church?

D What do you think pleases God the Father most of all? What grieves him most? Compare your findings with Luke 15:11-24.

6. God's Revelation

GOD REVEALS HIMSELF:

Supremely in Jesus

Throughout history God has been communicating to humanity. In the Old Testament God sent messengers and prophets to speak his messages, but it is in Jesus Christ that his revelation is complete and perfect. This is why Jesus is called "the Word". He is the fullest way in which God has revealed himself to us. Jesus' life, his teaching and his character portrayed God perfectly for he was God living as a man.

Through the Bible

Through a unique collection of writings brought together over a period of about 1,500 years, God has made plain his plan for humanity, using people he guided to convey his message.

Some men were chosen to write selected history, others to communicate wisdom and worship, yet others to unfold the future, or to give instruction for belief and conduct. Every book has its individual way of showing us God, within the unity of the Bible.

Through creation

The whole creation proclaims the glory of God. The universe holds together and finds its logic in the Eternal Logos (the Word – God the Son). He is the Light that lights every person in the whole world. On Judgement Day nobody will be wondering who their judge is, because he has confronted us in everything around us all our lives.

In history

The Bible shows us how to understand history. God has revealed himself in a powerful way through history. God's plan is revealed in the rise and fall of great empires,

Egyptian, Babylonian or Roman. Jewish history is seen in the Bible as the means by which the Messiah would finally come.

Furthermore, it cannot be a coincidence that the beginning of the Christian faith took place at a historically stable time, when communications were excellent in the Roman Empire, and when there was one common language – Greek.

In humanity

God also reveals himself in the very way in which we are made up. Human beings are made in God's image, and this image, although distorted through deliberate rebellion, is not obliterated. As a result, human nature can point to the work of the creator.

Human complexity and creativity is a signpost of God's revelation, as also is the power of the human conscience, instincts and emotions. It is evident that people were made to enjoy relationships and these very relationships show the character of the God who made us.

Through human experience

God continues to speak to us in the present. His voice is heard in many ways: through human friendship, through the arts and through our appreciation of all that is beautiful.

Christ's followers are also given the Holy Spirit, who speaks both to individuals and churches, and who progressively transforms those who listen to him. In these ways God continues to reveal himself to us in the present.

BIBLE CHECK

Jesus: Hebrews 1:1-4;
John 1:1-18; 14:8-10
Bible: 2 Peter 1:19-21;
Romans 16:25-27
Creation: Psalm 19:1-4;
Romans 1:18-20; John 1:9
History: Psalm 75:6-7;
Daniel 2:44
Humanity: Genesis 1:26-27;
Psalm 139:13-16; Romans
2:14-15
Experience: 2 Corinthians
3:17-18; Revelation 2:29

KEY TRUTH

"Revelation" means that God
has spoken to us so that we
can understand him and
respond to his love.

POSTSCRIPT

The creation proclaims the
glory of God – but it is only
through the written and
spoken gospel that God
shows his power to save.

BIBLE STUDY Psalm 19:1-14

This psalm of David is concerned with God's revelation, or
declaration, of himself. It is impossible for our fallen race to
discover God unless he does declare himself to us. Study this
passage, with the help of the following questions:

1 From the first section (verses 1-6), we may learn about God's
general revelation of himself. How would you describe this
revelation to someone else? What is its power? What is its
limitation? For a New Testament parallel, look up Romans
1:20.

2 From God's general revelation, the psalmist turns to his
verbal and special revelation (verses 7-11). In what does it
consist? List the terms by which it is described.

3 In what ways is this special revelation superior to the voice
of nature? From these verses, try to itemise its effects upon
us.

4 What is the psalmist's response to what he has learnt from
God's revelation? Verses 12-14 give the answer. Apply what
you find to yourself.

5 Look up the New Testament quotation of verse 4 in Romans
10:18. There the apostle Paul clearly sets the verse within the
context of the New Testament gospel of Christ. What are the
great implications of this?

6 How do the words of God's writers and the wonders of the
universe relate to Christ, God's personal revelation? Look up
Hebrews 1:1-3. Now spend some time in prayerful
application of these truths.

REFLECTION

A Consider carefully 2 Peter
1:16-21. What were the two
ways in which Peter witnessed
the truth of Christ? What
encouraging features can you
find in this passage about
God's revelation? Compare
verse 19 with Psalm 119:105.
B According to Romans
16:25-27, what is the purpose
of God's revelation?

C Why does not everybody
accept God's revelation in the
various forms in which it
comes? What does his
revelation mean to you?
See 2 Corinthians 4:3-6.
D How do you explain
kindness and bravery in
people who have no belief in
God at all?

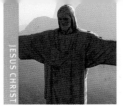

JESUS CHRIST
1. His Incarnation

Christ was Son of God before time and space

The Bible teaches that Jesus did not come into being when he was born, but that he has always existed as the Son of God. It was through him that God created the universe, and in him all things hold together.

It was by a supernatural conception

The circumstances of Jesus Christ's birth help us to understand that he was born without sin. The human bias to sin is inherited from our parents. Because of the unique conception of Jesus he was born without this bias.

While Christ's birth was as normal as that of any human, his conception occurred through the intervention of the Holy Spirit. Because of this Jesus was both God and man.

It upholds Christ's full deity

As the New Testament unfolds, the fact that Christ is God is increasingly revealed. The hints turn to signposts and the signposts turn to bold acclamation.

The signposts are: Christ's character (his sinlessness and purity), his claims (to be the centre of all truth, to be the world's judge, and to have a unique relationship to the Father), and his conduct (in performing miracles, forgiving sins and accepting worship).

It establishes Christ's full humanity

The New Testament shows that Christ was fully human born into a Hebrew family and subject to the Hebrew law.

He experienced all the problems that people have to face. He was exposed to hunger and thirst, fatigue and sorrow, and he faced the full force of temptation – yet without ever giving way. Although he was still fully God, Jesus (as a man) shared completely all human weaknesses. Because of this he was perfectly qualified to be the unique go-between, bringing humanity and God together.

It explains Christ's unique personality

Jesus Christ is without parallel, for he is both God and man, in two distinct natures, and one person for ever. It was the same Jesus who declared that he was thirsty, who also referred in a prayer to the glory which he shared eternally with the Father.

The New Testament writers do not try to explain as a philosophy how one personality could be both human and divine. But the portrait they give us identifies him both with human beings and with God.

It validates Christ's saving ministry

There are aspects of the incarnation that are beyond our understanding. But one thing is clear. We know enough to realise that in Jesus Christ, truly God and truly human, is found the one Saviour that the human race needs.

By laying aside his eternal splendour, and involving himself in humanity's burdens – even to the point of death on the cross for our sins – he becomes the reconciler between God and humanity, and by his resurrection he brings our humanity to heaven.

BIBLE CHECK

Before time: John 1:1-3;
Colossians 1:15-17
Supernatural: Matthew
1:18-25; 1 Peter 2:22;
Hebrews 4:15
Upholds: John 8:46,50-58;
Luke 5:20-21;
John 20:26-29
Establishes: Galatians 4:4-5;
Hebrews 2:14-18; 5:7
Explains: Matthew 8:24-27;
John 19:28; 17:5
Validates: 1 Timothy 2:5;
Philippians 2:5-11

KEY TRUTH

The word "incarnation"
means "to become human".
The New Testament tells us
that God became a human
being. This person, Jesus
Christ, was fully God and
fully human.

POSTSCRIPT

Errors have arisen in Christian
history when either Christ's
deity or his humanity has
been neglected. It must be
understood that in every way
he is fully God and fully
human.

BIBLE STUDY Colossians 1:15-20

The apostle Paul is writing, around the year AD 55,
to Christian believers in Colossae, a city situated in present-
day western Turkey. He writes from prison,
to counteract false teaching that threw doubt upon the
divinity of Jesus Christ. The following questions will help in
the understanding of this passage, and in a stronger grasp of
the nature of Christ.

1 This passage has been called the "Creed of Christ's Pre-
  eminence" (Handley Moule). As you scan these sentences
  what particular phrases in them point to such a description?
2 Try to understand Christ's relationship to creation. Why is it
  that the term "firstborn" (or "heir", verse 15) does not imply
  that Christ is a created being? Look carefully at verses 15-17
  and compare with Hebrews 1:2-3.
3 A university student once asked, "Is Jesus Christ the ultimate
  – or is there something yet bigger than him that I must
  seek?" This passage gave him his answer and he became a
  Christian. What is there in these verses that would have
  helped him?
4 In what sense may we say that Christ is the explanation and
  the goal of the whole universe?
5 There are those who will say, "Let us try to find the best from
  all traditions and reconcile them into a final, ultimate
  synthesis." How should we reply to this theory? Verses 19
  and 20 will help.
6 Establish from verse 18 the relationship of Jesus Christ to
  the church. Where is the one and only place that God will
  meet with us, and where we can find peace with him? What
  does this say to the message that we communicate to the
  world?

REFLECTION

A Consider Colossians
1:15-20. How does this
passage portray Christ in his
relationship to creation, to
the church, to God and to the
cross?

B People have argued over
almost every aspect of
Christ's incarnation. His full
deity and full humanity have
come in for particular attack.
Why do you think this is, and
what are the reasons for the
limit to our understanding of
this teaching?

C In what ways should we
follow the example of Jesus'
life as a man? See Hebrews
12:2-4 for one possibility.

D What do we gain from the
fact that Jesus is, like us, a
man? And what do we gain
from the fact that, unlike us,
he is God?

2. Main Events in the Gospels

His humble birth

Jesus was born, during the reign of the Roman emperor Caesar Augustus, into an extremely poor family. He was born in alien surroundings during a Roman census, and he was born into immediate danger – as King Herod searched to kill him.

These two elements, the humility and insecurity of Jesus' birth, were to set the pattern of his whole life.

His sinless baptism

The baptism of Jesus marks the beginning of his ministry. John the Baptist was calling his hearers to a baptism of repentance. Jesus, however, had no sin of which he could repent. But by his submission to John' s baptism, he showed his identification with sinful humanity. The descent of the Spirit like a dove and the Father's words of acceptance which accompanied the baptism came as God's approval of the ministry that was to follow.

His prolonged temptation

Immediately following his baptism Jesus went into the desert for a period of forty days during which he fasted, and was tempted by the devil.

The temptations that are recorded for us took the form of challenging Jesus to bypass his mission. Jesus successfully resisted these and all the other temptations that occurred throughout his life.

His revealing transfiguration

Towards the end of his public ministry Jesus took three of his disciples to a mountain-top where he became brilliantly irradiated before them. Moses and Elijah appeared and spoke

with Jesus about his coming ordeal in Jerusalem. The disciples also heard a voice of divine approval as at Christ's baptism. The event was clearly a preview in miniature of Christ's glory that lay ahead.

His obedient death

The tide of events turned against Jesus after his triumphant entry into Jerusalem. The Passover meal that he celebrated with his friends was swiftly followed by his betrayal, by a series of unjust trials, by death on a cross and by burial.

It was a dark hour but it was the hour for which Jesus had come into the world. He made it clear that he had come, not only to teach and heal, but also to suffer and die for all humanity.

His victorious resurrection

36 hours after the burial, Jesus' tomb was found empty, except for the discarded graveclothes. It was sufficient for John who "saw and believed".

Then Jesus began to appear to his friends over a period of 40 days. This was not an illusion, for he took food, could be touched, and was seen alive by hundreds of people. And yet he was uniquely and powerfully different – the victor over death.

His glorious ascension

The last time the disciples were to see Jesus was on the Mount of Olives. He commanded them to make disciples everywhere and he promised them the gift of the Spirit who would give them the power to do this.

He was then taken from them visibly. He would not be seen again until his return.

BIBLE CHECK

Birth: Luke 2:1-7; Matthew 2:1-18; Luke 9:57-58

Baptism: Matthew 3:13-17

Temptation: Matthew 4:1-11

Transfiguration: Luke 9:28-36

Death: Matthew 26 and 27; Luke 22:53

Resurrection: John 20 and 21; Luke 24:36-43

Ascension: Matthew 28:16-20; Luke 24:44-53

KEY TRUTH

The four Gospels present the reader with selected significant events in Christ's life. The events listed here are of particular importance.

POSTSCRIPT

It is rewarding to compare the accounts of Christ's life in the four Gospels and to see how the writers, from their differing viewpoints, complement one another.

BIBLE STUDY John 2:1-11

This passage follows the great first chapter of John, with its majestic teaching about the coming of Christ as the Word, as the life, as the light and as the Son.

The chapter ends with Jesus' prediction of heaven being opened and the angels of God ascending and descending upon the Son of Man. We would expect chapter 2 to take us into the realms of glory and the spectacular! But read on:

1 A tiny village in a very minor Roman province – together with a small crisis in a wedding reception. How can this be John's first "sign" of Christ's incarnate glory? Discuss this point.

2 If Mary, the mother of Jesus, had heard the ringing testimonies of chapter 1 (eg verse 49), it is possible that she spoke here, in verse 3, expecting Jesus to indicate that the hour of his emergence as Messiah had come. How then are we to understand Jesus' reply in verse 4? Compare John 17:1 and Mark 14:41-42.

3 Look at verses 5-10. How do these verses illustrate the truth that, through the Incarnation, Jesus takes hold of the ordinary, the ordinary becomes better – and the best is yet to come? What signal was being given to the disciples?

4 Can we learn something here about miracles and their purpose – from one who refused to turn stones into bread for himself. Who refused to perform miracles for Herod's benefit? Verse 11 gives a clue.

5 Not everybody got the point. The toastmaster can only joke with the bridegroom. "Fancy keeping the best wine until the end!" Why should this happen?

6 Look again at verse 11. Reflect on all that was to follow: the travels, the miracles, the transfiguration and the cross. What was this first revelation of Christ's "glory" hoping to achieve?

REFLECTION

A Read John 17:1-5. What exactly was the 'work' that Christ was given to do? How did the main events in his life contribute towards it?

B From what we know, how did Jesus prepare himself for his main work? How did he prepare his disciples?

C Jesus Christ had no home of his own, never travelled outside Palestine and never wrote a book. To what, then, do you attribute the impact that he has made upon the world?

D "If only Christ were on earth today." How do you react to this wish when it is expressed? Look at John 16:5-7.

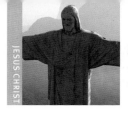

JESUS CHRIST
3. Main Aspects of His Ministry

Authority that convinced

The authority with which Jesus taught amazed the people who heard him. The prophets of old repeatedly declared "The Lord says ..." But Christ's frequent phrase was "But I say to you ..." He directed his hearers towards himself.

The Jewish leaders of Jesus' day took their authority from the great teachers of the past, but Christ taught in his own name and authority.

Parables that provoked

The teaching of Jesus Christ was given in terms and images understood in daily life, and this is particularly true of his unforgettable parables which both concealed and revealed truth.

People would often be captivated by the story of the Runaway Son or the Rich Fool, only to discover that the parable had been about themselves.

Miracles that confirmed

Christ's authority was further demonstrated by his miracles. The wind and the waves were obedient to his command, and even the dead were brought back to life.

But most of his miracles were acts of healing that were part of his mission of love. They also pointed to his identity as the Son of God and to the coming of God's kingdom.

Compassion that attracted

Christ's deep concern for people was born from his understanding that humanity is created in God's own image, but that we are also fallen and live in a fallen world.

Because of this Christ showed care and concern for the individual.

This can be seen in his many encounters with the bereaved, the sick and the demon-possessed. The crowds were quick to recognise the high value that Jesus placed on the individual, and they came to him in large numbers.

Training that prepared

Towards the beginning of the second year of Jesus' public ministry, the twelve disciples were chosen to share in his work of teaching, preaching and healing. These men learnt from Christ's example and from the private instruction he gave them. He also trained them for their future work as they (and some 70 others) were sent out two by two to do his work.

The twelve did not understand all that was being taught them at the time, but their training was to be vitally important in the future development of the church.

Controversy that challenged

From the outset the words and actions of Jesus had a controversial cutting edge that finally provoked a collision between himself and the Jewish authorities.

Jesus clashed with the Jewish leaders over the following issues: that he mixed with sinners, challenged traditions, liberated the Sabbath, and that he claimed to be God.

BIBLE CHECK

Authority: Matthew
5:21-22,27-28,31-34;
7:24-29

Parables: Mark 4:2; Matthew
13:10-17; Luke 15:11-32

Miracles: Mark 1:23-28;
John 10:31-33

Compassion: Matthew
9:35-38; 15:32-39; John
11:30-44

Training: Matthew 10:1-15;
16:13-21; 1 John 1:1-4

Controversy: Mark 2:5-7,15,
16; Matthew 23:13-36;
26:62-66

KEY TRUTH

Christ was unlike any prophet
or religious teacher that ever
lived. By his authority and
deeds and by the power of his
teaching and his example, he
challenged his hearers to
believe in him as the unique
Son of God.

POSTSCRIPT

It is a remarkable fact that
while Jesus directed his
hearers towards himself, he
never at any time gave the
impression of being
conceited, arrogant or selfish.

BIBLE STUDY Matthew 5:1-16

There were crowds around Jesus, but it was basically to the
"disciples" that he addressed the Sermon on the Mount, as it
has come to be called. Jesus is preaching a sermon, but he is
also painting a portrait of the ideal believer. He is further
planning a mission, as he goes on to teach in terms of "salt"
and "light". The following questions will help in the
understanding of the challenging radicalism of Christ.

1 Scan verses 1-12 to understand a little of how the values of
  Christ's kingdom directly collide with those of society.
2 Some have criticised the Sermon on the Mount as being
  beyond the average person. Now ask yourself whether it was
  ever intended for an "average" person! How different is the
  member of Christ's new society to be?
3 In verses 3-10, are these the differing qualities of eight
  separate people, or do they form a photo-fit of one person?
  Compare your findings with Galatians 5:22-23.
4 The qualities we are looking at are all inward in nature.
  Why?
5 If you are in a group, let each member "adopt" one of the
  virtues listed, and try to say, from what they already know of
  the Scriptures, what is meant by it, and how we would
  recognise its expression today.
6 What can be learnt from verses 11 and 12 about persecution
  of the believer; its cause, its history and our right reaction?
7 Verses 13-16 feature two illustrations of the outward and
  visible difference that Christians should make in society.
  Apply them to your own fellowship and church, and pray
  around them.

REFLECTION

A Consider Jesus' teaching in
Matthew 5:1-12. In what way
did his words overturn the
world's values? Try to list the
blessings that belong to the
members of Christ's
kingdom.

B How can a Christian best
put into practice that attitude
of Jesus to individuals? How
can this be done in your own
area?

C The true Christian cannot
avoid controversy. What
issues need to be faced at
present in the name of
Christ?

D What parable of Jesus has
spoken to you recently?
Discuss this with some of
your friends.

JESUS CHRIST
4. His Names

Son of God

As no one else, Jesus taught his disciples to think of God as their Father in a particularly intimate way. But because of his use of the terms "my Father'" and "your Father" it is clear that he saw his own relationship to the Father in a quite different way from that of his followers.

The Jewish authorities recognised this and accused Jesus of making himself equal with God. The term "Son of God" occurs most frequently in John's Gospel.

The Word

The Old Testament tells us that God created all things by his word. He spoke and it came to be. The apostle John shows that this word was in fact God's Son, without whom nothing would exist.

The Word is also involved in God's creation in another important way. He is the perfect expression of God to humanity. Because Christ is the Word, he did not merely bring us God's good news, but he is himself that good news.

High Priest

This title, given to Christ in the book of Hebrews, is drawn from the Old Testament system of sacrifices. A sacrifice had to be made every year by the High Priest on behalf of God's people to atone for their sins.

Christ, by his sacrificial death (never to be repeated) is the perfect mediator and High Priest.

Messiah

For centuries the Jews had looked for a future King who would be a descendant of David. This person was called the "Messiah" by the Jews (which in the Greek language is *Christos*, from which we get "Christ").

He would have God's authority and power to bring in the end of the age and establish the kingdom of God.

It was Simon Peter who made the first clear declaration that Jesus was the Christ, but it is important to note that Jesus totally rejected the popular idea of the Messiah as being a political deliverer from the Roman Empire. He saw his messianic role as one of suffering and death for the salvation of humanity.

Son of Man

Jesus used this name more than any other to describe himself. Although it seems to speak of his humanity, in reality it is a pointer to his deity, for the term is drawn from the book of Daniel, where the Son of Man rules an everlasting kingdom.

Jesus used the title in three ways – when speaking of his earthly ministry, his death and his coming glory. It is suggested that he favoured this title because it carried no nationalistic associations, it implied an identification with humanity, and it had both "overtones of divinity and undertones of humanity".

Lord

To call Jesus "Lord" was, in the New Testament church, the mark of a true Christian. To use this name invited opposition – from the Jewish authorities on the grounds of blasphemy, and from the Romans on the grounds of treason against the Emperor. This was the name that ascribed all authority to Jesus.

....

Son of God: John 20:17;
5:18,25; 20:31
Word: Psalm 33:6-9; John
1:1-4,14; Revelation
19:11-13
High Priest: Leviticus 9:7-8;
Hebrews 7:23-28
Messiah: Matthew 16:16,21;
John 4:25-26
Son of Man: Daniel 7:9-14;
Matthew 8:19-20; 20:17-19;
24:30
Lord: 1 Corinthians 12:1-3;
John 13:13; Philippians
2:9-11

KEY TRUTH

....

The many different names of
Jesus Christ reveal the
distinctive characteristics of
his person and the work that
he came to do.

POSTSCRIPT

....

The very fullness of Christ
defies human imagery and
thought. The six titles
described here are not the
only ones the Bible gives to
him. It is encouraging to list
the numerous other titles
given to Jesus.

BIBLE STUDY Revelation 19:6-16

This book. written in about the year AD 96, at a time when the
emperor Domitian tyrannised the Roman empire, has
encouraged believers, "the saints of God" down the ages, and
particularly at times of stress and opposition. It portrays the
victory of Christ, despite the terrifying ordeals that confront
his people. In this piece of futuristic writing, the apostle John,
alone in exile, has just described the end-time collapse of the
world of evil. Here Christ is identified through vivid imagery
and by a variety of titles. Be encouraged!

1 In verses 6-10, the rule of God is portrayed as supreme amid
   the acclaim of his people. What is the significance of the
   form of the celebration described?
2 The "Lamb" is also the bridegroom of his bride the church.
   What is so special about the Lamb? Compare Revelation
   12:11.
3 "Jesus" (verse 10). When did that name first begin to become
   important and treasured within your group? Reflect upon
   the world-wide family of believers who "hold to the
   testimony of Jesus".
4 The vision changes at verse 11. "White" consistently stands
   for purity and heaven in the book of Revelation. Think
   through the implications of following the Rider on the
   white horse (eg verse 14; see also verse 8)
5 Come now to the specific "names" of verses 11-16. There are
   four of them (verses 11, 12, 13, 16). What can be learnt about
   Christ himself from these four "names"? What caution
   should we be aware of. In what way should the unknown
   name of verse 12 caution us?
6 Spend some time in worship and intercession, applying the
   lessons of these and other names of Christ, as you pray.

REFLECTION

A Read Matthew 16:13-28.
Jesus praises Peter for
recognising him as Messiah,
but then forbids that the
identification be made public.
Why? In what other ways is
Jesus described in this
passage, and how does he see
his role?
B In what ways is Christ
superior to the Old
Testament priesthood? Look

at Hebrews 7:23-28.
C Why do we bother about a
title for Jesus Christ? What is
the danger today in simply
referring to him as "Jesus"?
Compare your answer with
Mark 13:5-6.
D Which, of Jesus Christ's
many titles, has meant a lot to
you? What new aspect of his
person has come to light
through this study?

5. His Atoning Death

CHRIST'S DEATH ...

Initiated a new relationship

The Bible teaches that human sin has created a barrier of guilt between him and his creator. However, Jesus accepted the responsibility for human sin and willingly took its penalty on the cross. The Bible calls this propitiation – Jesus became a sacrifice to turn away the anger of God. A new relationship is now available for those who respond to the good news that their sins can be forgiven.

Hostility has been replaced by friendship. Those who become united to Christ are viewed by God as though they had never been rebels at all. Indeed the Christian is seen as a new person altogether.

Fulfilled Old Testament Scripture

The Old Testament showed that God and humanity could not be reconciled unless a sacrifice was made. Only then could the guilt of sin be removed.

The Old Testament animal sacrifices could not in themselves take away sin nor could they be a final solution to the problem of sin. The New Testament sees them as illustrations of the perfect sacrifice Jesus was to make.

Destroyed Satan's kingdom

The power of Satan's kingdom was broken through the death and resurrection of Jesus Christ. The final destruction of the devil is yet to be. The Christian is aware of his activity and influence – but is confident of victory and protection through the power of the cross.

Reversed sin's dominion

In the Bible, the idea of redeeming (or "buying back") a person who is enslaved is very strong. Christ is presented as the one who, by his death, redeems his people from the penalty of God's moral law.

Because Christ has taken our guilt upon himself, sin no longer has the power to dominate the life of the Christian.

Provided a way of victory

With the power of the devil limited (and ultimately doomed) and with the guilt of sin removed, the cross of Jesus Christ has set the Christian free.

The Christian is not set free from the fight for moral purity – rather he is set free for the fight. The 'tenses' of salvation are as follows: we have been saved from the penalty of sin by a crucified Saviour; we are being saved from the power of sin by a living Saviour; we shall be saved from the presence of sin by a coming Saviour. From the cross onwards, the message is one of victory.

Guaranteed an eternity with God

The cross is the guarantee that God has set his eternal love upon his people; there could be no stronger demonstration than the death of his Son.

Death is still an enemy, but it is an enemy that is defeated because of the death and resurrection of Christ. Like the devil, death will face ultimate annihilation. The cross assures the Christian of a promised inheritance in God's eternal kingdom.

BIBLE CHECK

Initiated: 2 Corinthians 5:15-19; Romans 5:8-11
Fulfilled: Hebrews 10:1-12; Isaiah 53:4-12
Destroyed: Colossians 2:15; 1 John 3:8
Reversed: Galatians 3:13; Romans 6:6-11
Provided: 1 John 1:7-9; Titus 2:14
Guaranteed: Romans 8:31-39; Hebrews 2:14-15

KEY TRUTH

The word "atone" was coined by bringing the two words "at one" together. This expresses its meaning. By dying for the sins of the world, Jesus Christ has made it possible for all humanity to be made "at one" with God.

POSTSCRIPT

A great proportion of the four Gospels is taken up with the events surrounding Christ's death. The cross was not a tragic accident – it was the event to which Christ's whole life was directed.

BIBLE STUDY Matthew 27:32-56

Here is a passage, obviously the work of an eyewitness, stripped of all embroidery, yet notable for its sometimes ironic fulfilling of Old Testament prophecy. It was a very public death, watched by the soldiers (verse 36), visible to the passers-by (verse 39), to the religious hierarchy (verse 41), and witnessed by the centurion and many women (verses 54 and 55). As the passage is read, let the old spiritual raise the very personal question. Were you there, when they crucified my Lord?

1 Let each member of the group try and establish the central or key thought of the passage, and then compare notes. What is the biggest thing this passage is saying?
2 "Simon" (verse 32) was father of Alexander and Rufus, according to Mark 15:21. Does this mean that by the time of writing these two were already known Christians? Romans 16:13 gives us a further hint that this may be so. Ponder the effect that the cross would have had on Simon.
3 Let a member of the group read Psalm 22:1,7-8,14-18, and then discuss the bearing that this psalm has upon Matthew 27.
4 "If you are the Son of God" (verses 40,43). When had Jesus heard those words before? Look up Matthew 4:5 – was that a similar challenge to by-pass the ordeal of the cross? What was the irony of verse 42? Compare verse 40 with verse 54.
5 Read on about the death of Jesus and then reflect on verses 51-53, "when a shudder ran through nature" (Alfred Edersheim). What confidence do these events give us (compare Exodus 26:33 with Hebrews 10:19-22)? What did the cross do to death itself? See 2 Timothy 1:10. Now spend time in prayer and worship.

REFLECTION

A Read Matthew 27:32-54. Consider Christ's death in terms of its fulfilment of the Old Testament (for example Psalm 22).
B Just before he died, Jesus cried out, "It is finished!" (or "accomplished") – John 19:30. What was the significance of this saying? After thinking about this, read John 12:27 and 17:4.

C What is the best response that a Christian can make to the sacrificial death of Jesus Christ?
D In 1 Corinthians 1:18-25 we learn that the message of the cross is an offence to many. Why should this be so?

JESUS CHRIST
6. His Triumphant Resurrection

The foundation of the Christian faith

The resurrection of Jesus Christ lifts Christianity from the level of philosophy, or a mere code of conduct, to the supreme stature of God's good news for the human race.

In the resurrection God set his seal of approval upon Christ as Son of God, and underlined the value of his death. It was the resurrection that transformed the followers of Jesus, and sent them out into the world to preach the good news. The resurrection is the pivot of the Christian faith.

An event supported by evidence

If we enquire into the evidence for the resurrection, we are confronted first by the factual evidence. There is the empty tomb, containing only the abandoned grave clothes, and the persistent failure of all explanations other than that Christ had risen. Also to be faced are the numerous reported appearances of the risen Jesus, at different times and before different people.

There is also the psychological evidence. For example, there are the transformed disciples, the conviction of the early church in the face of persecution, and the change from Saturday to Sunday as the Christian day of worship (after centuries of Sabbath worship).

A promise of ultimate victory

If Christ had not been raised from the tomb, his death would have been evidence enough of the failure of his mission.

Thus the resurrection gives positive assurance that the Christian believer has not believed in vain. The mission of Jesus did not end in failure but in triumph. Ultimately all things, even the 'last enemy,' death itself, must submit to the victory and rule of Jesus.

The power of Christian experience

To the Christian, the resurrection of Christ is far more than a past event of history. It plays a vital part in Christian living in the present and colours the outlook, hopes and motives of every believer.

The New Testament teaches us that Christians must be ready to be like Jesus Christ in his life and death. This means that since we have died to self-interest (as Jesus died), it follows that we live a new life (as Jesus rose to new life). The Christian lives and works in the very power by which God raised Jesus from the dead.

The assurance of eternal security

Christ's victory over death has made immense changes in the area of sorrow and bereavement. The finality has been taken out of death.

All those who die can know that Christ has been through this experience before them, and will bring them through it to be with him.

Furthermore, because Christ's body was raised from death, the Christian has the guarantee that he too will receive in eternity a resurrection body of beauty and strength. This new body will be related to the old but without weakness or decay.

BIBLE CHECK

Foundation: 1 Corinthians
15:12-19; Romans 1:4
Event: John 20:1-29;
1 Corinthians 15:1-8
Promise: 1 Corinthians
15:24-28; Acts 17:30-31
Power: Philippians 3:10-11;
Romans 6:5-14
Assurance: John 11:25-26;
1 Corinthians 15:20,42-57

KEY TRUTH

The Bible says that God raised
Christ from the dead. By
doing this God declared that
his Son was the Saviour of the
world. The historical event of
the resurrection is also the
foundation of Christianity.

POSTSCRIPT

It is worth remembering that
Jesus would never have risen
from the dead so
triumphantly if he had not
first been willing to give up
his life. We only receive God's
new life when we give up the
control of our own lives.

BIBLE STUDY 1 Corinthians 15:1-11

The Christian faith welcomes every attempt to investigate, and
even "disprove" the resurrection of Jesus Christ; in many
instances, the attempt has resulted in the convincing of the
critic that the story is true. In this chapter, Paul expands upon
this key-stone of the apostolic gospel. The following questions
will help in an understanding of the passage selected.

1 From verses 1 and 2, how important are the truths that Paul
is writing about?

2 In verses 3-5, Paul is establishing the common ground of
belief throughout the church. Identify the four events listed
in these verses. What is significant about the fact that all
four events occur in a single sentence?

3 Stay with verses 3-5. How do they answer the theory that
Christ was only raised spiritually? What is the significance
of such phrases as "he was buried", "on the third day" and
"according to the Scriptures"?

4 How do verses 5-8 meet the hypothesis that perhaps the early
Christians were suffering from hallucinations?

5 Paul writes of his own change of heart and subsequent work
in the gospel (verses 9-11). What is the significance of the
four pronouns of verse 11 – "I", "they", "we", "you"? Why
should we not be satisfied with Scripture interpretations
that are out of harmony with each other – or even in
collision? What does belief in the bodily resurrection of
Jesus Christ do:

(a) to your view about your own future, and

(b) to your present lifestyle?

REFLECTION

A Consider 1 Corinthians
15:1-11. What are the main
points of emphasis in the
gospel proclaimed by Paul?
Try to list the evidences for
the resurrection put forward
by Paul, including the change
in himself.

B How has the message of
Christ's resurrection affected
your own view of death and
the future?

C On the evidence available,
what kind of body did Jesus
possess when he appeared
to his disciples after his
resurrection? Read Luke
24:39-43.

D Look at Galatians 2:20.
What does this mean, in
practical terms?

THE HOLY SPIRIT
1. His Person

He is the third person of the Trinity

The Holy Spirit is presented in the Bible as a person fully worthy of worship. Not only is he included in the Christian formula of baptism and in the apostolic blessing, but his works are described as the works of God.

He was associated with the work of creation; he gives the Christian new life; he is the source of all knowledge, the guide and helper of the church in all ages; and he makes salvation a real experience to individuals. Also, the apostle Peter equated lying to the Holy Spirit with lying to God (Acts 5:3-4).

When Christ had left the world, the Spirit was given his most specific work. The book of Acts (which is the account of the early church) portrays the Spirit as directing and controlling the new Christian movement.

He knows as a person (mind)

The Holy Spirit is more than a force; he is a person, with a character of his own. The Bible teaches that it is through the Holy Spirit that God knows us completely. It is the mind of the Spirit that helps to shape the life of the Christian.

Jesus declared that the Holy Spirit would remind the apostles of his words and teaching. The Spirit speaks (as in the letters to the seven churches of Revelation), intercedes and assures Christians that they belong to Christ.

He feels as a person (emotion)

Because the Holy Spirit is a person, it is no surprise to discover that he can feel emotion, as we understand the term, for human beings have been made in God's image.

As a result, it is possible to make the Holy Spirit sad. He can also be insulted – and therefore we must be careful, in what we say and do, not to insult the Spirit who lives in us. The Bible challenges us to bring glory to God by the quality of our lives and characters. In this way we will please the Holy Spirit.

He acts as a person (will)

The same Spirit who was involved in the creation, who equipped God's leaders in the past and inspired the prophets, is the Spirit who came in power upon the early church, and acted in it and through it. Throughout the Bible we can see his active personality.

For example, the New Testament shows us that he convicts people of their sins (as happened on the day of Pentecost). He leads and instructs Christ's followers. At other points in the New Testament he forbids certain courses of action and appoints leaders for the church. In such ways we see that the Spirit is a person who acts decisively in executing God's plans.

BIBLE CHECK

Third person: Matthew
28:19; 2 Corinthians 13:14;
John 15:26
Mind: 1 Corinthians 2:10-12;
John 14:26; Revelation 3:6
Emotion: Ephesians 4:30-31;
Hebrews 10:29
Will: John 16:8,13; Acts 8:29;
16:6; 20:28

KEY TRUTH

The Holy Spirit is the third
person of the Trinity. He
comes from the Father and
the Son, and is equal with
them. He is the one who
actively carries out God's will
and who works in the lives of
Christians.

POSTSCRIPT

The ascension of Jesus and the
coming of the Spirit at
Pentecost meant that
although Jesus was no longer
visibly and physically present,
the Spirit would be invisibly
present with God's people
everywhere. Christ now comes
to every believer through the
Holy Spirit. In having the
Holy Spirit, we have Christ.

BIBLE STUDY John 14:15-27

Jesus is comforting his disciples and preparing them for the
time when, after his death, resurrection and ascension, he
would be bodily absent from this world. The disciples were
apprehensive, but Jesus has good news for them in his
reassuring teaching about the coming of the Holy Spirit. Use
the following questions to pinpoint the great truths he was
giving to them – and to us!

1 Look at verses 15-17 and reflect on the fact of all three
Persons of the Trinity being identified within a single
sentence. Where else in the passage do all three Persons
feature together?
2 What can we learn from the titles given to the Holy Spirit
in this passage? Counsellor, Spirit of Truth, Holy Spirit?
Why is it not correct to speak of the Holy Spirit as "It"?
3 Jesus has already spoken of his impending bodily departure.
How then are we to understand his words in verse 18? What
is the great encouragement that we may draw from these
words?
4 Who can receive the Holy Spirit? The answer is in verses
15,17,21,23 and 24. What is the state of the disobedient and
the unbelieving? Look up 1 Corinthians 2:14.
5 What reassurance was given to the apostles in verses 25 and
26 for their future responsibility in proclaiming and writing
the truth as it has come to us today.
6 Acts 2 reminds us of the historical fulfilment of Jesus'
teaching here. From Pentecost onwards forgiveness and the
gift of the Spirit would be granted to all who repented and
turned in faith to Christ. When did this first occur for
members of the group? See Acts 2:38-39.
7 John 14:27 is worth learning by heart. Learn it, with the
correct reference.

REFLECTION

A Turn to John 16:5-15. It
might have been imagined
that Jesus' departure would
be a disadvantage for his
people. Why is this not true?
From this passage, try to list
the advantages of Christ's
physical absence.
B When were you aware, for
the first time, that God the
Holy Spirit was acting in your
life? Compare your experience
with others.
C Why do we find that so
many Christian people focus
on Christ rather than the
Spirit? How do you react to
this? See John 16:14.
D How far is it possible for a
Christian to know when the
Holy Spirit has been pleased
or displeased by certain acts
or deeds?

THE HOLY SPIRIT
2. His Names and Descriptions

HIS NAMES

The Holy Spirit

The third person of the Trinity is best known by this name. It was the name used by Jesus in his final words of promise to his disciples, and by Peter in his sermon on the day of Pentecost. The name conveys the Spirit's holiness and opposition to sin.

The Spirit of God

This title is used many times in both Old and New Testaments. It signifies both that the Spirit is God, and that he has God's power. Jesus claimed it was by the Spirit of God that he confronted the demonic world of his day.

The Spirit of Christ

This title brings great comfort and assurance to Christians, because it shows us that Christ was true to his word by not leaving his followers desolate when he ascended to heaven. The Spirit was sent in fulfilment of Christ's promise: "I will come to you."

The Spirit of Truth

The apostles were assured that the Holy Spirit would enable them to remember Christ's teaching and lead them into all the truth. The reader of the Bible may be thankful for its trustworthy, divine authorship.

The Counsellor or Helper

The literal meaning of the term "Counsellor" is one who comes alongside. This name is reassuring for Christians facing temptation, doubt, demanding service or opposition.

HIS DESCRIPTIONS

Wind

This vivid description of the Spirit's activity is used often in the Bible. There is Ezekiel's vision of the dry bones being given new life; there are Christ's words to Nicodemus in John 3, and the sound of rushing wind at Pentecost. The key ideas conveyed are mystery, sovereignty and energy.

Water

The chief reference to the Spirit's work as water comes from some words Christ spoke. Jesus talked about streams of life-giving water flowing from those who believe in him. He was clearly talking about the life-giving activity of the Holy Spirit.

Fire

Malachi predicts the coming of God's messenger in terms of refining fire, and this picture is picked up in the New Testament. John the Baptist said Jesus would baptise with the Holy Spirit and with fire. It is possible that the tongues of flame at Pentecost were to show the Spirit's refining activity.

Oil

In the Old Testament, anointing with oil was a sign that God had chosen someone for a particular task, so priests or kings were set apart for God's service. The Bible tells us that Jesus was "anointed" by the Spirit, and this is also true of his followers.

Dove

The Spirit, in the form of a dove, descended on Jesus at his baptism. While Jesus undoubtedly possessed the Spirit already, this event pictures the gentleness associated with the dove. This gentleness would characterise Christ's work.

BIBLE CHECK

KEY TRUTH

The character and activities of the Holy Spirit are emphasised through the various names and descriptions by which he is known.

POSTSCRIPT

We must be careful not to press these images of the Spirit's work into being anything more than helpful pictures.

BIBLE STUDY Acts 2:1-21

"Pentecost" has had a new meaning ever since this passage was written by Luke. Until then it represented the Jewish "Harvest Festival", which took place just 50 days after the start of the Passover (Greek *penteconta* – fifty). But for New Testament believers "Pentecost" is the day associated with the giving of the Holy Spirit in full to all who repent and turn in faith to Christ. Use these questions in the exploration of this truth.

1 Try to picture the scene described in verses 1-4. To what degree was this experience foreseen? Let different members of the group look up Joel 2:28-32; Ezekiel 36:26-27; John 16:7-10; Acts 1:5.

2 What attributes and activity of the Holy Spirit are conveyed to us by the symbols of "wind" and "fire"?

3 Pentecost has been described as a unique event, a saving event, a universal event and an evangelistic event. How would you understand this from the passage?

4 What is the significance of the miracle described in verses 5-12? What can be learnt by comparing this event with that described in Genesis 11:8-9?

5 What has Pentecost achieved for you, in your relationship to Christ's disciples across the world?

6 Evidently, we are to understand "the last days" (verse 17) as referring to the period immediately following Christ's earthly ministry. How should this realisation affect (a) our priorities, (b) our prayers?

REFLECTION

A Read Acts 2:1-13. What impressions do you gain from this account? What three signs indicated that the era of the Holy Spirit had begun for the church? In what ways was Pentecost unique? What makes it the secret of the church's life?

B Which of the names of the Holy Spirit do you warm to most in your experience? Why?

C Single out one or more of the Holy Spirit's qualities, suggested by his description, and turn your discovery into prayer or thanksgiving.

D At Pentecost, the apostle Peter links the gift of the Spirit to the gift of forgiveness (Acts 2:38-39). What may we learn from this about Christian communication?

THE HOLY SPIRIT
3. His Work

He convinces of sin

Because the Holy Spirit knows as a person, it follows that the lives of individuals are open to his scrutiny. Our needs can be fully met by him, for he is God.

As Spirit of truth, his work is to convince the unbeliever of being wrong. This is not achieved by human means – it only takes place as the Holy Spirit makes the message of the Bible a living force in a person's heart and conscience. In this way, the Holy Spirit opens the eyes of men and women to their true spiritual condition.

He illuminates truth

As it was the Holy Spirit who inspired the writing of God's word, so it is he who shows us what the Bible means. He makes the words of the Bible understandable and relevant to our lives.

Without the enlightening work of the Holy Spirit, the truth of God's message remains misty, and can even appear nonsensical or offensive.

He reveals Christ

The apostles were taught that when the Spirit came in power upon them, his task would be to focus the spotlight, not on himself, but on Christ.

This is the pattern of Christian experience. From Pentecost, the disciples became aware, not so much of the Spirit who was now controlling their lives, but of Christ and his love. It was indeed the Spirit of Christ who now ruled them.

He lives in believers

The Old Testament recognises that the Spirit works in a selective way, limiting his activity to certain individuals and tasks. But the prophets predicted a coming time when God would put his Spirit permanently within the lives of all his people. This prediction was finally fulfilled on the day of Pentecost.

The apostle Paul writes of Christ making his home in the hearts of his disciples, for it is the Spirit's work to make Christ real to the Christian. No one who belongs to Christ is without the Spirit. He empowers and equips us for the whole of life.

He inspires prayer

Because the Spirit is the Counsellor or Helper, we may look to him for assistance in all forms of Christian service and spiritual warfare.

In particular, the Spirit helps us to pray, because he understands our weaknesses. He prevents prayer from degenerating into mere mechanical drudgery or powerless routine.

He prepares for heaven

The entire Christian life is a life that is directed by the Spirit. The Christian has been set free from the control of sin, and God no longer judges him for it. However, although sin no longer controls, the disciple of Christ faces a life-long battle to develop a holy character.

It is the Spirit who helps a Christian in this battle and prepares him for the glory of heaven.

BIBLE CHECK

Convinces: John 16:8-11;
Ephesians 6:17;
Hebrews 4:12
Illuminates: John 14:25-26;
16:13; 1 Corinthians 2:12-14
Reveals: John 15:26; 16:14;
Acts 7:55
Lives: Ezekiel 36:26-27;
Ephesians 3:16-17;
Romans 8:9-11
Inspires: Romans 8:26;
Ephesians 6:18
Prepares: Romans 8:1-4,
16-17; 2 Corinthians 3:18

KEY TRUTH

The Holy Spirit is mainly
featured in the Bible for his
work in the lives of men and
women.
He is responsible for all the
activities listed here.

POSTSCRIPT

It is vital that we do not
underestimate what takes
place when the Holy Spirit
enters a person's life and
personality. All Christian
growth happens because of
him.

BIBLE STUDY Romans 8:1-17

The eighth chapter of Paul's letter to the Romans is loved by
believers everywhere. One ancient writer observed, "If Holy
Scripture was a ring, and the epistle to the Romans a precious
stone, chapter 8 would be the sparkling point of the jewel."
Chapter 8 is a reassurance for the Christian who, having read
in the earlier chapters of all that God has done for us, is faced
with the unhappy realisation that we still sin, and we still die.
Has anything really changed, then? Paul makes the point that
there is a change.

1 In verses 1-4, how would you describe the new situation that
makes life "livable" for the believer?

2 Try to identify some themes that run through this chapter:
Life and Death, Spirit and Flesh, Sinful Nature, Past and
Future.

3 How do you make sense of these themes? We love Romans 8,
but we are not always quite sure why! Try to see from these
verses how the whole sweep of our lives and our discipleship
is taken into account and provided for by the work of God.

4 The work of God – through all three Persons of
the Trinity. Where, in this passage, do we learn that:
(a) through the saving act of Christ we can face death,
(b) through the indwelling work of the Spirit we can face
evil, and (c) through the accepting love of the Father we can
face the future? What is so special about verse 11?

5 The Spirit is at work in the believer – but what is our
responsibility? See, for example, verses 5,12-13.

6 When were you first aware of experiencing the truth of
verse 16?

REFLECTION

A Look at Romans 8:1-17,
which gives teaching on life
in the Spirit. List what is
accomplished by the Holy
Spirit. What is our duty
(verses 12-17)? And what are
our privileges?

B If Christian discipleship is
governed by the Spirit, what
is there left for us to do? Is
Christianity an active or a
passive affair? Check your
answer with Philippians
2:12-13.

C What attitude should we
have towards those who do
not appreciate, or respond to,
God's love? What is likely to
bring a change in their
outlook?

D How may our resources
for living be described?
Compare your answer with
2 Corinthians 4:16.

THE HOLY SPIRIT
4. His Activity in the Christian

Life – new birth by the Spirit

Without the power of God, an individual is considered to be 'dead' spiritually. He shows no signs of life as far as God is concerned. The Bible teaches that the gift of new life is available because of the death of Christ on the cross.

This new birth is brought about by the Holy Spirit in the life of a person who responds to the good news of Christ. According to the Bible, that person can be described as a new being and an inheritor of God's kingdom. The new birth is not earned by personal achievement – it is God's free gift.

Assurance – the witness of the Spirit

The Holy Spirit comes to assure the Christian of the reality of his new relationship with Christ. He confirms that Christ's death will always be sufficient to provide complete forgiveness for sins.

He also confirms that the new believer is a child of God, and that the Bible's promise of eternal life is to be believed. The changing life and desires of the new Christian are a part of this inner witness by the Holy Spirit.

Unity – fellowship in the Spirit

Every Christian has received the Holy Spirit, and is said to have been "baptised in the Spirit". "Baptism" includes the ideas of entrance and membership. The Christian is brought into the life of the Spirit at conversion and is united to all other Christians in the body of Christ's church.

Ownership – the seal of the Spirit

The presence of the Holy Spirit in a person's life is the invisible yet permanent stamp of God's ownership upon that life.

Two ideas are present here. First, we belong to God and therefore cannot be separated from his love. Second, we are given the guarantee that God will keep us securely. Eventually, God will claim his own people finally and completely.

Power – the fullness of the Spirit

Christians are commanded to be filled with the Spirit, as a continuous and regular experience. This is not something that only happens once. We are filled with the Spirit so that our lives may be holy and our work for Christ effective. To be filled, we must obey God and submit to his rule; we must turn from evil daily and depend upon God's power; we must give ourselves in the service of other people.

Confidence – the pledge of the Spirit

The Bible teaches that the Holy Spirit is given to the Christian as a foretaste of all that God has prepared for his people in the future.

As we experience a small part of the fullness of life that God will one day give us, the Holy Spirit encourages us to press on. He makes us more confident about the future God has planned for us.

BIBLE CHECK

KEY TRUTH

From the beginning of our
Christian discipleship, the
Holy Spirit lives within us. He
gives us the power to follow
Christ, confidence in
believing, and unity with
other Christians.

POSTSCRIPT

A great deal of our life in the
Spirit consists in living out
and developing what God has
already given us.

BIBLE STUDY Ephesians 3:14-21

Until now, in this letter to the Ephesian Christians, the apostle
Paul has been explaining how salvation through Jesus Christ
has been extended to non-Jews – Gentile believers. They have
been adopted into God's family and have received from him
an eternal inheritance. They have been made alive in Christ
(chapter 2), and now, with all God's people are no longer
treated as "foreigners", but as fellow citizens in God's
household. Now follow his prayer for these Gentile Christians.
These questions will help in understanding it.

1 Here is a prayer that simply pours out of Paul's spirit. What
are the give-away phrases and words that reveal Paul's
deepest desires for his Christian friends?

2 What parts of this prayer indicate its "Trinitarian" content?

3 Where does the prayer imply that to have the Holy Spirit in
our lives is the same as having Christ in our lives? Why is this
so? Compare John 14:17-18 and Romans 8:9.

4 Do all these phrases amount to no more than a hot-air
balloon? Try and tie some of them down. For example, if by
"his glorious riches" Paul means what God has already
bought for his people through Christ, then what is this?
Look back a little in this letter to 1:5,7,9,11,13-14.

5 Notice the word "power" (three times). In many non-
Christian philosophies, this is regarded as something to do
with the tangible or sensational. What are the indications in
this letter that Paul is referring to a moral and character-
transforming power, a power for effective service of others?
Look at 4:11-12,22,32.

6 Study the "doxology" (verses 20,21) and allow your
expectation to rise, as you now turn to prayer for the
Christian fellowship.

REFLECTION

A Read Paul's prayer in
Ephesians 3:14-21. What is
the "power" that he desires
for his friends? Where does
this power come from, and
what will it do for us?

B Look at verse 20 of the
same chapter. What instances
can you recall in Christian
history, or from your own
experience, that illustrate
these words of Paul?

C Which of the different
blessings of the Holy Spirit
has meant the most to you?

D Why is there no instance in
the Bible of any individual
claiming publicly to be filled
with the Spirit – although
this was sometimes stated
about an individual by those
who knew him? Read Acts
6:1-6.

THE HOLY SPIRIT
5. His Fruit

Love

Christ said that his "new" commandment was that we should love one another. It was new because the love he had in mind was modelled on his own – a selfless, sacrificial and practical love that is revolutionary in any age.

Joy

The person who is reading the Bible for the first time will be surprised to find that joy and persecution go hand in hand in numerous instances (eg Matthew 5:11-12; Acts 5:41; James 1:2-3; 1 Peter 4:12-14).

This kind of New Testament joy is totally independent of circumstances. It is the joy of Christ's reign in our lives, inspired by the Spirit.

Peace

The peace which "passes all understanding" was described by Jesus to his disciples as "'my' peace". It does not mean the absence of trouble, but the deep peace that protects the life that is hidden in Christ.

Patience

The apostle Paul longed for the readers of his letters to be tolerant and patient in the face of each other's faults. Peter pointed to the example of Christ's endurance and patience under suffering. The strongest kind of patience comes only from Christ.

Kindness

Wherever the Spirit of Christ is involved in a situation or person, kindness will be seen in action. We can see Christ's unique brand of kindness in his parables, in his breaking of conventions to help the outcast, and in the value he placed on the individual.

Goodness

It was the transparent goodness of Jesus that drew people to him long before his true identity was known. Goodness is love in action. It expects no rewards, and it stems from a heart of purity and openness. It points other people to God.

Faithfulness

God delights to give his servants responsibilities. As we are faithful in the small tasks God gives us, he will trust us to do greater things. The Bible reminds the Christian servant of the final day when the faithfulness of his service will be assessed.

Gentleness

Once again, the Bible shows us that true gentleness was seen in Jesus Christ. In the face of extreme provocation he never lost control and never flaunted his immense power. His disciples needed to learn this quality – notably James and John (Luke 9:51-56).

Self-control

Excess and a lack of discipline result from moral weakness, while self-control is a sign of strength and growth in character. Paul said that we should be like athletes, who go into strict training before a sporting event. Thus, when the Spirit is in control, we experience the difference he makes.

BIBLE CHECK

Love: 1 Corinthians 13
Joy: 1 Peter 1:3-9
Peace: John 14:27
Patience: 1 Peter 2:23
Kindness: Titus 3:1-5,8
Goodness: 1 Peter 2:11-12
Faithfulness: Matthew
  25:14-30
Gentleness: Matthew
  11:28-30
Self-control: 1 Corinthians
  9:24-27

KEY TRUTH

It is the work of the Holy
Spirit to transform our
characters. The qualities listed
here are developed in us by the
Spirit and are taken from
Galatians 5:22-23.

POSTSCRIPT

We should recognise that
natural gifts in the Christian
are enhanced, rather than
diminished, by the work of
the Holy Spirit.

BIBLE STUDY Galatians 5:13-26

Paul the apostle is writing to the Christians in what was
probably the south of present-day Turkey, around the year AD
48. He is aware that because of false teaching, his readers are in
danger of slipping back into a sub-Christian gospel that is no
gospel at all (Galatians 1:6-7). This would also affect the
character and behaviour of the church. Read the passage and
try, with the use of these questions, to understand more of
how the Holy Spirit produces Christ-like living.

1 Having read the passage, identify the two "combatants" at
  war in the life of the believer. They are named some five
  times. How aware are you of this conflict? When did you
  first become aware of it?

2 In what way does this passage contradict the theory that
  when someone becomes a believer and receives the Spirit,
  the fallen nature that they were born with is killed off or
  "eradicated"?

3 Is it a good sign, then, or a bad sign, when a new Christian is
  aware of temptation and conflict?

4 Now identify the two opposing lifestyles in this passage. The
  "acts" of verse 19 affect what realms of behaviour? And the
  "fruit" of verse 22 affect what areas of relationship?

5 Now identify the two contrasting daily attitudes that should
  characterise the believer in regard to the sinful nature and
  the Spirit. See verses 24 and 25.

6 How does this affect the discipline of the Christian?

7 Discuss how the fruit of the Spirit is produced in
  our lives – naturally (John 15:4-5), willingly (John 15:3-7),
  painfully (John 15:2).

REFLECTION

A Read and think about
1 Corinthians 13. Why is love
of this kind so vital, and so
revolutionary? How may it be
developed in an individual –
and in a fellowship?

B Go through Galatians
5:22-23 and discover whether
these qualities can be
grouped under different
categories. For example, fruit
relating to God, to others, etc.

C Try to list some people in
the Bible who had obviously
developed one or more of the
fruit of the Spirit.

D Why do the Bible
translations that mention
"fruit" in Galatians 5:22, not
make the word plural –
"fruits"? How does the
Christian develop these
qualities – one by one, all
together, instantaneously,
painfully?

THE HOLY SPIRIT
6. His Gifts

The gifts exalt Christ

While the "fruit" of the Spirit is concerned with character, the gifts of the Spirit relate to abilities and functions distributed among believers. All the fruit should be exhibited in every Christian but the gifts differ widely from person to person.

The hallmark of spiritual gifts is that they glorify Christ. The Holy Spirit was sent for this very purpose – to illuminate the Lordship of Jesus.

The gifts involve all

Four passages of Scripture list some of the gifts: Romans 12:6-8; 1 Corinthians 12:8-10; Ephesians 4:11-12; 1 Peter 4:10-11.

It is significant that the gifts of the Spirit are not restricted to outstanding individuals, or leaders in the church. Each believer has at least one gift, and these gifts are to be discovered and developed, for all God's people are to be involved in Christian ministry and service of some kind.

The gifts should unite all

The church of Christ is likened to a body, composed of many limbs and parts, each part relating to the whole.

The individual believers, then, should see the abilities and functions that God has given them as gifts available for the whole body. In this respect, Paul had to correct the divided Corinthian church.

Gifts lay foundations

The church of Christ is also likened to a building, built upon the unique and powerful ministry of the apostle and prophets, Christ himself being the stone that holds the whole building together.

The gifts which characterised the apostles may not be in evidence today in the highest sense of those callings, but there are Christians who in a secondary sense have been sent (as were the apostles) to establish the church across new frontiers, or who speak to the church in relevant terms (as were the prophets) to encourage and build it up.

Gifts build up the fellowship

There is a great variety of spiritual gifts featured in the New Testament. The Christian is to make careful use of every gift received, to build up harmony and unity in the fellowship.

It is important that individual believers are not jealous of the gifts of others, nor insist on the superiority of their own. As we use God's gifts, we should be humble and look for ways in which we can serve others.

Gifts promote mission

The gifts of the Spirit are given for more than building up the church – they are given to widen its boundaries.

However corrupt and challenging their environment, Christ's followers are called – individually and collectively – to use their gifts in proclaiming the good news, vigorously cooperating with the Spirit of God, making mature disciples.

BIBLE CHECK

Exalt: 1 Peter 4:10-11; John 16:14
Involve: 1 Corinthians 12:7-11
Unite: 1 Corinthians 12:12-26; Romans 12:4-5
Lay: Ephesians 2:19-22
Build up: Ephesians 4:11-13
Promote: Colossians 1:27-29; 1 Corinthians 14:24-25

KEY TRUTH

The Holy Spirit distributes among Christians a variety of spiritual gifts, which are to be used for the building up of Christ's body, the church. No believer is without a gift.

POSTSCRIPT

Everyone has "natural" gifts from birth, which are given by God. By giving these back to him, these can be enhanced and made use of by Christ as we learn to follow him.

BIBLE STUDY 1 Corinthians 12:4-20

Paul again! Here he is writing to the Corinthian Christians who, of all the New Testament churches, were the most unruly and confused; worldly (3:1), immoral (5:1) and divided (11:17-18). They were confused over virtually every aspect of Christian living. Now the apostle is trying to correct their thinking about the gifts of the Spirit. We have, then, to read between the lines a little in this passage, as we try to understand the main emphasis that the apostle is making.

1 What point is being made by the three-fold use of the words "same", "all" and "one" in verses 4-6,8-9,11?

2 What is the overall purpose of gifts, imparted by the indwelling Spirit of God, in the life of the church? Verse 7 gives the clue. How far is this recognised as the purpose of gifts among the believers in your church or fellowship?

3 It is obvious that the Corinthians were familiar with certain gifts of a miraculous nature. What does Paul say about the origin of these gifts? Where are they in evidence? How does he regulate their use in public, particularly their speaking in tongues? (14:26-28).

4 Look on at verses 12 and 13. "Many" ... "one". How should a church apply the idea of the "body" of Christ to itself?

5 In verses 14-20, what is the great lesson that believers across the ages need to take to heart?

6 Encourage group members each to look up other lists of 'gifts' in the New Testament; Romans 12:6-8, Ephesians 4:11-13, 1 Peter 4:10-11. Speaking gifts, prophetic gifts, serving gifts, administrative gifts; now spend time in prayer, giving thanks for the gifts and dedicating them back to the Giver.

REFLECTION

A Look at Romans 12. What does Paul teach us about the way in which we use our gifts, and our attitude to other Christians? What difference should this make to your local church?

B What is the best way of discovering what your gifts are, as a Christian? How can other Christians help you to do this?

C How far is your own fellowship using the gifts of everyone to promote Christ's mission in the world? Identify any gifts that are being neglected in this respect, and that can be encouraged.

D Why do certain abilities or gifts sometimes cause problems for a church, as they seem to have done at Corinth?

1. Our Uniqueness

HUMANITY IS:

A whole being, physical and spiritual

The Bible teaches that all humanity has a common origin and nature.

We were created as intelligent beings and we are recognised as the head of all living things. As such, humanity is to govern the earth and to use its resources responsibly.

Because of humanity's place in creation, God made us as physical beings, completely involved in God's world. But humanity is not merely physical. We also have a spiritual dimension – we can be fully aware of God and all that he demands. These two dimensions, physical and spiritual, make up the whole person.

This description of humanity is given in the biblical account of creation, which, in its scope, simplicity and dignity is without parallel anywhere in literature.

A spiritual being, made in God's image

What characterises humanity as unique is our creation in the image and likeness of God. We possess a similar nature to God and we are therefore capable of a relationship with our Maker.

Because humanity is made in God's image, this does not mean that we are God, or even that we are a part of God. The Bible clearly teaches that humanity is distinctly different from God. Therefore humanity is not God in disguise, nor are we an 'incarnation' of God. But there is in us a key element that sets us apart from, and above, the rest of creation. We have been made to love God, to worship him and to enjoy his company.

A personal being, with mind, emotion and will

Humanity is not only made for God. We are also made for a variety of personal and loving relationships within the human family – this shows how human life is to be the image of the loving relationship between the Father, Son and Spirit. The human spirit reveals qualities of tenderness, loyalty and self-sacrifice. We are capable of original thought and of intelligent choice. We are aware of ourselves, capable of humour, sorrow, or hatred. We appreciate beauty and enjoy recreation.

These qualities of humanity show that we are not mere animals or machines. Our instincts, affections and aspirations prove that we are far removed from being a mere collection of chemical reactions. The Bible recognises that we have the dignity of personality and freedom.

A moral being, responsible for our actions

The Bible assumes and teaches that humanity has a moral aspect, which relates us to our creator. This may be seen in the laws which govern even the most primitive societies. Humanity recognises the difference between right and wrong.

The animal kingdom behaves according to the drive of mere instinct. Humanity possesses a drive that makes us morally aware – a drive which says "I ought".

As a result, it is basic to the teaching of the Bible that we are not victims of our upbringing or circumstances. Rather, we are responsible for our actions and must answer for them. If we remove this concept from our understanding of our nature, we also remove any true content from such words as reward, merit, justice and even forgiveness.

Whole: Acts 17:26; Genesis 2:15,19-20; Matthew 4:4
Spiritual: Genesis 1:26-27; Psalm 8:3-6
Personal: Genesis 2:18; Luke 10:25-37
Moral: Romans 2:14-15; Psalm 51:1-3

KEY TRUTH

The Bible tells us that humanity is the summit of God's creation. We are the only beings who may enter into a personal relationship with the creator.

POSTSCRIPT

It is the dimension of God in human beings that raises us above the level of an animal, a machine or an accident.

BIBLE STUDY Genesis 1:27-28; 2:7-24

It would be hard to imagine that the vast creation existed for our sake, without the Bible's emphasis, first, of God-centredness in the creation; secondly, that creation is not the home of the human species so much as the home of a race of God-like beings; thirdly, that all creation centres in a Man who is heir to it all, and in whom everything holds together (Colossians 1:15-17). The Bible takes only two pages over the creation – "a week's work"! It requires over a thousand pages to tell our story.

1 Is it the creation that defines our size and identity? Reflect on the truth of 1:27 and 2:7.

2 "Image" but only an image. How can we counteract modern theorists who tell us that we are God and there is nothing we cannot do?

3 By contrast, we are told that we are no different from other living creatures; that a new-born child is simply an animal. How would we answer this, from 2:28 and from Psalm 139:13-16?

4 Look at 2:8-17. What do we learn here about human responsibility?

5 2:18-25 gives us our creation charter of sexuality, marriage and community. Discuss the point that it isn't singleness that isn't "good" but solitude.

6 "Helper" (2:18-21) – does that imply a second-class being? Discuss the fact that the Hebrew word *ezer* elsewhere describes the kind of "help" that only God can give – eg Psalm 121:2; Hosea 13:9.

7 Think through the creation principle (2:24) of a one-man/one-woman, publicly recognised contract for life, within which is expressed the God-given intimacy of physical union.

REFLECTION

A Read Psalm 8. What gives significance to humanity in the vastness of the surrounding universe? What do we learn of our status and of our responsibilities? In what way does this Psalm correct current errors of thinking?

B A famous film star once said, "I am just a piece of meat." From the Bible, how may we comment on and correct such a statement?

C Look at Genesis 1:26-27. In what ways do you think we are like God? In what ways are we unlike him?

D How do you react to the belief that wrong-doing is a kind of disease, for which there is, somewhere, a proper form of treatment? May this sometimes be true?

2. Our Diversity

Natural dimensions

God has given us the earth as a home to live in and to look after. It is a home that is teeming with life and overflowing with variety and colour. Its seasons are regulated and its resources are immense.

The world and matter are not evil (as various non-Christian teachings have maintained) but are part of God's good creation. Food and bodily health are the gifts of God and are to be received with thanks. Through agriculture, industry and creativity, humanity is to be productive in the home that God has given us.

Creative dimensions

In general it is true that when the Scriptures have been taken seriously, technology and science have flourished in a productive way. This is because the Bible encourages us to explore and develop the wonderful works of God. Mining, trade, manufacture and construction, performed responsibly, are all part of our task.

Cultural dimensions

Humanity possesses what the animal kingdom can never know – a capacity for the appreciation of what is beautiful for intellectual development, for literature and the arts, and for sport and recreation.

Life on earth is meant to be enjoyable, but cultural activity calls for as much discipline as any other part of life. Nevertheless, rest and recreation are a vital part of the programme of human life.

Social dimensions

Humanity was placed on the earth to live, not in isolation from our neighbour, but in the pattern of community and family that stems from God's own nature. God has made us for relationships.

The Bible points out the enormous value of friendship, and above all, marriage. The relationship between a husband and wife is seen as a gift from God. Through shared problems and pleasures, companionship and the joy of sexual intimacy, married partners are able to strengthen each other throughout life.

We have been created to show compassion and justice in the way we treat others. Only when humanity uses these qualities do our relationships in the family, in social care, in government and in work become what God meant them to be. God's desire for all people is that they should love one another.

Religious dimensions

Humanity was made by God and we have a spiritual capacity. As humans are far from God, we constantly search for our spiritual home. The search takes many forms which are seen in the great religions of the world, in the quest for oneness with God, and for an experience which materialism is unable to give.

Jesus confirmed both an Old Testament saying and the findings of the human heart when he declared that "Man does not live on bread alone" (Matthew 4:4). We need more than the physical essentials of life. It is the Bible that gives to searching humanity the answers that philosophers and sages of religion have always been unable even to guess at: that God was on a search himself – for humanity whom he loves.

Natural: Genesis 8:22; Psalm
104:5-30; 1 Timothy 4:3-4
Creative: Genesis 1:26-28;
9:1-3; Psalm 8:6-8
Cultural: Exodus 35:30-35;
Daniel 1:3-4
Social: Genesis 2:18-24;
Romans 13:8-10
Religious: Psalm 90:1;
Ecclesiastes 3:11

KEY TRUTH

The many different sides of
humanity show positively that
we are created by God, and
for God.

POSTSCRIPT

Humanity's immense powers
should inspire us to develop
to the full our potential for
creative service in our world.

BIBLE STUDY Psalm 139

The "brightness" of this psalm was described by the Baptist
preacher C.H. Spurgeon as being like that of a sapphire stone –
"It flames out with such flashes of light as to turn night into
day." As you read the psalm, ask yourself whether there is
anywhere in literature that such a vivid and moving portrait of
God has been given to us – by a man who found himself and
knew himself only in relationship to his creator.

1 Look at verses 1-6. List the areas of life that the psalmist
David recognises as coming under God's complete
knowledge. What is David's reaction to this insight?
2 Move on to verses 7-10. Can you think of others who
experienced God in this way? Compare Genesis 3:9; Jonah
1:3. What is the most encouraging discovery of these verses?
3 As you read verses 11-12, try to identify those aspects of life
that plunge human beings into "darkness". A journalist
once wrote, "I am frightened like a child in a dark room; I
look for a window, and Christ is the window." What has
been your experience?
4 How do verses 13-16 speak to the anxieties and dilemmas of
every generation – to the present generation? When did we
become human? What does God's "book" speak to you of?
5 Should we feel threatened ... or outraged ... at God's
sovereignty and control of our lives? How far can you
identify with David's reaction?
6 Verses 19-24: suddenly David is back to being king again,
and to the conflicts of daily life. But note the humility with
which he concludes his remarkable reflections.

REFLECTION

A Read 2 Corinthians 5:1-10.
How does the apostle Paul
view his physical existence;
his heavenly future; and the
experience of being linked to
both?
B What natural abilities has
God given you? How have
they enriched you as a
person? What is the danger of
having many natural
abilities?

C How do you see your role in
a society that is often
corrupt? As one of
involvement, separation,
compromise, condemnation?
Check your answer with John
17:15-16 and Matthew
5:13-16.
D At times in history,
Christians have looked
distrustfully at the arts. Why
is this so? What principle
should govern us in our
attitude to music, painting,
films and literature?

HUMANITY
3. Our Rebellion and Fall

Humanity's innocence gave us fellowship with God

"Innocence" is the correct word to use of our original moral state.

Adam and Eve were not righteous, in the sense of possessing a developed uprightness of character; rather they were child-like in the trusting and open simplicity of their walk with God.

However this innocence was not an in-built and unalterable characteristic. We were not programmed to obey our maker, in the way that a computer must function, for humanity was not like a machine. Adam and Eve were real people, living in a free relationship with God.

Unlike their descendants, that first human couple originally had no inward urge to sin. But whether or not they were to remain in a relationship with God depended upon the choices that they could freely make.

Humanity's freedom gave us the power of choice

The Bible reveals that humanity had real choices in regard to our relationship with God. We were not compelled to go God's way. In any true relationship, the people concerned must have the freedom of choice that raises them above the level of being robots or puppets.

God did not hide from humanity that we had the power of choice. The instructions given were clear enough and easy to do. The human race was free to choose.

Humanity's choice gave us true responsibility

Although we are influenced by other people in what we do, ultimately, we must take the responsibility for the decisions we make. To have the ability to choose between right and wrong means that we also have the responsibility to choose what is right.

In the story of humanity's fall, we see how people try to avoid their responsibility. Adam blames Eve, who in turn blames the serpent. In the way that God deals with each of them, he shows that they were all guilty for the sins that they had committed.

Humanity's decision led us into moral rebellion

Humanity's revolt against our creator cannot be described as an accidental slip. Our first parents questioned God's authority by disobeying him, and they doubted whether God really knew what was best for them. As a result, the human race deliberately rebelled against God and followed their own way.

What humanity thus became – sinful and fallen – we still are today. Estranged from the creator, the human race as a whole must be described biblically as a fallen race. It is not that the image of God in humanity has been completely destroyed. It is still there, although distorted and marred. But there is no area of our mind and personality that does not exhibit a degree of "fallenness".

The sin principle has become universal. Men and women today, from their actions and choices, underline their involvement with the fallen race.

. . . .

Innocence: Genesis 2
Freedom: Genesis 2:16-17;
   3:6-7
Choice: Genesis 3:8-19;
   Matthew 12:36-37
Decision: Genesis 3; Psalm
   51:5; Jeremiah 17:9

KEY TRUTH

. . . .

God in creation gave humanity the gifts and privileges that allowed us individuality and freedom. The wilful misuse of these led humanity into rebellion and his subsequent fall.

POSTSCRIPT

. . . .

The fallenness of humanity means that for the whole of our lives we have a tendency to rebel against God. All humanity is on the same level of need.

BIBLE STUDY Psalm 51

This is perhaps the best known of what are called the Penitential Psalms. Written by David, after committing both adultery and murder (2 Samuel 11 and 12), it portrays more vividly than anywhere in Scripture the heartfelt plea for mercy on the part of the fallen sinner. David's sin had begun with a look, then continued with a message, a meeting, adultery, deceit and finally murder. These questions may help in getting to the heart of our rebellion, fall and reinstatement.

1 Notice in verses 1-3 how wrong-doing is described: "transgression" (rebellion), "iniquity" (pollution, corruption) and "sin" (failing the standard). What does this tell us about our problem? Compare Jeremiah 17:9.

2 Look at verses 3 and 4. Why is it that we can never say that what someone does in private is their own affair?

3 Verse 5 expresses the truth of what is called "original sin". Read Romans 5:12 for further amplification. Reflect in your study on what this means for society, in the need for locks on doors, receipts on payments, tickets, passes, police, etc.

4 Verses 6 and 7 indicate that the cleansing has to be from inside out. What is the ground by which we can be put right? Look back at verse 1. Compare Romans 3:23-25.

5 In verses 2 and 7, David has asked to be made clean. Now in verses 10-12 three further prayers follow. What area of his life do they apply to? The clue lies in the word that is common to all three prayers.

6 "Willing", verse 12. How is their motivation to be strengthened, so that God's follower wants to live purely?

7 Can you make David's vow of service (verses 13-19) your own?

REFLECTION

A Read and study the Ten Commandments (Exodus 20:3-17). Why did we need the Law to be given at all? What areas of life do these commandments deal with? Why are they still relevant today? Do you know them by heart?

B Whose fault is it, when we do wrong? The devil's? God's – for having given us free choice? Our "fallen" nature?

Compare your findings with Genesis 3:11-13; Romans 1:20; 3:19-20.

C How can Christ's followers strengthen their desire to choose the good and not the evil?

D We are responsible for everything that we choose to do. Describe, in your own words, what responsibility means. What does this tell us about the God who made us?

4. Our Rebellion and Condemnation

Rebellion and guilt

God made us to live in relationship with all of humanity on a collective basis. Therefore it is not surprising that Scripture teaches that the whole race is involved in the original fall, although no one is condemned for the sin of any other person.

Because we have rejected goodness and follow our own way rather than God's, we are guilty before him. Guilt is both a feeling and a fact. It is a feeling because our consciences tell us when we have done wrong. We feel ashamed and guilty for what we have done. It is a fact because God knows that we have rebelled against him.

We are guilty in the same way that a criminal has been proven guilty.

We deserve God's judgement.

Guilt and condemnation

The effects of our revolt against the authority of God are inescapable. In Genesis chapter 3 Adam and Eve are sent away from Eden and are told that they will only be able to live off the earth by hard work.

God had no choice but to condemn humanity. Because of his justice and holiness he cannot tolerate evil. Therefore, when God condemns us he shows that he is taking our sin seriously. To be condemned is to experience the anger of God.

Condemnation and separation

Although humanity must face physical death and hardship as a result of our rebellion, the Bible emphasises that our main loss is spiritual. Our most precious privilege, that of free access to God and fellowship with him, has been forfeited.

Throughout human history, and that of God's people, it is sin that has created barriers between us and the holy God. We find ourselves confused by our own capacity for evil and out of place in the world because we are separated from God.

Estranged from God, we are ignorant of our Maker and of his ways and we are unable to fulfil our destiny. We cannot enter into peace with God, and we cannot undo the past.

Separation and death

"The Tree of Life" in Genesis 2 conveys the idea of the eternal life of God. When humanity fell out of fellowship with God we were deprived of such life. The Bible teaches that sin and death are linked to each other.

The apostle Paul declares that death is the payment we receive for sinning. The difference between death as a spiritual state, and death as the end of physical existence is not always clearly drawn in Scripture. Spiritually and physically, death is an outrage in the teaching of the Bible, because it is God's judgement upon sin. As such it could never be abolished but by the action of God.

The physical conquest of death by Jesus Christ overshadows all else in our understanding of this issue.

Rebellion: Romans 5:12-17;
Ephesians 2:1-3
Guilt: Psalm 14:2-3; 143:2
Condemnation: Genesis
3:23-24; Isaiah 59:1-2
Separation: Genesis 2:15-17;
Ezekiel 18:4; Romans 6:23

KEY TRUTH
. . . .

It is disastrous that humanity
has rebelled against the
creator, for God in his
absolute holiness will not
tolerate sin, but must
condemn the sinner. As a
result, humanity is guilty,
confused, and separated
from God.

POSTSCRIPT
. . . .

Because of the universality of
sin, it is all too easy to become
used to locks, keys and tickets,
and other daily reminders
that fallen humanity is not to
be trusted.

BIBLE STUDY Romans 3:9-20

In this passage we are coming in at the tail end of a careful
argument by the apostle Paul. Before the good news can come
into focus, it is essential that the news can be faced.

1 Theologians sometimes speak of our need in terms of "total
depravity" – it is not that we are necessarily as bad as we can
be, but rather that there is no part of our lives that is
untouched by sin. How far do the various quotations from
the Old Testament bear this out, in 3:10-18?

2 In the face of God's law, every mouth is to be silenced (verse
19). What argument does Paul use earlier against the
universal moralist? See Romans 2:1. Who are such people
today?

3 Next it's the turn of the "naturalist" – those who may not
know the commandments, but nevertheless have within
them a moral sense. What speaks to them? See Romans
2:14-15 and 1:20.

4 Move on to the Jewish legalist – Romans 2:25-29 (especially
verse 23). What is the problem here? What is its modern
counterpart?

5 Then there is the ritualist. See Romans 2:25-29 (especially
verse 29). Was this a problem for Paul's day only or do we see
it today? What is the flaw at the heart of this thinking?

6 To cap it all we have the hedonist – the lover of self-pleasing,
who hopes to take advantage of God's mercy (3:7-8). How
recognisable is this figure? How does Paul react?

7 Which of these different categories have members of the
group come from? Meditate and pray together around 3:9.

REFLECTION

A Read and examine Psalm
51, written by David after an
incident in 2 Samuel 11 and
12. How does David
understand God's attitude to
sin; the nature of sin; the
remedy (both short-term and
long-term – see Ezekiel
36:25-27); and his own right
attitude for the future?

B Why are terms such as sin,
guilt and the fall of humanity
not fashionable in some
circles today? Were they ever
fashionable?

C Christians are people with
joy in their hearts. How is it
possible to live with the
biblical concept of our
fallenness and yet to avoid
dwelling constantly on our
own failures?

D What are the practital
indications from our
surroundings that this world,
while still a good place to live
in, has lost its initial
perfection?

5. Our Quest and Dilemma

Our religious search

Humanity is continually torn between the revelation of God, culminating in the person of Christ, and the numerous attempts to make a path to God.

These attempts have taken many forms in history, ranging from primitive superstition and magic to powerful and sophisticated religious systems.

In Bible times, God's leaders were continually challenging their hearers to forsake the man-made ways to God, and to accept the revelation of the one and only Lord. Many of the New Testament letters highlight the issue of false teachers and religious trails that lead to idolatry and error.

Our philosophical wanderings

The way of philosophy is the age-old search for the elusive wisdom and knowledge about the ultimate reality of the universe. Most attempts arrive at different conclusions, and some arrive at none.

The conclusions of philosophy (when God's revelation had been left out of the picture) are perfectly mirrored in the Old Testament book of Ecclesiastes. The writer shows that the human mind, without the help of God, is unable to come up with convincing answers to the meaning of life.

Our psychological contradictions

Our true nature constantly comes into collision with our fallen and sinful state. Because we were created in the image of God, humanity was designed to enjoy the company of our Maker. Our instincts will not easily allow us to forget our origin and our capacity for rational and satisfying relationships.

However, our fallenness and state of enmity with God make us a mass of contradictions. For humanity is not only at war with God. History all too frequently has shown us to be at war with our neighbour, with our environment, within our family and with ourselves.

Our problems do not stem so much from our outward circumstances, as from our own inner state. Jesus taught this and so did his apostles.

True identity and significance continue to elude all those who do not know God. Hence the symptoms of disorder. Hence the need of a Redeemer.

Our physical drive

Besides the loss of harmony in our emotions, will and relationships, the Bible points to the abnormal predominance of our physical and sensual appetite as being a result of the fall.

Thus, history's periods of spiritual poverty have tended to coincide with a marked increase in society's dependence upon money, alcohol, promiscuity and dehumanised pleasure.

Humanity has great potential for creativity and technical advance, but when this is not controlled by a God-centred view of the world, indiscipline and slavery are the inevitable result.

BIBLE CHECK

Religious: Acts 17:22-23;
2 Timothy 4:3-4

Philosophical: Ecclesiastes
1:16-18; 1 Corinthians
1:20-21

Psychological: Mark 7:21-23;
James 4:1-4; Romans
7:18-24

Physical: Ephesians 4:17-19;
Titus 3:3

KEY TRUTH

The history of the human race tells us about our quest for the meaning of our existence. People will remain in confusion, unless they experience the light and life of God. This confusion is seen in the areas listed here.

POSTSCRIPT

The Christian who fails to grow spiritually is liable to be caught up in the very dilemmas that ensnare the world, losing our assurance of peace with God.

BIBLE STUDY Ecclesiastes 2:1-16

The book of Ecclesiastes paints a superb picture of what human life is really like when God is taken out of the frame. It stems from the time of King Solomon of the 10th century BC; indeed it may be based upon his own critique of life. It is presented as the experiences of the Philosopher or "Teacher", who deliberately places himself in the shoes of a godless person. The resulting world-view is one of empty meaninglessness (1:2). Put yourself in these shoes now, as you come to this selected passage.

1 "... during the few days of their lives" (verse 3) – describe the mindset that the writer is adopting in verses 1-3.

2 Read verses 4-6; what was the driving force behind the expenditure of effort? Can you think of any of Jesus' teaching that has a bearing upon it? eg Luke 12:16-21.

3 Who or what is at the centre of the programme mapped out in verses 7-11? What is the great lesson to be learnt? How well is it being learnt among group members?

4 The writer seems to wonder whether anyone in the line after him can do better (verse 12). Try to understand the cynicism of the sentences that follow. What is it that gives rise to such apathy? Verse 16 gives the clue.

5 The writer is both teasing and tantalising at the same time – leading his readers along the line of their own godless logic. What is there to be said for the believer following his example, in the face of alien beliefs and outlooks?

6 Two ways to live! Which is it to be? Take a final glance at Ecclesiastes 12:1-2 and prayerfully encourage each other now.

REFLECTION

A Look at James 4:1-10, for a picture of people who are in open rebellion against God. What characterises their actions, and what explains them? What is the road to spiritual recovery, and what encouragements are there in this passage?

B What examples are there, in your own area, of people searching for religious answers to life? How can your church best contribute to their search? Compare your findings with 1 Thessalonians 1:5.

C As a Christian, can you recall what it was still to be in ignorance of God's friendship? How far did Revelation 3:17 describe you?

D List the ways in which people are at war with themselves, their neighbours, nature and God.

6. Our Enemies

Satan

The devil is not all-powerful or present everywhere at once, as God is. He is a created spirit or angel, who chose to rebel against the authority of God.

He is the enemy of humanity (the word Satan means "opponent" or "enemy"). His aim is to humiliate humanity, to separate us from God, and to destroy us. His power is immense, but limited. He is a deceiver, a liar, a tempter and a murderer. He is described in Scripture as a roaring lion and as a dragon.

His defeat was achieved through the death and resurrection of Jesus, and will be completed when he is finally judged and destroyed by Christ. Meanwhile, the devil is to be resisted (James 4:7).

Sin

Sin came into the world through the devil's temptation, and became universal in the life of humanity through the fall. Sin is defined in the Bible as breaking the law of God, as enmity with God, as rebellion, and as falling short of God's standard.

The outbreak of sin reveals itself in a great variety of ways, sometimes in gross acts, but equally powerfully in the subtle undermining of will, motivation and character. As a Christian focuses on Christ, so our determination to fight against sin is strengthened. With Christ's help sin is to be rejected (Hebrews 12:1-2).

The world

By the "world" the Bible frequently means the society, system and outlook which is hostile to God and limits life to earthly existence only. Those who live in this way limit their desires to gaining possessions and position, and exclude God altogether.

The results of living by this philosophy are all too evident in human life and Christians can be powerfully tempted by the things we see in the world. However, we can take courage in the defeat of the world by Jesus. Meanwhile we are to shine as lights in the world (Philippians 2:15).

The flesh

Apart from its usual meaning, "flesh", often termed "sinful nature" or "human nature" in modern Bible translations, refers to the sinful bias which every individual has. This sinfulness is found in both obvious and hidden selfish indulgence.

We all possess this fallen nature throughout life. As the Christian also possesses Christ's Spirit, but is still in the flesh as well, he becomes something of a battleground between flesh and spirit. However, we learn to live according to the Spirit and not the flesh (Romans 8:9).

Death

Death is our great enemy, pursuing us from infancy, disturbing our peace and haunting our hopes. However, the Christian recognises that Christ is the great destroyer of death and of the very fear of death. Like others, the Christian faces life's problems and trials, but we give thanks to God who gives us victory through Jesus Christ (1 Corinthians 15:57).

BIBLE CHECK

Satan: 1 John 3:8; 1 Peter 5:8-9; Revelation 12:7-12

Sin: 1 John 3:4; Romans 3:23; 8:10

World: 1 John 2:15-16; James 4:4; John 16:33

Flesh: Romans 7:18; Galatians 5:17

Death: 2 Timothy 1:10; Hebrews 2:14-15; Revelation 21:4

KEY TRUTH

As a result of our fall, we find ourselves faced by real and powerful enemies that can only be overcome by the greater power of God.

POSTSCRIPT

A subtle temptation for the Christian is to blame personal failures on the devil or on the pull of the world. When we sin, it is because we have chosen to do so.

BIBLE STUDY James 4:1-12

James, the earthly brother of Jesus Christ (Matthew 13:55), is writing a general letter to Christians everywhere. We are to be a credit to Christ in the consistency of our behaviour, despite the severity of the trials and temptations that confront the believer (James 1:2-3). Here we are urged to choose sides:

1 James addresses himself in verse 1 to the conflicts that have characterised all human history – both on the public and the private level. Why is it too shallow an explanation to say that such conflicts are the result of poverty, class distinction or tribalism?

2 At least seven symptoms of human disorder feature in verses 2-3. Try to list them, and ask yourselves to what extent our human race has advanced, morally combating these evils.

3 Why must we choose between "the world" and "God" (verse 4)? What is meant by 'the world'? For further help, see 1 John 2:15-16.

4 The issue condenses into a starker choice still, in verses 5-7, where James seems to be alluding to Proverbs 3:24 and Matthew 23:12. What is this choice now? What should encourage us in choosing rightly?

5 So far we have looked at the many projections of our inner turbulence, and at the two alternatives that demand our loyalty. What evidence is there today among God's people of the repentance described in verses 8-9; and of the mutual love that slander denies (verse 11)?

6 Verse 11 points to the only single ultimate authority. Commit yourself to God afresh in prayer now.

REFLECTION

A Read Ephesians 6:10-18, and think about the Christian's defences against spiritual opposition. List the commands in that passage – "Put on", etc. How do you interpret the various pieces of armour? Why may we expect to win?

B Whose world is it – the devil's – or God's? Compare your findings with 1 John 5:19; Matthew 4:8-9; 1 Samuel 2:8; Psalm 24:1 and Revelation 11:15.

C Specify different situations when the Christian should run from evil, meet it head-on, undermine it, or stand firm.

D In what ways is humanity always changing? In what ways do we remain the same?

1. Angels

Angels are worshippers around God's throne

Angels are part of the life of heaven, and in certain respects are superior to human beings; yet they are separate from God. They are not to be worshipped; their essential role is that of attending upon God, acclaiming his holiness and praising his Son.

At such limited times when angels have become visible (as in special visitations of God or in prophetic visions), they reflect the awesome holiness and harmony of heaven.

Angels are executors of God's will

They are numerous and may be known by different terms: "holy ones", "messengers" or "sons of God". The "cherubim" (plural of "cherub") are presented in the Scriptures as winged creatures flying to fulfil God's commands, guarding the way to his presence and acting as conveyors of his throned presence.

Angels are witnesses to God's saving acts

Angels are in evidence at the birth of Jesus; on the eve of his crucifixion; on the morning of his resurrection and on the occasion of his ascension. They will be Christ's heralds at his final return in glory.

They are said by Jesus to rejoice at the repentance of a sinner, and he speaks of them as gathering in his redeemed people at the end of the world.

Angels are messengers at times of revelation

At the beginning of certain great eras in God's redemption, angels have featured as announcers. Instances of this occur with the call of Moses the great lawgiver, with the commissioning of prophets, at the outset of the gospel story and with the momentous extension of Christ's salvation to the Gentiles.

These announcements were variously received with reactions of awe, fear, astonishment and holy joy.

Angels are protagonists at times of conflict

We learn from the Bible of an angelic rebellion and fall under the leadership of Satan, "the serpent", "the devil", "the father of lies", "the Accuser". Although his defeat was assured by the victory of Christ's death, the conflict with evil will not be fully over until Satan's final destruction.

Witness and prayer, then, are conducted on the part of God's saints in the light of a continuing angelic conflict with the demon world. Biblically, Michael is understood as heading the angel hosts.

Angels are ministers at times of crisis

At many points in God's dealings with his people – patriarchs, prophets, apostles and indeed Jesus himself received ministry and help from angels at particular moments of stress, temptation or danger.

But all inheritors of salvation are assured of the protection and support of God's angels. While we may be grateful for their presence, they are not to be reverenced as intermediaries between us and God. An undue attention to the angels can lead to distortions of the faith.

BIBLE CHECK

Worshippers: Psalm 8:5;
Daniel 7:9-10; Revelation
5:11-12

Executors: Psalm 89:5;
Genesis 3:24; Exodus
25:18-22; Ezekiel 1:4-24

Witnesses: Luke 2:8-15;
22:43; 24:4-8; Acts 1:10-11;
1 Thessalonians 4:16; Luke
15:10; Matthew 24:30-31

Messengers: Exodus 3:2;
Isaiah 6:1-7; Luke 1:28-38;
Acts 10:1-8

Protagonists: Luke 10:18;
Joshua 5:13-15; 2 Kings
6:17; Daniel 10:13; 12:1;
Revelation 12:7-9

Ministers: Genesis 19:15;
22:11-12; 1 Kings 19:5-7;
2 Kings 6:15-17; Matthew
4:11; Acts 12:7-10; Hebrews
1:14; Colossians 2:18

KEY TRUTH

Angels belong to a heavenly
order of spiritual, though
created, beings.
In their ceaseless worship,
they act as messengers of God
and as ministers to God's
people.

POSTSCRIPT

Certain errors are corrected by
the Bible truth that our future
human destiny is higher than
that of the angels, for our
final fulfilment will be in the
glorified Christ (Hebrews
2:5-9).

BIBLE STUDY Isaiah 6:1-8

Here is a vision of awesome holiness, given in 740 BC to the
young Isaiah, at the start of a long prophetic ministry that was
to span the reign of five kings. At that time, the average
Hebrew of the world, over which the sovereign Lord ruled, was
limited to an area no bigger than New Jersey or Wales. All that
changed with the rise in the east of the mighty Assyrian
empire that trampled down everything in sight in the name of
its ferocious gods. Suddenly, Israel and Judah looked tiny. Had
their God also become provincial? Not according to the
prophets! Let us learn from Isaiah's call:

1 Isaiah's world-view is shaped here in verses 1-4. What does it
centre in? Who, more precisely, is "the Lord"? See John
12:39-41.

2 If Isaiah's attention is riveted on the throne, what
is the apparent purpose of the angelic figures (verses 2-4)?
What do their appearance and their utterances point to?

3 To what extent should Isaiah's reaction of verse 5 be the
norm? Is our view of the Lord's glory and holiness greater or
lesser than his? Compare 2 Corinthians 4:6. Compare also
Isaiah's words with those of Peter the apostle in Luke 5:8.

4 Why should we be grateful for the ministry of angels? See
verses 6-7 and compare Luke 2:10-12.

5 Although angels feature many times in the Scriptures, why is
there no one major passage about them?

6 From verse 8, what was it that would "hold" Isaiah through
all his future trials? What holds any of us?

REFLECTION

A Turn to Hebrews 1 and
2:5-9. While there are
numerous references in Scrip -
ture to the angels, why is it
that there is no classical
"passage" that gives specific
detailed teaching on the
topic? Why is it that angels
seem to feature as ancillaries
to the main story line?

B As humans, we were made
"a little lower" than the
angels (Hebrews 2:7; see
Psalm 8:5). But the
implication of Hebrews
1:13-14 and 2:5-9,16 is that
our destiny lies higher than
the angels. How do you
explain this apparent
contradiction – a little lower
... eventually higher?

C Consider the nature and
status of angels in compari -
son to Christ, to human
beings and to the Holy Spirit.

D In the light of these
studies, how would you summarise the chief activities of
angels?

GOD'S MESSENGERS
2. Patriarchs

Forerunners of a new beginning

The patriarchal age began with God's call to
Abraham to leave his home in Haran and go
to the land of Canaan. Abraham and his
immediate descendants, Isaac and Jacob,
represent a new start in God's dealings with
the human race.

The first eleven chapters of the Bible end
in the confusion of the Tower of Babel, with
humanity scattered and sin spreading across
the world. What hope remained? The call of
the patriarchs is the beginning of the divine
answer.

Inheritors of a promised land

To the patriarchs and their descendants is
given the promise of a land that they are to
possess and occupy. In their own lifetime they
were not to see it; even so, the Old Testament
develops this theme of God leading his people
into a land of their own. The New Testament
shows how the patriarchs had their hope set,
not just on the land of Israel, but more
importantly on the coming new creation.

We must also recognise that the New
Testament language of inheriting a land, ties
in with the blessing of knowing Christ and
the new creation hope that we have in him.

Ancestors of a universal family

The patriarchs are foundational people for
the whole faith of the Bible. Their
descendants would be the world-wide family
of believers, and would be numbered like the
stars of heaven.

It is as we come to the New Testament that
we learn that the "seed" promised to Abraham
is Christ himself, for all God's promises are
fulfilled in him. Today all who belong to
Christ, both Jews and Gentiles, can be said to
be the descendants of Abraham and the
patriarchs.

Their message of the covenant

At several points, the divine contract – or
covenant – between God and Abraham was
confirmed and strengthened. By it, God
pledged himself to Abraham and his
posterity. His people, for their part, were to
separate themselves to God, as symbolised by
the outward rite of circumcision.

The "new covenant", inaugurated by
Christ, is not a new way of salvation; its basic
message was unchanged from patriarchal
times – the people of God must put their faith
only in Christ.

Their message of election

There was nothing about the patriarchs that
merited God's singling out of them for
blessing; Abraham came from a family of idol-
worshippers in Mesopotamia. Equally it must
be insisted that God did not choose this one
family for reasons of favouritism.

They were selected for a theological, moral
and missionary purpose – for the benefit of all
humankind. To the patriarchs were revealed
the distinctive names and character of God, for
the blessing of every nation.

Their message of obedient faith

Abraham, Isaac and Jacob (and their
descendants, known later as Israel) bequeathed
to their successors a model of how to walk with
Christ. In spite of their various failings, they
learnt the ways of prayer and sacrifice in a life
of nomadic travel.

Their trust in the faithfulness of God was
highlighted supremely in Abraham's
willingness to sacrifice his son Isaac. Their
God became defined as "the God of Abraham,
Isaac and Jacob".

BIBLE CHECK

KEY TRUTH

The patriarchs were the earliest heads of the representative family selected by God to receive his covenanted blessings, on behalf of believers in all generations.

POSTSCRIPT

In regard to the land promised to the patriarchs, chapters 9–11 of the letter to the Romans provide a full overview of the past, present and future, affecting this important topic.

BIBLE STUDY Hebrews 11:8-19

This chapter is God's "Hall of Fame". The apostolic writer is aware of a tendency among some to slip back into their old, pre-Christian way of thinking, and he points them to the "better" way provided now in the new covenant, centred in Christ. Here are some outstanding examples of those who have gone ahead of us. Among them, none was more prominent than the patriarch Abraham:

1 As you scan the passage, identify the main episodes that the writer emphasises as requiring the faith of Abraham.

2 Although Abraham received the promise of a "land" (verse 8) and of descendants as numerous as the stars and the sand (verse 12), in his actual lifetime he possessed no more than a single cave (Genesis 23:17-20) and one son, Isaac. One cave and one son. How does this bear out the truth of verse 13? What then does it mean to "see", in the language of verse 13?

3 The "city" (verse 10), the "better country" (verse 16). Try and understand salvation in terms of the original promise, the partial fulfilment, the universal extension in the gospel, and finally the eternal completion. Discuss these different facets of the one glorious truth.

4 Notice the New Testament commentary (verse 19) on Abraham's sacrifice of Isaac, narrated in Genesis 22. How was Abraham a true pioneer of faith in this respect?

5 Is it worth all the aggravation, being a believer in God?

REFLECTION

A Reflect on Hebrews 11:8-19 and the life of Abraham. Here is the beginning of the worldwide family of believers. Try and identify from the passage the various episodes that required the "faith" of Abraham.

B What was the motivation, the mindset, that kept Abraham on track? Verses 9,10,19 give clues. How does a right view of the future help us in the tensions of the present?

C Abraham's descendants are said to have "seen" something (verse 13). What have they seen? What does such a "seeing" mean for today's Christian?

D In what senses could it be argued that the hazardous life of faith is a blessing?

3. Priests

Although the principles of sacrifice and priesthood are laid down from the beginning of the Bible (eg Genesis 4:3-5; 8:20; 14:18-20), the truth that all people everywhere need a God-given mediator began to be taught in earnest when Israel was becoming a nation under Moses and Aaron. Through the priestly tribe of the Levites, and Israel's sacrificial system, spiritual lessons of everlasting importance are to be learnt:

We cannot come to God lightly

Washings, cereal offerings, sin offerings, burnt offerings, the Day of Atonement – the rituals associated with the worship tent of the tabernacle (and the temple that was to follow), fall strangely on the modern ear.

But the education was vital; access to God is impossible unless sin is dealt with.

We cannot come to God directly

A representative, a go-between, is necessary. The Levites were to act as priests on behalf of the people. They themselves underwent thorough ceremonial cleansing before they were counted fit for their task. Of all the priests, only Aaron the high priest could enter God's "Most Holy Place" – and then only once a year. The principle of mediation was basic for Israel.

We cannot come to God cheaply

The lesson sank in supremely through the feast of the Passover, instituted on the eve of Israel's deliverance from Egypt. The feast commemorated the application of the blood of a lamb to every Hebrew doorpost on the night that death took its toll of Egypt's first-born sons. Where blood was visible, life was spared. It was for the priests to continue this principle until the coming of Christ. Without the shedding of blood there is no deliverance.

Christ, the perfect Mediator

The Old Testament priesthood pointed to Jesus Christ and his atoning sacrifice for the sins of the world. Being both human and God, he is the ideal and unique go-between on behalf of sinful people. He is both sacrifice and High Priest. While Aaron had to offer repeated sacrifices both for himself and his people, Christ in his moral perfection offered a single sacrifice for sins, once and for all. Now as heavenly High Priest he provides open access to God the Father, interceding on behalf of all believers.

The cross, the final sacrifice

Until the time of Jesus' death, a heavy curtain in Jerusalem's temple separated the inner "Most Holy Place" (representing God's inaccessibility) from the rest of the building.

As Christ uttered his dying cry on the cross, an earthquake took place; simultaneously the temple curtain was ripped from top to bottom.

It showed that the death of Jesus, like the disintegrated curtain, had opened the way into God's presence for all believers. Never again would a sacrifice for sin be required.

Believers, the new priesthood

All this means that the whole Old Testament system of sacrifice and priesthood has been superseded and swept away by the one valid sacrifice of Jesus, described as "Christ our Passover lamb". A new priesthood has come into being; it is that of all believers everywhere. They offer, not a sacrifice for sins, rather sacrifices of praise and thankful service to God, and intercessory prayer on behalf of others. The temple now is spiritual, formed of "living stones". Christ's followers.

Not lightly: Leviticus 1:1-9;
16:20-22; Numbers 3:5-13

Not directly: Numbers
8:19-22; Leviticus 16:32-34;
Isaiah 53:6,12

Not cheaply: Exodus 12:7-14;
Leviticus 17:11; Exodus 24:8

Christ: 1 Timothy 2:5-6;
Hebrews 7:23-27; 4:14-16

The cross: Hebrews 9:1-4;
Matthew 27:50-51;
Hebrews 10:19-22

Believers: Hebrews 9:11-15;
1 Corinthians 5:7;
1 Peter 2:4-5

KEY TRUTH

. . . .

The priests of the Old
Testament nation of Israel
were the agents of mediation
through whom God was to be
approached. As such, they
foreshadowed Jesus Christ,
God's final and perfect
Mediator for all time.

POSTSCRIPT

. . . .

Christian elders and leaders
are required to set a Christ-
like example to the members
of the church, in the fulfilling
of their priestly duties.

BIBLE STUDY Hebrews 10:1-18

"In your beliefs, how do you get forgiven?" The speaker was a
Christian.

"Forgiven?" echoed the member of another faith. "Why ...
God just forgives. He is merciful."

"Really? Just like that? You mean that six million people
can be put through the gas chambers, and God says to the
perpetrators, 'All right, I'll forgive you, that's fine; we'll say no
more about it.' How can God do that without undermining
his own morality?"

"You've made me think," came the reply.

1 The story of the Bible is about this issue. Sin cannot be
lightly forgiven by the perfect and moral ruler of the
universe. Read the key of this passage, in verse 12, and reflect
on the wonder of what this one "priest" has achieved.

2 Shadows and realities (verse 1). Two systems are being
contrasted in this passage. Identify the various contrasts
between the many priests and their duties of the Old
Covenant, and the unique high priest of the New. What is
the special facet of the new covenant (verse 16)?

3 What is the greatest contrast of all? Verses 2 and 10 use the
same phrase.

4 The sacrifice of animals, though not representing God's
ultimate desire, nevertheless had a purpose. How would you
describe it, from verses 3 and 9?

5 "Never make perfect" (verse 1) ... "made perfect" (verse 14) –
had you noticed that contrast? If Christ's sacrifice of himself
has removed everything that blocked our approach to God,
how does this affect our life of prayer?

REFLECTION

A Study Hebrews 10:11-18.
Why can't God simply
"forgive" sins? And why the
need of a priest to be go-
between?

B Two systems are here being
contrasted: the old and the
new. List as many contrasts as
you can find in this passage.
What is the major thing that
stands out about them?

C "Made perfect" (verse 14) –
the meaning is that
everything that hindered our
approach to God has been
removed by Christ's sacrifice
of himself. What does that say
to us about the life of prayer?

D If every believer today is a
priest (1 Peter 2:5), what form
should our "spiritual
sacrifices" take? How does
this affect daily living?

4. Prophets

They received God's summons

From the beginning there were prophetic stirrings among God's people. Abraham himself was termed a "prophet" (Genesis 20:7). But it was supremely through Moses that the true nature and task of a prophet became established.

With many of the prophets we read of a direct "call", frequently from youth, sometimes dramatic. Some accepted reluctantly, in their recognition that they were being sent to uncaring listeners. It was, however, their awareness of having been in God's presence that stamped their ministry with authority. From Samuel's time there were "schools" of prophets; from Joel's period stemmed the great writing prophets. These were "men of God", "seers", "watchmen" and intercessors, standing in the breach on behalf of people under judgement.

They challenged God's people

The prophets were no mere product of Jewish life; they came into direct collision with Jewish ways, notably the repeated tendency to compromise the unique faith of Israel with that of other nations. It was Elijah's fearless stand against the prophets of Baal that placed him, in Jewish estimation, for ever on a level with Moses.

The issues were many: idolatry, syncretism, social injustice and spiritual apathy. These sins were confronted by prophets of God's kingdom of righteousness, peace, universality and permanence. Their moral authority exceeded that of even priests and kings. The exception was King David who, as the inspired psalmist, became classed as a prophet himself.

They revealed God's mind

The true prophets, as contrasted with the false, were concerned to speak out, however unpopular their message. They held firmly to five mighty concepts: that God is one with no rivals; that, as "the living God", he is active in redeeming and sustaining his people; that he is faithful to his covenant with Israel; that he is righteous and must judge evil; and that he is merciful and provides a blood-bought way by which sin can be forgiven.

They addressed God's world

The horizons of the prophets extended far beyond Israel's borders, taking in the time-span of world history. They were commentators on the past.

By their ministry, history became revelation. They were interpreters of the present, seeing current events as indications that God was executing his judgements on Israel and the nations alike. They were visionaries of the future. The prophecies of Daniel, like those of the book of Revelation, were given to comfort God's people at a time of great stress. Their ultimate fulfilment would only be realised in the era of the gospel, and even beyond at the end of the age.

They foretold God's Messiah

It was John the Baptist, the last prophet of the old era, who heralded the arrival of Jesus as the fulfilment of the long-awaited promise of a coming ruler whose kingdom would last for ever. Christ, as God's final "Word" to this world, is recognised as fulfilling the age-old expectation of a Moses-like "prophet" who must be listened to. Although there were New Testament prophets – a gift of the Spirit to the church – with the emergence of the New Testament Scriptures, their importance stays largely foundational, like that of the apostles.

BIBLE CHECK

Received: Exodus 3;
1 Samuel 3; Isaiah 6;
Jeremiah 1; Habakkuk 2:1

Challenged: Deuteronomy
34:10-12; 1 Kings 18:16-40;
Amos 5:21-24; Acts 2:29-30

Revealed: Jeremiah 20:9;
2 Peter 1:20; Deuteronomy
4:32-40

Addressed: Isaiah 5:1-7;
Daniel 2:36-46; 7:13-18;
Revelation 1:12-20

Foretold: John 1:19-34;
Isaiah 9:2-7; 53:1-12;
Deuteronomy 18:15; Acts
3:17-22; Ephesians 2:20

KEY TRUTH

The prophets of the Bible,
in their speaking and writing,
stood before their people
as those who had first been
called to stand in the presence
of God. As such, their inspired
utterances have been bound
up for ever in the Scriptures.

POSTSCRIPT

It is a loyalty to the Scriptures
and the gospel, and the ability
to make them relevant in
today's world that stamp a
church or a Christian leader
as "prophetic".

BIBLE STUDY Jeremiah 1:1-19

This most heroic of all the Old Testament prophets had a
remarkable and turbulent career that stretched from 626 BC to
the fall of Jerusalem in 587 BC, a ministry of 40 years.

At no time did he gain favour with his listeners. A true
patriot who loved his people, he was nevertheless called to
pronounce against them in God's name, and he suffered
throughout his career. Use these questions as you study this
passage:

1 How common to God's servants of any generation is the
hesitation expressed by the prophet in verse 6? Let different
group members look up Exodus 4:10; Isaiah 6:5; Jonah 1:1-3;
How did God compensate for the weaknesses of his
servants? (See verses 7-9.)

2 Jeremiah was sent to prophesy to the southern kingdom of
Judah. But his commission was wider. How wide? What does
this tell us about God's word throughout the ages?

3 Two visions come to Jeremiah (verses 11-15), one positive
with its message of blossom, spring and fulfilment; the
other negative, with its message of disaster pouring upon
Judah. What does this tell us about the "bitter-sweet" nature
of service for God? Compare Revelation 10:9-11.

4 Can you think of others of God's servants who, despite their
frailties, have mirrored the protection described in verses
18,19?

REFLECTION

A Take time to read Jeremiah
1. Jeremiah was called to be a
prophet for God in the year
626 BC. Why is it that the
message of the prophets has a
wider readership today than
that of Plato or other ancient
philosophers?

B What lessons can we learn
from the prophets as we face
God's call to service today?

5. Apostles

An apostle is one "sent" or "commissioned". In this sense Christ was the supreme Apostle, sent from his Father. The term is also applied to "representatives" of the gospel, sent by the churches. But in general, "apostles" describe the unique group, invested with Christ's authority in the early church.

Personally appointed by Christ

Originally twelve in number, they were chosen by Jesus to be with him, to go out preaching and exercising spiritual authority in his name. Outside of the twelve, certain others became recognised as apostles, either directly or by association, Paul being outstanding.

Historically acquainted with Christ

The great qualification was a first-hand knowledge of Jesus' earthly ministry, from the time of John the Baptist until the Ascension. In this way the apostles could "witness" to the fact that the resurrected Christ was the same individual that they had worked and travelled with. The apostle Paul had not been with Jesus from the beginning, but the revelation he received was direct, not second-hand, and his later encounter with the risen Christ was unique to him alone.

Supernaturally accredited by Christ

The work of a true apostle was to be authenticated by miracles. These stamped the apostle as a messenger of Christ. The future reliability of the apostles' teaching for the whole church was also guaranteed by Jesus' pledge of the Holy Spirit's promptings and inspiration in all their future work.

As far as the Christian fellowship was concerned, the calling of an apostle was a gift of the Holy Spirit to the church. But in this instance there would be no renewal of the gift in subsequent generations. Yet the entire church has benefited from Christ's apostles.

They provided the church's foundations

Here was a "foundational" gift to the church at its very beginning, and the growth and progress of the church ever since has been the superstructure. Across the ages, "twelve" and its multiple would be taken as a symbol of the people of God – standing both for the Old Testament tribes of Israel and the New Testament apostles of Christ.

They defined the church's teaching

Jesus assured the apostles that after his bodily departure the Holy Spirit would guide them into all truth. This meant that the apostles' teaching became definitive for the church, and was placed on a level with the rest of Scripture. It follows that the strongest warnings are given in the New Testament about the presence of false apostles. Indeed the greatest threat to the early church came from false teaching.

They inspired the church's mission

All the other ministries of the church flowed out of that of the apostles, the "pillars" who gave the new missionary movement its leadership and impetus. The call to minister to a dying world stems from the momentous commission given by Jesus to the apostles.

BIBLE CHECK

Personally: Mark 3:13-19;
Galatians 1:19; 2:9;
1 Corinthians 15:7-9

Historically: Acts 1:21-22;
Galatians 1:11-12;
1 Corinthians 9:1-2; 15:8-11

Supernaturally:
2 Corinthians 12:12;
John 14:25-26;
1 Corinthians 2:6-16

Provided: Ephesians 2:19-22;
Revelation 21:14

Defined: John 16:12-15;
Acts 2:42; 2 Peter 3:16;
2 Corinthians 11:13

Inspired: Galatians 2:9;
John 20:19-22

KEY TRUTH

The apostles, a group limited to those who had been originally selected by Jesus Christ to act in his name, have provided the church for ever with its unchangeable standard for belief and practice.

POSTSCRIPT

Although the apostles have no successors today, it is possible to speak of a church or ministry being "apostolic" provided it is proclaiming the apostles' teaching.

BIBLE STUDY Galatians 1:6-24

Sometimes goods have to be taken off the shelves of stores and supermarkets, because of malicious tampering. Even if only a little of the product has been affected, the remedy has to be swift and radical – for people's welfare is at stake.

So with the gospel. In this instance the gospel has been tampered with by false teachers, and the letter to the Galatians, written around AD 48, represents a strong defence of two things; God's pure gospel and Paul's true apostleship.

1 Paul has often been criticised for his strong condemnation of those who preach falsely. But is he any harsher than other apostles – or indeed than Jesus himself? Different group members can look up 2 Peter 2:17; Jude 12; Revelation 22:18 and Luke 17:1-2.

2 Paul has been attacked throughout history for preaching an invented gospel different from Christ's. The apostle makes two points in verses 11 and 12. What are they?

3 Look at verses 13-24, especially verse 20. Why this insistence that the gospel was revealed to him in independence from the other apostles; that he had not "consulted" anyone; that he had been in isolation in Arabia? The clue lies in 1:1.

4 Consider the fact that the apostles were all preaching the same truths (eg Galatians 2:6-8; 1 Corinthians 15:11). What does this say to those today who are content with a diversity of interpretations of the Scriptures?

5 How "apostolic" is your fellowship? Look up Acts 2:42; 1 Corinthians 15:3-5; Jude 3.

REFLECTION

A Turn to Galatians 1, and especially verses 11-24, where Paul takes up one of the major themes of his book – the genuineness of his apostleship. What main point is he making? The clues are in verses 11-12, 15-20, and relate to the fact that in the early days of his call to be an apostle, his contact with the other apostles was minimal.

B Consider the fact that the apostles were all proclaiming the same truths (Galatians 2:6-8; 1 Corinthians 15:11). What does this tell us about disharmony in some modern-day preaching? Where should churches see their priorities?

C "And they praised God because of me" (verse 24). Not everybody did in Paul's day, nor does everybody do so today. Why?

6. Evangelists

Their work is God's gospel

The term "evangelist" comes from a word that means gospel or good news. The evangelist is the announcer of such news. But it must be emphasised that the work of evangelism is primarily the work of God himself. It was God who first "evangelised" Abraham, and Jesus who was to be found "evangelising" in Jerusalem's temple.

It is therefore God's mission before it can ever be that of the evangelist. The evangelist is simply one who is caught up in the wonder and joy created by the gospel and who cannot remain silent.

Their home is God's church

The true evangelist is drawn from within the local church membership, for it is there that the Holy Spirit distributed his gifts. The believer who has been given the gift of evangelism is to work in harmony and unity with those of other callings in the church.

Thus the work of evangelism is one of those gifts of the Spirit by which the body of Christ, the church, may be built up. Whether they are evangelists at large, such as Philip, or those settled in the oversight of a church, such as Timothy, they are called, not to create their own following, but to serve the churches that send them.

Their message is God's salvation

The evangelist is called to proclaim that what sinful men and women under divine judge-ment cannot do for themselves, God has done for them in Jesus Christ. Christ has died for the sins of the world and is now raised and ascended as universal Lord and Saviour.

The work of the evangelist is to call people to repent of their sins and personally to accept Christ, for the forgiveness of their sins and the gift of the Holy Spirit.

Their confidence is God's word

A characteristic that has always marked out the true evangelist is a distrust of self or of natural gifts, and a reliance upon "the testimony about God". The New Testament evangelists were aware that their message was based upon the inspired word of God; they encouraged each other to preach and learn from the Scriptures that make people wise for salvation and equip them to serve God.

It was the work of the evangelist to take the words of Scripture and to apply them with urgency and relevance to people without Christ.

Their power is God's Spirit

Jesus had left his friends with the apparently impossible task of bringing his witness to the whole world. It was the promise of the coming Holy Spirit that made the difference. As the early followers of Christ were filled with the Holy Spirit they found the boldness to speak in his name.

Human oratory and tricks of persuasion can never be the power behind God's evangelists. Evangelism is to be a demonstration, through changed lives, of the power of God.

Their goal is God's glory

The need of unforgiven sinners facing the judgement of God will always weigh heavily upon the evangelist. But the highest motivation for evangelism is a passion for the glory of God.

The conversion of sinners is a grace of God alone.

The evangelists of the New Testament were sent out by the churches to proclaim Christ as Lord to all the world. When this is faithfully done, they are a glory to his name.

BIBLE CHECK

Work: Galatians 3:8;
Luke 20:1; Acts 4:18-20;
Romans 10:14-15
Home: Ephesians 4:11-12;
Acts 21:8; 2 Timothy 4:5
Message: 2 Corinthians
5:17-21; 1 Corinthians
15:3-5; Acts 4:12
Confidence: 1 Corinthians
2:1,13; 2 Timothy 3:14–4:2;
Acts 8:26-35
Power: Acts 1:8;
1 Corinthians 2:4-5
Goal: Galatians 1:23-24;
2 Corinthians 4:15; 8:23;
1 Corinthians 9:11-18

KEY TRUTH

While all Christians are
to share their faith, some
individuals are called to be
evangelists, with a special gift
from the Holy Spirit, to
announce the good news of
the gospel.

POSTSCRIPT

Although there is a place for
the evangelist to receive a
living for the service that is
given, a modest lifestyle and a
restrained discipline should
characterise the whole
ministry.

BIBLE STUDY 2 Corinthians 4:1-18

Both letters of Paul to the Corinthians are taken up with a
single theme, that of power through weakness. Of all the New
Testament churches, the Corinthian was the most confused
and the least mature. The false teachers had made a bid for the
soul of the church, and power-hungry bogus apostles were
promoting their own status and discrediting Paul.

When the thrilling work of proclaiming the gospel is
dishonoured by the power-grabbers, the peace-breakers and
the sheep-stealers; by self-promoting triumphalism and by the
wrenching of Scripture to bolster a dubious message ... the
Corinthian correspondence is the result.

1 This passage is full of fascinating paradoxes or contrasts.
Try to follow them through: weakness and power, mortality
and life, affliction and glory, etc. What does this teach us
about the ministry of making Christ known?
2 Why is it necessary to apply to ourselves the standards of
openness and integrity followed by Paul in verse 2?
3 Look at the discouragements! (eg verses 4,8-9). Why is it
then that "we do not lose heart" (verses 1 and 16)? What has
the answer got to do with the glory of Christ and the
message of the cross?
4 "Treasure ... jars of clay" (verse 7). Why this contrast between
the message and the messenger? If this is evangelism as it
should be, where do we see it at its best today?
5 Can you think of evangelists in the New Testament who
worked in the spirit and lifestyle of this passage? See Acts
8:26-40; 7:54-60. Spend time now in prayer for evangelists
you know.

REFLECTION

A Read 2 Corinthians 4. This
passage is full of paradoxes or
contrasts. Try to follow them
through: weakness and
power, mortality and life,
affliction and glory, etc. What
does this teach us about the
ministry of evangelism?

B Meditate on verse 5, and
identify evangelists and
missionaries who deserve our
support and our prayers in
the way they proclaim the
gospel.
C Verses 1-2 give important
guidelines to the evangelist.
What are they?

1. God's Plan for Humanity

God's plan – his will is sovereign

The Bible teaches that God is above everything, and he uses the most unlikely people to carry out his purposes .

Thus, Jacob and not Esau (who was the older of the two) was chosen to be head of the family which God would use to rescue humanity. Similarly David, the youngest of his family, was chosen as the one through whose descendants the Messiah would come. In the New Testament, those who were called to be God's people in Christ were called purely on the basis of God's own purpose and generosity.

God's plan – his work is eternal

The Bible teaches us that God's work of salvation, centred in Christ, has been planned from eternity.

The death of Jesus in Jerusalem at a fixed point in time was the result of the wilful act of angry sinners, but it must also be seen as an event planned by God from before the beginning of the world.

God's plan – his choice is specific

While the Bible is against the idea of "fatalism" (that is, whatever God decides for us, we are fated to do), it does teach that God's plan is more than simply a general call to all humanity. Those who freely respond to his call learn that God had chosen them from among many, according to his own purpose and will.

God's people – separated for holy living

Properly understood, the biblical teaching of predestination will never generate complacency in those who are chosen by God. For the people of God are called to be holy.

In the Old Testament, something that was specially set apart for the service of God was called "holy". So it is with the Christian. On freely responding to God's call, we learn that we have been predestined, from eternity, for a life of obedience and Christ-likeness.

God's people – called to good works

God's call of Abraham, of Isaac and Jacob, was for the specific purpose of bringing benefit to the world.

God's people, in the New Testament, are called to a life of good deeds and energetic mission. It is not for them to determine who are among the called. Their responsibility is to proclaim and reflect the goodness of God to all of humanity.

God's people – preparing for future glory

God's eternal plan for his people has a glorious future in view. From the beginning, the Christian has been chosen for salvation; this includes the future life of glory with Christ.

It is Christ who provides the key to God's plan. Without him, there is no salvation, and the Christian is nothing. It is only as we are identified with him that we can hope to share in his victory over death, and in the eternal home he has planned for us. The future glory begins now – in faithful service and obedience.

BIBLE CHECK

Will: 1 Corinthians 1:26-29;
Romans 9:10-18
Work: Acts 2:23; 1 Peter
1:18-20; Revelation 13:8
Choice: Matthew 22:14;
Romans 9:20-21,27
Separated: Romans 8:29;
Ephesians 1:4; 1 Peter 1:1-2
Called: Philippians 2:12-13;
Acts 9:15; 1 Peter 2:9-12
Preparing: 2 Thessalonians
2:13-14; Revelation 17:14

KEY TRUTH

God has always had a plan
for rescuing those who are in
rebellion against him. The
Bible tells us that although
we are free to respond to God,
he has already chosen us to be
his people. The word
"predestination" means that
God has selected and
separated a people for
himself.

POSTSCRIPT

The biblical emphasis
regarding God's sovereignty
and human free-will is not
found somewhere between
the two, but in both extremes.
If we over-emphasise free will,
then God will seem to be
powerless. If we over-
emphasise God's sovereignty,
then human beings will seem
to be denied any choice.

BIBLE STUDY Ephesians 1:3-12

Under the guidance of the Holy Spirit, the apostle Paul had
targeted Ephesus as a strategic growth point for the church of
Jesus Christ. He spent longer in Ephesus than in any other
church. The likelihood is that this was a "circular" intended
for all the churches on the Ephesus postal route, on the
seaboard of what is modern-day Turkey. Our passage before us
is, in the Greek original, a single unbroken sentence! Try to
take in the sweep of Paul's thought as he writes about God's
plan of salvation:

1 How impossible would the plan, as it is described in verse 10,
have looked to those inhabitants of a teeming pagan city?
What is the keystone of God's eternal plan? It features in
every single verse.

2 What can you learn from verse 3-6 about God's eternal plan,
on which we are to rest our confidence? Paul is working back
from salvation to ... what?

3 What can be learnt in this passage about the central work of
Christ – a second ground for our confidence? How does
verse 7 anchor the high-flown language in a concrete, earth-
bound way?

4 What can you trace here about the personal working of the
Holy Spirit – as a third ground on which the Christian's
confidence rests? The "seal" (verse 13) seems to stand for the
mark of genuineness, the stamp of ownership (Ephesians
4:30) and the guarantee of security (compare Matthew
27:66, same Greek word). Work out how this applies to the
Christian.

5 "Mystery" (verse 9) refers in this context, not to something
impenetrable, but to a secret, once hidden, but now blown
open – for everyone! When did this happen for you?

REFLECTION

A Read Ephesians 1:3-12.
What should be the reaction
of those who are called? What
is the immediate purpose of
this call, the future purpose
and the ultimate purpose?

B Meditate on John 6:37,44;
2 Peter 1:10-11, where God's
sovereignty and human free-
will are combined.

C Why should a true understanding of predestination
not stop us from urging those
we know to choose to become
Christians?

D Some may argue that they
are not called. Where does
Scripture teach that God's
redemption is offered to all?
Compare your findings with,
for example, 1 Timothy 2:4,6;
Titus 2:11.

SALVATION
2. Humanity's Need of Salvation

Humanity's need of a new direction

Although created by God, and for him, human beings have left the path of obedience to God. We are out of touch with God and all that he has planned for us, and without him life does not make sense to us.

Humanity is also under judgement. Jesus Christ's analysis was that the majority of humanity is treading the path of ruin and destruction. People are condemned for their rejection of God's truth.

Humanity's need of a new nature

Humanity is in bondage because of our refusal to follow God's commands. On our own, we are unable to change our nature as the sin principle dominates us, and our actions and habits show that we are in slavery.

We live our lives under the shadow of death, and over the ages no amount of philosophy, guesswork or moral endeavour has been able to remove the spectre of ageing and dying.

Humanity's need of a new motivation

The brevity and purposelessness of life without God are reflected in art and literature throughout history, particularly in times when society openly rejects God's standards.

The Bible indicates that we need the dimension of God if life is to be lived with dynamism and purpose. Without God we find no satisfying, alternative way of life.

Humanity's need of personal fulfilment

We are in urgent need of a sense of destiny and achievement in this world. Our aspirations will sometimes take the form of extreme materialistic ambitions; at other times they will shrivel into despair and aimlessness.

Jesus warned his hearers that a person's life should never be totally taken up with the accumulation of possessions. He taught that whoever spent his life and energies upon the material world would have made a bad bargain.

Humanity's need of social acceptance

From earliest times, as illustrated by the story of the Tower of Babel, human beings have been aware of the need for the friendship and acceptance of others. History illustrates our search for true fellowship, mutual trust and companionship.

But ideals, agreements and political arrangements all fall short of what we are searching for. The cynicism expressed in the book of Ecclesiastes shows us this clearly. Human beings are lonely.

Humanity's need of a spiritual dimension

As fallen people we cannot appreciate the spiritual side of life, left to ourselves. But because God made us, we feel incomplete without a Godward dimension.

Furthermore, we are unable to explore this dimension unaided, because we are described as being poor, weak, blind, and even dead. In the absence of spiritual awareness, our prospects appear to make a mockery of our once high position.

BIBLE CHECK

New direction: Hebrews 9:27; Matthew 7:13; John 3:19

New nature: Jeremiah 13:23; 17:9-10; John 8:34; Ecclesiastes 8:8

Motivation: Ecclesiastes 6:12; John 6:66-68

Fulfilment: Ecclesiastes 2:10-11; Luke 12:15; Mark 8:34-37

Social: Genesis 11:4; Ecclesiastes 5:8

Spiritual: 1 Corinthians 2:14; 2 Corinthians 4:4

KEY TRUTH

The human race is estranged and cut off from God. Humanity needs a new direction and nature, if we are to avoid permanent ruin and eternal judgement. We cannot bring about this change for ourselves.

POSTSCRIPT

Although we all need God's salvation, many people are unaware of their own need. A person may become so used to living in separation from God that conscience becomes dead. Such complacency is only further proof of our ruined nature.

BIBLE STUDY Ephesians 2:1-10

Paul outlines to his Christian readers in Ephesus the hopelessness of their case before the arrival of the gospel among them. Ephesus was a centre of idolatry, given over to the worship of Artemis (or Diana), whose temple was four times the size of the Parthenon at Athens. When salvation in Christ's name was preached at Ephesus for the first time, it rocked commercial interests and provoked a riot (Acts 19:23-41). This was the world out of which the new believers had been drawn:

1 "Dead" (verse 1). Dead in what way? Dead to what? Usually the doctor's work ceases at death. What then is the state of those without Christ? See end of verse 12.

2 "Transgressions and sins" (verse 1) – how popular would this description have been with a worshipper at the temple of Artemis? How are we to help those who say they have no needs at all?

3 In verses 2 and 3, identify those phrases that refer to the world, the flesh and the devil. Why is it wise to keep all three adversaries in view rather than transfer all the categories into a single camp – that of, say, the devil?

4 "Objects of wrath" (verse 3). How do phrases like this square with the teaching of Jesus? See Matthew 13:41-42; 18:6. Were members of the group ever aware that verse 3 once described them? If not, this serves as a useful reminder.

5 "But" (verse 4). This is the word that opens the door and lets in the light. As you read the remaining verses, think of the idolatrous Ephesians, raised in an instant to the situation of verse 6.

6 All this speaks to us of grace (verses 5,7-8). Discuss the meaning of this wonderful word. See Romans 3:24.

REFLECTION

A Study Ecclesiastes 2:1-11. Try to analyse this profile of a person without God. What drives him? What is his programme? What are his achievements and what does he get? Has verse 11 found an echo in other generations?

B How far are people in your own fellowship beginning to experience the answers of God to all these human needs?

C What makes Ecclesiastes so relevant to much of present-day society?

D How far have you experienced these needs in your own life? How far do you still experience them?

3. The Way of Salvation

The basis – the death of Jesus

The apostles proclaimed the death of Jesus Christ as the means by which God has dealt with the sins of humanity. They declared that without his death there could be no basis for salvation. On the cross, Christ accepted the judgement and separation from God brought about by the sins of the world.

This message directly fulfilled Old Testament prophecy, and the words of Christ himself. It was also taught in the New Testament letters.

The basis – the resurrection of Jesus

If the cross was seen as the means by which God had dealt with sin, the resurrection was proclaimed by the early church as the evidence and proof that Christ's death had been truly effective, and had been recognised by God the Father.

The message of Christ's resurrection was not taught merely as a point of academic discussion. The early witnesses announced it as a living reality.

The call – to repentance

The good news was recognised to have a distinctive moral challenge at its heart. The sinner who hears the gospel is called upon to "repent", which means to turn from the old life. This turning is more than a mere regret for the past. It is a change of attitude, leading to a change of direction.

The call – to faith

If repentance is seen as a turning from the old life, faith is to be understood in similarly active terms. It is turning towards the saving power of Jesus Christ.

There are three aspects to faith. There is belief in a fact, for true faith must start by believing with the mind. There is also belief in a word, or promise particularly as given by God. But, vitally, there is belief in a person – Jesus Christ. This requires a living relationship of love and trust with Christ. Without these three aspects faith is incomplete.

The promise – forgiveness

There is a finality and a completeness about the forgiveness of sins that is promised to all who respond to the good news of Christ.

Forgiveness is made available only at the price of Christ's death, and God gives it freely and permanently. To be forgiven does not merely mean the wiping away of our past sins – it means the beginning of a new way of life. Because God forgives us, we are able to enjoy his friendship and acceptance.

The promise – the gift of the Spirit

The forgiveness of sins and the gift of the Spirit go together as the promise of New Testament Christianity. God freely gives us the Holy Spirit when we repent and believe in him.

The gift of the Spirit makes the blessings of the gospel and the presence of Christ personal to the Christian. He gives us power for service and reassures us of the promise of eternal life. The Holy Spirit makes actual all that Christ's death made available.

BIBLE CHECK

Death: Acts 4:10-12; Isaiah 53:4-6; 1 Peter 3:18

Resurrection: Acts 2:32-36; Romans 8:11

Repentance: Acts 3:19; Luke 15:10; 24:46-47

Faith: Acts 13:38-39; 26:18; John 3:16; Revelation 3:20

Forgiveness: Acts 3:19; Psalm 103:11-12; Ephesians 1:7-8

Gift of the Spirit: Acts 2:38; Ephesians 1:13-14

KEY TRUTH

In all the preaching of the early church, as documented in the book of Acts, the way of salvation follows a distinctive pattern. First there is the basis of salvation – Christ's death and resurrection – followed by God's call; and then there is the promise to all who respond.

POSTSCRIPT

In becoming a Christian there is a part that only we can play and a part that only God can play. We repent and abandon our old way of life. God forgives us and empowers us through the Holy Spirit.

BIBLE STUDY Titus 3:3-8

Crete is the setting of this small but powerful letter from the apostle Paul to his trusted lieutenant Titus, around the year AD 62 or 63. Crete had become a part of the Roman Empire in 67 BC; it was a sizeable island, dominating the south of the Aegean Sea – mountainous, superstitious and tough to handle! Here Paul is concerned to hold his Cretan friends to the unchanging fundamentals of salvation's message. What was this message?

1 Somebody once said, "I didn't know I was lost until I was found." Why is it important to revisit our past, as Paul invited his readers to do in verse 3?

2 "Disobedient, deceived and enslaved" (verse 3) – how far do members of the group recognise these terms as describing their pre-Christian situation?

3 Now, in verses 4-8, the apostle reviews the process and wonder of salvation. What is the key word (verse 5)? What do you learn from the coupling of "God" (verse 4) and "Jesus Christ" (verse 6) as "Saviour"?

4 What are the phrases in this passage that speak of the new birth, participation in the out-pouring of the Holy Spirit at Pentecost, justification, and eternal life? Notice the word "washing" (verse 5). To what does this refer? For a clue, look up Ezekiel 36:25-26.

5 Think about the ground of our salvation. What is it, and what is it not?

6 The "appearing" of verse 4 can only refer, as in 2:11, to the coming of Christ and his self-giving at the cross (2:14). In the light of this, how do you define "grace" (verse 7)?

7 We know what we are saved from. What are we saved for? See verse 8.

REFLECTION

A Start reading half-way through Paul's sermon in Acts 13:22-41. What are the main elements in Paul's message? What is said about Jesus, and how is it said?

B Try to isolate one or more New Testament passages that helpfully sum up the message of salvation. Compare your findings with others. For instance, look at John 3, Romans 3, Ephesians 2, Titus 3.

C What is the relative importance of the mind, the emotions and the will in the response of the individual to the good news?

D What is the main goal in proclaiming salvation in Christ? Check your thoughts against Colossians 1:28 and Matthew 28:19-20.

4. Acceptance

God regenerates the believer as a new being

So radical is the renewing work of the Spirit that it is spoken of in terms of new birth, or "regeneration". It is described as birth "from above". As an individual repents and believes in Christ, so the Holy Spirit enters his life and personality and joins him to the family of God. The Spirit also gives him a new nature characterised by the hallmarks of a new moral outlook, love for the family of God, and faith in Christ.

God reconciles the believer in a new relationship

Until the good news is received and acted upon, a state of hostility exists between God and the individual. It is the death of Christ that specifically alters the situation. On the cross, Christ himself accepted the guilt and penalty for the sins of humanity. The way is opened for a repentant sinner to receive the reconciliation thus made available by God in Christ.

It is the cross that satisfies God's justice – for there God's anger against sin was fully poured out. This is why the cross is called a propitiation.

God redeems the believer through a new covenant

The old covenant was an agreement entered into by God with the Jews, primarily on the basis of the law of Moses. It established a way of life for them after their deliverance from Egypt. This old covenant was a shadow of the new covenant, pointing to the new covenant in all its details.

The new covenant (foretold by Jeremiah) was to achieve through the cross what the old could never do. The deliverance was of another kind, personal and internal, on the basis of Christ's shed blood, for the forgiveness of sins and the redeeming (or "buying back") of the sinner. This was a costly price indeed.

God justifies the believer for a new position

To "justify" is a legal term, which means to declare that a person is righteous. God has done this for the person who has responded to Christ, on the basis of the death of Jesus.

Justification is said to be by "grace" (which means God's undeserved favour), for it is a free gift. It is also by blood, for Christ's death is the means by which God could legally forgive the sinner. It is also by faith, for there is nothing the sinner can contribute to his new position of righteousness – nothing beyond accepting the gift in grateful faith.

God glorifies the believer for a new life

In the New Testament letters, it is noticeable that salvation is repeatedly expressed in three stages. First, there is the free grace of God as the initial act and base. Second, there is the growth of godliness in the Christian as a progressive experience. Third, glory is seen as the future goal and pinnacle. The Christian's great confidence is in the certain return of Christ, the promise of a resurrection body and a share in God's eternal glory.

BIBLE CHECK

Regenerates: Ezekiel
36:25-27; John 3:3-8;
Titus 3:4-5

Reconciles: 2 Corinthians
5:18-21; Romans 5:10

Redeems: Jeremiah 31:31-34;
Mark 14:24; 1 Peter 1:18-19

Justifies: Romans 3:23-26;
5:1; Titus 3:7

Glorifies: Romans 8:28-30;
Philippians 3:20-21

KEY TRUTH

The sinner is accepted by God
in Christ, and made a new
person. The benefits this
position and relationship
bring should make the
Christian eternally grateful.

POSTSCRIPT

New believers may be
confident that God has
accepted them because of the
promises in the word of God,
the finished work of Christ,
and the inward witness of the
Holy Spirit.

BIBLE STUDY Romans 5:1-11

The apostle Paul has been developing a logical argument as he
sets out God's way of salvation. He had argued for universal
guilt across the human race; he has outlined the way by which
people can be justified and placed in a right standing before
God, on the basis of Christ's death for us all (Romans
3:24-26). He moves on now to the wonderful consequences of
what it means to be justified.

1 Think through what is meant by peace with God,
   the first stated result of being justified. For Paul did not
   apparently have much "peace" in his turbulent career.
   However, as a preacher once said, "A dull bovine
   contentment is the stagnancy of life and not peace
   with God." What is this peace?

2 Linked with peace is a further benefit. How would you put
   verse 2 into your own words? Try and give a definition of
   "grace". Can one fall in and out of grace? See John 6:37.

3 In verses 2 and 3 there are two reasons given for rejoicing.
   How surprised are you that these two reasons are so close
   to one another? Why are they linked like this? (Compare
   1 Peter 1:11; 4:13; 5:1; 5:10.)

4 The unbelieving world does not think about trials in the way
   outlined in verse 3 and 4. How is it that the Christian can see
   affliction and adversity as productive?

5 Meditate on the sense of God's love, that he puts into the
   lives of all those who are justified (verses 5-8). Meanwhile
   what four words described us? (See verses 6,8,10).

6 Is the best yet to be? Give reasons for such thinking, from
   the rest of this passage.

REFLECTION

A Read Romans 5:1-11, with
its portrayal of the Christian's
new position in Christ. Look
for the key terms. List the
ways in which God has been
generous to us, and give
thanks to him for them.
B In what sense can we say
that we have been "justified
by grace / blood / faith"?

C Write down the qualities
you have enjoyed in a
relationship with one of your
friends. Write down the
demands such a relationship
makes. How is your
relationship with God the
same, and how is it different?
D Do the Christian's troubles
end, upon entering into peace
with God? What does
Romans 5:1-5 teach us?

5. Sanctification

A separation to God

While justification is the work of a moment – that of declaring the sinner righteous – sanctification is the process of a lifetime – that of making the sinner righteous in life and character.

Holiness means separateness. In the Old Testament, houses and animals were sometimes set apart for the special use of God. Christ's followers have been called by God to be set apart – so that they may become more like Christ and holy in character.

A separation from the world

The Christian is called to cooperate with the sanctifying purposes and power of God. There must be a willingness to abandon evil and impure ways; to be separate from all that could impede the development of Christ-like living.

Sanctification is not the separation of a hermit or recluse, because Jesus mixed with sinners and yet in his standards and character was "set apart" from sinners (Hebrews 7:26). His desire for his followers is that they remain involved in the world, while remaining free from its evil.

A separation for holy living

Success in Christian living is, to a great degree, dependent on our readiness to be given to God in total self-sacrifice and surrender.

The Christian who takes holiness seriously is viewed as a "slave" of righteousness; as a "living sacrifice" to God; as a clean household utensil.

A separation by the Holy Spirit

Although the Christian's cooperation is vital in the process of sanctification, the power comes from the Holy Spirit.

Throughout the Old Testament, the prophets challenge Israel to have circumcised hearts, hearts that have the law of God written upon them. The prophets called the people to not just know the law in their heads, but to love it from their hearts. This is what the Holy Spirit does in us. He gives us right desires and begins to change our characters so that we act in a way that pleases God.

A separation through the word of God

The Bible has a cleansing effect in the Christian's life. The Holy Spirit uses the Bible to enlarge the Christian's vision of Christ and strengthen his desire for holy living.

The Bible is also a guide to the way of life God wants us to live. It shows us what our priorities and attitudes should be. The Bible tells us that the words of God can be planted in our personalities. The Holy Spirit does this.

A separation that progresses throughout life

Sanctification is a process in which encouragement and challenge go side by side. The believer understands that we have been saved from the penalty of sin; that we are being saved from the power of sin that we shall be saved from the presence of sin.

BIBLE CHECK

To God: Leviticus 27:14;
2 Thessalonians 2:13
The world: 2 Corinthians
6:17–7:1; John 17:15
Holy living: Romans 6:19;
12:1; 2 Timothy 2:20-21
Holy Spirit: Ezekiel 36:27;
Galatians 5:16-18
Word of God: John 15:3;
17:17; Psalm 119:9;
James 1:21
Progresses: 2 Corinthians
1:10; 3:18; 1 Thessalonians
5:23

KEY TRUTH

The word "sanctification" describes the process that God wants every Christian to experience. God wants us to be sanctified, increasingly to become more like him in all that we think and do. Sanctification means to grow in holiness.

POSTSCRIPT

The fact that Christians become awake to their sins and failures is a sign of progress. We must go further, however, bringing our sins to God for his forgiveness, and enlarging our vision of Christ. In this way we shall increasingly want to be more like him. It is in the area of motives that the battle for holiness rages the strongest.

BIBLE STUDY 2 Peter 1:3-11

The apostle Peter was an old man when he wrote this, the second of two letters. This was written, mainly to non-Jewish readers, to encourage Christian people to keep on in their faith, and to resist the false teachers of the day who menaced them in their "precious" faith (1:1).

It is not just the start, but the continuing of the life of faith that is the mark of the genuine believer. Is there a good platform of knowledge for our growth as Christians? Are we holding onto the fact that we have been separated as a different, a holy people for God? These are the issues that this passage takes up:

1 Look at verses 3 and 4. How would you answer the fears of new believers who imagine that, having made a beginning with Christ, they are now out on their own and expected to manage?

2 We may "participate in the divine nature" (verse 4). This cannot mean that human Christians have become part of God. What then does it mean? Scripture interprets Scripture – John 1:12-13; 15:4-5 will help.

3 In verses 5-7 we are presented with a kind of "ladder of progress". If the power and resources come from God, what is required of us? In practical terms, how do you do this?

4 Go through these qualities that are looked for in the believer. Somehow they are all linked to knowledge (verses 2-3,5,8). How are you going to attend to this programme, and to fulfil Paul's prayer in Philippians 3:10?

5 "Short-sighted and blind ... forgotten ..." (verse 9). The remedy for this condition is in verses 10-11. Can you do that for yourself? Can you do it for each other in the fellowship?

REFLECTION

A Read 2 Peter 1:3-11. How are the Christian readers of this letter described, as regards their past state, their present responsibilities and their future goals?

B Forgiveness is always free. But to presume on God's mercy, in order to continue in sin, has no place in the Christian life. Why? See Titus 2:11-14.

C What are the tensions of staying involved in the world, and yet being separate from its evil (John 17:15)?

D Effort seems to be required of Christians who desire to grow (2 Peter 1:5-7,10). What kind of effort is needed? What are the rewards for such effort, as mentioned in the passage?

SALVATION
6. In the Letter to the Romans

It features the following themes:

Condemnation – Romans 1:1–3:20
Paul tells us that the theme of his letter is "the righteousness of God".

He then shows that the righteousness of the Gentile and Jewish world falls far short of God's standard and is therefore under his condemnation. All the world is guilty.

Justification – Romans 3:20–4:25
God's way of declaring the sinner to be righteous is independent of Old Testament law (although the Old Testament witnesses to it). It is provided freely, through the death of Christ, for all who have faith of the kind illustrated in Abraham.

Reconciliation – Romans 5:1–21
From the firm base of being put right with God, Paul amplifies the blessings and security of justification for the believer. He contrasts Adam with Christ – the new representative and Head of the human race, whose one righteous act is capable of setting free all humanity.

Identification – Romans 6:1–23
Paul defends the truth of justification against the charge that it encourages deliberate continuation in sin and in lawlessness. Paul argues that the believer has now been identified with Christ in his death and resurrection, and indeed has become a "slave" of righteousness.

Liberation – Romans 7:1-25
From justification and identification with Christ, Paul moves to a third privilege of the believer – freedom from slavery to the law. The Christian's slavery is now to Christ in the new way of the Spirit (verses 1-6). It is not the law, of course, that is to be blamed for human sin, but fallen human nature (verses 7-13). In his internal conflict, the Christian may know liberation and power (verses 14-25).

Sanctification – Romans 8:1-39
Now that the old legal slavery belongs to the past those who belong to Christ live by a stronger principle and power – the life of the Spirit.

Those whose life is controlled by the Holy Spirit fulfil God's laws from the heart. They are assured by the Spirit's presence in their lives that they are God's children. Nothing can now separate them from the love of Christ.

Election – Romans 9:1–11:36
Paul now faces the problem of the Jew's rejection of their own Messiah. He interprets this in the light of election – the truth that God chooses a people for himself. God is supremely sovereign, and uses even the disobedience of the Jews to divert his blessing to the rest of the world. Meanwhile God has not completely abandoned the Jews.

Transformation – Romans 12:1–15:13
Paul applies himself to the practical duties of Christian living. The life of the believer is to be a transformed life of service, sharing with other Christians, duty to the government, and respect for others' convictions.

BIBLE CHECK

Condemnation: Romans 3:9,19

Justification: Romans 3:24-25

Reconciliation: Romans 5:10-11

Identification: Romans 6:6

Liberation: Romans 7:6

Sanctification: Romans 8:11

Election: Romans 9:21-24

Transformation: Romans 12:1-2

KEY TRUTH

The letter to the Romans is the apostle Paul's "manifesto" of Christian truth, in which the way of salvation is clearly proclaimed and applied.

POSTSCRIPT

All who have encountered salvation will want to know more about the truth of their experience. Although the book of Romans may tax the reader's concentration, it is rewarding to read through it slowly and understand the truth of salvation at a deeper level.

BIBLE STUDY Romans 8:28-39

Running through all the first eight chapters of the letter to the Romans has been the unfolding plan of God. This great section now ends with one of the most inspiring passages of the New Testament, in which adversity is cut down to its true size, every accusation against the believer is destroyed, and God's love becomes a platform of confidence for time and eternity.

Read these verses, and use the following questions to help in the study of them:

1 Begin at the much-loved verse 28. It may be worth going round the group, and inquiring about the different circumstances in which the strength of this statement has so far been proved.

2 What is the ultimate "good" that God works for in us? Verse 29 gives the answer. How far do you recognise that this is the goal of all Christian living? Compare 2 Corinthians 3:18.

3 Predestination (verses 29-30) is not a topic for dry academic dispute; it is a comforting family secret for those who have responded to the claims of Christ. From these verses, what precisely is the comfort?

4 What great themes of the letter to the Romans can you trace in this passage? They are virtually all there.

5 Examine the five "unanswerable" questions of verses 31-36. Why is the word "if" so important in verse 31? What human predicaments do these questions relate to?

6 Is the language of verses 37-38 just a burst of purple oratory? On what reality is this based? Look back to verse 32. Compare 1 Corinthians 3:21-22.

REFLECTION

A Read Romans 8:28-39. In what way is God's purpose working on behalf of his people? What great themes of the letter to the Romans can you trace in this passage?

B In verses 31-39, what reasons does the apostle give for his triumphant confidence – in terms of the believer's relationship to God, to Christ, and to circumstances?

C Look at the question of verse 31. What do the themes of Romans mean to you, or what are they beginning to mean to you?

D A review question: in what way are justification and sanctification different from each other?

THE CHRISTIAN
1. Described

A sinner saved by grace

It was at Antioch that believers in Christ were first called Christians – probably as a term of abuse. However, Christians have always valued this identification, because of the immensity of the debt they owe to Christ, after whom they are called.

It is God's grace that has brought the sinner into union with Christ. Grace is the free, unearned favour of God towards the sinner. This grace is only possible because of the cross, and it is made real to us by the Holy Spirit. Salvation cannot be earned. It is a free gift to be received by faith.

A member of God's family

In his letter to the Roman Christians, the apostle Paul teaches that the people who did not belong to God at all are now, by his grace, called sons of the living God.

Such a title is not naturally ours. It is only given to those who receive Jesus Christ. It is by the power of God's love that this "adoption" into his family takes place. Being part of the church means to learn the discipline and joy of being in the family.

A disciple of Jesus Christ

A "disciple" in Jesus' day was a person who followed both his master's teaching and his way of life. Christ said that those who were willing to love him and obey him first above all else were his disciples. A Christian is a person who has responded to his call, "Follow me".

A temple of the Holy Spirit

In the Old Testament, the Jews were given special instructions on how to build the temple – and on it they lavished all their riches, craftsmanship and care, so that God should be glorified in every possible way. In his letter to the Corinthians, Paul tells us that our bodies are the temple of the Holy Spirit. This means that all our abilities and powers should be devoted towards glorifying God.

A pilgrim in an alien environment

Many of the Old Testament's great figures are described as people who had no permanent home of their own. Abraham, for example, left the security of his family home to live in tents in a foreign land. The writer to the Hebrews describes such people as those who saw that the earth was not their home. Similarly, the New Testament urges us not to put our trust in material possessions, and to guard against indiscipline. For we too must realise that this earth is not our true home. Christians are like foreigners and strangers, with their permanent home elsewhere.

A citizen of heaven

The Christian will not find permanence in this passing age – our permanent home still lies in the future. But the full membership and many of the privileges of that future home are with every Christian now.

As a result, the Christian is described as a citizen of heaven. We see ourselves as people who belong to another country and we are ambassadors of that country even in this present age.

Sinner: Acts 11:26; Ephesians
2:8-9; 1 Timothy 1:15
Member: Romans 9:25-26;
John 1:12-13; Ephesians
3:14-15
Disciple: Luke 14:26-27;
Matthew 9:9
Temple: 1 Kings 6; Acts
7:48-49; 1 Corinthians
6:19-20
Pilgrim: Exodus 22:21;
Hebrews 11:8-16;
1 Peter 2:11-12
Citizen: Ephesians 2:19;
Hebrews 13:14; Revelation
22:14

KEY TRUTH

A Christian is a person who
has received Jesus Christ as
Saviour and Lord, and has
submitted to the rule of God's
kingdom.

POSTSCRIPT

It is unwise, and untrue to the
Bible, to believe that a person
can receive Jesus Christ as
Saviour without receiving him
as Lord.

BIBLE STUDY Luke 5:1-11

Here is a story of utter simplicity. It occurred one fine
summer's day on a small lake, $12\frac{1}{2}$ miles long by $6\frac{1}{2}$ miles
wide – one of a string of lakes that stretches from Israel right
down into Africa and along the great Rift Valley, a scar on the
earth's face that is observable from the moon. In nearly all
those lakes tilapia fish are to be found, and Lake Gennesaret
(or Galilee) was no exception.

   Read the story carefully, because it is your story, the
beginning of the greatest movement and family of faith that
the world has ever seen, and which will never have an end.

1 What was the draw that day? What is always the draw? Is it a
   draw for you?
2 Jesus had met and called Simon and his colleagues before
   (Matthew 4:18-22). But it seemed to have been little more
   than a limited discipleship, a foot in the door? For what
   were the "disciples" doing, while the preaching was going on
   (verse 2)?
3 How common to you is the phenomenon that the real
   business often begins when the preaching has come to an
   end (verse 4)?
4 Reflect on the fact that the acknowledged lifetime fishing
   expert accepts advice on his trade from someone whose
   noted speciality was woodwork. What does this tell you
   about Christ? What is the key phrase of verses 5-6 – indeed
   of the whole passage?
5 Here in verse 6 is a catch that is going to get itself into the
   record books – better still, into the Bible. A whole new life is
   opening up for Peter (verses 8-11). Define it.
6 Could you have done what Peter and his companions did?
   After half a lifetime? Discuss this together, then pray.

REFLECTION

A Study Ephesians 2:1-10,19.
Reflect on the "but" of verse
4. In what way is it the shaft
of light that illuminates the
passage? If you were going to
speak on verses 8-9, what
major points would you
make?
B Two descriptions of the
Christian are given in
Ephesians 2:19. To what
extent have you experienced
the privileges implied by these
terms?
C What are the insecure
aspects of being a Christian?
What are the secure aspects?
D Try to think of some less
prominent biblical
illustrations of the Christian,
and of what they imply. (Clue:
look at 2 Timothy 2.)

THE CHRISTIAN
2. The Christian and the Bible

THE BIBLE ...

Directs the Christian for life

Biblically, a disciple of Jesus is recognised
by unashamed loyalty to Christ's person and
unquestioning obedience to his commands.
The Master cannot accept disciples who want
to establish their own method of instruction
or set their own course.

Jesus taught that those obedient to his
words would be characterised by stability;
the disobedient would be overthrown. This
is a principle throughout Scripture. The Bible
is like a lamp, guiding the Christian.

Equips the Christian for battle

The believer must learn from Christ, who
resisted the devil's temptations in the
wilderness with his knowledge of the Old
Testament. A working knowledge of the Bible
is a weapon of spiritual power.

Equally, in defending the Christian faith,
the Christian who enters the arena having
thought through the issues beforehand is at
an immense advantage. A biblically-trained
mind is a weapon of priceless value. The Bible
is like a sword, protecting the Christian.

Energises the Christian for service

The disciple is called to be fruitful in service,
bringing both the compassion and challenge
of Christ's message to bear upon a needy
world.

It is the inexhaustible supply found in
God's living word that gives Christian service
its vitality and freshness. The Bible's depths
can never be plumbed. The Bible is like water,
renewing the Christian.

Corrects the Christian from error

The Bible exposes and corrects many errors
and distortions of true belief. There is the
legalist – the victim of convention; the empty
ritualist – the victim of superstition; the
traditionalist – the victim of pride; the
rationalist – the victim of unbelief; and
the mere theorist – the victim of laziness.

The Bible is God's message to us. Because
of this, we should always be open to it to
correct our own wrong ideas, and to replace
them with God's truth. The Bible is like a
mirror, reforming the Christian.

Develops the Christian in the faith

The Bible is food for every Christian. We are
called upon to grow up from spiritual
childhood, strengthened by God's word.

As we advance towards maturity, we
should be able to see the great themes of
Scripture as a connected whole, rather than as
a collection of scattered thoughts. The Bible
is like milk, nourishing the Christian.

Informs the Christian of God's mind

The Bible is God's written revelation. It is
impossible to arrive at a knowledge of his
plan and will on the strength of our own
guesswork.

God has given us the Bible so that we
should not be in the dark about who he is,
and what he is doing.

The true wisdom that leads to salvation is
arrived at by a humble and careful study of
God's Word. The Bible is like treasure,
enriching the Christian.

BIBLE CHECK

Directs: John 8:31-32;
Matthew 7:24-27;
Psalm 119:105
Equips: Matthew 4:1-11;
1 Timothy 1:18-19;
Ephesians 6:17
Energises: John 15:16; Isaiah
55:10-11; Psalm 1
Corrects: Isaiah 29:13; Mark
7:9-13; James 1:23-25
Develops: 2 Timothy 2:15;
1 Corinthians 14:20;
1 Peter 2:2-3
Informs: Romans 11:33-36;
2 Timothy 3:14-15;
Psalm 119:162

KEY TRUTH

Through the Bible, the
Christian comes to an understanding of God's plan, and
receives nourishment for
Christian living.

POSTSCRIPT

To develop a balanced faith,
the Christian should read the
Bible regularly and
thoroughly. Unless we read all
of the Bible, we may distort or
over-emphasise some aspect
of its message.

BIBLE STUDY Matthew 4:1-11

Jesus has been baptised by the River Jordan, and in doing so
has identified himself with sinful humanity whom he had
come to save and redeem. In that moment he had also
received, with the Spirit's sign, God's endorsement of his
mission to the world.

This early landmark of his ministry was followed
immediately by a period of temptation in the solitude of the
wilderness. The testing was severe but Jesus was ready,
prepared – and armed with his knowledge of Scripture.

1 In the invitation to turn stones into bread – held out to one
whose kingdom was not of this world, yet who would one
day feed 5,000 people in the wilderness – what was the power
of this temptation? What was the significance of Jesus'
quotation from Deuteronomy 8:3 – given in the context of
God's miraculous sustaining of the Israelites in their
wilderness journeys?

2 Next comes the temptation, in the form of an offer of
round-the-clock protection. So the devil is not hesitant
about quoting the Scripture himself. But he has not quoted
it accurately. What was the significance of the omission? See
Psalm 91:11-12. Notice Jesus' answering quotation
(Deuteronomy 6:16) – again in the context of Israel in the
wilderness. Why was Jesus determined that he would not
win the world to himself by a spectacular deed?

3 The third temptation is in the form of a deal – a carve-up of
power. This time the answer comes in the form of
Deuteronomy 6:13. What was the principle at stake here?

4 Practically, how are you to be equipped to fulfil the
requirement of the 2 Corinthians 10:3-5?

REFLECTION

A Read 2 Timothy 3:14–4:5.
What is the nature of the
Bible's power, and what does
it achieve? What can regular
readers expect it to do in their
lives? What are the dangers
which may be avoided
through the Bible's message?
B What would be a good plan
and schedule for the reading
of the Bible? What plans have
your friends found helpful?

C Why is it vital to become
mature in the truth of the
Bible? Compare your findings
with Acts 20:29-32.
D Read Psalm 19:7-11. Try to
list the ways in which the
writer of this psalm delights
in God's word, and make this
passage a subject for praising
God.

THE CHRISTIAN
3. The Christian and Prayer

For communion with God

Christian prayer is not a technique. To try to manipulate God for our own purposes is the way of magic, and of the old cultic religions – when people are at the centre. With Christian prayer God is at the centre.

On the human level, we do not like to "use" those whom we love – and the same is true of those who have entered into a relationship with God of trust and acceptance. Jesus taught his friends to talk to God as to their heavenly Father, and not to use meaningless incantations characteristic of heathen worship. For prayer involves a relationship. We should learn from the example of Jesus, who would regularly go away and spend time alone with his Father.

For growth in God

Prayer is like breathing, in the life of a Christian. When we pray regularly, there takes place in our lives a steady growth in character and inner resources. Contrary to popular opinion, prayer is not a sign of weakness, but of strength and progress.

Prayer is an education. The disciples needed to be taught by Jesus, and he gave them a pattern of prayer that the church has never forgotten. The Christian of every age faces the same lessons, disciplines and privileges of growing in God.

For the service of God

God does not need our prayers. Prayer does not affect his will and overall purpose for us. But the Bible teaches, and our Christian experience confirms, that prayer does affect his specific actions in fulfilling his will.

The reason is that God has appointed prayer as a key way of involving his people in the carrying out of his will and service in this world. The Christian learns to pray in the name of Jesus – that is, with his interests at heart. He also learns to pray with the help of the Holy Spirit. Prayer is the most important form of service we can ever employ.

For the praise of God

The Christian is a temple of the Holy Spirit, and is therefore to glorify God in everything. Thanksgiving, joy and praise are key aspects in a Christian's attitude, according to the New Testament.

To praise God is to make great affirmations about him. This is evident in the book of Psalms, in which we repeatedly read of God's greatness and of what he has done for his people. As we meditate on the great themes of the Bible, so our praise of God becomes a vital part of prayer.

For the experience of God

Prayer can bring God into the heart of every human emotion and experience. The writers of the Psalms were able to look to God for guidance in times of uncertainty. The apostles were able to turn to him in praise and prayer when in prison. Paul was strengthened by God, even though his prayer for relief from affliction was not granted. Prayer allows God to mould and develop the new man in Jesus Christ.

BIBLE CHECK

Communion: Matthew 6:5-8; Mark 1:35; Luke 5:15-16
Growth: Ephesians 3:14-19; Matthew 6:9-13
Service: James 5:16-18; Ephesians 6:18
Praise: 1 Thessalonians 5:16-18; Psalm 34:1-3; Psalm 150
Experience: Psalm 57:1-3; Acts 16:22-25; 2 Corinthians 12:7-10

KEY TRUTH

Prayer is God's chosen way of communication and fellowship between the Christian and himself. It is the secret of spiritual growth and effective service.

POSTSCRIPT

There is a particular power and the promised presence of Christ when believers meet together to pray in his name, according to the promise of Matthew 18:19-20.

BIBLE STUDY Nehemiah 1:1-11

Nehemiah was a Jew, a child of the Babylonian captivity, now ended. Judah, however, was still under the overall rule of Persia. Certain stages of national reconstruction had been begun, but Jerusalem's city walls still remained to be rebuilt. It was 445 BC, and Nehemiah was still in Persia, as cup-bearer to the king. He feels the pull of Jerusalem, which he has never seen, and in frustration turns to prayer:

1 In the face of the grim news from Jerusalem, Nehemiah's is an example of prayer that weeps (verses 4 and 5). This was the prayer that settled a life's work – but there is no obvious request in it. What, then, is the strength of this prayer? (verses 5-11)
2 Despite Nehemiah's grief, note the absence of hysteria in the prayer. What do these words express about the character, the promises, and the redemption of God? Can we find a corrective here, in some of our modern praying, from this prayer that worships?
3 Nehemiah is praying far from the scene of Jerusalem. Yet what can be learnt here about prayer that watches and is vigilant? What can we learn about the hard work of intercessory prayer? Compare Ephesians 6:18.
4 Here, too, is prayer that waits. Notice the word "today" in verse 11. Yet how long did Nehemiah have to wait until his request was granted? The answer comes in 2:1-4 – four months later.
5 How does prayer help us in getting a right perspective on problems and people around us? Notice how prayer reduces the mighty king to the level of "this man" (verse 11).
6 "It is prayer and prayer alone that can make history" (Jacques Ellul). Discuss.

REFLECTION

A Think about the Lord's Prayer as recorded in Matthew 6:9-13. What pattern does it set out for us in our prayer life? What similar patterns have you established in your own praying?
B Why bother to pray? Try to list some convincing reasons.
C Why do most people find prayer not the easiest of activities? How can we help one another in this?
D A Scottish preacher has said, "We have actually got it all wrong when we speak about 'praying for the work,' because prayer is the work." How do you react to this statement?

THE CHRISTIAN
4. The Christian and Witness

Proclaiming a person

Because Christianity is concerned with a person rather than with a philosophy or religious system, the early disciples of Christ found little difficulty in witnessing. Whatever their education or background, they had all experienced the transforming power of the risen Christ.

Their witness was about him – and so Philip on the desert road spoke of Jesus to the Ethiopian official. This means that all who obey Jesus as Lord have something to share. Every Christian is a witness.

Explaining the truth

While it is Christ we proclaim, there are however, important facts in the Christian message which must be explained and understood if individuals are to become more than mere converts. The apostle Paul's aim was that men and women should grow to become spiritually mature in Christ.

In societies where there is little awareness of God or the Bible, it is vital that the truth should be taught, argued and explained.

Sharing a love

Behind the message of reconciliation is the motivating power of Christ's love. Christ sends us out into the world, not merely to talk about him, but to share his love and our love with others. Paul said that he preached because he was compelled by the love of Christ.

Witnessing consistently

Jesus said that the mark of his disciples was to be the presence of love in their fellowship. Their lives were to shine as lights in the world, through their words, their deeds and their life-style.

Such a witness is not a burdened, strained obligation. It springs naturally out of the life lived in union with Christ. Such witness is ready to seize and buy up the opportunities as they come; to give answers to those who are seeking, with humility and love.

Witnessing personally

When the early church experienced its first persecution, the believers were scattered throughout Judea and Samaria – except for the apostles. Although these Christians were without the leadership of the apostles, we learn that they went everywhere, witnessing about Christ.

It was a matter of standing out in unashamed and personal testimony. Earlier the apostles had declared that it was impossible for them to keep silent about Christ. When we are living close to the love of God, we find that we cannot keep the good news to ourselves.

Witnessing collectively

There is great strength and encouragement for all who join in combined witness. Jesus recognised the need to send his disciples out two by two.

On the day of Pentecost, as Peter rose to proclaim Christ, his eleven companions stood with him. The book of Acts repeatedly tells us that the first Christians worked together. Here was a unity in proclamation – a characteristic of any church which is working with Christ.

BIBLE CHECK

Proclaiming: Acts 1:8; 8:35;
Luke 24:46-48
Explaining: Colossians
1:28-29; Acts 18:4;
2 Timothy 2:2
Sharing: 2 Corinthians 5:14;
1 Thessalonians 2:7-13
Consistently: John 13:34-35;
Philippians 2:14-16;
1 Peter 3:15
Personally: Acts 8:1,4; Acts
4:18-20; Psalm 40:10
Collectively: Acts 2:14,42-47;
Philippians 1:27

KEY TRUTH

Christian witness is the means
by which God, through his
servants, continues the work
of his Son, in bringing the
message of salvation to the
world.

POSTSCRIPT

Witnessing should never be a
burdensome Christian duty,
but the grateful privilege of
those who have an experience
of Jesus Christ.

BIBLE STUDY Luke 10:1-16

This account of the sending of the 72 disciples only occurs in
Luke. It is different from the sending of the twelve apostles in
9:1. They formed a permanent group – parallel in idea to the
twelve tribes of Israel. Those called in Luke 10, by contrast are
called "others". While Christians today can never be apostles
in the strict sense, we can say that we are the obvious
successors to the "others".

1 Jesus was sending his representatives ahead of him, like
couriers of his kingdom (verse 1). What were they to
announce concerning his kingdom?

2 The kingdom is the rule of God, through Christ the King, in
the lives of his followers everywhere. But what is its impact?
Look at the definition in Romans 14:17. Is this any different
from the message of salvation? When did the kingdom of
God first touch you?

3 Couriers ... but there is a second piece of imagery that
describes Christ's witnesses. It is in verse 2. How should this
description of us affect our priorities and plans? On the
strength of this, how would you answer those critics who say
that Christians live such narrow lives? (Compare Matthew
13:38.)

4 A third piece of imagery is in verse 3. What aspect of
Christian service and witness does this highlight? Have you
modern examples?

5 While we cannot press pre-Pentecost situations into our own
era, we can learn a great deal from the style of verses 4-16.
What can we learn in our witness about travelling light; with
earnestness and modesty; with urgency and confidence?

REFLECTION

A Read the story of Philip and
the Ethiopian official in Acts
8:26-40. What can we learn
from Philip about bringing
others to Jesus Christ? What
qualities do we see in Philip?
How prepared was the official
for this encounter?
B Which is easier – to speak
to a stranger or to an
acquaintance about Christ?
Which seems to be the more
effective, and why?

C Read 1 Thessalonians
2:7-13. List the qualities of
Paul in this passage – his
motive, his efforts, his
persistence. How should
these verses affect our way of
spreading the good news?
D Bearing in mind your gifts,
what is there that you can do,
naturally and freely, to help
make Christ better known?

THE CHRISTIAN
5. The Christian and the World

THE CHRISTIAN IS ...

Called out of the world

"The world" means both this present, temporary age and the hostile system of thought and action that operates on this planet. This is our environment.

But the Christian's true home is not here. Whatever our physical situation – good or bad – all that we value most strongly (our heavenly Father, Jesus Christ, our inheritance, our hope) is elsewhere. The New Testament urges Christ's followers to set their hearts on the eternal and heavenly dimension.

Separated from the world

This thread runs through most of the New Testament letters. Christians, because of their heavenward calling, are to avoid the trends and evil associations of fallen society. Their ethical standards are to be the highest of all.

Separation, however, does not mean that the Christian is called to withdraw from society, but to be kept committed to Christ within it.

Sent into the world

The appeal of the New Testament is not simply that Christ's disciples should avoid being polluted by the world; rather they are to purify it.

The Christian's attitude to the world should never be one of contempt. It is God's world, and we are to be involved in its redemption.

To overcome the world

We must avoid judgemental views that simply dismiss the world as beyond the reach and care of God. But on the other hand, we should not fall into the trap of believing that the world is morally, socially or politically perfectible, however much may be done by Christians and others of good will to alleviate its problems. The true redemption of the world cannot be completed until the future glory of Christ is revealed.

Thus, the Christian is called upon to overcome the evil tendencies and pressures that the world brings to bear upon him. We are caught in a spiritual battle that involves every Christian in this dark age, and therefore we must be armed with spiritual weapons. Christ himself has given us the assurance of his strength for the fight, and of the ultimate victory of God over all evil.

To journey through the world

The Christian is a citizen of heaven, with relationships and privileges that are outside this world. We are like the Old Testament Jews, journeying towards a promised land, confident in the assurance of God's presence and guidance.

The pilgrim is required to exercise obedience and discipline. At times we are likened to a soldier who cannot afford to get entangled in civilian pursuits – or to an athlete who must observe the necessary rules.

Our Christian life is the story of a pilgrimage through a world that is staggering under its problems. But we travel on with faith as our lamp.

BIBLE CHECK

Called out: 1 Corinthians
7:29-31; Hebrews 10:33-34;
Colossians 3:1-2

Separated: James 4:4-5;
Ephesians 5:3-11;
John 17:15-16

Sent into: John 20:21;
Matthew 5:13-16;
John 3:16-17

Overcome: Romans 8:19-21;
Ephesians 6:10-18;
Romans 8:37

Journey: Philippians 3:20;
Joshua 1:9; Hebrews 11:16

KEY TRUTH

Christian witness is the means
by which God, through his
servants, continues the work
of his Son, in bringing the
message of salvation to the
world.

POSTSCRIPT

A true understanding of the
world that God loves will
strengthen the Christian's
calling to go into all the world
and proclaim Christ to every
person.

BIBLE STUDY Ephesians 6:10-20

The apostle Paul is writing from prison to the Christians of a
city which is already a thousand years old; sophisticated,
worldly and promiscuous. The believers must have felt the
challenge of being Christ's ambassadors in a hostile
environment, as they walked along the 70-foot wide
boulevard, running from the harbour of Ephesus to its great
theatre. And then there was the heathen temple of Artemis
which gave the 300,000-strong population its chief industry.

1 As you look at this passage, try to assimilate the strength of
the spiritual opposition that faced Paul's contemporaries.
Then think of your own setting. Who had the harder task?

2 Study the active verbs of this passage. What were the
Christians told to do? What do these verbs speak to you of?
How do they challenge us today?

3 How should we be encouraged when we think of the
spiritual powers that oppose the work of God? Look at
Colossians 2:15; 1 John 4:4; Revelation 12:11.

4 Let different members of the group "adopt" a piece of the
Christian's armour, described in verses 14-17, and then
compare notes as to the value and purpose of each piece, and
what they signify today.

5 Our problem is that we are not to isolate ourselves from the
world and it's affairs and standards. How does a Christian
prepare to "stand firm," while still being involved?

6 Verses 18 and 19 – the prayer life! What are your resolves,
jointly and privately, as a result of studying this passage?

REFLECTION

A Read and study 2 Timothy
4:1-22. Paul is in prison,
nearing the end of his
pilgrimage, in Rome. How
does he view the current
scene, his own situation and
the future, and his
acquaintances? Contrast the
careers of Demas and Mark
(compare with Acts 15:37-39).

B The Christian does not
regard the present world
system as perfectible. How
can we avoid adopting either
a judgemental attitude that
writes the world off, or an
extreme optimism that ends
in disillusionment?

C Read John 16:33. Why did
Jesus encourage his disciples
by saying these words? What
do they mean for them – and
us?

D How can we keep our
eternal goals clearly in view?

THE CHRISTIAN
6. The Christian Life

A vocation to be fulfilled

The New Testament overflows with phrases that speak of goals, aims and ambitions. The apostle Paul alone is an example. He wants to finish his course; he desires to win the approval of God; he longs to proclaim Christ to those who have never heard of him. All his ambitions were centred in Christ himself, who was to have first place in everything.

All Christians have a calling – to be God's own people. Such a vocation overrides all other callings in life and, indeed, enhances them.

A character to be developed

God's purpose for his people is that they should become like his Son Jesus Christ in the holiness of their living. To be a Christian does not mean only to believe in certain facts about Christ. Rather, it means to develop a Christ-like character. The Christian is to cooperate in this process, combatting sinful habits and attitudes through the power of the Holy Spirit.

A fellowship to be maintained

The Christian is given ways and means by which the relationship with Christ may be maintained. Two examples of this are prayer and the Lord's Supper.

The apostle John's first letter has much to say about the fellowship of the Christian life. It is a fellowship of life, for it centres in Christ, the Word of life. It is a fellowship of love, for all who are connected to Christ are connected also to each other. It is a fellowship of light, for there can be no darkness or hidden impurity where God is involved.

Energies to be harnessed

God has given us many natural gifts. When we become Christians we are not to give up these abilities. Instead, motivated by the truths of our faith, we are to devote them to God's use, that they may reach their full potential and power.

The quality of daily work, our relationships and service will be heightened by the dynamic of Christ's resurrection power. We should recognise that we are not placed on this earth simply for ourselves. We are to be used.

Minds to be developed

A Christian framework of thinking enables individuals to establish their relationship to the universe simply because Christianity is true.

By opening our intellects to the truth of God, we can be convinced about the deepest issues of life.

Each Christian must see to it that their mind is stretched to the limits of its capacity. Paul described those who were swept about with every shifting belief as "babies". His prayer was that the minds of younger Christians might be illuminated fully by the light of Christ. They were to be adult in their understanding.

A hope to be realised

It is the historic nature of the Christian faith – culminating in the resurrection of Jesus – that gives to God's people the eager expectation of their final inheritance in glory. The one who was raised will surely return; the past is forgiven; the present is covered, and tomorrow belongs to us.

BIBLE CHECK

Vocation: Philippians 3:14;
Romans 15:20; Colossians
1:18
Character: Romans 8:29;
2 Peter 1:5-8;
Ephesians 5:1-2
Fellowship: 1 John 1:1-7;
Ephesians 4:3-6; John 15:4
Energies: 1 Corinthians
15:58; Ephesians 2:10;
Colossians 3:23-24
Minds: 1 John 5:20;
Ephesians 4:13-14;
Ephesians 1:18
Hope: 1 Peter 1:3-9;
Titus 2:13; Revelation 22:20

KEY TRUTH

A Christian is reaching full
potential as progress in life
and faith is made. The
Christian life is seen in the
ways listed here.

POSTSCRIPT

It is vital that Christ's
followers should make, not
merely converts, but disciples,
men and women of mature
character and sound
judgement.

BIBLE STUDY Philippians 3:7-14

Paul had a special bond with the Christians at Philippi, for
this was the first church ever founded on European soil. We
read of its beginnings in Acts 16. This letter was written
around the year AD 61, and it forms another of Paul's prison
letters. In this passage, Paul is confiding his own testimony of
Christ, and outlining his goals and values for all of life. These
are among the most powerful and moving personal resolves
ever recorded in Scripture. The following questions may help
in the study of the passage:

1 In verses 7-9, the writer is doing his mathematics.
He is weighing up the best of what this world can offer
against the "hardest" aspects of Christian discipleship.
Which outweighs the other? What tips the balance? Who
else made a similar calculation? See Hebrews 11:25-26.

2 Look at verses 10 and 11. Can one have the "positive" aspects
of Christian experience, without the "negative"? What is it
about the death of Christ that exerts such a magnetic pull
upon the believer?

3 Verses 12-14 convey the idea of a race. Discuss the tensions
that Paul faced, between the start and the finish, between
the past and the future, between immaturity and perfection.
How do these tensions affect us today? How should we deal
with them?

4 "One thing I do"– verse 13. In fact Paul did many things; he
made tents, he lectured, he travelled, he founded churches,
he wrote letters. What did he mean by the "one thing"? Why
is it so vital to be a person with one main objective?

5 What is "the prize" of verse 14? The clues are in this passage,
and in 1:21.

REFLECTION

A Read John 15:1-17. Reflect
on what it means to be united
with Christ. How is this
achieved? What are Christ's
expectations of his people?
What are the privileges and
challenges of this
relationship?

B Bertrand Russell (who was
an atheist) once said of
Christianity: "There is
nothing to be said against it,

except that it is too difficult
for most of us to practise
sincerely." How accurate is
this assessment? Give your
reasons.

C How does your Christian
faith affect your daily work?
Discuss this with your
friends.

D How would you describe
your relationship with Jesus
Christ?

THE CHURCH
1. Its Characteristics

It is the church of Jesus Christ (historical)

Through the centuries it is only the church that has experienced the presence of Jesus Christ within its membership. This is because it is Christ's church, purchased for himself by his own blood, and cared for as a husband cares for his wife. Jesus declared that where two or three individuals meet in his name there his promised presence would be experienced. No matter how small the group – there is the church.

It is the company of all believers (universal)

This is the church of different eras: past, present and future – together, they form the church. It is the church of different cultures, found in countries scattered over the earth, but united by its common Lord. It is a church of different characteristics, abilities and temperaments, and it is a church featuring different levels of experience, from elderly Christians to the newest disciples – yet one church.

It is a unity of the Spirit (spiritual)

The unity of the Spirit, of which the apostle Paul wrote, is more important than the differences of groups and denominations. The church can only truly be one, because of the one Spirit who unites it.

Although all Christians are to work for unity and mend divisions, it is not uniformity nor unanimity that they are to seek. Rather, it is a recognition of all who exhibit the family likeness.

Its authority is God's word (scriptural)

Down the ages the church has had a vital relationship with the Scriptures; it is the scriptural revelation that is the basis of the church's belief and stability.

The church has been commissioned to defend this revelation, to proclaim it, and to submit to its authority. The Bible is the church's authority and tells us all that we need to know about salvation and Christian conduct. On these, the Bible has the final say. On other matters, however, such as church government, there is no clear blueprint – and this no doubt helps to explain the differences existing between churches even in New Testament times.

Its programme is worldwide (international)

The programme of the church is the programme of Christ. Jesus said that his task was to bring good news to the poor and liberation to the oppressed.

When Christ's earthly ministry had finished, he commanded the church to carry out his mission to the world. The book of Acts shows us the way in which the church's mission expanded from Jerusalem to Judea and Samaria, and then to the whole earth. Our task is one of evangelism and service and to do this, we are empowered by the Holy Spirit.

Its destiny is heaven (eternal)

The church on earth is living between two comings. It looks back to the birth and ministry of Jesus Christ, and it looks forward to his glorious return.

Meanwhile it works in the knowledge that Christ is preparing a future home. On a certain day, known only to God, the trumpet will sound and the church will be united to Christ.

BIBLE CHECK

Of Jesus Christ: Matthew 16:18; Matthew 18:20
Company: Colossians 3:11; Revelation 7:9-10
Unity: Ephesians 4:4-6; John 17:20-23
Authority: Jude 3; 2 Timothy 1:13-14
Programme: Luke 4:16-21; John 20:21; Acts 1:8
Destiny: Matthew 24:30-31; John 14:1-3

KEY TRUTH

The church of Christ is the whole company of redeemed people. Christ is present and active in the church, and uses it for his work in the world.

POSTSCRIPT

The biblical picture of the church, as described above, helps the church to keep the right priorities in its mission and worship. It also serves as an accurate test to show whether movements and sects which claim to be part of the church are true or false.

BIBLE STUDY Ephesians 2:11-22

Paul the apostle recognised Ephesus as a strategic centre for reaching out with the message of Christ into the whole Roman province of "Asia", now western Turkey. Ephesus was important as a cultural, commercial, political and religious centre. While in essence it was Gentile and heathen, it also had a sizable Jewish population.

It was in this letter to the Ephesian Christians that the New Testament's teaching about the church as God's new society reached perhaps its richest form – in a society that provided as hostile an environment for church growth as possible.

1 In verses 11-13, take up each of the terms that described the spiritual status of the Gentiles. How great was the gulf between them and the Jewish covenant? And what was the one factor that could possibly bring unity between the two alien groupings?

2 Did you notice the "but" of verse 13? (Compare 2:4.) Continue now with the "for" of verse 14. What was Christ's purpose? What were his achievements (verses 14-18)?

3 "One new man" (verse 15 ... "a single new humanity"). Notice that Jews do not become Gentiles, or Gentiles Jews. Here is an altogether new being. What conclusions do you draw from this passage as you view the world church scene? What corrections may we need to make?

4 Here, in verses 19-22 is described something to rival Ephesus' great temple of Artemis – but with many differences! Describe them.

5 Come back to the cross (verses 13 and 16), and rediscover your unity with the followers of Jesus everywhere.

REFLECTION

A Read Ephesians 4:1-16. What gives the church its essential unity (verses 4-6)? How is this preserved? How does this compare with the kind of unity that Christians should seek (verses 11-16). How is this achieved?

B A church leader once said, "The church is the only institution in the world which exists primarily for the benefit of non-members." How far do you agree with this statement?

C Some Christians strongly emphasise their own church tradition. Others treat denominations as unhealthy. Yet others are indifferent. What is your view?

D Read 1 Timothy 3:15. What can your own circle of Christian friends do to further the truth of God more?

THE CHURCH
2. Its Main Description

A firm building

The New Testament letters take up Christ's theme of "building" his church – although this idea is not to be confused in any way with literal buildings for Christian worship.

The apostles Paul and Peter, in particular, saw the church as a spiritual building, composed of "living stones" – Christians. This picture shows us how Christians depend upon each other and upon Christ as the building's cornerstone.

A virgin bride

A relationship of deep intimacy is suggested by the New Testament idea of the church "married" to Christ. We are told that Christ loves the church, and has made it pure and faultless by his death.

The apostle John's vision of the new heaven and the new earth describes the church as Christ's bride, prepared and ready to meet her husband.

A functioning body

The picture of the church as a body, with Christ as its head, emphasises that the church is a living organism and not an organisation.

As in the picture of the church as a building, the dependence of the church upon Christ is stressed, but we also learn the important truth that no member of the body is disposable – or of overriding importance.

A permanent city

The theme of the city of God is usually seen in the Bible as a future hope. God's people live as strangers in the world, and are looking for the city which is to come.

The city of God is mentioned a number of times in the book of Revelation, where the writer is speaking of the church. When God's chosen people are finally brought to completion, the city will be a vast community of purpose, life, activity and permanent security.

A stable family

The terms "family" or "household" of God point again to the relationship that exists in the church between the members and the head. And God's very fatherhood provides a pattern for family life now.

Great encouragement – particularly to Gentile converts in the early church – was found in the fact that all shared equally in the privileges of God's household, Jews and Gentiles alike. No longer was the Gentile an outsider or foreigner. This should also be true of the church today – because barriers spoil the family life God wants the church to have.

An active army

The references to the church as an army are not heavily pronounced in Scripture. However, the New Testament teaches that the church is involved in a spiritual warfare.

Intensity, activity and victory are the main ideas conveyed to us by this imagery; the weapons and the victory itself being God's.

Building: 1 Peter 2:4-5;
Ephesians 2:20-22
Bride: Ephesians 5:25-27;
Revelation 21:2
Body: 1 Corinthians 12:12-31;
Ephesians 1:22-23; 4:15-16
City: Hebrews 13:14;
Revelation 21:10-27
Family: Ephesians 2:19;
3:14-15; 1 Timothy 3:14-15
Army: Ephesians 6:12;
Revelation 12:11

KEY TRUTH

. . . .

There are a number of
different pictures of the
church in the New Testament.
Looked at together, these
pictures give us a full idea of
the nature and character of
the church and its mission.

POSTSCRIPT

. . . .

It must be emphasised that
the church is an organism
rather than an organisation, a
living fellowship rather than
mere buildings, a close family
rather than a collection of
individuals.

BIBLE STUDY 1 Peter 2:1-10

This wonderful letter, written by the apostle Peter in
AD 63 or 64, came out just in time to prepare the harrassed and
scattered Christians of Asia Minor for the great persecution
that erupted under the emperor Nero in the summer of 64. Its
message is one of hope and confidence despite "all kinds of
trials" (1:6).

Like Paul to the Ephesians, Peter in this passage uses vivid
terminology to describe the new society that God has brought
into existence through Christ. Use these questions to assist the
study:

1 Read verses 1-3. This was no time for believers to turn on
each other, but rather develop a healthy spiritual appetite.
How much are you praying for yourself and for each other in
this respect? "Make us hungry!"

2 In verses 4-5 the metaphor changes from babies to ... what?

3 In the spiritual and "invisible" temple of the church, what
place and function does Christ have in verses 4-8? Notice
from the Old Testament quotations how Christ is both a
source of confidence and a disaster. Why is this so?

4 Four descriptions of the Christian community follow in
verse 9. How are we to see ourselves in a largely unbelieving
society? What are our functions, in verses 9-12?

5 "The people of God" (verse 10). If no other group is classed
in this way, what is this saying to us in the church?

6 Animal sacrifices belonged to the past. What is a "spiritual
sacrifice" (verse 5)?

REFLECTION

A Read and think about 1
Peter 2:1-10. A number of
figurative expressions are
used of Christians in this
passage. Try to list them, and
consider their implications.
B Which of the various
descriptions of the church
have you found most helpful?
Why?

C Reflect on how much
Christ has done for his
church, as you consider each
picture of the church in turn.
D Look at 1 Corinthians
12:12-31. What do these
verses tell us about the
jealousy and pride in the
church? How do you regard
those in your fellowship who
seem more gifted, and those
who seem less gifted than
yourself?

THE CHURCH
3. Its Relationship to Christ

Christ died for the church

Christ's death is related not simply to individuals, but to the people of God, the church. The announcement to Mary about the impending birth of Jesus was that he would save his people from their sins.

It was clear, when Jesus took the cup and gave it to his disciples at the last supper, that he saw his death as bringing a new "Israel" or people of God into being. Ever since that time, the church has remembered in the Lord's Supper the cost Christ paid to found the church.

Christ builds the church

Jesus came to found, not a philosophy, but a community. It was basic to the early Christians' thought that new converts were immediately added to the fellowship; that all who had fellowship with the Father and the Son would be related to one another.

It was more than addition, however. Christ is the very source of the church's life, and so to be in the church is to experience Christ's life in a unique way. By his Spirit he directs the church, gives spiritual gifts to its members and creates unity and love.

Christ protects the church

In the Old Testament God's people were often protected by God, for example, in the story of the blazing furnace in the book of Daniel.

In the New Testament, we are told that Christ protects his people, the church. He defends the church from the attacks of Satan, and preserves it in adversity. More than this, he provides the power for the church to launch its own attacks against Satan. The church is not on the defensive – it is on the offensive.

Christ purifies the church

In the Old Testament, some of the prophets pictured Israel as a wife who had been unfaithful to her husband. God's people had been unfaithful to the promises they had made in their covenant with him.

The church is only seen as faithful and pure in the New Testament because of Christ. He has cleansed the church by his death, and continues to keep her holy. We are told that finally Christ will receive the church as a perfect bride: faithful and pure.

Christ intercedes for the church

The word "intercede" means to act on someone else's behalf as a peacemaker. It is encouraging to know that because of Christ's death on our behalf, he is now in heaven as a man, representing us before the Father.

Because Christ intercedes for us, we are assured of at least three guarantees. First, we are forgiven because of his death. Second, we have free access to God because of his presence in heaven. Third, we are protected against condemnation for our sins by his words spoken in our defence.

Christ prepares for the church

Jesus reassured his friends when he warned them of his departure that they need not be anxious about the future, as he would be preparing a home for them. This shows us that Christ loves the church, and longs to enjoy the company of those who believe in him. His work will not be complete until the church is in the place he has prepared for it.

BIBLE CHECK

Died for: Matthew 1:21;
26:26-29; Acts 20:28
Builds: Ephesians 4:11-16;
Acts 2:46-47
Protects: Daniel 3:19-27;
Matthew 16:18-19
Purifies: Jeremiah 3:6,14;
Ephesians 5:25-27
Intercedes: Hebrews 7:25-27;
1 John 2:1; Romans 8:34
Prepares: John 14:1-4;
1 Thessalonians 4:16-17

KEY TRUTH

The life, witness and
continuance of the church is
totally dependent upon its
relationship to Jesus Christ,
its builder and protector.

POSTSCRIPT

Christ's love for his church led
him to give up his own life for
her. The church is called to do
the same – to submit to the
interests of her Lord and to
fulfil his will.

BIBLE STUDY Ephesians 4:1-16

Paul is far from his friends, under house arrest in Rome,
awaiting trial under Nero. Yet he is able to remind his readers
of the soaring heights to which Christ has lifted the members
of God's New Society in Ephesus; men and women who have
been chosen in him, predestined, made alive with Christ,
reconciled through the cross, given access to the Father, made
fellow-citizens and built into a holy temple.

1 In view of the Ephesian Christians' high calling, how are
they now to live (verses 1-3)?

2 When it comes to unity, notice the frequency of the word
"one" (verses 3-6). What does this tell us about certain
unchangeable facets of the world-wide Christian church?

3 Move on to verse 13. If, in verse 3, there is already in
existence a spiritual unity to be maintained, there seems to
be a second unity that is yet to be attained. Try to establish
from verses 13-14 the nature of this unity and goal that still
lies ahead.

4 If the church at large – indeed any local fellowship – is
travelling from a unity that already exists towards a unity
that lies ahead, what lies between? What makes it possible to
negotiate this journey? The clue lies in verses 7-12.

5 If oneness was the earlier theme, now the diversity of
the gifts given by the incarnate and now ascended Christ
(verses 9,10) comes into prominence. What are the gifts for?

6 The Head ... the body (verses 15-16). How do we practise this
unique relationship?

REFLECTION

A Consider the message of
Revelation 3:1-6. John is
conveying Christ's message to
the church in Sardis (in
present-day Turkey). How is
this passage relevant to the
church in general, and to your
fellowship today? List the
accusations, the challenges,
and the promises of these
verses.

B "The Bible knows nothing
of solitary religion" (John
Wesley). Why should a
Christian bother about the
church of Jesus Christ?
C Look at Revelation 1:5-6.
What has Jesus done for his
church?
D Read Daniel 3:13-28. What
message is there in this story
for today's church?

THE CHURCH
4. Its Authority and Mission

Guarding the truth

The church is not to create truth, but guard it. It is described as the pillar of the truth; as contender for the faith that has been entrusted to God's people.

Thus the church must follow the apostles both in its standard of teaching and quality of mission. It must do more than guard the truth – it must proclaim it. Equally, it must do more than speak – it must speak the truth. The church is to be scripturally-minded and missionary-hearted.

Correcting the unruly

The Bible teaches that the authority of church leaders must be held in high regard if there is to be healthy discipline in the fellowship. On the other hand, leaders are to be held accountable for their standard of teaching and personal morality.

Indiscipline, immorality and division in the church are not to be condoned. However, all disciplinary measures are to be tempered by the desire to build up the offender and by the forgiveness that surrounds the family of Christ.

Challenging evil

Morally, spiritually and doctrinally, the church of God has always been surrounded by evil. The Bible teaches that evil can be overcome by the power of good. The church must challenge evil by its vigilance and by its determination to live and preach the truth.

Evangelising the world

Before he ascended, Jesus gave his disciples a specific command that is to be obeyed by the church in every age. They were to make disciples everywhere, spreading the good news of Christ throughout the world.

We are to announce that Jesus Christ, once crucified for the sins of the world, is alive, and that he is Lord; that forgiveness and the gift of his Spirit are for all who belong to him through repentance and faith. The message is to be proclaimed universally, obediently, relevantly, joyfully and yet urgently. We do it at his command.

Serving the world

Jesus never expected the church to be a proclaimer of words without being a performer of deeds. Christian service is a partner of evangelism, both activities being a necessary part of the mission of God.

Christ is the example for the service that his church is commanded to bring to the world. He fed the hungry, he healed the sick and he brought hope to the despairing. He identified with humanity in all its needs.

The same should be true of the fellowship he came to create.

Glorifying God

The church lives for the glory of God. In all that it does, it should direct attention and praise to God. It fulfils this purpose as it bears fruit in faithful service, and mirrors his love.

More particularly, following in the steps of Christ, it glorifies God as it suffers with him. Jesus said that the hour of his death was the hour of greatest glory. So the suffering and the glory of God's kingdom are combined in Jesus.

Guarding: 1 Timothy 3:15;
Jude 3; 1 Timothy 6:20
Correcting: Hebrews 13:17;
1 Corinthians 5:9-13
Challenging: Romans
12:17-21; Jude 19-21
Evangelising: Matthew
28:18-20; 1 Thessalonians
1:5-10
Serving: 1 John 3:17-18;
Titus 3:8; Philippians 2:5-7
Glorifying: John 12:27-28;
1 Peter 4:12-14;
Revelation 1:9

KEY TRUTH

. . . .

The church is not a passive
society in the world. It receives
its power and direction from
Jesus Christ, who has given it
his authority to fulfil his
mission.

POSTSCRIPT

. . . .

It is repeatedly in the very
weakness of the church that
its greatest power is seen.

BIBLE STUDY 1 Thessalonians 1:1-10

Thessalonica lay right across the Via Egnatia, a great Roman
trunk road which ran from western Greece right through to
Constantinople and the east. East and west met at
Thessalonica. As early as AD 49 Paul came to the city, and had a
three-week mission there, before Jewish opposition forced out
the evangelists. The account is written up for us in Acts 17:1-9.

But those three weeks were enough; a church had been
started! Some months later Paul wrote to the new church.
Had his mission failed? Evidently not, for good news had been
brought to him by Timothy (3:2). Paul writes this opening
passage with joy:

1 Thessalonica was a test case in heathen Europe. What are the
evidences that the mission had not failed? Look at verses
2-5, and list the graces. How typical are these of Christian
disciples?

2 Now analyse the experience in verses 6 and 7. To what extent
was this new church a model of New Testament patterns?
Compare Acts 14:22. In the world today where do we see
these same characteristics?

3 Now absorb the impact of this church, in verses 8-10. To
what extent had the Via Egnatia played a part? What was the
reputation of this young energetic church?

4 Your church could touch the world. The Roman roads have
given way to other communication aids, including the
Internet. But there are other resources open to Christians
across the centuries, chief of which is intercessory prayer.
What is your church or fellowship doing to make your faith
"known everywhere"?

5 Look back to the report of Thessalonica's mission in Acts 17.
What was the power that explained it all? See Acts 17:7.

REFLECTION

A Read Acts 12:1-19.
Consider the church's
situation. What were its
problems? Its mood? Its
influence? Its surprises?
B Where does the balance lie
in practice, for you, between
spreading the good news and
giving practical service? What
adjustments do you need to
make?

C How do you react to
disagreements in your
fellowship? How far do the
words of 2 Timothy 2:23-26
apply?
D To what extent are you able
to take a positive initiative
where you are, in being the
"salt" that improves society
(Matthew 5:13)?

5. Its Ordinances

BAPTISM

Admission to membership

Ever since Christ's command to make disciples and to baptise them in the name of the Trinity, baptism with water has been the outward distinguishing mark of the Christian.

More than a symbol

When an Ethiopian official was baptised by Philip the evangelist, he was full of joy, although his knowledge of Jesus was limited. Baptism is a powerful event. Received rightly, it becomes a means of God's grace to the Christian.

Death to the old life

Baptism is a farewell to the old life – it is a baptism into the death of Christ. It signifies that the one baptised has been crucified with him, and that the life of sin and self belongs to the past.

Rising to the new life

Baptism is the emergence to the new life; it speaks powerfully to Christians of being raised with Christ, of walking in the light, of peace with God.

Identification with Christ

In his own baptism, Jesus identified with sinful humanity. In our baptism we are privileged to identify with him, unashamed to be known by his name.

THE LORD'S SUPPER

We commemorate

Christ left us no monument or memorial; he never even wrote a book. What he left us was a fellowship "meal" by which we could draw close to him and remember the sacrifice of his body and his blood given for us in death. This is the *backward* look.

We communicate

It is not a dead Christ who is worshipped in the holy communion, but a risen Saviour. As his people share in the bread and wine, they give thanks and praise, and use the opportunity to renew their fellowship with the risen Lord. This is the *upward* look.

We appropriate

Jesus told his disciples to "take" the bread, as he sat with them. Here is no one-man drama. We are not spectators, but deeply involved; if we come to the Lord's Supper with a right attitude, we receive God's grace and strength for Christian living. This is the *inward* look.

We participate

The disciples all drank from the cup, as it was passed from one to another. It is, indeed, a sharing occasion. Believers do not come together in this way merely as individuals, but as a family. This is the *outward* look.

We anticipate

Christ told his disciples that the Lord's Supper should be observed regularly – until his return. Then our communion with him will be direct, face to face. Thus the service is a pointer ahead. This is the *forward* look.

BIBLE CHECK

Admission: Acts 2:41
More than: Acts 8:38-39
Death: Romans 6:3-4
Rising: Colossians 2:12
Identification: Galatians 3:27
Commemorate: Luke 22:19-20
Communicate: John 6:56
Appropriate: Mark 14:22
Participate: 1 Corinthians 10:16-17
Anticipate: 1 Corinthians 11:26

KEY TRUTH

Baptism and the Lord's Supper were both instituted by Jesus Christ as dynamic symbols of the gospel. The water of baptism signifies cleansing and entry into God's church. The bread and wine of the holy communion signify the receiving of Christ's body and blood, given for us in death.

POSTSCRIPT

It is important not to under-emphasise the value of these two ordinances, given by Jesus Christ. Through them we come to a deeper awareness of Christ's death and living presence.

BIBLE STUDY Luke 22:14-27

Jerusalem was the crossroads for all Judaism. People had flocked to the Holy City to celebrate the event that had propelled their nation into being – the passing-over of the angel of death and the dramatic deliverance from Egypt. This particular year it was more than routine that brought the extra crowds in. The minds of thousands were occupied with stories of a young Galilean preacher. Would this be the year when political deliverance from Rome would come from him?

1 Jesus himself was wishing the moment nearer. Why? Compare verse 15 with Matthew 26:18.

2 Why did Jesus choose the Passover meal as the occasion to institute what we know now as the Lord's Supper? The clues are all in the passage. Don't miss out on the word covenant. Look up 1 Corinthians 5:7 as a key verse.

3 It sounds strange to modern ears to speak of "eating the flesh" and "drinking the blood" of someone. For the meaning of these very Jewish terms take time to look up 1 Chronicles 11:1 and Psalm 27:2 – and we will see that these phrases refer to taking advantage of the life of someone else. Apply this now to the Lord's Supper for a very clear answer as to what we are doing in the eating and drinking.

4 Discuss the power of "remembrance" (verse 19) for a believer. What difference would it make to the church if there was no such event as the Lord's Supper?

5 Is it surprising that in history wrangles and controversy have arisen, even over this holy occasion? What evidence is there of wrong attitudes, even on the founding night?

REFLECTION

A Read Luke 22:14-27. Why did Jesus connect this event with the Old Testament Passover (see Exodus 12:25-27), and with the new covenant, prophesied by Jeremiah (Jeremiah 31:31-34)?

B Read Acts 16:29-33. In these verses, baptism is shown to be an important event in the Christian's life. Why do you think that baptism is important?

C As you attend the Lord's Supper or holy communion, in what frame of mind should you come – towards Christ himself, yourself, and your neighbour?

D Pick out the encouraging factors about that evening, and also the discouraging elements. What do they tell us about the gospel and ourselves?

THE CHURCH
6. Its Ministry and Order

Preaching and teaching

The acceptance of Christianity's revealed truth has never been an optional extra in the church. We read in the New Testament of the standard or form of teaching required for growth and discipleship.

The issue of false teaching is dealt with on page after page of the New Testament letters. What protected the infant church was its anchorage in the apostolic teaching, received not merely on an intellectual level, but practised in daily life.

Prayer and intercession

Prayer was the power-house of the early church. It was the unseen weapon that established bridgeheads for the gospel in areas dominated by idolatry and moral darkness.

Prayer is the way in which God's power becomes effective, unhindered by considerations of space, time, culture, or even the prison bars that people have erected.

Fellowship and caring

It has been pointed out that the early church was revolutionary. This was not because it roused slaves against their masters, but because it was more revolutionary still – it demolished the old distinctions altogether. The true liberation was freedom in Christ.

People divided by social status, religious background and language now became brothers and sisters in God's household. The apostles taught that widows are of importance in God's family; the sick are to be prayed for, and the hungry fed.

Worship and praise

Worship is the main purpose of the church. Jesus promised that even where only two or three met in his name, there he would be present with them. Praise and thanksgiving are the distinctive marks of the living church.

The worship of the Christian fellowship is not tied to a building or a structured order, although it is possible that "liturgies" (forms of worship) were developing by the time the New Testament letters were written.

However the New Testament clearly states that it is not only the leaders who worship God, but all God's people. There is a "priesthood of all believers", offering spiritual sacrifices.

Leadership and government

In the early church even the precise patterns and titles of ministry differed a little from church to church. Ephesus had "elders", while Philippi had "bishops" (both presumably describing the same function of pastoral oversight). There were also "deacons" who served in a helping capacity, while the apostles were in a class of their own.

Those in the pastoral ministry belong to the church; the church does not belong to them. They are God's gift to the church. They are to feed the flock, they are to be blameless in their beliefs and in their conduct and their ministry is to resemble that of Christ, who came to be a servant of all.

BIBLE CHECK

Preaching: Romans 6:17;
1 Timothy 1:3-7; Acts 2:42
Prayer: Acts 4:31; Romans
15:30; 1 Timothy 2:1-2
Fellowship: Colossians 3:11;
1 Timothy 5:1-2; James 1:27
Worship: Colossians 3:16;
Hebrews 13:15-16;
1 Peter 2:5-9
Leadership: Philippians 1:1;
1 Corinthians 3:5;
Titus 1:5-9

KEY TRUTH

The church is to maintain a
presence for God in the world,
proclaiming his message and
uplifting his name, under the
guidance of appointed
leaders.

POSTSCRIPT

It is important neither to
create a hierarchy, through
undue elevation of the
leadership, nor to endanger
truth and order in the church,
through devaluation of those
with oversight.

BIBLE STUDY Titus 1:1-16

Crete was the destination of this short but powerful letter,
written about AD 62, from Paul to Titus, his trusted colleague.
Crete had become a part of the Roman empire in 67 BC; it was
a sizeable island, dominating the south Aegean Sea,
mountainous, superstitious and tough to handle. The Greek
poet Homer said that it had 100 cities. The shaky and
inexperienced church needed a reliable leader, and Paul's letter
has much to say about true leadership and service:

1 "I left you in Crete" (verse 5). How many of the group know
   what it is to be left in charge? What were Titus' first tasks?
2 "Straighten out" (verse 5) – the same Greek word is used
   elsewhere for setting a broken bone. How disordered was the
   church in Crete? Scan the letter briefly for the give-away
   clues.
3 The appointed elders are to be "blameless", though as
   commentator John Stott states, "not flawless" – that is,
   without public blame in a public office. Discuss this
   insistence on high standards (compare 1 Timothy 3:1-7).
4 Examine both the vices and virtues listed here. How should
   we take similar precautions in public church appointments?
5 Notice too the doctrinal purity that is insisted upon (verse
   9). The message is "trustworthy", for God does not lie (verse
   2). What are the two duties required of the faithful teacher
   (verse 9)?
6 What are the chief characteristics of false teachers (verses
   10-16)? How are they to be blocked?
7 What is the main lesson that you can take from this study
   for your own fellowship?

REFLECTION

A Study 1 Peter 5:1-11. List
the qualities to be found in
one who shepherds God's
flock. What was the
association in Peter's mind
that prompted these terms?
Check your answer with John
21:15-17.
B What are the tensions that
the church of Christ
inevitably experiences (verses
5-9)?

C Look at 1 Timothy 4:11-16.
These are Paul's words to a
young church leader,
Timothy. What are the
responsibilities and rewards
of church leadership? In what
ways should we pray for our
leaders?
D Why is the church not a
"democracy"? And yet, why is
it not a hierarchy?

THE LAST THINGS

1. The Hope of the Christian

The promises to God's people

God is working in history. The Christian is confident in the righteousness of God, which is working through the events of this world towards the final glory that must eventually follow the ministry and sufferings of Christ. It is his personal return that will usher in the new age.

Resting on the predictions of the Old Testament, the promises of Christ and the conviction of the apostles, the Christian is assured of the sovereign control of God to the end of time.

The fulfilment of God's purposes

The preaching of the apostles demonstrated the Christian belief that the return of Jesus, to make all things new, would be the ultimate fulfilment of his work of salvation.

For the believer, the appearance of Christ will come as the longed-for conclusion and perfection of the salvation already won through the sacrifice of the cross.

The defeat of God's enemies

The outcome of the conflict between good and evil is already settled. The death and subsequent resurrection of Jesus has ensured the defeat of sin, death, and all the powers of evil.

But it will not be until Christ's public and powerful return in glory that God's righteousness will be finally upheld. God's victory will then be evident to all.

A living hope

It is Christ who fills the Christian with the confident expectation the Bible calls "hope". All the New Testament passages which describe the last things focus their attention on him.

It is in the resurrection of Jesus that we find particular encouragement. Our living hope is that like him we too shall rise from death to enjoy the new heaven and the new earth from which death and decay are banished. Christ's followers await a new body, incorruptible and powerful. This body will relate to the old existence, but Paul tells us that it will be significantly different.

A steadfast hope

The quality of Christian hope is that it imparts courage and patience for the present. It is not a vague desire for better times, nor is it a resigned and passive submission to life's problems while we wait for a new tomorrow.

The hope that is centred in Christ has kept the church through the ages during persecution and hardship. It is the hope that demolishes fear, and transforms pessimism into godly and practical optimism.

A purifying hope

Our hope in the return of Christ in the future should have a deep effect on the way we live now. Ours is not the hope of the curious who look only for the details of signs and dates while remaining detached and unaffected.

To the Christian, Christ's return is a reality. As a result, priorities, decisions and life-style will inevitably be shaped by the thought of his coming.

Promises: 1 Peter 1:10-12;
Isaiah 11:1-9
Fulfilment: Acts 3:17-21
Romans 8:18-23
Defeat: Philippians 2:9-11;
1 Corinthians 15:24-26
Living: 1 Peter 1:3-5;
1 Corinthians 15:20-23,
51-55
Steadfast: 1 Thessalonians
1:3; Romans 8:24-25
Purifying: 1 John 3:2-3;
Hebrews 10:23-25;
Jude 24-25

KEY TRUTH

The Christian's hope is a
confidence in the rule and
purposes of God, which find
their goal in the return of
Jesus Christ at the end of the
age.

POSTSCRIPT

Christian history indicates
that those who have their eyes
on the age to come are the
ones who are most effective in
this passing age.

BIBLE STUDY 1 Peter 1:1-12

It does not matter which country or century you are from –
the description of the Christians to whom the apostle Peter's
letter is addressed is all-embracing: "God's elect, strangers in
the world, scattered ..." These scattered – and soon to be
persecuted – believers had no New Testament; so the opening
greeting (verse 2) is packed with helpful reminders that their
conversion was no accident. Planned by the Father, achieved
by the Son in the sprinkling of his blood and applied by the
Spirit in sanctifying power – theirs was a Trinitarian faith.

1 Note the key words in this opening burst of praise (verses
3-8) ... hope ... inheritance ... salvation ... faith. What two
great events is this confidence based on – and we must
remember that Peter was a first-hand witness!
2 What are the phrases here that point to the believer's eternal
security – regardless of the impending suffering mentioned
in verses 6-7?
3 Identify the words of strong expectation for the future. How
does Peter refer to the final culminating point of all our
work and witness? How far is this mind set your own?
4 Why do joy and testing go so frequently together in the New
Testament? Look up James 1:2; 1 Peter 4:12-13. What should
we be teaching new believers about the trials they face?
5 Discuss the wonder of loving someone whom you have never
seen with your eyes (verse 8). When did this first begin to
happen to you?
6 Why is ours such a privileged era in which to live? Verses
10-12 give us the answer.

REFLECTION

A Read 1 Peter 1:1-12. What
were the circumstances of the
readers of this letter? How
can a Christian rejoice (verse
8) in the midst of adversity
(verse 6)? What is
the nature of the Christian
hope, and how is it created?
B Christians love someone
they have never seen (1 Peter
1:8). How is such love
generated and made a reality?
Check your answer with
Romans 15:4.

C In what ways do you look
forward to the future, and to
what extent do you fear it?
D How can the Christian's
view of the future make a
serious contribution to
society as it attempts to
grapple with the problems of
tomorrow?

THE LAST THINGS
2. The Prelude to Christ's Return

In the natural realm

It is extremely important that as we read in the Bible about the famines, earthquakes and plagues that will feature before Christ's return, we should not be too quick to identify such an era with our own.

The Bible's repeated use of the phrase "the last times" refers to the entire period between Christ's first and second comings. Therefore, before Christ's return we should not be surprised to see natural and even cosmic disasters.

In the social realm

Stress and social disorder are characteristics of the period before Christ's second coming. We are told that people will be arrogant and proud, materialistic and immoral. The Bible says that these will be terrible times when human sin is unchecked.

There will also be those who make a mockery of religion and of any talk of a return by Jesus Christ.

In the international realm

Jesus made it plain, as he taught his disciples, that wars, revolutions and political disturbances would characterise the coming age. These events would not mean that the end had come – they would be signs of the presence and advance of the kingdom. They would be the labour pains heralding the birth of the new order.

In the family realm

Hatred and division, even within families, were predicted by Jesus Christ as being features of the last times.

The family relationship would be endangered, and loyalties would be strained – in certain circumstances to the point of betrayal.

In the personal realm

During the last times, those who have no relationship with God will experience an increase in fear and insecurity.

Jesus predicted that the situation would be similar to that of Noah's generation. There would be aimlessness, with men and women eating and drinking, getting married and going about their daily business, yet estranged from God and with no real purpose for living.

In the spiritual realm

From descriptions in the book of Revelation we can see that the spiritual realm will be unrestricted in its rebellion. Paul describes the coming of "the man of lawlessness," who will declare himself to be God, and will demand worship. Also there will be numerous "false christs" who will attempt to lead people away from the truth.

The church, while exercising great influence through its proclamation of the gospel, will nevertheless face considerable pressure and persecution during the last times.

Natural: Luke 21:11,25;
Romans 8:22
Social: 2 Timothy 3:1-5; Jude
18; 2 Peter 3:3-4
International: Mark 13:7-8;
Luke 21:9-10
Family: Mark 13:12; Matthew
10:34-36
Personal: Luke 21:26;
Matthew 24:37-39
Spiritual: Matthew 24:4-14;
2 Thessalonians 2:3-10

KEY TRUTH

. . . .

Before Christ returns,
Christians may expect to see
varying degrees of disorder in
the world. This gives them an
opportunity to evangelise and
offer hope.

POSTSCRIPT

. . . .

In the Gospels, Jesus'
prediction of the destruction
of the Jerusalem temple
merges with his description of
the last times. Whatever our
interpretation, Christ's
prediction about the temple is
a prefigure of his further
prediction of the end.

BIBLE STUDY Matthew 24:1-35

Jesus is predicting the End – something that could never be
rehearsed – and he needs no rehearsal. But we do, if its reality
is ever to sink in. One such rehearsal of future glory occurred
in miniature at the Transfiguration (17). Here in this passage
Christ starts by telling his disciples about the "end" of
something they would be very familiar with – the temple.

1 Verses 1-3: It is vital to observe the nature of the disciples'
   questions – two questions in one! What were they assuming?
2 Now scan verses 4-21, as Jesus gives two answers in one. One
   is on the global and futuristic scale, the other on the local
   and immediate – with the division occurring at verse 15.
   Broadly, what are these two predictions about? Why does
   Jesus telescope them?
3 Rome's destruction of Jerusalem, and the temple, in AD 70
   (verses 15-21) was itself prefigured and "rehearsed" in 169 BC
   by the desecration of Jerusalem's temple by the Seleucid
   king Antiochus Epiphanes – the "abomination that causes
   desolation" predicted in Daniel 11:31. What is Jesus
   emphasising by alluding to this familiar and terrible episode
   of Jewish history?
4 The teaching is of an approaching catastrophe, the bitter
   memory of the past – both pointing to the march of history,
   referred to in verses 4-14 and 22-28. What is the general
   pattern of events in our own history that believers should be
   prepared for? Try and list them from these verses.
5 Jesus then speaks of the final end itself (verses 29-35) – of
   the whole chain of events that would begin to have
   happened in the lifetime of those present (verse 34). How
   should Christ's words affect our lives today?

REFLECTION

A Read Matthew 24:3-14. Try
to list the events and patterns
foreseen by the Lord as taking
place between his departure
from earth and his return. In
what way do you think they
apply to this generation?
B Why was Jesus not more
specific? Compare your
findings with Matthew
12:38-42 and Matthew 24:36.

C Reflect on the attitude that
we should have regarding
Jesus' warnings of world
events. How do his words
affect our lives today?
D What is faulty in the desire
to know the precise details
about the Lord's coming?
Compare your answer to
Matthew 24:42 and
Deuteronomy 29:29.

3. The Return of Christ

CHRIST WILL RETURN ...

Prophetically

There are numerous Old Testament passages that refer to the kingly rule of Christ – predictions that plainly will not be fulfilled until his return.

The New Testament prophecies are found throughout the Gospels, Acts, the letters and the book of Revelation. They refer to Christ's return as a Coming, as a Revealing, as the Day of the Lord and as his Appearing.

Personally

We are not, of course, to think of Jesus as absent from the world and from his people at the present time, for he promised to be with his followers until the end.

But while he is with the church invisibly at present, by his Spirit, Christ's coming at the end will be visible and personal. The assurance was given to the apostles, at the time of the ascension, that it would be the very same Jesus who returned.

Visibly

The return of Jesus Christ will be no secret, hidden affair. The Bible teaches that earth's entire population will see the event.

To some, the appearing of Jesus will be a glorious and wonderful sight, but we also learn from the Scriptures that many will be dismayed.

Suddenly

The Lord spoke of life in this world at the time of his coming as being very similar to life in Noah's day at the time of the flood. Marriage, eating and drinking – life would be continuing as usual.

But then, at a single stroke, everything would be interrupted. The Bible describes Jesus Christ's return as being like a lightning flash, like a thief in the night and like a master paying an unexpected visit on his servants. It is clear that people will be taken unawares, in spite of the many warnings of Scripture. All Jesus' parables relating to his coming include this aspect of suddenness.

Triumphantly

This second coming of Christ will be utterly different from the squalid obscurity in which he first came. The return will be accompanied by great power and splendour. In the face of the victorious majesty and power of Jesus Christ's appearing, every person will be forced to acknowledge that he is truly Lord.

Conclusively

The appearing of Jesus Christ will be the final chapter in the human story. His coming will bring governments, nations, authorities and every kind of enemy of God under his rule and judgement.

Death will be destroyed. Satan, and the whole empire of evil will be overthrown for ever. And Christ's people will be united to their Lord in the new creation that he has prepared for them.

BIBLE CHECK

Prophetically: Daniel 7:13-14; 1 Thessalonians 4:16-18
Personally: Matthew 28:20; Acts 1:11
Visibly: Matthew 24:30; Revelation 1:7
Suddenly: Matthew 24:27,36-51; 1 Thessalonians 5:2-3
Triumphantly: Luke 21:27-28; Philippians 2:9-11
Conclusively: 1 Corinthians 15:24; 1 Thessalonians 4:17

KEY TRUTH

All Christians look forward to the personal return of Christ at the end of the age, as predicted by the Bible.

POSTSCRIPT

History is full of examples of false predictions relating to the time of Christ's return. The Christian is best prepared for this event by being involved in active, obedient service.

BIBLE STUDY 1 Thessalonians 4:13–5:11

This was the church that had begun under the preaching of Paul in a mission of only three weeks (Acts 17:1-2). In that time they had been well taught, before Jewish opposition drove the evangelists out. Now however, that Paul is writing to the Thessalonians some months later, he is aware of a question that is puzzling the young Christians. If one of their members died before the second coming of Christ had taken place, would that person be at a disadvantage, in contrast to those who were still alive? This is the starting point of the passage. Read it now, and use these questions to help you:

1 How are we to understand the second coming in relation to the faithful departed (verses 13-18)? Would those who were "still alive" (verse 15) have precedence over them? How could the Thessalonians "encourage" (verse 18) the recently bereaved?

2 Scan the same verses again and establish the position of the church on earth, at the time of the Coming. Observe that Paul, naturally, classes himself among such.

3 Look more closely at verses 15-17, and consider the Coming in relation to the Lord himself. Paul's teaching is only "in accordance to the Lord's own word". Compare these verses with, say, John 14:1-3.

4 Consider 5:1-3 and the teaching about the Coming in relation to time. Compare Matthew 24:42-44.

5 Look at the same verses now, in relation to the unbelieving world. Compare these verses with 2 Thessalonians 1:7-9 and Matthew 24:37-38.

6 Lastly, consider the Return in relation to the Christian's present activities (5:4-11).

REFLECTION

A Study 1 Thessalonians 4:13–5:11. Why was this passage written? From these words, how may we understand the coming of Christ, in relation to Christians who have died, the Day itself, its timing and our right preparation for it?

B Compare John 14:3 with 1 Thessalonians 4:16-18. How does Paul's teaching relate to Christ's?

C What should be your attitude to readers of the Bible who, while believing in the main fact of Christ's coming, may not agree with you on every point of interpretation?

D What do your non-Christian friends think about the future of the world? How does their view differ from yours?

THE LAST THINGS
4. The Judgement

God will be declared as just

The final judgement is a definite future event that will take place at the second coming of Christ. The Bible says that it is unavoidable – as unavoidable as death itself.

At the judgement the balances of true justice will be set right for ever. There will be no excuse left to any who come under judgement – for it will be seen by everybody that the dealings of God are completely just and righteous.

Christ will be acknowledged as Lord

The judgement will signify the end of world history and the struggle between good and evil. Every power that has stood in opposition to God will be put under Christ's feet, and every tongue will confess that he is Lord.

At the judgement, Jesus Christ will receive the glory and worship that is due to him from his people, for he will have gathered them to himself from the whole earth. Their sins will not be counted against them, for by his death on the cross he has already taken their judgement upon himself.

Christians will be accountable for their service

While no Christian will be judged on the basis of the sins he has committed, it is taught in the Bible that Christ's people will be assessed for the quality of their service.

No Christian will ever be lost, but the coming Day will expose our work, which will be rewarded according to its worth. The faithful Christian is thus challenged to please his returning master throughout life's present opportunity.

The disobedient will be rejected for their unbelief

The basis of the judgement will be the response that individuals have made to the light that God has given them. The great sin of the New Testament consists in rejecting the light of Christ. When asked what the vital priority of life was, Jesus replied that it was to believe in himself.

The separation from God to which unbelievers are condemned is therefore no more than an underlining of their own choices regarding God's revelation to them.

Satan will be destroyed for ever

Satan is not all-powerful. The book of Revelation shows that he is very active in many different ways but he does not occupy the centre – for God never leaves his throne.

Thus, the judgement will bring the victory of the cross to completion. Satan and his allies will be overthrown and destroyed by God.

God: Hebrews 9:27; Psalm
96:13; Acts 17:31
Christ: 1 Corinthians
15:24-26; John 5:24;
Philippians 2:11
Christians: Romans 14:12;
2 Corinthians 5:9-10;
1 Corinthians 3:10-15
Disobedient: John 3:19;
6:28-29; 2 Thessalonians
1:7-9
Satan: Revelation 20:10

KEY TRUTH

The final judgement will be
the climax of this world's
events. It will set right the
injustices of history, underline the choices of individuals,
and demonstrate the
righteousness of God and the
victory of Jesus Christ.

POSTSCRIPT

Judgement is not a popular
theme in societies which have
become soft and indulgent.
However, we must recognise
that by the choices individuals
make, they sentence
themselves.

BIBLE STUDY 2 Peter 3:1-18

The apostle Peter is nearing the end of his life and
he knows it (1:14). His concern is that the next generation of
believers would hold on firmly to the apostolic truth.

These were difficult days for the Christian church, faced as
it was by spiritual and cultural pressures that threatened to
swallow it up. Use these questions to prompt your study of
this passage:

1 What main event is the apostle emphasising in this chapter?
Verses 7,10 and 12 allude to it. Where did Peter get this
concept from? Look up Matthew 24:29-31. Observe its
finality (verses 10,12).

2 What authority does Peter want his readers to rely upon for
his teaching? Look at verse 2, and compare Ephesians 2:20.

3 Verses 3-5 highlight the viewpoint of the critics with regard
to the last times. How similar is their argument to that of
every generation? Compare Jeremiah 17:15.

4 How does the believer resist the propaganda that we are just
part of a closed system and that nothing outside the life of
this world can affect it? The answer lies in 1:12-13,15 and in
3:1-2,8.

5 Answering the scoffers, the writer points to three "outside'
and unforeseen events affecting this world, two of which
had already happened. What are they (verses 5-7)?

6 How can we practically prepare for the final day? Look for
the references to patience, to godliness, to focusing and to
"growing".

REFLECTION

A Read Matthew 25:1-13.
What is the main thrust of
this parable of Jesus?
Contrast the two groups of
girls. What does this passage
teach us about the end times,
and about our choices in life?
B At the end, there will be a
separation between evil and
good. Is the world getting
better or worse? Compare
your thoughts with Matthew
13:24-30.

C What does 1 Corinthians
3:12-15 teach people about
their responsibilities and
opportunities?
D What does Christ's
teaching about judgement
tell us about the nature of
humanity?

THE LAST THINGS
5. The Resurrection

Christ its guarantee

Christianity presents the resurrection of the body as the final goal of our salvation – a supernatural event coinciding with the return of Jesus Christ.

This resurrection, which is the inheritance of every Christian, derives its pattern from Christ. The Bible says that Christ's resurrection is like the first sheaf of a large harvest, in which all Christians will be gathered. This is what the Bible means when it uses the word "firstfruits". Christ's resurrection is the guarantee of this event.

Nature its illustration

This expectation of a bodily resurrection is illustrated by Paul in his first letter to the Christians in Corinth.

Paul answers the objection that the resurrection is impossible, by referring to the miracle of sowing and reaping, in which a small seed is transformed into a plant. The resurrection does not mean a mere shadowy existence of the soul, but a glorious and transformed body.

Eternal life its outcome

The resurrection body is designed for a totally different environment from this passing, mortal age. When it is raised, it is a spiritual body, suited for life in the presence of God. There, believers will know an existence unlimited by the effects of the fall.

From humiliation to glory

Christians are assured in the Bible that when they finally see Christ, they will have a body like his. We are not given many details about the nature of the resurrection body, beyond that the believer's body is weak and ugly at death, but that when raised, it possesses marvellous beauty and strength.

Probably, the reason why we are only given a limited understanding of the resurrection body is that in this new life the focus will be on Christ himself and not on details of secondary importance. He will be at the centre, and that is what really matters.

From the natural to the spiritual

At death, the believer's body is physical; at the resurrection it is spiritual.

If Christ's resurrection body is the pattern, then we can understand that this body will be perfect in every way.

It will be a body that has continuity with the old body (and we will recognize one another in the new creation), and yet a body that is suited to that immortal, redeemed creation.

From mortality to immortality

All reminders of death, decay and disease will be banished from the new bodies of Christ's people. The apostle Paul seems to indicate that those believers who have died before Christ's return still await their resurrection bodies and for the present are without a body, although truly with Christ. They, like those who are still alive at Christ's return, will be raised to live for ever.

Christ: 1 Corinthians
15:20-23; Philippians
3:20-21
Nature: 1 Corinthians
15:35-38
Eternal life: 1 Thessalonians
4:16-17; John 5:24-26; 6:40
Humiliation: 1 Corinthians
15:43; 1 John 3:2
Natural: John 20:19;
1 Corinthians 15:44;
Luke 24:36-43
Mortality: 1 Corinthians
15:42,50-55; Philippians
1:21-24

KEY TRUTH

The Bible teaches that
Christians will be raised from
death to enjoy eternal life with
God.

POSTSCRIPT

The Christian's hope is not to
escape from the body, but to
be raised as a new body to live
the quality of life God has
always intended for us.

BIBLE STUDY 1 Corinthians 15:50-58

"The resurrection of Christ has altered the face of the
universe," writes David Gooding. "Not only is death not an
irreversible process; it is not even a permanent institution"
(*True to the Faith*, Hodder). Here in this passage the apostle Paul
has arrived at the stirring climax to his classic chapter on the
Resurrection. He has covered various difficulties and
objections; now he concludes with a ringing declaration:

1 In verse 50, Paul demolishes any idea of a crude return of a
   dead corpse to what it was before. How does he do this, with
   his use of terms? What was the difference between the
   raising of Lazarus and the resurrection of Christ? Compare
   John 11:44 with John 21:6-7.
2 Look on at verses 51-53. Discuss the nature of the "changed"
   bodies of Christ's followers. What clues do we have? Look
   back to verses 42-43 and Philippians 3:21.
3 "The last trumpet" (verse 52). To what does this refer? A
   parallel is found in Matthew 24:31 and 1 Thessalonians
   4:16. How much does this expectation make sense of the
   present for you?
4 Turn to verses 55-57. "The sting is not in death but in sin,"
   wrote Leon Morris (*1 Corinthians*, Tyndale Press). Relate this
   to the achievements of Christ on our behalf.
5 Apply verse 58 to the various callings and pieces of service
   represented in the study group.
6 How confident are you that your own body will one day be
   resurrected?

REFLECTION

A Read 1 Corinthians
15:20-28. How does Christ's
resurrection affect the future?
In what sense do we understand the defeat of death?
How is this confidence
reflected in Christian living
today?
B What difference, in
practice, does a Christian
faith seem to make to people
in the face of death?

C Turn to the Old Testament
passage of Ezekiel 37:1-14,
which relates to the message
of resurrection. Think and
pray about situations that
need this kind of
transformation.
D Because Christ is risen, we
too shall be raised from
death. In what ways does this
give the Easter story extra
meaning for you?

THE LAST THINGS
6. The New Order

The triumph of the Lamb

The Bible ends, in the book of Revelation, with an undisguised theme of victory, centred in Christ. Christ is described as the "Lamb" (which links him with the Old Testament sacrifices in which lambs were killed to take away sin). He is the Lamb who was killed, but is now worthy of receiving the praise of all creation.

It is through the shedding of his blood that complete victory over evil has been achieved.

The new creation

Revelation chapter 21 describes a new heaven and a new earth. The word "heaven" here means the rest of the universe, with all the stars and planets.

The old universe, with its weakness and decay, is radically redeemed. There are no more heartaches, pains or sicknesses. This new creation is made for God and his people to live in. There is a note of finality and triumph in the words of verse 6 "It is done."

The new Jerusalem

This chapter also describes the final home of those whom God has raised to eternal life. This walled city, the new Jerusalem, has been prepared by God for his people – for it comes from him.

The evil are excluded from the city, and inside it there will be perfect fellowship and worship of God. We are told that there will be no temple in the city, because God is the temple. The sun and moon will not be needed, because God's splendour will illuminate the city. This is the city of God.

Paradise restored

In the opening chapters of the Bible, Adam and Eve were placed in the Garden of Eden. At the centre of this garden was the tree of life. However, after the fall, Adam and Eve were driven out of paradise by God, and barred from the tree of life.

The last chapter of the Bible shows that God will restore humanity to paradise, and that we will have free access to the tree of life. Thus, at the very end of the story of God's redemption, humanity is back in fellowship again, in touch at last with the very life of God.

Jesus is coming

As John concludes with his portrayal of Christ as the returning bridegroom, the prophecy of the book of Revelation is witnessed to be true by the angel, by John himself and by Jesus. It is to remain unsealed, for the message is to be obeyed. It is not to be hidden, and it is not to be meddled with.

The concluding message is simple: "I am coming soon." The offer is free – that of the water of life for all who will come and accept it.

The final sentences of the Bible include a prayer for strength, offered on behalf of all God's people who are not yet within the security of the walled city. There is also a prayer of joyful hope and anticipation: "Come, Lord Jesus."

BIBLE CHECK

Triumph: Revelation 5:12-13; 7:17; 12:11; 17:14

New creation: Revelation 21:1-8; 2 Peter 3:10-13; Romans 8:18-23

New Jerusalem: Revelation 21:2-3,9-27

Paradise: Genesis 2:8-10; 3:22-24; Revelation 22:1-5,14

Coming: Revelation 22:6-21; Isaiah 40:9-10

KEY TRUTH

Christian people look forward to a new heaven and a new earth, where the dwelling place of God and his Christ are to be found.

POSTSCRIPT

In the new order, Christians will have new bodies, there will be a new Jerusalem and a new heaven and earth. All these things marred by sin, have to be changed. But we have the confident assurance that God himself, with his love and faithfulness, will not change.

BIBLE STUDY Revelation 21:1-14

Imagine that there was no book of Revelation. The impression then gained, at the close of the Bible would be of an unresolved conclusion, with God's saints contending valiantly for the faith, but with no apparent final verdict on the conflict between good and evil.

The verdict of this book is inescapable. You cannot read the last pages of this wonderful prophecy and stay in the camp of the pessimists! Let this final vision of the glory of God's kingdom inspire you in everything you are doing.

1 Verse 5 seems to be the key thought. What is its link with verses 1-2 and 4?

2 We are visualising a scene of glory (verses 10-14). How does this vision of the future make sense of the present turbulence, frailties and evils, mentioned in this passage?

3 How does our vision of the centre give shape to the whole? For the centre, see verses 3 and 5. How can we best transfer this thought into our own world-view?

4 "It is done" (verse 6) This is the tense of the "prophetic past" – it is as good as done already! How does this vision of the certain triumph of God add strength to the task in hand?

5 In the light of verses 7-8, discuss the statement, "God's judgement is the proof of his goodness."

6 What do the many "gates" of verses 12-14 speak to us of?

7 Why does God not achieve all this now, at a stroke?

REFLECTION

A Read Revelation 21. Try to put into your own words something of what this passage is telling us about God and his people. Would any kind of person feel at home in the new creation?

B "I am coming soon." What does this concept do to your priorities at present? What should you do about it?

C Read Revelation 22:17. What are the different thoughts in this verse? What effect should they have on your praying and witnessing?

D What are the suggestions and hints of a likeness between your own Christian fellowship and the perfection of the new Jerusalem? How can such a likeness be developed?

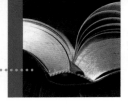

Focus on The Bible

ITS MAIN SECTIONS

A God who loves to bless
■ Genesis 12:1-3

A God who demands our allegiance
■ Joshua 24:14-15

A God for all the seasons of life
■ Ecclesiastes 3:1-8

A God who hates injustice
■ Amos 5:21-24

Time to receive the good news
■ Mark 1:14-15

Don't conform, be transformed
■ Romans 12:1-2

Jesus said, "I am the Alpha and the Omega"
■ Revelation 1:8-11

ITS INSPIRATION

The identity of its divine author
■ 1 Peter 1:20-21

The diversity of its human writers
■ Acts 18:3

The unity of its many themes
■ Matthew 5:17-18

The reality of its moral impact
■ Hebrews 4:12

It is ideal to meditate on
■ Joshua 1:7-8

All the Bible is inspired
■ 2 Timothy 3:16

Jesus said, "Come, follow me"
■ Matthew 4:19

ITS INTERPRETATION

Each part must be seen in its historical setting
■ John 13:14

Each part must be consistent with its surrounding passage
■ 2 Corinthians 4:2

Each part must be in harmony with the rest of Scripture
■ Matthew 22:29

Each part must be consistent with the purpose of God's revelation
■ Deuteronomy 29:29

Each part must be understood in changing cultures
■ Acts 8:34-38

Faithfulness in interpretation
■ Revelation 22:18-19

Jesus said, "Do not be afraid"
■ Matthew 28:10

ITS APPLICATION

Read prayerfully
■ Psalm 119:33-40

Listen personally
■ 1 Samuel 3:10

Look expectantly
■ 1 John 5:13

Apply regularly
■ Psalm 1:1-2

Act obediently
■ James 1:22-25

Read totally
■ 2 Corinthians 4:2

Jesus said, "Have faith in God"
■ Mark 11:22

ITS CENTRAL THEME

The continual conflict
■ Genesis 3

The promised Saviour
■ Jeremiah 31:31-34

The work of Christ
■ Luke 2:28-32

The new community
■ Ephesians 2:18-22

The ultimate victory
■ 1 Thessalonians 4:13-18

A useful summary
■ Titus 3:3-7

Jesus said, "Your sins are forgiven"
■ Luke 7:48

ITS CONTENTS

God's plan for his people
■ Genesis 1:26-28

The promise of freedom
■ John 8:36

A God of faithfulness
■ Psalm 36:5

A God of justice
■ Deuteronomy 32:4

A God of love
■ 1 John 4:10

Jesus is coming back for his own
■ 1 Thessalonians 4:16-17

Jesus said, "The Scriptures speak of me"
■ John 5:39

Focus on God

THE TRINITY

In the Old Testament
Genesis 1:26-27

Asserted in the New
Testament
John 14:15-26

Blessing the church
2 Corinthians 13:14

The Father commits his
works to the Son
Matthew 11:27

The Son revealed through the
Holy Spirit
John 15:16

God in the believer
Romans 8:9

Jesus said, "We will come to
him and make our home with
him"
John 14:23

THE CREATOR

In the beginning
Genesis 1

God the creator
Nehemiah 9:6

God the sustainer
Acts 14:17

God is achieving his purpose
Romans 8:18-25

Earth as a focal point
Revelation 21:1-3

What is man?
Psalm 8:3-8

Jesus said, "I will be with you
always"
Matthew 28:20

GOD'S BEING

God is everywhere
Jeremiah 23:23-24

God is all-powerful
Genesis 17:1

God knows everything
Hebrews 4:12-13

God is eternal
Isaiah 44:6

God is unchanging
James 1:17

Truths about God
Psalm 138:1-18

Jesus said, "Come to me"
Matthew 11:28

GOD'S CHARACTER

God's truth is inseparable
from his character
John 14:6

God's holiness reacts against
all impurity
Habakkuk 1:13

God's love extends to all
humanity
1 John 4:7-11

God's mercy holds back what
we deserve
Hosea 11:8-9

God's grace gives us what we
do not deserve
1 Corinthians 1:4-8

God's faithfulness provides
for daily life
Psalm 89:1-2

Jesus said, "I will give you
rest"
Matthew 11:28

THE FATHERHOOD
OF GOD

By creation – of all things
Acts 17:24-29

By covenant – of Israel
Isaiah 63:16

By adoption – of Christian
believers
Romans 8:14-17

From eternity – of Jesus
Christ
John 17:5

The Father's gifts
Galatians 4:4-7

The Father's delight
Luke 15:11-24

Jesus said, "Learn from me"
Matthew 11:29

GOD'S REVELATION

Seen supremely in Jesus
John 14:8-10

Seen through the Bible
Romans 16:25-27

Seen through creation
Psalm 19:1-4

Seen in history
Psalm 75:6-7

Seen in humanity
Romans 2:14-15

Seen through human
experience
Revelation 2:29

Jesus said, "Father, forgive
them"
Luke 23:34

Focus on Jesus Christ

HIS INCARNATION

Christ was Son of God before time and space
■ John 1:1-3

It was by a supernatural conception
■ Matthew 1:18-25

It shows Christ as fully God
■ John 8:46

It establishes Christ as fully human
■ Galatians 4:4-5

It explains Christ's unique personality
■ Matthew 8:24-27

It validates Christ's saving ministry
■ 1 Timothy 2:5

Jesus said, "Today you will be with me in paradise"
■ Luke 23:43

MAIN EVENTS IN THE GOSPELS

His humble birth
■ Luke 2:1-7

His sinless baptism
■ Matthew 3:13-17

His revealing transfiguration
■ Luke 9:28-36

His obedient death
■ Luke 23:26-43

His victorious resurrection
■ Luke 24:1-8

His glorious ascension
■ Luke 24:44-53

Jesus said, "Trust in God"
■ John 14:1

MAIN ASPECTS OF HIS MINISTRY

Authority that convinced
■ Matthew 5:21-22,27-28

Parables that provoked
■ Mark 4:2

Miracles that confirmed
■ Mark 1:23-28

Compassion that attracted
■ Matthew 9:35-38

Training that prepared
■ Matthew 10:1-15

Controversy that challenged
■ Mark 2:5-7

Jesus said, "Trust also in me"
■ John 14:1

HIS NAMES

Son of God
■ John 20:17

The Word
■ Revelation 19:11-13

High Priest
■ Hebrews 7:23-28

Messiah
■ John 4:25-26

Son of Man
■ Matthew 8:19-20

Lord
■ 1 Corinthians 12:1-3

Jesus said, "You are the salt of the earth"
■ Matthew 5:13

HIS ATONING DEATH

... initiated a new relationship
■ 2 Corinthians 5:15-19

... fulfilled Old Testament Scripture
■ Isaiah 53:4-12

... destroyed Satan's kingdom
■ 1 John 3:8

... reversed sin's dominion
■ Galatians 3:13

... provided a way of forgiveness
■ 1 John 1:7

... guaranteed an eternity with God
■ Romans 8:31-39

Jesus said, "I am the bread of life"
■ John 6:35

HIS TRIUMPHANT RESURRECTION

The foundation of the Christian faith
■ Romans 1:4

An event supported by evidence
■ John 20:1-29

A promise of ultimate victory
■ 1 Corinthians 15:24-28

The power of Christian experience
■ Romans 6:5-14

The assurance of eternal security
■ John 11:25-26

More evidence!
■ 1 Corinthians 15:1-11

Jesus said, "I am the light of the world"
■ John 8:12

Focus on The Holy Spirit

HIS PERSON

Part of the Godhead
■ Matthew 28:19

The very character of God
■ 2 Corinthians 13:14

He knows us through and
through
■ 1 Corinthians 2:10-11

He feels
■ Ephesians 4:30

He hurts
■ Hebrews 10:29

He guides
■ Acts 8:29

Jesus said, "… the Holy Spirit
… will teach you all things …"
■ John 14:26

HIS NAMES AND DESCRIPTIONS

The Holy Spirit
■ Acts 2:32-33

The Spirit of God
■ Matthew 3:16

The Spirit of Christ
■ Philippians 1:19

Wind
■ Acts 2:2

Water
■ John 7:38

Fire
■ Matthew 3:11

Jesus said, "I am the gate for
the sheep"
■ John 10:7

HIS WORK

He convinces of sin
■ John 16:8-11

He illuminates truth
■ John 14:25-26

He reveals Christ
■ John 15:26

He lives in believers
■ Romans 8:9-11

He inspires prayer
■ Romans 8:26

He prepares for heaven
■ Romans 8:1-4

Jesus said, "I am the good
shepherd"
■ John 10:11

HIS ACTIVITY IN THE CHRISTIAN

Life – new birth by the Spirit
■ John 3:3-8

Assurance – the witness of
the Spirit
■ Romans 8:15-16

Unity – fellowship in the
Spirit
■ 1 Corinthians 12:13

Ownership – the seal of
the Spirit
■ Ephesians 1:13-14

Power – the fullness of the
Spirit
■ Ephesians 5:18

Confidence – the pledge of
the Spirit
■ 2 Corinthians 5:5

Jesus said, "I am the
resurrection and the life"
■ John 11:25

HIS FRUIT

Love never fails
■ 1 Corinthians 13:8

Let God's peace rule
■ Colossians 3:15

Devote yourself to what
is good
■ Titus 3:8

God loves faithfulness!
■ Matthew 25:23

Gentle, like Jesus
■ Matthew 11:29

Personal discipline
■ 1 Corinthians 9:25-27

Jesus said, "… the Holy Spirit
… will teach you all things"
■ John 14:26

HIS GIFTS

The gifts exalt Christ
■ 1 Peter 4:10-11

The gifts involve all
■ 1 Corinthians 12:7-11

The gifts should unite all
■ Romans 12:4-5

Gifts lay foundations
■ Ephesians 2:19-22

Gifts build up the fellowship
■ Ephesians 4:11-13

Gifts promote mission
■ Colossians 1:27-29

Jesus said, "I am the way"
■ John 14:6

Focus on Humanity

OUR UNIQUENESS

I am a whole being, physical and spiritual
■ Deuteronomy 8:3

I am a spiritual being, made in God's image
■ Genesis 1:26-27

I am a moral being, responsible for my actions
■ Romans 2:14-15

I have natural dimensions
■ Psalm 104:5-30

I have creative dimensions
■ Psalm 8:6-8

I have religious dimensions
■ Psalm 90:1

Jesus said, "I am the truth"
■ John 14:6

OUR DIVERSITY

Created by God
■ Psalm 100:3

Created for God
■ Psalm 100:3

Created to glorify God
■ Psalm 100:4

Family is God's way
■ Genesis 2:18

Searching for God
■ Ecclesiastes 3:11

More than bread alone
■ Matthew 4:4

Jesus said, "I have come that they may have life, and have it to the full"
■ John 10:10

OUR REBELLION AND FALL

Humanity's innocence gave us fellowship with God
■ Genesis 2

Humanity's freedom gave us the power of choice
■ Genesis 2:16-17

Humanity's decision led us into moral rebellion
■ Genesis 3:8-19

Humanity's rebellion and guilt
■ Romans 5:12-17

Humanity's condemnation and separation
■ Isaiah 59:1-2

Humanity's separation and death
■ Romans 6:23

Jesus said, "I am the life"
■ John 14:6

OUR REBELLION AND CONDEMNATION

All have fallen short of the mark
■ Romans 5:12

The soul who sins will die
■ Ezekiel 18:4

All are guilty
■ Romans 5:18-19

All have turned away
■ Psalm 14:3

All are awaiting judgement
■ Romans 2:16

But thanks to God
■ Romans 8:1-2

Jesus said, "Whoever does not believe [in me] stands condemned already"
■ John 3:18

OUR QUEST AND DILEMMA

Looking for truth
■ Acts 17:22-23

Philosophy can be a blind alley
■ Ecclesiastes 1:17-18

Full of contradiction
■ Mark 7:21-23

God's workmanship, created in Christ Jesus to do good works
■ Ephesians 2:10

A spirit at war with God
■ James 4:5

Slaves to our emotions
■ Titus 3:3

Jesus said, "If the Son sets you free, you will be free indeed"
■ John 8:36

OUR ENEMIES

Satan
■ 1 Peter 5:8-9

Sin
■ Romans 8:10

The world
■ 1 John 2:15-16

The flesh
■ Romans 7:18

Death
■ 2 Timothy 1:10

Defence against enemies
■ Ephesians 6:10-18

Jesus said, "I am the true vine"
■ John 15:1

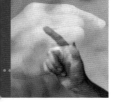

Focus on God's Messengers

ANGELS

Heavenly beings
■ Psalm 8:5

God's messengers
■ Luke 24:4-7

Rejoicing when a sinner repents
■ Luke 15:10

Revealing God's will
■ Exodus 3:2

Protecting God's own
■ 2 Kings 6:17

Attending Jesus
■ Matthew 4:11

Jesus said, "... their angels in heaven always see the face of my Father in heaven"
■ Matthew 18:10

PATRIARCHS

By faith Abraham obeyed
■ Hebrews 11:8

By faith Abraham offered Isaac
■ Genesis 22:7-9

By faith Isaac blessed Jacob and Esau
■ Genesis 27:27-29,39-40

By faith Jacob worshipped
■ Hebrews 11:21

God's promise to Abraham
■ Genesis 15:5

The promise fulfilled
■ Matthew 1:1-17

Jesus said, "Before Abraham was born, I am"
■ John 8:58

PRIESTS

Set apart
■ Exodus 28:1-5

The go-between
■ Leviticus 1:1-9

Past imperfect
■ Hebrews 7:11

Present perfect in Christ
■ Hebrews 7:26-28

The priesthood of believers
■ 1 Peter 2:4-5,9

Living stones
■ 1 Peter 1:5

Jesus said, "This is my blood of the covenant ... poured out for many"
■ Matthew 26:28

PROPHETS

Called by God
■ Isaiah 6:8-10

Challenging falsehood
■ 1 Kings 18:21

Revealing injustice
■ Amos 5:21-24

Revealing God's mind
■ 2 Peter 1:21

Showing the way forward
■ Daniel 2:36-46

Heralding the Messiah
■ John 1:29

Jesus said, "Watch out for false prophets"
■ Matthew 7:15

APOSTLES

Christ's authority
■ Matthew 16:18

Appointed by God
■ John 20:21-23

Witnesses to the resurrection
■ Acts 1:21-22

Evidence
■ 2 Corinthians 12:12

Foundation of the church
■ Ephesians 2:19-20

Teaching the truth
■ John 16:12-15

Jesus said, "You will be my witnesses"
■ Acts 1:8

EVANGELISTS

Good news to tell
■ Acts 8:5

Chosen by God
■ Ephesians 4:11

Proclaiming Christ
■ 1 Corinthians 15:3-5

Confident in God's word
■ Acts 8:35

God's power
■ Acts 1:8

Showing a changed life
■ Galatians 1:23-24

Jesus said, "He who receives you receives me"
■ Matthew 10:40

Focus on Salvation

GOD'S PLAN FOR HUMANITY

God's plan – his will is
sovereign
Romans 9:10-18

God's plan – his work is
eternal
Acts 2:23

God's plan – his choice is
specific
Matthew 22:14

God's people – separated for
holy living
Romans 8:29

God's people – called to good
works
Philippians 2:12-13

God's people – preparing for
future glory
Revelation 17:14

Jesus said, "Peace be with
you!"
John 20:21

HUMANITY'S NEED
OF SALVATION

Humanity's need of:
a new direction
Hebrews 9:27

a new nature
Jeremiah 13:23

a new motivation
John 6:66-68

personal fulfilment
Luke 12:15

social acceptance
Genesis 11:4

a spiritual dimension
1 Corinthians 2:14

Jesus said, "Remain in my
love"
John 15:9

THE WAY OF SALVATION

The basis – the death of Jesus
Acts 4:10-12

The basis – the resurrection
of Jesus
Acts 2:32-36

The call – to repentance
Acts 3:19

The call – to faith
Acts 13:38-39

The promise – forgiveness
Psalm 103:11-12

The promise – the gift of
the Spirit
Acts 2:38

Jesus said, "I chose you to go
and bear much fruit"
John 15:16

ACCEPTANCE

God regenerates the believer
as a new being
Ezekiel 36:25-27

God reconciles the believer
in a new relationship
2 Corinthians 5:18-21

God redeems the believer
through a new covenant
Jeremiah 31:31-34

God justifies the believer
for a new position
Titus 3:7

God glorifies the believer
for a new life
Romans 8:28-30

The Christian's new position
Romans 5:1-8

Jesus said, "I did not come to
bring peace, but a sword"
Matthew 10:34

SANCTIFICATION

A separation to God
2 Thessalonians 2:13

A separation from the world
2 Corinthians 6:17–7:1

A separation for holy living
2 Timothy 2:20-21

A separation by the Holy
Spirit
Galatians 5:16-18

A separation through the
word of God
John 15:3

A separation that progresses
throughout life
2 Corinthians 1:10

Jesus said, "The Son of Man
came to serve"
Mark 10:45

IN THE LETTER
TO THE ROMANS

Election
Romans 9:21-24

Transformation
Romans 12:1-2

God's working on behalf of
his people
Romans 8:28-30

Reasons for having
confidence in God
Romans 8:31-34

No separation from God
Romans 8:35-37

The love of God
Romans 8:38-39

Jesus said, "Give to God what
is God's"
Mark 12:17

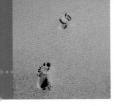

A THOUGHT FOR EACH DAY
Focus on The Christian

DESCRIBED

A sinner saved by grace
■ Ephesians 2:8-9

A member of God's family
■ John 1:12-13

A disciple of Jesus Christ
■ Luke 14:26-27

A temple of the Holy Spirit
■ 1 Corinthians 3:16

A pilgrim in an alien
environment
■ Hebrews 11:8-16

A citizen of heaven
■ Hebrews 13:14

Jesus said, "My words will
never pass away"
■ Mark 13:31

THE CHRISTIAN
AND THE BIBLE

The Bible:
equips the Christian for life
■ John 8:31-32

equips the Christian for
battle
■ Matthew 4:1-11

energises the Christian for
service
■ Psalm 1

corrects the Christian from
error
■ James 1:23-25

develops the Christian in the
faith
■ 1 Peter 2:2-3

informs the Christian of
God's mind
■ Romans 11:33-36

Jesus said, "Do not worry"
■ Matthew 6:25

THE CHRISTIAN
AND PRAYER

Prayer is:
essential for communion
with God
■ Mark 1:35

essential for growth in God
■ Matthew 6:9-13

essential for the service of
God
■ James 5:16-18

essential for the praise of God
■ Psalm 150

essential for the experience
of God
■ Psalm 57:1-3

God's special way of
communication
■ Romans 8:15

Jesus said, "Seek and you
will find"
■ Matthew 7:7

THE CHRISTIAN
AND WITNESS

Proclaiming a person
■ Acts 1:8

Explaining the truth
■ Colossians 1:28-29

Sharing a love
■ 2 Corinthians 5:14

Witnessing consistently
■ John 13:34-35

Witnessing personally
■ Acts 4:18-20

Witnessing collectively
■ Philippians 1:27

Jesus said, "Whoever will lose
his life for my sake will find
it"
■ Matthew 10:39

THE CHRISTIAN
AND THE WORLD

Called out of the world
■ 1 Corinthians 7:29-31

Separated from the world
■ Ephesians 5:3-11

Sent into the world
■ John 20:21

Sent into the world
■ Matthew 5:13-16

Sent to overcome the world
■ Romans 8:37

Journeying through the
world
■ Hebrews 11:16

Jesus said, "Love the Lord
your God"
■ Mark 12:30

THE CHRISTIAN LIFE

A vocation to be fulfilled
■ Philippians 3:14

A character to be developed
■ 2 Peter 1:5-8

A fellowship to be
maintained
■ Ephesians 5:1-2

Energies to be harnessed
■ 1 Corinthians 15:58

Minds to be developed
■ Ephesians 1:18

A hope to be realised
■ Titus 2:13

Jesus said, "Love your
neighbour as yourself"
■ Mark 12:31

Focus on The Church

ITS CHARACTERISTICS

It is the church of Jesus
Christ (historical)
▦ Matthew 16:18

It is the company of all
believers (universal)
▦ Colossians 3:11

It is a unity of the Spirit
(spiritual)
▦ Ephesians 4:4-6

Its authority is God's word
(scriptural)
▦ 2 Timothy 1:13-14

Its programme is worldwide
(international)
▦ Luke 4:16-21

The unity the church should
have
▦ Ephesians 4:1-16

Jesus said, "You must be born
again"
▦ John 3:7

ITS MAIN DESCRIPTION

A firm building
▦ 1 Peter 2:4-5

A virgin bride
▦ Revelation 21:2

A functioning body
▦ 1 Corinthians 12:12-31

A permanent city
▦ Hebrews 13:14

A stable family
▦ 1 Timothy 3:14-15

An active army
▦ Ephesians 6:12

Jesus said, "Love your
enemies"
▦ Luke 6:35

ITS RELATIONSHIP TO CHRIST

Christ died for the church
▦ Acts 20:28

Christ builds the church
▦ Ephesians 4:11-16

Christ protects the church
▦ Daniel 3:19-27

Christ purifies the church
▦ Jeremiah 3:6,14

Christ intercedes for
the church
▦ 1 John 2:1

Christ prepares for
the church
▦ John 14:1-4

Jesus said, "Be merciful"
▦ Luke 6:36

AUTHORITY AND MISSION

Guarding the truth
▦ 1 Timothy 6:20

Correcting the unruly
▦ 1 Corinthians 5:9-13

Challenging evil
▦ Romans 12:17-21

Evangelising the world
▦ Matthew 28:18-20

Serving the world
▦ Titus 3:8

Glorifying God
▦ 1 Peter 4:12-14

Jesus said, "What can a
man give in exchange for
his soul?"
▦ Matthew 16:26

ITS ORDINANCES

Baptism – admission to
membership
▦ Acts 2:41

Baptism – more than
a symbol
▦ Acts 8:38-39

Baptism – death to
the old life
▦ Romans 6

Baptism – rising to
the new life
▦ Colossians 2:12

The Lord's Supper –
we commemorate
▦ Luke 22:19-20

The Lord's Supper –
we anticipate
▦ 1 Corinthians 11:26

Jesus said, "God so loved
the world that he gave his one
and only Son"
▦ John 3:16

ITS MINISTRY AND ORDER

Preaching and teaching
▦ Romans 6:17

Prayer and intercession
▦ Romans 15:30

Fellowship and caring
▦ Colossians 3:11

Worship and praise
▦ Colossians 3:16

Leadership and government
▦ Philippians 1:1

Qualities for shepherds of
God's flock
▦ 1 Peter 5:1-11

Jesus said, "You will be my
witnesses"
▦ Acts 1:8

Focus on The Last Things

THE HOPE OF THE CHRISTIAN

Promises to God's people
■ 1 Peter 1:10-12

Fulfilment of God's purposes
■ Acts 3:17-21

Defeat of God's enemies
■ Philippians 2:9-11

A living hope
■ 1 Corinthians 15:20-23, 51-55

A steadfast hope
■ 1 Thessalonians 1:3

A purifying hope
■ Jude 24,25

Jesus said, "You will receive power when the Holy Spirit comes on you"
■ Acts 1:8

THE PRELUDE TO CHRIST'S RETURN

Before the return:

Disorder in the natural realm
■ Luke 21:11,25

Disorder in the social realm
■ 2 Timothy 3:1-5

Disorder in the international realm
■ Mark 13:7-8

Disorder in the family realm
■ Mark 13:12

Disorder in the personal realm
■ Luke 21:26

Disorder in the spiritual realm
■ 2 Thessalonians 2:3-10

Jesus said, "My sheep listen to my voice"
■ John 10:27

THE RETURN OF CHRIST

Christ will return prophetically
■ Daniel 7:13-14

Christ will return personally
■ Matthew 26:64

Christ will return visibly
■ Matthew 24:30

Christ will return suddenly
■ Matthew 24:27,36-51

Christ will return triumphantly
■ Luke 21:27-28

Christ will return conclusively
■ 1 Corinthians 15:24

Jesus said, "I give eternal life"
■ John 10:28

THE JUDGEMENT

God will judge everyone
■ Hebrews 9:27

Christians will not be condemned
■ John 5:24

Christians will be accountable for their service
■ Romans 14:12

The disobedient will be rejected for their unbelief
■ John 3:18-20

Satan will be destroyed for ever
■ Revelation 20:10

Separation between good and evil
■ Matthew 13:24-30

Jesus said, "I know my sheep"
■ John 10:14

THE RESURRECTION

Christ, its guarantee
■ 1 Corinthians 15:20-23

Nature, its illustration
■ 1 Corinthians 15:35-38

Eternal life, its outcome
■ 1 Thessalonians 4:16-17

From humiliation to glory
■ 1 John 3:1-2

From the natural to the spiritual
■ 1 Corinthians 15:44

From mortality to immortality
■ Philippians 1:21-24

Jesus said, "My sheep know me"
■ John 10:14

THE NEW ORDER

The triumph of the Lamb
■ Revelation 5:12-13

The new creation
■ Revelation 21:1-8

The new creation
■ 2 Peter 3:10-13

The new Jerusalem
■ Revelation 21:9-27

Paradise restored
■ Revelation 22:1-5

Jesus is coming
■ Revelation 22:6-21

Jesus said, "Let the little children come to me"
■ Matthew 19:14

Discovering God's Way

The aim of this section of the book is to give encouragement as you discover God's way for yourself. The key themes are:

· discovering Jesus Christ, for example his teaching, his claims and his death and resurrection
· discovering prayer. What is prayer? What should I pray for? Why are my prayers not answered sometimes? How can I overcome discouragement in prayer?
· discovering discipleship. How can I learn to follow Jesus Christ? What will this mean for my life?
· moving on as a Christian. How does being a Christian affect my priorities in life, for example my work and my speech?

Each study consists of teaching followed by an "Over to you" response for you to act on.

Discovering God's Way

CONTENTS

DISCOVERING JESUS CHRIST p.546

DISCOVERING PRAYER p.588

DISCOVERING DISCIPLESHIP p.614

The teaching of Jesus

JESUS THE TEACHER

His teaching was unique

"Well", said the big-wigs to the police one day, "why haven't you brought him in?" Their reply is striking: "There's never been anybody who has spoken like him" (John 7:46).

This testimony is even more impressive because of the ordinary way in which Jesus went about his teaching. Our teachers usually stand; in those days rabbis sat to teach, and that's just what Jesus did. You weren't really recognised as a rabbi unless a group of followers came round as learners or "disciples" to sit at your feet: exactly what happened to Jesus. It wasn't that he drew attention to himself, did press-ups or shouted; his method was low-key and in the common mould. But no one spoke as he did.

His teaching was astonishing

It was like that from the word go. They were astonished at his teaching, for he taught as one who had authority, and not as the scribes (Mark 1:22). The scribes were experts in what other people had said about Scripture over the centuries. With Jesus it was "I tell you," and for emphasis, "Truly, I say to you" (Matthew 5:18).

His teaching was biblical

Not that Jesus went against the Old Testament Scriptures; far from it. The words of Scripture are the words of God (John 10:35; 2 Timothy 3:16). Jesus won't surrender a single letter, or even part of a letter, of the Old Testament: see Matthew 5:17-19. He never contradicts it. His method is positive: he shows its true meaning, and he sweeps away the watering-downs and misunderstandings of centuries in order to confront people with the clear challenge of the original word: see Matthew 5:22,44; 15:1-9; 23:23.

His teaching confronted

"Confront": that was a hallmark of Jesus' teaching. People yawned as your average scribe informed them of the various interpretations of a difficult verse. They gasped, gripped and transfixed, as our Lord Jesus unleashed God's command into their consciences. When did you last obey Matthew 5:24,40 or 44-48?

And his stories! Unforgettable, and what's worse, uncomfortable! When Jesus speaks, God claims the whole of you in a way that allows no contradiction or evasion.

His teaching was momentous

Our Lord leaves us under no illusions as to the crisis we're left in by his teaching. To obey is to build our lives on a foundation that nothing will ever shake. To disobey will lead to the solemn verdict on a life: "great was the fall of it" (Matthew 7:24-27).

This is not to say that we are put right with God, or assured of getting to heaven, through what we do. That was the Pharisee's big mistake: see Luke 18:9-14. Jesus clearly taught that it is he alone who saves by giving his life as a ransom for ours (Matthew 20:28). All that we contribute to our salvation is the sin that makes it necessary! To receive and rely on Jesus to save us – faith in him as Saviour – is the "work" Jesus taught (John 6:29).

OVER TO YOU

Do you know the central truths of Jesus' teaching? Read through the Gospel of Matthew to remind yourself.

JESUS AND PRAYER

Friendship with God

God takes pleasure in our friendship: that's the heart of prayer. We really start praying when we regard prayer as a privilege not a duty! That's where the Lord's Prayer is so healthy: it starts with relating to God and admiring him ("Our Father in heaven") before it gets as far as asking anything. Let's take Matthew 6:5-18 as our guide to prayer and fasting.

Do you pray?

Notice that our Lord assumes we shall pray: it's "when", not "if"! Do you make it a regular, persevering part of your life? See Luke 18:1.

Then our Lord Jesus goes on to distinguish Christian prayer from two wrong sorts. Unlike hypocritical prayer – Matthew 6:5-6 – it makes God the only audience. And unlike pagan prayer – Matthew 6:7-8 – it is simple and plain, for it relies on the Father's willingness and not the prayer's wordiness!

Praying with others

God is the only audience: that doesn't speak at all against praying together. Jesus alternates the plural "you" with the private "you" in these instructions. We should pray alone, and we should pray with each other. Indeed, Jesus is present in an extra way, and gives extra power, to the united praying of Christians. See Matthew 18:19-20. But when we pray together, we are to pray to God!

Notice the value of *exclusion*: "go into your room and shut the door". Cut out all else to be with God.

Riches on offer

The word for "room" in Matthew 6:6 is a wonderful one. It indicates a store-room, a magazine where ammunition is kept ... and a treasury from which riches are handed out. Prayer brings the good things God has stored up for us, the spiritual ammunition we need against the devil's assaults, the riches that

Christ offers us in our neediness. Jesus also commends childlike confidence: "Your father knows what you need." See Matthew 6:8; Hebrews 11:6.

The Lord's Prayer

The prayer itself starts with worship: Matthew 6:9. This is tremendously important. It decentralises self and puts God back at the centre of our attention. Step two is to identify with God's concerns: his reputation, his reign and his will. See verses 9 and 10. Step three is that we may take to God all our concerns, great or small: our provision, our pardon and our protection (verses 11-13). The traditional ending probably wasn't said by Jesus or written by Matthew but it's thoroughly Christian for all that, praising God's kingship, power and glory.

Fasting

As with prayer, our Lord assumes we shall fast: Matthew 6:16. Fasting is going without food in order to devote ourselves to God. Again it's best seen as an opportunity rather than a duty. We could ask God so to burden us with particular needs close to his heart, that we'd *rather* be doing business with him about them than eating. Don't do it "because Christians ought to"! Try it when there are vital decisions to be made (Luke 6:12-13) or specific issues to see won for God (Ezra 8:21-23).

Issues won for God: that's what fasting and prayer are about. The sort of friendship with God that is effective for his reign and his honour.

OVER TO YOU

Have you chosen friendship with God as your greatest purpose in life? Giving priority to prayer is a good start.

JESUS AND FORGIVENESS

Our deepest need

When Jesus met a paralysed man he did something significant. He forgave his sins – something which, as the Pharisees were not slow to point out, only God can do (Matthew 9:2-6). That's very revealing. Jesus was telling us plainly what anyone with even half a conscience knows only too well: authentic, living forgiving is the deepest of our needs. It was an opinion he held to and lived by even in his darkest hour (Luke 23:34).

What is forgiveness?

There are three New Testament words for it and they each make their own contribution.

· The first and commonest (*aphesis*: verb *aphiēmi*) says that when he forgives us God sends our guilt and sin away. He and we abandon them and leave them altogether behind us. In most of the places we read "forgive" in the New Testament it will be this word.

· The second word for forgiveness (*charizomai*) is a word that means to be freely kind to. God freely pardons us, and we should do the same to each other: Ephesians 4:32.

· The third word (*apoluō*) says that in forgiving us God is releasing us from bondage or debt: he could hold our sins against us, but chooses not to. We open the tap of that release as we copy God and don't hold things against others: see Luke 6:37.

Forgiveness and Jesus' blood

In Matthew 26:28 we read, "This is my blood of the covenant which is poured out for many for the forgiveness of sins." The whole momentous good news of the Christian faith is encapsulated in those luminous words. As the hymn-writer has it:

> Bearing shame and scoffing rude
> In my place condemned he stood
> Sealed my pardon with his blood
> Hallelujah! What a Saviour!

Does "blood" seem a crude word for our Lord Jesus to use? Remember, Passover was a Jewish feast. All the Old Testament words for forgiveness are connected with their sacrificial system. "Blood" speaks of a life given up in atoning death with a view to forgiveness and reconciliation between God and humanity.

Why should that be necessary? It was laid down between God and humanity: the punishment for sin is death (Genesis 2:17; Romans 6:23). So sin can never be dealt with apart from a death (Hebrews 9:22), or God would be abandoning his own character. The wonder of the gospel is that God's love provided, in the death of Jesus, what his justice demanded.

How do I come by it?

How do we make this forgiveness our own? The parable of the Pharisee and the tax collector tells us (Luke 8:9-14). We come, as sinners, to the mercy God holds out to us in the person of Jesus Christ. Contrast the two men in the story. Forgiveness is something God never sells. It's something he gives to sinners; he never gives it to Pharisees who want to buy it by their good deeds. Since he only gives it to sinners, we need to take our place right there: we lay hold of the absolution he holds out to us, by laying hold (by faith) of the Saviour who purchased it. Then "if we confess our sins, he is faithful and just to forgive us our sins, and cleanse us from all unrighteousness" (1 John 1:9). A just God, and a Saviour! Could anyone ask for more?

OVER TO YOU

Do you practise forgiveness as the gospel calls Jesus' followers to do? Is there anyone you need to forgive today?

JESUS AND MONEY

Jesus worked among poor people

Working with poor people was part of the plan Jesus had at the outset of his ministry (Luke 4:18; see also Luke 1:52-53; 2:7). He said that it was the poor who were happy or blessed (Luke 6:20). Some people limit this to mean those who see themselves as spiritually poor (Matthew 5:3), but probably it means more than this.

The dangers of money

"You cannot serve God and money," declares Jesus (Luke 16:13). We will be either fully committed to God or money, but not both. What effects can money have on us?

- **Money can make us greedy.** A rich man was once asked how much money he would want to be really happy. The people waited to hear the fantastic amount. But the man just said, "More." The truth is, however much we have, we always want more. This can lead to a life that is self-centred and proud and neglects God. Look at Luke 12:16-21.
- **Money can make us blind to needs around us.** Consider the story of the rich man and Lazarus (Luke 16:19-31). We can be so busy showing off our latest acquisitions that we just don't notice the needs of people around us!
- **Money can blind us to our spiritual needs.** Getting more and more things can lead us to thinking that the visible, physical world is the only one. The result is that we can become totally hardened to anything spiritual (Luke 18:24).

How then should we live?

- **We should be honest.** Money should be earned honestly (Luke 19:2,8), and used for proper purposes.
- **We shouldn't trust in riches.** If we do, we're loving money more than God (Luke 6:24). Instead, we should trust God (Luke 12:27-34). Do you think a lot about money? Do you talk a lot about it? If so, you may be in love with it!
- **We should have what we need.** On one missionary journey the disciples took no money (Luke 9:3). On another, they did (Luke 22:36). We need to work out what having enough means to us individually. It may mean for example, buying second-hand, not new, consumer goods, or not having an expensive foreign holiday.
- **We should use the money we do have wisely.** We need to take care of our families. But we also need to remember that we belong to a world in which millions of people live in inadequate surroundings. So we may find it hard to justify spending a lot of money on ourselves. Our local church and missionary societies need support (Luke 8:3; 21:1-4).

And we can use our time and homes to be generous to others, even to those who cannot return our kindnesses (Luke 14:12-14,21). Some Christians may be more able to do this than others, but all have some responsibility. John Wesley's saying may be helpful: "Get all you can [honestly!], give all you can; save all you can."

OVER TO YOU

When did you last review your spending and your giving? Is it time to re-assess your priorities?

When Jesus spoke about the kingdom of God, he didn't mean a place. He meant God's reign – his rule or his kingship. We can look at this from two different points of view – as something that is here now and something that is still to come.

The rule of God: here and now

"The kingdom of God is within you," said Jesus (Luke 17:20-21). It had already come. These verses also tell us that this kingdom is something spiritual. And Jesus knew the reality of the battle between his kingdom and the power of the devil (Luke 11:20).

Get on with it!

The message that the kingdom is already here is meant to stir the church into action! The church should be:

- **a witnessing people.** Just as Jesus preached the kingdom (Luke 4:43; 8:1), with miracles supporting this (Luke 9:11), so he told his disciples to do the same (Luke 9:2,60).
- **a praying people.** When we pray, "Thy kingdom come" (Luke 11:2), we are asking for God's kingdom to be extended over more and more areas of life and society. In this way, slowly but surely, the kingdom will grow (Luke 13:18-21). We are also asking that God's control of our own lives will increase.
- **a faithful people.** When the people thought that the kingdom was going to come straight away, Jesus told them a parable (Luke 19:11-27). This can be summed up as saying, "Be faithful with what God has already given you."

The rule of God: still to come

The present kingdom won't turn into the future kingdom by itself. Dramatic events have to happen before this comes about (Luke 17:22-37; 21:5-33). But the kingdom of God will certainly come. One day there will be a new heaven and earth. This will be the complete and perfect realisation of God's power when Jesus Christ comes again. Jesus speaks of this kingdom as being something more than spiritual (Luke 13:28-29; 22:16,29,30).

Get ready for it!

The message that the kingdom of God is still to come is meant to make the world prepared and waiting expectantly (Luke 23:51). So we should be:

- **a humble people.** We must make sure that we are in the kingdom. Excuses are not acceptable; there will be judgement for those who aren't in the kingdom (Luke 13:28-29; 14:15-24). The kingdom must be received humbly (Luke 18:16-17).
- **a sacrificial people.** The rich young ruler's money came between him and following Jesus (Luke 18:18-25). Giving certain things up for the kingdom's sake is to characterise believers' lives (Luke 18:29-30). The rewards will be very great!
- **a reverent people.** Believers need to trust God to look after all their needs by seeking his kingdom. If we do this, we shall know the comfort of receiving the kingdom as God's gift (Luke 12:31-32).

OVER TO YOU

The kingdom of God is "now and not yet". How does this work out in your daily life?

The actions of Jesus

JESUS THE SON OF MAN

Jesus used this name more than any other to talk about himself. It tells us that he is a real man, yet much more than that – it also points to the fact that he is God's chosen King. The title comes from the book of Daniel, where the Son of Man comes at the end of history to inherit all the kingdoms of the world. So in the Old Testament, it was an accepted way of thinking about the coming Messiah.

A God of love

Jesus sums up the purpose of his life as, "The Son of Man came to seek and to save the lost" (Luke 19:10). Think of his authority in saying that he had God's right to forgive sins (Luke 5:24). Think of him declaring himself as Lord of the Sabbath (Luke 6:5). Think of him meeting people's needs (Luke 7:1-9; 8:40-56). He was no ordinary man!

The man of sorrows

When Jesus spoke about himself as the Son of Man he often pointed to the future: to the time when he would be betrayed (Luke 9:44) and have to suffer, and be rejected and killed – yet be raised again (Luke 9:22).

The Lord of glory

Jesus, the Son of Man, also spoke about a time when he would personally and gloriously return (Luke 9:26). This would be when it was least expected (Luke 12:40). Judgement would follow (Luke 21:35). As both Man and God, he is uniquely qualified to be God's judge of humanity.

"Who do you say I am?"

"Just who does he think he is?" was a question that was often heard when Jesus was around (Luke 5:21; 7:49; 9:9). And we must all answer the question, "Who is Jesus?" And if he is God, then we must face up to his claims upon our lives.

Come to the Son of Man

Jesus came to rescue us from our sins and the punishment that is rightly due to us. In his death, he took upon himself our sin and its guilt. This challenges us. We must come to him by calling upon him to save us (Luke 23:40-43).

As we think about the life and death of the Lord Jesus Christ, a deep sense of wonder, thanksgiving and praise should come over us (Luke 7:36-50).

Be like the Son of Man

God lowered himself to take on our human likeness. We should also be living lives of self-sacrifice, living for him. Being humble, devoting ourselves to holy living, and pleasing God should be marks of our lives. This will affect the way we spend our time and money. It will affect our friendships and relationships. But it is the way we will truly follow Jesus, the Son of Man (Luke 14:26-27).

OVER TO YOU

Are you living a life of self-sacrifice? Is God calling you to make any changes in the way you spend your time and money?

JESUS THE STORY-TELLER

There are about 40 parables in the Gospels and Luke includes the highest number of these – just under 30. A parable can be called "an earthly story with a heavenly meaning". Something that the listeners were familiar with, from nature (Luke 8:4-15) or their own customs (Luke 7:31-35), for example, is compared with a spiritual truth that Jesus is trying to explain.

What the parables were about

Two themes stand out in Luke's Gospel – what the kingdom of God is like and what discipleship is all about. We read about the growth of the kingdom (Luke 13:18-21), those who come into it (Luke 14:15-24), the joy as they do so (Luke 15), that there is a last chance to hear about it (Luke 13:1-9), and that people can reject Christ (Luke 20:9-19).

Various aspects of discipleship are described:

- **life in the Spirit:** forgiveness and prayer (Luke 7:40-50; 11:5-13; 18:1-8)
- **our inner character:** being alert, faithful and humble (Luke 14:7-11; 12:35-48)
- **thinking and acting** in the right way (Luke 14:28-33)
- **not loving possessions**, yet looking to the future (Luke 12:13-21; 16:1-13)
- **caring** for those in need (Luke 10:29-37; 16:19-31).

Why Jesus spoke in parables

Look at the "key" parable in Luke 8:4-15. According to verses 9 and 10, parables have two effects. First, they reveal the truth to some – those who have faith. To these people God shows what the kingdom is all about. To them, parables are more than just stories: they are different aspects of God's truth. But secondly, parables also have the effect of hiding the truth from those who have hardened themselves to receiving God's word.

While you're looking at this parable, read verses 11-16 and think about what the different responses to the good news mean to you.

How to understand the parables

It is probably best to look for the main lesson or lessons in a parable rather than push home a spiritual meaning to small details. (Think about the parable of the prodigal son in Luke 15:11-32 in this way.) Sometimes the situation in which Jesus spoke a parable is mentioned. This can throw light onto the teaching. See, for example, Luke 10:25-29.

Sometimes Jesus asked one of his listeners a question to see if they had understood (Luke 7:42). But often, because the point he was making was so clear, Jesus didn't need to say anything. The hearers were left to draw their own conclusions.

The impetus of Jesus' teaching in parables is to say, "Listen!" (Luke 8:8), and also, "Do!" (Luke 6:46-49). We need to remember that Jesus was not only teaching people then, he is also teaching us today! So the best way to understand a parable is to put its teaching into action! And the other point to realise is that we can also think of contemporary ways of communicating the Christian faith to today's society.

JESUS THE DISCIPLE-MAKER

The people he chose

Jesus chose ordinary people. The gospel of Christ is good news for ordinary people and Jesus chose ordinary men to communicate it. Four of them were Galilean fishermen (Mark 1:16-20), one was a tax-collector (Mark 2:14), one – Simon – may have been a political activist (Mark 3:18). They were hardly the television caricature of the effeminate cleric!

They were dedicated. Jesus' call was uncompromising: "Come, follow me." He chose them (Mark 3:14). They were prepared to give up everything else and give themselves totally to the work (Mark 1:18).

The methods he used

- **By example.** Fundamental to Jesus' training programme was the fact that he called the apostles to spend three years, all day every day, with him (Mark 3:14). Their teacher didn't meet them in the classroom or address them from the pulpit. They were constantly with him.
- **He didn't call them to do anything which he himself didn't do** (Mark 8:34; 10:38-39). He often took three disciples, who would later be most used to perform miracles of healing, with him as he healed (Mark 5:37-42; Acts 9:40).
- **By gift.** The Lord Jesus Christ didn't only encourage the talents the disciples naturally possessed, although he did this (Mark 1:17). He also gave them authority and power which they never had before (Mark 3:15; 6:7). This was essential, for they were to be in a spiritual battle (2 Corinthians 10:4-5; Ephesians 6:12).
- **By practice.** After being with Jesus and watching and learning from his work with people, the disciples were sent out by Jesus on their own for practical experience. They were to imitate his own ministry (Mark 6:12-13). After their tour they returned so that they could have the joy of telling Jesus

the things that had happened to them. This was good for "job satisfaction" (Mark 6:30; Acts 14:27). They felt they were a team; doubtless everyone picked up tips from others! And Jesus encouraged the disciples to learn from their mistakes (Mark 9:18,28-29).

Jesus didn't simply teach the disciples isolated lessons. He taught them a whole lifestyle. He taught them to have a realistic view of Christian work (Mark 4:13-20). He also taught them to live in utter dependence on God (Mark 6:8-10), and to beware of the teaching of the cynical, unbelieving religious leaders (Mark 8:14-21).

The way he communicated

Jesus gave a lot of time to teaching and preaching. He made great use of the opportunities of the moment, often thrown up by questions (Mark 12:28). His teaching was relevant – he scratched where people itched! He never tired of referring to the Scriptures as the word of God (for example, Mark 2:25; 4:12; 7:6; 9:48; 12:36). He also used a lot of common sense (Mark 3:4). Most ordinary people think in pictures, not in theoretical concepts. So his teaching was concrete rather than academic; it was full of familiar things from everyday life (Mark 2:21-22; 4:26-32). Many people don't grasp what they hear first time. Jesus wasn't afraid of repeating himself (Mark 8:31; 9:30-31; 10:32-34).

OVER TO YOU

Jesus used the opportunities of everyday life to talk to people about God. Can you do the same where you work or meet others?

JESUS AND WOMEN

Jesus' great respect for women

Of all the Gospel writers, Luke is the one who draws out most clearly the great respect Jesus had for women. Mary, his mother, was described as the most blessed woman on earth (Luke 1:42).

Women followed him

Some of the women who followed Jesus, such as Joanna (whose husband was the manager of Herod's household) and Susanna, used their own money to support Jesus and the disciples (Luke 8:3). Mary Magdalene was among such women, too. She was there when Christ's body was laid in the tomb (Luke 23:55) and with Joanna found the tomb empty after Christ had risen (Luke 24:10). Martha opened her home to Jesus and he ministered to her and her sister Mary (Luke 10:38-42).

Women worshipped him

The woman who had led a sinful life was deeply sorry for her sins and her thankfulness for Jesus' forgiveness "spilled over" into love and worship (Luke 7:36-50). Later, a woman in the crowd listening to Jesus spontaneously cried out how happy Jesus' mother must have been. But Jesus replied that an even greater happiness belonged to those who heard and obeyed God's word (Luke 11:27-28). When Jesus was taken away to be crucified, he had a word to say. But it was not a word of comfort – they should be weeping for themselves and their own children, as judgement was coming (Luke 23:27-31).

He cared for women

Jesus healed Peter's mother-in-law (Luke 4:38-39) and the woman bent double for 18 years (Luke 13:10-17). And we see his great compassion as his heart went out to the widow of Nain (Luke 7:13).

He mentioned women in his teaching

The peasant woman searching high and low for her lost coin speaks of God seeking out one sinner (Luke 15:8-10). In another parable a wicked judge finally gives in to a widow's constant demands for justice – how much more will a just, loving God judge in favour of his own faithful, praying people (Luke 18:1-8)? And then there is the story about the difference between the rich putting their "great" gifts into the temple treasury and the poor widow giving all she had (Luke 21:1-4).

So what?

How should all this affect our lives today? In those days, women were among the less

well-thought-of groups in society. Today, the situation of women has changed for the better – nevertheless we must be sure to respect men and women as equal. There may be groups in our society that are under-privileged and need our special attention. Jesus broke down barriers with his real compassion. We need, like Jesus, to show our love equally. We need to put our words into action and be involved with people. We could visit the elderly, sick or lonely, work with the young, get to know those from ethnic groups in our area or be involved in local government. The eyes and heart of Jesus were wide open – are ours?

Worship service in Bangladesh in the home of one of the fellowship. The congregation is growing so much that another member has donated part of a field where a church building will be built

OVER TO YOU

Are women treated equally and fairly in your society? Can you support those Christians who work for justice in other countries?

JESUS PERFORMS MIRACLES

John's Gospel tells us about miraculous signs that Jesus performed. At one level, they give instruction, warning or encouragement to faith. At a deeper level, they also show who Jesus really is and call for a response.

Water into wine (John 2:1-11)
The first miraculous sign was the changing of water into wine at Cana. Something physical illustrates a spiritual truth. Jesus showed he had absolute control over everything. This showed his glory, and it led to belief.

Miracles of healing (John 4:46–5:9)
The next two miraculous signs were miracles of healing. The first was that of an official's son. Jesus pointed out there were those who were always on the lookout for "signs and wonders" (John 4:48). This second miracle proved that distance was no obstacle to Jesus in the carrying out of his ministry. After the first sign his disciples believed in him. As a result of the second sign, not only did the court official believe, but so did his entire household (John 4:53).

The healing of a man at the pool of Bethesda (John 5:1-9) aroused great controversy because it was performed on the Sabbath (John 5:10).

The feeding of the 5,000 (John 6:5-13)
The three miraculous signs we have already mentioned are only recorded by John, but the feeding of the 5,000 is recorded in all four Gospels. Only John, however, follows it up with Jesus' talk on the bread of life (John 6:25-59). Notice the different reactions to what Jesus said. Some belittled both Jesus and his words (John 6:41-42). Some found it all too much to accept (John 6:60). But the inner group of the twelve disciples, represented by Simon Peter, confessed that Jesus really was the Holy One of God (John 6:68-69).

The man born blind (John 9:1-41)
Here is another miracle which only John records. He goes to great lengths to point out the reactions of the man's neighbours, of the Pharisees and of his parents. Most of all we're told how the man's faith developed. Read again John 9:11,17,24-38 for yourself.

The raising of Lazarus (John 11:1-44)
This story is also unique to John. In the discussion that Jesus had with Martha and Mary each of the sisters displayed her characteristic reaction. The miracle itself is simply and movingly told. Some came to believe (John 11:45), but there was the inevitable adverse reaction from some of the religious leaders (John 11:46-53).

Other miraculous signs
John tells us that he gives us just a selection of the miraculous signs that Jesus performed (John 20:30; 21:25). The resurrection itself is of course the greatest sign of all.

What was the purpose of the miraculous signs? To show who Jesus really was (John 2:11), to show that he is God, the Son of God, and the Messiah (John 3:2; 20:31). So Jesus wanted to draw attention away from the miracles to who was doing them.

But the miraculous signs aren't just meant to lead to an understanding in our minds of who Jesus is. They call for nothing less than a response of faith, trust, worship and commitment to the Lord Jesus Christ himself (John 9:38; 20:30-31).

And the final miracle in the Gospel, the catch of fish (John 21:1-11) reminds us again of the risen Lord Jesus' interest in his people and commission to them (John 21:15-22).

OVER TO YOU

Do you find it encouraging to read about the miracles that Jesus performed? Think about modern miracles and how God works wonders today.

The claims of Jesus

JESUS THE SON OF GOD

Why did John write about Jesus? He tells us in John 20:31 – that we might believe that Jesus is the Christ (the Messiah), the Son of God, and that through believing we might have life in his name.

Jesus Christ – the Son of God

John describes Jesus using a word that older versions of the Bible translate as "only-begotten". Newer translations have "one and only" or "only" in, for example, John 1:14,18. The word in the original Greek language is *monogenes*. It implies a number of things:

- **Jesus is equal with God.** He shares God's nature and fully expresses God's character. The Jews thought of this as blasphemy (John 5:18; 10:29-39; 19:7).
- **Jesus enjoys a unique unity of nature with God the Father.** He is one with the Father in the deepest possible way (John 10:30). He and the Father are inseparable in their nature, words, and actions (John 5:19-23).
- **Jesus is the only one who fully expresses and wholly represents God.** This is what John means by describing Jesus as "the Word" (John 1:1,18): he is the very expression of the mind of God.
- **Jesus is the Son of God for ever.** It has always been the nature of Jesus, and always will be his nature, that he is the Son of God. He didn't become the Son when he was born on earth (John 8:68).
- **Jesus is the unique Son of God.** He is the Son of God in a completely different way from his followers being called sons and daughters of God. Jesus spoke of God to his followers as "my Father" and "your Father" (John 20:17).

The love of God the Father

God shows that he loved the world so much that he gave Jesus, the only-begotten Son of God (John 3:16). Why did God do this? So that those who believe would not be condemned but have everlasting life (John 3:16-18,36).

A verdict is called for

We all have to make up our minds about who Jesus really is. Was he simply a great teacher? Was he sincerely mistaken? Was he a deliberate impostor? On three occasions in John's Gospel people came to the conclusion that he was indeed the Son of God: John the Baptist (John 1:34), Nathaniel (John 1:49), and Martha (John 11:27).

OVER TO YOU

Who do you think Jesus is? He has called us to follow him and as we come to know him better we will learn more about God.

THE CLAIMS OF JESUS

Jesus told the religious leaders of his day that even Abraham longed for the day when he, Jesus, would come. And he added, "Before Abraham was born, I am." To Jewish ears, he was claiming to be God and for this reason they picked up stones to stone him (John 8:56-59).

The Lord Jesus Christ was not only pointing to his existence before his birth but he took upon his lips the divine title "I am" (Exodus 3:14). To the Jews, God was the great "I am", the self-existent one. On at least seven different occasions Jesus claimed to be someone unique, introducing his claims with the words "I am".

"I am the bread of life" (John 6:35)

At Passover time, shortly after he had miraculously fed the 5,000, Jesus declared himself to be the bread of life, the living bread that came down from heaven (John 6:25-59). He was implying that the people needed more than material bread: they were in need of spiritual sustenance, which he alone could give them.

"I am the light of the world" (John 8:12)

At another festival, the Feast of Tabernacles or Shelters, Jesus claimed to be the light of the world (John 8:12). At such a time the people were celebrating the experiences of their forefathers who were led through the wilderness by a pillar of cloud by day and a pillar of fire by night. Jesus was assuming the whole world was in a state of spiritual darkness but he had come to bring the light. Jesus also told his disciples that they were "the light of the world" (Matthew 5:14).

"I am the good shepherd" (John 10:11)

In John, chapter 10, there are two "I am" sayings – "I am the gate for the sheep" (verse 7) and "I am the good shepherd" (verse 11). But there is really only one picture. An eastern shepherd usually stood in the doorway of the sheepfold as the sheep went in or out. He was the secret of their safety and he was responsible for the satisfaction of their needs. The sheep were utterly dependent on the shepherd. Jesus stressed he was the good shepherd and pointed out that not all shepherds could be described in that way.

"I am the resurrection and the life" (John 11:25)

Martha and Mary's brother, Lazarus, had just died and Jesus declared, "I am the resurrection and the life" (John 11:25). He had power even to raise the dead! And he had also come to demonstrate the reality of life after death.

"I am the way, the truth and the life" (John 14:6)

In answering a query from Thomas, Jesus declared himself to be the only way to God, to be the truth about God in person and to be the One to give to men the life of God.

"I am the true vine" (John 15:1)

The remaining "I am" was particularly relevant to the Jewish people. In the Old Testament the vine was used as a symbol of the Jewish nation (Psalm 80:8-19; Isaiah 5:1-7). He had come to them as the true vine and he showed the futility of trying to live apart from him (John 15:1-11).

OVER TO YOU

Jesus' claims about who he was were scandalous to some of his listeners. When we tell people that we are his followers why do some people today react negatively?

JESUS – THE PROMISED KING

Secret Messiah

Jesus arrived in the world at a tremendously exciting time. Jewish thinking was in ferment; Jews were awaiting their "Messiah": a Hebrew word meaning Anointed One (in Greek, "Christ"). As a result of passages like 2 Samuel 7:13; Daniel 2:34-45; 7:13-14, they were awaiting a conquering king from the family line of King David to smash all other empires and set up a world-leading kingdom that would last for ever. All it needed was a leader they believed in, and revolution against Roman rule in Israel would have spread like a fire in dry hay.

As a result, Jesus had to keep his Messiah-hood a secret: Mark 1:24-25,34,44; 3:11-12.

True Messiah

He was not the sort of Messiah they were expecting, but he was the Messiah! So from about the middle of his ministry Jesus told his disciples he was the Messiah – but immediately worked to re-channel their thinking (Matthew 16:13-27). Repeatedly from then on he drove home the nature of his kingship.

Three strands

We find three main strands in Jesus' being Messiah: he is a prophet, a priest and a king.

- **Prophet:** he speaks to us with God's voice. The role of the prophet is to speak God's message to people. Jesus' life story and teaching completed what God has to say to humanity (Hebrews 1:1-2). When in our own day he makes this come alive to us by his Spirit, Jesus is acting as a prophet.
- **Priest:** he leads us into God's presence. A priest's job is to make things right between God and people so they are friends. Before Jesus came, priests did this by praying for people and offering animal sacrifices to take away the guilt of sin and the anger which that raised in God (to sin is to break God's law). But our Lord Jesus offered up –

himself! See Hebrews 9:14; 1 Peter 2:24; 3:18. And he is always praying for us (Hebrews 7:25). None of us will ever fully realise just how much we have been spared and forgiven thanks to Jesus' working as our priest.
- **King:** he rules us with God's authority. The king in the Old Testament put into action God's rule over his people. Jesus does this in Christians' lives. He wins us to himself, rules and defends us. He will go on extending his reign until every atom in the universe relates to him as it ought: Philippians 2:9-11; Colossians 1:17-20.

Just what we need

The amazing thing is the way Jesus' Messiah-ship meets our deepest needs and heals the havoc caused in us by sin. We are ignorant; Jesus our prophet teaches us God's way of saving us. We are guilty; Jesus bore that guilt away when he was crucified for our sins. We are lost in this world; Jesus comes as King and restores order, identity and destiny to our lives.

> **OVER TO YOU**
>
> Jesus as prophet, priest and king; think about these different roles of the Messiah. Which one do you most associate with Jesus, and why?

DISCOVERING GOD'S WAY · JESUS CHRIST 559

COMMITMENT TO JESUS

The example of Paul

What effect are the claims of Christ to have on us? We can sum up the answer to that question in one word: commitment. What does that mean? What does the life of a committed Christian look like? If ever there was a committed Christian, then Paul certainly was one! Look how he describes his life in the letter to the Philippians. For him living means simply Christ himself (Philippians 1:21). Even his important background is worthless compared with knowing his Lord Jesus Christ (Philippians 3:4-8). His one aim is to know Christ (Philippians 3:10), and he strives onwards with an athlete's dedication (Philippians 3:13-14)!

The cost of commitment

Paul was committed to sharing the gospel (Philippians 1:7). Because of this, he writes chained to a soldier in Rome. He had endured all kinds of sufferings: frequent imprisonment, severe flogging, exposure to death, lashings (ordeals of 39 lashes experienced five times!), beatings with rods, stoning, dangers in travel including shipwreck, cold, hunger and thirst (2 Corinthians 11:23-28). He really knew that suffering, in some form or other, was the price of being fully committed.

The rewards of commitment

The Bible does say that we shall be rewarded for the good we do as Christians – see Matthew 25:34-36 and 2 Corinthians 5:10. But the reward we receive is linked with the glory of God in such a way that we could never boast. Every good thing we have done in Christ's name has been given to us. Whatever good we do, we do it with God's grace and help (1 Corinthians 3:10-15; 4:7).

Getting down to it

Believing in Christ involves wholehearted commitment to him. What does this mean in practice?

· Belonging to and playing a responsible part in a local fellowship of God's people (Philippians 1:1,27; 2:4-5).
· Reading God's word and praying regularly (Colossians 3:16; 4:2).
· Putting to death sinful attitudes and actions; becoming more like Jesus (Philippians 1:9-11; Colossians 3:5).
· Telling other people about Jesus (Philippians 1:5).

God is at work in us

How can we be fully committed? It isn't possible by ourselves. But God is already at work in us as Christians. We can be sure that, as we work out the salvation God has given us, he himself is at work in us, giving us the power to do what he wants (Philippians 2:12-13).

OVER TO YOU

Our commitment to Jesus is not measured solely by what we do on a Sunday. Pray that God would deepen your commitment day by day and show you how you can serve him in new ways.

JESUS GIVES HOPE FOR THE FUTURE

The word hope may suggest to us idle fantasy, a "brave face" or a cheerful but unrealistic optimism. New Testament writers like Peter, however, take this rather feeble-sounding word and give it a confidence and certainty which change it almost beyond recognition. So let's discover what 1 Peter says about hope.

Certain future

For a follower of Christ, the future is not a mist, a mystery, or a cause of fear and worry. For it is not the human race who will determine the future.

What lies ahead may well be a future shock for the world, but without doubt it is a future hope for the Christian. We dare to look forward and find that beyond death, life is described as a rich inheritance (1 Peter 1:4) and a glorious crown (1 Peter 5:4). These things are certain because we have been reborn spiritually: we have a "living hope" (1 Peter 1:3).

Good reason

The basis for this hope rests on an actual, historical event – the resurrection of Jesus Christ (1 Peter 1:3). Death no longer has to have the last word.

We believe in a God we cannot see (1 Peter 1:8), but we do so with good reason. The records of the resurrection offer evidence that we can explore for ourselves.

Firm ground

Human beings are used to disappointments – well-intentioned promises not kept. But it is different when our hope is fixed on God (1 Peter 1:21). He always:

· keeps his people safe, until the end of time (1 Peter 1:5)
· keeps his promise faithfully (1 Peter 4:19)
· keeps to his original purpose – calling us not only to follow him on this earth, but also to his eternal glory (1 Peter 5:10).

Clear incentive

A certain hope for the future leads us to be serious about the present. Living becomes no longer an aimless occupation, when what we do doesn't really matter.

Christian hope is the greatest spur and incentive to reaching high personal standards in the way we live. For Peter, this hope was automatically linked with an alert mind and active obedience to God (1 Peter 1:13-14). You can recognise Christians who know where they're going – by their lives!

Calm assessment

When we know that there is more to life than what we experience in this world, then:

· We have the right perspective on life; we don't see temporary pleasures, worldly security or material luxuries as being the most important things in our lives (1 Peter 2:11).
· We can afford to give way in our relationships with others (1 Peter 2:13,18).
· We are able to stand firm when the pressure is on (1 Peter 1:6).

As we put these things into practice, we can look forward with eagerness and patience to the return of the Lord Jesus Christ (1 Peter 1:13). We shall not be disappointed!

OVER TO YOU

What does the word "hope" mean to you? Our future hope does not rest on material security but in the person of Jesus Christ and in what he has done for us.

The good news of Jesus

BELIEVING IN JESUS

In John's Gospel, the word believe occurs many times. John speaks repeatedly of believing on Christ or of believing in the name of Christ (for example John 1:12; 3:16; 20:31). This conveys the idea of believing in all that he is in himself. The "name" summed up the whole personality: all that a person truly was. Believing is also often linked to Jesus doing miraculous signs (for example John 2:11,23).

Receiving Christ

It means trusting yourself to the Lord Jesus Christ by receiving him into your life (John 1:12). You can't use other people's experiences – you must believe for yourself (John 4:42). Eternal issues are decided in this life. Having faith is not a vague concept of a future eternal life. Faith is an assurance of eternal life now in this life (John 3:36; 5:24).

Believing in secret

John tells us that some believed in secret (John 12:42-43). They feared people's opinions, especially those of the Pharisees, and were not prepared to be thrown out of the synagogue. They didn't want to be singled out for criticism. It is a sad fact that fear of what friends will think often keeps people from openly confessing faith in Jesus.

Believing and knowing

Faith is an eye-opener; it leads us into knowledge. We tend to say, "Let me see and then I will believe." But God says, "Believe and you will see" (John 11:40). It is only by faith that we come to know God at all.

In a world of uncertainty, John is concerned that Christians should enjoy the assurance of salvation. To be a Christian, according to John, is to have been born of God (John 1:13), to know God, and to enjoy that intimate relationship with him which is the essence of eternal life (John 17:3). Such certainty is not arrogance or presumption but is the will of God for his children.

Knowing the Father

Jesus pointed out that believing in him implies believing in the One who sent him. Jesus and his sender are one (John 10:30; 13:20). It is impossible to accept the one and reject the other. Knowing Jesus, the Son, means knowing God, the Father (John 8:19; 14:6-7).

Refusing to believe

Sadly, in spite of the fact that through a simple act of faith anyone may be saved, many people cling to unbelief. On the face of it, unbelief on the part of those who had witnessed Christ's miracles was illogical (John 12:37), but it had been predicted by the prophet Isaiah (John 12:38-41). But Jesus describes the punishment that already falls on those who do not believe in the strongest possible way (John 3:16,18-20,36).

> ### OVER TO YOU
>
> Do you believe that Christ died on the cross for you? Thank God for the assurance that through his sacrifice you have salvation.

JESUS AND THE NEW BIRTH

"Born again"

The origin of the expression "born again" is John chapter 3. Basically, it describes the radical change that God makes in someone, to enable them to understand the things of God and to come into his kingdom. It's an inner, spiritual change that has widespread effects on outward behaviour.

How does the new birth come about?

The new birth is an act of God. God, not humanity, brings it about (John 1:12-13; 1 Peter 1:3). It is a work of the Holy Spirit (Titus 3:5-6). It's something that we cannot understand or control. The Holy Spirit's work is sovereign and mysterious, just like the wind (John 3:8). How does the Holy Spirit work? Through God's word – the Bible (1 Peter 1:23,25; 1 Thessalonians 1:5-6).

What does the new birth mean?

The new birth is not merely a psychological or emotional experience. It isn't turning over a new leaf. It doesn't come about by simply going to church, or being baptised or confirmed. It is something far more radical. Think about the amazing ways it is described:

- **a new life.** God gives life to those who are spiritually dead (Ephesians 2:1-5).
- **a new heart.** Believers are given a new heart – one that is responsive to God (Ezekiel 36:25-27).
- **a new creation** (2 Corinthians 5:17). As Christians, we have been born of God – we are his children (1 John 4:7). God the Holy Spirit lives in us (Romans 8:9).

What follows?

The new birth is the giving of a new nature, a new principle of life inside you. The first act of this new nature is turning to God, being deeply aware of sin (Acts 2:37-38), and believing (John 1:12-13).

In his first letter, John gives us some signs that follow the new birth. Someone born again still fights with sin but no longer habitually commits sin (1 John 3:9; 5:18). They recognise who Jesus is (1 John 5:1). Their great desire is to live a righteous life (1 John 2:29), wanting to please God in everything (Ephesians 4:22-24). And they will love their brothers and sisters in Christ (1 John 3:14).

Growing up

Babies don't stay babies for long! Sadly, it seems that some new Christians never go beyond the basics. How can we grow?

- **by praying.** Just as a baby cries, so will the new believer pray. It is the natural thing always to talk to your Father (Matthew 6:9; Romans 8:15).
- **by taking in God's word.** In Peter's first letter he writes that, as newborn babies, there is a longing for spiritual milk (1 Peter 2:2). But there should be more solid things to come! Read Hebrews 5:12-14.
- **by being active in God's church and his world.** Babies belong to a family, so it is important to play a responsible part in a local church. And he wants to use us in his world – to tell others about the new birth!

OVER TO YOU

Not all believers can identify the time at which they were "born again". Many, who have grown up in a Christian family, have always believed and have come to know Jesus gradually. Whatever your story, thank God that you have been reborn.

The facts of life

When we look at the book of Acts, we can see clearly that certain facts concerning Jesus had been established and were the grounds for everything else:

- **Jesus is God's Son** (Acts 9:20) and the Messiah, Israel's long-promised King (Acts 9:22).
- **Jesus was rejected** and crucified, although he was entirely innocent (Acts 3:13-15; 7:52). This was no accident but part of God's plan (Acts 2:23; 4:27-28), which he had foretold through the prophets (Acts 3:18; 8:32-35). He was also God's righteous Servant who suffered in the place of others (Acts 3:13; 4:27; 8:32-33).
- **God raised Jesus from the dead** (for example Acts 2:24; 3:15; 4:10), so showing that he really was his Son.
- **Jesus is now sharing God's glory** in heaven (Acts 2:33; 7:55-56).
- **One day Jesus will come again** to judge the world (Acts 3:20; 10:42; 17:31).

The promise of life

Because of what Jesus did, our sins can be forgiven (Acts 2:38; 3:19; 10:43). This is what is meant by *salvation* (Acts 4:12).

More than this, God promises to give us his power by the Holy Spirit (Acts 2:33,38). This enables us to live a life which pleases God, something we couldn't do on our own.

How come?

This new life does not come into being automatically. We have to respond to what Jesus has done for us.

- **We must repent** (Acts 2:38; 5:31; 11:18). This means that we must admit that we have sinned – broken God's holy Law – and, by God's grace, turn from our sins to him (Acts 3:19; 20:21).
- **We must believe** the good news for ourselves (Acts 8:12; 10:43; 16:31). This involves more than just saying that the facts

are true; it means resting our lives on them. If Christ is Saviour and Lord, we must *obey* him (Acts 5:32).

Remember too:

- The initiative in repentance and faith is really with God (Acts 13:48; 16:14). This does not, however, lessen our responsibility to respond but God does in fact lie behind our commitment.

What follows?

As we read through Acts, we see that when people turned to God and put their trust in Christ, they began to prove what God could do in their lives. They discovered that they had a great deal in common with everyone else who had responded, and this expressed itself in real caring and sharing.

Again and again we get a glimpse of the deep joy that these early Christians had, even when they had to suffer for what they believed. In fact, they discovered that they had so many blessings as Christians that they couldn't stop telling others and sharing the good news with them!

Today the facts, the promises, the conditions, and the blessings are just the same – and waiting for us to prove them for ourselves!

OVER TO YOU

Do you experience the blessings of the early church today? Look again at Acts 2 and pray for a renewed awareness of the Holy Spirit at work in your life.

Joy in worship.
Burkina Faso

JUSTIFIED BY FAITH IN JESUS

Paul's Letter to the Galatians is all about being justified (or put right) by faith in Christ (Galatians 2:16). Since justification is a theme Paul returns to again and again and also spells out in depth both in Romans and Galatians, it is important that we understand it.

The great crown court

The New Testament uses several pictures drawn from everyday life to explain what salvation is. Justification is one of them and comes from the law courts. We would say that a person who has been tried for a crime, found "not guilty", and has been restored to their full rights and privileges, has been justified. But when it comes to the Bible's teaching on justification that is only the starting point.

Humanity in the dock

God gave us a Law to live by, which we have broken. So we stand in the dock facing our judge, God, whom we have offended. We have every expectation of being condemned because we know that we are guilty. But somehow God arranges a way by which we can be found not guilty without justice being perverted.

More than that, not only are our sins forgiven through justification, but also our full freedom, privileges and status are restored to us as God's children (Galatians 3:26; 4:7). It is just as if we never sinned!

How was the verdict reached?

We could never have satisfied the offended judge, so how can we be set free? The answer is that the justice of God had its claims met by Jesus (Romans 8:3). This happened in two ways:

1. The Lord Jesus Christ himself kept the Law perfectly, and
2. The punishment that the Law demanded was taken out, not on us, but on Christ in his death on the cross.

So God justifies sinners:

- **by pronouncing on us** the verdict which Christ gained by perfectly keeping the Law. We are treated as if *we* had lived *Christ's* perfect life.
- **by pronouncing on Christ** the verdict which we deserved for breaking the Law. Christ is treated as if *he* sinned *our* sin.

Some regard that as unfair – even barbaric. So in a sense it is! But Jesus willingly did it to provide us with our freedom,

You are discharged!

What a relief those words must be to a person who has been on trial, as the judge frees them! God says the same – but not to everyone. Although there are no conditions for obtaining God's pardon, not all are in a position to receive it. Faith is the channel through which it comes into our lives (Galatians 2:20; 3:8). Faith means accepting God's word on trust and giving up trying to live our lives our way. Faith is like stretching out empty hands, offering God nothing, and asking him to fill them with his pardon.

Such mercy is almost impossible to imagine in our world, which constantly demands justice. But it is the way God works.

OVER TO YOU

Have you trusted in Jesus Christ to save you? Do you recognise the gracious gift of faith as a blessing from God?

The death and resurrection of Jesus

JESUS' ATONING DEATH

All for us

All that our Lord Jesus did, he did for us. He didn't have to come here on his own account – he came in order to save us. Whenever we read of an action of Jesus we can say, "He did that for me."

Nowhere is that more true than when we think about his death. He was the substitute God put forward for us. It would not have been the same if he had been killed in a mob riot. He had to be tried in our place. There had to be those particular charges, for they are God's fundamental charges against us as sinners.

Two basic sins

What are we all guilty of? Two basic sins. Back in the garden of Eden the devil's temptation was, "You will be like God!" (Genesis 3:5). When we de-throne God in our attitude and act like our own god – that's blasphemy. And when we revolt against his Kingship by sinning, that's treason.

Jesus in our place

And what do we find Jesus charged with? Blasphemy at the religious court; and at the civil court, treason! See Matthew 26:65-66 and Luke 23:2. Revelation 20:11-15 explains it. We are told about the Day of Judgement. And as we see Jesus standing before the Sanhedrin and before Pilate, we are seeing him taking the punishment, before God, for us.

Jesus' silence

This explains Jesus' silence, which Pilate just couldn't understand (Matthew 27:14). Why didn't he plead "not guilty"? He was accepting our sin on his shoulders, and as guilty in our place he had nothing to say for himself. Then came the verdicts and the execution. The punishment due to us had fallen on him.

> Thy grief and bitter passion
> Were all for sinners' gain;
> Mine, mine was the transgression,
> But Thine the deadly pain.
> (BERNARD OF CLAIRVAUX)

The heart of the gospel

Here we are at the very heart of the way Jesus is good news. "God made him who had no sin to be sin for us, so that in him we might become the righteousness of God" (2 Corinthians 5:21). Read Isaiah 53; Romans 3:25; Hebrews 9:27-28. Anyone who wants to be saved can be, through faith in Jesus Christ.

Claim it now!

Quick! How do we get the benefit? It reaches us when, content with this way of being saved, we give our consent to it. We know and agree that only Jesus is able to bring us to peace with God. Then, trusting his love and willingness, we receive and rely on him to do so, surrendering our lives to his control. See John 1:12 and Revelation 3:20. *Have you taken that step? If not, will you do so now?*

At-one-ment with God

Then be quite clear: the guilt which made us liable to God's punishment has been transferred on to Jesus!

OVER TO YOU

When you feel guilty, remember that because of Jesus' atoning sacrifice you are already forgiven and put right with God.

THE TRIUMPH OF JESUS' RESURRECTION

The resurrection story

By comparing the different Gospel accounts, we can arrive at a sequence of events.

- A group of women (Luke 24:10) were the first to visit the tomb early on the first day of the week (John 20:1). They went, hoping to embalm the body of Jesus (Luke 24:1) but as they approached the tomb, they found the stone was rolled away and the body was no longer there (Luke 24:2-3). The women hurried back to Jerusalem to tell the other disciples but were met, in the main, by sheer unbelief (Luke 24:8-11).
- Peter and John went to the tomb and discovered for themselves it was empty (John 20:2-8).
- Jesus appeared to Mary Magdalene and later to the disciples generally, apart from Thomas, who was not with them (John 20:11-23).

This much is common ground in the Gospels. We also see that after his resurrection Jesus could reveal himself and disappear at will.

John's own account

John gives his own personal account of various events connected with the resurrection of Jesus. After all, he was in a position to see for himself. John had seen the grave clothes and head cloth lying undisturbed, still in place (John 20:3-8). No one could steal a body and leave the grave clothes like that! John took careful note and believed (John 20:8).

John tells us at some length that Thomas wasn't there with the other disciples on that first Easter evening when the risen Jesus appeared to them. But a week later he was with them. Thomas demanded to see the nailprints in our Lord's hands before he would believe (John 20:25). Thomas was utterly convinced and cried out, "My Lord and my God" (John 20:28). This confession of faith illustrates supremely John's purpose in writing – to lead men and women to an assured and clear-cut belief in Jesus.

Only John gives the story of how Jesus met with Peter and some of the other disciples on the beach after a fishing expedition. It was there that Peter was able to affirm his love for his Master three times (John 21:15-24), in spite of the fact that earlier he had denied him three times.

Central to the Christian faith

The resurrection is absolutely essential to the Christian faith. 1 Corinthians 15:12-28 tells us this plainly.

- As Christians, we can have assurance that our salvation has been accomplished. The death of the Lord Jesus Christ on the cross was a sufficient sacrifice for the sins of God's people (Romans 4:25; 1 Corinthians 15:17).
- Everyone will rise when Jesus comes again. Christians will rise to life; those who do not believe will rise to judgement and condemnation (John 3:36; 5:29).
- The resurrection body of believers will be like Jesus' body and we will be completely free from all sin (1 Corinthians 15:42-57; 1 John 3:2).
- The resurrection of Jesus is to affect our lives here and now. We are to be concerned with the right sort of things (Colossians 3:1-4), knowing in ourselves the power that raised Jesus to life (Ephesians 1:18-20; Philippians 3:10). We are to be taken up with doing the work that Jesus wants us to do (1 Corinthians 15:58).

OVER TO YOU

The resurrection of Jesus is essential to Christian faith and Paul was clear about this (1 Corinthians 15:14). How does the promise of resurrection affect your life today?

THE MESSAGE OF THE RESURRECTION

You can't read Acts without seeing that resurrection was a key theme for the earliest Christians. Why did they insist on it?

What the Jews believed

Resurrection – rising bodily from death – was a Jewish belief. God made people with bodies in the first place so we would be incomplete without them. If God was really going to save his people, it had to be body and soul – not soul alone.

God led them to this truth slowly. Only in the later Old Testament books do we get a clear statement about it (for example Daniel 12:2). So the Sadducees, confining themselves to the first five Bible books, refused to believe in it (Acts 23:8). This was, no doubt, another reason why they persecuted Christians who preached it. Greeks believed in some kind of spiritual "out-of-the-body" after-life, so they had no time for resurrection either (Acts 17:32). Pharisees, however, were convinced that God would raise the dead on the last day (Acts 23:6-8).

What Jesus taught

Jesus obviously believed in resurrection too. He spoke about the general resurrection, when all would rise for judgement (John 5:28-29), and he even took on the Sadducees (Matthew 22:23-33). He also spoke about the special conditions for believers (John 11:25-26). But he promised that eternal life begins here and now for the person who trusts in him (John 5:24).

Jesus also predicted his own resurrection many times (for example Matthew 16:21), although both his death and his rising came as a surprise to his followers. So we find him explaining what had happened afterwards (Luke 24:44-48).

What the Christians preached

Jesus' resurrection wasn't an optional extra for the early Christians; it was an indispensable part of their message (Acts 2:24-32; 4:10; 10:40; 13:30-37; 17:2-3,18; 26:22-23). What is more, the first preachers were also eyewitnesses of the actual event (Acts 1:8,22; 2:32; 3:15; 4:20; 5:32; 10:41; 13:30-31). When Paul summed up his message, he pointed out that without the resurrection of Jesus, we have absolutely nothing to say (1 Corinthians 15).

So Christ's resurrection:

· **underlines** who Jesus really is: the Son of God, the Lord, the Messiah (Acts 2:32-36; 13:33)
· **assures us** that our salvation has been accomplished by Jesus' death on the cross (Romans 4:25; 1 Corinthians 15:17).
· **tells us** that Jesus is Lord and reigning now (Acts 5:31; 7:56).
· **reminds us** that Jesus will return to judge us (Acts 10:42; 17:31).
· **reassures us** that we too will rise one day (Acts 23:6; 24:15). Christians will rise to life; those who do not believe will rise to judgement and condemnation (John 3:36; 5:29).

The resurrection is meant to affect our lives today. Most of all, the resurrection and the following judgement call for an urgent response of turning away from sin and believing in the Lord Jesus Christ (Acts 2:29-41; 5:31; 17:30-31) to receive forgiveness.

OVER TO YOU

Just as in Jesus' day there are those today who do not believe in resurrection of the dead. What would you say to someone who does not believe?

THE ASCENSION OF JESUS

The return of Jesus to his Father, or the ascension as it is often called, is much more than a historical event. It also has a deep meaning for us today.

Luke is the only New Testament writer to give us an actual account of the ascension (Luke 24:51; Acts 1:6-11). 40 days after his resurrection, Jesus led his friends out to the Mount of Olives on the east of Jerusalem and was taken from them there.

Jesus returned to glory

Before Jesus went to the cross he prayed that his Father would restore him to the glory he left behind when he came into this world (John 17:5). The transfiguration gave his inner circle of disciples a glimpse of that glory (Mark 9:2-8). After his resurrection he was ready to reclaim it. That is why we are told that Christ was taken into heaven (Acts 1:10-11; 3:21).

Jesus reigns now

Jesus is now sharing God's rule in heaven. Peter quoted Psalm 110 in Acts 2:34. It could not have described David for the simple reason that David did not ascend, whereas Jesus did. To sit at God's right hand is to share his throne. Because of this, Jesus is to be honoured as both Lord and Messiah, the Christ (Acts 2:36).

It was extremely important for them – as it is for us – to remember that Christ is Lord and reigning now. We can be sure that he is in control of events even when they seem to us to be getting out of hand!

So the Lord Jesus Christ is now in the place of royal rule and authority (Ephesians 1:20-22). Because of his authority and his command to go (Matthew 28:18-20), Jesus the king sends us out into the world to tell others about him!

Jesus helps us now

In heaven Jesus is not only a king who rules but also a priest who intercedes for his people. He represents us before the Father (Romans 8:34; Hebrews 7:23-25; 9:24). Through him we can come with confidence and assurance right into God's presence, knowing the help of a sympathetic high priest (Hebrews 4:14-16).

His ascension is also proof that God fully accepted the sacrifice that Jesus made for our sins (Hebrews 1:3; 10:12). Our salvation is full and it is totally secure!

Jesus sends the Spirit

Jesus told his disciples that it was actually better for him to leave them, because if he did not, the Spirit would not come after him (John 16:7). Paul likened Jesus' return to heaven to a victorious general throwing gifts to the watching, cheering crowds (Ephesians 4:8), So the Spirit's activity on earth is proof that Christ is reigning in glory.

Jesus will return

Jesus' present reign in heaven is going to be temporary, that is, it will last only until he returns. The angels promised that this would happen in the same way in which he went (Acts 1:11). When God's plan for this world is finally worked out, then Jesus will return (Acts 3:20-21). That fact both encouraged and stirred up the early Christians. It should have a similar effect on us!

OVER TO YOU

What difference does it make to you that Jesus now reigns in heaven? He has triumphed over death and this enables us to live with joy and hope.

JESUS' RETURN

The early Christians were excited by the fact that Jesus was one day going to return to earth. 1 and 2 Thessalonians were written precisely because some of them had difficulty in understanding this truth.

How will he come?

This second time Jesus will not come as a vulnerable baby but as a universal judge. The style of his coming will be appropriate to his position (Matthew 25:31; 1 Thessalonians 4:16).

Why will he come?

· **To complete his work of salvation.** Christians have already begun to experience it but there is much more to experience yet. See 1 Thessalonians 4:17; 5:9; 1 John 3:2.
· **To bring about the resurrection.** Without this, death would appear to be the ultimate victor. Read John 5:28-29, 1 Corinthians 15:50-58 and 1 Thessalonians 4:16-17.
· **To judge the nations of the world.** Jesus told a dramatic parable about this in Matthew 25:31-46. Look up John 5:21-23 and 2 Corinthians 5:10 as well.
  All people will be divided into two groups: those who are declared right with God through faith in Christ will be with him for ever (end of 1 Thessalonians 4:17; 5:9-10) and those who do not believe will suffer the punishment of eternal destruction and exclusion from God's presence for ever (2 Thessalonians 1:8-9).
· **To usher in the new creation.** Peter talks about it in 2 Peter 3:10-13 and so does John in Revelation 20 and 21.

When will it happen?

Christians have spent a lot of time and energy disagreeing over the exact timetable of events. This is not surprising since the Bible is not written like a textbook and not all the details seem to fit easily with one another. What we can say is this:

  First, Mark 13 gives us a graphic picture of how the world will have degenerated before the end comes. 1 Timothy 4:1-3 and 2 Peter 3:3-7 speak of the same trends.

  Secondly, the return of Christ cannot come until the antichrist has shown himself. 2 Thessalonians 2:1-12 speaks of this. The identity of this person will be perfectly obvious when he unmasks himself. The same principle of evil is already at work (see 1 John 2:18) but it has yet to show itself in such intensity in one person.

  Thirdly, although we are already living in the last period of history before the return of Christ, none of us can predict when it will occur and nor should we speculate about it. Mark 13:32, Acts 1:7 and 1 Thessalonians 5:1-3 make that plain.

What difference does it make now?

· **We should be ready** (Luke 12:40), confidently expecting Jesus' return (Titus 2:13).
· **We should be holy** (2 Peter 3:11).
· **We should allow these truths to encourage us** (1 Thessalonians 4:18; 5:11).
· Far from being lazy (2 Thessalonians 3:6), **we should be all the more urgent and wholehearted in telling others throughout the world about Jesus** (Matthew 24:14).
· **We should be encouraged to see the church built up** (Ephesians 5:27; 1 Thessalonians 5:23; Revelation 21:2).

OVER TO YOU

Early Christians expected Jesus to return very soon but 2,000 years later we are still waiting. We are told in the Bible not to speculate about when this will happen, but to be ready. Are you?

Jesus and the church

JESUS AND HIS CHURCH

Some people are interested in Jesus Christ, but show little interest in the church. But this is to make a serious mistake. The assumption is that Jesus came to found a new philosophy but it was not a new philosophy that he came to initiate, so much as a new community!

The church is built by Christ

The story of the Bible may be seen as the story of a family. With the creation of humanity, in Genesis, the canvas is massive. But immediately the story begins to narrow down to the family and nation of Israel. It narrows further still as, through disobedience, much of the nation is carried off into captivity. A small, faithful remnant remains. As we come to the New Testament, the band narrows down to twelve men and their leader; then even they fail and we are left with a solitary individual, upon whose sacrificial obedience all depends.

From then on a widening begins, extending from Jerusalem, Judea and Samaria to the farthest parts of the world. The Jewish setting expands into a Gentile one. This is Christ's world-wide community – the church (Matthew 16:18; Colossians 3:11).

The church is bought by Christ

The death of Jesus Christ relates not simply to individuals, but to all of his people, all the church (Matthew 1:21; Acts 20:28). This was clear at the Last Supper, when he met with his friends and instituted a "new" Passover feast, the holy communion (Matthew 26:26-29). Forgiveness is promised to Christ's people through his death. We also learn that through his blood that was shed we have access to God, the Father (Hebrews 7:25-27).

The church is bound by Christ

It is Christ who holds us together and makes us one in spirit. Our traditions may vary between the various church communities. There may be variations in church government and ministry (Ephesus seemed to have "elders", while Philippi had "bishops" – both functions of pastoral oversight).

But these variations need not detract from the essential unity between Christians, centred in our common head, the Lord Jesus Christ. It was party divisiveness that caused scandals in the New Testament churches (1 Corinthians 1:10-15). Bitter competitiveness and refusal to recognise one another brings division into Christ's church. The New Testament pictures the church as a building – with Christ as the cornerstone (Ephesians 2:20-22); as a bride – with Christ as the Bridegroom (Ephesians 5:25-27); and as a body – with Christ as the Head (Ephesians 4:15-16). In every way we depend upon him.

The message of the book of Revelation is that Christ is speaking to his church, staying with his church, searching through his church and strengthening his church. Finally he will be returning for his church. It is the only community on earth to which he has solemnly pledged his presence.

OVER TO YOU

The church is pictured as the bride of Christ. Does this help you to appreciate how special and important to Jesus the church is?

THE CHURCH – GOD'S OWN PEOPLE

From the very beginning, Christians discovered that they had a great deal in common. They called each other "brother" or "sister", and shared their homes and possessions (Acts 2:44-47; 4:32-37). They called themselves the church, a word which means an "assembly" or "meeting", but which had also been used in the Old Testament of God's people.

Their gatherings

They met anywhere they could, in the covered temple porticos (Acts 2:46; 5:12,42) or in various houses (Acts 2:46; 5:42). Look up Acts 2:42 to see their priorities. They gathered for:

- **worship and prayer** (Acts 4:23-31; 12:5,12).
- **teaching** (Acts 11:25-26; 18:11; 20:20,27,31).

Jesus gave two special services as powerful symbols of the gospel. The early church practised both:

- **baptism** with water to show cleansing and entry into God's church (Matthew 28:19; Acts 2:4 1; 8:38:39; 16:29-33).
- **the Lord's Supper** or communion service. The bread and wine stand for Christ's body given for us in death (Luke 22:14-20; Acts 2:42; 1 Corinthians 10:16-17; 11:23-32).

Their leaders

Several sorts of leader are mentioned:

- **Apostles** comprised not only the original eleven remaining disciples, but also others: Paul and Barnabas (Acts 14:3).
- **Elders** had charge of churches (Acts 14:23; 20:17). At Jerusalem they operated alongside the apostles (Acts 15:4; 20:17-18). Paul also calls them overseers (sometimes translated "bishops") and shepherds or pastors (Acts 20:28). There was more than one in each church.
- **Prophets** are seen both in particular churches and travelling about, encouraging others and sometimes predicting what would happen (Acts 11:27-28; 13:1; 15:32; 21:9-10).
- **The seven** (Acts 6:1-6) chosen to look after administration have no particular title.

They could have been deacons (literally "servants"; see also 1 Timothy 3:8-13).
- We also have mention of an **evangelist** (Acts 21:8) who was also one of the seven, and of **teachers** (Acts 13:1), who may also have been church elders.

Their organisation

Early on, the Christian leaders at Jerusalem played an important role. They kept an eye on new developments (Acts 8:14-16; 11:1-18,22), and it was there that they thrashed out the terms on which Gentiles might join the church (Acts 15:1-33).

By the time that Jerusalem lost its importance, the church had grown to an international fellowship. There was not even any distinction between Jewish and Gentile church members.

What about us?

- Do we have a wholehearted commitment to teaching (Acts 2:42)?
- Is our worship really inspired by the Spirit rather than a routine (Ephesians 5:18-20)?
- Is everyone involved (Ephesians 4:12)?
- Do we care about new believers (Acts 11:21-23) and those in need (Acts 6:1-6)?
- How great is our vision (Acts 1:8)? And are we moved to put this vision into practice (Acts 13:1-3)?

OVER TO YOU

How does our own church life match up to some of these marks of New Testament churches?

GROWING TOGETHER IN JESUS

God wants healthy, growing churches! How can such growth be encouraged? Paul describes the work of the Bible as to teach truth, rebuke error, correct faults and train in holiness (2 Timothy 3:16). As we read Paul's letter to the Galatians, we see how these tasks are paralleled in the life and work of Paul, the pastor.

Teaching truth

The Galatians needed to relearn basic truths. They had forgotten what conversion was and, even more significantly, had misunderstood how to live the Christian life (Galatians 3:1-5; 4:8-19). They needed instructing so that they could be saved from disastrous courses of action. That's why Paul is so passionately concerned that they grasp his message; he does not teach in an indifferent manner. And today there are many Christians who are ignorant of basic Christian truths and need instruction.

Rebuking error

In a world where anyone's opinion is as good as another's, it's hard to grasp the difference between right and wrong! Granted that there are many issues where Christian opinion legitimately varies, there are also major truths which God has made known. To pervert these essential truths is not only mischievous but positively dangerous (Galatians 1:6-9).

So error must be exposed and rebuked in the church and those who persist in it must be disciplined.

Jesus recognised the need to preserve truth (John 17:17) and exercise discipline (Matthew 18:15-18), and the early church practised discipline. Look at 1 Corinthians 5; 2 Thessalonians 3:6-15; 1 Timothy 1:3-7,20.

Rebuking error is hard and requires loving firmness. But we dare not shy away from it.

Correcting faults

Error may take the form of wrong behaviour as much as wrong belief. The task of the Christian fellowship is to restore those who fall in this way. Often we pray for them, discuss them, or avoid them but we don't restore them! Active steps must be taken to bring them back into line and into fellowship.

Paul tells us how the task is to be done (Galatians 6:1-3; see also James 5:19-20).

You can only restore a fellow Christian if you act with gentleness, humility and understanding. To carry another's burden means that you will get underneath it and feel the full weight of the problem or pressure being borne. Superficial judgments from a safe distance are not allowed!

Training in holiness

Christian training concentrates on changing our character rather than filling our minds. God accepts us as sinners just as we are, but the Spirit motivates us as believers to be something different. Paul shows that the change has to do with our personal character (Galatians 5:22-23) and our social relationships (Galatians 5:26–6:6). To claim to be holy in one area while neglecting the other is a contradiction in terms. Training in holiness is training in maturity (Colossians 1:28)!

OVER TO YOU

God does not want huge churches full of one-day-a-week Christians; he wants committed followers who are eager to grow in faith.

What does the word fellowship suggest to you? A get-together in the church hall after a service? A social day out or weekend with other Christians? Let us try and see how these ideas match the Bible's picture of fellowship.

Sharing God's life

Real Christian fellowship begins not with us – but with God! Look up 1 John 1:3. To have fellowship with one another we must first have fellowship with God, through the Lord Jesus Christ. True fellowship is sharing our knowledge and experience of God – Father, Son and Holy Spirit – with one another.

Giving and receiving

How does this work out in practice? Fellowship is seen first of all in **what we receive** – as Christians, we share in the life of God by having fellowship with his Son (1 Corinthians 1:9). The first Christians devoted themselves to the apostles' teaching and fellowship (Acts 2:42). We share in a fellowship meal – the Lord's Supper, communion (1 Corinthians 10:16-17). We even share in suffering (Philippians 3:10; Acts 9:15-16).

Fellowship is also seen in **what we do**. See Philippians 1:4-5 where Paul prays with joy because of the Philippians' fellowship – their help or partnership in sharing the gospel (see also Philippians 1:27). The memories of sharing all the struggles and victories of a growing church gave him joy and stirred him to pray for them.

It is also important to remember that as Christians we need to have a **balanced fellowship**. We may be nearly always on the receiving end, only rarely putting into practice what we hear or read. Or we may be always serving others, never really opening up our own personal needs to anyone. True fellowship – and a growing Christian life – is seen in a balance between both giving and receiving. Look at the example of Paul in Romans 1:11-12.

Love in action

Love and fellowship go together because if we truly love others we will want to share with them. Fellowship is love in action! The richer and deeper our love, the greater the prospect of fellowship.

Here are some practical tips on how to have fellowship:
- **Be hospitable** (Hebrews 13:2; 1 Peter 4:9).
- **Encourage one another** (Hebrews 10:24-25).
- **Pray for one another** (Philippians 1:9-11) and get others to pray for you, too! It can be especially good to have a close friend with whom you can share every part of your life.
- **Bear one another's burdens** (Galatians 6:2).

Include everyone in your fellowship. Think about some of the people mentioned in Philippians – church leaders (Philippians 1:1), those with wrong motives (Philippians 1:15,17), even those at loggerheads (Philippians 4:2)! It is important that true Christian love and fellowship in any church should stretch across the barriers of race, class, colour, sex, status and culture that divide the world. Let our fellowship be real!

OVER TO YOU

Are you part of a loving, caring fellowship? Being a member of a church provides opportunities for serving others and receiving support in times of need.

THE UNITY OF THE CHURCH

What is unity?

Unity is exciting! It is one of the gifts that God gives his people (Ephesians 4:3; 1 Corinthians 12:13). Jesus thought of unity as based on a common commitment to himself. In John chapter 17 he longs for those who receive his words, those who believe (verse 8), to be truly one. In other words, he wants the unity of those who respond to the gospel, those who are true believers in the Lord Jesus Christ.

In John 17, we're told two other vital aspects of unity:

- the unity of believers is comparable to the unity in the Trinity. See verses 21-22. This is a far cry from an external, organisational unity. It is a spiritual unity.
- the unity of believers is based on truth (verse 17). There are certain central matters of biblical truth that Christians must hold onto at all costs, for example that Jesus was both fully God and fully man, that he died in our place to save us from the punishment due to us for our sins and that he rose again (see also Ephesians 4:4-6). There are other, secondary matters, on which Christians have different views. There must be room in churches to accept differences. As has been said, "In necessary things, unity; in doubtful things, liberty; in all things, charity!"

Unity begins at home

Unity, like charity, begins at home. Individual groups of believers would do well to ask themselves how united they are. We can express some of Paul's thoughts as questions:

- Are we standing firm in one spirit, fighting as one person for the faith of the gospel (Philippians 1:27)?
- Are we making every effort to keep the unity already given by the Spirit by means of the peace that binds us together (Ephesians 4:3)?
- Are we humble, gentle, patient and tolerant with one another (Ephesians 4:2)?

Expressing unity

If we answer these questions honestly, we'll probably realise that we've a long way to go. But unity is something that grows when everyone "pulls their weight" (Ephesians 4:11-16). Unity is the place where there is blessing; where Jesus reveals himself and prayers are answered (Psalm 133; Matthew 18:19-20). It is the place where things happen (Acts 4:32-35).

But the real purpose of unity isn't to make us inward looking, constantly taken up with ourselves. The purpose is that the world may know that God is a God of love who sent Jesus into the world (John 17:21,23). This means that we should seek occasions when churches can act together to declare the great message of Christ's salvation.

> ### OVER TO YOU
>
> What does "church unity" mean to you? Can you work in your area for greater cooperation between churches? This can be an impressive witness to those outside the church.

Making Jesus known

SHARING THE GOOD NEWS

What is evangelism?
It is offering people Christ with a view to their receiving and relying on him (John 1:12) and becoming part of his body the Christian church. It is announcing the Christian good news to people with this twofold hope in view, their conversion to Christ and their incorporation into his church (Matthew 4:19).

What is the good news?
God in his love has provided a Saviour for guilty sinners! Just as he promised, he has given his Son to be born as man, live a perfect life and die an atoning death – all for us. That Son Jesus is now alive for ever and reigning over this world. He will return to it to judge the living and the dead. He commands everybody to turn from the sin of running their own lives and surrender utterly to him. He is love incarnate, willing and able to save all who draw near to God through him. We gain that benefit when we make him our Saviour in faith.

Why evangelise?
- **Because Jesus commands it.** See Matthew 28:18-20.
- **Because we love our family and friends.** Having Jesus is the difference between fullness and emptiness of life (John 10:10) ... between heaven and hell (John 5:29; 6:29).
- **Because it hastens Christ's return.** The worldwide spread of the gospel is a factor in the fullness of human history. See Matthew 24:14; Acts 3:19-21; 2 Peter 3:12.
- **Because it glorifies God.** He ought to be honoured as the only sufficient Saviour. The more knees bow to Jesus, the greater is God's reputation as King and Redeemer: Philippians 2:10-11.

Who should do it?
We should share the good news in the way that fits each of us: Matthew 10:32-33 and Romans 10:9-10. What counts is the sort of Christian you are. "The Christlike heart is the chariot of God by which he comes to the world in grace and conviction" (Martin Luther).

How to do it
Bear three things in mind:
- **Pray.** Jesus is the person who actually does the effective work in evangelism. We may not presume on his Spirit's activity. We must ask him. "Prayer is evangelism shorn of its carnal attractions" (George M. Philip).
- **The church** is the proper base from which to work, whether on a personal or larger scale.
- We do well to consider **speaking out the message of the Bible** as the essential tool in evangelism: 1 Corinthians 1:18.

Given these three principles, Jesus can use any method that Christlike hearts and prayerful lives dream up. Public or private, indoors or open air, spoken word or written, formal preaching or informal testimony, lecture hall or kitchen teapot – all can count for Christ if the gospel and our friends really matter to us.

OVER TO YOU
Have you ever been involved in evangelism? You may not have spoken to strangers about your faith but telling friends how important Jesus is to you, and praying for the work of preachers and evangelists, is also important.

EVANGELISM – GETTING ON WITH THE JOB

The accounts in Acts are useful in telling us how the early believers got on with the job of sharing the good news with others and can help us today,

Know your audience thoroughly

· Sometimes they spoke to large crowds (Acts 2:14; 8:5; 21:40).

· Sometimes they shared with individuals (Acts 8:26-30; 13:7; 24:24) or with small groups (Acts 10:24; 16:13-15,32).

· When sharing with the Jews they began with the Old Testament Scriptures and claimed that Jesus had fulfilled them (Acts 2:16; 3:12-26; 13:16-41). When Paul and his friends went to a new place, they started work with those who were already aware of the Bible promises before going to the Gentiles.

· When sharing with the Gentiles they began much further back, starting with God and creation rather than with the Old Testament (Acts 14:15-17; 17:22-31).

So the early believers used the level of understanding that their audience had already reached as a starting point for what they wanted to say. We would do well to follow their example – to take time to think about what the people we speak to know and don't know about God, Jesus and the Christian message. It isn't "unspiritual" to think about what sort of culture we live in and adapt how we present the good news to fit in with this. No, it is acting responsibly towards God and his world.

Communicate your message clearly

The way we speak matters, too. Notice what happened when Paul started to speak to the people in a language they were used to (Acts 22:2). We too should speak words that our hearers understand. We mustn't expect them to grasp the full Christian meaning of words like *lost* or *saved*.

Notice too how Luke uses a great variety of words to describe the ways in which the

apostles shared the good news – look at Acts 17:1-3, for example.

So we need to do our best to communicate well in different situations: after all, we can really only claim to be communicating effectively if people understand what we say!

Explain the good news seriously

The gospel is good news from God – it isn't something that is human and to be played around with. There is a temptation to go overboard in presenting the gospel as attractively as possible and getting down to the level of our audiences; we can forget that life-and-death issues are at stake. Look at the awe-inspiring effects sharing the gospel had in Acts 9:31, for example. So we would do well to share the gospel seriously.

Rely on the Holy Spirit constantly

All that we have said so far assumes two things:

· that we are clear about what the good news is

· that we are relying on the Holy Spirit. He is indispensable (Acts 4:8,31; 6:10; 14:3) and the one who makes our evangelism effective.

> ## OVER TO YOU
>
> Ask God to provide you with opportunities to share your faith – and then be bold when he provides them.

People matter

Evangelism takes many forms, but no method is as effective as person-to-person contact. Although there were times when Jesus preached to great crowds the greater part of his work was spent with individuals. The story of his meeting with the woman at the well is a classic example. Look again at John 4:1-42.

One person matters

Jesus went out of his way to meet the woman. Good Jews normally avoided passing through Samaria because of the feud which existed between Jews and Samaritans (John 4:9), but Jesus felt constrained to do so for the sake of one needy woman whose path was going to cross his.

Notice the way he made contact with her. He was friendly, courteous and understanding in his approach. He simply asked for a drink (John 4:7) and so placed himself to some extent in her debt. He allowed an ordinary, everyday incident to provide an opportunity for a conversation which eventually led to the woman's conversion.

Jesus was fully aware that this woman was ignorant as far as spiritual values were concerned but he set her thinking when he mentioned the water of life (John 4:10). She had no idea what he meant but was intrigued by the expression. As she revealed her ignorance, he dealt gently with her (John 4:11-15).

Jesus then wanted her to see her responsibilities. While he did not reproach or scold her, he made her face up to her sin (John 4:16-18). At once she realised she was face to face with no ordinary man: look at John 4:19. Yet she didn't give in easily. She produced a "red herring" by bringing up a controversial religious issue regarding the mountain on which men ought to worship (John 4:20). But Jesus dealt with the issue firmly by pointing out that the important thing is to know the God we worship (John 4:21-24).

Clearly the woman now realised her sin and her need, and she recognised the One who was speaking to her. The first thing she did was to speak immediately with her old friends and associates, telling them she had found the Messiah (John 4:28-30). Look what happened (John 4:39-42)!

People are different

Jesus revealed himself as master of the art of personal evangelism. It always involves being interested in people, caring for them, being willing to take the initiative and being able to talk freely. There is an appropriate moment for getting to the point and pressing home the message. One conversation won't always be enough. Harm can be done if we try to accomplish too much too quickly. The great point we must always bear in mind is that people are different and we must avoid using a stereotyped approach or form of words. In the early church they passed on the good news in the course of ordinary conversation. That is really what it's all about.

OVER TO YOU

Some Christians are called to preach to large crowds – but *all* Christians are called to befriend other people and to love them.

LIGHTS IN THE WORLD

Let there be light!

At the dawn of creation, God created light (Genesis 1:3-4). Throughout the Bible, light is contrasted with darkness, which symbolises human sin. Whenever "light" is applied to people or things it has a favourable meaning.

God is light

John in his first letter writes that God is light (1 John 1:5). There is no darkness in him at all. Just as it is the nature of light to shine, so it is God's nature to reveal himself, and we see him as exalted and completely pure.

The light of the world

Jesus claimed to be the light of the world (John 8:12). He did so when the Feast of Tabernacles or Shelters was being celebrated in Jerusalem. Large branched, golden candleholders were lit in the temple court, and the city was flooded with light. This commemorated the pillars of fire and cloud that accompanied the Israelite people in their wilderness journey and which symbolised the divine presence.

The fact that Christ claimed to be the light of the world implies that apart from him there is darkness. Indeed, those who refuse to follow him are said to do so because they love darkness rather than light (John 3:19-21). As Jesus anticipated his death, he urged the crowds to turn to the light before darkness overtook them (John 12:35): they were to put their trust in the light. Paul describes the gospel as light since it leads people out of the darkness of sin and spiritual death (2 Corinthians 4:4).

Children of light

Those who trust Jesus, who is the light, become "sons" or "people" "of light" (John 12:36). In the Sermon on the Mount, Jesus told his disciples they were the light of the world, and they were to let their light shine before other people (Matthew 5:14-16). Paul wrote to the Philippians and told them they were to shine like stars in the sky (Philippians 2:15). Jesus is the light-bearer but his followers must reflect the light they have received from him.

So light also has to do with the way we live. John in his first letter speaks of "walking" or "living" "in the light" (1 John 1:5-7). This means living our lives in the light of the revealed will of God. This in turn means being open and honest, hiding nothing. Here is the secret of enjoying fellowship with one another.

If light is not followed, darkness comes and judgement is inevitable (John 3:19-20). Rejecting the light we have points to an evil character which shrinks from exposure, but a person who is honest and open by nature is responsive to the light (John 3:20-21). As any gardener knows, when you lift a large stone from a rockery, dozens of little creatures scurry off in all directions! They have always lived in darkness and cannot stand being exposed to the light. When the stone is replaced they return to the darkness.

How is all this to work out in practice? Look at Ephesians 5:8-14.

OVER TO YOU

Jesus wants us to be lights shining for him. Do we always behave in an open and honest way with other people or do we sometimes hide our light?

LOVE: THE NEW LIFESTYLE

What is love?

Three different Greek words may be translated by the one English word *love*. One refers to love in the sense of natural affection, another refers to love in the sexual sense, and the third word gives love its essentially Christian meaning – love that is self-giving.

Love is shown between the Father and the Son (John 10:17; 14:31; 15:9). The Father himself loves the followers of Jesus (John 14:21-23). In fact, the whole world is loved by God (John 3:16).

When we speak of love in the Christian sense, we have in mind something beyond natural human affection. It is essentially spiritual and Godlike. It is the fruit of the Holy Spirit rather than the expression of natural affection (Galatians 5:22). Christians should be able to love people they may not necessarily like. In our human state we shall not be drawn equally to everyone but the love of Jesus in us can reach out to everyone we come across.

Love speaks

Genuine love must express itself. Jesus said, "If you obey my commands, you will remain in my love, just as I have obeyed my Father's commands and remain in his love" (John 15:10). Our love for Jesus will be expressed by a desire to please him in all we do (John 14:15). One of the first things he requires of us is that we love other believers in a similar way to that in which he loves us (John 13:34; 15:12).

Jesus demonstrated how much he loved his disciples by washing their feet (John 13:2-17). It was an amazing example of divine condescension. To wash the feet of guests was normally a task assigned to the humblest slave in the household. The disciples had been quarrelling over which one would have the place of greatest honour (Luke 22:24) but their Lord was performing a task which probably none of them would have volunteered to do. And his disciples are to follow his example (John 13:15).

Genuine love will express itself in loving service, not a service done in a spirit of drudgery. Our love for Jesus is reflected in our love for people. What we do for others is seen by Jesus as serving him (Matthew 25:31-46). There is a danger we just love "nice" people, but Jesus even washed Judas' feet.

Love doesn't give up

Peter is an example of Jesus' love never giving up (John 13:1). He had protested loudly that whatever happened he would never deny his Lord (Matthew 26:33) but before long he was denying him three times over. He might well have imagined this was the end, that he could never again be trusted. But instead we find Jesus reinstating Peter and giving him a fresh commission. Just as Peter denied Jesus three times, so he is commanded three times to feed Christ's sheep (John 21:15-18).

Jesus has been described as the "one who knows the worst about us, yet loves us just the same". In his dealings with people he exemplified the love he wanted to see expressed in the lives of his followers. But Jesus' love found its greatest expression on the cross when he died (Romans 5:6-8).

OVER TO YOU

Pray for an opportunity to show Christ's love to someone you meet today.

Jesus in the Letter to the Hebrews

JESUS – GOD'S FINAL WORD

What is the book of Hebrews about? Three words can sum it up: prophets, angels and Jesus. Think of yourself standing at the interface between the Old and New Testaments. What do you see when you look back? Prophets and angels. And what do you see when you look forward? Jesus only. So this letter isn't about the greatness of Jesus in just a general way, it is about Jesus being the final word from God.

Prophets brought God's word to his people

The Old Testament prophets were among the greatest and most attractive men that ever lived – and among the most privileged. They were brought into God's close presence (Isaiah 6:8; Jeremiah 23:18; Amos 3:7) to such an extent that God's words became their words (Ezekiel 2:7-3:4). They were men speaking from God (2 Peter 1:21). But Jesus is God speaking to all the human race.

Angels brought God's word to his people

Now we look back beyond the prophets to the great man Moses, who founded the order of prophets. It was his privilege to go up to Mount Sinai and right into the darkness which shrouded God's very presence (Exodus 20:21). There he received God's basic Law for his people's daily life. From that point onwards the Lord lived and walked among his people as an angel (Exodus 23:20-23).

Many Old Testament passages speak of this special angel and many others of angels in general. From passages like Genesis 16:7,9,13, it becomes clear that this "angel of the Lord" is the Lord himself, graciously hiding the full brightness of his glory and keeping company with needy and sinful people.

The Son has brought God's word to us

We've thought about prophets and angels – and now we look at Jesus. He is the full, unveiled radiance of God (Hebrews 1:3). To see Jesus is to see the Father, to hear him is to hear the Father, to know him is to know the Father (John 14:7-10). The opening verses of Hebrews tell us that God has spoken to us by his Son (Hebrews 1:1-2): Jesus is unique. He is God's final Word to us. He brings in a new era of God's dealings with humanity.

Since Jesus is God's Word to humanity, we might have expected to read more about what Jesus said. But in fact the words of Jesus are not mentioned. Instead, we're told what Jesus has done and what he is doing.

Just as we stood between the Old and New Testaments, we can now stand at the cross of Jesus and look about us:

- **When we look at God**, we see that his anger towards our sin has been satisfied by the death of Jesus (Hebrews 2:17).
- **When we look at Satan,** we find he has been deprived of effective power (Hebrews 2:14).
- **When we look at ourselves**, we find that Jesus died in our place (Hebrews 2:9), purged us from our sins to bring forgiveness and cleansing (Hebrews 1:3), has brought us to share his glory (Hebrews 2:10) and lives to be our help when we are tempted in our lives (Hebrews 2:18).

OVER TO YOU

God's chosen people, Israel, had a special relationship with him but in Jesus Christ everyone can now know God in a personal way. Thank God for that privilege.

Jesus is our high priest

Good teachers don't plunge their pupils in at the deep end. They build up their teaching bit by bit, point by point.

As we read Hebrews, we discover that the central thought of the letter is that Jesus is our high priest. The theme has already been introduced (Hebrews 2:17–3:1), dropped and returned to (Hebrews 4:14-16). Its two main aspects have begun to emerge:

- **The high priest makes atonement** (Hebrews 2:17): he has a task towards God, to satisfy the demands of God regarding sin and sinners.
- **The high priest has a ready and sympathetic heart** towards people and helps those who are under trial (Hebrews 2:18; see also Hebrews 5:2).

Jesus sympathises with us

Let's think more about the high priest's gentle sympathy with our weakness. Hebrews makes a lot of the fact that Jesus actually lived a human life in this world. He became our brother (Hebrews 2:12), shared our humanity (Hebrews 2:14) and experienced our lot – suffering (Hebrews 2:10) and trials and temptations (Hebrews 2:18). So it follows that the One who has identified with us in this way will also identify with us in sympathy, understanding and help (2:18; 4:15-16; 5:2).

Jesus is without sin

But in one way, Jesus' experience was wholly unlike ours. He was without sin (Hebrews 4:15). Perhaps we might think then that his experience of life was unreal. How could his temptations be real if all the powers of a sinless nature were fighting on his side? This isn't how we should understand what Hebrews 4:15 is saying.

- It *doesn't* mean, "Though, of course, being sinless, Jesus was not after all quite like us in his trials and temptations."
- It *does* mean, "Remember this, that since he remained sinless in spite of temptation, Jesus knows far more of the ferocious strength and pressure of temptation than we ever will."
- Or, to put it another way: in our case as temptation increases its pressure, the more we resist. Over and over again, we give in at a certain point and there are therefore fires of temptation of which we know nothing. In our struggle against sin we have not yet resisted to the point of shedding our blood (Hebrews 12:4), but he did!
- The fact that Jesus is without sin, therefore, guarantees that whatever testing may come to us, he has been there – and beyond!

Jesus leads us to God

But we don't just have a sympathetic high priest; he is also the One who makes the way open for us to come into God's presence. We're encouraged to come with confidence to the throne of God (Hebrews 4:16). The appearance of a throne tells much about the sort of rule exercised there – more often than not pomp, pride and military power. But here is a throne of grace (Hebrews 4:16). God's kingship goes out in undeserved favour to those who come seeking mercy. He meets our needs.

OVER TO YOU

Jesus did not sin, but on the cross he experienced the conseqences of sin. Thank him that he knows what it is to be human and to be tempted.

GOING ON WITH JESUS

Can I be really sure?
What a book of if's Hebrews is! "If we ignore" (Hebrews 2:3), "if we hold on" (Hebrews 3:6), "if we hold firmly" (Hebrews 3:14), "if we keep on sinning" (Hebrews 10:26), "if we turn away" (Hebrews 12:25). There are many urgent warnings and cautions, too: "pay attention" (Hebrews 2:1), "look at our hearts" (Hebrews 3:12), "be careful" (Hebrews 4:1), "make every effort" (Hebrews 4:11), "hold firmly" (Hebrews 4:14).

All this may make us wonder if, after all, our salvation is such a sure thing as maybe we had thought. Can we be saved one day and – because we've slipped into sin or failed to be careful enough or slacked off – lose our salvation the next? This serious question becomes urgent when we read in Hebrews 6:4-8 of people who were once enlightened, experienced God's gift, shared in the Holy Spirit and the word of God and knew something of the powers at work in the new age brought in by Jesus – and yet fell away in such a manner that their restoration became impossible.

Clearly, a passage like this receives different explanations from different people and there are those who find no alternative to a "saved today, lost tomorrow" view. This is not, however, the view that we think is right

The experience of God's blessings
Look at Hebrews 6:7-8. Two pieces of land receive identical benefits; one responds in true fruitfulness; the other continues as though nothing had happened. The key ideas are fruitfulness and staying totally unchanged.

What does this mean in our spiritual experience? Numbers 13:21-25; 14:36 tells of a party of twelve going to spy out God's Promised Land. For 40 days they walked on its soil, breathed its air and gathered its fruits, but ten of them never actually possessed what they had experienced.

It takes nothing like 40 days to experience the blessings listed in Hebrews 6:4-5. It could be the work of a few minutes – a dawning recognition of the truth of the gospel, an awareness that salvation is God's free gift and a sense of the goodness of it, a touch of the Holy Spirit urging on towards faith in Jesus, an experience of responding to God's word and of a stirring of new life. This has happened to some as the gospel has been preached and a response encouraged. In this way, God's gracious rain has begun to fall – but what if some individual life goes on as if nothing had happened, re-crucifying the Son of God to their shame and loss, and subjecting him to public disgrace (Hebrews 6:6)?

The evidence of changed lives
We must not over-dramatise the blessings spoken of, for they need be nothing more than the first stirrings of blessing to come – the fruits of God's Promised Land designed to make us want to enter and possess it. Nor must we over-dramatise sins continued in, for they are the ordinary sins of the average non-Christian life. The fact of the matter is that claims to experience must be shown to be true by the evidence of a changed life. Our assurance of salvation is not related to claims to this experience or that but to the evidence of fruit: the things people see in us (Hebrews 6:9-10) and the goals of our lives (Hebrews 6:11-12).

OVER TO YOU
If you have accepted Jesus as your Saviour what difference has it made to your life? What differences in your speech and behaviour can be seen by others?

JESUS' DEATH: THE PERFECT SACRIFICE

Our great high priest

The high priest reached out to people in sympathy and understanding (Hebrews 2:18; 4:15-16; 5:2), but his major role was to represent people in matters related to God, to offer gifts and sacrifices for sins (Hebrews 5:1). How does Jesus fit into this aspect of priesthood?

Heavenly realities

Hebrews emphasises that Moses copied on earth what God had shown him (Hebrews 8:5; 10:1). Behind the tabernacle, its basic plan, detailed furnishings and officials and ceremonies, there are heavenly realities to which Hebrews refers as the true or real tabernacle (or tent) (Hebrews 8:2), the sanctuary "in heaven" (Hebrews 8:5), the greater and more perfect tabernacle (Hebrews 9:11; see also Hebrews 9:23-24).

How are we to understand all this? Is there a tabernacle in heaven? Is heaven "shaped" like a tabernacle? The meaning rather is this: the truths expressed by the tabernacle are truths dear to God; the requirements for approaching God in tabernacle worship are those which must be met if God is in reality to be approached. In this way, the tabernacle is an earthly copy of heavenly truth. When we read about Jesus as a high priest operating in the heavenly sanctuary (Hebrews 8:1-2), the meaning is that he has fulfilled ultimately, fully and eternally all that God requires.

A unique death

From the start, Hebrews has focused on the death of Jesus:

- in Hebrews 2:9, his death is the reason for his glory and a substitute for our death.
- in Hebrews 2:14-15, his death has rendered the power of the devil of no further significance and releases us from bondage.
- in Hebrews 2:17, his death makes atonement – "makes propitiation" for the sins of the people – it satisfies God's wrath against sinners.

But in the climax of Hebrews chapters 9–10, the meaning of Jesus' death is spelt out. Two passages are supremely important:

- Hebrews 9:12-18 uses the words *blood* and *death* interchangeably; the blood of Jesus is one way of speaking about his death, the laying down of his life.
- Hebrews 10:11-14 tells us clearly that the death of Jesus was once and for all. (See also Hebrews 7:27; 9:26; 10:10).

In my place

From the start, the Lord graciously provided substitutes to bear his people's sin. Sin and guilt were transferred from the guilty to the innocent (Leviticus 16:21-22), who bore the sin. The Old Testament looked forward to the coming of a sinless person who would fulfil this sin-bearing role (Isaiah 53:4-6,12) and Jesus was that person, voluntarily bringing God's lovely and merciful plan to completion (John 10:18; Hebrews 10:4-9).

Becoming more like Jesus

So complete is what Jesus has done that Hebrews speaks of us as already made holy, purified from sin (Hebrews 10:10). Hebrews 10:14 speaks of our being made holy or purified as ongoing. So we see that we have a lot of catching up to do before we express practically what we are really! But the truth is very important: Christian progress is not a vain and doomed attempt to become what we are not; it is the continual discovery and living-out of what Jesus Christ has already, by his death, achieved for us.

OVER TO YOU

Do you recognise that you have been made holy? This is a process that will not be complete until the kingdom of God is fully established, but rejoice that it has begun in your life.

COMING TO GOD THROUGH JESUS

How can we, as sinful, guilty people, come into the presence of the holy God?
Hebrews brings us the answer to the basic human problem of sin.

Restricted access

Turn back to the end of the book of Exodus chapter 40. What a blow to Moses when he could not go into the tabernacle (Exodus 40:35)! He had spent endless hours supervising its construction down to the smallest detail and now that it was complete, he was shut out. But read straight on into Leviticus. Leviticus 1:2 is full of "coming near" to the Lord. Though it does not make very good English we could translate it: "When anyone brings near that which brings people near to the Lord, you shall bring near the offering which brings you near ..." There it is: Moses was shut out, but could be brought near by the blood of sacrifice.

The tabernacle was planned by the Holy Spirit to create, in part, the sense of being shut out. For all the blessings it brought and the marvellous lessons of God's grace it taught, it was meant to provoke the people to say also, "God's tent is right in the middle of our tents and yet we cannot go to him. We are not allowed to visit him. He is 'in' but he is not 'at home to callers'." See Hebrews 9:7-8.

Open access

Jesus has not only gone into the Holy Place, he has also left the door open behind him! Where he has gone we can follow. The three curtains of the tabernacle were all the same, made of blue, purple and scarlet material and the whiteness of fine linen: the courtyard curtain (Exodus 27:16), the tent curtain (Exodus 26:36) and the sanctuary curtain (Exodus 26:31-34). Did the people ever wonder why they could go through one and not the others, even though they were identical?

Older writers saw these colours as describing the glories of Jesus: the blue speaking of his heavenly origin, the purple of his royal dignity, the scarlet of the blood of his cross and the white of his spotless purity. Be that as it may, Hebrews 10:20 identifies the torn curtain (Mark 15:38) with his torn flesh. Could we have a more dramatic demonstration than this that the death of Jesus has opened the way for us into God's very presence?

Direct access

Since, through Jesus and with him, we can enter into the Most Holy Place, he has not just given us priestly, but also high priestly privileges! And we are meant to make use of them, to enjoy them (Hebrews 10:19-22). In the original language, Hebrews 10:22 could be translated, "Let us keep on drawing near; let us be ever drawing near."

We should remember three things about this life of drawing near to God:

- We must cultivate a constant experience of the blood of Jesus cleansing us (Hebrews 10:22).
- We are to stand persistently for what we believe to be true (Hebrews 10:23).
- We are actively to develop and care for the fellowship of God's people (Hebrews 10:24-25).

OVER TO YOU

Drawing near to God is not just a matter of attending church. Do you seek God's presence every day through prayer and Bible reading? You may be able to meet with others during the week to help you in this.

Discovering prayer

Prayer is one of the most important parts of our lives as Christians. As we talk to God, our friend, we come to know him more and more. The miracle of prayer is that God listens to us! When we pray, we begin to discover what God is like. We respond to him in the right way. We become involved in what he's doing in the world. And we can draw on all the resources God has for us. Prayer is the secret of blessing, peace and power!

DISCOVERING PRAYER
Asking for others
GENESIS 18

In the very first book of the Bible we find people praying, but the outstanding thing about Abraham was that he was asking for others, not just for himself.

Others' needs

That's what "intercession" means. It's putting in a word for somebody else. The Bible tells us that this isn't just possible, it's our duty if we really love the Lord and are aware of his concern for people.

Asking as a friend

It's no good if you don't have any influence with the one you're asking, but Abraham did. God's plan for blessing all peoples was beginning to work out in Abraham's life, because one day, in the distant future, one of his descendants would be none other than Jesus Christ (verses 18-19). What's more, when we put our trust in Christ and what he did, we get right with God. That means that we have influence too!

Pleading for the undeserving

If anyone didn't deserve sparing it was the Sodomites. Their way of living was really bad (verse 20). Yet Abraham didn't self-righteously write them off. He unselfishly spoke up for them. After all, we all need God's grace and mercy.

Requesting justice

Abraham wanted to see justice done, and he knew he could ask for justice because a just God wouldn't contradict himself (verses 23-25). Even today our forgiveness is grounded in God's justice. Jesus paid the just penalty for our sins. That's why he can spare sinners like us without being unjust.

Looking for more

Abraham wasn't haggling with God; he was just taking one step of faith at a time. In practice we find that our prayers grow larger as we grow in faith. As we begin to see God's answers to our smaller requests we press on for more.

OVER TO YOU

God has called us to join him in working in the world; what response will you make?

Knowing God

EXODUS 33

Early on in their history, the Jews came up against the basic problem in prayer: how can people who are weak and sinful know God well enough to speak to him?

God is holy

God is morally upright and pure. There are no shades of grey with God. He is righteous, just, clean, true – everything, in fact, that we aren't. That's why he refused at first to go with the Israelites (verse 3). It was for their sake, not his. They would have found it too uncomfortable to have had him around. And he hasn't changed.

God is great

We use the word *God* so easily that we sometimes forget his sheer bigness. Remember, he put the world in place; he keeps the stars on course; he created the energy locked up in the atom; he lit the brilliance of the sun. God is simply too big for us to take in, let alone meet! Even Moses who knew him so well couldn't take the full glare of his splendour (look ahead to verse 20).

God is gracious

Here's the clue (verse 19). This same God is loving and kind, even towards those who don't deserve it. That's how he came to choose the Israelites, and that's how he stoops to deal with us. The cross tells us that God loves and forgives undeserving sinners who have gone their own way and broken his Law. That's how we get near enough to him to speak to him.

God is willing

Because we were made for him, the ultimate human experience must be to see him, something which we're promised will happen in heaven. But even now something in us wants to get to know him better, to understand his ways, to see him "face to face" (verse 18).

God makes sure that we only see as much of him as we can take. That's one of the reasons why his Son became a man and lived among us (John 1:14). But having seen all we can, we admit that there's so much we can't know here on earth – God's mystery which makes us wonder and worship.

OVER TO YOU

Spend a few minutes thinking about God's mercy and grace and worshipping and delighting in him.

DISCOVERING PRAYER
What is prayer?

All through the Bible, God's people – and Jesus himself – are described as praying. You might think of prayer as a basic spiritual exercise which everyone who has attempted to live the Christian life has had to learn. But many of us were taught that we must pray, without being given a reason.

Why pray?

After all, there are a number of arguments against praying. We could say to ourselves:

· "God surely isn't interested in me and my small needs; he has far more important things to attend to."
· "God has his plans all worked out beforehand, so my praying won't change anything."
· "Surely prayer is a bit pagan, as though we had to force God to do what we want?"
· "Prayer doesn't do anything as far as God is concerned, but it does make me feel better."

No doubt the Bible authors were aware of all these arguments, and others too, but that didn't stop them praying. Why? Because God himself had both told them and prompted them to do just that!

Our way to God

The Bible is about getting to know God. Although he is far greater than anything we can ever imagine, he has stooped – incredibly – to ask for our friendship! Prayer is one of the ways in which that friendship works out. When we pray, we talk with God, person to person, and we open our hearts and lives to him, listening for what he wants to say to us.

As Christians we can come to him freely and without fear because of what Jesus has done for us (Hebrews 10:19-20), What's more, all God's promises become available to us through him (2 Corinthians 1:20).

The secret of blessing

The fact is that God has pledged himself to hear and answer the prayers of his people. Again and again we are told – and Jesus reminded us – that what God wants to do in and with us is somehow dependent on our asking (Matthew 7:7-8; James 4:2). Prayer is the God-given way of letting him into our lives and needs.

In his word he has given us innumerable promises to take for ourselves, and he has committed himself to fulfil them when we take them seriously (for example, 2 Chronicles 7:14; Psalm 50:15; Jeremiah 33:3). Real prayer begins when we start taking God at his word.

Weapons for warfare

Jesus not only calls us to enjoy his blessings; he also involves us in a spiritual battle for which we need armour and weapons. Prayer is one of these (Ephesians 6:14-20). We see how this worked out in the book of Acts when the early Christians countered the devil's attacks with prayer (4:23-24; 12:5). It is by prayer that we cooperate with the Lord in the outworking of his plans for the world. So prayer isn't just a pleasant pastime; it's also work and warfare.

OVER TO YOU

"Prayer is the God-given way of letting him into our lives and needs." How can you make this even more real in your own life?

Right and wrong prayer
1 KINGS 18:16-46

Some people have strange ideas about prayer which have nothing to do with what the Bible teaches about it. Here is a good example of a common fault.

Pagan prayer

The prophets of Baal were certainly earnest in their praying. Seldom do we have so many words or so much sweat, tears and toil (verses 26,28). They were desperate for an answer, but they never got it because they were praying to the wrong God in the wrong way.

As Elijah pointed out, they pictured their god as human (verse 27). So they thought he would do what they wanted if they just "twisted his arm". That's a pagan idea, but too many people believe it today. They go to God when they want something, even though they have little idea of who God is, and they put in their demands. What's more, they're most hurt when they don't get an answer, and conclude that either prayer doesn't work, or that God doesn't exist.

True prayer

Elijah knew the God he prayed to. As his spokesman, it looks as though he had a pretty good idea of what God would do even before he asked, otherwise he would have been "tempting God" with such a prayer. What's more, it wasn't just his reputation that was at stake – it was God's (verses 36-37). So his prayer is simple, direct and trusting – and God answered in a dramatic way.

This is because the God of the Bible is the God who does things – not just a name or an idea or a shadowy figure somewhere "up there" – but a living, active God who hears the prayers of his people. But you must come to him on his terms, and you must ask for the right things.

Notice that Elijah's praying wasn't finished for the day when the fire fell (verses 41-44). Fire is all very well, but they didn't need fire; they needed water – and God gave them that too!

Burdened prayer

NEHEMIAH 1

Prayer is not just for the "heavenly-minded". In the Bible, prayer and action go side by side, as we see in Nehemiah's case.

Turning needs into prayers

It tells us something about what sort of man Nehemiah was that he could get worked up about happenings a long way away, and which he was unlikely to have anything to do with. This is what is called having "a burden" – a deep unhappiness and concern about God's work or God's people: look at verse 4. God sometimes burdens people today, either about the needs of their own land or about some missionary situations far away.

We learn more about Nehemiah in that he turned this need into prayer. But that's logical. If we are God's people, then God is concerned about us. Our needs are his, and we can turn them over to him.

Prayer as work

There was nothing slapdash about Nehemiah's praying. He almost adopted a strategy. He began by thinking what God was like (verse 5), and continued by confessing his sins (verses 6-7). He went on to remind God of his promises (verses 8-9) and he concluded by pleading the way that God had rescued them in the past. This was deliberate. It took effort, discipline and foresight. God has promised to answer prayer: people like Nehemiah set about proving that promise. Do we?

Prayer on impulse

Although Nehemiah would deliberately set time aside to pray, we also know that he threw prayers up to God whenever the need arose (see 2:4; 4:4; 6:9). He knew that God was always listening, even in the most ordinary circumstances.

But this also tells us something about his attitude of heart. Nehemiah was the kind of person who so trusted in God that it was natural – indeed it became a habit – to turn to God in time of need. For as we shall see, prayer isn't just an occasional venture into God's presence; it's a way of life.

OVER TO YOU

What particular people or situations has God given you a burden for? Don't become discouraged in continuing to pray for them.

DISCOVERING PRAYER
Why are my prayers sometimes unanswered?

God doesn't give us everything we ask for, but if we stop and think why he doesn't, we can learn something about how prayer works.

Sin in our lives
There's a fundamental rule in prayer: if there are things in my heart and life which God hates, I cannot expect him to hear or to answer my prayers (Psalm 66:18; Isaiah 59:1-2). So the first thing we need to do is to get right by confessing our faults and asking for forgiveness (1 John 1:9).

Wrong with others
You can't be right with God if you're wrong with your fellows (Matthew 5:23-24). And it isn't just a matter of saying sorry to God that things are as they are. We have to put them right. That may be costly as it hurts our pride when we have to apologise, but we must take the first step.

Selfish requests
There's a real difference between what we need and what we want, and sometimes we can't see it. Sometimes our requests are plain selfishness – and God's answer is a straight "No!" (James 4:2-3). God isn't an indulgent father who gives his children everything they cry for. He knows what's best for us. So we need to stop at times and ask ourselves just why we're praying for this or that.

Answers worked out
Sometimes we've already worked out what we think is going to be God's answer – but he thinks differently (2 Corinthians 12:7-10). At times we don't realise just what we are asking – if God gave it to us, it might be more than we bargained for!

Wrong approach
There are some people who don't get their prayers answered because they come in completely the wrong way. They barge in on God and tell him what he's got to do for them – and then they get hurt when he doesn't do it (Isaiah 45:11). Let's remember that we don't get heard because of who we are, but because of God's mercy and grace towards us.

Lacking faith
One reason why we may not get answers is that we may be coming to God doubting that he can really do anything about our needs. Jesus often demanded faith when he worked miracles (Matthew 13:53-58), and he taught that faith was necessary for answered prayer (Matthew 21:22). One of our added problems is that our culture doubts the reality and power of God, and we have to unlearn this if we are going to prove God in prayer.

Giving up
As we shall see, Jesus told his friends on more than one occasion not to give up but to go on praying till they got an answer (Luke 18:1). There may be several reasons why God delays his answers, but he knows best and sometimes, in his perfect, loving will for us, his answer is "Wait". It's often only as we carry on praying that we can see God's larger purpose for us or for our friends.

OVER TO YOU
Look back at the reasons given here why God may not answer your prayers. Have you given up praying? Talk to him honestly about your thoughts and feelings.

When God seems far away
PSALMS 42 & 43

There are times when we feel nothing like praying, when God seems to have left us. But those are the very occasions when we need to hang on as the psalmist did.

Depression

If you've ever been really depressed these psalms will speak to you. This poor man had trusted in God, and God seemed to have let him down. Things had gone badly. Unkind people were pouring scorn on his faith (42:3,10). He was far away from the temple where he used to worship God so gladly – the very memory of it depressed him all the more (42:4)! Worst of all, his own feelings were at rock bottom. He couldn't understand why he felt the way he did (42:5,11).

There might be all kinds of reasons for this – a good deal of depression is not spiritual at all but has to do with our health – but we all know something of it, sadly some more than others. And it affects our Christian lives. Is there any answer?

Hope

The psalmist begins by deliberately turning his thoughts to God (beginning of 42:6). God is still God whether we feel like it or not. And he is still in control. The flood of sorrow and circumstances that had overwhelmed this man were somehow part of God's purpose (42:7). God is still there and loving, even though he might be temporarily out of reach (42:8).

What's more, among the sadness and despair there's hope – a forward-looking faith which assured him that although he couldn't see why things were as they were, God would come to his rescue (42:11; 43:5). So he prays that the Lord would restore him and his happiness – the happiness which comes from worshipping and praising God (43:4).

In the meantime, although he still has no answer to his questioning, he trusts, as we must at times, in spite of his feelings, that God would bring him through. That's real faith.

OVER TO YOU

You may need to talk to yourself – to speak truth into your own life. Remind yourself who God is, what he has done and what he has promised to do, and allow these thoughts to affect your life.

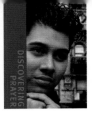

Getting right with God

PSALM 51

How can I pray if I have a bad conscience; if there are things in my life which offend God? Thank the Lord there is a way back: the way of confession and brokenness.

Confessing my sin

The psalmist uses several different pictures of sin here (verses 1-2). It's rebellion; it's uncleanness; it's falling short of what we should be. He's also aware that sin cuts us off from God, and that there's nothing we can do about it ourselves – except to acknowledge it (verses 3-5). This is hard because it hits at our pride. It means admitting that we are wrong and need to be put right, and doing that with real sorrow and grief that it ever happened.

Pleading his mercy

The very fact that a sinner can pray at all tells us something about the God of the Bible. God doesn't just wash his hands of us when we go astray. Our sins certainly hurt him and though he must condemn them for what they are, he is still a God who loves what he made. It's because of this that the psalmist throws himself on God's mercy (verse 1). Nothing he can do will earn forgiveness. And let's remember that this same mercy sent Jesus to the cross for us.

Asking for cleansing

Like the psalmist, all we can do is to ask God to clear the account (verses 1-2,7,9). That's the way to a clear conscience, to praise and to a fresh testimony to what God can do (verses 8,12-15).

But the psalmist asks for more than forgiveness. He wants a whole new attitude which will prevent him from making the same mistakes again (verses 6,10). That's real repentance, not just turning from your sins, but also breaking with them. And that's what God looks for on the part of those who want to get right with him.

> " *f or I know my transgressions, and my sin is always before me. Against you, you only, have I sinned and done what is evil in your sight.*"
>
> PSALM 51:3-4

OVER TO YOU

Spend some time thinking about Jesus Christ dying on the cross for you, to take away your sin. Turn back to him, confessing any sins, and thank him for his forgiveness.

DISCOVERING PRAYER
What should I pray for?

It's useful to study the Bible to see what the people of God prayed about in the past. It gives us some idea of what to ask for and how to ask.

People in need

These come high on the list, especially if we know them personally. We only have to remember that God loves people and that what hurts them hurts him too. Because Jesus came and suffered in the way we do, we are assured of a sympathetic hearing (Hebrews 2:17-18; 4:14-16). So we can ask him about people who are sick or troubled or hungry or out of work or tempted. Sometimes we don't know what to pray, but simply bringing them and their need to Jesus is enough. He knows what's best for them.

The land I live in

We may be members of Christ's kingdom now, but we still have strong natural links with those who live around us. Our first concern will be that they might come to know Christ too. It should begin with our neighbours; it ought to include our rulers and government. But we should also pray in more general terms that good may prevail and that evil might be restrained. So we can ask God to bring his gracious influence to bear on our lawmakers and our leaders in industry, our media and our writers, our business executives and our teachers (1 Timothy 2:1-2).

The church I belong to

When we come to know Christ, other Christians become family to us. They are, therefore, obvious people to pray for. We join some in thanksgiving for God's goodness, while we get alongside others in their troubles. Unfortunately, whatever church we belong to leaves a lot to be desired when we measure it by what God looks for among his people. That's why we pray, not just for our own fellowship, but for God's people at large, that he might make us what we really ought to be.

God's work in the world

Just as Jesus died for people of all nations, God is at present working throughout the world. We need to pray for those involved: for ministers, missionaries and Christian workers of various kinds, that we might see God's purpose fulfilled in our generation (Ephesians 6:19-20). We should have a special place in our prayers for those situations where it is extremely difficult to get a hearing for the good news – and for those Christians who are suffering for their faith.

And after all this ...

We can then bring our own personal needs to God!

Perhaps the task seems so big that we might be tempted to give up before we begin! So start by praying specifically about those needs and people that God gives you a special concern for. After all, only God can carry the troubles of the whole world.

OVER TO YOU

Look back over the people mentioned on this page. Who could you pray for whom you don't pray for usually?

DISCOVERING PRAYER
Pure praise
PSALM 103

There are times when it's good to stop asking God for things, and to start thanking him for who he is and what he's done. This psalm is praise from start to finish. It contains no requests at all.

Count your blessings
The psalmist begins by listing some of the ways in which God has helped and blessed him (verses 1-5). Notice that he reminds us to be thankful for material and physical blessings as well as for spiritual ones. They all come from God. Unfortunately we often take them for granted until we lose them.

God is kind and caring
That's the psalmist's conclusion. God looks after those who can't fend for themselves (verse 6). He guides his people in his own gracious purpose for them (verse 7). He forgives and restores us, even when we go astray (verses 8-12). The greatness of his love can only be compared with the distance he removes our sins from us!

Feeling weak?
God does not expect from us more than we can give. He is like a father making allowances for his little children (verse 13). He knows that we are "dust", pitifully weak, and so temporary (verses 14-16). Wonderfully, those who trust him can face both time and eternity (verses 17-18).

> " *Praise the LORD, O my soul; all my inmost being, praise his holy name. Praise the LORD, O my soul, and forget not all his benefits –* "
>
> PSALM 103:1-2

Praise God everybody!
Praise can't just be a private affair. Everybody must know and everybody must acknowledge the greatness of our God who is in absolute control. God deserves praise, honour, worship and thanksgiving from everything he made. *He deserves it from you!* (verses 19-22).

OVER TO YOU
Sit down and think of what God *has* done for you – not only specific answers to prayers, but all his gentle, powerful overruling in your life – often behind the scenes and out of sight. Spend some time thanking God for all this.

Prayer in earnest

DANIEL 9:1-19

Too often our prayers are half-hearted. It sometimes takes a crisis or a deep-felt need to make us really seek God. Daniel puts us to shame.

Meaning business

Daniel's concern arose out of his study of God's word (verse 2), and in the same way reading our Bibles often stimulates us to pray. What God has said, he will do, if we are prepared to cooperate. And Daniel was prepared (verses 3-4). He really meant to hold God to his word. God never disregards this kind of wholehearted prayer.

No excuses

Much of Daniel's prayer is an open, honest, no-excuses, confession of sin (verses 5-11). He felt the failings of his people so deeply that he included himself in that confession. He admitted that he was just as guilty even though he hadn't been involved in past events.

If we want answers to our prayers, we need to remember that there can be no self-righteousness where God is concerned. He sees us as we really are.

Real reasons

Why should God answer Daniel's prayers – or ours? Look at the arguments he used:
· God had given his promise in his word, and God does not contradict himself (verse 2).
· God himself had not changed; he was still faithful and loving (verse 4).
· God had delivered them in the past and could do so again (verse 15).
· God had committed himself to his people; they were his (verses 15-16,19).
· God was merciful, even though they did not deserve his love (verses 9,18).

And we can come to God with even greater confidence than Daniel, because we know that Jesus died to make it all possible.

" O LORD, listen!
O LORD, forgive!
O LORD, hear and act!"

DANIEL 9:19

OVER TO YOU

In this passage, we've seen how Daniel prayed according to God's will. God acts not only because he has promised to but also because his people pray. Here are three promises God has made that we can confidently ask him to fulfil:
· The gospel *will* reach to the ends of the earth (Matthew 24:14).
· God's word *will* have an effect on those who hear it (Isaiah 55:10-11).
· The Lord Jesus Christ *will* come again in glory and great power. "Come, Lord Jesus!" (Revelation 22:20).
  Pray over these promises now.

God's special recipe for prayer

We are discovering in our Bible readings that praying covers more than just asking for things and is even more than just about people. When we come to God there are a good number of other ingredients that make up prayer.

Acknowledge God's greatness

That's what we mean by "praise" or "worship". It's giving God something of the honour he deserves simply because of who he is (Psalm 95:1-7). He's the One who made us; the One who keeps this world going; the One who supplies our needs. His power is limitless. His splendour is utterly beyond us!

But he's more than great, he's holy, too. Just, righteous, faithful, true – a God who stirs our admiration and wonder to be expressed in adoration, especially when we think of the way in which he reached out to rescue us. Let's praise him!

Show you're grateful

Instead of just bringing an endless string of requests, stop and thank him for what he's done for you – and has given you – which is everything that's good and worthwhile in your life. We're so ungrateful that we can take his many generous gifts for granted, and even complain when things don't work out quite as we want them to. Come to him with heartfelt thanksgiving (Luke 17:11-19)!

Admit your faults

We are in no position to bargain with God. We have all broken his laws and gone our own way, asserting our independence from him. It's only because he is a merciful and gracious God that we dare approach him at all. We know this because of what Jesus had to do for us on the cross. That's why we come "in Jesus' name" – that is, on the basis of who he is and what he's done for us. Thank God that when we confess our sins, he has promised to forgive them for Jesus' sake (1 John 1:5-10).

Ask for others

As you become aware of the needs of other people – sometimes those near and dear to you, sometimes distant from you – bring them to a God who sees and knows and loves everyone (1 Timothy 2:1-6). Because he is God, we can ask for people on the other side of the world; because he's great we can ask for some whom others may have written off. As we pray for those involved in God's work, it's as though we were there, working alongside them. They feel it when we don't.

Bring your own needs

God is interested in *you* – not just in major crises or troubles, although we do come to him most readily and eagerly then – but in the ordinary round of our everyday lives. You can pray about anything and everything, about your spiritual, your physical and your material needs (Philippians 4:6-7). In this way you begin to let God into each and every aspect of your life, which, after all, is what Christian living is all about.

OVER TO YOU

Which actions in prayer do you find come most easily to you? Which do you find most difficult? Talk to God honestly about your response.

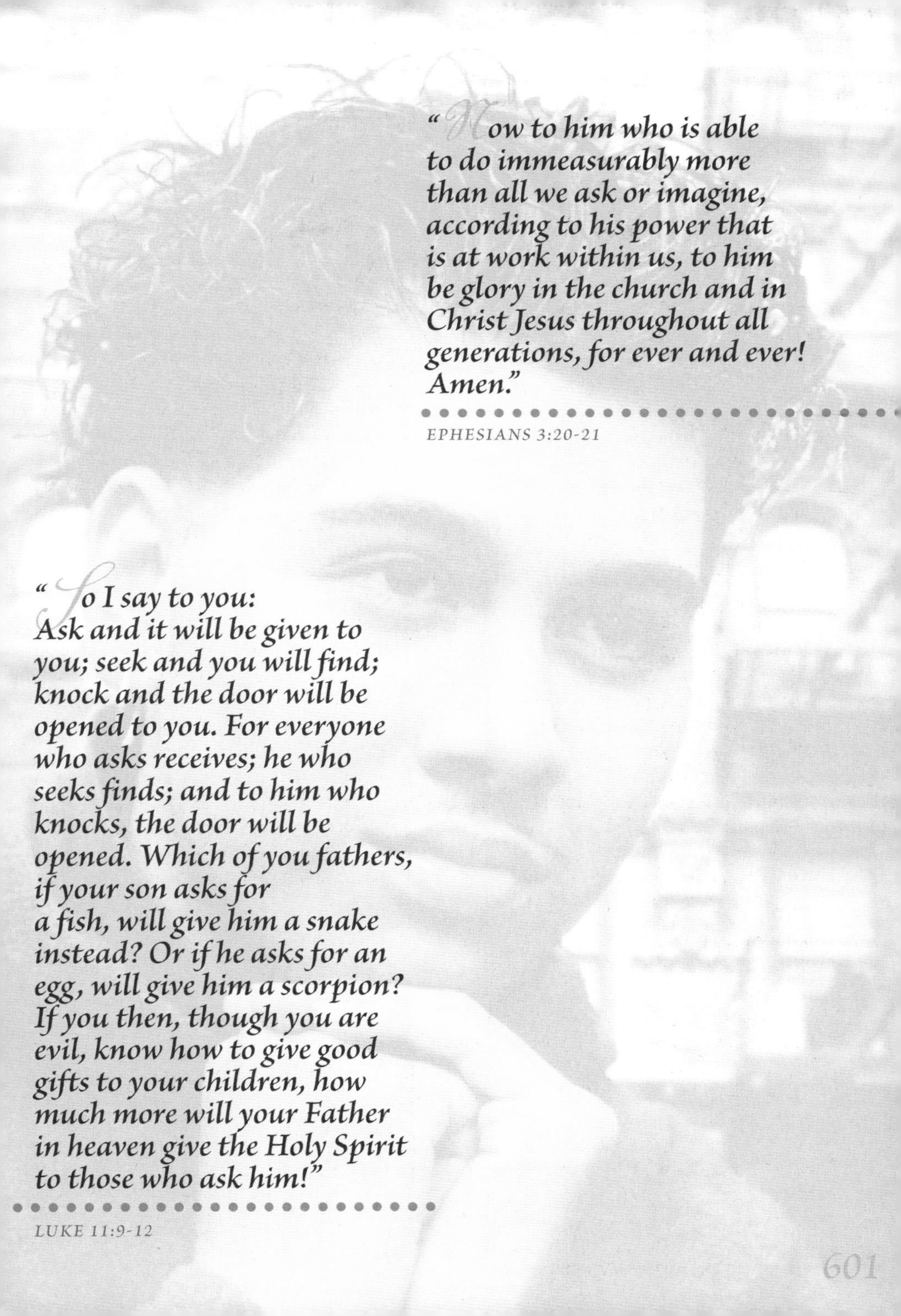

" ow to him who is able to do immeasurably more than all we ask or imagine, according to his power that is at work within us, to him be glory in the church and in Christ Jesus throughout all generations, for ever and ever! Amen."

EPHESIANS 3:20-21

" o I say to you: Ask and it will be given to you; seek and you will find; knock and the door will be opened to you. For everyone who asks receives; he who seeks finds; and to him who knocks, the door will be opened. Which of you fathers, if your son asks for a fish, will give him a snake instead? Or if he asks for an egg, will give him a scorpion? If you then, though you are evil, know how to give good gifts to your children, how much more will your Father in heaven give the Holy Spirit to those who ask him!"

LUKE 11:9-12

A wise and loving Father

MATTHEW 6:5-15

The Jews of Jesus' day thought they knew all about praying, but he had to put them right on some things just as he has to correct us.

Between you and God

The people Jesus criticised were those who were using their religion to make others think highly of them. In contrast, he tells us that it's a personal matter between God and ourselves (verses 5-6).

How deeply do you really know the Lord? How much time do you take to be with him on your own? Someone once said, "The secret of religion is religion in secret."

God knows

As we've already seen, praying isn't twisting God's arm. It isn't even a matter of using the right words, or a lot of them. Praying means coming in confidence to a heavenly Father who loves us and who already knows what we need. But as with any human father, our coming and asking – our personal relationship with him – is more important to him than just meeting our needs.

A pattern prayer

Jesus gives us an example of what prayer should be like. Notice how it's made up:
· It begins with acknowledging who God is and the fact that we must be prepared to do what he wants (verses 9-10).
· It goes on to list some very basic and simple requests (verses 11-13). Note that our physical needs are as important to God as our spiritual ones.

Between you and others

Praying may be private to you and the Lord, but others are involved too. It's a basic rule that we can't be right with God if we're wrong with someone else. Here the emphasis is on forgiving others (verses 14-15). If we know what it is to be forgiven ourselves, we will readily forgive those who have wronged us. And as we do, we open ourselves further to God's grace and mercy.

OVER TO YOU

Take one line of the Lord's Prayer and spend a few minutes thinking and praying about it. Tomorrow, move on to the next line and the day after, to the next and so on, so that you begin to take in more of the depth of Jesus' words.

DISCOVERING PRAYER
Pictures of prayer
LUKE 11 & 18

Jesus sometimes used parables – pictures from everyday life – to get across important lessons about praying.

The friend at midnight

Jesus is telling us here that, if we really want an answer from God, we must ask and go on asking. Sometimes it takes a while before we see answers to our prayers. We're tempted to give up and say that God doesn't answer prayer at all.

But there may be other, deeper reasons for delay that we can't understand. In the meantime we must get on with the job of praying. After all, he only ever wants to give us the very best. How much do we really want it?

The unjust judge

This is one of those stories which are meant to contrast strongly with the way God deals with us. God is not unjust. So if this unscrupulous man eventually gave in to this poor widow who had no influence with him, how much more will your heavenly Father hear and answer your prayers? So don't give up; go on!

The Pharisee and the tax-collector

Two men pray; one is heard while the other's prayers go no higher than the ceiling. Why?

The crowds who listened to Jesus would have expected the Pharisee's prayer to be heard. After all, he did all those things he claimed, while the tax-collector ... why, in those days, he was a complete outcast! But Jesus points out the fatal flaw in the religious man's efforts. It all came from himself. He had done it and he was proud of it.

> " *Then Jesus told his disciples a parable to show them that they should always pray and not give up ...*"

LUKE 18:1

But the good news is about God doing things for sinners, beginning with forgiving their sins. That's why the tax-collector knew peace with God, and why the Pharisee only went home with his own self-esteem.

God hears us when we realise that we are the spiritual bankrupts the Bible says we are.

OVER TO YOU

Which of these stories do you particularly need to take to heart and act on?

Jesus' path of prayer

One of the things which tells us just how human Jesus was is his prayer life. Although he enjoyed a special relationship with his Father, while he was here on earth he had fellowship with him through prayer.

A lifelong habit

From the beginning of his ministry we find Jesus making time for prayer. In the busyness of his crowded life he needed to commune quietly with his Father. So we find him getting away from the crowds, and even from his own disciples, to pray (Mark 1:35; Luke 5:16; Matthew 14:23). When he did pray with others around, there was something about him which made them ask him to teach them too (Luke 11:1). Remember this when you're tempted to put other things before your prayer time. If Jesus needed to pray, how much more do we?

Significant stages

We also find Jesus praying specifically at those turning points in his life when new things were about to happen. He prayed at his baptism (Luke 3:21), which marked the beginning of his public work; all night before he appointed the twelve disciples (Luke 6:12); and just before Peter confessed him to be the promised Christ (Luke 9:18).

We find him praying when his followers saw something of his real glory on the mountain (Luke 9:28-29), and just before he raised his friend, Lazarus (John 11:41-42). He had told his friends to pray for more workers to share the good news (Matthew 9:38), but he himself prayed when he got a glimpse of his worldwide ministry (John 12:27-28).

He prayed before he went out to his betrayal (John 17), and perhaps his best-known prayer was in the Garden of Gethsemane (Matthew 26:36-46). There Jesus wrestled as we often do with the choice between obeying his Father or taking an easier way (see also Hebrews 5:7).

All this adds up to an important lesson for us, and that is to take our major decisions, crises and problems to the Lord.

From the cross

It tells us a great deal about Jesus that his first prayer in the agony of being crucified was for those who had put him there (Luke 23:34). Are we as forgiving to those who hurt us? The best antidote to bitterness is to take that hurt or grief to God.

Throughout his life Jesus had addressed God as his Father. On the cross, bearing the load of human sin, he prayed, "My God ... why have you abandoned me?" (Matthew 27:46; Psalm 22:1). Remember what it cost him to put us right with God the Father.

At the very end he expressed a trust he had taught others about (Luke 23:46). In life and in death, Jesus left Christians an example to follow in prayer.

OVER TO YOU

What practical steps can you take to imitate the life of prayer of the Lord Jesus?

DISCOVERING PRAYER
Last requests
JOHN 17

We have one or two examples of Jesus' prayers, but the longest is his prayer for his friends just before he went to the cross. He was returning to glory; they were to be left in the world.

Jesus and his Father
All through this prayer we get glimpses of Jesus' close and intimate relationship with his Father:

- He had been with the Father sharing his glory, when the world was made, long before he came here (verses 5,24).
- He had lived out his life in perfect obedience to and oneness with his Father (verses 4,11,19,21).

" *Now this is eternal life: that they may know you, the only true God, and Jesus Christ, whom you have sent.* "

JOHN 17:3

This is what qualified him in a unique way to pray for others. He no doubt often prayed for his friends. However, on this occasion he seems to be praying out loud in order to reassure them (verse 13).

Jesus and his friends
It's interesting that, apart from asking to return to his Father, Jesus doesn't really pray for himself. He reserves that for the Garden of Gethsemane. Instead he prays for his friends – and we're told elsewhere that he's still praying for his followers. What did he want for them? After all, this would be the last time he would be with them before the cross. He asks:

- that they might be kept safe in a hostile world (verses 11,16), but not that they might be spared suffering.
- that they might be wholly committed to the Father and to doing his will just as he had been himself (verse 17).
- that others, who would believe because of their testimony, might find a loving oneness with them, and that in that way they might demonstrate Christ's power and glory to the whole world (verses 21-22).
- that one day, when all the troubles of this world are over, they might be with him in glory (verse 24).

I wonder if that's the kind of thing we would pray for the church or for our friends.

OVER TO YOU

Jesus' prayer in John 17 takes us to the heart of prayer: our relationship with God (verse 3). What effect should this have on you? Be practical.

Prayer in crisis

ACTS 4:1-31

Crises always drove God's people to prayer, and this example from the early days of the church puts trouble into its proper perspective.

The opposition

We can understand the authorities' action. Both the healing miracle and the boldness of the apostles pointed to the power of Jesus – and the authorities had put Jesus on the cross. Although they couldn't openly punish them, they could threaten them. But the disciples saw it in a different light.

The opposition was to be expected; it had been foretold, just as the cross had been. So these things didn't take them – or God – by surprise. In fact, he was in absolute control, working out his plan through their troubles. That's something we need to learn and which we often only come to when a crisis drives us to our knees. That problem of yours isn't yours at all – it's really his if you are his!

The response

What would you have prayed in their place? For rest and quietness? Beginning with the person of God himself, they then went on the offensive in prayer! They assumed that God was on *their* side, and they asked him for courage to go on doing exactly what they knew they should (verse 29). They asked for further miracles – not so that the people might think highly of them, but in order to enhance Jesus' reputation (verse 30).

> " *P*eter and John went back to their own people and reported all that the chief priests and elders had said to them. When they heard this, they raised their voices together in prayer to God. 'Sovereign Lord ...' "
>
> *ACTS 4:23-24*

The results

God answered their prayers: immediately, by a tangible surge of power through the place; and in the days that followed, by giving them courage to carry on where they had been told to leave off (verse 31). In time, it would lead to further troubles – but who cares as long as you are in God's will doing what he wants? Give your problem to God; it doesn't belong to you any more. And then get on with what he wants you to do!

OVER TO YOU

How does this reading affect your response to any problems you have at the moment?

The Holy Spirit and prayer

Left to ourselves, we might never pray at all, unless it was to bring selfish demands to a God we thought we could manipulate. It's the Holy Spirit who prompts us to pray properly, and who teaches us what prayer is all about.

Those first steps

When we first sensed that we needed God – or that we had miserably failed to be what we should be, it was the Spirit showing us ourselves as God sees us (John 16:8-11). This happened when Peter preached the first Christian sermon in the power of the Spirit (Acts 2:37). So it's the Spirit who prompts us to pray that first prayer of commitment to Christ. In fact, one of the signs that God is at work in our lives is that we begin to pray (Acts 9:11). It is he who gives us an appetite for spiritual things that we didn't have before, an appetite which expresses itself in prayer.

God's Spirit and God's word

It's the Holy Spirit who also brings God's truth to life for us (John 16:13). He not only makes Jesus real to us (John 16:14), he shows us that we can take and claim God's promises in the Bible. This is why studying the Bible often proves to be a good springboard for prayer. We see the ways in which God heard and answered prayer in the past; we learn about the kind of God we are coming to in prayer; and we are encouraged to expect prayer to work for us too. For many people Bible study and prayer form part of their daily routine. They let God speak to them by his Spirit through his word, and then they speak to him through the God-given channel of prayer.

Lessons in prayer

One of our most common problems in prayer is that we don't really know what God's will is, and therefore we don't know what to ask for. Once again the Holy Spirit comes to our aid.

He prompts our thinking and our speaking so that we begin to ask for the things God wants to give (Romans 8:26-27; Ephesians 6:18; Jude 20). What's more, he himself prays for us, expressing our needs perfectly.

God-given faith

As we've seen, we need faith if we're going to receive answers to prayer. But faith itself is a gift from God. Paul described it as part of what the Spirit produces in the lives of Christians (*faithfulness*, Galatians 5:22). As we grow nearer to Christ, we grow in our faith. Our hold on God and his promises becomes stronger, and we become more qualified to prove them for ourselves.

James seems to be saying a similar thing when he writes about praying in faith (James 5:16). Quite literally this means it is the divinely energised prayer of a good person that is effective.

OVER TO YOU

Looking back over your Christian life, express your thankfulness in prayer for what God's word the Bible and God's Spirit have meant to you personally. Let the Holy Spirit inspire your prayers!

DISCOVERING PRAYER
More than we ask for
ACTS 12:1-19

Sometimes when we pray, God's answers are so surprising that it's difficult to take in what he has done.

Grim outlook

Nothing sharpens our spiritual experience like suffering. That's why God sometimes allows opposition to come our way. It refines the church when believers have to stand up and be counted.

Although the early Christians had no fear of death, the removal of key leaders would have set the work back and hurt the church. So Peter's arrest led to desperate prayer (verse 5). In the circumstances they could do nothing else.

A lesson for us?

We should not pray for persecution – wanting to suffer is unhealthy. But we should be prepared for it and know how to respond to it. And when it comes, if it reduces us to earnest prayer, it can't be entirely bad for us!

Divine intervention

God can do the impossible. He can redeem a hopeless situation. He can work miracles (verses 6-11). We must begin with that fact when we pray. He is waiting for us to prove it for ourselves.

Unbelievable answer

We can sympathise with the people's reaction (verse 15) but it did betray something which we know all too well. The fact was, although they had prayed earnestly, they still could not believe that God would really answer as he had done.

God does sometimes stagger us with what he does, but we have to admit that, far too often, we do not really pray believing that he can do what we look for. Perhaps his surprises in this way are to encourage us to expect more when we ask. The possibilities really are unlimited where God is concerned!

OVER TO YOU

Prayer was the power-house of the early church. What practical steps can you take to know prayer as the way in which God's power becomes effective, overcoming the barriers of space, culture or even prison bars?

DISCOVERING PRAYER

Prayers from prison

EPHESIANS 1 & 3

Although in jail for his faith, Paul reminds his friends of the tremendous privilege of belonging to Christ – and then goes on to pray that the lesson might be driven home.

You're millionaires!

There is so much that God wants to do for us. Paul is praying here that his friends might realise this and allow the Holy Spirit to work it out in their lives (1:18). The power at their disposal was unlimited. It was the same power that operated when Jesus rose from the dead (1:19-20). They believed that Christ was risen and reigning now (1:21-22). Paul prays that they might see some evidence of that fact there and then in the lives of Christians in his church.

The challenge this presents

Do we really believe this? Do we expect God to work among us and our churches today as he did in New Testament times? Perhaps one of the reasons we often don't is that this way of living would be far too disturbing!

Scaling the heights

What is the *most* you could ever ask for yourself or someone else? Paul's requests here must come pretty near to that:

· that they might know the unlimited power of the Spirit at work at the very roots of their personalities changing them from the inside out (3:16).
· that the Lord Jesus may feel fully at home in their hearts and lives (3:17).
· that, beginning in that strong security which is God's love, they might go on to know its unknowable, limitless extent (3:18-19).
· that God himself might saturate them and all that they do or say or think (3:19).

Is this all too much to ask? But if God

> " *N*ow to him who is able to do immeasurably more than all we ask or imagine, according to his power that is at work within us, to him be glory in the church and in Christ Jesus throughout all generations, for ever and ever! Amen. "

EPHESIANS 3:20-21

almighty really is at work in our lives, there is quite literally no limit to what he can do for us (3:20-21)!

OVER TO YOU

What is the most you could ever ask for yourself or someone else? Name certain Christian friends to God and pray Paul's prayer in Ephesians 3:16-21 for them.

God's high-powered priority – prayer in the church

The early church began in a prayer meeting (Acts 1:14), and it's obvious from the rest of the story, as from the letters, that prayer formed a vital part of what they did in those exciting days.

Together and alone

Although they frequently gathered together for prayer, individuals also spent time with God on their own (Acts 10:9). We know that prayer meant a great deal to the apostle Paul. Prevented from visiting some of the churches, he prayed for them (Philippians 1:4,9-11; 1 Thessalonians 1:2; Philemon 4-6), and asked for their prayers for himself and his companions (Ephesians 6:18-20; Philippians 1:19; 2 Thessalonians 3:1-2).

The reason for this was that in those days they really believed that prayer achieved something (2 Corinthians 1:11)! In fact, part of the apostles' full-time work was to pray (Acts 6:4).

Prayer was taught

From the very beginning, new Christians were involved in praying (Acts 2:42), and there are many references in the letters to the need for continuing prayer:

· This was the way they had come to Christ (Romans 10:12-13), and this was how they were taught to go on (1 Timothy 2:8).
· They could now call God their Father (Galatians 4:6), and turn all their needs into prayers (Philippians 4:6; 1 Peter 5:7).
· Prayer was to become a habit (1 Thessalonians 5:17; 1 Peter 3:7).
· They were told to draw near boldly to a great God (Hebrews 4:16; 13:18), and to ask God for what they needed (James 1:5; 4:2,8).

On special occasions

Special needs draw out special prayer. As the leadership of the early churches was particularly important, we find that it was prayed about (Acts 6:6; 14:23). We also find Paul praying with church leaders (Acts 20:36). They also prayed as new stages of the work opened up (Acts 8:15). It was during a prayer meeting that Paul and Barnabas were singled out as missionaries (Acts 13:2-3). They prayed for the sick (Acts 9:40; 28:8; James 5:14-15), and saw their prayers wonderfully answered.

People in the early church prayed particularly in times of crisis and trouble (Acts 4:24-31; 12:5,12). As Stephen, the first Christian martyr, was stoned to death, he prayed to Jesus (Acts 7:59). Unfortunately, all too often, it's only when we face some crisis or illness that we really begin to pray. The first Christians put us to shame by their prayer lives, just as they make us envious of the blessings they enjoyed. But if we practised more of the former, we would know more of the latter!

OVER TO YOU

Think about times of prayer that you spend with other Christians. In what ways do you need to develop to become more like the Christians in the New Testament?

DISCOVERING PRAYER

Prayer for new Christians

COLOSSIANS 1:1-14

Paul couldn't visit this young church, but he could write – and he could pray.
Prayers span the miles just as surely as letters!

Thank you, Lord

The apostle was always thanking God for what God was doing by changing people's lives. Most of his letters begin with gratitude. Is there a lesson for us here?

In this case, Paul sums up the way they had responded to the good news as faith – their initial commitment to Jesus; as love – that new-found affection which God gave them for each other; and as hope – which grasped

" *For this reason, since the day we heard about you, we have not stopped praying for you and asking God to fill you with the knowledge of his will through all spiritual wisdom and understanding. And we pray this in order that you may live a life worthy of the Lord and may please him in every way: bearing fruit in every good work, growing in the knowledge of God, being strengthened with all power according to his glorious might so that you may have great endurance and patience, and joyfully giving thanks to the Father, who has qualified you to share in the inheritance of the saints in the kingdom of light. For he has rescued us from the dominion of darkness and brought us into the kingdom of the Son he loves, in whom we have redemption, the forgiveness of sins.*"

COLOSSIANS 1:9-14

God's plan for the future (verses 3-8). We should also be grateful for what we see God doing in the lives of others.

Take them on, Lord

Beginning isn't everything. They had to go on to prove even more of what God could do for them. What does Paul ask for these new Christians?

· that they might know what God wants, his will and plan for their lives (verse 9)
· that this might in turn lead to living for him daily. That would mean pleasing him and a radical change in their behaviour (verse 10)
· that they might not simply know about him, but that they might come to know him personally far better (verse 10)
· that he might give them strength to go on, facing the rough and tumble of life – not with resignation, but with joy at the privilege of being his (verses 11-12).

If we're honest, our prayers for other people seldom reach these heights. We ask that they might be kept safe or well or happy. Paul asked that his friends might really begin to work out what it means to be a citizen in Christ's kingdom – here on earth!

OVER TO YOU

Try and learn one of Paul's prayers, for example verses 9 to 14 of this reading. Then pray it for others ... and for yourself!

Praying in faith

JAMES 5:7-20

James gives us a valuable insight into how the church prayed in those days – and a valuable lesson in the art of praying.

Praise and prayer

These are natural outlets for the Christian's feelings (verse 13). Those who are happy realise that all their happiness comes from God – and praise him!

But we don't always feel like praising God. Sometimes we're pressed down with troubles, and then we just as naturally pray, bringing our needs to a God who can change things.

Praying for the sick

In those days when medical knowledge was limited, sickness was even more devastating

The praying prophet

God's answers to prayers in the past encourage us to take him at his word ourselves. Elijah was a wonderful example in this respect (verses 17-18). The point James is making is that he was no different from us. He was a weak human being like the rest, and yet, believing that God would answer, he saw what God could do in extraordinary ways. For prayer is God's own mysterious way of tapping his limitless resources. We may not understand how it works, but when we begin to take him at his word and put it into practice, we discover that it does. For the best way to learn about prayer is – by praying!

> " *The prayer of a righteous man is powerful and effective.* "

JAMES 5:16

than it is today – and there are times today when medical science can do nothing for our friends. But God can heal and restore if he chooses, so it's natural to ask him to do so (verses 14-15).

However, this is no blanket promise that God will heal every sick person. The wording here seems to say that God must also give the faith and prompt the praying. After all, there are times when God allows us to suffer, and even death itself has no terror for the Christian. Notice that James is as concerned here for their spiritual health as for their bodily fitness (verse 16).

OVER TO YOU

You might find it helpful to keep a note of what you have prayed for and also to note when God answers your prayers.

"Abiding" in Jesus

Our relationship with God is often an intermittent affair, and this is reflected in our prayer life. We may pray on Sundays or in times of trial, or even in daily times of prayer – and it stops there. But Jesus promised something far better than this.

What is possible

Jesus had a continuous relationship with the Father. Nothing ever came between them, and although Jesus had set times of prayer, he lived in complete, daily harmony with his Father. He promised that a similar relationship was possible for us (John 15:1-17). As long as a shoot remains united with a vine stem, the life-giving, fruit-forming sap can flow along it. In the same way, Christian living is Christ's life flowing through ours – and that depends on our maintaining that continuous, ongoing link with him. Paul also taught that each Christian was "in Christ", and that Christ was in him by the Holy Spirit, while elsewhere we find the idea of "walking with God" every day, which is the same thing.

What is important for our prayer lives is that Jesus told us that this is the way in which we get answers (John 15:7).

How it is done

Jesus linked this "abiding" or "remaining" with his "words" (John 15:7). This means filling our minds with what he has taught us, letting his teaching shape our attitudes and outlook (Colossians 3:16; 1 John 2:24-25). This will mean letting the Lord into everything we do, something that has been called "practising the presence of God". For the Lord is there not only in specific times of prayer and worship; he is also present as we go about our ordinary, everyday affairs, in our homes, at work or in our leisure time, and we can lift our hearts to him just where we are (1 Thessalonians 5:17). You can see why this leads to answered prayer. Living like that, we begin to think Christ's thoughts after him, so that when we pray, we ask for what he wants us to have.

The price to pay

Jesus pointed out that this kind of living was costly. The vine shoots need pruning in order to be fruitful (John 15:2). This means that things in our lives which he hates have to go, for there can be no abiding without obeying (John 15:10; 1 John 3:6). And John ties answered prayer to obedience (1 John 3:22). So if we want our prayers answered, we must deliberately break with those things which God shows us are sinful, and we must just as deliberately try to do what he wants (Colossians 3:5-10). For praying – opening ourselves, our needs, our concerns to God – is more than a practice, more than a religious exercise, more even than a devotional habit. It's a way of life!

OVER TO YOU

Think what God has been doing in your own life as you have read through these studies. Spend some time in worship and thanksgiving and enjoy his company as you share what you have learnt with him.

Discovering discipleship

Real disciples – isn't that what God wants ... and what the world needs?
Here are several specially chosen passages in the Gospels to help us see the master
disciple-maker, the Lord Jesus Christ himself, at work. For about three years the
first disciples followed him everywhere – observing, listening, asking, even
criticising and arguing with him!

They made mistakes, but they kept learning. We can identify with them
in their struggles to understand and follow Jesus. We will grow in our own
discipleship under him!

Come and see!
JOHN 1:35-51

Time to decide

What a strange opening conversation between the first two disciples and Jesus! Both sides seemed cautious. But the fact that they had been John the Baptist's disciples shows they were seekers. Jesus did not rush them into discipleship. Rather he invited them to "Come and see" (verse 39). He wanted only those disciples who would take seriously the decision to follow him all the way.

Time for a change

Exactly what Jesus and the two disciples discussed we are not told (verses 40-42). But the result was a strong enough conviction to tell others they had found the Messiah, the long-expected hope of their nation. Note how different Jesus' encounter with Simon was from that with the others. What do you think Jesus saw in him to give him a new name?

We've found him!

Like the first two encounters with Jesus, the next two were also different (verses 43-51). Here Jesus took the initiative to add Philip to his band of disciples. Philip's conviction about Jesus became like Andrew and John's – deep enough to make him tell someone else, "We've found the Messiah – Jesus of Nazareth!" (verse 45).

At first Nathanael seemed a tough nut to crack. But Philip was wise not to argue about his prejudice against Jesus' home town. Instead, like Jesus, he invited Nathanael to "Come and see" (verse 46).

Think about the conversation between Jesus and Nathanael. Nathanael's response to Jesus' description of him in verses 47-48 might seem a bit humorous, "How did you know I was such a good Israelite?" Was it flattery that made him change his mind about Jesus' identity? No, Jesus' commendation of his character was genuine.

But Jesus went on to challenge him to faith for a greater revelation of himself. In fact, Jesus in different ways had also commended and challenged the other four disciples to greater faith in him.

OVER TO YOU

How do you respond to Jesus' invitation to "come and see" for ourselves whether we are ready for a deeper commitment to himself as Lord? He sees in us good things, weak things – and vast potential for his kingdom.

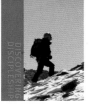

Jesus is Lord!

LUKE 5:1-11

Simon's first obedience

This lakeside event (verses 1-3) took place about one year after both the disciples' initial meeting with Jesus (John 1:35-51) and their first call to follow him (Mark 1:16-20). The present, second call shows that they had been following him only on and off. They had returned to their fishing business. They apparently followed him only when it was convenient!

Watch how Jesus caught these fishermen again for his business. First, he began naturally to involve Simon and his fishing partners in his growing ministry. This step of using Simon's boat was easy for the fishermen, like the first call to discipleship. Who wouldn't feel pride in helping the most popular preacher in town in full public view?

Simon's second obedience

But Jesus' second instruction (verse 4) was something else. Why, any fishermen knew that the best time to fish was at night, not in full sunlight! But to his credit, Simon obeyed Jesus, if reluctantly (verse 5). That was good enough for Jesus, who as a matter of fact knew more about fishing than Simon thought he did! His 51% obedience brought fishing results beyond his expectations – and beyond his ability to handle those results (verse 7).

Jesus had involved Simon. Simon now involved his partners. And everybody, including their families, benefited (verses 8-11)!

Simon's response

What a dramatic lesson for everyone (verses 8-11)! Jesus, the creator of fish and lakes, sunlight and fishermen, knew where the best fishing was. He knew well that the disciples' problems were material and personal:
· inadequate fish for their livelihood.
· inadequate faith in him.

He met a temporary need and an eternal need with one unforgettable act. See what this did to Simon Peter by comparing verses 5 and 8. Peter now began to see Jesus as Lord in an entirely new light. Jesus was worth following unconditionally!

OVER TO YOU

Look back at verses 4-7. When has your not obeying Jesus deprived others of God's benefits? What does your response to Jesus mean in your life (see verses 5, 8 and 11)?

Life in the Spirit

The Holy Spirit gives us new birth

As Christians we are born again by the working of the Holy Spirit (John 3:3-8; Titus 3:5). This comes about as our hearts and minds are convinced that we are far from God. So we repent – we turn from sin – and believe – by looking to the Lord Jesus Christ, trusting that his death on the cross is a sufficient sacrifice for our sin. As we commit ourselves to Jesus, he saves us, and the Holy Spirit comes to live in us.

The Holy Spirit glorifies Jesus

The great work of the Holy Spirit isn't to draw attention to himself, but to direct us to Jesus. Look up John 16:14-15. The Holy Spirit shows us the glory of God in Jesus, taking everything that is true about Jesus and making it real in our own lives.

The Holy Spirit assures us that we are God's children

The Holy Spirit assures us that we have a firm, unchanging relationship with Jesus. He confirms that we are God's children (Romans 8:15-17). Our faith would come alive if we knew the reality of such an assurance every day!

The Holy Spirit makes us more like Jesus

We should never forget that the Spirit of God is the *Holy* Spirit. He is pure and perfectly righteous. He is also the one who makes us clean: he clears up the pollution of sin in our lives (Ezekiel 36:25-27; 1 John 1:7,9).

As Christians, the power of sin no longer controls us. It does not rule in our lives because Jesus is our new "master" (Romans 6). But we find in practice that we still sin. Although we want to live a holy life, we find that we are frustrated by sin that still lingers in our bodies. We know the conflict that Paul

describes in Romans 7. We long to be completely free from sin!

Practically, this means that with the Spirit's help we need to put to death all traces of sin in our lives (Romans 8:13; Colossians 3:5). In this way we will become like Jesus and show the fruit of the Holy Spirit in our lives (Galatians 5:22-23).

The Holy Spirit gives gifts generously

God gives his gifts to every Christian (1 Corinthians 12), to build up the whole body of Christ (Ephesians 4:7-16). So, find out what your gift is and use it (Romans 12:4-8)!

Gifts are important, but they aren't the be-all and end-all of the Spirit's work. The church at Corinth had lots of gifts, but Paul had to write to tell them that holiness and love were even more important (1 Corinthians 6:19-20; 13).

The Holy Spirit gives us power

The Holy Spirit enables us to do what we could never do, if we were left to our own resources. He helps us give up bad habits, for example. He gives the power to tell others about Jesus, too (Acts 1:8; 4:33).

Being filled with the Spirit will affect our worship and relationships (Ephesians 5:18-21). And as we are filled with God's Spirit, we will keep in step with Jesus – our lives will be under the Spirit's control (Galatians 5:25).

> ### OVER TO YOU
> Which aspect of the work of the Holy Spirit do you need to know more? Turn your thoughts into prayer.

Radical discipleship

LUKE 5:12–6:11

Touching the untouchable

Lepers in that day were considered dead men, condemned to live among the tombs away from others. This man was full of leprosy – filthy, ragged, repulsive. Visualise Jesus' actions in verse 13, move after move. Such drama – and compassion! What "untouchable" does Jesus want you to reach out and touch for his sake?

Meeting the opposition

This event (verses 17-26) shows the beginning of opposition to Jesus. The religious leaders were in the house to criticise. Jesus was there to help. He knew they were accusing him of blasphemy, for which the penalty was death. Yet he went ahead to do the right thing – heal the man as a sign of his divine authority to forgive sins. He thus brought out their criticism and publicly challenged their doubt. How do you think his newly committed disciples felt?

Socialising with outcasts

The battle lines were now drawn (verses 27-32). This time the religious leaders attacked Jesus and his disciples by criticising their association with "low class" people. Jesus stepped right in to explain. By their friendships the disciples identified with his mission to call sinners to repentance, though they risked criticism from powerful leaders.

Celebrating new life

Jesus and his disciples became known more for having good times with people than for following certain religious traditions (verses 33-39). This offended people or at least provoked curiosity. Jesus again explained: in no way could those religious forms express the joyous new life he was bringing to people. Do you express his life in you with gloom or joy?

Celebrating God's goodness

The two incidents (6:1-11) here show how differently the Pharisees and Jesus viewed the Sabbath. The Pharisees had formulated hundreds of minute do's and don'ts for the Sabbath. Trying to follow them made people forget what its real purpose was – to celebrate God's care and goodness. Praise God that Jesus brings us back to that!

OVER TO YOU

Why did Jesus help so many needy people? What does this teach us about what we can do? How can we show a greater compassion and sensitivity towards the needs of other people? Try and think of practical things you can do!

From disciples to apostles
MATTHEW 10

Enormous risks

Look at verses 1-4. How amazing it is that Jesus committed his mission to such men as a self-inflated Simon Peter, hot-tempered brothers like James and John, an unimaginative Philip, a naïve Nathanael, a wavering Thomas, a fanatically nationalistic Simon and a treacherous Judas!

We're now at about the beginning of the third year in Jesus' ministry. During the second year, the twelve had followed, watched, absorbed, reacted and learned – but hadn't been assigned work by themselves. Now, Jesus delegates specific evangelistic work to them.

Practical instructions

The apostles' assignment (verses 5-15) was an immediate and temporary one, limited in area and time. So, it is not surprising that in verses 9-10 Jesus told them to travel lightly. Note also how practical he was in telling them what to do when people did not welcome the gospel. Jesus' instructions may seem irrelevant today. But remember that Jesus was challenging them and us to trust God for his provisions because it's his work.

Instructions for facing persecution

Jesus spared nothing in warning them of persecutions. He did not promise safety, but what did he promise? See verses 19-20,22-23. In sending his disciples into danger, Jesus was saying, "I've trained you. I've set you an example. I trust God for you."

Assurances about God's care

Jesus knew that after such solemn warnings, some of the timid disciples might be tempted to give up immediately. So he went on to assure them. Look especially at verses 28-31 for why we can be courageous.

Warnings and rewards

This temporary mission was to be a test case for the disciples' fitness to carry on his work (verses 32-42). The Lord Jesus challenges us equally today: Do we fear God or people? Would we risk family peace and loyalty for his sake? Would we follow him if it means death to self? If the answers are yes, Jesus promises us the rich rewards that come to obedient disciples.

> ## OVER TO YOU
> How can you encourage yourself – and others you know – to have a faith that is not only more real and fresh but also more outward-looking?

Growing up to maturity

They found fellowship

New Christians, like newborn babies, need special care. As we read through Acts, we see they found fellowship and received teaching; they were given direction as they became involved.

From the very beginning, new Christians were introduced to close sharing with other believers (Acts 2:42).

The Ethiopian official is the odd one out (Acts 8:26-40), for, generally speaking, the early church did not encourage isolated, individual Christians. Commitment to Christ obviously meant belonging to a church.

In the early church, new Christians were immediately baptised and identified themselves with a local fellowship (Acts 2:37–4:1; 9:17-19,26; 16:31-34). The way they met in those days – in homes – would have helped foster their fellowship. It is also reflected in the New Testament letters, where we see Christians belonging to one another, sharing with one another, encouraging one another – and so on. They were encouraged to share in very practical ways (Acts 2:44-45).

They received teaching

We read of new Christians being taught (Acts 2:42; 11:25-26; 18:11). Young Christians needed to know what they believed (Acts 18:24-26), because there were false teachers who could lead them astray, as there still are today (Acts 20:29-30).

The picture is filled out by the letters Paul wrote when he could not visit the churches. If these are shortened pieces of teaching, perhaps we'd be amazed at what his sermons must have been like! No wonder he could speak all night when he had important things to say (Acts 20:7,11)! But Paul does tell us that, at the beginning, he was prepared to

treat them like spiritual children, and to feed them with "milk" – that is, with the ABC of the Christian message (1 Corinthians 3:1-2).

They were given direction

New Christians needed help in the way they behaved – especially in the face of persecution, and especially as many had been converted out of a pagan background. Paul's visits to the churches he founded were to strengthen them (Acts 14:22; 15:36; see also 11:22-23).

This is why Paul appointed spiritually mature elders who could give a lead (Acts 14:23) and care for young Christians (Acts 20:28). Sometimes spiritual direction involved discipline (Acts 5:1-11; 8:18-24), but then it mattered how they lived. They had to learn, as we do, how to break with the past and follow Christ.

They became involved

From the letters, we also know that new believers were expected to be more than passengers. The church is like a body with everyone being a different part, so that everybody is expected to do something (Romans 12:3-8; 1 Corinthians 12:12-31). And from the way the gospel spread as Christians dispersed, it seems that they were also encouraged to share their newfound faith with others.

OVER TO YOU

Think how you can encourage yourself or others in what we have read about here: growing in deeper fellowship, putting into practice the teaching that has been received, giving or being given direction and becoming involved, to become mature in Christ (Colossians 1:28).

Discipleship and the cross

MATTHEW 16:13-28

"The Christ" acknowledged

The disciples were first drawn to Jesus because he spoke and acted with unusual authority and unusual compassion. They followed him for some time before they gradually recognised who he really was. For here it was about two and a half years after their first call when they finally made their clearest confession of him as the Messiah, God's Son.

So now Jesus knew he could share with them a great, new truth (verses 13-20). The church would be built on the rock of the great truth that he, Jesus of Nazareth, was "the Messiah, the Son of the Living God". Stop and think how great this declaration is!

Violence predicted

Simon Peter's confession was magnificent – more than he realised. But he was also ignorant of its practical implications which had actually been predicted about the Messiah in the Old Testament (verses 21-23). Like others, he believed that "the Christ" would soon lead them into Jerusalem to overthrow Rome's occupation troops and reestablish Israel as a nation. Jesus corrected that faulty thinking by saying that he first had to die before gaining power and glory. To Peter this was ridiculous, and he told Jesus so. Do you think that Jesus' reply to him (verse 23) is too strong?

Discipleship defined

"Then" (beginning of verse 24) introduces the immediate result of the disciples' open misunderstanding. Jesus had to explain carefully what kind of discipleship he expected of them. Look at verses 24-26 to see how radical Jesus' words were to his disciples. Jesus expected no half measures but total commitment to himself even if it cost them everything else in the world. Not everybody then and now wants that kind of discipleship. Yes, following Jesus on his terms is costly. But not to follow him on his terms is even more costly.

OVER TO YOU

Following Jesus every day (Luke 9:23) is where "the rubber hits the road". What practical steps can you take to help others you know to do this more effectively?

Discipleship on the road

MARK 9:9-50

Discipleship isn't learned in a classroom; it can really only be learned on the road of life. Many of Jesus' profoundest teachings were inspired by seemingly casual incidents or by spontaneous questions. Moreover, deep lessons arose from the tensions of the disciples' life together. All these Jesus naturally turned into learning situations, as we can see in this chapter.

Suffering, then glory

This private conversation (verses 9-13) followed Jesus' transfiguration. The disciples were still filled with ideas of immediate glory and grandeur, so they couldn't grasp his words about his death and resurrection. Yet they kept the matter to themselves. They asked him about something else (verse 11). Jesus willingly answered by taking them back to Scripture to show why suffering had to precede glory. That is a hard lesson for us to learn also.

Prayer, then power

We can also be sympathetic with the disciples' frustration here (verses 14-29). They had previously cast out demons. But now, in front of the hostile scribes, they failed. Try to identify with them as they afterwards privately discussed their powerlessness with Jesus. How do you suppose they felt as they listened to his explanation of the relation of prayer to power?

Humility, then greatness

Jesus again predicted his death to the disciples (verse 31). Why then couldn't they understand it? Verses 33-34 give the embarrassing answer: *self-assertion*. This could also be our situation. Put yourself in their shoes as they watched Jesus take a child in his arms to teach what true greatness is.

Surgery, then security

Jesus seems to be tolerant and broadminded in verses 38-41. But in verses 42-48 he sounds intolerant, using drastic language and violent illustrations! These are two sides of a Lord who has the complete view of life. He wants us to be free from narrow exclusivism (verses 38-41) and from disdain for seemingly unimportant people (verse 42). This calls for radical spiritual surgery for disciples who want a secure place in God's kingdom.

OVER TO YOU

Think about how Jesus taught his disciples in this chapter. Is there anything you'd not noticed before? Are there tensions between you and other Christians? Try and think how such tensions could be changed into something good for God's kingdom.

The good news is for sharing!

Hungry people around us

There are people all around us more hungry for God's security than they realise. Yes, the good news is for sharing. Yet some of us still hesitate to share Jesus with others. We want to, but somehow we find ourselves saying nothing when opportunities arise. We may be facing two areas where we are still uneasy: how to relate to outsiders, and what to say and when.

Relating to people as friends

How can we tell if a person is ready for the good news? How can we tell what kind of book or DVD, etc. to give a friend? Ah, there's a clue – "a friend"! Get to know other people as fellow human beings. This means establishing confident enough relationships where there is basic mutual trust. Generally, people will be as open and honest as you are. This may take a few minutes or a few meetings to develop (Acts 8:26-40).

Jesus, the friend of sinners

Jesus was accused of being a friend of sinners. He made time and effort to cultivate friendships (Luke 5:27-32; 7:34-35; 15:12). He loved them because he knew how precious each was to his Father (Luke 15:7,10,32). May more of us be accused of being friends of sinners for Jesus' sake – and theirs!

Focus on Jesus

What do you tell your friend who begins to show an interest in the Christian faith? In Acts 1:8, Jesus said we are to *witness* (not argue or philosophise). People are likely to see Jesus more clearly when we and our arguments get out of the way.

Peter's evangelism in Acts 10:34-43 is clear. His theme was "Jesus Christ is Lord of all" (verse 36).

- Jesus came as a man, one of us (verses 37-38).
- He was a good friend of the needy (verse 38).
- He died for our sins (verses 40-41).
- God raised him from death (verses 40-41).
- God has made him judge of all (verse 42).
- Only through Jesus can we be forgiven (verse 43).

Jesus, the courteous conversationalist

Not only is content important, manners matter as well! Jesus himself was an effective personal evangelist – sensitive yet firm and clear. Here are practical tips from his conversation with a woman in John 4:1-26.

- **Don't preach.** Try to make your conversation a natural, two-way discussion.
- **Use everyday language** and illustrations.
- **Ask questions** to give others opportunity to express beliefs, doubts or longings.
- **Don't condemn.** We are witnesses, not judges! God is the judge of sins.
- **Encourage questions.** People will ask questions if we have aroused their curiosity.

Our part in evangelism is important: faithfully to witness and to pray. But only God's Spirit can turn people around and bring new life to them (John 3:5). It's his work to bring understanding and conviction (John 16:8-11; Romans 8:14-16). Praise God! Pray that you and your fellowship will be bolder in sharing the good news of Jesus with others, and then get on with the sharing!

OVER TO YOU

Ask God to give you a few friends you can pray for, get to know and share Jesus Christ with. Be bold! Go for it!

Jesus' obedience as Son

JOHN 17

Mission accomplished

The hour in which Jesus would fulfil his life purpose had come. His death – a cruel, unjust, criminal death – was near. Yet what glorious calmness fills this prayer of Jesus to his Father for his apostles – and for us. Jesus had not yet died and risen again. Yet he spoke (verses 4-8) of this great work for our salvation in the past tense. Such confidence was based on two convictions:

· This act would bring the greatest glory to his Father and the Son.
· His death would be the only way for repentant sinners to have eternal life.

If we read verses 6-8 without knowing anything else about the people God had given Jesus (verse 6), we might think they were great characters. But Jesus had just predicted that all of them would deny and desert him (look back at John 16:32). Now listen to what he says of them in these verses! He committed himself totally to them.

Mission passed on

Moreover, Jesus repeatedly described them as the Father's gift to him (verses 9-19). No wonder he gave them his word, constantly prayed for them, kept them, protected them and finally entrusted his world mission to them.

What hope this should give all of us who have faltered and failed as we have tried to follow our Lord. We also are the Father's sacred gifts to his Son Jesus. So he wants to nurture and protect us also. He loves us and trusts us to obey his Father for his world mission.

> " *May they be brought to complete unity to let the world know that you sent me and have loved them even as you have loved me.*"
>
> *JOHN 17:23*

Jesus' greatest desire

Jesus then moved from praying for his apostles to praying for his universal church (verse 20), which they would help to establish. See how often Jesus repeated his great desire for the oneness of all believers (verses 21-23). He also often referred to his own oneness with his Father, not only because it was a superb example but even more so because there was such a beautiful mutual enjoyment of that oneness.

OVER TO YOU

Pray with other Christians for the unity Jesus prayed for. As Jesus himself said, it is the most powerful Christian witness to the world.

Jesus Christ our Lord

JOHN 20

Resurrection proof

Read verses 1-10. Of Jesus' many mighty works, his resurrection was the greatest sign that he was the Son of God and so humanity's only worthy Saviour. The first concrete proof of Jesus' resurrection was the empty tomb. The supporting details astounded Mary, Peter and John (the author). Read these verses again to see how vividly and lovingly each detail impressed these first eyewitnesses. What tremendous emotions must have flooded them!

Outside the tomb

But the empty tomb was just the start (verses 11-18). Greater evidence were the personal appearances of Jesus himself to individuals and groups not once but over and over again. What does it tell you about Jesus that he made his first appearance to someone like Mary Magdalene? (See Luke 8:2.)

Behind locked doors

What a contrast the ten disciples were to Mary on that first resurrection day! Her faith appeared immature as she tried to cling to Jesus, but at least she was at the tomb looking for him. These men were hiding behind locked doors (verses 19-23). Yet the risen Jesus came to them as before. Notice each move of Jesus as he helped them to believe he really was there with them.

What a contrast, too, between their cowardice and Jesus' confidence in them as he recommissioned them. He actually trusted these cowards to take over his great work. What greater confidence could any disciple have than to use all the resources of the triune God to reach others!

A special encounter

Despite all these assurances a week later the disciples were still behind locked doors. This time "doubting Thomas" was present. His love and loyalty for Jesus, however, were greater than his doubts. Jesus met him on his doubting terms, yet with a gentle rebuke (verse 27). Thomas' response was moving: he was the first disciple to respond to Jesus as personally and clearly as he did – "My Lord and my God!" (verse 28). May we learn that kind of awed worship of our risen Lord! And may we believe and carry on believing that Jesus really is the Messiah, the Son of God. This is the way of life (verse 31)!

OVER TO YOU

What can you learn from the response of the risen Lord Jesus to the different thoughts and emotions of the first disciples? Can you share in Thomas' declaration of faith, and if so, how do you show that in your daily living?

The reality of prayer

In this topic we'll focus mainly on how we approach God. Our examples are children, Jesus' disciples and Jesus himself. But first, a word about who it is that we pray to.

God is our Father

Our view of God affects our praying. Is he a stern judge? A doting grandfather? A distant creator? Old Testament people never addressed God as Father. They could only say God was *like* a father. So when Jesus told his disciples to begin their prayers with "Our Father" (Matthew 6:69) it was startling! It's difficult for us to imagine not praying like that.

Remember, too, that God is our Father "in heaven". He is not at all like some delinquent fathers on earth. "In heaven" also implies that though we may be intimate, we dare not be overfamiliar, because he is our holy Father.

A child's simple request

The short, simple, sometimes garbled sentences of a two-year-old child are more meaningful to his parents than is the eloquence of a doctor lecturing on child care! Relationships matter!

Jesus wants his disciples to pray like children. They keep asking, seeking and knocking (Matthew 7:7-8) because they trust their fathers to give them the good gifts they want. How much more is our heavenly Father ready to give even better gifts to his children (Matthew 7:10-11). Have you the simple persistence of a child trusting a generous Father?

The disciples' honest dialogues

Look back at some examples in these readings?. For instance, Matthew 16:13-20 suggests some guidelines for talking with Jesus. Notice that the two-way conversation requires mutual listening and response.

Notice, too, that Jesus encourages broad thinking and freedom of expression but that he has the last word!

In Mark 9 and 10 we see more guidelines for praying. First, the disciples asked Jesus about things that puzzled them (9:11,28; 10:10,26). Secondly, they learned to take his questions seriously (9:16,19,33). You see, in praying, God's part is not only to answer our prayers. He also asks us some questions – and makes comments! If you're puzzled about this kind of praying, try listening to God more when you pray.

The Son's deep prayer

The disciples show us the learning side of praying to God. Jesus' example in John 17 shows us how to pray for others. Intercession is not for our convenience. For instance "God, make my neighbour a Christian – she would be easier to have around" isn't intercession. Praying for others should always be for God's glory (verses 1,4).

In intercession we should learn to share Jesus' deepest desire for the unity of his church (verses 11,21-23).

OVER TO YOU

Look again at Matthew 6:9-10. Pray this prayer for others, eg "May ... acknowledge that your person is holy. May ... here and ... abroad keep working with you to make your rule more widely and deeply known." See how else you can adapt Jesus' great prayers and make them personal to yourself and people you know!

" Then he said to them all: 'If anyone would come after me, he must deny himself and take up his cross daily and follow me. For whoever wants to save his life will lose it, but whoever loses his life for me will save it.'"

LUKE 9:23-24

Lovely or radical?

MATTHEW 5:1-12

We now turn to look at Jesus' great "Sermon on the Mount" to see what kind of lives Jesus wants his disciples to live. This reading is on the statements Jesus made about the character of a real Christian – the beatitudes. "Aren't the beatitudes lovely?" a lady was once heard to exclaim. If she knew Jesus' revolutionary intentions she would not have said "lovely"! Jesus wants his disciples to turn the world upside down by being radically different from it.

The world says, assert yourself if you want to get ahead! Grab pleasure in any way, even if it means breaking God's laws of right living. Push and shove in the rat race. Forget about the welfare of others, if you want success. Be hardhearted; don't give in to soft feelings like mercy or people will step all over you.

Jesus says ...

Who's right – the world or Jesus? If you believe that Jesus is right, how might you help a puzzled Christian to really get hold of what these "hard sayings" (verses 1-9) are all about? One way is quietly to demonstrate their truth in your life. Another way is to discuss what happens to the character of people who live by the world's standards of self-pushing. Or you could point out:

· Our "small" part – having the right attitude to ourselves, to God and to others.
· God's huge part – sharing ownership of heaven and earth with such people!

Use a Bible in modern English for these verses. For instance, verse 3 in the Good News Bible is "Happy are those who know they are spiritually poor ...".

Try putting Jesus' sayings into your own words. Verse 4 could be, "Blessed are the people who are not just regretful about their sins, but sorrowful to the point of repentance, for then God can comfort them with his forgiveness." Use other verses that can throw light onto the meaning. Verse 5 could be illustrated with Jesus' own meekness (1 Peter 2:21-23).

Persecutions and promises

The beatitude in verse 10 is the climax of the whole progression of Christian attitudes from verse 3 to verse 9. It has the same promise as the first. All the other promises in verses 4-9 are different aspects of this one great promise!

Note in the beatitude in verses 11-12 that Jesus has switched from "they" to "you", making it more personal. Why do you think he comments only on this beatitude?

OVER TO YOU

Think honestly in God's presence about the distinctive character of the Christian as shown in these verses. Which attitude do you need to cultivate most? Pray for God's grace to help you display that aspect of being like Jesus.

DISCOVERING DISCIPLESHIP
Salt, light and the Law
MATTHEW 5:13-20

Power to preserve

Today we use salt mainly to flavour food. But in Jesus' day its main function was far more important – to preserve food.

Any chemist can tell us that salt can't be desalted. So, was Jesus ignorant when he spoke of salt losing its saltiness (verse 13)? No, he was referring to something common then – salt mixed with so many impurities that it was dangerous for preserving food and useless even for the manure pile!

Power to penetrate

A great similarity between salt and light is the power to penetrate. Another is their smallness compared to their environment. Yet both salt and light positively influence their surroundings with great penetration.

Picture verses 14-15 as Jesus makes his appeal for his followers to be where they should be and to do what they should do. Think of what happens to an oil lamp when it is put under a bowl. Only when Christians have penetrated their society with Jesus' light (verse 16) can they influence that world. What happens to Christians when they hide under a church bowl?

More obedient than Pharisees

Jesus' teaching on Christian character and influence was radical. Some of his listeners may have thought he was putting aside Old Testament teaching. Was he really telling his disciples to ignore Moses and the prophets? Not at all! His teachings gave the full meaning of what these great men taught.

By their narrow views the teachers of the Law and the Pharisees had blocked God's real aims from view. Jesus dared to show he had a higher view of Scriptures than they. Jesus also dared to challenge his "ordinary" disciples to go beyond the Pharisees' limited obedience to the Scriptures. How could respectable Scripture scholars like them have missed God's standards so badly?

OVER TO YOU

As Christians, we're called to "stop the rot" and to bring out what is good in our society. Can you think of ways that Christians should preserve good values in society?

Becoming involved in God's world

God is at work in his world in many different ways. But the world has many injustices and extremes of poverty and wealth. A lot of the world's problems are caused by the troubled relationships between countries and within countries. So how, amidst these tensions, can we act as salt and light (Matthew 5:13-16)?

Salt where it counts

As we have seen, salt adds flavour and acts as a preservative. As Christians, we are to add flavour to what is already good in our society. This means identifying ourselves with and supporting those who are working for greater harmony and humanity. And we must act as a preservative to try to arrest the rate of decay in society, combating all that prevents people from living according to their God-given potential.

The light of the world

Jesus challenges us to be the light of the world also (Matthew 5:14). So we need to take seriously what is good in our society and preserve it. But we also need to speak out against what is evil (Ephesians 5:11).

The whole gospel

There's a danger that we can so emphasise the spiritual aspects of the good news that we forget its social aspect. (Do you remember how the priest and the Levite paid no attention to the man who was attacked by robbers in the parable of the good Samaritan – Luke 10:25-37?) So following Jesus involves not only making a spiritual response but also being socially responsible (Matthew 25:31-46). It means helping people and supporting activities and policies that will lead to a more just world.

Here are some practical guidelines to follow:

· Be informed. Find out about the issues and needs. Read books and your newspaper more closely, and try to get behind the Internet headlines!
· Let the Bible speak to you about your own life.
· Pray about the right use of your time, talents and resources.
· Review your lifestyle. Could it be simpler? Could you share some of what you have with other people?
· Put into practice what you learn.

You could welcome people from a different culture into your home and listen to them. You could also support a group in your area that helps people in your community or is concerned for development or human rights.

Beware!

Look again at Matthew 5:13. At the end of this verse, Jesus adds a note of caution. In certain circumstances, there's a risk that salt can lose its saltiness, its purity. Jesus recognised such a risk, and this is why he asks God not to lead us into temptation but to deliver us from evil (Matthew 6:13).

OVER TO YOU

What practical steps can you take to follow the example of Jesus and show we care for all those in need?

Anger, adultery and divorce

MATTHEW 5:21-32

Jesus now uses six examples of how the Pharisees kept the letter of the law but lost its spirit.

The examples chosen by Christ illustrate principles. It is the spirit, not the letter, that is important; we can only live the Christian life in a vital relationship with God himself. Note in verses 21-22,26-28,31-32 Christ's claim to a higher authority than theirs.

Murder in the heart

Examine the three situations of anger in verse 22. Jesus used Jewish court procedure to picture how God judges anger against a brother. How is this anger different from the kind that Jesus sometimes expressed? In God's view, anger is as serious as murder, for the desire is the same – to get rid of the person.

Acts of worship cannot cover anger in our hearts. So in verses 23-26 Jesus instructs his disciples on what to do about it – settle matters of grievance with a brother as soon as possible, for unresolved anger has destructive effects on our relationship with God, with others and with ourselves. Have you hidden anger against someone? Pray for God's help to follow Jesus' command.

Adultery in the heart

In verses 27-30, Jesus is not talking about normal physical attraction to the opposite sex. He is describing a man who can think of nothing else save his desire for a woman's body. For this, Jesus prescribes radical spiritual surgery!

By his shocking analogies, Jesus wanted to emphasise that if we really want to belong to God's kingdom we must drastically discipline ourselves. We must act as though we had no eyes to see with and no hands to touch anything that feeds our lust. Strong words! Strong Lord!

Divorce, rabbinic style

Read verses 31-32. In Jesus' day, certain rabbinic traditions had permissive views of marriage. They made divorce easy for a man who wanted to get rid of his wife for selfish reasons, not for her unfaithfulness. See how Jesus sought to protect the woman and to stress the husband's responsibility. Above all he sought to bring people back to God's view of marriage: sacred and indissoluble. Pray that Christians will work harder at strong marriages that will glorify God.

OVER TO YOU

Keeping the spirit and not just the letter of the law is not easy. Examine your heart and seek God's help if you are tempted to be judgemental.

Oaths, revenge and enemies
MATTHEW 5:33-48

I swear

Verse 33 summarises the Mosaic laws about the seriousness of breaking oaths. A Pharisaic tradition taught that if an oath used a formula other than God's name, then breaking it was not serious. Look in verses 34-35 at four common formulas that Jesus named to show how ridiculous the Pharisees' literalism was: the first three were Jewish references to God, and even one's head is the creation of God!

Jesus' point is that his disciples should not have to use any oaths to convince others they spoke the truth. Rather, their credibility should rest on their character.

Getting even

This Pharisaic distortion of another law is from Exodus 21:24, which judges used as a limit to restrain vengeance. But the Pharisees took the law out of its civil context and applied it to personal relationships. This allowed them to take revenge in their own hands. Jesus said not retaliation but love for the evil person (not his acts) rules. He then applied the principle to different cases common to Israelites (verses 39-42).

Is it cowardice not to resist "the evil person" who takes advantage of you? No, it is the courage of love, which is more likely to restrain his or her evil than revenge. Revenge tends to worsen relationships and fosters our own unhealthy emotions.

Extraordinary love

In verses 43-48, Jesus now takes on one of the worst traditions of Scripture twisting. Referring to Leviticus 19:18, the rabbis omitted "as yourself" from "love your neighbour", then added "hate your enemy"! Jesus turned this teaching on its head and commanded his disciples to love their enemies and pray for them.

OVER TO YOU

How can you practically apply Jesus' teaching in these verses? What does your own personal credibility rest on? If you loved your enemies, how would you pray for them?

The Bible – God's word for life!

What makes the Bible unique

The Bible is the world's best-known book. It is the oldest book in common use. It has been translated into over 1500 languages and dialects spoken by 97% of the world's peoples. The Bible has influenced all great Western literature directly or indirectly. Its laws of justice and high moral codes have been the foundation of the free world for centuries.

But all these facts alone are not what makes the Bible the most exciting book in the world. The Bible stands in a class by itself because it is God's personal message to the human race. For thousands of years this message has changed millions of lives on every continent.

What the Bible says about itself

The writers used human effort (Luke 1:1-4) but they were conscious of the divine source of their writings. Over 3,800 times they say "The Lord said" or similar claims, for example Exodus 20:1; Jeremiah 1:4. Jesus clearly strengthened these claims of divine authority (Matthew 5:17-18; John 10:35). His apostles also recognised and submitted to that authority (Romans 9:25; 2 Peter 1:20-21). No wonder that at the end of his life's work, Paul could say with greater confidence than ever that the Scriptures are "breathed out by God" (2 Timothy 3:16)!

Why people read the Bible

Yes, the Bible is extraordinary. Even new readers sense this when they start studying it. Today millions of people read it because they want to hear God speak to them directly.

Through the Bible we come to know God the Father, his Son our Saviour and his Spirit who empowers us for living. It shows us how to live with ourselves and with others. We find that the Bible is practical and necessary (2 Timothy 3:16-17):
· for teaching basic Christian beliefs
· for rebuking wrong beliefs
· for correcting wrong behaviour
· for training in right behaviour.

How to get more out of your Bible

In trying to understand the Bible, your attitude is more important than your knowledge of its original languages or decades of "advanced theology" (Psalm 119:99-100). So come to the Scriptures:
· with reverence (Psalm 119:159-160)
· with eagerness (Acts 17:11)
· with submission (1 Thessalonians 2:13)
· with a willingness to obey (John 13:17).

It is possible to "know" the Bible but not understand it if you don't see Jesus Christ as its major message (John 5:39-40). Without him as the central thread, it makes little sense (Luke 24:27,32).

OVER TO YOU

Some practical steps in reading the Bible:
· **Find** the basic facts and start to link them together (Psalm 119:18).
· **Discover** their meaning by seeing hidden facts behind what you've already linked together (2 Timothy 2:7).
· **Reflect** on the message for today and listen to God's word for you (Joshua 1:8).
· **Apply** its lesson to your life (James 1:22-25).

True Christian worship

MATTHEW 6:1-18

For whose approval?

In chapter 5 Jesus laid the foundation of Christian character, from which comes Christian influence in the world, and which is expressed in Christian obedience that surpasses that of the Pharisees. Now Jesus logically follows with the topic of true Christian worship. Try rewording his teaching in verse 1.

Christian giving

Jesus could see beyond the outer acts of giving to the not-so-hidden motives. He also saw something else: those who give to be approved by others really get their satisfaction! But the question is whether that brings the highest kind of satisfaction. Why is God's approval the best of all (verses 2-4)?

Christian praying

Trumpeting your giving (verse 2) is a bit more understandable than parading your prayers in public. The first has to do with your relationship to others. But the second deals with your relationship to God. Desire for social approval hits us even in this private area! Christian praying is not to be moved by greed for human approval. Nor is it to be like that of the pagans who think the longer and more repetitious their prayers, the more impressed God is (verse 7).

That's why the model prayer Jesus gave his disciples is not for mere mechanical repetition. See if your prayers cover the same God-centred concerns that Jesus outlines here:

· for his praise (verse 9)
· for his purposes (verse 10)
· for his provisions (verses 11-13).

Christian fasting

Spiritual cosmetics – that's what Jesus said some of the religious leaders used to show they were fasting (verse 16). They applied a greyish colouring and drew lines on their faces to look pale and weak!

Fasting is a good practice. Of the three religious duties Jesus discussed it is the least practised today. Look at verses 17-18. What reasons for fasting would please God?

OVER TO YOU

When we pray, we must always remember that we come to the almighty, eternal, holy God. But we are also to realise that God, in Christ, has become *our Father*.

A passage in Hebrews encourages us to come confidently, yet humbly, into God's presence. Here is a place of real worship and thanksgiving!

"Therefore ... since we have confidence to enter the Most Holy Place by the blood of Jesus, by a new and living way opened for us through the curtain, that is, his body, and since we have a great priest over the house of God, let us draw near to God with a sincere heart in full assurance of faith, having our hearts sprinkled to cleanse us from a guilty conscience and having our bodies washed with pure water."
HEBREWS 10:19-22

Love God or hate him
MATTHEW 6:19-34

The first test

Look at verse 24: "Who's your boss – God or money?" Some may answer too quickly, "God, of course. I'm not greedy for money." But read verses 19-21. Where do your strongest mental energies go – towards thinking of ways to make your life more financially secure? Or, thinking of ways to help others to know God better? You don't have to be greedy for money to be distracted from God by it. Material possessions distract our hearts from God when we count on them rather than God as our basic security.

The second test

Some Christians complain that they don't understand this or that about life with God. They read the Bible and hear sermons, they say, but they don't see relevant applications to life. It may well be, as Jesus says, their eyes are more focused on material values.

Jesus' words in verse 23 are a sober warning. How can money (or materialism which money symbolises) be "light" that turns out to be darkness in the end?

The third test

No, most materialistic people are not greedy for money. But they worry about money – how to get enough for food and clothes. For many in poor countries this is certainly a valid anxiety. But for many in affluent countries, "necessities" means keeping up with others. They worry that their friends and neighbours may look down on them for not following the latest trends in foods and fashions.

But in *any* country, Jesus' disciples have the same heavenly Father, whose world has abundant proof of his loving care. He wants us to have material security – and a far greater and lasting security: his kingdom and himself. Read verse 33.

OVER TO YOU

The death and resurrection of the Lord Jesus Christ lie at the heart of the Christian gospel. Christ died for our sins: the way back to God is open. God now calls us to a total commitment to him every day – this is the only fitting response to the giving of himself on the cross. Stop and think about verse 33.

Onward, Christian soldiers!

In Jesus' great sermon there is no part where he doesn't assume strong opposition to his way of life. The forces against God's kingdom are a powerful combination of "the world, the flesh, and the devil". We must know which of these is directly attacking us at any one time. Otherwise we may be fighting the wrong enemy when the real enemy is attacking us from the rear!

The world

"The world" here means the social system operating apart from God (1 John 2:16-17). The world says indulge yourself, live for the moment, look after number one! In business, industry, government and elsewhere, people sometimes use underhand ways that badly hurt others in the long run.

Look at John 7:3-7. The world can even be in our homes! Jesus' own brothers opposed him, mocking his claim to be the Messiah (verse 4). Jesus' response? The world hates only those who hate the world (verse 7). His true disciples hate the world because like their Lord they say that its works are evil (verse 7). How closely do you identify with Jesus' standards in his warfare against the world?

The flesh

Jesus' great apostle, Paul, also knew the hatred of the world that opposed his Lord. He also knew how "the flesh" clashed with his desire to please God. Here "flesh" stands for the "me-first" tendency in us. We also recognise that same "me-first" power that tries to pull us away from obedience to our Lord.

This is why we need to know ourselves, so that we don't quickly blame others for our defeats. But this shouldn't lead to an inferiority or defeatist complex. Look at Romans 7, verses 24-25. Hang on to this stupendous truth: Jesus Christ is at hand 24 hours a day to deliver us from our weaknesses!

The devil

Ultimately behind all evil is the devil himself (Ephesians 6:12). We must not underestimate his power. But the Spirit of Jesus Christ who lives in us is far, far greater (1 John 4:4).

The devil does not hate us as much as he hates God. He wants to hurt God by hurting us. But Jesus by his death for us defeated him (Hebrews 2:14). This is now the time for the mopping-up operation before the battle is officially over. Satan knows this and wants in the meantime to deceive as many people as he can (John 8:44).

God's whole armour

Yes, defeated is the last word for Satan. But while we're still on earth we need to be totally prepared for his remaining warfare. Look up Ephesians 6:10-20 and note how often Paul repeats the words *all, full* or *whole*. Of the six parts of your armour and equipment (verses 14-17), are any in need of repair?

Paul's strong emphasis on prayer (verses 18-20) reminds us how important it is to keep in constant touch with God. He is our victorious general!

OVER TO YOU

Thank God that he has gained the decisive victory over the devil. Pray for the Lord's help to overcome forces that oppose God in your own life, the community in which you live and in the wider world.

Wise ways to help people

MATTHEW 7:1-12

This time, Jesus' key statement for the section comes at the end in verse 12. The "golden rule" is usually quoted alone. Let's see how its preceding text can deepen our understanding of it.

When to help

Verse 1 is sometimes quoted by itself to prove that Christians should never make any kind of judgement of people and their situations. But look at verses 5-6 to see that Jesus fully expects his disciples to make some kind of evaluation of people before they can help them!

Jesus wants to discourage the practice of people who want to help others with their problems when they have not yet taken care of their own (verses 3-5). How this can boost our ego! Think of the woman who thought her neighbour's laundry on the line was dirty till someone told her that it was her windows that weren't clean!

When to share

This time we have to judge whether other people are ready or not to receive the truth. That truth may be the good news. Or it may be any insight that could help them – if they are ready to appreciate it. Otherwise it's wasted (verse 6).

How to help

To help others we need to pray for God's help. Note the steps of praying – ask, seek, knock (verses 7-8).

- **Asking** is putting into words what we want God to do; for example, giving us wisdom to help someone.
- **Seeking** is moving into action; for example, spending time with that person to understand them.
- **Knocking** is persisting in spite of slow response.

As Jesus' picture of a child and father shows (verses 9-11), prayer expresses a personal and growing relationship between us and our Father. He delights to shower us with his gifts when we are ready.

Can you now see how verse 12 guides us in helping others?

OVER TO YOU

However long we have been Christians, we still have more to learn and experience of God's love and purposes. What active steps are you taking to become more like Jesus? Remember, the Holy Spirit helps you!

We don't have to wait until we reach a certain stage before we can be useful to God. In fact, as we have seen, serving him can be an important aid to our own growth. How can you become even more useful in your service for Jesus in the world? Try and share your ideas or plans with someone else.

Only two ways

MATTHEW 7:13-29

Two gates

Notice in this final part of the Sermon on the Mount how Jesus echoes major ideas he has been teaching. Read verses 13-14. The gate for entry into his kingdom is as "narrow" as the first four beatitudes (5:3-6). The road that leads to life is as "hard" as the next four that climax in persecution (5:7-10). But think of the alternative – the wide gate and the easy road that lead to hell!

Two kinds of trees

Wish as we may, the Christian life is never going to be easy. Notice the three contrasts in verses 13-14 between life with Jesus and life without him.

Jesus surely calls for judging those who are the false prophets (verses 15-20). Today the obvious ones are leaders of cults and sects. But in 5:21–6:18, Jesus has also warned about leaders within orthodox religion who mislead people. They too make the road to life hard. What kind of bad fruit do they eventually produce?

Two standards

It's scary to think that religious people who do certain impressive works (verses 21-23) can themselves end up being rejected by God. They have set their own standard for entry into God's kingdom. What delusion! God's standard is personal knowledge of him – being Jesus' friends who do the Father's will.

If verse 21 is true, how can you tell a real Christian? Supernatural experience or miracles (verse 22)? A single word in verse 23 says it all: *knew* speaks of a meaningful person relationship with Christ which involves obedience.

Two builders

Yes, true discipleship under Jesus' lordship is narrow and hard. It doesn't allow for the false and the artificial. Yes, the other way is easy – and self-destructive. No wonder Jesus calls the true disciple a wise builder (verses 24-27), the one who takes time to dig through the sands to the solid rock on which to build their life. That rock is the person and authority of Jesus himself. Building on that rock means unconditional obedience to him and his words.

Don't miss the punch-lines in Jesus' picturesque story; they are its first words and its last (verses 24,27). There is only one Bible translation you can't do without – yours, into action! There is no escape: Jesus' word comes with his authority: see verse 29. Have you surrendered to Jesus' authority?

Keep up the good work!

Realism and true glory

Many Christians don't like to listen to "negative" or "strong" subjects like endurance (perseverance, "stickability"). Maybe they're like Jesus' first disciples. In Matthew 24:1-2 we see their pride in the magnificent temple in Jerusalem. They were dreaming of how Jesus would overthrow the Romans and establish his kingdom. Then they themselves would be installed as his cabinet (Matthew 20:20-21).

Instead Jesus warned them that there would be greater opposition, growing persecution, betrayals and suffering (Matthew 24:4-29). But he promised that if they endured they would be saved for a far greater glory than they had imagined (Matthew 24:13,30-31).

Jesus' prediction of horror was fulfilled for many Christians then and since then. Today believers in some parts of the world are going through what Jesus described. Pray that they will see beyond present sufferings to the glory that Jesus promises.

Those who don't endure ...
and those who do

In other parts of the world, there are different challenging problems. Through a parable (Luke 8:5-15) Jesus pictured what kind of people don't endure and what kind do.

Some don't endure because they let God's word go in one ear and out the other (verse 12). Others don't endure because though God's word enters them, their hearts are too hard for it to take root. Tribulation and persecution prove that (verse 13). In the third group, God's word does take root, and they

start to bear fruit. But life's worries, riches and pleasures take over their hearts, and their fruit never reaches maturity (verse 14).

The fourth group of people (verse 15) face the same kind of opposition and temptations as the others. But they endure, Jesus says, because they not only hear God's word, they also persist in nurturing it in a good heart and in obeying it (verse 15). Pray for God's strength to persist until your fruit matures.

Jesus helps us to endure

We need not face temptations and other problems alone. Jesus fully understands and is praying for us right now (Hebrews 2:18; 7:25). In Luke 22:32 can you hear him saying your name instead of Simon's? Can you hear him expressing his confidence that you will endure in spite of failure?

Jesus had confidence in Simon's endurance because he saw that deep in his heart he had a basic loyalty to him as Lord. What does the Lord Jesus see in your heart?

OVER TO YOU

When you're experiencing suffering, think how much greater Jesus' suffering was and it was for our sake! Like Jesus, keep your eyes fixed not on the hardships but on what is beyond – the joy of sharing life with him in heaven for ever! Keep your eyes on Jesus! (Hebrews 12:2).

Moving on as a Christian

You may have been a Christian for a little while but perhaps have got stuck and don't think you are growing. This section contains 28 studies designed to help you grow and move on as a Christian.

The aim here is that you not only know more about what happened to you when you became a Christian but also that you are able to work out your faith in everyday life.

God's rescue operation

In the letter to the Romans, Paul clearly sets out God's plan of salvation – his rescue operation. The following themes stand out:

Everyone needs rescuing

The lives of both Jews and Gentiles fall far short of what God demands. Everyone is guilty and faces God's condemnation (Romans 3:9-19).

Getting right with God

This is the central point of Romans. We can't put ourselves right with God. But God himself has provided a way that is independent of keeping the Law. God's rescue is given freely, through Jesus' death on the cross, to all who believe (Romans 3:21-26). Abraham shows us what this faith is like (Romans 4).

Changed from enemies into friends

Being right with God is the launching pad for all the security in the Christian life. That never changes. We're no longer God's enemies, but his friends (Romans 5:10-11). Paul sets out the differences between belonging to Adam, before we became Christians, and belonging to Jesus, since we came to believe in him (5:12-21).

Living the new life

"Can we live how we want, then?" asks someone. "No way!" comes Paul's reply (Romans 6:1-2). Baptism reminds us that as Christians we've died with Jesus and have been raised with him. We're dead to the reign of sin in our lives and alive to the new ruler, Jesus (6:3-11). And this is to affect how we live. We have become "slaves" of righteousness (6:12-23).

Being free from the Law

As Christians we are set free from the Law's demands and its slavery, to be married to Jesus in a new way in the Spirit (Romans 7:6). But there's a conflict between what we know

is right and what we want to do, and how we actually behave (7:14-25).

Knowing the Holy Spirit's help

Slavery to the Law is past. As Christians we know the Holy Spirit in us as a stronger power (Romans 8:1-11). He assures us that we belong to God's family (8:15-16). Nothing can separate us from his love (8:35-39)!

God does the calling

Paul is sad as he thinks about the Jews' rejection of Jesus. Some parts of Romans chapters 9 to 11 are difficult to follow, but certain things are clear: God calls some and not others – and whom he chooses is entirely up to him (9:21-24). We can only become believers because of God's mercy (9:15) and because we've responded to God's word (10:14). The way for all, Jew and Gentile, is now open to all who believe (10:12-13).

Changed, to love and serve other people

How is all this to affect our lives? It's to work out in a life of giving ourselves to God (Romans 12:1-2), as members of a church (12:3-8), and a community (Romans 13). This love is strong: it takes other people into account (Romans 14:1–15:6). It'll mean hard work with affection for other Christians (Romans 15; 16) to spread the good news to others who need to know God's rescue operation for themselves!

OVER TO YOU

How does the knowledge that you have been rescued by God affect your daily life? The way you behave towards other people?

Conversion – the radical change

"A leopard cannot change its spots," the saying goes – people's characters cannot be changed. But it is different when God is at work. Conversion is a major turn-round in a person's life and it has two sides – repentance and faith, which go together.

Repentance – turning from sin

Repentance and sin are strong words, but Jesus used them. He came to call sinners to repentance (Luke 5:32). The story of the prodigal son tells us about repentance. It is a change of mind. The prodigal son recognised that he had sinned (Luke 15:18) – he had offended his father and God himself. You have to acknowledge that you have gone wrong, that you have broken God's good and holy laws, before you can be put right!

Repentance is also a change of heart. You may realise that you have broken God's laws, but not react further. True repentance is being deeply sorry for your sin. Notice in Luke 15:21 that the prodigal son was gravely affected by his sin, because he saw it in its true light. He knew he was justly condemned and could only throw himself at the mercy of his father. And so it is with us and God.

Repentance also involves a change of will. With the prodigal son, there was action (Luke 15:20). He was willing to turn from his old life to lead a changed life in the future. This is having a clean break with a past life.

Faith – turning to God

Faith is knowing certain facts: that Jesus Christ is the Son of God and that he died for our sins and on the third day rose again. But it is more than knowing them in your mind. Faith is also believing them to be true, becoming convinced of them, in your heart. And then true faith is resting your whole life on these realities.

This means there is a way out from the punishment we deserve as children who have turned away from the Father, because he has provided the way. God sent his Son to die to suffer the punishment due to us and he raised him from the dead to show that his death had met all of God's demands. We can only respond to this by receiving what Jesus Christ has already done. We cannot add to it – by performing good works or by going forward at the end of a meeting. Only Jesus can save us.

What follows?

If you have repented and believed, your sins have been forgiven (Luke 5:18-20; 24:47) and you will live for ever (18:30). The Holy Spirit has been given to you (3:16). But Jesus was equally clear on what happens if you do not repent – you will die (13:3,5).

The New Testament gives the ordinance of baptism as the sign that the old life has been washed away to bring in a new life. This is bound to affect the way you live (Luke 3:7-14; 9:23-25). Look at what Zacchaeus did (19:8)! Peter also had a task to do (22:32).

John the Baptist was to turn God's people back to God (Luke 1:16), and Jesus Christ came to bring this message (5:32). Conversion was at the heart of the message the first disciples were to speak about urgently (24:47). And so it is with us.

OVER TO YOU

Do you live each day in the knowledge that you have been forgiven? What difference does it make?

The sovereignty of God

Why the Lord Jesus Christ came

As you read through Luke's Gospel, it is clear that Jesus had a definite sense of why he came to earth. We can trace this right through his life: in the temple, he had to be in his Father's house (Luke 2:49); he had to preach the good news (4:43) – calling sinners to repentance (5:31-32) – and to continue doing so (13:33), to be involved with people (19:5), and to die and be raised (24:7). In fact, it is his death and resurrection at Jerusalem that appear increasingly in focus (for example 9:22,51).

What God has said

Prophecy – and its fulfilment – also play an important part in the Gospel. Think back to the prophecies about John the Baptist (Luke 3:4-6) and Jesus (4:17-21) from Isaiah. There are also other times when the prophets are mentioned, especially in connection with salvation (for example 1:69-75; 16:29-31) and, again, Jesus' death and resurrection (22:37; 24:25-27,44-47). Prophecies about the future of Jerusalem and Jesus' second coming also feature (Luke 21).

God is in control

Both prophecy and the purpose that Jesus had in coming speak to us of a plan that God has. This plan is intended for his glory and also our good. It covers absolutely everything – from the biggest things in our lives to the smallest. All this is very different from some modern thinking. God's plan isn't fatalism – the teaching that says that what will happen will happen, and nothing we do or don't do will make any difference. "Man is not a pawn on a cosmic chess board, with mechanistic forces moving the pieces" (Wayne Detzler). Chance is wrong, too; there is a plan and God is behind it.

This doesn't mean that as human beings we are not responsible for our actions. We follow our own wills. And when we sin, the responsibility lies fully with us. Yet even our sin brings God's purposes to pass (Luke 22:22).

What is our response?

Like the disciples on the road to Emmaus, we tend to be slow to believe these things (Luke 24:25-27). But if we do believe, we shall be blessed indeed (1:45)!

This teaching calls upon us to be submissive and humble. We may think we are important in our school, college, office or factory, but God is the real boss – he's on top of everything! Or we may be unemployed. Without wanting to offer any clichés, the Bible still firmly says that God is in control.

This teaching comforts us in great difficulty or distress. We can seek comfort in a heavenly Father's almighty and perfect care (12:6-7,22-32; 18:7). He knows all about our situation. He's never taken by surprise.

This teaching isn't meant to make us always refer tiny details of life (such as which tin to choose in a supermarket!) directly back to God's guidance. It is intended so that we can live our lives in quiet confidence in God (1:38), seeking to bring glory to him.

OVER TO YOU

Do you have complete confidence in God's plan for your life? If not, turn to prayer and ask God to reassure you.

Amazing grace!

What is grace?

Grace is one of the ways of describing how God acts. There are a number of important strands that belong to this great Bible theme:

· God chose a people for himself, Israel. God was in no way obliged to do this; he did it out of grace (Deuteronomy 7:7-8).
· God made an agreement, a covenant of friendship, with his people. His grace meant that he remained loyal to them, even when his people were unfaithful to him (Psalm 25:14; Hosea 11).
· God's grace is seen most of all in his "rescue operation", his salvation of sinners (Ephesians 2:5).
· God's grace is known by sinners when their sins are pardoned and forgiven. Again, this grace is totally undeserved. It is "love shown to the unlovely" (Ephesians 2:1-10).
· God's grace moves sinners to respond to God and to be changed people (Acts 2:37-41). And sinners, saved by grace, know more and more of God by grace (beginning of Galatians 4:9).

Grace and salvation

Let's focus on God's act of salvation, because that's where we see grace most wonderfully displayed.

· The grace of the Lord Jesus Christ is what is important, especially the grace shown in his death on the cross (Galatians 1:3-4; 2:20-21).
· We are called by grace. We come to know this salvation because in his grace God chooses us (Galatians 1:15). The way we lay hold of such grace is by faith (Galatians 2:16). So we are saved by grace to become new people (Galatians 6:15).
· We are kept by grace. Grace preserves us (John 10:27-29). One hymn puts it like this:

My name from the palms of his hands
Eternity will not erase;
Impressed on his heart it remains,
In marks of indelible grace.

So God keeps us by his grace. As we have seen in Galatians, Paul has written repeatedly that keeping the Law in order to stay right with God is not God's way at all (Galatians 5:4).

Grace and the Law

If we are kept by grace, can we behave how we want to, then? No, it matters how we live. As Christians we don't keep the Law to commend ourselves to God to make us right with him, nor do we irresponsibly set aside the Law. No, we try to keep the Law out of a devotion to our new Father (end of Galatians 5:6). As children of the Father, it's only natural that we want to please him. That is why the encouragements of, for example, Galatians 5–6 are important: we need the Law as principles to show us what a godly life is like. And we know the Holy Spirit helping us live such a life (Galatians 5:22-23), as we obey Jesus and follow his example.

OVER TO YOU

You can't think about the theme of grace for long without being amazed! As we see that we are lost, corrupt and sinful in God's sight and deserve only his righteous punishment, we're bound to marvel at the costly grace that meant that the Son of God himself died on the cross for us!

"*But* I pray to you, O LORD,
  in the time of your great
    favour;
in your great love, O God,
  answer me with your sure
    salvation.
Rescue me from the mire,
  do not let me sink;
deliver me from those who
    hate me,
  from the deep waters."

PSALM 69:13-14

We can be sure – that the Christian faith is true

We live in an age of uncertainty, a time when people are afraid to say anything for sure. How different from the letters of John! Their whole atmosphere is one of certainty. There are two things in particular about which we do not need to have any doubt at all. We can be sure that the Christian faith is true. We can also be sure that we have eternal life. Turning to 1 John, let us see what John says about the first of these.

What we know

We do not know *everything*, for there are some things which God has not told us (1 John 3:2). But the things which have been told us are true through and through, and we know them to be so. The things we believe are not lies or fairy stories.

· We know the truth about the state of this world (1 John 5:19; see also 2:18).
· We know the truth about ourselves – how we must live, and where we are going (1 John 2:10-11; 3:2,18).
· We know the truth about God and Christ (1 John 5:20). In fact we know them (2:13-14; 3:1,6; 4:6-7)!
· We know the truth about what caused Christ to come (1 John 3:16; 4:16), and what his coming achieved (3:5).

How we know it

We can point to actual historical events that took place. Sent by the Father (1 John 4:9-10), Christ came (1 John 5:20) and showed himself on this planet (1 John 3:5,8) in real human flesh (1 John 4:2; 2 John 7). It was here that he was baptised and shed his blood (1 John 5:6).

There can be no doubt about all this, because everything concerned with our Lord Jesus Christ was witnessed (1 John 1:1-3; 4:14).

In addition, we believers have received the "anointing" or "pouring out" of the Holy Spirit, which means that we can tell truth from error (1 John 2:20,27). The Holy Spirit is within us (1 John 5:10) and convinces us in

> " *We can be sure of what we believe, and need never doubt the basis of our faith*"

our hearts that when we hear of the events of Christ's life, we are hearing the truth (1 John 5:6-9).

What this means

We are Christians who live in the 21st century, but we are no less sure of the truth of the Christian faith than those who lived in the 1st century. Our faith is rooted in historical events that actually took place, and the passing of the centuries cannot alter the facts. When we trust what eyewitnesses of those events tell us, the Holy Spirit within our hearts assures that we are not being led astray.

We need not be disturbed by the "antichrists" (enemies of Christ) who do all they can either to ignore or to deny the facts on which our faith is built (1 John 4:3; 2 John 7). We can be sure of what we believe, and need never doubt the basis of our faith.

OVER TO YOU

Are there things or people in your life that would try to deny the facts that underpin your Christian faith? How do you react to them?

We can be sure –
that we have eternal life

The word "know" occurs over 30 times in John's letters. We have already seen that we can know that the Christian faith is true. But we can also be sure that we ourselves have been saved by that Christian faith and, therefore, that we have eternal life. The very reason that John wrote his first letter was to bring believers to this point of certainty (1 John 5:13).

Five ways of putting it

Did you notice the five different ways in which John talks of this certainty?

· We know that we know God (1 John 2:3).
· We know that we are in him, and that he is in us (1 John 2:5; 4:13).
· We know that we are children of God (1 John 3:1; 5:19).
· We know that we have passed from death to life (1 John 3:14).
· We know that we have eternal life (1 John 5:13).

Christians need never doubt that God has accepted them. Those who say that it is boastful or cocky to claim to be sure of being saved are wrong.

Three ways of finding out

Some people claim to be sure of their salvation when they have no right to be. Their assurance is without foundation. True Christian assurance comes by asking whether you have the three essential marks of a true believer. If you do, you can be completely certain that your faith is genuine.

1. Do you love God's commands and make an honest attempt to keep them? Deliberately continuing to sin is inconsistent with the nature of God (1 John 1:5-6), the reason Jesus came (1 John 3:5), and being born again with a spiritual nature (1 John 3:9).
2. Do you love fellow believers? (1 John 2:9-10; 3:14; 4:20). God is love, and the loveless person obviously does not know him (1 John 4:7-8). If you are truly born of God

then you will love those who are your spiritual brothers and sisters (1 John 5:1). Believing and loving go hand in hand (1 John 3:23).

3. Do you believe the truth about Jesus Christ that he is the Son of God (1 John 3:23; 5:5,10,13) who walked this earth as a human being (1 John 4:2; 2 John 7)? Nobody who denies this is in touch with God (1 John 2:23).

Words alone aren't enough

It is possible for people to say that they are Christians without actually being so. He who says he is a believer, but does not have all three marks of one, is a liar (1 John 2:4,22; 4:20).

Each one of the marks is definite evidence of the new birth (1 John 2:29; 4:7; 5:1), and no one could possibly answer "Yes" to these three questions unless the Holy Spirit had worked in their life. If you have all three marks you can be perfectly sure that you have eternal life (1 John 2:3; 3:14; 4:2).

> ### OVER TO YOU
>
> Do you pass the test of the three questions above? If so, you can go into the week ahead with fresh certainty and with a fresh boldness in your witness to others.

Three key words – light, life and truth

The New Testament writings of John contain four key words: light, life, truth and love. Let's look now at how three of them are used in his letters.

Light

John uses the imagery of light to speak to us of the absolute purity and unspoiled holiness of God (1 John 1:5). He is entirely without sin and untruth. We cannot be light ourselves, but when we come to have fellowship with God we can be said to be walking or living "in the light" (1 John 1:7). Those who do not know God, and whose lives are therefore unchanged, are still in darkness (1 John 2:9) and do not know where they are going (1 John 2:11). The pictures of light and darkness also stress how different from each other believers and unbelievers are (1 John 2:8-11) and that there is no middle ground between them.

> "*Being a Christian is a matter of believing and behaving in line with the truth which God has revealed*"

Life

God is not only light, he is also life. He exists from eternity to eternity, and is the source of his own existence. His Son Jesus Christ, who is equally "the true God and eternal life" (1 John 5:20) is the way that God has expressed himself and made himself known (1 John 1:1-3). He came to give us spiritual life (4:9), and God promises that whoever receives his Son receives with him eternal life (1 John 2:25; 5:11-12). Christian conversion can therefore be described as passing from death to life (1 John 3:14-15). Again we see the enormous difference between the converted and the unconverted. The unconverted person boasts about this life (1 John 2:16), while the Christian knows that the life that has been received from God is eternal (1 John 5:13).

Truth

We are not being led astray. The God whom we have come to know through Jesus Christ is the true God (1 John 5:20). His Holy Spirit within us is the truth (1 John 5:6), and he has given us a "sixth sense" which means that we know that the Christian faith is true, and that errors which come to us in the name of truth are not to be followed (1 John 2:20-21,27; 4:6).

Being a Christian, then, is a matter of believing and behaving in line with the truth which God has revealed (2 John 2; 3 John 3,4). People whose lives are ruled by the truth have an automatic family feeling of love towards each other (2 John 1; 3 John 1). They are keen to help those who spread God's truth (3 John 8), and measure each other's characters by seeing how it compares with the standards God has revealed (3 John 12).

Some people, measured against what God has said about the belief and behaviour of a true Christian, are seen to be devoid of truth (1 John 1:6,8; 2:4). The same test, applied to believers, brings them to be sure that their faith is genuine, and that they "belong to the truth" (1 John 3:19).

OVER TO YOU

Does your behaviour always reflect your belief? Pray that God would help you to live in accordance with your belief in Jesus.

God's love – and ours

In his letters, John's fourth key word is love. There is a lot of talk about love today – and a lot of singing about it too! But how did "the apostle of love" use the word?

Only Christians love

John tells us that the source of true love is God, because he, in his very nature, is love. This means that the only people who can really love are those who have been spiritually reborn, and who know God (1 John 4:7-8). It is true that unconverted people have a sort of love, but this is not the love of which John speaks. They love this world, and the way that it runs its affairs without God (1 John 2:15). True love is found only in the hearts of those who know that God loves them (1 John 4:19). It loves others because it loves God first (1 John 4:19-21; 5:1).

Loving the unlovely

Again and again John rejoices in God's love (1 John 4:16). It is this love that has made us God's children (1 John 3:1)! His love did not depend on our loveliness. No, he freely sent his Son to lay down his life for sinners (1 John 3:16; 4:9-10). It is this sort of sacrificial love, which does not depend on the loveliness of the person being loved, that Christians should show to each other (1 John 3:16; 4:10-11).

Not an optional extra

Such love is not something we may, or may not, choose to show. We are commanded to behave in this way to each other, and we must make sure that we do (1 John 3:11,23; 2 John 5). If we do not, it is because we have not been truly born again. Brotherly love is found in every Christian without exception, and it is only non-Christians who do not have it (1 John 3:14; 4:7-8,12). And there is no middle ground. We either love our brothers or we hate them (1 John 2:8-11).

Love can't be hidden

Love is not simply an attitude. It can be seen. Love towards God is seen in the fact that we do not cringe in terror before him (1 John 4:17-19), and that we live a life of glad obedience to his commandments (1 John 2:5; 5:2-3). Love towards others does not stop at words, but feeds and clothes the needy (1 John 3:16-18) and provides hospitality to fellow Christians (3 John 6). This, of course, does not mean that love does not use words to express itself. John himself writes to his readers in the most affectionate terms (1 John 3:2; 4:1; 2 John 1; 3 John 1,11).

Love also shows itself in a firm attitude towards error. We know that error damns people. We cannot therefore idly stand by and do nothing. We must speak out against error in forthright terms (1 John 2:18-19,22; 4:13; 2 John 7-9), and we must not even have false teachers in our houses (2 John 10). God's truth matters this much.

Finally ...

To sum up, then, what is love and what does it mean for us? "This is love, not that we loved God, but that he loved us and sent his Son as an atoning sacrifice for our sins. Dear friends, since God so loved us, we also ought to love one another" (1 John 4:10-11).

OVER TO YOU

Do you display sacrificial love to your fellow Christians? Ask God to help you show by all you do that you know God's love in your life.

Setting new priorities

Following the Lord
Disciples feature in 15 out of the 24 chapters in Luke. The word disciple means "someone who learns through teaching or experience". A Christian disciple is someone who responds to the call of the Lord Jesus Christ by following him completely.

Counting the cost
When crowds followed him, Jesus took great care to point out that there was a great cost involved in becoming a disciple (Luke 14:25-33). "It will mean changing established loyalties to your family and even to yourself. You must sit down and think whether you will continue to the end." All this may be too great a sacrifice to make, as it was for the rich young ruler (16:13; 18:22-23).

Setting new priorities
"Follow me," said Jesus, explaining discipleship (Luke 9:59). "Don't look back – look at me!" (9:62; 17:32). On the one hand this means giving up the right to choose your own way in life (9:23). On the other hand it means:
· becoming like Jesus (Luke 6:20-22)
· really recognising Jesus as Lord by faithfully obeying him (Luke 6:46-49; 19:12-27)
· being loving (Luke 6:32-35; 10:27-37)
· being a witness to Jesus (Luke 5:10; 24:48)
· being fruitful (Luke 6:43-44; 8:8,15)

Discovering the rewards
The rewards of being a disciple are great: a relationship with God (Luke 8:19-21), fellowship with God and entrance into his kingdom through the Lord Jesus Christ (12:32), joy (10:20), eternal life and much more now and in the future (18:29-30).

The committed believer will also suffer (9:23). "When Jesus tells you to take up your cross daily, he is not telling you to find some way to suffer daily. He is simply giving forewarning of what happens to the person who follows him" (John White).

Learning from the teacher
Jesus was the master disciple-maker. He carefully and prayerfully chose the twelve disciples (Luke 6:12-16). He lived his life openly before the group of closer disciples and taught crowds, "sharing his spirit until they caught his vision" (Ada Lum). In private to the smaller group, he explained things

> " *He shared his spirit until they caught his vision*"

further to develop their understanding (8:9-15; 11:1-13). He sent them out on practical assignments (9:1-5; 10:1-16) and evaluated them when they returned (10:17-24). And he prayed about them and for them (10:21-22; 22:31-32). We are the disciples of today. We still need to learn humbly (6:40; 14:11) by hearing his word and responding in prayer (11:2-4) and obedience, to carry out the work he has given us (24:45-49).

OVER TO YOU
Spend some time in prayer, thinking about what is stopping you from becoming a closer follower of Jesus Christ. Ask for the Lord's help to overcome those difficulties as you set new priorities before him.

The beauty of holiness

About halfway through many of Paul's letters, deep theology gives way to practical, everyday application. We need the good foundation first, on which we can build Christian characteristics.

There is nothing weak about holiness! A holy person is someone who has been transferred from the control of sin to the control of Jesus Christ. To be holy is to be distinctive; it is to be different. First of all our attitudes must change, and then our behaviour will become clearer and more Christlike.

There are two sides to living holy lives: God working in us and us working with him.

God works in us

This is the work that God, the Holy Spirit, does in us. He gives us peace and he uses the word of God – the Bible – to make us holy (Colossians 3:15-16). It's up to us to allow God to change us.

We work with God

God expects us not only to cooperate with his Holy Spirit who works in us but also to make a deliberate attempt to avoid sin and to act as Christians (Philippians 2:12-13).

It is this aspect of living holy lives that Paul spells out in Colossians 3:1-5.

The readjusted mind

The way we behave is decided by the way we think. What goes on in our minds is important! Jesus Christ is not only our high example, he is also our Lord and master. Our pattern is based not on the world below, but on the world above, where Christ now lives (Colossians 3:3). We need to readjust our thinking, not just when we become Christians, but regularly.

The redirected life

Certain aspects of our "old self" need to be put to death: see Colossians 3:5,8-9. It's very easy to see these horrible vices in others, but much more difficult to get rid of them in our own life! Again, a constant pruning is needed to get rid of these harmful weeds which choke healthy growth.

But look at Colossians 3:12-14 and see how beautiful the "new clothes" are that we are to put on. Love is the holiest virtue of all (verse 14).

Out with sin!

So Paul writes about putting to death sin in our lives (Colossians 3:5). How can we deal with sin? Quite simply – stop doing it! We are to get rid of sin in every shape or form. Of course this also means being watchful and prayerful (Matthew 26:41; James 1:13-15), Putting to death all sin is to be our aim throughout life, even though we know we shall only be completely free from all traces of it when we get to heaven.

Remember that we're not alone in the struggle! The Holy Spirit lives in us, and as we put sin to death, we know God's power at work in our lives (Romans 8:13).

OVER TO YOU

How can we deal with sin? Quite simply – stop doing it! Pray for strength from God to put this into practice.

Coping with temptation

The Bible uses the term "temptation" to describe two processes: any way in which God puts our Christian resolution to the test and any way in which we are incited to do wrong. Often these two aspects meet in a single experience. Thus, when our Lord Jesus was tempted (Matthew 4:1-11), the devil wanted him to do wrong and God was testing his recent commitment to rescue us.

It's not wrong!

It is very common to feel ashamed of being tempted, so let's notice at once that it's not wrong to be. Jesus was! It's wrong to put ourselves in a place where we are liable to be tempted, and we are to pray against such times (Matthew 6:13). But a favourite tactic of the devil is to put temptation our way and then make us feel sinful about it! He's really rotten. Another very important thing to remember is that God never tries to get anyone to do wrong (James 1:13).

Why then does he let the devil do that? James tells us: "Consider it a sheer gift, friends, when tests and challenges come at you from all sides. You know that under pressure, your faith-life is forced into the open and shows its true colors. So don't try to get out of anything prematurely. Let it do its work so you become mature and well-developed, not deficient in any way"(James 1:2-4, *The Message*). Good can come from being tempted. Anything that simultaneously develops our strength and promotes our growth is worth the closest attention.

Know your enemy

Step one is to discern the devil's presence. Often he uses the pull of the world. Or he plays on the pull of the "flesh", as the Bible calls our incarnate egotism and our natural drives. And we need to recognise that he quite simply attacks us directly, enticing us to do wrong.

Know the Christian response

The second step is to develop the coping strategy taught in Scripture. When we know that we are never tempted beyond what we can take (1 Corinthians 10:13), when we know that the Jesus in us is stronger than the devil who assaults us (1 John 4:4) and when we live by "resist the devil and he will flee from you" (James 4:7), then we are mastering the principles of Christian resistance.

Now do it!

A little girl was asked what she did when Satan knocked at her heart. "Why", she said, "I send Jesus to the door."

OVER TO YOU

How serious are you about temptation? Pray that God would help you to master the three strategies that Jesus taught (Matthew 4:1-11) for coping:

· Know your Bible
· Instant rejection
· Constant resistance

Real service

Christian service has transformed the world throughout history. The fight to destroy poverty and injustice, to get good education and hospitals has often had its roots in the good news of Jesus.

Israel – God's servant

When God delivered the people of Israel from slavery in Egypt and made them his special nation, they promised to obey and serve the Lord (Exodus 24:7). Israel was God's servant. But down the years of history, the nation failed dismally to live up to that promise, turning away from God on many occasions.

Against this background Isaiah the prophet wrote about God's perfect servant, who would fully carry through all God's plans. There are four sections of Isaiah which are known as the "servant songs": Isaiah 42:1-9; 49:1-13; 50:4-9; 52:13–53:12.

Jesus – God's perfect servant

Look at Mark 1:11. When Jesus was baptised, the voice of God the Father was heard. This can be understood as a combination of two Old Testament verses: Psalm 2:7 and part of one of the servant songs: Isaiah 42:1. God identified Jesus as the true servant. The New Testament church saw Jesus in the same light (Acts 8:30-35). As God's perfect servant, Jesus fully pleased God and through Jesus God fulfils all his plans for the world.

The New Testament teaches the marvellous truth that Jesus died for us (Mark 10:45). And he also lived for us. Not only did the sacrifice of his death take away our sins, but the perfect life lived by Jesus is accounted to Christians in the sight of God. God treats those who have faith in Jesus as if they themselves had perfectly obeyed and served God as Jesus did. Look at Romans 3:22. It says God gives us a righteousness: he puts people right with himself. Through Jesus, God's

personal data files record that each Christian has lived perfectly! Now look at Romans 5:19. This says that through the obedience of Jesus, many people will be counted as totally obedient in God's sight. There is no more need for struggling to please God to get ourselves right with him! It is all done for us, by Jesus; salvation is God's free gift!

Serving God today

Jesus taught his disciples to imitate his great example of service. At the Last Supper Jesus performed the servant's job of washing the disciples' feet. (See John 13:13-17.)

In Mark's Gospel Jesus often took time with the disciples to underline this point. The job of looking after children is often despised by the world, but look at what Jesus said about this in 9:33-37. The church isn't to operate like the power pyramid of an earthly kingdom or business empire. The greatest in the kingdom of God is accessible to all, and is the slave of all (Mark 10:41-45). From this priority of service flows all Paul's teaching about every part of the church body having some function in serving the rest: 1 Corinthians 12:12-31; Ephesians 4:11-16. And service is to be worked out in areas of family life, employment and social concern (Ephesians 5:22-33; 6:5-9; James 2:14-17).

OVER TO YOU

How do you serve others? Is it time to review areas of your life where you could do more to demonstrate Christian service?

MOVING ON AS A CHRISTIAN
Sunday – have a good day!

Made for humanity

At creation, God's pattern of action was that he worked for six days and on the seventh he rested (Genesis 2:2). We are made in the image of God and so it is both right and good for us to follow the same pattern of six days' work and one day for rest and fellowship with God (Exodus 20:8). Although the weekly pattern had special significance for the Jews, notice what Jesus said in Mark 2:27 – it was given for the good of all humanity. God's power in people's lives was often demonstrated by Jesus choosing to do many of his miracles on the Sabbath (Mark 3:2; Luke 13:16; John 5:9).

Jesus – Lord of the Sabbath

The Jewish Sabbath was the last day of the week, Saturday. Keeping the day holy out of real love for the Lord would bring delight to both God and people (Isaiah 58:13-14). But a mere outward keeping of the day was offensive to God (Isaiah 1:13-14). The Pharisees introduced many of their own do's and don'ts for the Sabbath and turned it into a day to be endured rather than enjoyed (Mark 2:24). More often than not they used it simply as an opportunity to find fault with other people (Mark 3:2; John 9:16). Sadly, this same spirit of Sabbath legalism has often been adopted by the church.

But Jesus is Lord of the Sabbath and it is for each Christian with freedom of conscience under his Lordship to decide how to use the blessing of this one day in seven (Mark 2:28; Romans 14:5-13). Feeling unable to take part in the final of his race during the Olympic Games of 1924, because it was being run on a Sunday, the Christian Eric Liddell took a stand which had a great impact for Christ: perhaps you have seen the film *Chariots of Fire*?

The Lord's day

At the beginning of the New Testament church some believers continued with a Saturday Sabbath, but this soon fell away (Colossians 2:16). The first day of the week became a special day for Christians, so continuing the pattern of the one in seven (Acts 20:7; 1 Corinthians 16:2). The reason for this was that God by his actions made Sunday a special day. All the Gospels note that Jesus was raised from the dead on the first day of the week (Matthew 28:1; Mark 16:2; Luke 24:1; John 20:1). Jesus appeared to the disciples on that day (John 20:19,26). The day of Pentecost was a Sunday (Acts 2:1).

The day of rest

We need time to meet with God. Our spiritual lives need to be developed. In God's pattern we find the origins of the weekend which we all value so much. But this rest has a greater significance. It is a picture of the gospel by which we are called to stop trying to come to God by depending on our own good deeds, and trustfully rest on Jesus to bring us to God. It is also a picture of the rest that awaits us in heaven (Hebrews 4:1-13).

OVER TO YOU

Do you keep the Sabbath as a special day? It may not be a Sunday – especially if you work in the church – but taking a day each week away from your working routine and spending more time in prayer and reading the Bible than you do the rest of the week or in enjoying God's creation can really help you to grow as a Christian.

The occult – hidden danger!

Demons

Although the possibility of angels has been frowned upon, Mark's Gospel tells us clearly that they exist: Mark 1:13; 12:25; 13:32; 16:5. There are beings in the universe besides ourselves. Angels are not limited by physical bodies, but are spirits invisible to the human eye. There are good angels (Hebrews 1:13-14) and there are evil angels (2 Corinthians 11:14) which the Bible calls demons or evil spirits. Satan himself is a fallen angel.

Occult practices

The word occult means "hidden". Some people, knowingly or unknowingly, have contact with God's enemies in the hidden, invisible dimensions of the universe. Seeking to discover the future by astrology and fortune-telling has become acceptable but it is, in fact, demonic (Acts 16:16-18). Even the seemingly innocuous newspaper horoscope leads people to rely less on the God-given gifts of mind and reason, and instead to take decisions based on lies (John 8:44). Trying to contact the dead, the Ouija board, séances, Satanism, faith healing other than in the name of Jesus, all these and more potentially involve contact with demons and are forbidden by God (Deuteronomy 18:10-11).

Occult practices are unspeakably dangerous and can even seriously impair the spiritual life of any Christian who foolishly gets involved with them (1 Corinthians 10:20-22). Jesus can deliver those who are caught up with the occult, but drastic action has to be taken to finish with the practice (Acts 19:17-20).

Demon possession

Jesus taught that when an individual life is empty of God it is in danger. Demons can gain a hold over people (Matthew 12:43-45). Jesus often met and dealt with people who were possessed by demons (eg Mark 1:32; 3:11; 5:1-20). Discernment is required. The Gospels carefully distinguish demon possession from epilepsy (Matthew 4:24). Throughout Mark's Gospel people who are possessed by demons show very negative and often violent reactions to the presence of the Holy Spirit and Jesus (Mark 1:24; 5:7; 9:20). Spiritual authority is required to help demon-possessed people (Mark 3:15). Such authority only comes from strong faith and transparently righteous living, which are the fruits of walking close to Jesus (Acts 19:13-16).

Jesus and Satan

On the cross, Jesus didn't only deal with our sins. The cross also marks the climax of the battle between Jesus and Satan. There, Satan was utterly defeated (Colossians 2:14-15; 1 John 3:8). His defeat at the cross seems to have led to a drastic reduction in the number of cases of demon possession. Compare the Gospels and Acts.

Satan is beaten. This means as we as Christians stick close to Jesus, we can know his power to defeat Satan and his ways (Ephesians 6:10-20). We should be careful of Satan, but needn't be scared out of our wits by him (James 4:7; 1 Peter 5:8-9).

OVER TO YOU

Have you ever had contact with practices that the Bible describes as demonic? Do you know people who are still involved? If so, pray for deliverance from evil influences (seeking help from a Christian minister) and for a fresh start with Jesus.

Saying "no" to ourselves

The way of the cross

When Jesus calls us to take up the cross (Mark 8:34-35), he is calling us to do at least two things:

- He is calling us to leave sin. As Christians, we are called upon to do all in our power, God helping us, to kill every sin in our lives (Romans 8:13).
- He is calling us to put aside our personal comfort and ambition to meet the needs of his kingdom. A regular job is a blessing. But Jesus gave up his carpentry to preach, and to meet the needs of the kingdom of God. Similarly, during his ministry Jesus had no permanent home (Mark 6:3; Luke 9:58). His prayer in Gethsemane shows his attitude (Mark 14:36). Jesus calls us to do the same. How do you think this applies to you, the needs of your fellowship, and the need of those around you to hear the gospel?

Words of encouragement

If we're honest, the idea of the cross frightens us. We naturally shy away from giving up the right to our own lives, A life of straining towards a goal, of being in harness to Jesus, doesn't appeal to us! But Jesus is sympathetic. He does not lower his demands, but he does go out of his way to encourage us, and urge us lovingly forward in this matter.

- He promises us that through following him in this way we will know the joy of growing and having effective Christian lives (John 12:24-26; 15:2).
- He warns us that the way of selfishness ends in tragedy (Mark 8:35-36).
- He promises us that heaven will more than make up for the difficulties we may experience for Christ (2 Corinthians 4:17-18). One day God the Father will honour us just as he has honoured Jesus (John 12:26).
- We become more like Jesus. Jesus loved us and gave himself for us (Galatians 2:20). Giving yourself to people is at the heart of God's personality. As we follow him we will find ourselves (Matthew 10:39).

Saying "yes" to God

Why did Jesus deny himself and go to the cross? Why did he leave the comforts of heaven to live the harsh and difficult life that he lived? Why did he put himself into the position where he was forsaken by God? Why did he allow himself to fall into the ground like a seed to die (John 12:24)? For you. For me. That we might have life. When we look at Christ's love we feel constrained to serve him and follow him (2 Corinthians 5:14-15).

So saying "no" to the way we want to live isn't something to do for a few days every year. Saying "no" to ourselves is something we are all called upon as Christians to do. It isn't an end in itself, but leads to the greater glory of God and the growth of his kingdom. If we are to say "yes" to God, we will often have to say "no" to ourselves. We cannot serve two masters!

OVER TO YOU

How often do you say "yes" to God – even when it means saying "no" to something you want for yourself? Ask God to give you a clearer vision of the blessings that he has in store for those who follow him selflessly.

Suffering and healing

The problem: suffering in the world

In the world we live in, everyone suffers in some way. "Man is born to trouble as surely as sparks fly up from a fire" (Job 5:7). And believers in God and Jesus don't have lives that are free from difficulty and suffering.

The origin: what causes suffering?

Some of the suffering in the world can be put down directly to people. Think of the air crash where the pilot was negligent or the hotel fire where proper precautions were not taken. Think also of places with bad hygiene or where there are serious economic difficulties because of uneven distribution of wealth. People are responsible. It can fairly and squarely be attributed to human sin. But the earthquakes, the "natural" disasters remain. Who is responsible for these?

The reason: why does God allow suffering?

There are no easy, slick answers. But the Bible says that the effects of human sin are some- how so devastating that even the created world itself suffers. The natural world creaks and groans (Genesis 3:17-19; Romans 8:20-22). This is a clear reminder that humanity is weak and sinful in the sight of a holy God.

When the tower in Siloam fell down, killing 18 people, some critics asked Jesus whether they had sinned more than other people. Why did it happen? Jesus gave a pointed reply: "These people weren't worse sinners. But if you don't turn from your sins, you will die as they did" (Luke 13:5).

The purpose: what is our response?

There's a purpose in suffering. It's how we react to it that's important. God may be developing our character (Romans 5:3-4; James 1:2-4). So instead of indulging in self-pity, we need to remember that God understands what we're going through.

God's answer: the cross

The good news that Jesus brought is that God is concerned about people – concerned enough to send his only Son into the world, to take the judgement – the suffering and death due to us for our sins – upon himself on the cross (Isaiah 53:4-6; see also Luke 9:22).

Jesus' life: the healer

Healing was part of the life and work of Jesus. Doctor Luke gives us many examples of this (Luke 4:40; 6:17-19). Together with preaching the kingdom of God, healing was part of the commission given to the first disciples (Luke 9:2; 10:9). Today, miracles of healing occur, often to accompany and confirm the preaching of the gospel. And of course it is clear that God also works through the normal means of medical help to bring about healing.

We can pray for the healing of those who are ill, in body, mind or spirit (Luke 7:1-9; 11:2). Leaders in local churches have special responsibilities (James 5:15). Whatever God's will is with individual people, we can know that he does care (1 Peter 5:7).

OVER TO YOU

Do you recognise the hand of God in healing today? Pray for anyone you know who is suffering in any way, that they might know such healing from God.

The gift of work

The gift of work

Work is one of the original intentions that God had for humanity, even before the fall (Genesis 2:15). It comes as part of the Ten Commandments (Exodus 20:9). What else does the Bible say?

· We should use the different skills and gifts that we have: there is no difference between "spiritual" and "secular" work (Exodus 31:2-11; Matthew 25:14-30; Luke 19:11-27).
· We're intended to enjoy our work (Ecclesiastes 5:18-19).
· It is right to receive reasonable pay for work (Luke 3:14; 10:7).
· With the money earned, we can support ourselves, our families and those in need (1 Timothy 5:8; 2 Corinthians 8, 9).
· There are harsh words for those who refuse to work (2 Thessalonians 3:6-15).

Frustration at work

Much of this might seem a far cry from the real world. Work can become boring and we can find ourselves just living for evenings, weekends and holidays. Relationships with people at work can be tough, too. Why is this?

At the fall (Genesis 3:17-19), it seems that the conditions in which work is carried out (not work itself) suffered the judgement of God's curse. So work becomes a toil, and there is drudgery, monotony, disappointment and frustration. But it is how we respond to this that is important.

Out of work

For some people the difficulty is not the problems of working in a job, but not having a job at all. If work is part of God's plan for people, then it must be wrong to deprive people of work. If we are unemployed, we can become bitter and weaker and weaker in

morale. But God knows; he understands. He still has a plan for the lives of his people, and with him something good can be found in everything (Romans 8:28). Christian friends can be a great help and encouragement too, and maybe there's work that we can do in our local church.

Rest from work

Work is not intended to become the be-all and end-all in life! Look at Luke 12:16-22 for a man whose life centred on his work. Rest and leisure are also part of God's plan. And one day in seven, a Sabbath, is to be a special day free from necessary work, given over to serving God (Exodus 20:8-11; Nehemiah 13:15-18).

Working for God

If Jesus was our boss, how would we work? We would probably be more punctual, more careful and more hard-working! Well, according to Colossians 3:22–4:1, he *is* our boss! (And even if you are a boss, he's still *your* boss!) So instead of being irritable and grumbling, we should be calm, patient and content to do an honest good day's work! Think what a difference that would make to us all (Ephesians 6:5-9)!

OVER TO YOU

Do you regard your work as a gift from God? Even if you feel sure that you are not doing the work that God intended for you – perhaps because you are currently unemployed – there will be some aspect of what you are doing in which God is using you. Rejoice that you can serve him in this.

Mind your language!

Again and again James refers to the way we use our tongue. Speech is a wonderful gift of God, but like all his gifts it can be used for good or ill. How tragic it is that the same tongue may one moment be praising God and the next cursing a fellow human (James 3:9)!

Empty words

It is not exactly a compliment when someone is said to be "all talk". The talk may all be kind and true, but if it's not backed up by action, it's not much use. Someone cold and starving does not want to be wished well – he wants help (James 2:15-16). Words are no substitute for work either (look up Proverbs 14:23).

A forest fire

Few situations can be more frightening than a raging forest fire when it gets out of hand. It may begin with only a little spark and yet cause devastation (James 3:5-6). Think of how one lie leads to another in an endless cover-up operation. Or a piece of gossip spreading like wildfire, getting more and more distorted each time someone reports it.

Slander, especially of our fellow Christians, is a terrible abuse of the tongue (4:11). So is boasting and bragging, as if we were masters of our own fate (4:13-16). The sad thing is that a word once spoken cannot be retracted. When mud is thrown, some of it sticks, however much we try to clear it up afterwards. Why not use the prayer in Psalm 141:3?

"Put your tongue out"

That's what the doctor says! The tongue is also like a thermometer for our spiritual health. If you can't control your tongue, your religion is worthless (James 1:26). But the fact is that without God's help we cannot tame it (3:8)! The reason does not lie simply in the power of speech, but in the way the tongue betrays the real state of our heart and mind. Jesus summed it up very crisply in Matthew

12:34. (Just think what you say when someone suddenly treads very hard on your toe in the supermarket!)

Sometimes our words give away our real attitudes and beliefs. It may be social discrimination (James 2:3-4), racial prejudice or pride. By this test, what is my spiritual temperature today?

Winged words

As Christians, we are entrusted with words of life. How will people hear the good news, unless someone tells them? Spiritual growth requires regular teaching of the truth God has revealed.

Our new life as Christians will be detected in our manner of speech as well. It will be so trustworthy that it will require no oaths to support it (James 5:12). It will not be rash and thoughtless, but gracious and wholesome (see Proverbs 17:27-28 and Colossians 4:6).

OVER TO YOU

The psalmist said that his tongue was the pen of a skilful writer (Psalm 45:1). Does what you say "write skilfully" about your Christian life or does it sometimes betray aspects of your life that are still "work in progress"? Pray that you will speak good words to others that will encourage them.

MOVING ON AS A CHRISTIAN
Called to be free

When an embassy is besieged, a plane is hijacked or families are held hostage, the world holds its breath, following the news anxiously until the hostages are free. We set tremendous store by freedom, not just in terms of physical liberty but also in terms of human rights. The same value is fundamental in our relationship with God.

Hostages held

Paul, in Galatians, identifies three potential "terrorists" that seek to deprive us of our liberty.

- **The Law which we break.** Since we have no chance of keeping the Law in the present and we are guilty of breaking it in the past, we have little hope. The verdict having been passed, the Law demands that a heavy sentence be imposed (Galatians 3:10-13).
- **The religion which others impose.** Part of the Law that receives special emphasis has to do with religion. The requirement to go through some ceremony like circumcision or to keep some day sacred, plus a thousand and one other rules, is burdensome (Galatians 4:10; 5:3).
- **The sin we indulge.** As well as outside forces, there are also threats from within. Sinful desires of all kinds are strong, and as we give in to them so our own conscience traps us and our own characters become more subject to them (Galatians 5:13-21).

God's Law, others' expectations and personal failure all combine to form a strong prison from which we cannot escape.

Set free

Christ comes to give us the freedom (Galatians 5:1) that we cannot achieve ourselves. That is the good news of justification – of being put right with God!

Freedom fighters

Now you are free, you must fight to stay free. How?

> " *A* Christian is a perfectly free lord of all, subject to none. A Christian is a perfectly dutiful servant of all, subject to all."
>
> *MARTIN LUTHER*

- **Live in freedom.** The subtle temptation to go back to prison and make external rules more important than they are, assuming that they can keep us in God's favour, is always present (Galatians 3:1-6; 4:8-10).
- **Live in forgiveness.** The sin of the past is dealt with and the Law's condemnation no longer has any hold over us. Then why let our consciences remain in bondage (Galatians 3:25; 4:1-7; 5:18)?
- **Live in purity.** Freedom has brought with it the gift of the Spirit so that we can have the power to reject the lure of our sinful natures and live holy lives (Galatians 5:13-16,22-24).
- **Live in love.** Freedom is not self-centred but puts the interests of others first (Galatians 5:26–6:10).

OVER TO YOU

Are you really free? Ask God for the strength and insight to live in freedom, forgiveness, purity and love.

Enjoying God

"Man's chief end is to glorify God, and to enjoy him for ever," says the opening instruction in the *Shorter Catechism*. How much do we enjoy God?

The joy of believing

As Christians, we can really know joy. Our sins are forgiven, we are declared right with God, the way into God's presence is open and we are children of God. True joy follows coming to believe in the Lord Jesus Christ. This was the experience of people in the Acts of the Apostles (Acts 8:39; 16:34). It also comes out in the teaching of the apostles (Romans 5:11; 1 Peter 1:6,8).

The joy of knowing God

As Christians, we know the joy of fellowship with God and God himself. Read Psalm 16:11. Such a joy is experienced when believers are together (Isaiah 35:10). This can be maintained even in times of great difficulty (Habakkuk 3:17-18).

The joy of receiving gifts from God

God wants his people to enjoy life – everything that he has made, the things he has given. God's gifts can of course be abused, but fundamentally he wants us to accept and enjoy all the good things he has given us in a spirit of thankfulness (1 Timothy 4:4; 6:17). Think of things that you can thank God for.

What is joy?

Joy can't really be defined (1 Peter 1:8), but we can describe it in some ways. It isn't a superficial, artificial happiness. It doesn't come from foolish, irreverent jesting. It is more a quality of life than an emotion. According to the Bible, it comes *from* God!

Joy from the Holy Spirit

"The disciples were filled with joy and with the Holy Spirit" (Acts 13:52). Joy is part of the fruit of the Spirit (Galatians 5:22). See also Luke 10:21; Romans 14:17; Ephesians 5:18-19. Are we being filled with the Holy Spirit?

Joy from the Lord Jesus Christ

As we stay close to Jesus, acknowledging our constant dependence on him, we will know his joy (John 15:1-11). As we do what he wants us to do (John 14:23), pray and receive his answers to our prayers (John 16:24), we will know his joy. Paul's letter to the Philippian church was all about joy. The people were to rejoice in Jesus (Philippians 4:4). It was as the disciples saw the risen Jesus that they knew joy (John 20:20). As we worship him, so we will know joy, too.

Joy from God the Father

Nehemiah encouraged the people, "The joy of the Lord be your strength" (Nehemiah 8:10). He was reminding them that their God and his joy would make them strong. What does this mean for us? The psalmist in Psalm 119 had a great delight in the Scriptures (see for example verses 14 and 162). As we think about what God has done for us and what he wants to do with us, we need to be open to God to allow him to fire our hearts, to turn aside to worship and pray, and then to put his word into action.

OVER TO YOU

Is the joy of the Lord your strength? Spend some time in studying John 15:1-11 and pray for a real sense that you are part of the vine that is Jesus Christ, so that "your joy may be complete".

The Holy Spirit is vital!

The Holy Spirit is a divine person
He is linked with the Father and the Son in the great commission Jesus gave to his disciples before his ascension (Matthew 28:19) and also in the apostle's closing blessing in the final verse of 2 Corinthians 13.

Jesus repeatedly referred to the Holy Spirit as "he" (John 14:26; 15:26; 16:8,13-14). He is not a vague influence but a living person. We should never speak of the Holy Spirit as "it". New Testament writers speak of him as possessing the elements of personality: mind (Romans 8:27), feeling (Ephesians 4:30) and will (1 Corinthians 12:11).

He carries out the work of the Godhead. He does the will of the Father and applies the work of the Son. Yet he himself is God and not merely an agent who acts on God's behalf. Qualities that clearly belong only to God are attributed to the Holy Spirit. He is one of three Persons in the eternal Godhead.

We are born again through the Holy Spirit
It is the Holy Spirit who convicts us of our sin and who causes us to see that Jesus Christ is the answer to our need to be right with God (John 16:8-11).

It is the same Holy Spirit who brings about the new birth in the believer. Becoming a Christian is from start to finish the work of the Holy Spirit (John 3:5-8). Every Christian has the Holy Spirit living in him (Romans 8:9). Although we may not always be conscious of his presence within us, we could not be Christians apart from him.

We are guided by the Holy Spirit
Jesus promised that the Holy Spirit would guide his followers into all truth (John 16:13). He is called the Spirit of truth (John 14:17). This speaks to us of our understanding of God's word but it also applies to guidance.

Christians are those who are led by the Spirit of God (Romans 8:14). The Holy Spirit is a teacher and he delights to unfold to us the truth concerning Jesus (John 14:26). So this means asking for his help. In John 14–16, we see that John describes the Holy Spirit as "Counsellor" or "Helper". Sometimes this word was used for an advocate, the counsel for defence or even for a cheerleader who encouraged dispirited troops!

We become more like Jesus by the Holy Spirit
The great work of the Holy Spirit is to glorify Jesus (John 16:14) and one of the ways he does this is by producing a Christlike character in the lives of his followers – this is "the fruit of the Spirit" (Galatians 5:22-23).

We are equipped for service by the Holy Spirit
Jesus assured his disciples that they would be enabled to do even greater works than he did (John 14:12). He clearly had in mind the part the Holy Spirit would be playing in the hearts and lives of his followers. How we need to know the work of the Holy Spirit in our lives to have a sense of God, to come to know him and to have power to do his will!

OVER TO YOU
If you are not aware of the presence of God's Holy Spirit in your life, pray for a fresh experience of the truth that he is with you. Spending time identifying the gifts that God has given you so that you can work for him – whether in preaching, teaching or in very practical things like organising or catering – can be a useful way of reminding yourself that his Spirit is active in your life.

"Whoever believes in me,
as the Scripture has said,
rivers of living water will flow
from within him."

JOHN 7:38

God's people – army of the Spirit

The many references to the Holy Spirit in Galatians make clear how vital he is. The church is the great task force of the Spirit, born, directed, sustained and assured of victory by the Spirit. Let's look at what Paul says about the Spirit.

The Spirit represents Jesus (Galatians 4:6)

The Holy Spirit does not "do his own thing". He is the Spirit of Jesus (see also John 14:26; 16:7-15), which means he continues the work of Jesus, reflects the character of Jesus and makes Jesus real to people.

The Spirit creates life (Galatians 4:29)

Being a Christian is quite simply to be "born by the power of the Spirit". To receive the Holy Spirit as God's gift is like starting life from scratch in a totally new way (Galatians 3:2-5). Just as the Spirit was involved in the creation of the world (Genesis 1:2) so he is involved in the Christian's new creation. God promised centuries ago that he would do this (Galatians 3:14).

The Spirit gives assurance (Galatians 4:6)

When we are tempted to doubt, the Spirit reminds us of the incredible relationship that we have with God by giving us a strong inward conviction that God is our Father. *Abba*, the word for "Father" used in many versions, stresses the intimate nature of our relationship but it is also a term of great respect.

The Spirit gives strength (Galatians 5:5)

The full potential of our salvation cannot be realised in this world. Sometimes when we are under pressure or discouraged we may be tempted to give up. But the Spirit holds on to us and helps us to endure the hardships until our full victory can be finally enjoyed.

The Spirit provokes conflict

(Galatians 5:16-18)
Some of the hardship comes because of the Spirit's life within us. The Spirit is holy and so is strongly opposed to our fallen natural desires. So the new life of the Spirit fights a civil war with our sinful desires. What matters, though, is that the Spirit has the upper hand and increasingly wins. He cannot do otherwise.

The Spirit produces fruit:

(Galatians 5:22-23)
Just as an apple tree produces apples because it has the source of life of an apple inside it, so we have the source of the life of Jesus inside us and can now reproduce his character in our personality. No better description of Jesus' character could ever have been given than the fruit of the Spirit.

The Spirit expects obedience

(Galatians 5:25)
We have seen what the Spirit does for us. But it is obvious that we need to express the Spirit's life. We are to live our life under his control. We do this through obedience to God and love for others. We cannot expect the Spirit to work in us if we are not prepared to express his work. All input and no output makes for a stagnant pool!

OVER TO YOU

Are you expressing the life of the Spirit? Pray that God would help you to live in obedience to him, so that everything you do and say is increasingly an expression of the life and resources of God's Spirit in you.

MOVING ON AS A CHRISTIAN
Facing up to persecution

A suffering church

From the very beginning, Christians have had to suffer for their faith. Early on, the opposition came from the Jews. They were jealous of the church's success, and they were frightened in case the movement upset their national security and comfort. This had been their main fear about Jesus. They were also quite sincere at times, regarding the good news about Jesus as a form of blasphemy. They felt that they were doing God a service by persecuting Christians (John 16:2). Paul tells us later that this is what Christianity had meant to him (Philippians 3:6).

At the outset, the Roman authorities thought that Christianity was another version of Judaism, and they left Christians alone, except when the Jews falsely accused them of disturbing the peace. Later on, when it became clear that Christianity was a new faith, and therefore illegal, the empire took a hand in persecuting Christians, especially when they refused to call the emperor "Lord".

Why persecution?

The church is persecuted:

- **because the world is a hostile place.** Human nature is fallen and rebellious. Men and women are blind to God's truth (John 16:3).
- **because people don't want the truth.** It hurts because it shows their sin. Believing would cost them too much. It would mean altering their views (John 15:20-25).
- **because the devil wants to spoil God's work.** He is the one who stirs up opposition and persecution, as well as provoking internal problems in the church (1 Peter 5:8-9).

Why does God allow persecution?

God uses persecution:

- to show he is in control and that whatever people do to Christians, his plans cannot be frustrated. We are on the winning side (John 16:33; see also Acts 2:23-24).
- to sharpen up Christians, making us more sure of what we believe and, as we suffer for it, making us value it more (Romans 5:1-5). In this way, our faith will be proved (1 Peter 1:6-7).
- to give us an opportunity to share our faith (Acts 8:1,4). Jesus promised that God would even give us the words we need when having to answer for what we believe (Matthew 10:16-20).
- to teach his people to rejoice in trouble (Acts 16:25), something only the Holy Spirit can do (1 Thessalonians 1:6).

Persecution now

Christians are still being persecuted in the world, and we should remember to pray for them. Most Christians in the West can thank God that they have never known serious persecution. However, many of us do face mockery and minor forms of hostility, and we can gain God's help and blessing in these situations. In fact, the Bible says that all Christians are bound to suffer in some way or other (Matthew 5:10-12; John 15:20; 2 Timothy 3:12).

OVER TO YOU

Pray for those who are being persecuted for their Christian faith. Think about your own life. Are there ways in which you suffer or are "persecuted" because of your faith? Draw strength from the fact that God understands, is with you and will give you opportunities to witness for him in these circumstances.

Make yourself at home!

The importance of house groups

From the day the church was born at Pentecost, believers used their homes as a place for regular meetings (Acts 2:42-46). They used a very simple formula for their meetings. They concentrated on:

- the teachings of the apostles – now the New Testament
- the fellowship – sharing and caring
- the breaking of bread – the communion service and, more widely, sharing a meal together: what the New Testament calls *hospitality*
- prayer

All this was done in conjunction with public gatherings.

When Paul reviewed his ministry (Acts 20:17-35), he spoke about his teaching in public and in homes (verse 20). The public ministry was threatened by the religious leaders from the beginning (eg Acts 5:40) and this was still persisting years later when Paul preached in Asia (Acts 20:19). By AD 64 this persecution included political abuse, when Nero blamed the Christians for the burning of Rome. By AD 80, Christianity was declared illegal in all the Roman Empire, almost ending public preaching.

The ministry in the homes of the Christians became the chief means of building up the believers in their faith and reaching others for Jesus. So meetings in homes are mentioned several times in the New Testament, for example, 1 Corinthians 16:19; Colossians 4:15; Philemon 2.

Caring and sharing Christians

From the beginning of Acts the spirit of the early church was that of serving one another. Bearing one another's burdens was the hallmark of Christian conduct (Galatians 6:2). This was so evident to outsiders that a common reference to Christians was, "See how they love one another!" To fail in this respect brought severe criticism from Paul (1 Corinthians 11:20-22).

Jesus said, "Everyone will know you are my disciples, if you love one another" (John 13:35). This loving behaviour grew out of the close-knit sharing and caring house groups in the early church.

Reaching others through the home

It is interesting to see that the winning of converts to the faith is connected both with public meetings and house meetings (Acts 2:46-47; 5:42). The early Christians were as much given to real personal interaction as to public teaching. Paul wrote to the Thessalonians: "We loved you so much that we were delighted to share with you not only the gospel of God but our lives as well, because you had become so dear to us." Opening up our homes can mean opening up our lives too as we share the good news of Jesus and also our own lives.

Many churches today are realising what is to be gained from having small fellowship meetings in people's homes in addition to large public meetings. What the church needs is Acts 20:20 vision!

OVER TO YOU

Are you part of a small fellowship group? The mutual support and encouragement that come from sharing and praying together can be an invaluable part of your Christian life.

MOVING ON AS A CHRISTIAN
Living out God's word in his world

Jesus told his followers that they would be like salt and light in the world (Matthew 5:13-16). We certainly see the early Christians spreading the light, but what about the salt? Salt was used as a preservative to stop meat rotting. What impact did Christians in Acts have on society at large?

Earning respect

First of all, the very lives Christians lived made them highly respected (Acts 5:13). Paul's defence to both Jews and Romans was that he knew the Law and had a clear conscience (Acts 22:3; 23:1; 24:16).

Christians stood out as kind and caring people, for example, Tabitha (Acts 9:36). They were expected, in a very permissive society, to be sexually moral (Acts 15:20). Paul set an example of self-supporting work (Acts 18:3; 20:33-35; 2 Thessalonians 3:6-12). Morally, Christians stood head and shoulders above the rest. What is more, they were concerned for everyone, reflecting Christ's compassion for people in need (Acts 10:38; 20:35),

Upholding law and order

Christians were law-abiding people (Romans 13:1-7). They were only prepared to break the law when it cut clean across what they knew to be true (Acts 4:19-20; 5:29). Although the Romans later persecuted them, in Acts they are pictured as having no quarrel with Christians. And although preaching often led to civil disturbances, these were usually started by the Jews.

Roman government was very different from our own, but the citizen did have certain rights – which Paul claimed more than once (Acts 16:37-39; 22:25-29). He also used the system when it was to the advantage of the gospel (Acts 25:11). In a democratic society we have even greater opportunities of making Christian views known and the Christian presence felt.

Affecting society

Jesus likened the kingdom to yeast in dough, working from the inside (Matthew 13:33). Generally speaking, Christians were expected to carry on doing what they did, bringing their influence to bear on society where they were. And along with the many who responded to the gospel in Acts, there were some who occupied very influential positions (Acts 8:27-39; 13:12; 16:14; 17:4,12). The most striking example of what the gospel can do happened at Ephesus (Acts 19). As Christians grew in number, the whole of the local economy felt the impact.

The early preachers called a special people together by the gospel. They did not attempt to Christianise society. But when the gospel does its work, its influence is inevitably felt by all who come into contact with genuine Christians. The principles we see in Acts can change the face of whole communities, affecting laws and morality and promoting the good and welfare of all men and women.

For us there is a danger that we can be so taken up with our own church life that we are not affecting different areas of society. We need to be encouraged to apply biblical principles to contemporary political and social issues.

OVER TO YOU

What do you feel about Christians being involved in politics? Think about whether it is a good thing for Christians to be involved in the way society is run, either at local or national level.

"*I am not ashamed of the gospel, because it is the power of God for the salvation of everyone who believes: first for the Jew, then for the Gentile.*"

ROMANS 1:16

A pastor shares his faith with a villager, Bengal

MOVING ON AS A CHRISTIAN
Transforming God's world

Paul's letter to Philemon is about slavery – so let's think about this some more and see if there are any lessons that we can learn today.

Slavery – an ancient practice

Slaves are people who are owned by a master and who have no rights of their own. Slavery has been practised since earliest times, the main source of slaves being captives in war. Laws in most societies made provision for the treatment of slaves. The Hebrew laws given through Moses adopted a much more humane approach than those of other societies at that time. The Hebrew people were themselves slaves in Egypt, and God brought about their liberation.

Slaves ... and friends

Treatment of slaves varied widely – from harsh cruelty to the giving of positions of trust and even freedom. By New Testament times, the commonest practice was that of owning household slaves. They were usually treated fairly leniently.

Jesus himself likens the relationship of disciples to himself as that of slaves to a master. But he goes on to show that the relationship is a far more intimate one – that of friends (John 13:16; 15:15).

Slaves as Christians

Many early churches contained masters and slaves. This was so in the church in Philemon's house and also in Ephesus and Colossae, where Paul gives instructions to masters and slaves (Ephesians 6:5-9; Colossians 3:22–4:1). So Paul doesn't expect Christianity to introduce any immediate legal changes – but he does expect inner, moral changes in relationships on both sides.

Because Paul doesn't argue strongly for the abolition of slavery, did he want things to stay as they were? If we read 1 Corinthians 7:21; Galatians 3:28; Colossians 3:11, we see Paul saw such institutions as irrelevant – not the most important thing. True freedom is freedom in Jesus, which transcends human relationships and institutions.

What about today's problems?

The apostles saw slavery as part of the order that was passing away. Rather than seeking revolutionary changes, they tried to change the system from within, with tact and courtesy. They looked for a change of heart brought about by the conversion of slave-owners.

So what does this mean for us today?

- **We should be concerned for our society.** As Christians we should seek reforms wherever there is injustice and cruelty. The leaders of the movements to abolish slavery were Christians. What is God calling us to do? Whatever it is, tact and patience should be the hallmarks of our action.
- **We should be concerned for individuals around us.** Paul had a real concern for the slave Onesimus. Look again at Philemon verses 10-12,16,17. How concerned are we for individuals whom we meet day by day? And does our concern lead to action?

OVER TO YOU

Does "slavery" exist today? It is a fact of life for many people around the world, whether they are child labourers or young people, female and male, trafficked between countries and exploited in the sex industry. As a Christian you can pray for such people and also seek ways of providing practical support.

MOVING ON AS A CHRISTIAN
The power of praise

The triumph of the resurrection
What a triumphant note Luke ends his Gospel on – read Luke 24:50-53! Look how the mood of the people involved in this last chapter changed dramatically:

- the women – from being so frightened and utterly dejected to urgently and eagerly sharing the news (Luke 24:1-10)
- the two on the road to Emmaus – from being sad and downcast to having a heartfelt burning in their spirits (Luke 24:13-32)
- the disciples – from being mournful, desperate and disbelieving to being so joyfully amazed. Worship was then ever so natural (Luke 24:9-12,33-52).

Why did all this come about? Simply because: Jesus wasn't dead but had risen!

The joy of the good news
Looking back quickly over the whole Gospel of Luke, we can see how the theme of joy stands out:

- the five opening songs of praise in the first two chapters
- the message that the angel brought to the shepherds was good news of great joy (Luke 2:10)
- believers can rejoice that they are known personally in heaven, and indeed God and the angels rejoice when a sinner turns back to God (Luke 10:20; 15:7,10).

Praise – a God-centred experience
The disciples showed that they were joyful and thankful by praising God (Luke 24:52-53). Here was a spontaneous burst of adoration. The risen Lord was with them. He really opened their minds to understand the Scriptures. Sometimes when we try and tell God how great we think he is, our praise becomes dull and dry. We need the Holy Spirit's help; and because we are worshipping God, our praise must also be reverent (10:21).

Praise – a shared experience
Look how Jesus came to the disciples when they were together (Luke 24:36). And naturally, they stayed with each other to worship (24:50-53). Is this relevant to us? Should we only worship with brothers and sisters in Christ when we feel like it? (What would happen if ministers did this?) No – our worship together matters far more than our feelings. We encourage one another by coming together. And hearing the Bible being read and explained is an important part of our worshipping God together (4:16-22).

Praise – a living experience
Praise isn't just something we are meant to do on Sundays! Praise is an attitude we are made to live for every day! Praise is meant to overflow into a living that gives over our will to God and what he has in mind for us. "If Jesus Christ be God and died for me, then no sacrifice can be too great for me to make for him," said the pioneer missionary C. T. Studd. Think of what Jesus told the first disciples to do (Luke 24:47) and how the resources of the Holy Spirit would be provided for them (24:49). Better start doing something about it, then!

OVER TO YOU
How can you cultivate an attitude of worship that is part of each day? Reading particular Bible passages, prayer or listening to – or singing along with – worship music can all be part of your daily worship of God.

MOVING ON AS A CHRISTIAN
Living for Jesus every day

You can't read through Acts as a Christian without getting excited and without wondering if those things could happen again today. What did they have in those early days?

They had an experience that was real

They knew the life-changing power of the good news. It wasn't a dead set of beliefs or a shallow profession of faith. It was real and personal.

What is more, they knew it together in a sense of belonging and sharing which changed their whole lifestyle (Acts 2:42-47).

They had a faith worth sharing

All these early Christians seemed to have been ready to speak about what had happened to them. They were witnesses, testifying to what they had seen and heard.

But they also had the power to do things. The Holy Spirit gave them boldness, worked miracles and turned the hearts of men and women to God (Acts 4:31; 11:21; 14:3).

They were willing to suffer

They didn't mind what it cost them. They were prepared to stand up and be counted – and to suffer for it. They were ready to face physical violence, to go to prison, even to face death, rather than keep quiet about the truth. And they did it gladly, thanking God for the privilege of suffering for Christ (Acts 5:40-41).

They knew a God who was in control

What they did, they did as God directed them. This was true of individual lives, of the work of the church, and equally true of their evangelism. They did, said or went as God told them to.

This, in turn, generated tremendous trust and confidence that God was looking after their affairs – and that they need not worry.

Instead, they readily brought their needs, and their praise, to him (Acts 4:24-31).

They knew a gospel that was unstoppable

The Acts story is the story of the spread of the good news – both to those who had been prepared for it and to those who had no background at all. In spite of opposition and persecution, including plots directed against the church leadership, the word of the Lord kept spreading and growing stronger (Acts 19:20). Because God was in this, they were on the winning side – and they knew it!

And today?

What goes on in many churches today seems light years away from Acts: dead, outward religion; dull worship; poor teaching; a lack of interest in unbelievers; a lack of real care for the believers; powerlessness. Thank God this isn't always so; there are those who are dissatisfied with such coldness and deadness and who are looking to God to provide something better.

There is no reason why God couldn't do it for us – he has done it before! Let us ask him to do it again – and we will see more of what Jesus is doing in our own day.

OVER TO YOU

How fresh is your Christian life? Can you be more engaged in developing real friendships with those who are not yet Christians, to help them draw closer to Christ? Take a reality check and pray honestly to God about what he wants you to do ... and then get on and do it!

Living the Christian Life

This part of the book is for those who not only want to "understand" but also to "live" the Christian life to their fullest capacity. It is for participants, for those who really want to be involved and make progress in the Christian life.

To be a participant we have to start, and the best place to start is at the beginning! But starting at the beginning does not mean stopping there. We must move on if we are going to know the real thrill of participating in this adventure with God.

We shall make many mistakes as we progress. Indeed, the mistakes we make will in themselves encourage us to depend more on God, realising that he is only too willing to help us. Real, lasting progress is always the result of this partnership with God.

Each section is like a journey. Starting with the first section, we move on through a further eight areas of practical Christian living until we come to the final section: "Arriving".

These nine sections each have six complete studies, giving to the individual or group 54 studies in all.

Living the Christian Life

CONTENTS

Living the Christian Life
Contents continued

WINNING p.752

Jesus is king
He conquered sin
He conquered death
He conquered evil
He will conquer the
world
Bible summary:
Jesus' cosmic plan

Victory is certain
No need to sin
No need to fear
No need to doubt
No need to falter
Bible summary:
He is able

Right in the heart
Jesus comes first
Thinking straight
Pure motives
Love determines
action
Bible summary:
Not I, but Christ

Overcoming evil
Be sure of your
ground
Depend on God's
power
Learn to say no
Tell Satan to go
Bible summary:
The armour of God

Resisting pressure
The pressure to
conform
The pressure to
compromise
The pressure to
complain
The pressure of
complacency
Bible summary:
United we stand

Onward Christian soldiers
Building the kingdom
Salt in the world
Light for the world
Winning enemy
territory
Bible summary:
What is the
kingdom of God?

SERVING p.764

Called to serve
Called by God
Compelled by love
Committed through
faith
Concerned for others
Bible summary:
Pictures of service

Power to serve
Sharing God's work
Filled with his Spirit
Controlled by his
word
Equipped with his
gifts
Bible summary:
Doing what comes
naturally

Serving in the church
The first shall be last
Lending a hand
Caring for the needy
Speaking God's word
Bible summary:
Building
community

Into the world
A life that is different
Lips that are pure
Little things count
Loving our enemies
Bible summary:
Pilgrims in a
strange land

Sharing good news
A message for
everyone
Talking about Jesus
Letting God work
Telling the
neighbourhood
Bible summary: All
things to all people

Service for life
Ready for change
Giving everything to
Jesus
Supporting his
workers
Praying for God's
servants
Bible summary:
Paul, a servant of
God

Living the Christian Life
Contents continued

HOW TO USE THIS MATERIAL

The material has been arranged for maximum flexibility of use, and for a wide range of situations and readers.

Use it in personal study
This material may be used as a companion to the Bible. It may be used as a reference to the teachings of the Bible, but it may also be used for personal, regular study of the Scriptures. It is made up of 54 studies, and if one main section is studied each week, the total material will be covered in the course of just over a year.

By using a reference Bible or concordance, each study may be extended. The passages given in the "Bible Check" can serve as a starting point for readers' own discovery of the Bible. In this way a comprehensive view of each theme can be built up. It would be useful for you to keep your own notebook handy.

Use it in a group
The material in this section will be of particular value wherever Christian people meet together. Study groups of all ages will greatly profit from the teaching they will discover for themselves as they follow the guidelines given here. It will also prove beneficial where newcomers to the Christian faith are eager to learn the practical implications of their belief.

Group leaders are encouraged to make the following preparations before using this material in any discussion. First, they should become familiar with the Bible passages provided, and be prepared to support these with cross references. Second, they should carefully read through the study material itself. Third, they should be prepared to use the questions as a basis for discussion, and to prepare further questions of their own.

Use it in a church programme

Ministers, pastors and teachers will find this material an invaluable reference source for subject material when preparing programmes for the church. For example, the six studies could be used as the basis for a six-week course of Sunday sermons or midweek meetings.

The headings are designed to capture the truth of the Bible. It is hoped that this will be helpful to preachers and teachers alike.

Use it in schools and colleges

The teaching material, Scripture passages and questions will help to stimulate those involved in religious education, as well as members of informal religious discussion groups and forums. The material has been planned as a comprehensive aid so that students from many different backgrounds of worship and tradition may learn together from the Bible's teaching in a way that prepares them for life.

Some extra features about this material:

1. Each study has four divisions which help in retaining the key truths presented.

2. Key Bible passages and references are provided with every study so that you can see what God's word actually says about it.

3. Included in each study are questions ("To think about..."). We trust this will be a real help, especially for group discussion.

4. Each main study is introduced with a "Key truth" and concludes with a "Postscript". Again, this is provided to help you to retain important truths.

5. Beside the 54 main studies there are "Bible summaries". Each summary follows a main study and is complete in itself. We encourage you to supplement the main study by looking up the references and Bible passages in the "Bible summary".

There is one thing that we have not provided and that is the help of the Spirit of God to all those who seek to live for him. We do with confidence, however, commend to you a dependence on him as you seek to live and make progress as a Christian.

The Christian life is for all of us a matter of progress, and each day brings new opportunities for growth. It is our sincere prayer that you will find this section a useful guide in living the Christian life.

STARTING
What it's all about

KEY TRUTH

Being a Christian consists of a close personal relationship with God, and not just of following a certain code of behaviour.

A life lived with God

Many people think that being a Christian is a matter of living in a certain way: being kind to others, giving to charities, going to church services, and not committing crime or fraud.

The Bible sees it differently, however. While all these things are part of living a Christian life, the essence is called "faith". That means trusting God personally, as well as believing certain truths.

Jesus complained that some of the religious people of his day had become so tied up by rules and regulations that they were neglecting their relationship with God. The gospel, or good news, is that ordinary people can once again know God personally and live in harmony with him.

A life given by God

Since the world began, people have tried to find God and have invented all kinds of ways to please him. But the whole Bible shows how futile these attempts are. Because people have refused to obey God's commands, the whole world is now cut off from him.

The only way people can make lasting contact with God is to welcome Jesus into their lives. He was God's perfect Son, who became a man in order to explain God's purposes to the world. And when he died, he took on himself the punishment for human rebellion, and opened up the way for us to God.

No one can create a new relationship with God for themselves. He has already done everything necessary; his way can only be accepted – or rejected.

A life dependent on God

Trusting Jesus is not like wearing a lucky charm. It is not simply a way of getting on the right side of God and making sure of a place in heaven.

Being a Christian is a matter of trusting God all the time. It involves staying in touch with him so that we receive his instructions and do what he asks each day.

It can bring a whole new dimension to our lives. But the Christian life will not always be easy. Saying "no" to wrong things is often difficult. Facing unexpected problems can be shattering. But he promises to help all who follow him.

A life lived for God

Most important of all, being a Christian means living for God. Some people throw

TO THINK ABOUT

Make a list of the different attitudes and activities that are often associated with being a Christian.

· Which of these are really important, if being a Christian is about having a close personal relationship with God?

· Are there any that are simply human rules and regulations? Why are these dangerous?

· Think about which is easier: to follow a set of rules, or to develop a friendship. Now think about which is more *worthwhile*. Why do we sometimes try to turn Christianity into a set of rules?

everything into work, family life or special interests. Christians are called to put all their energy into serving and pleasing God.

That does not mean that they are expected to stop what they are doing and become preachers or missionaries! Each person has talents and abilities which God wants to be fully used, with love and care. He wants each person's faith to influence all their relationships and activities.

BIBLE CHECK

A life lived with God John 17:3;
  2 Timothy 1:12
A life given by God John 14:6; Acts 4:12
A life dependent on God Luke 9:23-25;
  John 15:1-5
A life lived for God Matthew 6:24;
  James 2:14-18

POSTSCRIPT

The Bible never separates "believing" from "doing". Faith and work go together. If you emphasise one more than the other you may have a philosophy or a lifestyle, but you will not have true Christianity.

Our friends often have an important influence on our lives.

· How important is your relationship with God? Is he just another friend, or does a relationship with him come before everything else?
· How does your relationship with God shape your life?

Thank God that your relationship with him is based purely on his love for you, and not on your own attempt to reach him. Ask God to forgive you for the times when you have let other things become more important. Pray that he will help you to grow in your relationship with him.

BIBLE SUMMARY
WHAT GOD HAS DONE

The Bible describes how the first people who knew God refused to do what he asked. Ever since, humanity has been disobeying God's laws. So people are out of touch with God in this life, and prevented by death from enjoying eternal life in heaven (Ephesians 2:1-3).

A picture of hope

The Old Testament tells how God showed people how they could get in touch with him again. He told them to obey his laws. And he said that their sin was so serious that the only remedy for it was an innocent victim – an animal in those days – who would carry the death penalty on their behalf (Leviticus 16:6-10).

But that was only a picture of God's greatest act of love. Animals could not provide a permanent solution. The New Testament says: "God so loved the world that he gave his one and only Son, that whoever believes in him shall not perish but have eternal life" (John 3:16).

An act of love

Jesus Christ was the only person who has ever lived who was sinless. Even his enemies could not fault him. And he saw his death as "a ransom for many" (Mark 10:45); the innocent suffered the sentence passed on the guilty. John the Baptist called him, "The Lamb of God, who takes away the sin of the world" (John 1:29).

But because he was God as well as man he conquered death by rising to life again and promised that all who welcomed him would receive eternal life (John 3:36). That life was to begin at once. Eternal life is knowing God for oneself and enjoying his presence for ever (Romans 8:38-39).

STARTING
Making a new start

KEY TRUTH

Becoming a Christian is like starting life all over again, by handing over the control of our lives to Jesus Christ.

Seeing the need

God is a person almost beyond our imagination. He is the powerful creator of everything which exists, yet he also knows just how each individual thinks and feels. He is holy, too – he can do nothing wrong.

By contrast none of us is perfect. We have not always kept God's laws. We have done things which even our conscience knows are wrong. And above all, we have left God out of our thinking.

As a result, we are separated from God by a barrier largely of our own construction: self-will, self-indulgence and self-confidence. The Bible calls this barrier sin: it prevents us from knowing God personally.

Saying sorry to God

None of us likes to admit that we have been wrong. It is even harder if we have to admit that the whole direction of our life so far has been off course – going our way instead of God's.

But we cannot get to know God for ourselves without first telling him we are sorry for having neglected him and for the wrong things we have done. And that includes thoughts and words as well as actions.

Perhaps we also need to say sorry to other people whom we have hurt along the way.

Saying no to sin

We often teach children to say sorry when they do wrong, but watch them blunder on in the same way moments afterwards! Saying sorry is not enough; we have to show we mean it, too.

God knows what we are really like, and words never fool him. We must put all our sin behind us, and promise him not to go wilfully our own way again. This is what the Bible calls "repentance".

For some people this may involve a very radical change in the way they live. For others the change will be more inward, in the way they think and speak. God promises to help us, whatever is involved.

Saying yes to Jesus

Jesus has already done everything necessary to restore our relationship with God by dying on the cross and rising from the dead. He offers the gift of eternal life to any who will accept it.

But we cannot be half-hearted about it. We cannot ask God for his forgiveness if we are not also prepared to let him take charge of our life from then on.

TO THINK ABOUT

Take some time to think about the direction of your life.
- Do you think the direction of your life pleases God?
- What does "repentance" mean? What effect should repentance have on the direction of your life?
- Have you ever made a new start by confessing your sin to God and receiving his forgiveness? If you haven't, are you ready to do so now?

When we make a new start, we come into God's family for the first time. The Bible gives us three pictures of this: birth, adoption and coming home.

If you have never made a fresh start with Jesus, or if your Christian life has become stuck in a rut, you can use a simple prayer like this: "Dear God, I am sorry I have left you out of my life, and sinned against you in thought, word and deed. Thank you for sending Jesus to die on the cross so that I could know you for myself. Forgive my sin, and give me the power of your Spirit to live for you every day until you bring me to be with you for ever in heaven. For Jesus' sake, Amen."

BIBLE CHECK

Seeing the need 1 John 1:5-8; Romans 6:23
Saying sorry to God 1 John 1:9-10; Psalm 51:1-4,10-12
Saying no to sin Matthew 4:17; Ephesians 4:22-24
Saying yes to Jesus Revelation 3:20; Matthew 11:28-30

POSTSCRIPT

Jesus called people to follow him just as they were, without trying to reform themselves first. But he also said that once they had begun to follow him, he himself would change them.

· How do these pictures relate to your own relationship with God?
· What is new about your life now that you have made a fresh start? Have you let Jesus take control of the direction of your life?

Thank God that he has made it possible for you to belong to his family. Confess to him all the sin that you want to put behind you, and ask him to fill you with his Spirit so you can live a brand new life.

BIBLE SUMMARY
WHAT HAPPENS WHEN YOU START

There are a number of pictures in the Bible which illustrate what happens when a person welcomes Jesus into their life. Three of them have one thing in common: they refer to a family (see Ephesians 2:19).

A happy event

The first picture is of a baby born into the family. When a person accepts Jesus as the one who has cleared away their sin and opened up the way to God, they are "born again" (John 3:3). They have become a true child of God, because God's Spirit has given them a new, eternal life (John 1:12-13). Like a human baby, the new Christian has a lot of learning to do and they can easily make mistakes or even be led astray (1 Peter 2:1-2).

A new status

The next picture is that of adoption, when a child of one family is accepted as a true son or daughter of another. No one has the right to belong to God's family. Everyone is by nature shut out of it; they belong in the devil's domain. But God adopts those who trust Jesus into his family, welcoming them as his own children (Romans 8:15-16).

Where we belong

Finally, there is the well-known picture of "coming home". In Jesus' parable of the lost son, a rebellious child decides to come home, sorry for having run away, wasted his life and brought shame on the family (Luke 15:11-32). His father (God) sees him from a distance, goes out to meet him and welcomes him home. His sin is forgiven, and the family celebrates his return.

STARTING
A new way of living

KEY TRUTH

**Living as a Christian means enjoying
and experiencing life in a totally new
way.**

A new life

Before Jesus Christ enters our lives we are
spiritually dead – unable to know God and
draw on his help. But once we have
committed ourselves to him, he promises to
make everything fresh and new.

He gives a new quality of life which is open
to God and lasts for ever. It includes new
hope, peace and joy, and power and patience
to cope with difficulties.

It has new standards of conduct, and new
attitudes, too. But all these things are given to
us by God, and cannot be created by our own
efforts.

A new relationship

To the Christian, God is no longer a distant,
shadowy figure. He is a real person who can
be known, loved and worshipped.

He is like a new friend, always ready to help
and strengthen us. But the Bible usually calls
him "Father", because like the best of human
fathers he promises to provide all we need to
carry out his purposes.

Sometimes he will tell us off. But he never
bullies his children. And for our part, it will
take time to get to know him better.

A new family

If the Christian were an only child of our
heavenly Father, life would be very lonely. But
in fact we are born into the worldwide family
of God. In every town and district we have
"brothers" and "sisters" who love the Father.

This family is generally known as the
church. It may be large or small in a local
situation, and like human families it is not
always perfect. But it has important
functions.

It exists to help each Christian grow in the
faith. God has provided it so that we can find
the support and encouragement we need.

A new friend

When Jesus was on earth, his followers were
upset when he spoke of leaving them. But he
promised to send "The Comforter" (the Holy
Spirit) to be with them.

The Holy Spirit is God active in the
Christian's life. He points us to Jesus and
helps us understand the Bible and speak to
God in prayer. He shows up what is wrong in
our lives, and gives power to put it right.

And he promises to give us abilities to help
other Christians, using God's strength, not
our own.

TO THINK ABOUT

The Christian life is a new way of living
because God now lives in relationship with
us as Father, Son and Holy Spirit.

· What does it mean to call God "Father"?
  How are human fathers like our Father
  God? How are they unlike him?
· What role does Jesus have in your life?
· Do you think the Spirit is essential for
  your Christian life? Why should he be?
· Why does our new relationship with God
  change everything?

Many other people across the world also
share this relationship with God through
Jesus Christ and the Holy Spirit.

BIBLE CHECK

A new life 2 Corinthians 5:17-18; Colossians 3:12-17

A new relationship John 14:23; 1 Peter 5:7

A new family 1 Peter 2:9-10; Ephesians 2:19-22

A new friend John 14:26; 1 Corinthians 12:4-11

POSTSCRIPT

The new life is a gift from God. Some people only allow him to make superficial changes to their lives, but Jesus wants to change us right through.

· How should we think about these other people? Are they just friends, or do we have a closer connection with them?
· Why is it important that we belong to a worldwide family of believers?

Thank God for the excitement of a new way of living with him and with other believers. Pray that you will be filled with his Spirit to equip you for this new life.

BIBLE SUMMARY
THE FULLNESS OF GOD

When we describe what God does for us, we use different names for him: Father, Son (Jesus), and Holy Spirit. Sometimes people mistakenly think they are different gods, or that only one has any relevance to us today.

In fact, God reveals himself as three "persons". Each is fully God, but has a different function. But when we talk about God being "in" a Christian's life, all three persons are involved (John 14:23).

Christ in you

Jesus, the Son of God, lives in us from the moment we receive him as the one who takes away our sin and gives us eternal life (Colossians 1:27). He promises never to leave us (Hebrews 13:5).

Filled with the Spirit

The Holy Spirit also enters our life at the same time (Ephesians 1:13-14). But the Bible also speaks of other times during the Christian life when he "fills" a person, usually when they face a special task (eg Acts 4:31). However, we should always be filled with the Spirit, his life flowing into and out of us to others (Ephesians 5:18).

When we specially need the Spirit's blessing to help us worship or serve God, Jesus tells us to ask the Father and we will be given the power of the Holy Spirit (Luke 11:13).

But he never gives his power in advance of its being used. And there are times when he cannot fill us, because sin has crowded him out (Ephesians 4:30).

STARTING
God's unbreakable promises

KEY TRUTH
God promises to help us in many ways, and he never breaks his word.

The promise of security
We do not know what will happen tomorrow. We may face entirely new circumstances: poverty or wealth; illness or tragedy; hard decisions; unexpected opportunities; changes in relationships.

Because life is to some extent uncertain, we are often tempted to find a sense of security in familiar objects or people. But they can change too. Only God offers perfect security.

He promises never to let go of his children. He will never abandon us even if we forget him. He holds us secure in his love all through this life, and into the next.

The promise of support
We are most conscious of the need for God's help when we face difficulty or temptation. But if we are to do everything God wants, we need to draw on his power all the time.

In fact, we need his support just as much when life is running smoothly. Then it is easy to forget him, and so to fail him by something we do or say.

God promises his help at all times. But he never promises to brush aside our problems. In fact, problems often become opportunities to experience and demonstrate his power.

The promise of guidance
For many people, the journey through life is rather like stumbling through a dark forest. It is hard to find the way which will be most rewarding.

God, because he knows both us and the circumstances of our life in every detail, promises to show us the right thing to do at each step along the way.

He also has a special purpose for each person, and he promises to lead us to it. So as we go in the direction he has prepared, we experience a new harmony with him.

The promise of his presence
Sometimes Christians complain that life for the very first followers of Jesus must have been much easier than it is now, because they could see and touch their master.

But in fact it was harder. Jesus could only be in one place at a time. Now he promises to

TO THINK ABOUT
Make a list of some of God's promises as you find them in the Bible.

· Does God keep his promises? Are there reasons why you can believe that he does? Are there promises he has already kept in your life?

· Do you find it easier to believe God's promises when times are difficult or when times are easy?

· What stops you from depending upon God? Do you think he will fail you, or do you prefer to control your own life?

· How should you respond to God's promises?

be with everyone everywhere who loves and serves him.

We may not always feel him near us, but the Bible is never in any doubt. Jesus said, "I will be with you always, to the very end of the age" (Matthew 28:20).

He stays on hand to help, teach and guide us.

BIBLE CHECK

The promise of security John 6:37-39; Romans 8:38-39

The promise of support Matthew 11:28 30; Philippians 4:11-13

The promise of guidance Psalm 32:8; Isaiah 30:21

The promise of his presence Psalm 139:7-12; Matthew 28:19-20

POSTSCRIPT

Human beings will often break their promises because they are weak and imperfect; God can never break his promises because he is all-powerful and perfect.

Think of the situations you are facing in life at the moment.

· Can you think of any of God's promises that are especially relevant?

· How will trusting God to keep these promises change the way you live? How will it change the way you pray?

Thank God that he always keeps his promises, even when it is difficult for you to see how he will do so! Thank him that he is always with you. Tell God that you are willing to depend on his promises today.

BIBLE SUMMARY
GOD KEEPS HIS WORD

Some people will promise anything but never do what they say. God is not like that. He cannot change his mind and let us down. In the Old Testament he was specially known as a God who made solemn promises (or "covenants") and kept his word (Deuteronomy 7:9).

Two-edged promises

But as the nation of Israel soon found out, God's promises are two-edged. We can only enjoy all that he offers if we continue to obey him (Deuteronomy 7:10-11). Some of his promises, of course, are unaffected by our sin. He does not rob Christians of eternal life when they do not obey him (John 6:39).

That truth is, however, intended to inspire us to loving devotion, not to encourage us to be careless. God is so gracious that he loves us even when we ignore him (Romans 6:1-4).

Three special promises

The Bible stresses three special promises of God:

· He promised Noah that he would never again destroy the earth by flood in his anger at human sin (Genesis 9:15).

· He promised that Abraham would be the father of many nations, and have a special close relationship with God. And in believing that promise Abraham demonstrated what faith really is (Genesis 17:7-8).

· And he made a "new covenant" with the Christian church through the death of Jesus: that he would be our God and we would be his people for ever (Hebrews 8:6-13).

STARTING
The help which God gives

KEY TRUTH
God has provided four special ways in which we can receive his help.

Help through prayer
We often have lots of questions to ask God. Prayer is the way in which we can tell him how we feel, what our needs are, and share with him the problems and opportunities we face.

The Bible tells us that God is always ready to listen to our prayers, and loves to answer them. But sometimes we ask for things which will take us away from his purposes, so he will not give us these. We may be so full of requests that we never stop to ask what he really wants.

And he frequently waits for us to ask before giving us what we need, because only when we ask humbly are we ready to receive gratefully.

Help through the Bible
Our relationship with God is always two-way. We talk to him in prayer, and one of his ways of speaking to us is through the Bible (sometimes referred to as his "word").

The Bible authors were guided by God as they wrote down their experiences of him and the truths he revealed. All God wants us to know about himself and how to live for him are contained in its pages.

And the Holy Spirit will make it come alive to us and apply it to our circumstances, if we seek his insight.

Help from God's people
We have already seen that God has made us members of his family. Our "brothers" and "sisters" in Christ have special gifts and insights which God uses to help us. In fact, he intends that we should be almost as dependent on each other as on him, for we all lack wisdom.

Some people will be able to help us understand God's truth and the Bible better. Others will be able to advise us about our problems. We can talk and pray with them, and learn together from the Bible, sharing with all what God shows to each.

And it is always a good idea to talk to other Christians before making important decisions, to receive both advice and support.

Help through worship
Worship happens when a group of Christians meet together to express love and gratitude to God for all that he is and all he has done. They may sing and even shout; they may be quiet and thoughtful. And, of course, we can worship God on our own, as we think about his love to us.

TO THINK ABOUT
We need God's help at all times, so these four ways of receiving his help are not just for special occasions! Think about how you can build them into your daily life.
- How much time do you spend in prayer? Do you make sufficient time and space away from distractions so that you can be open with God? How does prayer help?
- How does the Bible bring God's help? Should that affect the way you read the Bible?
- Do you acknowledge the help that other Christians can give you? Why is it wrong to try to be a Christian on your own?

Praising God helps us in two ways. First, it reminds us of how great he is. The things which concern us then seem smaller, and our confidence grows in God's ability to deal with them. Secondly, it opens us to the Holy Spirit, making us more able to hear and obey him, and to receive his power.

BIBLE CHECK
Help through prayer John 16:24; Matthew 7:7-11

Help through the Bible 2 Timothy 3:16-17; John 16:12-15

Help from God's people Ephesians 4:11-14; Romans 12:4-8

Help through worship Acts 4:31; Psalm 29:1-4,10-11

POSTSCRIPT
Make a list of all the things you could praise God for, then praise him!

· Why is worship important? Do you allow yourself to genuinely worship God, or are you always thinking about the problems you need help with?

Take time to bring your own life before God in prayer. Ask him to speak to you through the Bible, and through other Christians. Worship him for his kindness and care.

BIBLE SUMMARY
EVERYONE HAS NEEDS

Even Jesus himself, his closest followers and all the great characters of the Bible, needed to use prayer, the Scriptures, "fellowship" with God's people and worship, to keep themselves in harmony with God.

Prayer often preceded important events. Jesus prayed all night before choosing his twelve apostles (Luke 6:12-13). And they and their close friends "devoted themselves" to prayer after Jesus left the earth, before the Holy Spirit filled them with power on the Day of Pentecost (Acts 1:14).

A weapon for battle
Jesus used the Scriptures as a weapon to fight off the subtle and powerful temptations he received in the desert before he began his public ministry (Matthew 4:3-11). The psalmist said that the way to lead a pure life was to store God's word in his memory so that he could draw on it at a moment's notice (Psalm 119:11).

Caring for each other
Paul often writes appreciatively of the help he was given by other Christians (eg Colossians 4:7-11). The Bible records the ways in which God's people cared for each other. It was a care which sometimes meant rebuking and challenging, as well as encouraging, each other.

As for worship, it seems to have been such a natural desire and thing to do (eg Acts 20:7) that only in extreme cases is it actually commanded (Hebrews 10:24-25).

STARTING
A permanent life

KEY TRUTH
The Christian life never stops; there is always more to learn, and heaven to look forward to.

A joyful life
Jesus promised his followers the two things which everyone wants but few ever find: inner peace and joy. Neither depends on an easy life. Rather, they stem from the confidence that our loving Father is in control of it, whatever happens.

Christian joy is a sense of thankfulness for God's care and love. We are no longer tied down by our sin but are free to be the people he intended us to be. We really have something to celebrate!

Joy is a gift from God, however, and not something we can just turn on or manufacture by a certain technique. And it always focuses on him, and is not a feeling to be enjoyed for its own sake.

A growing life
The Christian life has only just begun when a person becomes a member of God's new family. Just as a human child has many things to learn, and takes a long time over it, so too does a child of God.

There is always something new to learn about God and his ways. And Scripture tells us to go on to perfection – which is a long way ahead! Growing in faith can be an exciting, as well as an exacting, adventure.

Sometimes we will only grow more like Jesus when we face difficulty and apply our faith to it, just as he did. But he also promises to renew our old, sinful nature, so that we steadily move forward in our Christian life.

A giving life
Christian faith is not meant to be kept to ourselves. The first followers of Jesus couldn't stop telling others of what God had done for them.

We have something to give to others – a "gospel", or "good news" – which transforms people's lives, attitudes and relationships.

And we have something to share with each other, too: love and concern, some new gift or ability, a possession – anything which will help build up others' faith and minister to their needs. Only as we give in faith will we grow in it.

An everlasting life
Some Christians are laughed at as being "too heavenly-minded to be of any earthly use". We are not meant to be useless. Our ultimate home is heaven, but our feet are to be firmly on the ground.

TO THINK ABOUT
Think about the eternal life that God promises to give his people.
· Does "eternal life" refer to the future? Or the present? Or both? How does your present Christian life relate to the future God has promised?
· Do the things you do now have eternal significance?
· What aspects of your life today will also be part of life in God's future kingdom? What aspects will not?
· Do you think a Christian should strive to be perfect, like Jesus?

But, in fact, sometimes we may not be heavenly-minded enough. We have been promised eternal life in heaven with Jesus for ever. That is meant to inspire and encourage us in our life now.

We know that death is not the end for us. We have nothing to fear for the future. We have hope, and we shall not be disappointed in the wonderful place God has waiting for us.

BIBLE CHECK

A joyful life John 15:11; Psalm 95:1-7
A growing life Philippians 3:12-16; Ephesians 4:13-14
A giving life John 13:34-35; Luke 6:38
An everlasting life Revelation 22:1-5; Philippians 1:21-24

POSTSCRIPT

Jesus said that the Christian life is a narrow path, compared to the broad road of self-indulgence followed by many other people. But his way leads to abundant life now and for ever.

· In which areas of life do you know you need to grow?
· Which Christian characteristics do you need to develop? Do you need to be more joyful? Or more giving?

Thank God that his love for you will never fail – and that your relationship with him will continue in God's new creation. Ask for the Spirit's help to become more like Jesus, so that you will already live the type of life that God wants you to have in his eternal kingdom!

BIBLE SUMMARY
HOW PERFECT CAN YOU GET?

Jesus told his followers that they should be "perfect" (or mature) Christians (Matthew 5:48). Although God's word promises forgiveness for the sins Christians commit, it does not expect them unconcernedly to commit them (1 John 2:1-2). Jesus himself was perfect, and we are to follow his example (1 Peter 2:21-23).

But we are not instantly made perfect when we receive Jesus, even though our sin is swept away and is no longer a barrier between us and God. His life enters us, his power is available to us, and we have to learn to make use of it. This takes time, and we will make mistakes (James 3:1-2).

Becoming perfect

The Bible tells us to become perfect by obeying God's will (1 Peter 1:14-16). As we do so, we become more skilled in understanding and knowing what God wants us to do (Hebrews 5:12-14).

Sometimes we will get frustrated, because our own human nature, which still retains its imperfections and limitations, never quite manages to be as good or do as well as God's Spirit within us is urging us to. There is a battle going on inside us between the old and the new (Romans 7:15-25).

Battling against evil

And there is a battle against evil, too, as we are tempted, mocked and unsettled by evil forces which come sometimes from the most surprising quarters (Ephesians 6:12-13). But Jesus' people are promised victory over them (1 John 5:4-5).

KNOWING
Know yourself

KEY TRUTH

We can only fully appreciate all that Jesus has done for us when we see ourselves as he sees us.

A spiritual person

God has made every human being a unique person. But we all have certain things in common, such as a similar physical shape, and abilities like speech, thought and emotion.

We also have a natural desire to seek God. Unlike other creatures, we can know him in a personal way, although many people have a substitute "god" to which they devote their lives.

God gave us this ability so that we would live in harmony with him. Lives which include worship and love of God through Jesus Christ start to become what God intended they should be.

A sinful person

Nobody except Jesus himself has lived a fully perfect life. It was because of people's failure to obey God's laws (our "sinfulness") that Jesus had to die on the cross.

But even Christians, who have accepted Jesus' death on their behalf as the way to knowing God, remain sinful. Every part of us is still less than perfect – our thoughts, knowledge and actions.

That is why sometimes we fail to live the Christian life as fully as we intend. It is still easy to fall into the old ways of living. But Jesus always gives us his power to avoid sinning if we ask for it.

A saved person

Christians often talk about being "saved from their sins". To some people that sounds like the language of another culture. But everyone knows people are saved from burning houses, or from drowning in rivers.

So a Christian is a person who has been saved from a terrible fate – living without God for ever. And we are "saved" the moment we receive Jesus into our lives, just as a drowning person is saved the moment they are grabbed by their rescuer.

But being saved is not just a past experience. Having been saved is a constant fact and a continuous experience; we have been given a new life.

A separated person

Jesus has called us to set aside the ways of the world. This does not mean going into seclusion, but abandoning the attitudes to life and other people which are common in our society when these conflict with Jesus' love and purposes.

TO THINK ABOUT

Make a list of what you think makes human beings different from the rest of God's creation.
- What aspects of being human does society around you usually think are most important?
- Does God see things differently? What aspect of human life do you think he sees as most important?

Christianity is about becoming the true human being God intended you to be.
- What does the life of Jesus teach you about being human?
- In what ways do you fall short of this (sin)?

Sometimes that will mean saying "no" to things we once liked or enjoyed, because they would hinder our relationship with him.

But more important, it means saying "yes" to what he wants. When the Bible uses the word "holy", it means being dedicated to doing God's will. It involves caring for others, sharing Jesus' love and avoiding sin.

BIBLE CHECK

A spiritual person Acts 17:26-27; Philippians 2:9-11

A sinful person Romans 3:23; 1 John 2:1-2

A saved person 1 Timothy 1:15; Matthew 1:21

A separated person Matthew 6:24; Ephesians 2:8-10

POSTSCRIPT

While we all have certain characteristics in common, God made us with quite different personalities. We are not meant to look or feel the same, nor to do the same things as others, and he deals with us just as we are.

· What does "salvation" mean? How is it related to your whole life – body, mind, heart, soul and spirit?

· How do you think the Christian life is more truly human than other ways of living?

Thank God that he has made you as you are. Ask him to forgive you for the times when you don't live as he intended, and pray he will help you by his Spirit to live a properly human life – just like Jesus.

BIBLE SUMMARY
A WHOLE PERSON

Sometimes people talk about parts of the human personality as if they were all quite separate. They speak as if the body had a mind of its own! Although the Bible does distinguish between different parts, it never regards them as separate. When it refers to one part, it intends us to see the whole person from that angle.

The mind or heart

"Mind" and "heart" often mean the same in Scripture. They refer to a person as a thinking, feeling being. Emotion is part of the Christian's life (Romans 12:15). Even Jesus wept (John 11:35-36). But God gave us minds so that our reactions would always be based on an understanding of God's truth (Romans 12:2).

The body

The Bible never regards the body or its functions as sinful, even though sinful things are done with it (Romans 12:1). It is to be cared for (1 Corinthians 6:19-20). After death we will be raised to life by God who will then give us a new body which will never decay or grow old (1 Corinthians 15:42-44).

Soul and spirit

The "soul" refers to the whole living person. The word is often translated as "life" (Mark 8:35-36). Often soul and spirit are used interchangeably. Spirit, however, sometimes has a more precise meaning. It can refer to our inner motives. So the Egyptian king who refused to let Moses leave his country was hardened in spirit (Exodus 7:14). And when Paul prayed with his spirit (1 Corinthians 14:14) as well as with his mind, his whole being was involved in that prayer.

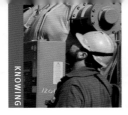

KNOWING
Knowing God

KEY TRUTH
God is a person with whom we can have a lasting, growing relationship of love and trust.

A personal God
All through the Bible, God is thought of as a person. He is never regarded merely as a force or power, like for example electricity, which only works in set ways.

Of course, he is not entirely like a human person. He does not forget his promises, he never stops loving, and he does not lose his temper!

But he is personal. The Bible has many accounts of how he spoke to people, showed them his plans, and taught them how to respond to him. Its central message is that he can be known by anyone at any time and in any place.

A holy God
Although God loves and cares, there is another side to his character. He can do nothing wrong himself, and he cannot accept wrong-doing by others.

He is often described as holy. That means he is perfect in himself, and separated from all that is imperfect. That is why Jesus had to die on the cross: the perfect man suffered the just punishment for our sins so that we could know this holy God.

Each time a Christian does something which is against God's holiness, the relationship with God is hurt, although not destroyed – just as when a close friend lets down the person they love.

A loving God
God's love is so much greater than human love because it continues when it is not deserved, or even when it is rejected. And because it is a pure, holy love, it does not depend on what we are like, nor does it spring from favouritism.

The Christian encounters God's love first at the cross. In his love for us, God sent his Son to live and die in the world. But we can experience it every day, too, as we ask for and receive his help and guidance, as we discover his power, and as we see all he has done. Even in the darkest times, his love still shines through.

A purposeful God
The world is very old, and there have been many generations of people living in it. God, who created it, has long-term plans which he has worked out over many centuries.

TO THINK ABOUT
Note down the ways people normally describe who (or what) God is.
- How are these ways different from the revelation in the Bible that God is personal?
- Do you ever think of God as an impersonal force or power rather than as a personal friend and Saviour? Why?
- If God is personal, how can you get to know him better? What sort of attitude towards him should you have?

The best example is the long time he took preparing the Jewish nation for the birth of Jesus. For us, it means we live at a point in history when what we do for God, however small it seems, contributes to the fulfilment of his purposes in the future.

And that also means that he has specific things for us to do: perhaps a career to follow, a person to help, or a spiritual gift to use.

BIBLE CHECK

A personal God John 17:3; 2 Timothy 1:12
A holy God 1 Peter 1:14-16; Leviticus 11:44-45; Isaiah 6:1-5
A loving God John 3:16; 2 Thessalonians 2:16-17; 1 John 4:10-12
A purposeful God Ephesians 1:9-12; 3:3

POSTSCRIPT

Knowing God personally involves learning about him from the Bible as well as experiencing him in our lives.

We have seen that God is holy, loving and purposeful.
· What other characteristics could be used to describe the God of the Bible?
· Now think of stories from the Bible to illustrate each of these characteristics.
· Do you have any experiences of these aspects of God's nature from your own life?

Thank God that he has made himself known to you, and to the whole world, in Jesus Christ. Pray that the Spirit will enable you to know him more and more – not as a distant object, but personally.

BIBLE SUMMARY
WALKING WITH GOD

"Enoch walked with God" (Genesis 5:22). "Walking with God" means keeping him always in mind, aware of his purposes and reflecting his character. It implies patience too, in not running ahead to do something which might seem right but is wrong in God's timing.

Walking in faith

Abraham is a good example of a faithful relationship to God. He believed God when he was told his wife would have a son, even though it was many years before the boy was born (Hebrews 11:8-12).

Then, later on, he obeyed God even at extreme times of testing, for example when God told him to prepare to sacrifice his son Isaac. God saved the boy at the last minute and praised Abraham for his faith (Hebrews 11:17-19; Genesis 22:1-19).

Walking in light

John, one of Jesus' closest followers, said we should "walk in the light, as he [Jesus] is in the light" (1 John 1:7). "Light" means "God's truth and holiness".

As we allow his "light" to expose our sinfulness and make clear how we should live, we begin to enjoy deep Christian friendship (or "fellowship") with others and experience the forgiveness and help of God.

Walking by the Spirit

Paul said that a Christian could either "gratify the desires of the sinful nature" or walk "by the Spirit" (Galatians 5:16). Our natural tendency towards self-centred living is not God's way, he said. So in order to overcome it, he told his readers to live in daily dependence on the Holy Spirit who dwells in their lives (Galatians 5:25).

KNOWING
Know your enemy

KEY TRUTH

Christians are confronted by forces which threaten to hinder or destroy their relationship with God.

The world

The physical universe was created by God, and although it shares in the effects of human sinfulness, it is not itself an evil place as some people have thought.

However, the world which people have created, the world of social, business and political life, is often organised without any concern for God and his laws.

The Bible warns us that this "world" has attitudes and beliefs contrary to Christianity. It is frequently more concerned with getting than giving. It may regard as right what God says is wrong. Jesus said that although we do not belong to this world but to his kingdom, we are nevertheless called to serve him in it.

The flesh

Whenever the New Testament refers to "flesh" as something sinful, it does not mean the physical body, but our natural selfishness. It is often translated "sinful nature". This is the "old nature" which Jesus seeks to replace with his love.

Sometimes, when there is an opportunity to do something positive for God, we feel lazy or tired, or try to get it done easily by not doing it properly. That feeling is the "flesh" resisting the Holy Spirit within us.

And sometimes we will feel a strong urge just to indulge ourselves no matter what the cost is to us or others. That, too, is a fleshly desire which God wants us to resist.

The adversary

The Bible is in no doubt about the existence of a personal evil spirit called the devil (see Bible Summary). Some forms of opposition to the Christian life are especially associated with him.

First, there is temptation to do wrong, or perhaps to use wrong means to achieve God's purposes. Then there are doubt and lack of faith, which hinder our effectiveness for God. And finally there is personal conflict in the church which ruins our witness of love.

Sometimes, other people do the devil's work for him by ridiculing our faith, opposing the work of the church, and even persecuting Christians.

The last enemy

Death is described in Scripture as "the last enemy". It is a barrier through which we have to pass before we can enter eternal life in God's presence.

TO THINK ABOUT

The enemies of the Christian life are the world, the flesh, the devil and death.

- What does "the world" mean for you? What systems of thought or behaviour try to influence you and distract you from the Christian life? What are the main influences in the wider world today?
- How does "the flesh" affect your life with God? What are your particular temptations and sins? Why are they dangerous?
- Why is it important that we acknowledge the existence of the devil as a personal evil spirit?
- How is death an enemy of the Christian life?

Jesus has already passed through death and come back to life again – he has defeated this enemy so that it cannot prevent us entering heaven.

But we must still die. The Christian has nothing to fear from death itself, although the act of dying is often a sad and sometimes a frightening occasion. It reminds us of the weakness of human life which will only be restored in heaven.

BIBLE CHECK

The world John 17:15-18; 1 John 2:15-17
The flesh Matthew 26:41; Galatians 5:15-25
The adversary Mark 8:31-33; 1 Peter 5:8-9;
  Ephesians 6:11-12
The last enemy 1 Corinthians 15:53-58;
  Philippians 1:21-24

POSTSCRIPT

Although Christians face opposition from many directions, they need never be defeated because the power of God is greater than all their enemies.

Christ has already defeated all these enemies by his death and resurrection.
· How does this knowledge help you to face the world? the flesh? the devil? and death?

Pray that God will help you to see the areas of your life and the society around you that are influenced by these enemies. Ask for his strength to stand up to evil, defeat temptation, fight against the devil and face death with confidence in Christ's resurrection life.

BIBLE SUMMARY
THE DEVIL STILL ROARS

The devil, sometimes called Satan or the adversary, appears right at the start of the Bible narrative, when he tricks Adam and Eve into disobeying God (Genesis 3:1-7). He is always around, prompting people into wrong courses of action (eg 1 Chronicles 21:1,7), until he will be finally destroyed at the end of time by God (Revelation 20:10).

The spiritual being

The Bible does not speculate about the origin of Satan. The main clues are in Isaiah 14:12-17, Luke 10:18 and 2 Peter 2:4, which imply that he is a spiritual being (or angel) who rebelled against God. Sometimes he is shown as being in God's presence, opposing his plans (Job 1:6-7; Zechariah 3:1-2).

An evil being

His sole purpose is to destroy or hinder God's work (1 Peter 5:8-9). So he tried to make Jesus stray from God's path (Matthew 4:1-10).

Sometimes he tempts people in subtle ways, disguising his real motives and character by plausible-sounding ideas (2 Corinthians 11:14). At other times his opposition is clear and his attack direct, as when he takes total control of people as in Mark 5:1-13.

A dying being

He cannot possess those who are already indwelt by God's Spirit, although he can tempt them and if they are not careful, defeat them. But Jesus' death on the cross has already sealed his fate. His power is limited – like that of a wild animal tied to a rope – and he will never get what he wants. He is no match for God.

KNOWING
Knowing where you stand

KEY TRUTH

God wants us to be sure about the permanence of his love.

Saved for ever

A person who saves someone from drowning does not let go of them if they struggle in fear. Neither will God let go of us, even if at times we struggle to get away from him.

Because we have been "born again" or adopted into God's family, we have become new people. We will never be the same again. We were "saved" when we received Jesus, and all who receive him have been given the unbreakable promise of eternal life.

We cannot lose that life; it cannot be taken from us. It depends, not on us living perfectly, but on God who cannot lie.

Kept from falling

God's promise does not refer only to life after death. He does not keep us safe just for heaven. He wants to keep us close to him all through our lives, too.

He promises to protect us in situations which we could otherwise not cope with, although he will often allow us to be stretched beyond what we believe our limits to be. And when we are tempted, he offers the strength to say "no".

The Bible often refers to God as a fortress. Those who trust him are safe and will not be defeated, however hard the battle around them.

Equipped for victory

All we have thought about may make the Christian life sound negative and passive. Certainly, we do need to be realistic about the strength of the opposition we face and the impossibility of our withstanding it unless we depend entirely on God.

However, being a Christian is in fact a very positive way of living. It is actually an assault on the enemies of God. Having got our defences in order, we can go on the attack.

Jesus promises victory – over temptation, difficulty, and all opposition. We can work for these victories through prayer, by applying the truth of the Bible, telling others about Jesus, and by careful avoidance of sin.

Constantly forgiven

It was hot and dusty where Jesus lived and people would wash the feet of visitors when they entered the house. Once, when Jesus did this to his closest followers, he said, "A person who has had a bath needs only to wash his feet; his whole body is clean."

Christians have "had a bath" in the forgiving love of God before setting out on

TO THINK ABOUT

Think about a time when you sinned and failed God after you became a Christian.

· How did the sin affect your relationship with God? How did you respond?
· What does the Bible say about sin in the life of a Christian? Can it be forgiven?

God assures you of his love and care for you, even when you sin. Your salvation depends entirely upon him, not your own efforts.

· How does this assurance affect the way you live your life? Does it give you more strength to do what God wants you to do?
· What will you do next time you face temptation?

the Christian life. But like the travellers, they can pick up "dust and dirt" – sin along the way – which needs to be forgiven and regularly washed out of their lives.

God promises to keep on forgiving and renewing us throughout our lives. But he also expects us to avoid sin as if it were a horrifying disease.

BIBLE CHECK

Saved for ever John 6:38-40;
  Romans 8:1-2,38-39
Kept from falling Matthew 6:13; Jude 24;
  Psalm 59:9,16-17
Equipped for victory Psalm 98:1-2;
  1 Timothy 6:11-12; 1 John 5:4-5
Constantly forgiven John 13:8-11; 1 John
  2:1-2; Matthew 6:14-15

POSTSCRIPT

Because we can be confident about our relationship with God, we can serve him boldly and confidently, too.

Thank God for his constant love for you, and for his forgiveness available in Jesus Christ. Tell him that you want to have victory over temptation, difficulty and opposition, and ask for his Spirit to give you the strength to remain faithful to him in these times.

BIBLE SUMMARY
THE UNFORGIVABLE SIN

Occasionally some Christians become convinced that they have committed such a bad sin that they can never be forgiven. However, their very concern shows they can still be forgiven, because they know they have done wrong and are concerned about it. The only person whom God cannot forgive is the one who will not admit his need of that forgiveness (1 John 1:6).

Blasphemy against the Spirit

Jesus did say that there was one unforgivable sin (Matthew 12:31). He called it "blasphemy against the Spirit".

Blasphemy against the Holy Spirit is deliberately (not just mistakenly) attributing to Satan the work of God. Only a person totally opposed to God can say that. They will never want forgiveness, and so will not receive it.

Apostasy

Hebrews 6:4-8 says that a person who has experienced Jesus' new life cannot be forgiven if they commit "apostasy". This is much more than, say, Peter's denial of Jesus (Mark 14:66-72). Peter was forgiven.

Apostasy describes the action of a person who leaves the family of God (of which they were not true members) and then seeks to destroy it. Such a person is unable to receive anything God offers.

Not guilty

Sometimes, Christians become depressed because their feelings of guilt are so strong and they feel they cannot be forgiven. Jesus not only forgives, but washes away our guilt. We need to forgive ourselves, and not sink under a weight of guilt. (See Psalm 103:1-14.)

KNOWING
Knowing the truth

KEY TRUTH

The Christian life is based on the truth God has shown to us, and he wants us to put that truth into practice.

Set free by truth

Jesus once said, "You will know the truth, and the truth will set you free" (John 8:32). When we have accepted God's truth about ourselves, our needs, and Jesus' death, we are set free from the prison of sin: it cannot separate us any longer from God's love.

We are also set free from ourselves. Jesus offers us the help we need to overcome the faults and failings which hurt others but which we have been powerless to change.

And he sets us free from Satan's clutches, too. The powers of evil may attack us, but they can no longer harm us.

Surrounded by truth

Everyone knows that there are right and wrong ways of doing certain things, like building a house. If the rules are not followed, the house will fall down.

God created people to live according to certain rules. They are summarised in the Ten Commandments. They are like a moral and spiritual guidebook. They tell us to love God, care for others, and look after the things he has given us.

Far from being restrictive, preventing us from doing what we would like, God's truthful laws are like the fence at the top of a steep cliff. They prevent us from harming ourselves and each other.

Taught by the truth

The best way to find out the truth about someone is to question them personally and compare their answers with what others say about them.

God promised that because Christians know him personally, they will also understand and know the truth about him, his world and his purposes. But we do not suddenly receive a whole library of knowledge when we become Christians.

As God teaches us in our experience, we have to check that experience against what the Bible says. God's word always reflects God's truth, whereas our experience – or our understanding of it – may be imperfect.

Inspired by truth

Jesus often found himself in difficult situations. So, too, did his first followers. But they never tried to get out of them by telling lies.

When Peter lied about his relationship with Jesus (he denied he knew him just when

TO THINK ABOUT

Write down some of the things about God, the world and yourself that you have learned as a Christian.

· How did you learn these things? Think about the different ways God uses to teach you the truth about himself, his world and yourself.

· Do you find some aspects of the truth uncomfortable? Do you find other aspects encouraging?

· How does the truth set you free?

Jesus needed his support), he deeply regretted it. King David in the Old Testament used trickery and murder to get what he wanted, and he was punished by God.

The whole Christian life is based on truth. God never does wrong, nor does he lead his people to do wrong. He expects us to think, speak and act honestly, even if others around us do not.

BIBLE CHECK

Set free by truth John 8:31-36; John 14:6; Galatians 5:1
Surrounded by truth Exodus 20:1-17; Matthew 5:17-20
Taught by the truth Psalm 119:9-16; John 17:17; 1 John 2:20-22
Inspired by truth Ephesians 4:25; 1 Peter 2:22

POSTSCRIPT

It is easier to be truthful in practice if we are also thinking truthfully in our minds.

Truth is not just about knowledge; Christians must live truthfully as well.

· How does God's law help you to live truthfully? Is it simply a list of rules and regulations?
· Are there any situations in which you find it difficult to speak or live truthfully? Why do you find them difficult? What can you do to be more truthful?

Thank God for his truth which sets you free. Ask him to forgive you for the times when you try to avoid the implications of his truth. Pray that his Spirit of truth will help you today.

BIBLE SUMMARY
LAW AND GRACE

Paul's letter to the Galatians, like most of the New Testament letters, was written to meet a special need. The Christians in Galatia had started to make fresh rules for new converts to follow (Galatians 1:6-9). So Paul explains the uses and limits of rules in the Christian life.

Faith is the key

The Christian life begins by trusting (or having faith) in Jesus Christ and in all he has done. We cannot have a right relationship with God just by keeping his rules, because in fact we have broken at least some of them already (2:16; 3:6).

Jesus has saved us from the law which demanded that we pay in full the punishment for our sins (3:10-14).

The law came first

God's law was given centuries before Christ came to earth. It was meant to help people understand God's nature and how they should live (3:19,23-26). It was a temporary measure until Jesus came to deal with it and give God's final teaching to humanity (4:4-7).

Rules out; obedience in

The Christian life is not the product of detailed human rules about behaviour, or of superstitious ritual (4:8-10). However, that does not mean that Christians can do anything they like; the Holy Spirit helps us to live in obedience to God's will (5:1,13-24).

KNOWING
Knowing your privileges

KEY TRUTH
God has given us many privileges to inspire and encourage us in our Christian lives.

Belonging to God's family
The "family" of God – all those who love and serve him – is not restricted to one place. It extends across the whole world. And it stretches right back into history.

Belonging to such a well-established group is a privilege because we know that as members of it we are right at the centre of God's purposes for the world.

And it is an encouragement because we can look back on how other Christians have triumphed over temptation and conquered evil. From their example we can learn how to live Christian lives, and know that what we face has been faced before – and God's power seen in it.

Being an ambassador
An ambassador is a person chosen to represent their country's interests in a foreign land. They tell people what their country believes, and they help their compatriots when they visit that land.

Every Christian is an ambassador for Christ, representing his kingdom in a "foreign" land – a society which does not care much for him.

That means our first loyalty is to Jesus. Christians will always try to live as he wants, rather than follow the standards of the world around them. And their duties never stop; they are ambassadors wherever they go. People will judge our Lord by what we do and say.

Bearing good news
The Christian is a messenger as well as an ambassador. We have been given a message to pass on to other people; the message, or good news, of Jesus' life, death and resurrection.

The Christian faith is not something to be kept secret. Jesus told us to proclaim it to all who will listen. God is concerned for everyone, everywhere.

Not all Christians have a special gift for preaching or teaching. But everyone can tell others the simple facts that God cares for them and can be known by them. It is a message the world badly needs to hear, because so many people feel lost or anxious, and do not have the joy of knowing God.

Becoming a saint
People often think of saints as very holy men and women who did miracles and who have statues or pictures made of them.

TO THINK ABOUT
Many companies and organisations give special privileges to their valued customers or employees.

· What kinds of privileges are available in the society around you? Do you belong to any clubs or groups that give you special benefits?

· Now make a list of the privileges you have because you are a child of God (eg you can pray to your heavenly Father). How do these privileges compare with those that the world offers?

Privileges are closely connected with responsibilities.

· Do you have any new responsibilities now that you belong to God? What are they?

But the Bible calls every Christian believer a saint. One of our privileges is being regarded so highly by God. The trouble is, we are not always very saintly people!

So we are called to live as saints – to grow in our faith and understanding so that we shall actually be what God has intended we should be. It is not a matter of whether or not we feel saintly, nor of adopting an artificial air of other-worldliness. Rather, we are simply to reflect the love of Jesus through our daily lives.

BIBLE CHECK

Belonging to God's family Romans 8:15-16; Hebrews 11:32–12:2

Being an ambassador 2 Corinthians 5:20; Ephesians 6:18-20

Bearing good news Acts 8:4; 2 Kings 7:3-10; Luke 8:38-39

Becoming a saint Colossians 1:1-4; Philippians 2:1-13

POSTSCRIPT

It is easy to take our privileges for granted, so it helps if we thank God for them regularly.

· Ambassadors receive all they need to live on from the country they represent. Why are Christians called ambassadors for Christ?

· How will you tell someone the good news about Jesus this week?

Thank God for the privilege of being his child. He provides all you need to be a holy, faithful ambassador for Christ. Tell him that you don't want to take these privileges for granted, and pray for opportunities to serve him.

BIBLE SUMMARY

WHO IS ON THE LORD'S SIDE?

Joshua had what seemed to be an impossible task ahead. Moses, the man who led Israel out of slavery in Egypt, was dead. And Joshua had the job of helping a vast number of people settle into a new country (Joshua 1:1-5).

But he was promised the power of God, who had not failed Moses (1:5). His own courage was to be strengthened by reading the Scriptures (1:8-9).

Promises, promises

As God's people moved into the new land, they were told to keep God's commands and do things his way. At first they promised to do so (1:16-18), but they soon forgot what they had said (7:10-15).

But not Joshua. At the end of his life, having gone through many difficulties and suffered many disappointments, his faith remained as strong as ever. "Choose for yourselves this day whom you will serve," he said – either the false gods or the real God. "But as for me and my household," he added, "we will serve the Lord" (24:15). The privilege of serving God dominated his whole life.

The need for growth

KEY TRUTH

However long a person has been a Christian, they still have more to learn and experience of God's love and purposes.

Growing into Christ

If anyone wants to know exactly what living a Christian life involves, they need only read the accounts of Jesus' life. Neither his enemies nor his closest friends could point to any wrong actions or words.

He is the example we are to follow, the standard by which our words and deeds can be measured. When faced with a difficult decision, it is often helpful to ask, "What would Jesus have done if he was here?"

But we are not only to grow more like him. The Bible reminds us of the need to grow closer to him personally: to love him more dearly and serve him more faithfully.

Growing in faith

As a friendship develops between two people, so too does trust. Christians learn steadily how to trust Jesus and so their faith grows stronger.

God has given us many promises: to help, provide, lead, teach and protect his followers. Most Christians find it helpful to take God at his word in one or two small things. Then, as they learn to trust him and apply his truth, they can move on to bigger things.

But God is not like an automatic machine giving us whatever we ask. His promises relate to his purposes for us, so growing in faith also involves discovering his will.

Growing in knowledge

"Knowledge" in the Bible often means "understanding" or even "experience", rather than simply "knowing facts". Knowing God involves growing not only in Bible knowledge, but also in understanding his will.

In a human friendship a person may know instinctively how the other feels or what they want. The aim of the Christian life is to develop a deep awareness of God's general purposes, so that we can discover more easily what he specifically wants in each situation.

This understanding grows through prayer, Bible reading, worship, and the willingness to put Jesus first in everything.

Growing in love

One of the hardest parts of the Christian life is allowing Jesus to change our habits and attitudes, and especially our relationships with other people. The selfishness which prefers to dominate others, rather than submit to them, dies hard.

So every Christian has to grow in love, by

TO THINK ABOUT

Think about a family member or friend who is very close to you.

· Has your relationship with that person developed over time? Why is it important that friendships and relationships grow?

· How is your relationship with God similar? Does it need to grow in some of the same ways?

learning how to say sorry, how to care for others, and how to be kind even to those who hate or despise in return.

The rule for Christian living is God first, others second, and self last. And to apply that, we need the help of the Holy Spirit. The standard is too high to achieve on our own.

BIBLE CHECK

Growing into Christ Ephesians 4:15;
1 Peter 2:21-23

Growing in faith Luke 17:5; 2 Corinthians 10:15; 2 Thessalonians 1:3

Growing in knowledge Colossians 1:9-10; 2 Peter 3:18

Growing in love 1 Thessalonians 3:12-13; 4:9-12

POSTSCRIPT

A growing person does not have to wait until they reach a certain stage before they can be useful to God; serving him is in fact an important aid to growth.

Make a list of the areas of your life with God that have already grown since you became a Christian.

· Has your relationship with God stopped growing? If so, why?

· Are there particular areas of your Christian life that you need to grow in right now?

· What practical steps will you take to grow in these areas?

Thank God that he is so immense that you will never stop growing in your relationship with him – there will always be more of his love and will to discover. Pray that he will challenge you to grow in your Christian life.

BIBLE SUMMARY
BECOMING LIKE JESUS

Christians are sometimes – and usually wrongly – accused of being a closed group of people who conform to certain customs. Like the rest of God's creation, there is enormous variety among Christians. As we grow in our faith, we begin to conform not to each other but to the character of Jesus.

Our nature renewed

The Bible teaches that every human being is created in the image of God (Genesis 1:26). But human sinfulness has damaged and distorted our likeness to God.

During the Christian life the damage is slowly repaired by the Holy Spirit (Colossians 3:9-10), and our whole self is finally and completely renewed in heaven (1 John 3:2).

God's will for us

Every Christian aims to be like Jesus – and every non-Christian expects us to be like him. The process of becoming like him – honouring God in all that we do – is sometimes called "sanctification", or growth in holiness (1 Thessalonians 4:3). The Holy Spirit will point out things in our lives which need correcting (John 16:8). And, like growing children, there are certain things we can do to aid this process.

The Bible is called "food" or "milk", and so we can draw spiritual nourishment from it (1 Peter 2:2). Using the gifts which God has given us is like exercising our bodies (1 Corinthians 9:26-27; Ephesians 4:11-16). And keeping in touch with God through prayer is like breathing fresh air (Ephesians 6:18).

The source of growth

KEY TRUTH

The Holy Spirit is the source and inspiration of all Christian growth.

The Spirit lives in us

The Christian is like a house with many "rooms" – he or she is a person with many interests, relationships and talents. When we become a Christian, the Holy Spirit enters our house – our life. Slowly he moves from part to part clearing away the dust of sin, opening up the windows of the mind so that God's light can shine in, filling us with new life.

But he does not always break down locked doors. He dwells within us, but may not have access to every part, unless we invite him in to do his work, and help us grow as Christians.

The Spirit sanctifies us

The Holy Spirit wants to make us "holy" – people reflecting the love and goodness of God. He does this in three ways.

· First, he points out what is wrong in our life, perhaps through our conscience, some Bible passage, or even through another person.
· Then he gives his help and strength to overcome that sin or habit.
· And thirdly, he replaces sinful words and actions with what the Bible calls the "fruit of the Spirit". These are positive attitudes like love and patience which are expressed in practical service to God and other people.

The Spirit empowers us

The New Testament word for the power the Holy Spirit gives us is *dunamis*, from which comes the word for dynamite. His power can be explosive!

Sometimes he will blast away things that stand in the way of God. He will break down barriers which other people set up in order to protect themselves from the gospel of Jesus Christ.

But often, his power is also experienced when he gives us patience to endure suffering, or strength of character and wisdom to do a difficult task. He can be powerful as dynamite; he can also be gentle as a dove.

The Spirit unites us

Each Christian is a member of God's family, but like an ordinary human family, the members do not always get on well with each other. In fact, the family is made up of many differences of opinion.

But the Holy Spirit is concerned to help us show our faith by working together despite our differences. That is why he gives special abilities or "gifts" to Christians, so that we can both give to and receive from each other some spiritual truth.

TO THINK ABOUT

God gave you his Holy Spirit when you became a Christian.
· What does the Bible say about the Spirit's role in the Christian life?
· Are you aware of the Spirit's work in your life, or do you find him too mysterious and so ignore him?
· Are there any areas of your life that you try to keep away from God's Spirit? Perhaps you don't want these areas to change, or perhaps you would like to change them in your own strength.

The Spirit also "reconciles" people: he helps to heal broken relationships, and brings love and peace to situations where before there was hate and discord.

BIBLE CHECK
The Spirit lives in us Revelation 3:20; John 14:16-17
The Spirit sanctifies us Ephesians 4:30; 1 Peter 1:14-16
The Spirit empowers us Romans 15:13,17-19; Ephesians 3:20; 2 Timothy 1:7
The Spirit unites us Ephesians 4:3; 1 Corinthians 1:10-13

POSTSCRIPT
Growing in the Christian life involves submission to the Holy Spirit, and also willingness to learn from other Christians.

The Spirit's work is not just to clean up our lives; he is also the source of positive growth.
· Which part of the fruit of the Spirit is most needed in your life right now?
· Why is it important that the Spirit unites you with other believers?

Thank God that he has given you the gift of his Spirit. Allow the Spirit to flow through your life and transform you. Ask for his power and strength to cultivate every part of the fruit of the Spirit.

BIBLE SUMMARY
THE FRUIT OF THE SPIRIT

One of the simplest, most beautiful but also most demanding descriptions of the Christian is found in Paul's letter to the Galatians (5:22-23). He lists nine virtues, which he calls "the fruit of the Spirit", which cannot be produced merely by our own effort but are the result of God's work in our lives (compare John 15:18). This is what they mean:

Love towards God
"Love" means self-sacrificing devotion to God. "Joy" refers to our thankfulness for all that he has done for us through Jesus, and "peace" reminds us of our healed relationship with him. As the fruit grows in us, we are likely to become more loving, joyful and peaceable people, bringing a sense of God's presence to others.

Patience towards people
"Patience" is the virtue of keeping calm with people who are aggressive or thoughtless in their attitude towards us. "Kindness" means being thoughtful and sensitive about people's needs. And "goodness" is the willingness to help people practically with no thought about the cost to ourselves.

At peace with ourselves
The Christian becomes "faithful" in the sense of being someone others can trust not to let them down. They are "gentle" too, which implies being humble, reasonable, considerate and unselfish. And finally, the Christian is self-controlled", experiencing the power of God's Spirit in every area of human weakness.

GROWING
The evidence of growth

KEY TRUTH
Christian growth can be measured by the steady changes which take place in a person's life.

A growing experience
Jesus is alive! That has been the cry of Christians in every generation. They believe it for two reasons. One is that they can point to the historical certainty that Jesus rose from the dead. And the other is that they can see evidence of his influence in their lives. Looking back, they can see how he has helped them overcome sin and temptation. But above all, they can recall times when God has acted in some way in their lives: answering prayers, using their words or actions to encourage other Christians or to bring people to Christ, and showing he is in control in some difficulty or problem.

A growing confidence
As we begin to see God at work in our own lives and in the lives of others around us, our confidence in God's promises and power will increase and our fears will decrease. As that happens, we will be encouraged to ask him to do greater things.

The New Testament often speaks of boldness in approaching God and in attempting things for him.

But of course, Christian confidence is always in what God is both able and willing to do. There is no place in the Christian life for the kind of over-confidence which is not humbly depending on God at all times.

A growing usefulness
God has something for each Christian to do. It may be a specific job within the church – for example preaching, or counselling others. It may be showing his love in appropriate ways in our day-to-day life.

The Holy Spirit has showered all kinds of "gifts" on the church, which those who receive them are to use for the benefit of everyone else. Teachers and preachers, artists and administrators, people who can organise and others who can help.

One of the Bible's most touching stories of usefulness is that of John Mark. He found the going too hard while travelling with Paul, who later refused to take him back, even though others trusted him. But at the end of his life Paul called for Mark, saying how useful he was.

A growing battle
Shortly after Jesus was baptised by John the Baptist at the start of his public ministry, he experienced severe temptation. It is a common experience: great blessing is

TO THINK ABOUT
Your Christian life is living evidence of the power of God.
· What experiences or characteristics could you point to in your own life to show that Jesus is alive and is now your Saviour and Lord?
· Do you have more "evidence" now than when you first became a Christian? Should you?
· How does this evidence affect your confidence in God?

sometimes followed by tough spiritual warfare and testing. It has been said that the devil only concerns himself with those who threaten his temporary hold on the world. A Christian determined to serve Jesus is just such a threat.

So growing Christians may also find themselves fighting Christians; the battle gets hotter as faith grows stronger.

BIBLE CHECK

A growing experience 1 Corinthians 15:3-8; Acts 12:5-11

A growing confidence Ephesians 3:12; 6:19-20

A growing usefulness Acts 13:13; 15:37-40; 2 Timothy 4:11; Romans 12:4-8

A growing battle 2 Corinthians 2:10-11; 1 Thessalonians 2:17-18

POSTSCRIPT

The Christian will be encouraged by becoming aware of growth, but the person who spends time looking for growth is likely to become self-centred.

Sometimes you may not even notice that you are growing until you look back over a period of your life and see what God has done. At other times, the changes will be clearer.

· Are there new ways you could serve within your local church?

· Are you aware of any spiritual battles in your life? Are these the result of your growing faith?

Thank God that your faith in him brings real changes in your life. Pray that his Spirit will help you to become more like Jesus, so that everyone will be able to see that he is your living Saviour and Lord.

BIBLE SUMMARY

THE BATTLE FOR THE MIND

A verse in the Old Testament book of Proverbs is translated in one Bible version as: "As he thinketh in his heart, so is he" (Proverbs 23:7, KJV). Throughout the Bible the mind – our inner attitude and real beliefs – is seen as the key to spiritual growth. If our thoughts are wrong, our actions can never be right (Matthew 7:17-20).

Become a non-conformist

Every group of people tends to have its own agreed standards and way of looking at things. In some cases these are quite opposite to Jesus' teaching. The world around may say, "Take all you can get." But Jesus said, "Give all you have." So if we are to lead a Christian life, we cannot always think in the same way as others (Romans 12:2). Jesus said that our old, sinful approach to life was to be finished with for ever (Mark 8:34-37).

Let your mind be renewed

The Bible never says "don't" without also saying "do". So God remoulds our minds from the inside (Romans 12:2), putting in them his love and laws (Hebrews 10:15-16). At the same time, he tells us to concentrate on what is good, holy and of God (Philippians 4:8), and thus to develop renewed minds (Ephesians 4:22-24).

Our new way of thinking is characterised by the humility and concern which Jesus himself showed (Philippians 2:3-9). In fact, the Christian has the privilege of being given insight into Jesus' own mind (1 Corinthians 2:15-16).

GROWING
The secret of growth

KEY TRUTH
Prayer is the chief means by which Christians maintain and develop their relationship with God.

In touch with God's purposes
A person taking part in a major activity involving many others needs to keep in touch with the organiser. The participant needs to know exactly what job the organiser wants them to do.

Prayer is a way of keeping in touch with what God wants us to do. If we pray in accordance with his purposes, then he promises to give what we ask at the right time. But if we neglect prayer, it is easy to stray from his plan.

Prayer is nothing more or less than conversation with God. It is a natural and important part of our relationship with him. What is more, he really wants to hear us!

Aware of God's presence
If you are talking to a person, it is impossible not to be aware of their presence! But when we pray, it is sometimes helpful to repeat Jesus' promise, "I am with you always"; he is present, although we cannot see him.

Sometimes, when we pray, we will feel him near us, perhaps almost with a physical sensation, or by a deep awareness inside. But what we feel is less important than what prayer actually does. It brings us close to God. Jesus, through his death, has broken down the invisible barrier of sin which once had barred us from God's presence. Now, the simplest prayer is like having a personal audience with a king, who cares for us and longs to help us.

A source of God's power
Some remarkable things happened when Jesus' early followers prayed. Many people became Christians through their preaching. Others were healed of their diseases. Peter and Paul were both released from prison by God's powerful intervention as a result of prayer.

Even Jesus prayed, sometimes all night, and he told his followers that some works of God could only be achieved by concentrated periods of prayer which were not stopped even for food.

It is often true that the prayerless Christian is a powerless Christian. God sometimes chooses to channel his power to us and others when we pray.

Taking time to pray
Jesus sometimes looked for a quiet place away from all disturbances so that he could pray to his heavenly Father. His example is a good one to follow.

TO THINK ABOUT
Keep a note of the amount of time you spend in prayer over one week, and what you pray for.

· Do you find prayer exciting, boring, invigorating, difficult, or something else? Do you think this relates to your understanding of what prayer is?

· If prayer is the secret of Christian growth, why do we sometimes think we can get by without praying?

· Can you identify common themes in your prayers? Are there aspects you are missing?

There is so much to talk to God about. And human nature (and the devil's tempting) can find all sorts of excuses for avoiding it. So it is often helpful to set aside a convenient time on most days to pray, just as you set aside time to eat. And keeping a list of things to pray about will help you to forget nothing.

Paul also reminded his readers to pray at all times. A brief prayer in the middle of the day, when we are especially conscious of our need for God's help, or when we are thinking of someone else, is important and effective.

BIBLE CHECK

In touch with God's purposes 1 John 5:14-15; 1 Timothy 2:1-6

Aware of God's presence Ephesians 3:11-12; Hebrews 10:19-22

A source of God's power Mark 9:28-29; Acts 4:31-33

Taking time to pray Psalm 5:1-3; Luke 6:12

POSTSCRIPT

Every decision we take, every situation we are in, is a legitimate subject for prayer. But we are also told to pray for others, that they too may know God's power.

Consider how you can establish a regular time of prayer in your life. If you have never done this before, start by setting a realistic goal – perhaps ten minutes every day. In time, you will want to increase this!

· How can you be aware of God's presence in your prayer times? What distractions do you need to deal with?

· How does prayer bring change and growth?

Thank God that he is listening to you now. Bring him your concerns for yourself and for the world around you.

BIBLE SUMMARY
WHAT IS PRAYER?

Prayer is often hard to understand, as well as to practise. But there are two important facts on which it depends.

Open to God

People sometimes ask why God wants us to pray for things when Jesus has said that he already knows our needs (Matthew 6:8). The main reason is that the act of asking implies a humble dependence on God, which is the basis of the Christian life (Matthew 6:8). God delights to give good gifts to those who ask him.

If we are able to receive his gifts humbly, we will be more likely to use them properly. Besides, while we pray we may realise we are asking for the wrong thing, so our prayers can be modified (James 4:3-10).

Deeply concerned

Prayer is, in a sense, very easy: just telling God, aloud or silently, how we feel or what we need. We don't even have to use special words. But in other ways it is hard; the prayer which God answers is often hard work, because it is part of our spiritual battle (Ephesians 6:18).

Also, in our praying it is important to mean what we say, sincerely asking for what we believe is his will for us – and to trust that God is actually able to do what we ask (Mark 11:22-25; James 1:6).

Some prayers consist of deep longing and groaning inside our hearts and minds, and cannot be fully expressed in words. But God still understands and answers them, because they are inspired by his Spirit (Romans 8:26-27).

A pattern for growth

KEY TRUTH

Prayer consists of praising and thanking God, and being sorry for our wrongdoing, as well as asking for things.

Love prayers

The friendship between God and the Christian is marked by love. Love grows between two people as they learn to express their feelings for each other. So Christians grow as they experience God's loving care and learn to express their love for him.

Our love prayers, or "adoration" and worship, tell God we love him for all that he is and for all that he has done for us through Jesus Christ.

Such prayers help us to grow closer to him, deepen our appreciation of him, and keep us open to receiving his help and his gifts. The Psalms are full of love prayers, and many Christians find them helpful as a basis for their own.

Sorry prayers

The wrong things we do can grieve God, and make our relationship with him more difficult.

Each time we pray it is a good idea to start by telling God we are sorry for the sins we have committed. We can then experience his forgiveness in a fresh way, and can clear away the blockages which prevent us knowing his power.

We also need to be willing to say sorry to other people whom we have offended, and to forgive those who have wronged us. We can hardly be open to God's forgiveness if we are bitter and resentful towards other people.

Thank-you prayers

These are like love prayers, but they are a response to specific things that God has done for us or others.

We can thank him for answering our prayers, for providing for our needs, including things we take for granted yet still depend on him for, like a meal we are about to enjoy. We can also thank him for helping or guiding us, and for intervening in some situation.

Saying thank you before we ask for other things can help to increase our faith. It is a reminder of how much God has done already.

Asking prayers

These are the easiest and most common of all prayers but they should really come at the bottom of the list. It is a limited relationship which is expressed only in a series of requests or demands.

The Bible tells us to ask for three things.

TO THINK ABOUT

Think about the four elements of prayer mentioned here.

· Does your prayer time usually include all these elements? Are there any that are often missing?

· Why is it important to express praise and adoration to God? Why do we tell God how great he is?

· Do Christians still need to say sorry to God?

· What things can you thank God for today?

· How can you stop your asking prayer from becoming simply reciting a list of demands?

One is the spiritual resources and blessings God wants to share with us: deeper faith, knowledge of his will, the ability to obey him. Another is our daily needs – food, drink, clothes and shelter – because in many parts of the world people do not think of them as God's provision but as an automatic right.

And finally we are to ask for specific things: that someone we love will come to Jesus; that God will act in a situation, and for whatever he knows is good for us to have and enjoy.

BIBLE CHECK
Love prayers Psalm 31:23; 95:1-7; 113:1-9
Sorry prayers Matthew 6:14-15; Psalm 51
Thank-you prayers Psalm 116; Philippians 1:3-11
Asking prayers Luke 11:9-13; James 1:5-7

POSTSCRIPT
As we grow in the Christian life, prayer becomes more natural and spontaneous. It may sometimes grow stale unless we give each element its proper place.

· Why is it important to have a balance of these four elements of prayer?

The Lord's Prayer that Jesus taught his disciples can be used as a prayer itself, as well as a pattern for praying in our own words.

· Do you use the Lord's Prayer on a regular basis? Should you?

Think about what the words of the Lord's Prayer mean. Then turn it into your own prayer, thanking God for this way to grow in your life with him.

BIBLE SUMMARY
JESUS' PATTERN FOR PRAYER

Jesus did not in fact teach a great deal about prayer; he told his followers to get on with it, because it is natural to talk to our heavenly Father. However, in the "Lord's Prayer" (Matthew 6:7-15) he gave a summary of how to pray and for what: not just a prayer to be recited.

Children and servants
First, we approach God as his children, remembering his greatness – "Our Father in heaven ..." and his holiness – "hallowed be your name". Then we ask that people all over the world will come to love, honour and serve him – "your kingdom come", and that we ourselves may serve him faithfully – "your will be done".

Beggars and debtors
The next phrase reminds us to ask God to provide for our daily needs – nothing is too small for him – and to pray for the hungry and homeless – "Give us today our daily bread". Then we ask his forgiveness, and tell him we forgive those who have wronged us, just as Jesus forgave his murderers before his death – "Forgive us our debts, as we also have forgiven our debtors."

Guarded and kept
Finally, there is a reminder of our weakness: a prayer that God will protect us from the trials which will crush our faith – "lead us not into temptation", and that he will release us from the power of Satan – "deliver us from the evil one".

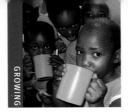

GROWING
The problems of growth

KEY TRUTH

The Christian life is not an escape route from difficulty, but a way through difficulty.

Exercising faith

Jesus said that even a tiny amount of faith was all that was needed for God to work powerfully. But he also made it clear that he would not do great things if people did not believe he could.

Faith is not certainty, but trust. Growing as a Christian through prayer depends on our trusting God entirely to do what will most honour him, in his way and in his time.

Actually believing he will answer our prayers is not easy, but if we are too timid to ask, we may not see him work powerfully.

Waiting for answers

God is not always in a rush to do things, for he stands beyond time and is working out his purposes over many centuries. Sometimes we will have to wait a while before he answers our prayers.

This in itself can be a test of our faith: do we really want what we are asking for, and do we really believe Jesus can give it? He told us to keep on asking until we receive.

There are two things to do while we wait. One is to keep looking for an answer, which may be different from the one we expect. The other is to make sure that all our prayers, and our whole life, are lined up with his will.

Keeping alert

The person who wants to do things for Jesus Christ will always find opportunities – a word of explanation about their faith, an act of kindness, a job within the church. There will be challenges, too, and unexpected problems.

The Christian who is constantly in touch with God through prayer will be able to make the most of these opportunities and challenges. A short silent prayer at the time will keep our mind focused on him and help prevent us from relying on our own lesser abilities.

The example of Nehemiah in the Old Testament is a good one to follow. He and his helpers prayed quickly about their needs, then worked hard and sensibly at their jobs.

When God seems silent

Many Christians experience times when God seems very far away, when their prayers seem to be unanswered, and when living the Christian life becomes hard and laborious.

It might be that they have sinned against God. Maybe something in their life – a personal relationship, for example – needs resolving. Or they may just be tired, or unwell.

TO THINK ABOUT

Think about some of the difficulties that children face as they grow up.

· Does this help you to understand why growing as a Christian can sometimes be difficult or frustrating?
· Are there any aspects of the Christian life that you are finding challenging at the moment? Can you think why?
· What does it mean if God doesn't seem to be answering your prayer?
· How can you learn to be patient?

But it might also be that God himself is leading them through what some have called "the dark night of the soul" – a time when their longing for God deepens and their faith is eventually strengthened, through being tested. Growing up in the Christian life, just like growing as a human person, is not all fun and games.

BIBLE CHECK
Exercising faith Luke 17:5-6; Matthew 13:57-58
Waiting for answers Luke 18:1-8; James 5:7-11
Keeping alert Nehemiah 2:4-5; 4:7-15; Proverbs 3:5-8
When God seems silent Psalm 38:9-22; 42:1-11

POSTSCRIPT
The Bible says Jesus was made perfect (or complete) through suffering. Those who obey him and follow him may find that he calls them to suffering, too, and through it to discover more of his love.

When you face difficulties in your Christian life, God doesn't ask you to pretend there are no problems. If you are sure there is no sin in your relationship with him, then sometimes you must simply wait and trust.
· Is it possible to praise God and trust him, even when you don't understand what he's doing? Why?

Thank God that he knows the problems you face. Tell him that you are trusting him to help you, and ask him to give you enough strength for each day.

BIBLE SUMMARY
GOD'S MYSTERIOUS WAYS

When something unexpected occurs, people often ask, "Why has God allowed this to happen?" Usually it is a sort of complaint; they regard the event as undeserved punishment. But for the Christian, whatever happens can provide an opportunity to move forward in the Christian life, though the question "Why?" may remain.

God's ways are different
Everyone knows that God is greater than any human being, so it is hardly surprising to read in the Bible that his ways and thoughts are beyond human understanding (Isaiah 55:8-9). They are too complex for us to work out (Ecclesiastes 3:11). That is why the Bible encourages us to pray carefully before making major decisions (see Jesus' example in Luke 6:12-16).

Human wisdom is limited
People usually do what they believe is right, but human wisdom can be very far from God's truth because it is not always informed by his law and will (1 Corinthians 2:3-10). Even Christians can be misled and mistaken (1 Corinthians 1:10-13; Galatians 1:6-9).
Despite this, God promises to give us wisdom to know how to act correctly in each situation (James 1:5-6).

A new set of values
In fact, Jesus' teaching is often opposite to the accepted wisdom of the people around us. They usually say it is a sign of God's blessing to be rich; Jesus said it was a sign of his gracious love to be able to give to those in need at whatever cost to oneself (Matthew 5:42). We are so used to our godless ways, that the Christian life can seem very strange and different.

DISCOVERING
Discovering a new life

KEY TRUTH

The Christian life is like a journey in which there are many things to be discovered.

Journey into life

When Jesus first called a group of twelve men (known as the apostles) to follow him, they literally set off on a journey. Together they travelled around the land, teaching God's truth to all who would listen.

Jesus used the picture of a journey to illustrate the Christian life. He said it is like turning off the broad, easy road of self-indulgence that leads away from God.

Instead, the Christian way is a narrow, steep path. It has many obstacles and is sometimes hard going. But it leads to new life: a life lived in harmony with God, full of new joys and discoveries, which goes beyond death.

A constant companion

The Christian never walks alone. Even when we feel very lonely – perhaps when we are the only Christian in a place where others are hostile to our faith – God is always there.

He promises never to leave us. He will show us what he wants us to do, and how to do it.

He is like an expert guide. He knows the way through the difficulties which lie ahead. And he has many new things to show and teach us as we follow him into the sort of life he wants us to lead.

New every morning

From time to time, ever since the days of the early church, people have claimed that God has given them a completely new teaching. They offer a new, improved version of Christianity. They either allow something which was previously forbidden in the Bible, or they insist on some custom being added to the gospel before a person can be fully recognised as a Christian.

But they are always wrong. God's purposes for his people, and his teaching, never change. Neither do his laws, nor the simple way of faith in Jesus through which we come to him.

His truths are always fresh, however. They never grow stale, and come to us "new every morning". Because Jesus is alive, he is always doing new things in us and for us.

I know where I'm going

Some people who rightly recognise how great God is find it hard to understand that he is concerned with the details of their lives.

But he is – just how great he is! He not only forgives our sins and gives us eternal life, but he also has a special purpose for us in this life too.

TO THINK ABOUT

Think of a time when you went on a journey to a new place.

· Were you excited about going somewhere new? How did you feel about leaving familiar places behind?

The Christian life is rather like that. Although Christians leave many things behind, they have an exciting journey ahead of them.

· How does it make a difference to understand faith as a journey, rather than as having already arrived at a destination?
· How can you be sure that you are travelling in the right direction? Where do you look for guidance?

That means the path we follow on our "journey into life" has already been prepared by God. Life is not just a series of accidents; there is a plan to it. That plan is always good, although not always easy.

BIBLE CHECK

Journey into life Matthew 7:13-14; John 10:9-10

A constant companion Psalm 23; Ephesians 3:14-21

New every morning Ecclesiastes 1:9; Lamentations 3:22-23; Galatians 1:6-9

I know where I'm going Ephesians 2:10; Romans 12:2; Hebrews 13:20-21

POSTSCRIPT

Although there are many things to discover in the Christian life, the end is never in doubt. Jesus has prepared a place for us in heaven.

· Is it significant that Christians follow Jesus? What does it mean for you that Jesus has gone ahead of you on the road of life?

· What are the costs in following Jesus?

Thank God for the excitement of the journey of faith. Thank him for your companions on the journey – Jesus ahead of you, the Spirit with you, and fellow Christians around you. Ask for his help to follow faithfully.

BIBLE SUMMARY
BECOMING A DISCIPLE

The word "disciple" means a follower, one who learns from their teacher. Jesus does not want passive converts, but active disciples, people who will go on to discover the richness of the Christian life.

Jesus comes first

Jesus said that nothing should come between him and the Christian. Even family relationships would weaken our discipleship if they interfered with it (Luke 14:26).

However, he made it clear that families were not to be neglected (Mark 7:9-13; John 19:26-27).

A rich person once asked what he had to do to become a follower of Jesus. Jesus told him to sell all his possessions and give the money to the poor. In his particular case, he would have done anything for Jesus except that. But Jesus made it clear that there can be no exceptions; love for Jesus is the Christian's priority. He wants us to put all that we have and are at his disposal (Luke 18:18-30; compare 9:23-25).

A willing sacrifice

Jesus does not require his followers to make sacrifices or give to the church in order to gain acceptance by God. Jesus' death was the ultimate sacrifice which brings God and people into harmony with each other (Hebrews 10:11-18).

But God does call us to offer ourselves as living sacrifices (Romans 12:1-2). That does not mean committing suicide, but being willing to do whatever Jesus wants, in the sure knowledge that his way is always best.

DISCOVERING
Discovering God's way

KEY TRUTH

God has shown us his unchanging purposes in several ways, so that we may be sure of what he wants.

Shown through conscience

One aspect of being made "in the image of God", as the Bible describes us, is that we know there are such things as right and wrong.

Unfortunately, the human conscience can be mistaken in what actually is right or wrong. It can be influenced by local custom and what we have been taught to believe.

But the Holy Spirit renews and revitalises the Christian's conscience. God's law slowly becomes more perfectly "written on our hearts" so that we learn to tell instinctively what we should or should not do.

Shown through God's law

God has not laid down many rules and regulations for the Christian life. He wants us to love, serve and honour him freely, because we wish to and not because we feel we have to.

However, he has given a basic moral code, not just to Christians, but to all humanity. It is set out in the Ten Commandments (see Bible Summary).

These reflect the way God has made the world. They are the "Maker's instructions" on how human life is designed to operate. We cannot expect to find peace and happiness if we break these laws, because we are destroying the very structure of peace and happiness itself.

Shown through Jesus

Jesus Christ was God's final and most complete revelation of who he is and what he wants. In Jesus' life we find an example of how everyone should live, and in his teaching we discover God's principles for daily life.

Jesus showed that God's way has two vital elements:

· The first is loving and serving God at all times, and never compromising our faith.
· The second is to love other people with the same kind of self-giving love which Jesus showed in his life, and particularly on the cross. That means putting their interests before our own.

Shown through the Bible

In the past, God revealed his will through people, often called prophets, and through Jesus' closest friends, the apostles. Their words are written in the Bible, through which God speaks today.

In the Bible we see how God's people in the past discovered his will, which never changes

TO THINK ABOUT

It is easy to say that you want to do what is right. It is often much more difficult to discover what is right in some situations.

· Can you think of an occasion when you were unsure what was the "right" way? How did you decide? Do you think you made the right choice?
· How effective is your conscience? Is it always wise to be led by your conscience?
· Do you think the Ten Commandments are still relevant today? Why?
· How did Jesus show God's way?
· How can the Bible help you to know the difference between right and wrong?

in principle, even if today's circumstances seem different.

The Bible is a permanent record of what God has said and done. Through it we can find out how he wants us to live, and what he wants us to avoid.

BIBLE CHECK

Shown through conscience Romans 2:14-16; Hebrews 9:13-14; 10:19-22

Shown through God's law Exodus 20:1-17; Matthew 5:17-20

Shown through Jesus John 13:15-17,34-35

Shown through the Bible Romans 15:4; 2 Peter 3:1-2

POSTSCRIPT

God has promised to help us keep to his ways. If we trust our own abilities, we will fail, but if we draw on his power we can succeed.

. . . .

Jesus showed the world that it is always right to love God first and then love others.

· How can you put this into practice? Are there any situations you are facing at the moment where this would affect your actions?

Thank God for the ways in which he shows his purposes to the world. Thank him especially for Jesus, and ask for the help of the Holy Spirit to live more and more in line with Jesus' life.

BIBLE SUMMARY
THE TEN COMMANDMENTS

These ten brief instructions in Exodus 20:1-17 are the core of the Bible's teaching about our relationship with God and with one another. They fall into two sections:

Duty to God

The first four concern our approach to God. He is a God who saves his people (verse 2; compare Jesus' work on the cross, Matthew 1:21). He cannot have any rival (verse 3).

Because God is the mighty creator of the earth and is Lord over all creation (verses 5-6) people cannot, and should not, try to show what he looks like. Nor should we treat the power which belongs only to God as if it came from a lesser source (verses 4-5). An "idol" is anything we put in the place which God alone should have.

God is holy, and therefore is to be respected in word and deed (verse 7). He has created people in such a way that they need to take one day in seven off work to relax and enjoy their God (verses 8-11).

Duty to others

Family life is something precious and to be preserved (verse 12), because it is the basis of a stable society. That is why casual sexual relations are forbidden (verse 14); they weaken the family bond and deny the deep unity created between a married couple who share everything.

Human life is sacred and not to be taken (verse 13), and the same applies to property belonging to others (verse 15). We are not to lie for the sake of personal comfort or gain (verse 16). And, as Jesus pointed out, inner attitude is as important as outward act (eg Matthew 5:21-30). So wrong desires which could lead to theft, murder or adultery must be shunned.

DISCOVERING
Discovering God's will

KEY TRUTH

God promises to guide us in every situation, so that we can do his will.

Praying it through

When we want to find out God's specific purpose for us – whether it concerns the job we are to follow, a task to take on in church, or a problem we have to face – the first thing to do is pray specifically about it.

Jesus did this shortly before his crucifixion. Knowing he was about to be betrayed, and that death as a sacrifice for our sin would certainly follow, he prayed that God would spare him.

But he was determined to do only what God wanted, so he submitted to the Father's will. Through prayer, our will can be guided so that it matches God's will, and we can be strengthened to do it.

Searching the Scriptures

The Bible is often the means God uses to guide us. Our reading of it will make us familiar with his general purposes.

But there will be times when a particular passage "speaks" to us in a very clear way. It seems to fit exactly our situation. It may be a word of challenge to change something, or a word of encouragement to go ahead with a decision we are about to make.

It should not be used like a horoscope or magic oracle, however. People who dip into it at random can sometimes get a shock. One person who is supposed to have done that hit on the verses "Judas went ... and hanged himself" (Matthew 27:5) and "Go and do likewise" (Luke 10:37)!

Talking it over

Big decisions are often made more easily after we have discussed them with an experienced Christian friend – perhaps a church leader.

Some people have a special insight into God's plans and our circumstances. Others are able to help us think through a situation, on the basis of their deeper experience of God. Sometimes their invitation to us to do something might in itself be sufficient guidance for us.

Even a casual remark, or perhaps a talk given at a church service or meeting, can be used by God to challenge and guide us.

Making up your mind

When the time comes to make a decision, some doubt may still remain in our minds. This might be for various reasons: our incomplete knowledge of the situation or even because God is testing our faith and our love for him.

There is no infallible rule. If the doubt

TO THINK ABOUT

Think of a few situations for which you need the specific guidance of God – they may be major life changes or seemingly insignificant decisions.

· How do you find out what God wants in each of these situations? Is there only one way to find God's will, or does it differ according to the specific circumstances?

· If God can show you his will in different ways, what should you be looking out for? Where should you be looking?

· Do you think God's guidance is always clear? If it is not, is that because you are

persists, however, it is usually best not to act in the way proposed. Christians frequently – but not always – experience a sense of inner "peace" when they reach a right decision. God's Spirit gives them the assurance that they are on the right track.

But such feelings should not be accepted on their own, because they can be wrong. And even with them, we still have to act "in faith", trusting God to take us through to the next stage.

BIBLE CHECK

Praying it through Luke 22:39-46; Acts 10:9-16,27-29
Searching the Scriptures Romans 15:4; 2 Peter 3:15-16
Talking it over Acts 15:6-23; Galatians 2:11-16
Making up your mind Acts 15:23-28; Romans 1:9-15

POSTSCRIPT

Sometimes our sin or self-will makes us unable to receive God's guidance. Then we need to ask him to make us willing to do whatever he says.

not listening properly, or because God is not giving a complete answer?
· Can you think of other Christians who can help you to discover God's will? Are you willing to listen to them?
· Are there times when we have to act without being sure of God's will?

Ask God to help you to be alert for his direction. Thank him that he will always go with you, and is ready to forgive you even if you go astray.

BIBLE SUMMARY
LIVING THROUGH FAITH

The Bible reminds us that Christians live by faith in Jesus rather than with certain, clear knowledge about the future (2 Corinthians 5:7). This means some decisions are made when we believe that they are what God desires, even if they seem unusual at the time (Hebrews 11:8). But faith is not folly; it is confidence that God has led us so far and will lead us on in the future (Hebrews 11:1-2). It does not mean we should stop using our minds!

God's common sense

One of the most obvious ways God guides us is through the circumstances we are in. The Good Samaritan did not need to ask for guidance in Jesus' parable. He saw a man who had been beaten up and knew that, because of his need, God wanted him to stop and help (Luke 10:33-34).

Similarly, Paul was often hindered from visiting Rome because of pressures to work in other places, although he longed to go there. In addition, the gospel had been preached in Rome already, so it would have been wrong to duplicate the effort (Romans 15:22-29).

Using our gifts

Jesus once told a parable about the use of gifts (or talents) given to those who follow him (Matthew 25:14-30). It was clear that whether his servants had many or few gifts, they all had the ability to use them in the events of daily living.

He looks to us, also, to use the gifts and abilities we have. Even if they seem insignificant to us, they are important to him (Matthew 10:40-42).

DISCOVERING
Discovering God's word

KEY TRUTH

The Bible is the permanent record of God's revelation to humanity, and contains all we need to know for our new life in Jesus.

A book of truth

The Bible is a unique book. Although it tells the stories of ordinary people and their experiences of God, it is much more than a religious biography.

It is uniquely "inspired" by God. That means he guided the people who wrote it so that what they put down was a true record of God's nature and purposes.

Although the Bible contains 66 books written over some 1,500 years by more than 40 authors, it does not contradict itself. It contains different emphases, of course, and we see how God's revelation grew clearer through the years, but the truth it teaches is consistent.

A book of example

Although the Bible contains passages of pure teaching – some of Paul's letters, for example – mostly it is about people.

Their surroundings were different from ours, but our feelings and problems are much the same as theirs were. So we can read stories of men and women who knew God well, and discover how they coped and remained faithful to him. They will challenge, excite and encourage us.

There are also examples of how not to live, and what mistakes to avoid. The people in the Bible were really human, ordinary people – warts and all!

A book of warning

The Bible includes books of "prophecy" including Isaiah, Jeremiah, Ezekiel, Daniel and Amos in the Old Testament, and Revelation in the New Testament.

Occasionally, they foretell the future. Some of these prophecies have been fulfilled, some have yet to take place, and many apply to more than one period of history.

But the prophets were also God's messengers who warned his people that God was holy and just. They reminded them that they could not lead sinful lives and still receive God's help and favour, and they often spoke of God's judgement or punishment given even to those who claimed to serve him but who, in fact, were evil.

A book of challenge

The Bible presents us with two kinds of challenge. One is through great men and

TO THINK ABOUT

Note down the parts of the Bible you have studied recently, or heard talks about.

· Are there any sections of the Bible that you have not looked at recently?

It is often easy to fall into the habit of only reading the same passages.

· Is it important to read from the whole of the Bible – both Old and New Testaments? Why?

· What practical steps can you take to make sure you are reading the whole of the Bible, and not just your favourite parts?

· If the Bible is God's word, how should that affect the way you read it?

women of God, who challenge us by their total devotion to him.

The other is more direct. We are challenged by some of the writers to believe the truth which they have written down and to live lives which are worthy of God.

We are also challenged to take his message out into the world which prefers to ignore it. The Bible contains the truth which has brought us to faith in Jesus Christ, and it challenges us to take that message to others.

BIBLE CHECK

A book of truth John 17:17; 2 Timothy 3:14-17

A book of example Hebrews 11:29-40; 12:14

A book of warning Jeremiah 17:1-10; Revelation 2:1-7

A book of challenge Mark 8:34-38; Luke 24:45-49

POSTSCRIPT

The Bible is not a book to be read like any other. To hear God speaking to us through it, we will need to pray for the help of his Holy Spirit.

· Is it possible to understand the Bible's message without the help of the Holy Spirit?

Thank God that he speaks to make himself known. Thank him for the richness and diversity of the Bible. Pray for the help of his Spirit to understand what the Lord is saying to you today.

BIBLE SUMMARY
ALL WE NEED TO KNOW

The Bible contains all we need to know about God, Jesus, ourselves, and the world, in order to live Christian lives (2 Timothy 3:16-17). But it has often been ridiculed or questioned, even by Christian scholars.

Entirely trustworthy

The phrase "inspired by God" in 2 Timothy 3:16 means "breathed out by God" (NIV "God-breathed"). God did not dictate his Bible to its authors, but guided their thoughts so that what they wrote was true and would encourage us to know, love and serve him.

The Bible contains all that we need to know in all matters of belief and behaviour (2 Timothy 3:15). If we follow what it says we can discover the reality of Jesus. It is also "useful for teaching"; we do not need to add any human laws to it. The Holy Spirit who inspired it will interpret it to us (John 16:13-15; 2 Peter 1:20-21).

Not an encyclopaedia

The Bible does not contain all that there is to be known; about science, sport or sociology, for example. It does not even tell us everything about God; the universe would be too small to contain such knowledge!

Paul was dismayed that people were speculating about details which the Bible did not refer to (Colossians 2:8). The Bible speaks with authority about being a Christian and the content of Christian belief. Where it is silent, we are encouraged to trust God's wisdom in not revealing everything to us (1 Peter 1:10-12).

DISCOVERING
Applying God's word

KEY TRUTH

The Bible is a basic tool for the Christian life; by using it carefully we will keep close to God.

Equipment for the journey

Just as no explorer would dream of leaving home without food, maps and a survival kit, so God does not expect us to go through life without some basic equipment which we will need on the way.

Our chief piece of equipment is the Bible. It provides wisdom for dealing with difficult situations, insight into the real needs of the world, and understanding of both God and his ways.

Above all, it provides us with spiritual "food". Our relationship with Jesus is nourished and enriched when we read and apply his word. It draws us closer to our Guide.

A light for dark paths

The Christian life takes most of us into situations where God's way is far from obvious. Besides, we are travelling through a world which the Bible says is "in darkness" because its affairs are not illuminated by the life and light of Jesus.

So the Bible helps to shed light on things. It explains why people are awkward, why evil exists and how it can be overcome or avoided.

Through our regular reading of it, God will often provide us with just the illumination we need to cope with a situation or to answer a difficult question.

A sword for hard battles

Paul the apostle called God's word the "sword of the Spirit" (Ephesians 6:17). This is because

it has a sharp, powerful action. It penetrates beneath the protective layers of pride, selfishness and deceit which people sometimes use to keep God's truth out of their lives.

Sometimes we need to use the Bible like a sword, to cut down opposition to Jesus. When arguments with non-Christian friends fail, the Bible will sometimes succeed in convincing them – but we have to learn to use it carefully, not clumsily.

And when we face temptation, the words of Scripture read, spoken and applied can help us to victory over Satan.

Strength to keep going

The Christian life is like a long expedition through different kinds of country. Sometimes the going is quite easy, like walking on level ground.

At other times it is hard, like climbing a

TO THINK ABOUT

God's word is relevant to all situations and seasons of life.

· When do you turn to the Bible most often? Is it when times are good, or when times are difficult? Why?

· How do you feel your life is going at the moment? What do you think the Bible's message is for you just now?

· How have you used the Bible recently to fight temptation? To discover guidance? To gain strength? To help you worship God?

steep rocky hill or struggling through a fast-flowing river or dense forest. It is then that Christians can become disheartened.

The Bible provides encouragement and strength to keep going. Sometimes the hardest thing to do is actually to open the Bible; the devil does all he can to make us doubt its power and so stop us using it.

BIBLE CHECK

Equipment for the journey
Psalm 119:97-104; 1 Peter 2:1-3
A light for dark paths
Psalm 119:105-112,130; 1 John 1:5-7
A sword for hard battles
Psalm 119:9-11,113-115; Ephesians 6:17; Hebrews 4:12-13
Strength to keep going
Psalm 119:25-40,73-80; 2 Timothy 2:15

POSTSCRIPT

The Bible does not group together all its teaching about specific issues. To find out what it says, we need to get to know it well.

God gives the Bible to help you in your Christian life. He also gives it to you so that you can help others.

· Can you think of a situation involving other people in which you could use the Bible to offer guidance, comfort or even rebuke?

Thank God for the ways in which his word is relevant and useful for your life. Ask the Holy Spirit to apply God's word to you more and more.

JESUS' VIEW OF THE BIBLE

Although Jesus was the Son of God who came to reveal God's truth to humanity (Hebrews 1:1-4), he used the Bible of his day, the Old Testament, a great deal.

A weapon to fight with

When he was confronted by the devil in the desert before the start of his public ministry, Jesus answered his temptations by quoting the Bible (Matthew 4:1-11). He found in Scripture a perfect and simple answer to his temptations. He did not argue; he just showed what God's word said and stood by it.

Evidence of God's work

Frequently Jesus, and the apostles, quoted the Old Testament to show how events in their experience had been foretold, and to prove that God was still at work. For example, he said John the Baptist was the prophet foretold several centuries earlier by Malachi (Matthew 11:10). And he applied the Bible to those who refused to listen to what he said. As the prophets had warned, they had refused to listen just when God was trying to speak to them in a new way (Matthew 13:14-15).

Support for his actions

Jesus was often challenged by people to justify what he was doing, especially when it conflicted with their customs. So, when he was accused of breaking the Old Testament law about observing the Sabbath, he quoted a precedent – the action of King David – for what he was doing (Matthew 12:1-8).

DISCOVERING
Handling God's word

KEY TRUTH

To discover the truth of God's word, we need to approach it in several different ways.

Reading it regularly

Most Christians find it helpful to spend some time each day reading the Bible, usually just before their prayer time, perhaps first thing in the morning or last thing at night.

This helps to focus our thoughts on God and gives us subjects to pray about. Some lesson from the Bible can be used as a basis for prayer for ourselves or others, or for worship and praise.

Using the Bible in this way, we can read steadily right through it. It is easiest to start with one of the Gospels, say Mark, then move on to some of Paul's letters (Ephesians is a good one to begin with), before turning to the Psalms in the Old Testament. That way, we get a broad taste of the different parts of the Bible.

Soaking it up

In countries where there are few books, or where many people are unable to read, God's word has always been memorised. The habit of learning passages by heart is a good one, even for those who have a Bible readily available.

There are two reasons for this:

· One is that, like Jesus, we then have an instant reply to the devil's temptations. We can answer him back quickly and decisively.
· The other is that we will know exactly what we believe at any time of need. A few basic verses such as John 3:16 will remind us of the basic gospel, and promises such as Matthew 11:28 will help us when we are under pressure.

Studying its teachings

There is much to learn from the Bible about God, the world, ourselves, and what Jesus has done and will do for us.

So in reading the Bible, we also need to fit together the teachings we get from its different parts. Then we can build up a picture of God's truth and will not be prey to false teachers who try to unsettle our faith.

If you have a Bible with cross references in the margin, or if you have a concordance, you can follow through a subject more easily. If not, make some notes as you go along and build up your own index of subjects. There are also some helpful books on Bible teaching available.

Discovering its characters

The Bible has many rich descriptions and accounts of people who learned the hard way to do God's will.

It is thrilling to read about some of them,

TO THINK ABOUT

Make a list of the different ways you can learn (eg listening to a lecture, discussing in a group).
· Which ways of learning do you find most helpful?
· Can you think of ways of studying the Bible that correspond to your different methods of learning?
· How can you put these together into a regular pattern of Bible reading and study?

like the young shepherd who became King David. Others are tragic figures, like Samson: physically strong and courageous but morally weak. Yet all of them have both achievements and failures.

They have much to teach us, because we see ourselves and others in them. Time spent gathering stories about such people from the different Bible books in which they appear can be rewarding and enjoyable.

BIBLE CHECK

Reading it regularly Joshua 1:8; Psalm 119:97; 1 Peter 2:2; 2 Timothy 3:16-17
Soaking it up Psalm 119:11; James 1:22-25
Studying its teachings Matthew 7:15-23; 1 Timothy 4:6-10; 6:3-5
Discovering its characters Hebrews 11:24-28; 12:1-3

POSTSCRIPT

When you come to a "difficult" passage in God's word, try to interpret it in the light of other related statements in the Bible in which the meaning is clear. Usually the obvious, most simple explanation is the right one.

Getting to know the Bible is not just about having the right methods. In fact, it is more important to have the right attitude!

· What is the right "heart condition" for reading the Bible? Are there other conditions that might affect this, like location or time of day?
· How can you prepare yourself to read the Bible and receive God's message through it?

Pray that the Holy Spirit would prepare your heart to hear God's word. Tell God that you want to handle the Bible wisely and truthfully, and that you are ready to respond to him.

BIBLE SUMMARY
UNDERSTANDING GOD'S WORD

Some people have claimed that you can make the Bible say what you want it to. That is true, if you take statements or sentences out of their context. There are three things to ask about any passage which will help you understand it. Take as an example the parable of the Good Samaritan in Luke 10:25-37.

What sort of passage?

This is clearly not an historical event, nor is it a closely argued piece of Christian doctrine. It is a parable, a story designed to teach one point. Jesus shows this at the end (verses 36-37). It is a story which was, of course, quite plausible. Something like it probably had happened.

What does it say?

The main elements are that first and foremost we must love God (verses 25-28) but that loving our neighbour goes hand in hand with it as an expression of that love. And our neighbour can be anyone in need, not just someone we happen to like – Jews did not like Samaritans.

What does it mean for me?

Jesus' command to the lawyer (verse 37) is always applicable. This is not a nice story to be enjoyed, but an example to be applied.

BELONGING
Belonging to God's family

KEY TRUTH

All Christians are members of God's international family, the church, because of their shared faith in Christ.

One Father

There is only one God. Despite all the different religions and different ideas about him, only one God truly exists. And he, says the Bible, so loved the world that he sent his Son Jesus Christ into it so that we could be reunited with him.

God becomes our "Father" in a special way when we receive the risen, living Lord Jesus into our heart and home, giving them over to his control.

And he is "Father" to all Christians, everywhere. Because we belong to him, we also belong to one great "family", his church.

One Lord

Christians are not only worshippers of the one true God – they are servants of Jesus Christ, too.

Jesus was unique. While being fully human, though sinless – his physical needs and emotional feelings were like ours – he was also fully God. Through him, God took on the limitations of human life in order to reveal himself to us and to bring us back to himself.

That is why the Bible calls Jesus "Lord", a title it usually reserves for God. Jesus is king over the whole world, and he becomes our king, or Lord, when we first trust him. All Christians share this relationship with him.

One Spirit

The Christian church was "born" when God sent his Holy Spirit on the first followers of Jesus. It was six weeks after Jesus' final resurrection appearance (his "ascension"), on the Jewish festival of Pentecost.

The Holy Spirit is active in every Christian: we could not even have come to trust Jesus without the Holy Spirit first showing us our need of him.

So he binds us together in one family. He is the invisible bond who creates unity and friendship between Christians. He gives us "gifts" or talents, to equip us to help each other grow in faith.

One faith

Christians differ widely from one another not only in personality but also in the aspects of the faith they emphasise, and in the ways they express it. But there is really only one Christian faith. It is summed up in the basic truths which all members of God's family share, and which centre on what Jesus did for us.

TO THINK ABOUT

Make a list of as many different Christian denominations or movements as you can. Find out about the way Christians worship in another part of the world.

- When you look at all these forms of Christianity, is it easier to note the similarities or the differences? Do Christians often stress their differences from each other? Why do they do this?
- How is it possible that all Christians belong to the same family?
- Think of a time when God's Spirit created unity between you and another Christian. Why is it important that the Spirit does this?

He became a man, died so that our sins could be forgiven, rose from the dead, and now promises eternal life to all who trust him. And those who teach differently, says the Bible, do not belong to the family.

BIBLE CHECK

One Father Acts 17:22-31; Romans 1:18-23;
  1 John 3:1
One Lord John 8:51-59; Philippians 2:5-11
One Spirit Acts 1:1-5; 2:1-4; Ephesians 4:1-7
One faith 1 Corinthians 15:1-8;
  Galatians 1:3-9

POSTSCRIPT

It is important to distinguish between those truths which are essential to genuine Christian faith, and those which, while important, can be interpreted and applied in different ways. Christian unity is based on the former, not the latter.

· What do you think are the essentials of the Christian faith? Compare these with the things you often emphasise in your own faith and church.
· How can you show that you belong to a worldwide Christian family this week?

Thank your Father God that he has called Christians together from all parts of society and everywhere in the world. Pray for the Spirit's help to serve, love and believe together.

BIBLE SUMMARY
ALL ONE IN CHRIST

Christianity is the only faith or ideal which has consistently achieved what all others seek: genuine unity and equality of people while continuing to respect and value their different abilities.

Rich and poor

The first Christians came from a variety of backgrounds. Many were poor and uneducated, working as slaves (1 Corinthians 1:26-29). But some came from the rich and ruling families (Philippians 4:22), and others were evidently well-off householders who gladly opened their homes as meeting places for the church (Romans 16:3-5).

Jew and Gentile

Perhaps the greatest miracle in the early church was the discovery by the first believers, who were Jews, that God's purposes in Jesus included non-Jews (Gentiles) as well (Acts 10:9-16,34-38).

They met to discuss this, and decided that no Jewish customs should be imposed on others (Acts 15:12-21). Later, Paul was to describe how God had broken down the wall of hostility between the groups, something people, not God, had erected (Ephesians 2:11-22).

No distinction

The church knows no sexual, social, racial or cultural barriers (Galatians 3:28). But such distinctions have not been destroyed; so everyone retains their personal identity. Our differences have been put into perspective by something greater: the love of Jesus for all who know they are sinful and need his forgiveness and new life (Colossians 1:15-23).

BELONGING
Belonging to each other

KEY TRUTH
Because Christians all belong to God's family, there is a special bond of love between them.

Baptised into Christ
The one thing above all others which binds Christians together is the fact that we all have to start the Christian life at the same place – the cross of Jesus Christ.

For there, humanity and God were reconciled. From the cross comes the possibility of new, eternal life. Jesus' death shows that we all have the same basic need: we are all sinful, and we need his "salvation".

Baptism, in whatever form it takes, is a symbol of our submission to Jesus Christ through faith in him as our personal Saviour. Being put under, or sprinkled with, water, symbolises death to our old self; rising from the water signifies the new life the risen Jesus gives; the water itself is a sign of the washing away of our sins. By entering God's family in the same way through faith – we are united to each other.

A club for sinners
Sometimes the church is made out to be an exclusive club for good people. In fact, it is just the opposite. It is where people meet who know they are not good, and who need the help of Jesus.

Every Christian already belongs to the family of God, so it is a natural thing to join with others to share our faith, encourage and help each other, and worship God together.

Each person will find some churches more helpful than others. Try to find one where the Bible is clearly taught and believed, and where the people are wanting to learn and grow together.

A new set of friends
When some people become Christians, their old friends (or even relatives) do not want to know them any more. And even if they do, they may not understand their new approach to life.

Within the church, however, will be people whom we can learn to love and trust. They will be able to help us – and we may be able to help them.

Making new friends takes time. It calls for openness and tact by all concerned. But because you already have the bond of faith, do not wait for others to approach you first!

En route for heaven
There is a good answer to those who say it does not matter if Christians don't get on with each other. We will have to get on with each other – in heaven!

Jesus has promised us eternal life. In heaven, which is the visible presence of God,

TO THINK ABOUT
Think of which group of people in your life you feel you belong to the most.
- Is this the church? Why or why not? Should it be the church?
- Most clubs or societies gather around a common interest or goal. What should be the basis of the church's fellowship?
- Why has baptism been so important for the church all through its history?

the whole church is gathered together to worship and praise Jesus.

Therefore he wants us to make every effort to express and enjoy our oneness on earth. Besides, if the world sees our love for each other, it will be encouraged to take our message seriously.

BIBLE CHECK

Baptised into Christ Romans 3:21-26; Galatians 3:23-28

A club for sinners Ephesians 2:1-7; Hebrews 10:23-25

A new set of friends Romans 16:1-16; 2 Timothy 4:11-22

En route for heaven Revelation 7:9-14; John 13:35

POSTSCRIPT

We should never expect a local church to be perfect – because no single member of it is perfect. And we should expect to find needy people in it, who find only in Jesus the answer to their needs.

Just like any human group, belonging to the church can sometimes be frustrating!

· Have you ever been frustrated with your church? What did you do? What should you do?

· If the church today is a glimpse of life in God's new creation, what things are you looking forward to?

Pray for the group of Christians that make up your church. Thank God for bringing you together, and ask for his Spirit's help to become more open to each other and to new Christians.

BIBLE SUMMARY
A UNIVERSAL CHURCH

The church of Jesus Christ does not consist of human structures or "denominations", so far as God is concerned. So no single group can claim to be "the one true church". The real church is made up of people throughout the world who have submitted their lives to Jesus' control. Jesus cares for and develops their relationship with one another (Ephesians 5:25-27).

Different in emphasis

The differences in human personality are not eliminated by faith in Jesus. They are not meant to be. But they have led to churches which cater for a certain kind of person, which emphasise certain doctrines more than others, or which worship in a certain kind of way.

Paul condemned divisions in the church at Corinth (1 Corinthians 1:10-13), but he did not insist that the separate groups always met together or did everything in the same way. Differences are allowed in the Bible, divisions are not.

United in truth

The New Testament knows nothing of close-knit international "churches". It only knows of a loose federation of local churches, which are joined together by mutual love and concern, and kept in touch with each other by the apostles and other teachers.

What united them was their concern for the truth of the gospel (Philippians 1:3-11). Christians who are agreed on the basic truths of the gospel are able to witness powerfully together in their community, even if they worship in different buildings.

BELONGING
Worshipping together

KEY TRUTH

Worship is a natural expression of a Christian's love for God; sharing with others in worship can stimulate our faith.

The reason for worship

"God is worthy to be praised!" That is what the writers of the Psalms – which are like hymns – conclude.

There are many aspects of God's character which inspire worship. He made, and continues to uphold, the physical universe. He loves, cares and provides for his people. He sent Jesus to die on the cross for our sins. He promises to bring justice and peace to the new world he will make when Jesus returns to earth.

These things give the Christian a sense of thankfulness for his goodness, and wonder at his greatness. They are the basis for Christian worship.

The object of worship

Every human being needs to worship someone or something outside themselves. That is part of being made in the image of God: he has built into human nature the need to worship him.

Worship is simply concentrating our whole mind, heart and life on something in which we find satisfaction. So in some places people build statues to please the spirits which they believe will help or hinder their life.

Elsewhere, people devote themselves to jobs, political ideals, pastimes, and so on. But for the Christian, Jesus, the Father and the Holy Spirit alone are worthy of worship. They alone hold everything together and give meaning and purpose to life.

The source of worship

There are times when we feel more like worshipping God than at others. We may be conscious of some special help he has given us, or, by contrast, we may be anxious about something.

But Christian worship is not dependent on our feelings. It focuses on God who never changes.

And it is inspired at all times by the Holy Spirit within us. He alone can lift our hearts to God. Otherwise we could easily become self-satisfied or depressed.

The value of worship

Worship has three important effects. The first is that it reminds us of how great God is. We need that reminder because daily events can blind us to him, just as a small object in front of our eyes blocks out the sun.

TO THINK ABOUT

Make a list of the common elements of your worship with other Christians.

- What does your worship say about who God is and what he has done?
- How is Christian worship different from people's "worship" of other things in their lives?
- Do you find it easier to worship with other Christians, or on your own? Why is it important that you do both?

Secondly, it lifts our spirits. It can restore to us the joy of knowing Jesus, even when we find life difficult. Worship with other people can be very stirring.

And finally, it can open us to the power of God. He loves a cheerful giver, the Bible says; if we give ourselves in wholehearted worship, we are more ready to receive his gifts of love.

BIBLE CHECK

The reason for worship Psalm 147:1-11; 150:1-6

The object of worship Romans 1:20-23; Revelation 4:8-11

The source of worship Ephesians 5:18-20; Philippians 3:3

The value of worship Psalm 96; Acts 16:25-34

POSTSCRIPT

There are many styles of worship. We need to find a church whose worship style suits our personality, and where we can feel part of God's family.

Hymns, songs, prayers and liturgies were all written to express a living, loving relationship with God.

· Are there any elements in your worship that have simply become a routine? Is this good or bad?

· Is it a good thing to worship in different forms, even if some may not be natural to you? How could this be helpful, or unhelpful?

· What practical steps can you take to ensure that your worship is always genuine and fresh?

Worship God now!

BIBLE SUMMARY
MAKE A JOYFUL NOISE!

There are many elements in Christian worship. It is helpful to use all of them, in private as well as in church.

The need for order

Most churches have a structure for their worship. People often find this helpful, because they know what is happening all the time. Paul stressed the need for order, but he also allowed for spontaneous contributions as the Holy Spirit prompted them.

God, he said, is "not a God of disorder but of peace" and people should be helped (or "edified") in worship, not confused. (1 Corinthians 14:26,33,40.)

Songs and silence

Music has always been a vital ingredient in worship (see Psalm 150). A catchy tune and stirring words can unite people in praise, perhaps with hand-clapping (Psalm 47:1; James 5:13), and a quieter, moving hymn can strike a note of wonder.

But silence is helpful, too, when we can sit and remember God's presence with us, think about a passage from the Bible or something which has just been said, and "listen" for God to teach us through it (Psalm 62:1; Ecclesiastes 3:7; Zechariah 2:13).

Body, mind and spirit

Every part of our personality can be used in worship of God. He looks for whole-hearted love and service, rather than outward ceremonies which can sometimes be meaningless (Amos 5:21-24; Romans 12:1-2).

In Bible times, people would stand up to pray, sometimes lifting their arms into the air (Psalm 141:2; Luke 18:10-14). It does not matter what position we take up, so long as God is really worshipped.

BELONGING
Sharing together

KEY TRUTH

Worship in church meetings is a time not only for meeting with God, but also for sharing with each other in fellowship.

Praying together

When we meet with other Christians to worship God, it is easy to treat the meeting as if it were our own personal time of worship or prayer which we have when other people happen to be having theirs.

Worship together, however, is really a time when the whole family of God brings its joint praises and requests to the Father.

Coming to the Father with things we are all agreed about can be a powerful way of drawing still closer to each other in love and unity. And God has made a special promise to answer our prayers when we are united in our requests.

Learning together

The Bible is, under the guidance of the Holy Spirit, an open book. Anyone can read and understand it. At least, they can up to a point. But God has appointed some members of his family to be teachers so that we can understand its truth more adequately.

Such people have a special gift of understanding, explaining and applying God's word. Through their ministry the rest of us can grow closer to God and serve him more effectively.

It is therefore helpful to listen to, or read, their teaching. But it is also helpful to meet in groups to discuss each other's insights into the Bible and how we can apply it locally.

Giving together

Part of our worship of God is giving gifts of money or goods to those who work in the church full-time to teach us and to win others for Jesus. Gifts for other members of the family of God who may be in special need are important, too.

In some churches, the collection of gifts (or the "offertory") becomes part of the worship. In others, a container for gifts is placed by the door. And some people prefer to give directly to people or church agencies of their choice.

There are no set rules about how much to give. But many Christians find that the Old Testament standard of one tenth of their income is a helpful one to follow.

Eating together

The night before he was crucified, Jesus had a meal with his closest friends. During that meal he took a loaf of bread, broke it into

TO THINK ABOUT

God did not only give his new life to you; he gives it to all who follow him.

· How should this change your attitude towards other Christians?
· How important to you is your fellowship with others? Why?
· Can you be a Christian on your own?

Make a list of the ways you already share together with other Christians.

· Are there other things you should or could be doing together?
· Is there a prayer concern you have which you could share with someone else or a group?

pieces and passed it round. Then he passed round a cup of wine for all to drink.

He said that those two staple food items symbolised his broken body and shed blood on the cross, through which we can be reconciled to God.

Ever since, the "breaking of bread", "Holy Communion" or "Eucharist", has been central in the worship of Christians. By eating bread and drinking wine together, we recall all that Jesus has done for us. That physical act is a powerful reminder of our unity with him.

BIBLE CHECK

Praying together Matthew 18:18-20; Acts 4:31; 12:6-12

Learning together Acts 2:42; 1 Timothy 4:13

Giving together Malachi 3:8-12; Acts 4:32-37; 1 Corinthians 16:1-2

Eating together Matthew 26:26-29; 1 Corinthians 11:23-32

POSTSCRIPT

Sharing together also includes sharing our joys and sadnesses with those who can appreciate them and who will pray or rejoice with us.

· Why is it important to listen to other people's understanding of the Bible?
· What happens when the church gathers around the Lord's Table to eat bread and drink wine together? Do you think this is a shared experience or a private experience? Or both?

Thank God for the Christians you share with on a regular basis. Pray for them now, and ask the Spirit to make your fellowship more joyful and meaningful.

BIBLE SUMMARY
ONE IN FELLOWSHIP

"Fellowship" is a biblical word which means "sharing together". The original word, *koinonia*, is sometimes used because it is well known. It sums up the love and concern we are encouraged to show to each other.

Centred in Jesus

If we trust him and live as he wants us to, said Jesus' closest friend, John, we have fellowship with him (1 John 1:2-7). This is the basis for fellowship with other Christians. It reminds us of the incredible fact that we are Jesus' friends, and not just servants (John 15:14-15).

Sharing together in Jesus

Our fellowship with each other is therefore a loving expression of gratitude that God has drawn us to himself (1 Corinthians 1:9-10). It is shown in our caring for one another's needs (1 John 3:14-18), by being sensitive to and sharing in one another's joys and sorrows (Romans 12:15), and loving in the same self-giving way as Jesus loved us (John 13:34).

BELONGING
Ministries for each other

KEY TRUTH

God has provided a number of different functions or "ministries" within the church so that it can grow and work smoothly.

The need for leaders

Jesus once looked at the crowds of people who followed him everywhere, and felt sorry for them. He said that they reminded him of sheep without a shepherd. They appeared aimless and confused.

Throughout history, God has always provided leaders who can see where God wants his people to go, and who are able to encourage and inspire them to follow.

That does not mean they have the authority to push people around, however. But there is both a human and spiritual need for people with genuine vision and God-given enthusiasm and confidence who will act as responsible leaders. Otherwise, we might do nothing at all for him.

The need for pastors and teachers

A pastor is one who is able to help people in a personal way; a teacher is one who can explain the truths of Christianity clearly. Sometimes, but not always, the same person has both gifts.

We need people who are able to help or "counsel" us because everyone faces problems or difficult situations from time to time. The pastor's advice should be based on the Bible, and coupled with deep human and spiritual insight.

The need for teachers is that we may grow in the faith and avoid errors of belief, which will weaken our effectiveness for God. We can never learn enough about him, but such knowledge will strengthen our faith.

The need for organisers

During the first exciting months of the Christian church, after the Day of Pentecost, the twelve apostles found they were doing everything: preaching, teaching, counselling, organising meetings and distributing gifts.

They felt this was wrong, so they appointed some "deacons". These were strong Christians and had a gift for organising things and handling money. They took over the practical work, leaving the apostles to do their own work unhindered.

There will always be people to do this today, to save the church minister from becoming overworked.

The need for submission

The leader, the pastor, the teacher, and others with different gifts, such as prophets and evangelists, can only exercise their ministries if the rest of the church allows them.

Paul said that when people claim to speak

TO THINK ABOUT

Make a list of as many different tasks within the church as you can – they can be very visible (eg preaching) or seemingly small (eg tidying chairs).

· Do you think they are all "ministries"?
· What makes something a "ministry" rather than simply a job to do?
· Does God use people because of their natural talents, abilities and personalities, or despite them?

God's word, we should test what they say by the Scriptures, and think it over. But if we have already acknowledged their gifts, then it is natural for us to submit to their judgement. Otherwise, chaos will ensue. God told the prophet Ezekiel that people would praise his words but not apply them. They refused to follow God's leading through the prophet, and so their witness became weak and ineffective.

BIBLE CHECK

The need for leaders Matthew 9:35-38;
Joshua 1:1-6
The need for pastors and teachers
1 Timothy 4:11-16; 2 Timothy 4:1-5
The need for organisers Acts 6:1-7;
Romans 12:6-8
The need for submission Ezekiel 33:30-33;
1 Corinthians 14:29; Hebrews 13:17

POSTSCRIPT

The church is neither a dictatorship, with one person making all the decisions, nor a democracy, where everyone takes part in decision-making. Rather, it is a fellowship, with all sharing as God enables them.

Think about the person you are, and the special gifts God has given you.
· Why does God give talents and gifts to his people?
· How are you serving in the church? Are there ministries you should be offering to help with? Are there ministries you should be letting other people share, or even stepping away from yourself?

Thank God for who you are, with your personality, abilities and gifts! Pray for opportunities to use them to serve in his kingdom, and for wisdom and strength to take the opportunities!

MINISTRY IN THE NEW TESTAMENT

The main emphasis in the early church was that every Christian had some ministry from which others could benefit (Romans 12:4-6). There is no such thing as a one-person ministry in the New Testament, with a single person trying to do everything. But there are certain leadership functions outlined.

Apostles and prophets

The apostles had unique authority from God to establish churches and teach the truth (Romans 1:1; 1 Timothy 2:7). Prophets were often used to bring a direct word from God to the people (Acts 11:27-30). Christians today are not agreed on exactly how, or even if, the equivalent of the first apostles and prophets exists.

Elders or bishops

It would seem as if each church had several elders (the Greek word is sometimes translated "bishop") – the "shepherds" or "overseers" of the church. They were the local leaders, who encouraged the church, and probably often acted as teachers as well. They are described in 1 Timothy 3:1-7.

Deacons and other organisers

Paul also describes deacons, in 1 Timothy 3:8-13. It is clear that he expected those who took any responsibility to be people that others respect (compare Jesus' statement in Luke 12:48).

Other ministries in the church included helpers, who assisted in practical tasks (Romans 12:7); people with the gift of healing (1 Corinthians 12:9); some who could speak or interpret other languages inspired by God in worship or prayer (1 Corinthians 12:10); and those who performed acts of mercy or kindness (Romans 12:8).

Working together

KEY TRUTH

The church is often called "the body of Christ", because like a body it consists of many parts all working together for the good of the whole.

The local church

The church of Jesus Christ exists on three levels:

· There is the worldwide church of all true believers, which does not have a single, recognisable structure.

· Then there is the regional or national church, which may have its own customs.

· And there is the local church, to which we belong. That local expression of "the body of Christ" is truly Jesus' hands, feet and voice in the local community, taking his love and message to those who need it.

Most local churches function to an extent independently, although many are also linked to other churches, in a "denomination", which have a similar outlook.

A caring church

The church is more like a hospital than a hotel. Rather than offering shelter to the spiritually rich, it offers help to the spiritually poor and sick.

A church which is being faithful to Jesus will attract all kinds of people, some of whom no one else cares for. They may have personal problems, or be difficult to get on with. But Christians are told in the Bible to welcome one another in the Lord. Such care is not always easy, but it is an expression of, and response to, God's love to us.

A witnessing church

The good news about Jesus is too good to be kept to ourselves. Indeed, there is no other hope for human beings to find God except through Jesus.

So we also have a duty to tell others about him. That is partly an individual matter. We can share our faith, however difficult we find it to put into words, with our families and friends.

But the church as a whole also proclaims the gospel. Often it can do so more effectively than the individual because we can pool all our resources to make a united impact with our message and new life.

A growing church

The church, like a human family, is always growing. New members are being born into it. Some members may leave the area and set up a new branch of the family where none existed before.

There are two sorts of growth we can expect to see:

TO THINK ABOUT

Think about the ways in which the parts of the human body all work together.

· What does this tell you about the way the church lives and works?

· Does "the body of Christ" refer to the worldwide church, the regional church, the local church, or the church throughout all the ages? Or is it all or some of these?

Make a list of the things Christians can do together.

· Is cooperation more or less effective for each of these activities?

- One is growth in numbers, as people become Christians and join in the life of the family.
- The other is growth in holiness. Together we can look for ways in which we can come closer to Jesus as a group, and discover how we can be more effective in our witness for him. He always has something fresh for us to do and learn.

BIBLE CHECK

The local church Matthew 5:14-16; Revelation 2:12-17

A caring church Matthew 5:46-48; Colossians 1:3-8

A witnessing church Matthew 28:18-20; 1 Thessalonians 1:8-10

A growing church Acts 2:46-47; Ephesians 4:15-16

POSTSCRIPT

Because the church consists of more than just our local group of Christians, the Bible encourages us to learn about others and to help them whenever possible.

· ·

- What barriers often prevent Christians from working together? Are these good reasons?
- What could you or your local church do to work with other Christians in your area to spread the good news of God's kingdom? What could you do in the wider world?

Christ is the head of the church. Pray that the Holy Spirit will keep you and your church close to him, so that he can direct you to work together with others to do his will.

BIBLE SUMMARY
THE CHURCH ACROSS THE WORLD

From its spectacular beginning in Jerusalem around the year AD 33, the Christian church spread right across the Roman Empire, westwards into Europe and eastwards towards India, by the end of the first century. Indeed, it was an international church from the beginning, because many turned to Christ from the wide variety of nationalities present in Jerusalem on the Day of Pentecost (Acts 2:7-13).

Sharing our riches

The church soon learned to share its blessings. For example, when there was a famine in Jerusalem, the churches of Asia Minor, hundreds of miles away, organised a collection and sent money, so that their brothers and sisters in Christ would not go hungry (Acts 11:29-30; 1 Corinthians 16:1-4). Through Paul and the other apostles, news about various churches spread, so that all were encouraged (Colossians 1:3-8).

A missionary church

But above all, the church has a message for the world. Jesus has called us to go to every race, tribe and language with the gospel, so that all have an opportunity to hear it before Jesus returns to earth (Matthew 24:14; Revelation 7:9-10).

For Peter, Paul and their friends no distance was too great, no hardship too severe, to prevent them going to strange lands with the only message which can unite, save and renew men and women everywhere. Paul's example remains a challenge to this day (2 Corinthians 11:23-33).

TESTING
The reality of testing

KEY TRUTH

Every Christian's faith is tested so that we may grow stronger.

It happens to everyone

Think of the most famous people in the Bible: Abraham, Moses, David, Jesus, Paul. They all went through times of testing, when living for God seemed especially hard.

Sometimes they faced opposition when people tried to stop them doing God's work. Sometimes they had to battle with strong personal desires to leave God's way.

And at times it seemed that everything was against them as problems and difficulties mounted up. But they became famous, partly because they showed how to overcome the difficulties everyone faces.

It may not seem fair

When people suffer in some way, they sometimes complain that they do not deserve such an experience. They feel that God is wrongly punishing them by inflicting trouble on them.

But suffering is not usually a matter of deserved or undeserved punishment. We simply live in an imperfect world – one which has been made imperfect by generations of human sinfulness – and everyone inevitably faces problems.

Sometimes it seems that bad people get away with their sin while Christians find the going very hard. That is not always true, and God promises that all sin will be punished eventually. But as Christians are opposed to evil, we can expect the devil to try hard to upset us.

It is allowed by God

The things which test our faith most are often those we least expect to happen. So it is easy to assume that they have taken God by surprise, too.

In fact, they have not. Nothing which happens to us is outside of God's purposes. He does not, however, always stop unpleasant things happening. To do that he would have to be constantly interfering in the natural processes he has created, for example, to stop fire hurting someone.

This does not mean that God deliberately plans to hurt us. He wants us to let his love shine through to us always, and he never lets us be tested beyond the ability he gives us to cope.

It can teach us more about God

Everything in the Christian life can be used to draw us closer to God, and teach us more about him.

TO THINK ABOUT

Christians are not sheltered from problems or opposition. In fact, sometimes the Christian life might seem to bring more problems!

· How do you react to difficulties? Do you try to ignore them, explain them, or something else?
· Do you think your life would be better or worse without difficulties? Why?
· How does God use these times to strengthen your faith?

In fact, Christians sometimes find that in a time of testing they are made to realise just how far they have wandered from God, or just how great and loving he is.

Above all, it reminds us of just how weak and inadequate we are, and how much we need his help and power. We appreciate his help most when we most need it.

BIBLE CHECK

It happens to everyone 1 Peter 4:12-16; 5:8-11

It may not seem fair John 16:32-33; Revelation 21:5-8

It is allowed by God Romans 8:28-30; 1 Corinthians 10:13

It can teach us more about God 1 Thessalonians 1:4-8; 1 Peter 1:6-9

POSTSCRIPT

Although everyone desires a comfortable, trouble-free life, such an existence is not always as good for us as we imagine: it can lead to self-satisfaction and spiritual laziness.

Think of a difficulty that you have faced recently or are facing at the moment.

· How is this difficulty a test of your faith? Do you think all difficulties test your faith?

· What particular thing are you learning about God through this situation?

· Do you think God wants you to be tested? Why, or why not?

Tell God about the situations and circumstances you find hard, and how they test your faith. Pray that he will give you the strength he promised, so that your relationship with him will grow stronger.

BIBLE SUMMARY
THE PATIENCE OF JOB

Job is an Old Testament character who was rich and well-respected. He was a godly man, too, who tried to pass on his faith to his children (Job 1:1-5). But then his world fell to pieces.

The role of Satan

The book of Job reveals that Satan sometimes has access to God (1:6). He told God that Job worshipped him only because life was easy (1:10-11). So God gave Satan permission to test Job's faith by attacking his possessions and family (1:12), and then, later, by making him ill (2:5-9).

Job's faith stayed firm

Job's faith had two aspects. There was his faith in God, which remained unshaken. He still trusted God even when people around him said he was mad to do so (1:20-22; 2:9-10). But he was also very upset (3:1-26), cursing the day he was born.

His friends told him he must have sinned, to bring such awful things on himself (eg 11:1-6). But his faith in his own integrity before God also remained firm; he knew he was not being punished, so his suffering remained a mystery to him.

Job's faith was deepened

But good as he was, and undeserved as his sufferings were, Job still had something to learn. God later revealed his true greatness to him (38:1-21, etc.), and Job realised that even his strong faith had still been rather shallow (42:1-6). The story had a happy ending – Job became wealthy again – but he was wiser after his experience.

TESTING
Testing through doubt

KEY TRUTH
Doubt can be a means God uses to draw us nearer to him, but it can also paralyse the Christian's life if it is not dealt with.

A touch of humility
There are two kinds of doubt:

· One is usually called "scepticism" – the harsh unbelief of someone who does not wish to know and trust Jesus.
· The other is the uncertainty which sometimes hits a Christian. It may be a lack of confidence about whether we truly belong to God's family, or about God's willingness to do something in our life.

Such doubt can arise from genuine humility: we know ourselves to be sinful and do not expect God to be lenient. But such an attitude forgets the enormous love and power of the one who came not "to call the righteous, but sinners to repentance" (Luke 5:32).

A touch of opposition
Doubt is one of the chief causes of inaction among Christians. If we doubt whether something is right, or whether God wants us to act in a particular way, we are unlikely to go ahead. If a doubt is an instinctive reaction prompted by the Holy Spirit to something which is wrong or unwise, that can be good. But if the proposed action would honour God and help others, doubt is bad.

So the devil often sows doubts in people's minds to stop them doing God's work, and to cause confusion in the church. Doubts, like weeds, stop the fruit of the Spirit from developing properly.

A touch of faith
Doubt and faith are closer to each other than many people think. After all, faith, although firmly based on what God has said in the Bible, is not total knowledge.

Therefore faith can easily slip into doubt: the kind of uncertainty which the devil sowed in Eve's mind in the garden of Eden – "Did God say ...?" – grows worryingly larger.

When that happens, it is helpful to do two things. One is to recall the ways in which God has helped us or others in the past. The other is to remember the unchanging facts on which our faith is based: the total revelation of God's word. His plan will never be inconsistent with this.

A touch of confidence
God does not always clear away our doubts as soon as we ask him. He may want us to think through our doubts, and return to faith much stronger as a result. That process can be lonely and painful. We need the support of

TO THINK ABOUT
Make a list of things you have doubts about from your daily life (eg that it won't rain!).
· Is doubt always bad? How can it be helpful in some situations?

Now think about doubt in the Christian life. Note something you have doubted about the faith or your own Christian life.
· Is it wrong for a Christian to doubt?
· Can you think of a situation where doubt might be helpful? On the other hand, can doubt be sinful? When?

friends with whom we can talk things through – or to offer them our support, and try to understand them, when they have this experience.

But in the end, doubt, if it persists for a long time and grossly hinders our Christian life, may have to be labelled sin: it could be a refusal to take God at his word. If that is the case, then we need to confess the sin and accept, in faith, his forgiveness. That act of confidence will lead to many more!

BIBLE CHECK

A touch of humility Luke 18:9-17; 1 Timothy 1:12-17

A touch of opposition Matthew 13:24-30,36-43; James 1:6-8

A touch of faith Genesis 2:15-17; 3:1-22; John 20:24-29

A touch of confidence 1 Timothy 1:3-7; 2 Timothy 1:11-14

POSTSCRIPT

Doubt can lead to faith, but it can also become an excuse for not pressing on in the Christian life, and accepting a comfortable existence in which God is unable to work powerfully.

- How can you move through doubt to a clearer faith and stronger trust in God? What practical steps would you need to take to do this?
- Are there any doubts you need to let go of at the moment? Are there any aspects of your faith that God is prompting you to consider more carefully?

Thank God that you can be utterly confident in his love for you. Pray that the Spirit would help you to discern God's will and ways more clearly.

BIBLE SUMMARY
THE NATURE OF FAITH

Jesus' friends once asked him to increase their faith. His reply was unexpected. If they had faith as small as a grain of mustard seed, he said, they could move mountains (Luke 17:5-6; Matthew 17:20).

It depends on God

The disciples had in fact asked the wrong question. Faith is not something which grows in quantity. It is not something we can possess more or less of; that would make it dependent on ourselves. Rather, our faith is in what God can do. So what seems "a little" faith can achieve much, because it knows that nothing is too great for God (Genesis 18:14).

The disciples should have asked, "Improve our faith". We need to learn how to trust God simply, without reservation. See Matthew 8:5-13, where a soldier recognised that Jesus needed only to utter a word of command and his request would be granted.

It submits to his will

Jesus taught his followers to pray, "Your will be done" (Matthew 6:10). God's will is always good (Romans 12:2), but he will often only work through people who trust him (Mark 6:5-6; 9:23-24). So faith requires boldness which expects God to work, and humility to ask only for that which will fit in with his purposes.

While it is often right to qualify our requests with "If it is your will" (Matthew 26:39), such a prayer can be a veiled form of unbelief. There are many occasions when we can be sure that what we ask is God's will, and so we can pray with conviction and confidence (John 14:14)!

Testing through temptation

KEY TRUTH

Every Christian faces temptations to disobey God, but the power of God is always greater than the temptation.

An ever-present danger

Because many people do not acknowledge Jesus as their king, the world is full of temptations for the unwary Christian. The Christian life is like walking along a jungle path where there are dangers everywhere.

Some people will deliberately try to make us disobey God, saying he won't notice or that no harm can come from, say, a petty theft or lie.

The lifestyle of others will itself be a source of temptation, because it may blind us to God's better way of living. Plus of course, Satan will try to trip us, and our own human nature will want to take the easy way out of a situation without asking what God wants.

Sometimes our own fault

Jesus taught us to pray, "Lead us not into temptation." Another way of putting it would be, "Do not let us stray into tempting situations."

While we cannot avoid temptation altogether, we can often avoid people and places which are likely to provide a strong source of temptation to us personally.

Everyone is different, so there cannot be a set of rules covering every situation. But, for example, a person who gets drunk easily should obviously avoid situations where they will be able or expected to drink a lot of alcohol. While God promises to help and protect us, we should not expose our weaknesses unnecessarily.

Often subtle and cunning

Some temptations are very obvious – to disobey God, to lie, to steal – but others are more subtle. Instead of being tempted to do something which is clearly wrong, we may be tempted to do something which is only wrong because it is not God's will for us, or because we are doing it from wrong motives. King David learned that when he tried to count the people of Israel – an act which stemmed from his pride.

And other temptations show up Satan's cunning even more; they may be half right. He simply tries to steer us gently off course, and so reduce our effectiveness for God.

Always a way out

Facing temptation is never easy; often it is a test of whether we really want to do what is right and experience God's power, or to be self-indulgent.

Sometimes, as we battle with temptation, the pressure to give in increases. Normally,

TO THINK ABOUT

Think about the different temptations you face in your life.

- Are you only tempted to do what is wrong? Can you be tempted to do the right thing for the wrong reason?
- Where do these temptations come from?
- Are there particular situations that you should avoid? If you can't avoid being tempted, what steps can you take that will help you reject the temptations when you face them?

however, each refusal to give in makes victory over the temptation easier.

There are times, too, when Satan seems to leave us alone after we have resisted him, only to come back with a renewed attack when he gets an opportunity.

Although God has promised always to give us the ability to overcome temptation, we have to admit that sometimes we prefer the "pleasures of sin". Without our cooperation God's help is limited.

BIBLE CHECK

An ever-present danger Luke 17:1-4;
  1 John 2:15-17
Sometimes our fault Matthew 6:13; 18:7-9;
  James 1:12-15
Often subtle and cunning 1 Corinthians
  6:1-6; 2 Corinthians 11:12-15
Always a way out 1 Corinthians 10:12-13;
  James 4:7; 2 Peter 2:9

POSTSCRIPT

Human will-power is not enough to overcome temptation. We need the Holy Spirit to strengthen our will so that we can resist temptations to sin.

While some temptations may be familiar to you, others will come unexpectedly.
· What does the Lord's Prayer mean by "lead us not into temptation"? Does God ever tempt you?
· Are there things you can do *before* you face temptation so that you will be prepared, even if it surprises you?

It is best to decide in advance that you want to withstand temptation. Tell God this, and ask him to give you the wisdom and strength of his Spirit to identify temptations and then reject them.

BIBLE SUMMARY
JESUS' TEMPTATIONS

Jesus was often tempted, so he understands and can help us when we are tempted (Hebrews 2:17-18). Few of his temptations are recorded, but those he experienced before he began his three-year teaching ministry are given in detail in Matthew 4:1-11.

Jesus was feeling weak

Jesus' temptations came when he was very tired and hungry, and so least able to resist (verse 2). That is how Satan often attacks us; his only thought is to overthrow God's people by any means. Jesus became the object of Satan's attack because he knew the importance of Jesus; he tries to crush all who represent even the smallest threat to his evil ways.

Satan twisted the Bible

Satan began by trying to make Jesus doubt his calling: "If you are the Son of God ..." (verse 3). Then he twisted the Bible, quoting it at Jesus and telling him to apply its promises for the wrong reason – for the sake of a spectacular stunt, rather than out of obedience to God (verse 6). Then he made Jesus a promise he had absolutely no power to fulfil (verses 8-9).

Jesus stood firm

Jesus responded in two ways. First, he quoted the Bible at Satan (verses 4,7,10). He did not argue: he simply faced Satan with the real truth. But he also trusted himself entirely to God at the same time. He was hungry, but he knew that God would provide bread for him without his having to misuse his own powers in a selfish way. He really did want to serve God only (verse 10), and when Satan saw that, he left him alone for a while (verse 11).

Testing through failure

KEY TRUTH

Sometimes God allows us to make mistakes, so that we may learn to let him guide us in the way we should use our freedom.

The gospel for failures

Jesus once told his followers that he did not come to call righteous people, but that he came to call sinners to turn back to God. That is why some people find the Christian faith unpleasant: they have to admit they have been wrong.

We begin the Christian life by admitting that in God's sight we are failures. We have not obeyed and loved him with all our heart.

God deals with us as we really are, not as we would prefer other people to imagine us. And that is true all through the Christian life: he wants us to be honest with him – and with each other.

The weakness of human nature

Despite all our good intentions and our prayers, we sometimes fail God. We give in to temptation. We fail to do something we know we should have done.

Sometimes we are just plain wrong. We are lazy or uncaring. Sometimes we are blind to the opportunity to experience God's power or show his love until it is too late.

That is because we are still weak even though God's Spirit dwells in our lives. Our human nature can still stray from God's path.

God's promise of success

When Nehemiah, an important official in the government of Babylon, went to see the king with an important request, he prayed for success. Later, when he was back in his native

Jerusalem, helping to build up the ruined city, he kept praying that God's work would get done despite the opposition.

His is one of many examples in the Bible of people who faced difficult tasks, who prayed that God would help them overcome, and who eventually achieved what they set out to do. Sometimes God does ensure that despite our mistakes we still do what he wants. That reminds us of just how great he is!

The gospel of new beginnings

When we do fail God, our faith in his love can be severely tested. We may feel very guilty or depressed because we know we have let him down.

While it is right that we should not take our failure lightly, we should not let it cripple our Christian life.

The promise of forgiveness with which we began the Christian life still holds true. God

TO THINK ABOUT

Think about a time when you fell short of God's standard for your life.

· How did you react? Was it easy to be honest with God about your sin, or did you want to make excuses for yourself?
· How did it make you feel about God? What does God feel about you? Does God accept you back completely after you have failed?
· What counts as a "failure" in the Christian life? Is it worse to do something wrong, or not do something that is right?

sets us on our way again, as we tell him that we are sorry for our failures. And he continues to give us the power of his Spirit with which to love and serve him.

BIBLE CHECK

The gospel for failures Luke 5:29-32; 1 John 1:5-10

The weakness of human nature Romans 7:15-20; James 3:2-10

God's promise of success Nehemiah 1:4-11; 4:9,15-20

The gospel of new beginnings Romans 6:1-11; 1 John 2:1-6

POSTSCRIPT

While God understands and forgives our failures, we cannot excuse them. He is always ready to help us do what is right.

Make a list of some well-known characters of faith from the Bible (eg Abraham, Jonah).

· Can you think of a time when each of them fell short of God's standard or failed in fulfilling God's purpose for them? What happened next? Did God stop using them?

· Can failure help you to grow in your faith?

Thank God for his grace and forgiveness. Tell God that you want to do what is right, and ask for his help each day.

The Bible is not full of success stories which seem entirely beyond our abilities. It has many accounts of ordinary people's failures, too, which help us to see that their successes were very much the result of God's work, and not their own special ability.

Full of promise

Peter, one of Jesus' closest followers, who was also called Simon, was always full of big promises. He boasted that he would never let Jesus down (Matthew 26:33-35). He was convinced that Jesus held all the answers to his need (John 6:67-69) and was the first to recognise Jesus as being the Son of God (Matthew 16:13-16).

A total let-down

Peter even tried to protect Jesus from going to the cross, not realising that it was part of Jesus' work to do so (Matthew 16:21-23; John 18:10-11). But when Jesus was put on trial, Peter was frightened. The servants of the high priest were talking over the day's events by a fire when one of them recognised Peter as a follower of Jesus. Peter panicked and denied he had known Jesus (Mark 14:66-72). He soon realised his mistake, and broke down in tears of regret.

Back to normal

After his resurrection, Jesus made a point of talking specially to Peter, to encourage him and give him a new job to do (John 21:15-19). There was no word of rebuke; he understood, and knew that Peter was deeply sorry. From then on, Peter became a pioneer preacher introducing many people to Jesus (Acts 11:1-18).

TESTING
Testing through pain

KEY TRUTH

Suffering is a universal experience from which Christians are not always free, but through which they can still experience God's love.

Pain in the world

In one sense, pain is a good thing: it is a warning that something is wrong in our body, or that danger, such as fire, is near.

But there is much suffering which in itself has no virtue: suffering from illnesses, accidents and natural disasters which everyone can experience.

Some suffering stems directly from human sinfulness: murder, war, theft. Other forms of suffering occur because the whole world is imperfect. The Bible says everything has been affected by the sin of the human race.

Coping with suffering

It is natural to complain when we suffer: no one likes the experience, and we may feel it is unfair of God to allow it. But the first thing we have to learn is to accept that for the time being this is the state in which we have to serve God.

However, during our suffering, God may seem far away. It may be hard to pray; we may not be able to concentrate on the Bible.

Therefore Christians have a great responsibility to visit and help in every possible way all those who suffer.

What is more, we have the unfailing promise that Jesus is always with us even in our sufferings – and that his love never dries up. He knows from personal experience what suffering is about.

Healing is possible

Both Jesus and the apostles not only preached the gospel, they also healed the sick. There is no record that they healed everyone, and Paul, for example, appears to have had a long-standing problem which God did not remove (see Bible Summary).

There are two ways in which God heals people today. One is through normal medical treatment – because he is still the Lord of our bodies and their functions. And the other is as an answer to special prayer on our behalf, with or without medical treatment.

We are told to pray for healing. But healing may not always be sudden; God may have a lot to teach us as we slowly get better. The inner healing of mind and spirit is as vital as that of the body.

The end of all suffering

The Bible paints a beautiful picture of heaven, the place where all Christians will spend their

TO THINK ABOUT

Think about a Christian you know who is suffering pain at the moment.

· Why is there pain in the world? Why are Christians not exempt from experiencing pain?

Many of the people who were healed by Jesus had been excluded from worshipping God in the temple because of their illnesses. After they were healed, they could worship God again.

· What does this tell you about the nature of healing? Do you think God heals people for the same reasons today?

lives after death in the close presence of Jesus. In heaven, it says, there will be no more death, disease, hatred, war or any other suffering. Everything will be made new and perfect.

It is a picture which is meant to encourage and inspire us in this life. We know that one day all that we long for will happen. Meanwhile, we are not to stop our efforts to ease or remove suffering. Part of being a Christian is to bring a touch of heaven to earth.

BIBLE CHECK

Pain in the world Luke 13:1-5; Romans 8:18-23

Coping with suffering 2 Corinthians 1:3-11; Hebrews 12:7-11

Healing is possible Mark 1:32-34; Acts 5:14-16; James 5:14-15

The end of all suffering Romans 8:18; Revelation 21:1-4

POSTSCRIPT

Sometimes, it is only through suffering that the deep things of God become clear to us, and the work which God has given us to do is completed – just as Jesus had to suffer in order to do his work.

· Why do you think Jesus heals some people and not others?

· How can you help other Christians who are suffering? What encouragement can you give to them? What is the best thing to pray for in times of pain?

Thank Jesus that he has experienced intense suffering, so he knows the pain you and others go through. Pray that pain will bring new experiences of God's love.

BIBLE SUMMARY

PAUL'S "THORN IN THE FLESH"

Paul was a remarkable person. He, above all others, spelt out Jesus' teaching in detail for the benefit of the church. He travelled thousands of miles in sailing ships, on horseback and on foot to take the message of Jesus to new countries or districts.

A life of suffering

In doing that task Paul suffered a great deal. He lists some of his sufferings in 2 Corinthians 11:23-33 as he uses his experience to prove his genuineness. No one would be shipwrecked, beaten up, robbed, starved and overworked unless he believed in his calling!

Paul also wrote that he was prepared to suffer for Jesus, because Jesus had suffered much for him. He remembered, too, how he made Jesus' followers suffer before he became a Christian (Philippians 3:7-11).

Weakness becomes strength

There was, however, one particular pain from which Paul wanted to escape. He had what he called a "thorn in the flesh" (2 Corinthians 12:7-10). No one is sure what this was. It may have been a physical deformity or very poor eyesight.

Paul felt that it hindered his work, so he prayed for healing. But God answered, "My grace is sufficient for you, for my power is made perfect in weakness."

Three times Paul prayed for healing, and each time God gave him the same answer. After that, he accepted his disability. He was more open than ever to receiving God's strength for his work and he proved that God could use weak people to do his will (1 Corinthians 1:25).

TESTING
Testing through persecution

KEY TRUTH

In every generation some Christians are ridiculed, hurt or even killed by other people simply because they love and serve Jesus Christ.

The gospel offends people

The message of Jesus brings truth to light, but some people prefer their world of lies and wrongdoing. They therefore try to stop the spread of the Christian faith or hinder Christians from living it out.

Others will ridicule the faith because its simple message seems nonsense to them. They do not believe there is a God, or if there is, they claim he has not revealed himself finally and completely through Jesus Christ.

In some countries, people regard Christianity as a threat to their political ideals, so they pass laws limiting its activities, or banning it altogether.

The ways they attack

Sometimes, the pressure on us will come from those closest to us – our families or special friends. They may have a different faith, or simply not understand what has happened to us. They may accuse us of being disloyal to them; some Christians have been thrown out of their families as a result.

Persecution can be violent. Christians have been imprisoned and tortured for their faith. They have been banned from certain jobs, or banished to special hospitals.

But often the pressure is less obvious. People may pick arguments, or try to make us sin. They may exclude us from their social circle, or just laugh at our faith.

The call to be faithful

The taunt which Satan made against Job was that he would do anything to save his own skin. In fact that was not true, and Job remained faithful to God despite his suffering.

The threat of persecution can be more frightening than any other suffering, but the apostles and many Christians since have shown that it is just as possible to remain faithful to God under these conditions.

God wants us to remain faithful to him, even if that means not doing what other people want. He promises to give us wisdom to know what to do, and has said that he is always honoured when we stand up for him.

Resisting, even to death

Being faithful to God meant death on the cross for Jesus. In fact, that was why he came to earth – to die for our sins.

But for some of his followers death came

TO THINK ABOUT

Take some time to find out about Christians in another part of the world who are being persecuted because of their faith in Jesus Christ.

· What can they teach you about following Jesus? How does persecution affect the faith of Christians?

Now compare their situation with your own experiences as a Christian.

· Have you ever experienced persecution or intense pressure to give up on your faith? What forms of persecution might you face today?

· Do you find it difficult or easy to stand up for Jesus?

early, too, because they loved him. Stephen was stoned to death for sharing his vision of Jesus with the religious leaders, and became the first Christian martyr.

Ever since, people have willingly been murdered rather than deny the truth of Christianity. For most of us, it will not come to that, but the challenge to remain faithful, under pressure, right up to the moment we die, remains.

BIBLE CHECK

The gospel offends people John 15:18-27; 1 Corinthians 1:20-25

The ways they attack Matthew 10:16-39; Acts 4:1-4

The call to be faithful Acts 4:16-20; Mark 13:9-13

Resisting, even to death John 16:1-4; Acts 7:54-60; Hebrews 2:1-4

POSTSCRIPT

Sometimes, Christians can bring persecution on themselves by being tactless or by making too much of secondary or less important truths.

· How can the Spirit help you?
· Do you ever think it would be easier to face death than the ridicule of friends and relatives, or the indifference of society? Is it harder to remain faithful to God when the persecution is subtle?

Thank God for the glorious hope of living with him eternally in his new world! Ask him to help you be faithful to him, whatever situation you are in, so that you will hear his "well done" at the end of your life.

BIBLE SUMMARY
THE PROMISE OF PEACE

"Cast all your anxiety on him because he cares for you" (1 Peter 5:7) is one of the most memorable of the Bible's many guidelines. One of the strongest witnesses to the reality of our faith is the inward peace which Jesus gives when we obey that instruction.

A peace beyond words

Jesus promised his peace to his followers before he died (John 14:27). He said it would be unlike anything the world had to offer. It would not be like the temporary release from anxiety which drugs or strong drink may give, because they deal only with our feelings, and not with the real problem.

Rather, his peace would be an underlying sense of confidence that all our circumstances are in God's capable hands, and that his purposes for us are always good even if very hard or even painful.

A peace despite trouble

The Jewish word for peace, "shalom", means "wholeness" as well as "tranquillity". It reminds us that peace is dependent on our relationship with Jesus. We already have peace with God (Romans 5:1-5) in the sense that everything which makes us his enemies has been dealt with by Jesus' death on the cross.

So, whenever there is turmoil around us, we have an opportunity, firstly, to experience the peace which is the gift of God's Spirit within us (Galatians 5:22). But, secondly, we can also use that sense of peace to help us become peacemakers in that situation, helping others to be reconciled to each other (Matthew 5:9).

WINNING
Jesus is king

KEY TRUTH
The whole universe is already in Jesus' power, and he will one day bring all its rebellious parts to order.

He conquered sin
"Sin" describes both the attitude and actions of people which go against God's laws and purposes. People are cut off from God by sin.

Jesus conquered sin in two ways. First, by living a perfect life on earth, he showed it was possible for people to avoid sinning and obey God.

But most of all, he conquered it through his death on the cross. There, he suffered the punishment – death itself – which each sinful person deserved, so that we could know God and receive his new life which lasts for ever.

He conquered death
"The soul who sins is the one who will die": that was the Bible's judgement until Jesus came to earth. Here more than physical death was implied: it involved spiritual separation from God.

But death could not defeat Jesus, because he was the creator of life! Although his body died completely, God raised him from the dead to demonstrate his total victory over the grave.

In so doing, God broke the curse which had plagued the human race for centuries. He opened up the way to heaven, so that although we, too, will have to pass through death, it cannot hold us in its clutches and keep us from everlasting life.

He conquered evil
Because God gave every person freedom to choose whether or not they would obey him, some people have chosen to do what is wrong. In addition, there are evil powers in the world trying to overthrow God's kingdom.

When he died on the cross, Jesus mortally wounded the forces of evil, because he conquered their ultimate weapon, death.

Now Satan is in his last days. He knows he will be totally destroyed when Jesus returns to earth. Meanwhile, he attempts to hinder God's people, but he can never harm those who trust themselves entirely to Jesus.

He will conquer the world
In three of Paul's letters – Ephesians, Philippians and Colossians – he bursts into exclamations of praise at the greatness of Jesus' victory.

Jesus promises to do nothing less than

TO THINK ABOUT
Make a list of some of the people, movements and ideas that seem to be in charge of the world today.
· How do they try to control the world? What powers do they use?
· What does it mean for these "rulers of the world" that Jesus is king?

Jesus' rule over the world was established by his death and resurrection.
· What was so important about Jesus' death and resurrection? What did Jesus accomplish by them?
· How can Jesus' rule as king be seen today? How can your life show that Jesus is king?

conquer the whole world with his love and his truth.

He will do it in two ways. First, he will do it through his people. We are called to take and live out his message in every place. Secondly, he will do it completely when he returns to earth to create a new world in which peace, love and truth are supreme.

BIBLE CHECK

He conquered sin Matthew 9:1-8;
Romans 8:1-3; 1 Peter 2:21-25
He conquered death Luke 24:1-9;
1 Corinthians 15:20-28
He conquered evil Luke 13:10-17;
Colossians 1:13-14; Revelation 20:7-10
He will conquer the world Philippians 2:9-10

POSTSCRIPT

Because Jesus is king, nothing happens which he cannot use in some way for his own good purposes, even if events stem from evil sources rather than from him.

· What does Jesus' rule mean for the future of the world? What will that mean for you personally?
· Do you find it easier to accept Jesus' rule as a present or as a future reality? Why is it important that he is king both now and then?

Thank God that in Jesus he has conquered the powers of sin, death and evil. Pray that the Spirit would help you to let Jesus rule as king in your life.

BIBLE SUMMARY
JESUS' COSMIC PLAN

Sometimes, Christians talk as if God's plan to give them eternal life was simply a personal, individual matter. In fact, it has a much greater dimension. His plan includes the whole world, which he loves and cares for (John 3:16-18). It has been slowly unfolding through the years (Colossians 1:19-20).

The role of the church

The church may seem weak and powerless in the world today, but in fact it is God's new family (1 Peter 2:9). Jesus is its head, and God's new world will be filled by those who have loved and served him in this life (Ephesians 1:18-23). Those who seem great in the world will not be there, unless they too have trusted Jesus (Matthew 19:28-30; 20:1-16).

The rest of creation

The whole universe will be renewed (Ephesians 1:9-10), held together by Jesus with a new perfection and beauty. All things are out of harmony with God because of the massive impact human sin has had on the physical world. But one day everything will be reconciled to God, just as we have to believe in him (Romans 8:22; Colossians 1:19-20).

In other words, God plans a whole new creation (Revelation 22:1-5, compare 2 Corinthians 5:17-19), in which everyone will know that he is the true king, the creator of all things who alone is worthy to be worshipped and served (Revelation 4:11).

WINNING
Victory is certain

KEY TRUTH

Because Jesus has already shown his power in conquering evil and death, we can be certain of his ability to help us to honour God in every situation.

No need to sin

We are faced with all kinds of temptations to disobey God every day. Sometimes those temptations come from our own weakness, from our circumstances, or directly from Satan.

But whatever their source, and whatever their strength, those temptations are never more powerful than the Holy Spirit who is active in our lives. He is steadily making us more like Jesus, who resisted all temptations.

Prayer helps in overcoming temptation. We can ask God to make us more alert and sensitive, so that we see temptation coming. Also, we can pray for the Holy Spirit's power at the time we need it: to claim Jesus' victory over sin as our own, and to act as if we have already overcome it – and we will!

No need to fear

Fear of any kind can cripple a Christian as much as a physical handicap. Like one animal being attacked by another, we may be paralysed by fear and therefore do nothing until it is too late.

But Christians have nothing to fear, even in frightening situations, for two reasons. First, Jesus is always there, ready to help. Second, he can deal with the fears of those who love and trust him fully, so that they can serve him effectively.

No need to doubt

One of the most remarkable stories of Jesus' life was when he stayed behind while his closest followers crossed a lake in a boat. A storm blew up, and Jesus walked across the water to them.

Peter, impulsive as ever, asked if he too could walk on the water. Jesus said yes, but as soon as Peter had taken a few steps, he saw the waves and felt the wind, doubted, and began to sink.

Yet his own experience had already proved that he could walk on the water – and Jesus had told him to! Our past experience (and that of others) and Jesus' own instructions encourage us to do whatever he wants.

No need to falter

Many Christians are tested almost to breaking point. It might be constant temptation; it could be human suffering of some kind.

TO THINK ABOUT

Think of times when you have faced temptation, fear, doubt or suffering.

· When these times come, what happens to your faith in God? Do you become anxious? Why?

· What does Jesus' victory mean in each situation?

Make a list of some promises God makes to the Christian. Note down what situations they would be appropriate for (eg 1 Corinthians 10:13 for temptation).

· Is it possible not to sin? How does God promise to help you? How can you live in the light of this?

It is easy to grow tired, not only physically, but spiritually, too. Battling with evil can be very wearing.

But the Spirit within us will carry us through. He will give that energy we need, that extra will-power and determination to press on. God's love for us never falters, so we, too, can love and serve him consistently.

BIBLE CHECK

No need to sin Mark 11:24; Luke 11:13; 1 John 4:4

No need to fear Psalm 34:4-6; Matthew 10:26-33; 2 Timothy 1:6-7

No need to doubt Matthew 14:22-33; 21:18-22

No need to falter Isaiah 40:27-31; Galatians 6:9; Hebrews 12:3

POSTSCRIPT

There can never be any excuse for not enjoying Jesus' victory. Yet if we do fail him, we know he will not fail us, but will always forgive and renew us.

· Why do you not have to fear the enemies of the Christian life?

· Are you ever like Peter? In what situations do you find it difficult to keep trusting Jesus' power?

· Should your Christian life be marked by victory or defeat? Why?

Memorise some of God's promises you noted down so you can pray them in your times of need. Thank God that he has already won the victory, and is ready to help you when you call on him.

BIBLE SUMMARY
HE IS ABLE

The New Testament is full of confidence about all that God can do. Here are some of its assertions.

Able to keep us

We know that he is able to forgive our sins and give us eternal life; Hebrews 7:25 reminds us that he is able to do this for ever. No matter what century people live in, God can save them.

And once we belong to him, he is able to keep us from falling away (Jude 24). That means victory over sin, and a certain place in heaven.

Able to help us

Jesus reminds Paul in 2 Corinthians 12:9-10 that the strength he is able to give is wholly adequate.

We experience that strength when he enables us to overcome temptation (Hebrews 2:18), and when he keeps his promises to us (Romans 4:20-21).

Able to support us

God shows his power especially by doing all kinds of things for us, through us and within us – things we often do not even expect (Ephesians 3:20-21).

He is able to provide us with whatever we need – spiritual resources and physical resources, too – so that we can do his work in his way (2 Corinthians 9:8).

WINNING
Right in the heart

KEY TRUTH

The secret of living a successful Christian life is to ensure that our thoughts and attitudes reflect those of God.

Jesus comes first

During his life on earth, Jesus frequently told people that if they really wanted to be his followers, he had to have first place in their lives.

Just as the Old Testament commandment said, "You shall have no other gods before me," so Jesus cannot fully work out his purposes for us if we value anything or anyone more highly than him.

And although that may sound a hard requirement, it is in fact the gateway to success. With Jesus first in our lives, he is free to do many great things, and we are free to enjoy them.

Thinking straight

Proverbs 23:7 is a difficult verse to translate and appears in one Bible version as, "As he thinketh in his heart, so is he." In other words, what we are like inside is what will show outwardly, however much we try to hide it. Jesus said the same thing.

Living a Christian life is not about doing certain good deeds and avoiding bad ones. It is about being in a right relationship with God, from which certain ways of behaving will come naturally.

So the Bible encourages us to let God's Spirit set our thinking straight. To help him do this, we can concentrate our thoughts on God, his goodness and his purposes.

Pure motives

It is perfectly possible to do the right thing for the wrong reason. We can try to help someone, for example, not so much out of concern for them, but because we want to exercise power over them.

Or we can do something right in order to persuade others that we are good, unselfish people, while in fact we are just the opposite, and know it.

Ananias and Sapphira were like that. They sold some land and pretended to give all the money to the church, but held some back. They did not need to give it all, in fact, but the act of pretence was seen to be very serious.

Love determines action

Love for others is the golden rule of the New Testament. Our actions are to be determined by it; we are to do for others only – and everything – what we hope they would do for us.

So before doing something, it is often worth asking both what Jesus would do in the

TO THINK ABOUT

Read Paul's list of excellent Christian qualities in Philippians 4:8.

- Why does Paul tell his readers to fill their minds with these things? What will the result be (see Philippians 4:9)?
- Do your thoughts ever stray from these qualities?
- What practical steps can you take to keep your mind on these things?
- How do you think your thoughts influence your actions and attitudes?

situation and what we would like done if we were on the receiving end.

But love is not soft. It sincerely desires only what will help, encourage and benefit others. Sometimes that may mean gently helping them come to terms with some sin or fault in their life or faith. Love stems from a deep and genuine concern for the other person's welfare.

BIBLE CHECK

Jesus comes first Exodus 20:3; Luke 9:23-26,57-62; 1 Timothy 6:6-16
Thinking straight Proverbs 23:7(KJV); Mark 7:14-23; Philippians 4:8
Pure motives Acts 5:1-11; 1 Peter 2:1-3
Love determines action Luke 6:27-36; 1 Corinthians 13

POSTSCRIPT

Developing right attitudes is a good example of how we are to cooperate with God: he promises to change our attitudes, but we have to recognise where they need changing, and ask him to deal with them.

Jesus told his disciples that the greatest commandment was love for God, along with love for others.

· What does "love" mean in this context?
· What are some of the motives that drive your life? How can you make sure that you do everything out of love for God and others?
· Would it be helpful to describe the Christian life as "single-minded"?

Thank God that his Spirit transforms your life by renewing your heart. Pray that the Spirit will fill you with love for God and for others, and give you strength to keep your mind focused on all that is excellent.

BIBLE SUMMARY
NOT I, BUT CHRIST

A mistake which many make is to try to live a Christian life largely by their own efforts, and only sometimes drawing on God's help. Paul's example was rather different: for him, being a Christian was to allow Jesus' life to fill and flow through him at all times (Galatians 2:20).

Many things are beyond our complete understanding, and this is one of them. "Christ in you, the hope of glory" (Colossians 1:27), is a mystery, says Paul, but it is true just the same.

So he prays that the Christians in Ephesus may know Christ dwelling in their hearts, and so base their lives firmly on love, and begin to understand the immensity of God's purposes (Ephesians 3:14-19).

Christ changing us

When we allow Jesus to "live through us" we are relying totally on him, but also need consciously to clear away the things which will hinder him (Ephesians 4:22-24). We are encouraged to live consistently with the new nature he has already put in us to make us like him (Colossians 3:5-17).

WINNING
Overcoming evil

KEY TRUTH

God wants his people to share practically in Jesus' conquest of evil, and to conquer it in their own experience.

Be sure of your ground

We cannot effectively fight evil if we are unsure either about the nature of evil itself, or of the resources we can draw on.

That is why it is important to grow in our knowledge of the Bible. Through it we discover just what a Christian can believe and do, and what is untrue and wrong.

The most effective fighters in any battle are the ones who have the confidence that they will never be defeated. We can have that confidence, because despite the intensity of our fight against evil, God can never be defeated – and nor need we be.

Depend on God's power

With God, nothing is impossible. Furthermore, he wants to show how great and powerful he is, by doing things which we could never do ourselves.

In fact, the person most able to receive and enjoy God's power to overcome evil is the one who is most conscious of their need and weakness. God is then free to work, without being hindered by our self-confidence.

Whenever we face temptation or opposition as Christians, we need to renew our trust in Jesus, rely on his promises, and receive in faith his power to speak or act wisely.

Learn to say no

One of the problems about some kinds of sin is that they seem very attractive. They do not always appear bad. Sometimes they appeal to our natural desire for comfort or excitement.

The secret of conquering any kind of temptation is never to argue about it, or even consider it to be a possible course of action.

If we learn to say no in small things, it will be easier to stand against bigger ones. But saying no to them is only part of our saying yes to Jesus and the far better things he offers.

Tell Satan to go

Satan is sometimes like a very noisy dog. He barks loudly to frighten us away from doing God's will, but in fact if we press on in God's power, Satan will not be able to harm us.

Sometimes, a word of command will make him stop his activity when it is seriously endangering God's work. But we can order

TO THINK ABOUT

Name the different types of evil you recognise today. Some evil may be personal or local; other evil may be a worldwide problem.

· How powerful is evil? How does it influence you?
· What does God think about evil?

Jesus dealt decisively with evil in his death and resurrection.

· If Jesus has already defeated evil, why does it still remain in the world?
· What does God want you to do when you are faced with evil? Should you simply run away from it in order to keep yourself

him to stop interfering only in the name of Jesus Christ, God's Son, praying for his authority and victory.

We must be specially careful about tangling with the forces of evil, expecially if a non-Christian appears to be controlled by them. In those cases, the way forward may be for several mature Christians to pray for that person's release from Satan's hold.

BIBLE CHECK

Be sure of your ground 1 Corinthians
  3:10-15; 1 Timothy 6:11-16
Depend on God's power Mark 13:9-11;
  Luke 18:27; Philippians 4:13
Learn to say no Matthew 16:21-23;
  1 Peter 5:8-9
Tell Satan to go Luke 10:17-20; Acts 13:4-12;
  19:11-20

POSTSCRIPT

Fighting evil is not a game, but a deadly serious business. We need not fear evil forces, but we should not belittle their strength or intentions.

pure, or does God want you to fight it in some way? Is every situation the same?
· Are you able to fight evil on your own? What resources does God give?
· How can you fight evil in God's strength this week?

Even though you may fight against evil, it is only God who can give the ultimate victory. Thank him for his power, and pray for help to overcome evil in your own life, the society around you, and even in the wider world.

BIBLE SUMMARY
THE ARMOUR OF GOD

In Ephesians 6:10-20 Paul reminds his readers that the battle Christians face is not against people so much as against great armies of spiritual forces which influence many people (often without them knowing it) and which control many of the world's institutions and governments (verse 12).

In order to deal with them effectively, he tells us to "put on the full armour of God" (verses 11,13). Then he lists the spiritual resources we can draw on, using the picture of a Roman soldier, ready for battle.

Hold to the basics

The basic armour for the soldier was a breastplate, helmet, belt and shoes. For the Christian, our basic protection against evil is the truth of God, his righteousness, and the complete salvation Jesus gives, together with the good news which brings us peace with God and eternal life (verses 14-15,17).

Keep alert and active

In battle, the flaming arrows that were shot at soldiers were intercepted by their shields. So, our faith is something which can be held up to deflect the dangerous arrows of temptation which will be flung at us (verse 16).

We also have a "sword" which will cut the enemy to pieces more effectively than any real weapon of war. It is the Bible, which contains God's word for every situation (verse 17). And as we use these two pieces of battle equipment, we also need to keep in touch with God our commander through prayer, ready to receive and obey his instructions (verse 18).

WINNING
Resisting pressure

KEY TRUTH

The Christian is called by God, not only to overcome any opposition, but also to resist subtle pressures which would weaken our witness.

The pressure to conform

No one likes to be different from others. We all want to be considered part of a community, club or group of friends. And so we usually adapt our behaviour to what is acceptable to that group. But that may not always be acceptable to God. If we follow him faithfully, we shall sometimes want to be different from other people.

There is also a temptation to conform to the world around us by not bringing the Bible to bear on every aspect of our life. So, for example, some Christians tried to prevent the abolition of slavery in the nineteenth century, simply because it was a part of the society they knew.

The pressure to compromise

There are two dangers here. One is to water down our beliefs under the pressure of teachers or preachers who deny some important truth or to modify our behaviour to include something which God has clearly forbidden, just because it is easier to do so.

The other danger is for us to bring pressure on others by insisting that our way of doing things or our understanding of some problems is the only one possible. However, Christians do sometimes differ, in love, over secondary matters.

In the first case, we must simply stand our ground and obey God: in the second, we should obey our conscience, and learn to respect those who differ.

The pressure to complain

It is always easier to complain about something or someone than to try to put matters right. It is also easy to complain against God or our church leaders when things become difficult.

The new nation of Israel complained bitterly once they had left Egypt under the leadership of Moses and found themselves hungry and thirsty in the nearby desert. They had been keen enough to set off, but were not prepared to follow God through the hard ways as well as the exciting ones.

But the Christian way is always to show love, consideration and faith, rather than shout slogans. In his own kind way, Jesus tells us to get on with our business of living and serving him. We can let him be the judge of what is best for us, and of other people's actions.

The pressure of complacency

Sometimes, the Christian life is quite straight-

TO THINK ABOUT

Pressures can be so subtle that often you may not be aware that you are giving in to them. Spend some time thinking about your life and try to identify what pressures you face.

· Do you think pressures are as dangerous for your Christian life as temptations and opposition? Why, or why not?

· Are there any situations in which you find it easier to conform to an accepted pattern of behaviour, rather than living according to the pattern of Jesus' life?

· When you meet people who believe or act differently from you, what things are you

forward. There are no big problems to face, no great temptations bearing down on us.

That is just the time when we can slip into complacency. We can become content with our comfortable life and so miss all kinds of opportunities to serve Jesus, by caring for others or speaking for Jesus.

And older Christians, too, can sometimes ease up after many years of devoted service to Christ. To all comes Paul's challenge to press on.

BIBLE CHECK

The pressure to conform Romans 12:1-2; Ephesians 2:1-7

The pressure to compromise 1 Corinthians 8:7-13; 10:23-31; 1 Timothy 4:1-10

The pressure to complain Exodus 17:1-7; Matthew 18:15-22

The pressure of complacency Proverbs 6:6-11; Luke 17:7-10; Philippians 3:12-14

POSTSCRIPT

The example of Jesus, who loved even unlovable people, and for whom nothing was ever too much trouble, is the one we are called to follow, even when many subtle pressures may put us off.

tempted to compromise on? What should you hold to firmly?

· Do you ever complain? What steps can you take to make your words more peaceful and encouraging?

· What is the difference between rest and complacency?

· How can other Christians help you to resist pressure?

Ask the Spirit to help you identify the pressures on your life. Pray for strength not to give in to them, and receive the Spirit's power into your life.

BIBLE SUMMARY
UNITED WE STAND

One of the functions of the church – the local group of Christians who meet together for worship and fellowship – is to help one another stand firm in the faith (Philippians 1:27-28).

That cannot happen if we are always arguing among ourselves, and the weaker brother or sister may easily slip away from God because of our neglect of their spiritual or other needs (1 Timothy 5:13-15; 2 Timothy 2:22-26).

So the New Testament is always urging us to offer support to one another, so that we may win our battles and overcome the dangers which face us as a group (1 Thessalonians 5:14).

The need for wisdom
In order to stand together on the truth of Jesus, we need to be "wise about what is good, and innocent about what is evil" (Romans 16:17-20).

That means growing in our knowledge of how to live according to the Bible, and at the same time giving evil a wide berth (Ephesians 5:3-6).

It also means sorting out our differences swiftly and maturely, so that we can get on with our main task of proclaiming God's word in the world (1 Corinthians 6:1-8). Jesus promised that, in united prayer, God is able to work mightily when we are all agreed (Matthew 18:19).

WINNING
Onward Christian soldiers

KEY TRUTH

The Christian life consists, not only in overcoming evil, but also in doing important things in the world for God.

Building the kingdom

The "kingdom of God" was a phrase used by Jesus to describe the extent of God's direct rule on earth over his people, and of their influence for him in the world.

This kingdom is slowly growing in size and extent. Jesus said it was like a tiny seed which grows into a large shrub.

It is also growing in effectiveness. Its members are like seeds sown in good, fertile soil, said Jesus in one of his parables. Each one yields a crop of the "fruit" of his Spirit: we each have some influence for God in our community.

Salt in the world

Salt is an important ingredient in almost everyone's diet. A small amount has a great effect.

Salt was used in Jesus' time to preserve foods like meat in order to stop them going bad when they were stored. It was also used to bring out the flavour of foods.

Jesus said that was how he wanted his people to be in the world. Our influence will help prevent human society going completely bad. For example, God promised to hold back his judgement of Sodom in the Old Testament because of the righteous people there. And we can bring joy and hope into the world, where they are so often lacking.

Light for the world

Light is often used in the Bible as a picture of God, because of the total contrast with sin and evil, which is often described as "darkness".

Jesus said he was the light of the world. He came to show up the deeds of evil people, and to make clear the way to God.

We are to reflect his light, share his love and reveal his life wherever we go. Then others will see that his ways are good and his laws right.

Winning enemy territory

In human warfare, armies not only defend themselves against each other, but also try to capture each other's territory.

In the spiritual battle, God has called us to go with him into the world which is under Satan's influence, and see God himself slowly extend his kingdom.

TO THINK ABOUT

Make a list of some parables that describe what the kingdom of heaven is like.
- What does "the kingdom of heaven" mean? Is this just another way of talking about the church, or is it something more?
- What does the kingdom of heaven do in relation to the world?

Think of a particular area or situation where you especially want God's kingdom to appear.
- How does God's kingdom grow? Is the growth the result of God's activity, or your activity, or both?

Together with all God's people we can take the good news of eternal life in Jesus Christ to those who have never known him. We may see people who were once in Satan's grip released to serve God. We may see individuals, families and even whole communities changed by the power of God's word.

BIBLE CHECK

Building the kingdom Matthew 13:1-9,24-32
Salt in the world Genesis 18:26-33;
   Matthew 5:13; Colossians 4:6
Light for the world Matthew 5:14-16;
   John 1:4-13; 8:12
Winning enemy territory Acts 8:4-8,26-40

POSTSCRIPT

We have been told to expect to see God at work through the witness of our churches. If nothing seems to be happening it may be because we are not obeying him fully.

· If Jesus is the king of this kingdom, who are you?
· What tasks do all Christians share in as part of this kingdom?
· How might God's kingdom begin to grow in the area or situation you thought about just now? Are there any special tasks that God wants you to do?

Thank God that he uses you to bring his life to the world. Ask for his kingdom to come through your prayers and actions, on earth as it is in heaven.

BIBLE SUMMARY

WHAT IS THE KINGDOM OF GOD?

The kingdom, or rule, of God, was what Jesus came to proclaim (Matthew 4:17), and he sent his followers out to proclaim it, too (Luke 10:8-9).

His kingdom is not a country as we know it, however (John 18:36), and does not have actual land. Rather, it consists of people all around the world who love and obey him (Luke 14:15-24).

Parables of the kingdom

Many of Jesus' parables were about the kingdom of God. It would grow, he said, like seed in the ground (Matthew 13:1-9, 31-32). However, there would be people who did not really belong to it but who seemed to be part of it (Matthew 13:36-43).

The kingdom would have a good but often unnoticed effect on the world, like yeast in a loaf of bread (Matthew 13:33). It is like a precious stone, or treasure; it is worth selling everything in order to get into it (Matthew 13:44-46).

Present and future

The kingdom of God already exists (Luke 17:20-21) wherever God's people are. But it also has a future dimension, and Jesus will establish it finally at the end of time (Matthew 25:31-40).

SERVING
Called to serve

KEY TRUTH

God wants every Christian to take part in his work in the world.

Called by God

When we became Christians by asking God's forgiveness for our sins and trusting him to give us eternal life, we also became Christian workers.

God has brought us into his worldwide family of people who love him. As in every family, there are lots of jobs to be done if life is to run smoothly. No one is expected to be lazy and do nothing.

God has also put us in the place in the world where he wants us to show his love and spread his truth. We are called by him to be his servants, to do his will wherever we are.

Compelled by love

The first Christians could never have been accused of being halfhearted. They were almost reckless in the way they threw themselves into their service for Jesus. The reason was quite simple. They were so amazed at the love of God for them, that nothing was too hard or too much trouble for them to do in gratitude to him.

The love that resulted in Jesus laying aside all the beauty and perfection of heaven, to share in the limitations of human life, and then to be killed without cause by sinful people, is so great that he rightly deserves all our energy and devotion.

Committed through faith

Part of being a Christian is a willingness to do whatever God wants.

He wants to change our lives so that we become more like Jesus. For this to happen we need to accept his instructions and rebukes.

Since we are already committed to letting him work in our lives, he now wants us to follow his instructions one step further, and commit ourselves to serving him in the world.

Concerned for others

There are many people in every community who have physical or spiritual needs. Some of them may need help just to live more comfortably – people such as the poor and disabled.

Others are lonely and need human friendship; most probably the majority of them still need to find Jesus as their Saviour and friend.

It is easy for us to be so concerned with ourselves that we are blind to the needs of others. But God wants us to grow more sensitive to the needs of others and to help them whenever we can.

TO THINK ABOUT

Read the story of Jesus washing his disciples' feet in John 13:1-17.

- How does it make you feel that the Lord of all creation did the work of a household servant?
- How is this a pattern for all Christians? Does it mean you should literally wash feet?
- Why is it important that you see yourself as God's servant? How is this different from being God's employee?
- Are you excited to be a servant, or does it sound like a chore?

PICTURES OF SERVICE

The New Testament writers use a number of pictures to describe God's people as they seek to serve him. Here are a few of them.

Employed on God's business

A frequent description is that of a slave, or servant. In Bible times, slaves were common in society. They worked for one man, and while some of them had a great deal of personal freedom, they were "bound" to their master – they could not leave his service.

Paul regarded himself as the slave of Jesus (Romans 1:1; 1 Timothy 1:12), and said that all Christians were to live as if they were the slaves of God (Ephesians 6:6). Another similar description he uses is that of "stewards", managers of houses and estates, who were required to be honest and faithful to their employer (1 Corinthians 4:1-2).

Working for God's kingdom

Paul sometimes thought of himself as a builder, laying the foundations of faith in Jesus (1 Corinthians 3:10-15), or a farmer who plants seed (the word of God) which others tend and help grow to maturity (1 Corinthians 3:5-9).

He also pictured himself as a soldier, fighting both to defend the truth and defeat evil by bringing others into God's kingdom (1 Timothy 6:12; 2 Timothy 4:7).

Following Jesus' footsteps

Perhaps the most helpful picture is of a "disciple", one who follows in their master's footsteps, always willing to learn and to obey. Jesus' disciples were his pupils and fellow workers (eg Luke 8:9-10; 9:1-6; 11:1).

BIBLE CHECK

Called by God Romans 6:15-19; Ephesians 2:8-10

Compelled by love John 13:34-35; Romans 5:3-5; 2 Corinthians 5:14-15

Committed through faith Matthew 24:45-47; Romans 12:1-2

Concerned for others Matthew 9:36; 14:14; 1 Peter 3:8

POSTSCRIPT

There are many things we could do for God, so we need to pray for his guidance to know exactly what tasks he has for us.

Make a list of the people you meet on a regular basis, and the places you go.

· Have you ever thought of yourself as God's special servant to these people and in these places?

· How would this change the way you behave? Are there things you need to start doing or saying?

Thank God for the privilege of serving him. Pray for the people and places he has called you to serve. Keep praying for them regularly.

Power to serve

KEY TRUTH

It is possible to do God's work in God's way only by relying entirely on the power given to us by his Holy Spirit.

Sharing God's work

Christians are called to share in the work God has been doing, and will continue to do, in the world. It is his continuing work, not ours.

That does not mean we can lay aside the skills and knowledge we have gained in the world. But it is easy to assume that God must approve anything we do in connection with telling others about Jesus, or helping in the life of the church. In fact, we can only be sure of what is his work by regularly seeking his guidance. Sometimes, things are done in churches only because they have always been done.

Filled with his Spirit

Whenever the first Christians set out on a new venture, they asked for God's Spirit to fill their lives with the power and wisdom they needed to do his work.

And as they went out in faith, they often discovered that God had already gone ahead, preparing people to receive their message.

When we take part in God's work, we need to do it in his way, and not depend merely on human ideas and methods. Only as we allow the Holy Spirit to flow through us, will we see the results of God's love working in our community or church.

Controlled by his word

God does not want us to go into the world to teach our own ideas about him. He has given us his word – the truth of his nature and our needs – to proclaim and to live out.

That word carries the authority of God himself. However people react to us and our message, we need never doubt its truth and relevance. The living God has stamped it with his power.

However, we are not to be like parrots, repeating key phrases in answer to every question, as some non-Christian sects teach their members. God's word is big and powerful enough to be explained and applied in ways which make sense in our society without losing its truth and authority.

Equipped with his gifts

Jesus told a story about a man who gave his servants money (the coinage was called "talents") to gain profit for the man while he was away on business.

All except one were faithful, and made use of their gifts with varying degrees of success. All were praised, except for the servant who buried his gift in the sand.

TO THINK ABOUT

Make a list of the opportunities for service that you have.
· Would you be able to do all or any of them without God's help?
· What would happen if you tried?
· Does God ask you to take every opportunity for service that you come across, or should you learn also when to leave a task for someone else?

God has given us personal abilities to use for him. There are natural talents he gave us when we were born, and there are spiritual gifts he wants us to seek, too. We always have the resources to do whatever he calls us to.

BIBLE CHECK

Sharing God's work John 14:12-14; 2 Corinthians 6:1

Filled with his Spirit Acts 8:26-30; 13:1-4; Ephesians 5:18

Controlled by his word John 17:14; Acts 4:31; 1 Corinthians 2:1-5

Equipped with his gifts Matthew 25:14-30; Ephesians 4:7

POSTSCRIPT

Christian service is as much an act of faith as anything else in the Christian life. We are not called to be timid, but faithful and bold, trusting in God's power.

The Holy Spirit provides you with both the guidance and the strength to use opportunities for service.

· What particular gifts has the Spirit given to you to help you serve God effectively?

· Just because the Spirit gives these gifts, does that mean you have nothing to contribute yourself?

· What can you do to work along with God's Spirit this week?

God equips you for the things he has called you to do. Thank him for his help, and spend some time praying for your opportunities for service.

BIBLE SUMMARY
DOING WHAT COMES NATURALLY

The church is sometimes pictured by Paul as a body. Each person has a particular job to do, just as each part of the human body has its own function.

Working together

So, says Paul, chaos would rule if the foot thought itself useless because it was not a hand, or if the head told the feet they were not needed (1 Corinthians 12:14-21).

In fact, he goes on, God has given the apparently weaker parts of both the human body and "the body of Christ" an indispensable role (verses 22-26). The Bible gives no justification for creating a hierarchy of jobs in Christian service according to the power or status they are thought to carry. We have one master – Jesus – and all are called to serve him (Matthew 23:8-12).

Being ourselves

Everyone likes to be well thought of by others, and respected for their abilities. Christians are to respect one another for what each has to offer, recognising that all have something of value to give (see Philippians 2:3-4).

Therefore we can be free to do whatever God wants – whether it is leading a church or counting the money, speaking at meetings or providing refreshments – without feeling at all inferior or superior.

And that means the hypocrisy which Jesus so strongly condemned need never appear in our churches (see, for example, Matthew 23:1-7,13-15,23-28). God is then free to do just what he wants through us – which is always a great deal!

SERVING
Serving in the church

KEY TRUTH

There are as many things to do for one another in the church as there are members of it.

The first shall be last

When two of Jesus' twelve apostles came to him to ask for the best seats in heaven, the rest of the group were naturally upset.

Jesus took the opportunity to explain to them all that, in his kingdom, the greatest person was in fact the one who was slave to the rest. In other words, service to God is more important than human praise.

Jesus taught that the really great people are often those who are despised by others because they are humble rather than ruthless or ambitious, or because they are not very fortunate or gifted.

Lending a hand

Some churches probably have too much organisation – too many committees and planning meetings and administrative tasks. Such things can easily get in the way of our calling to teach and live out the simple message of God's love.

But every church must have some organisation, because God wants us to reflect his character, which brings order out of chaos.

There are all kinds of things to be done today, just as there were in the early church. Everyone can help with cleaning or making things, looking after buildings or children, and arranging activities or meetings.

Caring for the needy

Love, expressed by caring for the poor, the ill, the disabled, the sorrowful, the weak and the homeless has always been a characteristic of the Christian church.

There are people in every congregation who have needs which others can meet. They may require help to buy food or keep their homes tidy. They may be lonely, sad or afraid, and need the comfort and security of someone else's friendship.

Sometimes, this care demands special skills of counselling to help people apply Jesus' truth to their deepest needs. But often it is just a matter of being available to others to let the love of Jesus flow through us.

Speaking God's word

This is often, and wrongly, regarded as the most important aspect of Christian service. It is important, but should not be allowed to overshadow other aspects.

There are many ways we can speak God's word. Some will have opportunities to teach

TO THINK ABOUT

Spend some time thinking about your local church.

- Who is the most important person in the church? Should there be a "most important person" in the church?
- Are there any jobs in your church that no one ever wants to do? Why do people avoid them? Could you serve in this way?
- Are there any people in your church who are often overlooked? Do they have needs that you could help with? Could you at least talk with them and pray for them?
- Why is it wrong to leave the communication of God's message only to "the professionals"?

or preach at meetings. Others will be able to contribute to discussions. A few may be given, by the Spirit, God's special word of encouragement or warning to the church, which others must test by the Scriptures.

But there are also gifts of singing, writing, acting, dancing, painting and so on, which can all speak God's word in some way. And above all, so too can our daily conversations with friends, neighbours and work colleagues.

BIBLE CHECK

The first shall be last Mark 9:35-45; Matthew 19:29-30
Lending a hand Acts 6:1-3; Romans 12:7-8,13
Caring for the needy 1 Thessalonians 5:14; James 2:14-17
Speaking God's word 1 Corinthians 14:3-5,29-32; 2 Timothy 4:1-5

POSTSCRIPT

Just as each person has something to give, so we also each have something to receive. Christian service is mutual: we must be as willing to be helped as we are to help.

The Christian life calls for mutual service.
· Are you willing to let other people serve you? If not, why not?
· What needs do you have that could be opportunities for service for others in your church?

Thank God for the care you receive from other Christians. Ask him to show you ways that you can serve him and bless others in your local church.

BIBLE SUMMARY
BUILDING COMMUNITY

God intended that all human beings should live in a community of giving and receiving, and of mutual sharing; it is not possible to live a fully human life alone (Genesis 2:18).

The world has long since become a very selfish place, in which everyone fends for themselves, and rarely helps others at their own expense (Luke 11:37-42; 16:19-31).

The church, however, is meant to be the place where God's new community, his kingdom, is made visible to the world as an example of true love and care (see 1 Peter 2:9-10).

Growing together

This ideal can only be reached as Christians learn to share their lives together as fully as possible. That involves more than meeting together regularly, important as that is (Hebrews 10:23-25).

In addition, we need to get to know one another in such a way that we can function like a fit and mature body, without limping or stumbling (1 Corinthians 12:25-27). To achieve this, our church life will become much more than a pastime; it will be the centre of our life.

SERVING
Into the world

KEY TRUTH

God wants his people to show
through their behaviour, speech and
church life the difference Jesus has
made to them.

A life that is different

A Christian is a human being like everyone
else. That means we all share the same
emotional, spiritual and physical needs. If we
pretend to be above these needs, we shall
appear cold and inhuman – something Jesus
never was.

But at the same time we are different.
God's Spirit is active in our lives. We belong to
God's kingdom, which has a different set of
values from our human society.

The Christian life is based on love for God
and our neighbour. This is meant to result in
caring deeply for others, and in avoiding all
kinds of sin. We will not need to be like the
Pharisees in Jesus' day who tried to impress
people by their good deeds. People will simply
see Jesus in us.

Lips that are pure

It is always much easier to speak harshly than
kindly. And it is easier to curse than to bless,
to lie than to tell the truth.

But all these easier things spring from our
selfish nature and not from God. We are his
representatives in the world, so our
conversation should reflect his attitudes. This
means that swearing, boasting, lying (even
small, "white" lies) and impatient anger are
out. Rather, he wants us to be loving,
gracious, truthful and patient.

Little things count

There is a false idea that the only things that
really count for God are the big, important
actions and decisions.

That is the devil's own lie; with God little
things are extremely important. Only when
we are faithful to him in them can we hope to
be faithful in larger issues.

So Jesus and his followers said that the
little actions of love, and seemingly
unimportant words of help or
encouragement, are vital. They are ways of
showing God's care for the details of life.

Loving our enemies

Christian love is demanding and far-reaching.
Jesus said that most people love those who are
kind to them, but that his followers were to
love their enemies as well.

This kind of love was to take two forms.
There was "going the second mile" – doing

TO THINK ABOUT

Think of someone you know or meet
regularly who is not yet a Christian.

· Do you think they notice anything
  different about your life? What makes you
  different?
· Do any of the differences in your life point
  people to Jesus? Or do they just make you
  seem strange?

Living a Christian life in the world is not
just about avoiding certain things, but also
about living a distinctive life that radiates
the life of Jesus!

· How should your Christian faith affect
  the way you speak with other people?

more for people than they insisted on. And there was also the attitude of being kind and forgiving towards those who insulted or persecuted Christians. Jesus showed us an example of that by praying for the forgiveness of those who were nailing him to the cross.

BIBLE CHECK

A life that is different Matthew 6:1-14; Ephesians 5:3-20

Lips that are pure Ephesians 4:25-32; 1 Peter 3:8-12

Little things count Matthew 10:40-42; Colossians 3:17

Loving our enemies Matthew 5:38-48; 26:48-54; Luke 23:34

POSTSCRIPT

The Christian life does not consist simply of following set patterns of conduct; God wants our total lifestyle to reflect his character so that the world may truly recognise him.

· What actions can you do this week to express your love for God?
· Do you have any "enemies"? How can you follow Jesus' command to love them?

Thank God that the world is his world. Pray that he will help you to live as he intended you to live – full of his life, peace and joy! Pray that God's Spirit will use your life to point others to Jesus.

BIBLE SUMMARY
PILGRIMS IN A STRANGE LAND

Every Christian is a member of God's kingdom. The rest of the world is not. We are, therefore, in this life like "strangers and pilgrims" in a foreign land. Our way of life reflects the love and laws of God (see 1 Peter 2:11-12).

Residents of the world

We are not told to form our own separate communities – cut off from the rest of the world (John 17:15; 1 Corinthians 5:9-13). That would be almost impossible, and would restrict our witness for God.

The Bible encourages Christians to observe the laws of the land and pay their taxes, always bearing in mind they cannot obey a law which prevents them doing what God commands, or orders them to do something wrong. (See Jesus' example in Matthew 17:24-27; his teaching in Matthew 22:15-22, and in the apostles' application of it in Romans 13:1-7; 1 Peter 2:13-17.)

Citizens of heaven

Despite this, Jesus reminds us that we are not of the world (John 17:16) – our citizenship is now in heaven (Philippians 3:20). Therefore we are God's "ambassadors" on earth (2 Corinthians 5:20), living out our new life in a sometimes hostile environment among people who do not know God. But at the same time, we are to tell them about him.

SERVING
Sharing good news

KEY TRUTH

Jesus has told his people to take his message of new, eternal life and forgiveness to the whole world.

A message for everyone

There is no message the world needs to hear more than the message of Jesus. Everyone needs to hear about him. Their only certain hope of enjoying his love now and for ever is to trust him, just as we have done.

No one is too old, young, clever or illiterate to be able to know Jesus for themselves. His death on the cross was for everyone who would accept it.

So important is the "gospel", the good news, that one of the last things Jesus told his followers was to travel everywhere to proclaim it.

Talking about Jesus

After the first wave of persecution in the early church, the followers of Jesus scattered across several countries. Wherever they went, they told people about Jesus.

In some ways it is natural to tell people about things that mean a lot to us – special events which have happened, new people we have met. So it should be natural to tell them about Jesus and what he has done for us.

Some Christians find it hard to put their faith into words, because it is a deeply personal thing. But there is usually something we can say, at the right moment – a comment, perhaps, about how Jesus promises to deal with some difficulty people are talking about, or just a verse from the Bible which is relevant to a conversation.

Letting God work

There is "a time to be silent and a time to speak", advises a wise Old Testament writer. While most of us probably do not speak enough about Jesus, sometimes we may choose the wrong moment or manner.

God uses our words, but sometimes we need to be patient, and let his word, through his Spirit, work in a person's mind or heart.

God has gifted certain people in telling others about Jesus and leading them to him. They need our prayers and financial support. We may just be able to interest someone enough to encourage them to meet or hear an evangelist.

Telling the neighbourhood

Paul, in the New Testament, is well known for his missionary strategy. He did not work without a plan. He went to important places and people to proclaim Jesus, leaving behind him a group of Christians who would be able to tell others in their district and beyond.

TO THINK ABOUT

Think of a recent event that you were eager to share with other people.

· Do you find it easier to share your own good news or the good news of Jesus Christ? Why do you think this is?
· Do you need special skills to tell people about Jesus?
· Are words the only way to pass the good news on?

The good news of forgiveness and new life in Jesus Christ is for everyone!

· Are there any people in your area who have no Christian witness at the moment? Is there a reason for this?

His example is a good one to follow. There may be groups of people in an area who will be specially open to the gospel. Or there may be areas where there is no witness, to which we could reach out.

The work of evangelism – telling the good news – is something we can all share in by our own personal witness, by delivering leaflets, visiting the homes of others, helping with special church services, and so on.

BIBLE CHECK

A message for everyone Matthew 28:18-20; John 3:16-17; Acts 4:11-12
Talking about Jesus Acts 8:4-8; 9:10-19
Letting God work Ecclesiastes 3:7; John 12:20-23; Luke 1:76-79; 3:4
Telling the neighbourhood Acts 17:16-18; 18:1-4

POSTSCRIPT

It is easy to be discouraged by a lack of response to our efforts, and so concentrate on our church fellowship. But Jesus calls us to keep on proclaiming him, with the methods which are most appropriate in our area.

- What could you do to share the good news with these people?
- How does the Holy Spirit help when you are sharing the message about Jesus? Why is the Spirit's work essential?
- What should you do if there seems to be no response from people?

Thank God for his immense love for you. Pray for those who do not yet know him as Saviour and Lord. Pray for opportunities to share the good news with them, and the courage for you to do so.

BIBLE SUMMARY

ALL THINGS TO ALL PEOPLE

Paul told the Corinthians that in his task of proclaiming the good news of Jesus, he became "all things to all men" (1 Corinthians 9:22). The phrase is sometimes used to describe people who are unreliable; just as a chameleon changes the colour of its skin to blend in with its surroundings, they adapt their words or actions so they will always be accepted.

Identifying with people

However, that was not what Paul meant. Rather, he did all he could to identify closely with the people he went to, so that he could make his message totally relevant to their needs or culture.

So to the Jews, he proclaimed Jesus in the context of being the "King of the Jews", the promised Messiah (1 Corinthians 9:20). To non-Jews, he emphasised the fact that Jesus came to save the whole world, and that God is not concerned with racial differences (1 Corinthians 9:21).

To people in personal need, Paul preached the tenderness and care of Jesus, which he himself knew and experienced (1 Corinthians 9:22). His reason was not to change the message, but to adapt the way he taught it to the needs of the moment.

Jesus' own example

In doing this, he was following Jesus' own example. His favourite name for himself was "Son of Man" (eg Luke 5:24), through which he closely identified with us. He, too, adapted his methods. He used parables for some people and direct teaching for others (for example Matthew 13:10-18).

SERVING
Service for life

KEY TRUTH

Every Christian is in full-time service for Jesus; there are no part-timers or reservists in God's "army".

Ready for change

The Holy Spirit is dynamic – he is always on the move, always working. We, on the other hand, usually prefer a quiet life which is secure and stable.

When Jesus spoke to the church in Ephesus, he said that while they had been faithful to him, they had lost their first love. They needed to be open to change, ready to follow him wherever he led, just as they had once done.

That has always been a challenge to Christians. We need to ask frequently, "Lord, what do you want me to do?"

Giving everything to Jesus

In one sense, we have already given everything to Jesus – our whole selves, our lives, in return for his forgiveness and new life.

But there may be a further way in which he wants us to give ourselves to him; by being willing to give up our jobs and join the staff of a church or missionary society, or enter some other form of Christian work.

Our commitment to him may also be expressed in our willingness to give up more of our spare time to take on church responsibilities. However, if we have families, it is important not to neglect them.

Supporting his workers

"The worker deserves his wages" is a New Testament principle which reminds us that church leaders and workers, some of whom have given up well-paid jobs to serve Jesus in the church, need food to eat and clothes to wear. And if we do not provide those things for them, they will be hungry and cold. God expects us to share their ministry to us by sharing our earnings and goods with them.

Paul considered that such support was a right. In Corinth, however, he did not exercise that right, to avoid being a burden on the church. Instead, he earned money by making tents. But that was his personal decision, and did not alter the principle on which he usually worked.

Praying for God's servants

Some people do not seem to have much to give in the way of Christian service. They may be old, infirm, poor or with little time to give to the church.

But of course, they can love and care about others. And above all, as with everyone else, they can give time to prayer.

TO THINK ABOUT

· How has your Christian service changed already over the time you have been a believer? What caused those changes?
· What is your service like at the moment? Do you need to find fresh ways to serve God? Or do you need to renew your enthusiasm for your current activities?
· Is God calling you to some form of Christian work? How can you test this call?

You should also look for opportunities to support other Christian workers.

· Are there any people you know who need your support at the moment?

God works the world over through the prayers of his people. Moses, the Jewish leader, once needed someone to support him physically as he led Israel in battle; through prayer, we support spiritually those who are on the front line of spiritual warfare. Without us, the going would be tougher.

BIBLE CHECK

Ready for change Revelation 2:17; John 3:8
Giving everything to Jesus Jeremiah 1:4-10; Luke 10:1-12; Romans 10:14-17
Supporting his workers Luke 10:7; 1 Corinthians 9:3-18
Praying for God's servants Exodus 17:10-13; Colossians 1:9; 4:2-4

POSTSCRIPT

Christian service is a work of love. It is hard work, and it is more effective when it stems from our love for Jesus and his people.

· What steps can you take to find out about their needs, so that you can pray for them and give to them more effectively?

In the world of work, retirement comes when a person reaches a certain age.
· Does a Christian ever retire? How does this make you feel?

Thank God that he will always have work for you to do, whatever stage of life you are at. Pray for strength to serve him faithfully to the end.

BIBLE SUMMARY
PAUL, A SERVANT OF GOD

In some respects Paul the apostle was an exceptional person. The amount of work he got through would have killed a lesser person (2 Corinthians 11:23-29)! But despite that, his service for Jesus remains an inspiring model for us to follow.

Dedicated to Jesus

Paul did not believe in doing things by halves. Jesus had given everything for him, so he gave everything for Jesus (Galatians 2:20). Such was his dedication that he never slackened, right up to when he died (2 Timothy 4:6-8). That is the basis of all Christian service – we cannot expect to achieve great things for God unless we are ready to follow him fully.

Controlled by God's word

Before his conversion, Paul was a Jewish scholar (Galatians 1:14) with a good knowledge of the Old Testament Scriptures. After his conversion, God revealed the full truth about Jesus to him (Galatians 1:11-12), which was in full agreement with what the other apostles had been teaching (Galatians 2:1-2).

All his teaching was firmly built on the basic facts of who Jesus was and what he had done on the cross, and Paul firmly resisted all attempts to alter that gospel or add to it (Galatians 1:6-9; 2 Timothy 1:11-14). That is a key to effective Christian service; we cannot expect to win others for Jesus or to help other Christians to grow, if we ourselves are not firmly teaching and applying his truth.

ARRIVING
On the road to heaven

KEY TRUTH

Christians always have heaven in their sights.

Heaven on earth

Every person who has recognised that Jesus Christ's death on the cross was God's way of offering forgiveness and eternal life and who has personally asked for that forgiveness and life will without doubt go to heaven when they die.

For us, eternal life has already begun; God's love has broken into our earthly life. His Holy Spirit has started the process of turning our sinful nature into something pure and perfect which will be completed in heaven.

And the Spirit brings the life of heaven to us by giving us both confidence (or assurance) that we belong to Jesus and his power to overcome sin and evil. Sometimes, too, in our prayers we will become specially conscious that we are no longer bound to earth but are bound for heaven.

Life in perspective

Most people live as if this life were all that mattered. They spend lots of energy and time gathering possessions or working to achieve status or recognition in the world. But Jesus taught that life on earth is important, precisely because it is the period of time we have been given to come to terms with God's purposes for us.

Those purposes embrace the whole world and the whole of eternity. That gives our life now a small but still significant place in his plans. And it puts a comparatively short earthly life into a new perspective: eternity never ends!

Aiming for the goal

We all need an aim in life, otherwise we drift about and are never satisfied. The aim of the Christian life is to please Jesus.

But there is also another goal to aim for, which we cannot miss, but which should determine how we go about pleasing him. That goal is to spend eternity in his presence. If that is where we are going, then every thought, word and deed in this life deserves to be worthy of his presence.

Ready for Jesus

Human nature is the same all over the world. Jesus was aware that a Christian could be as lazy as anyone else. So several of his parables about the end of time showed how we should live now in readiness for the next life.

In one story he showed how five girls did not bother to prepare themselves for a

TO THINK ABOUT

Think about the things that people hope for in their lives. Perhaps you could ask a few of your friends for their thoughts on this.

· What do Christians hope for? How is this different from other hopes and dreams for your life?
· How will eternal life in God's new creation be different from the eternal life you have now in Jesus Christ? How will it be the same?
· What are you especially looking forward to?

marriage festival, so that when it happened, they were not allowed in.

And in another, a servant decided to live selfishly and to hurt others, because his master was away and seemed to delay in returning home. He thought it would not matter, but he was punished. Jesus concluded. "You must be ready, for you do not know when the Son of Man is coming."

BIBLE CHECK

Heaven on earth Ephesians 3:14-21; Titus 3:3-7
Life in perspective Luke 9:24-25; 16:19-31
Aiming for the goal 1 Corinthians 9:24-27; Philippians 3:8-17
Ready for Jesus Matthew 24:45–25:13

POSTSCRIPT

There are two uncertainties in life: one is the time of our death, the other is the time of Jesus' return to earth. The Bible tells us to be ready for both.

The Christian faith is not "a heavenly train ticket", so that all you have to do is wait around on earth for heaven to come along.
· What do Jesus' parables teach about the time of waiting?
· What things should you do this week because of your Christian hope?
· How does the thought of eternal life with God put your life now in perspective?

Thank God for the wonderful future he has for you and for all believers. Pray for his Spirit to help you live in hope now, and bring you safely to his eternal kingdom.

BIBLE SUMMARY
HOPE SPRINGS ETERNAL

When hope dies, life becomes almost impossible (Job 19:10). Everyone needs something to look forward to, to work for, to spur them on. Whether the Christian life for us is very hard or comparatively trouble-free, the hope of eternal life with Jesus is said in the New Testament to be the spur we need in order to be faithful to him, who is faithful to us.

Hope in God's promises

Hope is closely linked to faith in the Bible (eg 1 Corinthians 13:13). Hope, like faith, is confidence that God will fulfil his promises. "Against all hope, Abraham in hope believed" that God would make him, a childless husband, the ancestor of many nations (Romans 4:18-21). Similarly, when we experience difficulty or testing, hope is strengthened as we endure suffering by the power of God: we see what he can do, and his love gives hope that he will continue to sustain us (Romans 5:1-5).

Hope in God's provision

Most of all, hope is something the New Testament writers link to eternal life (Titus 1:2). Hope is the basis of our faith in Jesus (Ephesians 1:18-20; 1 Peter 1:3); we look forward to what God has prepared for us in heaven, which is far better than the best things the world has to offer. Therefore, our life now can be one of self-sacrifice (Colossians 1:4-5), because our hope outweighs any inconvenience we may experience. We cannot see our hoped-for home with Jesus (Romans 8:24-25), but we wait for it patiently, while Jesus' life within us fuels that hope and keeps it alive (Colossians 1:27).

ARRIVING
Coping with bereavement

KEY TRUTH
Jesus brings a new perspective of hope to the sad experience of bereavement.

Coping with our grief
"Jesus wept." That is the shortest verse in the Bible. But the words sum up the deep feelings of Jesus at the tomb of one of his closest friends, Lazarus.

The customs of showing grief in public vary from country to country, but the feelings of grief are very natural and it is not weak or un-Christian to mourn the death of those we love. After all, they have given much to us, for which we are deeply grateful.

But Christians need not grieve "like the rest of men, who have no hope". Sad though the loss is to us personally, we can also rejoice that a believing person has gone to be with the Lord for ever. Yet the loss of unsaved loved ones is an agony beyond words.

Coping with our loss
A time of bereavement is a time of conflicting emotions. The bereaved person wants to be alone, yet they also want the company of friends.

It can easily turn into a time of bitterness when we complain that God has robbed us of someone we love. But of course, our loss means their blessing in his presence.

His perfect plan has allowed for the right time of death for each person, hard as that may sometimes be to understand. One day those who belong to Christ will be reunited; meanwhile, we have the loving presence of Jesus.

Coping, with Jesus' help
Because Jesus has experienced both bereavement and death itself, he knows how to comfort those who mourn. He always showed deep concern and sympathy with the bereaved. Because he never changes, he offers his peace to the troubled, his joy to the sorrowful, and his presence to the lonely.

That does not mean we will suffer no pain at all. But it does mean that because he has kept us here in this life for a little longer, he still has something useful for us to do.

Helping others to cope
In New Testament times, the church always had a special place for widows. This was partly because there was always a welcome for the lonely, but mainly because without husbands they would become very poor.

So the church organised collections to help pay for food, clothes and shelter. There

TO THINK ABOUT
Read the story of Jesus at the tomb of Lazarus in John 11.
· Why did Jesus weep (11:35)? What does this tell you about what he thought of death?
· What comfort did he give to Lazarus' sisters?
· How is it different to cope with the death of a Christian and someone who did not believe in Jesus? Should this affect Christian funeral services?

are always things which the bereaved need help with, even in countries where they are not short of money. Most of all, they need fellowship – the deep caring and sharing of Christians who are able to love and grieve together, and offer human spiritual support.

BIBLE CHECK

Coping with our grief John 11:28-37; 1 Thessalonians 4:13-18

Coping with our loss 2 Corinthians 5:1-8; Revelation 7:9

Coping, with Jesus' help Lamentations 3:19-33; Luke 7:12-13; John 14:27

Helping others to cope 1 Timothy 5:3-16; James 1:27

POSTSCRIPT

An important element in coping with bereavement is being prepared to surrender those we love to Jesus, just as we have surrendered ourselves.

Bereavement can last a very long time. Even though life may go on, you may still feel the loss of a loved one deeply.

· What continued comfort does God offer to those who mourn?

· Are there people who can share your loss? Are there others in your church who need your support and prayers at the moment?

· How is the fellowship of the church important? What can you do to increase this depth of fellowship in your church?

Ask God to give comfort to those you know who are feeling the pain and sadness of bereavement.

BIBLE SUMMARY
WHY MUST WE DIE?

Death is unpleasant, sometimes painful, and always sad. And that in itself partly answers the question as to why it happens. Death is a result of the imperfection and fallenness of humanity (Genesis 3:19; 1 Corinthians 15:56).

No exceptions

Because we all share in the sinfulness of the world, we all have to die (Ezekiel 18:4; Romans 6:23). Death has been called the great leveller; the best and the worst people all have to go through it.

The Bible records only a couple of instances of "translation" – the sudden transformation from this life to the next without death. One was Enoch (Genesis 5:24; Hebrews 11:5) and the other Elijah, who was seen being taken into heaven in a whirlwind (2 Kings 2:11).

The only other exceptions will be when Jesus returns to earth. Christians who are alive then will be taken direct to heaven (1 Corinthians 15:51-52; 1 Thessalonians 4:17).

Death defeated

Death is no longer the unconquerable enemy it once was. Jesus has defeated it by dying and being raised to life. While we must still experience death, a continued life with Jesus is waiting beyond it for all who have accepted his death as God's way of dealing with their sins (See Romans 5:12-21).

Facing death

KEY TRUTH

Because of Jesus' death and resurrection, we can face our own death with confidence rather than fear.

Life completed

There is no guarantee that a person will live for a certain length of time. Sometimes people die from disease, accident or violence long before we think they should.

That is part of the tragedy of a sinful world. Some people do not have the opportunity to do all they could usefully accomplish. Therefore, we always need to be ready to return to God who made us.

But he alone knows how useful we really are, and his purposes will never be defeated by premature death. When he calls us to be with him for ever, we know that we will have done our part for him on earth.

Saying goodbye

Our attitude to death will depend very much on our attitude to life – which is as good a reason as any to prepare ourselves for it.

If we have been largely selfish, allowing ourselves to be dominated by possessions, wealth, privileges and human status, it will be very hard to let go of these things as death approaches.

But if our life his been characterised by giving, sharing and loving, then it will not be so hard to say goodbye. We can be sure that the Lord who will look after us in eternity will also look after the people we leave behind.

A place for repentance

Sometimes, when death approaches, people are very conscious of all the wrong things they have done in their life. They remember the hasty words, the unkind actions, the forgotten promises and neglected duties. While it is never too late to repent and be saved or experience restored relationships with God or others we have wronged, it is sad to learn so late the joy that reconciliation brings.

The aim for every Christian should be to confess each sin as it happens all through life, in order to keep close to Jesus and experience his love and help.

The doorway to heaven

Death, for the Christian, is not the end of life but, as it were, the gateway through which they pass to experience a new phase of the eternal life Jesus has given. Much of the fear of death arises because both it, and what lies beyond it, are largely unknown.

But Jesus has been through it – and come back again. The heaven he spoke of, and

TO THINK ABOUT

Many people talk about the things they want to do before they die.

- Are there certain things you want to accomplish in your life? Why are they important to you? How would you feel if you knew now that you would be unable to do them because of infirmity or death?

Psalm 31:15 says, "My times are in God's hands".

- What does this tell you about the length of your life? Does it necessarily mean your life will end without trouble or pain?

which was revealed to some Bible writers, is not a place to fear but to look forward to.

BIBLE CHECK

Life completed Philippians 1:19-26;
  2 Timothy 4:6-8

Saying goodbye Job 1:21; Psalm 68:5-6;
  Mark 10:17-31

A place for repentance Psalm 103:1-14;
  Isaiah 53:1-12

The doorway to heaven 1 Corinthians
  15:3-19; Revelation 7:16-17

POSTSCRIPT

Death, like life, is God's gift. The Bible does not allow us to take our own or anybody else's life even though, as believers, we may be certain of eternal life.

· How can you be prepared for death? What
  do you need to change about your
  behaviour or speech so that when you die,
  you will have lived a life to the praise of
  God? Are there any things you need to put
  right, or arrangements you need to make?
· Should a Christian be afraid of death?

Thank Jesus that he has already gone ahead of you, through death, into God's resurrection life. Pray for the Spirit's help to live your life well, so that whenever and however it ends, your life and death will point others to God.

BIBLE SUMMARY
LIFE'S LAST CHANCE

Jesus once told a story about men who were employed to work in the fields. Some were hired in the morning, others at midday, and still others only a short while before dusk. Yet each received the same wage (Matthew 20:1-16).

The story was intended to show that it does not matter when a person becomes a Christian. All receive the same gift of eternal life, however much of their life has been spent working for Jesus. Christ made the point strongly when he promised that same gift to the thief who was crucified beside him, and who repented just before his death (Luke 23:39-43).

No second chances

However, it is in this life that we are called on to turn away from our sins and look to Jesus for eternal life. There is only one verse in the Bible which implies that those already dead may have a second chance, and it seems to apply only to those who lived in the years before Jesus came to earth (1 Peter 3:18-20).

Because the date of our death is uncertain, and because Jesus came into this world precisely to tell us the way to God in this life, the Bible message is always "now is the day of salvation" (John 1:10-13; 3:14-18; 2 Corinthians 6:2).

Action replay

KEY TRUTH

Every person who has ever existed will have their life judged by God at the end of time.

Nothing is hidden

Adam and Eve tried to do the impossible by hiding themselves from God. And Jesus once said that some religious leaders of his day were like whitewashed tombs – seemingly clean on the outside, but rotten inside.

What we really are, and what we really have or have not done, will be brought to light when the world is judged by God.

Christians need not fear this judgement, because it cannot cost them their place in heaven – that is already secure. But it does remind us that we cannot abuse our gift of eternal life by living carelessly.

The fire test

The major test for everyone is not how they have lived, because no one can enter heaven just because of the good things they have done. The question God will ask each one is, "How did you treat my Son? Did you receive him or reject him?"

However, all Christians will have their lives assessed by God, to see how valuable they have been for him. Paul says some people's lives will be like wood, hay and stubble: they have done nothing worthwhile for God and his kingdom, and it will be as if their work just goes up in smoke.

Others' lives, however, will be like gold, silver and precious stones. They will survive the "fire test" – the searching scrutiny of God's pure love and law – and will be built into the new heavens and earth.

Well done!

Christians will be spared the detailed judgement that others will face. Instead, after their assessment spoken of above, they will be welcomed and praised by Jesus himself.

The detail of Jesus' parables cannot be pressed too far, but in one of them God is pictured as giving his faithful servants degrees of responsibility in heaven, as a reward for their service on earth. Each reward exactly suits their abilities and achievements.

Paul also speaks of another reward – a "crown", a symbol of victory and conquest over evil, which everyone will receive.

A place for you

Heaven is beyond imagination. Some people feel terrified at the thought of a huge mass of people all together; others cannot understand how we shall get on with each other! But Jesus' promise to the individual is that there is

TO THINK ABOUT

Many people, if they believe in heaven at all, think that they will "get in" because they have been nice people or done good things.

- Why is this a dangerous idea?
- What will God's standard of judgement actually be?
- Does it matter what you do in your life, or only what you believe?
- What do you think will happen to those who have never heard about Jesus Christ?

a tailor-made place actually waiting for us to fill. He has gone ahead to get it ready for us.

One day, he is coming back to earth. Then, all Christians who have died will be raised from the dead, and they and the Christians still alive will be taken to be with Jesus.

BIBLE CHECK
Nothing is hidden Luke 12:1-3; 2 Corinthians 5:6-15; Hebrews 9:27-28

The fire test 1 Corinthians 3:10-15; 1 John 4:16-19

Well done! Matthew 25:14-30; 1 Corinthians 6:2-3; 2 Timothy 4:8

A place for you John 14:1-7; 1 Thessalonians 4:16-17

POSTSCRIPT
Although this part of our Christian life lies in the future, it will be no less real than our current experience. The Bible is full of predictions which have come to pass, and we can be confident these will too.

....

Make a list of as many different aspects and activities of your life as you can. Now read 1 Corinthians 3:10-15.

· Which parts of your life are "wood, hay and straw"? Which parts are "gold, silver and costly stones"? How do you think your life will stand in God's refining fire?

· What can you do this week to build your life with quality material?

Thank God for the assurance of his acceptance of you in Jesus Christ. Confess to him the parts of your life that are poor quality, and ask for the help of his Spirit to become more like Jesus.

BIBLE SUMMARY
THE EVENTS OF THE END

The precise order of events surrounding Jesus' return to earth, and the end of the present world, is not entirely clear in Scripture. This has led some people to do precisely what Jesus warned us against: attempting to predict the precise date, and speculate about certain events (Matthew 24:4,36,44; 2 Thessalonians 2:1-4).

Short of grappling with the symbolism of Revelation, the best basic guide to "the end" is Jesus' teaching in Matthew 24 (and parallel passages in Mark 13:1-31 and Luke 21:1-33). Other teaching can then be fitted into that structure.

A time of suffering
The end days will be characterised by great suffering in the whole world (Matthew 24:6-8). This will be followed by intense persecution of Christians (verses 9-13), with false accusation, torture and murder. But the gospel still has to be preached in every part of the world before Jesus can return (verse 14).

The "abomination that causes desolation" (verse 15) could relate to the anti-Christ spoken of by Paul (2 Thessalonians 2:3-12), a figure of great power who claims to be divine (see also verse 24), but who is very evil.

Jesus takes over
After that "great tribulation" the coming of Jesus will be seen by everyone (verses 27,30). He will come to judge the world, and demonstrate his great power in gathering to himself all his own people (verse 31). Then he will create a new heaven and new earth, to be occupied only by those who have trusted him as their Saviour from sin and Lord of their life (Revelation 21:1).

Welcome home!

KEY TRUTH

Heaven is the Christian's final home, where we shall live for ever with Jesus and all his people.

A place of peace

Heaven is a real place. Paul teaches that all Christians go straight to be with Jesus when they die, but that we do not take our final place in heaven until it is finally established at the end of the world.

But peace reigns as soon as we die. Our struggles are over. We are with Jesus in a closer, more personal way than we have ever experienced on earth.

In heaven, there is no war. There are not even any arguments. And that is not because people have lost their personalities; it is because they have become perfectly human, as Jesus was when he lived on earth.

A place of joy

Heaven is a very joyful place. There is nothing there to be sad about!

But the joy is not a selfish kind of relief that evil and sin and suffering are a thing of the past. Rather it is rejoicing in the greatness, glory and love of God, which fill heaven.

Worship will be a major activity. It will not be like an unending church service; rather it will be genuine praise from the hearts of people who have come to see more clearly the wonderful gift of eternal life given to them because of Jesus' death on the cross.

A place of beauty

Heaven is a brand-new creation by God for his people. It will replace everything which existed before, although nothing that God originally made will be wasted.

It is therefore hard to imagine. Whenever the Bible writers describe it, they use picture language.

It is certainly a place of beauty and perfection – far better than anything humanity has ever built. It is full of light and colour. Beyond that, we cannot imagine it – but no one will be disappointed by it!

A place of justice

Heaven is where justice will be seen to have been done. Everyone who truly belongs there will be there. And no one who has rejected Jesus and lived in selfishness and evil will be allowed to enter.

TO THINK ABOUT

Make a list of the things that make somewhere a "home".
· Will these things be present in God's new creation? How will they be different from your experience of them here and now?

The Bible speaks of a new heaven and a new earth. Have a look at the word picture of this new world in Revelation 21–22.
· What does this tell you about the eternal life you will enjoy for ever?

God's presence in this eternal home will transform everything! He promises to dwell with his people for ever (see Revelation 21:2-3).

Then we shall see that wrongs have been put right – that will be part of our "reward" – and that wrongdoers have received the punishment they deserved.

That state of peace, joy, beauty and justice will never end. No one can imagine what eternity really means, except that it makes our human life and all its concerns seem quite small.

BIBLE CHECK

A place of peace Compare Philippians 1:23 with 1 Thessalonians 4:17; Revelation 21:4-7

A place of joy Revelation 4:8-11; 7:9-12

A place of beauty Revelation 21:9-27; 22:1-5

A place of justice Romans 12:17-21; Revelation 20:11-15; 21:8,27; 22:12-15

POSTSCRIPT

People who believe in heaven are not excused from working to create peace, joy, beauty and justice on earth, where the first signs of God's kingdom are to be built.

· Are you excited by this prospect? Why?
· How will God's new creation be a place of justice and healing?
· Do you often think about this hope? Should you? Why?
· Is it true that some Christians can be so heavenly-minded that they are no earthly good?

Thank God that he is preparing a home for you and for all Christians, in which he will live with you for ever. Pray that he will prepare you to live in this new home for ever!

BIBLE SUMMARY
WHAT HAPPENS TO NON-CHRISTIANS?

Despite the beauties and attractions of heaven, Jesus spent much time talking about the fate of those who rejected him. He did not paint a very pretty picture.

Excluded from God's presence

Jesus often used the picture of "outer darkness" where there will be "weeping and gnashing of teeth" (eg Matthew 24:30). It is a picture of people cut off for ever from the presence of God, from the warmth, love, peace and joy of heaven.

He also used the picture of an unquenched flame. It speaks of a place of frustration and unfulfilled desire, with people consuming themselves with anguish and sorrow. (See Mark 9:42-48; Luke 16:23-24,28; Revelation 20:14-15.)

The implication is that this state, usually called hell, lasts for ever. Certainly its effect is everlasting because there can be no transfer from it to heaven (Luke 16:26).

Jesus, the hope for the world

There is only one certain way of receiving eternal life, and that is to trust our lives entirely to Jesus Christ (John 14:6). That is why we are told to preach the gospel everywhere.

As for those who die without hearing about Jesus, Paul reminds us that God is always just and fair in his judgement of them (Romans 2:14-16). We cannot assume, however, that sinful people can attain that level of total faithfulness to what they have perceived of God's nature; hence the urgency of the missionary task.

Life's new beginning

KEY TRUTH

The Christian's life has no end; death is the beginning of a new experience of life, love, peace and joy.

All things new

"I am making everything new!" Those are some of the last recorded words of Jesus in the New Testament.

And "everything new" means what it says: the physical earth, no longer corrupt and subject to decay; the organisations and systems which have controlled people's lives, no longer oppressive but creating order and freedom.

Everything which has existed will in some way be renewed and restored, for God wastes nothing. Only truly evil things will be totally destroyed. And this new creation depends as much on Jesus' death on the cross as our own eternal life does.

A new body

When Jesus appeared to his closest followers after his death, he was usually recognisable. Some people even saw the marks of the nails which had fixed him to the cross. But his body was different, so that he seemed no longer bound to the earth by natural laws.

His resurrection body is the prototype of ours. The Bible says we will receive new bodies in heaven. Through them we shall express our true self; without them we would be frustrated spirits, like those in hell who do not receive new bodies.

It seems as though we shall recognise one another in heaven – but of course, all the old disabilities and infirmities will have been taken away.

A new understanding

If you add up everything that is known in the world, it still only comes to a tiny proportion of what could be known. And each one of us only knows a tiny amount of the knowledge which does exist.

We are promised that when we get to heaven, we will understand much that has puzzled us on earth. However, even then we are not promised that we shall know everything – only God can be like that.

We may well understand some mysteries of our life – why God allowed this problem, or seemed not to answer that prayer – unless such issues are no longer of significance!

A new kind of life

Heaven has often been wrongly pictured – usually by those who make fun of it. Some people think of it as an unending holiday, or an everlasting party.

TO THINK ABOUT

Think of some of the ways people talk about, and often caricature, heaven.

- How have some people missed the real point of eternal life with God?
- Can you think of anything that you say or do as a Christian that gives a misleading image of what God's future is all about?

God's new creation may still be in the future, but Jesus' resurrection has already given Christians a glimpse of what it will be like.

- What can you learn by looking at the risen Jesus? What will be absent in heaven? What will be present?

In a sense it is, but that is only a part of the truth. The person who never wants to work will not be happy in heaven.

There will be lots to do, see, learn and experience. We will not cease to be human – in fact, we will have become truly human for the very first time. That means our life will be truly satisfying and stimulating – which a long period of idleness could never be. It is certainly something to look forward to!

BIBLE CHECK
All things new Romans 8:19-23; Colossians 1:19-20; Revelation 21:5-7

A new body John 20:19-29; 1 Corinthians 15:35-54

A new understanding 1 Corinthians 13:12; 1 Timothy 3:16; Revelation 7:13-14

A new kind of life Matthew 22:1-13; Revelation 21:22-27

POSTSCRIPT
If Jesus is to make all things new in the future, he will not be content to leave us unchanged in the present; the change starts now.

· Will you have a body in the new creation? Is this important?
· Why do you think God wants to reconcile and renew the world, rather than start from scratch? What does this tell you about creation?
· What will you be doing for eternity?

Praise God for his great plan to renew the whole creation! Thank him for including you in his plan, and for the sure hope of living with him for ever. Pray that you will begin to live today in the power of Jesus' resurrection.

BIBLE SUMMARY
HE IS RISEN!

If Jesus did not rise from the dead, there is no guarantee that we shall rise either. That is Paul's confident – and logical – comment in 1 Corinthians 15:12-20.

Paul believes in eternal life because he is convinced by the evidence that Jesus really did rise.

The empty tomb
The major piece of evidence is the empty tomb (John 20:1-8). The disciples saw the head bandages had been lifted off, and the rest of the bandages were undisturbed – and empty.

The Jews had placed a guard over the tomb (Matthew 27:62-66). At least they took seriously Jesus' prophecy about rising from the dead, even if the disciples did not! But the guards saw nothing criminal, although Matthew 28:4 says they saw something supernatural. So the Jews spread a rumour that the disciples had stolen the body (Matthew 28:11-15). But no one was able to produce it to prove that the resurrection was false.

Many witnesses
Jesus appeared several times to his followers (eg Luke 24:28-53). Once, he appeared to over 500 people at once (1 Corinthians 15:3-8) – no vision or delusion!

Notice what happened to the disciples after the Day of Pentecost (Acts 2:14,37-41). The cowards who had run from the cross now fearlessly preached that Jesus was risen from the dead. They could never have continued with that message if they had known it to be a lie.

Jesus is risen: and his love and power have been poured out through his Spirit to all who trust him and who ask for it – whoever they are.

Congregation outside their hillside church,
West Bengal

Resources for the journey

The final section of his book provides further reference material to help in understanding and communicating God's word, the Bible. It contains:

· an alphabetical listing of key Bible themes, giving not only practical and teaching help but also Scripture references
· a guide to using the studies in this book on PowerPoint
· and an index to the subjects in this book.

Bible Themes

Accepting the will of God
Humbly responding and submitting to God's purposes and depending on his grace to do his will.
Exodus 4:10-12
Job 13:15
Psalm 119:71
Proverbs 3:11-12
Matthew 6:10; 26:39
Romans 9:19-21
2 Corinthians 12:9
1 Peter 4:12-13
See also **Comfort; Contentment; Submission**

Access
The privilege of entering God's presence on the basis of Christ's death.
Psalm 24:3-4
John 14:6; 17:24
Romans 5:2
Ephesians 2:13,18; 3:12
Hebrews 10:19-22
James 4:8
1 Peter 3:18
See also **Adoption; Assurance; Prayer**

Adam
The first human being and the Hebrew for "mankind; humanity".
Genesis 1:27; 2:7,18
Romans 5:12,18-19
1 Corinthians 15:22,45
See also **Fall, the; Man**

Adoption
The believers' privilege of becoming member of God's family through Jesus Christ.
Matthew 5:44-45; 6:9,31-33
John 1:12
Romans 8:14-17
2 Corinthians 6:18
Galatians 4:5-6
Ephesians 1:5
1 John 3:1-2
See also **Access; Assurance; Confidence**

Adultery
See **Marriage**

Advice
See **Counsel**

Angels
Unseen spiritual beings who serve God and his people, especially in salvation and in communicating his word to people.
Psalm 91:11
Daniel 3:28; 12:1
Matthew 18:10; 25:31
Luke 1:26; 15:10
Acts 7:53
1 Corinthians 6:3
Ephesians 3:9-10
Hebrews 1:14
Revelation 5:11-12

Anger
(of God) God's displeasure shown against sin and evil; (human) displeasure that can be acceptable or unacceptable as a justified response to sin, but it can be destructive.

of God
Psalm 103:8-9
Isaiah 5:24-25
Habakkuk 3:12
Matthew 3:7
Mark 3:5
John 3:36
Romans 1:18
Ephesians 2:3
1 Thessalonians 1:10
Revelation 6:16
See also **Punishment**

of humanity
Proverbs 14:29; 15:18; 16:32
Matthew 5:21-22
1 Corinthians 13:5
Galatians 5:19-20
Ephesians 4:26-27,31
James 1:19-20

Antichrist
One who is directly opposed to Jesus Christ.
Daniel 7:8,25
Matthew 24:5,24
2 Thessalonians 2:3-4,6-10
1 John 2:22; 4:3

Apostles
Those appointed and sent to represent Jesus Christ; the word refers especially to the twelve disciples Jesus sent out to take his good news to the world.
Matthew 10:1-4
Acts 1:21-22; 14:14
1 Corinthians 9:1-2; 12:28

Ephesians 2:19-20
Hebrews 3:1
Revelation 2:2

Ascension
See **Jesus Christ, Ascension**

Assurance
Certainty of a person's faith
in Jesus Christ.
John 6:37; 10:28
Romans 5:1-5,9-10; 8:1,31-35,
   37-39
Philippians 1:6
2 Timothy 1:12
Hebrews 10:22
1 John 1:7,9; 4:13; 5:12
See also **Adoption; Comfort;
Victory**

Atonement
A "making at one": a word
that describes how God
makes sinners right with
himself through Jesus Christ.
Leviticus 1:4
Isaiah 53:4-6,10-12
Mark 10:45
Romans 5:8
2 Corinthians 5:14,21
Ephesians 5:2
Hebrews 1:3
1 Peter 2:24; 3:18
See also **Blood; Jesus Christ,
death; Redemption**

Authority
The right to act or speak in a
certain way; ultimately all
human authority comes
from God and is to be used
responsibly.
Malachi 2:7
Matthew 7:29; 8:9; 9:6; 10:1;
   28:18
Mark 1:27
Luke 12:5
John 1:12; 5:27; 10:18; 17:2

Romans 13:1
See also **Power**

Backsliding
See **Falling away**

Baptism
A dipping or immersing in
water, symbolising the
cleansing and washing of
believers from sin through
God's grace.
Matthew 3:11,16; 28:19
Acts 2:38,41; 8:36,38; 16:33;
   19:4-5

Romans 6:3-4
1 Corinthians 12:13

Beatitudes
See **Matthew 5:1-12**

Bereavement
See **Comfort, in bereavement
and sorrow**

Bible
Coming via Latin from the
Greek for "books", the word

**A student takes time with her
devotions, Kerala, India**

refers to the Bible as a collection of 66 books.
Isaiah 55:10-11
Matthew 4:4
John 5:39-40; 14:26
Acts 17:11
Romans 3:2
Ephesians 6:17
Colossians 3:16
1 Thessalonians 2:13
2 Timothy 2:15; 3:15-17
Hebrews 4:12
2 Peter 1:20-21
See also **Law; Revelation; Will of God**

Bishops
See **Elders**

Blasphemy
An action or act of speaking that dishonours or reviles God's name.
Exodus 20:7
Isaiah 52:5
Ezekiel 20:27
Matthew 12:31; 26:63-65
2 Timothy 3:2
James 2:7
See also **Vow**

Blessing
A material or spiritual gift given by God that is to be received with joy; act by which such gifts are provided; also the response of believers to God's actions.

Genesis 12:1-3; 32:26
Numbers 6:24-26
Deuteronomy 28:2
Malachi 3:10
Mark 10:16
Romans 12:14
2 Corinthians 1:11
Ephesians 1:3
1 Peter 3:9
See also **Christian life, character of the Christian**

Blood
The symbol of life; the atoning death of a sacrificial victim; giving up of life. Jesus Christ shed his blood as he gave his life to gain redemption and forgiveness for sin and sinners.
Leviticus 17:11
Matthew 26:28
Romans 3:25; 5:9
Ephesians 1:7
Colossians 1:20
Hebrews 9:22; 10:19; 13:20
1 Peter 1:18-19
1 John 1:7
Revelation 1:5-6; 12:11

Body
The physical substance of a person, created by God, but liable to sin and suffering, that can be offered to God in worship and will ultimately be changed at the resurrection.

Matthew 26:26
Romans 12:1
1 Corinthians 6:19-20; 12:27; 15:44
Colossians 1:18

Boldness
See **Confidence**

Bribe
A reward, usually of money, that is dishonestly or illegally offered to gain an action in favour of the giver.
Exodus 18:21; 23:8
Proverbs 15:27; 17:23
Micah 7:3

Celibacy
The state of not being married.
Matthew 19:10-12
1 Corinthians 7:7,32

Children
See **Family**

Christian life
The way of life of those who have turned away from sin to trust in Jesus Christ personally. Christians are to remain close to Jesus Christ in obedience and dependence on God's grace, his power and the Holy Spirit.

calling of the Christian
Isaiah 43:1
Matthew 5:13-16
Acts 1:8
Romans 8:28,30
1 Corinthians 1:9
Ephesians 4:1
2 Timothy 1:8-9
1 Peter 1:15; 2:9,20-21
1 John 3:1
Jude 1

"*But you will receive power when the Holy Spirit comes upon you; and you will be my witnesses in Jerusalem, and in all Judea and Samaria, and to the ends of the earth.*"

● ●

ACTS 1:8

See also **Church; Disciples; Election**

character of the Christian
Psalm 1:1-3
Matthew 5:3-11
Galatians 5:22-23
2 Peter 1:3-8

coming to faith
Isaiah 55:6-7
Matthew 11:28
Luke 14:25-27
John 1:12; 3:16; 6:37; 14:6
Acts 2:37-38; 16:30-31;
   17:30-31
Romans 10:13
2 Corinthians 5:20-21
1 Peter 3:18
See also **Conversion**

continuing in the faith
John 8:31,51; 15:5,9; 17:11
Acts 2:42; 14:22
Philippians 1:6
Colossians 1:28
Hebrews 10:23; 12:1-2
1 Peter 1:5
2 Peter 1:10
Jude 21,24
Revelation 3:11
See also **Endurance**

longing for God
Exodus 33:18
Psalms 27:4; 42:1-2; 63:1-2;
   73:25; 84:2
John 12:21
Romans 7:22
1 Peter 2:7
See also **Worship**

Church
The group of people who are
committed to Jesus Christ
and who are to praise God,
establish Christ's kingdom
and declare the good news of

Jesus Christ to the world.
Matthew 16:18; 18:17
Acts 2:42; 9:31; 14:23; 20:28
Ephesians 5:23,25-27
Hebrews 10:25

Circumcision
The practice of cutting off
the foreskin on males.
Genesis 17:10-13
Jeremiah 9:25-26
Romans 2:28-29
1 Corinthians 7:19
Galatians 5:6
Philippians 3:3

Comfort
The reassurance of people
who are suffering, worried or
needy.

when afraid
Genesis 15:1
Psalms 27:1; 34:4; 46:1-2
Proverbs 18:10
Isaiah 43:1-2
Matthew 14:26-27
Luke 2:10; 12:32
John 14:27
Hebrews 2:14-15

when anxious
Matthew 6:25-33; 10:19; 11:28
Galatians 6:2
Philippians 4:6-7
1 Peter 5:7

in bereavement and sorrow
Job 1:21
Psalm 23:4
Matthew 5:4
John 11:25-26; 14:3
Romans 12:15
1 Corinthians 15:20,53
1 Thessalonians 4:13,16-18

in despair
Psalms 34:18; 40:1-2; 42:5-6;
   51:11-12

Isaiah 42:3
Lamentations 3:21-23
2 Corinthians 4:8

when lonely
Psalms 25:16; 102:7
Isaiah 41:10; 49:14-16
John 14:18
2 Timothy 4:16-17

in suffering
Exodus 2:24-25
Deuteronomy 33:27
Job 13:15
Psalm 73:26
Isaiah 40:1-2; 53:4
Habakkuk 3:17-18
Romans 8:28,35-39; 12:12
1 Corinthians 10:13
2 Corinthians 1:3-4; 4:16-18;
   12:9
Hebrews 4:16; 12:2
1 Peter 4:12-13
Revelation 21:4

Commitment
See **Covenant; Disciples;
Obedience**

Communion
The remembrance of the
meal Jesus Christ ate with his
disciples the night before he
died. Other words for this
commemoration include
"Eucharist".
Matthew 26:26-28
Acts 2:42
1 Corinthians 10:16-17;
   11:23-30
See also **Fellowship**

Compassion
See **Mercy**

Confession
Making known in public of
personally trusting Jesus
Christ, accepting that he is

God and Lord;
acknowledging your sin, as
part of turning away from it
and turning to Jesus Christ,
leading to receiving God's
forgiveness.
Matthew 10:32
Romans 10:9-10
Philippians 2:11
1 John 4:15

of sin
Leviticus 5:5
Psalm 32:3-5
Proverbs 28:13
James 5:16
1 John 1:9
See also **Repentance**

Confidence
Assurance of who you are or
what you can do that is to be
based on God's promises
rather than human abilities.
Psalm 27:3-4
Proverbs 14:6; 28:1
Acts 4:13
Hebrews 4:15-16; 10:19; 13:6
1 John 2:28; 3:21; 4:17; 5:14
See also **Access; Assurance;
Courage**

Conscience
The inner ability given by
God to discern right from
wrong.
1 Samuel 24:5
Acts 24:16
Romans 2:14-15; 9:1
1 Corinthians 8:7
Titus 1:15
Hebrews 10:22
1 John 3:20-21
See also **Guilt**

Contentment
A state of happiness that
comes from a certain and

secure knowledge of God
Psalm 37:3
Isaiah 58:10-11
Luke 3:14
John 6:35
1 Corinthians 10:10
Philippians 4:11-13
1 Timothy 6:6-8
Hebrews 13:5
See also **Joy**

Conversion
The turning of a person to
Christ in repentance and
faith.
Psalm 22:27
Matthew 18:3
Mark 4:12
Luke 22:32
Acts 14:15; 26:18
1 Thessalonians 1:9
1 Peter 2:25
See also **Faith; New birth;
Repentance**

Conviction of sin
A strong awareness of guilt
before God because of your
sin.
Psalm 51:3-4
Isaiah 6:5
Luke 5:8
John 16:8-9
Acts 2:37

Counsel
Advice, which is necessary
for wisdom and guidance on
right living; however, you
cannot always trust human
advice.
Psalms 1:1; 32:8-9; 33:10-11
Proverbs 12:15; 19:20
Isaiah 9:6; 25:1
Acts 20:27
See also **Guidance; Way**

Courage
Being able to act bravely in
the face of suffering,
difficulties or opposition;
boldness in doing dangerous
or risky things for God, for
example declaring the gospel
to others.
Joshua 1:6-9
2 Chronicles 32:7-8
Psalm 27:14
Matthew 9:2,22
John 16:33
Acts 4:29
Philippians 1:27-28
2 Timothy 1:7
See also **Comfort;
Confidence**

Covenant
A commitment or contract
between individuals or
groups; main word in the
Bible to describe the
relationship between God
and his people.
Genesis 17:7-10
Exodus 24:8
Psalm 25:14
Matthew 26:28
Ephesians 2:12
Hebrews 7:22; 8:10; 9:15; 13:20
Revelation 21:3

Covetousness
See **Desire, wrong**

Creation
The action of God in
bringing the universe into
being; created order itself.
Genesis 1:1,27
Psalms 8:3-4; 95:6
Isaiah 40:26,28
Mark 16:15
Romans 1:20; 8:19-23
2 Corinthians 5:17

Working hands that pray and a Bible that is read and loved. The hands of a pastor who is discipling young men under his care

Ephesians 2:10
Colossians 1:15-16
Revelation 4:11
See also **Providence;
Revelation; World**

Cross
See **Jesus Christ, death**

Deacon
A New Testament term for a church leader who "serves" in the Christian community alongside elders or overseers (bishops).
Acts 6:1-4
1 Timothy 3:8-13
See also **Elders; Service**

Death
The ending of life; general experience of every living thing, but the opposite of what God originally planned.
Genesis 2:17; 3:19
Psalm 116:15
Proverbs 14:12

Ezekiel 18:32
John 8:51
Romans 6:7-8,11,23; 8:10-11;
　14:8-9
1 Corinthians 15:22,26,54-55
2 Corinthians 5:8
Ephesians 2:1
Philippians 1:21,23
Colossians 3:5
1 Thessalonians 4:16-18
2 Timothy 1:10; 2:11
Hebrews 2:14; 9:27
James 1:15
Revelation 2:10; 21:4
See also **Comfort; Last
things, resurrection; Life**

Deliverance
See **Redemption; Salvation
and Saviour**

Demons
Evil spirits, over which Jesus Christ has authority.
Matthew 8:16,31; 25:41
Mark 3:11,22
Luke 8:27; 10:17; 11:14
Ephesians 6:12
Colossians 2:15
James 2:19
See also **Devil; Occult**

Depression
A severe sense of low vitality, discouragement and sorrow.
Job 3:2-3
Psalms 6:6-7; 13:1-2; 32:4;
　42:3,7
Proverbs 18:14
Lamentations 3:17,19-24
See also **Comfort**

Desire
See **Christian life, longing
for God**

Desire, wrong
Wrongly wishing for things; greed.
Exodus 20:17
Psalm 119:36-37
Proverbs 15:27
Jeremiah 6:13
Luke 12:15
Ephesians 5:5
1 Timothy 6:9
James 4:2
1 John 2:15-16

Devil
Satan, also known as "the enemy" or "the accuser", who opposes God's person and will. Satan is known especially for his deceit and temptation to try to turn believers away from God.
Genesis 3:1
Job 2:7
Matthew 4:1; 13:19
John 8:44
Acts 26:18
2 Corinthians 2:11; 4:4; 11:14
Ephesians 2:2; 6:11
Hebrews 2:14
1 Peter 5:8-9
1 John 3:8; 5:19
Revelation 12:9-10; 20:10
See also **Demons; Victory**

Diligence
See **Work**

Discernment
Insight that enables people to see what God is doing or the true circumstances of life; ability to make right decisions based on God's wisdom.
1 Kings 3:9
Isaiah 11:2
1 Corinthians 2:14; 12:10; 14:29
Philippians 1:9-10
Hebrews 4:12; 5:14
See also **Self-examination; Wisdom**

Disciples
Learners or pupils; those who are called to follow Jesus Christ.
Matthew 10:1; 28:19-20
Luke 14:26-27,33
John 8:31; 13:35; 15:8

Discipline
Corrective training of character that God exercises in his love and which produces maturity and responsibility.
Proverbs 3:11-12
Matthew 18:15-18
2 Timothy 4:2
Hebrews 12:7-11
See also **Family, children and the whole family**

Disobedience
Refusing to obey God and his word.
Deuteronomy 28:15
Jeremiah 7:24-26,28
Romans 5:19
Ephesians 2:2
2 Thessalonians 1:8

2 Timothy 3:2
See also **Obedience; Punishment; Submission**

Divorce
See **Marriage**

Doubt
Uncertainty about the truth of spiritual matters; lack of trust in God.
Genesis 18:12-14
Psalm 31:22
Isaiah 40:27-28
Matthew 11:2-3; 14:31; 21:21; 28:17
Mark 9:24
John 20:25
James 1:6
Revelation 12:10
See also **Assurance; Comfort; Unbelief**

Dreams
A sequence of images thought in your mind while sleeping, sometimes associated with divine communication.
Genesis 28:12; 37:5
Deuteronomy 13:1-5
Psalm 126:1
Jeremiah 23:32
Daniel 2:27-28
Joel 2:28
Matthew 1:20
Acts 16:9

Drunkenness
The abuse of drinking alcohol.
Proverbs 23:29-30
Isaiah 5:11; 22:13; 28:7
Romans 13:13
Galatians 5:19,21
Ephesians 5:18
See also **Temperance**

Education
See **Teachers and teaching**

Elders
Senior leaders among God's people, recognised for their mature experience.
Exodus 3:16
Acts 11:29-30; 14:23; 20:28
1 Thessalonians 5:12-13
1 Timothy 3:1-4; 5:17
Titus 1:5
Hebrews 13:7,17
James 5:14
1 Peter 5:1-3
See also **Deacon; Pastor**

Election
God's sovereign choice of his people, because of his love for them.
Matthew 11:27; 25:34
John 6:37,44; 15:16; 17:6
Acts 13:48
Romans 8:29-30,33; 9:15-16
Ephesians 1:4-5
Colossians 3:12
2 Thessalonians 2:13
1 Peter 1:2; 2:9
2 Peter 1:10
See also **Christian life, calling of the Christian; Grace**

Encouragement
Giving people reassurance and confidence.
Acts 2:40; 4:36; 11:23; 14:22; 15:32
Romans 12:8
1 Thessalonians 2:11-12; 5:14
2 Timothy 4:2
Hebrews 3:13; 10:24-25
See also **Comfort; Fellowship**

Endurance
The ability to persevere in the Christian faith in the face of

difficulties or opposition.
Matthew 10:22; 13:21
Romans 5:4
1 Corinthians 10:13
Ephesians 6:11,18
Colossians 1:11
2 Timothy 2:3,12
Hebrews 12:2
James 1:12
See also **Christian life, continuing in the faith; Victory; Zeal**

Enemy

Forces of opposition that threaten people; the main enemies of God's people are the human heart with its tendency towards sin and the unseen forces of wickedness led by Satan.
Exodus 23:4-5
Proverbs 16:7; 24:17; 25:21-22
Matthew 5:43-44
Romans 5:10

Enjoyment
See **Joy**

Envy

A desire to have the gifts, possessions, etc that another person has; associated with jealousy.
Psalms 37:1; 73:3
Ecclesiastes 4:4
Matthew 27:18
Galatians 5:19,21
1 Peter 2:1
See also **Jealousy**

Eucharist
See **Communion**

Evangelism
See **Witness**

Evangelists
People called by God to

declare the good news of Jesus Christ; task originally given to the apostles and then to other believers as a gift of the Holy Spirit.
Acts 8:1,4-5,12,35; 21:8
Ephesians 4:11
2 Timothy 4:5
See also **Witness**

Evil

The presence and force of wickedness and depravity in the world that is opposed to God; result of the fall of humanity and God's punishment of human disobedience.
Genesis 3:5
Amos 6:3
Habakkuk 1:13
Matthew 6:34; 27:23
Mark 7:21
John 3:19
Romans 7:19; 12:9
1 Thessalonians 5:15,22
1 Timothy 6:10
1 John 2:13

Faith

An attitude of trust towards God, in which we give up depending on our own selves and put our complete confidence in God and his word.
Genesis 15:6
Psalms 18:2; 37:3-5
Proverbs 3:5
Habakkuk 2:4
Matthew 8:26
Mark 9:23-24; 11:22,24
John 1:12; 3:16,18; 6:29; 14:1; 20:31
Acts 6:5; 16:31
Romans 3:25; 5:1; 10:9-10,17
1 Corinthians 13:13

2 Corinthians 5:7
Galatians 2:20
Ephesians 2:8; 6:16
Hebrews 11:1,3,6
James 2:14,22,26
1 John 5:1,4
See also **Conversion; Repentance; Righteousness**

Faithfulness, faithful

Commitment in human relationships; also an important aspect of God's constant love towards his people.
Deuteronomy 7:9
Proverbs 20:6
Lamentations 3:22-23
Matthew 24:45; 25:21
Luke 16:10
1 Corinthians 10:13
Galatians 5:22
2 Timothy 2:2,13
Hebrews 2:17
Revelation 2:10
See also **Mercy**

Fall, the

Adam's first sin and its results.
Genesis 3:1,4,6-8,16-19
Romans 5:12,15-19
See also **Adam**

Falling away

A general turning away from God; denial of the faith by those who once claimed to hold it.
Proverbs 14:14
Jeremiah 7:24; 14:7
Malachi 3:7
Matthew 26:31
John 15:6; 16:1
1 Timothy 4:1
Hebrews 6:4-6; 10:26

Family

People connected by marriage or physical descent; Israelite concept of the extended family is far wider than the modern Western family of two parents and their children.

children and the whole family

Exodus 20:12
Deuteronomy 6:7
Joshua 24:15
1 Samuel 1:11
Psalm 127:3-5
Proverbs 13:24; 17:6; 22:6
Matthew 10:37
Mark 7:10-12; 10:13-16
Luke 2:51-52
Ephesians 6:1-2,4
Colossians 3:20
1 Timothy 3:4; 5:8
See also **Teachers and teaching**

husbands and wives

Proverbs 12:4; 18:22; 31:10
1 Corinthians 7:14; 11:3
Ephesians 5:21-25,28
1 Peter 3:1-7
See also **Marriage**

Fasting

The practice of abstaining from food and sometimes drink, especially for a limited period of time as a sign of religious commitment and devotion or to show repentance from sins.
Leviticus 23:27
2 Samuel 1:11-12
Isaiah 58:3-4,6
Joel 2:12-13,15
Matthew 4:2; 6:16-18; 9:15
Luke 18:12

Acts 13:2-3

Father

See **Family**

Fear

A feeling of anxious distress, caused by concern for a threat to yourself, the future, death or judgement.
Genesis 3:10
Exodus 3:6
Joshua 7:5
Psalm 55:5
Matthew 10:26,28,31
Mark 4:40
Luke 21:26
John 7:13
Romans 8:15
1 Corinthians 2:3
1 John 4:18
See also **Comfort**

Fear of God

See **Reverence**

Fellowship

The sharing of a common life; on the basis of a mutually acceptable agreement between the parties involved; believers have fellowship with one another because of their relationship with God.
Acts 2:42,44
1 Corinthians 1:9; 10:16-17
2 Corinthians 13:14
Galatians 2:9
Philippians 1:5; 4:15
1 Peter 4:13
1 John 1:3,6-7
See also **Love; Unity**

Fool, foolishness

A person without wisdom or understanding, especially in matters concerning God.

Sisters, being sisters

1 Samuel 25:25
Psalm 14:1
Proverbs 12:15; 26:11
Isaiah 32:6
Matthew 7:26
Luke 12:20
Romans 1:22-23
1 Corinthians 1:18,27; 2:14
See also **Wisdom**

Forgiveness

The freeing of a person from guilt and its results; act of love that restores a broken relationship.
Psalms 32:1-2; 51:1-2; 103:12; 130:3-4
Jeremiah 31:34
Micah 7:18
Matthew 6:12,14-15; 9:6; 12:31
Acts 2:38; 10:43
Ephesians 1:7; 4:32
Hebrews 9:22
1 John 1:9

See also **Atonement; Repentance; Sin**

Freedom, free
The state of liberty of not being oppressed or slavery; only Christ can make people truly free.
Isaiah 61:1
John 8:31-32,34-36
Romans 6:22; 8:2-4,21
1 Corinthians 8:9
2 Corinthians 3:17-18
Galatians 5:1,13
Hebrews 2:14-15

Friends
People that you are close to, especially those who give support in difficulties.
Exodus 33:11
Psalm 25:14
Proverbs 17:17; 18:24; 27:6
Matthew 11:19; 26:50
John 15:13-15
James 2:23

Fruit
Christian character produced by the Holy Spirit, showing spiritual life, growth and health.
Deuteronomy 7:13
Matthew 3:8; 7:16
John 15:5,8,16
Galatians 5:22-23

Fullness
The totality of something, as brought to completion by being filled. Jesus Christ expresses the full nature and purposes of God.
Psalm 24:1
John 1:14,16
Ephesians 1:23; 3:19; 5:18
Colossians 2:9-10

Gentiles
The word derives from Latin for "nations"; in common usage those who were not Jews.
Psalm 2:8
Isaiah 11:10
Luke 2:32
Acts 9:15; 10:45; 11:18
Romans 2:14
Galatians 3:28
Ephesians 2:11-19
Revelation 7:9

Gentleness
An attitude and action of compassion that God shows towards the weak and which Christians are to show in their relationships with other people.
Matthew 11:29
2 Corinthians 10:1
Galatians 5:22-23; 6:1
1 Thessalonians 2:7
2 Timothy 2:25
James 3:17
1 Peter 3:4

Gift
Something presented to you freely and without payment, especially salvation as freely given by God; also special spiritual gifts given by the Holy Spirit to every believer.
John 3:16
Acts 2:38; 5:31
Romans 6:23; 12:6
1 Corinthians 12:4-7,11; 14:1
2 Corinthians 9:15
Ephesians 2:8
1 Timothy 4:14
James 1:17

Giving
Offering or dedicating

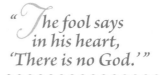

something or yourself to others or to God. Believers are to respond to God's generous gift of his Son for sinners by loving God and other people.
Genesis 14:20
1 Chronicles 29:14
Malachi 3:10
Matthew 6:2-3
Mark 12:42-44
Luke 6:38
1 Corinthians 16:2
2 Corinthians 8:1-5; 9:7
See also **Stewardship**

Glory
The majestic and powerful splendour of all God's qualities, revealed through creation, God's acts in history and especially in the life and resurrection of Jesus Christ.
Exodus 33:18
Numbers 14:21
1 Samuel 4:21
Matthew 17:2
Mark 8:38
John 2:11; 17:5
Romans 3:23; 8:18
1 Corinthians 10:31; 11:7
2 Corinthians 3:18
Hebrews 1:3

God
The creator and Redeemer of the world. He has made himself known in Scripture and in Jesus Christ. He is to

be worshipped. God is personal and is completely trustworthy. God is the Father of Jesus Christ and of all believers.

all-knowing
Psalm 139:1-6
Romans 11:33
Hebrews 4:13

all-present
Psalm 139:7-10

almighty
Job 42:2
Luke 1:37
Revelation 19:6

eternal
Psalm 90:2
1 Timothy 1:17

faithful
Deuteronomy 7:9
Lamentations 3:22-23
1 Corinthians 1:9

good
Psalms 34:8; 136:1
Mark 10:18
Romans 2:4

holy
Isaiah 6:3
Habakkuk 1:13
Revelation 15:4

infinite
1 Kings 8:27
Isaiah 57:15
Jeremiah 23:24

just
Genesis 18:25
Deuteronomy 32:4
Acts 17:31
1 John 1:9

loving
Deuteronomy 7:7-9

John 3:16
1 John 4:10

merciful
Exodus 34:6-7
Psalm 103:4
Ephesians 2:4-5

self-existent
Exodus 3:14
John 5:26

spiritual
John 4:23-24

unchangeable
Numbers 23:19
Malachi 3:6
James 1:17

wise
Psalm 104:24
Daniel 2:20
See also **Creation; Providence; Sovereignty of God**

Godlessness
An outlook that does not acknowledge God.
Job 20:5; 27:8
Psalms 2:2; 119:78
Proverbs 11:9
Isaiah 55:7
Romans 1:18; 5:6
See also **Unbeliever**

Goodness
God's perfection, which is made freely available for the whole world to benefit from. Good works are acts that benefit others; salvation does not depend on good works, but leads to them.
Genesis 1:31
2 Chronicles 5:13
Psalm 51:18
Mark 10:18

Acts 10:38
Romans 7:12,18; 8:28;
   12:2,9,21
Galatians 5:22
Ephesians 2:10
1 Timothy 4:4

Gospel
The good news of God's redemption of sinful humanity through the life, death and resurrection of his Son Jesus Christ.
Matthew 24:14
Mark 1:14-15; 16:15
Luke 4:18-21
Acts 20:24
Romans 1:16-17
1 Corinthians 9:16; 15:1,3-5
2 Corinthians 4:3-4
Galatians 1:11-12; 3:8
Ephesians 6:19
Philippians 1:27
1 Timothy 1:11

Grace
God's undeserved favour, revealed through Jesus Christ, and seen most clearly in the redemption and forgiveness of sinners through their faith in Jesus Christ.
Deuteronomy 7:6-8
John 1:14,16-17
Acts 4:33; 13:43
Romans 3:24; 5:2; 5:20–6:2
1 Corinthians 15:10
2 Corinthians 8:9; 12:9; 13:14
Ephesians 2:4-5,8
Hebrews 4:16
2 Peter 3:18

Greed
See **Desire, wrong**

Grief
Great sadness; human

Sincere worship in morning chapel service, West Bengal

Psalms 32:5 ; 51:1-4
Isaiah 6:7
Romans 8:1
1 Corinthians 11:27
James 2:10
See also **Conscience;**
Conviction of sin;
Forgiveness

Happiness
See **Joy**

Hardness
A persistent inner refusal to hear and obey the word of God.
Exodus 4:21
Deuteronomy 15:7
Proverbs 28:14
Isaiah 6:9-10
Matthew 19:8
Mark 3:5
John 5:40
Acts 7:51
Romans 2:5
2 Corinthians 3:14
Ephesians 4:18
Hebrews 3:15
See also **Falling away;**
Rejection; Unbelief

Hate, hatred
An attitude and feeling that is the opposite of love; associated with sin. Scripture asserts God's hatred of sin and evil.
Psalm 139:21-22
Proverbs 6:16-19; 15:17
Amos 5:15
Habakkuk 1:13
Matthew 24:9
John 3:20; 7:7; 15:18-19

response to pain and distress, especially those involving loss.
Psalms 23:1-6; 31:10; 51:17
Ecclesiastes 3:4
Isaiah 6:5; 53:3-4
Jeremiah 8:22
Matthew 8:12; 26:37-38
Luke 19:41-42; 22:45,61-62
John 11:35
2 Corinthians 6:10; 7:10
See also **Comfort;**
Repentance

Growth, spiritual
See **Christian life, character of the Christian**

Guidance
God has purposes and plans for his people. Believers are to seek God for his direction in their lives.

Psalms 23:2-3; 37:3-5,23
Isaiah 58:10-11
John 16:13
Acts 15:22,28
Romans 12:2
James 1:5
See also **Counsel;**
Sovereignty of God

Guilt
The state of being in the wrong, often including the emotion that comes from being aware of being at fault. Human guilt arises from sin before God, and can only be cleansed through accepting the forgiveness offered through the death of Jesus Christ.
Genesis 3:8,10
Exodus 20:7

Healing

Bringing about of a state of physical or spiritual health.

1 Kings 17:21-22
2 Kings 5:14
2 Chronicles 7:14
Psalms 103:2-3; 107:20
Matthew 4:23; 10:1
Acts 3:6-7
1 Corinthians 12:9
James 5:14-16

See also **Comfort; Illness; Suffering**

Heart

The inner being of God or human beings. The inner person, though fallen, may be changed by the Holy Spirit and is to show evidence of renewal.

Deuteronomy 6:5
1 Samuel 13:14; 16:7
Psalm 51:10
Jeremiah 17:9-10
Ezekiel 36:26
Matthew 5:8; 6:21
Mark 7:21-22
John 7:38-39
Romans 6:17; 8:27; 10:9
Colossians 3:15
1 Peter 1:22
1 John 3:19-21

See also **Hardness; Mind; Spirit**

Heaven

See **Last things**

Hell

See **Last things**

Help

Aid or assistance as given by God or other people.

1 Samuel 7:12
Psalms 46:1; 121
Matthew 15:25

Acts 18:27; 20:35
Romans 8:26
1 Corinthians 12:28
2 Corinthians 1:11
Galatians 6:2
Hebrews 13:5-6

See also **Comfort; Kindness; Service**

High priest

See **Priest**

Holiness

The quality of God that sets him completely apart from his world, especially in his purity. His holiness is also seen in the work of Jesus Christ and in the Holy Spirit. Believers are to become like God in his holiness.

Exodus 3:5; 20:8
Leviticus 11:44
Isaiah 6:3
Romans 6:22
2 Corinthians 7:1
1 Thessalonians 4:7
Hebrews 7:26; 12:10,14
1 Peter 2:9

See also **Sanctification**

Holy Spirit

One of the three persons of the divine Trinity who is the unseen presence of God in the world. He inspired Scripture and brings new life to the people of God.

Genesis 1:2
Exodus 31:3
Judges 3:10
Psalm 51:11
Isaiah 11:2
Ezekiel 36:27
Joel 2:28
Zechariah 4:6
Matthew 3:11,16; 12:31

Luke 1:35; 11:13
John 3:5-6; 7:38-39; 14:16-17,26; 15:26; 16:7-11,13-14
Acts 1:8; 2:1-4,38; 4:8; 5:3-4; 7:51; 13:2; 15:28
Romans 5:5; 8:5-6,9-11,13-16, 26-27; 12:11
1 Corinthians 2:4,10; 12:7
2 Corinthians 3:17-18
Galatians 5:22-23
Ephesians 4:30; 5:18-21; 6:17
1 Thessalonians 5:19
2 Peter 1:21

Homosexuality

The forbidden practice of sexual relations between two people of the same sex.

Leviticus 18:22; 20:13
Romans 1:24,26-27
1 Corinthians 6:9-10

See also **Sex**

Honesty

Behaviour, in action and words, that conveys truth; essential aspect of God's own character and is required of his people.

Proverbs 11:1
Luke 8:15
2 Corinthians 4:2; 8:21
Ephesians 4:28
2 Thessalonians 3:7-8

See also **Lying; Truth**

Hope

A confident expectation for the future, based on God's character and promises.

Psalm 42:5
Romans 4:18; 5:2,5; 8:23-25; 15:13
1 Corinthians 13:13
Ephesians 2:12
Colossians 1:27

Hebrews 6:18-19
1 Peter 1:13

Hospitality
Acts of generosity, practical Christian love and friendship towards strangers.
Matthew 25:35
Acts 16:15
Romans 12:13
1 Timothy 3:2; 5:10
Hebrews 13:2
1 Peter 4:9

Humility
An attitude of lowliness and obedience, based on the

> *"But God demonstrates his love for us in this: While we were still sinners, Christ died for us."*
>
> *ROMANS 5:8*

proper recognition of your relationship with God and other people.
Isaiah 66:2
Matthew 5:3; 18:4
Mark 10:43
John 13:3-5,14
Philippians 2:3,5-8
1 Peter 5:5-6
See also **Pride**

Husband
See **Marriage**

Hypocrisy, hypocrite
An outward pretence that hides an inner reality; practice of saying one thing

but doing another; condemned in Scripture.
Matthew 6:2,5,16; 7:5; 15:7-9
Luke 6:46
2 Timothy 3:5
See also **Pharisees; Teachers of the law**

Idolatry
The worship of anything or anyone other than God himself; especially the worship of images of gods made of wood, metal or stone.
Exodus 20:3-5; 32:4
Psalm 115:4-7
Galatians 5:19-20
1 Thessalonians 1:9
1 John 5:21

Illness
A diseased condition that prevents people or animals from reaching their full potential or adversely affecting their abilities.
2 Chronicles 16:12
Job 2:7
Psalm 38:3
Mark 3:10
John 11:3
See also **Suffering**

help in
Psalm 41:3
Isaiah 53:4
Matthew 8:2-3
James 5:14-16
See also **Comfort; Healing**

Immigrants
People who settle in a foreign country; Israelite law encouraged a hospitable caring attitude towards foreigners, but prohibited acceptance of their religious

practices that detracted from God's standards.
Exodus 22:21
Leviticus 19:33-34
Deuteronomy 10:18-19
Psalm 146:9
Matthew 25:35
Hebrews 13:2

Incarnation
See **Jesus Christ, Jesus, the man**

Inheritance
A birthright or endowment, often personal possessions or land, that is passed from one generation to the next; Scripture considers eternal life and other privileges of faith as an inheritance from God.
Matthew 25:34
Acts 20:32
Romans 8:17
1 Corinthians 6:9; 15:50
Galatians 4:7
Ephesians 1:11,13,14,18
Titus 3:7
Hebrews 1:2
1 Peter 1:3-4; 3:7

Injustice
The unjustified ill treatment of others, by false accusation or inflicting pain or punishment; originating in Satan, injustice works through the sinful human heart and is revealed in every sphere of life.
Exodus 23:1
Leviticus 19:15,35
2 Chronicles 19:7
Psalm 82:2
Proverbs 20:10
Jeremiah 22:13

Zephaniah 3:5
See also **Justice; Oppression**

Israel

A name, meaning "he struggles with God", which was given to Jacob as he wrestled with God. Also, from the time of the exodus, the usual term for the twelve tribes. God called Israel out of Egypt to be his own treasured possession and his covenant faithfulness with them is maintained, despite their persistent disobedience.
Genesis 32:28
Micah 5:2
Matthew 19:28
John 19:19
Romans 2:28-29; 9:6-7; 11:25-26
Galatians 6:15-16
Philippians 3:3
See also **Gentiles**

Jealousy

A strong sense of possessiveness; (of God) a passionate commitment to his people; (human jealousy)
a destructive feeling seeking to avoid the possible loss of something that is yours.
Exodus 20:5; 34:14
Proverbs 27:4
Luke 15:25,28-30
1 Corinthians 13:4
Galatians 5:19-20
James 3:14,16; 4:5
See also **Envy**

Jesus Christ

The co-equal and co-eternal Son of the Father, who became a man in Jesus Christ for the redemption of the world. The Bible emphasises both the divinity and the humanity of Jesus Christ, and the necessity and total sufficiency of his atoning death for human salvation. Through his resurrection and ascension, he intercedes for believers at the right hand of God.

Ascension
Luke 24:26,51
John 7:39; 20:17
Acts 1:9; 2:33

Ephesians 1:20-23
Philippians 2:9

authority
Matthew 7:29; 9:6; 28:18
Luke 4:36
John 5:27; 10:18

death
Genesis 3:15
Isaiah 53:3-9
Matthew 16:21
John 10:11
Acts 2:23; 3:15
Romans 4:25; 5:6-8
1 Corinthians 1:18,23-24; 15:3
Galatians 2:20; 6:14
Colossians 2:15
Hebrews 2:14-15
See also **Atonement; Reconciliation**

eternal son of God
Proverbs 8:22-23
John 1:1-2; 8:58
Colossians 1:15-19
Hebrews 1:2-8; 13:8
Revelation 1:8

holiness
John 8:46
Hebrews 4:15; 7:26
1 Peter 2:22

humility
Zechariah 9:9
2 Corinthians 8:9
Philippians 2:6-8

Jesus as king
Psalm 110:1
Jeremiah 23:5
Daniel 7:13-14
Zechariah 9:9
John 18:36; 19:19,21

Lake Galilee, Israel, at dusk. Scene of many of Jesus' miraculous acts

Hebrews 1:8
Revelation 12:10

Jesus, the man
Isaiah 7:14; 9:6
Luke 2:7
John 1:14; 3:16-17
Galatians 4:4
Philippians 2:5-8
1 Timothy 2:5; 3:16
Hebrews 2:9,14; 4:15
1 John 4:2

Jesus, the one to be worshipped
Matthew 2:11; 16:16
Luke 5:8
John 20:28
Revelation 5:12

Jesus as priest
1 Timothy 2:5
Hebrews 4:14-15; 5:5-6;
    7:24-26; 9:15; 10:11-12

Jesus as prophet
Deuteronomy 18:15
Matthew 21:11
Luke 7:16; 24:19

love
Matthew 9:36
John 13:1; 15:9
Romans 8:38-39
Ephesians 3:17-19
Revelation 1:5

obedience
Psalm 40:8
Matthew 26:42
John 4:34; 8:29
Philippians 2:8
Hebrews 5:8

Resurrection
Psalm 16:10
Isaiah 53:10-12
Matthew 16:21; 28:6
Acts 2:32; 17:31

Romans 4:25; 6:4-5,9-11
1 Corinthians 15:4,12-21
Colossians 3:1
Revelation 1:17-18

second coming
See **Last things**

seven words from the cross
Matthew 27:46
Luke 23:34,43,46
John 19:26-28,30

Joy
Delight and happiness,
ultimately from God as
Father, Son and Holy Spirit;
attitude that comes from
being fully accepted by God.
Nehemiah 8:10
Psalms 16:11; 118:24;
    119:162; 126:3,5-6
Isaiah 12:3; 35:10
Matthew 5:3; 13:20-21
Luke 15:7
John 15:11; 16:24
Acts 13:52
Romans 5:1-2; 15:13
2 Corinthians 12:9
Galatians 5:22
Philippians 4:4
1 Timothy 6:17
Hebrews 12:2
1 Peter 1:8
3 John 4

Judgement
See **Last things**

Justice
A concern to act rightly;
quality of God that is to
affect every aspect of human
society.
Leviticus 19:13
Deuteronomy 16:20
Psalm 72:1-2
Proverbs 21:3

Isaiah 1:17; 59:11,14; 61:8
Amos 5:24
Micah 6:8
Colossians 4:1
See also **Injustice;
Righteousness**

Justification
The acquittal, or declaration
of being righteous, by
which God declares people
"righteous"; central aspect of
the salvation that God
accomplished through the
death and resurrection of
Jesus Christ.
Genesis 15:6
Job 9:1-2
Psalm 32:1-2
Isaiah 50:8-9; 61:10
Luke 18:13-14
Romans 3:24; 4:5; 5:1,9,19;
    8:30,33-34
2 Corinthians 5:21
See also **Atonement; Faith;
Righteousness**

Kindness
Compassion and generosity
that is a quality of God that
he shows towards everyone,
and especially the weak and
poor; quality that is
demanded of believers.
Isaiah 58:10
Matthew 25:35-36,40
Luke 10:30,33-35
Acts 20:35
Galatians 5:22
Ephesians 4:32
Hebrews 10:24
See also **Love; Service**

Kingdom, kingdom of God
The kingly rule of God,
recognising his authority
and especially the ministry of

Jesus Christ; in Matthew's Gospel, the "kingdom of heaven".

Matthew 5:3; 6:10,33; 7:21; 25:34
Mark 1:15; 10:15
Luke 17:20-21
John 3:3
Acts 14:22
Romans 14:17
1 Corinthians 4:20; 6:9; 15:24
Colossians 1:13
Hebrews 12:28
Revelation 11:15

Knowledge
Awareness and understanding, seen as a gift from God; God knows all things; his people are to know his will and purposes for them.
Genesis 2:9
Job 19:25
Psalms 46:10; 119:125; 139:1-6
Isaiah 11:9
Hosea 6:3
Matthew 11:27
John 10:14-15; 17:3
1 Corinthians 8:1; 13:2,12
Ephesians 3:19
Philippians 3:10
Colossians 1:9-10
2 Timothy 1:12
1 John 2:3
See also **Discernment; Understanding; Wisdom**

Land
Area of territory; possession of land was considered to be a sign of security and prosperity.
Exodus 23:10-11
Leviticus 25:10-11,23
Deuteronomy 26:9-10; 28:2-4

2 Chronicles 7:14
Psalm 24:1
Acts 4:34-35

Last Supper
See **Communion**

Last things
Events associated with the second coming of Jesus Christ when he will return visibly and gloriously at the end of history to raise the dead, judge the world, destroy all evil and opposition to God and consummate his kingdom.

events before the second coming
Matthew 24:6,9-14,21-22,29
2 Thessalonians 2:3-4,8
Revelation 20:2-3,7-8

heaven
Psalm 73:25
Isaiah 66:1
Matthew 6:9-10
John 14:2-3; 17:24
Acts 2:2
1 Corinthians 2:9
Philippians 3:20
Hebrews 9:24
Revelation 7:9,15; 20:4; 21:3; 22:3-5

hell
Matthew 7:13; 8:12; 10:28; 25:41,46
Luke 16:26
2 Thessalonians 1:9
Revelation 14:9-11; 20:10,15; 21:8

judgement
Matthew 10:32-33; 25:31-33
Acts 17:31
1 Corinthians 4:5; 6:2-3
2 Corinthians 5:10
Hebrews 9:27
Jude 6
Revelation 6:16-17; 20:11-15

renewal of all things
Matthew 19:28
Acts 3:21
Romans 8:21
2 Peter 3:10-13
Revelation 21:1-5

resurrection
Isaiah 66:24
Daniel 12:2-3
Matthew 22:32
John 5:28-29; 11:24-25
1 Corinthians 15:42-44,52
Philippians 3:20-21
1 Thessalonians 4:16
Revelation 20:10

second coming of Jesus
Daniel 7:13
Matthew 24:27,29-30,36
John 14:3
Acts 1:11
1 Thessalonians 4:14-17; 5:2
2 Thessalonians 1:7,10
Hebrews 9:28
Revelation 1:7

state between death and resurrection
Psalm 9:17
Luke 16:23-24,26; 23:43
John 11:26
2 Corinthians 5:8
Philippians 1:23
1 Thessalonians 4:14
Hebrews 12:23
Revelation 6:11; 14:13

Law

The God-given regulation of the life of God's people that affects their relationship with him and the relationship between fellow human beings.
Psalms 19:7; 119:18
Matthew 5:17
John 1:17
Romans 3:19-20,31; 6:14; 7:7,12,22-23; 8:2-4; 13:10
Galatians 2:16; 3:24; 4:4-5
Hebrews 8:10; 10:1
James 1:25; 2:8
See also **Bible; Will of God**

Laying on of hands

A symbolic action concerning God's blessing, especially for healing, a blessing or setting a person apart for God's service.
Genesis 48:14-15
Leviticus 16:21
Deuteronomy 34:9
Mark 6:5; 10:16
Acts 6:6; 13:2-3; 19:6
1 Timothy 4:14; 5:22
Hebrews 6:1-2

Laziness

Idle unproductiveness; attitude that is consistently discouraged.
Proverbs 6:6,9; 15:19

2 Thessalonians 3:6-8,10-12
1 Timothy 5:13
Hebrews 6:12
See also **Work**

Leadership

Giving guidance and direction, based ideally on individuals being called and appointed by God to guide God's people into his purposes for them.
Exodus 18:22-23
Numbers 13:1-2
1 Samuel 13:14
Jeremiah 5:1
Mark 10:43
Romans 12:8
2 Corinthians 11:28
1 Thessalonians 5:12-13
1 Timothy 3:1
2 Timothy 2:2
1 Peter 5:3
See also **Deacon; Elders; Service**

Life

The state of being alive, marked by vitality and growth. In Scripture, life includes more than mere physical existence; it also includes humanity's relationship with God. Human beings come to life spiritually through personally trusting Christ.
Genesis 2:7,9
Exodus 20:12
Deuteronomy 8:3; 30:19
Job 19:25
Psalms 63:3; 91:16
Proverbs 8:35
Isaiah 55:3
Ezekiel 37:3
Hosea 1:10

"Do not think I have come to abolish the Law or the Prophets; I have not come to abolish them but to fulfil them."

ROMANS 5:8

Matthew 6:25; 7:14; 16:26; 22:32; 25:46
John 5:24; 6:35,68; 10:10,28; 11:25; 14:6,19; 20:31
Acts 17:28
Romans 6:23; 8:6,13
2 Corinthians 4:10
Galatians 2:20
Ephesians 2:5
Philippians 1:21; 2:16
Colossians 3:4
1 John 3:14; 5:12
See also **Adam; Death; Last things**

Light

The brightness that enables sight in the darkness, created by God; symbol of the saving presence of God in a dark sinful world.
Genesis 1:3
Psalms 27:1; 119:105,130
Isaiah 9:2; 49:6; 60:1
Matthew 5:14-16
John 1:4-5,7-9; 3:19-21; 8:12
Acts 26:18
2 Corinthians 4:6; 6:14
Ephesians 5:8-9,13-14
Philippians 2:15
1 Timothy 6:16
1 Peter 2:9
1 John 1:5,7
Revelation 22:5

Loneliness

Unhappy feeling of being unwanted and isolated; from the beginning, the Bible shows it is not good to be alone: God wants human beings to live together in harmony and to respect one another.

Genesis 2:18
1 Kings 19:10
Job 19:13-14
Matthew 26:38,56; 27:46
2 Timothy 1:15
See also **Comfort**

Love

The deepest expression of God's nature. Although God loves all people, he is especially committed to sacrificial, faithful relationships with his people; God's love is fully revealed in the life and death of Jesus Christ.

of God

Deuteronomy 7:7-8
John 3:16
Romans 5:5,8; 8:35-39
Galatians 2:20
Ephesians 2:4-5
1 John 4:8-10
See also **Faithfulness; Grace; Mercy**

of humanity for God

Deuteronomy 6:5; 10:12
Psalm 116:1
John 14:15,21
Romans 8:28
1 Corinthians 2:9; 16:22
1 Peter 1:8
1 John 4:20-21
See also **Christian life, longing for God; Worship**

of human beings for other human beings

Exodus 20:12
Leviticus 19:18,34
Matthew 5:44-46; 7:12; 18:10
John 13:34-35; 15:13
1 Corinthians 13:1-7,13
Galatians 5:22
Ephesians 5:25
1 John 4:7,11; 5:2
See also **Kindness**

Lying

Telling untruths and giving false witness, which is especially associated with Satan and the antichrist.

Exodus 20:16
Numbers 23:19
Psalm 120:2
Jeremiah 9:5
John 8:44
Acts 5:3-5
Colossians 3:9
1 John 2:4,22

Man

Human beings are the most important part of God's creation; only they are created in his image. As a result of sin they have become separated from God and from one another and are by themselves unable to change this situation. The salvation of humanity depends completely on the atoning death of Jesus Christ, received by grace through faith.

Genesis 1:26-27; 3:17; 6:5
Psalms 8:4-8; 103:15-16
John 2:25
Romans 5:12
See also **Responsibility, human; Woman**

Marriage

The union of a man and a woman living together in a permanent relationship. God's relationship with his people is described in terms of the marriage bond.

Genesis 2:18,24
Matthew 19:6; 22:30
1 Corinthians 7:39
Ephesians 5:22-33
1 Timothy 3:2; 4:1-3
Hebrews 13:4
See also **Family; Sex**

adultery

Exodus 20:14
Proverbs 6:32
Matthew 5:27-28

divorce

Malachi 2:15-16
Matthew 5:31-32; 19:7-9
1 Corinthians 7:10-11

Maturity

See **Christian life, character of the Christian; Perfection**

Meditation

The quiet pondering of God's word, his creation, his powerful works or other aspects of his revelation to draw close to him.

Joshua 1:8,
Psalms 1:2-3; 4:4; 19:14; 37:7; 119:15; 143:5
Luke 2:19
2 Corinthians 3:18
See also **Mind; Thought**

Mercy

A quality of love and compassion, seen especially in God's forgiveness of human sin; in his mercy, God protects sinners from what

they deserve.
Exodus 34:6-7
Psalms 25:10; 51:1; 89:33;
  136:1
Lamentations 3:22-23
Daniel 9:18
Hosea 6:6
Micah 6:8
Matthew 5:7
Luke 6:36; 18:13
Romans 12:1
Colossians 3:12
See also **Grace**

Mind

The seat of a person's
thought, desires and
consciousness; believers'
minds are to be shaped by
God, so that their behaviour
becomes more like that of
Jesus Christ.
Isaiah 26:3
Matthew 22:37
Acts 17:2-4
Romans 1:21; 8:5-6; 11:33-34;
  12:2
1 Corinthians 2:16
Philippians 2:5; 4:7
Colossians 3:2
See also **Heart; Meditation;
Understanding**

Ministry
See **Service**

Miracles

Extraordinary events that
cannot be adequately
explained on the basis of
natural laws, especially those
associated with the Jesus
Christ; evidence of the
presence and power of God
and as showing authority by
his people.
Exodus 14:21,31

1 Kings 18:37-38
Psalm 72:18
Matthew 24:24
Luke 1:37
John 2:11; 14:12
Acts 4:30; 9:40
1 Corinthians 12:10
2 Corinthians 12:12
Hebrews 2:4

Money and material goods

A conventional means of
payment that can be used to
build God's kingdom; it can
also ensnare people. Jesus
taught that people cannot
trust God and money at the
same time.
Ecclesiastes 5:9
Matthew 6:19,24; 22:17-21
1 Timothy 3:3; 6:6-7,10
Hebrews 13:5
See also **Giving; Rich and
riches**

Mother
See **Family**

Murder

The unlawful taking of
another person's life,
forbidden by God and
carrying the threat of severe
punishment.
Genesis 4:8-10; 9:6
Exodus 20:13
Deuteronomy 19:4-6,11-12
Matthew 5:21-22
1 John 3:15
Revelation 21:8

Name

The title given to a person;
person's name may reflect
special characteristics of a
person or the hopes or
wishes for that person by the
one giving the name.

Genesis 2:19-20; 12:8
Exodus 3:13-15; 20:7
Proverbs 18:10
Matthew 6:9; 18:20; 28:19
Luke 24:47
John 14:13,26
Acts 3:6; 4:12; 19:17
Philippians 2:9-10
Colossians 3:17

Neighbour

A person such as a friend or
fellow Christian with whom
you have a natural relationship and to whom you owe
an obligation of love and
support.
Exodus 20:16-17
Leviticus 19:18
Luke 10:29-37
Galatians 5:14
See also **Love, of human
beings for other human
beings**

New birth

The radical spiritual renewal
of a person's inner being by
the work of God's Spirit.
Psalm 51:10
Ezekiel 36:25-27
John 3:3-8
2 Corinthians 5:17
Ephesians 2:1-5
Titus 3:5
1 Peter 1:23
1 John 3:9

Obedience

A willingness to submit to
the authority of someone else
and to do what you are asked
or told to do; central aspect
of the relationship between
human beings and God.
Genesis 22:18
Numbers 14:24

Deuteronomy 28:2
1 Samuel 15:22
Matthew 7:21
John 14:15
Acts 5:28-29,32
Romans 6:17
Philippians 2:8
Hebrews 5:8
James 1:22
1 Peter 1:14-15
1 John 3:22; 5:2
See also **Blessing;**
Disobedience; Submission

Occult
Supernatural or magical
powers or practices, such as
divination, astrology, necro-
mancy and magic rituals;
expressly forbidden by God.
Leviticus 19:26,31; 20:27
Deuteronomy 18:10-12
1 Chronicles 10:13-14
Isaiah 8:19; 47:13-14
Acts 8:9; 19:19
Galatians 5:19-20

Old age
Living for a relatively long
time; generally associated
with God's blessing,
although it also brings
physical weakness.
Leviticus 19:32
Job 12:12
Psalms 31:15; 71:9; 90:10,12;
    92:13-14
Proverbs 17:6
Luke 2:36-37
2 Corinthians 5:2
Philippians 1:21
Titus 2:2-3

Oppression
The unjust or cruel
treatment of individuals or
nations that prevents them

from having the same rights
or freedom as others.
Exodus 22:21
Deuteronomy 24:14
Psalms 9:9; 103:6
Proverbs 14:31
Isaiah 38:14; 53:7
Zechariah 7:10
James 2:6

Parent
See **Family**

Passover
An important annual Old
Testament feast that
commemorates the exodus
from Egypt as an act of God's
deliverance.
Exodus 12:3,5-8,11-13,24
Luke 2:41; 22:13
1 Corinthians 5:7
See also **Communion**

Pastor
A church leader who guides,
protects and feeds his people
spiritually.
Ephesians 4:11-12
1 Thessalonians 2:11
2 Timothy 4:5
See also **Elders; Shepherd;**
Teachers and teaching

Patience
The quality of forbearance
and self-control that is seen
especially in being willing to
wait on God for him to act,
and in personal
relationships.
Psalm 37:7
Proverbs 14:29
Isaiah 40:31
Romans 2:4; 12:12
1 Corinthians 13:4,7
Galatians 5:22
1 Thessalonians 5:14

James 5:7-8
Revelation 2:2
See also **Endurance**

Peace
The state of harmony that is
available to believers
through being in a right
relationship with God and
other people; associated
especially with the Holy
Spirit.
Numbers 6:26
Isaiah 9:6-7; 26:3; 48:22
Matthew 3:16; 5:9; 10:34
Mark 4:39
Luke 2:14,29; 10:5-6
John 14:27; 16:33; 20:19
Romans 5:1; 8:6; 12:18
1 Corinthians 14:33
Galatians 5:22
Ephesians 2:14; 6:15
Philippians 4:7
Colossians 3:15
2 Thessalonians 3:16
See also **Reconciliation**

Perfection
The state of completion and
absolute self-sufficiency,
characterised by an absence
of any fault. Although only
God is naturally without
fault, human beings may also
achieve perfection. It is a
status given to all who
believe in Christ because
their sins have been
completely forgiven.
2 Samuel 22:31
Psalm 19:7
Matthew 5:48; 19:21
Romans 12:2
1 Corinthians 13:9-10
Ephesians 4:11-13
Philippians 3:12,15
Colossians 1:28

2 Timothy 3:17
Hebrews 5:8-9,14; 10:14

Persecution

Forms of suffering, eg hardship, ridicule and oppression, from individuals and state authorities, because of a person's faith. Believers are encouraged to remain faithful in the face of such persecution and to draw strength from the example of Jesus Christ.
Matthew 5:10-12,44; 13:21
Luke 21:12
John 15:20
Acts 8:1; 9:4
Romans 8:35,37; 12:14
2 Timothy 3:12

Perseverance

See **Christian life, continuing in the faith**

Pharisees

A Jewish religious group who insisted on strict adherence to the ritual law and to the traditions of their predecessors. They were hostile to Jesus Christ, whom they considered as having compromised their interpretation of the law.
Matthew 12:14; 22:15; 23:13
Luke 5:17,30-31; 7:39;
    11:38-39; 18:9-12
John 12:42
Acts 23:6
See also **Hypocrisy; Teachers of the law**

Possessions

See **Money and material goods**

Poverty

The state of being without material possessions or wealth; a state that is contrary to God's intention for his people. Although Jesus taught that poverty was inevitable in human society, he also stressed the importance of having compassion in providing for poor people.

> " *You will keep him in peace*
>   *whose mind is steadfast,*
>   *because he trusts in you.*"
>
> *ISAIAH 26:3*

Exodus 23:6
Deuteronomy 15:7
1 Samuel 2:8
Proverbs 14:31; 19:17
Matthew 5:3; 26:11
Mark 12:43-44
Luke 4:18; 14:13
2 Corinthians 8:9
James 2:5-6
See also **Justice; Rich and riches**

Power

The quality that enables individuals to achieve their aims. Absolute power comes from God; all other forms of power are dependent on his authority. Scripture asserts the power of God, as seen in Jesus Christ's resurrection and given through the Holy Spirit.
Isaiah 40:31
Matthew 6:13; 22:29; 24:30

Mark 5:30
Luke 4:14
Acts 1:8; 4:33
Romans 1:16; 15:13
1 Corinthians 1:23-24
2 Corinthians 4:7; 12:9
Ephesians 1:19-20; 6:10-11
Philippians 3:10; 4:13
1 Thessalonians 1:5
2 Timothy 3:5
1 Peter 1:4-5
See also **Authority**

Praise

Worship of God, giving him the honour due to him as creator of all and the Saviour of his people.
Psalms 34:1,3; 50:23; 100:1-4
Isaiah 43:21; 61:1,3
Acts 2:46-47
Ephesians 5:19
Hebrews 13:15
Revelation 5:12
See also **Prayer; Worship**

Prayer

A vital part of a personal relationship with God through Jesus Christ, as expressed in worship, thanksgiving, confession and intercession, through which believers draw near to God. The Holy Spirit plays a significant role in stimulating and guiding prayer.

answers to prayer

Psalm 34:6
Mark 9:28-29
2 Corinthians 1:11; 12:8-9
Ephesians 3:20-21
Philippians 4:6-7
Hebrews 4:16
James 4:3; 5:16

encouragements to pray

1 Chronicles 16:11
Psalms 34:15; 62:8
Isaiah 65:24
Matthew 6:6
Luke 18:1
1 Thessalonians 5:17
Revelation 3:20

how to pray

Matthew 6:7-13; 26:41
Romans 8:26
Ephesians 6:18-19
1 Timothy 2:1-2
James 1:5-6

promises in prayer

2 Chronicles 7:14
Psalms 37:4; 66:18
Matthew 7:7-8; 18:19-20;
   21:22
John 14:13; 15:7; 16:23-24
1 John 3:22; 5:14
See also **Praise; Worship**

Preaching

The public spoken
declaration of God's word,
especially the good news of
Jesus Christ.
Isaiah 52:7; 61:1
Luke 24:47
Acts 20:27
Romans 10:14-15
1 Corinthians 1:21,23; 9:16
1 Thessalonians 1:5
1 Timothy 4:13; 5:17
2 Timothy 2:15; 4:2

See also **Teachers and
teaching**

Pride

An excessively high opinion
of yourself; sense of
overconfidence and
arrogance that is
unacceptable among
believers, whose lives are to
be marked by humility.
Deuteronomy 8:17
Proverbs 16:18
Matthew 23:12
Mark 7:21-22
Luke 1:51
Romans 12:3,16
1 Corinthians 1:31; 10:12;
   13:4
2 Corinthians 12:7
See also **Humility; Self-
righteousness**

Priest

A person with direct access
into God's presence and has
the responsibility of
mediating between God and
his people, ensuring proper
worship, and maintaining
the spiritual health of the
people of God.
Exodus 19:6; 28:1
Deuteronomy 18:3; 21:5;
   33:10
Mark 14:53
Luke 22:4
Acts 6:7
Hebrews 5:1-4; 8:3; 10:11-12
1 Peter 2:5,9
See also **Jesus Christ, Jesus as
priest**

Promise

Binding offer or
commitment by one person
or people to another. The
value of such promises
depends on the faithfulness
of the person who makes the
promises. God's promises
reveal his eternal purposes to
which he is committed and
on which believers can totally
depend. These promises are,
however, conditional on
obedience on the part of
believers.
Luke 24:49
Romans 9:8
2 Corinthians 1:20
Ephesians 1:13; 2:12
Hebrews 8:6; 10:23
James 1:12
2 Peter 1:4; 3:9,13

Prophets and prophecy

People, male or female, called
and empowered by God to
declare his will to his people,
including revealing his
future intentions to save and
judge his people.
Deuteronomy 18:22
Jeremiah 7:25-26
Matthew 7:22-23; 24:24
Acts 2:18; 11:27-28
1 Corinthians 12:28; 13:8;
   14:1,31-32
Ephesians 2:20
1 Thessalonians 5:20-21
2 Peter 1:21

Propitiation

The satisfaction of the
righteous demands of God in
relation to human sin and its
punishment through the
sacrificial atoning death of
Jesus Christ on the cross, by
which the penalty of sin is
cancelled and the anger of
God turned aside.
Isaiah 53:10

Luke 18:13
Romans 3:25
Galatians 3:13
Hebrews 2:17; 9:5
1 John 2:2; 4:10
See also **Anger, of God;
Atonement; Reconciliation**

Providence

God's loving provision of
the good things of life for
everyone, alongside his often
unseen actions in human
events to fulfil his purposes.
Genesis 8:22; 22:14
1 Chronicles 29:14
Nehemiah 9:6
Psalm 135:6-7
Proverbs 16:1,33
Matthew 10:29-31
Acts 17:28
Ephesians 1:11
Colossians 1:17
Hebrews 1:3
See also **Sovereignty of God**

Punishment

A form of physical pain or
deprivation, usually in
proportion to the offence
that leads to it. Punishment
is the just consequence of
breaking God's law. The
Bible emphasises the reality
of punishment by God for
sin, while urging that human
punishment should be
humane. Punishment
generally involved
retribution, correction and
vindication, and sometimes
included compensation for
the victim.
Exodus 2:12
Numbers 32:23
Ezekiel 33:8
Matthew 25:46

**Open air evening filmshow at a
village school in Maharashtra, India,
organised by local students training
for the mission field**

John 3:18
Romans 2:8-9; 6:23; 13:4
2 Thessalonians 1:9
Hebrews 10:29
See also **Anger, of God;
Discipline; Last things, hell**

Purity

An absence of blemish or
stain, especially sin. The
standard of life that God
requires and which is
characteristic of God himself
and also an expected
distinguishing mark of the
church.
Psalm 19:8
Habakkuk 1:13
Matthew 5:8
Ephesians 5:25-27
1 Timothy 5:22
Titus 1:15
James 3:17; 4:8
1 Peter 1:22

Race (ethnic)

A division of humanity

that shares common
characteristics.
Genesis 1:27-28
Acts 10:34-35; 17:26
Galatians 3:28
Revelation 7:9
See also **Immigrants**

Reconciliation

The restoration of fellowship
between God and humanity
and the resulting restoration
of human relationships,
which has been brought
about by the death of Jesus
Christ.
Isaiah 2:4
Matthew 5:23-24
Romans 5:10-11
2 Corinthians 5:18-20
Ephesians 2:16
Colossians 1:20,22
See also **Atonement; Peace;
Propitiation**

Redemption

The buying back or release of
someone or something from
some form of bondage or
imprisonment; especially
God's ransoming of believers

through the death of Jesus
Christ on the cross.
Exodus 6:6
Job 19:25
Isaiah 35:10; 43:1
Mark 10:45
Romans 3:24; 8:23
1 Corinthians 1:30; 6:20
Galatians 3:13; 4:4-5
Ephesians 1:7
Colossians 1:14
1 Timothy 2:5-6
Titus 2:14
Hebrews 9:12
1 Peter 1:18-19

Regeneration
See **New birth**

Rejection
The deliberate conscious act
of turning away from
someone, or refusing to
accept something being
offered. On the cross, Jesus
felt God had rejected him.
1 Samuel 15:23
Psalm 118:22
Isaiah 50:5-6; 53:3
Jeremiah 5:23
Matthew 10:14; 27:46
Mark 7:9
John 1:11; 12:48
1 Peter 2:4
See also **Hardness; Unbelief**

Repentance
A change of mind and heart
that leads to a change in
action; sincere turning away
from sin to God. Repentance
towards God and faith in
Jesus Christ form the basis
on which people can know
God for themselves.
2 Chronicles 7:14
Isaiah 55:7

Ezekiel 18:30
Joel 2:12-13
Matthew 3:8
Mark 1:15
Luke 5:32; 13:3; 15:7,17-18;
   24:47
Acts 3:19; 11:18; 17:30; 20:21
Romans 2:4
2 Corinthians 7:10
2 Peter 3:9
Revelation 2:5
See also **Conversion; Faith;
Grief**

Responsibility, human
Accountability towards God
for our actions; the
responsibilities that believers
and the church have come
from their privileged
relationship to God.
Ecclesiastes 12:13
Micah 6:8
Matthew 22:37-39
Acts 4:27-28; 13:48
Romans 14:7-8
1 Corinthians 10:31
Philippians 2:12-13
2 Peter 1:10
See also **Service; Sovereignty
of God**

Rest
The need for physical and
spiritual relief and stress; the
true resting place of
humanity lies in God, the
creator and Redeemer.
1 Kings 19:3-8
Psalm 127:2
Isaiah 30:15
Matthew 11:28-30
Mark 6:31
Hebrews 4:1,3-11
See also **Sabbath**

Resurrection
See **Jesus Christ; Last things**

Retaliation
Personal revenge; it is wrong
to strike back or to repay evil
for evil; justice must be left
with God or with the
authorities he has ordained.
Leviticus 19:18
Deuteronomy 32:35
Proverbs 20:22
Matthew 5:38-42
Romans 12:19-21

Revelation
The making known of God's
person, nature and deeds in
the Bible, history and
especially Jesus Christ. An
essential element of biblical
faith is that people can know
God only because he has
revealed himself to them, not
because they can discover
him by themselves. God is
also revealed, to a limited yet
important extent, through
his creation.
Psalm 19:1-2
Isaiah 55:8-11
Matthew 11:27; 16:16-17
Acts 14:17
Romans 1:19-20
1 Corinthians 2:9-10
Galatians 1:11-12
2 Timothy 3:16
Hebrews 1:1-2
See also **Bible; Will of God**

Reverence
The proper sense of awe and
respect that is inspired and
called for by an encounter
with the living God.
Deuteronomy 6:2
Psalms 19:9; 103:11; 111:10

Proverbs 8:13
Ecclesiastes 12:12-13
Isaiah 11:2
Mark 4:41
Acts 9:31
Romans 3:18
2 Corinthians 5:11; 7:1
Philippians 2:12-13
Hebrews 12:28
1 Peter 3:15
See also **Worship**

Revival

A period of special evidence of God's sovereign activity, in which he renews his people in vigour.
2 Chronicles 7:14
Psalm 85:6
Isaiah 64:1-2
Ezekiel 37:3-5
Joel 2:28
Habakkuk 3:2
Acts 3:19; 4:31; 6:7

Reward

Recompense for services given. The Bible emphasises that although salvation is a gift of God, all believers will be rewarded with the blessings of heaven.
Genesis 15:1
Psalm 19:11
Matthew 5:11-12; 19:27-29; 25:46
Luke 6:35
1 Corinthians 3:13-14
1 Timothy 5:18
Hebrews 11:6
See also **Last things, heaven; Obedience**

Rich and riches

Material possessions and wealth. The Bible emphasises that these come from God

and are to be used wisely to lead to a blessing; if they are used foolishly, they can turn people away from God.
Deuteronomy 8:17-18
Psalm 73:3
Amos 6:1
Luke 1:53; 16:19-28; 18:22-25
Ephesians 3:8
1 Timothy 6:17
James 5:1-5
1 John 3:17
See also **Desire, wrong; Money and material goods; Poverty**

Righteousness

Righteousness usually combines two main emphases: being faithful to an established relationship and conforming to a recognised standard of law. The Bible identifies a close link between righteousness and faith. Part of being right with God is trusting in him. The New Testament does not see faith simply in terms of moral righteousness, but also in terms of a living trusting relationship with God. The Bible affirms the righteousness of God and Jesus Christ in all their activity.
Genesis 6:9; 15:6
Proverbs 14:34
Isaiah 32:17; 64:6
Amos 5:24
Matthew 5:6,20; 6:33
Acts 17:31
Romans 1:17; 3:10,21-26; 5:17-21
1 Corinthians 1:30
2 Corinthians 5:21

Ephesians 6:14
Philippians 3:8-9
James 3:18
1 Peter 3:18
See also **Justification**

Ritual

The ceremonial regulations governing Israelite religious life and worship, especially sacrifices, ritual cleanliness and food laws. By the sacrificial death of Jesus Christ these rituals have been fulfilled and are not part of the new covenant.
1 Samuel 15:22
Isaiah 29:13
Amos 5:22,24
Malachi 1:13
Matthew 23:25-28
Romans 2:29
2 Timothy 3:5

Sabbath

A Hebrew word meaning "rest"; day of rest for the people of God. The Old Testament considered the seventh day of the week (Saturday) as the Sabbath. The Christian church, in recognition of the importance of the resurrection of Jesus Christ, observed a day of rest on the first day of the week (Sunday).
Exodus 20:8-11
Nehemiah 13:15-18
Isaiah 58:13-14
Matthew 12:11-12
Mark 2:27-28
Acts 20:7
1 Corinthians 16:2

Sacrifice

The Old Testament pattern

of worship required the offering of gifts to God on an altar. The Old Testament describes many sacrifices, but the New Testament announces the fulfilment of sacrifices in Jesus Christ.

Genesis 8:20
Exodus 12:5-7
Leviticus 1:4
1 Samuel 15:22
Psalm 51:16-17
Amos 5:21-24
Matthew 9:13
Romans 12:1
Hebrews 10:11-12; 13:15-16
See also **Blood; Passover**

Sadness
See **Grief**

Salvation and Saviour
God's eternal plan to deal with human sin that reaches its climax in the person and work of Jesus Christ. Salvation is the transformation of a person's nature and relationship with God because of repentance and faith in the atoning death of Christ. All humanity stands in need of salvation, which is only possible through faith in the Saviour Jesus Christ.

Psalm 27:1
Joel 2:32
Matthew 1:21; 19:25-26; 24:13
Luke 2:11; 13:23-24; 19:10
John 3:17
Acts 4:12; 16:30-31
1 Corinthians 1:18
2 Corinthians 6:2
Ephesians 2:8
Philippians 2:12-13
1 Timothy 2:3-4
2 Timothy 3:15

Hebrews 2:3
1 Peter 1:5
1 John 4:14
Revelation 7:10
See also **Atonement; Christian life, coming to faith; Sin**

Sanctification
Being set apart or consecrated to God; the process of being made holy through the work of the Holy Spirit, which depends ultimately on the sacrificial death of Jesus Christ.

John 17:17
Romans 6:19; 7:22-23; 12:1-2
1 Corinthians 1:30
1 Thessalonians 4:3; 5:23
1 Peter 1:2
See also **Christian life, character of the Christian; Holiness**

Satan
See **Devil**

Second coming
See **Last things**

Self-denial
A willingness to put your own interests and ambitions aside for the sake of following Christ, to grow in holiness and commitment to God.

Mark 12:42-44
Luke 9:23-24
John 3:30; 12:25
Galatians 5:22-23
See also **Disciples; Service**

Self-examination
Reflection on your own life, character, motives and actions, in order to judge

whether they fully accord with true Christian values.

Psalm 119:59
Haggai 1:5
1 Corinthians 11:28-30
2 Corinthians 13:5
Galatians 6:3-4

Self-righteousness
A moral self-confidence and superiority arising from satisfaction in your own achievements.

Deuteronomy 9:4
Proverbs 16:2
Matthew 6:1; 23:28
Luke 18:9-14
See also **Hypocrisy; Pride; Righteousness**

Service
Ministry rendered to God or to people; official service of individuals who have been specially set aside by the church.

Exodus 3:12
Matthew 4:10; 10:24
Mark 10:43-45
John 12:26; 13:12-14
Romans 12:7
Galatians 6:10
Colossians 3:23
1 Peter 4:11
See also **Help; Kindness**

Sex
God created human beings as male and female; human sexuality is a gift from God and part of what it means to be human. Sexual relations are an aspect of God's good creation which can be corrupted through sin.

gift of
Genesis 1:27-28; 2:24-25

1 Corinthians 7:3-5
See also **Marriage**

misuse of
Genesis 39:6-9
1 Corinthians 6:9-10,15-19
Galatians 5:19
Ephesians 5:3
See also **Homosexuality**

Shame
Feeling of guilt and
humiliation after having
done or thought something
wrong.
Genesis 2:25; 3:10
Psalm 34:5
Mark 8:38
Romans 1:16
2 Timothy 1:12
Hebrews 11:16; 12:2
1 Peter 4:16
1 John 2:28

Shepherd
The one who leads, protects
and feeds a flock; metaphor
for the task of leadership of
God's people. God is the
Shepherd of his people.
Psalm 23:1
Isaiah 40:11
Jeremiah 50:6
Ezekiel 34:1-2,23
Matthew 26:31
Luke 2:20
John 10:11
Hebrews 13:20
1 Peter 2:25; 5:4

Sin
Primarily a wrong relationship with God, other people,
possessions or the environment. Sin is expressed in
wrong attitudes, actions,
words or thoughts. The Bible
emphasises that this

condition is deeply rooted in
human nature, and that only
God is able to break its
penalty, power and presence,
through the death and
resurrection of Jesus Christ.
Numbers 32:23
Psalm 51:4-5
Isaiah 1:18; 53:6; 59:2
Habakkuk 1:13
Matthew 1:21
John 1:29; 8:34
Romans 3:23; 5:12; 6:1-2,23
2 Corinthians 5:21
Ephesians 2:1-3
1 Timothy 1:15
Hebrews 9:22
1 Peter 2:24
1 John 1:7-9; 3:4-5,9
See also **Forgiveness;
Repentance; Salvation and
Saviour**

Son of God
See **Jesus Christ**

Sorrow
See **Grief**

Soul
The psychological,
emotional and intellectual
areas of a person's life;
innermost part of human
nature.
Psalms 23:3; 42:2,5-6; 103:1-2
Ezekiel 18:4
Matthew 10:28; 11:29; 26:38
Luke 1:46
See also **Heart; Spirit**

Sovereignty of God
God's freedom and ability to
do all that he wills; his reign
over all creation and his will
as the final cause of all
things.
Deuteronomy 4:39

Job 1:12
Proverbs 19:21
Luke 22:22
John 3:8; 6:37
Acts 2:23
Romans 8:28
1 Corinthians 12:11
Ephesians 1:11
Philippians 2:12-13
See also **Election;
Providence; Responsibility,
human**

> *"The LORD is my
> shepherd, I shall
> not be in want."*

ROMANS 5:8

Speech
The human capacity of
speaking to express yourself
and communicate with other
people. We are to guard the
words we speak.
Psalm 141:3
Proverbs 25:11
Matthew 12:36
Ephesians 4:15,29
Colossians 4:6
James 3:6,8-10
1 Peter 3:10,15

Spirit
The innermost part of
human nature.
Psalm 51:10
Proverbs 16:2
Matthew 5:3; 26:41; 27:50
John 4:23-24
Romans 8:15-16
1 Corinthians 2:11,15;
14:14-15
See also **Heart; Holy Spirit;
Soul**

State, responsibility to
Submission to the civil authorities as God's means of maintaining law and order.
Matthew 22:21
Acts 5:28-29
Romans 13:1-7
1 Timothy 2:2
1 Peter 2:16-17

Stealing
Unlawfully taking the property that belongs to another person without their permission; thieves could become Christians if they changed their ways.
Exodus 20:15; 22:1
Matthew 21:13
Mark 7:21
John 12:6
1 Corinthians 6:9-10
Ephesians 4:28
Titus 2:9-10
1 Peter 4:15

Stewardship
The careful use and management of the possessions of another that have been entrusted to you; responsible use of wealth, material possessions and skills when considered as gifts from God, for which we are accountable to him.
Matthew 25:14-15
Luke 16:1-3
1 Corinthians 4:1-2; 9:16-17
Ephesians 3:2
2 Timothy 1:12,14
1 Peter 4:10
See also **Giving; Time**

Strength
See **Power**

Submission
A humble attitude of obedience in a relationship, to God, authorities or other people at work, in the church, in marriage or in the family.
Romans 13:1
Ephesians 5:21-22,24; 6:1-2,5
Hebrews 13:17
James 4:7
See also **Obedience**

Suffering
The experience of pain or distress, physical and/or emotional; the Bible considers that suffering did not occur outside God's authority and was ultimately the result of human disobedience.
Job 5:7
Matthew 13:21; 24:9,21
Luke 24:26
Acts 14:22
Romans 2:9; 8:18-21
1 Corinthians 12:26
2 Corinthians 4:8-9
Colossians 1:24
1 Peter 5:9

purposes of
Job 36:15
Psalm 119:71
John 9:1-3
Romans 5:3
2 Corinthians 1:4; 12:7
Hebrews 12:10
1 Peter 1:6-7
See also **Comfort**

Sunday
See **Sabbath**

Swearing
See **Blasphemy**

Talents
See **Gift**

Teachers and teaching
People who are responsible for instructing others, especially concerning faith and life. In the Bible teachers are parents in the home; priests and teachers of the law in Israel, and apostles, prophets, pastors and teachers in the church; Christians should also seek to teach one another informally.
Deuteronomy 6:7
Psalm 119:33
Matthew 28:19-20
John 7:16; 14:26
Acts 2:42; 20:20
1 Corinthians 12:28
Colossians 3:16
2 Timothy 3:15-16
See also **Family; Pastor; Preaching**

Teachers, false
People who deny or distort the gospel; their origin is either human error or demonic inspiration; God's people are warned to be watchful against such people.
Deuteronomy 13:1-3
Matthew 7:15-16; 15:9; 24:4-5
Romans 16:17
Galatians 1:6-8
1 Timothy 4:1
Titus 1:16
2 Peter 2:1
1 John 4:1-2
Jude 3,4

Teachers of the law
Scholars of the Jewish law,

sometimes called "scribes"; they opposed Jesus Christ, who condemned their hypocrisy.
Nehemiah 8:1
Matthew 5:20; 7:29; 8:19; 21:15; 23:2-7
Mark 14:43
See also **Hypocrisy; Pharisees**

Temperance
Moderation; self-control; ability to do God's will by controlling your selfish desires and living a disciplined life.
Romans 14:19,21
Galatians 5:22-23
1 Thessalonians 5:7-8
1 Timothy 3:8,11; 5:23
See also **Drunkenness**

Temptation
Pressure to give in to influences that can lead people away from obeying God and to turn to sin. The Bible urges believers to resist temptation and gives them encouragement to face it.
Deuteronomy 8:2
Job 1:12
Proverbs 6:27
Matthew 4:1; 6:13; 26:41
Luke 17:1
2 Corinthians 11:3
Galatians 6:1
Hebrews 11:17
James 1:13-14

help in
Psalms 19:13; 141:3
Proverbs 4:14
Luke 22:31-32
Romans 6:2
1 Corinthians 10:13
Ephesians 6:11

Refugee camp, Darfur: a result of civil war and international inertia

Hebrews 2:18; 4:15
James 1:2-3
1 Peter 1:6-7; 4:12-13; 5:8-9
See also **Victory**

Tests of faith
See **Temptation**

Thanksgiving
The offering of thanks, especially for gifts received. The Bible stresses the importance of giving thanks to God for all his gifts and works, to express our dependence on him and our gratitude to him.
Psalms 50:14; 136:1
Luke 17:16-18
1 Corinthians 15:57
2 Corinthians 9:15
Ephesians 1:16; 5:4,19-20
Philippians 4:6
1 Thessalonians 5:18
See also **Joy; Praise; Worship**

Thought
The human ability to reason and reflect. Believers are called to consider the words and works of God as they are revealed through Scripture and to avoid speculation that

is based only on mere human reason.
Psalms 48:9; 139:17-18,23-24
Isaiah 55:8-9
Matthew 22:42
1 Corinthians 2:11; 14:20
2 Corinthians 10:5
Philippians 4:8
See also **Meditation; Mind**

Time
The regular flow and duration of life, which is created by God and is measured by changes in the created order. The flow of time is directed by God who appoints particular times within his unfolding purposes. Because human life is brief, time should be used properly, making the most of every opportunity.
Genesis 1:14
Exodus 20:8
Ecclesiastes 3:1-2
Mark 1:15
John 7:6; 11:9
Acts 1:7; 3:21
2 Corinthians 6:2

Galatians 4:4
Ephesians 5:16
Colossians 4:5
2 Peter 3:8
See also **Old age; Youth**

Tiredness
A natural result of work and stress for which God has provided relief, rest and renewal. Scripture recognises that tiredness may have spiritual, as well as physical, causes.
Ecclesiastes 12:12
Isaiah 40:28-31; 50:4
Matthew 11:28
John 4:6
2 Corinthians 4:16
Galatians 6:9
Hebrews 12:3
See also **Power; Rest**

Tithing
See **Giving**

Tongues, gift of
The divine enabling of a believer to use a language, unknown to the speaker. The gift of tongues may be used to praise God or to declare a message from God that, supplemented by the gift of interpretation of tongues, builds up other believers.
Acts 2:4; 19:6
1 Corinthians 12:28,30; 13:1,8; 14:2,4,13-14,18-19, 21-22

interpretation
1 Corinthians 12:10; 14:5,27-28

Trinity
God's personhood as clearly expressed in terms of a unity of three persons in one, as Father, Son and Holy Spirit. The Son and the Holy Spirit are equal to God the Father in eternity, nature and status. Within the Trinity, the Father is head, first among equals; the Son and the Holy Spirit do the Father's will, glorifying him and making him known; and the Holy Spirit glorifies and makes known the Son.
Deuteronomy 6:4
Matthew 3:16-17; 28:19
1 Corinthians 12:4-6
2 Corinthians 13:13
Ephesians 4:4-6
1 Peter 1:2

Trust
See **Faith**

Truth
Truth in Scripture is more than mere veracity. In the Old Testament, it is a moral concept, grounded in the being of God himself and includes faithfulness and reliability. In the New Testament, the concept widens to include reality and completeness. Ultimately, truth is an attribute of God that is fully revealed in the person of Jesus Christ and is communicated in the world primarily through God's word.
Jeremiah 10:10
John 1:14; 3:21; 8:31-32; 14:6; 16:13; 17:17; 18:38
Ephesians 4:15; 6:14
1 Timothy 3:15
2 Timothy 2:15

Unbelief
A failure to trust God that challenges his being and truthfulness: expressed in disobedience and rebellion.
Psalm 78:19,32
Matthew 13:58; 17:17
Mark 6:6; 9:23-24; 16:14
Luke 8:12
John 16:8-9; 20:25,27
Hebrews 3:12
See also **Doubt; Faith; Hardness**

Unbeliever
A person who is unwilling to believe and trust in God, especially as he has revealed himself in and through Jesus Christ.
John 3:18-19; 8:24
Romans 1:21
1 Corinthians 2:14
2 Corinthians 4:4; 6:14
Ephesians 2:1-3,12
1 John 5:12
See also **Godlessness; Sin**

Understanding
The God-given perception of the nature and meaning of things, resulting in sound judgement and decision-making; in particular the ability to discern spiritual truth and to apply it to human behaviour.
Psalm 32:9
Proverbs 2:3-6; 3:5; 9:10
Jeremiah 4:22
Matthew 13:19,23
Acts 8:30-31
Ephesians 5:17
Philippians 1:9-11; 4:7
Hebrews 11:3
See also **Knowledge; Thought; Wisdom**

Unity

The bringing together of separate or fragmented parts into a unified whole. God's ultimate purpose is to unite everything under the lordship of Christ. God's desire for unity is also evident in the lives of his people.

Psalm 133:1
Ecclesiastes 4:12
Amos 3:3
Matthew 18:19-20
John 17:21
Acts 4:32
Ephesians 4:3-6
Philippians 2:2

Vengeance

See **Retaliation**

Victory

The conquest of, or gaining a decisive advantage over, an enemy. God's decisive victory against those who oppose him was achieved when Jesus Christ defeated the devil and all forms of evil through his death and resurrection.

Isaiah 41:10
John 16:33
Romans 8:31,37; 16:20
1 Corinthians 15:57
2 Corinthians 10:4; 12:9
Colossians 2:15
1 John 4:4; 5:4
Revelation 12:11
See also **Endurance**

Vow

A promise made to God to be fulfilled at a later time, usually in the context of worship or religious practice. There was no requirement on any Israelite to make vows,

but once made, they were binding and had to be kept.

Genesis 28:20-22
Deuteronomy 23:21-23
Psalms 22:25; 50:14
Proverbs 20:25
Nahum 1:15
See also **Blasphemy**

War

The state of taking up weapons against an opposing nation or people. War was an accepted reality of human life, whose origin is explained as envy and hatred in the human heart.

Exodus 15:3
Deuteronomy 20:1
2 Chronicles 20:12
Psalms 27:3-4; 33:16
Isaiah 10:5-6
Matthew 24:6-7
Romans 8:35-37; 13:4
James 4:1
For "Spiritual warfare" see also **Christian life, continuing in the faith; Endurance**

Water

The colourless, odourless liquid that is essential for sustaining life in human beings and animals. God is described as the spring of living water, being the source of life and salvation to those who come to him.

Isaiah 11:9; 12:3; 55:1
Jeremiah 17:13
Ezekiel 36:25
Matthew 3:11
John 3:5; 4:14; 6:35; 7:37-39
Ephesians 5:25-26
Titus 3:5
Hebrews 10:22

Way

A term used metaphorically to refer both to the Christian faith (especially in Acts) and to Jesus Christ himself (especially in John's Gospel).

"I am the way and the truth and the life. No-one comes to the Father except through me."

JOHN 14:6

Faith in Jesus Christ is the only way of salvation for sinful human beings.

2 Samuel 22:31
Psalms 1:6; 25:8-9
Proverbs 14:12
Isaiah 30:20-21; 40:27-28
Ezekiel 33:11,17
Matthew 7:13-14
John 14:6
Acts 24:14
Hebrews 10:19-20
See also **Guidance**

Weakness

A lack of strength, whether physical or spiritual. Scripture attributes weakness to human sin and foolishness and urges believers to find their true strength in God alone.

Psalm 62:1
Isaiah 35:3; 40:28-31; 41:10

Jonah 2:7
Matthew 11:28-30; 26:41
Acts 20:35
Romans 14:1; 15:1
1 Corinthians 1:27; 8:9; 9:22;
  15:43
2 Corinthians 12:9; 13:4
See also **Power**

Widows

God's special concern for
bereaved wives is declared
throughout the Bible He
defends their rights and
expects his people to do the
same.
Deuteronomy 10:18; 14:29
Psalm 146:9
Isaiah 1:17
Mark 12:41-44
Luke 2:36-37
Acts 6:1
1 Corinthians 7:39
1 Timothy 5:5,10,13-14
James 1:27

Wife

See **Marriage**

Will of God

The intention and purpose
of God, both generally and in
relation to individuals, as
revealed in Scripture. A
central aspect of the will of
God is that his people are to
be faithful and obedient.
Psalm 40:8
Isaiah 53:10
John 4:34
Romans 12:2
Ephesians 1:9-10; 5:17
1 Thessalonians 4:3; 5:16-18
1 John 2:17; 3:23
See also **Accepting the will of
God; Guidance**

Wisdom

The quality of knowledge,
discernment and under-
standing characteristic of
God himself. True wisdom,
seen in the ministry of Jesus
Christ, is a gift of the Holy
Spirit. The Bible affirms that
true human wisdom is a gift
from God and points out the
folly of trusting in mere
human wisdom.
1 Kings 4:29-30
Psalm 111:10
Proverbs 3:13,15-18
Isaiah 11:2
Matthew 7:24; 10:16; 11:19
Luke 2:52; 16:8
Acts 6:3
Romans 11:33
1 Corinthians 1:21,30; 2:6-7;
  12:8
Ephesians 1:17
Colossians 2:3
James 1:5; 3:17
See also **Fool; Knowledge;
Understanding**

Witness

An individual who, having
observed something take
place, is able to give an
accurate and full account of
what has happened.
Witnesses were of central
importance to Old
Testament law. The theme of
giving account is also of
major importance to
evangelism, which rests upon
believers explaining the
impact of Jesus Christ upon
their lives.
Isaiah 6:8
Matthew 4:19; 9:37-38;
  28:19-20

Luke 24:46-48
John 15:26-27
Acts 1:8; 4:20
2 Corinthians 5:20
Ephesians 6:19
See also **Evangelists;
Preaching**

Woman

God created both women
and men in his image and
likeness. Scripture shows
women in a variety of roles,
playing an important part in
God's salvation plan. In
Christ, there is no
fundamental distinction
between believers on account
of gender, race or social
status. Women played a
significant part in the life of
Jesus Christ and in the early
church. The New Testament
both records their role and
faces the questions thereby
raised.
Genesis 2:18,21-23; 3:16,20
Matthew 27:55
Mark 16:9
Luke 1:42; 8:1-3; 23:55–24:12
John 4:1-39
1 Corinthians 11:3,8;
  14:33-34
Galatians 3:28
1 Timothy 2:11-12,14-15
See also **Man**

Word of God

See **Bible; Jesus Christ**

Work

Work was ordained by God
as a means of fulfilment,
service and praise. It is to be
supplemented by rest,
following the pattern of
God's creation of the world.

Despite the effects of sin, work can still be honouring to God.

Genesis 2:15; 3:19
Exodus 20:9-10
Psalms 104:23; 127:1
Proverbs 16:3
Ecclesiastes 9:10
Matthew 20:1
Luke 10:7
Ephesians 6:5-9
Colossians 3:17
1 Timothy 5:8,18
See also **Laziness**

Works, good

Acts designed specifically to benefit others, which are characteristic of God. He requires and enables his people to do good, although this is contrary to their sinful human nature. Salvation does not depend on good works, but leads to them.

Matthew 5:16
Luke 6:46
John 6:28-29
Acts 26:20
1 Corinthians 15:58
Ephesians 2:8-10
2 Timothy 3:17
Hebrews 10:24
James 1:22; 2:14,17-18,22,24, 26
See also **Service**

World

The Bible understands "the world" in a number of senses. It refers to the world as God's good creation. This world, has, however, now fallen into sin, with the result that it can be a threat to believers. Believers are called to live in the world,

maintaining contact with it, while remaining distinct from it, and avoiding being contaminated by it.

created universe
Psalm 24:1
Acts 17:24
Hebrews 1:2
See also **Creation**

humanity
John 3:16-17

humanity rebelling against God
John 15:18-19; 17:11,16
1 John 2:15-17

Worry
See **Comfort, when anxious**

Worship

The praise, adoration and reverence of God, both in public and private. It is a celebration of the worthiness of God, by which honour is given to his name.

Exodus 20:3-4
1 Chronicles 16:29
Psalm 95:6
Matthew 2:11; 4:10
John 4:23-24
Acts 2:46-47
Philippians 2:10
Colossians 1:10; 3:16-17
Revelation 4:11
See also **Praise; Reverence; Service**

Youth

The Bible characterises youth as a time of vigour and strength. It also speaks of the pressures and expectations of youth, warns about the temptations facing young people, and instructs the

young about what is expected of them.

Exodus 20:12
Psalms 34:12-14; 119:9
Proverbs 17:25
Ecclesiastes 12:1
Isaiah 40:30-31
Lamentations 3:27
Matthew 19:21
Luke 15:11-24
1 Timothy 4:12
2 Timothy 2:22
1 John 2:14
See also **Family**

Zeal

A single-minded desire marked by enthusiasm and devotion. In Scripture it is often directed towards God, but God is also credited with zeal for his people and for the honour of his name. Misdirected or inappropriate zeal can degenerate into fanaticism.

Exodus 20:5-7
Numbers 25:11
Psalm 69:9
Romans 10:2-3; 12:11
1 Corinthians 9:16; 15:58
Galatians 6:9-10
Philippians 3:6-7,14
Titus 2:14
1 Peter 1:22
Jude 3
Revelation 3:19

Using PowerPoint in your presentations

In the next few pages, we give examples of PowerPoints from the various main sections of this book. See page 8 for details of how to access PowerPoint material on DVD or website. There you will find summaries of the teaching studies of this book in Word format so that you can add to them or adapt them in your own teaching context.

Here are a few guidelines to using PowerPoint effectively in your presentations.

1 Your aim in creating presentations is to communicate your message, not to show off all the effects that you know how to use. With a wide range of fonts, backgrounds, animations and transitions available, it is tempting to want to incorporate them all – but that communicates only confusion! A simple uncluttered appearance says more.

2 Don't put too much on one slide. Especially, resist the temptation to put too much text on one slide. It's better to break text up onto more than one slide. For example, in the sample PowerPoints for the Bible Book-by-Book section, we have put the Key Themes and Relevance for Today material onto separate slides, rather than trying to amass everything onto one.

3 Don't try to reproduce the whole of your talk on PowerPoint. Keep your PowerPoint as simple as possible. Use PowerPoint for the main headings and even then shorten them as much as possible.

4 Keep your PowerPoint consistent with the content of your presentation. Some people may look at the screen and become confused with what is written as they listen to you. Have a consistent message.

5 Keep headings consistent, eg begin with simple verbs. For example in the Bible Book-by-Book section at Joshua: Be obedient, Be strong, Be radical, Be fair. It can also help to have headings beginning with the same letter. For example, in the Bible Book-by-Book section at Esther: Aligning your life, Accepting your delays, Affirming your joy. Beware of overdoing this, however.

6 Keep to one main font, maybe using a second font for contrast, eg for a subtitle. Use a large font (28 to 36 points) and aim to have no more than six to ten lines per page. PowerPoints with many more lines do not communicate at all. Use a sans serif font where possible as this is easier to read on a screen than a serif one. Headings and subheadings should be aligned left and ragged (unjustified) on the right; these are easier to read than headings that are centred. Generally speaking, capitals with lower-case letters are easier to read than all capitals.

7 Use clearly distinguished colours, eg red on grey, yellow on blue, or black on white.

8 Don't put the most important items at the foot of a slide – people at the back of the room may not be able to see them above the heads of others.

9 If you are confident and can use them well, use clear and helpful (not just decorative!) pictures, screenshots and video clips. A small picture on some slides alongside the text helps to keep your presentation alive –

see for example the small illustrations at the top of many pages in this book, but make sure the pictures are relevant.

10 Check everyone can read the PowerPoints. If in doubt, ask someone whose eyesight is less than perfect.

11 Try to develop consistency within a presentation for a day's talk, or over a weekend conference or for a series of talks, in colours, fonts and headings.

12 Rehearse your presentation beforehand by yourself if you possibly can in a quiet place until you feel confident in knowing the ins and outs of your whole presentation. Time yourself and if necessary cut out parts that are not essential to your main message.

13 Arrive early at the site of your presentation so that you can check the equipment, to avoid late technical errors and embarrassment if the technicalities don't work properly. Print out the slides, especially if someone else is working the computer, and even if you are yourself – this serves as a visual reminder of where you are up to in your presentation. If someone else is working the computer for you, then go through your presentation with them beforehand with your script. This means that you should not need to say "Can we have the next slide, please."

14 You could print out your slides at say four slides on the front of one A4 page and four slides on the back and give this paper to your listeners. This will give them a hard copy and they can make notes on the presentation as you are speaking rather than rushing to copy everything down. It also gives you peace of mind if modern technical aspects fail.

15 When giving your talk, keep eye contact with your audience, not with the screen and not with the computer.

We wish you well as you teach and explain the Bible, making it clear to those listening so that they can understand what you are teaching (Nehemiah 8:8).

AVOIDING TECHNICAL PROBLEMS

1 Be careful if you are adding a movie to your presentation and do not intend to use the same computer for your presentation. Test your presentation on another computer with a CD or memory stick, just in case.

2 Back up your presentation to your email in case your CD or memory stick gets lost.

3 If you are using Microsoft Office PowerPoint, make sure you save your final presentation in two formats if you are giving your presentation from a different computer. Save as PowerPoint 2003 and PowerPoint 2007 in case there are compatibility problems with the other computer.

SAMPLE POWERPOINTS

KNOWING JESUS
A selection of the 24 PowerPoints in section 01

Each of the eight major sections in this book is structured in a way that can be easily adapted for PowerPoint presentation. There are ready-made PowerPoints of all the material on the DVD, arranged section-by-section, which are freely available for use. You may prefer to create your own presentation. You will find text in Word format available for this purpose on the DVD.

The examples here show just one way to present material in a structured fashion.

JESUS' UNIQUE IDENTITY
Jesus in history

The world of Jesus
- Jewish writings
- Dead Sea Scrolls
- Josephus
- Roman historians
- Archaeology

The life of Jesus

The Gospels about Jesus

The Word became flesh and made his dwelling among us. We have seen his glory, the glory of the One and Only, who came from the Father, full of grace and truth.
JOHN 1:14

Knowing Jesus 01

JESUS' UNIQUE IDENTITY
Jesus the Messiah

Old Testament promises

Jewish expectations

The reality of Jesus
- The birth of Jesus
- John the Baptist
- Jesus' ministry
- Peter's declaration
- The Messianic secret
- and crucifixion
- ction

thing of the early

"But what about you?" he asked. "Who do you say I am?" Simon Peter answered, "You are the Christ, the Son of the living God."

JESUS' UNIQUE IDENTITY
Jesus, the true human

The man from Nazareth
- Physical, emotional and spiritual life
- Jesus' miraculous power
- Death and physical resurrection

The Son of Man

The second Adam

The image of God

That which was from the beginning, which we have heard, which we have seen with our eyes, which we have looked at and our hands have touched – this we proclaim the Word

JESUS' UNIQUE IDENTITY
Jesus the Lord

"Jesus is Lord"

Lord of creation

Lord of salvation
- Miracles
- Suffering and death
- Resurrection and return

Lord of the Spirit

Lord and God

Thomas said to him, "My Lord and my God!"
JOHN 20:28

Knowing Jesus 03

JESUS' UNIQUE IDENTITY
Jesus, Wisdom and Word

Words of wisdom

The Wisdom of God
- Wisdom and creation
- Wisdom and salvation
- Jesus embodies wisdom
- Wisdom and God

The Word of God

In the beginning was the Word, and the Word was with God, and the Word was God. He was with God in the beginning. Through him all things were made; without him nothing was made that has been made.
JOHN 1:1-3

Knowing Jesus 05

THE BIBLE BOOK BY BOOK
A selection of the 134 PowerPoints in section 02

Genesis
GREAT BEGINNINGS

KEY THEMES

God and humanity
- God is eternal, unique, and all-powerful
- Human beings are made to know him

Creation and sin
- Taking care of God's good creation
- Adam and Eve's disobedience

Covenant and election
- God's covenant with Abraham
- God chooses his people out of love

"You intended to harm me, but God intended it for good to accomplish what is now being done, the saving of many lives."
GENESIS 50:20

Genesis
GREAT BEGINNINGS

RELEVANCE FOR TODAY

Sin is always exposed
- Don't hide sin, but confess it

Faith is always rewarded
- Keep faith in God's promises

Obedience is always blessed
- Respond to God's call

"You intended to harm me, but God intended it for good to accomplish what is now being done, the saving of many lives."
GENESIS 50:20

Matthew
THE DISCIPLES' GOSPEL

KEY THEMES

Jesus the Messiah

Jesus the King

Jesus the fulfilment and foundation

Jesus the Teacher

Jesus the Judge

"Jesus went throughout Galilee, teaching in their synagogues, preaching the good news of the kingdom, and healing every disease and sickness among the people."
MATTHEW 4:23

Matthew
THE DISCIPLES' GOSPEL

RELEVANCE FOR TODAY

Using God's word

Depending on God's word

Teaching God's word

Following God's word

Trusting God's word

Sharing God's word

"Jesus went throughout Galilee, teaching in their synagogues, preaching the good news of the kingdom, and healing every disease and sickness among the people."
MATTHEW 4:23

Psalms 1
THE HEARTBEAT OF FAITH

SONGS OF PRAISE AND THANKS

KEY THEMES

Praise for who God is
- God is the awesome Creator
- God is the great King

Thanks for what God has done
- The salvation of Israel
- Personal deliverance

"Shout with joy to God, all the earth! Sing the glory of his name; make his praise glorious!"
PSALM 66:1-2

Psalms 1
THE HEARTBEAT OF FAITH

SONGS OF PRAISE AND THANKS

RELEVANCE FOR TODAY

Joining with creation in praise

A celebration of praise

"Shout with joy to God, all the earth! Sing the glory of his name; make his praise glorious!"
PSALM 66:1-2

1 Corinthians
ADVICE TO A DIVIDED CHURCH

KEY THEMES

Church unity

Personal morality

Freedom and responsibility

Public worship

Resurrection hope

"I did not come with eloquence or superior wisdom ... so that your faith might not rest on men's wisdom, but on God's power."
1 CORINTHIANS 2:1,5

1 Corinthians
ADVICE TO A DIVIDED CHURCH

RELEVANCE FOR TODAY

Don't split your church over secondary matters
- More important: Christ's death and resurrection

Recognise God-given boundaries to sex
- The effects of ignoring these boundaries

The impact of public worship
- Orderly worship showing the reality of God

"I did not come with eloquence or superior wisdom ... so that your faith might not rest on men's wisdom, but on God's power."
1 CORINTHIANS 2:1,5

BIBLE TEACHING

A selection of the 61 PowerPoints
in section 03

DISCOVERING JESUS

A selection of the 39 PowerPoints
in section 04

THE BIBLE
Its main sections

The Old Testament
- History
- Poetry and wisdom
- Prophecy

The New Testament
- History
- Letters
- Prophecy

THE TEACHING OF JESUS
Jesus the teacher

Unique

Astonishing

Biblical

Confronting

Momentous

"No one ever spoke the way this man does."
JOHN 7:46

JESUS CHRIST
His triumphant resurrection

- The foundation of the Christian faith
- An event supported by evidence
- A promise of ultimate victory
- The power of Christian experience
- The assurance of eternal security

THE ACTIONS OF JESUS
Jesus performs miracles

Water into wine

Miracles of healing

The feeding of the 5,000

The man born blind

The raising of Lazarus

Other signs

"The first of his miraculous signs, Jesus performed at Cana in Galilee. He thus revealed his glory, and his disciples put their faith in him."
JOHN 2:11

GOD'S MESSENGERS
Patriarchs

- Forerunners of a new beginning
- Inheritors of a promised land
- Ancestors of a universal family
- Their message of the covenant
- Their message of election
- Their message of obedient faith

THE DEATH AND RESURRECTION OF JESUS
Jesus' return

How will he come?

Why will he come?
- To complete his work of salvation
- To bring about the resurrection
- To judge the nations of the world
- To usher in the new creation

When will it happen?

What difference does it make now?
- We should be ready and holy
- We should be urgent in telling others about Jesus

"Since everything will be destroyed in this way, what kind of people ought you to be? You ought to live holy and godly lives as you look forward to the day of God and speed its coming."
2 PETER 3:11,12

THE LAST THINGS
The judgement

- God will be declared as just
- Christ will be acknowledged as Lord
- Christians will be accountable for their service
- The disobedient will be rejected for their unbelief
- Satan will be destroyed for ever

JESUS IN THE LETTER TO THE HEBREWS
Going on with Jesus

Can I be really sure?

The experience of God's blessings
- two pieces of land
- not possessing what has been experienced
- going on as if nothing has happened

The evidence of changed lives
- claims to experience must be confirmed by what people see in us

"We must pay more careful attention, therefore, to what we have heard, so that we do not drift away."
HEBREWS 2:1

DISCOVERING PRAYER

A selection of the 24 PowerPoints
in section 05

DISCOVERING DISCIPLESHIP

A selection of the 24 PowerPoints
in section 06

DISCOVERING PRAYER
Asking for others

Others' needs

Asking as a friend

Pleading for the undeserving

Requesting justice

Looking for more

"Is anything too
hard for the LORD?"
GENESIS 18:14

DISCOVERING DISCIPLESHIP
Come and see!

Time to decide

Time for a change

We've found him!

The first thing
Andrew did was to
find his brother
Simon and tell him,
"We have found the
Messiah" (that is,
the Christ).
JOHN 1:41

DISCOVERING PRAYER
Why are my prayers sometimes unanswered?

Sin in our lives

Selfish requests

Wrong approach

Lacking faith

Giving up

If I had cherished
sin in my heart,
the LORD would not
have listened.
PSALM 66:18

DISCOVERING DISCIPLESHIP
From disciples to apostles

Enormous risks

Practical instructions

Instructions for facing persecution

Assurances about God's care

Warnings and rewards

He called his twelve
disciples to him and
gave them authority
to drive out evil
spirits and to heal
every disease and
sickness.
MATTHEW 10:1

DISCOVERING PRAYER
The Holy Spirit and prayer

Those first steps

God's Spirit and God's word

Lessons in prayer

God-given faith

"Exalted to the right
hand of God, he has
received from the
Father the promised
Holy Spirit and has
poured out what you
now see and hear."
ACTS 2:33

DISCOVERING DISCIPLESHIP
The reality of prayer

God is our Father

A child's simple request

The disciples' honest dialogues

The Son's deep prayer

"This, then, is how
you should pray:
'Our Father in
heaven,
hallowed be your
name,
your kingdom come,
your will be done
on earth as it is in
heaven.'"
MATTHEW 6:9-10

DISCOVERING PRAYER
Praying in faith

Praise and prayer

Praying for the sick

The praying prophet

And the prayer
offered in faith will
make the sick person
well; the Lord will
raise him up. If he
has sinned, he will be
forgiven.
JAMES 5:15

DISCOVERING DISCIPLESHIP
True Christian worship

For whose approval?

Christian giving

Christian praying

Christian fasting

"But when you pray,
go into your room,
close the door and
pray to your Father,
who is unseen. Then
your Father, who
sees what is done in
secret, will reward
you."
MATTHEW 6:6

MOVING ON AS A CHRISTIAN
A selection of the 28 PowerPoints in section 07

MOVING ON AS A CHRISTIAN
God's rescue operation

- Everyone needs rescuing
- Getting right with God
- From enemies into friends
- Living the new life
- Being free from the Law
- Knowing the Holy Spirit's help
- God does the calling
- Changed, to love and serve other people

> For if, when we were God's enemies, we were reconciled to him through the death of his Son, how much more, having been reconciled, shall we be saved through his life!
> ROMANS 5:10

MOVING ON AS A CHRISTIAN
Three key words – light, life and truth

- Light: the purity and holiness of God
- walking in the light
- Life
- passing from death to life
- Truth
- believing and behaving

> This is the message we have heard from him and declare to you: God is light; in him there is no darkness at all.
> 1 JOHN 1:5

MOVING ON AS A CHRISTIAN
The Holy Spirit is vital!

- The Holy Spirit is a divine person
- Born again through the Holy Spirit
- Guided by the Holy Spirit
- More like Jesus by the Holy Spirit
- Equipped for service by the Holy Spirit

> But the fruit of the Spirit is love, joy, peace, patience, kindness, goodness, faithfulness, gentleness and self-control. Against such things there is no law.
> GALATIANS 5:22-23

MOVING ON AS A CHRISTIAN
Living for Jesus every day

- An experience that was real
- A faith worth sharing
- A willingness to suffer
- A God who was in control
- A gospel that was unstoppable
- And today?

> The Lord's hand was with them, and a great number of people believed and turned to the Lord.
> ACTS 11:21

LIVING THE CHRISTIAN LIFE
A selection of the 54 PowerPoints in section 08

STARTING
What it's all about

A life lived with God
- John 17:3; 2 Timothy 1:12

A life given by God
- John 14:6; Acts 4:12

A life dependent on God
- Luke 9:23-25; John 15:1-5

A life lived for God
- Matthew 6:24; James 2:14-18

> Being a Christian consists of a close personal relationship with God, and not just of following a certain code of behaviour.

GROWING
The secret of growth

In touch with God's purposes
- 1 John 5:14-15; 1 Timothy 2:1-6

Aware of God's presence
- Ephesians 3:11-12; Hebrews 10:19-22

A source of God's power
- Mark 9:28-29; Acts 4:31-33

Taking time to pray
- Psalm 5:1-3; Luke 6:12

> Prayer is the chief means by which Christians maintain and develop their relationship with God.

WINNING
Right in the heart

Jesus comes first
- Exodus 20:3; Luke 9:23-26,57-62; 1 Timothy 6:6-16

Thinking straight
- Proverbs 23:7(KJV); Mark 7:14-23; Philippians 4:8

Pure motives
- Acts 5:1-11; 1 Peter 2:1-3

Love determines action
- Luke 6:27-36; 1 Corinthians 13

> The secret of living a successful Christian life is to ensure that our thoughts and attitudes reflect those of God.

ARRIVING
Welcome home!

A place of peace
- Compare Philippians 1:23 with 1 Thessalonians 4:17; Revelation 21:4-7

A place of joy
- Revelation 4:8-11; 7:9-12

A place of beauty
- Revelation 21:9-27; 22:1-5

A place of justice
- Romans 12:17-21; Revelation 20:11-15; 21:8,27; 22:12-15

> Heaven is the Christian's final home, where we shall live for ever with Jesus and all his people.

DELIVERING A POWERPOINT PRESENTATION

There are many ways of delivering a presentation using PowerPoint. One simple approach is to introduce elements and topics as the presentation progresses. This page shows the development of one PowerPoint item from the Knowing Jesus section.

Index

A

Aaron 143
"abiding" in Jesus 613
Abraham 131
   journeys of (map) 132
Abram 130
Absalom, rebellion of 171
acceptance 488
   social 484
accepting God's will 790
access 587, 790
accountability 524
acknowledgement, Christ's 524
action,
   determined by love 756
   God's, John, relevance of 325
   James, relevance in 385
   Jesus', Mark, relevance of 310
   obedient 416
actions of Jesus 551
Acts 326
acts of healing 72
Adam 790
   second 29
administration, Nehemiah, relevance of 198
adoption 430, 790
adultery 631, 790, 808
   spiritual, Hosea, theme of 255
adversary 696
advice 790
   parental 147
afraid,
   comfort when 793
   feeling 684
aiming 776
alignment, Esther, relevance of 202
alone, Jesus 94
ambassador, being an 702
Amos 260
   visions of 260
ancestors, patriarchs as 472
angels 470, 790
   Daniel, theme of 252
anger 631, 790
   God's, 790
   God's, Zephaniah, theme of 284
   humanity's 790
   Jonah, relevance of 270
answer, unbelievable 608
answers,
   awaiting 714
   worked out 594
anticipation 438
antichrist 790

B

backsliding 791
baptism 516, 791
   into Jesus 730
   Jesus' 436
battle 496
   God of, Joshua, theme of 154
   growing 708
battles, hard 724
Beatitudes 49, 301, 791
beauty,
   of holiness 651
   place of 784

anxious, comfort when 793
apocalypse, Joel, theme of 258
apocalyptic, Ezekiel, relevance of 249
apology 712
apostles 478, 790
   to disciples 619
application 416
approach, wrong 594
appropriation 514
argument,
   Galatians, relevance of 347
   Habakkuk, relevance of 281
armour, God's whole 636
army, active 508
arriving 776
ascension, Jesus' 436, 570, 791
asking
   for others 589
   prayers 712
assurance 444, 646, 647, 791
   Holy Spirit gives us 617
   of eternal life 647
   of truth of Christian faith 646
   Romans, relevance of 336
   work of Holy Spirit 452
assurances about God's care 619
Atonement, Day of 139
atonement 442, 791
atoning death of Jesus 567
attack 750
   Satan's, 2 Thessalonians, theme of 366
authorities and opponents, Jesus' 88
authority 791
   Jesus' 438
   Jesus', Mark, relevance of 309

B

backsliding 791
baptism 516, 791
   into Jesus 730
   Jesus' 436
battle 496
   God of, Joshua, theme of 154
   growing 708
battles, hard 724
Beatitudes 49, 301, 791
beauty,
   of holiness 651
   place of 784

beginning 130, 231, 472, 680, 746,786
   2 Corinthians, relevance of 344
being,
   moral 458
   new 488
   personal 458
   spiritual 458
   whole 458
belief,
   care about, 2 Thessalonians, relevance of 367
   James, relevance in 385
believers 474
   company of 506
believing in Jesus 562
belonging 702, 728
bereavement 791
   comfort in 793
   coping with 778
Bethlehem 312
betrayal by Judas 92
better,
   Moses 48
   Torah 88
Bible 410, 633, 722, 791
   and Christian 496
   and God's will 720
   application of 416
   applying 724
   authority of 12
   book by book 117
   consistency of 414
   contents of 420
   corrector 496
   developer 496
   director 496
   discovering 722
   discovering characters of 726
   divine author of 412
   energiser 496
   equipper 496
   God's revelation in 432
   handling 726
   harmony of 414
   help through 688
   historical setting of 414
   how to get more out of 633
   human writers of 412
   informer 496
   inspiration of 12, 412
   inspired truth of 412
   interpretation of 414
   listening to God 416
   looking expectantly 416
   main sections 410
   message of 14
   moral impact of 412
   obedience to 416, 418

   prayer and 416
   read carefully 416
   read regularly 726
   revelation through 718
   soaking up 726
   studying teachings of 726
   teaching 406
   teaching, discovery of 406
   theme of 418
   understanding the message 14
   uniqueness of 633
   unity of its themes 412
   why people read it 633
   word for life 633
Bildad 203
birth,
   Holy Spirit gives new 617
   Jesus' 436
   Jesus and new 563
   new 452
bishops 792
blasphemy 792
blessed 49
blessing 792
   secret of 591
blessings 230
   counting 598
blood 792
Boaz 161
body 693, 792
   functioning 508
   new 786
boldness 792
bones, dry, Ezekiel, relevance of 249
book,
   of challenge 722
   of example 722
   of truth 722
boundary, God's, 1 Samuel, relevance of 169
bribe 792
bride of Christ, Hosea, relevance of 256
bride, virgin 508
builders, two 638
building 194
   firm 508
building the kingdom 762
business, meaning 599

C

calendar, Jewish 122
call 152
   to discipleship 70
   to faithfulness 750
calling 502, 764
   Colossians, relevance of 359

final word of 583
fullness of 685
future kingdom of 230
generosity of, Joel, relevance of 259
Genesis, theme of 132
gifts of 766
glory of 480
good 618, 800
gospel of 480
grace of 386, 428
grace of, Exodus, relevance of 138
grace of, Ruth, theme of 163
greatness 600
guidance of, Exodus, relevance of 138
hating 635
heart of, 2 Chronicles, relevance of 190
help from people of 688
help of 688
his king, 1 Chronicles, theme of 184
his king, history of 182
his knowledge 602
holiness of 428
holiness of, Deuteronomy, theme of 149
holy 694, 800
Holy One, Isaiah, theme of 231
hope, of Exodus, relevance of 138
house of, 2 Chronicles, relevance of 190
image of 30
infinite 800
is caring 598
is gracious 590
is great 590
is holy 590
is kind 598
is willing 590
Jesus Son of 32, 557
judgement of 282, 333, 401
judgement of, Jude, theme of 399
judgement of, Revelation, theme of 402
just 800
justice of 271
justice of, Job, theme of 205
justice of, Nehemiah, theme of 197
justice of, 2 Thessalonians, theme of 366
kingdom of See kingdom, of God
kings of, 2 Chronicles, theme of 189
knowing 590
knowledge of 426, 694
law of 718
law of, 2 Chronicles, theme of 189
Law of, Nehemiah, theme of 197

law of, revelation through 718
lessons through testing 740
letting him work 772
life dependent on 680
life given by 680
life lived for 680
life lived with 680
life with, 1 John, relevance of 394
Lord and 43
love of 428, 649
love of, Deuteronomy, theme of 149
love of, John, relevance of 325
love of, 2 Kings, relevance of 181
love of, Malachi, theme of 294
loving 635, 694, 800
making known 56
man of, Nehemiah, theme of 197
merciful 800
mercy of 268, 428
mercy of, Jonah, theme of 269
message of, John, relevance of 325
messengers of 470, 472, 474, 476, 478, 480
Messiah of 476
mind of 476, 496
nature of, Micah, relevance of 274
omnipotence of 426
omnipresence of 426
omniscience of 426
our way to 591
parallels of, Esther, theme of 201
people of 476, 482, 518, 574, 664
people of, pray 52
people of, 1 Chronicles, theme of 184
people of, Esther, theme of 201
people of, Ezra, theme of 192
people of, 2 Kings, relevance of 181
personal 694
perspective of, 2 Kings, relevance of 181
plan of 482, 753
portion of, 2 Kings, relevance of 181
power of 76, 426, 710, 758
power of, Exodus, relevance of 138
power of, Galatians, theme of 347
power of, Jude, theme of 399
power of, Revelation, relevance of 404
presence of 426, 710

presence of, Esther, theme of 201
presence of, John, relevance of 325
priests of, 2 Chronicles, theme of 189
promise of success 746
promises of 686
promises of, 2 Chronicles, relevance of 190
promises of, Exodus, relevance of 138
promises of, Hebrews, theme of 380
prophets of, 2 Chronicles, theme of 189
protection of 698
protection of, Esther, theme of 201
purpose of, 1 Chronicles, theme of 183
purposeful 694
purposes of 350, 518, 710
purposes of, Genesis, relevance of 133
purposes of, Habakkuk, theme of 280
purposes of, Micah, theme of 273
redemption of, Ruth, theme of 163
remnant of, Nehemiah, theme of 197
remnant of, Ruth, theme of 162
rescue operation 641
resources of, 2 Chronicles, relevance of 190
restoration of, John, relevance of 325
revelation of 432
salvation of 480, 482
seems far away 595
self-existent 800
servants of 774
severity of, Nahum, theme of 276
silence of 714
Son of 321
sovereign will of 482
sovereignty of 643
sovereignty of, Ezra, theme of 192
sovereignty of, Obadiah, theme of 265
specific choice of 482
Spirit of 448, 480, 766
Spirit of, John, relevance of 325
spiritual 800
summons of 476
supremacy of, Romans, theme of 334
teaching about 56
temple of, 1 Chronicles, theme of 184
temple of, 2 Chronicles, theme of 189
temple of, Ezra, theme of 192

timing of, 1 Samuel, relevance of 169
Trinity 422
trusting, Judges, relevance of 160
truth of 428
truth of, 1 John, theme of 393
truth of, 2 Timothy, theme of 373
unchangeable 800
uniqueness of, Deuteronomy, theme of 149
voice of, 1 Samuel, relevance of 169
walking with 695
ways of, Job, relevance of 206
will of, accepting 790
wisdom of 37
wise 800
word of 38, 480, 490, 506, 607, 633, 667, 766, 768
word of, Ezra, theme of 192
word of, Matthew, relevance of 302
work of 60, 350, 597, 766
world of 476, 630, 669
worthiness of, Psalms, relevance of 211
godlessness 398, 800
gods, Judges, theme of 159
going on with Jesus 585
golden rule 637
good news *See* gospel
good work 639
good works, Titus, relevance of 378
goodbye, saying 780
goodness 800
  celebrating God's 618
  fruit of Spirit 454
  Titus, relevance of 378
gospel 49, 369, 750, 800
  application of 333
  applying, Galatians, relevance of 348
  bearing 702
  comprehensive 318
  for failures 746
  for life 564
  God's 480
  heart of 332
  inclusive 318
  of Jesus 562
  of new beginnings 746
  sharing 578, 579, 580, 623, 772
  spread of (map) 348
  summary, Titus, theme of 377
  whole 630
Gospels,
  about Jesus 22
  main events 436
  sinners in 84
government, leadership and 516

Authors and Contributors

Creative 4 International

Tony Cantale, designer, is passionate about communicating the message of the good news in print and has spent his working life exploring ways to present the gospel in relevant forms to ordinary people. He is an elder at his local church in Woodford, Essex, UK.

Robert Hicks' first career was as a senior executive in retailing before he moved into publishing, in which he has concentrated on creativity and marketing as well as initiating national enterprises. He has led the distribution of over 100 million Gospels and Gospel extracts, and initiated the annual "Back to Church" campaign which involves thousands of churches.

Martin Manser has been a professional reference book editor since 1980. He has compiled or edited over 180 reference books, particularly English-language dictionaries and Bible-reference titles. He is also a language trainer and consultant with national companies and organisations.

Larry Stone has been vice-president for Thomas Nelson Publishers and president of Rutledge Hill Press (USA). He has edited and published such biblical reference books as *Nelson's Illustrated Bible Dictionary* and *The Bible Almanac*, and published more than a dozen *New York Times* bestsellers. He has recently written *The Story of the Bible*. A graduate of Moody Bible Institute and the University of Iowa and a former missionary to Zambia, he now lives in Nashville, Tennessee and Katskill Bay, New York.

Contributors

John Balchin (*Discovering God's Way*) pastored many churches and was lecturer at London Bible College 1972–85. He returned to pastoral ministry at Purley Baptist Church and at Above Bar Church, Southampton, until retirement in 2002. His popular books include include *The Church* (Kingway), *Let the Bible Speak* (IVP), *Reader's Guide to the Bible* (SU), *Out of This World* (Kingsway), *What Christians Believe* (Lion), *The Bible in Outline* (SU), *The Bible User's Manual* (IVP). He contributed to a number of other works including *NIV Thematic Bible* (Hodder and Stoughton).

David Barratt (*The Bible Book by Book*) was for many years senior lecturer in English at the University of Chester. He has also taught in Pakistan and the United States, and is the author of a book on C.S. Lewis. One of his concerns is the interplay of literature and the Christian faith.

Mike Beaumont (*The Bible Book by Book*) is a pastor, lecturer, author and broadcaster. Based in Oxford, he travels widely in many nations and has over 30 years' experience equipping pastors, churches and seminaries. He contributed to the *NIV Thematic Study Bible* and is the author of *The One-Stop Bible Guide* (Lion).

John Benton (*Discovering God's Way*) is pastor of Chertsey Baptist Church, Guildford and managing editor of the monthly newspaper, *Evangelicals Now*.

Richard Bewes OBE (*Bible Teaching, Discovering God's Way*), – formerly at All Souls Langham Place, London – travels widely, has written 20 books and is known for his hosting of the on-screen programmes *Open Home: Open Bible* and *Book by Book*.

Rosalind Bradley (*Discovering God's Way*) lives in Australia and is involved in interfaith dialogue from a Christian perspective. Her first book *Mosaic* is a compilation of prayers chosen by inspiring Australians; she is currently compiling a global version.

Nicola Bull, editorial assistant, is an Oxford University science graduate and freelance editor, working mainly on Christian books. She is active in her local Baptist church, and is also involved in ecumenical and environmental groups.

Julian Charley (*Discovering God's Way*) was a member of the Anglican Roman Catholic International Commission (ARCIC), a warden of Shrewsbury House, Liverpool, and vicar of Great Malvern Priory from 1987–97. He retired in 1997.

Peter Grainger (*Discovering God's Way*) is pastor at large, Charlotte Chapel, Edinburgh. He spent 20 years with Wycliffe Bible Translators in India, Pakistan and Nigeria. He then served as pastor of a church in West Swindon. He was the senior pastor at Charlotte Chapel from 1992–2009 before moving to wider pastoral ministry among the church mission family.

Erroll Hulse (*Discovering God's Way*) is associate pastor of Leeds Reformed Baptist Church, editor of *Reformation Today* magazine and full-time organiser of African Pastors' Conferences.

Gilbert Kirby (*Discovering God's Way*) was minister of two Countess of Huntingdon's Connexion churches and General Secretary of the Evangelical Alliance before becoming principal of London Bible College. He died in 2006.